THE
TRIGGER

EXPOSING THE LIE THAT CHANGED THE WORLD
– WHO *REALLY* DID IT AND WHY

ickonic
publishing

First published in September 2019.

ickonic
publishing

1a Babbington Lane,
Derby,
DE1 1SU
UK

Tel/fax: +44 (0) 1983 566002
email: info@davidicke.com

Cover Design: Gareth Icke

British Library Cataloguing-in
Publication Data
A catalogue record for this book is
available from the British Library

ISBN 978-1-9160258-0-6

Printed and bound by CPI Group (UK) Ltd, Croydon, CR0 4YY

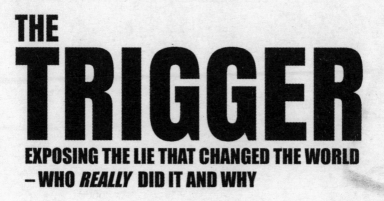

THE
TRIGGER

EXPOSING THE LIE THAT CHANGED THE WORLD
– WHO *REALLY* DID IT AND WHY

DAVID ICKE

Dedication:

To all those who lost their lives on September 11th
and to their loved ones left behind.

To all those who have lost their lives in the 'war on
terror' and to their loved ones left behind.

To all those truly behind 9/11 – may you one day
have mercy on your *own* soul.

Other books and DVDs by David Icke

Books

Everything You Need To Know But Have Never Been Told

Phantom Self

The Perception Deception

Remember Who You Are

Human Race Get Off Your *Knees* - The Lion Sleeps No More

The David Icke Guide to the Global Conspiracy (and how to end it)

Infinite Love is the Only Truth, *Everything* Else is Illusion

Tales from the Time Loop

Alice in Wonderland and the World Trade Center Disaster

Children Of The Matrix

The Biggest Secret

I Am Me • I Am Free

… And The Truth Shall Set You Free – 21st century edition

Lifting The Veil

The Robots' Rebellion

Heal the World

Truth Vibrations

DVDs

Worldwide Wake-Up Tour Live

David Icke Live at Wembley Arena

The Lion Sleeps No More

Beyond the Cutting Edge – Exposing the Dreamworld We Believe to be Real

Freedom or Fascism: the Time to Choose

Secrets of the Matrix

From Prison to Paradise

Turning Of The Tide

The Freedom Road

Revelations Of A Mother Goddess

Speaking Out

The Reptilian Agenda

Details at the back of this book

and through the website **www.davidicke.com**

RENEGADE

THE FEATURE LENGTH FILM

/ˈren·ɪˌɡeɪd/

noun

a person who abandons the religious, political,
or philosophical beliefs that he or she used to have,
and accepts opposing or different beliefs.

Twas always so ...

Why of course the people don't want war. Why should some poor slob on a farm want to risk his life in a war when the best he can get out of it is to come back to his farm in one piece? Naturally the common people don't want war: neither in Russia, nor in England, nor for that matter in Germany. That is understood.

But, after all, it is the leaders of the country who determine the policy and it is always a simple matter to drag the people along, whether it is a democracy, or a fascist dictatorship, or a parliament, or a communist dictatorship ... Voice or no voice, the people can always be brought to the bidding of the leaders. That is easy. All you have to do is tell them they are being attacked, and denounce the peacemakers for lack of patriotism and exposing the country to danger. It works the same in any country.

Nazi Hermann Goering

The Answer

When humanity remembers we are all one consciousness having different experiences the illusional fault-lines that divide us will fall and peace will come.

David Icke

The Answer

What is needed is the right to print what one believes to be true, without having to fear bullying or blackmail from any side.

George Orwell

Contents

What happened on September 11th?

Ask Alice ...

Nothing would be what it is,
Because everything would be what it isn't.
And contrary-wise – what it is, it wouldn't be.
And what it wouldn't be, it would.
You see?

Lewis Carroll

Eyes Wide Shut

We ought to be thankful not for our eyes but for our ability to see
– Mokokoma Mokhonoana

The highly-symbolic title of director Stanley Kubrick's final film is a good place to start with an exposure of the extraordinary Mega-Lie that is the official story of what happened on September 11th, 2001.

Two years before the 9/11 attacks Kubrick's last movie was released with its strange inverted title which said everything about human society in three short words: *Eyes Wide Shut*. Okay, eyes can't be literally wide shut, but they can be open and see nothing which is the same in outcome and consequence. I have written at length in other books about the life-long perceptual download imposed through 'education', media and peer-pressure which programs people to sleep-walk through life seeing only what they are told to see and thinking only what they are told to think. This doesn't apply to everyone, of course, but enough to allow a very few to dictate the lives of the very many by hijacking individual and collective perception and manipulating the subsequent myopia that can enslave a mind for life. Downloading a perception of what happened on 9/11 to great swathes of the human population has been essential to the transmutation of global society that we have seen in its wake. If more human eyes had been wide-open instead of wide-shut this would not have been possible. The attacks of September 11th were the perceptual trigger that launched a sequence of events still unfolding that are transforming the world into an Orwellian state. Therefore, this book will be both exposing the Big Lie of 9/11 and putting those catastrophic events within the context of a vastly bigger picture of human control – a context in which perception is all.

Never has incessant perceptual programming been more obvious than today with fascistic/communistic screaming mobs driving the mass censorship of political correctness and insisting that you either agree with them or be intimidated and abused into silence by those who believe they are the 'progressive' chosen who have the right to edit, censor and dictate the lives of everyone else. I say fascistic/communistic because I see fascism and communism as basically masks on the same face, terms for the same thing. Both are centralised tyrannies and the detail is simply window-dressing. I'm sure Russians would have felt so much better if they had been under Hitler's mass-killing fascist control and Germans the same under Russia's mass-killing Karl Marx-inspired communism. The extreme 'progressive' mind-set seeking to impose its will on society today through the deletion of free speech and opinion is only Marxism wearing a very thinly-veiled disguise. Marxism ('left') and fascism ('right') share techniques of control and manipulation because they are both tyrannies and so use the same *tools* of tyranny. Here you have the reason why extreme 'progressives' (Marxists) employ classic techniques of fascism while claiming to be 'anti-fascist'. Marxism was the creation of the banking and business elite to fool the masses into handing over power to a 'government of the people' controlled by ... the banking and business elite. Karl Marx was the elite's man as will become very clear. This is why 'radical', 'anti-establishment progressives' are cheered on today by mega-rich owners of giant corporations who censor opposing views on their behalf. This is why 'arch-capitalist' billionaires such as George Soros hand over tens of billions to parties and organisations promoting a Marxist society under the smokescreen of 'progressive' and 'social justice'. Marxism is not and never was an ideology to throw off human oppression but an ideology to impose oppression for the benefit of the elite it is supposed to be designed to overthrow. Transformation of society via the conflict of the Marxist 'class struggle' has been replaced by the conflict of the Marxist 'self-identity struggle'. Self-identity is the new 'class' and as ever more self-identities are systematically invented so the potential for 'struggle' between them is constantly expanded. Playing one group off against another is still the technique of the New Marxism and only the names and forms of division have changed. Self-identity struggle replacing class struggle has removed the divisions between masses and elite because now if the elite support your self-identity struggle they are 'on your side' and no longer oppressors. Of course they *are* still oppressors, but they are not perceived as such while they appear to share the same goals or what are today called 'values'. Thus a multi-billionaire financial manipulator like George Soros becomes a hero of the 'progressive' (fake) left in ways that would never have happened before when class was the source of division and not, as now, self-identity. Ongoing transformation through conflict and the destruction of cohesive community including the family unit are classic Marxism (Elite-ism) on the road to a global state of total and merciless centralised control. September 11th was an historic day on that nightmare journey because of where it has led us so quickly and exposing the lies on which the 9/11 narrative is founded is a historic day in changing direction.

Control is not about what is true or not true; it's about what the target population can be manipulated to *believe* is true. Purveyors and promotors of a Marxist/fascistic society can be manipulated to believe they are anti-fascist, anti-establishment 'radicals' while building a world that gifts power over the many to the very, very few. They will think they are seeking equality while preparing the way for extreme and systematic inequality – precisely what is happening day after crazy day. The imposition of belief I am describing here can most certainly be seen in the case of 9/11 and the scale of perceptual programming involved is made even more extraordinary by the evidence that I will present to expose the official story as a work of utter fiction. A more obvious lie – or indeed mountains of them – would be hard to imagine and the same with blatant contradictions and impossibilities that include the suspension of the laws of physics. Yet somehow this global fairy tale has survived largely intact all these years in the perceptions of the populous – or many of them, anyway, *far* from all. There are a number of reasons for this. One is that people overwhelmingly get their information (thus perceptions) from mainstream sources where government narratives dominate and by their very nature mainstream organisations employ mainstream minds. Most of these are so completely enslaved they actually think they are free. As Johann Wolfgang von Goethe said: 'None are more hopelessly enslaved than those who falsely believe they are free.' Mainstream minds are mantra-minds battered into submission by the constant repetition of official reality, but still convinced they are free because of either self-delusion or in a desperate bid to retain some self-respect and avoid facing the truth that the state is in their head.

'Progressive journalist' George Monbiot at the London *Guardian* rails against 9/11 'conspiracy theorists' with comments that include: 'Why do I bother with these morons?' He accepts the official story of 9/11 while bizarrely believing he's somehow anti-establishment and a 'radical thinker'. Does he know that those who told us the official version of 9/11 were the *same people* who lied about weapons of mass destruction in Iraq to justify a catastrophic war? Does he know that experts from a stream of relevant professions have created organisations to highlight the lies, miracles and inconsistencies of the official garbage? They include Pilots for 9/11 Truth; Architects & Engineers for 9/11 Truth; Firefighters for 9/11 Truth; Scientists for 9/11 Truth; Intelligence Officers for 9/11 Truth; Military Officers for 9/11 Truth; Veterans for 9/11 Truth; Medical Professionals for 9/11 Truth; Scholars for 9/11 Truth; Political Leaders for 9/11 Truth; Lawyers' Committee for 9/11 Inquiry and more. Does he know that the terms 'conspiracy theory' and 'conspiracy theorists' came into widespread use as a form of abuse and dismissal after the CIA contacted major media organisations in 1967 to urge them to use those labels to discredit anyone exposing the official story of the

Kennedy assassination? Too right – we must discredit those strange, misguided nutters who didn't buy the claim that a single bullet went through several people while changing direction at crazy angles or that a bullet which so clearly came from the front and hit Kennedy in the forehead miraculously came from behind. Do we have U-turn bullets now, then? Does Monbiot and his media mind-set think the CIA took that action to protect the truth about what happened to Kennedy or to protect the lie they were seeking to sell? Yet here we are all these decades later with the mantra-minds of the mainstream media simply repeating as a form of abuse the very terms circulated for its own ends by the CIA. How pathetic is that?

It really is a head-shaker to see how the so-called 'progressive left' is the most resistant of all to questioning 9/11 and statements by the very authorities they claim to be challenging. My God, what's going on in there? You can't trust authority except when they tell you what to believe about a world-changing event which triggered a sequence of other events that have left millions dead and injured, countries turned asunder and shredded civil liberties and basic freedoms across the globe. It must be sheer coincidence that this very sequence of human catastrophe and censorship had been provably planned for decades and by September, 2001, only the excuse to launch the sequence remained to be found. The stance of these 'progressive' system-servers goes like this: 'You crazies who question, think for yourself and don't have a naivety addiction, should shut up and leave the revolution to those of us who live in the real world.' Or, as Alexander Cockburn at the 'progressive' *Counterpunch.org* put it: 'The Conspiracy Nuts have combined to produce a huge distraction.' But from what, pray – that the state tells us the truth? David Corn at the 'progressive' AlterNet website urged readers to stop sending him emails 'suggesting, or flat-out stating, the CIA and the US government were somehow involved in the horrific September 11 attack.' Corn was adamant: ' ... the notion that the US government either detected the attacks but allowed them to occur, or, worse, conspired to kill thousands of Americans to launch a war-for-oil in Afghanistan is absurd.' This is what I mean by terminal naivety – terminal in the sense of being the death knell of real change, real justice and real comprehension. I would say to this mind-set before we start: You will never change the world until you understand how it works and unless you open your eyes-wide-shut you never will.

The rhetoric of the Monbiots, Cockburns and Corns is not based on whether something is right or wrong, happened or didn't happen, but is simply a reflection of their capacity or incapacity to *perceive* that it could happen. This or that could not have happened because my imagination cannot *perceive* the possibility. Er, that's it. Facts should lead perception. Instead people allow the limits of their own imagination to dictate their sense of the possible and what they believe to be 'real'. I cannot imagine what you say is happening and so it can't be happening. This arrogance of ignorance holds humanity in ongoing perceptual, thus 'physical', servitude. Are we really to be imprisoned in our sense of the possible by the limits of a *Guardian* or *Counterpunch* mind? Or by some professionally-biased joker at CNN or the BBC? Now *that* would be absurd. Day after day, hour by hour, you see mainstream 'journalists' of every background making definitive statements about subjects and situations they know absolutely nothing about because they have never crossed the perceptual Rubicon to breach the illusions of the box or bubble they have allowed to define them. This myopic perspective then blocks all motivation to research possibility beyond the mantra-norms because why would you research something that your software mind tells you cannot be? Why in this perceptual Alcatraz would you take seriously or show respect to those who *do* seek out truth in realms of possibility that you cannot imagine? Therefore: 'I cannot conceive that what they are saying is true, so it can't be true, and they must be weirdos and crazies' – Monbiot's 'morons' and Cockburn's 'Conspiracy Nuts'. The mentality of *I am right* and so anyone saying something different must by definition be wrong is a human disease now reaching epidemic proportions across global society. Such self-inflicted perceptual ignorance among the media masses of *all* shades in this unquestioning *'I am right'* society creates a dependency on official pronouncements which they can only repeat and call it 'news' and 'journalism'. They have no idea what is really going on and so have no questions that would reveal and uncover the lies and deceit. How can the clueless question the ruthless and come out with the truth? This is even more so when their continuing income depends on conformity to 'norms' and not free thought and investigation.

The dictionary definition of 'conspiracy' is 'a secret agreement made between two or more people or groups to do something bad or illegal that will harm someone else.' On that basis there are conspiracies everywhere in government, banking, business, intelligence agencies, the military, and every-day experience. Lies about weapons of mass destruction in Iraq to justify mass murder that wouldn't otherwise have happened is *not a conspiracy*? The same people who told us those lies that have killed and maimed millions would not kill 3,000 on 9/11 and then lie about it? The very idea that anyone would do this is 'absurd'? *Why* – because the dead were mostly Americans and Americans wouldn't do that to Americans? You think that psychopaths that kill millions without a second thought care about little details like the birthplace of their victims? Blimey, the childlike naivety is breathtaking and, anyway, who said that the 9/11 conspiracy was only perpetrated by Americans? I certainly don't – as we will see – and I am not talking about Muslims either. Irony of ironies ... what is the *official* story of 9/11 except a *conspiracy theory* and a crazy one at that? A theory that includes incompetent pilots of one-engine planes miraculously flying wide-bodied jets in ways that pilots who have flown them for decades say they could not have done; a theory that depends on the suspension of the laws of physics for the buildings to collapse as they did without the use of explosives. You will see as we proceed that there is no provable evidence that the alleged Muslim hijackers boarded those planes and some of the 'hijackers' named certainly didn't because they were still alive after the attacks. What did they do – parachute? You will further see that no provable evidence has been produced to confirm that the planes which left the airports that morning were the ones that struck the buildings and this evidence would be easy to produce from serial numbers of surviving parts if in fact they were the same aircraft. Did you know that the FBI has said there was not enough evidence against Osama bin Laden to make a case that would stand up in court? The list of such anomalies is almost endless and so are the outrageous lies of key government players on 9/11 such as Vice President Dick Cheney and Defense Secretary Donald Rumsfeld. But, no, the idea that a bunch of psychopaths in government would lie to you about what happened to justify a series of *very* long-planned wars and societal redirections is simply 'absurd'. What *is* absurd is the belief that even the possibility is absurd and this is the mentality that allows the few to control and direct the lives of the global population. Programmed myopia you might call it, or myopian naivety – *eyes wide shut*.

The moment I heard about the 9/11 attacks shortly after the first plane struck I was sceptical of the fast-emerging official story and the very speed with which that narrative was circulated amid the chaos and confusion was a big red flag in itself. How could they explain what happened so quickly while at the same time claiming they had absolutely no clue beforehand what was being planned? As days turned to weeks the bare-faced lies and daily contradictions confirmed that we were looking at an horrific event orchestrated by horrific people for horrific ends – which have played out ever since – and those responsible were not 19 Muslim hijackers answering to Osama bin Laden. I gave the subject most of my waking moments through what was left of 2001 and the first half of 2002 to expose the official story for the mendacious nonsense that it is. The result was the book *Alice in Wonderland and the World Trade Center Disaster – why the official story of 9/11 is a monumental lie*. It was, at least to my knowledge, the first major book challenging the full-of-holes narrative being sold to the world by every mainstream source. *'Alice'* was published a year to the month after the attacks. I began this book as an update of that one, but soon the scale of evidence researched and compiled in the two decades since the attacks by so many dedicated people made it clear that a whole new book starting basically from scratch was necessary. *The Trigger* is, however, infinitely more than a book about 9/11. I will dot-connect information that exposes the lies and identifies the networks and people really behind what happened, but also put 9/11 in the context of what has happened since and what is happening *now*. None of the society-transforming events we have seen since 2001would have been possible in the way they have happened without the essential trigger of 9/11 which supplied the initial excuse and momentum to impose a long-planned sequence of overseas wars and domestic oppression that have literally changed the world. Indeed the world today cannot be understood without awareness of the force that was really behind the attacks of that sunny September morning. Identifying this force will take me in to seriously controversial areas, but sod it – the truth is the truth and it needs to come out.

I want to make it clear before we start that I am not seeking to prove exactly *what* happened on 9/11. There are far too many smoke and mirror diversions and cover stories to be definitive about that although we will see the themes very clearly and I will let different opinions have their say on how they believe the various elements were orchestrated and made possible. *What* happened is less important in the greater context than what *didn't* happen. I am going to show that (a) the official story *definitely* didn't happen, and (b) who and what was really behind what *did* happen. We only have to show that the official story *cannot be true* to prove the conspiracy and from that everything else will follow.

PART 1

Demolishing the official story

CHAPTER 1

Lord of the Flies

Laws, like the spider's web, catch the fly and let the hawk go free
– Spanish proverb

Human life – let alone 9/11 – cannot be understood without awareness of The Spider and The Web. I may seem to be talking metaphorically, but not really. The symbolism describes precisely the dynamic and organisational structure that allows the very few to dictate the lives of the very many and pull off attacks like those of September 11th while others get the blame.

I have written at enormous length over the last 30 years about the nature of 'The Spider' – a force that hijacked human society thousands of years ago with the goal of complete control of human perception (thus behaviour) and ultimately the assimilation of the human mind into its own. The current race to connect the human brain to Artificial Intelligence is its endgame. I have exposed all this in detail in a stream of books including *All You Need To Know But Have Never Been Told* and for a deeper understanding of The Spider and its ultimate nature the information is there to be read. In most of this book I am going to stay focussed on the attacks of 9/11 and the background to who was really behind them and why. An appreciation of the basic dynamic of The Spider and The Web is, however, essential to putting those events in their wider context and to answer often-asked questions like how could anyone carry out such a massive attack on the American mainland and then make the world believe that someone else was to blame? It sounds fantastic at first hearing, but it's not – because of The Web. Standing at the centre is The Spider from where the direction of human society is dictated with its demand for the constant centralisation of power in all areas of life. The more you centralise power the more power the few at the centre have over the many, and the more power is centralised and concentrated the more power you have to centralise even quicker. The whole process therefore accelerates and that's exactly what we have seen. Humans once lived in tribes that made decisions about the tribe; then lots of tribes were brought together to form nations and countries through which a few people could then dictate to *all* the former tribes;

1

these nations are now being absorbed into superstates like the European Union and 'trading groups' which allow a few to dictate the lives of all the nations and all the former tribes. The overall effect of this power-grab was given a name a long time ago – globalisation – which is simply the incessant centralisation of power I am describing playing out in plain sight. I see protests about the consequences of globalisation which allows a tiny elite (currently dubbed 'the one percent') to exploit the poorest and most desperate in the human family. Yet many of the *same people* have been protesting against the 'Brexit' disconnection of Britain from the European Union. It is testament to the scale of systematic perceptual programming that they don't realise the obvious fact that globalisation and the constant and unelected centralisation of power in the EU are different expressions of the *same* agenda. This is why the all-party political class in the UK and EU bureaucrats worked so hard to block the Brexit that a public referendum voted for. More than 7.7 billion people can only be directed and dictated by a relative handful through the concentration of power because devolved diversity of decision-making would make it impossible for a few to call the shots and control the game. I have been exposing this for three decades and alerting people to where it is all meant to end. The attacks of 9/11 have allowed an enormous leap forward in this agenda – which is why they happened. This is the planned structure of global dictatorship that I first warned about here decades ago:

> A world government imposing tyrannical control over everyone everywhere on Planet Earth; a world army imposing the will of the world government on those who resist; a world central bank controlling all finance; a single global electronic currency with all cash deleted; and a microchipped population connected to a global computer system.

Look at the money situation alone and what has happened since I first wrote those words in the early 1990s. Digital money via cards and technology is taking over and cash fast disappearing from circulation. Oh, but it's so *convenient?* Really? How convenient will it be when the computers say 'no' to your digital 'money' and there is no longer cash to pay any other way? The cashless society, as I have warned from the start, is primarily about control, not finance. Digital money is only 'convenient' while cash still exists. When cash has gone what is left is only control by dictating who is allowed to use cashless money and who isn't. You want to challenge our authority? Oops, your card suddenly won't work – or your microchip as it is meant to be. We have seen the constant centralisation of power in politics, finance and military since I warned about this all those years ago and we are fast heading for a microchipped, nano-chipped population connected to Artificial

Intelligence which is planned to replace the human mind. The technological 'revolution' is another example of the famous poem *The Spider and the Fly* and the line: '"Will you walk into my parlour?" said the Spider to the Fly.' The idea from the start has been to manipulate or force the population to accept under-the-skin microchips they can see and nano-chips they cannot. People were first made addicted to technology they can hold – smartphones and tablets etc.; then came technology they could wear – Bluetooth, Apple watches and endless other gadgets; now technology is being inserted into the body as microchips which was the aim step-by-step all along. This process of addicting people to screens and introducing more and more sophisticated technology until human brains are connected to Artificial Intelligence has been coldly calculated and is moving fast towards its goal. Insiders like Google's Ray Kurzweil predict that this will be happening by 2030 and while this may not appear at first to be connected to 9/11 those attacks and their aftermath triggered a series of multiple events that have driven the speed of change across all areas of human society and led us to where we are now on the brink of total human control.

Children and the young have been prime targets because they will be the adults when AI-controlled humans will be full-blown reality unless we wake up like *now*. Human microchips are being introduced with ever-greater speed. At the time of writing more than 3,000 people in Sweden have been microchipped to interact with technology and both the British employers' organisation, the Confederation of British Industry (CBI) and Trade Unions have publicly expressed their concern at companies planning to microchip their staff. You mean that guy Icke they dubbed a 'crazy nutter' has turned out to be right? My God – some mistake, surely. How is it possible to impose and coordinate this global agenda in every country? How is it possible for political correctness – getting the population to silence itself – to be hatched in California and then go worldwide? How can the same be done with the transgender explosion which began with the premise of protecting transgender people from discrimination but has become a global phenomenon dedicated to creating widespread confusion about gender which has led to a thousands of percent increase in the number of those wishing to change from birth gender to perceived gender? The young are again the prime targets. There are big picture reasons why all this is happening that I reveal in other books, but how they can happen and be so coordinated worldwide is simple to explain: The Web. The same is true for how a relatively small number of people could plot, prepare, carry out and cover up the biggest terrorist event in history on American soil.

The Web

Human society is controlled by a hierarchy that we don't see which inflicts its will on the population through the hierarchy that we do see. They are, in fact, the same seamless hierarchy but divided into two forms – the seen and the unseen. The former is given labels such as the 'one percent', global elite, the establishment, and so on, while the latter works from the shadows through a global network of secret societies and connected groupings (Fig 1). Each 'strand' in The Web represents a secret society, semi-secret group or organisation in the world of the seen including governments and their agencies, corporations, the banking system, media etc. The strands closest to The Spider are the most exclusive secret societies which almost no one will have heard of. Many don't even have names to make them harder to uncover and track and they have among their membership those initiates deep in the shadows who know exactly what is really going on, why, and to what end. Many

Figure 1: The Spider's Web structure that allows the Hidden Hand few to control the many. Strands around the Spider are the most exclusive secret societies and further out – still in the hidden – are the secret societies that people will have heard of, but have no idea of their agenda – the inner circles of the Freemasons, Knights Templar, Knights of Malta, Jesuit Order, and so on. Next are the 'cusp' organisations where the hidden meets the seen and from here the Spider's agenda plays out into mainstream society as 'random' events and decisions. The vast majority of those who actually implement the decisions have no idea there even is a Spider let alone that they are imposing its will.
© Neil Hague 2019

of these names will be unknown to the public despite their power to influence events. They will certainly never have been troubled by a ballot box. Further out from The Spider, still in the unseen, we have the secret societies that most or many people will have heard of – the Freemasons, Knights of Malta, Knights Templar, Opus Dei, the inner-circle of the Jesuit Order and so many more. The last four are connected to the Roman Church which itself is a hierarchical secret society and the successor to the religion and secret society network of ancient Babylon (a key historical foundation of The Web). The inner core of Zionism (a political philosophy, not a race) is also a secret society which connects via The Web with the inner sanctums of the Roman Church and the other secret societies. No one will be more surprised to hear this than most Jewish people who are systematically kept in the dark about what Zionism really is. They think it's a political movement supporting a homeland for Jews in today's Israel, but that is only to mislead them into supporting an agenda they are not supposed to understand. Some far-seeing Jewish people – brave ones, too – have looked beyond the propaganda and worked to expose the truth while the great majority are subjected to life-long perceptual programming which is fierce and constant from the earliest age and leaves them at the mercy of the manipulators in their midst. Talk to Jewish people about how the indoctrination instils from birth a cultural self-identity 'norm' which includes the claim that the rest of world 'hates the Jews'. In fact we *don't*, but when the inner-core few want to secure the support of a majority in any situation then fear of a perceived enemy is always on page one of the training manual. I will call this inner-core elite of Zionism '*ultra-*Zionism' and later 'Revisionist Zionism'. This is the extreme and much manipulated version that is driven though secret society Zionism. The difference can be likened to mainstream Islam and the Saudi Arabia-based version called Wahhabism which manifests as crazies like ISIS or Islamic State. Mainstream Zionism and *ultra-*Zionism are absolutely not the same and no one needs to understand the difference more than the mass of Jewish people from whom this knowledge is hidden. I will be going much deeper into this background towards the end of the book and its fundamental connection to what happened on 9/11. Ultra-Zionism, a relatively modern phenomenon, wants to replace the Al-Aqsa Mosque on what Jews call Temple Mount in Jerusalem with a rebuilt 'Solomon's Temple'. You might look at the Jewish connection and say, well, I can see why they would want that. But, hold on. Rebuilding 'Solomon's Temple' on that spot has also been the goal of the Knights Templar secret society since it was established in the *12th century*. One of the major symbols of Freemasonry which emerged in its present form centuries ago are the twin pillars said to have been at the entrance to 'Solomon's Temple' (Figs 2 and 3 overleaf). Ultra-Zionism is part of a far

Figure 2: The twin pillars said to stand at the entrance to 'Solomon's Temple'.

Figure 3: The twin pillars of Solomon's Temple became the twin pillars of Freemasonry. The six-pointed 'Star of David', or hexagram, is a symbol of Saturn which will be significant much later in the book. This image is from the 'Mother Lodge' of Freemasonry in London.

bigger and more ancient picture and agenda than it appears to be and the body of Jewish people are to this day its unknowing pawns. Today's Israel with its total population of around just eight million has so much power and influence in the world because of the part played by ultra-Zionism in the global web and the connections that come not least through the House of Rothschild which largely created modern Israel in the land of Palestine in 1948. There is a point on The Web where the hidden meets the seen and I refer to this as 'The Cusp'. Here you find semi-secret groups and organisations that gather together people from American, European and global politics, intelligence, military, business, banking and media to form common policies and approaches to current events and longer term agendas for the world.

These 'cusp organisations' include a group spawned by a London-based secret society called the Round Table established by the Rothschild dynasty at the end of the 19th century and headed by Rothschild agent Cecil Rhodes who plundered southern Africa for gold and diamonds to add still more to his masters' phenomenal wealth (Fig 4). The Round Table was behind the 'Balfour Declaration' in 1917 when the British government formerly announced its support for a homeland for Jewish people in Palestine. The 'declaration' was actually a letter sent by Lord Arthur Balfour, British Foreign Secretary and inner circle member of the Round Table, to Lord Lionel Walter Rothschild, funder and founder of the Round Table and described as 'a leader of the British Jewish community'. You can see with this example alone how events in the seen can be so easily orchestrated from the unseen while the public are told a

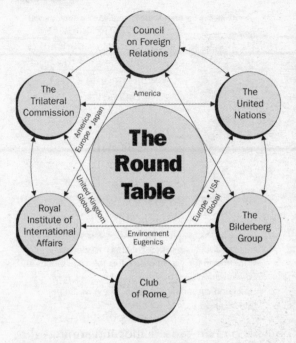

Figure 4: The London-based Rothschild Round Table secret society and the network of organisations it created both sides of the Atlantic.

very different story. Keep that in mind when we get to the details about 9/11. The Round Table created a series of cusp organisation satellites which include the following: Royal Institute of International Affairs (also known as Chatham House) in London (1920); Council on Foreign Relations (CFR) in New York (1921); Bilderberg Group (1954); Club of Rome (1968); and the Trilateral Commission (1972). The Rothschild and Rockefeller families were the major force behind their creation together with other connected elite families and they are known by various descriptions including 'non-governmental discussion groups', 'non-governmental organisations' (NGOs) and the all-encompassing title of 'think tanks'. You will see later the essential part played in 9/11 of 'think tanks' which are a means to group together like-minded people in pursuit of a common outcome while also persuading necessary outsiders to come to your view of what should be done. In this way think tanks are incredibly influential in manipulating policies decided in the hidden to become public reality. This Round Table cusp network was also responsible for the establishment of the United Nations which is a stalking horse for fully-fledged world government. The Rothschild-Rockefeller-dominated Council on Foreign Relations has been a major manipulating force behind United States foreign policy from 1921 to present day. America's delegation at the founding of the UN included 74 of its members making it what one insider called 'a roll call of the CFR'. The land on which the UN building stands in New York was donated by the Rockefellers such was the determination of The Web to establish a global body which they could eventually transform into world government. The Bilderberg Group has been behind so much manipulation of European, American and world affairs. It was intimately involved in the creation of the European Union as it replaced the former Common Market and in the introduction of the single-currency euro as so many European countries replaced their own unique version of money (a major step on the road to a single global currency). A secret society that works closely with the Bilderberg Group is Le Cercle which will later become relevant to 9/11. Another cusp entity to mention is the Club of Rome established in 1968 with the specific task of exploiting environmental issues to justify global transformation in line with The Spider

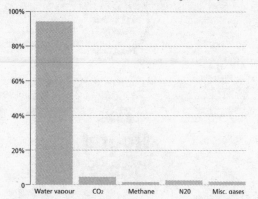

Contribution to the Greenhouse Effect (including water vapour)

Figure 5: This graph of greenhouse gases puts the hysteria about carbon dioxide into perspective. If you want to stop the greenhouse effect then ban clouds and condensation and, by the way, without a greenhouse effect and carbon dioxide (C02) there would be no human life.

agenda and from this has come the human-caused 'global warming' hoax which is being used to do just that. Greenpeace co-founder Patrick Moore described it as 'the greatest scam in history', but he's a rare sane voice in the mob-rule that the environmental movement has become. American meteorologist Joe Bastardi said that billions of years of climate fluctuations are being judged by the time equivalent of six seconds in the life of an 80-year-old. 'It's like one scene in a movie of five seconds determining the whole movie.' The overwhelming contribution to 'greenhouse gases' comes from water vapour and clouds and the majority of carbon dioxide (without which we'd all be dead) is naturally-occurring (Fig 5). I have been warning again for decades that 'climate change' blamed on human activity is the manufactured excuse to justify fascistic/communistic centralisation of control through United Nations deceptions known as Agenda 21 and Agenda 2030. Elite stooge Alexandria Ocasio-Cortez, the extraordinarily narcissistic New York congresswoman, launched her 'Green New Deal' in 2019 which demands what I said years ago would be the societal transformation that 'climate change' would be used to justify. What was the justification that Ocasio-Cortez gave for her plan? Human-caused climate change is going to kill us all. It's just a coincidence, nothing to worry about.

The mushroom technique

So the Spider dictates the policies and direction of the world and these play out through the upper levels of secret societies into the cusp organisations and on into mainstream society where we see apparently random decisions and legislative changes that appear to be made by

The Masonic Structure

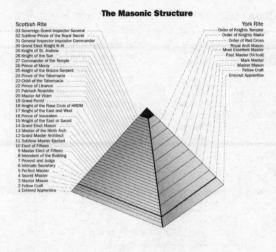

Scottish Rite
33 Sovereign Grand Inspector General
32 Sublime Prince of the Royal Secret
31 General Inspector Inquisitor Commander
30 Grand Elect Knight K-H
29 Knight of St. Andrew
28 Knight of the Sun
27 Commander of the Temple
26 Prince of Mercy
25 Knight of the Brazos Serpent
24 Prince of the Tabernacle
23 Child of the Tabernacle
22 Prince of Libanus
21 Patriach Noachite
20 Master Ad Vitam
19 Grand Pontif
18 Knight of the Rose Croix of HRDM
17 Knight of the East and West
16 Prince of Jerusalem
15 Knight of the East or Sword
14 Grand Elect Mason
13 Master of the Ninth Arch
12 Grand Master Architect
11 Sublime Master Ejected
10 Elect of Fifteen
9 Master Elect of Fifteen
8 Intendent of the Building
7 Provost and Judge
6 Intimate Secretary
5 Perfect Master
4 Secret Master
3 Master Mason
2 Fellow Craft
1 Entered Apprentice

York Rite
Order of Knights Templar
Order of Knights Malta
Order of Red Cross
Royal Arch Mason
Most Excellent Master
Past Master (Virtual)
Mark Master
Master Mason
Fellow Craft
Entered Apprentice

Figure 6: The structure of secret societies is the blueprint for human societies. Each lower level is compartmentalised from higher levels and so only the few at the top know what is really happening and why.

governments and their agencies, the military, corporations, banks, medicine, Silicon Valley and all the rest. In fact, the society-changing decisions are not random. They are originally made by The Spider and transform human society through its agents/gofers/serfs while the overwhelming majority of them have no idea there even is a Spider let alone they are doing its bidding. This is possible because of the technique of 'compartmentalisation' or 'the need to know' which is the same system employed by secret societies to keep most of their members blind to what the few at the top know and are doing (Fig 6). Look at any sizable organisation, no matter what it may be, government, corporation, university, anything, and you will see a compartmentalised pyramid in which a few at the top know what's going on while everyone else is only aware of their particular contribution in compartmentalised isolation from what others are doing. If you make an isolated piece of technology you don't necessarily know what it will be part of once all the other components made elsewhere are fitted together. This is the principle I am talking about and it means that people daily contribute to their own and their family's enslavement while having no idea that this is what they are doing. The structure of isolated contributions means that very few are needed to control the actions and direction of giant organisations, multiple actions and global events. In that one sentence I have described the structural basis of 9/11 and how its cover up was possible. Each compartmentalised strand in The Web, governments and their agencies, corporations, banks, military, intelligence, media are overwhelmingly staffed by those who don't know there *is* a Web or what their organisation is ultimately being used to achieve. Go deep enough into these hierarchies and you'll reach the point where they attach to The Web or to use another analogy all the pyramids fuse into one global pyramid (Fig 7 overleaf). At this level of the global network governments and their agencies, corporations, banks, military, intelligence, media are operating as *one unit* in pursuit of the *same end* – the complete control of human society. It is important to remember that The Web has no borders and operates as one global

The Pyramid of Manipulation

The Spider & Hidden Hand

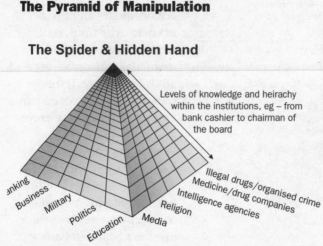

All the major institutions and groups that affect our daily lives connect with the Global Elite, which decides the coordinated policy throughout the pyramid.

People in the lower compartments will have no idea what they are part of.

Levels of knowledge and heirachy within the institutions, eg – from bank cashier to chairman of the board

anking
Business
Military
Politics
Education
Media
Religion
Intelligence agencies
Medicine/drug companies
Illegal drugs/organised crime

Figure 7: The Hidden Hand – where all compartmentalised pyramids meet.

entity.

The Web dramatically increases the potential for covert coordination between apparently unconnected people and organisations and their hidden connections allow so much to be secretly orchestrated while a totally different cover-story is presented to the public by the elite-owned (and largely clueless) media. For example, people see governments, major corporations, cartels like Big Pharma, Big Biotech, Big Oil, Big Tech and Big Media, world events and political happenings, and they are perceived a certain way. In and of themselves they all appear as individual entities making apparently random decisions made by random individuals; but if you go deep enough or high enough in these organisations they all attach to the same Web and a very different perspective emerges. Internet media near-monopolies like Facebook, Google, YouTube, Twitter, Apple, Amazon, PayPal, Reddit, GoDaddy, Shopify and others become one unit at that level and respond in unison to attack and destroy the Internet presence of alternative information and social media platforms dedicated to free speech – cheered on by the Marxist elite-controlled 'progressives' who are an insult to the civil rights movement of the 1960s they so wrongly claim to succeed. Inner-circle initiates and funders driving this 'progressive' response are also attached to The Web and serve its interests while the mass of mindless repeaters and followers think they are challenging the established order. How easy it is to have Web-controlled governments, newspapers and Web-funded and manipulated 'progressives' to demand in unison that free speech be deleted from those they want to silence and then Web-controlled Internet companies to say they are censoring people in response to public opinion and government pressure. The Web is used to promote giant corporations and limit their tax bills while government agencies that supposed to protect the public from the activities of those corporations are attached to the same Web and so let them get away with it. They target the opposition in the form of small independent businesses that face incessant regulation and far higher levels of taxation. The potential for manipulation through The Web is endless and coordinating actions between elements of government, military, intelligence agencies and law enforcement on 9/11 would have been quite straightforward with such a structure in place.

Spider bloodlines

The concept of 'royalty' and 'aristocracy' did not appear out of nowhere. I reveal in other books how bloodlines were seeded in the ancient world that believed themselves to be the bloodlines of the 'gods' – hybrids or 'demigods' of entities in bands of frequency unseen to human sight or what is called 'visible light'. Most people don't realise that the band of frequency that we can see is so tiny it is laughable. According to mainstream science the electromagnetic spectrum is 0.005 percent of what exists in the Universe (some say more but not much) and 'visible light', the only frequency band we can see, is a *fraction* of the 0.005 percent. Everything else we *cannot see* – the almost entirety of the Universe and all of infinite reality beyond. These 'gods' as they were perceived operate in these unseen realms and some of them comprise The Spider ultimately behind world events and the hierarchical control system in the realm of the seen. We see this theme of humans interbreeding with 'gods' most famously with the biblical sons of God who are described as interbreeding with the daughters of men and producing the hybrid Nephilim; but this is not unique to the Bible. The theme can be found in ancient cultures all over the world with the 'gods' referred to as 'Archons' (Gnostic), 'Jinn' (Islam and pre-Islam); 'Anunnaki' (Sumer/Babylon); 'Chitauri' (Zulu); and so many more around the world. I have had the same story confirmed to me many times by whistleblower insiders of the government-military-intelligence complex. When native shamans and dark suit insiders speak the same language and tell the same story it is worth listening if you have a mind of your own. I have been researching and tracking this bloodline 'Nephilim' network since the early 1990s and it makes so much sense of the world. 'Royal' families have claimed the 'Divine Right to Rule' and this is taken to mean 'Divine' in the meaning of the Christian God. In fact the word 'divine' originates from early Vedic literature in India and their word 'Deva' which meant 'supernatural beings'. 'Divine' Right to Rule becomes the right to rule at the behest of supernatural beings, not the Christian God. This certainly fits with the Old Testament concept given that 'sons of God who interbred with the daughters of men' translated originally as 'sons of the *gods*' plural. These hybrid 'royal' bloodlines and families saw themselves as special and chosen above the rest of humanity and for thousands of years they were seen in the same way by their 'subjects'. Some shockingly still do. Rule by bloodline became a common method of leadership and dictatorship until humanity began to grow up and demand far more representative government. Some overtly royal families survived – as in Britain where the head of state is bizarrely still decided by who had sex with who and in what order to dictate the line of succession. Why is the present monarch on the British throne and not someone else? The answer is *bloodline* and only bloodline. Most of the formerly open royal families and their offshoots around the world rebranded themselves and headed into politics, business, banking and other influential areas of society. Their attire may have changed with the transformation but they still consider themselves special and 'of the gods' which they have worshipped in their rituals since ancient times.

One group of bloodlines very relevant to the world today can be picked up thousands of years ago in Sumer and Babylon, in what today is Iraq, and in the Egypt of the Pharaohs. I have charted their movements and background in other books but basically they eventually headed north into Europe under various names and some established Rome and the Roman Empire which allowed for further infiltration into Britain and northern Europe. This was only one flow of people and their 'royal' leadership, however, and others went north

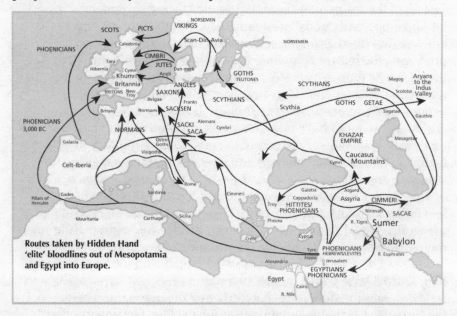

Figure 8: The march of Hidden Hand control out of the Middle East that seized the reins of power in Europe before expanding across the world through 'colonisation'.

Figure 9: Virgin mothers and their holy child abound throughout the ancient world from reptilian figurines found in of the Ubaid culture in the land that became Sumer and Babylon to Egypt's Isis and Horus and on to Christianity's Mother Mary and Jesus.

through the Caucasus and into Eastern and Western Europe by various routes (Fig 8). The bloodlines that established Rome would go on to found Christianity as we know it today which was a milder version of the religion their ancestors brought out of Babylon which today's bloodline family elite still follow under what is now called 'Satanism'. In Babylon they worshipped a trinity of Nimrod, the father god; Tammuz, the virgin-born son; and Queen Semiramis, the virgin mother. It was said that when Nimrod died he became the sun-god Baal and impregnated Semiramis with the rays of the sun through which came the virgin-birth of Tammuz. Roman Emperor Constantine the Great decreed what Christians must believe at the Council of Nicaea in what is now Turkey in 325AD. Constantine worshipped Sol Invictus, the 'Unconquered Sun', and so had no problem encompassing a new religion in which Nimrod became 'The Father', Tammuz became 'Jesus' and Semiramis became the 'Holy Spirit'. Christianity symbolises the Holy Spirit as a dove which was the symbol for Semiramis in Babylon. Other Babylonian attributes of Semiramis like virgin mother and mother of God were given to the Christian figure of Mother Mary. The virgin mother and child story is ancient and can be found all over the world long before Christianity inherited the story and presented it in a new historical context (Fig 9). Symbols of the bloodline religion with its origins in Babylon and beyond are all around us. Symbolism is their secret language and they believe that very few will ever work it all out. The symbol of the Babylonian goddess Semiramis was the dove and the name Colombia comes from a Latin root-word meaning 'dove'. Washington DC is located in the District of Columbia or the District of the Dove – the Babylonian goddess. This was supposed to be named after Christopher Columbus, but that's a diversion. Another Babylon goddess symbol is the owl and so you have the street plan around Capitol Hill in the District of the Dove clearly made to depict an owl

Figure 10: The owl and pyramid street plan in Washington DC symbolising the Babylonian goddess with Capitol Hill so appropriately in her belly.

Figure 11: The 'Statue of Liberty' is really a depiction of the Babylonian goddess given to New York by French Freemasons in Paris. Under the satanic law of inversion Statue of 'Liberty' means Statue of Control.

with the Congress Building in its belly (Fig 10). How utterly appropriate and indicative of how things are. The Statue of Liberty is also the Babylonian goddess holding the torch of the 'Illuminated Ones', 'Illuminati' or bloodline elite (Fig 11). The Liberty statue was given to New York by French Freemasons in Paris who knew what it really represents and there is a mirror-image 'Liberty' on an island in the River Seine in the French capital (Fig 12). The woman holding the torch in the logo of Columbia Pictures is the same symbolism and in London the 'Mother Lodge' of Freemasonry (established in 1717) is located in Great Queen Street because 'Great Queen' was a title of Semiramis in Babylon (Figs 13 and 14). Freemasonry was introduced into America by the Mother Lodge where it has been

Figure 12: The other Statue of Liberty on an island in the River Seine in Paris.

Figure 13: The Babylonian goddess again as the famous logo of 'Columbia' (the dove, goddess) Pictures. See also Washington DC in the 'District of Columbia'.

Figure 14: The Mother Lodge of Freemasonry in London with the twin pillars of 'Solomon's Temple'. The building is located in Great Queen Street – a title given to the Babylonian goddess. It was from here that Freemasonry was established in the United States.

central to the creation and direction of the United States.

Bloodline Satanism

While Christianity became the publicly acceptable version of the religion of Babylon the real deal involving human sacrifice and other unspeakable horrors has continued to be worshipped in secret by the bloodlines and their offshoots and lackeys which is why my research into such people invariably leads to Satanism and its fundamentally-connected paedophilia. I explain in other books why the two are so connected and what Satanism really is. Very briefly we don't live in a 'world' so much as a band of frequency that our senses can decode. You can symbolise this as a television channel. Tune the TV to one channel and that is what you get – it is all you are aware of on the screen. However, all the other channels exist at the same time although they can't be seen and you can access them if you tune the set to their code or frequency (switch the channel). Our reality is like that. The five senses tune us to a particular and tiny band of frequency and beyond five-sense reality is infinite reality teeming with life of every conceivable kind and then some. Skilled psychics and mediums can tune to some of these unseen realms – unseen to the human senses – and Satanists perform their rituals specifically to interact with those realms and entities that we know as demonic. This is where they get their power and source of unimaginable evil. American Freemasonic and occult historian Manly P. Hall wrote in *The Secret Teachings of All Ages:*

> By means of the secret processes of ceremonial magic it is possible to contact these invisible creatures and gain their help in some human undertaking. Good spirits willingly lend their assistance to any worthy enterprise, but evil spirits serve only those who live to pervert and destroy ... The most dangerous form of black magic is the scientific perversion of occult power for the gratification of personal desire.

Interacting with these 'evil spirits' and being 'possessed' by their demonic power is what elite Satanism is all about. I had correspondence some years ago, which I published in books at the time, with a man who said he was the unofficial son of the late Baron Philippe de Rothschild of the Mouton-Rothschild wine estates in France (Fig 15). He told me that his half-sister is the Baron's daughter, Baroness Philippine de Rothschild, who inherited the wine empire (see *Children of the Matrix*). He said his Rothschild name was Phillip Eugene de Rothschild and he was living in the United States under another name after fleeing the horrors of what he called the 'grand conspiracy' of his family which had given him a role of infiltrating the Christian Church for the satanic Rothschild Death Cult. This will be extremely significant later on. Phillip Eugene told me how the Rothschilds have hundreds of thousands of children produced through sperm bank breeding programmes to ensure survival and expansion of the hybrid bloodline. These children then come to power in many and various fields under different names and appear to have no genetic or other connection to the Rothschilds and bloodline families. He said that incest within the elite families was considered normal and something to be admired – something my own research has confirmed again and again. Phillip Eugene de Rothschild described the elite obsession with Satanism and its sacrifice rituals:

Figure 15: Baron Philippe de Rothschild.

I was present at my father's death in 1988, receiving his power and the commission to carry out my destiny in the grand conspiracy of my family. Like their other children, I played a key role in my family's revolt from God. When I watch CNN, it startles me to see so many familiar faces now on the world stage in politics, art, finance, fashion and business. I grew up with these people, meeting them at ritual worship sites and in the centres of power. Financiers, artists, royalty, and even Presidents ...

... I can recall the Rockefellers and the Bushes attending rituals, but never having the supremacy to lead them. I still regard them as lackeys and not real brokers of occult power. Except for Alan Greenspan [long-time head of the US Federal Reserve], most of these fellows were camp followers in the occult, primarily for the economic power and prestige. Greenspan, I recall, was a person of tremendous spiritual, occult power and could make the

Bushes and the younger Rockefellers cower with just a glance.

Ex-CIA Director Casey (as were most of the CIA leadership for the past forty years), Kissinger, and [former US Secretary of State] Warren Christopher were in attendance at non-ritual gatherings and some occult rituals as well, but well back in the gallery.

Ultra-Zionist Alan Greenspan held an incredibly powerful position as chairman between 1987 and 2006 of the Federal Reserve, a *privately*-run operation that serves as America's central bank directing the US economy with its global implications and consequences. Phillip Eugene said that others he met at rituals included Bill Clinton, who would become President of the United States, and Al Gore, Clinton's vice president who would be chosen as the elite's frontman for the global warming hoax aimed at manufacturing an excuse to transform global society with great support from the Round Table's Club of Rome. A Swiss banker described the same theme in an anonymous interview in 2011 for the Russian magazine, *NoviDen*. He said of elite bankers:

> ... These people are corrupt, sick in their minds, so sick they are full of vices and those vices are kept under wraps on their orders. Some of them ... rape women, others are sado maso, or paedophile, and many are into Satanism. When you go in some banks you see these satanistic symbols, like in the Rothschild Bank in Zurich. These people are controlled by blackmail because of the weaknesses they have. They have to follow orders or they will be exposed, they will be destroyed or even killed.

Paedophilia and Satanism are fundamentally connected and this is why so many people in positions of royal, political, corporate and religious influence are both paedophiles and Satanists. I highlight this because it provides an insight into the mentality of those in power with regard to 9/11. To these sick and perverted psychopaths 9/11 would have been a mass sacrifice ritual – just as wars are to them. I hear it said that political, military and intelligence leaders would not be evil enough to kill thousands of people that day and use the attacks to justify their agenda of wars and deletion of freedom. The truth is that those who would sacrifice children or watch them be sacrificed are hardly going to suddenly become empathetic and emotional over dead men, women and children on 9/11. Not only *would* they do it – they would be sexually aroused by it. They feed off human death and suffering and to them the death and destruction of war is something to celebrate. I have exposed many rich and famous names involved in human sacrifice, paedophilia and violent abuse of children – it is rampant at 'elite' levels of society. When you see what they will do to children and in manipulated wars of mass murder you may appreciate that the calculated killing of nearly 3,000 people on September 11th would be of no consequence to these psychopaths – for that is what they are. Robert D. Hare, a Canadian criminal psychology researcher, developed the 'Hare Test' listing the traits of psychopaths and if you have enough of them you are considered psychopathic. They include no empathy; no remorse; no shame; parasitical behaviour; pathological lying and doing whatever it takes to get what they want. I have read that psychopaths are considered to be born that way whereas sociopaths are the result of life experience. These bloodlines are largely *born* psychopaths with an incapacity to process empathy – the ability to connect with the feelings of those they adversely affect. Without empathy there is no fail-safe mechanism of human behaviour because there are no emotional consequences, no shame or remorse, no matter what you do. This is the mentality running our world and the one behind 9/11. To understand those who orchestrated the attacks you have to get into their minds and then their capability to do what they did becomes clear.

The former overtly royal and aristocratic bloodlines now employing their new dark-suit disguise set about the work of building a global structure of control that would allow for their domination of human society. They were behind the European empires of conquest and colonisation led by Britain where the centre of this assault on the world was located. The British Empire was vast because that was the centre of bloodline activities along with Rome. They remain so today in the shadows if not publicly while the spotlight has turned to America and its modern-day global empire. Bloodlines out of Britain and to an extent France invaded Native American lands and seized them as their own fiefdom. This was a pattern that happened across the world as Planet Earth became Global Babylon through colonisation and centralisation of power or what is today called globalisation. They created a money system to control and suppress choice that involves lending people 'money' that doesn't exist called 'credit' and charging interested on it. If you don't pay back the loan of fresh-air 'credit', often through no fault of your own and actions taken by bankers and financiers, those same people can take your wealth that does exist like your home, land, business and resources. By this means the bloodlines and their networks have absorbed the wealth of the world by simply exchanging non-existent 'credit' for the real wealth of the world. We haven't reached the point by accident where six people own collectively the same wealth as the poorest *half* of the human population. It's been done by design and they are far from finished yet. They want *everything*. One of their most productive scams is to issue non-existent 'credit' for the amount that you borrow, but never create even with fresh-air 'money' the amount of *interest* you will have to pay. This means that there is never ever enough money, credit or otherwise, in circulation to pay back all the principle and *interest* on the outstanding debt. Losing your home, land, business and resources is built into the system on purpose to achieve just the outcome I have described. Talk about psychopaths and parasites. Control of money means control of choice and choice means freedom. Control money in the way that society is currently structured and you go a long way to controlling freedom and dictating who has it and who doesn't. People fall for the idea that the hysterical pursuit of money by this 'elite' is all about greed, and that is true to an extent, but its bottom line is really *control*.

Permanent Government

The financial system is an essential part of the Permanent Government which by definition is a government that is always there no matter what political personality or persuasion comes and goes every few years. I have been writing about the Permanent Government for decades and now we have the widely-used term of the 'Deep State' to describe agencies of government pursuing their own agenda often at odds with that of elected officials. The Deep State consists of intelligence agencies, military personnel, law enforcement and government administration that transcend the comings and goings of politicians and work to undermine and obstruct political agendas that threaten the interests of its own. The Permanent Government, of which the Deep State is a part, also consists of the banking and financial networks, major corporations, mainstream media (and parts of the 'alternative'), legal system and courts as well as the Deep State intelligence agencies, military personnel, law enforcement and government administration (Fig 16). Weaving through all of these agencies and subject areas are the secret societies into which key players are initiated. They pledge allegiance in their initiation rituals to The Spider and The Web under various guises and this allegiance overrides any publicly-spoken pledge to the people they are supposed to represent or, in the United States, to the Constitution. Compared with this edifice of permanent power the here-today-gone-tomorrow politicians and parties are small fry controlled either

Figure 16: Structure of the Permanent Government which really dictates global events. Politicians and 'elected' governments that come and go are a hoax and diversion to protect the real rulers from exposure. The 'All-Seeing Eye' is a prime symbol used by the Hidden Hand to portray its perceived 'omnipotence'.

HYBRID BLOODLINE
SECRET SOCIETIES
FINANCE/BANKING
MILITARY/INTELLIGENCE
CORPORATIONS
GOVERNMENT ADMINISTRATION
LAW/COURTS
MEDIA
POLITICS AND ELECTED GOVERNMENTS

directly or by manipulating circumstance through the Permanent
Government and Deep State. This is why that no matter what party or
politician comes and goes the same agenda continues with them all.

The American political system is a clear and perfect example of how
the scam works in every country. There are usually two or three political
parties that have any chance of forming a government and if the
Permanent Government controls all of them it controls events whichever
one a 'democratic vote' puts temporarily in office. In America the
Republican and Democratic parties take it in turns to form the
government although it is planned for the Democrats to be permanently
in office eventually through the transformation of American
demographics. For now we have a one-party state with two masks that
claim to be independent and in opposition. The Republican Party is
controlled by a group known as the Neocons or neoconservatives (big-
time involved in the 9/11 story) that ran the Boy Bush presidency and
now dictate to Trump. The Democrats have a similar group behind the
scenes which I call the Democons. They include people like billionaire
manipulator extraordinaire George Soros. Neocons and Democons are
the Permanent Government's representatives ensuring control of the
political parties and dictating who runs for office and who doesn't.
Whether it be 'Democrat' Bill Clinton, 'Republican' Boy Bush,
'Democrat' Barack Obama or 'Republican' Donald Trump the same force
is in charge because the Neocons and Democons control the parties and
both groups answer one step deeper into the shadows to the same
Permanent Government (Fig 17). This is why no matter who you vote
into office, and no matter what they promise to do, human society

continues in the same
direction – the
direction dictated by
the Permanent
Government.
Presidents, prime
ministers, parties in
political office, just
come and go while the
Permanent
Government is always
in control. An
essential diversion is
to focus attention of
the population on the
political level of the
structure and program
perception that this is

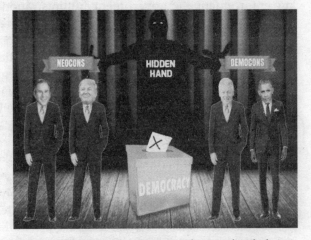

Figure 17: The one-party state masquerading as political 'choice'.
They appear to be 'different' politicians from 'different' parties –
but they answer to the same masters. This is why the direction of
the world doesn't change no matter who is in illusory political
'power'.

where the power lies to change events and direction. It isn't. The political level is largely there only for show and to officially implement in the form of legislation what the Permanent Government has decided. I read one dismissal of 9/11 conspiracy 'poison' by 'progressive' journalist David Corn at AlterNet which said that 9/11 president Boy Bush was 'not that evil', 'not that ballsy' and 'not that competent'. The level of ignorance it takes to write that sentence is breathtaking. Bush was a gofer, mate. He did not have to be that 'ballsy' and 'competent', only do what he was told and as far as possible stay out of the way – hence he was nowhere near Washington DC on 9/11 leaving Dick Cheney to control the White House.

Permanent Governments in each country are connected by The Web to form essentially a Permanent Global Government. Of course it doesn't always work as they would like with a few mavericks here and there pushing back and not everything always goes to plan. The idea is to so increase the level of control that eventually even the mavericks are squeezed and forced out. You can imagine The Web as like a transnational corporation with a corporate headquarters and subsidiaries in each country which operate in line with the centrally-dictated corporate brand, mode of working and business plan. The Web has centres of power in places like London, Rome, Paris, Berlin, Tel Aviv/Jerusalem, New York and Washington and in each country there is a subsidiary secret society network and bloodline family hierarchy whose job it is to implement in their sphere of operation the plan dictated from the centre. This is how the same things can suddenly happen all over the world pretty much at once or certainly in a close time period. The Web and the US Permanent Government were crucial in coordinating 9/11 with other Web assets, most notably the ultra-Zionist network and its military intelligence arm, Mossad, which I will come to much later in the book.

Global mind game

The numbers dynamic between manipulators and manipulated is absolutely shocking. A comparative few are controlling and directing a population of beyond 7.7 billion. This can only happen if the few control key positions of power either directly or through proxies and place people. It is remarkable how few positions you need to control to dictate events through an entire structure or system. You only have to dominate the big decision-making and hire-and-fire roles and then you can select personnel who will do what you want either through those in awareness of the game (the very few) or through compartmentalised ignorance (everyone else). Another essential is to control to the greatest extent possible the perceptions of the target population by control of information. Perceptions dictate behaviour and what people will do or not do, support or not support, challenge or leave alone, and perceptions are formed from information received. This can be through personal experience (some) or mass media (most of the rest). By controlling information you are controlling perception and through that you dictate behaviour. It is a simple cause and effect and so many people ('journalists' especially) simply believe what the authorities tell them. We have already seen classic examples of this with the response to questioning 9/11 from those 'progressive' journalists who think they are 'anti-establishment'. Perceptions are formed not only through the media but also the 'education' system in which children only four years out of the womb begin a process of perception programming throughout their entire formative years as day after day they download the state's official version of everything. The idea is to give them an initial foundation download of 'normal' which they have topped-up for the rest of their lives by the mainstream media and peer-pressure friends and associates who have been through the very same process. 'Normal' becomes a self-fulfilling prophecy in the absence of query and questions – an 'everybody knows that' when a few questions and a bit of independent research would reveal so many norms to be nonsense. September 11th is an example almost like no other. There has been a short window in the developing years of the Internet when people had access to other sources of information and this has had such an affect in changing perceptions of the world that a frenzy of censorship has been launched by Web organisations such as elite-owned Facebook, Google and Google-owned YouTube, Twitter and so on to protect official narratives from demolition by factual investigation. Justifications for this include 'fake news' (see mainstream media that isn't censored), and 'hate speech' (an Orwellian term meaning a different opinion). They had to allow the Internet to be free from censorship to start with to get people hooked and make the Internet the foundation of modern society. Now that point has been reached and Internet Web corporations have achieved near-monopolistic power they can transform the Internet into the information controller and suppressor it was always intended to be (see *Everything You Need To Know But Have Never Been Told* for the detailed background). I have noticed how Google and others make it far more difficult to locate specialist information questioning 9/11 than it did when I researched *Alice in Wonderland* in 2001 and 2002. A perfect example is the information gathering website, Reddit. Those seeking out content on Reddit exposing the official story of September 11th are met with this notice:

> Are you sure you want to view this community? This community is quarantined. It may contain a high degree of misinformation. If you are seeking historic information about the September 11th attacks, please visit the

National Commission on Terrorist Attacks on the United States (https://www.9-11commission.gov).

What a message to encapsulate the times we are living in and if anyone wants to make a statement about that they can always boycott Reddit in protest and tell them they are doing so. You will see in this book that the official 9/11 Commission 'report' on the attacks recommended by Web servants Reddit is the biggest fairy story since Cinderella. No, make that Sleeping Beauty because you have to be asleep to believe it, as American comedian George Carlin famously said of the 'American Dream'. I coined the terms 'Problem-Reaction-Solution' and the 'Totalitarian Tiptoe' for the two most used and most powerful techniques of perception manipulation. I will be brief here because I will expand on both with regard to 9/11. Problem-Reaction-Solution (P-R-S) is a term I began using in the 1990s to describe the technique that specifically creates a problem to justify a solution that would otherwise be difficult to sell. It goes like this:

(1) The Problem: Covertly create a problem that would provide the excuse for your desired 'solution' or change. This could be a terrorist attack, war, government or financial collapse or a long list of other 'problems'. Crucially you produce a fake story about who or what is behind the problem to hide the fact that it was you all along. Your fake 'villain' is designed specifically to lead to your pre-planned 'solution'. If you want to invade Afghanistan, for example, then blame Osama bin Laden based in Afghanistan for what happened on 9/11.

(2) The Reaction: Tell the public through an unquestioning mainstream media the version of the 'problem' you want them to believe and you are looking for the 'reaction' of fear, outrage and a demand that you 'do something' about what has happened. Even if people don't demand what you want to do they will be more open to it – 'We don't want our freedoms taken away but we've got to fight terrorism'.

(3) The Solution: Once you have the problem and reaction you then offer the solution through which you introduce new laws, policies and changes that advance your agenda for human control, deletion of freedoms and centralisation of power.

There is another version that I call NO-Problem-Reaction-Solution in which you don't need a real problem only the *perception* of one. Lying about weapons of mass destruction in Iraq to justify an invasion that would not otherwise have happened is a perfect example of this technique. The modus operandi of P-R-S is also known as a 'false flag' operation as with covertly carrying out a terrorist attack and then blaming the people you want to target. The partner-in-crime of P-R-S is a technique I refer to as the 'Totalitarian Tiptoe' which often connects different P-R-S events together to drive society in a particular direction. You start at 'A' and you want to go to 'Z', but you know that if you move too quickly the change will be such that many people might see the pattern of where they are being taken. So you go in steps that move you towards 'Z' at the fastest speed you can while not moving so fast that the pattern is too clear. In this way a European 'free-trade area' became step-by-step a centralised bureaucratic dictatorship called the EU. Globalisation and the deletion of freedoms, not least freedom of speech, has been achieved through the Tiptoe. You will be seeing both techniques in action with regard to 9/11.

One more thing before we proceed. I will refer to The Spider and The Web from hereon as the 'Hidden Hand' to keep it simple. I will use the term to describe any person or organisation doing The Spider's work, knowingly or otherwise.

CHAPTER 2

Rule by psychopaths

Liberty cannot be preserved without a general knowledge among the people, who have a right and a desire to know; but besides this, they have a right, an indisputable, unalienable, indefeasible, divine right to know that most dreaded and envied kind of knowledge, I mean of the characters and conduct of their rulers – John Adams

Public incredulity is a key defence mechanism protecting the Hidden Hand and its agents and gofers from exposure. This is captured in the reaction: 'They would never do that'. Oh, but they *would* and the more horrific and unspeakable the better. The Bush family is a classic case.

Point number one to stress again: Those truly behind 9/11(not 'Arab hijackers') and all the war, poverty, deprivation, hunger and human suffering of every conceivable kind are full-blown in-extremis psychopaths on a scale that is almost unfathomable for those who are not psychopathic. They have no empathy and so no limits to the depths of depravity to which they will descend. If you view those that direct and manipulate world events – in this case 9/11 – through your own sense of morality, conscience and behaviour then read no more. If you judge them through your own lens of possibility there is no way you will grasp the sheer undiluted evil that is at work among us. These people do not see the world and human beings as you do. They are what have been described through history as the 'soulless ones' and their depravity has no limits because they have no emotional or empathic consequences no matter what they do. Suffering to most of the human population is something to be avoided, but to the Hidden Hand and its operatives *maximising* suffering is the whole point of their existence. It is their very 'life-force', their energetic sustenance, and the bloodline families born into psychopathy select their foot soldiers from non-bloodline psychopaths. They constantly scan the universities and the world of business and Satanism looking for potential recruits. A re-evaluation of what evil means is urgently required to understand the forces driving human society into a global Orwellian nightmare that even Orwell himself understated.

To put this into perspective I am going to outline the background to some of the public players in the mass murder of 9/11 to give you a feel for the mentality that I'm describing. Then there will be no doubt that they *would do that* in terms of the mass murder of thousands of innocent people. I emphasise the term 'public players'. Most of those that you see with political and military titles and the calculated liars in the media were not the real architects of what happened on September 11th – as they are not the real power running America and other countries. They are merely the front men and women who play their compartmentalised parts like actors on a stage to deliver their script and then cover up what really happened. Writer David Corn, who has trashed any idea of a 9/11 conspiracy or 'inside job', personified this misunderstanding when he wrote in *Mother Jones* magazine that the Bush administration was 'not that evil', 'not that ballsy' and 'not that competent'. The idea Boy George Bush with all his intellectual limitations orchestrated 9/11 is a joke. He was just an empathy-deleted pawn, a peripheral player, to those in the shadows who *are* that evil, ballsy and competent. Clearly Corn like all the others of his ilk doesn't appreciate the difference. Political and military leaders had to *officially* make decisions that allowed 9/11 to happen because that was the law while the engineers in the shadows decided *what* decisions their puppets appeared to make. Most of the

Figure 18: Brutal Bush.

high-profile public names involved in the attacks are the oil-rags and not the engineers of 9/11. Two exceptions I would make to that are Father George Bush, the three-times President of the United States (two of them officially given to Ronald Reagan while Bush was his deputy) and Dick Cheney who was 9/11 vice president to Boy George Bush while being de-facto president the whole time alongside his bewildered and clueless official 'superior' (Fig 18 and 19). Both were the puppet-masters of Boy Bush, the little boy in short trousers way out of his depth (Fig 20). Father Bush and Cheney have appeared in my books since the 1990s for their unspeakably disgusting actions and behaviour and both give

Figure 19: Brutal Cheney.

personification to the term 'psychopath' (see *And The Truth Shall Set You Free, The Biggest Secret* and others). Neither are anywhere near the top of the hierarchy behind 9/11, but they were higher than other American politicians. Father Bush died in 2018 aged 94 and it's a pity he didn't get to read this book. Mind you, there were plenty of others I wrote exposing him before he left us for that darkest of dark places which evil calls home.

The Bush crime family (see also the Clintons)

The Bushes have been one of the most active Hidden Hand families (but still servants of the real power) since at least Father Bush's own father, the Nazi-supporting-and-funding politician and banker Prescott Bush (1895-1972). The family has produced two US presidents, both called George Bush, and I will overcome the potential confusion in the text by referring to George H.W. Bush as 'Father George' (de-facto president and official president from 1981 to 1993) and his son George W. Bush (president from 2001 to 2009) as 'Boy George'. The latter is more than appropriate because a little boy is all he was while the adults ran 'his' presidency – including the White House/Pentagon contribution to the events of September 11th, 2001. Father George and his wife Barbara were both descendants of Godfroi de Bouillon (also known as Godfrey of Bouillon) who led European noblemen in the successful Crusade in 1099 to recapture Jerusalem from Islam and then occupied the King's palace at what Christians and Jews call Temple Mount where the Al-Aqsa Mosque stands today. This is the alleged site of 'Solomon's Temple' and rebuilding this temple with its perceived twin pillars at the entrance has been a long Hidden Hand obsession going back at least to the Knights Templar in the 12th century. Plans by ultra-Zionist extremists to replace

Figure 20: Boy George Bush: 'What did you tell me say again?'

Al-Aqsa in East Jerusalem with a new Solomon's Temple are not unique to the relatively recent Rothschild-engineered Zionism movement. A new Solomon's Temple is a 'Web' ambition and moving the American Embassy from Tel Aviv to Jerusalem (Al-Quds to Muslims) in 2018 while continuing the systematic ethnic cleansing of Palestinian Arabs in East Jerusalem are stepping-stones to this end. The long obsession of the Hidden Hand with Jerusalem, Temple Mount and Solomon's Temple explains so much about the terrible events over centuries in that city and the focus on Jerusalem by Christianity, Judaism and Islam. Godfroi de Bouillon was the first ruler of Jerusalem after the First Crusade and Duke of Lower Lorraine in France which remains a major region to this day for the Hidden Hand bloodline (see *The Biggest Secret*). Boy Bush, a descendant of de Bouillon through both his mother and father, talked of a 'Crusade' against Islamic terrorism after September 11th and this was no slip of the tongue or unfortunate gaffe as reported. He knew exactly what he was saying and why (or those who told him to say it did). Godfroi de Bouillon became the first ruler of the Kingdom of Jerusalem and 20 years later the Knights Templar secret society was formed to protect Christian pilgrims visiting Jerusalem – or so it officially claimed. The Knights Templar grew into a vast network that became fantastically wealthy and established the basis for today's banking and financial system. Monarchs were in debt to them and in 1307 they were purged in France by King Philip IV ('Philip the Fair') who owed them lots of money. The Templars seemed to disappear after that, but that was only in public. They went underground in locations like Portugal and Scotland where they re-emerged on one front as the Scottish Rite of Freemasonry. Today they remain a major arm of the Hidden Hand with their initiates involved in global politics, banking, business and media. Modern-day Templars control the City of London financial district, one of the world's premier centres for manipulating the world financial system. Part of the 'City' or 'Square Mile' within the greater expanse of London is known as The Temple after the Templar's still-surviving original temple established there in the 12th century and featured in the 2006 movie, *The Da Vinci Code*. The centre of the English legal system (and in many ways the world's) is located in The Temple district on land once owned (and still controlled by) the Knights Templar. Freemasonry, the world's biggest secret society in terms of membership, largely emerged from the Knights Templar and forms a highly-significant strand in The Web. You can see that in bloodline terms the Bush family meet the criteria for positions of power which serve the agenda of the Hidden Hand although they are far from the top and today in decline.

George and Barbara Bush were from the Pierce bloodline that changed its name from Percy after fleeing England in the wake of the Gunpowder Plot of Guy Fawkes to blow up the English Parliament and kill King James I in 1605. This event is still celebrated in the UK every November 5th when effigies of Guy Fawkes are burned on bonfires. Bush ancestor Thomas Percy was one of the main plotters. George and Barbara Pierce Bush (of Merrill, Lynch, Fenner and Smith) are from the same bloodline as US President Franklin Pierce who was in the White House from 1853 to 1857. Other Bush relatives include the Grosvenor families of England and America, the Tafts of Ohio, who produced

William Howard Taft, president from 1909 to 1913, and the Delano-Roosevelts who gave us President Franklin Delano Roosevelt (in office from 1933-45) and Theodore Roosevelt (1901-1909). It's true then – *anyone* can be President of the United States! The English Grosvenors are the Dukes of Westminster who own prime properties in London and the City of London financial district. The Grosvenors of America founded National Geographic which is notorious for removing the archaeological treasures of the world, especially those with religious significance, and relocating them at the Smithsonian Institute in Washington DC. The Institute is controlled by Grosvenor cousins, the Smithsons, who in turn are descended from the Percys – the Pierce bloodline that produced the Bushes. Ancestry of both George Bushes can be traced to England's Alfred the Great and to Charlemagne, a very notable figure in the Hidden Hand bloodline story from whom the great majority of US presidents are descended. Charlemagne, also Charles the Great, was King of the Franks and then Holy Roman Emperor from 800AD. Rome was a major centre for the bloodline and remains so today. Charlemagne was a hero of Adolf Hitler. With both his father and mother having such serious royal and aristocratic ancestry Boy George has a mass of bloodline connections as documented by the bible of 'elite' genetics, *Burke's Peerage*. The Bushes are related to the British royal family who are big-time Hidden Hand.

Dark secrets galore

The bloodlines manipulate and recruit through their secret society networks and so you would expect the bloodline Bushes to be heavily involved in secret societies. They have long been pillars of the infamous Skull and Bones Society based in a windowless mausoleum known as 'the Tomb' alongside the campus at Yale University at New Haven in Connecticut (Fig 21). The skull and bones is an ancient Hidden Hand symbol and the Knights Templar were accused of using skulls in their rituals. They certainly flew the skull and bones flag on their ships which became associated with the flag of pirates. 'The Order of the Skull and Bones' was co-founded by bloodline operatives Huntington Russell and Alphonso Taft in 1832 and appears to have its origins in Germany. Elite universities have secret societies that recruit initiates to be future Hidden Hand agents to serve the agenda for human control in politics,

Figure 21: Skull and Bones Society headquarters across the street from Yale University where the elite of tomorrow, called 'Bonesmen', are initiated into the Hidden Hand network.

banking, business, military, intelligence, media, and so on. Another secret society at Yale is the Scroll and Key. Every year 15 bloodline or other elite students are initiated into the Skull and Bones Society and the ratio of 'Bonesmen' who end up in positions of power is enormous compared with the general student population. They span the arenas of politics, banking, business, media, military and intelligence agencies, both in front of the camera and behind the scenes. Father and Boy Bush were initiated into Skull and Bones and so was their father and grandfather Prescott Bush who has a particular claim to fame in The Order. He and five other Skull and Bones initiates raided and ransacked the grave of Native American Apache leader Geronimo at Fort Sill, Oklahoma, in May, 1918. They took turns to stand guard while others robbed the grave and took away artefacts and Geronimo's skull. This was taken to the Skull and Bones headquarters at Yale where it was used in their sick rituals and ceremonies. This horrible story is told in an internal history of the Skull and Bones Society and was quoted to Ned Anderson, Tribal Chairman of the San Carlos Apache tribe, when he was negotiating to have Geronimo's remains returned to tribal custody. A 1989 article in *The New Yorker* said: 'One Bonesman ... recalled during the early 70s seeing perhaps 30 skulls, not all of them human, scattered about the Tomb.' Initiates of university and other secret societies pledge allegiance to the goals of the secret society above all else – and this includes those that become President of the United States or head of the CIA. The public they supposed to be serving are irrelevant compared with their allegiance to their 'Order' which, in turn, locks into The Web. Initiation rituals for new members of Skull and Bones involve lying naked in a coffin within 'The Tomb' headquarters and spilling your sexual secrets to all assembled. Chanting is also part of the ritual as the initiate is taken out of the coffin, clothed in a symbol-festooned robe and said to be 're-born' into the Society. This is what Father and Boy Bush would have been through before going on to be US president. Such is the mentality of the people running our world and in power at the time of 9/11. The presidential 'election' in 2004 was between Skull and Bones Boy Bush and Skull and Bones John Kerry – the statistical chances of that with so few Bonesmen in the American population are absolutely fantastic (Fig 22).

Redwood rituals

Bush family men have a long association with the diabolical rituals performed by Hidden Hand bloodlines and lackeys every summer at Bohemian Grove, a ritual and sexual playground for leading American and foreign politicians, mobsters, bankers, businessmen, media owners and editors, top entertainers, etc., who are Hidden Hand initiates or serve the agenda in some form. Bohemian Grove is located in 2,700 acres

Figure 22: The 2004 Skull and Bones election for US President between Boy Bush and John Kerry. The one-party state personified.

Figure 23: Ronald Reagan and Richard Nixon either side of the speaker at the 'elite playground' of Bohemian Grove in a picture dated 1947. This was taken long before either became President of the United States. Presidents are not elected by the public – they are chosen by the Hidden Hand. Yes, including Trump.

of very secluded redwood forest near the hamlet of Monte Rio in Sonoma County, 75 miles north of San Francisco. Attendees have included presidents Father Bush, Boy Bush, Jimmy Carter, Bill Clinton, Ronald Reagan, Richard Nixon, (Fig 23); 9/11 vice president Dick Cheney; Secretaries of State Henry Kissinger, George Shultz, Casper Weinberger and Bush family crony, James Baker; Alexander Haig, former US Defense Secretary; Alan Greenspan, long-time head of the Hidden Hand's Federal Reserve and 'a person of tremendous spiritual, occult power'; David Rockefeller, grandson of Standard Oil tycoon J. D. Rockefeller and Hidden Hand manipulator for most of his life who was responsible for the building of the World Trade Center; Walter Cronkite, television news anchor; David Gergen, author and adviser to presidents for 30 years and editor-at-large at *US News and World Report*; newspaper tycoon William Randolph Hearst and presidents of major media operations like CNN and Associated Press. Dirk Mathison, San Francisco bureau chief of *People* magazine sneaked into the Grove three times in July, 1991. On the third occasion he was recognised by an executive of Time Warner which owned the magazine and he was thrown out and the story suppressed. Mathison said that John Lehman, a former Secretary of the Navy, delivered a lecture at the Grove which revealed how the Pentagon estimated 200,000 Iraqis had been killed a few months earlier in the US-Iraq Gulf War – a figure not made public. Another speaker was Al Neuharth, founder of American daily, *USA Today*, who was identified in the official programme as chairman of the

Freedom Forum – a $700-million foundation
dedicated to a 'free press'.

Whistleblower Cathy O'Brien was held
captive in US government mind control
programmes for 30 years (see *The Biggest
Secret*) and she describes in her book, *Trance-
Formation of America*, how she and her fellow
mind-slaves were forced to serve the
perversions of their famous abusers at
Bohemian Grove (Fig 24). These included
satanic rituals, child sacrifices, torture and
blood drinking. I have known Cathy since

Figure 24: Cathy O'Brien.

1996 and spoken to her and her late partner Mark Phillips at great length
about her experiences in an 'elite' mind control programme called
Project Monarch (after the butterfly which symbolises part of the brain).
Monarch was an offshoot of the publicly-exposed MKUltra which was
(and still is under other names) a huge CIA-military operation to
develop techniques of mind control and 'Manchurian candidates' that
would carry out assassinations and other horrors when programmed to
do so. MKUltra involved some 80 institutions, including universities,
and was overseen by the CIA's Office of Scientific Intelligence working
with military organisations like the US Army Biological Warfare
Laboratories. Drugs, sensory deprivation, hypnosis, torture, sexual
abuse and other violence were inflicted upon adults and children to
make them literally lose their minds. Prison inmates were used in drug
experimentation and even dogs. The unspeakable abuse of children in
MKUltra and Project Monarch is testament to the level of psychopathy
that drives the Hidden Hand and was at work on 9/11. President Gerald
Ford, who was involved in MKUltra, appointed his vice president
Nelson Rockefeller (also involved) to head an 'inquiry' into the project in
the 1970s when it was exposed to public attention. The idea was to have
the 'Rockefeller Commission' appear to reveal what happened while
covering up the most extreme aspects of it. Father George Bush, Dick
Cheney and the Clintons were seriously involved in the abuse of
MKUltra and Monarch mind-slaves long after the projects officially
ended with the emphasis in Father Bush's case on *children*. Still more
details of this horrendous programme came to light in 2018 through
documents released under the Freedom of Information Act.

Cathy O'Brien says of Bohemian Grove in her book: 'Slaves of
advancing age or with failed programming were ritually murdered at
random in the wooded grounds of the Grove and I felt it was only a
matter of time before it would be me.' She says the Grove has a number
of rooms for different perversions, including a Dark Room, Leather
Room, Necrophilia Room (sex with dead bodies) and one known as the

Figure 25: The 40-foot stone owl at Bohemian Grove is symbolic of both the Babylonian goddess and the ancient god Moloch or Molech to whom children were sacrificed in fire. Moloch/ Molech is also a symbol of Saturn which is a focus of Hidden Hand satanic rituals.

Underground Lounge, spelt as U.N.derground on the sign. I know this sounds seriously far out to peoples' 'normal' sense of reality, but you will see the enormous evidence to support all this if you read *The Biggest Secret, Children of the Matrix* and many books by other researchers and victims. The bloodlines have been involved in sickening human sacrifice rituals since Babylon and before and this still continues in secret and on a scale that beggars belief. Robed and hooded men conduct the opening ritual at Bohemian Grove standing alongside a large fire and a 40-foot stone owl – symbolic of the Babylonian goddess and also with male 'god' symbolism relating to Moloch or Molech to whom children were sacrificed by fire in ancient times (Fig 25). Molech is mentioned several times in the Old Testament as in Jeremiah 32:35: 'They built the high places of Baal in the Valley of the Son of Hinnom, to offer up their sons and daughters to Molech, though I did not command them, nor did it enter into my mind, that they should do this abomination, to cause Judah to sin.' These world famous initiates at Bohemian Grove burn and sacrifice a human 'effigy' under the owl at the start of their 'summer camp' every year during a Babylonian-type ritual called Cremation of Care. Put 'Bohemian Grove' into YouTube and you will see footage of the owl ritual filmed secretly by talk show host Alex Jones. The film clearly shows the bizarre opening ritual and the sound quality is particularly good. At one point an 'effigy' is floated on a boat across the lake at Bohemian Grove where it is placed under the giant owl and set on fire. At this point you hear very clearly a bloodcurdling scream and one of two things are happening here. They are either sacrificing a human being in the guise of an 'effigy' or they broadcast the sound of the scream of agony as part of the ceremony. Either way, these are the people running our world. Jones was too far away to see if the sacrifice was an 'effigy' or real, but human sacrifice rituals go on among the elite of the elite in much more secret and secluded locations during the 'camp'. Boy Bush is a Bohemian Grove member like his father and grandfather were and he arrived at the Grove in 2000 shortly after the Jones video was shot.

Skull and Bones drug network

Among the most important functions of the Bush family and Skull and Bones Society has been circulating drugs like cocaine and heroin on the streets of America and around the world. Global trade in drugs, weapons and children are orchestrated from the shadows by Hidden Hand families along with Satanism and paedophilia. The vehicle for all these crimes against humanity are the global secret society networks which lock into government, military, intelligence agencies, law enforcement and the rest of the Permanent Government. Drug-trafficking generates incredible amounts of money to spend on secret so-called 'black budget' projects (including 9/11) and this doesn't appear in official government and military bookkeeping. Another source of funding is simply to make trillions in the US military budget disappear and then have a 'terrorist attack' strike the very offices at the Pentagon where civilian accountants were seeking to track the trillions. In doing so all evidence of what you have done is destroyed. This is what happened on 9/11 as we shall see and news of the missing trillions was announced by the Pentagon on September 10th, 2001, because of what they knew was coming the following day to divert attention. Very wealthy aristocratic and other Hidden Hand bloodline families in Britain and the United States launched the global drug trade and they still control it with the Bushes and Clintons – drug and business associates not political 'opponents' – very much involved in the United States before and across 9/11. Hidden Hand drug networks use their government agencies to 'bust' the opposition and leave the field clear for themselves. This is worth remembering when you hear reports of a 'big drug find' or some villain or network exposed for trafficking. The real players never get caught because they control law 'enforcement' and intelligence agencies. The Hidden Hand drug-running network destroys lives on a monumental scale and creates fear and divide and rule through the division and crime generated by those who rob and steal in a desperate attempt to feed their addiction. This in turn justifies greater police powers and deletions of freedom and privacy to 'fight' the problem that has been systematically created.

The Skull and Bones Society is owned by the Russell Trust which is controlled by the drug-running Russell bloodline family. They flew the skull and bones flag on their ships as they transported drugs for the British Empire from Turkey to China and elsewhere during the Opium Wars of the 19th century. Samuel Russell (1789-1862), an American 'entrepreneur', launched Russell and Company in 1824 and within seven years it had absorbed the Perkins opium syndicate based in Boston. Russell's head of operations in Canton, China, was Warren Delano Jr, grandfather of Franklin Delano Roosevelt, a Bush family relative and US President during the Second World War. Roosevelt was also a cousin of fellow wartime leader, British Prime Minister, Winston Churchill. Other famous families (Hidden Hand bloodline) were partners in the Russell drug network – names like Coolidge, Forbes, Perkins, Low and Sturgis. In the background behind all of them was the ever-dominant force and overseers of The Web at one level, the House of Rothschild. Railroad magnate John Murray Forbes (1813-1898) was involved with the drug-running Russell and Company and he was the great-grand uncle of American politician, John Forbes Kerry, who was Secretary of State to the fraud, Barack Obama, during the ongoing 'war on terror' that followed 9/11. Kerry is descended from a line of Austro-Hungarian Jewish immigrants and ran against Boy Bush in the 'Skull and Bones' presidential election of 2004. Both were asked during their election campaigns about the Skull and Bones connection, but they refused to go there. It was a 'secret', they said. *What* – a secret from the American people you are asking to vote for you?? Yes, *especially* them. A member of the public who stood up at an event to ask Kerry about his Skull and Bones membership was Tasered by police and thrown out. If you are new to all this perhaps you are now getting a feel for how the world really works and how something like 9/11 could be both pulled off and the truth hidden.

Bush and Kerry are not rare examples of the connection between Skull and Bones and positions of power. Skull and Bonesmen and initiates of other secret societies are strategically placed across the range of influential positions including the law and judiciary. Henry Stimson, US Secretary of War for the whole of World War II, was a Bonesman and so were Henry Luce, founder and publisher of *Time, Life, Fortune, and Sports Illustrated*; Frederick W. Smith, founder of FedEx; Harold Stanley, co-founder of Morgan Stanley and families that have dominated American politics, business, banking, and covert intelligence operations – the Rockefellers, Harrimans, Tafts, Lords, Kelloggs, Goodyears, Whitneys, Vanderbilts, Bundys, Sloanes, Perkins and others. Skull and Bones initiates have always had a very close association with the US intelligence community and they include the infamous James Jesus Angleton and Father George Bush. Angleton was a major figure in the creation of the CIA structure after the agency was formed in 1947 under Nazi supporter Allen Dulles and he specialised in liaising with Israel's Mossad and Shin Bet intelligence agencies. Both will become prominent in the 9/11 story much later on. Bonesman Father George Bush was Director of the Central Intelligence Agency between 1976 and 1977 before becoming the 41st President of the United States. He was replaced by his drug-running associate, oops, sorry, political opponent, Bill Clinton, president between 1993 and 2001 when Boy Bush took over for the next eight years during which came 9/11 and the 'war on terror' justified by 9/11. This is clearly all just another coincidence and nothing to worry about. I'll come to the Bush-Clinton drug operation in more detail shortly. Clinton was a member of DeMolay International, an organisation for men 'of *good character*' between 12 and 21 which is named after Knights Templar Grand Master Jacques de Molay who was burned to death during the Templar purge in France in the early 14th century. Walt Disney was another DeMolay member.

Prescott Bush, funder of Hitler, and Rockefeller 'race-purity'

Prescott Bush, father and grandfather to the Bush presidents, was a Senator for Connecticut, home of the Skull and Bones Society. He was a golf partner of President Dwight D. Eisenhower, a military man who, like 9/11 Secretary of State Colin Powell, enjoyed a fantastic rise to prominence because of his Hidden Hand sponsors; but Eisenhower disappeared from view after he warned about the dangers to freedom posed by the 'Military-Industrial Complex' (the Hidden Hand) in the closing days of his presidency. Prescott Bush was a keen and active supporter of the eugenics (master race) movement along with his bloodline associates, the Rockefellers and Harrimans. This clique led by the Rockefellers and ultimately by the Rothschilds funded the work of Adolf Hitler's race 'purity' expert, Ernst Rudin. Their money allowed Rudin to occupy an entire floor at the Kaiser Wilhelm Institute for Genealogy and Demography in Berlin. Soon after Hitler had abolished elections and become dictator of Germany in 1933, the Rockefeller-funded, Bush and Harriman-supported, Dr Rudin was commissioned to write the Law for the Prevention of Hereditary Diseases in Posterity which involved the forced sterilisation of anyone considered genetically inferior. President Father George's enthusiastic funding of 'population control' programmes was another modern example of this family obsession. The detailed and sickening story of the master race movement supported by the Bushes, Harrimans and Rockefellers (with the Rothschilds) is told in *And The Truth Shall Set You Free*. Both sides in the World Wars were funded by the same people via Hidden Hand-controlled Wall Street and the City of London financial district. Prescott Bush supported eugenics and Hitler's crazed master race 'philosophy' and helped to fund the Nazi war machine. He brought up his son with the same psychopathic mentality as his own and ditto with Father Bush and his sons including the 9/11 president. Wars are instigated to transform society and create the excuse and opportunity to centralise global power through the Problem-Reaction-Solution perception manipulation technique. Nations are manipulated into conflict and all sides funded until the status quo is destroyed and another status quo – the Hidden Hand's version – can replace it. This is what the two world wars of the 20th century and endless other conflicts have really been about – transforming societies and the world map in ways that are

irreversible. See also Afghanistan, Iraq, Libya, Syria and the post-9/11
'war on terror'. Prescott Bush helped to finance Hitler to this end
through a company run by German Nazi-funder Fritz Thyssen called the
Union Banking Corporation (UBC). Thyssen, a German steel
entrepreneur and banker, was funding the Nazis from the early 1920s.
His banking operation in Germany was affiliated through a subsidiary
with the W.A. Harriman Company in New York (Brown Brothers
Harriman after 1933), which in turn was funded by the House of
Rothschild. The Harriman family was also prominent in supporting the
Russian Revolution, Adolf Hitler and the master race insanity of the
eugenics movement. E. Roland Harriman (Skull and Bones Society) was
on the board of Fritz Thyssen's Union Banking Corporation in the US
along with known Nazis and Nazi financial backers. Prescott Bush was
also on the UBC board and owed his wealth to the Harrimans. The trio
of Brown Brothers Harriman, the Sullivan and Cromwell law firm,
headed by Rockefeller cousin John Foster Dulles, and the Union Banking
Corporation of Prescott Bush and George Herbert Walker (Father
George's grandfather) represented the interests of Nazi business cartels
in the United States at the time of the Second World War. The golf
trophy, the Walker Cup, is named after Father Bush's Nazi-supporting
grandfather. John Foster Dulles would become US Secretary of State
while his brother, Allen, was the first head of the CIA. In 1942 the US
government seized UBC assets under the Trading with the Enemy Act
and stopped George Walker and Prescott Bush pouring money into
Hitler's regime – at least in theory. Eight days later two other Bush-
managed companies, the Holland-American Trading Corporation and
the Seamless Steel Equipment Corporation, were seized for the same
reason. These were followed by another Bush-Harriman operation, the
Silesian-American Corporation. Thanks to their Hidden Hand
connections they were able to not only avoid prosecution, but secured a
massive pay-out when the bank was liquidated.

The Bush-Nazi connection was highlighted by John Loftus, president
of the Florida Holocaust Museum, who pointed out that Prescott Bush
derived a portion of his personal fortune from his affiliation with a Nazi-
controlled bank. Loftus, a former prosecutor in the [In]Justice
Department's Nazi War Crimes Unit, confirmed that Prescott Bush was a
principal in the Union Banking Corporation in Manhattan in the 1930s
and 40s, and that leading Nazi industrialists secretly owned the bank at
the time. Loftus said they were moving money into the UBC through a
second bank in Holland even after the United States declared war on
Germany. He said the bank was liquidated in 1951 and Boy Bush's
grandfather and great-grandfather received $1.5 million as part of that
dissolution. Loftus said he possessed a file of paperwork linking the
bank and Prescott Bush to Nazi money. 'That's where the Bush family

fortune came from: it came from the Third Reich,' Loftus said in a speech during the Sarasota Reading Festival. He documented in his book, *Unholy Trinity: The Vatican, The Nazis and the Swiss Banks*, how Swiss bank accounts harboured funds confiscated from concentration camp victims and the involvement of Italian priests in smuggling Nazi war criminals to safe havens in Canada, Central and South America and the United States after the war. This is also detailed in the earlier *And The Truth Shall Set You Free*, which, like Loftus, exposes the Nazi connections of other prominent American Hidden Hand families, including the Rockefellers and Kennedys in the form of Nazi-supporting Joseph Kennedy, the father of President JFK. Nancy Krauss, a member of the audience who heard Loftus in Florida, said:

> I am absolutely shocked. I wish this would have come out before the election. My husband voted for Bush. I don't think he would have voted for him if he would have known.

If people knew what the Bush family had really done – and did with regard to 9/11 and other human catastrophes – they would all have long been in jail with the key hurled into a very deep ocean. Hidden Hand control of the mainstream media and the clueless and gutless nature of the great majority of alleged 'journalists' has protected them and their Web associates from widespread exposure. Another important question here is why the Zionist and Nazi-hunter organisations and networks have never sought to expose the Bush family for their Nazi funding and support for Hitler's race-purity programme when all you have to do – especially these days – is to factually expose the government of Israel to be instantly labelled a 'Nazi', 'anti-Semite' and 'Holocaust denier'. There is a simple answer to that, however. Those calculated slurs are used by the inner core of ultra-extremist Zionism and its gofers and agents to silence exposure and opposition while the Bush family and so many other bloodline families have served the interests of the ultra-Zionist (Hidden Hand, Web) agenda and so they get away with supporting Hitler and his race purity insanity. It is essential to understand the ultra-Zionist modus operandi that the inner core has as much contempt for Jewish people as they do for everyone else. They are there to serve the Web, not Jewish people. I will be explaining much more about this in due course. The two totally manipulated World Wars cost the lives of an estimated more than 120 million people if you include deaths from war-related disease and famine. More than 60 million were civilians. Hey, but 'they would never do that' to 3,000 more on 9/11, right? The Second World War came to a close with the atomic bombs dropped on Hiroshima and Nagasaki in 1945 after which Japan surrendered on the same terms they had offered before the nuclear strikes which killed

105,000 after impact and who knows how many since through the effects of radiation? The order to drop the bombs came from President Harry S. Truman, a Freemason and Rockefeller cousin. Truman was also the first world leader to recognise the State of Israel under Jewish rule amid extreme levels of terrorism that caused 750,000 Palestinians to flee their homeland never to return. Truman did this despite opposition from his own administration and while the United Nations was discussing other options. The need to drop those bombs on Japan related to the next stage of the long-planned Hidden Hand sequence of events to transform human society into a global fascist/communist tyranny – the Cold War. This would be founded on the fear of nuclear destruction and that would be far easier if the public had experience of what atomic bombs can do rather than trying to sell a concept that had never been seen. These are real nice people and the very psychopathic mentality that orchestrated 9/11.

Funding the Russian Revolution

The sequence of events to change the face of global society is planned long in advance of each stage and ahead of the Cold War had to come the creation of 'the Baddy' in the form of the Soviet Union. Once again the same bloodline crowd was involved. The Harriman family and their close associate, Prescott Bush, helped to fund the Russian Revolution. E. Roland Harriman was the brother of W. Averill Harriman (Skull and Bones Society), a director of a company called the Guaranty Trust when it was financing Lenin and Trotsky to trigger the Russian Revolution (another Hidden Hand Problem-Reaction-Solution). Half the board members of Brown Brothers Harriman and their fellow Russian Revolution financers, J.P. Morgan, were Skull and Bones initiates. Roland Harriman, Prescott Bush and Percy Rockefeller were in the same Bonesmen group. Global manipulator Averill Harriman, the Henry Kissinger of his day, would later make big profits from Russian ventures and be appointed US ambassador to the Soviet Union to advance Hidden Hand interests there. American and Soviet governments were on different 'sides' in the 'Cold War'? Not at the Hidden Hand level they weren't. It was all yet another game to dupe the people. Averill Harriman was a controlling voice in the Democratic Party and dictator to President Franklin Delano Roosevelt of the drug-running Hidden Hand bloodline related to the Bushes. Harriman's wife, Pamela, who died while US ambassador to Paris in 1997, was extremely influential in Bill Clinton's rise to the presidency and he made her ambassador to France as a pay-back. In turn, her husband, Averill, a 'Democrat', was very much a mentor to Prescott Bush and the Bush family in general who were 'Republicans'. As one headline at the time of Bill Clinton's run for president put it: 'Bush Camp Finances Clinton Campaign.' The

United States, as with the UK and other countries, is a one-party state masquerading as a free society. Whoever you vote for the same government gets in – the Hidden Hand Permanent Government. Pamela Harriman was also married to Randolph Churchill, son of Britain's wartime Prime Minister, Winston Churchill (bloodline and cousin to Franklin Roosevelt) and she had affairs with the Italian Fiat boss Giovanni Agnelli (bloodline and Hidden Hand operative) and Baron Elie de Rothschild (bloodline and Hidden Hand operative) among a string of others. When you move in Hidden Hand circles, it is a very small world. The network of support for the Russian Revolution in the United States that I have described was a subordinate group controlled by the House of Rothschild and I will come to their central involvement in the revolution and the connection to 9/11 later in the book.

Father George – the psychopath's psychopath (one of so many)

This was the background into which George Herbert Walker Bush – Father George – arrived in this world on June 12th, 1924. He was groomed from birth to serve the Hidden Hand in a long list of roles, including US Ambassador to the United Nations, Chairman of the Republican Party at the time of the Watergate hearings, Director of the CIA, and Vice President and President of the United States. The Herbert Walker in his name comes from his grandfather, George Herbert Walker (Skull and Bones Society), who was heavily involved with Prescott Bush in the funding of the Russian Revolution, expansion of the eugenics movement and Adolf Hitler. Wherever you look in Father Bush's life you find bloodline operatives, human sacrificing Satanists, child abusers and orchestrators of genocide. Father Bush was all of these, as my books and others have long detailed. He was very much a power behind the throne during the 9/11 presidency of his son along with Daddy Bush's long-time friend and associate Dick Cheney who was his Defense Secretary during the 1991 Gulf War and would be vice president (de-facto president) during the reign of Boy George. Cathy O'Brien was designated to 'serve' Bush and Cheney during the Reagan and Bush presidencies and told me how Boy George was treated as little more than a 'make-the-tea' servant to his father and Cheney while he was growing up. Well, trying to. One of Boy Bush's roles was to get his father home in often paralytic drunken states. The same dynamic continued when Boy Bush was president – he was the tea-maker and gofer for Cheney and his dad – and that included what happened before, during and after the attacks of September 11th.

I will summarise here just a few of the crimes against humanity inflicted by Father George Bush and his dominant partner and fellow genocidal maniac, the ultra-Zionist Rothschild/Rockefeller asset, Henry Kissinger. It will give you further confirmation of the true mentality behind September 11th and the subsequent 'war on terror'. Bush served the Hidden Hand in China while Kissinger and the Chinese were supporting Pol Pot in the genocidal war on Cambodia that led to the extermination of millions of Cambodians. Bush returned home in 1975 when he received a telegram from Kissinger saying that he was being nominated by President Ford (Kissinger in other words) to be Director of the CIA. Bush held the post in 1976 and 1977 and he has been so fundamentally involved in CIA activities officially and unofficially that in 1999 its headquarters compound at Langley, Virginia, was named the George Bush Center for Intelligence. The CIA is part of the so-called 'Inner Fed' of the secret government or 'Deep State' that consists of the CIA, National Security Agency, FBI, NASA and the Federal Reserve 'Central Bank of America'. Through 'umbrella' network structures like the 'Inner Fed' a coordinated policy and response can be conducted between apparently unconnected agencies and organisations. Much of the funding of this cartel of manipulation in secret projects comes from its involvement in the drugs trade. Father Bush was not new to the intelligence game and his connections with the CIA would appear to go back to the 1950s or even much earlier given the Skull and Bones Society connection to the US intelligence community. Among Bush's CIA operatives in South America was the infamous Nazi 'Butcher of Lyon', Klaus Barbie, who had escaped from Europe thanks to US (Hidden Hand) intelligence. It was he who masterminded the so-called 'cocaine-coup' in Bolivia in June, 1980, and used the profits from CIA-supported drug networks to finance the neo-Nazi overthrow of the government in Argentina. Mike Levine, a former US Drug Enforcement agent, said the coup was achieved by troops wearing Nazi armbands. The contacts George Bush made at the CIA would be invaluable when he became vice president to Ronald Reagan in January, 1981. Reagan's personal fortune dated from a time shortly after becoming Governor of California when he bought some land cheaply and sold it at a massive profit to a group of benefactors who have never been publicly identified. Reagan, a former B-movie actor, was a long-time member of Bohemian Grove and an initiate of the Knights of Malta, another very significant strand in The Web. Reagan was 70, the oldest man to be inaugurated as President. His mind was failing and he needed long afternoon naps each day. Almost everything Reagan said, even in relatively off-the-cuff situations when greeting foreign leaders, was written for him by his aides on cue cards. Father Bush was president in all, but name.

Iran-Contra

It was strictly illegal under US law for the government to supply arms to Iran or to fund and arm the Nicaraguan 'freedom fighters' (terrorists) called the Contras in their war with the Sandinista government. It was certainly illegal to accept payment with drugs in return. The Reagan-Bush administration would do all of these things. They would fund the Contras through Honduras in an operation involving Oliver North, an official of the National Security Council. On January 18th, 1985, the Bush-appointed Felix Rodriguez is known to have met his namesake (but not thought to be a relative), Ramon Milian Rodriguez, an accountant and money launderer who worked for the Medellin drug cartel. This meeting was confirmed by Felix Rodriguez and reported in the *Miami Herald* on June 30th, 1987. From his cell in Butner, North Carolina, Ramon told investigative journalist, Martha Honey:

> …[Felix offered] … in exchange for money for the Contra cause he would use his influence in high places to get the [cocaine] cartel US goodwill … Frankly, one of the selling points was that he could talk directly to Bush. The issue of goodwill wasn't something that was going to go through 27 bureaucratic hands. It was something that was directly between him and Bush.

This could easily be done given that Felix Rodriguez was working from Bush's office. A memo in early September, 1986, sent to Oliver North by retired Army Major General John K. Singlaub, said that Felix Rodriguez was talking of having 'daily contact' with Bush's office and this could damage President Reagan and the Republican Party. Oliver North would write in his notebook: 'Felix has been talking too much about the VP [Vice President].' Former *CBS News* producer Leslie Cockburn presents devastating evidence in her 1987 book, *Out Of Control*, of Bush's involvement in Iran-Contra and drug running. She says that planes chartered by the CIA and packed with cocaine flew directly into the Homestead Air Force Base in Florida using a CIA code signal. Drug-running through Florida will enter the 9/11 story later with alleged leader 'hijacker', Mohamed Atta. Colonel Albert Carone, who was later murdered, said in a sworn statement that he remembered seeing Oliver North make more than 20 entries in his diary detailing how drug profits were being used to buy weapons for the Contras. Carone said that an entry for July 5th, 1985, noted that '$14 million to buy arms came from drugs'. North was made president of the influential US National Rifle Association in 2018 and was acclaimed as a 'national hero'. Cathy O'Brien writes in *Trance-Formation of America* that she witnessed drug parties in which the drug-running North was among the guests. The Reagan-Bush administration admitted in 1986 that Adolfo 'Popo' Chamorro's Nicaraguan Contras, terrorists supported by the CIA, were helping a Colombian drug-trafficker to transport drugs into the United States. Testimony by John Stockwell, a former high-ranking CIA official, revealed that drug smuggling was an essential component of the

CIA operation with the Contras. North was up to his neck in this. George Morales, one of South America's biggest traffickers, testified that he was approached in 1984 to fly weapons to the Contras. In return, he says, the CIA helped him to smuggle thousands of kilos of cocaine into the United States via an airstrip on the ranch of John Hull, a self-confessed CIA agent and associate of Oliver North. As Michael Ruppert, a former drugs specialist with the Los Angeles Police Department, said:

> The CIA and Ronald Reagan and [CIA Director] Bill Casey and vice president George Bush were running the whole operation, we know that now. They circumvented the will of Congress and there was an explosion of drug trafficking all throughout Central America, coordinated by the CIA.

Meanwhile, the other aspect of Iran-Contra was continuing to illegally trade arms for American hostages held by Iran and Oliver North was heavily involved again. Weapons were being shipped via close associates in Israel. Release of hostages was explained in part by the efforts of Terry Waite, the representative of Britain's Archbishop of Canterbury. 'Negotiator' Waite was being used without his knowledge by North who was quite happy for him to take the credit for the release of hostages when, in fact, they were the result of illegal arms sales. Waite would eventually as a consequence be taken hostage himself. Father Bush was telling the American people throughout all of this: 'We will make no concessions to terrorists' – just as his son said after 9/11. Father Bush negotiated with the Iranians even before Reagan was elected to delay release of hostages until after the presidential election of 1980 to ensure that Jimmy Carter, the sitting tenant, would not get the kudos before polling day. This worked so perfectly that 52 hostages flew out of Iran after 444 days in captivity minutes after Reagan was inaugurated. No doubt the promise of arms sales to Iran by a future Reagan-Bush administration was fundamental to the deal. I know it's hard for us to imagine how anyone could coldly ensure that American hostages would spend months longer in captivity just to serve a political agenda, but that's the mentality we are dealing with here – the same mentality that was behind September 11th and what followed. The Iran-Contra scandal blew in late 1986 and Ronald Reagan had to admit some, though only some, of what was happening. He said:

> A few months ago I told the American people I did not trade arms for hostages. My heart and my best intentions still tell me that is true but the facts and evidence tell me it is not.

Put another way – I lied. Father Bush should have been bang-to-rights for his involvement in Iran-Contra with the evidence so overwhelming, but I want to highlight how he got away with it because this will be useful later in appreciating how the true perpetrators of 9/11 could have been protected from exposure and a prison cell for life. On October 5th, 1986, a plane left the Ilopango Air Base in El Salvador with arms and ammunition for the Contra terrorists in Nicaragua. The flight had been coordinated by officials within George Bush's office. As the plane came low to make the drop, it was grounded by a Sandinista missile. Three people died in the crash while cargo handler Eugene Hasenfus parachuted into the hands of the Sandinistas. Bush was alerted in a call to his office by his long-time friend, drug-runner and assassin Felix Rodriguez. The truth was out. Or some of it was. The power of the Hidden Hand network can be the only explanation for how, despite the overwhelming evidence against him, Father Bush evaded prosecution even though Buz Sawyer, the pilot of the crashed plane, was found to have Bush's private office phone number in his pocket. Hasenfus also stated that Father Bush knew about the whole thing. Bush denied involvement or knowledge of what happened. Subordinates like Donald Regan, Admiral John Poindexter, Oliver North, Robert McFarlane, and Major General Richard Secord, were sacrificed and scapegoated instead. They were very much involved, but Bush got away with it, as did Reagan and his Secretary of Defense Casper Weinberger. North, who was up to his eyes in the intrigue, faced hearings with other small-fry and staggeringly emerged in the eyes of many as an American hero. Bush still had a problem, however, with former Defense Secretary Casper Weinberger, who was indicted with others in 1992 for lying to Congress over what happened. This could have been disastrous for Bush with his presidency coming to an end and so he pardoned Weinberger and the others to ensure there would be no trial. The pardon came on Christmas Eve, 1992, in the dying days of his presidency after he had lost the November election to Bill Clinton and a matter of weeks before Weinberger and company were due to face a trial that would have implicated Bush. The presidency passed from Father Bush to Clinton in January, 1993, who continued the cover-up because – as I expose at length in *And The Truth Shall Set You Free* – he was also involved with the Contra drug operations in Arkansas when he was Governor. It is actually possible to coordinate a drug-running and arms-running operation from the White House and get away with it. Where were the media while all this was going on? Nowhere as usual – with rare exceptions. One proper reporter, Gary Webb at the San Jose Mercury News, did have the guts to expose how the CIA and the Father Bush-controlled White House had poured crack cocaine into African-American communities to raise money for the Contras and create more addiction and the consequences that follow. Webb and his newspaper were not only attacked by the authorities when the stories appeared. At the frontline of condemnation were their fellow 'journalists' and major papers like the Hidden Hand-owned *Washington Post, New York Times*, and *Los Angeles Times*. The United States was convicted by the World Court in 1986 for its war crimes against Nicaragua and later faced censure for its actions against the people of Panama; but nothing happened. Governments claim immunity for colossal crimes while holding the 'little people' to account for minor ones.

The Gulf War

At the time of 9/11 in 2001 we had the Bush family in the White House, Dick Cheney as Vice President, Colin Powell as Secretary of State, and a United States international 'coalition' went to war in the Middle/Near East. In 1991 the Bush family was in the White House, Cheney was Defense Secretary, Powell was head of the US forces as Chairman of the Joint Chiefs of Staff and a United States international 'coalition' went to war in the Middle East. The 1991 Gulf War was over a border dispute between Iraq and Kuwait. Father Bush sent US forces – or a 'UN coalition', including the UK – to intervene in what was called Operation Desert Storm. Add together the casualties from the initial conflict in 1991, the brutal sanctions that followed and the 2003 US invasion and Iraqi casualties were numbered in millions. What happened during the Gulf War and after offers clear insight into the mentality later involved in 9/11 and the 'war of terror' and how 'they *would* do that'. First of all, the Gulf War wasn't exactly a war. My understanding of a 'war' is that you need two sides and under that definition the Gulf War was not a 'war'. It was the military equivalent of putting Mike Tyson in the ring with your granny. American soldiers have described this 'war' as a 'turkey shoot' which is precisely what it was. The Iraqi army, mainly conscripts who had no choice, may have been armed over the years by the US and Britain, but it was still like trying to stop an elephant with a pop gun. While the media was showed us pictures provided by the US military of 'smart bombs' that could target a building and go through a toilet window a very different reality was happening beyond the military censors. At least 93 percent of the bombs that rained down were not 'smart' – that's according to the Pentagon's own numbers – and 70 percent missed their military target. Writer Wade Frazier's excellent study of the Gulf 'War' revealed the background to just one of the devices used against the Iraqi people:

> The [fuel-air] bomb works thus: there are two detonations; the first spreads a fine mist of fuel into the air, turning the area [about the size of a football field] into an explosive mix of vast proportion; then a second detonation ignites the mixture, causing an awesome explosion. The explosion is about the most powerful 'conventional' explosion we know of.

At a pressure shock of up to 200 pounds per square inch (PSI), people in its detonation zone are often killed by the sheer compression of the air around them. Human beings can typically withstand up to about a 40-PSI shock. The bomb sucks oxygen out of the air, and can apparently even suck the lungs out through the mouths of people unfortunate enough to be in the detonation zone. Our military used it on helpless people [in the 1991 Gulf Slaughter].

People who would order the use of such weapons without a care for the consequences would not kill 3,000 people on 9/11 with the same empathy-deleted nonchalance? The Iraqi people, living, breathing, human beings like you and me, were subjected to a lovely piece of hardware called a 'Big Blue' which produces a shock wave only eclipsed by nuclear weapons. As Wade Frazier points out, the power of the shock wave can turn a body into a hamburger. So-called 'bouncing bombs' were also deployed. These are designed to 'bounce' to waist height before exploding and ensure a better chance of splattering people into a thousand pieces. These are called 'antipersonnel' weapons in the sanitised Orwellian 'Newspeak' of Hidden Hand front men. Then there was the 'Beehive' which explodes 8,800 pieces of razor-edged shrapnel in all directions, cutting through a human body like the proverbial knife through butter. All these weapons were used against civilian men, women and children in the Gulf 'War' and others since – including the 'war on terrorism'. In an oh, so rare excursion into reality by the media, John Balzar of the *Los Angeles Times* reported in 1991 on the fate of Iraqi conscripts. Balzar saw night-vision 'gun sight' footage from the US military briefing room:

> They looked like ghostly sheep flushed from a pen – Iraqi infantrymen bewildered and terrified, jarred from sleep and fleeing their bunkers under a hellish fire. One by one, they were cut down by attackers they could not see or understand. Some were blown to bits by bursts of 30-millimeter exploding cannon shells. One man dropped, writhed on the ground, then struggled to his feet; another burst of fire tore him apart ... Even hardened soldiers hold their breath as the Iraqi soldiers, as big as football players on the television screen, run with nowhere to hide. These are not bridges exploding or airplane hangers. These are men.

The same reporter wrote:

> The mechanics of death and destruction are a grim affair. The military's scientific approach and its philosophies – for example, its preference for wounding vital organs over blowing off limbs – can be deeply disquieting to anybody who imagines such matters are left to chance. Many people would

rather not know about the gruesome details.

The psychopaths of the Hidden Hand behind the Gulf War and 9/11 enjoy the gruesome details because for them it's a sexual high.

'Nuke 'em, kill 'em all'

This was not a war, it was a mass slaughter by the very forces and their controllers that would wage a 'war on terror' justified by 9/11 that would include a full-blown invasion of Iraq. These protectors of 'freedom' and 'liberty' used the same rhetoric then as they do now to justify the mass bombing of civilians. They hide the truth behind the lies so eagerly repeated by excuses-for-journalists and large swathes of the public that has long forgotten not only what to think, but even how to think. Then, as now, no dissent was allowed against the genocide of the innocent by the criminally insane. Talk show hosts, without two brain cells acting in unison, called for nuclear attacks on Iraq and anyone who challenged the 'war' was either stupid or a supporter of evil. While the sheep and chickens followed the fox, or Fox, the US government and their British allies were targeting civilian bomb shelters, killing hundreds of fathers, mothers and children because 'intelligence told us that the bomb shelter was actually a military headquarters'. *Bullshit*. On the ground thousands of Iraqi soldiers were buried alive as 'UN' forces used bulldozers to fill in their trenches in shocking contravention of international law. Nothing better sums up the mentality of the deeply sick people behind 9/11 and still waging the 'war on terror' than the almost unimaginable attacks on the 'Highway of Death'. The Iraqi army was in retreat in the wake of the air bombardment and headed out of Kuwait across the border to Basra in Iraq. With them were civilians and prisoners. US pilots attacked the vehicles at the front and back of the seven-mile *retreating* human convoy, so forcing it to a standstill on the open road. They then bombed the convoy while constantly racing back to their aircraft carrier to re-arm and return to continue the mass murder. One pilot said that it was like 'shooting fish in a barrel' and thousands died at the hands of the very people who promote themselves as morally superior to those they target. Barry McCaffrey, one of the generals involved in this mass murder, was later appointed by President Clinton to head his 'war on drugs'. Father George Bush's approval ratings soared as he conducted these crimes against humanity – just as they did for his son when he continued the long, long, family association with genocide. The blatant defiance of the Geneva Convention on the Highway of Death produced no action against the Father Bush administration because there is one law for America, Britain, France and Germany, etc., and a very different one for those they choose to bomb, kill, and mutilate. An International War Crimes Tribunal found

President Father Bush, Vice President Dan Quayle, Defense Secretary
Dick Cheney, Secretary of State James Baker, and military leaders, Colin
Powell and Norman Schwarzkopf, guilty of war crimes. What was done
as a result? Nothing – *as always*. When Bill Clinton replaced Bush he
imposed sanctions on Iraq so severe that by 1995 his evil Secretary of
State Madeleine Albright was forced to admit on the US *60 Minutes*
television programme that sanctions had already cost the lives of *half a
million* Iraqi children and that was only up to then. This was the
exchange:

> Lesley Stahl: 'We have heard that half a million children have died. I mean,
> that's more children than died in Hiroshima. And, you know, is the price
> worth it?'
>
> Albright: 'I think this is a very hard choice, but the price – we think the price is
> worth it.'

The figure continued at some 5,000 dead children a month and passed a
million in total. Albright's answer was one which only a psychopath
could deliver. This mentality would not orchestrate 9/11?

Burying the truth

Crimes for which the Bush family and their masters and associates are
responsible rarely come to light because the corporate media is
controlled by the Hidden Hand and most journalists either don't realise
they are pawns in a game or silently accept that they are to protect their
careers. Accounts are legion of how evidence and footage that would
expose the lies, especially in wartime, are banned or confiscated as they
are with regard to 9/11. One example during the 1991 Gulf War was
when American TV networks NBC and CBS refused to air pictures shot
in Iraq of the destruction of civilian areas which revealed Bush
government and military accounts to be a grotesque fiction. The story
was blocked by the President of NBC Michael Gartner and producers
offered it to CBS where Tom Bettag, Executive Editor of the CBS *Evening
News*, said he would run the story the following day. That evening
Bettag was sacked and the story buried. This is the real background to
TV news and today the Internet information giants, too, all of which
ultimately answer to the Hidden Hand. Footage of the Highway of
Death was suppressed and US casualties caused by the enemy were
claimed to be 'training accidents'. Father Bush's lies about Iraqi troop
deployments in Kuwait, provable by satellite images, were never shown.
This satellite 'loophole in the lies' was the reason why the US
government purchased all rights to satellite pictures of Afghanistan
while that country was subjected to another insane American and British

bombing onslaught after 9/11. We should remember that having said in 1991 that CIA-installed dictator Saddam Hussein was a threat to the world, and with the Iraqi 'army' destroyed, Father Bush suddenly called an end to the 'war' and pulled the troops out leaving Saddam still intact. Norman Schwarzkopf said with an air of disappointment: 'We could have completely closed the door and made it a battle of annihilation ... [it was] literally about to become the battle of Canaan, a battle of annihilation.' This is what I wrote at this point in *Alice in Wonderland and the World Trade Center Disaster* published in 2002:

> Ah, never mind, Norman, but you see your President and those who controlled him wanted Hussein to stay put, or at least appear to, so they could play that card over and over. I suspect, however, that the Saddam story is going to lead to some kind of climax eventually.

A few months later it did with the invasion of Iraq in 2003.

Evil begets evil

Hidden Hand operatives like Father Bush and his associate Henry Kissinger are mass murderers on a scale that is almost incomprehensible. They and their associates and successors have a record of genocidal horror that spans the world in Vietnam, Cambodia, Laos, Korea, Nicaragua, Panama, Grenada, Indonesia, Bosnia, Kosovo, Iraq, Afghanistan, Libya, Syria and that's only a partial list. The dead, maimed, starving, destitute and dispossessed that have ensued can be numbered in billions of our fellow men, women and children. Nothing captures the 9/11 mentality of empathy-deleted psychopathy behind all this more powerfully than Father Bush's sexual abuse, torture and murder of children held in captivity in the mind-control and sexual abuse programmes of this depraved beyond belief Hidden Hand network. I explain in other books why these bloodlines are obsessed with paedophilia, but the why is less important here than the fact that it happens at all as we explore the depths of evil to which these extreme psychopaths daily plunge. If you read *The Biggest Secret, Children of the Matrix*, and other books by researchers and victims of this network, you'll see that what I am saying is no fantasy. Father Bush was a notorious paedophile, torturer and child killer among those who have researched this subject. I first outed Bush in 1998 as a rampant paedophile who tortured children and while I was writing this book more than two decades later Washington and Republican insider Dr Steve Pieczenik also exposed Bush in an Internet video. Pieczenik is a former US Department of State official and a Harvard-trained psychiatrist who served as Deputy Assistant Secretary of State under Henry Kissinger, Gerald Ford, Jimmy Carter, Ronald Reagan and Father

Bush. He confirmed from his own knowledge the paedophilia of Father Bush and how prevalent it is among the power elite – what I have been exposing for so long. Pieczenik said:

> It has been rampant in our government, if you remember Bush Sr. had a whole group of young Hispanic men who he groomed and played with. At the same time, Hillary and Bill Clinton along with their friend Mr. Epstein went down to the Bahamas and they were molesting and utilizing young girls and boys to have sexual pleasures, but nothing was done about the fact that Jeffrey Epstein had been guilty and convicted of that crime.

Paedophile billionaire Jeffrey Epstein was not only a buddy of the Clintons. Among the names and phone numbers in Epstein's 'little black book' were Donald Trump, Tony Blair and his close friend Prince Andrew of the British royal family. Epstein's friends arranged an outrageous plea deal that allowed him to avoid the long jail sentence which the paedophilia charges against him should have involved. Alex Acosta, the US attorney in Miami who agreed the deal on behalf of the government, was appointed US Labor Secretary by Trump. A judge ruled in 2019 that Acosta broke the law by not informing Epstein's victims of the plea agreement which allowed the paedophile to get off basically scot-free for running a child-trafficking ring. What a cesspit. Even by these 'standards' Father Bush was at the far end of extreme. Cathy O'Brien, a mind-controlled slave of people like Bush and Dick Cheney for the first 30 years of her life, reveals in *Trance Formation of America* the staggering levels of abuse inflicted on her and her daughter Kelly by Father Bush and his like. Kelly was only a small child literally born into captivity when Bush began his sexual and violent abuse of her – abuse and torture that her mother had long suffered. This is just one of her experiences with President George H. W. Bush, father and controller of 9/11 President Boy Bush. The Alex Houston she mentions here was her and Kelly's CIA handler in the US government mind-control programme known as MKUltra:

> Kelly became violently, physically ill after her induction into George Bush's 'neighborhood' and from every sexual encounter she had with him thereafter, she ran 104-6 degree temperatures, vomited and endured immobilizing headaches for an average of three days. These were the only tell-tale evidences aside from the scarring burns left on her skin. Houston forbade me to call a doctor, and Kelly forbade me to comfort her, pitifully complaining that her head 'hurt too bad even to move'. And she did not move for hours on end. Kelly often complained of severe kidney pain and her rectum usually bled for a day or two after Bush sexually abused her. My own mind-control victimization rendered me unable to help or protect her ...

... Kelly's bleeding rectum was ... one of [the] ... physical indicators of George Bush's pedophile perversions. I have overheard of him speak blatantly of his sexual abuse of her on many occasions. He used this and threats to her life to 'pull my strings' and control me. The psychological ramifications of being raped by a paedophile president are mind shattering enough, but reportedly Bush further reinforced his traumas to Kelly's mind with sophisticated NASA electronic and drug mind controlled devices. Bush also instilled the 'Who ya gonna call?' and 'I'll be watching you' binds on Kelly, further reinforcing her sense of helplessness. The systematic tortures and traumas I endured as a child now seem trite in comparison to the brutal, physical and psychological devastation that Bush inflicted on my daughter.

Father Bush pledged during his 1987 presidential election campaign to build a 'kinder, gentler, America'. This man was in the White House for twelve years followed by his friend and associate Bill Clinton, whom Cathy also exposes, and then his son and tea-maker, Boy Bush. Such a mentality would not plan and execute what happened on September 11th, an event that has so massively advanced the Hidden Hand agenda for a global fascist/communist state? 'They would never do that'? You must be joking. It is their modus operandi in every way.

CHAPTER 3

The Gofer Gang

It is better to remain silent and be thought a fool than to open one's mouth and remove all doubt – Voltaire

Boy George Bush would have been well aware that the attacks of September 11th were not the work of 'Arab hijackers' answering to Osama bin Laden, but to claim that he had any direct involvement in planning them is to miss the entire point. Politicians – even US presidents – are agents and stooges of the Hidden Hand and not its centre of power and organisation.

The very idea that Boy Bush with such a glaring lack of intelligence would be an organiser of 9/11 is patently ridiculous and for those who bravely call themselves mainstream 'journalists' to dismiss evidence of a conspiracy on the grounds of Bush's limited grey matter shows just how clueless they are about how the world works. Why do they think he was down in Florida at a long-arranged school visit when all hell was breaking loose in New York and Washington? Why do they think he was then whisked away to two Air Force Bases and kept well clear of the White House until 7pm that evening? The real orchestrators wanted him out of the way where his gaff-prone lack of intelligence could do no harm as initial events and responses were underway. There are basically three types of political 'leader': (1) those who knowingly work for the Hidden Hand; (2) those who want power for power's sake and will do and say whatever it takes to secure funding and other support; (3) those who are not very bright and puppets of their Hidden Hand-appointed advisors and aides. Boy Bush was a combination of (1) and (3) when he took office in January, 2001. He could not possibly be a member of the Bush family or a Skull and Bones initiate and not know about the Hidden Hand and its plans for humanity. Nor did he have the mind that could be any more than a hapless frontman while his father and vice president Dick Cheney ran the White House and he took only official responsibility. 'Sign this, George' – 'Okay, dad'. 'Do this, George' – 'Okay, Uncle Dick'. These are just a tiny selection of his stupendous intellect:

'I know the human being and fish can coexist peacefully.'

'More and more of our imports come from overseas.'

'Well, I think if you say you're going to do something and don't do it, that's trustworthiness.'

'We cannot let terrorists and rogue nations hold this nation hostile or hold our allies hostile.'

'I'm telling you there's an enemy that would like to attack America, Americans, again. There just is. That's the reality of the world. And I wish him all the very best.'

'I remember meeting a mother of a child who was abducted by the North Koreans right here in the Oval Office.'

So, no, Boy George Bush was not an organiser of 9/11. This is not to excuse him from responsibility in any way because he played his part and should be in jail with the rest of them. I am saying we have to look elsewhere for the real orchestrators both close to him and much further away – start with Dick Cheney who utterly controlled every aspect of the Boy Bush government and then pan out until you are no longer within the borders of the United States. Boy Bush was born in 1946 in New Haven, Connecticut, home of Yale University and the Skull and Bones Society, and was raised in Texas. He was groomed and moulded from birth, like his father, to serve the Hidden Hand cause with all the open doors, protection, financial support and privilege that come with that. He attended Yale University and avoided the draft to Vietnam, as did Dick Cheney. Send others to kill and be killed while you stay home safe and sound. People like Bush, Obama and Trump say 'We will do this or that' when they threaten countries with the US military and yet the 'We' they talk about are the men and women in uniform they send into battle. The political 'We' sits back in Washington sipping coffee while carnage is delivered on the other side of the world. The same applies to all the other 'We' psychopaths like Tony Blair in Britain. None of them has ever seen a bullet fired in anger or war. *Washington Post* staff writers George Lardner Jr and Lois Romano revealed in an article in 1999 how two weeks before he was due to graduate from Yale, Boy Bush arrived at the offices of the Texas Air National Guard at Ellington Field outside Houston and said he wanted to sign up for pilot training. This was on May 27th, 1968, when the Vietnam War was at its peak with some 350 Americans dying every week and goodness knows how many

Vietnamese. Another twelve days and he would have lost his student immunity from the draft and so he grasped, with his father's help, an escape route from combat by joining the National Guard. Father George was at this time a Congressman for Houston and a supporter of the Vietnam conflict and the policy of sending American soldiers to suffer and die. Many of the American elite were trying to pull the same trick for their sons and the National Guard had a long waiting list. Not only that, Boy George had scored only 25 percent in a pilot aptitude test and that was the lowest acceptable grade. This will surprise no one who witnessed his presidency and all these factors should have prevented his admission and, therefore, made him available for Vietnam. Instead Boy George was sworn in as an airman with the Texas Air National Guard on the *same day* that he applied. Colonel Walter B. 'Buck' Staudt, commander of the 147th Fighter Group, even staged a special ceremony later so he could be photographed administering the oath for Bush instead of the captain who had officially sworn in Bush earlier. Staudt did the same when Boy Bush was commissioned as a second lieutenant. Lloyd Bentsen Jr, a major Texas Democrat, ensured that his son, Lloyd Bentsen III, was enlisted into the National Guard by Staudt around the same time as Bush. When obvious questions were asked during Boy Bush's run for the presidency, Staudt said that no favouritism had been shown to him. Boy Bush claimed he did not join the National Guard to avoid the Vietnam War which he and his father supported, but rather because he wanted to be a fighter pilot. Okay, insult my intelligence some more. Even on his National Guard application forms he ticked the box saying, 'do not volunteer' when asked if he wanted to go overseas. Not only did he avoid going to Vietnam, he was even able to live in his then home town of Houston while learning to be a pilot who was never to face a conflict. He served as an F-102 pilot with the Texas Air National Guard to avoid the draft to Vietnam and became a hard-drinking, cocaine-snorting, womaniser before 'discovering Jesus' (I know, I know, but this is the official story). Bush's drug habit was brought to public attention – and then buried by the media – with the publication of the 1999 book, *Fortunate Son: George Bush and the Making of a President*. Author J.H. Hatfield was subjected to a national campaign of character assassination after he claimed Bush was arrested on drug charges in 1972 while serving with the National Guard and that this had been wiped from the record by a Republican judge and friend of his father in exchange for Bush's participation in a community service programme called Project PULL in Houston's inner city. What is for sure is that suddenly, and for no credible reason, this hard-drinking playboy felt an overwhelming desire to volunteer to work with black inner-city kids in Project PULL.

Bush drug family

Michael C. Ruppert, a former Los Angeles Police Department narcotics investigator, went further in his newsletter, *From The Wilderness.* He said that Boy Bush and his brother, Jeb, Governor for Florida across 9/11, were filmed in a 1985 'sting' by the US Drug Enforcement Administration (DEA) at Tamiami airport outside Miami. Ruppert quotes statements made by Terry Reed who took part in drug operations for the CIA and the Bush family involving the notorious self-confessed drug smuggler Barry Seal who was murdered when he began to talk too much (see *And The Truth Shall Set You Free* and Reed's book, *Compromised: Clinton, Bush and the CIA.*). Ruppert said the Bush brothers arrived from the Intermountain regional airport at Mena, Arkansas (Governor Bill Clinton), to pick up two kilos of cocaine from Seal. This was the location of the infamous and well-documented Mena airstrip drug operations involving the Clintons and Bushes which would see a number of people murdered including two young boys who saw too much (again see *And The Truth Shall Set You Free*). There is no way that the Bush sons could not have been involved in drug trafficking when their then vice president father was one of the most active drug barons in America working for Hidden Hand networks. CIA drug operative Terry Reed quotes a conversation with drug pilot Barry Seal about the Bush family drug operations. Seal was the son of a Ku Klux Klan member and involved in covert off-the-books operations from the 1950s. His wife, Deborah, said he 'flew a getaway plane out of Dallas after JFK was killed'. Seal once met alleged JFK assassin Lee Harvey Oswald and certainly had connections to characters like Clay Shaw and David Ferrie who New Orleans District Attorney Jim Garrison believed were involved in the assassination plot. Seal's association with Father Bush and family fit this scenario with Bush also reported to have had a role in Dallas that day in 1963. Barry Seal was played by Tom Cruise in the 2017 film *American Made* in which a lot of poetic licence was used. Terry Reed wrote that Seal told him:

> Ever hear the old expression, it's not what ya know, it's who ya know? Well, whoever said that just hadn't caught the Vice President's kids in the dope business, 'cause I can tell ya for sure what ya know can definitely be more useful than who you know ...

Reed asked Seal if he was saying that Father Bush's sons were in the drug business:

> Yup, that's what I'm tellin' ya. A guy in Florida who flipped for the DEA [Drug Enforcement Administration] has got the goods on the Bush boys. Now I heard this earlier from a reliable source in Colombia, but I just sat on it then,

waitin' to use it as a trump card, if I ever needed it. Well, I need ta use it now. I got names, dates, places ... even got some tape recordin's. Fuck, I even got surveillance videos catchin' the Bush boys red handed. I consider this stuff my insurance policy ... Now this is real sensitive shit inside of US Customs and DEA and those guys are pretty much under control.

Barry Seal's 'insurance' did not prove too effective, however, because he was silenced before he could tell his story to a bigger audience. Soon after he began to speak out in February, 1986, he was murdered at Baton Rouge, Louisiana. The murder was blamed officially on two Colombian hitmen with Mac-10 machine guns and while they may or may not have been the actual killers the assassination was ordered by the highest levels of the United States government to stop his revelations about Bush and Clinton family involvement in the drug racket through Mena, Arkansas (Fig 26). Bill Clinton said at a press conference at the time that he knew very little about Seal when a number of people reported seeing them dining together at Fu Lin's, one of Clinton's favourite restaurants in the Arkansas capital of Little

Figure 26: Political 'opponents' Bill Clinton and Father Bush who were in fact close associates involved in the same drug-running operation – Hillary, too.

Rock. Noelle Bush, the then 24-year-old daughter of Jeb Bush, was arrested in January, 2001, for prescription drug fraud involving an anti-anxiety drug similar to Valium. I understand her need for that after being brought up by the Bush family and living with Jeb at the governor's mansion in Florida. Jeb Bush said at the time with stunning hypocrisy: 'Unfortunately, substance abuse is an issue confronting many families across our nation ...' Yes, but not every family has made billions from making those substances available on the streets of America. Private investigator Stewart Webb uncovered Bush family connections to the drug trade and major American financial firms who laundered the money for them. He said:

George Jr., Jeb and Neil Bush were all party to the crimes involving drugs and gun money laundering through Silverado Savings in Denver. They were all aware of 'poppy' George's schemes using CIA, Israeli Mossad, Homestead Air Force Base and Mena, Arkansas to import drugs and ship weapons.

Yep, weapons to terrorists. The significance of 'Israeli Mossad' to drug-running and 9/11 will become clear later because Mossad was both centrally involved in 9/11 and is a major player in the global drug trade. The closeness of the Bush family to Mossad will make a lot of sense of 9/11 as the story unravels. Investigator Stewart Webb highlighted Bush family involvement in financial fraud and murder while his calls for a grand jury investigation into his findings were ignored – of course they were when the Hidden Hand controls the decision-making levels of law enforcement and the courts. Mind control whistleblower Cathy O'Brien reveals from personal experience how the drug operation involving the Clintons extended into human-trafficking in Haiti. Cathy, who was often sexually abused in her mind-controlled state by Hillary Clinton, writes:

> Bill Clinton's infamous Mena cocaine operations that I'd been exposed to since the late 1970's extended internationally to include Haiti and expanded into related criminal activity such as human trafficking. Bill and Hillary's complicity in crimes against humanity are rooted deeply with absolute power corrupting absolutely.

> The Clintons are no strangers to charities being used as cover for their criminal operations. Charities like World Vision and various Christian 'missions' collecting money under the guise of helping Haitians instead notoriously lined pockets while funding black ops. Churches including the Lord's Chapel in Brentwood, Tennessee and Hendersonville, Tennessee's Mormon church are among those 'missions' I had experience to know merged with CIA cocaine ops. Like many others, these cult churches sent their mind controlled followers out on 'missions' to Haiti as cover for muling cocaine for the CIA.

You can read the full article and much more at Cathy's website *Trance-formation.com*.

Buffoon in the White House (not the first or last)

Boy Bush was somehow elected Governor of Texas in November, 1994, after which he became the most enthusiastic enforcer of capital punishment in America. I wonder if he wanted the electric chair for drug-traffickers? The plan soon became clear that another Bush was being groomed for the presidency. He was re-elected governor in 1998 with 68.6 percent of the vote and two years later he was the 43rd President of the United States as I had predicted he would be some three years earlier. You only had to know his family background and the way his political profile was being raised to realise that he was the chosen one. Presidents are not elected by the public except in theory – they are selected by the Hidden Hand with the candidate they want the most pitched against a candidate that is still acceptable if things don't go

according to plan. In this case the other one was Hidden Hand asset to
his fingertips, the 'Democrat' Al Gore, who would later front-up the
hoax about human-caused 'global warming' as an excuse to transform
global society through de-industrialisation and other restructuring of
human life (see *The Perception Deception* and other books for the detailed
background). Boy Bush's election campaign broke all records at the time
for fundraising as Hidden Hand companies and assets pitched in with
the cash to win the presidency for their first choice. Gore's insider
knowledge of the Bush family could have destroyed Boy Bush, but then
Bush could have done the same with Gore so they both stayed quiet. The
result all came down, infamously, to the outcome in Florida, the state
governed by Bush's brother, Jeb, another mega-crook. The Florida vote
was so obviously rigged (to anyone with a brain cell) and yet Al Gore
meekly accepted it in the end and slipped quietly away as a Bush
family-controlled Supreme Court awarded the election to Bush. Gore
knew what had happened and he knew why. He also knew better than
to cause trouble serious enough to stop Bush taking the throne. What I
have revealed is only a fraction of the grotesque background to the Bush
family that produced the 9/11 president and it is worth concluding
before I move on to other 9/11 'personalities' with a quote from Al
Martin, a retired Lieutenant Commander with the US Naval Reserves
and Naval Intelligence, and author of *The Conspirators: Secrets of an Iran-
Contra Insider*. Martin claimed to have seen at first hand government
drug trafficking, illegal weapons deals and an 'epidemic of fraud' –
corporate securities fraud, real estate fraud, insurance fraud and bank
fraud. He said of the Bush family:

> You have to look at the entire Bush Family in this context – as if the entire
> family ran a corporation called Frauds-R-Us. Each member of the family,
> George Sr., George Jr., Neil, Jeb, Prescott, Wally, etc., have their own specialty
> of fraud. George Jr.'s speciality was insurance and security fraud. Jeb's
> speciality was oil and gas fraud. Neil's specialty was real estate fraud.
> Prescott's speciality was banking fraud. Wally's speciality was securities fraud.
> And George Sr.'s specialty? All of the above.

This is the family of President Boy Bush who said there must be 'a
new era of integrity' in American corporate life. Anyone still think these
guys have told you the truth about September 11th?

'Big Dick'

The Bushes have always surrounded themselves with crooks, killers and
deeply disturbed friends and associates. They like to feel at home. There
are few better examples of this theme than their fellow Bohemian
Grover, Dick Cheney, the White House Chief of Staff to President Ford;

Father George's Defense Secretary at the time of the 1991 Gulf War; and vice president to Boy Bush across 9/11 and the launch of the 'war on terror'. Cathy O'Brien describes in *Trance Formation of America* her almost unimaginable experiences of Cheney when she was a victim of the Hidden Hand/CIA mind-control programmes and Cheney was Defense Secretary to Father George – the violent sexual abuser of her daughter, Kelly. Cathy details how she was involved in drug running operations under instructions from Cheney, some of which involved Bandar bin Sultan (Cheney called him 'the Sultan'). Bin Sultan was the deeply corrupt US ambassador to King Fahd of Saudi Arabia, the George Bush puppet and close associate of the Bin Laden family and terrorist financiers such as Bush family friend and Saudi billionaire Khalid bin Mahfouz. We will see later that Father Bush – indeed the Bush clan in general – also had close connections with the Bin Laden family. Cathy describes the constant and sickening brutality that she and her daughter suffered from Cheney and Father Bush. This was just one occasion:

> Bush attempted to sell Cheney on the idea of pedophillia through graphic descriptions of having sex with Kelly. Both were already sexually aroused from drugs and anticipation. Cheney demonstrated to Bush why he did not have sex with kids by exposing himself to Kelly and saying: 'Come here'. Upon seeing Cheney's unusually large penis, Kelly reeled back in horror and cried 'No!' which made them both laugh. Bush asked Cheney for his liquid cocaine atomizer as he got up to take Kelly to the bedroom. When Cheney remarked how benevolent it was of Bush to numb her with it before sex, Bush replied: 'The hell it is. It's for me.' He described his excited state in typical vulgar terms and explained that he wanted to spray cocaine on his penis to last longer.
>
> Cheney said: 'I thought it was for the kid.'
>
> Bush explained: 'Half the fun is having them squirm.' He took Kelly's hand and led her off to the bedroom. Cheney told me that since I was responsible for Bush's assault on my daughter ... I would 'burn' (in hell). He burned my inner thigh with the fireplace poker and threatened to throw Kelly in the fire. He hypnotically enhanced his description of her burning to traumatize me deeply. As he sexually brutalized me, I heard Kelly's whimpers coming from the bedroom. As her cries grew louder, Cheney turned on classical music to drown out her cries for help.

Cathy tells of what happened another time when she asked Cheney, amid yet another brutal beating session, if she could go to the toilet:

> Cheney's face turned red with rage. He was on me in an instant, slamming my back into the wall with one arm across my chest and his hand on my

throat, choking me while applying pressure to the carotid artery in my neck with his thumb. His eyes bulged and he spit as he growled: 'If you don't mind, I will kill you. I could kill you – kill you – with my bare hands. You are not the first and you won't be the last. I'll kill you any time I goddam well please.' He flung me on the cot-type bed that was behind me. There he finished taking his rage out on me sexually.

This was the same Dick Cheney who became de-facto US President during the official tenure of Boy Bush. Cheney controlled every aspect of the Bush administration and lied, lied and lied again about what happened on 9/11 as we shall be seeing. This brutal man, an extreme psychopath, would give a damn about the consequences for 3,000 people and their loved ones in attacks in which he played a very significant part? These people have no empathy, remorse or shame – the latter confirmed by Boy George, son of a serial paedophile and associate of Cheney, announcing an initiative in 2002 to 'protect America's children'. Richard Bruce Cheney was born in Nebraska in 1941 and brought up in Casper, Wyoming. He is yet another of the clique to hail from Yale, home of the Skull and Bones Society, but he dropped out before eventually securing a degree in political science at Wyoming University. Cheney then headed for Washington where he joined the Nixon administration as a special assistant to Donald Rumsfeld, the 9/11 Defense Secretary and yet another professional liar. Rumsfeld at that time was the first director of the Office of [Hidden Hand] Economic Opportunity. President Richard Nixon resigned over the Kissinger-engineered Watergate scandal in 1974 (see *And The Truth Shall Set You Free*) and Rumsfeld joined the White House staff as assistant to the new president, Gerald Ford, another abuser of Cathy O'Brien, and a man who, thanks to Watergate, never had to be elected and never would have been if the voters had been given a say. This was another coup on America. Ford's intellectual capacity was akin to that of Boy Bush. The famous saying that Ford couldn't walk and chew gum at the same time was right on and here was another combination of someone well aware of the Hidden Hand he served while fulfilling the role of I-do-what-they-tell-me. Cheney moved to the White House with Rumsfeld and eventually became Ford's Chief of Staff between 1975 and 1977 when he was still in his early thirties and gained experience of controlling and nursing an idiot president. Cheney had the first of several heart attacks (how did they find it?) and recovered to be elected as Congressman for Wyoming where he remained until Father George made him Defense Secretary after the presidential election of 1988. Cheney is yet another of the bloodline clique who are keen to send others into battle so long as they never have to go. He avoided the draft to Vietnam when he was given deferments because he was a student and a 'registrant with a child'. He told his Senate confirmation hearing that (just like Boy Bush) he 'would have been obviously happy to serve had I been called'. What a coincidence that they never are. Cheney's wife, Lynne, who he married in 1964, was another Hidden Hand Washington insider who would be at his side in the White House during the 9/11 attacks while Boy Bush was kept out of the way. She was head of the National Endowment of the Humanities from 1986 to 1993 under Reagan and then Father Bush (or under Bush and then Bush in other words) and later became a senior fellow at the seriously Hidden Hand American Enterprise Institute (where Dick Cheney was also involved between 1993 and 1995). Mrs Cheney was on the Hidden Hand Lockheed Martin board from 1994 until January, 2001 – a company that has benefited in billions from the war on terror that followed 9/11. Dick Cheney became widely known during the Gulf Slaughter in 1991 when he worked to ensure the mass murder of Iraqis which reached more than a million when you include the sanctions that followed under Bill Clinton and Madeleine 'We think the price is worth it' Albright. Alongside Cheney in the Father George government was Bush family associate, Secretary of State James Baker, who would later serve as chief legal adviser to Boy Bush during the Florida election controversy.

Big Dick and big business

Cheney moved into 'private business' to serve the Hidden Hand in another way after Father Bush's pre-arranged defeat to his subordinate associate Bill Clinton in 1992 and became fantastically wealthy as a director of elite companies like Morgan Stanley, Union Pacific and Procter and Gamble. His most important business appointment came in 1995 when he was named Chairman and Chief Executive of the Texas-based Halliburton Oil in the Bushes' home state. This was founded in 1919 and owned a highly relevant subsidiary called Brown & Root. Cheney had no experience in the oil industry, but that's not why Halliburton offered him the job. He had other 'qualities' that would expand their business. While Cheney was Defense Secretary (and before and afterwards) Brown & Root was awarded hundreds of millions of dollars' worth of construction contracts in war zones in countries devastated by US bombing and/or manipulation. The technique is this: you control the political decisions to start wars that suit your agenda; you hand over taxpayers money for your military to buy armaments from your companies; then, when all this has devastated the target country and its population you get yourself awarded the contracts to rebuild what you have destroyed. Cheney was the biggest shareholder in Halliburton with a stake of some $45.5 million and the company's board included Lawrence Eagleburger who held State Department posts under President Father George and was an executive of the notorious

Kissinger Associates. Halliburton and Brown & Root had long used
political patronage and funding to expand business and profits. Brown
& Root's ticket to the top came through its political contributions to
President Lyndon Johnson from the time he ran for the Senate in 1948.
The *Austin Chronicle* once called him 'the candidate from Brown & Root'.
Thanks to Hidden Hand puppet Johnson they made billions on
government contracts including those relating to the Vietnam War after
Johnson reversed the policies of the assassinated JFK and plunged
America deeper into the conflict. Johnson further gave his personal
funders contracts for airports, pipelines and military bases. Biographer
Ronnie Dugger, author of *The Politician: The Life and Times of Lyndon
Johnson*, said much of the money he was paid by Brown & Root arrived
in cash. 'It was a totally corrupt relationship and it benefited both of
them enormously,' Dugger said. 'Brown & Root got rich, and Johnson
got power and riches.' Using the same tactics, contracts continued to
flow from government not least thanks to Dick Cheney. Michael C.
Ruppert, a former Los Angeles police officer, wrote in a study of Brown
& Root:

> From Bosnia and Kosovo, to Chechnya, to Rwanda, to Burma, to Pakistan, to
> Laos, to Vietnam, to Indonesia, to Iran to Libya to Mexico to Colombia, Brown
> & Root's traditional operations have expanded from heavy construction to
> include the provision of logistical support for the US military. Now, instead of
> US Army quartermasters, the world is likely to see Brown & Root warehouses
> storing and managing everything from uniforms to rations to vehicles.

Both Halliburton and Brown & Root were funders of a now infamous
company called Permindex, a British Intelligence front organisation
headed by the Canadian Louis M. Bloomfield, which, it is now well
documented, was a central coordinating network behind the
assassination of President Kennedy in Dallas in 1963. Permindex also
ran death squads in Europe, Mexico, Central America, the Caribbean
and the United States. Clay Shaw, who ran a division of Permindex in
New Orleans, is the only man to be tried for involvement in the
assassination. New Orleans District Attorney Jim Garrison failed to
secure a conviction because key prosecution witnesses had this strange
habit of dying from less than natural causes. Shaw was a British
intelligence operative who worked for Winston Churchill during the
Second World War. We should not let any of this deflect attention,
however, from the involvement of Mossad, Israeli intelligence, in the
Kennedy assassination which I detail in *And The Truth Shall Set You Free*.
Connections into Permindex involved a stream of famous companies,
banks and personalities. Among them were the Bush family and ultra-
Zionist Bronfman gangster family in Canada through its Seagram liquor

operation. Halliburton, at Cheney's say-so, bought and merged with Dresser Industries in an $8 billion deal in 1998 to create the biggest oil-drilling services company in the world. Boy Bush's grandfather Prescott Bush was on the board of Dresser Industries for 22 years in his capacity as a partner in Brown Brothers Harriman, funders of Hitler and the eugenics movement, which owned Dresser. President and Chairman of the Dresser board was Henry Neil Mallon who was among those involved in the raid on the grave of Apache leader Geronimo at Fort Sill, Oklahoma, in 1918 to steal his skull and take it back to Skull and Bones headquarters at Yale. It was Mallon, apparently, who burned the flesh and hair off the skull after Prescott Bush and friends had stolen it. Father George's crooked son, Neil Mallon Bush of Silverado Savings and Loans corruption fame, was named after the Skull and Bones Dresser president.

Snouts in the trough

Dick Cheney said he stood for small government and against government handouts. What he meant, naturally, is he believed in that for everyone else and absolutely not for himself. Thanks to Cheney Halliburton received in five years some $4 billion (at least) in government contracts and loans insured by the taxpayer. The Clinton government guaranteed credits worth $489 million through the US Export-Import Bank to a Russian oil company to the benefit through Brown & Root of Halliburton. This company, according to Russian and American sources and documents, was connected to drug trafficking and organised crime. Halliburton's business with the US Defense Department before Cheney arrived was worth around $300 million a year. Under Cheney, the former Defense Secretary, government contracts soared to more than $650 million, according to the *Baltimore Sun*. It's the same story with loans and guarantees from the Clinton government's Export-Import Bank and the Overseas Private Investment Corporation: $100 million in the five years before Cheney, but at least $1.5 billion under his leadership. In return for political support and loan guarantees, Halliburton donated big sums to political candidates and parties after Cheney's arrival and the lobbying budget doubled: $300,000 a year on lobbying politicians before Cheney and $600,000 with him at the helm. Halliburton has also benefited from US 'aid' to various countries, which was then spent by the recipients on hiring Halliburton. The *Los Angeles Times* obtained State Department documents that showed how government officials helped Halliburton to win major contracts in Asia and Africa. This is the way the Hidden Hand families and their agents operate. They control government decisions through the Hidden Hand one-party state and operate companies like Halliburton which benefit from those government decisions and policies. This is how, once Cheney took over, Halliburton was able to expand so rapidly and become the fifth largest defence contractor in the US and benefited enormously from the 'war on terror' which followed Cheney's clear involvement in 9/11. Halliburton developed a worldwide operation involving 130 countries and became America's biggest non-union company. No wonder Cheney was given a $34 million 'retirement package' when he left in the summer of 2000 to be the running mate of Boy George. This was after five years on a salary of $1.3 million a year, plus bonuses of millions more, stock options worth some $45 million, and his sale of 100,000 Halliburton shares that netted him $5.1 million. Remember these are year 2000 figures and values. Cheney's Halliburton has worked closely with some of the most appalling terrorist dictatorships on the planet because this psychopath would work with anyone at any price to ensure more money, power, and the advancement of the Hidden Hand agenda. Cheney was Defense Secretary in the Gulf Slaughter supposedly aimed at Saddam Hussein in 1991 and yet made big profits for himself and Halliburton after 1998 through deals with ... Saddam Hussein's Iraq. The London *Financial Times* reported that Cheney oversaw $23.8 million worth of contracts for the sale of 'oil industry' technology and services to Iraq and he used Halliburton subsidiaries in France, Italy, Germany and Austria to hide the Cheney-Halliburton connection. Among these companies were Dresser Rand and Ingersoll-Dresser Pump. These contracts together were worth more than any other US company doing business with Iraq. A Halliburton spokesman admitted that its Dresser subsidiaries had sold oil-pumping equipment to Iraq via their European agents. So get this: Cheney's Halliburton contracts were helping to rebuild the oil infrastructure of Iraq destroyed by the bombs dropped by United States aircraft in 1991 commanded from the Pentagon by Defense Secretary Dick Cheney. Then, after 9/11 and the invasion of Iraq in 2003, he blew them up again while controlling the White House of Boy Bush.

Donald Rumsfeld – integrity not a speciality

Boy Bush's 9/11 Defense Secretary was Donald Rumsfeld, a long-time insider with an impeccable record of service to the global agenda (Fig 27). He began his career in Washington DC as an administrative assistant after attending Princeton University and serving in the Navy and was elected to Congress from his home state of Illinois in 1962.

Figure 27: Donald Rumsfeld: 'So I lied – it's what I do.'

Rumsfeld joined the Richard Nixon administration (controlled by
Hidden Hand Secretary of State Henry Kissinger) in 1969. He was a
member of the Nixon cabinet from 1971 to 1972 – the year of the
Watergate break-in, the sting on Nixon orchestrated by Kissinger which
caused Nixon to resign. Rumsfeld went to Europe in 1973 as US
Ambassador to NATO while the Watergate storm blew out before
returning the following year when Nixon had been ousted. He became
chairman of the transition to the presidency of the unelected, Watergate-
imposed Gerald Ford. Rumsfeld joined the Ford cabinet as Chief of Staff
at the White House (which means he must have been very acceptable to
the despot Kissinger) and he became US Secretary of Defense for the first
time between 1975 and 1977. He then went into private business while
maintaining a close involvement in politics. He was Chairman and Chief
Executive of G.D. Searle, the pharmaceutical company later owned by
the despicable Monsanto, and was given a long stream of appointments
in and by government. These included a role as the Reagan-Bush 'envoy'
sent to meet Iraqi dictator Saddam Hussein to arrange for the shipment
of chemical and biological weapons for Saddam to use in the US-Iraq
instigated war against Iran throughout most of the 1980s. The war began
the year that Reagan and Bush took office. A declassified CIA report in
1991 estimated that Iran had suffered more than 50,000 casualties from
these chemical weapons, but the Organization for Veterans of Iran said
the figure didn't include all the civilians affected or the children of
Iranian troops that developed 'blood, lung and skin complications'. A
figure closer to 100,000 is believed to be more accurate with some 20,000
Iranian soldiers killed instantly by the chemical weapons shipped from
America to Iraq with Donald
Rumsfeld operating as the
facilitator and middle man (Fig
28). These facts were confirmed
by thousands of State
Department documents
declassified and released under
the Freedom of Information
Act. Among the biological
weapons that Rumsfeld
arranged to be shipped were
viruses including anthrax and
bubonic plague. This is the
empathy-deleted psychopath
who became Boy Bush's
Defense Secretary across 9/11
and the subsequent war on
terror in which American

Figure 28: 9/11 Secretary of Defense Donald
Rumsfeld greets Iraqi President Saddam Hussein in
Baghdad on December 20th, 1983, as he arranged
for the shipment of chemical and biological
weapons to Saddam for use against Iran. Rumsfeld
was acting as an envoy for President Ronald Reagan
(Father Bush).

troops invaded Iraq on the lie about 'weapons of mass destruction'. Rumsfeld even had the nerve (psychopaths have no capacity for shame) to say that 'ruthless and brutal monster' Saddam had to be removed because he used chemical weapons on his own people – yes, the ones that Rumsfeld arranged for him to be shipped. When he said 'ruthless and brutal monster' he must surely have been looking in a mirror. Rumsfeld is another who would 'never do that' with regard to 9/11? He was appropriately head of a pharmaceutical company when he did the business with Saddam and how helpful all his government connections proved at Searle in other ways. Rumsfeld used his Washington insider contacts to ensure that the Food and Drug Administration (FDA) gave the go-ahead to market the infamous brain- suppressing artificial sweetener aspartame (now known by other names). He was to Searle what Cheney was to Halliburton. FDA documents released under the Freedom of Information Act in 1995 revealed that according to scientists the consequences of this horrendous aspartame substance included blindness and death; brain tumours, brain lesions, headaches, mood swings, skin polyps, insomnia, depression, suppression of intelligence and effects on short-term memory. Investigative author and food specialist Carol Guilford described aspartame a 'molecular holocaust'. This is the mind suppressant (sorry 'sweetener') for which Donald Rumsfeld was hired by Searle in 1977 to win government approval. In January, 1981, with the Rumsfeld's friends in power under Bush and Reagan, he could get the job done. According to one attendee, he told a sales meeting that he would 'call in his markers' and get aspartame approved by the end of the year. The Commissioner of the Food and Drug Administration was then fired and the job was given to Dr Arthur Hull Hayes, a professor and contract researcher for the Defense Department. His first major decision was to approve the use of aspartame in dry foods and his last, in 1983, was to approve it for soft drinks. This was despite all the evidence of its consequences and the opposition of his own board of inquiry. Hayes then left the FDA to become a senior adviser to the public relations firm of ... Rumsfeld's Searle. Rumsfeld earned millions for manipulating aspartame into widespread use and he picked up a $12 million bonus when Searle was bought by Monsanto, promoter of genetically modified (GM) food. Monsanto has since merged with Bayer which was once part of I.G. Farben that ran the concentration camp at Auschwitz. What a shower – what a Web. Donald Rumsfeld, a life-long manipulator with a missing integrity gene, was the Defense Secretary on 9/11 and during the subsequent war on terror and he would lie his way through the official explanation of what happened before, during and after the attacks. He was the official top man in the Pentagon although he was really a version of Boy Bush in that his deputy, the Israel operative, Paul

Wolfowitz, was the real point of power.

Other psychopaths

There are three other characters to mention to set up the background to
the 9/11 Bush administration key personnel – John Ashcroft, Michael
Chertoff and John Negroponte. Ashcroft was Bush's 9/11 Attorney
General and another with his snout in the corporate trough with
Monsanto, Microsoft, corrupt energy company Enron and the alcohol
industry among his benefactors. When Boy Bush's biggest funder –
again Enron – collapsed amid corruption and scandal we had the farcical
situation in which Attorney General Ashcroft could not take part in the
subsequent investigation because he had taken money from them.
Ashcroft was so disliked that when he ran for the Senate in the 2000
election he even failed to beat a dead man. His opponent, the Missouri
Governor Mel Carnahan, died in a plane crash with his son and
campaign adviser while flying in a Cessna to a campaign rally.
Carnahan's name stayed on the ballot paper and more people voted for
him than Ashcroft. It was the first time anyone had posthumously won
election to the Senate. While he couldn't beat a dead man Ashcroft was
soon back in Washington when Bush named him US Attorney General.
This is the man who began dismantling basic human freedoms in the
United States in the wake of September 11th with an enthusiasm and
glee that can only be described as orgasmic. Attorney General is another
big Hidden Hand-nominated post. Ashcroft described himself as a
Christian conservative who didn't smoke, drink or dance. He was
against abortion because it takes a human life created by God and yet
supported the death penalty and the murder of men, women and
children in their thousands every month in the war on terror. Ashcroft's
claim to fame before he joined the Bush administration was his 'war on
drugs' and addictive substances and he demanded the death penalty for
drug offences. Shit, bad news for the Bushes and Clintons then, but
somehow they survived. Much more powerful and significant than
Ashcroft in the 9/11 [In]Justice Department was ultra-Zionist fanatic
Michael Chertoff, son of a rabbi father and reportedly a Mossad agent
mother, who was named by Bush (those that controlled him) as head of
the Criminal Division of the Department of [In]Justice overseeing the
entire criminal investigation into 9/11. Chertoff is a central player in the
9/11 story and there is *much* more about him to come. One other
psychopath I want to mention is John Negroponte who became
Bush's 9/11 Ambassador to the United Nations which was a vital role in
selling the post-attack 'war on terror'. Negroponte knew all about terror
from his days as US ambassador to Honduras between 1981 and 1985
under Reagan-Father Bush where he helped to coordinate America's
covert war against the Sandinista government in Nicaragua. US aid to

Honduras soared from $3.9 million in 1980 to $77.4 million in 1984 during his time there. This funded so many US bases and so much weaponry that the country became known as *USS Honduras*. I can see why Boy Bush (Cheney) chose him, then. Among the characters aiding and abetting Negroponte in his Central American genocide was Elliot Abrams who was named as 'special envoy' by Donald Trump in 2019 to take charge of the so transparent attempted US coup in Venezuela. The same soul-sellers turn up everywhere.

I wanted to lay out right at the start some essential background to key players involved in 9/11 to dispel the myth that they would not be evil enough to coldly play their part in the deaths of 3,000 people that September morning. The 'not that evil', 'not that ballsy' and 'not that competent' nonsense had to be addressed first for those new to this information because it is such a block on the opening of minds to the reality of what really happened and who was responsible. Yet even most of these US government operatives were relatively bit-part players compared with the prime orchestrators that I will come to much later in the book. The rabbit hole goes so very, very deep and before I finish we will be exploring – and exposing – those depths of almost unspeakable malevolence.

CHAPTER 4

Play it again, scam

The best kept secrets are those in plain sight – George Banister

Problem-Reaction-Solution (P-R-S) events abound throughout history that mirror in their themes and often detail what happened in New York, Washington DC and Pennsylvania on September 11th. They have been orchestrated by the same networks – even the same people in recent times – that played their central or peripheral parts in 9/11.

The P-R-S technique is so simple yet so devastating in the way it seizes and hijacks public perception and opens the collective mind to accept 'solutions' to 'problems' that have been covertly created by the very same people and networks promoting the said 'solutions'. Such connections, however, are hidden by the essential cover-story concocted beforehand to pin the blame on others for the 'problem' – a cover-story sold to the public by a compliant and pitiful mainstream media that simply parrots without question what the authorities tell them about what happened and who was responsible. If we had a mature, grown-up media these P-R-S mega-scams would not be possible because the cover-story would be taken apart very quickly; but we don't. We have overwhelmingly clueless people called 'journalists' who know nothing about how the world really works being string-pulled by the few that own and control media corporations and set the limits on what can be investigated or reported. Employment is swiftly concluded for those who cross the line. The Hidden Hand secret society network crucially extends into the media to install the owners, executives and keyboard fodder that dictate what you see – and don't. This is absolutely vital because you can't control perception if you don't control information. Ironically, the same clueless, gutless media then ridicule and dismiss as 'conspiracy theorists' those who do have the intelligence and backbone to question the cover-stories and show them to be riddled with blatant lies and contradictions. This essential cluelessness – essential for the cover-ups and the survival of their careers – extends even to the terms 'conspiracy theorists' and conspiracy theories' which are used as labels of derision to discredit those that question unsupportable and unsustainable official narratives. As I said earlier, these terms came into widespread use in the 1960s when the CIA contacted major media organisations in the United States as part of a campaign to discredit those questioning the assassination of President Kennedy in 1963 and later those of his brother, Bobby, Martin Luther King and Muslim leader Malcolm X. The document can still be found on the Internet in which the CIA suggested that the labels 'conspiracy theorists' and 'conspiracy theories' could be effective in making the public ignore what was being uncovered. All these decades later today's 'journalists' continue to repeat these CIA-circulated terms of derision while having no idea how they came into such widespread use. Cover stories go on being repeated without question in accordance with the ancient technique of perception control – repeat something often enough and people will believe it. Fortunately, and more than ever before, the 'suckers' as the Hidden Hand perceives them are not buying the lies on the scale we have seen before and this is driving both the censorship of the alternative, questioning media, and public contempt for the systematically mendacious mainstream.

A perfect example of Problem-Reaction-Solution is NATO's Operation Gladio which operated throughout Europe after the Second World War. Gladio was primarily the work of British and American intelligence and involved operatives from many countries – especially in Italy where they were responsible for terrorist attacks and kidnappings that were blamed on target groups they wished to demonise to justify increased government powers. Operation Gladio was behind the Bologna railway station bombing in 1980 which killed 85 people and was blamed on a terrorist group called the Red Brigades to discredit communists. An Italian parliamentary investigation in 2000 heard that the bombing was actually carried out by 'men inside Italian state institutions and ... men linked to the structures of United States intelligence'. Former Gladio agent Vincenzo Vinciguerra, a neo-fascist serving a life-sentence for a deadly car bombing in 1972, said in testimony:

> You had to attack civilians, the people, women, children, innocent people, unknown people far removed from any political game. The reason was quite simple. They were supposed to force these people, the Italian public, to turn to the state to ask for greater security. This is the political logic that lies behind all the massacres and the bombings which remain unpunished, because the state cannot convict itself or declare itself responsible for what happened.

This is the foundation methodology behind 9/11 and there are so many Problem-Reaction-Solution 'false flags' which have remained unquestioned to this day by the very same media – sometimes even the same 'journalists' – that have told you what to believe about the attacks of September 11th. Here are just a few:

Oklahoma bombing

There was a 'rehearsal' for what happened on September 11th six years earlier on April 19th, 1995, when a massive bomb, or bombs *plural* in truth, destroyed the Alfred P. Murrah Building in Oklahoma City and killed 168 people, many of them children at a day care centre (Fig 29). All the classic features were there: the *Problem* of a 'terrorist attack' on a US federal building and the villain or 'patsy' named immediately as Timothy McVeigh; the *Reaction* of understandable outrage from the public when they saw the devastation and believed the government's version of events; and the *Solution* that followed with a series of measures that deleted civil liberties and targeted the so-called Christian Patriot or militia movement that had been having considerable success exposing the global conspiracy at least on one level. The Oklahoma cover-story from the government of Bush family associate Bill Clinton and law enforcement agencies like the FBI claimed that McVeigh was connected to the militia underground. He was executed by lethal injection on June 11th, 2001, and became the first federal execution for 38 years (Fig 30). Terry Nichols, his alleged accomplice, was portrayed as a white supremacist and racist even though his two marriages had been to a Mexican and Filipino. Go figure. McVeigh was executed and Nichols was sentenced to 161 consecutive life terms without parole – a Guinness world record. 'Anti-terrorism' bills were rushed through Congress in days and at least some had clearly been written and printed before the bombing. They included all the elements of destroying civil liberties that have been still

Figure 29: The devastated Murrah Federal Building in Oklahoma City. No way that this scale of damage was caused by a truck bomb as claimed by the official story.

Figure 30: Timothy McVeigh, executed patsy of the Oklahoma bombing.

further extended as a result of 9/11 with the 'white supremacy' card being played today with ever-growing hysteria. President Clinton was calling within 24 hours of the carnage for '... an easing of restrictions on the military's involvement in domestic law enforcement'. He also used the bombing to urge the media to ban 'anti-government extremists' from their newspapers, screens and microphones, and he attacked alternative talk radio shows which were giving the public a rare opportunity to hear and communicate information that differed from the official line.

The bombing was said to have been a response by McVeigh to the murder of men, women and children by the Clinton government at Waco, Texas, two years earlier to the day on April 19th, 1993. One of the government agencies blamed for Waco (along with the FBI) was the Bureau of Alcohol Tobacco and Firearms (ATF) which had offices in the Murrah Building. The official story said they were the target. A bill proposed in response to the bombing by Democrat and ultra-Zionist Charles Schumer, who became a senator for New York, included five-year prison sentences for publicly engaging in 'unseemly speculation' and publishing or transmitting by wire or electronic means 'baseless conspiracy theories regarding the Federal government of the United States'. Naturally, the government would decide if it was 'baseless'. Schumer, one of a stream of ultra-Zionist agents batting for Israel within the US political system, had also vehemently dismissed evidence of the mass murder by the FBI in Waco in a way that had sane people gasping for breath. His fascistic bill never became law, but it was part of a long-planned trend to target alternative information and opinion that is in overdrive today. The FBI 'Joint Anti-Terrorism Task Force' issued flyers urging the public to call the authorities with information about possible 'terrorists' in the United States. They warned people to particularly watch for those who were 'defenders' of the US Constitution against the federal government and United Nations; people who make 'numerous references to the Constitution'; those who 'attempt to police the police'; and 'lone individuals'. The FBI, the main [non]investigation agency for the September 11th attacks, is deeply corrupt at its controlling core and its primary goal is not to find the truth but to support official cover-stories by hiding the truth. My goodness you will see this recurring theme so clearly before the end of the book. You can appreciate from the 'solutions' to the Oklahoma City bombing how a Big Brother state was being prepared that would be expanded so much further and quicker after 9/11 and through Facebook/Google etc. and other censorship in current times.

There is a clear tell-tale theme with these set-ups and stings, be it Oklahoma, the Kennedy assassination or September 11th: The official story is so full of untruths and glaring contradictions that anyone with a smear of intelligence could take them apart. The cover narratives are just that – a cover. They don't describe what happened, only what they want you to believe happened, and so by definition they have to weave a web of lies. With such a deluge of mendacity required to hide the truth there are inevitably lies that contradict other lies, and the bigger the event and the more elements and people involved the more lies have to be employed which lead to even more contradictions. If 'A' is true, then 'B' can't be true, and so on. This is certainly the case with 9/11. The Clinton government and FBI claimed that a fertiliser and fuel oil bomb in a Ryder truck parked outside by McVeigh destroyed the Murrah Building. McVeigh had said he was microchipped while serving with US forces and to understand why he would not vigorously defend himself we would need to know what was going on in his head. Why would someone not mount such a defence when he could not possibly have been responsible for that scale of death and devastation by himself and possibly even at all? Once a person is in government captivity the potential for mind and perception control is limitless with the techniques available then and even more so today. They can be made to say and think almost anything. A 'confession' from his jail cell by Terry Nichols in 2004 – eleven years after the bombing – should be viewed with that in mind although his claim that he didn't know what was really going on rings true of the way these attacks are set-up using 'patsies' – people who are manipulated to take the blame for something others have really done. They are tricked and misled to be in the wrong place at the wrong time by thinking they are there for a completely different reason. It was highly significant with regard to mind control that when McVeigh was first arrested he was given a 'mental assessment' by Louis Jolyon West from the University of California. What newspaper reports about this did not say is that West was one of the most notorious CIA mind controllers in America and heavily involved in MKUltra. West performed the psychiatric evaluation of Jack Ruby who killed Lee Harvey Oswald so the Kennedy assassination would not see an open court where the truth could be told. This mentally ill psychiatrist once killed an elephant with a massive dose of LSD. Another interesting coincidence is that two years before the Oklahoma bombing, Martin Keating, brother of Oklahoma Governor Frank Keating, wrote a novel called *The Final Jihad* which described a terrorist attack on the 'Oklahoma City Building' by a man called Thomas McVeigh. Keating dedicated the book to the 'Knights of the Secret Circle'. Days before the attack a Ryder truck was photographed from the air within a secure a military compound near Camp Gruber-Braggs, Oklahoma.

Provable lie

The FBI said the Murrah Building was destroyed by a single ammonium

nitrate truck bomb in a 20-foot Ryder rental truck parked outside by
McVeigh. The problem is that this was impossible. Lies can do the
impossible, but truth can't. You have only got to see the small crater left
where the truck was standing to see that the explosive power could
never have brought down the Murrah Building. There are other little
details like the fact that while some pillars closer to the truck bomb did
not fall, others further away did. This was a prelude to the stunning
contradictions and impossibilities with regard to the collapse of the
World Trade Center buildings. Retired Brigadier General Benton K.
Partin said from the start that a fuel-fertiliser device in the Ryder truck
could not possibly have brought down the Murrah Building. He said
that too many facts simply didn't add up. Partin was no anti-
government 'extremist', although that was the way he was portrayed to
discredit his devastating testimony. He was chairman for four years of
the Republican Party in Fairfax County, Virginia, and among a long list
of US Air Force appointments he was Commander of the Armament
Laboratory, a top research and development facility at Eglin Air Force
Base in Florida. During his 31 years of active duty he became a highly
acclaimed expert in weapons systems and explosives and his Air Force
and civilian career record was extremely long and impressive. Partin's
detailed assessment of the bombing was widely quoted in the alternative
media while virtually ignored in the mainstream even though it
destroyed the official story. Actually, make that *because* it destroyed the
official story. Partin's report, dated July 30th, 1995, said that serious
damage and demolition to supporting columns inside the building
could *only* have been caused by devices attached to, or placed within,
the columns. He said it was impossible for that to be achieved by an
explosion from outside the building. The truck bomb could have
shattered windows and scattered considerable debris, but the laws of
physics did not make it possible to bring down concrete pillars that
distance away. The laws of physics were also suspended by the official
story of 9/11. Partin pointed out that '... most people fail to appreciate
how inefficient a blast is in air and how dramatically its destructive
potential drops off just a few feet from the explosion'. The main columns
in the Murrah Building were constructed to survive pressure of more
than 3,000 pounds per square inch. There is no way, as Partin's report
pointed out, for a fuel-fertiliser bomb that far from the building to
generate more than a fraction of that pressure. By contrast, Partin said
the fantastic damage to the Murrah Building could have been caused by
a total of just 150 pounds of explosive if it was located in the right places
on the right support columns. Dr Rodger Raubach, a PhD in physical
chemistry and member of the research faculty at Stanford University,
said:

General Partin's assessment is absolutely correct. I don't care if they pulled up a semi-trailer truck with 20 tons of ammonium nitrate; it wouldn't do the damage we saw there.

The 'McVeigh bomb' began to miraculously increase in size once the government and FBI were faced with these facts about the impossibility of a truck bomb causing the damage – the same way the 9/11 story changed once elements of the earlier version were revealed to be impossible. The Bureau of Alcohol, Tobacco and Firearms and other government agencies originally said the bomb contained 1,200 pounds of ammonium nitrate and fuel oil; but, as if by magic, it was to become 4,000 pounds and eventually 4,800. I even heard 7,000 pounds quoted in the media around the time of McVeigh's execution in 2001. It really didn't matter to the laws of physics even if it was 20 tons although it did provide confirmation that we were dealing with a cover-story lie. A study by the US Air Force confirmed that even at 4,800 pounds the story does not make sense:

> It is impossible to ascribe the damage that occurred on April 19th, 1995, to a single truck bomb containing 4,800 pounds ... In fact, the maximum predicted damage of the floor panels of the Murrah federal building is equal to approximately 1% of the total floor area of the building. It must be concluded that the damage at the Murrah federal building is not the result of the truck bomb itself, but rather due to other factors such as locally placed charges within the building itself.

This report was not presented at McVeigh's trial and neither were 4,000 pages of other evidence that the corrupt-to-its-core FBI claimed to have 'lost'. FBI agents interviewed General Partin but did nothing when he showed them that the official story was impossible (this is the same FBI that was the lead investigating agency of 9/11). Partin sent copies of his detailed engineering analysis, including colour photographs, to every member of Congress and more than a thousand media organisations. Only a handful of replies came back. They would rather the orchestrators of mass murder remain at large than reveal that the government and its agencies were lying at every turn. People still say that if the conspiracy I am exposing were true *the media would tell us* about it. Talk about fully-paid-up members of Naivety Anonymous. Researcher J. Orlin Grabbe and others have revealed that a secret Pentagon report on the bombing came to basically the same conclusions as Partin. Grabbe said the Pentagon commissioned nine explosives experts to write reports and accepted two of them as the 'official' report. He said he spoke to both experts, but they declined to be interviewed because of 'confidentiality agreements with the Pentagon'. Grabbe revealed that sources familiar with the Pentagon report told him that the conclusions were the same as those of General Partin, except that the Pentagon report concluded there were demolition charges placed on five columns and not the four suggested by Partin. These findings were supported by the science and witness accounts. Many said they heard more than one explosion. A 500-page report by the Oklahoma City Bombing Investigation Commission said that many witnesses 'have testified to hearing a second bomb' and that 'explosives experts contend that the extent of the damage to the building could not have resulted from a single truck bomb ...' The seismographic record at the Oklahoma Geological Survey (OGS) at the University of Oklahoma recorded two 'seismic events' at the time the Murrah Building was hit and a geophysicist at the OGS, Dr Raymon L. Brown, told *New American* that the simplest explanation for this was 'two separate explosions'. Witnesses support this. After rescuers arrived on the scene there were many reports of other bombs being found and defused and the area was evacuated several times. Volunteers at the site and television viewers remember how police and fire authorities warned that another device, or devices, had been found in the rubble. Television reporters and witnesses that morning said there were other bombs on the site that had not exploded. Oklahoma Governor Frank Keating told one interviewer: 'Reports that I have is that one device was deactivated, apparently there's another device ...' A television report quotes the FBI as saying the explosion was caused by a 'very sophisticated device and had to have been done by an explosives expert'. A spokesman for the rescue teams said that they were not able to get into the wreckage to retrieve the injured because of unexploded bombs still in the building. A reporter with KWTV said that he had just seen a bomb squad truck going towards the Murrah Building to defuse another device. Senator Charles Key's Oklahoma Bombing Investigation Committee confirmed these reports and said there were at least four sightings of other bombs in the building. The Bureau of Alcohol, Tobacco and Firearms (ATF) removed these unexploded bombs from the scene according to police logs and firefighter witnesses. This is the ATF that was supposed to have been McVeigh's target in the official cover story. We were told at different times that other bombs were found, that no other bombs were found, and that bombs were found, but they were 'dummies' used for training by the ATF. Soon all of this was forgotten and the official version of what happened dominated the media. The Oklahoma Bombing Investigation Committee also concluded:

> There is sufficient evidence to confirm that law enforcement agencies in Oklahoma City, as well as Washington DC, had sufficient prior knowledge of the impending disaster, yet took minimum measures to avert the bombing.

Documents and witnesses support this conclusion.

What a precursor that statement was to what happened on 9/11. On the subject of which ... rubble from both the Murrah Building and the World Trade Center was swiftly removed to prevent a proper analysis that would reveal the truth of what happened.

Rubble trouble

Rubble from the Murrah Building contained the proof of where the bombs were really located, what they were, and how many there were. All that was required to establish what had happened beyond doubt was for explosives experts to go in and do their analysis. General Partin made this very point and requested that the site be protected until this investigation could take place. He wrote to Oklahoma Senator Don Nickles and delivered the letter personally to his Washington office and to those of some 23 other senators and 30 congressmen on May 18th, 1995. He wrote:

> I am concerned that vital evidence will soon be destroyed with the pending demolition of the Federal Building in Oklahoma City. From all the evidence I have seen in the published material, I can say with a high level of confidence that the damage pattern on the reinforced concrete superstructure could not possibly have been attained from the single truck bomb without supplementing demolition charges at some of the reinforced column bases.

> The total incompatibility with a single truck bomb lies in the fact that either some of the columns collapsed that should not have collapsed or some of the columns are still standing that should have collapsed and did not.

Instead of listening to Partin the government hired a company called Controlled Demolition to bring down the rest of the building and take the rubble to a private landfill site operated by BFI Waste Systems. Here the remains of the Murrah Building were kept under guard by the Wackenhut Corporation, one of the Hidden Hand's many private armies which helped to ship chemical weapons equipment to Saddam Hussein before the Gulf War thanks to middleman Donald Rumsfeld. George Wackenhut, a former FBI operative, started the company with other FBI associates in 1954. Recruits from the FBI, CIA, and military dominated its board. Wackenhut was a long-time friend of Father Bush and funded his political campaigns along with those of Boy George and Florida governor Jeb Bush. McVeigh's defence team and independent explosives experts were refused access to the rubble that would have revealed all and represented a glaring admission that there was something to hide. Controlled Demolition said this about the Murrah contract on its website: 'When a crime scene involves the detonation of explosives, and the possibility of undetonated materials exist, an experienced contractor is needed to preserve evidence critical to ongoing investigations while dealing with any explosives discovered.' So why was McVeigh's defence team not allowed access to any virgin remains to conduct such investigations? The removal of the Murrah Building rubble before it could be analysed was repeated with the remains of the World Trade Center after 9/11 as I will detail.

Clear prior knowledge

The Bureau of Alcohol, Tobacco and Firearms was supposed to be McVeigh's target so how strange then that no ATF agents were killed or injured because they were miraculously not in the office that morning. We'll see that key players on 9/11 were also miraculously not where they would normally have been on that morning and survived as a result. There were no badge-carrying federal agents in the Murrah Building, only civilian workers. The ATF wheeled out agent Alex McCauley when this fact became known and he told of heroic efforts to rescue victims by himself and a fellow agent who was said to have fallen three floors in an elevator and lived; but Duane James, the building maintenance supervisor, proved that technically and logistically the story was a lie. He said that it was 'pure fantasy' and the ATF had to retract the story and admit that McCauley was nowhere near the building – let alone in it. Remember that when reading the official story of 9/11. The ATF would not say where McCauley or any of their other personnel actually were. Federal Judge Wayne Alley was not in his chambers across the street from the Murrah Building either. He told the *Oregonian* newspaper that he had decided not to go to work that day because 'there had been talk'. He said:

> Let me just say that within the past two or three weeks, information has been disseminated ... that indicated concerns on the part of people who ought to know, that we ought to be a little more careful ... My subjective impression was there was a reason for a dissemination of these concerns.

Alley was warned off in other words and took the advice because the authorities had prior knowledge of what was going to happen – the same would be the case on 9/11. Witnesses who spoke with ATF agents at the scene were told its personnel were not in the building because they had been tipped off through their pagers not to go to work that day. These witnesses included Tiffany Bible, a paramedic who was at the Murrah Building within minutes of the blasts. She swore in an affidavit that she found the ATF in full combat gear (which apparently takes half an hour to put on) and they said they had been pre-warned. Another major question: Why was the bomb squad on site *before* the bombing? Glenn and Kathy Wilburn who lost two small children in the bombing worked constantly and passionately for years to uncover the truth. They conducted and documented more than 300 hours of interviews and persuaded people to talk who had remained silent for fear of the consequences. They established beyond question that a heavily armed bomb squad had been in downtown Oklahoma near the Murrah Building that morning *before* the bombs exploded. Many people saw them, including Oklahoma lawyer Daniel J. Adomitis, who was heading for a charity board meeting at 7.30am, an hour and a half before the explosion:

> There was this fairly large truck with a trailer behind it. It had a shield on the side of the door that said 'bomb disposal' or 'bomb squad' below it. And I really found that interesting. You know, I'd never seen anything like that in person.

Parents saw these people in their bomb squad uniforms when they dropped their children off at the day care centre at the Murrah Building – children they would never see alive again. The Sheriff's Department had to admit after months of denial by the FBI and other government agencies that the bomb squad *had* been there. Glenn and Kathy Wilburn were bitterly attacked by other bereaved families as they challenged the government story and they were denounced as 'conspiracy theorists'. Such is the scale of 'they would never do that' programming. We are dealing with extreme psychopaths and 'they' will do whatever it takes to get what they want. In the end other families also became convinced that the authorities had prior knowledge of the bombing, just as they did about 9/11. The Wilburns and many other families filed legal claims against the US government alleging they had 'detailed prior knowledge of the planned bombing of the Murrah Building yet failed to prevent the bombing from taking place' and claimed that ATF agents were 'alerted not to go to work on April 19th, 1995'.

FB-LIE

Danny Colson, the FBI's director of the terrorist task force, told *Time* magazine in 1999 that when he heard about the blast he had driven to Oklahoma from his home in Dallas at speeds of 100 miles an hour to support the rescue operation and 'investigation'. In fact, Colson checked into the Embassy Suites Hotel in Oklahoma at 12.20am on April 19th which was nine hours *before* the bomb went off. *Why?* The FBI said McVeigh's truck rental agency was tracked from a vehicle identification number (VIN) on the Ryder truck's rear axle. This axle was somehow found both in the bomb crater (mayor of Oklahoma press statement) and

three blocks away (FBI). It must have been one heck of an axle. The FBI
story is another provable lie because rear axles of vehicles manufactured
in America were not imprinted with a VIN and the Ryder rental
company did not add them to the axles either. McVeigh was claimed to
have rented the truck with both his real ID and a false ID and the same
FBI had to admit shortly before McVeigh's first scheduled execution that
they had withheld 4,304 documents from his defence team. He was
given a month-long stay of execution because of this. I can hardly say
often enough that this is the agency that told you the official story of
9/11 and is completely controlled from its highest levels by the Hidden
Hand. The foundation, motivation and nature of the FBI's upper
hierarchy were dictated from the start by that epitome of psychopathic
evil, J. Edgar Hoover. He became director of the FBI's forerunner, the
Bureau of Investigation, in 1924 and was key man in the founding of the
FBI in 1935. Hoover was appointed its first director and remained in the
post until his death more 37 years later. FBI headquarters in Washington
DC is named after him. Hoover created the FBI blueprint of corruption
and deceit and was most definitely involved in the assassinations of the
two Kennedys, Martin Luther King and Malcolm X in the 1960s. That is
not to say that all FBI agents are corrupt – far from it and often quite the
opposite. I am talking about those that control the organisation and the
lower-level assets who choose to do their bidding.

McVeigh stitch-up

The FBI's 'star witness' against McVeigh was Michael Fortier who
admits doing a deal to testify for the prosecution in return for lighter
sentences for gun offences. He told the court that he and McVeigh had
made themselves familiar with the Murrah Building weeks before the
bombing to establish the location of the ATF offices. Well, in that case
why did McVeigh stop at a gas station in the Ryder truck that morning
and ask the way to the building? Why would he do that anyway when
he knew he would be recognised and reported after the bombing? In
that one moment he connected himself to the Ryder truck and the
Murrah Building. Why? If he had spent so much time locating the ATF
offices, why did he park the truck on the side of the Murrah Building
furthest away from the ATF section when he could have left it directly
underneath? We are also asked to believe – and depressingly many do –
that having connected himself with the Ryder truck and the Murrah
Building before the bombing by stopping at the gas station he then
proceeded to 'get away' undetected in a highly visible yellow car
travelling at nearly 100 miles an hour with expired licence plates. We are
further asked to accept that when he was stopped by police for a traffic
violation a man who had just murdered 168 people and maimed
hundreds made no attempt to avoid arrest even though he was armed

and a highly trained soldier. McVeigh was arrested so conveniently for a traffic offence immediately after the bombing for the same reason that Lee Harvey Oswald was arrested in a cinema immediately after the Kennedy assassination and Osama Bin Laden was named as the culprit immediately after 9/11. They are the patsies required by Problem-Reaction-Solution to hide the real orchestrators so name your fake villain as fast as you can. Lee Harvey Oswald was a US agent who was placed in the right place at the right time (wrong for him) without being told exactly why he was there. He realised this after Kennedy was shot and he ran. When he was arrested he said he was a patsy, a stooge, and would have said so in court. This is why he was paraded in public through a parking lot to allow another government agent, Jack Ruby, to shoot him and kill the evidence (see *And The Truth Shall Set You Free*). Ruby was mentally 'assessed' by the same MKUltra psychiatrist Louis Jolyon West who 'assessed' McVeigh – when he wasn't killing elephants with LSD. In the same way, very possibly, McVeigh was a government stooge who parked the Ryder truck without knowing the full story. This would explain why he saw no problem in stopping at the gas station to ask the way to the Murrah building and why he made such a 'getaway' and offered no resistance to the police officer. It would further explain why witnesses saw another man with McVeigh and the Ryder truck who became known as 'John Doe 2'. This mystery man appeared briefly in news reports and was then forgotten. I present evidence shortly that the FBI have security video of 'John Doe 2' which they have kept from public view. McVeigh apparently said that he was not told what the project was really all about and had been trapped, 'framed', and made a patsy to cover up high-level US government complicity. Years later Terry Nichols would say that McVeigh misled him about the nature of what they were doing – which would make sense if McVeigh didn't know either. It would be the blind leading the blind. Your patsies don't have to know the real story – it is essential they *don't* – and you only have to make sure they are where they need to be to manufacture your story of fake villains and give cover to the real ones.

Father Bush and the Iraqi connection

I almost completed a section without mentioning the Bush family, but naturally that couldn't last. It will stagger Americans to learn that at the end of the Gulf War in 1991 President Father Bush arranged for around 4,000 officers from the military and intelligence agencies of Iraq, mostly from Saddam's Republican Guard, to relocate in the United States and 2,000 of these officers became resident in ... *Oklahoma.* Another 500 went to Lincoln, Nebraska. Father Bush arranged for their funding, housing and employment, and this was continued by Bill Clinton and Boy Bush. Jayna Davis, a former reporter with NBC affiliate KFOR-TV in

Oklahoma, worked tirelessly after the bombing to uncover the true story. In 1996 the ultra-Zionist *New York Times* bought her television station and stopped her reports, but she continued to uncover devastating information. She established that more than 70 witnesses saw McVeigh with other men and that more than 20 of these sightings involved people with Middle Eastern features. A sketch of a man with 'olive skin' seen with McVeigh was released by the FBI immediately after the bombing and this was 'John Doe 2'. Jayna Davis was represented by lawyer David Schippers, one of the lead investigators in the impeachment proceedings against Bill Clinton over allegations of perjury and obstruction of justice in 1998/99. Schippers would later represent FBI agents who said their investigations into terrorist suspects were blocked by their superiors before 9/11. He described how the FBI manipulated witness evidence relating to Oklahoma:

> Some of these people who gave affidavits were interviewed by the FBI during the course of the investigation. They were interviewed about the second person they saw and the agents tried to make them say that the second person was Nichols. Every single one of these people said absolutely not, it was a Middle Eastern type individual. Now, listen to this, none of those 302s [interview documents], none of those investigative reports, have ever surfaced.

Reporter Jayna Davis produced a detailed dossier and interviewed witnesses who said they would testify that they saw McVeigh with a former Iraqi soldier who lived in Oklahoma City at the time of the bombing. This man surrendered during the Gulf War and was resettled in the United States from a detention camp in Saudi Arabia. The FBI issued an All-Points Bulletin immediately after the blast for Middle Eastern-looking suspects seen fleeing the scene in a brown Chevrolet pickup with tinted windows and a bug shield. James Patterson, an editorial writer on the *Indianapolis Star*, remarked: 'Something here doesn't pass the smell test.' FBI agents seized all security camera footage in the area that would have shown what happened and who was involved – exactly what they did on 9/11. Their excuse was that the videos were 'part of the investigation' (the traditional excuse also used with 9/11), but TV reporter Brad Edwards located a source who had seen parts of them. Edwards presented a reconstruction for the UK's *Channel 4 News* of what his source claimed to have seen:

> The source said that the tapes show two men inside [the Ryder truck]. One strongly resembling Timothy McVeigh gets out of the driver's side, steps down, he then appears to have dropped something on the step up into the truck. He bends down and appears to pick something up off the step. Then he turns and

walks directly across this street towards the General Electric building. All this time John Doe number 2 is still inside the Ryder truck's cab sitting on the passenger side.

Time passes. The surveillance tape is time-lapse photography. Without knowing exactly the time interval between shots our source can't be sure how long John Doe number 2 sat in that cab. What was he doing all that time? Then the tape shows John Doe number 2 getting out of the passenger side of the Ryder truck. Again the tape shows that a bombing witness accurately described what happened next ... the tape shows John Doe 2 getting out, shutting the passenger side door. He steps towards the front of the truck and is momentarily out of the frame of the surveillance camera. But shortly he appears back in frame walking towards the rear of the truck, still on the sidewalk in the front of the Murrah Building.

The source said that 'John Doe' wore a baseball cap, was taller than the man resembling McVeigh, and had an olive complexion. This was supported by many witnesses, including a man interviewed with a blacked-out face and featured in the report by Brad Edwards:

 I was standing in the building and I looked out the window and I seen the Ryder truck and I seen a man get out of the Ryder truck. He was olive complexion and he was ... he had black curly hair. He was wearing a baseball cap, but his curls were sticking out of his hat. It was very short in the back, but you could still see the curls in his hair. He was not American, he was foreign, you could tell by his skin, his face, and the way his face was ...

Senator Charles Key, who helped to produce a report on Oklahoma, said his understanding was that there is a video showing McVeigh and John Doe 2 getting out of the Ryder Truck and into another pick up. 'Where is that video ... are we going to get to see it?' he asks. Er, you must be joking, the FBI replies. Incidentally, I was on a radio show in McVeigh's home town in America in 2002 talking about the way the FBI had refused to release these surveillance camera tapes. A bloke claiming to be a former FBI agent came on the line saying loudly and vehemently that he worked on the case and there were no surveillance tapes. It took a member of the public to come on to tell him that not only did the tapes exist the FBI had admitted this on the national news. The FBI said in 2001 the tapes were not going to be released at all because of 'national security' (the security of the official lie). When McVeigh went on trial the FBI did not use the tapes in prosecution because they would have destroyed its story. If only McVeigh and no one else had been on the tapes the world would have seen them within hours of the blast. Rule number one of cover stories: if letting the public see something that would support your cover story you let them see it. If the public seeing something would destroy your cover story you don't let them see it. Surveillance cameras are part of the Hidden Hand system of control, but they are also a problem for them when they carry out their public operations. Therefore we have a clear red flag test on these occasions – are we allowed to see the surveillance camera tapes of the scene in question? There were 17 surveillance cameras working 24 hours a day along the route of the last journey taken by Princess Diana between the Ritz Hotel and the Pont de l'Alma tunnel in Paris in 1997, but at that time, of all times, every single one of the 17 *cameras* was 'not working' – or so we are told. This scenario has been repeated again and again including with the London bombings of 2005, the police killing of an innocent Brazilian electrician shortly afterwards and most certainly with 9/11. James Patterson of the *Indianapolis Star* described how critical evidence that several Middle Eastern men may have been connected to the Oklahoma bombing appeared to have been kept from the public by the FBI. He said:

> Officially, the FBI has dismissed the possibility of a John Doe No. 2, an olive-skinned man whose sketch they released immediately after the bombing, or other suspects. But current and former FBI agents in Oklahoma City say they received documents pointing to another person or even a cell of Middle Eastern operatives. At a minimum, Congress should question one former FBI agent who says he obtained 22 affidavits and more than 30 witness statements describing sightings of Middle Easterners with McVeigh.

Hoppy Heidelberg, a prominent Oklahoma horse breeder, was dismissed from the grand jury 'investigating' the case when he went public with his complaints that the 'investigation' was a sham. He said he was not allowed to ask for witnesses, even though it was his lawful right, and one of the areas he wanted to explore was the reports about 'John Doe 2'. He said he was visited by FBI agents brandishing guns who said that if he knew what was good for him he would shut up. Apparently local, state and federal police detained dozens of Middle Eastern men after the bombing as they tried to leave the United States and these included members of the Iraqi Republican Guard brought to the US by Father Bush. Some reports claim that Bush-buddy President Clinton insisted they were released despite being found in possession of bomb-making materials. You are going to see that this behaviour was repeated in the aftermath of 9/11. Do these 'Middle Eastern men' brought to the United States from Saddam's Iraq by Father Bush connect with the 'Middle Eastern men' that form the basis of the 9/11 story? They had enough to choose from – 4,000 – and it would make far more sense than the official make-believe. David Schippers, lawyer for

Oklahoma reporter Jayna Davis, said the same team that carried out the Oklahoma bombing was also responsible for the September 11th attacks. He said that he understood a former Iraqi Republican Guard officer called Al-Hussaini Hussain, who had been mentioned by Jayna Davis as a possible John Doe 2, later worked at *Boston Logan Airport where two of the 9/11 flights took off.* Larry Johnson, a former Deputy Director of the State Department's Office on Counterterrorism, told Fox News the same. He said he believed that Al-Hussaini Hussain was John Doe 2 in Oklahoma and he added: 'The thing that really concerns me relative to 9/11 [is that] when he left Oklahoma, around 1996 and 1997, he went to work at Logan Airport in Boston. We don't know where he is now.' The involvement of Father Bush's Iraqi soldiers is highly possible – if not probable – in the 9/11 story, but only at a bit-part level. The force really orchestrating everything will become obvious much later in the book. Jayna Davis has testified under oath before a grand jury about the Oklahoma bombing and in 1997 she attempted to hand over a large part of her evidence to the FBI which didn't want to know. The Deep State agency showed a similar lack of interest when offered information about Osama Bin Laden which would have dismantled the official 9/11 story. Former FBI agent Dan Vogel offered to testify at a hearing of Terry Nichols, the man convicted with McVeigh, to say that he had received from Jayna Davis affidavits from witnesses who had seen McVeigh with Middle Eastern men in the months, weeks and days before the attack and on the morning of the bombing. Vogel wanted to testify that he had sent the package to FBI agent Henry C. Gibbons and yet the witness statements were not made public. However, a judge ruled that Vogel could not make this devastating testimony because the [In]Justice Department did not want the evidence to be heard and would not authorise the testimony. The Oklahoma bombing was a blueprint for how 9/11 was covered up by the same people.

Waco revisited

The FBI and the Bureau of Alcohol, Tobacco and Firearms (ATF) were lead players in the mass murder of men, women and children at the ranch or 'compound' of the Branch Davidians community, a Bible-based apocalypse cult located 13 miles from Waco, Texas, on April 19th, 1993. The Oklahoma bombings were claimed to be retaliation two years later to the day for what happened to the Davidians. The ranch was known as Mount Carmel from the reference in the Old Testament to a mountain of that name in Israel. Authorities claimed the group were stockpiling illegal weapons and the ATF secured a warrant to search the compound and arrest the group's leader David Koresh and some other members. If they had something on Koresh they could have arrested him months earlier when he often left the ranch, but these deeply mentally disturbed psychopaths wanted a ritual sacrifice by bullets and fire. Perhaps not coincidentally Adolf Hitler and the Nazis, serious malevolent occultists, chose the same day, April 19th, to burn the Jewish ghetto in Warsaw in 1943. They torched the ghetto block by block and then flooded and smoke-bombed sewers when Jews tried to use them to escape. What the ATF and FBI did at Waco was pretty much the same. April 19th and 20th are days of blood sacrifice through fire according to satanic occult law followed so slavishly by the Hidden Hand and its agents. April 19th is the first day of a 13-day satanic ritual period dedicated to the fire god, Baal, Molech/Nimrod, also known in Rome as Saturn, and sacrifice by fire on April 19th/20th has an emphasis on children – as with the Oklahoma bombing on April 19th when 19 children died mostly in a day care centre and the 26 dead children at the Branch Davidian compound on April 19th. The Columbine High School shooting at Littleton, Colorado, was on April 20th, 1999, and also involved the ATF and FBI. I cannot stress enough the obsession these people have with occult ritual and its calendar and I explore this in detail in *The Biggest Secret* and other books. Wars to these satanic psychopaths are mass blood sacrifice rituals. The ATF eventually tried to raid the Davidian compound in a seriously over-the-top manner that included three Army National Guard helicopters and an 80-vehicle convoy stretching back a mile. The raid was resisted and a siege began with the authorities having little interest in negotiation, a fact later criticised by an [In]Justice Department report. Janet Reno, Clinton's recently-appointed Attorney General, gave the go-ahead for a final assault on the Mount Carmel compound using *tanks and gas* to force them out on April 19th. Her main excuse was that children were being abused and Reno's solution was to *kill 26 of them.* The FBI Hostage Rescue Team would later deny they had such evidence of child abuse. Two documentaries, *Waco: The Rules of Engagement* (1997) and *Waco: A New Revelation* (1999) devastatingly exposed calculated mass murder by the FBI and ATF and the involvement of the highest levels of the US government. *The Rules of Engagement* won an Emmy award for best investigative journalism. *Waco: A New Revelation* was narrated by former FBI Special Agent Dr Frederic Whitehurst who detailed the criminal manipulation of evidence and stunning 'incompetence' at the FBI crime laboratory. The documentaries reveal how the authorities used 'flash-bang' devices to start the fire that engulfed the Branch Davidians after filling their compound with high explosives and poisonous gas. The devices were found at all locations where the fires started, but were claimed to have been silencers and gun parts. The documentaries show how 'shape' charges were placed by military operatives at the top of a concrete structure that became a 'bunker' where women and children sought to escape from lethal concentrations of CS gas. The 'shape' charges blew a hole in the concrete roof killing everyone inside and caused the partial disintegration and fusing together of some of the bodies of the women and children because of the pressure and heat from the blast. Military explosives expert General Benton Partin supported this version of events and shape charges were also identified by some researchers in relation to the Murrah Building in Oklahoma. Gene Cullen, a CIA service officer, was among the sources that confirmed how Delta Force, an elite (and brain dead) unit of the US military, was at the compound during the 'siege'. Delta Force fired on anyone who tried to flee the compound through the only escape route and the Davidians either died this way or in the inferno. The FBI claims to have tapes of the Davidians planning to set the compound alight which they have never produced because they are lying. That's what FBI chiefs do – lie. It's their job (see 9/11). Cult leader David Koresh was among 76 Davidians who died that day including all those children. What were the consequences for the FBI and ATF after Waco? *Their funding was increased.* After Oklahoma? *Same.* After September 11th? *What do you think?*

Pearl Harbor – the first 9/11

President Boy Bush called the attacks of September 11th 'our Pearl Harbor' and 'the Pearl Harbor of the 21st century' and for once he was right although not in the way he wanted us to believe. Months earlier a Hollywood blockbuster movie had been released amid widespread promotion that marked the 60th anniversary of the attack by the Japanese Air Force on Pearl Harbor, Hawaii, in 1941. This was the attack that took the United States into the Second World War. To this day popular accounts of history portray President Franklin Delano Roosevelt, a Bush family relative, as a man who 'strove in vain to ward off war' and this is yet another gross misrepresentation. The Roosevelts and the Delanos are Hidden Hand bloodline and I mentioned earlier that President Roosevelt's grandfather, Warren Delano, was a major operator in the drug-running operation of the Russell family, founders of the Skull and Bones Society. Delano also worked in the drugs networks of the British government in Asia, China and the Far East in general. When Franklin Roosevelt was seeking re-election as president in 1940 he repeated the same mantra:

> ... while I am talking to you, mothers and fathers, I give you one more assurance. I have said this before but I shall say it again and again and again; your boys are not going to be sent into any foreign wars!

Roosevelt even had the nerve to add: 'You can therefore nail any talk about sending armies to Europe as deliberate untruth.' He was re-elected because that is what people wanted to hear and this is another example of how psychopaths are pathological liars. Roosevelt, a Hidden Hand stooge to his fingertips, knew that the sons and many daughters of America were going to war again across the ocean very soon. What he needed was an event of such magnitude that America would go to war while, at the same time, Roosevelt would be cleared of any responsibility for going back on his constantly-repeated pledge in the election campaign. The Hidden Hand plan, known all along by Roosevelt, was to engineer an attack on the United States that would so anger public opinion that people would agree to go to war against the aggressor and also join the European conflict. Roosevelt would have been well schooled in manipulating public opinion with engineered events as a member of President Woodrow Wilson's administration in the First World War. I have described in detail in *And The Truth Shall Set You* Free how America was manipulated into that so-called 'Great War' by ultra-Zionist agents of the Rockefellers and Rothschilds. Senator Gerald Nye of North Dakota said in 1939 that he had seen a series of volumes called *The Next War*. These included one entitled *Propaganda in the Next War* and they were written before there was any talk of a Second World War. The material, Nye revealed, included the plan for manipulating public opinion into accepting American involvement in a second global conflict which the documents revealed was coming. Wars don't happen spontaneously – they are long planned. This *Propaganda in the Next War* document originated in Britain (a global Hidden Hand centre). It said:

> To persuade her [the United States] to take our part will be much more difficult, so difficult as to be unlikely to succeed. It will need a definite threat to America, a threat moreover, which will have to be brought home to every citizen, before the Republic again take arms in an external quarrel ... 'The position will naturally be considerably eased *if Japan were involved,* and this might and probably would bring America in without much further ado. [My emphasis.]

> At any rate, it would be a natural and obvious effect of our propagandists to achieve this, just as in the Great War, they succeeded in embroiling the United States with Germany ... Fortunately with America, our propaganda is on firm ground. We can be entirely sincere, as our main plank will be the old democratic one. We must clearly enunciate our belief in the Democratic form of government, and our firm resolve to adhere to ... the old Goddess of Democracy routine.

Sound familiar in the months after September 11th and so many times since? The Council on Foreign Relations (CFR) is a Hidden Hand front organisation in the United States established by the Rockefeller/Rothschild-connected elite in 1921 which has driven so much of American foreign policy to this day. The CFR is part of a web of satellite organisations that I highlighted earlier spawned by a London-based secret society called the Round Table which includes the Bilderberg Group, Trilateral Commission, London-based Royal Institute of International Affairs (also known as Chatham House), and the Club of Rome which was specifically created in the 1960s to exploit fears about the environment to justify the transformation of human society. The Council on Foreign Relations devised the plan to antagonise Japan to such an extent that it would attack the United States so providing the excuse for the US to enter the Second World War with Roosevelt in the clear despite his election promises. CFR founder Henry Stimson, Roosevelt's Secretary of War, wrote is his diary: 'We face the delicate question of diplomatic fencing to be done so as to be sure that Japan is put into the wrong and makes the first bad overt move.' The CFR's War and Peace Studies Project sent a memo to Roosevelt suggesting that aid be given to China during its conflict with Japan and that Japanese assets be frozen in the US, a trade embargo imposed and Japan refused access to the Panama Canal. George Morgenstern's excellent book, *Pearl Harbor, The Story of the Secret War*, reveals how Japan was goaded to attack Pearl Harbor on December 7th, 1941. Roosevelt, who was wholly-owned by the Council on Foreign Relations, set about provoking Japan into an attack with a number of measures and sanctions that included targeting Japanese oil supplies. The Hidden Hand circle controlling Donald Trump have employed the same techniques against Russia, China and other targets. Roosevelt's administration had been intercepting and decoding secret Japanese messages for four years before the Pearl Harbor attack. They knew the Japanese intended to alert diplomatic centres around the world of a decision to go to war through a false weather report during the daily Japanese-language short-wave news broadcast. The forecast of 'east wind rain' indicated war with the United States; 'west wind clear' would mean a decision to go to war with Britain, and British and Dutch colonies in the east; 'north wind cloudy' meant war with Russia.

A Congressional investigation heard in 1945 that messages indicating a decision to go to war with the United States and Britain, though not with Russia, were intercepted and decoded on December 3rd, 1941 – four days before Pearl Harbor. These messages subsequently went 'missing' from Navy files. Other decoded messages gave Roosevelt prior warning of the attack, but the public were not told and nor were the sitting targets in Hawaii. Joseph Grew, US Ambassador to Tokyo, had written to Roosevelt on January 27th, 1941, to say that Pearl Harbor would be the first target in the event of war and Roosevelt had information in total from eight different sources indicating a probable attack. Historian Robert Stinnett revealed the results of 17 years of research into the Pearl Harbor conspiracy in his book, *Day of Deceit: The Truth About FDR and Pearl Harbor.* His research included more than a million documents obtained under the Freedom of Information Act which show that prior knowledge of Japanese plans was kept from US commanders in Hawaii – the very same men who were later made scapegoats for what happened. Stinnett uncovered a memo written on October 7th, 1940, by Lieutenant Commander Arthur McCollum who headed the Far East section of US Naval Intelligence. McCollum confirmed the policy of systematically provoking the Japanese to attack the United States in order to provide the political and public motivation for the declaration of war. The attack was purely to manipulate American public opinion into agreeing to take part in another Hidden Hand war that had long been planned and no one was more duped than the Japanese. They had been tricked into attacking the US both by the Americans and the Germans. Nazi Foreign Minister Joachim von Ribbentrop had been pressing the Japanese to attack the United States. Hitler had added to the Japanese resolve on December 6th, 1941, by indicating that German forces were about to enter Moscow. On December 8th, the day after Pearl Harbor, the Germans were found to be in retreat from the Russian front. More than 3,000 people were killed at Pearl Harbor, about the same as the official death toll on September 11th, and they were still more victims of the Hidden Hand agenda.

The network that coldly allowed 3,000 Americans to be killed at Pearl Harbor to secure a political end would not kill 3,000 others on 9/11 to do the same?? Allen Dulles, the Hidden Hand agent, Hitler supporter and Rockefeller cousin, was appointed to the staff of the Office of the Coordinator of Information the day after Pearl Harbor. This later became the Office of Strategic Services (OSS) and then the CIA which Dulles would lead. The Pearl Harbor plan worked brilliantly as public opinion reacted exactly as required to an attack on American soil – or soil the US had stolen from native Hawaiians. Now the United States was involved in another war in Europe and 'our boys' were on their way across the ocean again, many of them to die, despite Roosevelt's election promises to their mothers and fathers. Roosevelt was in the clear, though, because, well, circumstances had changed. This is how Problem-Reaction-Solution works. You get what you want with none of the responsibility. Winston Churchill, the Hidden Hand bloodline Prime Minister in Britain and a relative of Roosevelt and the Bushes, said of the news: 'That is what I have dreamed of, aimed at, and worked for, and now it has come to pass.' He might have added: 'And I always knew it was going to.' The influence on Roosevelt of the Hidden Hand Council on Foreign Relations, with its membership throughout government, banking, commerce, media and military, cannot be overestimated. Roosevelt's son-in-law, Curtis Dall, said:

For a long time I felt that [Roosevelt] ... had developed many thoughts and ideas that were his own to benefit this country, the USA. But he didn't. Most of his thoughts, his political 'ammunition', as it were, were carefully manufactured for him in advance by the Council on Foreign Relations-One World Money Group. Brilliantly, with great gusto, like a fine piece of artillery, he exploded that 'ammunition' in the middle of an unsuspecting target, the American people – and thus paid off and retained his internationalist support.

A committee known as the Informal Agenda Group packed with members of the CFR wrote the proposal for the United Nations and handed it to Roosevelt who made it public on June 16th, 1944, as if he was the architect. Henry Louis Mencken wrote in *The American Language* that the term 'United Nations' was first mentioned by Roosevelt in a meeting with Churchill at the White House in December 1941 – the month of Pearl Harbor. Some 74 members of the Council on Foreign Relations were in the US delegation at the founding meeting of the United Nations which was created from the start to be a stalking horse for the Hidden Hand's planned world government. The UN building in New York today stands on land donated by the Rockefeller family at a location formerly occupied by a slaughterhouse (how apt). The Rockefellers were also responsible for two other famous buildings in Manhattan ... the twin towers of the World Trade Center.

Gulf of Tonkin

The 'incident' that triggered the full-blown Vietnam War (plus the related conflicts in Laos and Cambodia) was another example of P-R-S. It was also confirmation that often you don't even need a real problem only a public perception of one – as with 'weapons of mass destruction' in Iraq. This is the technique that I call NO-Problem-Reaction-Solution. President Lyndon 'Brown & Root' Johnson, the man who replaced (without an election) the assassinated John F. Kennedy, announced on August 4th, 1964, that Communist North Vietnam had attacked American destroyers in the Gulf of Tonkin off the Vietnamese coast. The official story claimed a US destroyer on 'routine patrol' was targeted by North Vietnamese torpedo boats in an 'unprovoked attack' on August 2nd and that this action was repeated against US ships on August 4th. The media, as usual, reported this as fact simply because Johnson and the Pentagon said it was. The truth is there was no second attack on August 4th and the first was not 'unprovoked' against a US ship on 'routine patrol' as many studies and investigative books have revealed. The destroyer *Maddox* was actively involved in intelligence gathering to support attacks on North Vietnam by the US-backed South Vietnamese Navy and Laos Air Force. Captain John J. Herrick, head of the task force in the Gulf of Tonkin, sent cables to Washington that talked of 'freak weather effects' and an 'overeager sonarman' who was 'hearing [his] ship's own propeller beat'. Squadron Commander James Stockdale, a famous prisoner of war and later a vice-presidential candidate, was flying over the scene that night. Years later he said that he had 'the best seat in the house to watch that event'. He said there was no attack by North Vietnamese gunboats: '... Our destroyers were just shooting at phantom targets – there were no PT [North Vietnamese] boats there ...There was nothing there but black water and American fire power.' President Johnson said the year after he had used this non-existent attack to escalate the conflict into the Vietnam War: 'For all I know, our Navy was shooting at whales out there.' Tom Wells, author of *The War Within: America's Battle Over Vietnam*, said the government was able to deceive the American people because of the media's 'almost exclusive reliance on US government officials as sources of information' and their 'reluctance to question official pronouncements on national security issues'. This happens every time and never more so than after 9/11. Daniel C. Hallin wrote in *The Uncensored War: The Media And Vietnam* that journalists had a great deal of information available that contradicted the official version of events in the Gulf of Tonkin, but it was ignored. He said that it was '... generally known ... that "covert" operations against North Vietnam, carried out by South Vietnamese forces with US support and direction, had been going on for some time.' Journalists and media watchers Jeff Cohen and Norman Solomon described the responsibility of the media in what followed the non-incident in the Gulf of Tonkin:

> By reporting official claims as absolute truths, American journalism opened the floodgates for the bloody Vietnam War. A pattern took hold: continuous government lies passed on by pliant mass media ... leading to over 50,000 American deaths and millions of Vietnamese casualties.

Journalists, or those who pass for them, love to deny responsibility for their actions. They say 'we are just the messenger; don't kill the messenger because you don't like the message'. This is bullshit. If the messenger accepts the message without question they cease to be some neutral, 'independent' courier for information and allow themselves to become an essential tool in the propaganda war against the population. At this point, which was reached a long time ago, they are not 'journalists' at all. They are PR people for the official version of everything – propaganda tools of the Hidden Hand which ultimately owns them. President Johnson went on national television to lie about the Gulf of Tonkin and announce 'retaliatory air strikes' that became the insane Vietnam War. The media praised his speech and said the North

Vietnamese had only themselves to blame. Politicians are overwhelmingly influenced by the media, their perceived public image and financial backers and only two votes were cast against the Gulf of Tonkin Resolution that went through Congress three days after a US ship was *not* attacked by the North Vietnamese. Another lie = another war.

One interesting aspect of the Gulf of Tonkin was the part played by Rear Admiral George Stephen Morrison who was in command of the Carrier Division during the controversial 'incident'. He was the father of Jim Morrison, lead singer of The Doors, one of the most iconic 'anti-establishment' bands in the Flower Power 'counter-culture' era of the 1960s. It is simply fantastic to realise how many key bands and artists central to the 60's 'revolution' came from military-intelligence families in the Washington DC/Pentagon area and how they suddenly headed in the same period to California and especially a location outside Los Angeles called Laurel Canyon. From there the 'counter-culture' was basically launched on the world and one of the effects with its free-love, 'drop out' drug culture was to hijack the anti-Vietnam War movement and allow the carnage on both sides to continue for much longer than a feet-on-the-ground response may have done. Copious amounts of the mind-altering drug LSD that formed such a foundation of Flower Power came courtesy of the CIA. I can most strongly recommend the book by the late David McGowan, *Weird Scenes Inside the Canyon: Laurel Canyon, Covert Ops & the Dark Heart of the Hippie Dream*. I loved 60's music, but nothing, but *nothing*, is what it seems.

History is awash with Problem-Reaction-Solution events set up to justify a course of action that could not otherwise be justified. Another was when the Nazis burned down the Reichstag parliament building in Germany and blamed others for this mega-arson. Adolf Hitler became Chancellor of Germany on January 30th, 1933, and on February 27th the parliament building was torched. The attack was blamed on Marinus van der Lubbe, a mentally-challenged Dutch communist who was later executed for a crime he did not commit. Hitler invoked Article 48 of the Weimar Constitution the day after the fire which allowed civil liberties to be suspended during a 'national emergency'. This Decree of the Reich President for the Protection of the People and State brought an end to freedom of speech and the press, the right of assembly and association, privacy in postal and electronic communications, protection against unlawful searches and seizures, individual rights to property and the rights for states to be self-governing. A further decree created federal 'police' agencies, the SS or 'Special Security' and the SA or 'Storm Troops'. The rest, as they say, is history and look at what has happened as a result of 9/11. What Hitler introduced to fight 'communist terrorism' has been repeated by American presidents and what has been signed into law since the September 11th attacks. Problem-Reaction-Solution is a technique that spans the entirety of known human history and it is time to get wise to it.

Okay, now with all this essential background laid out we shall turn our attention to what happened and didn't happen when America awoke to the clear blue skies of September 11th, 2001. Strap in – it's an extraordinary story that will get progressively more extraordinary the deeper we go.

CHAPTER 5

What didn't happen

If the freedom of speech is taken away, then dumb and silent we may be led, like sheep to the slaughter – George Washington

The attacks of September 11th and their consequences of war and deletion of freedom are a textbook example of Problem-Reaction-Solution. This becomes obvious when you observe the blatantly mendacious official story and what it has been used to justify. I will briefly outline in this chapter the foundations of the utter claptrap we have been asked to believe and then begin to take it apart lie by lie. I should stress that many of the 'facts' in this official version depend on which spokespeople or agency you speak to because they have contradicted each other over and over.

The US government and its 'security' agencies like the CIA and FBI say they had no idea that a terrorist attack was being planned as tens of thousands of people began their working day in the office complexes of Manhattan and at the headquarters of the American military at the Pentagon across the Potomac River from Washington DC. These 'security' agencies employed together some 100,000 people in the United States and worldwide and devoured tens of billions from US taxpayers every year (and that's only the official funding). Yet they claim not to have uncovered one single piece of information to suggest that '19 Arab terrorists' were planning to simultaneously hijack four US commercial aircraft in American airspace and crash them into the very symbols of US military and financial power. The first they knew, so the story goes, was when it was far too late to respond. This is an outrageous lie to be filed with all the rest under 'n' for nonsensical. Anyway, this is the official fairy tale that they want us to believe:

Arab terrorists answering to al-Qaeda 'terror-chief' Osama bin Laden conspired to hijack four commercial aircraft in United States airspace to fly them into iconic American landmarks over a period of some two hours. The 19 hijackers included pilots who took over the controls and gave their lives – and everyone else's – for the glory of Allah. At 7.59am that Tuesday morning, American Airlines Flight 11, a Boeing 767, took off from Logan International Airport in Boston heading for Los Angeles. On board were 81 passengers, two pilots and nine flight attendants.

Following along the runway soon afterwards was United Airlines Flight 175, another Boeing 767, which departed at 8.14am, also for LA. This flight was carrying 56 passengers, two pilots and seven flight attendants. At 8.01am, and more than 200 miles to the south, United Airlines Flight 93 pulled back from the gate at Newark, New Jersey, and the Boeing 757 began its routine journey across America to San Francisco with 38 passengers, two pilots and five attendants. The take-off was delayed apparently by runway congestion and Flight 93 did not leave the ground until 8.42. Meanwhile, at 8.20, American Airlines Flight 77 was leaving Washington's Dulles International Airport for Los Angeles with 58 passengers, two pilots and four attendants aboard a Boeing 757.

American Airlines Flight 11

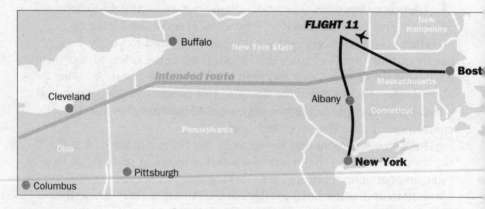

The official story claims that shortly after Flight 11 took off from Boston the plane was hijacked by Arab terrorists using small knives and box cutters. The pilot and co-pilot were John Ogonowski and Tom McGuinness, a former F-14 Navy Tomcat pilot described as 'big and burly'. About 14 minutes into the flight they were instructed by air traffic control to make a 20-degree turn to the right. The pilot replied in the normal way of ground to air communications by repeating the instruction and giving the flight code: '20 right, AAL11'. Very soon after this, the pilot was asked to climb to 35,000 feet, but there was no response. The following is claimed to be a transcript of the exchange published in *The New York Times* that took place from approximately 8.13am:

Boston Control Center: AAL11 turn 20 degrees right.

AAL11: 20 right AAL11.

Controller A: AAL11 now climb maintain FL350 [35,000 feet].

Controller A: AAL11 climb maintain FL350.

Controller A: AAL11 Boston.

Controller A: AAL11, ah, the American on the frequency how do you hear me?

Controller B: This is Athens.

Controller A: This is Boston. I turned American 20 left and I was going to climb him; he will not respond to me now at all.

Controller B: Looks like he's turning right.

Controller A: Yeah, I turned him right.

Controller B: Oh, O.K.

Controller A: And he's only going to, um, I think 29.

Controller B: Sure that's fine.

Controller A: Eh, but I'm not talking to him.

Controller B: He won't answer you. He's nordo [no radar] roger. Thanks.

So the first sign of a problem on 9/11 was shortly after 8.13am and at 8.24am a controller is officially reported to have heard a voice from the cockpit which said:

> We have some planes. Just stay quiet and you will be okay. We are returning to the airport. Nobody move.

The controller is said to have replied: 'Who's trying to call me?' There was no response. This was another 'radio transmission' reported to have been heard by controllers at 8.33am:

> Nobody move please. We are going back to the airport. Don't try to make any stupid moves.

Two minutes later another instruction was heard:

> Everything will be okay. If you try to make any moves, you'll endanger

yourself and the airplane. Just stay quiet.

If all this is true the pilots or 'hijackers' had switched on the microphone in the cockpit, which, the official version says, allowed air traffic controllers to hear the hijackers. Strangely, the four-digit alert code that warns the ground that a plane has been hijacked was never sent and that's the first thing a pilot is meant to do in such circumstances. Even more inexplicably no hijack code was sent by any of the four 9/11 aircraft. The official story says there was only one further contact between Flight 11 and air traffic control. This was when controllers were asked for a route, or air corridor, to John F. Kennedy International Airport in New York, although by whom is not clear. The transponder, or IFF beacon, which allows an aircraft to be more easily tracked on radar and supplies detailed information, was switched off at 8.20am and Flight 11 turned sharply and headed for New York. Losing the transponder makes it harder to track a plane with the more basic conventional radar that bounces a signal off the body of the aircraft, but it is still trackable so long as it is not blocked by mountains or low altitude. Without a transponder signal the plane's location can be tracked although not its height or identity.

We are told that flight attendant Madeline Amy Sweeney (known as 'Amy'), a 35-year-old mother of two, made calls from the plane and spoke to American Airlines Flight Services Manager Michael Woodward at Boston Logan Airport who had known her for ten years. She said hijackers had stabbed two flight attendants, we are told, and that 'a hijacker cut the throat of a business class passenger and he appears to be dead'. She added that terrorists 'had just gained access to the cockpit'. This begs the question of why the pilots had not punched in the hijack code of 7500 (known as 'squawking') if things were happening on the plane before the hijackers gained entry to the cockpit. The action takes two seconds and this would have alerted air traffic controllers to what was going on, but none of the pilots initiated this absolutely basic hijack procedure. Sweeney first spoke with Evelyn Nunez, a passenger service agent for American Airlines, then to staff assistant James Sayer before the most publicised of her conversations with Michael Woodward. An FBI media report said the men were storming the front of the plane even as Sweeney was relating to Woodward details about the hijackers. If all this was happening on the plane why no hijack code from the cockpit and why wasn't the cockpit door immediately secured from the inside? According to Woodward when the plane changed direction and began to descend Sweeney called the cockpit and got no reply. Sweeney told James Sayer the plane was over New York when at that time it was still around 150 miles from the city. She is reported to have told Woodward the seat numbers of the hijackers and that the plane was going down.

Her final words were given as: 'I see water and buildings. Oh my God. Oh my God.' I met with Michael Woodward at Boston Logan Airport when I was researching *Alice in Wonderland and the World Trade Center Disaster* but he said he could add nothing to what had been reported.

American Airlines later released an account of a conversation it says took place during the flight between attendant Betty Ong and airline staff on the ground. They say that Ong pressed number 8 on a seatback Airfone and got through to an American Airlines reservations agent who called the system operations control centre in Fort Worth, Texas. Airfone was an air-ground radiotelephone service embedded in seatbacks and marketed under the names Airfone, GTE Airfone and Verizon which allowed passengers to make in-flight calls. Ong is said to have made her call at 8.27am which was about twelve minutes after the cockpit first failed to respond to air traffic instructions. She said she was on 'Flight 12' before correcting to Flight 11. Amy Sweeney also said 'Flight 12' in her call from the plane to American Airlines passenger service agent Evelyn Nunez. Sweeney then called Flight Services Manager Michael Woodward and in his notes taken at the time the flight number 12 is overwritten with 11 suggesting a third mention of 'Flight 12'. Craig Marquis, the American Airlines manager on duty, said that Betty Ong told him that two flight attendants had been stabbed and one was being given oxygen. A passenger had been slashed in the throat and looked dead and the hijackers were in the cockpit. She said passengers had been sprayed with something that made her eyes burn and she was having difficulty breathing. Ong reported there were four hijackers (not the five the FBI claims) and she said they were in the first-class seats, 2A, 2B, 9A, and 9B. These numbers were slightly different to those given by attendant Sweeney and both were different to those given by the FBI. I asked the FBI in 2002 why there was a discrepancy and they said they could not answer questions because of the 'ongoing investigation'. I would have to apply through the Freedom of Information Act in years to come to find the information I wanted, a spokesman said. Craig Marquis asked Betty Ong if the plane was descending. 'We're starting to descend. We're starting to descend,' she is said to have replied.

At 8.46am, 48 minutes after leaving Boston, the official story says that Flight 11 crashed into the North Tower of the World Trade Center at the 96th of the 110 floors. Some may question why I am saying 'the official story says' Flight 11 struck the building when everyone saw that this was the case. But was it? The building was hit, yes, of course, but was the impact from Flight 11? There is much to question about that. The FBI later listed five hijackers on Flight 11 although two separate attendants on the plane both said four. I will use 'hijacker' names and spellings from the official 9/11 Commission report into the attacks published in 2004 because names have come and gone and varied in spelling. Among those listed by the FBI as a hijacker of Flight 11 was Egyptian Mohamed Atta who is claimed to have been at the controls and the overall leader of the 9/11 terrorists. Other alleged hijackers on Flight 11 were named as Saudi Arabians Abdulaziz al-Omari, Wail al-Shehri, Waleed al-Shehri and Satam al-Suqami.

United Airlines Flight 175

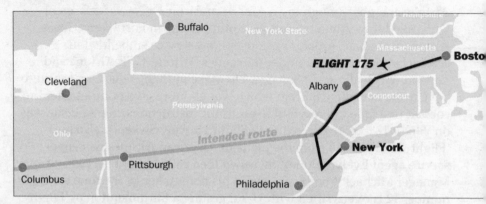

Captain Victor J. Saracini, aged 51, and 38-year-old first officer Michael R. Horrocks were at the controls of Flight 175 when it pushed back from Gate 19 at Boston's Logan Airport. This was seven gates along from Flight 11 which had left from Gate 26 about 15 minutes earlier. Official stories of what happened to the two planes are very similar. Flight 175 took off about 8.14am and nothing seemed amiss in the initial climb. At 8.37, with Flight 11 now known to be in trouble, a controller is said to have asked Saracini and Horrocks if they could see American Flight 11 ahead of them.

> **Controller:** Do you have traffic? Look at, uh, your twelve to one o'clock at about, uh, ten miles south bound to see if you can see an American seventy six seven out there please.

> **UAL175:** Affirmative we have him, uh, he looks, uh, about twenty, yeah about twenty nine, twenty eight thousand.

> **Controller:** United 175 turn five turn thirty degrees to the right. I [want to] keep you away from this traffic.

We are told there were no further communications between the ground and Flight 175 until 8.41, that's just five minutes before Flight 11 crashed into the World Trade Center. At this time one of the pilots on Flight 175 is reported to have called the controller and said, using the pilot code for Boston: 'We heard a suspicious transmission on our departure from B-O-S. Sounds like someone keyed the mike and said: "Everyone stay in your seats".' Just 90 seconds after that communication with air traffic control Flight 175 veered off-course over northern New Jersey and headed south before turning back in a U-turn towards New York at some 400 miles an hour. Think about that – *90 seconds* between no problem and the plane being taken over by hijackers and flown off-course? Once again the transponder was switched off and there was no hijack code from the pilots. Howard Dulmage, an aviation attorney and pilot, said: 'You think four times in one morning one of those crews would have done that – that means they had to be upon them before they could react.' Well, that's one way of trying to explain it, but there are others as we'll see. I mean, *four* pilots on *four* planes did not do the first thing they are supposed to do when a hijack is happening? A female flight attendant is said to have spoken to a mechanic at an airline maintenance centre in San Francisco that takes in-flight calls from attendants reporting items that need replacing or repairing. We are told the mechanic reported the conversation at about 8.50am to Rich 'Doc' Miles, manager of the United Airlines System Operations Center in Chicago. Miles said the mechanic told him the attendant had said: 'Oh my God. The crew has been killed; a flight attendant has been stabbed. We've been hijacked.' The line then went dead. If this is all accurate then, according to the official timeline, the hijackers stormed the cockpit, killed the crew, took over the controls, a flight attendant rang the airline mechanic, and he called Rich Miles to report what she said – all in the space of around seven minutes. Messages were sent to the cockpit computer without reply. Passenger Peter Hanson, a software salesman, is said to have used his cell phone to ring his parents in Easton, Connecticut, at about 9am, some 45 minutes after take-off, and told her that hijackers with knives had taken over the plane and stabbed a stewardess. He is reported to have called again and before the line was lost he is said to have told his father Lee that the plane was 'going down'. Hanson's wife Sue, son Peter, and their two-year-old daughter Christine were also on the plane. At 9.03am what is a claimed to have been 'Flight 175' smashed into the South Tower of the World Trade Center on live television amid a fireball that no one who saw it will ever forget. The FBI said hijackers on Flight 175 were led by Marwan al-Shehhi of the United Arab Emirates who is claimed to have been a close friend and associate of Mohamed Atta. Others named are Fayez Banihammad (United Arab Emirates), Mohand al-Shehri (Saudi Arabian), Hamza al-Ghamdi (Saudi Arabian) and Ahmed al-Ghamdi (Saudi Arabian).

American Airlines Flight 77

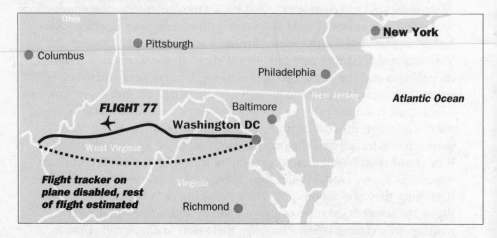

In the cockpit that morning as Flight 77 took off from Washington Dulles at 8.20am for Los Angeles were 51-year-old Captain Charles F. 'Chic' Burlingame III and first officer David Charlebois, who was 39. Burlingame was a graduate of the 'Top Gun' fighter pilot school and was such a perfectionist that one colleague said that he would carry a set of small paint brushes to dust the instruments. He had once worked at the Pentagon while a Navy reservist not far from where his flight would be said to have crashed that morning. Once again – *said* to have crashed? I'll explain as we proceed why there is good reason to question that claim. Burlingame's father was in the Navy and Air Force for 23 years and he and his wife are buried in the Arlington National Cemetery close to the Pentagon. Among the passengers on Flight 77 was a former American Airlines pilot called Wilson 'Bud' Flagg, a retired Navy Admiral once posted to the Pentagon; Brian Jack, a head of fiscal economics in the office of Defense Secretary Donald Rumsfeld at the Pentagon, where he had worked for 25 years; three engineers from plane makers, Boeing; and Barbara Olson, an on-air contributor to CNN and wife of the US Solicitor General, Theodore 'Ted' Olson. About 8.50am we are told that the cockpit stopped responding to controllers and six minutes later the transponder was turned off. A controller is said to have called the aircraft repeatedly asking: 'American 77 Indy radio check, how do you read?' At 9.02am, still nearly 40 minutes before impact, a controller is reported to have told American Airlines:

> We lost track control of the guy, he's in coast track [no transponder] but we haven't – we don't really know where his target is and we can't get a hold of him.

An 'unidentified' aircraft was then picked up on radar headed for

Washington at some 500 miles an hour. A military C130 took off from Andrews Air Force Base near Washington to identify the plane and reported it was a Boeing 767 (Flight 77 was a 757) moving low and very fast. This was Flight 77, or so we are told, with the Pentagon as its target. One of the alleged terrorists is said to have told passengers that they were going to die and they should phone their families. The official story claims that former federal prosecutor and CNN contributor Barbara Olson rang her husband, US Solicitor General Ted Olson, at his office in the [In]Justice Department at about 9.25am. He said he was watching television coverage of the World Trade Center when his secretary told him: 'Your wife is on the phone.' Olson said that Barbara, his third wife, told him that her plane had been hijacked using box cutters and knives. She said nothing about the number of hijackers or their nationality. There appear to be several published versions of their conversation and in one she said the pilots were with her at the back of the plane. Ted Olson told her about the World Trade Center and she said: 'What should I tell the pilot?' before the line went down. Olson said he called the [In]Justice Department command center staff who told him they had no idea the plane had been hijacked. His wife rang back and said the plane was circling, but the line was lost again, Olson said. We will see that the validity of Ted Olson's story is *seriously* open to question. He was the lawyer who argued the case before the Supreme Court for George W. Bush to be elected president after the Florida voting fiasco and he was a vehement advocate of Bush's anti-terrorism laws after September 11th. Ted Olson defended the United States before the Supreme Court in March, 2002, against charges that the CIA committed murder (which it does). He said that day:

> It's easy to imagine an infinite number of situations where the government might legitimately give out false information. It's an unfortunate reality that the issuance of incomplete information and even misinformation by government may sometimes be perceived as necessary to protect vital interests.

The official story claims that some *80 minutes* after take-off Flight 77 was seen approaching Washington DC. The plane is said to have made a sharp turn and descended very steeply from 7,000 feet to near surface level, crossed a highway and clipped street lamps, before striking a helicopter pad and exploding into a five-storey section of the Pentagon (one of the world's biggest buildings) at 9.43am. Defense Secretary Donald Rumsfeld was in an office at the opposite end of the Pentagon to the impact and such is the size of the Pentagon he said that he felt only a 'jarring thing'. We are told that a total of 190 people died in the plane and the Pentagon. The FBI said five hijackers were on board Flight 77 led by Hani Hanjour, a notoriously poor pilot of tiny one-engine aircraft, who is said to have been at the controls when the wide-bodied jet struck the Pentagon. He was a Saudi and so were the other 'hijackers' claimed to have been on the plane: Khalid al-Mihdar, Majed Moqed, Nawaf al-Hazmi and Salem al-Hazmi.

United Airlines Flight 93

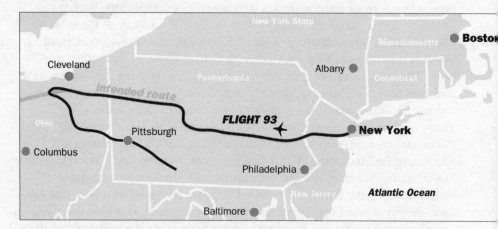

Flight 93 left Gate 17 at Newark International Airport at 8.01am bound for San Francisco and took off at 8.42am after its long delay. At the controls were 43-year-old captain Jason Dahl, from Littleton, Colorado, and the 36-year-old first officer LeRoy Homer of Marlton, New Jersey. They flew west over Pennsylvania and into northern Ohio where they received a message from United Airlines warning all pilots of a potential 'cockpit intrusion'. Flight 93 pilots confirmed receipt of the message and because of its late departure this was the only one of the four planes that had prior warning of possible trouble. It is said that Flight 93 was hijacked some 30 minutes after take-off, that's around 9.10am, and after two planes had crashed into the World Trade Center. The official story says that it was not until 9.40 that the transponder signal was lost. Hijackers are said to have forced their way into the cockpit and one of them warned he had a bomb attached to his waist. Hijackers told passengers they were taking the plane to another airport according to the official story. Air traffic controllers apparently said they heard two short radio transmissions around the time the 'cockpit was stormed' and in one they heard a pilot say: 'Get out of here'. An unnamed government official quoted in the media said there were at least four radio transmissions in which the phrases 'bomb on board', 'our demands' and 'keep quiet' were heard. *ABC News* claimed to have secured a tape of these transmissions in which a hijacker says:

We'd like you all to remain seated. There is a bomb on board. And we are going to turn back to the airport. And they had our demands, so please remain quiet.

We are told that passengers used their cell phones and seatback Airfones to call friends and family and they heard about the planes crashing in New York and Washington. This, it is claimed, led to passengers getting together to challenge the four hijackers who were armed once again with small knives and box cutters. At 9.45am Todd Beamer, a 32-year-old employee of the computer software company Oracle, is said to have spoken to Airfone supervisor Lisa Jefferson after his credit card was refused when he tried to call his family. A summary of the 15-minute conversation was faxed by the Verizon phone company to his wife in which he said that the pilot and co-pilot appeared to be dead and the hijackers were flying the plane. Another passenger, Lauren Grandcolas, is reported to have phoned her husband Jack in San Francisco to say: 'We have been hijacked.They are being kind. I love you.' Beamer is said to have stated that one hijacker was guarding 27 passengers at the back of the aircraft while having what was claimed to be a bomb around his waist. He is reported to have said that two other hijackers were in the cockpit and another was guarding first class. Beamer sent love to his wife, who was five months pregnant, and his two small sons. The last words the phone supervisor is said to have heard him say were: 'Are you guys ready? Let's roll.' His wife Lisa, never spoke to him directly. The official story says that at 9.42am Mark Bingham, a 31-year-old rugby player and an enormous man at six-feet-five, called his mother, Alice Hoglan, from the plane:

> Mom, this is Mark Bingham. I want to let you know that I love you. I'm calling from the plane. We've been taken over. There are three men that say they have a bomb.

Jeremy Glick, a former national judo champion, is reported to have talked with his wife, Liz, on an Airfone and asked if it was true about planes crashing into the World Trade Center. He said the passengers were taking a vote over whether they should try to take back the plane. 'Honey, you need to do it,' she told him. Glick's mother-in-law told CNN that he also called her to report that 'one of the hijackers had a red box he said was a bomb and one had a knife of some nature'. She said Glick left the phone for a while and then returned to say; 'The men voted to attack the terrorists.' Thomas Burnett Jr, a 38-year-old father of three girls, is said to have called from the plane four times and in his last call told his wife that they planned to challenge the hijackers. 'I know we're all going to die,' he is said to have told her. 'There's three of us who are going to do something about it. I love you, honey.' Flight attendant Sandy Bradshaw called her husband Phil, a US Airways pilot. 'Have you heard what's going on?' she said. 'My flight has been hijacked. My flight has been hijacked with three guys with knives.' Note again that the FBI says four, just as it names five for Flight 11 and 175 when attendants were reported to have said four. Bradshaw reported she was in the galley filling jugs with boiling water and she ended: 'Everyone's running to first class. I've got to go. Bye.' The official story is that passengers attacked the hijackers and the plane crashed into a field at Shanksville, Pennsylvania, at 575 miles an hour. The aircraft is said to have hit the ground at 10.03 or 10.06 depending on the information you believe. This is more than two hours after the first hijacked plane left Boston. By now thousands of people were dead and the world was in trauma at the unspeakable horror of what had happened. Four alleged hijackers on Flight 93 were named as: Ziad Jarrah (Lebanese), Ahmed al-Haznawi (Saudi Arabian), Ahmed al-Nami (Saudi Arabian), Saeed al-Ghamdi (Saudi Arabian).

Television brought the shocking scenes to hundreds of millions of people as the North Tower burned from the collision with 'Flight 11'. Then, 18 minutes later, as people were watching those live pictures, 'Flight 175' careered into the South Tower amid an enormous explosion of flame. An estimated 20,000 people could have been working in each of the towers at that time in the morning and the official death toll was a little under three thousand. At 9.59am, 56 minutes after impact from 'Flight 175', the South Tower collapsed as a horrified world looked on. Half an hour later the North Tower went the same way an hour and 42 minutes after impact from 'Flight 11'. The official explanation for the imploding collapse was that the fuel fire had weakened steel supports and the floors above the impact began to fall, creating an ever more powerful chain reaction as floors crashed upon floors until the whole building collapsed. Among the dead were 341 fire fighters together with other rescuers who had rushed into the buildings to help and been killed in the sudden collapse. We will see that the official story of why the towers collapsed in a provable lie that would have required the suspension of the law of physics.

This is a basic outline of the official story of 9/11 which has been used to justify mass death, destruction and slaughter in the Middle and Near East, a frenzy of mass surveillance 'to stop the terrorists' and the deletion of fundamental freedoms. From hereon we shall dismantle this impossible version of events and show that all the world-changing happenings that have followed have been founded on a Big Lie.

CHAPTER 6

House of cards

Let us never tolerate outrageous conspiracy theories concerning the attacks of September the 11th – George W. Bush

The official story of 9/11 is an obvious and transparent fantasy and the unspeakable atrocities were yet another version of Oklahoma and Pearl Harbor.

Problem-Reaction-Solution attacks are not only *made* to happen but *allowed* to happen and this is the combination you see in all these Hidden Hand false flags. First they arrange for their agents in government, military and intelligence networks, and sometimes terrorist groups they control, to execute the plan and then ensure the plan is allowed to happen by blocking the usual response by law enforcement and other security agencies. A proper investigation is suppressed in the aftermath and this, together with a pathetically compliant mainstream media, means the real perpetrators are never exposed. The perpetrators and those protecting the perpetrators are both assets of the same Hidden Hand Web. In fact, they are often the very same people and certainly were with 9/11. Colonel Leroy Fletcher Prouty was a man with long experience in covert operations working with the US security apparatus. He worked with the Office of Strategic Services, the forerunner for the CIA, and established Air Defense Command in 1950. Prouty went on to work with the CIA then led by its notorious first director, Allen Dulles, and for nine years he served at the Pentagon as Briefing Officer for the Secretary of Defense, Chairman of the Joint Chiefs of Staff and Chief of Special Operations. He revealed in his 1973 book, *The Secret Team*, that the CIA was a tool of a 'high cabal' of industrialists and bankers (the Hidden Hand). Prouty revealed the existence of the CIA Executive Action programme which specialised in removing foreign leaders 'unfriendly' to American (Hidden Hand) interests. Prouty said this group was behind the assassination of President Kennedy in 1963 under the direction of its head, Edward Lansdale, who was in Dallas acting '... like the orchestra leader, coordinating these things'. Prouty later wrote and lectured about many clandestine operations and authored the book, *JFK, The CIA, Vietnam And The Plot To Assassinate John F. Kennedy*. The

Donald Sutherland character called 'X' in the Oliver Stone movie *JFK* was apparently based to an extent on Prouty who died just three months before September 11th. This guy operated for decades in the shadowy world from which came the real orchestrators of 9/11. This is what he said about assassinations and it applies just as much to what happened that September day:

> No one has to direct an assassination – it happens. The active role is played secretly by permitting it to happen. This is the greatest single clue. Who has the power to call off or reduce the usual security precautions?

If you look at the evidence detailed in books by myself and others, Fletcher Prouty's words are true in the assassinations of John F. Kennedy, his brother Bobby, Martin Luther King, Princess Diana, Israeli Prime Minister Yitzhak Rabin, Swedish Prime Minister Olaf Palme ... the list could go on for pages. The same is also true of September 11th in that the usual security and response systems were nowhere to be seen. I am going to present the information layer-by-layer going deeper and deeper as we progress and what appears to be the case at one point will look different as more and more layers are revealed. Only at the end of the book will my presentation of the evidence (so far) be complete and even then there will be more to know. There always is. I will start with the most obvious question of how four commercial airliners could be hijacked in highly-protected American airspace and crashed into iconic buildings and a field without a military response over nearly two hours that in any way affected events.

NORAD and Cheyenne Mountain

The organisation charged with the task of protecting North American airspace in both the United States and Canada is NORAD, the North American Aerospace Defense Command, headquartered at the Peterson Air Force Base in Colorado with its operational centre in the nearby Rockies known as Cheyenne Mountain. This was the organisation that did nothing to effectively respond to the attacks in the very American skies it is their job to protect. Consider the scale of their operation and capability even in 2001. NORAD was created by an agreement signed by the US and Canadian governments on May 12th, 1958. NORAD's brief, to quote its own website at the time of 9/11, involves:

> ... the monitoring of man-made objects in space, and the detection, validation, and warning of attack against North America whether by aircraft, missiles, or space vehicles, utilizing mutual support arrangements with other commands. Aerospace control includes ensuring air sovereignty and air defense of the airspace of Canada and the United States.

NORAD has an agreement with the civilian Federal Aviation Administration (FAA) to respond to civil aviation emergencies when commercial aircraft are hijacked, lose contact with air traffic controllers or stray off-course. What happened on 9/11, therefore, was exactly what NORAD is there to deal with. The President of the United States and the Prime Minister of Canada officially appoint NORAD's commander. This means, of course, that the US President appoints him – on the recommendation of others. Another quote from the NORAD website in 2001: 'Cheyenne Mountain serves as a central collection and coordination facility for a worldwide system of sensors designed to provide ... the leadership of Canada and the US with an accurate picture of any aerospace threat.' Ah yes, Cheyenne Mountain. It was not long into my research of the global conspiracy in 1992 that I first came across Cheyenne Mountain. There have been many mysterious animal mutilations in that area, including some at the nearby Cheyenne Mountain Zoo, and researchers into 'UFO' activity have long had their eyes on the Cheyenne Mountain complex (Fig 31). What we know for sure is that this is the vast super-secret headquarters for the 'defence' of North America which acted as the early warning and response centre during the (manufactured) 'Cold War' with the Soviet Union. Cheyenne Mountain is also the location of so much more that we are not told about. The complex is mounted on more than 1,300 half-ton springs that allow it to sway up to a foot horizontally in any direction should it be struck by an earthquake or nuclear attack. The two main doors consist of 25 tons of baffled steel, three feet thick, and the complex is located 2,000 feet inside the granite mountain. In the same region are other major military and technology centres like Ent Air Force Base, Fort Carson Army Base, Peterson Airfield, Lowry Air Force bombing range, US Air Force Academy, Buckley Air National Guard and Naval Air Station, and Rocky Mountain Arsenal. A Scripps Howard News Service survey reported in 1998 that about 7,000 people were employed within Cheyenne Mountain and that spending on the facility was substantially increased by the best part of $2 billion after the 'Cold War' was over. This would seem to be a

Figure 31: The fantastic global tracking facility at Cheyenne Mountain, Colorado.

strange contradiction if you didn't know that the enormous network of underground bases and tunnel systems that connect them across the United States are not there primarily to protect the population at all. Their role is to *control* the population and operate as part of the secret Permanent Government with an agenda that US Presidents know nothing about. Inside Cheyenne Mountain are some of the most brilliant technological minds in the world using and developing technology that is light years ahead of anything you will see in the public arena. It is a big mistake to judge what is possible only on the basis of technology you know about. These guys aren't working with that.

The following information came from the official Cheyenne Mountain website in the period across 9/11 and represents only a fraction of what really goes on there. The excavation of Cheyenne Mountain near Colorado Springs began in May, 1961, and was completed in around a year, according to the official story. The NORAD command centre was located here and became fully operational on April 20th, 1966, when its duties were transferred from Ent Air Force Base. NORAD has since been joined inside Cheyenne Mountain by other 'early warning and response' organisations tasked with defending North America from air attack. One is the Air Force Space Command that is supposed to provide protection from space and missile attack and this operates the Space Defense Operations Center. From here personnel and 'their worldwide sensors, under the direction of Air Defense Command', supported the first flight of the space shuttle in April, 1981. Cheyenne Mountain continued to support every subsequent shuttle mission. General Ralph E. Eberhart, commander of NORAD during 9/11, was also commander of Space Command and took over in February, 2000, from General Richard B. Myers who was Deputy Chairman of the Joint Chiefs of Staff at the Pentagon and acting chairman when the attacks were happening. Myers was appointed chairman soon afterwards and became head of the uniform level of the Pentagon hierarchy. Eberhart and Myers both served at the 'CIA' Air Force Base at Langley near Hampton, Virginia, from where, it is claimed, jets were scrambled (far too late) to intercept Flight 77 as it headed for Washington. Eberhart was Commander, Air Combat Command, from June 1999 to February 2000 when he replaced Myers at NORAD. I'll have much more about Myers' behaviour on September 11th and his bizarre lies in due course. I'm not finished with Eberhart either.

This defence network could not respond on 9/11?

The website for Cheyenne Mountain operations in 2001 described the role of NORAD and its capabilities – none of which were on view on 9/11 when events happened over a period of some two hours without a NORAD intervention that was routine every other day. The website said that the Air Defense Operations Center employed its air defense network 'to provide surveillance and control of air operations to North America and unknown traffic'. NORAD's Combat Operations Center evolved into the Cheyenne Mountain Operations Center which collected data 'from a worldwide system of satellites, radars, and other sensors and processes that information on sophisticated computer systems to support critical NORAD and US Space Command missions'. Cheyenne Mountain Operations Center provided warning of ballistic missile or air attacks against North America, assisted the air sovereignty mission for the United States and Canada, and, if necessary, was the focal point for air defense operations to counter enemy bombers or cruise missiles. The website said that Cheyenne Mountain provided a day-to-day picture of precisely what was in space and where it was located and 'supported space operations, providing critical information such as collision avoidance data for space shuttle flights and troubleshooting satellite interference problems'. Cheyenne Mountain operations were conducted by six centres manned 24 hours a day, 365 days a year – the Command Center; Air Defense Operations Center; Missile Warning Center; Space Control Center; Combined Intelligence Watch Center; and the Systems Center. The Command Center was 'the heart' of operations 'monitoring, processing, and interpreting missile, space or air events which could have operational impacts on our forces or capabilities, or could be potential threats to North America or US and allied forces overseas'. The Command Center was linked directly to National Command Authorities of both the US and Canada as well as regional command centres overseas. NORAD and US Space Command assessed missile, air, and space events and a response and direction were then 'properly conveyed and executed ...' *Except on 9/11*. The website said:

> ... The Air Defense Operations Center provides command and control for the air surveillance and air defense network for North America. In 1994, they monitored over 700 'unknown' radar tracks entering North American airspace. Many of these were subsequently identified as friendly aircraft that had erred from flight plans or used improper procedures. Yet nearly 100 were identified as illegal drug-carrying aircraft that were subsequently prosecuted by the US and Canadian Drug Enforcement Agencies.

The technology located within Cheyenne Mountain was state of the state of the art for 2001 and the Missile Warning Center employed a 'worldwide sensor and communications network to provide warning of missile attacks, either long or short range, launched against North America or our forces overseas'. The technology provided information 'regarding missile launches anywhere on earth which are detected by the strategic missile warning system and which could be a potential threat to Canada or the US'. The Space Control Center at Cheyenne Mountain, opened in March, 1994, had highly sophisticated technology that 'supports the space control missions of space surveillance and protection of our assets in space' and its primary objective was to perform 'the surveillance mission ... to detect, track, identify, and catalog all manmade objects in space'. The Center has a computerised catalogue of 'all orbiting space objects, charts objects, charts present position, plots future orbital paths, and forecasts times and general locations for significant objects re-entering the Earth's atmosphere'. The Space Control Center was tracking some 8,000 'in-orbit objects', and this information was used to provide NASA with collision avoidance information during space flights. Cheyenne Mountain was also home to the Combined Intelligence Watch which served as North America's 'indications and warning center for worldwide threats from space, missile, and strategic air activity, as well as geopolitical unrest that could affect North America and US forces/interests abroad'. Put another way, they have a satellite surveillance network that could read your licence plate from space wherever you may be. Combined Intelligence Watch gathered 'intelligence information to assist all the Cheyenne Mountain work centers in correlating and analyzing events to support NORAD and US Space Command decision makers'. There was a Systems Center that ensured 'continuity of operations throughout the Cheyenne Mountain Operations Center by providing communications and computer systems management for over 100 computer systems and 600 communications circuits in support of NORAD and US Space Command missile warning, space control, and air defense missions'. This is the organisation that failed to intervene in the 9/11 attacks.

'Most unique installation'

Cheyenne Mountain called itself one of the most unique installations in the world in 2001 and no doubt still does. The complex allowed for cooperation and coordination between apparently unconnected organisations because it employed staff from the Army, Navy, Marine, Air Force and Canadian Forces. Cheyenne Mountain operated military communication and navigation satellites that directed and guided 'western' armies during their bombardments of Iraq, Afghanistan and elsewhere. Major Mike Birmingham, an Army spokesman for the Colorado base, said: 'Space support basically allowed US forces to perform that famous 'left hook' operation [employed during the Gulf War] – the Iraqis assumed no one could navigate that well in the desert.' Despite all of this amazing technology and response capability four commercial airliners hijacked in American airspace proved too much for them on September 11th and absolutely nothing was done that made any difference to events. *Why?* If anyone is still in any doubt about the technological and coordination capability we are talking about here and its instant communications network throughout the United States government, military and air traffic surveillance, the official Cheyenne Mountain website said at the time:

> The Cheyenne Mountain Operations Center comprises the largest and most complex command and control network in the world. The system uses satellites, microwave radio routes, and fiber optic links to transmit and receive vital communications. Two blast-hardened microwave antennas and two underground coaxial cables transmit the bulk of electronic information. Most of this information is data sent from the worldwide space surveillance and warning network directly to computers inside the Mountain. Redundant and survivable communications hotlines connect the Command Center to the Pentagon, White House, US Strategic Command, Canadian Forces Headquarters in Ottawa, other aerospace defense system command posts, and major military centers around the world.

I am outlining all these capabilities because this is the same organisational network of surveillance and security that we are told could not respond even *once* to the 9/11 hijackings and attacks over a period of nearly two hours that in any way impacted on the outcome. Flight 77 alone was in the air for more than *80 minutes* and is officially reported to have performed a U-turn from its authorised course more than *40 minutes* before it is claimed to have struck the Pentagon.

Colonel Prouty again:

> No one has to direct an assassination – it happens. The active role is played secretly by permitting it to happen. This is the greatest single clue. Who has the power to call off or reduce the usual security precautions?

Exactly.

Federal Aviation Administration (FAA)

The civilian (US government) Federal Aviation Administration has a joint response procedure with NORAD to react to hijackings. The FAA has been accused of large-scale corruption over the years and being steeped in the culture of cover-up. I am not referring to most of the employees, but the controlling core of the FAA. The late Rodney Stich, a former navy and airline pilot and FAA crash investigator, documented some of the corruption that he experienced directly and through his own investigations. He was author of the book *Unfriendly Skies* which charged the FAA with a catalogue of corruption, cover-ups and lies putting the safety of passengers at risk. Stich accused one FAA

administrator of covering up testimony and dozens of government
documents supporting charges of corruption within the FAA relating to
fatal airline crashes. It might be worth keeping that in mind when
assessing the trustworthiness of the FAA leadership over 9/11. Stich said
that information about FAA corruption had been repeatedly given to the
'politically-appointed' National Transportation Safety Board (NTSB)
which investigates air disasters. He said the information had been
covered up and 'fraud-related' air disasters were allowed to continue to
happen. Stich accused the NTSB of 'falsifying accident reports that
covered up for their own duplicity in the crashes and deaths'. He cited
the FBI, US attorneys and 'the main Justice Department personnel' as
other people and government agencies which had been given the facts
about FAA corruption involving major aircraft disasters, but ignored it
and even retaliated against him and other former federal agents who
tried to expose what was happening. He said federal judges blocked his
efforts to expose FAA corruption through the courts. It is sobering to
think that the FAA, NTSB, FBI and [In]Justice Department were all
involved in the [non]-investigation of 9/11. Government agencies are
pliable to what is expedient to government and financial interests and
we will see obvious lies and diversions from all these agencies and the
military with regard to September 11th. I saw a documentary about an
air accident that happened in 1989 when parents of a passenger
tenaciously pursued the truth and secured documents that the National
Transportation Safety Board (NTSB) themselves possessed. These clearly
showed that the problem was a faulty mechanism on a United Airlines
cargo door which had long been known about. The NTSB gave a
different reason for the door's failure which cleared airlines, aircraft-
maker Boeing and the FAA from responsibility. In fact, *all* of them knew
about the problem, but the FAA had allowed airlines 18 months for
economic reasons to fix the problem when it needed to be sorted
immediately and disaster followed. The parents were later proved to be
right as the NTSB was forced to admit. We need to keep in mind that
while these agencies have many genuine people in their ranks those in
charge cannot be trusted without question to tell us the truth as history
has confirmed so many times. Crash investigator Rodney Stich told his
story about lax air safety to members of Congress who he said ignored
documented evidence of 'hard-core corruption' within the FAA:

> These are the same members of Congress, and the secretary of the
> Department of Transportation, whose crocodile tears cover up for the fact that
> they were repeatedly offered evidence of the corruption that resulted in a
> series of fatal airline crashes, fatal hijackings, and who helped insure the
> success of the September 11, 2001, terrorist hijackers. The cover-up of these
> matters by members of Congress following the September 11 tragedies will

insure the protection of the guilty and continuation of the tragic consequences, as documented for the past 40 years ...

What the hell happened to normal procedure?

This is the corrupt-at-its-core network that told you what happened when the planes were hijacked on September 11th. The FAA was the other organisation, with NORAD and the Pentagon, that was responsible for responding to what happened that day. An example of the FAA-NORAD response procedure can be seen in the case of the private Learjet carrying professional golfer Payne Stewart and his friends on October 25th, 1999. Air traffic controllers lost contact with Stewart's plane after it took off from Orlando in Florida heading for Dallas. When they realised all was not well the FAA contacted NORAD and fighter jets were *immediately* scrambled to check out what was happening. The Learjet had suffered a pressurisation failure and was flying on autopilot while the real pilot and passengers were unconscious. An *ABC News* report quoting the Air Force said that after contact was initially lost two F-15s from Tyndall Air Force Base in Florida were sent to track the Learjet. The F-15s pulled back and two F-16s from Florida's Eglin Air Force Base took over. When the Learjet reached the Midwest, the Eglin F-16s withdrew and four others along with a mid-air refuelling tanker from the Tulsa Air National Guard replaced them. Finally, two F-16s from Fargo, North Dakota, moved in close to look into the windows to see if the pilot was slumped over and to help clear airspace. 'Officials hoped that the F-16s could provide assistance to anyone on board who might have helped land the plane safely', *ABC News* said. The Learjet ran out of fuel and the F-16 pilots watched the plane fall to the ground on unoccupied land. White House spokesman Joe Lockhart said the National Security Council monitored the doomed flight, fearing the jet might crash in a populated area. President Bill Clinton could have ordered fighters to shoot down the plane to avoid that potential tragedy, but Lockhart said no such recommendation had been made. Clinton told reporters at the time: 'I am very grateful for the work the FAA did, and for the two Air Force pilots, and the others in the Air Force that monitored this plane and made every effort to try to make contact with it.' The Pentagon's National Military Command Center (NMCC) and military big-wigs of the Joint Chiefs of Staff were also monitoring the Payne Stewart plane and that will become very significant when we get into the detail of the (systematic) non-reaction to the 9/11 attacks.

There's another important point to stress here. If you were 'highly trained' Arab terrorists from this 'brilliantly organised' network of Osama bin Laden, a network we are told was capable of hijacking four commercial aircraft simultaneously in American airspace, one of your obvious calculations would be the possible NORAD reaction time once it was known that the planes had been seized. So why did they choose to hijack planes in Boston to strike the World Trade Center in New York with a distance well in excess of normal every-other-day NORAD reaction time and why would they have allowed Flight 77 to fly way out from Washington towards the Midwest before turning around and going all the way back to Washington? This meant they had to fly for 45 *minutes* from the time the plane was known to be hijacked to the moment it was alleged to have struck the Pentagon. By any criteria, and the most minimal study of NORAD and FAA procedures on the Internet, they would have known that Air Force jets would be scrambled long before they reached their target. They would have further known that these procedures involved the shooting down of aircraft that threaten US cities. Had Payne Stewart's plane threatened people on the ground that would have been taken out. Any idiot putting this plan together, with the aim of crashing planes into the World Trade Center and the Pentagon, would have been aware that under NORAD's every-other-day reaction times they would have to complete the mission as fast as possible. Taking off from New York and Washington and crashing them immediately into those buildings would have been the ideal plan for them, surely? Instead, Flight 77, which actually took off from Washington, was allowed to fly away from the city for around three quarters of an hour before the hijack happened and then had to be flown all the way back. This is clearly ridiculous. It would make sense only if those truly behind the attacks – not 19 Muslim hijackers – knew that NORAD would not be reacting that day. I suggest this is exactly what happened with the evidence to follow.

Reacting to the hijackings should not have been a problem with the fantastic technology available to NORAD and the Cheyenne Mountain operation in general. Technology allows aircraft to be located and safely navigated and communicated with from almost anywhere on or above the earth thanks to the satellite network known as the Global Positioning System (GPS). This was created for use by the US military and provides 'incredibly accurate position information to end users'. I'll just give you that again: it provides 'incredibly accurate position information to end users' and I am quoting from descriptions of what was possible in 2001. What's more this system was controlled by NORAD and the rest of the gang at Cheyenne Mountain. Yet they could not track those hijacked planes and follow what was going on? Besides all the ground-based and satellite-based sensors and surveillance NORAD also directed AWACS aircraft which are in the air 24 hours a day while refuelling from flying tankers. AWACS (airborne warning and control system) were a modified Boeing airframe from a 707-320 with the 30-foot rotating radar dome on the top. They were the premier 'air battle command and control' aircraft in the world and provided surveillance to NORAD from the earth's surface to the stratosphere over land and water. One was involved in the Payne Stewart case. AWACS radar has a range of more than 250 miles (375.5 kilometres) for low-flying targets and further for those at higher altitudes and has a 'friend or foe' identification system that can detect, identify and track friendly or 'enemy' low-flying aircraft by eliminating 'ground clutter' that can confuse other radar systems. There is, to put it mildly, no credible excuse imaginable for what happened – or rather didn't – on 9/11 if normal procedures had been followed. Why and how they weren't will become clear much later in the book.

What should have happened

The hijack response protocol is made very clear in official regulations and procedures of the FAA. Chapter 7 of the procedures in 2001 deals with the 'escort of hijacked aircraft'. It says that an FAA 'hijack coordinator' on duty at the Washington DC headquarters will request the military to provide an escort aircraft for a confirmed hijacked plane to: (a) assure positive flight following (that's staying on the authorised course to you and me); (b) report unusual observances; and (c) aid search and rescue in the event of an emergency. The escort service, the regulations said, will be requested by the FAA hijack coordinator by direct contact with the National Military Command Center (NMCC) at the Pentagon (which monitored the Payne Stewart Learjet in real-time when alerted by the FAA). NORAD escort aircraft will normally take the required action, the document said:

> The center/control tower shall coordinate with the designated NORAD ... military unit advising of the hijack aircraft's location, direction of flight, altitude, type of aircraft and recommended flight plan to intercept the hijack aircraft.

Escort aircraft were told to position themselves five miles directly behind the hijacked plane and to approach from the rear to avoid the possibility of being observed. The escort plane should take the same altitude, speed and heading as the hijacked aircraft. When a hijacking happens within the continental United States, the procedures said, the 'appropriate NORAD ... Senior Director' is forwarded reports of the aircraft's call sign of position, latitude, longitude, heading, speed and altitude. An escort mission could be terminated by FAA headquarters, the National Military Command Center at the Pentagon or major military command authority – in other words NORAD. Air traffic controllers could, through the FAA, call for military planes to escort or 'intercept' a commercial aircraft if contact is lost with the pilot, the plane strayed from its designated course or anything inexplicable was happening. NORAD scrambled jets 125 times in such circumstances the year before 9/11. An intercept does not require the approval of the US President or some high-up government official. It is a routine response to check what is going on and who is flying the plane. The intention was not to blow the plane from the sky which needed presidential approval or, since 9/11, the approval of the head of NORAD and other designated military chiefs. There was an agreed procedure and code in place for communicating between intercepting NORAD jets and commercial aircraft. For example:

> Rocking wings from a position slightly above and ahead of, and normally to the left of, the intercepted aircraft and, after acknowledgement, a slow level turn, normally to the left, on to the desired heading = You have been intercepted, follow me; circling aerodrome, lowering landing gear and over flying runway in direction of landing ... = Land at this aerodrome.

There was, likewise, a series of coded replies for the other aircraft. If the hijacked plane did not follow these orders the interceptor could 'make a pass in front of the aircraft' and eventually 'fire tracer rounds in the airplane's path' or 'down it with a missile', according to Marine Corps Major Mike Snyder, a NORAD spokesman quoted in the *Boston Globe*. Snyder confirmed that fighters intercepting aircraft was 'routine'. For example, after 9/11 when a small private Cessna flew near to President Bush's ranch at Crawford, Texas, the FAA activated a response through NORAD and two jets were dispatched immediately. They tuned to the pilot's frequency and ordered him to land. Another similar incident was reported in Wood County, Texas, where Rodney Mize, the Sheriff's Senior Dispatcher, confirmed that a private plane carrying four reporters from the *Houston Chronicle* was forced down by two military pilots in A-10 Warthog jets. They flew above and below the plane and it landed at Wisener Field near Mineola. Bush's ranch, it seems, was far more important than the Pentagon and the World Trade Center. Such incidents are happening week after week as the FAA and NORAD activate the normal response system.

Hijack procedure

If a problem with an aircraft is considered a possible hijack by an air traffic controller a much higher level of command is activated. FAA spokeswoman Alison Duquette explained: 'The air traffic controller would notify the supervisor on the floor who would then immediately notify the FAA's regional operation center who would notify NORAD, as well as others.' In these cases, according to the regulations: 'The escort service will be requested by the FAA hijack coordinator by direct contact with the [Pentagon] National Military Command Center (NMCC).' The

Defense Department (DOD) manual covering plane hijackings said:

> In the event of a hijacking, the NMCC will be notified by the most expeditious means by the FAA. The NMCC will, with the exception of immediate responses ... forward requests for DOD assistance to the Secretary of Defense for approval.

CNN described how '... officers on the Joint Chiefs were monitoring the [Payne Stewart] Learjet on radar screens inside the Pentagon's National Military Command Center'. This was the normal response system in action as the FAA alerts the Pentagon and the military respond immediately. None of this happened on 9/11. FAA regulations left air traffic controllers in no doubt that they must never take chances. They were told that if there was an unexpected loss of radar or radio communication they must consider that 'an aircraft emergency exists'... and ... 'If ... you are in doubt that a situation constitutes an emergency or potential emergency, handle it as though it were an emergency.' An Air Defense Liaison Officer, a top FAA official, was located within Cheyenne Mountain to coordinate between the FAA and NORAD in these situations. All these personnel and procedures were in place on September 11th. Yet look at what happened, or rather didn't. Robin Hordon, an air traffic controller who had worked at the Boston Air Traffic Control Center involved in 9/11, said:

> I knew it was an inside job by 4 or 5 o'clock that afternoon [because] we got the information to kind of say roughly where the aircraft went [and] if they knew where the aircraft went and they were talking to them at a certain time ... normal protocol is to get fighter jet aircraft up to assist ...

Hordon said he had information provided by those he knew at Boston Center that hijack response protocols were fulfilled from their end – 'the controllers were not asleep, they did their job' – and the only way the planes could not have been intercepted was through a major systems failure such as a power crash which stopped all communication – 'but that did not happen'. Much later in the book we will see how this communication system could have been scrambled by those *truly* behind the attacks. Hordon said that information provided to the public by the FAA was enough for him to know that all the systems at the centres were working well and that if the usual protocols had been acted upon there was no way the planes could have reached their alleged targets. He added that once a hijack is confirmed or suspected this information is communicated throughout the FAA and military system. To put it simply this was the procedure that should have been followed – but wasn't – on 9/11: The civilian FAA should have contacted the National

Military Command Center (NMCC) at the Pentagon as soon as a plane
was suspected – *suspected*, not confirmed – to have been hijacked. The
NMCC should have then contacted NORAD to immediately scramble
fighters to locate and pursue the aircraft involved. The NORAD centre
for the region where the 9/11 planes were flying was the Northeast Air
Defense Sector or 'NEADS' which was based in a rural location called
Rome in northern New York State about 45 miles from Syracuse.
NORAD chief General Ralph Eberhart said in 2002 that from the
moment the FAA suspects a problem it takes 'only about one minute' to
contact NORAD which can have fighters in the air 'within a matter of
minutes to anywhere in the United States'. There is no evidence to
suggest that the same situation was not the case a few months earlier on
9/11 – so why the NORAD no-show?

NORAD timeline

I asked both NORAD and the FAA in 2002 for the sequence of events
and the timeline for what occurred that morning. Both said that only at
8.40 did the FAA notify NORAD that American Airlines Flight 11 had
been hijacked (this was changed to 8.38 in the official 9/11 Commission
report of 2004). Yet contact was lost with the aircraft at 8.13 and at the
very latest it was clear by 8.20 that something was seriously wrong. We
should know why it took up to 27 minutes (25 in the Commission
version) for Air Traffic Control through the FAA to alert NORAD. *The
New York Times* reported that Flight 11 maintained its authorised course
for only 16 minutes after take-off and 'just past Worcester, Mass., instead
of taking a southerly turn, the Boeing 767 swung to the north at 8.15. It
had been taken over ...' Let's give the controllers another five minutes
before they were sure the aircraft was in trouble. This still means that the
FAA waited 20 minutes from the point of confirmed lost contact to
report that a commercial airliner was not responding to instructions and
had changed course with a deactivated transponder over an area of high
population and in skies criss-crossed by intensive air traffic. Either that
or the military ignored the FAA alert. I asked the FAA in 2002 to confirm
when exactly it was known that Flight 11 was in trouble and why it took
so long to contact NORAD, but the spokesman would not answer. Let us
make it clear again: FAA regulations instructed air traffic controllers that
if there was an unexpected loss of radar or radio communication they
must consider that 'an aircraft emergency exists'... and ... 'If ... you are in
doubt that a situation constitutes an emergency or potential emergency,
handle it as though it were an emergency.' This could not be clearer. For
goodness sake, the official story says that at 8.24 the controller heard
from the cockpit of Flight 11:

We have some planes. Just stay quiet and you will be okay. We are returning to the airport. Nobody move.

This is said to have happened *16 minutes* before we are told the FAA
alerted NORAD that the plane had been hijacked. None of this makes
sense. The FAA would seem to be in the dock here right from the start,
but the finger of responsibility is going to point in other directions, too,
as we unpick the cover stories protecting cover stories protecting cover
stories. Nothing with 9/11 is what it first appears to be. Flight 11's
transponder was switched off at 8.20 – around *20 minutes* before
NORAD was informed. We should not forget that through all of this the
Air Force was constantly monitoring the commercial air traffic system as
it does 24 hours a day. This has to be done to prevent collisions between
commercial and Air Force planes. Flight 11 attendant Betty Ong is said
to have used a seatback phone to call an American Airlines reservations
agent who contacted the system operations control centre in Fort Worth.
Ong is reported to have made that call at 8.27 – more than *ten minutes*
before NORAD says it was told of the hijack. Even five minutes before
the first alleged contact with NORAD the controllers are claimed to have
heard another cockpit transmission that said:

> Nobody move please. We are going back to the airport. Don't try to make any
> stupid moves.

The FAA-NORAD timeline therefore is simply ridiculous. NORAD said
it scrambled fighter jets at 8.46 from Otis Air National Guard Base on
Cape Cod in Massachusetts 153 miles from New York. This is eight
minutes after it says it was told of the Flight 11 hijack (9/11 Commission
timings). At the very moment the jets were officially scrambled, and
seven minutes before they were airborne, 'Flight 11' (or something) was
crashing into the North Tower. An F-15 departing from Otis can reach
New York City in 10 to 12 minutes, according to an Otis spokeswoman,
and can fly three times the speed of a 767. If you take the journey to be
ten minutes that means the jets would be flying at around 918 miles per
hour and well within their top speed of in excess of Mach 2.5 (more than
1,600 mph). Some sources even quote a top speed of 1,800 mph and yet a
NORAD spokesman estimated the speed of the scrambled F-15s to me at
only between 603 and 675 miles per hour. Why not faster? I did read one
report that the Otis standby jets had been ordered by Colonel Robert
Marr, battle commander at NORAD's Northeast Air Defense Sector
(NEADS), to carry missiles and extra fuel for monitoring a Russian Air
Force exercise taking place over the North Atlantic, Pacific, and Arctic
Oceans and this was why their speed was reduced. One of the pilots told
a BBC 'documentary' *Clear The Skies* on September 1st, 2002, that they
did fly supersonic and this statement added to the contradictions

emerging from different spokespeople for the US military. But wait. It gets sillier. The Pentagon told CNN that NORAD was 'informed of the plane striking the World Trade Center at 8.47'. *Informed?* We are talking about the most sophisticated military surveillance operation on the planet which, in its own words, is 'the largest and most complex command and control network in the world', utilising a vast network of satellites and cutting-edge air tracking and surveillance technology. Cheyenne Mountain can tell you if a missile has been launched on the other side of the world and it has to be 'informed' that a commercial airliner one of its agencies had already belatedly scrambled jets to intercept had hit the World Trade Center? Ah, but the military response to 9/11 aircraft was basically isolated within NORAD's Northeast Air Defense Sector (NEADS) in New York State while Cheyenne Mountain was nowhere to be seen. Isolating NEADS with far less sophisticated technology was very important in negating effective response. We are told that at 8.53am the two F-15 Eagles took off from the Otis base 153 miles from New York to intercept the second hijacked plane from Boston – Flight 175 – although the pilots say they didn't know that as we'll see. About ten minutes later, at 9.03, Flight 175 crashed into the South Tower (so says the official story) with the F-15s still 70 miles away, so they tell us. Why did it take the planes seven minutes to get airborne from a scramble at 8.46 to take-off at 8.53 when the Air Force apparently claims response times of scramble to 29,000 feet in two and a half minutes? The collective suspension of normal procedures in so many ways meant that nothing intervened throughout the entire period of the attacks to make any difference to the outcome.

What about no-fly zones?

Another major point is that of no-fly zones (also 'prohibited airspace') where access is barred to unauthorised aircraft which can be shot down if they fail to broadcast the code that allows them to enter. The World Trade Center is said by one of its first tenants to be a 'no-fly zone'. If that is so (and you would have expected it to be) there has to be a system of air response very close to New York or the no-fly zone would be unenforceable. What would be the point of it? Ken Smith, a tenant of the World Trade Center back in 1979, said on Radio Free America that when he was there it was well known by tenants that the WTC was a no-fly zone. Smith said that any plane off-course within 12 miles of the buildings was given a warning to change direction and he added: 'If you came within five miles they would threaten to shoot you down ... If you came within three miles, they could shoot you down.' Former US Secretary of Defense Casper Weinberger told US television about the Washington DC no-fly zone and how it was policed:

The city is ringed with Air Force Bases and Navy bases and the ability to get defensive planes in the air is very, very high [and you would close] off the entire airspace so in effect the whole Washington area is a no-fly zone so that any planes that can't identify themselves and get into that are shot down. Those were the orders and that was the response that was always contemplated.

Well, *except* on September 11th. Robin Horton, a former air traffic controller at the Boston Center responsible for Boston Logan, said: 'No untracked aircraft get near the Pentagon and near the White House, it just doesn't happen.' Again – except on September 11th. Restricted airspace around Washington DC – known as P-56 – is the best-defended airspace in the world (on every other day). Horton said that no unknown aircraft are supposed to go through there: 'It's like an aviation no-man's land, nobody.' P-56 is an air-identification zone within a 50-mile radius of Washington with a 17-mile protected zone around the Washington Monument with an inner-protection zone of three miles around the capital. Yet somehow all this was breached simply through the non-action by the air defences that would normally respond. Then there are the ground-to-air missiles that defend Washington. Barbara Honegger served in high-level federal government posts including White House Policy Analyst and Special Assistant to the Assistant to the President for Domestic Policy during the Reagan administration. She was also a Senior Military Affairs Journalist at the Naval Postgraduate School, the leading science, technology and national security affairs graduate research university of the Department of Defense. Honegger became a member of Political Leaders for 9/11 Truth after seeing the nonsense of the 9/11 narrative and she has been one of many government, military and intelligence officials calling for a new 9/11 investigation. She said of Pentagon defences:

If a plane, any kind of plane, was coming into the Pentagon why didn't its anti-aircraft missile batteries that are there, why didn't they fire to protect the building? This is, after all, the most protected building on the planet.

The Pentagon and the White House are defended by ground-to-air missile systems – *of course they are*. So why weren't they used on 9/11? Even at the G-8 Summit in Genoa, Italy, only weeks earlier in July, 2001, airspace was closed over the city and defended with ground-to-air missiles. I was shown around the parliament building in Canberra, Australia, by a man who worked with the nation's air-defence computer system. He showed me the hidden positions around the building where the ground-to-air missiles are located and said that when a plane enters the restricted airspace over the Australian capital the computer system demands that pilots tap in a four-digit code that gives them permission to be there. If this is not done quickly enough missiles automatically launch, I was told. This is what happens in Canberra while the same or better technology is not in place at the Pentagon and White House? My Australian contact said he knew for a fact that the Pentagon, and Washington in general, are defended by an even more sophisticated missile system than Canberra which works in basically the same way. It is obvious that this would be the case and it has been openly accepted that a ground-to-air system is in place to defend the White House. The *Globe and Mail* newspaper in Canada provided one of the rare mentions of the Pentagon system:

> Meanwhile, there was no explanation of how four airliners could be hijacked and flown – in at least two cases hundreds of kilometres and for nearly an hour – without being successfully intercepted. That one ploughed into the Pentagon, supposedly protected by surface-to-air missiles, dramatically demonstrated US vulnerability. Why weren't those missiles launched to stop the Pentagon crash?

They weren't meant to be launched because the 9/11 attacks were both *made* to happen and *allowed* to happen.

The whole system went AWOL

After I had originally completed this chapter I came across an investigative website that claims to have conducted a phone interview on December 9th, 2001, with a member of the US Air Force based in New York. The source said he was ordered to the crash sites in New York, Pennsylvania and the Pentagon within days of 9/11 as part of an Air Force investigation. What he and others discovered, the website claims he told them, was that the standard response procedures were fully in effect that morning and were followed to the letter as usual by FAA air traffic control and that Air National Guard and Air Force units were alerted immediately that it was clear that something was amiss with the four aircraft. He said that after these alerts and requests for action were received from the FAA, orders from the 'highest level of the executive branch of the federal government were received, demanding that the Air Force stand-down and not follow through with established scramble-intercept procedures that morning until further notice'. This Air Force contact was unnamed, but then, to be fair, how could he have been? People will just have to decide for themselves if what he is claimed to have said rings true. It is a scenario that does fit what happened and makes sense of the apparently nonsensical lack of response. No fighters were scrambled to intercept the hijacked planes and no ground-to-air defences were activated to save the lives of those who died inside the Pentagon and the World Trade Center. Some would call this incompetence and, staggering as that alone would be, what happened on September 11th is far more than that. It was calculated mass murder by psychopaths so extreme they stretch comprehension to its outer-limits. Any unidentified aircraft heading into the protected airspace over Washington and the Pentagon should have been *automatically* shot down before it would cause harm on the ground. The only way that this could not happen is for the system to have been purposely disarmed or stood down. This just gets crazier and crazier when you look at Flight 77.

The official timeline says the FAA notified NORAD at 9.24am (often reported as 9.25) that American Airlines Flight 77 from Dulles Airport near Washington DC to Los Angeles may have been hijacked when it was known at least *20 minutes* earlier that Flight 77 was hijacked. *The New York Times* published what it claimed was a partial transcript of the communication tapes with Flight 77. When contact was lost with the cockpit at 8.50am the plane would have been under the control of the Indianapolis Air Route Traffic Control Center. This is one of 20 regional centres that track flights between airports. At 9.02, still 40 minutes before 'impact with the Pentagon', a controller is reported to have told American Airlines the latest news on Flight 77: 'We lost track control of the guy, he's in coast track but we haven't – we don't really know where his target is and we can't get a hold of him.' Yet it was only at 9.34 – *44 minutes* after contact was lost – that the FAA told NORAD that Flight 77 was *'missing'* and not that it was hijacked (according to the official story). Four minutes after that FAA communication 'Flight 77' was said to have hit the Pentagon. Oh do come on, this is the land of clouds and cuckoos. On air safety grounds alone there should have been an immediate response to Flight 77 because of the lethal dangers to other aircraft of flying off-course. 'Flight 77' did a 180-degree turn near the Ohio border and headed back towards Washington, but *still* no alert even with two hijacked planes buried in the World Trade Center and with controllers apparently unable to locate Flight 77 on their radar screens for ten minutes. FAA regulations for air traffic controllers said:

> Consider that an aircraft emergency exists ... when: ... There is unexpected loss of radar contact and radio communications with any ... aircraft [and] If ... you are in doubt that a situation constitutes an emergency or potential emergency, handle it as though it were an emergency.

An MSNBC television report the day after 9/11 detailed how seriously air traffic controllers and their bosses at the FAA are supposed to take aircraft that deviate from their agreed route:

If a plane deviates by 15 degrees, or two miles from that course, the flight controllers will hit the panic button. They'll call the plane, saying 'American 11, you're deviating from course.' It's considered a real emergency, like a police car screeching down a highway at 100 miles an hour. When golfer Payne Stewart's incapacitated Learjet missed a turn at a fix, heading north instead of west to Texas, F-16 interceptors were quickly dispatched.

So why not on *four separate occasions* on 9/11? A *Newsday* report said: 'The record suggests that teenagers on instant-message networks communicate faster than some federal officials did during the crisis.' Or, as *The New York Times* put it:

> ... despite elaborate plans that link civilian and military efforts to control the nation's airspace in defense of the country, and despite two other jetliners' having already hit the World Trade Center in New York, the fighter planes that scrambled into protective orbits around Washington did not arrive until 15 minutes after Flight 77 hit the Pentagon.

Even beyond all this, there is a more fundamental question that needs to be answered. Why, when two hijacked airliners had been crashed into the World Trade Center, weren't fighter jets deployed immediately to guard the skies over Washington? Surely the first thing you would do after what happened in New York is to instigate air defence for your other most likely targets – Washington DC being the most obvious. The *Miami Herald* talked to air traffic controllers who said they could not understand why there was no reaction to what was happening in the skies that morning. Why no response from the FAA and the military? A controller in Miami told the *Herald*:

> That's a question that more and more people are going to ask. What the hell went on here? Was anyone doing anything about it? Just as a national defense thing, how are they able to fly around and no one go after them?

The *Herald* quoted controllers who said that even with the transponder silent the plane would have been visible on radar to controllers who handle cross-continent air traffic and to an FAA command centre outside of Washington. The FAA would not discuss with the *Miami Herald* the track of Flight 77 or what happened in air-control centres while it was in flight and nor would American Airlines. Air traffic controllers said the trouble should have been instantly noticeable. Flight 77, as with all such planes, would have first showed up on radar screens as a short solid line, the *Herald* reported, with a readout that identifies the plane and gives its altitude and speed. When the transponder shuts down, the short line vanishes. The speed number goes away too. 'It's just something that catches your eye', one controller said. The first move when a transponder goes down would be to contact the pilot and tell him the transponder wasn't working and even if the plane remained silent controllers could still find it – by switching their screen display to the old fashioned radar that bounces a signal off the plane's metal skin, the *Herald* said. The report went on:

> Military jets are routinely scrambled in the case of hijackings and 'runners,' planes that do not answer or do not heed air traffic controllers. But FAA officials would not say when controllers detected the errant Flight 77 or whether any fighter jets were able to get into the air to confront it. Fighter jets are based nearby, in Virginia, and could have reached the White House within minutes, aviation sources say ...

> ... The FAA has a detailed hijacking manual: Supervisors are notified. The FAA command center near Washington and the FBI are put on alert. Military jets are scrambled to follow the plane. Air-traffic controllers try to figure out where the hijacker wants to go and, if necessary, clear an air space of other traffic.

The 'why' will become increasingly obvious as we traverse the rabbit hole. Vice President Dick Cheney told NBC's *Meet the Press* that from the time that Flight 11 struck the World Trade Center the Secret Service travelling with President Bush on a public engagement in Florida had 'open lines' with the FAA. He said: 'The Secret Service has an arrangement with the FAA. They had open lines after the World Trade Center was ...' He didn't finish the sentence, no doubt because he realised he had said too much, and it is worth pondering the wider implications of that statement. The FAA had open lines with the Secret Service after the World Trade Center was hit? That happened at 8.46, about the time that Flight 77 was known to be in trouble, and yet the FAA said they did not tell NORAD and the Pentagon Command Center about Flight 77 until 9.24 when they had already established open lines to the Secret Service. Are we being told that the Pentagon and NORAD did not have open lines also with the FAA and were able to follow in real time the communications and non-communications from the cockpits long before any fighter jet was deployed? Indeed the FAA and NORAD both confirmed to me in 2002 that they had open lines to discuss Flights 77 and 93. I asked the FAA when exactly these open lines were established, but its spokesman would not say. Surely in any sane system these would have been established, as Cheney indicated, at least from the moment the first plane struck the World Trade Center. So, again, why the delay in responding?

The NORAD tapes

The official 9/11 Commission 'investigation', which produced a laughable 'report' in 2004, was established to hide the truth of what happened, as I will detail later. It did, however, at least subpoena audiotapes of exchanges claimed to be between the control room of NORAD's Northeast Air Defense Sector, or 'NEADS', and the FAA air traffic control system. Recordings were made at both NEADS and FAA ends of the conversation. They exposed the lies told to the Commission earlier by senior military figures about what happened that morning with response to the hijackings. Military chiefs who misled the Commission were brought back to testify under oath (shockingly they were not under oath for their original statements) and I will cover that in due course. What the tapes claim to record destroys the official NORAD version that was first issued on September 18th, 2001, and repeated to the 9/11 Commission before the tapes came to light in 2004. They reveal the confusion and diversion faced by NEADS operatives in reacting to the attacks. I would say this was instigated confusion and diversion from deep in the shadows and much further on in the book I will highlight how 9/11 computer systems could have been manipulated in real time. Remember compartmentalisation. A series of 'exercises' were happening on that day of all days in the skies over the Eastern Seaboard that mirrored the themes of what actually happened and this created (I say calculated) confusion from the start. I will address these exercises in more detail shortly. Information communicated to NEADS about real-time events by the FAA led to more confusion and diversion in the form of false reports of possible hijackings including one that said *Flight 11 had not struck the World Trade Center* and was instead still in the air heading for Washington DC. Delays in the FAA informing NEADS of problems with 9/11 flights was a consistent and massively significant factor in the lack of response if you believe the official timeline. Just one example on the tapes was after 8.57am when Flight 175 veered off course near Allentown, Pennsylvania, and set a course for New York. Air traffic controllers at New York Center are heard speculating on its target – maybe the Statue of Liberty – and one calls out the plane's rate of descent every twelve seconds as the radar refreshes. Even so the FAA didn't alert the military at NEADS about Flight 175 until *seconds from impact* (according to the official story). Flight 175, or at least a large plane, struck the South Tower at 9.03. The first military version of events that stood between September 18th, 2001, and 2004 when the tapes came to light claimed that the FAA notified NORAD about Flight 77 at 9.24am and jets from the CIA-connected Langley Air Force Base in Virginia, 130 miles from Washington, were immediately scrambled to protect the US capital from 'Flight 77'. By contrast the NORAD tapes reveal that NEADS was not told of the hijacking of 'Flight 77' until just before impact 'with the Pentagon' and 'Flight 93' (Pennsylvania) until *after* it is said to have crashed. They reveal that fighters had been scrambled from Langley, Virginia, not in response to Flight 77, but to the *false report that Flight 11 had passed over New York and was flying towards Washington.* The official story had also claimed that Air Force jets were tracking Flight 93 and could have shot it down if the order had come while the tapes record a very different scenario. The information about the 'still-flying' phantom Flight 11 came from Colin Scoggins, civilian military liaison at the FAA's Boston Center, from a still-unknown source apparently resulting from an FAA teleconference call. None of this appeared in official reports until the tapes were released in 2004. Scoggins said American Airlines refused to confirm for several hours that Flight 11 had hit the World Trade Center and this caused confusion as the attacks continued. Well, it certainly appears to have done so for him. Scoggins told *Vanity Fair* magazine:

> When we phoned United [after the second tower was hit], they confirmed that United 175 was down, and I think they confirmed that within two or three minutes. With American Airlines, we could never confirm if [Flight 11] was down or not, so that left doubt in our minds.

The report of the 'phantom Flight 11' flying past New York towards Washington turned out to be nonsense and they weren't even tracking a plane heading for Washington at the time; it was all supposition. The tapes reveal that NEADS wanted to direct more jets to protect New York airspace to join the two from Otis that had arrived too late, but the FAA, which has the final say when civilian airspace is involved, refused. The excuse was that it would put civilian aircraft in danger in crowded airspace, but they clearly already were. Given that NEADS was the central hijack reaction centre to launch fighter jets in response to events the more confusion and misinformation that could be generated there the better. Keeping NEADS personnel out of the loop of information they required would have been essential and it is clear that the public watching live television knew more about some of what was going on than those in the NORAD hijack operations center. NEADS personnel said they were working with limited and outdated technology and couldn't track the planes efficiently when transponders were turned off. This is extraordinary given the state-of-the-art tracking technology their colleagues within Cheyenne Mountain were claiming to have. Where was the Cheyenne Mountain operation in all this? Are we saying that all Soviet planes had to do to access the United States airspace during the Cold War was to turn their transponders off? Jets from the Otis base had been scrambled, but too late to reach New York before 'Flights 11' and '175' and now the second scramble from Langley had been launched in pursuit of a 'Flight 11' that didn't exist. In fact, it gets even crazier. The fighters were scrambled to Washington from Langley at 9.24am, but they didn't head for the capital at all. *They flew east into the Atlantic because as one pilot said: 'No one told us why we were being scrambled'!* The 9/11 Commission heard that the Langley pilots were not told what was happening and assumed they were scrambled to protect the American mainland from attack from the Atlantic to the east in line with the procedure during the Cold War. 'I reverted to the Russian threat – I'm thinking cruise-missile threat from the sea', a pilot told the 9/11 Commission. By 9.24am two commercial airliners had crashed into the World Trade Center, much of humanity was watching on live television, and the Langley pilots didn't know what they were being scrambled for? The Otis pilots said that they were similarly kept in the dark about much of what was happening, including the crash of Flight 175. Major Dan Nash, one of the Otis pilots, said they were shocked to see billowing smoke appear on the horizon as they approached New York because no one had told them what was occurring. They had only been told they were scrambled to intercept and escort Flight 11. Nash said:

> From 100 miles away at least, we could see the fire and the smoke blowing. Obviously, anybody watching CNN had a better idea of what was going on. We were not told anything. It was to the point where we were flying supersonic towards New York and the controller came on and said, 'A second airplane has hit the World Trade Center' ... My first thought was 'What happened to American 11?'

Chaos and confusion was being instigated everywhere. Back at NEADS, a NORAD Staff Sergeant William Huckabone saw the Langley jets were going the wrong way and out to sea. At 9.34am this exchange took place involving him, Master Sergeant Steve Citino, and Naval Air Traffic Control, or 'ATC':

9:34:12

Navy ATC: You've got [the fighters] moving east in airspace. Now you want 'em to go to Baltimore [Washington]?

Huckabone: Yes, sir. We're not gonna take 'em in Whiskey 386 [military training airspace over the ocean].

Navy ATC: Okay, once he goes to Baltimore, what are we supposed to do?

Huckabone: Have him contact us on auxiliary frequency 2-3-4 decimal 6. Instead of taking handoffs to us and us handing 'em back, just tell Center they've got to go to Baltimore.

Navy ATC: All right, man. Stand by. We'll get back to you.

Citino: What do you mean, 'We'll get back to you'? Just do it!

Huckabone: I'm gonna choke that guy!

The misdirection and delayed scrambles meant the Langley fighters would not make it to Washington before 'Flight 77' which NEADS found out about *by accident.* Tech Sergeant Shelley Watson was frantically ringing all possible sources to establish the position of the long-crashed 'Flight 11' that was supposedly still flying and when she contacted Washington Center air traffic at 9.34 the operations manager told her that Flight 11 was lost. Why had no one told NEADS? Why didn't NEADS know with all the tracking and surveillance technology available to their colleagues at Cheyenne Mountain? On one section of the NORAD tapes this exchange can be heard with Washington Air Traffic Control when NEADS heard about Flight 77 for the first time:

9:34:01

Washington Center: Now, let me tell you this. I – I'll – we've been looking. We've also lost American 77.

Watson: American 77? ... Where was it proposed to head, sir?

Washington Center: Okay, he was going to LA also.

Watson: From where, sir?

Washington Center: I think he was from Boston also [it was actually Washington Dulles]. Now let me tell you this story here. Indianapolis Center was working this guy.

Watson: What guy?

Washington Center: American 77, at flight level 3-5-0 [35,000 feet]. However, they lost radar with him. They lost contact with him. They lost everything. And they don't have any idea where he is or what happened.

It was *40 minutes* before this conversation, at 8.54 am, that Indianapolis controllers lost radar contact with American 77 and, in line with regulations, told their superiors at the FAA that the plane was probably hijacked. According to the tapes no one at the FAA told NORAD, or the military didn't tell their NEADS centre, and only *by chance* did Tech Sergeant Shelley Watson find out from Washington Air Traffic Control. At 9.35, Colin Scoggins at the FAA's Boston Center told NEADS that they had a report of a low-flying aircraft six miles southeast of the White House, but 'moving away'. This was the alleged Flight 77. The following exchange involves Major Kevin Nasypany, NEADS mission crew commander:

9:36:23

Nasypany: Okay, Foxy [Major Fox, the Weapons Team head]. I got an aircraft six miles east of the White House! Get your fighters there as soon as possible!

Male voice: That came from Boston?

Huckabone: We're gonna turn and burn it – crank it up.

Male tech: Six miles!

Huckabone: All right, here we go. This is what we're gonna do ...

Nasypany: We've got an aircraft deviating eight miles east of the White House right now.

Fox: Do you want us to declare A.F.I.O. [emergency military control of the fighters] and run 'em straight in there?

Nasypany: Take 'em and run 'em to the White House.

Fox: Go directly to Washington.

Citino: We're going direct DC with my guys [Langley fighters]? Okay. Okay.

Huckabone: Ma'am, we are going A.F.I.O. right now with Quit 2-5 [the Langley fighters]. They are going direct Washington.

Navy ATC: Quit 2-5, we're handing 'em off to Center right now.

Huckabone: Ma'am, we need to expedite that right now. We've gotta contact them on 2-3-4-6.

They thought the White House was under threat, but it turned out to be the Pentagon. One of the NEADS staff spotted the plane, or whatever it was, on radar.

9:37:56

Male tech: Right here, right here, right here. I got him. I got him.

Nasypany: We just lost track. Get a Z-point [coordinate] on that ... Okay, we got guys lookin' at 'em. Hold on ... Where's Langley at? Where are the fighters?

The answer was that they were more than a hundred miles away after being allowed, through lack of information, to fly in the opposite direction out into the ocean. This would explain why they took so long and why their average speed from take-off to arrival in Washington appeared to be so pedestrian. At 9.38 the Pentagon was struck. This was 15 to 20 minutes depending on the report before the Langley planes arrived. Immediately after the Pentagon strike, Colin Scoggins at Boston air traffic called with yet *another* false alarm, a Boston plane heading for Las Vegas. Then, at 10.07am, came a call to NORAD's NEADS centre from Cleveland air traffic control in Ohio:

10:07:16

Cleveland Center: We got a United 93 out here. Are you aware of that?

Watson: United 93?

Cleveland Center: That has a bomb on board.

Watson: A bomb on board? And this is confirmed? You have a [beacon code], sir?

Cleveland Center: No, we lost his transponder.

Nasypany: Gimme the call sign. Gimme the whole nine yards ... Let's get some info, real quick. They got *a bomb?*

Four minutes before this conversation took place the plane, or *a* plane, had *already crashed* in Pennsylvania at 10.03 – some reports say it was 10.06. It was *35 minutes* earlier that John Werth, a Cleveland air traffic controller of long experience, had heard suspicious noises from the cockpit of Flight 93 and believed it had been hijacked. It was, by now, a familiar tale. Werth had reported his suspicions through the FAA chain of command, as per regulations, but according to the tapes they did not pass this information to the NEADS centre until the plane and its passengers and crew were already no more. Or the FAA *did* tell the Pentagon, but they didn't tell NEADS. This happened despite the fact that two planes had hit the World Trade Center before John Werth's report, and the Pentagon was also hit some 25 minutes before Cleveland air traffic informed NEADS about Flight 93. By 10.03 when that plane is officially reported to have crashed it was an hour and 11 minutes since fighters are said to have been scrambled from Otis AFB to New York. We should remember, too, after outlining the 'scrambled planes' response here, that for *a week* after 9/11 the official story from the Pentagon, NORAD and the White House was that *no planes* were scrambled at *all from anywhere* until the Pentagon was hit. I will come to that in the next chapter.

Military special operations commander was head of FAA 'security'

Everyone involved in the chain of command at the FAA that day who is still alive should be subject to an independent public inquiry into what on earth happened and the same with other civilian and military agencies. This is not to condemn the operational level of air traffic controllers and nor does this pin all the responsibility on the FAA. It is clear when you study statements and evidence that a big effort has been made to pile the blame onto FAA personnel and away from the military. There is much evidence to suggest that higher levels of the military were kept informed of events by FAA operatives including an FAA memo presented to the 9/11 Commission which said that an FAA-military teleconference had begun within minutes of the first tower being struck at which real-time information was shared on 'all flights of interest'. Highly significantly this very important memo was not included in the final report of the cover-up Commission. The head of FAA security on 9/11 was Major General Michael Canavan. His title was Director of Civil Aviation Security for the FAA and, according to the 9/11 Commission report, the hijack coordinator on September 11th was the 'Director of the FAA Office of Civil Aviation Security, or his or her designate' – Major General Canavan or whoever he designated. I asked the FAA in 2002 who the hijack coordinator was that day, but they didn't reply. Canavan is reported to have been in San Juan, Puerto Rico, on 9/11 and headed for Washington by military jet. So who was his designate as FAA hijack coordinator and why are we not being told given the importance of this position that day? Look again at the official hijack regulations with regard to the FAA alerting the military:

The escort service will be requested by the FAA hijack coordinator by direct contact with the National Military Command Center (NMCC) [based at the Pentagon].

The Defense Department (DOD) manual covering plane hijackings says:

> In the event of a hijacking, the NMCC will be notified by the most expeditious means by the FAA. The NMCC will, with the exception of immediate responses ... forward requests for DOD assistance to the Secretary of Defense for approval.

Why didn't this happen? Where was the 'hijack coordinator', *who* was the 'hijack coordinator', when air traffic controllers were reporting suspicious planes and passing this information up the FAA chain of command while NORAD operatives at the NEADS response centre were apparently not being told until it was too late? Why wasn't Director of the FAA Office of Civil Aviation Security Major General Michael Canavan publicly questioned on this obvious issue by the 9/11 Commission? Personnel at the National Military Command Center (NMCC) in the Pentagon also have major questions to answer about the non-reaction as will become clear. General Canavan has a considerable background in US Special Operations, which, according to the Department of Defense's *Dictionary of Military and Associated Terms*, are defined as: 'Operations conducted by specially organized, trained, and equipped military and paramilitary forces to achieve military, political, economic or psychological objectives by unconventional means in hostile, denied or politically sensitive areas'. In short: Operations that are above the law and off the record and involved the manipulation of *perception*. Canavan had been stationed at Fort Bragg, home to the US Army 4th Psychological Operations (PSYOPS) Group which had operatives working in the news division at CNN's headquarters in Atlanta in the final days of the Kosovo War, according to media reports, and also staffed the National Security Council's Office of Public Diplomacy (OPD), a shadowy government propaganda agency that planted stories in the US media supporting the Reagan-Bush administration's policies in Central America. The *Miami Herald* of July 19th, 1987, quoted a 'senior US official' as describing the OPD as a 'vast psychological warfare operation of the kind the military conducts to influence a population in enemy territory'. These are the sorts of operations that Michael Canavan, head of FAA security on September 11th, would have been involved with in his high positions in Special Operations Command. Canavan was Commanding General, Special Operations Command, Europe, and Commanding General, Joint Special Operations Command, at Fort Bragg, North Carolina, with its centre for psychological warfare which is defined thus:

> The use of propaganda ... intended to demoralise the enemy, to break his will

to fight or resist, and sometimes to render him favourably disposed to one's position ... The twisting of personality and the manipulation of beliefs ... by brainwashing and related techniques can also be regarded as a form of psychological warfare.

Problem-Reaction-Solution is psychological warfare. Major General Canavan had further been involved with a plan by the elite Delta Forces to capture Osama Bin Laden. Canavan, a one-time Chief of Staff of the US European Command in Stuttgart, Germany, became FAA Director of Security in late 2000, just before Bush was sworn in as president, and he announced his departure less than a month after September 11th.

Calculated confusion

The NORAD NEADS tapes subpoenaed by the 9/11 Commission provide far more questions than answers. Why would NORAD issue a false timeline in September, 2001, that posed so many questions about its lack of response and competence when the timeline on the tapes directs the blame on the FAA? Why would NORAD officers repeat the same story to the 9/11 Commission right up to the tapes being revealed and open themselves to accusations of deliberately misleading the inquiry? General Larry Arnold, commander of NORAD's Continental US Region from 1997 to 2002, confused matters even more when he told the Commission: 'We launched the aircraft out of Langley to put them over top of Washington DC, not in response to American Airlines 77, but really to put them in position in case United 93 were to head that way.' Where the heck did that come from? The official story is a mass of contradiction and confusion, added to by the NORAD tapes and of course confusion and chaos were absolutely essential to the attacks playing out without challenge. Who had the power to call off the normal response to hijackings that day – *Osama bin Laden* or the American Deep State? The first position taken by the authorities is that there was nothing they could have done. That is what they really want you to believe. The second, when that doesn't work, is to let you think they were incompetent. Both positions are designed to hide the truth – the truth that what we are looking at here amid the explosion of lies and diversions is not incompetence at all. This was *orchestrated* incompetence in which forces at, and behind, the highest levels of the United States government and military were intervening to stop the system working as it normally would. To stop thousands of people going home to their families that September day because it suited the sick agenda for those people to die and for the world to watch it all live on television. Genuine people at the FAA and within the military did their job as best they could, but another force was intervening and before this book is complete you will see what that force was and how it could have been done. The claim that the military didn't know what was happening because the FAA didn't tell them does not stand up to scrutiny. Not only were there open lines between the FAA and the Pentagon we are told by Ben Sliney, operations manager at the FAA Air Traffic Control System Command Center, they had a 'military cell' on site for FAA-military liaison and they were present throughout the 9/11 attacks. The military clearly *did* know what was happening, but the response was sabotaged.

Why not Andrews?

Fighter jets were scrambled and arrived too late from Langley (130 miles from Washington) and Otis (153 miles from New York City), but why did NORAD choose those bases when Andrews Air Force Base, the one designated to defend Washington DC, is little more than *ten miles* from the capital and Andrews pilots could have had breakfast and still intercepted Flight 77 with time to spare? Andrews Air Force Base is a minute or so by fighter jet from Washington DC and that's why it is the capital's first line of air defence (Fig 32). In the name of sanity, the airspace above the Pentagon and the White House is a *no-fly zone* and of course, short of complete and utter insanity, there are going to be fighter jets on standby at the nearest Air Force base to defend the area. Mike Kelly of the North Jersey Media Group reported in December, 2003, that two F-16s from 177th Fighter Wing at Atlantic City International Airport were taking part in bombing run practice 'just eight minutes away' from Manhattan. Boston Air Traffic Control Center contacted the Atlantic City base to ask for air response to the hijacking of Flight 11, but were unaware that its NORAD reaction role had ended after 1998. Even so – they had planes *in the air* eight minutes from the World Trade Center.

The disgusting 9/11 Commission didn't mention the Atlantic City planes in its pack of lies, distortions and omissions (sorry, 'report') compiled in 2004 specifically to defend the official story from the truth. Colin Scroggins, military liaison at the FAA's Boston Center, said fighters at

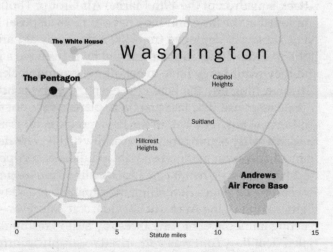

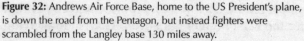

Figure 32: Andrews Air Force Base, home to the US President's plane, is down the road from the Pentagon, but instead fighters were scrambled from the Langley base 130 miles away.

Burlington, Selfridge, Syracuse and Toledo would have been ready to respond while the District of Colombia Air National Guard may not have been on stand-by they did fly every morning and NORAD 'could have grabbed' those aircraft to react to events. The Commission claimed that the entire United States had only seven bases on scramble alert and each had only two fighters in that mode at any time. They blamed 'the end of the Cold War'. The Commission asked us to believe that NORAD'S Northeast Air Defense Sector (NEADS), the one responsible for the 9/11 skies, had only two bases on alert to cover more than half a million square miles of airspace – Otis and Langley. There was no other choice and that explains everything. Doubles all round. This is either mendacity or incompetence on a scale that beggars belief. New York airspace with all those commercial planes coming and going all day is 'defended' from a base in Massachusetts *153 miles away*? The Washington-Pentagon no-fly zone is policed from the Langley base *130 miles away* when the major base at Andrews is only *ten miles* away? The very idea is as crazy as the mainstream media is pathetic for not challenging this nonsense.

Former ABC investigative producer James Bamford reported that in truth NEADS had a choice of on-alert planes at least four other locations. Among them was Andrews, one of the most famous bases in America and home of the US President's plane Air Force One with foreign heads of state often passing through. Are you going to locate the presidential plane at a base that does not have fighters ready to move at a moment's notice? Andrews, in fact, has two major squadrons on what are officially termed 'the highest possible state of readiness'. These are the 121st Fighter Squadron of the 113th Fighter Wing and the 321st Marine Fighter Attack Squadron of the 49th Marine Air Group. Thousands of people are employed at the base and they have at their disposal the very F-16s that NORAD says it deployed from 130 miles away at Langley, plus F/A-18 fighters. Sidewinder missiles carried by F-16s have a range of 18 miles and they would only have to get off the ground, lock in and fire to stop a plane crashing into the Pentagon even if there was no ground-to-air missile response. The fact that these planes were not scrambled from Andrews at any time before the Pentagon was hit is stunning and fundamentally significant. The Andrews AFB website went down immediately after September 11th and did not reappear until around mid-November. When it came back online it no longer had a link to the Air Force web pages describing the capabilities and mission of 113th Fighter Wing of the Air National Guard at Andrews – the capability of reacting immediately to any threat by air to Washington. A website called dcmiltary.com was authorised to supply information to those employed by US forces. It reported *before* 9/11 that Andrews is the base for the 121st Fighter Squadron, 113th Fighter Wing, and it confirmed the role:

> ... as part of its dual mission, the 113th provides capable and ready response forces for the District of Columbia in the event of a natural disaster or civil emergency. Members also assist local and federal law enforcement agencies in combating drug trafficking in the District of Colombia. [They] are full partners with the active Air Force.

The website said of the 321st Marine Fighter Attack Squadron of the 49th Marine Air Group at Andrews:

> In the best tradition of the Marine Corps, a 'few good men and women' support two combat-ready reserve units at Andrews AFB. Marine Fighter Attack Squadron (VMFA) 321, a Marine Corps Reserve squadron, flies the sophisticated F/A-18 Hornet. Marine Aviation Logistics Squadron 49, Detachment A, provides maintenance and supply functions necessary to maintain a force in readiness.

These units are operated by the District of Colombia National Guard, headquartered at Andrews, which provide combat units in 'the highest possible state of readiness' and describe themselves as the 'Capital Guardians'. Well, as long as jets are on standby 153 and 130 miles away. NORAD spokesman Barry Venable told me in 2002 that NORAD fighters were 'not standing alert, nor even stationed, at Andrews AFB on 11 September':

> The USAF did indeed have fighters stationed at Andrews AFB on 11 September, but not for the purpose of standing air sovereignty alert – a role NORAD performs.

Then how come fighters from Andrews were in the sky over Washington immediately *after* the Pentagon was hit? *USA Today* sought to explain away the 'Andrews mystery' by reporting that 'Andrews Air Force Base, home to Air Force One, is only 15 miles [by road not military jet] away from the Pentagon, but it had no fighters assigned to it. Defense officials won't say whether that has changed.' Not even NORAD claims there were no fighters at Andrews and what kind of journalism is it that prints this story when the truth is only a search-engine away? The same *USA Today* edition said in direct contradiction: 'The District of Columbia National Guard maintained fighter planes at Andrews Air Force Base, only about 15 miles from the Pentagon, but those planes were not on alert and not deployed.' The *San Diego Union-Tribune*, however, told the truth about Andrews when it reported:

Air defense around Washington is provided mainly by fighter planes from Andrews Air Force Base in Maryland near the District of Columbia border. The DC Air National Guard is also based there and equipped with F-16 fighter planes, a National Guard spokesman said. But the fighters took to the skies over Washington only after the devastating attack on the Pentagon ...

Other media sources reported that fighters from Andrews AFB were deployed over Washington. NBC *Nightly News* said: 'It was after the attack on the Pentagon that the Air Force then decided to scramble F-16s out of the DC National Guard Andrews Air Force Base to fly a protective cover over Washington, DC.' The UK *Daily Telegraph* said:

> Within minutes of the attack [on the Pentagon] American forces around the world were put on one of their highest states of alert – Defcon 3, just two notches short of all-out war – and F-16s from Andrews Air Force Base were in the air over Washington DC.

Surely it is common sense that Washington DC and its no-fly zone would be defended from air bases in and around Washington DC and not from 130 miles away. A 'former Pentagon Air Traffic Controller' quoted, but not named, is reported to have said:

> All those years ago when I was in the Pentagon, this wouldn't have happened. Air Traffic Control Radar images were (and are) available in the understructures of the Pentagon, and any commercial flight within 300 miles of DC that made an abrupt course change toward Washington, turned off their transponder, and refused to communicate with ATC, would have been intercepted at supersonic speeds within a max of 9 minutes by a fighter out of Andrews. Period. Why these planes weren't, baffles me. If we could get fighters off the ground in two minutes then, we could now.

Yet Pentagon spokesman Rear Admiral Craig Quigley made this astonishing statement: 'Planes come up and down the Potomac all the time. You can hear them in the building. There was no warning.' John A. Koskinen, the Washington DC City Administrator, said the District was 'largely helpless' to stop such attacks'. Utter garbage. There were apparently bases contacting NORAD *offering help* after the attacks began. William Scott wrote about this in a 2002 edition of *Aviation Week and Space Technology*. He described offers of air support made to NORAD NEADS Commander, Colonel Robert Marr:

> Calls from fighter units ... started pouring into NORAD and sector operation centers, asking 'What can we do to help?' At Syracuse, N.Y., an ANG commander told Marr, 'Give me 10 minutes and I can give you hot guns, Give

me 30 minutes and I'll have heat-seeker (missiles). Give me an hour and I can give you slammers.' Marr replied, 'I want it all'.

But *nothing happened.*

I asked FAA media spokesman Fraser Jones in 2002 who was responsible for policing no-fly zones like the ones over Washington and New York and what was the procedure when they were threatened. What aircraft were used and where were they based? What happened on September 11th when there was no effective response? What is the point of a no-fly zone if there is nothing to defend it? Mr Jones replied:

> The FAA monitors prohibited airspace and would be aware if a pilot blundered into such an area. Our mission is not civil defense. We would help coordinate the appropriate response given the circumstances.

What on earth does that mean? NORAD told me that it is not responsible for policing the no-fly zone over Washington and it was a matter for the civilian FAA. The FAA tells me it 'monitors prohibited airspace' and would be aware if a pilot blundered into such an area and would then help to coordinate the appropriate response in the circumstances. Oh, really, well take your time, no rush. How long does it take for a plane to enter restricted airspace over Washington before it parks itself in the White House, Capitol Hill or the Pentagon? So where would the immediate air response come from? Langley, Virginia, 130 miles away? What use would that be? The FAA and NORAD were either not telling me the truth or there was no system for protecting no-fly zones. However, we know there *was* – in the name of sanity there *had* to be or a no-fly zone would be pointless. Why wasn't it activated on 9/11?

Another astonishing ''coincidence' – the wargame ''exercise drills'

What are the chances on this of all days that a series of 'training exercises' were happening in the same airspace at the same time as the 9/11 hijackings? Or that among these 'exercises' was a training scenario involving *a plane flying into a building in Washington?* This meant that radar screens were potentially infected with simulated 'hijacked planes', as well as genuine ones, which confused the system that morning – as planned. The wargame exercises also gave cover to the force in the shadows manipulating events. Jeremy Powell, a technical sergeant at the NORAD Northeast Air Defense Sector (NEADS) dealing with the hijackings, assumed at first like his colleagues that reports about a problem with Flight 11 were part of the exercise scenarios. He asks on the NORAD tapes: 'Is this real world or exercise?' This was a question asked many times that morning. Lieutenant Colonel Kevin Nasypany, mission-crew commander on the operations floor at NEADS, said that when he was told about a hijack his first reaction was 'somebody started the exercise early'. He had said out loud: 'The hijack is not supposed to be for another hour.' Now we can see one reason why lower-level NORAD operatives dealing directly with the attacks were so confused. They didn't know initially when the actual 9/11 planes were hijacked if this was for 'real' or part of an exercise. This was not by accident, but design. There were many exercises happening that day and among them were those code-named Vigilant Guardian; Global Guardian; Northern Vigilance; Northern Guardian; Vigilant Warrior; Amalgam Warrior; Amalgam Virgo; Crown Vigilance; Apollo Guardian; and Whisky 105. They were supported by AWAC reconnaissance aircraft in the skies over Washington and elsewhere. The exercises had the added effect of relocating fighter planes to Alaska, Canada and a list of other locations that would normally be defending the East Coast. General Eberhart, commander of NORAD, said: 'It took about thirty seconds to make the adjustment to the real-world situation.' But this was an obviously ridiculous statement when the 'exercises' were clearly confusing the hijack response system. His mate, General Myers, acting uniform head of the military, said something similar and so they had one song-sheet in sync at least.

Eberhart was the man who ordered that an series of 'exercises' which normally take place in October and November each year were instead to be held across September 11th with enormous implications for confusing the response when real hijacks were happening that morning. Eberhart's decisions meant that at least *twelve* aerial exercises were happening at the same time that 9/11 planes were being hijacked – a move described as unprecedented. If that is a coincidence then I'm a pair of curtains and I should pull myself together. Scenarios included hijackings of two 747 passenger aircraft. Operation Vigilant Guardian involved the simulation of hijacked planes in 9/11 airspace and the same NEADS centre dealing with 9/11 hijacks. One Vigilant Guardian scenario was a plane hijacked to target New York City. The exercises focused attention of many agencies within Cheyenne Mountain including Eberhart's Space Command. The Whisky 105 exercise was centred on Otis Air Force Base and six of their F-15s took off for exercise duties in the Atlantic at 9am on 9/11 – eight minutes after the two F-15s were said to have been scrambled for New York. Vigilant Guardian was supervised by NORAD's airborne and warning officer, Lieutenant Colonel Dawne Deskins at NEADS. Newhouse News Service reported Deskins as saying that when she was called by Boston Air Traffic Control about the hijacking of Flight 11 the belief was that 'it must be part of the exercise'. FAA and military officials had difficulty discerning the war game operations from the actual attacks – as they were meant to – and this was most importantly the case with NORAD's NEADS centre which was directly responsible for responding to the 9/11 aircraft under its commander, Colonel Robert K. Marr. 'Everybody' at NEADS thought at first that the attacks were part of Vigilant Guardian, according to NORAD's Lieutenant Colonel Deskins.

Other US air defence fighters were occupied in Canada and Alaska on another exercise and staff at Cheyenne Mountain were heavily focussed on this and other drill scenarios when reports of genuinely hijacked aircraft began to come in. Canadian Lieutenant General Rick Findley, Battle Staff Director in the Cheyenne Mountain Operations Center, told the 9/11 Commission that there was 'confusion as to how many, and which aircraft, were hijacked'. General Larry Arnold, NORAD commander of the Continental US region, said: 'By the end of the day we had 21 aircraft identified as possible hijackings.' Despite all of this we are expected to believe that simulated hijackings in the same airspace did not affect the response to the real hijackings? The claim by General Eberhart and General Myers that the exercises didn't adversely affect the reaction time to the 9/11 attacks is beyond belief. Myers even said they 'enhanced the response' and Eberhart said the exercises 'cost us no more than 30 seconds'. How can that be when the normal raft of fighter aircraft at Andrews Air Force Base was seriously reduced by taking part in an exercise in the Las Vegas area? They left before the first plane struck the World Trade Center and didn't return until 2.35 in the afternoon when the attacks were well over. James Ampey, an FAA air traffic controller at Andrews, told the 9/11 Commission that an unusually high number of aircraft were taking off and landing on 9/11 morning because of the exercises and radar screens were depicting 'emergencies all over the place'. This is explained by an *absolutely vital* aspect of 9/11 that must be understood. At least some of the exercises like Vigilant Guardian involved 'sim over live' procedures in which the *simulated hijacks appeared on the live screens of air traffic controllers* both civilian and military. Imagine the potential for confusion, chaos and havoc that this would have wreaked once the real hijackings began – just as the orchestrators planned. Radar operators at Cheyenne Mountain demanded during the attacks that NEADS 'get rid of the goddam sim'. This is a major reason why NEADS, genuine operatives at Cheyenne Mountain and FAA air traffic controllers and others became so confused about what was real and what was exercise. What a coincidence that *twelve hours* before the attacks NORAD chief General Eberhart had reduced the protection for Pentagon communication networks to its *lowest level.* The Information Operations Condition (Infocon) system consists of a series of levels dictated by the perceived threat to military information and computer networks and is employed to defend against computer attacks. In a period where multiple wargame exercises were

happening and simulated hijackings were to be visible on real-time air
traffic screens Eberhart directs that Infocon be put on its *lowest level* of
alert and protection? *What*? Much later in the book when I get down to
the fine detail of who was behind 9/11 you will see how fake
'hijackings', simulated events and even phantom planes could have been
inserted in real-time onto air traffic screens by those who were not even
directly working with NORAD, the Pentagon, Cheyenne Mountain or
the FAA. It's quite a story and the lower the Infocon level the better.

A closer look at Eberhart

General Ralph E. Eberhart has not been a high-profile figure in the 9/11
story compared with people like Bush, Cheney, Rumsfeld and Myers,
despite being the commander-in-chief at NORAD and as such the man
with overall responsibility for protecting America from the 9/11 attacks.
His behaviour that day and before deserves far more public scrutiny
than has been the case so far. Red flags fly for me when someone is
lauded as a 'hero' when the opposite should be the case and people like
Eberhart enjoy post-event promotion for what should have seen them
fired. Flashing lights should also be activated when people and events
crucial to uncovering the truth about 9/11 are either ignored or made
peripheral in the final report of the official 9/11 Commission. All these
things happened with Eberhart. You may think that calling him a '9/11
hero' might just require some re-evaluation in the light of the following.
Eberhart both rearranged exercises so they would all be happening on
September 11th and reduced the level of Pentagon computer protection
to its lowest level at the time of the attacks and so why has he not come
under serious scrutiny? Eberhart began his day on September 11th at his
office at Peterson Air Force Base in Colorado about 20 miles from
Cheyenne Mountain. Peterson was the headquarters of another Eberhart
operation, the US Air Force Space Command and according to
Lieutenant Colonel Dawne Deskins at NEADS in evidence to the 9/11
Commission: 'NORAD planning exercises are mostly held at Peterson.'
Colorado was in a different time-zone to New York, but I will use East
Coast time to avoid confusion. The official version tells us that Eberhart
was contacted from Cheyenne Mountain at 8.45am to be told of a
suspected hijacking (Flight 11) that was 'not exercise' and he then saw
on television the stricken North Tower. Eberhart said there was
confusion in the system and that's not surprising after he had sanctioned
– and re-scheduled – so many exercises across America and Canada and
in the skies above the eastern United States that simulated aircraft were
all over air traffic screens. He said that he recognised after the second
plane struck that they were dealing with 'an ongoing and coordinated
terrorist attack' (such brilliant insight). His words and response,
however, might appear very strange to many. We are told that he spoke

with General Myers and said there were 'several hijack codes in the system' – meaning that pilots were punching in the hijack code; but 9/11 planes *weren't* and this is one of the great mysteries of the hijackings. Where was he getting that from? Eberhart informed Myers that he was going to stay at Peterson because he didn't want to be out of communication and then soon afterwards headed for Cheyenne Mountain, a usually 30 minute car journey that took him 45 minutes, and throughout that time he was not able to take calls because apparently his cell phone didn't work. He is reported to have missed a call from Dick Cheney while on the road. At the same time as claiming he was out of communication he says he ordered fighters to 'battle stations' at 9.49am. Ugh? Battle stations is an on-alert status when pilots sit in their planes with the engines off waiting for orders and he didn't order planes in the air as per standard practice in hijacking situations as we have seen in official regulations. Eberhart said he drove to Cheyenne Mountain because 'things had quieted down' when obviously they hadn't. Two planes were still hijacked and while he was on the road the Pentagon was hit. What's more he was a commander on a military base – why wasn't he rushed to Cheyenne Mountain by helicopter? Eberhart could have triggered a response plan known as Security Control of Air Traffic and Air Navigation (SCATANA) to clear the sky of commercial aircraft and give the military control of airspace. NORAD staff had urged him to do so, but he refused. He said NORAD radar were not sophisticated enough to do this while his staff clearly didn't see this as a problem. Two hours after Flight 175 hit the South Tower at 9.03 a 'modified' SCATANA was implemented when the attacks were well over. Eberhart also allowed his wargame exercises to continue despite what was happening until 10am when the attacks ended and the 'sim' or simulated attacks were allowed to stay on air traffic screens until the Pentagon was hit. We will see a clear pattern with major players on 9/11 like Bush, Cheney, Rumsfeld, Myers and Eberhart all with concocted out-of-the-loop cover stories for what they were doing before the Pentagon was hit and to within minutes of Flight 93 going down. In other words – *until it was all over*. Fighter response failed to effectively react *until it was all over* and the confusion and diversion of wargame exercises were continued *until it was all over*. Colonel Prouty:

> No one has to direct an assassination – it happens. The active role is played secretly by permitting it to happen. This is the greatest single clue. Who has the power to call off or reduce the usual security precautions?

Groundhog Day

Exercises began the day before 9/11 and were due to last a week and

who was in political charge of these wargames that confused the
response system on 9/11? Well, well, well: *Dick Cheney*. Others involved
were Donald Rumsfeld and acting Chairman of the Joints Chiefs of Staff
that morning, General Richard Myers. It is important to remember this
when you read the accounts of Rumsfeld and Myers in the next chapter
and Cheney later in this one. 'Exercises' and drills have been used again
and again as a cover for the scenario they are 'practising' to happen for
real. We saw this with the London '7/7' bombings in 2005 when three
tube trains and a bus were bombed while an exercise was going on at
the same time that mimicked what actually happened. Peter Power, a
former police officer in the anti-terrorism branch of London's Scotland
Yard, was running the exercise staged by his crisis management
company, Visor Consultants, in conjunction with an unnamed company
'of over a thousand people'. He told BBC radio that his London training
drill was 'based on simultaneous bombs going off precisely at the
railway stations where it [actually] happened this morning, so I still
have the hairs on the back of my neck standing up right now'. Power
said that they 'had to suddenly switch an exercise from fictional to real
which is what we have heard many times before – not least from
NORAD commander General Eberhart after 9/11. It is highly doubtful
that Power would have been initially so open about the stunning
'coincidence' if he had been knowingly involved in using the exercise as
cover for the real thing. Who did have prior knowledge and make the
exercise fit so perfectly? Somebody did because when you see how
many exercises happen at the same time as the real thing don't give me
that 'it's just a coincidence' crap. Power would tell ITV News: '... we
chose a scenario – with [the company's] assistance – which is based on a
terrorist attack because they're very close to, er, a property owned by
Jewish businessmen, they're in the city and there are more American
banks in the city than there are in the whole of New York.' The *Jerusalem
Post* ran an article that same day by Efraim Halevy, former head of
Israel's military intelligence agency, Mossad, which described the
'multiple, simultaneous explosions that took place today on the London
transportation system'. A little problem there is that London police did
not know they were 'simultaneous' at the time of the article and
believed they happened one after the other at 7.51, 7.56, and 8.17am.
Halevy called in his article for a world war against Muslim terrorism in
the wake of the attacks. Israeli Prime Minister Benjamin Netanyahu –
then Finance Minister – was in London at the time and so was New York
9/11 Mayor Rudolph Giuliani. An Associated Press correspondent in
Jerusalem reported that the Israeli embassy in London had been warned
by Scotland Yard of an imminent terror attack (how did they know?) and
Netanyahu was warned by the embassy not to attend an economic
conference at the Great Eastern Hotel near to the Liverpool Street

underground station where one of the bombs went off. Giuliani was staying at the Great Eastern Hotel where the conference had been arranged by the Tel Aviv Stock Exchange, the Israeli embassy and Deutsche Bank. See *Terror on the Tube, Behind the Veil of 7/7* by Nick Kollerstrom for more on the London attacks.

Rudolph Giuliani, who knew Netanyahu, also had a Peter Power-type security company – Giuliani Security and Safety – that ran 'mock terror drills' and so on, and it would appear that Power knew Giuliani personnel such as Richard Sheirer, Senior Vice President of Giuliani and Partners. Sheirer was formerly Commissioner at the New York Office of Emergency Management (created by then Mayor Giuliani) from February 2000 to March 2002 which included 9/11. Sheirer was also Director of New York City Homeland Security. He was called 'Ground Zero's Jewish Knight' after 9/11, but was later widely criticised for 'crucial failures of communication, especially between the Fire Department and the Police Department, which may have led to unnecessary deaths of scores of firefighters'. Pasquale J. D'Amuro, the FBI inspector in charge of the 9/11 [non]-investigation under Director Robert Mueller, left the Bureau after 26 years to become chairman of Giuliani Security and Safety. You will see that the world of 9/11 is a very small one indeed. 'Terror drills' that are near carbon copies of what happens for real in the same place at the same time, or very soon afterwards, have been identified many times. Among them have been the sinking of the ferry *Estonia* in the Baltic Sea en route from Estonia to Sweden (1994); the Madrid train bombings (2004); Oslo bombing (2011); Boston bombings (2013) and a long list of other terror attacks and mass shootings. Many police officers who took part in the *Estonia* terror drill died on their way home on the ship. When the part of the vessel officially responsible for the sinking was raised from the seabed the lead investigator was reported to have ordered it to be thrown back. 9/11 anyone?

Cheney tracks "missing plane" from White House "bunker"

Vice President Dick Cheney was given control of all 9/11 exercise operations just four months before the attacks in a presidential executive order in May, 2001. Executive orders are an outrageous system by which the President decrees law without the complication of a vote or debate. Cheney is a brutal and deeply imbalanced man. His computer program must have been written by a sadist and he was the real power in the White House in the Boy Bush years. Cheney told the media on September 12th, 2001, that he only heard of the 9/11 attacks from a clerical secretary who was watching television in his Washington office. Yes, and pigs are flying in formation. He said the Secret Service took him to the Presidential Emergency Operations Center, an underground bunker at the White House, and he began to direct the response – or lack of it – to what was happening. It was no accident that Boy Bush was arranged to be out of the way at a school in Florida and then to be flown between military bases until the evening. Bush was only a figurehead president and he would have got in their way. Go fetch the tea, George – Dick is thirsty. What happened in that White House operations 'bunker' was described by Secretary of Transportation Norman Mineta who witnessed a highly significant exchange. Mineta described what happened before the Pentagon was hit in evidence to the 9/11 Commission:

> During the time that the airplane was coming in to the Pentagon, there was a young man who would come in and say to the Vice President, 'The plane is 50 miles out, the plane is 30 miles out'. And when it got down to 'the plane is 10 miles out', the young man also said to the Vice President, 'Do the orders still stand?' And the Vice President turned and whipped his neck around and said, 'Of course the orders still stand. Have you heard anything to the contrary?

Here is devastating evidence from a member of the Bush-Cheney administration which the official 9/11 Commission shockingly censored and *did not include in its final report*. Mineta was confirming that Cheney and the Hidden Hand he represented were tracking Flight 77, or whatever hit the Pentagon, all the way into Washington, while the official story claims that air traffic controllers had 'lost' the aircraft and NEADS wasn't told of a problem until just before impact. There were two levels of tracking going on all the time. One was the day-to-day operational staff at the NEADS operation in New York State and the FAA (or at least the operational levels). The other was the tracking system that Cheney, the hierarchy at Cheyenne Mountain and Pentagon top brass were operating. *They* were tracking all the planes all the time and directing events while the rank-and-file FAA/NORAD system was having spanners hurled in the works and again towards the end of the book I will explain how this could be done and who by. Cheney was still relatively 'yes sir' and bit-part compared with the real orchestrators. The evidence presented by Norman Mineta has the 'young man' asking Cheney if 'the orders still stand', as the plane hurtles towards Washington with Cheney replying: 'Of course the orders still stand. Have you heard anything to the contrary?' What orders were these then? Mineta indicated that he didn't know what they referred to, but appeared to take them to mean they were to shoot down the plane. This makes no sense at all because, despite the obviously detailed tracking that was going on, the plane or projectile was *not* shot down before the Pentagon was struck. The only explanation that makes sense of what

Mineta said he witnessed is that the orders were *not* to shoot down the plane or whatever it was and allow it to reach its target. No wonder Mineta said the 'young man' sounded so anxious and wanted more confirmation. In other words there was a 'stand-down' order in place that would explain the absence of an effective military response in every aspect of 9/11. Charles E. Lewis, who worked on a project involving the Airport Operations Area at Los Angeles airport, or LAX, until two months before 9/11, described what happened when he returned to the airport after the happenings in New York to see if he could help in some way given his experience of new security systems. He said:

As on other days, there was 'chatter' on LAX Security walkie-talkies and I could easily hear what Security was saying when they were outside the guard shack (they would go in and out, but they were mainly outside). On some of the walkie-talkies, I could hear both sides of the conversations; on others only one.

I do not know who was at the other end of the walkie-talkies, but I assumed that it was LAX Security dispatch or command. At first, LAX Security was very upset because it seemed to Security that none of the FAA's Air Traffic Controllers (ATCs) tracking the hijacked airliners had notified NORAD as required. More chatter revealed that ATCs had notified NORAD, but that NORAD had not responded, because it had been 'ordered to stand-down'.

This report made Security even more upset, so they tried to find out who had issued that order. A short time later the word came down that the order had come 'from the highest level of the White House'. Security was puzzled and very upset by this and made attempts to get more details and clarification, but these were not forthcoming while I was still there.

Another piece of information that I heard, shortly after my arrival, was that the Pentagon had been 'hit by a rocket'. It's possible that the word was 'missile', although I'm quite certain it was 'rocket'. I was, in any case, quite surprised when I later got home and learned that the media were reporting that an airliner had hit the Pentagon.

Apparent chaos is wonderful camouflage for calculation. As I've said, there were two communication networks operating on 9/11. One involved the 'people on the ground', the operatives at air traffic control centers and those at NEADS. These communications were systematically disrupted and sabotaged by those working for the other communication networks that day. This was the one involving the Joint Chiefs of Staff Command Center in the Pentagon (which I am about to discuss), the highest level of NORAD and associated agencies at Cheyenne Mountain,

Dick Cheney and other Hidden Hand and Web operatives. Something similar was planned in the 1960s by the Pentagon Joint Chiefs of Staff, as I will be explaining. Some researchers have confused the more basic NEADS operation in New York State with NORAD's operational headquarters in Cheyenne Mountain where incredible tracking technology exists, much of it unknown to the public arena. This second network, operating to its pre-arranged plan, had access to state-of-the-art technology while NEADS was kept confused and bewildered about what was going on as they tried to make sense of what was happening amid, among other things, Pentagon 'wargame exercises' that also involved simulated hijackings. These wargames were under the ultimate authority of Dick Cheney.

It was this Cheney-Pentagon-NORAD network that was orchestrating the attacks on one level and sabotaging the normal speed and efficiency of response but even they were only artisans in a network of even deeper control that I will expose in detail towards the end of the book.

CHAPTER 7

Where were you on 9/11?

Without censorship, things can get terribly confused in the public mind
– General William Westmoreland, Commander US forces in Vietnam

Our attention turns next to the National Military Command Center (NMCC). This is the Pentagon command and communications operation that is supposed to oversee and respond to emergencies and threats like 9/11 under the authority of the Chairman of the Joint Chiefs of Staff who officially answers to the Secretary of Defense and US President.

General Richard B. Myers officially took over as Joint Chiefs chairman, the highest uniform post in the US military, two weeks after the attacks and was acting chairman while they were happening (Fig 33). He was appointed deputy chairman in 2000 and before that he was commander of NORAD. Myers, therefore, knew precisely what the procedures were for reacting to unexplained happenings with planes in North American airspace. FAA regulations say: 'The escort service will be requested by the FAA hijack coordinator by direct contact with the National Military Command Center (NMCC).' The Department of Defense manual says:

> In the event of a hijacking, the National Military Command Center will be notified by the most expeditious means by the Federal Aviation Administration. The NMCC will, with the exception of immediate responses ... forward requests for DOD [Department of Defense] assistance to the Secretary of Defense for approval.

This is the same National Military Command Center that claims it had no warning that an airliner was about to

Figure 33: General Richard Myers was somehow in two places at the same time on 9/11.

151

crash into its own building some 45 minutes after it deviated off course! Where was General Myers while all this was going on and what were the top brass in the Pentagon doing all this time? What was Defense Secretary Donald Rumsfeld doing? Where was President Bush? Myers knew the response procedures. He knew that Andrews Air Force Base little more than ten miles down the road had all that was necessary to respond to Flight 77 as it headed for Washington. Yet nothing was done. *The New York Times* tried to explain what was happening at the Pentagon that morning:

> During the hour or so that American Airlines Flight 77 was under the control of hijackers, up to the moment it struck the west side of the Pentagon, military officials in a command center on the east side of the building were urgently talking to law enforcement and air traffic control officials about what to do.

[No, you didn't misread that.]

> But despite elaborate plans that link civilian and military efforts to control the nation's airspace in defense of the country, and despite two other jetliners' having already hit the World Trade Center in New York, the fighter planes that scrambled into protective orbits around Washington did not arrive until 15 minutes after Flight 77 hit the Pentagon [reported elsewhere as 20 minutes].

What? Military chiefs in the Pentagon Command Center were 'urgently talking about what to do?' These are the guys who are supposed to protect the United States from nuclear attack! Officials in the Command Center were talking to air traffic officials (FAA) during the hour in question and so why no response from NORAD? Why are we told that NORAD's NEADS center, which is under Pentagon command, was not alerted about Flight 77 when Pentagon officials were 'urgently talking to law enforcement and air traffic control officials about what to do' during 'the hour or so that American Airlines Flight 77 was under the control of the hijackers'? Given what had happened in New York why weren't planes scrambled to patrol the skies over Washington as a matter of course anyway? Here we have the nexus from which the two tracking operations were coordinated – one that was feeding countdown information to Cheney in his White House bunker and the other (run by NEADS and lower-level FAA) was being systematically isolated and sabotaged. General Myers told his Senate confirmation hearing when he became Chairman of the Joint Chiefs of Staff that he pledged '… to keep our armed forces at that razor's edge'! Pentagon spokesman Air Force Lieutenant Colonel Vic Warzinski even had the audacity to tell *Newsday*: 'The Pentagon was simply not aware that this aircraft was coming our way …' The Cheyenne Mountain official website said of the NORAD Command Center supplying real-time information to the Pentagon:

> Redundant and survivable communications hot lines connect the Command Center to the Pentagon, White House, US Strategic Command, Canadian Forces Headquarters in Ottawa, other aerospace defense system command posts, and major military centers around the world.

Where were these 'hot lines' on 9/11 when Pentagon chiefs claim they *didn't know that a hijacked plane heading for their own city for more than 45 minutes was coming their way??* CNN reported that while golfer Payne Stewart's plane was flying on auto pilot '... officers on the Joint Chiefs were monitoring the Learjet on radar screens inside the Pentagon's National Military Command Center'. Of course they were, that is what they are supposed to do. Why are we told they did not do this on September 11th when four planes were hijacked and how come they didn't know one was heading in their direction? The lies would be laughable if the consequences had not been so tragic. CNN also quoted officials at the Pentagon as saying they were never made aware of the threat from hijacked United Airlines Flight 93 until after it crashed in Pennsylvania at 10.03am. The FAA is reported to have informed NORAD at 9.16 that Flight 93 may have been hijacked and the transponder was turned off at 9.40. NORAD and the FAA both told me that open lines between them were established to discuss Flight 93. There is no way that the Pentagon's National Military Command Center with open lines to the FAA and NORAD (in Cheyenne Mountain) was not aware of the hijack of Flight 93 until we are told that it crashed after 10am. The Pentagon's entire story is nonsense and it is designed to hide the simple truth – at the highest levels within the US government and military these attacks were being both orchestrated and allowed to happen. 'Flight 77' crashed into the Pentagon on the west side of what is the biggest office complex in the world. This is the opposite side of the building to where Rumsfeld, military top brass and the National Military Command Center were located. The targeted section had been the first of five to undergo renovations and strengthening to protect the Pentagon from terrorist attacks and yet this is the very section these 'highly trained, highly professional' terrorists aimed for?? Such is the size and strength of the Pentagon that Rumsfeld said that he only felt a 'jarring thing' when the plane hit. If you were really a crazed Islamic fanatic dedicated to attacking the 'Great Satan America' why would you aim the plane at the very opposite side of a 29-acre, six million-square-foot building to where your real targets are? The answer I guess is the same as why Timothy McVeigh parked the Ryder truck as far away as he did from his alleged target, the offices of the Bureau of Alcohol, Tobacco,

Firearms and Explosives (ATF).

Where was Myers?

General Myers was acting chairman of the Joint Chiefs of Staff on
September 11th in the absence abroad of the outgoing General Hugh
Shelton. Myers would be confirmed as Shelton's successor at a Senate
hearing only two days later. Chairman of the Joint Chiefs is the highest-
ranking uniformed military post and third in command of US forces.
Surely this is a man who would have been at the centre of events with
America 'under attack' from terrorists. Where was Myers while the
nightmare was being unleashed? It turns out, and I'm not kidding, that
he was having a meeting with Senator Max Cleland of Georgia on
Capitol Hill. Or, at least that's what he claims. I think it's best if you sit
down while you read the following and breathing deeply might help,
too. This is Myers' account of his movements that morning described in
an interview with the Armed Forces Radio and Television Service:

 I remember it was like watching a bad movie. I was on Capitol Hill. I was
 about ready to meet with Senator Cleland. I was meeting with him in
 preparation for my hearing, my confirmation hearing to be the Chairman of
 the Joint Chiefs of Staff. And I remember before we walked in there was a TV
 that was playing and somebody has said, 'An airplane has hit one of the
 World Trade Center towers'.

 They thought it was an airplane, and they thought it was a small airplane or
 something like that. So we walked in and we did the office call with Senator
 Cleland.

The highest-ranking uniformed officer in the US military on American
soil that day hears that a plane has hit the World Trade Center and
instead of checking it out he goes into a routine meeting with a senator
about confirmation hearings? *Come again?* And it gets worse:

 Sometime during that office call the second tower was hit. Nobody informed
 us of that. But when we came out, that was obvious. Then right at that time
 somebody said the Pentagon has been hit.

Hold on, let me sit down here and fasten the seat belt. No one
informs the acting chairman of the Joint Chiefs of Staff, the top military
man in America at the time, that a second airliner has hit the World
Trade Center (or even the first) when down in Florida White House
Chief of Staff Andrew Card was telling President Bush that 'America is
under attack' according to the official story? General Myers' account
makes no rational sense whatsoever. Do they really think we are all so

stupid that we would believe that the acting chairman of the Joint Chiefs of Staff is not contactable at all times and that he would not have been told by the Pentagon about the second plane – indeed the first also – as a matter of course? Myers then says that 'right at the time' when he and Cleland came out of their meeting 'somebody said the Pentagon has been hit'. We can therefore add a timeline to his story. Myers' account puts him in the meeting with Cleland at no later than around 9am before the second plane crashed and he did not come out until about the time the Pentagon was struck. This means no earlier than 9.38-9.40 and even later given reaction time. How amazing that this meeting took place across precisely the period that the attacks were happening – if indeed there was such a meeting given evidence that follows. *The New York Times* tells us that 'during the hour or so that American Airlines Flight 77 was under the control of hijackers, up to the moment it struck the west side of the Pentagon, military officials in a command center on the east side of the building were urgently talking to law enforcement and air traffic control officials about what to do'. All this was happening and they didn't inform their ultimate boss that day who claims to have been in a meeting down the street on Capitol Hill? Smell a rat? I smell a whole species. General Myers says that when he emerged from the meeting to be told what most of the world already knew he launched into action:

> Immediately, somebody handed me a cell phone, and it was General Eberhart out at NORAD in Colorado Springs talking about what was happening and the actions he was going to take. We immediately, after talking to him, jumped in the car, ran back to the Pentagon.

I have detailed the fantastic technology and communications network at the disposal of NORAD and the Pentagon yet NORAD's commander contacts the acting military head of US forces only *after* three hijacked planes had crashed over nearly an hour and when somebody handed him a cell phone? NORAD commander General Eberhart – the man who replaced Myers at Cheyenne Mountain – is telling him 'the actions he is *going* to take' after three airliners are embedded in three of America's biggest buildings? What in God's name had Eberhart and his NORAD operation been doing all this time? And why did Eberhart wait until three aircraft had crashed into buildings before calling the acting Chairman of the Joint Chiefs of Staff? If you feel you can stand any more General Myers also told Armed Forces Radio and Television:

> The Chairman [General Shelton] had left that morning to go to Europe, so he was somewhere over the Atlantic. As I got to the Pentagon I noticed a lot of people were coming out of the Pentagon. Of course they'd been told to evacuate. My concern was where can you best discharge your duties? ... [My]

battle station was in the National Military Command Center. I asked if it was still running, they said it sure is, so I went back in the building to the Command Center and was joined shortly thereafter by the Secretary of Defense [Rumsfeld]. The Deputy Secretary [Wolfowitz] actually went to another location at that point. We did what had to be done in terms of the command and control of the day ...

The interviewer asked Myers if he could believe that it was actually a terrorist attack:

I didn't know what to believe at the time. That was the problem. We had these events, and then subsequently the airplane went down in Pennsylvania. We were trying to tie this together, what does this mean? General Eberhart was working with the Federal Aviation Agency trying to figure out the logical steps at this point. We had some fighters airborne at that time in case we had some hijacked airplanes that were possibly a threat to other institutions or structures, but it was initially pretty confusing. You hate to admit it, but we hadn't thought about this.

They hadn't thought about this when they had been performing practice drills over years based on just this scenario? Given what is claimed to have happened, the voices said to have been heard from cockpit radios and reports by passengers and attendants on 'cell phones' and 'Airfones' that morning it is an unbelievable misrepresentation to say they didn't know this was a 'terrorist attack'. Only with three planes down and a fourth soon to crash in Pennsylvania did the top military officer on duty that day walk into the Command Centre at the Pentagon which, as we have seen, has clear and set procedures for reacting to hijackings or aircraft anomalies and would have had open lines throughout to the FAA and NORAD in Cheyenne Mountain. Only then did the Defense Secretary Donald Rumsfeld appear and he was in the building from at least before the time that Flight 11, the first hijacked plane, was leaving its gate at Boston Logan. More about Rumsfeld shortly, but let us stay with General Myers because this guy really is something else. You may have seen him at the time, a grey-haired chap in uniform giving news conferences at the Pentagon while his forces bombed innocent civilians in Afghanistan and elsewhere justified by what is alleged to have happened on September 11th. Two days after 9/11 Myers appeared before the Senate Armed Services Committee hearing that confirmed his appointment as Chairman of the Joint Chiefs of Staff. Committee Chairman Senator Carl Levin questioned him about what had happened while the attacks were taking place:

Levin: Was the Defense Department contacted by the FAA or the FBI or any other agency after the first two hijacked aircraft crashed into the World Trade Center, prior to the time that the Pentagon was hit?

Myers: Sir, I don't know the answer to that question. I can get that for you, for the record.

[He didn't know?]

Levin: Thank you. Did the Defense Department take – or was the Defense Department asked to take action against any specific aircraft?

Myers: Sir, we were ...

Levin: ... And did you take action against – for instance, there have been statements that the aircraft that crashed in Pennsylvania was shot down. Those stories continue to exist.

Myers: Mr Chairman, the armed forces did not shoot down any aircraft. When it became clear what the threat was, we did scramble fighter aircraft, AWACS, radar aircraft and tanker aircraft to begin to establish orbits in case other aircraft showed up in the FAA system that were hijacked. But we never actually had to use force.

Levin: Was that order that you just described given before or after the Pentagon was struck? Do you know?

Myers: That order, to the best of my knowledge, was after the Pentagon was struck.

[He doesn't know?]

The highest-ranking military man in America, third only in military authority to the President and the Defense Secretary, and himself a former Commander of NORAD, does not know two days after 9/11 if his own Defense Department was contacted by the FAA or FBI or any other agency after the first two hijacked aircraft crashed into the World Trade Center and before the Pentagon was hit? He didn't ask at any time after he claims to have rushed to his 'battle station', the National Military Command Center in the Pentagon, where they would have known everything that had happened? What utter tripe. He knew exactly the procedure and lines of communications as both the acting chairman of the Joint Chiefs of Staff and a former head of NORAD. He knew that the Defense Department, NORAD, and the FAA work closely in hijack situations and that the Pentagon would have normally been notified before the first plane crashed never mind after two had done so. He knew that fighters are deployed as a matter of course to seek out rogue aircraft. Myers said that 'to his knowledge' no order was given to scramble jets in response to the attacks until after the Pentagon was hit. 'To his knowledge'? He didn't ask that question either when he arrived at the Pentagon or *for two days afterwards?* In that time no one told him? This question of whether jets were indeed scrambled before the Pentagon was struck is interesting because not only did Myers say to his knowledge that military jets were *not* scrambled until after the Pentagon strike this was NORAD's position for several days also. New York Mayor Rudolph Giuliani said that he called the White House just before 10am and asked Chris Henick, Bush's deputy political director, about air cover over New York. Giuliani said he was told that jets had been scrambled twelve minutes earlier which would have made that after the Pentagon was hit. This is a common theme. NORAD spokesman Barry Venable told me in 2002 that this was not the case and sent me an Associated Press report of September 11th in which NORAD spokesman Colonel Mike Perini is quoted as saying: 'NORAD controllers did track one of the hijacked planes, but it crashed into the World Trade Center even as fighters were scrambling.' Other NORAD spokesmen said the very opposite, as did General Myers. Major Mike Snyder, a spokesman at NORAD headquarters, said that no fighters were scrambled before the Pentagon was hit. This was exposing outrageous incompetence (at best) and the story was about to change.

No fighters were scrambled? *What??* Cue Dan

The 'we did scramble planes' story only began to circulate after a report by Dan Rather, a Council on Foreign Relations member and CBS News 'anchor'. Rather is the man who told talk show host David Letterman:

> George Bush is the President. He makes the decisions. Wherever he wants me to line up, just tell me where.

You are a *journalist*, man – or supposed to be. It was Rather who announced to the nation on September 14th that jets had been scrambled while quoting no sources. From this 'Rather exclusive' the 'we scrambled jets, but they were just too late' story became official history. In fact Rather himself had asked CBS military consultant Colonel Mitch Mitchell on September 12th why the Pentagon didn't have a system in which fighters were used to defend against attacks like 9/11. Rather's revelations that jets *were* deployed on September 11th before the Pentagon was hit came the day after the disastrous testimony of General Myers to the Senate Armed Forces Committee in which he had made the shocking statement that no fighters had been ordered to intercept the first three hijacked airliners that morning. Myers made no mention of planes scrambling from Otis or Langley, the CIA Air Force base where he was stationed for three years in the late 1980s. Then, hey presto, the following day the scrambled fighter jets story suddenly appeared on CBS. Dan Rather said that night:

> CBS News has learned the FAA alerted US Air Defense units of a possible hijacking at 8.38 Tuesday morning, and six minutes later, at 8.44, two F-15s received a scramble order at Otis Air Force Base on Cape Cod. But two minutes later, at 8.46, American Airlines Flight 11, the first hijacked jet, slammed into the World Trade Center. Six minutes later, at 8.52, the F-15s were airborne and began racing towards New York City, but the fighters were still 70 miles away when the second hijacked jet, United Airlines Flight 175, hit the second Trade Center tower. Shortly after that blast, the F-15s reached Manhattan and began flying air cover missions over the city.

> But to the south, a new danger and a new response. At 9.30, three F-16s were launched out of Langley Air Force Base in Virginia, 150 miles [130] south of Washington. But just seven minutes later, at 9.37, American Airlines Flight 77 hit the Pentagon. The F-16s arrived in Washington just before 10am and began flying cover over the nation's capital.

The contradictions can be clearly observed in two reports in the *Boston Globe* just four days apart. On Saturday, September 15th, reporter Glen Johnson highlighted the opposing accounts of CBS and NORAD. After repeating Rather's CBS 'exclusive' the night before, he wrote that NORAD at that stage still denied scrambling any jets before the Pentagon was attacked even though a NORAD spokesman, Marine Corps Major Mike Snyder, said they 'routinely' intercept aircraft (it was happening about 100 times a year). Go figure. The *Globe* quoted Snyder as saying:

> We scramble aircraft to respond to any aircraft that we consider a potential threat. The hijacked aircraft were normal, scheduled commercial aircraft on approved flight plans and we only had 10 minutes prior notice to the first attack, which unfortunately was not enough notice.

But he also confirmed that none were scrambled for the next hour either! The *Globe* story said:

> ... Snyder, the NORAD spokesman ... said the command did not immediately scramble any fighters even though it was alerted to a hijacking 10 minutes before the first plane, American Airlines Flight 11 from Boston to Los Angeles, slammed into the first World Trade Center tower at 8.45am Tuesday.

Never before had a hijacked airliner been steered into a skyscraper, Snyder noted, in trying to explain the lack of immediate response [exercise scenarios had been happening for years to practice for just such a situation].

The spokesman said the fighters remained on the ground until after the Pentagon was hit by American Airlines Flight 77 at 9.40am, during which time the second Trade Center tower was struck by United Airlines Flight 175, which also originated in Boston and was destined for Los Angeles. By that time, military authorities realized the scope of the attack, Snyder said, and finally ordered the jets aloft.

Vice President Cheney was still telling this same story five days after the attacks on September 16th when he told the NBC show *Meet the Press* that it was Bush who personally made the decision to send up interceptors and Cheney suggested this was only done after the Pentagon was hit. How does all this square with the later (and since official) story about having fighters in the air heading for hijacked airliners before that time? Suddenly the story changed, new song sheets all round at Cheyenne Mountain and the Pentagon. By September 19th – *eight* days after 9/11 – Glen Johnson and the *Boston Globe* were reporting a very different version of events from NORAD. Johnson wrote:

Two fighter jets dispatched from Otis Air National Guard Base on Cape Cod had closed to within 71 miles of New York last week when the second of two hijacked airliners slammed into the World Trade Center towers, the military confirmed Tuesday.

Similarly, two F-16 fighters that had scrambled from Langley Air Force Base in Virginia streaked toward Washington as a third airliner bore in on the Pentagon, but both were still about 12 minutes away when the commandeered plane struck the nation's military headquarters.

The timeline, provided by NORAD, had miraculously changed. Johnson rightly pointed out:

The account contradicted earlier statements from a defense command spokesman and the incoming chairman of the Joint Chiefs of Staff [Myers]. Both said the military did not launch its planes until after the Pentagon had been hit.

NORAD spokesman Army Major Barry Venable said the previous statements were based on 'inaccurate information'. What – *for more than a week?* I met with the *Boston Globe's* Glen Johnson and he told me he had called the public affairs office at Otis Air Force Base to ask them to confirm that they did scramble planes that morning, but they refused to comment for reasons of 'operational security' even though their bosses at NORAD had now issued a press release saying that they had. Johnson told me that eventually they would not return his calls. What goes on? I asked NORAD if I could speak with the pilots of the planes that were said to have been scrambled from Otis. I was told they had 'elected not to speak with the media'. They had no problem, however, speaking with the BBC programme *Clear The Skies* that unquestioningly repeated the official line and enjoyed great cooperation and access to Cheyenne Mountain and other military establishments as a result. The blatant contradictions in the official story are constant and obvious everywhere you look. Anyway, even according to this new timeline of NORAD and the Pentagon, no fighter jet got within 100 miles of even the fourth aircraft, Flight 93, before it 'crashed in Pennsylvania'. The *Globe's* Johnson highlighted the obvious point that these 'scrambled' jets flew to their targets at well below their potential speed. Why? We had the same contradictions with Flight 93 almost two hours after the problem was first identified with Flight 11. Major General Paul Weaver, director of the Air National Guard, said that 'no Air National Guard or other military planes were scrambled to chase the fourth hijacked airliner, United Airlines Flight 93'. This is a staggering statement in itself, but Defense Secretary Rumsfeld's deputy Paul Wolfowitz was quoted in the *Boston Herald* telling a very different story. He said: '... the Air Force was tracking the hijacked plane that crashed in Pennsylvania on Tuesday after other airliners slammed into the Pentagon and World Trade Center and had been in a position to bring it down if necessary.' General Myers was questioned by Senator Bill Nelson during his Senate confirmation hearing on September 13th and his shocking mendacity was there for all to see:

Nelson: The second World Trade tower was hit shortly after 9am. And the Pentagon was hit approximately 40 minutes later. That's approximately. You would know specifically what the timeline was. The crash that occurred in Pennsylvania after the Newark westbound flight was turned around 180 degrees and started heading back to Washington was approximately an hour after the World Trade Center second explosion.

You said earlier in your testimony that we had not scrambled any military aircraft until after the Pentagon was hit. And so, my question would be: Why?

Myers: I think I had that right that it was not until then. I'd have to go back and review the exact timelines. [He *thinks* that's right?]

Nelson: Perhaps we want to do this in our session, in executive [secret] session. But my question is an obvious one for not only this committee, but for the executive branch and the military establishment. If we knew that there was a general threat on terrorist activity, which we did, and we suddenly have two trade towers in New York being obviously hit by terrorist activity, of commercial airliners taken off course from Boston to Los Angeles, then what happened to the response of the defense establishment once we saw the diversion of the aircraft headed west from Dulles turning around 180 degrees and, likewise, in the aircraft taking off from Newark and, in flight, turning 180 degrees? That's the question. I leave it to you as to how you would like to answer it. But we would like an answer.

Myers: You bet. I spoke, after the second tower was hit, I spoke to the commander of NORAD, General Eberhart. And at that point, I think [*think?*] the decision was at that point to start launching aircraft.

In his interview with Armed Forces Radio and Television Myers said that when he came out of his meeting on Capitol Hill with Senator Max Cleland he was told of the second plane crashing into the WTC *and* that the Pentagon had just been hit. Only then, he said, did he talk to Eberhart. Myers is changing his accounts in response to Nelson's questions as they expose the inexplicable non-reaction of Cheyenne Mountain and the Pentagon. What Myers is therefore saying here again is that no planes were scrambled until after the Pentagon was hit.

Myers: One of the things you have to understand, senator, is that in our posture right now, that we have many fewer aircraft on alert than we did during the height of the Cold War. And so, we've got just a few bases around the perimeter of the United States.

What about the fighters a minute's flying time from Washington at Andrews AFB, which were deployed after the Pentagon was hit?

Myers: So it's not just a question of launching aircraft, it's launching to do what? You have to have a specific threat. We're pretty good if the threat's coming from outside. We're not so good if the threat's coming from inside.

Two planes have hit the World Trade Center and another hijacked aircraft is heading for Washington and he says you have to have a 'specific threat' before scrambling fighters? And 'launching to do what?' Launching to do what they do every week of the year and as a former commander of NORAD he well knew that. Why were planes not deployed over Washington as soon as the World Trade Center was attacked? If it was felt right to do that after the Pentagon was hit why not before?

> **Myers:** In this case, if my memory serves me – and I'll have to get back to you for the record – my memory says that we had launched on the one that eventually crashed in Pennsylvania. I mean, we had gotten somebody close to it, as I recall. I'll have to check that out. [Remember this is the top-ranking uniformed military officer in America speaking two days after the attacks.] I do not recall if that was the case for the one that had taken off from Dulles. But part of it is just where we are positioned around this country to do that kind of work because that was never – it goes back to Senator Collins' issue. Is this one of the things that we'll worry about. You know, what's next? But our posture today is not one of the many sites and the many tens of aircraft on alert. We just have a handful today.

Let us not forget that General Myers said that he headed straight for the Command Center in the Pentagon after he came out of his meeting on Capitol Hill. The idea that he did not know that morning, never mind two days later, what fighter jets had been, or not been, scrambled is simply insulting to the American public. Of course he knew and what he said until he was faced with uncomfortable questions is that they did not scramble jets until the Pentagon was hit. When you have someone presenting such a travesty of the truth and dithering around unable to answer the most basic of questions – answers he would clearly have known – the alarm bells begin to explode. Senator Nelson later emphasised his point again to the committee:

> Mr Chairman, may I, just for the record? Commenting from CNN on the timeline, 9.03 is the correct time that the United Airlines flight crashed into the South Tower of the World Trade Center; 9.43 is the time that American Airlines Flight 77 crashed into the Pentagon. And 10.10am is the time that United Airlines Flight 93 crashed in Somerset County, Pennsylvania. So that was 40 minutes between the second tower being hit and the Pentagon crash. And it is an hour and seven minutes until the crash occurred in Pennsylvania.

What a [coordinated] shambles

The whole official story is a mess and the 9/11 Commission, the official cover up of what really happened, would produce *a third* FAA/NORAD response timeline when it reported in 2004 in another desperate attempt to hide the truth that normal procedures were sabotaged to allow the attacks to happen unchallenged. *Three* separate report and reaction timelines were issued all contradicting each other over a period of three years? Yep, sounds credible. The Commission described a 'they-called-them-who-called-them' chain of command to explain delays in response that totally contracted hijack reaction procedures in the official manuals which are based on problem-report-scramble. Military chiefs were exposed in Commission hearings for lying in their previous statements, but don't worry there's not a scam going on or anything. In the Commission's timeline for Flight 11 the FAA was aware of a hijacking at 8.25am and yet waited seven minutes to alert the NORAD'S NEADS response system in New York State where NEADS Battle Commander Colonel Robert Marr only put Otis planes on alert and called Major Larry Arnold, commanding general of NORAD's US Continental Region, to consume another eight minutes before Arnold gave the go-ahead to get them airborne. Forty seconds later, according to the Commission timeline, Flight 11 hit the North Tower. From the FAA realising the plane was hijacked to the fighters being scrambled to respond took *21 minutes* in this timeline. It should have taken less than five and if that had happened the fighters would have travelled the 153 miles to New York before the building was struck. Yet another misdirection is that NEADS required higher authorisation before jets could be scrambled. Regulations say that in an emergency action can be taken before higher authority is secured. While FAA top brass have fundamental questions to answer the 9/11 Commission version of events hung out to dry the rank and file FAA and cleared the top brass military to hide the existence of stand-down/don't respond orders until after the Pentagon strike.

NORAD or SNORAD?

General Ralph Eberhart, Commander in Chief of NORAD and Space Command at Cheyenne Mountain, appeared on October 25th, 2001, before the Senate Armed Services Committee Hearing on the 'Role of Defense Department in Homeland Security'. By now the new song sheets had been circulated. Eberhart said that the FAA did not notify NORAD or the Department of Defense that Flight 77 was 'probably hijacked' until 9.24am even though it had changed course and turned back at about 8.55 – after the first plane had already crashed into the World Trade Center. The plane was 'probably hijacked'? Can it get any sillier? Eberhart said:

> I show it as 9.24 that we were notified, and that's the first notification that we received. I do not know, sir, why it took that amount of time for FAA. I hate to say it, but you'll have to ask FAA.

Did anyone ever bother? It should also be pointed out the claim that NORAD was told about Flight 77 at 9.24 was exposed as untrue three years later by the NORAD tapes. Eberhart was asked if they had now improved the communication system:

Sir, I assure you that we have, and we practice this daily now, and now it takes about one minute from the time that FAA sees some sort of discrepancy on their radar scope or detects a discrepancy in terms of their communication before they notify NORAD. So that certainly has been fixed.

I think at that time, the FAA was still thinking that if they saw a problem it was a problem that was a result of a mechanical failure or some sort of crew deviation. They weren't thinking hijacking. Today, the first thing they think is hijacking, and we respond accordingly.

You can see from the evidence presented in the last chapter about the normal reaction procedures of the FAA and NORAD before September 11th that we are being seriously misled here. If you look at what happened to those planes it was clear to air traffic controllers that the aircraft were not suffering a 'mechanical failure or some sort of crew deviation' and so why is Eberhart talking such nonsense? Senator John Warner said he was 'a little bit stunned' that Eberhart didn't know six weeks after the attacks why there was such a delay in the FAA informing NORAD/NEADS about what was happening. Warner asked him if the FAA and NORAD had not rehearsed the possibilities of an aircraft being seized by terrorists. Eberhart replied: '... although we practice this, day in and day out, the FAA sees on their scopes scores of problems that are a result of mechanical problems, switch errors, pilot errors, et cetera, and that's what they think when they see this'. Oh do come on. Contact was lost with the cockpits, transponders were turned off, there were serious changes in course and planes were crashing into buildings. Then we are told there were calls from passengers on the planes and 'terrorists' heard in the cockpits. Nothing to worry about, Ralph, must be a mechanical fault. Note that he says they 'practice this, day in and day out ...' and uses the pre-September 11th tense if you read the sentence. He was, after all, speaking only weeks after the attacks. Eberhart continued:

Although we have exercised this, we have practiced it, in most cases it's a hijacking like most of the hijackings, all of the hijackings I'm aware of, where we have plenty of time to react, we get on the wing, and we follow this airplane to where it lands and then the negotiations start. We were not thinking a missile – an airborne missile that was going to be used as a target – a manned missile if you will – the origin of this flight was from overseas and we did not have the time-distance problems that we had on that morning. We had plenty of time to react.

[Nonsense – exercise drill scenarios for just this plane-as-a-missile situation had been practiced for years.]

We were notified that for sure there was a hijacking and we were notified that they were holding a gun to the pilot's head and telling him to fly toward New York City or Washington, DC. So that's how we had practiced this, sir. I certainly wish we had practiced it differently, but I really think that, for sure in the first two instances, and probably in the third, the time and distance would not have allowed us to get an airplane to the right place at the right time.

A few months later he said that from the moment the FAA suspects a problem it took 'only about one minute' to contact NORAD and fighters are in the air 'within a matter of minutes to anywhere in the United States'. He claimed this was a new procedure when it was nothing more than the previous policy – suspended on 9/11 – that said if there was an unexpected loss of radar or radio communication it must be considered that 'an aircraft emergency exists'... and ... 'If ... you are in doubt that a situation constitutes an emergency or potential emergency, handle it as though it were an emergency'. Eberhart's operation within Cheyenne Mountain had access to the most sophisticated tracking and surveillance technology on earth – and in space – known to man and this is a point missed (of course it was) by the 9/11 fake Commission which said that NORAD was struggling to locate Flight 11 because its transponder was turned off. Author and researcher David Ray Griffin points out in *The 9/11 Commission Report, Omissions and Distortions* that NORAD's tracking systems are far more advanced than civilian technology and did not need a transponder to track a plane and its altitude. Griffin rightly adds that if all Soviet planes had to do to avoid detection during the Cold War was to turn off their transponders what kind of state-of-the-art defence system was that? It's all nonsense and another diversion to cover the military response stand-down/sabotage on 9/11. Two planes had hit the World Trade Center and Eberhart claims they didn't have the time to intercept a plane that turned back towards Washington 40 minutes before it struck the Pentagon? He says that they 'were not thinking a missile – an airborne missile that was going to be used as a target – a manned missile if you will', but two such 'missiles' had already crashed into the World Trade Center before the non-reaction to Flight 77 in Washington by the FAA-NORAD system. Senator Wayne Allard asked Eberhart if they had aircraft 'at least up in the air with the second plane to hit the twin towers'. He replied, 'Yes sir.' The following exchange then took place:

Allard: And so what I'm interested in knowing is, what was the process there and then, how was that followed-up with the other aircraft that you identified that were coming or heading toward Washington, and how you responded? And how was the FAA interacting with NORAD in that whole situation, starting with that first plane that you deployed heading toward New York City?

Eberhart: Yes, sir. The first flight I think was American Flight 11. [He thinks?] The FAA, once they notified us and we issued a scramble order almost simultaneously to the first crash, tragically. That flight of two out of Otis Air Force Base, out of Cape Cod ...

Allard: Let me understand – so right at the time the first aircraft was hitting the Twin Towers, you were being notified by FAA that you had another plane headed toward the Towers, you just routinely brought another aircraft ...

Eberhart: No, they notified us of the first hijacking just about the time that that airplane was hitting the tower.

Allard: Okay.

Eberhart: And at that time, we issued a scramble order for the two F-15s out of Otis Air Force Base [even though NORAD was denying this for a week]. We continued to send those airplanes toward New York City because initially, as we worked with the FAA, we weren't sure if that was the hijacked airplane [a ludicrous statement]. I mean, I hate to admit this, but I'm sitting there hoping that someone has made a mistake; there has been an accident; that this isn't the hijacked airplane, because there is confusion. We were told it was a light commuter airplane. It didn't look like that was caused by a light commuter airplane.

[With NORAD's technology at Cheyenne Mountain they would have known exactly what it was.]

So we were still trying to sort this out, so we're moving the two F-15s and we continue to move them. They're flying toward New York City. In fact, they are eight minutes away from New York City when the second crash occurs. We didn't turn around. We didn't send them back.

Allard: They hadn't made a sighting of that ...

Eberhart: Again, it's time and distance. It took them only six minutes to get airborne. [The Air Force claimed a potential response time of 2.5 minutes from scramble to 29,000 feet.] Once we told them to get airborne, it took them six minutes to get airborne. I think this talks about the professionalism and training of these individuals. Tragically, there was just too much distance between Otis and New York City to get there in time to ...

Allard: Did FAA then notify you that you had a second hijacked plane somewhere in there, and the planes up there were ...

Eberhart: During that time, yes, we were notified, and again we'll provide the exact time line for the record.

Allard: I'm not interested in exact time lines as much as I am just how the FAA reacted with NORAD during this time period. And then you had the other two planes heading out. Then FAA continued to notify NORAD that you had two other potential hijackings, these headed for Washington; is that correct?

Eberhart: Yes, sir. The initial hijacking of the one, I think [think?] it's 77 that crashed into the Pentagon, we were working that with the FAA and we launched the airplanes out of Langley Air Force Base as soon as they notified us about hijacking.

At that time it took those airplanes, two F-16s, again, six minutes to get airborne. They were approximately 13 minutes away from Washington, DC, when that tragic crash occurred. Six minutes to get airborne, but still 13 minutes to it.

I don't want to worry you, but this guy was the head of the operation that is supposed to protect the United States from attacks from air and space. Better get that shelter dug pronto. Eberhart's claim about scrambling planes in pursuit of Flight 77 would later be shown to be untrue – the Langley planes were scrambled according to the NORAD tapes in response to a false report that Flight 11 didn't crash and was heading for Washington. He also doesn't mention that the Langley fighters first headed the wrong way into the Atlantic because no one told them where to go. Eberhart revealed that NORAD helped to provide the radars used by the FAA to track aircraft in US airspace and that NORAD had 'moved manpower of the order of about 200 people over the years to the FAA to operate these radars'. I wonder if any NORAD staff were on FAA duty that day? We can't know because no one is saying and if they did would you believe them? Eberhart said that he could not discuss in an open session who had the authority to order a commercial plane to be shot down even though the White House had confirmed it was the President before 9/11 and that the head of NORAD and a list of other named military men could now issue such an order. Oh, by the way, after questioning Eberhart and being given pathetic answers Senator Allard said:

Well, I just want to thank you and your people for, I know, I think a tremendous effort in light of some totally unexpected circumstances. And at least, I, for one, appreciate, you know, the readiness that was displayed.

I know, incredible isn't it? These are the people running our world.

Where was Rumsfeld?

We have established where General Myers was that morning – nowhere to be seen according to his own account (but more about that shortly). What about the Defense Secretary Donald Rumsfeld, the number two in the United States military command structure behind the president? He said that he was working on the east side of the Pentagon from before the time that Flight 11 took off from Boston. He told CNN talk show *Larry King Live* on December 5th, 2001, that he was in his office and was given no warning whatsoever that Flight 77 was heading for Washington before it crashed into the Pentagon. Can the official story get any more insane? Unfortunately it can. This is the headquarters of the US military with open lines to NORAD at Cheyenne Mountain with all its satellites, AWACS and ground-based surveillance and with open lines by now with the FAA. Two planes had already crashed into the World Trade Center and the US Defence Secretary was given no warning that an aircraft was about to crash into the building he was in, albeit a long, long, way from impact? This is an extraordinary statement and more transparent tosh. Larry King failed to ask a single question about the Defense Secretary's ridiculous story which will surprise no one. If he'd have asked the questions a proper journalist would have asked that would have been career over. The money's too good, right, Larry? He has since been employed by Russian station RT – what are they thinking of? Rumsfeld related to King that earlier on 9/11 morning he had told a congressional delegation in his office at the Pentagon:

> Sometime in the next two, four, six, eight, ten, twelve months, there would be an event that would occur in the world that would be sufficiently shocking that it would remind people, again, how important it is to have a strong, healthy Defense Department that contributes – that underpins peace and stability in our world. And that is what underpins peace and stability.

How amazingly prophetic. Then came another outrageous statement that Rumsfeld made to King. He said that during this meeting in his office ...

> ... someone walked in and handed me a note that said that a plane had just hit the World Trade Center. And we adjourned the meeting. And I went in to get my CIA briefing right next door here, and the whole building shook within 15 minutes. And it was a jarring thing.

Now hold on here. The first plane hit the World Trade Center at about

8.46. The Pentagon wasn't hit until around 9.38. Yet Rumsfeld tells King
he was handed a note saying a plane had 'just' hit the WTC and within
15 minutes Flight 77 crashed into the Pentagon? Are we being asked to
believe that the Defense Secretary wasn't told about the first plane
crashing until some *40 minutes* after it happened when he had been
sitting in his own office at the Pentagon all this time? This is the only
way that the Pentagon strike 'within 15 minutes' can be explained. Most
of America and hundreds of millions across the world were watching
events unfold live on television well before 9am and yet the Defense
Secretary, number two only to the President in the US military
command, *didn't know until about 9.20?* Where does that leave the 'just'
hit the World Trade Center in the Rumsfeld story and why was he not
told about the second hit on the WTC at the same time which happened
at 9.03? Rumsfeld's own Department of Defense manual said:

> In the event of a hijacking, the [National Military Command Center at the
> Pentagon] will be notified by the most expeditious means by the FAA. The
> NMCC will, with the exception of immediate responses ... forward requests
> for DOD assistance to the Secretary of Defense for approval.

Given this procedure alone the Secretary of Defense would surely have
been told immediately the first plane hit the North Tower – more than 50
minutes before the Pentagon was hit and not 15. In fact, he would have
had to be told under the Pentagon's own procedures immediately it was
known that the first plane had been hijacked. That would have been
around 8.20 – an hour and 20 minutes before the Pentagon was hit. The
lies are just so breathtaking and we will see shortly that what Rumsfeld
said he did that morning is pure fantasy. *The Washington Post* reported
that after Rumsfeld was informed of the World Trade Center attack by
his Chief of Staff he 'stayed in his office on the east side of the Pentagon
for a scheduled CIA briefing' – note 'scheduled' – while 'several of his
senior aides rushed to the Pentagon's Command Center deep within the
five-sided complex, where a crisis action center [no-action center] was
being set up'. If you only believe the *ludicrous* official version that
Pentagon officials were given twelve minutes' warning of the plane
heading their way, why would no one tell the Defense Secretary before
he felt his 'jarring thing'? Why wasn't evacuation of the Pentagon begun
and how come Rumsfeld claims he didn't know a potentially hostile
plane was heading towards Washington when Dr Thomas Mayer, the
top Department of Emergency Management official and medical director
for Fairfax County Fire and Rescue, said that he was told by air traffic
controllers that 'something was headed towards the national capital
area' and 'we knew we needed to get ready'? John Darrell Sherwood, a
Navy historian, said that a Park Police helicopter working that day from

the helipad close to where the building was hit was dispatched to 'try to distract the plane' and try to stop it going into the Pentagon. This was confirmed by the pilot's girlfriend, Stephanie Hughes, who went to meet pilot Keith Bohn at his workplace that morning but she said he had left a note saying: 'Got called into the air, there is another plane headed this way, go home and wait for me to call.' *But Rumsfeld and the military chiefs didn't know??* Nowhere, but nowhere, do the official pieces fit and there is a very good reason for that. It's a pack of lies. I contacted the Pentagon with the following list of questions, but officials chose not to answer them.

1. With the capability of United States air defence, how can a hijacked airliner, Flight 77, be allowed to fly for 40 minutes towards Washington, with communication lost with air traffic control and the transponder turned off, approach a no-fly zone and hit your headquarters without any challenge whatsoever?

2. Why was the Defense Secretary Mr Rumsfeld unaware that the plane was approaching until the Pentagon was actually struck?

3. Why was Secretary Rumsfeld not told of the first plane striking the WTC until around 15 minutes before Flight 77 struck the Pentagon (thus about 9.20am to 9.25am)? Why was he not told at this time that a second plane had struck the World Trade Center?

4. Why was Richard Myers, the acting chairman of the Joint Chiefs of Staff, not informed that two planes had struck the WTC and that another was heading for Washington while he was in a scheduled meeting on Capitol Hill and available throughout? Why did he only learn of what was happening when he emerged from the meeting to be told that the Pentagon had been hit? Is there not a constant communication link between the Chairman and the Pentagon?

5. Why were the ground to air defences at the Pentagon and the White House not activated when Flight 77 approached?

6. Why is there no surveillance camera footage of Flight 77 from much closer to the point of impact? The pictures released by the Pentagon seem to be a long way away for a building that must be guarded by a very large number of cameras, many of them looking outwards.

The questions were not answered because those questions are unanswerable without lifting the lid on the endless flow of lies that are the official story of 9/11. The government released just five frames of distant footage that claim to show the plane striking the building but we will see later that what it appears to portray is actually impossible. Five distant frames are all they have when the Pentagon must be drowning in security cameras?? A Freedom of Information request led to the Department of [In]Justice revealing that 85 security camera videos were in its possession retrieved at or close to the Pentagon where officials refused to make them public because they were exempt from Freedom of Information laws. Why didn't the 9/11 Commission (a) subpoena them and (b) even mention them? Dan Philbin from the Office of the Assistant Secretary of Defense (Public Affairs) Directorate for Public Inquiry and Analysis merely referred me to transcripts of Pentagon press briefings on the Internet which did not address my listed questions. I told him so and asked for direct answers. He did not respond. Rumsfeld's response to the 'jarring thing' and his fake realisation that two airliners had struck the World Trade Center and another smacked into the Pentagon was to head outside to help with rescue efforts. Yes, that's just what you want an elderly man to do who happens to be US Secretary of Defense in the middle of a national catastrophe when there were thousands of service people to deal with rescue. It keeps you out of the official loop, though. Rumsfield's story is a lie as we shall see.

Where was Bush?

So to George W. 'Boy' Bush: Where was he when his country needed a decisive President? Boy Bush was not in Washington on September 11th which doesn't surprise me at all. They would have wanted him to be where his legendarily-limited intelligence couldn't get in the way. Bush was in Florida, then governed by his brother, Jeb, for a pre-publicised photo opportunity at the Emma E. Booker Elementary School in Sarasota. What he did that morning and when and how he heard about 'Flight 11' striking the World Trade Center depends very much on which official account you want to believe. There are several different versions claimed by Bush, Cheney and Ari Fleischer, the presidential press secretary. Sonya Ross, an Associated Press reporter, said she knew of the first crash even before Bush had reached the school:

> My cell phone rang as President Bush's motorcade coursed toward Emma E. Booker Elementary School in Sarasota, Florida. A colleague reported that a plane had crashed into the World Trade Center in New York. No further information. I called the AP desk in Washington, seeking details. Same scant information. But I knew it had to be grim. I searched for a White House official to question, but none was on hand until 9.05am.

If her office knew and enough time had passed for her to call them then

Bush must have known well before he arrived at the school that an aircraft had crashed into the World Trade Center and he must have known even earlier there was a hijack in progress on Flight 11. Contact was lost with the aircraft at 8.13am and the president travels with a staff in instant contact with the National Military Command Center (NMCC) at the Pentagon, which coordinates with NORAD, the FAA and the government Secret Service intelligence and security network. Dick Cheney let this slip – well almost – in a post-9/11 interview when he said:

> The Secret Service has an arrangement with the FAA. They had open lines after the World Trade Center was ...

He stopped the sentence abruptly at that point because he was about to demolish the 'Bush didn't know' story and it was left to Richard Clarke, the Bush administration counterterrorism advisor on 9/11, to basically complete the sentence in his 2004 book, *Against All Enemies*. Clarke wrote: 'Secret Service had a system that allowed them to see what the FAA's radar was seeing.' The Secret Service had open lines with the FAA when the World Trade Center was hit – of course they did, it was normal protocol – and who was looking after Bush in Florida? The *Secret Service*. Clarke also said that he had an open line with Deborah Lower, director of the White House Situation Room, who was ... *in Florida travelling with Bush and his entourage*. The claim that Bush didn't know what was going on is another lie and another insult to those who died and lost loved ones that day. John Cochran, an ABC journalist, was reporting Bush's visit to Florida. He told anchor Peter Jennings:

> Peter, as you know, the President's down in Florida talking about education. He got out of his hotel suite this morning, was about to leave, reporters saw the White House Chief of Staff, Andy Card, whisper into his ear. [A] reporter said to the President, 'Do you know what's going on in New York?' He said he did, and he said he will have something about it later. His first event is in about half an hour at an elementary school in Sarasota, Florida.

We have it confirmed that Bush was asked by reporters as he left his hotel about what was happening in New York because those reporters already knew that a plane had struck the World Trade Center. From that knowledge alone the Bush cover story that would later be sold to the public can be seen to be a whopping lie. At the very least from about 8.46am when 'Flight 11' crashed the Secret Service which looks after the safety of the President had 'open lines' with the FAA. Open lines would surely have been activated earlier than that when 'Flight 11' began to act very strangely and dramatically change course. The Bush team in

Florida knew precisely what the FAA knew by that time – indeed suspected from about 8.20 – that 'Flight 11' had been hijacked. It would have been the most basic security response to keep the President away from a pre-publicised event at a school only five miles from the Sarasota-Bradenton International Airport. Especially after 'Flight 11' struck the World Trade Center the thought that the President could be a target for a similar attack must have occurred to them and at the very least you would delay the school visit until you knew what was happening. Dick Cheney said he was whisked away to an underground bunker at the White House by Secret Service agents who wouldn't take no for an answer but here was Bush, President of the United States, allowed to continue his trip to the school. Did they know something we didn't? Oh, just a little bit. What about the potential danger to the children in these circumstances if you take them on face value?

'There's one terrible pilot'

Despite the journalist eye-witness reports of when Bush must have known about 'Flight 11', he completely contradicted this – and earlier accounts of his own officials – in an extraordinary performance on December 4th at a 'town meeting' at the Orange County Convention Center in Orlando, Florida, where he was answering non-challenging questions from a sycophantic audience. I actually watched this happen live on CNN in a hotel bar in America. I sipped my beer and despaired at the hero worship being enjoyed by a village idiot when Bush made a startling statement about September 11th. For the next two days I scanned the newspapers, Internet mainstream 'news' sites, including CNN, but there was no mention of the amazing statement Bush had made. Weeks later a Belgian visitor to my website sent me the text of what Bush said which was posted on the White House website and hidden away in the full and long transcript of the meeting. Bush was talking about what happened on 9/11 and how he heard of the atrocities in New York in response to a question from a young boy called Jordan:

> Well, Jordan, you're not going to believe what state I was in when I heard about the terrorist attack [well, it didn't show]. I was in Florida. And my Chief of Staff, Andy Card – actually, I was in a classroom talking about a reading program that works. I was sitting outside the classroom waiting to go in, and I saw an airplane hit the tower – the TV was obviously on. And I used to fly, myself, and I said, well, there's one terrible pilot. I said it must have been a horrible accident. But I was whisked off there; I didn't have much time to think about it. And I was sitting in the classroom, and Andy Card, my Chief of Staff, who is sitting over here, walked in and said, 'A second plane has hit the tower, America is under attack.

A few facts are urgently required. There was no live television coverage of the first plane hitting the North Tower – how could there be? Recorded footage of the first crash did not air until long after Bush went into the classroom where he was told of the second crash by Card. Live pictures were of the *second* plane when the television networks were already broadcasting shots of the burning North Tower. How could Bush, therefore, claim to have seen the first plane strike? This is simply not possible, so what on earth was he talking about? What about his reaction of 'there's one terrible pilot'? A passenger jet crashes into a 110-storey building full of people and all the President of the United States can say is 'there's one terrible pilot'! We have already seen that Bush must have known about the first crash before he even arrived at the school and he wants us to believe that the President of the United States, Commander-in-Chief of US forces and 'homeland' defence, had no idea what was going on? Bush, remember, said before leaving his hotel for the school that he would 'have something' later about what was happening in New York and the Associated Press reporter said she knew of the first crash before Bush had even arrived at the school. Yet he says that he saw the plane crash on a television at the school (not possible) and his reaction was: 'I used to fly myself, and I said, well, there's one terrible pilot.' Lies, lies and still more lies. Bush's story is also in direct contradiction to the earlier official version that he was told about Flight 11 in a call at the school from his National Security Adviser Condoleezza Rice before he went into the classroom. This, in turn, contradicts the accounts of reporters who made it clear that Bush must have known what was happening before he arrived at the school. Then, knowing what had happened and knowing the plane had been hijacked the President of the United States walks into a classroom to hear children from the second grade read him a story about a pet goat! As the children read to him he said: 'Really good readers – whew!' Bush interrupted at one point, saying: 'This must be sixth grade.' God help us. There had just been a catastrophe in New York, Mr President, involving and eventually killing thousands of people and you know the cause is a hijacked airliner. *Hello?* Andrew Card came into the classroom and is said to have whispered in Bush's ear that a second plane had hit the World Trade Center and 'America is under attack'. This was the picture seen all over the world along with headlines like: 'The Moment Bush Knew' (Fig 34 overleaf). What does the President do then? He continues to sit there listening to a story about a pet goat. If you were writing this as fiction they'd say it was a ridiculous story. It is certainly ridiculous, but unfortunately it's *fact* not fiction. Associated Press reported on September 12th:

In Sarasota, Florida, Bush was reading to children in a classroom at 9.05am

Figure 34: Andrew Card tells Bush about the second plane.

Figure 35: Satanic symbol Baphomet – the Hidden Hand's 'pet goat'.

when his chief of staff Andrew Card whispered into his ear. The president briefly turned somber before he resumed reading. He addressed the tragedy about a half-hour later.

He 'briefly' remained somber, or sombre, as we spell it in Britain? He was supposedly just told that a second commercial airliner had struck the World Trade Center. Death and destruction on a massive scale was already obvious, but he turned 'briefly somber' before continuing to focus on the adventures of a pet goat. Goat symbolism is very much part of the Hidden Hand's satanic language – see the satanic symbol known as Baphomet – and anyone who has studied their staggering obsession with symbolism will note the 'coincidence' (Fig 35). They leave their symbolism signature everywhere if you know what to look for because it's their hidden language which insiders understand. What is ancient hieroglyphics except the language of symbolism? Jenna Heath of Cox Newspapers' Washington Bureau reported that Bush 'did not appear preoccupied' as he introduced Education Secretary Rod Paige inside the classroom and shook hands with teacher Sandra Kay Daniels. 'There was no sign that [Condoleezza] Rice had just told Bush about the first attack on New York's World Trade Center during a telephone call,' Heath wrote (repeating the official story). Look at his reaction when Card 'whispered in his ear' before he left his hotel? 'He did not respond,' said witnesses. Is this really a natural reaction from a man who had been told of such extraordinary events in the country he is supposed to be leading? Or is it the response of someone who knew full well what was going on even if he was only a figurehead while those really in power were doing their dastardly deeds? Bush told the Florida town meeting on December 4th:

But I knew I needed to act. I knew that if the nation's under attack, the role of the Commander-in-Chief is to respond forcefully to prevent other attacks from happening. And so, I've talked to the Secretary of Defense; one of the first acts I did was to put our military on alert.

Bush says he knew he needed to act when the indisputable truth is that he didn't. What's all this about calling Defense Secretary Rumsfeld? When did he do that? Rumsfeld told Larry King that even though he was in his office in the Pentagon he didn't know anything was happening until he was handed a note while meeting a congressional delegation in his office little more than 15 minutes before the Pentagon was struck at about 9.38am. We are being told here that although the President knew well before 9am, the Defense Secretary was not told until at least half an hour later even though he was in the Pentagon. Wherever you look there is a deluge of lies and contradictions. Either Bush didn't talk to Rumsfeld, which means Bush was lying, or he did and Rumsfeld was lying. Actually, both of them are – and big time. Bush said that he put the military on alert when he could not have done this until he was finished with the goat story and left the classroom shortly before 9.30 – more than 40 minutes after the first plane hit. The official tale (official version 99933/S11/666/update/updated/updated) is that Bush was taken to a private room before he went into the classroom and spoke on the phone with National Security Adviser Condoleezza Rice who told him about Flight 11. We are asked to believe that at this point the crash of 'Flight 11' could have been considered just a 'terrible accident' – an obvious lie. If Bush talked to Rice before 9am how come Defense Secretary Rumsfeld says he didn't know anything for another 25 minutes? Why was Rice not in immediate contact with Rumsfeld? Why wasn't the President? Why wasn't anyone? It was 9.30 – *26 minutes* after hearing of the *second* crash – before Bush went into the school library to announce:

Ladies and gentlemen, this is a difficult moment for America. Two airplanes have crashed into the World Trade Center, in an apparent terrorist attack on our country. I am going to conduct a full-scale investigation and hunt down and find those folks who committed this act. Terrorism against our nation will not stand.

Those folks? *Those folks?* Bush's behaviour that morning was at the very least criminally inept and incompetent, but it was more than that as I shall highlight later. 'Those folks' were not 'Muslim hijackers', but very much closer to home as Bush well knew. The disgraceful cover-up known as the 9/11 Commission official [non]investigation of the attacks claimed despite the all the evidence laid out here: 'No one in the [president's] travelling party had any information during this time that other aircraft were hijacked or missing.' Filmmaker Michael Moore highlighted Bush's inaction in his movie, *Fahrenheit 9/11* (executive producer ultra-Zionist women-abuser Harvey Weinstein), but as usual with Moore he missed the real point completely and failed to ask all the key questions while not challenging the official story about Muslim hijackers taking down the planes. This is typical of the work of fake-radical Moore and his productions which appear to be challenging the establishment while again and again promoting what that very establishment wants people to believe. I don't say for a moment that he is doing this knowingly – he's just incredibly uninformed about how the world works and enslaved by his 'progressive' addiction to virtue-signalling.

The lie about Scare Force One

Bush was taken to the presidential plane, Air Force One, and even the official story says that he did not call Vice President Cheney and put the US military on high alert status until at least 10am – by which time the Pentagon had been hit (a constantly recurring theme of no effective action until the Pentagon strike). Bush took off about 9.55 and headed for Barksdale Air Force Base, Louisiana, and the US Strategic Command at Offutt Air Force Base in Nebraska. He did not arrive at the White House, via Andrews Air Force Base, until shortly before 7pm. This was more than ten hours after the first strike on the World Trade Center. When understandable questions were being asked about why Bush did not head straight for Washington to lead his country at such a terrible time the White House propaganda machine said a phone call had been received giving a secret code to warn that Air Force One was the next target. *No it wasn't* – that was yet another lie. Attorney General John Ashcroft, a man who delivered 'justice' to others, also said the 'government had credible evidence that the White House and Air Force One were targets'. Lie again. Reports were circulated through the news agencies on September 12th that quoted a White House spokesman as saying: 'There was real and credible information that the White House and Air Force One were targets of terrorist attacks and that the plane that hit the Pentagon was headed for the White House.' Bush press secretary Ari Fleischer confirmed this the same afternoon. The Secret Service had 'specific and credible information' that the White House and Air Force One were potential targets, he said. Bush's chief political strategist, lie-for-a-living Karl Rove, was quoted the following day as confirming that the threat came in language that proved the terrorists had knowledge of the president's 'procedures and whereabouts'. So why did they allow him to attend a publicised appearance at a school in the circumstances of that morning and why, if there was a specific threat to Air Force One, was Bush taken straight to the airport to take off in that very plane after he had finished with the pet goat story? And why did it take off *with no military air cover*?? There were Air Force bases only 185 miles away (Homestead) and 235 miles (Tyndall) with fighters that could have responded to a call in minutes; but the call never came. Once again – what did they know that we didn't? Maureen Dowd wrote in *The New York Times* that Karl Rove had 'called around town, trying to sell reporters the story'. Then two weeks later the White House was forced to back down on the whole fantasy and on September 25th *CBS Evening News* reported that the threat 'simply never happened'. Most newspapers did not even report this exposure of the lies spewed out daily by the Bush administration and *The Washington Post* only ran the story on an inside page. Ari Fleischer, the same White House press spokesman who repeated the lies about Air Force One, also told us how Flight 77 was heading for the White House before it 'veered off' and aimed at the Pentagon. Dick Cheney said the same on NBC's *Meet the Press*. Cheney confirmed that the plane was being tracked (so why no response?) and then produced this lie: 'When it entered the danger zone and looked like it was headed for the White House was when they grabbed me and evacuated me to the basement ...' They waited, he claims, until the aircraft was 'in the danger zone' before evacuating the vice president when in truth they had been tracking a plane's progress towards Washington for some 40 minutes after two planes had already crashed into the World Trade Center. *CBS News* Transportation Correspondent Bob Orr reported that the recorded flight path of Flight 77 does not support what Cheney and Fleischer claim:

> Eight minutes before the crash, at 9.30am EDT, radar tracked the plane as it closed to within 30 miles of Washington. Sources say the hijacked jet continued east at a high speed toward the city, but flew several miles south of the restricted airspace around the White House.

Once again I sent a list of questions to the White House media office relating to these events. They were faxed in May, 2002, but they chose not to answer any of them:

1. When did the President know that Flight 11 was in trouble or there could be a problem? When did the FAA, NORAD, and the Pentagon communicate this information to the President's support team in Florida that morning?

Would not respond.

2. Why, when he was told of the first plane striking the WTC, did the President continue with his engagement and go into a reading class at

the Emma Booker School?

Would not respond.

3. Why when told by Andrew Card in the classroom that a second plane had struck the WTC and that 'America is under attack', did he continue to stay in the classroom for some time?

Would not respond.

4. When did the President put the United States military on high alert?

Would not respond.

5. Why did the President not go back to Washington immediately when we now know that the story of the telephone warning that Air Force One was the next target never happened?

Would not respond.

6. Why did the President tell a public meeting that he saw the first plane strike the WTC and said 'There's one a terrible pilot', when he could not possibly have seen that happen before he entered the classroom? That footage was not aired until much later.

Would not respond.

7. Why was the President not considered to be in danger when the attacks began, and thus removed from the school and a pre-announced visit when the school was only a short distance from an airport?

Would not respond.

Why no evacuation?

Another piece of criminal negligence – in truth more than that – was the failure to evacuate the Pentagon, White House and other major Washington symbols until the Pentagon was struck. This was despite a warning apparently issued to the Pentagon by the FAA. 'Defense Department officials', quoted by CNN, said that no action was taken for at least 12 minutes despite warnings that an airliner 'appeared' to be heading towards Washington. In fact the aircraft must have been tracked heading in that direction for more than 40 minutes. American Forces Press Service reported that personnel at the Pentagon realised they could be a target long before they were hit: 'We were watching the World

Trade Center on the television,' said a Navy officer. 'When the second plane deliberately dove into the tower, someone said, "The World Trade Center is one of the most recognizable symbols of America. We're sitting in a close second".' Top people in the Pentagon, apparently, could not see what everyone else could. Or maybe, I would suggest, some of them could see very clearly, but did nothing because a pre-planned series of events had to be played to their conclusion. Officials at the Pentagon, quoted by CNN, said that 'no mechanism existed within the US government to notify various departments and agencies under such circumstances'. *No mechanism to evacuate the Pentagon with a flying bomb heading in its direction??* Pentagon spokesman Glenn Flood contradicted this when he said that 'to call for a general evacuation, at that point, it would have been just guessing ... We evacuate when we know something is a real threat to us.' Clearly something is only considered a 'real threat' when it smashes into the building. Oh, it was a real threat then; better evacuate, I guess. So there *was* an evacuation procedure (of course there was) – it just wasn't activated. *Newsday* reported that many of the building's 20,000 workers were still sitting at their desks when the plane struck and some said they heard the crash but didn't know the plane had hit the Pentagon until they saw it on TV! 'The first thought everyone had was that it had been a bomb,' said Victoria Clarke, a spokeswoman for Defense Secretary Rumsfeld (maybe it was, at least in part, but that's for later). Only with a hole in the side of the building and 125 employees and workers dead was the Pentagon evacuated followed by the White House, Capitol Hill and elsewhere. None of the Pentagon leadership were killed or injured because they did not work in the part of the building that was struck. They were on the opposite side as far from impact as you can get. The segment of the colossal building that was hit was where civilian accountants were working to track down the missing trillions from the Pentagon budget publicly announced the day before. Many of the money-trackers were killed. General Richard Myers, Chairman of the Joint Chiefs of Staff, had the unbelievable nerve to say at a memorial ceremony for the victims that they were 'serving their country' in the course of doing their jobs at the Pentagon 'and on September 11 were called to make the ultimate sacrifice'. Sacrifice, I think, was the only appropriate word. They were allowed to die as the recorded facts make so plain. All this was coldly calculated by those running the 9/11 operation because the more death and destruction they could cause the bigger would be the problem, the bigger the reaction and therefore the bigger the solution that could be offered – a war without end and the dismantling of basic freedoms. The families of those who died in the Pentagon have an open and shut case for a lawsuit against the US government for the gross negligence that cost the lives of their loved ones. It is, however, as I continue to stress, far more than 'negligence' that is behind all this.

Where was 'Big Dick'?

Representatives of government, 'security' agencies and the military at the highest levels constantly lied over and over about what did and did not happen on 9/11 which brings me to mega-liar Dick Cheney. Where was the vice president all this time? He told the media on September 12th that a clerical secretary watching television in his White House office alerted him to the attacks. Oh really, Dick? The Cheyenne Mountain official website said of the NORAD Command Center: 'Redundant and survivable communications hotlines connect the Command Center to the Pentagon, White House, US Strategic Command, Canadian Forces Headquarters in Ottawa, other aerospace defense system command posts, and major military centers around the world.' Yet Cheney, sitting in the White House, says he learned of the attacks when a clerical secretary comes in and says: 'Hey, you'll never guess what I've just seen on the telly.' The whole story is a joke, but look at the common denominator here between Bush, Rumsfeld and Myers, the 1, 2, 3, in the military command structure, and Cheney. You can throw in NORAD's Eberhart as well. Their (cover) stories and actions all ensured that they were not in a position to react immediately to events until after the Pentagon was hit. Or rather they had an excuse why they didn't do so. Bush was occupied with the goat story until shortly before the Pentagon was hit and then went straight into another room to make a statement to the media. Rumsfeld gave Larry King a tale that he knew nothing about the World Trade Center until 15 minutes before the Pentagon was hit and claims no one told him that a plane was coming his way before his 'jarring thing'. 'So how could I order a response?' is the obvious implication. Myers says that he was in a pre-arranged meeting with a senator on Capitol Hill throughout the period between the first strike on the World Trade Center and the Pentagon strike almost an hour later while the actual Joint Chiefs chairman at the time was on a plane mid-Atlantic. The cover-story narratives about the movements of Cheney, Rumsfeld and Myers all have them otherwise engaged until about the same time – around 10am and crucially after the Pentagon was hit (by something). Isn't that all so terribly convenient? These transparently false cover-stories were accepted by the 9/11 Commission cover up. Another key question is where was *Father* George Bush, the orchestrator, with Cheney, of the Boy George 'presidency'? Daddy Bush, like Cheney, was a disgusting man, the depths of which are almost indescribable. He admitted himself that he was at the White House the night before 9/11, but said he flew the next morning to St Paul, Minneapolis. What time the next morning? The first plane to be hijacked was Flight 11 at about 8.15. Two planes had crashed into the World

Trade Center by 9.03 and, if Flight 93 had not been delayed well over
half an hour before take-off, it is highly probable that all four aircraft
would have hit their targets by around 9.40. What were Father Bush and
Cheney doing while all this was going on? How did he take a plane out
of Washington amid what was happening? One place Bush was reported
to have been by the mainstream media on September 10th and 11th was
at Washington's Ritz-Carlton Hotel in a business meeting for the Carlyle
Group with Osama bin Laden's brother, Shafiq bin Laden, and other
members of the family. I'll have more later about the Bush-Carlyle
Group-Bin Laden family connection. Also at the meeting were Carlyle
executives, former Secretary of Defense Frank Carlucci and former
Father Bush Secretary of State James Baker, who played a crucial role in
getting Boy Bush the presidency in 2004 amid the controversy over the
vote in Florida.

Clarke's bombshell

Richard Clarke, Boy Bush's counterterrorism advisor at the time of
September 11th, published a book, *Against All Enemies,* in 2004 that
demolished the accounts of Myers, Rumsfeld and Cheney about what
they were doing that morning and where they were. Clarke said he was
at a conference when he heard about Flight 11 and in the five minutes or
so it took him to get to the White House he ordered a secure
teleconference to be organised with the Counterterrorism Security
Group. This included key personnel in government counterterrorism
and security agencies. When he heard that the second tower had been
hit, he said: 'I want the highest level person in Washington from each
agency on-screen now, especially the FAA.' Clarke immediately made
contact with Dick Cheney and National Security Adviser Condoleezza
Rice who were in Cheney's White House office. Cheney told him: 'It's an
al-Qaeda attack and they like simultaneous attacks. This may not be
over.' What prophets were on duty that day. These events happened
according to Clarke just a few minutes after the second tower was hit at
9.03. How on earth could Cheney make such a statement to Clarke
when, according to the official story, everyone else was running around
in confusion about what was happening? As with all Problem-Reaction-
Solution events, the false villain story is prepared and waiting when the
'problem' occurs. Hence, minutes after the first attacks, Cheney was
already selling his manufactured culprits – Osama Bin Laden and 'al-
Qaeda'. Remember, too, that Cheney was the man with ultimate
responsibility for the wargame exercises going on in the skies at this
same time and he claims he didn't know about 'Flight 11' hitting the
World Trade Center? *Utter bollocks.* Richard Clarke's revelations expose
Cheney's monumental lies about what he did that morning and what he
knew. Clarke said he told Cheney and Rice that he was instigating 'a

secure teleconference to manage the crisis'. He said that as he left he saw both of them gathering papers and preparing to leave for the Presidential Emergency Operations Center (PEOC) in the East Wing of the White House. This was about 9.10 and David Bohrer, a White House photographer, says that he saw Cheney head for the bunker just after 9am. This supports Clarke's version while Cheney and the official account accepted by the 9/11 Commission [non]investigation says he didn't leave until 9.30. Cheney told NBC's *Meet the Press* that Flight 77 was being tracked and 'when it entered the danger zone and looked like it was headed for the White House [Secret Service agents] grabbed me and evacuated me to the basement [the White House 'bunker'] ...' Yeah, sure Dick, and there were fairies there to help them?

By the time this made-up story was supposed to have happened Cheney was already in the Presidential Emergency Operations Center (PEOC) and not his office, as confirmed by both Richard Clarke and Transportation Secretary Norman Mineta who said that when he arrived at the PEOC at 9.20 Cheney was already there. Secret Service documents and accounts confirm the same. Cheney's false account was concocted to help him claim ignorance about events in the sky and especially Flight 77. His wife, Lynne Cheney, a member of the Hidden Hand's American Enterprise Institute, was to join him along with Rice in the White House operations room. What was Cheney's *wife* doing there? What authority did she have to be there? Also assembled were Cheney's Chief of Staff Lewis 'Scooter' Libby and Deputy White House Chief of Staff Josh Bolton. Richard Clarke described Cheney's East Wing command operation as 'decidedly more political' than the one he was running and Cheney was constantly hanging up the line to Clarke's teleconference. Clarke says it was about 9.10-ish when he arrived at the Secure Video Conferencing Center next to the Situation Room in the West Wing and began to direct and discuss a response to the attacks with leading military and FAA officials. I emphasise the time – about *9.10*, or just after. Clarke says that others taking part in this teleconference were CIA Director George Tenet, FBI Director Robert Mueller, FAA Administrator Jane Garvey, Deputy Attorney General Larry Thompson, Deputy Secretary of State Richard Armitage and ... here we go ... *Defense Secretary Donald Rumsfeld and acting chairman of the Joint Chiefs of Staff, General Richard Myers*. Well, well, bloody well. Both men, Clarke said, were 'surrounded by generals and colonels' the whole time. Rumsfeld had said 'I am too goddam old to go to an alternate site' when a relocation had been suggested. Robert Andres, Principal Deputy Assistant Secretary of Defense for Special Operations and Low Intensity Conflict, said in 2007 that he knew Rumsfeld had gone to Clarke's video conference and went to find materials that Rumsfeld would need. Andres said: 'I was there in the Support Center with the secretary when he was talking to Clarke on the White House video-conference, and to the President.' So what happened to Rumsfeld's account on *Larry King Live* that he was handed a note in his office about 9.25 telling him that the first plane had hit the World Trade Center, but not the second, and that he felt a 'jarring thing' when the Pentagon was hit in an attack for which he was given no warning? What happened to the General Myers story of being in a meeting on Capitol Hill until the Pentagon was hit? Of course Myers would have been at the Pentagon. For a start he would have been involved in the long list of simultaneous wargame exercises going on that morning. Transportation Secretary Norman Mineta told the 9/11 Commission that he was in Cheney's East Wing bunker as the 'young man' was giving Cheney regular reports of the progress of 'Flight 77' heading for Washington, but Defense Secretary Rumsfeld in a teleconference with open voice lines to Cheney's and Clarke's operations didn't know? If Cheney knew, the military knew, so why didn't Rumsfeld? Richard Clarke said that Rumsfeld joined the teleconference minutes after the second plane crashed in New York and remained throughout. Clarke had said about the moment when the Pentagon was struck: 'I can still see Rumsfeld on the screen, so the whole building didn't get hit.' What happened to Myers' story that he was on Capitol Hill having a meeting with Senator Max Cleland while all this was going on? He said he had seen that a plane had hit the first tower (8.46am), but had still gone into the meeting with Cleland and did not come out until about the time the Pentagon was hit (9.38am). He said that in the interim no one had told the top uniformed commander in the US military on duty that day that a second plane had crashed at 9.03. Yet here he was all along, according to Richard Clarke, taking part in a teleconference with Rumsfeld and company at the Pentagon. Joint Chiefs Chairman General Hugh Shelton, on his plane heading for Europe, also indicated that Myers was where Clarke said he was during the attacks (even Shelton's own account of his return to Washington later that day is fraught with inconsistencies – did anyone tell the truth that day?). I tried to contact Max Cleland while researching *Alice in Wonderland* to ask about his alleged meeting with Myers which provided the cover story of where Myers was before the Pentagon was hit, but I received no reply. Cleland later indicated that he was indeed with Myers, but *he could not have been*. Richard Clarke even recounts one exchange he had with Myers at 9.28 – before the Pentagon was struck. He told Myers that he assumed that NORAD had already scrambled fighters and AWAC recognisance aircraft. Clarke asked how many and where? Myers had replied:

Not a pretty picture, Dick. We are in the middle of Vigilant Warrior, a NORAD exercise, but ... Otis has launched two birds toward New York. Langley is trying to get two up now. The AWACS are at Tinker and not on alert.

AWACS were actually in the air taking part in the exercises and could have been immediately diverted to real events – but weren't. Clarke asked 'how long to CAP [Combat Air Patrol] over Washington?' Myers replied: 'Fast as we can.' Looking around at other generals he asked: 'Fifteen minutes?' This is Myers who claimed that (a) he was on Capitol Hill at this time and (b) said he didn't know if fighters were airborne in response before the Pentagon strike. He told a hearing on Capitol Hill two days later that 'to the best of my knowledge' no fighters were scrambled before the Pentagon attack when he must have known the details on the day given that he was involved in making those decisions. Rumsfeld and Myers outrageously lied about where they were and what they were doing and their lies were meant to hide what really happened that morning. The idea was to sell the public a story of apparent confusion to hide coldly-calculated design. Look at the other implications in what Clarke describes. He was on the line with NORAD and he confirmed that FAA Administrator Jane Garvey was also there. This teleconference alone, starting around 9.10, connected NORAD, the FAA and the Pentagon via Rumsfeld and Myers and their 'generals and colonels'. What is all this stuff from NORAD and the military about the FAA not telling them in time to react? We are told in one mendacious diversion that air traffic was not sure if Flight 11 had crashed into the North Tower because American Airlines would not confirm it. How can this claim stand up when Clarke opened his teleconference, not long after 9am, by asking FAA Administrator Jane Garvey what she knew? Clarke said she replied: 'The two aircraft that went [into the WTC] were American Flight 11, a 767, and United 175, also a 767 – hijacked.' Where is the confusion in that? NORAD NEADS operatives were not told about Flight 93 until after it crashed, according to the tapes subpoenaed by the 9/11 Commission, but Flight 93 was being mentioned in the Richard Clarke teleconference at 9.35 when the FAA's Jane Garvey reported it among possible hijacked flights. This was *28 minutes* before it officially crashed.

The criminal '9/11 Commission', which was set up *not* to find the truth, said of this teleconference: 'It is not clear to us that the teleconference was fully under way before 9:37, when the Pentagon was struck'. This false time is in the Commission report purely to obscure fundamental contradictions in the official story. The Commission report goes on: 'We do not know who from Defense participated, but we know that in the first hour none of the personnel involved in managing the crisis did.' Excuse me. A Commission that held months of hearings could not establish 'who from Defense' participated in this crucial teleconference? *Didn't they ask?* Or are the Pentagon top brass and everyone else who took part with Clarke suffering from mass amnesia? No – the Commission is laying a diversion. To tell the truth and list the people from the Pentagon who participated and the time they were there, including Rumsfeld and Myers, would destroy the official story – and that of Cheney. When you see who was involved in the compilation of the Commission's 'report' you'll appreciate why it cannot be taken seriously. The report says that none of the information conveyed in the White House teleconference, at least in the first hour, was being passed to the NMCC [National Military Command Center]'. The Command Center is located in the Joint Chiefs of Staff department of the Pentagon and, in its own words, is responsible for 'generating Emergency Action Messages to launch control centers, nuclear submarines, recognisance aircraft and battlefield commanders worldwide'. The NMCC is essentially the control centre for the entire military and described as a central clearinghouse. It provides continuous monitoring and coordination of worldwide military operations and supports commanders, the Chairman of the Joint Chiefs, Secretary of Defense and the President, in the command and control of US armed forces in peacetime, contingencies and war. Well, if you believe the 9/11 Commission, and no one with half a brain will do so, all this is happening 24 hours of every day – *except* on September 11th. The Commission report says that Richard Clarke's teleconference was not connected into the area of the NMCC from where the crisis was being managed, and 'the director of the operations team who was on the phone with NORAD did not have the benefit of information being shared on the teleconference'. *Nonsense.* Clarke confirms that the Secretary of State for Defense and the acting chairman of the Joint Chiefs of Staff, the second and third in command of the entire US military, were surrounded by generals and colonels during the conference. But still the Pentagon Command Center didn't know what was going on?? *Lies, lies, lies.*

Dick Cheney left the White House after the attacks and relocated to Site R, or the 'Underground Pentagon', a top-secret complex of buildings inside Raven Rock Mountain, near Blue Ridge Summit, Pennsylvania. This is about seven miles north of the presidential 'retreat' at Camp David. Site R is also known as the Alternate Joint Communications Center. Journalist James Bamford, a former ABC investigative producer and an intelligence specialist, said that hours after the attacks five helicopters arrived at Site R together with a convoy of vehicles with black-tinted windows. One of the first people to arrive was Paul Wolfowitz, Deputy Secretary of Defense and the real power at the Pentagon where Rumsfeld was window dressing. Wolfowitz went on to head the World Bank before corruption finished him. He was the Bush administration's liaison to the American Israel Public Affairs Committee

(AIPAC), one of Washington's biggest lobby groups which campaigns for policies favourable to Israel. AIPAC is an extension and agent of the Israeli government at the heart of American political affairs and the Israel connection to 9/11 will become very clear later on. Cheney would disappear for long periods in the wake of the attacks to top secret locations preparing for the next stage of the attack on human freedom – the 'war on terror' justified by 9/11.

CHAPTER 8

Contradictions, anomalies and mystery men

Many are destined to reason wrongly, others, not to reason at all; and others, to persecute those who do reason – Voltaire

Accepted versions of 'truth' and 'history' are rarely the result of factual information. They are formed by simple repetition. Tell people something often enough and they will believe it.

In this way it has become accepted truth and official history that 19 hijackers working for Osama Bin Laden hijacked four commercial aircraft, took over the controls, and flew them into the World Trade Center and the Pentagon while the fourth crashed when passengers attacked the Arab pilots. These hijackers, we are told, learned to fly on simulators and at schools in the United States where they trained on small one-engine light planes like the Cessna. Keep that in mind as you read the next two statements. First a report on what happened when Flight 77 is said to have crashed into the Pentagon:

> The hijacker-pilots were then forced to execute a difficult high-speed descending turn. Radar shows Flight 77 did a downward spiral, turning almost a complete circle and dropping the last 7,000 feet in two-and-a-half minutes. The steep turn was so smooth, the sources say, it's clear there was no fight for control going on. And the complex maneuver suggests the hijackers had better flying skills than many investigators first believed. The jetliner disappeared from radar at 9.37 and less than a minute later it clipped the tops of street lights and plowed into the Pentagon at 460 mph.

Now the remarks of Rick Garza, a flying instructor at Sorbi's Flying Club in San Diego, who remembers trying to teach Khalid al-Mihdhar and Nawaq al-Hamzi, two of the Arab 'pilots' alleged to have been on Flight 77:

> It was like Dumb and Dumber. I mean, they were clueless. It was clear to me they weren't going to make it as pilots.

A 'hijacker' named by the FBI as Hani Hanjour is said to have been at the controls of the wide-boded 757 of 'Flight 77' performing that incredibly skilled manoeuvre to approach the Pentagon and yet instructors at Freeway Airport in Bowie, Maryland, banned him from renting a one-engine plane because he was such an incompetent pilot only *weeks* before 9/11. He took three flights with instructors in the second week of August, 2001, and flew so badly his application for plane rental was refused. A *New York Times* story headed 'Trainee Noted For Incompetence' described how Hanjour was reported in February, 2001, by instructors at his flying school in Phoenix because his piloting and English were so poor. The instructors questioned if his pilot's licence was genuine. *The Washington Post* ran a story the month after 9/11 headed 'Hanjour: A Study in Paradox' which said that how and where Hanjour obtained a pilot's licence remained 'a lingering question that FAA officials refuse to discuss'. Descriptions of Hanjour's ineptitude as a pilot of one-engine planes include 'a trainee noted for incompetence' and this from a former employee of his flying school: 'He could not fly at all.' One thing can be stated without question: Hani Hanjour was not at the controls of Flight 77 as the authorities claim. Clearly there's something seriously wrong here with these official stories – there is at every turn. I am going to explore the official story of the 9/11 'hijackers' in this chapter and we know the identity of at least one without a modicum of doubt because we have his passport. Yes, in one of those amazing little miracles that so often turn up in government narratives the always-truthful FBI and New York police revealed that the paper passport of one of the hijackers was found in a New York street even though it was supposed to be in a plane that crashed in a fireball into the World Trade Center. Who said God is not on our side? The 'passport' was spotted by an 'unnamed passer-by' a few blocks from the WTC 'in the vicinity of Vesey Street' (Fig 36).

Figure 36: A paper passport survived the impact with the World Trade Center and a subsequent fireball and was not even damaged? Yes, and I'm Dolly Parton.

Was it singed? FBI Assistant Director Barry Mawn told a news conference that the passport was found 'several blocks' from the World Trade Center and a 'grid search' of the whole area had been launched in the hope of finding other important evidence about the hijackers. At the same conference it was said to be unlikely that remains of the hijackers would be conclusively identified since nothing was likely to be available for use as a DNA match. *Phew* – thank goodness they found the passport then. We are told that no aircraft black boxes survived the World Trade Center crashes to tell us what happened, but a paper passport that one of the 'hijackers' was carrying somehow survived a fireball and wafted back to earth. The passport story surviving a fireball and a skyscraper collapse turned out to be too ridiculous even for the 9/11 fairy tale and by 2004 the story had changed to it being found before the towers fell. Oh, that makes sense now, thank you, except there is still the problem of the fireball, if I may be so bold. The passport was claimed to belong to Satam Muhammed Abdel Rahman al-Suqami, an alleged hijacker on Flight 11. Lead Counsel Susan Ginsburg, in testimony to the waste-of-space 9/11 Commission which 'investigated' the attacks, said the passport had been 'manipulated in a fraudulent manner in ways that have been associated with al-Qaeda'. Yawn. A year after 9/11 when a British television news team were filming for a first anniversary programme they asked New York police about the passport. They replied that it was 'a rumour that might be true'. This was a 'rumour' reported as fact immediately after 9/11 at a news conference for no other reason than to sell the validity of the official story in the immediate aftermath. Passports belonging to 'hijackers' Ziad Jarrah and Saeed al-Ghamdi were said to have been found at the alleged crash site of Flight 93 which would be a little more credible were not the story of that crash awash with contradictions. Mark Twain said: 'When you tell the truth you don't have to remember anything.' The official story is founded on so many lies told so often that it has to remember everything it has previously lied about and you therefore have an endless stream of contradictory stories and claims. Given a mainstream media with a modicum of willpower and courage to establish the truth there would be famous people in jail by now and they would not be Arabs. There are so many lies that every aspect has to be questioned to see if its stands up to scrutiny.

Hijacking the 'hijackers'?

The CIA and FBI claimed they had no prior warning of the September 11th attacks which is clearly baloney and has been shown to be so; but let's run with that for a moment. Let's say it was really true that they didn't know. This incompetence in failing to trace any orchestration of such a multi-faceted and long-planned attack on US soil would, in any sane society, lead to wholesale sackings and inquiries. Instead President Bush rewarded the CIA and FBI for their 'incompetence' by greatly increasing their budgets. Again the contradiction can be explained by the realisation that these agencies were not meant to stop the attacks before they happened, just as the elite inner core of the FAA, NORAD and the Pentagon were not meant to stop them while they were underway. Having failed, or so they say, to track any sign whatsoever of the 'terrorists' and their plans before September 11th the FBI was able to name the 19 men it claims were responsible almost immediately afterwards. What brilliance. There has been much controversy over the identity of the 'hijackers' officially named with claims at various times that seven and up to ten were still alive amid stories of identity theft and mistaken identity. We cannot be sure that all the people named are accurate even before we examine if they were actually to blame for what happened. The list of the 'guilty 19' was released by a highly-politicised FBI 'investigation' led by Boy Bush appointee Robert Mueller who took over the Bureau only two weeks before September 11th. The same Mueller was wheeled out in 2018 to lead the highly-politicised 'investigation' into alleged Russia collusion with the Trump election campaign and predictably found no evidence but still disingenuously gave Democrats encouragement to impeach the President. Even Mueller told CNN in 2002 there was 'no legal proof to prove the identities of the suicidal hijackers' and yet the same names went on being used. In the light of the staggering untruths told by the FBI and other government agencies decade after decade, and never more so than since 9/11, you'll understand if I don't take the official information released on the 'hijackers' at face value. Such 'information' is so often of two-face value (Fig 37). The most famous of them and the 'poster man' of the 9/11 attacks is Mohamed Atta, an Egyptian

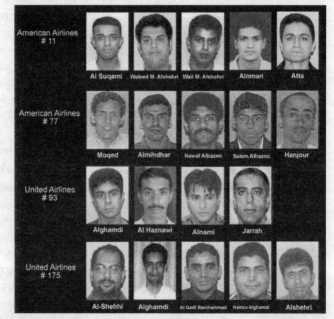

Figure 37: The alleged 9/11 'hijackers'.

Figure 38: Mohamed Atta, 'lead hijacker' on 9/11 – or maybe not.

national who is said to have been the leader of the hijackers and the 'pilot' who directed Flight 11 into the World Trade Center (Fig 38). Atta – or the person claimed to have been him – grew up in Cairo and used the name Mohamed El-Amir. His full name was Mohamed El-Amir Awad el-Sayed Atta. He became an electrical engineering student at the Technical University of Hamburg-Harburg in Germany where his tutor Dittmar Machule said he didn't know the name Mohamed Atta until after 9/11 because his pupil didn't call himself that. 'Atta' was described in very different terms by those who met him to the Islamic extremist profile promoted by the official story. Machule said the Germany 'Atta' – Mohamed El-Amir – was very religious, prayed often and never touched alcohol. He said his student would not even shake hands with a woman when introduced. Ralph Bodenstein, a fellow student who spent three months with El-Amir on a field study in 1995, said:

> The Mohamed I know was not a terrorist. But the photo they show in the press, that is the person, that is the same person I knew. He was a very complex person. On the one hand, he was a very religious person. He was growing a beard, he had just come back from a small hajj. He did pray five times a day.

> On the other hand, he was very full of idealism and he was a humanist. He was very much interested in social work. The person I knew then is not a person who could do what he is said to do now ... I knew him as an idealist who had great dreams about people living together.

Descriptions of Mohamed El-Amir's personality by his father, retired Cairo lawyer Mohamed al-Amir Atta, matched those who knew him in Germany. He said: 'Oh God! He is so decent, so shy and tender. I used to tell him "Toughen up, boy!"' El-Amir's father said in a statement to the London-based *al-Sharq al-Awsat* newspaper on September 22nd, 2001, that his son was in Germany and had phoned him after the attacks. The father claimed that on September 12th he was at his holiday home on the Mediterranean coast without radio or television and was unaware of the attacks in America the previous day. He said his son called him there and they talked about 'normal things'. Only later did the father hear

what had happened in the United States. He also dismissed the
suggestion that El-Amir was a supporter of al-Qaeda:

> Mohamed, my son, hates Osama Bin Laden like he hates the sinner. Do not
> forget that Osama Bin Laden is behind the attack on our embassy in Pakistan.
> Mohamed is a real Egyptian. All this talk is nonsense.

He said he believed that his son's identity had been stolen and that
El-Amir 'Atta' didn't know how to fly a plane. In fact, he was frightened
of flying and always vomiting when he travelled by air. 'He was a
donkey when it came to politics. I advised him, like my father advised
me, that politics equals hypocrisy,' he said. Mohamed El-Amir's tutor
Dittmar Machule supported this theme. He told the *Wall Street Journal*: 'I
never heard any anti-Zionist, anti-American or anti-Christian statements
from him.' For sure the 'Atta' in America was not frightened of flying
and although he had no experience whatsoever on wide-bodied jets he
could pilot one-engine planes. Mohamed El-Amir was remembered in
Germany as tolerant of other religions and 'not a radical thinker'.
Friends said he condemned terrorist attacks on tourists in Egypt and in
1999 he presented his thesis on the restoration of the old quarter of the
city of Aleppo in Syria with his 152-page study arguing that urban
planning should reflect the traditional coexistence of Muslims and
Christians. He appears to have registered with *Bab Souria*, formerly
known as *Syria Online*, in 1997 under the name Mohamed El-Amir
asking for information about Aleppo. His alleged transformation into
'American Atta' is claimed to have happened when according to *The
New York Times* he disappeared from the university from mid-1997 to
October, 1998, and when he returned he had changed. He now wore a
beard and persuaded the university to provide a prayer room for
himself and other Arab students including his 'hijacker' friend Marwan
al-Shehhi and one other 'suspected hijacker', a Lebanese student named
Ziad Jarrah or Jarrahi, who studied aircraft design. There has been
confusion about the spelling of the name with the FBI first saying Jarrahi
and then Jarrah. The man they claim to be Jarrahi/Jarrah liked
nightclubs and was due to marry his Turkish girlfriend two weeks after
September 11th which sounds like we have a real Muslim extremist on
our hands. I don't buy the convenient 'Atta' personality transformation
and there is the rather relevant matter of Germany-based 'Atta' being a
very small man, no more than five-feet-four, while American 'Atta' was
said to be between five-feet eight and ten. Mohamed El-Amir's father
said that the 'Mohamed Atta' seen on security video at an airport in
Portland, Maine, did not look like his son. The UK *Guardian* recognised
the personality contradictions days after the attacks. It said of Atta:

He repeatedly switched names, nationalities and personalities. If in Egypt, and later in the US, he was Mohamed Atta, then at the Technical University of Harburg, he was Mohamed el-Amir. For the university authorities, he was an Egyptian, yet for his landlord, as for the US authorities, he was from the United Arab Emirates.

And while it is not hard to see Atta, whose face gazes out from the passport photograph released by the FBI, as that of the mass murderer of Manhattan, el-Amir was a shy, considerate man who endeared himself to Western acquaintances. Such indeed was the gulf between the two that some people, notably his father, insisted last week that Mohamed Atta's identity must have been stolen by the hijackers' leader.

Does that description of 'America Atta' sound more like an intelligence operative than a urban planning student?

Booze-drinking, cocaine-snorting 'Muslim hijackers'

Germany 'Atta' was described by friends and acquaintances as polite, reserved, introverted, never aggressive, always smiling, 'very nice', and a Muslim so devout that he would not shake hands with a woman. Contrast this with the description and life-style of America-based Mohammed Atta who was often dubbed rude, aggressive and arrogant and was anything but devoutly religious. Amanda Keller, a lingerie model escort and pizza restaurant manager, said she lived with Atta for a short time in early 2001 in the Sandpiper Apartments in Venice, Florida, close to the airport where he is said to have trained at a flying school. Stephanie Frederickson, a neighbour of Keller, remembered Atta living there with Keller and so did apartment manager Charles Grapentine. Frederickson said:

Amanda moved in next door first, saying she had come from Orange Park. Then one day in the middle of March she brought home Atta ... Amanda said to me, 'I'd like you to meet my friend Mohamed Atta. He's from France.' I looked at her to see if she was joking, but I guess she wasn't.

We are told the 9/11 attacks were carried out by Islamic fanatics as part of a Jihad, or Holy War, against the United States and two most basic tenets of the Muslim religion are that you never drink alcohol and never eat the meat of a pig. Atta, according to Amanda Keller, was a heavy drinker, regularly snorted cocaine and his favourite food was pork chops. He and other alleged hijackers are reported to have made at least six trips to Las Vegas with all its non-Islamic recreational activities including handing hundreds of dollars to lap dancers at the Pink Pony strip club. Islamic fanatics *they were not*. Why would he be the 'lead hijacker' in a suicide attack on behalf of an Islamic 'holy war'? Was the Germany 'Atta' the same man as the American 'Atta'? It's highly unlikely unless he went through a remarkable transformation in which he ditched his Muslim beliefs, carried out a suicide attack in the name of his Muslim beliefs and grew several inches. The 9/11 cover up doesn't want us to know this background because their fairy tale starts to unravel. Amanda Keller was tracked down by investigative journalist Daniel Hopsicker for his book, *Welcome to Terrorland: Mohamed Atta and the 9-11 Cover-Up in Florida,* and she described anything but the 'Islamic extremist' the authorities want us to believe he was. Keller eventually retracted her story after being subjected to what she called FBI intimidation. Neighbour Stephanie Frederickson and manager Charles Grapentine said they experienced the same from the FBI after speaking publicly. Frederickson said:

> The question they asked was always the same. You aren't saying anything to anybody, are you? At first, right after the attack, they told me I must have been mistaken in my identification. Or they would insinuate that I was lying. Finally they stopped trying to get me to change my story, and just stopped by once a week to make sure I hadn't been talking to anyone.

Charles Grapentine described the same experience:

> They called me a liar, and told me to keep my mouth shut. Nobody likes to hear that; that they didn't see something they know they saw.

This is how the truth stays hidden and FBI operatives are long-time experts at this in the mould of their psychopathic former leader, J. Edgar Hoover (assassinations of 'threats to the state' like Martin Luther King a speciality). Amanda Keller is quoted by Hopsicker as saying: 'They told me not to talk to anybody, to keep my mouth shut.' The 'Muslim extremist' 'Mohamed Atta' named in the official story was, in fact, a hard-drinking, cocaine-snorting pork-eater with a white, seriously non-Muslim American girlfriend and frequented strip clubs and lap-dancing joints. No wonder the FBI sought to intimate witnesses telling this story. The enormous difference in personality and lifestyle, plus the distinct difference in height, between Mohamed El-Amir in Germany and Mohamed Atta in America make it clear that they were not the same people. Amanda Keller said that Atta had pilot licences from many countries – flying experience confirmed by his flying school owner in Florida. There is no evidence it seems that Mohamed El-Amir knew how to fly and his father said he had been frightened of flying. If the American 'Atta' was not the German 'Atta' then who was he?

Where are the 'hijackers'?

American and United Airlines released 'partial' passenger lists ('manifests') for the four hijacked planes and not one contained any of the 'terrorists' named by the FBI, nor even anyone with an Arabic name. The airlines said that some passengers were not listed because their next of kin had yet to be informed. This would not have applied to the hijackers, though, surely, so why were they not there? To this day we have not seen the original passenger manifests which were immediately confiscated – like all video surveillance footage – by Robert Mueller's FBI which then produced a list of 19 alleged 'hijackers' three days after the attacks. The first list (later changed) was revealed by CNN a day after the attacks but four names alleged to have been on Flight 11 would be replaced by the FBI in a subsequent version. Adnan Bukhari, Ameer Bukhari, Abdulrahman al-Omari and Amer Kamfar would be replaced by Abdulaziz al-Omari, Wali al-Shehri, Waleed al-Shehri and Satam al-Suqami. How can this be? Either the first four were on the passenger manifest lists or they weren't. They could not have been because Ameer Bukhari was killed a year to the day before 9/11 in a mid-air crash while Adnan Bukhari was still alive and living in Florida. Abdulrahman al-Omari and Amer Kamfar were alive in Saudi Arabia. This is extraordinary. The FBI identified 'hijackers' from the flight manifests (legal documents) and the names were either there or they weren't. You can't name people from passenger lists and then change your mind when evidence emerges that they could not have been on board. Hani Hanjour, the supposed 'hijacker pilot' of Flight 77, was not named in a list of 18 hijackers and then appeared hours later replacing another name reported by CNN that was never mentioned again or appeared in print which sounded something like 'Mosear Caned'. *The Washington Post* reported that Hanjour was not on the original passenger list 'because he may not have had a ticket'. How did he get on the plane, then – teleportation? A letter from American Airlines to the 9/11 Commission in March, 2004, said: 'We have not been able to determine if Hani Hanjour checked in at the main ticket counter.' What they mean is there is absolutely no proof that he was on the plane. This is the bloke who was supposed to have flown Flight 77 into the Pentagon. Despite all of the above Hani Hanjour was named on an official passenger list produced for the trial of alleged '20th hijacker' Zacarias Moussaoui in 2006, of whom more later.

The FBI released photographs on September 27th of men they believed, note believed, were the hijackers and emphasised that 'attempts to confirm the true identities of these individuals are still underway'. We appear to have heard no more so how are they getting on? The family of alleged 'hijacker' Hamza al-Ghamdi said his photograph looked nothing like him. I met with Michael Woodward, the American Airlines Flight Services Manager at Boston Airport, who says he took the call from attendant Amy Sweeney shortly before Flight 11 crashed. He told me that when he took the call from the plane he punched up the passenger list for Flight 11 on his computer screen and Atta's name was there in the seat that Sweeney had mentioned. A BBC report, *The Last Moments of Flight 11*, pointed out that Sweeney said there were only four hijackers while the FBI says there were five and that 'the seat numbers she gave were different from those registered in the hijackers' names'. Flight 11 attendant Betty Ong gave other different seat numbers for the hijackers in her alleged call from the plane. I asked the FBI to explain these inconsistencies, but it would not give me an answer. In fact five passengers were missing from the list released for American Airlines Flight 11 and eight for Flight 77. It was the same story with the lists issued by United Airlines. Nine names were absent from Flight 175 and twelve from Flight 93. There is much confusion and contradiction about the authenticated passenger lists or manifests – again *legal documents* – which have never been released by either the airlines or the FBI. They have all steadfastly resisted doing so despite endless requests directly or through the Freedom of Information Act. What they have made public are alleged lists of passengers with no authentication. The question of who was on the planes reached new levels of farce in 2004 with a report by American Airlines to the 9/11 Commission claiming that some passengers had boarded Flight 11 'after the plane had pushed back from the gate'. Now that is a feat I would love to hear explained. Take your time. Robert Bonner, former Administrator of the Drug Enforcement Administration (DEA) and Commissioner of US Customs and Border Protection, told the 9/11 Commission that within an hour of the attacks 'US Customs Office of Intelligence had identified the 19 probable hijackers as well as the complete lists of passengers on the aircraft'. Many questions come from this. For example – why then have we never to this day seen the original authenticated legally-binding passenger lists and how did they access them so quickly and identify the 'hijackers' within an hour amid multiple confusions about which flights had been hijacked and crashed.

Atta is said to have flown to Boston that morning from Portland, Maine, and according to a US Air ticket agent in Portland, Michael Tuohey, he would have had to go through check-in and security again at Boston to board the American Airlines Flight 11. Tuohey said Atta gave him an icy stare when he refused to give boarding passes to him and his associate for their connecting flight in Boston. He warned the pair they had to hurry to avoid missing their flight and they left for security. If the 'hijackers' were on those planes out of Boston then surely check-in staff would remember them. When you travelled by air inside America in

2001 you didn't tend to see that many Arabic people and as these guys were supposed to have flown in business class and first class they would have had their own check-in desks and attendants with far fewer passengers to deal with than those checking in economy passengers. There were very light passenger loads on all four planes anyway – remarkably so. We are told that Atta was in first class and if he was on board there is no way the first class check-in attendant or boarding gate attendant would not have remembered him especially as he would have had to present a photo ID that matched his face and name with his ticket. Why have we never seen the boarding card clips of the 'hijackers' that are removed by staff at the boarding gate? When Michael Woodward was asked if he could put me in contact with the check-in staff that dealt with Atta and company that morning he paused and said: 'I don't know who that would be.' Maybe it's just me, but I found that a strange statement five months after the attacks. If you had taken a call from someone on a hijacked airliner that then crashed into the World Trade Center wouldn't you want to know from your colleagues what exactly happened that morning and who did what? Was there never any conversation between staff in five months about who checked in these guys, what happened and what they were like? I find that bewildering. Woodward said he would find out the name of the check-in person for me and when he did not reply over the next three days I returned to Boston Airport in search of the person who checked in Atta and his fellow hijackers. I talked to a check-in staff supervisor on duty at American and asked him about speaking to the check-in staff in business and first class on September 11th. The man became very agitated and would not even tell me his name. He went over to a check-in computer while refusing to enter into any conversation to find the number of the American Airlines media centre in Texas. Asked why he couldn't, or wouldn't, speak to me he said it was 'for personal reasons' and would say no more.

'Ask the FBI'

I asked staff at American Airlines corporate headquarters in Fort Worth, Texas, if they could confirm that the alleged hijackers passed through their check-in systems at Boston Logan and Washington Dulles. Tim Kincaid, Manager of Communications Planning, American Airlines Corporate Communications, replied that I would have to ask the FBI. I asked if I could speak with the check-in staff that dealt with the 'hijackers' to confirm that they went through. Kincaid replied: 'Sorry, no.' Rich Nelson, media spokesman for United Airlines based in Chicago, told me the same. When I asked if he could confirm that the men named as hijackers passed through United's normal check-in procedures at Boston Logan and Newark, New Jersey, Nelson also referred me to the FBI. He said that I couldn't speak with the check-in staff involved out of respect for their privacy. However, I heard a very different story from Stanley Hilton, the San Francisco lawyer who filed a $7 billion lawsuit against Bush and other members of his administration on behalf of 9/11 families and others claiming Bush administration complicity in allowing the attacks to happen. The case was dismissed in 2004 when the judge ruled that US citizens do not have the right to sue a sitting President because of the Doctrine of Sovereign Immunity which degrees that a 'sovereign or state cannot commit a legal wrong and is immune from civil suit or criminal prosecution'. Hilton told me that clients who worked as flight attendants and pilots for American Airlines had been subjected to 'very tough gag orders' and were threatened with 'immediate termination if they talk about any of this publicly'. That would certainly explain my own experience with AA staff at Boston Logan and why should we think it would be any different at United? I said to Tim Kincaid at American Airlines that when they released passenger lists for Flights 11 and 77 there were five names missing on Flight 11 and eight for 77. I said I understood the original reason given for some of the passenger names not being there – next of kin not yet notified – but why were there no names for the hijackers on those lists? Kincaid's reply: 'Sorry, you'll need to contact the FBI.' I said that given next of kin for all the passengers will now long have been informed could I have complete passenger lists for Flights 11 and 77? Kincaid referred me to the American Airlines website for news releases for September, 2001, which merely had the original lists with the names missing. I went back to ask if the incomplete passenger lists released on September 12th were the only ones they had published. He said that the news release 'is the only one we put out and is as complete as we could make it'. He explained that 'some families asked that their loved one's name not be listed, and [they had] honored their wishes'. This is not the reason originally given for the missing passengers which was that next of kin had not been informed. Are we to believe that by some fantastic coincidence the very same next of kin who had not been informed soon enough for their loved ones to be included in the first list are the very same next of kin who decided they did not want the names of their loved ones to be published? Where are the hijackers? I contacted Kincaid again: 'What do you mean by 'as complete as we could make it? Why no hijackers anywhere?' His reply: 'That's as much as we can share. Call the FBI.' A year later at the time that *Alice in Wonderland and the World Trade Center* was published we had still not had a full passenger list for the 9/11 flights nor seen authenticated airline ticket and boarding pass documentation of the 'hijackers' who are claimed to have been on those planes. Nearly two decades later we *still haven't*. I asked Kincaid, a pleasant guy merely doing his job, if I could I see copies of the paperwork detailing the calls made by Betty Ong and Amy Sweeney to AA ground staff from Flight 11, but it was the usual reply: 'Contact the FBI.' Rich Nelson, media spokesman for United Airlines, told me that they only released the names of those whose families authorised them to do so.

Why so few passengers?

Then there is the matter of the passenger numbers on the four flights involved. Okay, it was a Tuesday, the slowest day of the week the airlines claimed, but these were pan-America flights leaving at a time to coincide with the business day on the West Coast in the major cities of Los Angeles and San Francisco. According to airline figures Flight 11 had only 81 passengers on a plane that could carry 158; Flight 175 had 56 passengers on a plane with a capacity of 168; Flight 77 was carrying 58 passengers when the capacity was 176; and Flight 93 had just 38 on a plane capable of holding 182. We have four aircraft leaving from three airports, all hijacked in well under two hours, all left to their fate with no effective reaction from the FAA-NORAD response system, the Pentagon or government, Bush administration complicity in allowing the attacks to happen and all remarkably low on passengers. I asked American Airlines for the average number of passengers on Flights 11 and 77 throughout the year 2000. They told me: 'This information is proprietary and not available, sorry.' At least I wasn't told to contact the FBI. Rich Nelson at United Airlines said that, beyond saying that Tuesdays are typically light days, he couldn't tell me the average passenger numbers for those flights because it was considered to be 'proprietary information'. So 'proprietary information' was more important to these people than being open about what happened on 9/11? Even with the small number of passengers we are still told that between four and five hijackers without guns could overpower and control two pilots in each plane and between 43 and 90 passengers and flight attendants, using box-cutters and small knives. *The Washington Post* reported that attendant Michelle Heidenberger on Flight 77 had been 'trained to handle a hijacking':

> She knew not to let anyone in the cockpit. She knew to tell the hijacker that she didn't have a key and would have to call the pilots. None of her training mattered.

The question is – why? What could have happened? There were some big guys on these planes both in the cockpit and among the passengers. Mark Bingham, a 31-year-old, six-feet five rugby player, and Jeremy Glick, a former national judo champion, were both on Flight 93. Judo is an art of self-defence that includes dealing with people who have knives. I contacted the FBI where everyone kept referring me and was asked to fax a list of my 47 questions to Rex Tomb, a representative for the FBI's Fugitive Publicity and Internet Media Services Unit. Many of the questions were the ones I had asked the two airlines and other organisations which they told me could only be answered by the FBI. A few days later I received a faxed reply from Ernest J. Porter at the Office of Public and Congressional Affairs saying that Tomb had given my questions to him. Porter said he regretted being the bearer of disappointing news, but it was not possible for the FBI to answer any of my questions. The news was not, in fact, 'disappointing', just depressingly predictable. Porter told me: 'It will be some time, perhaps years, before the FBI's investigative files on this case may be available through vehicles such as the Freedom of Information Act. The answers to your questions may be found in the files at that time.' One of my questions was: 'When did Robert Mueller officially become head of the FBI?' The propaganda and cover-up technique comes clearly into focus. It is the same technique used with all such set-ups: (1) you give the media the 'information' about the event that tells the public the story you want them to believe; (2) you tell everyone with any knowledge or relevant information about the event that they must pass all inquiries to the FBI; (3) the FBI then says it cannot answer questions about its official story because of the 'ongoing investigation'. It's funny how the 'ongoing investigation' didn't prevent the FBI from promoting its version of events. It only becomes a problem when the Bureau is questioned about that version. There are many decent, dedicated people working for the FBI, but when it comes to key positions of power they are not there to uncover the truth only to stop it ever being known.'

'Ringleader' Atta

The FBI claims that Mohamed Atta first arrived in the United States with fellow 'hijacker' Marwan al-Shehhi on June 3rd, 2000, but the FBI in Miami reported that in *April*, 2000, a 'Mohamed Atta' approached a Farm Loan Manager at the Florida Department of Agriculture seeking a loan 'to buy a six-passenger, twin-engine airplane that he wanted to convert into a crop-dusting plane'. The loan officer was Johnelle Bryant who told the FBI what happened after 9/11 and she went public in June, 2002. Bryant confirmed in a television interview that this 'Mohamed Atta' was in the United States before the official entry time and that 'Atta' told her he came from Egypt, studied in Germany, had moved to Afghanistan, admired Osama bin Laden and wanted to find recruits in America for al-Qaeda. Why would you reveal that unless it was part of the cover story being constructed? Who was this guy? 'Atta' was also sighted in Portland, Maine, in the same April, 2000, ahead of 'his' official arrival. The *Portland Press Herald* reported that Spruce Whited, head of security at the Portland public library, claimed to have seen Atta several times at the library using computers with al-Shehhi. Reference librarian Kathy Barry said the same: 'It was either him or his twin brother.' Yep, but which one was it?? Then there was the strange report of the two 'Atta's' arriving in Florida at the same time. The *Miami Herald* reported on September 22nd, 2001:

> INS [immigration] documents, matched against an FBI alert given to German police, show two men named Mohamed Atta [arrived] in Miami on January 10 [2001], each offering different destination addresses to INS agents, one in Nokomis, near Venice, the other at a Coral Springs condo. He [or they] is admitted, despite having overstayed his previous visa by a month.

> The double entry could be a paperwork error, or confusion over a visa extension. It could be Atta arrived in Miami, flew to another country like the Bahamas, and returned the same day. Or it could be that two men somehow cleared immigration with the same name using the same passport number.

There was certainly more than one 'Atta'. The FBI said that in November and December of 2000 Atta purchased flight deck videos for the Boeing 747 Model 200, Boeing 757 Model 200, Boeing 767 Model 300ER, Airbus A320 Model 200 and other items from a pilot store in Ohio. This is thought to be Sporty's Pilot Shop at the Clermont County Airport, about 20 miles from Cincinnati, although the owners wouldn't confirm that except to say they had spoken with the FBI. Nawaf al-Hamzi, who is alleged to have been on Flight 77, is said to have bought similar videos from an 'Ohio pilot store' along with Zacarias Moussaoui, a 33-year-old (at the time of arrest) French national and so-called '20th hijacker' who would be jailed for life for playing a part in 'the plot'. Officials said that Atta was given his visa at the US Consulate in Berlin on May 18th, 2000, and landed at Newark, New Jersey, on June 3rd on a flight from Prague in the Czech Republic. He overstayed his visa by more than 30 days, but was allowed back for another six months when he returned to the US with no questions asked by immigration. This is not normally the case when previous visas have been overstayed. Some who claim to have met Atta and rented him rooms in America were quoted in the media as saying he was cold, distant and secretive. They talk of his stare like the one portrayed in the driving licence picture distributed by the FBI. Atta is a real mystery man in that we don't know where he came from or what his background was and so many diversions have been thrown in the path of anyone trying to find out. I know what the authorities say about him, but that's not where you find the truth. We actually know very little about the 'Atta' who lived in the United States.

There have been many false or unsubstantiated claims about Atta and much 'information' has been presented as 'proof' when it was nothing of the kind. He was said to be wanted for the bombing of an Israeli bus in Jerusalem in 1986 and one newspaper report said: 'He was so brazen that he crisscrossed US and European borders under his own name while listed as a suspect in a 1986 Israeli bus bombing.' Brigadier General David Tsur, Chief of Staff of the Israeli Ministry of Public Security, said that Atta was not the man suspected of the bombing. The wanted man was Mahmoud Atta (also known as Mahmoud Abad Ahmad), a 33-year-old (in 1986) Jordanian who ambushed a bus in the West Bank. Mohamed Atta was said to have met with an official of Iraqi intelligence in Prague in April, 2000, and this was used to implicate Iraq with the 9/11 attacks. Iraq denied this and, once again, no evidence was produced except for Secretary of State Colin Powell saying the information came from Czech Prime Minister Milos Zeman. *The International Herald Tribune* reported a senior Bush official in May, 2002, as saying there was no evidence that Atta met the Iraqis in Prague. The whole story is claimed to have come from Czech 'intelligence' which thought that a man seen on surveillance camera footage was Atta when he wasn't. See how 'history' and 'truth' are created from utter crap? What people retain, however, is not the detail that destroys the story, but a perceptual 'image' compiled from the sum total of lies and false statements presented to them.

Atta was reported by 'witnesses' to have been at the Professional Aviation Flight Training University in Punta Gorda, California. When the FBI checked the story he had never attended that flying school. Atta was claimed to have been seen in Norfolk, Virginia, in the winter of 2000 where he 'might' have been surveying the US naval base as a possible target. Who says so? The FBI through *Newsweek*. He 'might' have been 'casing' Boston's Logan Airport more than six months before. Who says so? *Newsweek*. Sources? The usual. The *Chicago Tribune* said that he was a member of the Egyptian Jihad group with ties to Osama bin Laden. Who said so? 'Sources'. The FBI claimed that Atta flew from Miami, Florida, to Madrid, Spain, on July 9th, 2001, and picked up a rental car ordered through the Internet. The *Observer* newspaper in London claimed to have seen hotel records confirming that Atta spent at least one night at the Montsant hotel in the resort town of Salou on Spain's eastern coast during this trip and he returned his Hyundai Accent rental car to Madrid airport on July 18th, less than two months before the 9/11 attacks. The paper claimed that he went to Salou to meet with four unidentified Muslim extremists. Who says so? A Spanish newspaper. Sources? 'Investigators'. Oh, them again. Now I am not saying that any of this is true or not true, just that all the 'evidence' we have with regard to 'Muslim extremism' is from agencies with a genetic condition widely known as 'lying through your teeth'. The FBI claims that Atta met an 'al-Qaeda' operative called Ramzi bin Shibh in Salou. Shibh is said to have once shared an apartment with Atta and 'the authorities believe' he may have been involved in the planning of 9/11 from Germany. *The International Herald Tribune*, reporting *The New York Times*, said that investigations in Salou by the FBI and Spanish intelligence had found no one who saw the two together at the resort. Another point to highlight here: Atta and Marwan al-Shehhi were alleged by the FBI in a court indictment in December, 2001, to have bought a knife in Zurich, Switzerland, on July 8th, 2001. How could Atta do that if, as the FBI also claims, he didn't fly from Florida to Spain until July 9th?

'Mr Nice Guy' or not?

The official story says that Atta drove some 3,200 miles in rental cars in America between August 6th and September 9th, 2001. He and al-Shehhi apparently walked into Warrick Rent-A-Car in Pompano Beach, Florida, on August 6th and owner Brad Warrick said that Atta carried a briefcase, was polite and looked like a businessman. Many witnesses remember him as a slick dresser who wore jewellery – another no-can-do for Muslim men. Warrick said: 'He didn't spend money like there was an unlimited source. He squabbled a little bit over mileage.' Atta had switched to a Ford Escort after renting a Chevy Corsica for a week because it cost ten dollars less. He was by contrast said by various witnesses and people who knew him to have unlimited funds and wads of notes in his pocket. Warrick described the two Arabs as 'uncommonly polite' and always '... had a briefcase and books in the trunk'. This description of Atta's demeanour is at odds with reports from flying schools where he is described as anything but polite. Warrick said that on one occasion Atta phoned from Venice, Florida, to say that the oil light had flickered on and reminded him about the problem when the car was returned on September 9th. 'The only thing out of the ordinary was that he was nice enough to let me know that the car needed an oil change,' Warrick said. 'That was odd since he was planning to die in a matter of days.' Or was he? Warrick said he found it strange that Atta had been concerned about the condition of the car when he returned it just two days before the 9/11 attacks. 'I mean, if you're going on a suicide mission, why not leave the car at the airport?' You'll never get a job with the FBI, Mr Warrick. The car rental owner also revealed that when the car was returned – again two days before 9/11 – al-Shehhi asked for the charge to be transferred from Atta's credit card to his own. Warrick said: 'If you're going on a suicide mission who cares who pays for what?' How about if you're not?

Atta was lucky not to be stopped by a traffic cop (very easy, as I know, when travelling those distances in cop-happy America) because

in the April, 2001, he had been given a ticket for driving without a
licence and didn't show for a court hearing. The bench issued a warrant
for his arrest which the police failed to act upon. He overstayed his visa
and no action was taken. Lucky man, or was he? Patsies and intelligence
assets are always protected to allow them to serve their purpose. Atta is
said to have rented a Piper Archer single-engine plane at Palm Beach
County Park Airport in Lantana, Florida, on August 16th, 17th and 20th,
2001, or on three consecutive days from August 19th, depending on
which report you read. The manageress told the media that Atta said he
wanted to complete 100 flying hours. On August 28th he is reported to
have used a Visa card on the Internet to buy two one-way tickets for
Flight 11 ... quoting a frequent flyer membership number obtained only
three days before! Anyone who has frequent flyer membership knows
how long it takes to build up enough free miles to make it worthwhile –
in Atta's case that would have been long after September 11th had
passed. Why is he collecting air miles if he plans to kill himself days
later? The other ticket, we are told, was in the name of Abdulaziz Al-
Omari, or whoever that was because the real Al-Omari was still alive
after 9/11. A man by that name turned up alive in Saudi Arabia and said
his passport was stolen in 1995 when he studied at the University of
Denver. The FBI released the man's details claiming he was a hijacker,
but the accompanying picture was not him. 'I couldn't believe it when
the FBI put me on their list,' the real Abdulaziz Al-Omari said. 'They
gave my name and my date of birth, but I am not a suicide bomber. I am
here. I am alive. I have no idea how to fly a plane. I had nothing to do
with this.' The Wikipedia page of the fake 'Al-Omari' named as a
hijacker with Atta on Flight 11 sums it up really: 'Little is known about
al-Omari's life, and it is unclear whether some information refers to
Omari or another person by that name.' But we *know* he did it – *we know*.
Now go back to sleep and stop asking questions.

Atta was said to have been at Shuckums Oyster Pub and Seafood
Grill in Hollywood, Florida, 30 miles from Miami, with Marwan al-
Shehhi and another man on September 8th with three days to go before
the 9/11 attacks. Night manager Tony Amos said they stayed from
around 4.30pm until about 7pm. Waitress Patricia Idrissi told the media
that one of them went to play a video machine at one end of the
restaurant while Atta and al-Shehhi sat drinking and arguing. Al-Shehhi
drank rum and coke, she said, while Atta downed five Stolichnaya
vodkas with orange juice. The bill was $48 and Atta argued with the
manager about it. This is a guy with a pocketful of notes who, we are
told, was only three days from flying a plane into the World Trade
Center? 'You think I can't pay my bill?' Atta is said to have shouted. 'I
am a pilot for American Airlines. I can pay my fucking bill.' *Mmmm*. Did
he really mention American Airlines? It seems very convenient to the

official narrative. Atta paid the bill from a 'thick wad' of $50 and $100 bills, staff said, and so why the argument about the cost only days before September 11th? This is just silly. The *St. Petersburg Times* and other media reported that FBI agents arrived at Shuckum's 'soon after the attack' (what fantastic detective work so quickly) to interview staff and show them pictures of 'several Middle Eastern men' to see if they were the drinkers they were talking about. Amazingly they *were*. FBI documents submitted to the 9/11 Commission and released in 2009 contain three agent reports of these interviews in which some witnesses recognise Atta but not al-Shehhi and others do the opposite. The reports also play down the alcohol consumption which was bad for the official story. Islamic law strictly forbids drinking alcohol. 'Atta's' father, or the father of Mohamed El-Amir, said:

If my son sees you with a beer, he'll cross the road' and he was 'very shy, very polite, would never swear'. He said it was '... like accusing a decent, veiled religious girl of smuggling prostitutes into Egypt. It is nonsense, imagination!

Other reports have said that al-Shehhi did all the boozing, which, if true, casts still more doubt on the 'American Airlines pilot' statement that Atta is said to have made according to the same witness who claims he drank five vodkas. Whether it was al-Shehhi or both of them hitting the bottle these people are supposed to be Islamic fanatics willing to kill themselves and thousands of others for their faith while drinking in public such a banned substance? It doesn't add up – none of does. Azzan Ali, a friend of Atta and al-Shehhi when they were students at a Florida flying school, said: 'They were very religious.' Clearly they weren't – *if they were the same people*. The *Longboat Observer* at Longboat Key, Florida, reported in November, 2001, that bartender Darlene Sievers had seen Atta four days before 9/11 at the Holiday Inn Hotel & Suites drinking rum and coke at the bar. She said she remembered him because of the big tip he left and other staff recalled al-Shehhi drinking there. A similar story emerged from the other side of the world when *The New York Times* reported the month after 9/11 that Atta and al-Shehhi had been seen drinking whisky during visits to the Philippines between 1998 and 2000 when they stayed at the Woodland Park Resort Hotel, dined at a Middle Eastern-style restaurant and al-Shehhi hosted a party for 'six or seven Arab friends'. The FBI story is that Amir ('Atta') disappeared from his German university from mid-1997 to October, 1998, and returned as a religious extremist. Now witnesses were telling us where he was for some of that period – getting pissed with women in the Philippines. Woodland Park waitress Gina Marcelo recalled:

They drank Johnnie Walker Black Label whisky and mineral water. They barbecued shrimp and onions. They came in big vehicles, and they had a lot of money. They all had girlfriends ... [but] they never tipped. If they did, I would not remember them so well.

Money no problem and lots of booze appears to be the common theme of these 'Islamic fanatics'. Then there were the reports of other 'Islamic fundamentalists' drinking in a strip bar the night before September 11th. Associated Press reported on September 13th: 'Three men spewed anti-American sentiments in a bar and talked of impending bloodshed the night before the terrorist attacks.' John Kap, a strip club manager in Daytona Beach, told FBI investigators that the men in his bar used credit cards to spend $200 to $300 each on lap dancers and drinks, the report said. 'They were talking about what a bad place America is.' Kap is quoted as telling the FBI: 'They said "Wait 'til tomorrow. America is going to see bloodshed".' It's all so convenient. Kap said that he gave the FBI the men's credit card receipts, photocopied driver's licences, a business card left by one of the suspects and 'a copy of a Koran that one of the men had left at the bar', the Associated Press report claimed. Pardon me? A Muslim 'fanatic' would take a Koran into a strip bar, knock-back the booze and leave it there? Oh, do let's be sensible here. These alleged 'hijackers' and 'accomplices' (diversion agents) seem to have left copies of the Koran everywhere they went in cars, hotel rooms and bars – how perfect for the cover story. What were these guys, the Islamic version of the Gideons? The Associated Press article said the FBI told Kap not to reveal the names of these men. The *Arab News* of Saudi Arabia asked:

How could the hijackers themselves have been 'Islamists' if they frequented bars, drank in some cases beer and wine, and one even attended an evangelical Christian school and stated that he would not have minded marrying a non-Muslim? How can we have faith in the investigations when almost half of the original list of hijackers have turned out either to be dead [before the event] or alive and well in other parts of the world?

A writer on the Liberty of Freedom website said:

Ziad Jarrahi, the alleged Lebanese hijacker of the plane which crashed in Pennsylvania, had a Turkish girlfriend in Hamburg and enjoyed nightclubs and drinking. Yet at the same time, we are being told that these same hijackers spent the night before the attack getting drunk in bars, making noise, screaming insults at the 'infidels', and doing everything they could to attract attention to themselves.

They used the credit cards issued in their stolen names, allowed their driver's licenses with the stolen names to be photocopied, and used public library computers to send emails back and forth using their stolen names signed to unencrypted messages about their plans to steal aircraft and crash them into buildings, then decorated their apartments with absurdly obvious props such as a crop dusting manual to the point where the whole affair reads like a low budget 'B' detective movie from the 1930s. In short, these men did everything they could to make sure everyone knew who they were, or more to the point, who they were pretending to be.

Pretending to be is a highly relevant point and so is attracting attention to themselves. You will see by the end of the book that many people with clear connections to events acted in ways that made people remember them. A cover story was being concocted before the attacks that could be 'uncovered' the moment they happened. This is very easy because the mainstream media simply accepted the official story without question. I remember seeing a television 'documentary' about Mohamed Atta on the UK ITV channel in which Jonathan Dimbleby, one of Britain's best-known current affairs presenters, repeated the FBI story without question from start to finish. Unbelievable.

Doubles all round

A staple technique of intelligence agencies such as the CIA, Mossad and British Intelligence is the use of doubles and we should add this into the mix. Even plastic surgery can be used when necessary. Some of the alleged hijackers using their alleged names were credibly sighted and/or recorded on official documents in different locations at the same time – some in very different locations on different sides of America and even in different countries. This can only be achieved by the use of doubles and false identity documentation for which intelligence agencies are legendary. We will see later the extent to which Mossad for example goes to produce credible fraudulent passports and other documents. The Florida *Sun-Sentinel* reported 17 days after the 9/11 attacks:

> At least six of the suspected terrorists had two sets of driver's licenses issued by Florida, which would have allowed two or more people to use the same identity ... Many of the suspected terrorists, it is becoming increasingly clear, swapped identities as part of their preparations for the Sept 11 attacks on the World Trade Center and the Pentagon, according to a *Sun-Sentinel* review of documents, interviews and published reports.

They swapped identities or their handlers and manipulators did? Lee Harvey Oswald, the patsy wrongly accused of the assassination of President Kennedy, is an example of someone who appeared to be in more than one place at the same time and if doubles were used for that we have another reason why Oswald was killed to head off a public court hearing. We should also keep in mind the around 4,000 Saddam Hussein Republican Guard operatives brought from Iraq to the United States to settle after the Gulf War of 1991. Anyone think Father Bush did that out of the kindness of his heart? He didn't have one. They were brought to the United States to be used and exploited, but why? Well, for a start here were thousands of 'Middle Eastern looking men' with the potential to pose as would-be terrorists and their doubles. At least one has been connected to the Oklahoma bombing as 'John Doe 2' and it would not have ended there. Look-a-likes can pose as the target person while doing different things in different guises and claiming different background histories. When someone of the same name and appearance is reported to be a guilty party all these different appearances and personas of the real person and the double or doubles are fused together into a composite 'history' which then becomes the official one. In this way people can be described as having different personalities when they are not the same people. I am sure this is what happened with 'Atta'. Doubles can be put on terrorist watch lists when the target they are standing in for has (a) no idea he has a double and (b) has never done anything to deserve being on a terrorist watch list. Then when an attack happens the authorities say the patsy 'was on a terrorist watch list' and so give public credibility to their false narrative. Using doubles with the target party's identity is a common way to set someone up to take the rap for something they didn't do. Real people set up by doubles are often liquidated to stop them proving they could not have been responsible. What's the point of having a fake Mohamed Atta and then allow the real Mohamed El-Amir to turn up and prove it wasn't him? The authorities can try to explain away dead hijackers turning up alive as 'identity theft', but Atta was such a central character on which so much of the official narrative depends that Mohamed El-Amir would have had to be taken out. His father said in 2005: 'My son is gone. He is now with God. The Mossad killed him.' He probably got the assassins right as we will explore much later. Ziad Jarrah, a friend of El-Amir in Germany and the alleged hijacker pilot of Flight 93, is another victim of the doubles hoax. Lebanon-born Ziad Jarrah was no Muslim extremist. He was educated in Christian schools, liked to dance, party and drink beer and had a reputation for knowing the best night clubs and beaches in Beirut. Jarrah had a Turkish girlfriend in Germany and they were planning to marry in the summer of 2002. His father said:

He never expressed any religious thoughts or ideas. He never changed in his appearance, or behaviour. He was still the same person we know since he was born, and throughout all his life.

FBI claims about Jarrah's background turned out to be false and there have been inconsistencies about where he was supposed to have been. 'Jarrah' was said to have been questioned in Dubai on January 30th, 2001, when he admitted to his inquisitors spending the previous two months and five days in Pakistan and Afghanistan where Osama bin Laden operated a terrorist training camp; but what this fake 'Jarrah' said in Dubai is impossible. The real Jarrah was registered with a flying school in Venice, Florida, near the one attended by 'Atta'. The school confirmed that he continuously attended until January 15th and his family confirmed that he then flew to Lebanon where he arrived on January 26th to visit a hospital every day until the 30th where his father had undergone open heart surgery. He could not have been in Dubai. Fake 'Jarrah' in Dubai (a major intelligence centre for the CIA) was playing his role in preparing the post-9/11 cover story. He told his questioners that he was going back to Florida to connect him to the real Jarrah, but then flew to Europe and how could someone who had just indicated possible terrorist connections then be allowed to head for the airport? CNN reported that the Dubai interrogation of 'Jarrah' was conducted at the request of the CIA and provided the only confirmed link (a lie) between any of the alleged 'hijackers' and Afghanistan. Another fake Ziad Jarrah made an appearance years earlier when he leased a home in Brooklyn, New York, between March 1995 and February 1996. His landlords recognised the picture of the real Jarrah/Jarrahi circulated after the 9/11 attacks, but while what would appear to be his double was in New York the real Jarrah was completing his education at a Catholic high school in Beirut. He didn't leave Lebanon until April, 1996, when went to study in Germany. Fake Jarrah had his rent paid by a house-mate called Ihassan Jarrah and claimed to be a photographer. His New York landlord said he would sometimes come home with a prostitute. Charles Lisa, a landlord of Jarrah in Florida in 2001, said he had a German passport. Why would that be when he was supposed to be a Lebanese citizen? Lisa was reported as saying that Jarrah 'was too happy a man for a guy who knew he was going to die in the next ten days or so.' Most of those who met the alleged hijackers appeared to be astonished that they could have carried out such attacks. Many were described as 'ordinary' people or, as one article put it: 'Friendly neighbors, serious students and model dads: the men suspected of hijacking the jets that carried out history's deadliest terror strikes looked a lot more like the guy next door than the incarnation of the devil.' Another aspect of the patsy operation on the real Ziad Jarrah was his alleged 'suicide letter' to his girlfriend in Germany 'hours before the attacks' in which he is alleged to have said:

I did what I had to do. You should be very proud of it, it is an honor, and you will see the result, and everybody will be happy.

Somehow – just a coincidence – 'Jarrah' wrongly-addressed the package to a location he knew very well and just by chance it was returned to the United States where it ended up in the hands of the FBI. Oh do fuck off. This alleged 'suicide note' mentioned future meetings and contained references to scuba diving instructions. The real Jarrah of course disappeared at just the right time to go the same way as the real Mohamed El-Amir ('Atta'). Jarrah's family offered to provide DNA for a test with fragmentary alleged remains of 'hijackers' on Flight 93, but the FBI turned it down. I can't for the life of me think why. Doubles would explain how devout Muslims became booze-swilling, cocaine-snorting pork eaters and womanisers and how in reverse people who had no interest in Islamic extremism suddenly began behaving like Islamic extremists. Atta's English and accent were described by Florida rental car owner Brad Warrick as that of someone resident in the United States for a long time. By contrast 'Atta' (which one?) would be denied flying tuition at Jones Aviation in Sarasota, Florida, because he and al-Shehhi were aggressive, rude, and ... *couldn't speak English*. The question might be asked about why doubles would allow themselves to pose as people and then be killed on crashed airliners. The answer is two-fold. Often the doubles themselves don't know the big picture and can be manipulated into the wrong place at the wrong time and secondly, in the case of 9/11, there is *no confirmation they were on the planes*. I say that because if the 'hijackers' that are claimed to have crashed the planes actually boarded them, even as patsies who didn't know what was going to happen, *multiple* surveillance pictures around the airports and their boarding pass stubs would have been made public immediately after the attacks. All these years later we are still waiting. There would appear to be two different 'Attas' in Germany and America, but how many 'Attas' were there in America? How many doubles of other alleged 'hijackers' were there when they could not possibly have been in different locations, even countries, at the same time? Confusion is the key to diversion from the truth and with 9/11 we are drowning in it. We have had apparently credible sightings of 'Atta' all over America from coast to coast – and in Canada and Germany – and he and other alleged 'hijackers' were seen or located in different places at the same time.

Evidence presented by investigative journalist Daniel Hopsicker and in highly detailed books like the excellent multi-authored *The Hidden History of 9-11* clearly show that Atta and others in the alleged 'Islamic plot' were being both closely watched by military intelligence assets and protected from investigation or arrest. Mossad and the Israeli military will seriously enter the story with regard to this. The same Hidden Hand operatives were guiding the cover story and preventing those involved in the cover story (knowingly or otherwise) from being stopped or exposed – operatives of the same agencies that claimed after 9/11 that they were taken completely by surprise and had no idea what was coming. A double could explain reports that Atta was seen with his father in the United States. Either that or the father of Mohamed El-Amir has been lying to us. Numerous witnesses in Venice contacted the FBI office in Sarasota after El-Amir's father appeared on television after 9/11 to say they had seen him in Venice with Atta two weeks before the attacks. The usual FBI intimidation of witnesses telling the wrong story then followed to pressure them to shut up. Both the FBI and the 9/11 Commission have sought to air-brush and delete Atta's months of residence in Venice, Florida, and you can see why with what happened there demolishing their 'radical Islamist' script. I will focus further on Venice, this key centre of 9/11 activity, later in the chapter. Another Atta location in Florida was the town of Hollywood about 30 miles from Miami and a three-hour drive from Venice. Hollywood is going to be centrally-important to the 9/11 story much later in the book. One other point about identity is that technology can fabricate photographs or fuse two people into a face that resembles both. That is obviously true today and even in 2001 intelligence networks had technology way ahead of what was available to the public. On the subject of pictures – why have we not seen many more of Atta and his alleged accomplices who would have been caught on camera all over the place? Why did the FBI turn up at the LA Fitness gym in Coral Springs, Florida, where Atta was a member for some weeks, and remove his picture from the computer – as confirmed by employee José Serraz? Why haven't we ever seen it? All we see is basically the same single image of his period in the United States from his driving licence.

'Atta' everywhere

On September 8th a man of Middle Eastern appearance (they had so many to choose from thanks to Father Bush) is reported to have walked into the control tower at Boston Logan Airport. Some speculated that this was Atta, but the FBI claim that he flew from Florida to Boston via Baltimore the following day, September 9th. Well, that's one FBI timeline, anyway. Other FBI reports have him flying out of Fort Lauderdale-Hollywood airport on September 7th on a flight to Baltimore at a time he was seen drinking at Shuckum's bar while also booking a one-way ticket on September 5th from Florida to Boston, not Baltimore. Still another timeline has Atta and al-Shehhi checking out of the Panther Inn in Deerfield, Florida, on September 9th which would fit returning the hire car to Brad Warrick on the same day. An FBI document compiled on September 12th, 2001, has a man identified as Atta selling his 1989 red Pontiac Grand Prix to Wynn Errico at the Wynn Motor Company in North Lauderdale for $800 on September 7th. Another version of that car-selling story, with differences, appeared in an FBI document dated September 17th and still another has the car sold for $800 but to Sun Auto Leasing and Sales on September 8th. Whatever the discrepancies why would you go to so much trouble selling your car when you already had lots of money and were planning to die in four days? To add still further to this Twilight World an FBI document has Atta, Hani Hanjour (the alleged pilot of Pentagon Flight 77) and possibly other 'Middle Eastern men' photographing passports on September 7th at a Kinko shop in Laurel, Maryland, 20 miles from Baltimore which is more than a thousand miles from where he is supposed to have sold his car in the early afternoon on the same day. Amid all these conflicting timelines came another in May, 2002, when CNN and the *New York Daily News* sourced reports to the FBI which said credit card receipts appeared to locate Mohamed Atta in Manhattan, New York, on September 10th, 2001.What he is supposed to have bought was not mentioned. It's crazy stuff and fuels the confusion and contradiction that hides the truth.

Several hours before the 'Atta' figure showed up at the Boston Airport control tower on September 8th we are told that four 'Middle Eastern men' had asked a controller how to get into the tower. This begs the question of what 'Atta' and these other men expected to gain by getting into the tower. What would it have told them? It wouldn't have helped them hijack the planes three days later in any way. What it would have done is attract attention to them and suspicion. This is the last thing they would have wanted so close to their 'big day' at the very airport where they were acting suspiciously. On the other hand if you were setting up a cover story for September 11th you would want 'Middle Eastern men' acting suspiciously at the airport where the first two planes were to be hijacked. I asked the FBI about the 'Atta' man and the other four at the control tower when I was researching *Alice in Wonderland,* but they refused to answer my questions. Forbes.com quoted frequent flier Janice Shineman in a 2016 article as saying she saw Mohamed Atta at the American Airlines terminal at Boston Logan on September 9th – the day his rental car was returned in Florida. She said he 'stared menacingly' into her car when she arrived and then cut in front of her inside the airport to ask a question of an American Airlines agent. Shineman said he held a red file folder and wore pink and blue flowered gym pants. The word 'Nantucket' was on the back of his purple T-shirt. She said 'Atta' took notes while standing in front of gate agents and she planned to say something to the pilot about him, but he did not board the flight. The *Forbes* article went on:

An FBI chronology of the hijackers' movements states that Atta rented a car at

Logan on Sept. 8, 2001 – which coincides with Shineman's observations the next morning – but it also states that Atta flew to Logan from Baltimore on Sept. 9. The FBI could not explain the discrepancy or why the time-line lists two different flight numbers for Atta's Baltimore-Boston flight.

There are so many discrepancies in the 9/11 story I don't wonder people have trouble keeping up with them and while Atta was hiring a car in Boston he was being seen drinking heavily in a Florida bar. The main focus of the 2016 *Forbes* article was an even more bizarre story in which Delta Airlines captain Pat Gilmore claimed that he had flown from Baltimore to Atlanta on a Boeing 757 on July 26th, 2001, with Mohamed Atta in the jump-seat behind him posing as an American Airlines pilot. *You are kidding me?* No – Gilmore told the American Media Institute that Atta showed him a standard pilot's FAA Class 1 medical certificate and a jump-seat request form that pilots typically present when riding as cockpit passengers on their own or competing airlines. The documents bore the name 'Atta' and his picture was on the company ID. Atta had worn an American Airlines pilot uniform and 'cast a pall over the flight deck'. Gilmore claimed: 'He gave me a stare in the cockpit at cruise altitude that was bone-chilling.' Forbes noted that the story conflicts with the FBI Atta timeline (but then what doesn't?) and reports how Gilmore was 'just one of several witnesses who say they saw the mastermind of the attacks on New York and Washington while the clock ticked toward the largest terrorist attack in US history'. How many 'Attas' were there and how many sightings were accurate? Gilmore said he called the FBI who told him there was no way to confirm the story and it probably had nothing to do with the attacks. Surely unless this 'Atta' was protected he was taking a massive chance scamming himself into the cockpit when if he had been caught his alleged contribution to 9/11 would have been over. WTF?

'Quick – we'll miss it!'

The FBI timeline says that on September 10th Atta and Abdulaziz Al-Omari rented a Nissan Altima from Alamo at Boston Logan Airport and drove just over 100 miles to Portland, Maine. They are said to have stayed overnight at a Comfort Inn before heading the next morning for Portland Airport and a plane back to Boston to pick up Flight 11. Why on earth would they take such a chance of missing the flight they were supposed to be targeting when even a short delay could have been crucial? Why would the leader of the biggest plane hijack in history, an attack years in the planning, risk flying to Boston that morning and giving himself so little time between landing in Boston from Portland and the departure of Flight 11? The Portland plane arrived in Boston at 6.45am and Flight 11 was scheduled to leave at 7.45am. Atta and Al-

Omari are said to have been caught on video at Portland as they
boarded a Colgan Air commuter flight to Boston. Well, for a start, that
wasn't the real Al-Omari on the
videotape because he was
still alive after the attacks and
which 'Atta' was it? On the
videotape released by the FBI
of 'Atta' and 'Al-Omari'
going through security at
Portland is the time-code 05-
53-41 (Fig 39). That's just 19
seconds short of six minutes
to six. I know you can work
that out, but it is worth
emphasising because the
flight they took from Portland
to Boston that morning,
USAir Flight 5930, was
scheduled to depart at ... 6am.
That's only *six minutes* after
'Atta' and 'Al-Omari' were
'captured' on videotape

Figure 39: "Atta' and 'Al-Omari' rush through security
at Portland airport. The time-code at the bottom (where
you would expect it to be) shows six minutes to flight
departure (hence the rush) while the one in the middle
(the last place you would normally put a time-code on
a security video) shows 15 minutes to departure. Most
of the media cropped this image to show only the
middle time-code.

passing through security! No wonder they were described as 'rushing'
for the plane. Airline worker Michael Tuohey who described how he
checked-in Atta and Al-Omari said they wore 'ties and jackets'. By the
time they appeared on security cameras immediately afterwards rushing
to the gate they had open neck shirts and no jackets. The FBI timeline
said that Atta and Al-Omari checked out of their hotel in Portland at
5.33am, just 27 minutes before their plane was due to depart and they
then had to park their rental car, check-in and get to the gate. Atta was
described as 'sweating bullets' and said he was running late. 'His
forehead was drenched,' an airline witness said. Anyone who travels by
air knows that if you leave it that late you are highly likely to miss the
flight. Not only did the leader of the biggest plane hijacking in history
take the chance of flying into Boston from a connecting flight that
morning he arrived so late that the Portland plane departed only
minutes after he got to the gate. All that planning and he took those
risks of not even getting to Boston? What was that *The Washington Post*
said about the '... astonishing degree of organization and planning
undertaken by the terrorists'? Hilarious. It was more like the Keystone
Cops. No, sorry, that's the FBI (or what decent and intelligent agents in
the FBI are forced to be by their superiors). I asked the FBI about all
these anomalies and contradictions, but, of course, officials refused to
answer my questions. On the Portland airport security video a second

time-code appears in the *centre* of the screen – the last place you would put a time-code on a surveillance video. This code reads 5.45 and appears to be only there to hide the ridiculous contradiction of a 'highly professional' leader of the hijackers running to his plane at six minutes to departure when if he missed the flight he missed his hijack connection. The way the shot was framed by most of the media only the second time-code in the middle of the screen was visible. The true one at the bottom of the frame was cropped off. If this second, centre-of-the-screen, time-code was correct, it means that Atta and friend must have checked out of their hotel, taken their car to the airport car park, checked in and passed through security to the gate all in 12 minutes. I rang Ruth Dudley, a very nice lady, who was Head of Security at Portland Airport. I asked her why there were two time-codes – one of them slap bang in the middle of the screen. She said she didn't know and would have to see it to give me an opinion. Unfortunately, she said, they didn't have those tapes anymore because they were immediately confiscated by the FBI – as were all the tapes relating to 9/11 and all such attacks, including Oklahoma. I asked the FBI why there were two time-codes on the video and why one was in the middle of the screen, but officials refused to answer.

Other 'hijackers' are said to have arrived at Boston Airport in a white Mitsubishi Mirage with Virginia licence plates. The car contained 'five' Arab men (three in other reports) and the FBI said that in one window was a pass allowing access to restricted areas at the airport. Media reports and official statements claimed that (unidentified) witnesses remembered the men because there was an argument with an unnamed driver over a parking dispute. I have seen the 'hijackers' arrival time as anything between 06.45am and 07.15am, but if we take the now official time of between 06.45 and 06.52 they are still leaving it very late for a departure at 07.45 that they apparently meant to hijack. David Boeri on *NewsCenter 5* in Boston reported: 'Sources say at least four suspects, described as Middle Eastern men, arrived late to the airport, purchased one-way tickets and paid in cash for them, all of those factors being known security risk flags.' He said security personnel were trained to question late-arriving passengers who pay in cash for tickets. Surely 'highly trained' hijackers would know this? There are so many conflicting reports of what happened in this period – the hijackers paid cash at the time or booked their tickets earlier, airline and staff remember them and they don't. The 9/11 Commission said none of the checkpoint supervisors recall seeing any of the 'hijackers' or report anything untoward. If there were no hijackers and nothing happened untoward that would explain it.

Camera shy

I have noticed that many people seem to believe they have seen video
footage of Atta and friend going through security at Boston Logan. This
is because people tend to get an impression from a news item and not
the detail. We have been shown no pictures of any of the alleged
hijackers getting on any of the 9/11 planes. We have seen 'Atta' and 'Al-
Omari' alleged to be passing through security on the time-code-doctored
images from Portland airport but nothing in Boston. *Three years* after the
attacks footage was released of the alleged hijackers of Flight 77 passing
through security at Washington Dulles (more about this later). Even this
was not released voluntarily, but through a Freedom of Information Act
request from a law firm representing some 9/11 families. If the footage is
real and authentic why wasn't it revealed much earlier and not on the
day before the 9/11 Commission presented its report? That's it – the
extent of footage confirming the 'hijackers' boarded the planes and you
can bet that if proof existed it would have been all over the media on
September 11th-12th. Staggeringly, Boston Logan, of all the airports in all
the world, did not have surveillance cameras and so we have no proof
that Atta and company boarded Flights 11 and 175. A *Boston Herald*
article said: 'In perhaps the most stunning example of Massport's lax
security safeguards, Logan International Airport is missing a basic tool
found not only in virtually every other airport, but in most 7-Elevens'.
Massport ran Boston Logan Airport and almost every other transport
operation in the city it would seem. I went to see its media spokesman
when I was speaking in Boston in February, 2002, and he said that
Massport was not responsible for security. I'll come to who was at the
most relevant time in the latter stages of the book. He confirmed there
were no video cameras in the departure lounge, but by the time I spoke
with him they did have face-recognition cameras taking still pictures to
ensure that the person who checked in was the person getting on the
plane. The *Boston Herald* article pointed out that the lack of cameras in
the departure lounge has prevented the FBI from definitively identifying
the men who boarded the planes. How strange that when airport
cameras were already ubiquitous they did not have them at an
international airport when they did at a small regional jetport at
Portland. Therefore Boston was the perfect airport if you wanted to hide
the truth. Cameras had been in widespread use in airports for some 15
years before 9/11 and Michael Taylor, President of American
International Security Corp in Boston, said: 'It's not rocket science,
convenience stores employ them, why wouldn't Massport?' The absence
of cameras when you would find them at almost every other similar
airport is another one of those endless coincidences that you find
everywhere in the 9/11 story. This means that the evidence is simply not
there to prove that the 'hijackers' named by the authorities were on the

Boston planes – even those that were not still alive. Charles Slepian, a New York security consultant, said:

> You have names, but the FBI has said it hasn't been able to match the faces of those who were on the flights. Who boarded at Logan? You don't have pictures, and that's a problem. And are those suspects the ones who actually got on at Logan or are they still alive? Who knows? That's one of the big questions the cameras would have been able to answer.

How convenient that at Boston Airport of all places they couldn't do that. Funny, too, how there were 17 surveillance cameras constantly filming the roads between the Ritz Hotel and the Pont de L'Alma tunnel in Paris which would have proved beyond question what happened to the car in which Princess Diana died in 1997. For reasons never explained none of them was working the night she died (see *The Biggest Secret*). Cameras are very important to the Hidden Hand when they want to keep surveillance on the public, but they can be a real problem when they need to hide their own activities. Still, hold on: Boston did have cameras in parking garages, ramp areas and on Logan's roadways to monitor traffic. Why haven't we been shown video pictures of these 'Middle Eastern men' who arrived in the car park that morning and had the argument with an unnamed driver? What about the men we are told arrived at the car park in their vehicle several times in the days before September 11th? Where is the footage of the other hijackers arriving that morning? Surely the 'Middle Eastern men' who asked how to get into the control tower must be on tape somewhere as well as the one who seems to have got in 'unaccompanied'. The *Boston Globe* reported on September 13th:

> When they reviewed videotape of the parking lot's surveillance camera, investigators found that the car had entered the lot up to five times between last Wednesday and Tuesday, according to sources. Those sources said the constant presence of the car over the last week suggested that the terrorists had scouted the airport, or performed dry runs for the daring attack.

Who was on the tape and where is it? Where is the recording of the 'Middle Eastern men' arriving in the white Mitsubishi on the morning of September 11th and having the argument over a parking space with an unidentified driver? I asked the FBI all these questions, but officials refused to answer. Michael Taylor, president of American International Security Corp, said he had worked for the Port Authority of New York and New Jersey and confirmed that Newark, New Jersey, from where Flight 93 departed, has video cameras in the departure lounge. Why haven't we been shown footage of the 'hijackers' boarding that flight? I put this same point to Tara Hamilton, a very pleasant woman in the media office at Washington Dulles Airport. She replied:

> I've checked with our airport police department and they inform me that the FBI is in charge of all information regarding September 11th and the specifics about the men who came to Dulles Airport. In regard to questions about our airport cameras, those are part of our security system and we're not able to discuss that. I'm sorry we're not able to provide the information you are seeking but am sure you understand our situation.

Well actually, no I don't. If releasing video footage of 'Atta' and friend at Portland airport was okay, what was the problem with letting us see other 'hijackers' boarding planes at other airports? Very questionable footage was released in security at Dulles in 2004, but nothing from the departure lounge. Tara Hamilton, like all of these media spokespeople, was just saying what she was told to say, and the idea that asking for confirmation that 'hijackers' were caught on camera would in any way affect the airport security system is ridiculous. They don't want to discuss it, that's the truth. I asked the FBI why these pictures had not been released, but officials refused to answer. Police said that after the attacks they found Atta's red 1989 Pontiac Grand Prix in the parking lot of Logan Airport and the rented Altima in Portland. Why would Atta rent the Altima at Boston Airport to drive to Portland if he had another car already at Boston? Where did this car come from when he had been at the other end of America, in Florida, with another rental car until September 9th? Florida police understandably appealed for anyone who might find the Grand Prix in the area where Atta was said to be living. Instead it turned up in a Boston car park 1,673 miles away and yet Atta went to car rental companies in Florida on the 9th and Boston on the 10th, according to the official story. Do the sums and you find that even if Atta maintained a speed of 100 miles an hour for the entire journey (no chance, he would have had so many speeding tickets) it would take nearly 17 hours to complete the journey with no hold ups or stops whatsoever. Not worth even going there, it's so stupid. Yet the *Chicago Tribune* said:

> Sometime before the attack, Atta, perhaps accompanied by al-Shehhi, made his way up the Eastern Seaboard. After Tuesday's attack, police found Atta's Grand Prix in the parking lot of Boston's Logan International Airport.

The reporters would have seen how ridiculous that was if they had only stopped to think instead of taking the official story without question. How can they find a car so far away from Florida where FBI reports said Atta sold it for $800 on September 7th or 8th? What about the FBI reports that said Atta flew to Boston via Baltimore? Oh, and would you believe it? The Mitsubishi left by other 'hijackers' in the car park at Boston Airport was found to contain a ramp pass allowing access to restricted areas, a copy of the Koran, a fuel consumption calculator and a flight training manual written in Arabic on how to fly a 767. *Wow!* What synchronicity. All this was 'discovered' at the very time the Bush government was preparing to pin the blame on Arab terrorists working for Osama bin Laden. Shit, thank you God. Just a thought, though: Maybe a note signed by Osama bin Laden saying 'all the best with your mass murder on my behalf today by flying those planes into the World Trade Center and the Pentagon' might have been a nice touch, just to cover all bases. Perhaps they could have placed the note inside the hijacker's passport that was 'found' a few blocks from the World Trade Center. Nicely charred at the edges, you know the sort of thing. Add all this to the 757 flying manuals and 'eight inch stack of East Coast flight maps' that were claimed to have been found in hotel rooms rented by 'hijackers' and the story is complete. Oh yes, not to forget the reports that al-Shehhi and Atta were spotted in Switzerland that summer buying pocket knives and box cutters the day before the FBI says Atta flew from Florida to Spain. 'Hey Mohamed, we need box cutters and pocket knives, better fly to Switzerland to buy them, eh?'

Yet another miracle (they keep on coming)

Even without cameras at Boston the gods clearly wanted to help the FBI and other government 'investigators' to find those responsible. Of all the luggage of all the passengers on all the airlines on that day of all days, it was *Atta's* bags that didn't make it on to Flight 11. The FBI found inside a note dated five years earlier in which Atta said he was willing to martyr himself in a holy war against infidels. Yeah, of course he did. The contents were first reported to have been found in a rental car left by Atta at Boston airport and when the narrative changed to him driving a rental car from Boston to Portland we were told his bags were found at Boston airport because they didn't get on to Flight 11. The contents were the same, though, and oh my God! They only found in Atta's bags a copy of the Koran, a Saudi passport, correspondence from the university he attended in Egypt, Abdulaziz al-Omari's international driver's license and passport, a folding knife and pepper spray and ... *yes, yes* ... a video of how to fly a wide-bodied airliner. *Bingo!* Game, set, and match, all sorted, case closed. What use a knife and pepper spray were in a bag planned for the hold was not explained. The find was described by former FBI agent Warren Flagg as 'the Rosetta stone enabling FBI agents to swiftly unravel the mystery of who carried out the suicide attacks and what motivated them'. Red Flagg said:

How do you think the government was able to identify all 19 hijackers almost immediately after the attacks? They were identified through those papers in the luggage. And that's how it was known so soon that al-Qaeda was behind the hijackings.

Well blow me down, you don't say. Extraordinary – what a piece of luck! Another document was claimed to give instructions for Atta's burial and what should be done with his possessions 'when I die'. The *Los Angeles Times* reported: 'Authorities said Atta instructed that he be buried 'next to good Muslims,' with his body pointed east toward Mecca, that strict Muslim traditions were to be followed for his burial and that no women be allowed at his funeral. The document, dated April 11th, 1996, suggested that 'Atta may have been considering a suicide attack for several years before he carried it out'. This included the request that he wanted to 'go to heaven as a martyr'. How they can produce this stuff without laughing is beyond me. It's not even a B-movie script. The letter and 'will' 'found' in the baggage of Mohamed Atta was claimed to include a five-page message to his fellow hijackers. The FBI said that essentially the same letter was found in the wreckage of 'Flight 93' in Pennsylvania. *'Essentially'* the same document? Did Atta, or whoever, hand-write basically the same five-page instruction to all of them then? Had he not heard of photocopiers? I mean, he was at a Kinko's copying store near Baltimore while selling his car in Florida. Attorney General John Ashcroft also told an [In]Justice Department news conference on September 28th that another copy of the 'letter' had been found at Washington Dulles Airport 'in a vehicle used by Nawaf al-Hamzi, one of the hijackers on American Airlines Flight 77'. Ashcroft said the letter was a disturbing and shocking view into the mind-set of these terrorists: 'The letter provides instructions to the terrorists to be carried out both prior to and during their terrorist attacks.' The FBI released 'extracts' of the letter 'found' in 'Atta's luggage' via *The Washington Post* on September 28th and it was claimed to be originally written in Arabic by someone alleged to be an Islamic fanatic. The original Arabic text was not released until later by the FBI. A number of various translations have been circulated over the years and the document has been questioned in terms of its Islamic authenticity. These are some instructions for the hijackers in the Atta 'letter' according to a translation for *The New York Times*:

Pray during the night and be persistent in asking God to give you victory, control and conquest, and that He may make your task easier and not expose us.

Shouldn't we take advantage of these last hours to offer good deeds and obedience?

Nah, let's just get pissed like we did in Florida.

> Bless your body with some verses of the Qur'an (done by reading verses into one's hands and then rubbing the hands over whatever is to be blessed), the luggage, clothes, the knife, your personal effects, your ID, passport, and all your papers.

Why would fanatical Muslims have to be told how to bless something?

> Check your weapon before you leave and long before you leave. (You must make your knife sharp and must not discomfort your animal during the slaughter).

Oh yes, and don't sleep in so you have to run your arse off to get on the Portland plane.

> Tighten your clothes [a reference to making sure his clothes will cover his private parts at all times], since this is the way of the pious generations after the Prophet. They would tighten their clothes before battle. Tighten your shoes well, wear socks so that your feet will be solidly in your shoes.

Didn't your mum ever tell you that? Mine neither. Remember – don't let your dingle dangle.

> When the taxi takes you to (M) [this initial could stand for matar, airport in Arabic] remember God constantly while in the car. (Remember the supplication for entering a car, for entering a town, the supplication of place and other supplications).

I think it is more important to remember that the FBI says these guys travelled to the airports in hire cars, not taxis.

> When you have reached (M) and have left the taxi, say a supplication of place ('Oh Lord, I ask you for the best of this place, and ask you to protect me from its evils'), and everywhere you go say that prayer and smile and be calm, for God is with the believers.

Say a prayer, smile and be calm? I thought they were supposed to have had an argument with a guy over a car space immediately they arrived? They ought to listen more.

In his 'will' Atta also asks that his body be washed and buried. What, after flying a plane with a 20,000 gallon fuel capacity into the World

Trade Center? That's one heck of an embalming job. It should also be noted that while they produced this 'letter' to the hijackers, which talks of everyone fearing death, the FBI also said that 11 of the 19 hijackers named did not know they were on a suicide mission, but believed themselves to be preparing for a conventional hijack. Not if they read Atta's letter they weren't. 9/11 was like the worst type of Hollywood movie in terms of the official storyline and the miraculous and implausible happenings required for it to be true.

Venice – City of Mirages

This title may be awarded to the most famous Venice in Italy, but it could equally apply with regard to 9/11 to the small city of the same name on the Florida coast. A key strand of the official story is that all the pilots named by the FBI attended American flying schools in preparation for hijacking four commercial airliners and taking over the controls. They did this by practising on single-engine planes and some extremely incompetently at that. The main centre for this flying tuition was the little airport in Venice which is not far from Sarasota where Bush visited the school on the morning of 9/11. Three of the four alleged pilots trained at flying schools at Venice airport – Mohamed Atta (Flight 11), Marwan al-Shehhi (Flight 175) and Ziad Jarrah (Flight 93). Hani Hanjour, alleged hijacker pilot of Flight 77, attended schools in Arizona and briefly experienced a flight simulator. Venice is a seaside resort and retirement centre on the Gulf of Mexico on Florida's south-western coast with a population of some 23,000. Venice airport was mentioned during the Iran-Contra hearings when Oliver North was being questioned and the subject involved gun running from the airport to the Contras in Nicaragua. The airport was also a conduit for the CIA drug-running operation into the United States out of South America aided and abetted by the Bushes and Clintons. Funnily enough, small as Venice may be, close Bush family associate Jackson Stephens had a long association with the place. Stephens was an investor in George W. Bush's Harken Energy together with Khalid bin Mahfouz, the man named by the US State Department as a financial backer of Osama bin Laden. Bin Mahfouz and Stephens had something else in common, too – their involvement in the corrupt and criminal Bank of Credit and Commerce International (BCCI) in which the Bush family and the Saudis were also seriously implicated. Stephens was a close friend and financial backer of Father George and funded Bill Clinton's campaigns to be governor of Arkansas and US President. He has further been linked by researchers to the National Security Agency (NSA), the major overseer of the US intelligence network and boss to the CIA. Some government officials have accused the NSA of destroying data relevant to the 9/11 investigation, but why wouldn't they when destroying evidence of government-military-intelligence criminality is their job? Stephens was also a roommate of President Jimmy Carter at the US Naval Academy. To put it mildly, this guy had massive 'connections' and has been named in relation to a number of scandals including the corrupt Whitewater land deals which involved the Clintons and the Iran-Contra gun-running and cocaine smuggling operation through the Mena airstrip in Arkansas while Clinton was governor and Bush/Reagan were in the White House. A block away from Venice Airport and the 'hijacker' flying schools was the former national headquarters of the Stephens company, Beverly Enterprises. At the time of 9/11 it was home to his former law firm, Boone, Boone and Boone, and a Stephens executive still had an office there. Boone, Boone and Boone, it seemed, pretty much ran the place. Venice was a 'Boone town', you might say.

Florida is a major centre of drug trafficking and CIA, Mafia and military activity, all of which go together. I have seen the Saudi royal family mentioned for its connection to the Florida elite and criminal networks and 15 of the 19 alleged hijackers were from Saudi Arabia. Drug-trafficking and 9/11 are intertwined. Florida-based journalist Daniel Hopsicker said the son of Jewish gangster Alvin Malnik from the Miami Mafia was married into the Saudi royal family through a daughter of a Saudi prince. The king of Saudi Arabia would regularly send his private 747 to Florida to allow Malnik and gang to do business with the Saudis away from public view, Hopsicker reports. Three 9/11 'pilots' ended up at Venice flying schools even though Florida had hundreds of schools to choose from. The fact that Venice airport was a conduit for transporting drugs in the CIA operation was not a coincidence it is safe to say. American 'Atta' was involved it seems in the drug racket as a pilot and attending the flying school was a front. He already knew how to fly small planes and had licences from many countries. Being an operative in the CIA drug trade would also explain his many movements and long distances in hire cars and his wads of cash. There is a very good chance that he was set up by the 9/11 cover-story creators while he thought he was working for 'them' on other business. 'Mohamed – we need you to go to Boston and then on to Portland to stay overnight and return to Boston the next day.' Or he could have known what he was doing. Either is possible. The Venice flying schools had both changed hands shortly before Atta and company arrived there and both were purchased 'independently' by Dutch nationals within a month of each other. Rudi Dekkers bought Huffman Aviation and Arne Kruithof bought the Florida Flight Center. Atta and al-Shehhi went to Huffman and Jarrah to the Flight Center. Atta and al-Shehhi also attended Jones Aviation flying school at Sarasota Bradenton International Airport half an hour from Venice and five miles or so from the Emma E. Booker Elementary School where President Bush was on the morning of September 11th. Dekkers launched an aggressive European 'marketing' campaign not long before the 'hijackers' turned up at Huffman. He told the local *Venice Gondolier* at the time:

> The world is my working place. I won't forget Venice, but I'm going to market throughout the world, Germany, France, Belgium. That's our goal, to get people to come in here from all over the world.

So it proved. Foreign nationals soon made up 80 percent of student pilots at the school. Hundreds a year were paying thousands of dollars while it was reported that Dekkers was falling behind with the rent. Daniel Hopsicker, author of *Barry and the Boys: The CIA, the Mob, and America's Secret History*, said that Huffman Aviation was one of the schools authorised by the Immigration and Naturalization Service to issue I-20M immigration forms. These helped foreign students to secure US visas as vocational students. Arab would-be pilots began to arrive at both Venice schools in unprecedented numbers. The schools were connected to an elite international 'exchange' programme. This was a 'joint venture' between the American and German governments and run by a little-known private organisation, Carl Duisberg International (CDS). Hopsicker said this had close ties to Hidden Hand figures like David Rockefeller and Henry Kissinger and was supported by the Clintons. The usual suspects in other words and what a coincidence that is – or rather isn't. Hopsicker quotes an 'observer' at Venice Airport as saying of Rudi Dekkers:

> I've always had some suspicions about the way he breezed into town out of nowhere. Just too many odd little things. For example, he has absolutely no aviation background as far as anyone can tell. And he evidently had no use for, nor knowledge of, FAA rules and regs.

Dekkers claimed to have extensive aviation experience, but Richard Boehlke, a former business associate who fell out with him, said: 'He was an oxymoron the day I met him. I can't believe anyone handed him millions of dollars to run a business he had no experience in.' That could be explained if we were talking about a business for which the flying schools were only a public cover for very different activities. The joint owner of Huffman Aviation, along with Dekkers, was a guy called Wally Hilliard and on July 25th, 2000, while Atta was attending the school, Hilliard's Learjet was found to have 43 pounds of heroin on board when searched by the Drug Enforcement Administration in Orlando. *The Orlando Sentinel* called it 'the biggest drug seizure in central Florida history'. Hopsicker said it is no coincidence that Atta was, allegedly with Hilliard's help, selling Afghanistan opium and heroin that was financing the Taliban in league with the CIA and Pakistan's Inter-Services Intelligence (ISI). The CIA and ISI were running the opium/heroin operation in Afghanistan and creaming off profits for Bin Laden and the training and arming of Islamic terrorism – as I have exposed in other books. The *Times of India* revealed that Atta was wired $100,000 just before 9/11 on the orders of then ISI chief General Mahmoud Ahmed who was in Washington DC on September 11th meeting with CIA Director George Tenet and other intelligence figures. This money was believed to be connected to 9/11, but with Atta involved in the ISI-CIA drug operation this is far more likely to have been the reason. Amanda Keller, Atta's one-time girlfriend, said he had a constant supply of cash and drugs:

> These guys had money flowing out their ass. They never seemed to run out of money. They had massive supplies of cocaine. Whenever they'd run out, they'd go over to the flight school. I followed them one day with Sabrina [a German friend of Atta's] to see where they were going, and saw them go into Florida Flight Training.

Dekkers and Hilliard were also flush with money despite apparently losing a fortune on the flying school. One observer said of Dekkers: 'He didn't even have the money to buy gas for an airplane ... and yet a year later he shows up and plops a million seven, a million eight or two million dollars on the table as if it were paper money.' Hopsicker said this can be explained because Dekkers was a CIA asset and the CIA was running the whole operation. He said in a radio interview:

> I discovered that we were dealing with flight school owners who are CIA assets ... Mohamed Atta was in this country as a result of a program being run through the Central Intelligence Agency.

Hopsicker says the FBI lied to protect Dekkers and, in turn, Dekkers lied to Congress about his relationship with Atta. The 9/11 Commission, set up to whitewash the whole story, basically ignores the flight schools in Venice along with anything else that is relevant to the truth. Whenever you are dealing with a CIA connection you'll almost always find drug trafficking and the same with Israel's Mossad. This is one of the main ways CIA 'black ops' (Hidden Hand ops) are financed without using official funds that can be traced and the Bushes and Clintons have been heavily involved in this. The FBI systematically covered up the Florida connection and claimed it had no idea where Atta was located between leaving the flying school (according to Dekkers about Christmas 2000) and when they officially pick him up again in May, 2001. This is nonsense, as Hopsicker reveals. Numerous witnesses told them where

Atta was in that time – in Venice, Florida. He lived in nearby North Port from January, 2001, until early March and then moved in with Amanda Keller in the Sandpiper Apartments. All this was happening four months after the FBI tells us that Atta left Venice and they lost track of him. Rudi Dekkers claims he never saw Atta again after he left in late 2000 and yet several witnesses saw them together in Venice two weeks before 9/11. These included Venice licenced cab drivers who reported taking Atta to and from Huffman Aviation and other Venice locations in August, 2001, and on two occasions with Rudi Dekkers. Another witness said Atta bought a sandwich from her in Venice one week before the attacks. Why is the FBI covering up what happened in Venice and why has Rudi Dekkers not been held to account for his false testimony?

Trained by the United States?

Florida is home to the Naval Air Station in Pensacola where the US military operates exchange programmes for overseas officers. Within days of September 11th reports appeared in *Newsweek, The Washington Post*, and Knight Ridder newspapers that five of the hijackers named by the FBI were trained at secure US bases in the 1990s including three at Pensacola. *Newsweek* quoted a 'high-ranking US Navy source' as saying that three of the alleged hijackers listed Pensacola Naval Air Station for their driver's licence and car registration addresses. The report said these men were believed to be Saeed al-Ghamdi and Ahmad al-Nami, both allegedly on Flight 93, and Ahmed al-Ghamdi from Flight 175. It was claimed that their training at Pensacola was paid for by Saudi Arabia with its close connections to the Father Bush Carlyle Group which also had direct connections to the Bin Laden family. *Newsweek* claimed that military records showed that three men used the address of 10 Radford Boulevard, a base roadway where the residences of foreign-military flight trainees are located. Saeed al-Ghamdi listed this address in March, 1997, to register a 1998 Oldsmobile, *Newsweek* said. Five months later he used it again to register a late-model Buick. *Newsweek* said that driving licences were believed to have been issued to the other two suspects in 1996 and 1998 and also listed the barracks as their residences. An FBI spokesman was quoted as saying the hijackers could have stolen identities of people who trained at the bases. Mohamed Atta was reported by *Newsweek* to have attended the International Officer School at Maxwell Air Force Base in Montgomery, Alabama. In response to these reports Florida Democrat Senator Bill Nelson faxed a request to Attorney General John Ashcroft demanding confirmation or otherwise of this story. A spokesman for the senator said:

> In the wake of those reports we asked about the Pensacola Naval Air Station but we never got a definitive answer from the Justice Department. So we

asked the FBI for an answer if and when they could provide us one. Their response to date [five months later] has been that they are trying to sort through something complicated and difficult.

A Pentagon spokesman responded on September 16th, 2001, by saying that 'name matches may not necessarily mean the students were the hijackers and that discrepancies in biographical data indicate that 'we are probably not talking about the same people'. *'May not necessarily?' 'Probably'?* You mean they don't know? Of course they do so why don't they simply reveal the background to those foreign trainees with the same names as those claimed to be hijackers? A Pentagon spokesman denied that the Mohamed Atta who attended the International Officer School at Maxwell was the same man named as leader of the hijackers while refusing all requests for the biographical background of the Mohamed Atta at the school. The spokesman told reporters: 'I do not have the authority to tell you who attended which schools.' Did some of the alleged hijackers, including Atta, attend military training schools in the United States? I asked the FBI this question, but officials refused to answer. Investigative journalist Daniel Hopsicker said the wife of a former CIA pilot at the base told him:

I have a girlfriend who recognized Mohamed Atta. She met him at a party at the Officer's Club. The reason she swears it was him here is because she didn't just meet him and say hello. After she met him she went around and introduced him to the people that were with her. So she knows it was him. There were a lot of them [Saudi/Arab pilots] living in an upscale complex in Montgomery. They had to get all of them out of there. They were all gone the day after the attack.

The *Los Angeles Times* quoted a 'defense official' as saying that two of the hijackers were former Saudi fighter pilots who had attended two prominent US military programmes, the Defense Language School at Lackland Air Force Base, Texas, and the Air Force's Air War College at Maxwell Air Force Base, Alabama. There were and are extremely close connections between the US and Saudi military. The United States Military Training Mission operated – and still does – a joint training mission under the command of United States Central Command at MacDill Air Force Base in Florida. Could some of these alleged 'hijackers' have been trained by the United States? There is certainly a massive Saudi connection to the 9/11 official story and Michael Springman, former head of the American visa bureau in Jeddah from 1987 to 1989, told the BBC *Newsnight* programme:

In Saudi Arabia I was repeatedly ordered by high level State Department officials to issue visas to unqualified applicants. These were, essentially, people who had no ties either to Saudi Arabia or to their own country. I complained bitterly at the time there. I returned to the US, I complained to the State Department here, to the General Accounting Office, to the Bureau of Diplomatic Security and to the Inspector General's office. I was met with silence.

The BBC also quoted 'a highly placed source in a US intelligence agency' as saying there had always been 'constraints' on investigating Saudis and that under President George W. Bush it had become much worse. Patsies from military and intelligence backgrounds taking the blame for a much wider plot are numerous and this could well have been the case with the American 'Atta' or 'Attas'. The Kennedy assassination was blamed on US-trained CIA operative Lee Harvey Oswald and the Oklahoma bombing patsy was highly-trained US soldier Timothy McVeigh. 'Middle Eastern men' could easily have been recruited from the thousands of Iraqi Republican Guard officers who were relocated to the United States – Oklahoma in particular – by Father George Bush after the 1991 Gulf War. Operatives from nations with 'Middle Eastern' features can be trained and directed to work on Problem-Reaction-Solution scenarios and unknowing witnesses report seeing 'Middle Eastern men' at relevant places at relevant times. 'See – it was Islamic terrorists!' Al Martin, a retired US Navy Lieutenant Commander, said that one of the Iranians involved in the bombing of the World Trade Center in 1993 was trained at the Redstone Arsenal in Huntsville, Alabama, and completed an explosives course in the guise of a Pakistani officer. Not just anyone can qualify to attend these US military training schools. You need connections with foreign governments 'friendly' with the United States – governments like Saudi Araba, Egypt etc., – in league with Hidden Hand elements that control the United States. Foreign nationals who are accepted for military training in the United States are not squaddies, foot soldiers or guys off the street and nor could Atta have been if he did attend such a school at Maxwell. A former Navy pilot at the Pensacola base in Florida said in the *Newsweek* article:

We always, always, always trained other countries' pilots. When I was there two decades ago, it was Iranians. The Shah was in power. Whoever the country du jour is, that's whose pilots we train.

The American military's country of choice for such trainees in the 1990s turns out to be ... *Saudi Arabia* – a country that weaves through the 9/11 narrative while never having consequences for that. We will see in due course that the inner core elites of the United States, Saudi Arabia and Israel are all on the same side and form *one* elite. The way the world is truly controlled, directed and manipulated cannot be understood while perceiving divisions of country borders, race, culture or apparent religion. Those are there to keep the little people in line and fighting each other while the Hidden Hand and The Web operate beyond them in common cause to the same common outcome of global dictatorship. Many connections between Saudis and 9/11 players and families have already been highlighted. Father Bush's Carlyle Group were 'advisers' to the Saudi royal family and controlled them, according to insiders. The Saudi Arabian Bin Laden family were investors in the Carlyle Group and Boy George's Arbusto Energy. At least eleven members of the family (some report more) were allowed to fly home in a 747 from Boston Logan Airport after the 9/11 attacks while all non-military aircraft were grounded. Who would soon be named as the overseer (patsy) of the attacks? Osama bin Laden. Bush family Saudi associate Khalid bin Mahfouz was a major player in the Bank of Credit and Commerce International (BCCI) through which drug money was laundered, weapons trafficked, terrorism supported, including 'al-Qaeda', and off-the-books intelligence operations funded. Jackson Stephens, another BCCI player and close friend and funder of the Bush family, had a liking for the little city of Venice in Florida where the flight schools were located. The overwhelming majority of those named as 'hijackers' were Saudi nationals and even Atta, an Egyptian, was reported to have a Saudi passport. Men with the same name as some alleged hijackers, including Atta, attended US military training schools at secure bases in the 1990s at the time when Saudi Arabia was the country of choice for such training.

Able Danger

Army reserve Lieutenant Colonel Anthony Shaffer who worked for the Defense Intelligence Agency (DIA) revealed how a classified military operation called Able Danger had identified Mohamed Atta and 'al-Qaeda cells' in the United States more than a year before the attacks. Able Danger was a joint project between the DIA and the Pentagon's Special Operations Command (SOCOM) and was established in 1999 on the orders of the Pentagon Joint Chiefs of Staff then headed by Chairman Hugh Shelton who was on a plane mid-Atlantic during the 9/11 attacks and replaced by General Richard Myers. The goal of Able Danger was said to be 'developing targeting information for al-Qaeda on a global scale'. They should have just called the *creators* of al-Qaeda at the CIA and other levels of the Pentagon and saved themselves a lot of work. Anyway, Shaffer said that the Pentagon's Special Operations Command intervened to stop Able Danger operatives from telling the FBI what they knew and no action was taken against 'Atta and the cells'. Shaffer said that when he leaked the information to the FBI and demanded the arrest of Atta the alleged 9/11 'terrorist ringleader' was protected by Pentagon lawyers who stepped in and blocked any response by the FBI. Why on earth would a Pentagon operation that was told about Atta and 'al-Qaeda cells' a year before the attacks want to stop action being taken against them? Why did the official 9/11 Commission report omit to mention Able Danger and this blocking of FBI intervention when Lieutenant Colonel Shaffer said that he told Commission Executive Director Philip Zelikow all about what happened? Who was 'Mohamed Atta' *really?* Insider attacks like 9/11 are orchestrated by a fiercely compartmentalised Hidden Hand structure with on one side those organising the event and developing the cover story to blame the wrong people and on the other genuine people in law enforcement and intelligence that want to stop such attacks happening. Positions of power are secured by the Hidden Hand group to plan, prepare and carry out attacks or whatever Problem-Reaction-Solution scenario it might be. When genuine law enforcement/intelligence operatives begin to uncover the plot believing it to be an external plot, in this case from 'al-Qaeda', the same positions of power step in and stop the investigation or actions that would expose the conspiracy and stop it happening. Genuine officers are then bewildered at why their power hierarchy stops them doing their job – why would they do that? They do it because it protects the assets and patsies playing out the cover story that will later be sold to the public and media (easy) and divert attention from the real perpetrators. There is considerable evidence that not only Atta but others named in the cover story were protected so what happened *could* happen. Very few people need to be in on these plots and manipulations so long as they control decision-making positions that can take action to advance the plan and stop action that would expose it. I am not only talking about Hidden Hand networks in America here, but also the global reach – especially in the United States – of Israeli intelligence arm Mossad. I'll have *much* more about its involvement later on.

Expert scepticism

Former German Defence Minister Andreas von Bulow told me that the CIA, German intelligence and Mossad are extremely closely connected and the same certainly goes for British intelligence. Were Atta and company knowingly or unknowingly constructing the cover story, but never boarded the planes? Were they set up to be in the wrong place at the wrong time? Are these stories of the 'hijackers' trained at US military establishments simply a diversion? Any of these situations is possible. In fact, the one story that is truly *im*possible is the one told by the FBI and the American government. Von Bulow was German Minister of Defence and Minister for Research and Technology in the government of German

Chancellor Helmut Schmidt and he wrote a book, *Im Namen des Staates (In the Name of the State)*, which used his knowledge and experience of government investigations to expose the methods employed by intelligence agencies. He said that the official version of what happened on 9/11 is ridiculous and that 95 percent of the work of intelligence agencies is deception and disinformation communicated through the mass media to create an acceptable 'virtual' version of events. Von Bulow should know. He was a member of a parliamentary commission responsible for oversight of the Germany Secret Service. He told *Der Tagesspiegel* that the planning of the 9/11 attacks was technically and organisationally a master achievement. To hijack four huge airplanes within a few minutes and within one hour to drive them into their targets with complicated flight manoeuvres was unthinkable without years of support from 'secret apparatuses of the state and industry'. He said there were 26 intelligence services in the United States with a budget then of $30 billion – more than the German defence budget – and yet they were not able to prevent the attacks and 'for 60 decisive minutes the military and intelligence services let fighter planes stay on the ground'. Then within 48 hours 'the FBI had presented a list of suicide attackers, seven of which turned out to be alive'. Von Bulow went on:

> If this Atta was the decisive man in the operation, it's really strange that he took such a risk of taking a plane that would reach Boston such a short time before the connecting flight. Had his flight been a few minutes late, he would not have been in the plane that was hijacked. Why should a sophisticated terrorist do this? One can, by the way, read on CNN (Internet) that none of these names were on the official passenger lists. None of them had gone through the check-in procedures. And why did none of the threatened pilots give the agreed-upon hijack code over the transponder to the ground station?

> In addition: The black boxes which are fire and shock proof, as well as the voice recordings, contain no valuable data ... [and] ... assailants ... in their preparations, leave tracks behind them like a herd of stampeding elephants. They made payments with credit cards with their own names; they reported to their flight instructors with their own names. They left behind rented cars with flight manuals in Arabic ... They took with them, on their suicide trip, wills and farewell letters, which fall into the hands of the FBI, because they were stored in the wrong place and wrongly addressed. Clues were left behind like in a child's game of hide-and-seek, which were to be followed!

Researcher Christopher Bollyn, who has been on the case of 9/11 from day one, writes that Von Bulow told him he believed that Israel intelligence was involved in the form of Mossad to demonise Arabs in the public mind. I agree and I'll be coming to that. Eckehardt

Werthebach, former chief of German domestic intelligence, said that a major intelligence agency had to be involved and the attacks could have required years of planning. Werthebach told *American Free Press* that the magnitude of the planning and the 'deathly precision' could not have been achieved without support from a state intelligence organisation and could not have been the work of a 'loose group' of terrorists by themselves. He said the lack of prior warning would also indicate intelligence agency involvement. Horst Ehmke, who supervised German intelligence in the 1970s, said the same – an intelligence organisation had to be involved. He said the events of September 11th looked like a 'Hollywood production'.

This is precisely what it was – a deadly production for nearly 3,000 people – and there certainly was an intelligence agency involved ... in fact *more* than one.

CHAPTER 9

Searching the maze
(with smoke and mirrors)

The elementary principle of all deception is to attract the enemy's attention to what you wish him to see, and to distract his attention from what you do not wish him to see – General Sir Archibald Wavell, Memorandum to the British Chiefs of Staff, 1940

If you know about Operation Northwoods you know basically what happened on 9/11. This Pentagon document from 1962 includes all the major elements of the colossal scam and hoax that played out on live television 40 years later.

People need to know before I come to Northwoods that there are two levels of technology as there are two levels of knowledge: One for the Hidden Hand and the other for the public. Whatever appears to be the technological cutting edge to the public gaze is light years behind what is possible in the shadows. This is how it was in 2001 and remains so today. As technological possibility advances in the world of the seen so it advances still faster in the world of the unseen. The often chasm of difference is widely exploited to make something happen with secret technology and when researchers seek to expose what happened and how it was done they are met with – 'That's ridiculous, it's not possible.' Not with technology we know about, maybe, but that is not the limit of the Hidden Hand which, by definition, keeps its activities and potential *hidden*. Much of what is now called technologically-advanced was being used in the shadows decades and more ago and when you look at publicly-known technology today what on earth is possible away from public sight? If you read *Everything You Need To Know But Have Never Been Told* you will get an idea. At least some of the 'flying saucers' or UFOs that people report are flown by humans from secret projects and underground bases that even US presidents are not allowed to know about. They are flown with anti-gravity technology that the elite have been working with for decades. You want a fake 'alien invasion' to secure an outcome? 'Okay, sergeant – scramble the fleet!' Presidents and prime ministers don't run countries – the inner core of the military-intelligence-industrial complex does. The rest is window-dressing to make the population believe they have choice and freedom.

A front-line Pentagon vehicle for developing this secret beyond-the-cutting-edge technology is the Defense Advanced Research Projects Agency (DARPA) which was established under another name by President Eisenhower in 1958. This truly despicable organisation makes lovely contributions to human society such as death rays, soldiers controlled by artificial intelligence (AI) and ever more sophisticated ways to kill as many people as possible without damaging the architecture. DARPA was behind the technology that became the Internet and is the real power behind major search engines, social media platforms and AI developments in Silicon Valley or what I call the Devil's Playground (see again *Everything You Need To Know But Have Never Been Told*). Well, on one level it is. Silicon Valley is actually controlled by something much deeper in the rabbit hole beyond DARPA as I will be revealing. DARPA's work in seed-funding and overseeing technologies to advance the Hidden Hand agenda is supported by the CIA and its technology development operation In-Q-Tel. The 'Q' is a reference to the 'Q' character in the James Bond films who provides Bond with his amazing gadgetry. These organisations – and others – develop technological capability that the public dismiss as a sci-fi fantasy when it actually exists. Technology frontrunner Amazon was created to control the American and then global retail market and monopolise book circulation to ensure its pivot role as the censor of books the Hidden Hand doesn't want people to see – just like the Nazis did. Amazon, however, goes much deeper in its relevance to the Hidden Hand than that. The grandfather of Amazon multi-billionaire Jeff Bezos, from whom he says he learned 'business skills', worked for the Pentagon's Advanced Research Projects Agency, or ARPA, which was renamed DARPA – creator of what became the Internet. Today Bezos and Amazon have phenomenal contracts and connections with the Pentagon and the CIA to provide 'cloud services'. It's all smoke and mirrors, wheels within wheels. I wonder where all the personal information accumulated by the Amazon Echo ends up? I can't think.

Operation Northwoods

We can see an example of this development of secret military-Hidden Hand technology with Operation Northwoods in which the Joint Chiefs of Staff in the Pentagon (supported by the US intelligence networks) planned to use a pilotless aircraft flown from the ground to create the illusion of an attack by Cuba to justify an invasion of that country to remove its leader Fidel Castro. In the wake of 9/11 Boy Bush called for a system to be developed that would allow controllers on the ground to assume remote control of a hijacked aircraft and direct it to a safe landing at the nearest airport. *The New York Times* quoted him as saying that the new technology 'probably far in the future' would allow air traffic controllers to land distressed planes by remote control. This was a gross misrepresentation of the truth. I have pointed out many times in my books and talks how Hidden Hand operatives speak to each other during public speeches and announcements in code that only they understand. Language and statement reversal is one technique where you say the opposite of what is true and those who know the system will simply reverse what you say. Streetwise members of the public always do this with politicians. In this instance the 'we must develop remote control technology' could easily mean in the hidden code of language reversal that 'we already have remote control technology' with all the implications to a Web insider of how 9/11 was pulled off. The statement was also a diversion from any questions about the planes being remotely controlled by emphasising that this was not technologically possible at the time – when it *was*. How could Bush credibly say that such technology was 'probably far in the future' when the existence of remotely-controlled aircraft had been in existence for at least 40 years? A few weeks after 9/11 remotely-controlled aircraft were being flown over Afghanistan under the term 'surveillance drones'.

The Operation Northwood documents were appropriately first made public in 1997 by the John F. Kennedy Assassination Records Review Board. Kennedy's assassination was another military-intelligence 'Deep State' hit. A more complete version of Northwoods was posted online by the National Security Archive on April 30th, 2001, only five months before the same script was delivered on 9/11. The contents came to wider public attention with the publication in late April, 2001, of a book by James Bamford, a former Washington Investigative Producer for *World News Tonight* on ABC Television. The book was called *Body of Secrets* and revealed from official government archives the Northwoods plot hatched by America's top military leaders to commit acts of terrorism in US cities, kill civilians and blame it all on Cuban president, Fidel Castro. This plan was devised by the Pentagon Joint Chiefs of Staff under their chairman, Army General Lyman L. Lemnitzer, after President Dwight Eisenhower, who preceded Kennedy, had earlier asked the CIA to produce a plan that would create an excuse for the invasion of Cuba. Latter-day Joint Chiefs were in the Pentagon Command Center orchestrating events on 9/11 (or at least allowing them to happen). Operation Northwoods was designed to win public and international support for an invasion of Cuba that would remove Castro while the September 11th attacks were engineered to justify an Orwellian state and the 'war on terror' which has devastated the Middle East and elsewhere. James Bamford was researching the National Security Agency (NSA) when he came across official documents detailing the Northwoods operation. They revealed plans to blow up an American ship and blame Cuba and they say: '... Casualty lists in US newspapers would cause a helpful wave of national indignation.' I emphasis again that to understand those behind these plans and what happened on 9/11 it is vital to appreciate that we are dealing with mentally-deranged psychopaths that should be in a very secure psychiatric hospital and not in the Pentagon or White House. The Joint Chiefs also proposed to kill astronaut John Glenn during the first attempt to put an American into orbit and blame that on Cuba, the documents reveal. If Glenn's rocket exploded 'the objective is to provide irrevocable proof ... that the fault lies with ... Communist ... Cuba', say the Northwood documents. James Bamford wrote:

> ... the plan, which had the written approval of the Chairman and every member of the Joint Chiefs of Staff, called for innocent people to be shot on American streets; for boats carrying refugees fleeing Cuba to be sunk on the high seas; for a wave of violent terrorism to be launched in Washington DC, Miami, and elsewhere.

> People would be framed for bombings they did not commit; planes would be hijacked. Using phoney evidence, all of it would be blamed on Castro, thus giving Lemnitzer and his cabal the excuse, as well as the public and international backing, they needed to launch their war.

The plan was to stir up so much hatred for Cuba in the United States (see Muslims post-9/11) that the people would support an invasion and even demand that it was done. They intended to explode plastic bombs, arrest Cuban agents and release previously prepared documents falsely substantiating Cuban involvement. The plan included attacks on the now infamous US base at Guantanamo Bay in Cuba where, since the invasion of Afghanistan, the 'Land of Freedom' has detained untried and uncharged 'terrorists' in disgraceful, inhuman, conditions and despite the promises of the mega-fraud Barack Obama the evil of Guantanamo continues to this day. Planned Northwoods attacks on the base would be blamed, once again, on Castro and the documents speak of 'a series of well-coordinated incidents ... in and around Guantanamo to give the genuine appearance of being done by hostile Cuban forces'. A Memorandum of July 27th, 1962, says that the operation would mean an enormous increase in Cuban and American casualties. The techniques to be used included:

Starting rumours; using clandestine radio; landing friendly Cubans in uniform 'over the fence' to stage 'attacks' on the base; capturing (friendly) Cuban 'saboteurs' inside the base; starting riots near the base main gate using friendly Cubans; blowing up ammunition inside the base and starting fires; burning aircraft on the base and blaming Cuba; throwing mortar shells into the base; capturing assault teams approaching from the sea or Guantanamo City; capturing a militia group which storms the base to sabotage a ship in harbour; sinking a ship near the harbour entrance; blowing up an unmanned vessel in Cuban water and blaming it on Cuban aircraft that would naturally come and investigate what had happened; issue false casualty lists to the US media to whip up public opinion against Cuba; and, look at this ...'conduct funerals for mock victims'.

You can see now the origins of fake terrorist attacks (fake in the sense that those blamed didn't do them) and 'chemical attacks by President Assad' in Syria which have been really carried out by US/UK/NATO proxy terrorists or are 100 percent staged for the cameras with no chemicals involved at all. Even mainstream media 'journalists' have had to admit long after the event that chemical attacks in the Damascus suburb of Douma blamed on Assad were staged by Western-backed anti-Assad 'activist groups' and the terrorist front known as the White Helmets: Problem-Reaction-Solution. Wars can be started in this way – see the Gulf of Tonkin [non]-'incident' and what followed in Vietnam. Northwoods documents call for the use of Soviet Union MIG-type look-alike aircraft flown by US pilots to harass civil aircraft, attack surface shipping and destroy US military remotely-controlled drone aircraft to give the impression it was all done by Cuba. 'An F-86 properly painted would convince air passengers that they saw a Cuban MIG ...' one document says. It was further planned to stage the mock shooting-down of a US Air Force plane in international waters by simply getting the pilot, using a made-up name, to report that he was under attack and stop transmitting. He would then fly back to his base where the plane would be repainted with a new tail number and the pilot would resume his real name. A US submarine would send aircraft to search for planted wreckage in the sea and this would be found to confirm the 'Cuban' attack. Bamford said the plans for these terrorist acts against American targets had the written approval of all the Joint Chiefs of Staff and were presented to President Kennedy in March, 1962, by Defense Secretary Robert McNamara. Eventually, the 'civilian leadership' rejected them and three days later Kennedy told Lemnitzer there was virtually no chance of ever using overt force to take Cuba. Operation Northwoods remained secret for four decades until these documents came to light and they mirror what really happened on 9/11 – and since. Bamford told his former employers at *ABC News*:

These were Joint Chiefs of Staff documents. The reason these were held secret for so long is the Joint Chiefs never wanted to give these up because they were so embarrassing. The whole point of a democracy is to have leaders responding to the public will, and here this is the complete reverse, the military trying to trick the American people into a war that they want, but that nobody else wants.

Bamford revealed the Northwoods plan to the mainstream media, but when Northwoods Mark 2 came along weeks later with 9/11 that same media believed and promoted every word of the government narrative and have done so ever since. Even more than that they condemn and dismiss all those who asked questions about the government's fairy story as 'conspiracy theorists'. Had the same excuses-for-'journalists' been around in 1962 and had the Northwoods plan gone ahead they would have done precisely the same. Bamford writes that even after the original plans were rejected others continued to be developed, such as creating a war between Cuba and another Latin American country to allow the US to intervene. The highest levels of the military and intelligence plan these Problem-Reaction-Solution operations and they connect into organisations like the National Security Agency (NSA) and CIA along with overseas assets of the Hidden Hand such as British intelligence and Israel's Mossad. It is no good people claiming their leaders could not have been behind the horrors of 9/11 when the documents exist to show that the Pentagon had planned in detail something so very similar in the 1960s. The good news is that Kennedy blocked the execution of Operation Northwoods and sacked Chiefs of Staff chairman Lemnitzer. The bad news is that he was then appointed *Supreme Allied Commander of NATO*.

2001 in 1962

The most profound point about Northwoods in relation to 9/11 was the plan to *hijack civilian aircraft*, land them at an Air Force base and *replace them with pilotless drones* that would then be shot down and the attack blamed on Cuba. Northwoods documents say it was possible to create an incident that would convince the public that a Cuban aircraft had shot down a chartered civil airliner on a flight from the United States to Jamaica, Guatemala, Venezuela or Panama. The destination would be chosen so the route would cross Cuba. The 'real' plane (actually a CIA aircraft) would carry 'selected' passengers boarded under 'carefully prepared aliases' and take off from a civilian airport. It would be replaced in the sky south of Florida with a *remotely-controlled* aircraft and this would then be flown over Cuba, send out a distress signal, and be destroyed by radio signal. The original plane would be landed at an Air Force base where the make-believe 'passengers' would get off. All this was planned *40 years* before 9/11. Imagine what the remote-control technology was like by comparison in 2001? Bamford quotes from the Northwoods documents in *Body of Secrets*:

> An aircraft at Eglin AFB would be painted and numbered as an exact duplicate for a civil registered aircraft belonging to a CIA proprietary organization in the Miami area. At a designated time the duplicate would be substituted for the actual civil aircraft and would be loaded with the selected passengers, all boarded under carefully prepared aliases. The actual registered aircraft would be converted into a [remote-controlled] drone. Take off times of the drone aircraft and the actual aircraft will be scheduled to allow a rendezvous south of Florida.
>
> From the rendezvous point the passenger-carrying aircraft will descend to minimum altitude and go directly into an auxiliary field at Eglin AFB where arrangements will have been made to evacuate the passengers and return the aircraft to its original status. The drone aircraft meanwhile will continue to fly the filed flight plan. When over Cuba the drone will be transmitting on the international distress frequency a 'May Day' message stating he is under attack by Cuban MiG aircraft. The transmission will be interrupted by destruction of the aircraft, which will be triggered by radio signal. This will allow ICAO [International Civil Aviation Organisation] radio stations in the Western Hemisphere to tell the US what has happened to the aircraft instead of the US trying to 'sell' the incident.

I have said for many years that the staged 'hijacking' of planes and their remotely-controlled replacements planned by Operation Northwoods were eventually carried out on the day known forever as 9/11. I say the planes that left the airports were taken over in-flight from the ground and were not the planes that hit the buildings. I will outline detailed evidence to support that view as we go along. I emphasise that not only was remote-control possible in 2001 the technology had been around since at least 1962 when Northwoods planned to use it. In fact remote-control had been available to the military since the 1950s.

No pilot necessary

I wrote in *Alice in Wonderland*, published in 2002, that a US Air Force fact sheet available to anyone on the Internet at the time of 9/11 detailed the capabilities and background of a remotely-controlled aircraft technology called Global Hawk. This was an Unmanned Aerial Vehicle (UAV) providing Air Force battlefield commanders with near real-time, high-resolution, intelligence, surveillance and reconnaissance imagery flying at extremely high altitudes to survey large areas with pinpoint accuracy (Fig 40 overleaf). The fact sheet said that once the 'mission parameters' were programmed into Global Hawk the aircraft could 'autonomously

Figure 40: Global Hawk remotely-controlled aircraft technology was being used by the military in 2001.

taxi, take off, fly, remain on station capturing imagery, return and land'. Operators on the ground could alter flying instructions during flight as necessary. *Airman* magazine summarised the control systems of the Global Hawk:

The bird's 'pilots' stay on the ground. Its flight control, navigation and vehicle management are independent and based on a mission plan. That means the airplane flies itself – there's no pilot on the ground with a joystick manoeuvring it around. However, it does get instructions from airmen at ground stations. The launch and recovery element provides precision guidance for take-off and landing, using a differential global positioning system. That team works from the plane's operating base.

Such technology is commonplace today, but the point is that it was operating in the public arena in 2001 and therefore far more advanced technology was available to the Hidden Hand. The Global Hawk in service at the time of 9/11 was 44 feet long with a wingspan of 116 feet (equivalent to a Boeing 737) and a range of 12,000 nautical miles. Global Hawk could fly at up to 65,000 feet at speeds approaching about 400mph for as long as 35 hours. The plane was developed through the 1990s and the principal contractor was Hidden Hand-controlled Northrop Grumman at its Ryan Aeronautical Center, San Diego, California. Communications systems were provided by L3 Com, Salt Lake City, Utah. Global Hawk began tests and exercises in 1999 sponsored by US Joint Forces Command. Boy Bush-appointed James Roche, who was US Secretary of the Air Force in 2001, held many executive posts with Northrop Grumman. These included corporate vice president and president, Electronic Sensors and Systems Sector, before leaving to join the Bush administration. Roche was a member of the Hidden Hand's Council on Foreign Relations and Center for Strategic Studies and responsible for Air Force 'functioning and efficiency ... formulation of ... policies and programs' and those responsibilities encompassed NORAD. Colonel Wayne M. Johnson became manager of the Global Hawk Programme at the Reconnaissance Systems Program Office, Aeronautical Systems Center at Wright-Patterson Air Force Base at Dayton, Ohio, which assumed total programme control on October 1st, 1998. This is about 200 miles by road from where Flight 93 was 'hijacked' and turned around. A Global Hawk deployed to Eglin Air Force Base in Florida (where the Operation Northwoods drone was planned to take-off) was flown across the Atlantic to Europe by remote control to take part in NATO exercises. In April, 2001, the pilotless aircraft was flown non-stop the 7,500 miles across the Pacific from the Edwards Air Force Base in California to the Royal Australian Air Force Base at Edinburgh, South Australia. This set (officially) new world records for remote-controlled aircraft. Global Hawk was also deployed in the grotesquely-named Operation Enduring Freedom which after a translation from the Orwellian meant the mass murder of civilians in Afghanistan justified by 9/11. The Predator, another remotely controlled aircraft capable of reaching 25,000 feet, was deployed to Afghanistan and had seen action in the former Yugoslavia. Technology to remotely-control planes from the ground as per Operation Northwoods was far more advanced by 2001 and NORAD, so central to what happened on 9/11, had been using remote-control capability in many different aircraft over more than 40 years. An article by Alan Staats published in *Quill* magazine in 1998 detailed the history and development of remote control technology. Staats writes:

> Controlling the aircraft from the ground is nothing new. The military has been flying obsolete high performance fighter aircraft as target drones since the 1950s. In fact, NORAD (the North American Air Defense Command) had at its disposal a number of US Air Force General Dynamics F-106 Delta Dart fighter aircraft configured to be remotely flown into combat as early as 1959 under the auspices of a program known as SAGE. These aircraft could be started, taxied, taken off, flown into combat, fight, and return to a landing entirely by remote control, with the only human intervention needed being to fuel and re-arm them. To this day, drone aircraft are remotely flown from Air Force and Naval bases all over the country to provide targets for both airborne and ground based weapons platforms.

Staats goes on to say that the technology existed (writing in 1998) that would allow a ground crew to override and direct the flight path of a hijacked plane and that *the military has employed this capability since the 1950s*. So much for Bush and his claim that remote-control from the ground was 'probably far in the future' and as someone who flew with the Texas National Guard to avoid the draft to Vietnam he did not have the excuse of ignorance (for once) for this pathetic misdirection. Staats wrote three years before 9/11 that from an engineering point of view modifying and implementing the technology for use on passenger-carrying aircraft in the United States to fly them and land them by remote control *'is a relatively simple matter'*. He said 'autoland' systems had been in wide commercial use in different parts of the world since the 1980s. Auto landings were routinely performed thousands of times a day throughout the world and Staats continued:

> It is technically possible to create a system to perform remotely commanded return flights of a hijacked airliner. On-board digital command, control and display equipment can easily share data with, and accept commands from, ground control stations. Little input beyond the initial command to enter safe return flight and the ultimate destination are needed.

Commercial aircraft are largely flown by computers today and the pilot can have comparitively little to do with the actual flying once it's off the ground and programmed with a route to follow. In 2001 a flight plan agreed with the FAA, or its equivalent around the world, was entered into the aircraft computer system or Flight Management System (FMS). This could be done through direct programming or a disc. The flight programme included the planned height and speed throughout the flight as it travelled between points in the sky known as waypoints. When the plane had taken off it aimed for the first waypoint and the computer would execute changes to head for the next point and so on to its destination. The system is highly-advanced today and the point I am making is that it was happening in 2001. Alan Staats wrote three years earlier:

> Because all the components of controlling the aircraft communicate with each other digitally through a central unit, the FMS, activating such a 'safe return' system would be a matter of uploading commands to the FMS to fly the aircraft to the nearest airport. Controlling the aircraft's speed, altitude and course, the FMS would guide it back to land.

In other words to remotely-control any commercial airliner at the time of 9/11 all you needed to do was get control of the Flight Management System (FMS) computers and override the ability of pilots to have an input. Do that and you could fly a plane wherever you like with the pilots in the cockpit unable to do anything about it. You could also turn the transponder off and control the entire system, including blocking the pilot's ability to send the normal hijacking alarm code which, remarkably, none of the pilots on September 11th managed to do. But there's more – the very act of hacking the flight computers could *automatically turn off the transponder.* I'll have more about this shortly.

Remote-control and DARPA

Staats said that the data links to remotely-control digital airborne flight control systems in commercial aircraft was already widely used in 1998. They were called ACARS (Aircraft Communications Addressing and

Reporting System) and these communicated a long list of data including position, fuel consumption, weather and flight plan information to ground stations. ACARS also has the ability to send data to the aircraft from the ground. Staats said that this link allowed 'both uploading digital control inputs to control the aircraft as well as the potential to download and remotely monitor the digital aircraft displays'. These are only technological possibilities before 9/11 that were known in the public arena – the military's capability would have been far in advance of this. If you look at what is publicly possible *today* you can get a feel for what the military could do then. Stanley Hilton, the lawyer who filed a lawsuit against Bush and associates over 9/11, told me he had spoken with a mechanic with United Airlines who personally worked on this remote-control system of taking over aircraft from the ground. If you can fly a plane from America to Australia and back without a pilot you will have no trouble directing one into the World Trade Center. Australia-based investigator Joe Vialls wrote in the wake of 9/11 about the connection to the Pentagon's technology-development arm, DARPA:

> In the mid-seventies ... two American multinationals collaborated with the Defense Advanced Projects Agency (DARPA) on a project designed to facilitate the remote recovery of hijacked American aircraft. [This] ... allowed specialist ground controllers to ... take absolute control of [a hijacked aircraft's] computerized flight control system by remote means. From that point onwards, regardless of the wishes of the hijackers or flight deck crew, the hijacked aircraft could be recovered and landed automatically at an airport of choice, with no more difficulty than flying a radio-controlled model plane ... [This was] the system used to facilitate direct ground control of the four aircraft used in the high-profile attacks on New York and Washington on 11th September 2001.

Vialls referred to the technology as 'Home Run' and said that top-secret computer codes were hacked on 9/11 to allow control of the planes from the ground:

> In order to make Home Run truly effective, it had to be completely integrated with all on-board systems, and this could only be accomplished with a new aircraft design, several of which were on the drawing boards at that time. Under cover of extreme secrecy, the multinationals and DARPA went ahead on this basis and built 'back doors' into the new computer designs. There were two very obvious hard requirements at this stage, the first a primary control channel for use in taking over the flight control system and flying the aircraft back to an airfield of choice, and secondly a covert audio channel for monitoring flight deck conversations. Once the primary channel was activated, all aircraft functions came under direct ground control, permanently

removing the hijackers and pilots from the control loop.

The term 'back-doors' into computer systems is going to be crucial to understanding 9/11 and current world events before the end of the book. Vialls said the system began with the best of intentions – to save lives – but 'finally fell prey to security leaks, and eventually to compromised computer codes'. My own view is that it was originally sold under the guise of saving lives with a very different agenda going on higher up. Vialls said the technology 'piggy-backs' on the plane's transponder and this is why the pilots were unable to send the hijack code from any of the many activation points on the aircraft. The 'takeover' technology locked into the frequency of the transponder's communication channel overriding its use by the pilot and no hijack code was sent because before the pilot realises there is a problem the channels are down through which communication with air traffic control can be made. This has been confirmed by many aeronautical sources and this would be one explanation for why transponder transmissions went down. Hidden Hand hackers on the ground were using transponder channels to make a connection with the plane's computers. It should be mentioned, however, that the official story has some transponders turned off some time after the planes began to act strangely, but we shall be exploring how accurate that flight path information really is. Joe Vialls said that the cockpit listening capability of 'Home Run' technology intercepted microphones in the cockpit which normally feed the pilots' conversations to the Cockpit Voice Recorder (CVR) in the black box. The CVR would therefore be blank because microphones would have been de-activated once remote control took over. He claimed that German national airline Lufthansa removed 'Home Run' technology:

> As long ago as the early nineties, a major European flag carrier [Lufthansa] acquired the information and was seriously alarmed that one of its own aircraft might be 'rescued' by the Americans without its authority. Accordingly, this flag carrier completely stripped the American flight control computers out of its entire fleet, and replaced them with a home grown version. These aircraft are now effectively impregnable to penetration by Home Run, but that is more than can be said for the American aircraft fleet.

Brian Desborough, an American scientist/engineer who worked for Boeing and a conspiracy researcher since the 1960s, told me after 9/11:

> Unlike earlier airliners such as the Boeing 747, which are equipped with conventional hydraulically-operated flight controls, the Boeing 757 and 767 aircraft that were involved in the 9/11 incidents, and the Airbus 300 which

crashed at Queens [New York], have fly-by-wire flight control systems as a weight-saving measure. These aircraft types are equipped with a special black box that was developed by the US Department of Defense Research Agency, DARPA. If terrorists attempt to hijack a fly-by-wire aircraft and deviate off course, the black box prevents whoever is piloting the aircraft from sending flight commands to the flight control surfaces and engines. Instead, the aircraft is remotely flown from a land-based covert Federal facility.

In all probability, a Global Hawk remote surveillance aircraft was circling at 60,000 feet over New York on 9/11 in order to provide the ground command center a real time image of the aircraft. At 60,000 feet, the surveillance aircraft would be invisible to people on the ground. I'm aware of a very covert research company in California engaged in the development of advanced engines for tanks. A remote surveillance plane circles overhead every day as a security measure, yet is invisible from the ground.

So it was possible to take control of those planes from the ground on September 11th and fly them wherever the controllers wanted them to go. Does this not make more sense than incompetent Dumb and Dumber pilots who had struggled to fly a Cessna at American flying schools? Also, looking at this in another way, if these planes did have 'anti-hijack' remote control technology why were they allowed to crash as claimed? Why were they not landed safely?

Missing evidence (a common theme)

Clearly there's something seriously wrong with the official narrative wherever you look. Still, no problem, no worries. What happened on those four flights and who was in the cockpits can be revealed by the information secured by their black boxes (orange, not actually black). Aircraft have two black boxes: The Flight Data Recorder (FDR) which records the plane's speed, height, course and mechanical operation; and the Cockpit Voice Recorder (CVR) which retains at least the last 30 minutes of cockpit conversations and activity. Black boxes are designed to survive fantastic impact and heat, but even with two in each plane we are told that those in the World Trade Center aircraft did not survive and were lost while the Cockpit Voice Recorder was destroyed in 'Flight 77'. Information allegedly gleaned from flight data black boxes for 'Pentagon' Flight 77 and 'Pennsylvania' Flight 93 do not support the official story of what happened peddled by the US government as I will detail. The cockpit voice recording claimed to be from Flight 93 is also inconclusive. We will see there is no published data to show the black boxes were even from the aircraft that left the airports when it would be simple to prove if they were. The *Counterpunch* website ran a story in December, 2005, that in fact black boxes for the World Trade Center planes *were* found by firefighters and analysed by National Transport Safety Board (NTSB) air-crash investigators before being confiscated by the FBI. New York firefighter Nicholas De Masi and rescue worker Mike Bellone claimed in a 2003 book, *Behind the Scenes: Ground Zero*, to have found three of the four black boxes before January, 2002. They said federal agents took them away and told the men not to say they had found them. Nicholas De Masi has since died of 9/11-related cancer connected to toxins breathed in from the dust. Thousands of others living and working around Ground Zero that day have perished the same way and some 10,000 are estimated to have been affected by a 'cesspool of cancer' among responders and residents. A painstaking clean-up of the World Trade Center site would surely have located the black boxes at some point and they emit a location signal for some time after a crash. How is it credible to find fragments of bone and human tissue but not bright orange boxes emitting a location signal in a relatively small area when finding them would (should) have been a major priority? *Counterpunch* ran the article after they said a source at the National Transportation Safety Board told them the black boxes were recovered and analysed by staff at the NTSB. 'Off the record, we had the boxes', the source said. 'You'd have to get the official word from the FBI as to where they are, but we worked on them here.' This makes far more sense than 'they were never found'. Ted Lopatkiewicz, NTSB director of public affairs, said: 'No recorders were recovered from the World Trade Center.' But he added the rider: 'At least none were delivered to us by the FBI.' He also said it was extremely rare that boxes were not found and he could not recall another domestic case in which the recorders were not recovered. Meanwhile the FBI has officially contended the boxes were never found, but, again, spokesman Stephen Kodak added a caveat: 'To the best of my knowledge, the flight recording devices from the World Trade Center crashes were never recovered – at least we never had them.' What a strange attitude to knowing what happened to them when they should have been crucial to any investigation. *ABC News* reported on the survivability of black boxes:

Although investigators look for an entire black box, sometimes the only parts of the device that survive are the recorder's crash-survivable memory units (CSMU). The CSMU is almost indestructible. It is housed within a stainless-steel shell that contains titanium or aluminium and a high-temperature insulation of dry silica material. 'It is designed to withstand heat of up to 2,000 degrees Fahrenheit for one hour [greater on both counts than they would have experienced in the World Trade Center crashes], salt water for at least 30 days, immersion in a variety of liquids such as jet fuel and lubricants, and an impact of 3,400 Gs. By comparison, astronauts are typically exposed to up to six Gs during a shuttle take-off.

With a beacon transmitter the black boxes can be, and have been, located deep under the ocean and under piles of rubble when buildings have been struck. The *ABC News* information was confirmed by the National Transportation Safety Board (NTSB) on its official website which also said:

> Both the Flight Data Recorder and the Cockpit Voice Recorder have proven to be valuable tools in the accident investigation process. They can provide information that may be difficult to obtain by other means.

What a pity, then, that so many black boxes were 'destroyed' or 'inconclusive' from four aircraft in four separate crashes. FBI spokesman Bill Crowley said the Cockpit Voice Recorder (CVR) of Flight 93 'found at the Pennsylvania crash site' was in 'fairly good condition' and yet was sent to CVR manufacturer Honeywell for help in extracting information after officials with the National Transportation Safety Board could not get sound from the device. The 'Flight 93' CVR was alleged to have been found on September 14th some 25 feet below the 'impact crater' when the entire area had been cleared of public and media for miles around. Reports say there are no known witnesses to this 'find' and no serial number for the CVR has been published to confirm the plane to which it belonged. The FBI later claimed to have played this cockpit recording to relatives of those who died on Flight 93, but was it the real one? These questions need to be asked after the scale of lies revealed only this far. What was heard certainly appeared to be inconclusive and unclear and Deena Burnett, wife of passenger Tom Burnett, said she heard one hijacker telling another how to fly the plane and shouting that he was touching the wrong buttons. He demanded the pilot be brought back to the cockpit to turn off the alarms. Oh, a well-drilled operation, then. Hey, Abdul, what does this knob do? The tragedy is unspeakable and matched in that enormity only by the farce of the official story. I guess the 'hijackers' were supposed to be speaking in English given that Deena Burnett knew what they said and there was no transcript provided to families. Why weren't they speaking in Arabic? Two other later publicly-reported versions of the tapes contradicted each other and the version the families said they heard. Elias Davidsson notes in *Hijacking America's Mind On 9/11* that an alleged transcript of the 'Flight 93' cockpit tapes produced for the Moussaoui '20th hijacker' trial lacked the following: Date, time and location of crash; aircraft tail number; CVR serial number; name of transcript agency; names of transcribers; date of transcription; signature of the person responsible for production. All this information and more is included in normal transcriptions of CVR recordings. Every procedure considered normal and routine seems to have been ditched for anything to do with 9/11. The FBI said the voice recorder on Flight 77 'recovered' at the Pentagon could yield no information because it was too severely burned. A black box can survive heat of 2,000 degrees Fahrenheit for an hour and is located in the tail furthest away from impact. I asked the FBI at the time for details of the black boxes and their condition and I was told this information could not be given because of the 'ongoing investigation'. Every other question about the official story was met with the same response. The *Counterpunch* article rightly observed of the New York black boxes:

> Why would the main intelligence and law enforcement arm of the U.S. government want to hide from the public not just the available information about the two hijacked flights that provided the motivation and justification for the nation's 'war on terror' and for its two wars against Afghanistan and Iraq, but even the fact that it has the devices which could contain that information? Conspiracy theories abound, with some claiming the planes were actually pilotless military aircraft, or that they had little or nothing to do with the building collapses.

> The easiest way to quash such rumors and such fevered thinking would be openness. Instead we have the opposite: a dark secrecy that invites many questions regarding the potentially embarrassing or perhaps even sinister information that might be on those tapes.

Selling the impossible

I am grateful for much of the information about the aircraft background in this chapter to Pilots for 9/11 Truth. This is an organisation which has brought together a long list of professional commercial and military pilots with extensive collective experience to forensically examine the alleged aeronautical happenings on September 11th. Pilots for 9/11 Truth is one of many groups of experts in specific fields including architects and engineers, firefighters, flight controllers, doctors, academics, intelligence operatives and FBI employees who are questioning the official story of 9/11 because from their area of expertise it makes no sense to them. I am not an aviation expert or a pilot and so I will ask the questions here and highlight the anomalies that pilots – some of whom flew in the same aircraft involved in 9/11 – have asked and noted. Firstly this is the organisation's mission statement:

> Pilots for 9/11 Truth is an organization of aviation professionals and pilots throughout the globe that have gathered together for one purpose. We are committed to seeking the truth surrounding the events of the 11th of September 2001. Our main focus concentrates on the four flights, maneuvers performed and the reported pilots. We do not offer theory or point blame.

However, we are focused on determining the truth of that fateful day since the United States Government doesn't seem to be very forthcoming with answers.

Rob Balsamo, a commercial airline pilot, co-founded Pilots for 9/11 Truth with Glen Stanish, a commercial pilot with American Airlines, ATA, TWA and Continental. Balsamo became interested in 9/11 research in 2006 after watching then CNN host Glenn Beck accept without question that five frames of very dodgy footage claiming to be a plane striking the Pentagon was genuine and beyond question. 'You can see a 757 in 10 seconds flat!', the great mind that is Glenn Beck observed. 'Either that or a naked Michael Moore heading for the buffet!' Beck added that this should put all the 'conspiracy theories' to rest. Pilot Balsamo didn't see a 757 and set out to investigate unresolved questions surrounding the 9/11 attacks from an aviation perspective to see if the government narrative could be confirmed. 'I didn't want to believe our government might have had something to do with 9/11', he said. Balsamo soon had his mind blown when he came across Operation Northwoods and contrasted this with a statement by Thomas Kean, chairman of the set-up-to-fail 9/11 Commission. Kean said that 'the greatest failure of 9/11 was lack of imagination' about the possible nature of a terrorist attack which echoed claims by the military. Here was Balsamo reading about the Northwoods plan from 40 years earlier which included the themes and elements of September 11th and was compiled by the same US military that pleaded 'lack of imagination' for its failure to stop the attacks. Soon after Pilots for 9/11 Truth was established in 2006 they secured Flight Data Recorder information about 'Flight 77' which is claimed to have hit the Pentagon. Analysis revealed that the contents did not support the official story and Pilots for 9/11 Truth has grown consistently ever since with more pilots joining the group bringing with them thousands of hours of experience. All these years later Balsamo says: 'I'm frustrated because we haven't been able to find *anything* to confirm the government's story and what's worse is that the FBI and NTSB refuse to even discuss with us the many obvious problems we found in the Flight 77 Flight Data Recorder.' The FBI refuses to comment or explain? See my own experience with them and that of all other 9/11 researchers when asking the most basic questions. Pilots for 9/11 Truth say they don't publicly express their own conclusions about what happened on 9/11. They focus purely on exposing the fact that the official story surrounding the aircraft and their alleged pilots is simply not possible, or, as I would put it, a crock of shit. The organisation has produced a series of videos explaining their case which you can see at Pilotsfor911truth.org and the site includes many articles updated with new information.

Pilots against 9/11 nonsense

These are some of their findings and conclusions with regard to the planes claimed to have hit the North Tower (Flight 11) and South Tower (Flight 175) of the World Trade Center. Claims that the black boxes were never found obviously make analysis far more difficult although far from impossible. The pilots have considered, for example, radar data, information provided by the National Transportation Safety Board (NTSB) and the speeds that it claims the planes were travelling at low altitude approaching the towers. They say this makes no sense either with the structural integrity of the airframe (why it didn't fall apart?) or the ability of novice and next-to-useless small plane pilots to control a wide-bodied jet. Novice pilots on small aircraft would have had to somehow strike buildings with only a tiny margin for error – a feat that has been described by pilots as like parking your car in a one-car garage at 150 miles an hour without hitting the sides. The NTSB data claims that Flight 11 was travelling at 430 knots (about 494 mph) and Flight 175 at 510 knots (about 586 mph) which is way higher than the Boeing safety limit at those near-ground altitudes before the plane enters the zone in which structural failure becomes possible and increasingly likely the faster you go. The pilots cite the example of Egypt Air Flight 990 in 1999, a Boeing 767 which went down in the Atlantic on route from Los Angeles to Cairo via New York. The NTSB report claimed a deliberate ditching of the plane by the pilot although Egypt Air disputed this. The plane broke up on decent after breaching the Boeing safety speed limit and reached its fastest speed at about 22,000 feet when air pressure on the plane's structure is far less than it would have been for the near-ground 9/11 aircraft. There were two major fields of debris from Flight 990 indicating a break-up in the air. Black boxes and the transponder stopped transmitting seconds after the plane reached its maximum speed indicating a loss of power and communication connection. You would obviously expect this if the plane was disintegrating.

The impact on the structure is far more destructive at low altitudes where air density is much greater. Boeing therefore lists two maximum safety speeds before the structure may be compromised – VMO (Velocity Max Operating) at lower altitudes and MMO (Mach Max Operating) at higher altitudes measured in Mach. This is based on the relationship to the speed of sound in air which is termed 'Mach 1'. The VMO for a Boeing 767 is 360 knots and the MMO is Mach 0.86. There is also a third measurement known as EAS (Equivalent Air Speed) which projects the speed in MMO to what it would be in VMO, or translates Mach to knots while taking into account the very different air densities at the two altitudes. EAS is measuring the speed at near sea level that would produce the same potential structural effects experienced at higher levels. Air pressure means that the near sea level speed must necessarily be considerably less than high altitude flying. An example: 522 knots at 22,000 feet for a 767 is equivalent to just 360 knots at near sea level in terms of the structural effect on the aircraft. This is highly significant because according to data from the National Transportation Safety Board (NTSB) the 767 on Flight 175 struck the South Tower at near sea level at a speed of 510 knots. Boeing have refused to share wind-tunnel footage and information to show at what speed a 767/757 would break up and Pilots for 9/11 Truth calculated the likely speed window from the data available for Egypt Air Flight 990. NTSB official data says the Egyptian plane fell apart at .99 Mach at 22,000 feet and that speed translated to the equivalent at near sea level would be about 425 knots – 65 knots above Boeing's safe operating limit and Flight 175 was said to be doing close to 150 knots above the limit. Pilots for 9/11 Truth point out the following in the video *9/11 World Trade Center Attack*:

> According to the NTSB, Flight 175, the aircraft which allegedly struck the World Trade Center, reached a speed of 510 knots – 150 knots over its max operating and the equivalent of 85 knots [faster than] Egypt Air 990. Using Egypt Air 990 as precedent, it is impossible for the alleged Flight 175 to have reached 510 knots. Period.
>
> We now know an unmodified 767 cannot reach speeds reported for the South Tower strike but it's also impossible for Flight 175, an unmodified 767, to have continued controlled flight at 150-plus knots over its max operating limit according to precedent set by Egypt Air 990 ...

The reported speed of 'Flight 175' of 510 knots before impact is the equivalent, in terms of effect on the plane structure, of 722 knots at 22,000 feet or Mach 1.19 – *above the speed of sound or supersonic speed for a Boeing 767*. Flight 11, another 767, would also have faced 'dynamic pressure' above Mach 1 if the NTSB data is correct, the pilots' analysis concluded, although its reported speed was lower at 430 knots. Flight 77 which allegedly stuck the Pentagon would also have breached the equivalent of Mach 1. So, the pilot video asks, if these weren't stock 767/757s what were they? Were they beefed up or 'modified' to attain such incredible speed? If so, did '19 Islamic extremists' do the modifications?? The very strong possibility that someone much closer to home 'beefed up' other aircraft to replace the ones that left the airports will be considered later on. Pilots for 9/11 Truth members with vast experience, many flying 767s and 757s, are incredulous at what is claimed to have happened that day in terms of speed and other factors. United Airlines captain Ross 'Rusty' Aimer piloted the actual planes that were Flight 175 (N612UA) and Flight 93 (N591UA). He said: 'I think it's impossible to get to that kind of speed [at near sea level] on a commercial airplane – any pilot that has been in a commercial jet would probably laugh if you said 510 knots' (Fig 41). International captain Ralph Kolstad said that such speeds were 'physically impossible' – 'To come up with 510 knots is pretty insane, [it] defies all laws of physics.' Boeing spokeswoman Leslie Hazzard was asked if it was possible for a 767-200 to reach speeds of 500 miles per hour at 700 feet and she laughed as she replied: 'Not a chance – not that fast.' Dwain Deets, a retired NASA Senior Executive, published his concerns about these questions and anomalies with regard to 'Flight 175' at the American Institute of Aeronautics and Astronautics (AIAA):

Figure 41: An animation of a plane heading for the Twin Towers. Pilots say it is not possible for controlled and stable flight at the speed and altitude claimed by the official story.

> The airplane was UA175, a Boeing 767-200, shortly before crashing into World Trade Center Tower 2. Based on analysis of radar data, the National Transportation and Safety Board reported the groundspeed just before impact as 510 knots. This is well beyond the maximum operating velocity of 360 knots, and maximum dive velocity of 410 knots. The possibilities as I see them are: (1) this wasn't a standard 767-200; (2) the radar data was compromised in some manner; (3) the NTSB analysis was erroneous; or (4) the 767 flew well beyond its flight envelope, was controllable, and managed to hit a relatively small target. Which organization has the greater responsibility for acknowledging the elephant in the room? The NTSB, NASA, Boeing, or the AIAA?
>
> Have engineers authored papers, but the AIAA or NASA won't publish them? Or, does the ethical responsibility lie not with organizations, but with individual aeronautical engineers? Have engineers just looked the other way?

Even if the planes had remained intact they would have been virtually impossible to control for an experienced pilot let alone those who were supposed to be at the controls. What if the planes that struck the buildings had been modified to fly at those speeds and they didn't need the skill of an on-board pilot because they were remotely-controlled from the ground? If they were specially-designed for the job would they not also have specially-designed 'black boxes' or none at all? A simulator test based on the more manoeuvrable 737 was set up for a group of experienced pilots to see if they could have hit the World Trade Center towers at the reported speeds and none of them could do it despite multiple attempts. However, for 'hijackers' trained to fly one-engine Cessnas (some were poor pilots even at that level) could somehow pull it off. Pilots for 9/11 Truth put all these points to various agencies of government, including the National Transportation Safety Board (NTSB), but they all refused to comment – the usual story. I had a long conversation in 2002 with a German pilot who had flown commercial airliners for Lufthansa for 28 years and trained as a military pilot before that. He dismissed immediately the idea that 'hijacker-pilots' could have taken over controls of the four planes from their computer systems and flown them manually. His view would have been that they would have crashed the planes for sure long before they reached their targets such is the complex nature of modern airliners. It is this very complexity which requires that computers make the calculations, he told me. He did say, however, that hijackers would not need to know how to fly the plane to hit a target. They would only need to know how to reprogram the Flight Management System to make the computer do it for them. I take the point, but this begs more questions. If that is the way it was done why would the 'hijackers' have trained at flying schools on Cessnas and similar small planes when the Lufthansa pilot told me this would be utterly useless and irrelevant to flying a 757 or 767 and equally so for knowing how to reprogram a Flight Management System? This doesn't make sense at all. Although he said the reprogramming could be done pretty quickly by someone who knows what he's doing, Flight 175 dramatically changed course only 90 seconds to two minutes after the last communication from the real pilots with air traffic control. The 'hijackers' would have had to seize control of the cockpit, disable the pilots and reprogram the computer system in less than two minutes. This is so ridiculous it can be ruled out. By contrast if the plane's controls were suddenly taken over externally from the ground or another aircraft and all communications from the cockpit were blocked by remote-control technology these circumstances could be explained. One second you are flying a plane and talking with air traffic controllers, the next the aircraft is flying off course and when you tell air traffic control they do not respond because they can't hear you and you can't hear them.

9/11 planes have never been officially identified

This sub-heading may appear to be a fantastic statement although the whole official story depends on the fantastic and miraculous. No, it's true. The planes have not been officially and publicly identified when this could have been done quite easily. For a start the amount of wreckage against the size and content of the planes is another big question that needs addressing because 767s and 757s are big aircraft with a maximum take-off weight of 300,000 lbs and 255,000 lbs and think of all the parts that would be potential wreckage. What we have been shown is a fraction of each plane. Even with the small amount publicly recovered the confirmation that parts and debris came from the planes allegedly involved is very straight forward. All aircraft have maintenance logs and all parts have serial or part numbers (including black boxes) which can be compared with the serial numbers on the maintenance logs. Shockingly this has *never been done*. Aircraft have certain parts replaced on a time basis and if they are not replaced within that period the plane is grounded. These 'time-change' parts have serial numbers that are logged with the identification number of the aircraft and checking one against the other in the event of a crash proves the identity of the plane. Aircraft also have their own serial numbers and tail numbers to make the process of identification very simple. NTSB air crash investigators always seek to match the black box serial number with that of the doomed aircraft so why has this not happened with any of the planes alleged to have been involved on 9/11 with its national and global importance? *Why?* I suggest that this basic procedure of identification has not been done because it would reveal the truth – they were not the planes that left the airports that morning. Glen Stanish, then a 16-year member of the Air Line Pilots Association (ALPA), had flown with USAir Express, Jetstream International (later PSA Airlines), TWA, ATA and he was a First Officer with Continental Airlines. He sent a letter to ALPA with his observations about plane identity in the case of Flight 77. Stanish wrote in October, 2006:

[Flight 77] ... was reported to be a Boeing 757, registration number N644AA, carrying 64 people, including the flight crew and five hijackers. This aircraft, with a 125-foot wingspan, was reported to have crashed into the Pentagon, leaving an entry hole no more than 16 feet wide.

Following a cool-down of the resulting fire, this crash site would have been very easy to collect enough time-change equipment within 15 minutes to positively identify the aircraft registry. There was apparently some aerospace type of equipment found at the site but no attempt was made to produce serial numbers or to identify the specific parts found. Some of the equipment removed from the building was actually hidden from public view.

If an aluminum Boeing 757 had struck that fortified building, there would have been more aluminum on the ground outside than what went inside, yet there was little visible evidence of an airplane crash on the outside. What physical evidence that could have been of some value, was immediately carted away under cover ... With all the evidence readily available at the Pentagon crash site, any unbiased rational investigator could only conclude that a Boeing 757 DID NOT fly into the Pentagon as alleged.

The plane registration/tail numbers are the identity of the actual aircraft while the 9/11 Commission and media talk only of 9/11 flight numbers. These do not identify the plane – they identify the flight number of the route and time designated to the plane on that one day. Aircraft can change flight numbers on the same day and if you want to identify a specific aircraft this has to be done by the registration/tail number. If you want to identify a particular bus would you do it by the number of the route on the destination board or by the registration plate? Former FAA accident investigator Colonel George Nelson explained that 'time-change' parts such as hydraulic flight surface actuators, pumps, landing gears, engines or engine components are virtually indestructible. 'It would be impossible for an ordinary fire resulting from an airline crash to destroy or obliterate all of these critical time-change parts or their serial numbers', he said. Nelson stated that in his entire career as an accident investigator he 'never witnessed nor even heard of an aircraft loss, where wreckage was accessible, that prevented investigators from finding enough hard evidence to positively identify the make, model, and specific registration number of the aircraft'. If the FBI and company were telling the truth they certainly had enough wreckage to positively identify the aircraft, but if they were *lying* they could never make a match between wreckage and planes which do not match. So why have they never tried?? The fact that they haven't is on the public record. Assistant US Attorney Patrick A. Rose, responding to a Freedom of Information request about proving the identity of 9/11 aircraft, said:

> Federal Defendant [FBI] has determined that there are no responsive records. The identities of the airplanes hijacked in the September 11 attacks was never in question, and, therefore, there were no records generated 'revealing the process by which wreckage recovered by defendant, from the aircraft used during the terrorist attacks of September 11, 2001, was positively identified by defendant ... as belonging to said aircraft ...'

This is such mendacity. The identity of the aircraft was absolutely in question and even more so now that we know they were never positively identified using simple procedures employed in every other air crash. Not only that – there was never an investigation into any of the 9/11 air disasters by the National Transportation Safety Board (NTSB) which is the very body designated to identify why planes crash and confirm their identity. Corrupt-to-their-DNA FBI 'investigators' ran the whole show to ensure one-stop-shop control of what was investigated and what conclusions were agreed.

Wrong engines? Military planes?

We have seen relatively few pictures of plane wreckage in the rubble of the World Trade Center complex. Among them was an alleged piece of landing gear from Flight 11 and part of the fuselage from Flight 175 (Fig 42). Who says this is so? The authorities do. Proof? None. An aircraft engine was found in Murray Street near Ground Zero and claimed to be

from a 767 – 'Flight 175' that struck the South Tower judging by where it came to rest. A Pilots for 911 Truth video suggests that this does not belong to a standard 767. They say the South Tower 767 carried the tail number N612UA and according to its logs the plane was powered by two Pratt and Witney JT9D-7R4D engines. The pilots' video points out that the Murray Street engine

Figure 42: A Federal Emergency Management Agency (FEMA) image of what is alleged to be wreckage from 'Flight 175'.

includes a curved tube structure known as Tobi-Ducts which cool the turbine within the engine and it claims that this comes from a different engine to that carried by Flight 175 – one called the JT9D-7A/JF/7J. The pilots say the cooling duct for the 175 aircraft looked very different and that the engine found in Murray Street is fitted on 747 Jumbo Jets which can travel at much higher speeds (Fig 43). We have the same theme at the Pentagon with an alleged engine part that the Pilots for 9/11 Truth video says could not have come from Flight 77 – plane identification number N644AA. This aircraft carried two Rolls Royce RB211 engines and the pilots' video says the slotted disc on the engine part at the Pentagon doesn't come from a Rolls Royce RB211 (Fig 44). They say the disc is a feature of the Pratt and Whitney JT8D, versions of which have been used in large military aircraft. Others have said the engine parts do match those of a 767 and 757 and Rob Balsamo, co-founder of Pilots for 911 Truth, agrees that the engines can't be definitely identified without physically examining the parts which would require a congressional inquiry. In fact, all it would take to solve this question and many others is for the authorities to match the serial numbers of the parts found at the crash scenes with the maintenance logs of the aircraft just as it would end all questions about what hit the Pentagon if the FBI released the footage from surveillance videos they immediately confiscated on 9/11

Figure 44: The Pentagon engine part questioned by Pilots for 9/11 Truth.

Figure 43: The engine found in Murray Street near the World Trade Center. Does the 'Tobi duct' prove that the 'Flight 175' engine did not come from a standard 767? Some say yes, but others challenge that.

and have never made public. Some had to have captured what caused the damage at the Pentagon, Flight 77, another large jet, a small plane, missile or bomb. It's that simple and yet we are now closing in on 20 years since 9/11 and neither has been done. For goodness sake – *why?*

It is no good attacking those who question the official story of 9/11 when the authorities refuse to take such simple steps to confirm their story with evidence in their possession all this time – if their story is true. The FBI and other agencies have been questioned about why they have never matched plane part serial numbers with the maintenance logs, but as always they refused to comment. Both the FBI and National Transport Safety Board rejected requests to identify the planes that crashed on 9/11 through their component serial and part numbers. What if the planes which struck the buildings after replacing the ones that left the airports – as described in Operation Northwoods – were modified versions with reinforced airframe and fitted with more powerful engines for greater performance and structural strength than the standard 767/757 could have achieved? Another point is that commercial airliners are upgraded in this way as a matter of course ... by the US military. This would certainly make sense of the experience of Mark Burnback, an employee of Fox Television, who was close to the World Trade Center when 'Flight 175' crashed into the South Tower. He told WCBS in a live interview from the scene that the aircraft definitely did not look like a commercial plane. 'There was a blue logo on the front of the plane,' he said. 'I did not see any windows on the side – it was not a normal plane that I've seen at the airport.' The interview was never repeated. Voices from onlookers who had seen 'Flight 175' strike the tower can be heard on video footage saying:

> No, wasn't no commercial airliner ... The second wasn't, no, the second definitely wasn't ... It didn't have any markings on it that I saw, no emblems, no markings ... It was a military plane, a military plane.

Interviews with witnesses at the scene had the same theme. One man said of 'Flight 175': 'The plane wasn't no airliner or anything. It was a two-engine big grey plane.' Another said: 'The plane ... smashed into the World Trade Center, it was grey to be honest with you.' A big military aircraft with airframe reinforcement and advanced capability would explain how it performed manoeuvres that a bog-standard 767 would not be able to do.

Is it a bird? Is it a plane? No – it's Superscam

Pilots for 9/11 Truth secured through a Freedom of Information Act request to the National Transportation Safety Board (NTSB) what is claimed to be the Flight Data Recorder (FDR) for Flight 77 which left Washington Dulles and is said to have crashed into the Pentagon. The Cockpit Voice Recorder (CVR) was destroyed in the crash according to the authorities. FDR information secured by the pilots included radar data, air traffic control recordings and an animation of the plane's alleged path. Pilot and aviation engineer analysis conducted by Pilots for 9/11 Truth found that the supplied data did not match the official story of what happened. Pilots and engineers concluded that the data for 'Flight 77' was not actually from Flight 77. The plane recorded in the data didn't even depart from the gate at Washington Dulles that is claimed. I don't mean Flight 77 didn't leave that gate, but whatever plane the data really belongs to didn't. Latitude and longitude coordinates had to be entered into a plane's computer at the gate or the entire flight navigational information was thrown out of sync. American Airlines operating manuals for this aircraft type, confirmed by pilots familiar with the procedure, said that all flights had to be aligned in terms of latitude and longitude at the gate through the IRS, or Inertial Reference System, and the plane had to be stationary for ten minutes or more for this to be completed. American Airlines grounded aircraft if this couldn't be done and even if an error was noted on route to the runway the pilot would have to return to the gate to realign the system. American Airlines captain Ralph Kolstad, who had piloted the Flight 77 aircraft (N644AA), said that if the IRS failed in flight or seriously malfunctioned then an emergency was declared. Flight 77 may have departed from Dulles gate D26, but the pilots say that for sure the plane featured in the fake '77' Flight Data Recorder did not. Commercial jets like the 757 were not able to realign in-flight if the gate data was incorrect, but *military* aircraft could do so through the Global Positioning System (GPS) which was not available to commercial aircraft at the time (remember what I said about the Hidden Hand and its military having technology ahead of anyone else). Now – *here we go* ... Pilots for 9/11 Truth point out that flight data information which the government says is from Flight 77 shows that its GPS system was operational. Problem is ... the 757 that was Flight 77 *didn't have a GPS system*. The data further shows that the plane was navigationally auto-aligned in-flight which cannot be done without a GPS system which Flight 77 did not have. All this could have been done, however, by a *military aircraft or military modified commercial aircraft*. Another point: The flight data decoding system which was specifically designed for American Airlines aircraft could not fully decode the data in the (fake) Flight Data Recorder claimed to be from American Airlines Flight 77 and nor could the Boeing system from the company that built the plane. They should have asked for help from the military – I'm sure they would have had the technology that synced with it. A military aircraft would also explain why ground-to-air missiles defending Washington and the Pentagon did not launch. Barbara Honegger, Senior Military Affairs Journalist who worked for the Department of Defense, said: 'That craft had to have been a military craft because only military craft put out a signal – it's called an identify friend or foe (IFF) device – and only a military craft would be allowed to approach the building.' Former Boston air traffic controller Robin Horton said the two radar systems which military radar defensive systems read are a civilian aircraft transponder and a military transponder:

> The military transponder is called IFF, civilian aircraft do not have an IFF transponder – they are not given that capability, okay? So if there was an American 757 that went into the Pentagon, for example, and it turned off its transponder, it didn't have an IFF military transponder on it, so it was a primary target going into that airspace – pooh, pooh, pooh, pooh, pooh. Should have been shot down.

John Judge, a 9/11 researcher for former Congresswoman Cynthia McKinney, a rare questioning voice on Capitol Hill, captured the situation:

> What I am describing to you is a breakdown in proper operating procedure by FAA, NORAD, P-56 [Washington no-fly zone] and the Pentagon all on the same day in the middle, after 9.05, what was known nationally to be a terrorist attack and it makes no sense.

No, mate, because it's all bollocks.

Hani Hanjour: Puddle-jump incompetent

According to the government's Cuckoo Land version of events, hijackers broke through the cockpit door of Flight 77, threatened the pilots with box-cutters and small knives and ordered them to the back of plane while taking over the controls – and all executed in three minutes. The 'hijacker pilot' was claimed to be Hani Hanjour who had been banned by instructors at the Freeway Airport in Bowie, Maryland, from renting a small plane six weeks before 9/11 because he was such an incompetent pilot. He must have been a quick learner because the government said that he now turned around the 757 and headed back for Washington. Hanjour was a small man of around five-feet tall with a slight build (just the man to overpower flight crew with cardboard box-cutters) and had a poor grasp of English. How strange when fluently speaking, writing and understanding English is essential to securing a pilot's licence. Somehow he got one anyway while being next-to-useless. Hanjour was dropped by his first two schools in Oakland, California, and Scottsdale, Arizona. Duncan Hastie, owner of the Scottsdale school, said Hanjour was 'a weak student' who was 'wasting our resources'. Hanjour then enrolled with the nearby Sawyer Aviation which Wes Fults, a Sawyer instructor at the time, described as a 'school of last resort' – '... it was a commonly held truth that, if you failed anywhere else, go to Sawyer.' Fults said that Hanjour got overwhelmed with the instruments on the flight simulator. 'He had only the barest understanding of what the instruments were there to do', Fults recalled. Hanjour had used the simulator three or four times, then 'disappeared like a fog'. This is the man the official story claims took over the controls of Flight 77. Captain Russ Wittemberg, a commercial and military pilot for 30 years, said: 'There is no way you could possibly come out of a [one-engine] 172 and fly a jet that you've never flown before – that's like showing me how to carve up a Christmas cookie and then say go make a heart transplant.' The plane's autopilot was turned on throughout the flight, the National Transportation Safety Board data says, until 9.08. It was then turned off for three minutes before being restored. There's another teeny-weeny problem with the story of the cockpit being stormed and the pilots overwhelmed and forced to retreat to the back of the plane ... according to Pilots for 9/11 Truth the alleged Flight Data Recorder of 'Flight 77' shows that *the cockpit door remained closed throughout the flight*. This is just incredible in every sense unless the 'hijackers' went through demanifestation training to walk through doors, but then you still have the problem of how the pilots were able to go the other way to the back of the plane. Maybe they were given a swift instruction on how to demanifest in the three minutes that little Hanjour was taking over the plane. That's crazy? Oh, really – any more so than a hijacker's passport floating down undamaged from a fireball or a next-to-useless puddle-jumper 'pilot' taking over a 757? Important note here – soon after this 'hijacking' total radar contact is said to have been lost and the plane disappeared from the screens until *36 minutes* later when a plane was picked up again. It is claimed that Flight 77 was lost to radar at 8.56am and suddenly reappeared at 9.32am when seen by Danielle O'Brien, an air traffic controller at Dulles International Airport, moving at a speed she didn't understand. There is more about her recollections coming up. This missing time is when the switch would have occurred – as per Operation Northwoods – because there is no evidence from 8.56 onwards that what was spotted heading for Washington was Flight 77 and indeed all the evidence says that it wasn't. Captain Russ Wittemberg, a 30-year commercial and military pilot, said:

> If Flight 77 really did go off the radar screens for 36 minutes ... then the plane is no longer flying, or it was low enough it was out of radar coverage – one or the two. So was the airline landed at some place, some remote field? Then it makes sense that they lost the airplane for 36 minutes. Other than that there is very little explanation for that.

If it was landed – and I say at least three and possibly all were – then it was right in line with the scenario of Operation Northwoods. Whatever happened Cheyenne Mountain would not have lost the plane for 36 minutes.

Little 'hijackers, big pilots

The pilot of Flight 77 was Charles 'Chic' Burlingame, an aeronautical engineer and honours graduate from the Navy's Top Gun fighter pilot school in Miramar, California. Kent Hill, an American Airlines captain on European routes and a life-long friend of Burlingame, seriously questioned the official story. The two were graduates of the Naval Academy, flew in Vietnam and had flown with American Airlines for 28 years. Hill could not understand why there was no hijack code sent from any of the planes. He said they were all trained 'on the old type of hijack' where the hijacker is treated cordially, the pilot punches a four-digit code into the transponder to alert ground control that the plane has been hijacked and then takes hijackers where they wish to go and puts the plane on the tarmac. 'However, this is a totally new situation,' Hill said. 'Not one of the planes alerted ground control that they were being hijacked. How come?' Well, this can be explained if the planes were hijacked remotely in a way that would override the transponder channel and block all communication with air traffic controllers including the four-digit hijack code. With no hijack taking place *on* the plane, but *from the ground*, the pilots might even have believed, at least for a time, that there was a mechanical fault when the plane did not respond to cockpit commands. Kent Hill said he was sure that none of the pilots had control of the aircraft when they crashed because no pilot would do that. 'Even if I had a gun at my head, I'd never fly a plane into a building. I'd try to put it in anywhere – a field or a river – and I'd be searing the hell out of them by flying upside down first. 'Chic' Burlingame's sister, Deborah, said that he would 'never, never have entrusted a stranger with that airplane when he had lives at stake' – and would never have easily conceded control of the cockpit. How does this all square with claims that CNN contributor Barbara Olson rang her husband, Boy Bush Solicitor General Ted Olson, to say that the pilot of Flight 77 was at the back of the plane with her and to ask her husband what she should she tell him? Pilots and an entire crew just went to the back of a 757 leaving hijackers in the cockpit after being threatened only by what Olson described as knives and box-cutters and they managed to do this without the cockpit door ever opening?? Burlingame was a weightlifter and boxer, described as a tough man. How would he have been overpowered by little men with box-cutters when they were described in a statement to the 9/11 Commission as 'not physically imposing, as the majority of them were between 5-5 and 5-7 in height and slender in build'? If they had messed with Burlingame they would have been eating their next meal through a straw. His brother Mark said they would have had to incapacitate or kill him for Burlingame to have allowed the plane to be taken over. If either had happened he would not be at the back of the plane while Olson is said to have asked her husband: 'What do I tell the pilot?' Crazy, crazy stuff. Retired Colonel Donn de Grand Pré, a friend of Burlingame's life-long friend, Kent Hill, said he gathered together a group of experienced civilian and military pilots, including combat fighter pilots and commercial airline captains, to discuss what could have happened during what he described as a 'so-called terrorist attack [that] was in fact a superbly executed military operation against the United States, requiring the utmost professional military skill in command, communications and control'. He said the pilot group concluded:

> ... the enemy is within the gates, that he has infiltrated into the highest policymaking positions at the Federal level, and has absolute control, not only of the purse strings, but of the troop build-up and deployment of our military forces, including active, reserve and National Guard units.

Colonel Donn de Grand Pré reported that the group of highly experienced pilots was not impressed by claims that the four aircraft were flown by hijackers who had trained in planes like the Cessna. He said one officer remarked: 'I seriously question whether these novices could have located a target dead-on 200 miles removed from take-off point – much less controlled the flight and mastered the intricacies of 11FR [instrument flight rules] – and all accomplished in 45 minutes.' The pilots said that the way the planes were flown ruled out the level of experience and competence reported for the 'hijackers'. An Air Force officer, who flew more than 100 sorties over North Vietnam, is quoted as saying: 'Those birds either had a crack fighter pilot in the left seat, or they were being manoeuvred by remote control.' Stan Goff, a former Special Forces sergeant turned conspiracy investigator, said this about Flight 77:

> Now, the real kicker. A pilot they want us to believe was trained at a ... puddle-jumper school for Piper Cubs and Cessnas, conducts a well-controlled downward spiral, descending the last 7,000 feet in two-and-a-half minutes, brings the plane in so low and flat that it clips the electrical wires across the street from the Pentagon, and flies it with pinpoint accuracy into the side of this building at 460 knots.

> When the theory about learning to fly this well at the puddle-jumper school began to lose ground, it was added that they received further training on a flight simulator. This is like saying you prepared your teenager for her first drive on I-40 at rush hour by buying her a video driving game. It's horse shit! There is a story being constructed about these events.

Captain Russ Wittemberg, a military and airline pilot, said 'the story of how the plane hit the Pentagon just doesn't make any sense at all'. American Airlines captain Ralph Kolstad said that even with 6,000 hours of flying time in 757s and 767s he could not have done what incompetent Cessna pilot Hani Hanjour is claimed to have done. Nila Sagadevan, a pilot and aeronautical engineer, said:

> I challenge any pilot, any pilot anywhere: give him a Boeing 757 and tell him to do 400 knots 20 feet above the ground for half a mile. CAN'T DO. It's aerodynamically impossible.

But, of course, it *is* possible if you are a government script-writer.

CHAPTER 10

'Plane strikes the Pentagon' – or did it?

An illusion is an illusion. Reality always exists despite the façade
– Kasie West

If Flight 77 was really hijacked by 'highly-trained Islamic terrorists' they would have known the defence procedures to protect Washington airspace and so why would they (a) allow the plane to fly so far out of the city before turning back, and (b) not hit the Pentagon directly in their approach instead of flying the plane in a fantastic spiral to strike the building at the precise spot which had recently been re-enforced in a Pentagon upgrade to protect the building from just such an attack?

Why would they not have targeted the plane directly at the offices of Secretary of State Rumsfeld and military leaders of the Joint Chiefs of Staff located on the very opposite side of the building to where the Pentagon was hit? Instead the building was struck in the offices where the computer systems were located that held the key to uncovering how $2.3 trillion had disappeared from the Pentagon budget ($8,000 for every man, woman and child in America) which Secretary Rumsfeld had announced the day before the attack was unaccounted for. What a coincidence that he revealed this to the media on September 10th and by lunchtime the following day a 'plane' strikes the building precisely where now-dead civilian accountants, bookkeepers and budget analysts were investigating where that money went. Bryan C. Jack, who headed the Pentagon's programming and fiscal economics division and was responsible for crunching America's defence budget, was also on Flight 77 which is said to have hit the Pentagon where his budget accountants and analysts were working. How predictable, if appalling, that an aide of then British Prime Minister Tony Blair would tell government colleagues on 9/11 that this was 'a good day to bury bad news'. If you wanted to bury the announcement of the missing $2.3 trillion it could not have been better timed than Monday, September 10th, 2001. Monday is normally the last day you announce news you want to hide with another five working days for the media to discuss and expand on the story and the weekend for more in-depth analysis. Late Friday is when you bury bad news unless you know that something is coming along to make it disappear – which they did. What happened to that money and trillions more since bringing the total officially missing at the time of writing to *$21 trillion?* One answer is that attacks like 9/11 and other so-called 'black budget', off-the-books Hidden Hand projects can be extremely expensive. Investigative journalist David Lindorff described how the scam works:

> ... they submit the financial statements from prior years showing falsely that it's spent all its money and then asking for more. And so Congress obligingly gives them more. But the money that they don't spend each year gets stashed away in secret places within the Pentagon and gets used without any accountability at all.
>
> This means that they are able to do black operations that get no oversight. It means that they could use it for corrupt purposes. There are all kinds of things they could do with it. And that fund could be now as large as $100 billion which I would note is larger than Russia's entire military spending, close to Chinese entire annual military spending. And that is a slush fund.

'Islamic fanatics on Flight 77' could have targeted the gigantic Pentagon roof or even more spectacularly that part of the building where Rumsfeld and the military big-wigs were located (which was publicly known). Instead they aim for a point at the very opposite side to where they had their offices and bang on the spot – known as Wedge 1 – which had recently been seriously upgraded and strengthened to protect from just such a terrorist attack but where the accountants were searching for the missing trillions. A CBS report on November 28th, 2001, said: 'In an astonishing stroke of luck, the terrorists had hit the only section of the Pentagon designed to resist a terrorist attack.' Hey Abdul, you sure this map is the right way up? Another relevant question is why 'Islamic fanatics' bent on maximum death and destruction did not target a nuclear power station instead of the most reinforced part of the Pentagon? 'Flight 11' and 'Flight 175' passed close to the major nuclear power installations at Indian Point about 24 miles from New York City with the potential to turn that whole region of the United States, including New York, into an uninhabitable wasteland and kill millions of 'infidels' through radiation poisoning in the months and years to come. Was it really more effective to target a newly-reinforced section of the Pentagon on the opposite side from Rumsfeld and the military chiefs where the smallest number of people were working because of the on-going work on reinforcement? This building work, of course, would be a great cover for planting explosives.

Questions without answers – official ones, anyway

'Flight 77' is supposed to have struck five lamp posts as it approached the Pentagon and you can see pictures of these poles on the ground, but the route and approach of the 'plane' in the National Transportation Safety Board (NTSB) Flight Data Recorder information analysed by Pilots for 9/11 Truth has the aircraft on a route and height that makes striking those lamp posts impossible. A Navy Annex building and a gas station were under the path of the aircraft and according to the Flight Data Recorder it passed to the north of these buildings, or the left from a pilot's view, while the flight animation supplied by the NTSB had the plane flying to the south or right of them (Fig 45).

The latter would have taken the plane towards the lamp posts, but it is very clear from multiple witness testimonies, with the buildings as an obvious guide, that the plane did indeed pass the Navy Annex and

Figure 45: The official flight path of 'Flight 77' came in low from the right of the Citgo gas station and struck lamp poles before smashing into the Pentagon. The Flight Data Recorder information from the National Transportation Safety Board (NTSB) – along with eyewitness reports – has the plane arriving from the left of the gas station with a direction and height that could not have struck the lamp poles or even the Pentagon in the way the official story claims.

gas station to the left and could not have struck the lamp posts. Pilots for 9/11 Truth highlight serious discrepancies between the alleged hard data from the Flight Data Recorder of the plane as it approached the Pentagon and the animation based on that data provided by the NTSB. Jim Ritter, head of the Vehicle Performance Division at the NTSB, who signed off on the flight data, refused to even discuss these discrepancies. The arrogance of the NTSB and other government agencies like the FBI in not answering legitimate questions and the contempt they therefore have for the truth and victims is sickening.

Pilots for 9/11 Truth point out that the altitude indicator in the

Figure 46: A few frames of a 'security' video at the Pentagon which pathetically claims to show a plane striking the building – but doesn't. There were more than 80 surveillance cameras located at the Pentagon and surrounding business premises. Why were they confiscated on 9/11 and kept from the public ever since?

Figure 47: If a plane came in at ground level and struck the Pentagon why no damage to the lawn?

animation shows the plane 300 feet lower than the hard data and when the aircraft's true height is factored in the lamp posts would have had to be 440 feet high for the plane to hit them. The 'Flight 77' Flight Data Recorder does not have the plane careering across the Pentagon lawn to strike the building level to the ground yet the five-frame Pentagon distant 'security video' images claiming to show the impact depicts a 'plane' hitting the wall while level to the ground across the – *undamaged* – Pentagon lawn (Figs 46 and 47).

Slightly longer footage including the five-frames released under a Freedom of Information Act request in 2006 was also inconclusive and claimed to depict a distant blurry 'plane' doing something considered near impossible by professional pilots let alone by Cessna incompetent, Hani Hanjour, and it's a manoeuvre not to be found on the 'Flight 77' data recorder. Pilots for 9/11 Truth flight simulator tests using the same data provided by the NTSB showed that the plane would have flown over the building or, with the same vertical speed but positioned low enough to hit the lamp posts, it would have crashed into the ground long before it reached the alleged impact point. One postured scenario that would bring the flight data and the explosion together was that the plane – not, of course, Flight 77 – came in low and unleashed a missile that caused the explosion. Could the release of a missile have been what Air Force Master Sergeant Noel Sepulveda witnessed when he saw the plane come in low over a nearby hotel and 'drop its landing gear'? This would also explain the dearth of aircraft wreckage at the scene and the size of the main hole in the building. People remember the collapsed wall of the Pentagon, but the collapse only happened some 30 minutes *after* the alleged impact (Fig 48). I have seen estimates of between 20 minutes and 45 minutes and I will use a mean figure of 30 which is the approximate period widely quoted. The point is that the wall fell long after impact. The main damage point was described as between 16 and 20 feet across and is supposed to have swallowed a passenger jet with a wing-span of 125 feet (Figs 49 and 50). Witnesses near the Pentagon described seeing 'like a white commuter plane'. One described 'maybe a 20-passenger corporate jet, no markings on the side, coming in at a shallow angle like it was landing right into the side of the Pentagon'. Witness Kelly Knowles described a 'second plane':

Figure 48: This is the image that people remember of the collapsed wall of the Pentagon, but this didn't happen until half an hour or more after 'impact'. Before that time the hole was tiny compared with the size of a 757.

Figure 49: This is what the impact point looked like with the wall still standing when a 757 is supposed to have struck the Pentagon.

> Thank god somebody else saw that. There was most definitely a second plane. It's so frustrating because nobody knows about the second plane, or if they do, they are hiding it for some reason.

A second plane, or a plane and a missile? Or, some researchers ask, could the whole 'second plane' story actually be the same plane seen twice or multiple times? A few witnesses talk of a second plane close to 'Flight 77' as it came into the Pentagon while many others say there was

Figure 50: A 757 with this ratio size to the Pentagon is supposed to have disappeared through the entry point that you see.

definitely only one, including a few right under the flightpath. Some 'second-planers' could be systematically disinforming for reasons I will come to while others could have been deceived by seeing the plane coming low towards the Pentagon followed by a massive explosion from a bomb inside the building and the 'second plane' (the only plane) climbing steeply away. Some witnesses describe a single plane lifting sharply to climb over the Pentagon and others say they saw the 'second plane' climbing away from the Pentagon after the explosion. Pentagon police officer Roosevelt Roberts said that he was a few steps inside the Pentagon loading dock during the explosion and immediately ran outside to see a 'large aircraft liner', a commercial jet, very low and flying away. 'You could see that plane as clear as day', he said. 'You couldn't miss it.' He described the plane as silver in colour and flying 'at no more than 100 feet'. Roberts gave a recorded interview for the Library of Congress after the attacks. He didn't see a plane hit the Pentagon and only assumed that one had. He therefore believed the aircraft he saw was a 'second plane' when it could easily have been the only one. People *assuming* the two-plane theory is understandable by associating a plane coming in low towards the Pentagon with the explosion about the same time. What better cover for a plane climbing quickly away than an enormous explosion to focus attention? Imagine if you saw the house across the road explode. What else would you see in your peripheral vision when it was happening? Nothing. If this was the case with the explosion caused by a bomb inside the building or missile it was beneficial to the interests of the cover-up that the second plane story began to circulate.

To confuse matters still further two other aircraft were in the sky over Washington and the Pentagon area at the time. Five minutes before the Pentagon explosion Air National Guard Lieutenant Colonel Steve

O'Brien and his crew were told to take off from Andrews Air Force Base down the road (while the fighter aircraft stayed on the ground) in a C-130 cargo plane headed for Minnesota. This was six minutes after all planes in the United States had been grounded following the attacks in New York. O'Brien said that when he took off he was unware of what had happened at the World Trade Center even though this was 46 minutes after 'Flight 11' and 29 minutes after 'Flight 175' met their fate. That is quite a statement given that he was on an airbase at the time which should have been on stand-by to defend Washington DC. O'Brien said that when they were airborne they saw 'Flight 77' make a close pass of his aircraft and he identified what he said was an American Airlines plane. He said he was told to follow the plane and report on its movements but he couldn't keep up with it in a slow cargo aircraft. Then he saw an explosion on the ground. It was reported in the media that he saw the plane hit the Pentagon. This is not the case – he said he didn't know what the explosion was at first. O'Brien continued his journey to Minnesota and in what is claimed to have been an extraordinary coincidence he was contacted by air traffic controllers over Pennsylvania to ask if he could see another aircraft in trouble – 'Flight 93' – and he said he saw smoke from the 'crash' two minutes after alleged impact. O'Brien may have been an innocent dupe in all this, but I cannot see myself that these events were actually a fantastic coincidence. There are far too many of those in the 9/11 story. The C-130 over Washington added to the confusion of witnesses and the 'second plane' stories as did reports of a 'mystery white jet' seen circling the White House and central Washington which appears to have been an E-4B National Airborne Operations Center (NAOC) plane – a highly modified Boeing 747 which operate as military command posts in the sky. This was airborne at least immediately in the wake of the explosion at the Pentagon and may have been involved in one of the 'exercises' or, some suggest, the orchestration of the Pentagon attack.

There are witnesses that claim to have seen an American Airlines 757 strike the Pentagon although most are military or other 'establishment' figures and their evidence is contradictory or even impossible as with one account by retired Army officer Frank Probst. He claimed that one of the plane's engines passed within six feet of him. Given the turbulence created by an aircraft that big passing him so close at the reported speed let's just say it's yet another miracle that he survived to tell his tale. I am not saying that 'I saw the plane hit' witnesses shouldn't be believed if that's what people feel to do – only that seeing and saying are not necessarily the same thing. A warning to take great care with the 'evidence' of 'witnesses' supporting the official story is provided by the case of cab driver Lloyde England who claimed on television that one of the lamp poles 'struck by Flight 77' crashed through his car windscreen.

There are no photographs of the car in this state and there was no damage to the car's hood or bonnet which he said had been struck by a 20-foot light pole with the heavier end landing on the hood (Fig 51). England said the pole came through the windscreen to the backseat and 'the large piece was sticking out across the hood'.

Figure 51: Taxi driver Lloyde England said a lamp pole struck by 'Flight 77' smashed into his windshield and came to rest on his car bonnet or hood. The hood being undamaged – indeed pristine – should in no way discount the story.

Clearly it is impossible for a heavy and sturdy metal street light pole to be hurled through a windscreen and smack onto the hood without causing even a scratch. Bizarrely there was a copy of my book *Children of the Matrix* on the back seat at the time which he said he was reading. England said that his wife Shirley Hughes-England worked for the FBI 'for a long time': 'She don't talk about it – I don't talk about it.' Neither England nor his wife would discuss her role even off camera when questioned in 2008. Two years later he said she was 'a cleaner'. There are many discrepancies in his story about what he claims to have happened and he would be captured on camera saying that 9/11 was an event for the 'rich people' and it was bigger than him – 'I'm a small man':

> You know what history is?... It's not the truth, it's his story ... It has nothing to do with the truth, it's his story ... This is too big for me man, this is a big thing ... you know this is a world thing happening, I'm a small man ... I'm not supposed to be involved in this. This is for other people. People who have money and all this kind of stuff. I'm not supposed to be involved with this ... This is their thing. I'm not supposed to be in it ... we came across the highway together. It was planned.

We should also watch out for people coming into what is called the '9/11 Truth Movement' and claiming out of nowhere to be, for example, the 'foremost authority on 9/11'. There are many possible scenarios to mislead and discredit real researchers including disinformation. Circulating total disinformation doesn't work very well because seasoned researchers will see through it very quickly. The most effective method is to promote information that is partly inaccurate and partly true because then the truth can be discredited with the lies. There is also a method whereby the person comes forward with a narrative that is basically true, but then the person themselves is discredited (as planned) and with that so is the truth they were disseminating. Weaving a path through the smoke and mirrors requires eyes to be constantly wide open.

It was Flight 77? Okay, prove it

The fundamental diversion and cover up technique in these scenarios is confusion. The more conflicting stories there are flying around after 'false flag' or Problem-Reaction-Solution events the better from the Hidden Hand's point of view. The way to avoid this is to focus on the impossibility of the official story which is the point of this book. A lot of very good research is offering possible explanations for *what* happened, but that does not have to be established to prove that 9/11 was a government-military-intelligence conspiracy or 'inside job'. All that is necessary to expose the Big Lie is to show that the official story of what happened could not have happened and that is already clear. The lies are constant wherever you look. While I am including informed speculation and solid evidence about what *did* happen it is what *didn't* happen – the government's version of events – that holds the key to exposing the 9/11 hoax. One thing is absolutely clear – the NTSB 'Flight Data Recorder' information released in 2006 purporting to come from Flight 77 is fraudulent and there are witnesses that also put into question the 'Flight 77' radar data released by the Air Force 84th Radar Evaluation Squadron (84 RADES) after a Freedom of Information Act request in 2007. Multiple witnesses report seeing the plane purported to be Flight 77 heading for the Pentagon from a different direction to the NTSB and RADES data. They describe the plane coming from the East crossing the Potomac River between Washington DC and Virginia while the NTSB/RADES data does not have the plane crossing the Potomac and tracks it coming from the west. The RADES data further shows a plane pulling away from the Pentagon after the explosion and this is said to be the C-130 transport plane. This is at odds with the route that pilot Steve O'Brien said he flew. Once again with Flight 77 we have the recurring theme with 9/11 of serial numbers and part numbers of black boxes and alleged debris from the plane (albeit very little) that were not publicly matched with the serial numbers of the aircraft and part logs. This is done in every case of air crashes where black boxes and debris are found although not with the planes alleged to have crashed on September 11th. Boston air traffic controller Robin Horton said:

> There is nobody, anywhere, in this entire investigation that has said that is positively American 77. They suppose it, they presume it, they assume it, they say this is what we think it is.

The amount of wreckage we have been shown at the Pentagon site has been described as little more than could be carried in the back of a truck. CNN's then senior Pentagon correspondent Jamie McIntyre said this in a dispatch from the scene:

From my close-up inspection, there is no evidence of a plane having crashed anywhere near the Pentagon ... The only pieces left that you can see are small enough that you could pick up in your hand. There are no large tail sections, wing sections, a fuselage, nothing like that anywhere around which would indicate that the entire plane crashed into the side of the Pentagon and then caused the side to collapse. Even though if you look at the pictures of the Pentagon you see that the floors have all collapsed, that didn't happen immediately, it wasn't until almost about forty-five minutes later [other reports have differing times] that the structure was weakened enough that all of the floors collapsed.

Even Defense Secretary Donald Rumsfeld said there were no big pieces of wreckage only small pieces and 30-year pilot Captain Russ Wittemberg said:

I have been at some accident investigation sites in the Air Force. And I have never come across any accident scene where there is no tell-tale evidence of the plane that crashed.

Seismic evidence, or lack of it, also supports this theme with five seismic recording stations between 63 and 350 kilometres from the Pentagon failing to measure a clear seismic signal for the impact – the only one of the four 9/11 planes not to do so.

An expert view

Albert N. Stubblebine III, a retired Major General in the United States Army, was commanding general of the United States Army Intelligence and Security Command from 1981 to 1984. Stubblebine, who died in 2017, was outspoken in his contention that no plane hit the Pentagon. He believed the official story at the time until he saw the hole in the Pentagon and his response was: 'Something's wrong. There is something wrong with this picture ...' Stubblebine should know. He was in charge of Army Imagery Interpretation for Scientific and Technical Intelligence during the Cold War measuring pieces of Soviet technology from photographs. He said that he took measurements of the Pentagon and the depth of the damage and did the same with a 757 in terms of the length of the nose and wings and concluded from 30 years military experience and his time in military intelligence that an aircraft did not make the hole: 'The plane does not fit in that hole. So what did hit the

Pentagon? What hit it? Where is it? What's going on?' This is an understandable assessment given that we are told a 125 foot wide 757 with a 40-foot high tail passed through an entry hole 16-20 feet wide. Stubblebine noted that a turbine that he saw at the scene looked like one from a missile. 'I can't prove that, I don't know ... there was something there that did not look like the engine from an airplane, but did look like a turbine from a missile.' He said of the five-frames claimed by the Pentagon to be the plane hitting the building:

> Later I saw another photograph taken by one of the sensors [cameras] on the outside of the Pentagon. Now, all of the sensors **had been turned off**, which is kind of interesting – isn't it? That day, why would all of the sensors around the Pentagon be turned off? That's strange. I don't care what the excuse is. That's strange.
>
> There happened to be one that did not get turned off, and in that picture, coming in, flying into the Pentagon, you see this object, and it obviously hits the Pentagon. When you look at it, it does NOT look like an airplane. Sometime later, after I'd gone public, that imagery was changed. It got a new suit around it that now looked like an airplane. But, when you take the suit off, it looks more like a missile – not like an airplane.

Surveillance footage and images have not been published from a building that was awash with security cameras except for those highly-dubious out of focus frames of a distant explosion claiming to be the plane's impact. Researchers who slowed down the footage revealed that 'something' appears on the right hand side of the frame and then basically stops until the explosion happens and then miraculously shoots forward at incredible speed into the explosion which came *first*. The footage had clearly been seriously doctored and frames taken out. Let us see the real pictures from all the relevant cameras – they must exist unless they were turned off – and put an end to all this. If they *were* turned off – WTF? The FBI confiscated surveillance camera footage immediately after the crash, just as it did at Portland airport and all the others. We saw the same with the Oklahoma bombing. Major General Stubblebine also said that all defence systems in the region of the 9/11 attacks were deactivated that day:

> All of the air defence systems had been turned off ... Why would you turn off all of the air defence systems on that particular day unless you knew that something was going to happen? It's a dot. It's information. But, it's strange that everything got turned off that day.

There was an exercise that was designed for the air defence systems that was an attack on the towers by airplanes. Isn't that strange that we had an exercise that mimicked what really happened? Strange that we had planned an exercise that was exactly what happened. And, at the same time, the air defence systems were turned off. Don't you find that strange? I find that really strange.

Stubblebine believed himself to be the highest-ranked military officer to go public with the view that the official story is not true.

Pentagon witnesses

Pentagon employee April Gallop was at her computer inside the building when it was rocked by the explosion which sounded like a bomb. She said the only fire was from computers bursting into flames, as another witness reported. Witnesses said people shouted that a bomb had exploded and these included Don Perkal, deputy general counsel for the Secretary of Defense, who said that he immediately began to smell cordite, a bomb-making constituent. 'Then I knew explosives had been set off somewhere', he said. The Pentagon is constructed with five concentric rings of buildings dubbed A, B, C, D and E from inside to outside. Claims of a bomb were supported by the deaths of people in the inner A and B rings which were not affected by the 'plane' that caused damage only between the E, D and C rings going from the outside in (Fig 52). Severe damage was reported in the B ring and Robert Andrews, Acting Assistant Secretary of Defense, said he felt an explosion and then had to 'walk over dead bodies' as he left the innermost A Ring furthest from the impact point and way beyond where the 'plane' reached. Pentagon worker April Gallop escaped through a hole in the Pentagon wall with her baby son who was about to go to the day-care centre. They went to a grassed area before being taken to hospital. At no time did she see any wreckage from a plane or smell any jet fuel from what would have been still well-filled fuel tanks after a relatively short journey. Gallop saw no

Figure 52: The ring system at the Pentagon. 'Flight 77' is said to have penetrated the first three.

steel, luggage, human remains or anything to indicate that a plane had crashed there. Then came the usual intimidation from the 'Feds' – a common theme – who came to see Gallop in her hospital bed:

> They never identified themselves or even said which agency they worked for. But I know they were not newsmen because I learned that the Pentagon told news reporters not to cover survivors' stories or they would not get any more stories out of there. The men who visited all said they couldn't tell me what to say, they only wanted to make suggestions. But then they told me what to do, which was to take the money [from the Victim Compensation Fund] and shut up. They also kept insisting that a plane hit the building. They repeated this over and over. But I was there and I never saw a plane or even debris from a plane. I figure the plane story is there to brainwash people.

Gallop's point about lack of evidence that a plane had crashed was a common story from a list of witnesses including firefighters who saw the impact site immediately after the 'hit'. Major Dean Eckmann, a military pilot flying over the Pentagon to assess the damage, believed that a truck bomb had been responsible because of the lack of aircraft wreckage and he only found out later about an 'airliner' after the military told the media that this is what happened. Park Police helicopter pilot Ronald Galey said in an interview with the Naval Historical Center that he couldn't believe that a 757 could have struck the building and he arrived within no more than four minutes of the explosion. He also pointed to a truck from where most of the fire seemed to be coming and there was no large fire. 'There's absolutely nothing you could identify as an aircraft part anywhere around there. Nothing. Just couldn't have been', he said. Galey emphasised what a relatively small hole was in the building before the larger collapse some time later. Fellow Park Police pilot Keith Bohn made the same point about a 'small slit' that he could not believe a 757 could pass through. 'I could not see any aviation parts. I could not see an engine or a wing. There was just rubble, pieces, small pieces.' Where did the little amount of debris come from that later appeared in photographs? Colonel George Nelson, a former US Air Force aircraft accident investigator and expert in airplane parts, a former airframe and power plant mechanic, gave his verdict:

> The government alleges that four wide-body airliners crashed on the morning of September 11 2001, resulting in the deaths of more than 3,000 human beings, yet not one piece of hard aircraft evidence has been produced in an attempt to positively identify any of the four aircraft. On the contrary, it seems only that all potential evidence was deliberately kept hidden from public view.

The hard evidence would have included hundreds of critical time-change aircraft items, plus security videotapes that were confiscated by the FBI immediately following each tragic episode. With all the evidence readily available at the Pentagon crash site, any unbiased rational investigator could only conclude that a Boeing 757 did not fly into the Pentagon as alleged.

Two large planes, Bashkirian Airlines Flight 2937 and DHL Flight 611, a Boeing 757 cargo jet, collided at around 36,000 feet the year after 9/11 and crashed to the ground in Germany with many major pieces of wreckage still visible and intact (Fig 53). No-plane advocates point to pictures of a twelve foot wide hole punched when an object, whatever it

was, exited on the other side of three rings of buildings within the five-ring Pentagon (Fig 54). The official story claimed this hole was made by the nose of the 757, but the nose of an aircraft is extremely fragile and made only of carbon fibre to allow electromagnetic waves to freely emit from navigation systems located there. The idea is

Figure 53: Two planes collided in mid-air and careered to the ground from 36,000 feet, but very large and recognisable wreckage can be seen.

ridiculous that the nose could have ploughed intact between the point of impact (where it would have been crushed) and through three rings of buildings in an area of the Pentagon that had just undergone serious steel-concrete reinforcement to protect against terrorist attack. Defense Secretary Rumsfeld said the plane 'penetrated three of the five concentric rings of the building' which means the plane had to smash through six outer walls. Could an aircraft score through three reinforced rings of buildings and the nose still be so intact that it could have caused the hole on the other side? Even if an engine caused the hole as some claimed – where are pictures of that engine? The official story is an

Figure 54: The round C-Ring exit hole some twelve feet across made by whatever struck the Pentagon.

absolute blaze of apparent contradictions and it claims that the following happened simultaneously: The plane struck the building and 'pulverised'; engines and other solid components disappeared because they 'melted'; 100 tons of melted metal were not found because the inferno was so hot at more than 2,500 degrees centigrade that everything 'evaporated'; the small exit hole, around twelve feet across, was caused by the nose or engine of the aircraft which had penetrated three reinforced buildings despite all of the former. For sure all of those statements can't be true. The ludicrous official story was summed up by a French website that highlighted the contradictions in the wake of the Pentagon crash:

> The aircraft thus disintegrated on contact with the Pentagon, melted inside the building, evaporated at 2500°C, and still penetrated two other buildings via a hole two and half yards in diameter.

Black box re-run

Dick Bridges deputy manager for Arlington County, was quoted by Associated Press as saying that both black boxes for Flight 77 were found '... right where the plane came into the building'. If that is the case where was the rest of the wreckage if much of the plane and the black boxes in the tail section only made it that far? How could it also have ploughed through those three rings of buildings? 'Flight 77' black boxes were reported to have been found at 4am in the morning on September 14th so why was the Pentagon file detailing the content of the Flight Data Recorder created more than four hours *before* it was found – at 11.45pm on September 13th? Navy Captain Glenn N. Wagner, director of the Armed Forces DNA Identification Laboratory in Rockville, Maryland, said a team of forensic pathologists, odonatologists, a forensic anthropologist, DNA experts, investigators and support personnel worked for more than two weeks to identify victims of the attack on the Pentagon. He said they had identified 184 of the 189 who died in the plane and the building. You either believe this or you don't, I guess, while taking into account government claims that the plane 'vapourised' and 'melted' and that evidence points most strongly to the fact that whatever caused the explosion could not have been Flight 77. Captain Daniel Davis is a former US Army Air Defense Officer and NORAD Tactical Director, former Senior Manager at General Electric Turbine Engine Division and founder of Turbine Technology Services Corp, a turbine services and maintenance company. In short, he knows a lot about jet engines and aircraft. Davis said:

> As a former General Electric Turbine engineering specialist and manager and then CEO of a turbine engineering company, I can guarantee that none of the

high tech, high temperature alloy engines on any of the four planes that crashed on 9/11 would be completely destroyed, burned, shattered or melted in any crash or fire. Wrecked, yes, but not destroyed. Where are all of those engines, particularly at the Pentagon? If jet powered aircraft crashed on 9/11, those engines, plus wings and tail assembly, would be there.

Additionally, in my experience as an officer in NORAD as a Tactical Director for the Chicago-Milwaukee Air Defense and as a current private pilot, there is no way that an aircraft on instrument flight plans (all commercial flights are IFR) would not be intercepted when they deviate from their flight plan, turn off their transponders, or stop communication with Air Traffic Control. No way! With very bad luck, perhaps one could slip by, but no there's no way all four of them could!

Finally, going over the hill and highway and crashing into the Pentagon right at the wall/ground interface is nearly impossible for even a small slow single engine airplane and no way for a 757. Maybe the best pilot in the world could accomplish that but not these unskilled 'terrorists'. Attempts to obscure facts by calling them a 'Conspiracy Theory' does not change the truth. It seems, 'Something is rotten in the State'.

Engines de-manifested when they could not have done so while somehow two pieces of a driver's licence survived allegedly belonging to 'hijacker' Majed Moqed. As the song goes ... 'I believe in miracles – since you came along, you sexy thing.' The song should be renamed 'Ode to the FBI'.

Evidence for a missile strike

We would do well not to dismiss anything out of hand before looking at the facts very carefully after what has been done and planned in the past. Many researchers – myself included – continue to believe that no 757 crashed into the Pentagon and the explosion was caused by a bomb, missile or possibly a remote-controlled military aircraft. I think a missile/bomb is favourite. A commercial airliner flying low towards the Pentagon and then climbing sharply over the building would have been the perfect cover and created what we have – witnesses galore describing an airliner, two planes, small plane, missile and bomb. All of which = confusion – the currency of cover up. Winged missiles were used at the time by the US military and guided to their target by computer with often pinpoint accuracy (Fig 55 overleaf). This is an Internet profile in 2001of a Cruise missile used by the US military:

Cruise missiles are jet-propelled pilotless aircraft designed to strike distant targets with great accuracy. Travelling at hundreds of miles an hour, cruise

Figure 55: A winged cruise missile had the capability in 2001 of travelling at jet plane speed and striking the Pentagon in the way officially described for 'Flight 77'.

missiles use the global positioning system, inertial guidance, optical scenery correlation, and terrain comparing radar to find their targets. Their accuracy makes them especially useful in attacking military targets in urban areas with limited damage to nearby civilian facilities.

Once airborne, its turbojet engine starts, its wings spread, and it noses over to hug the surface at about 500 miles (800 km) per hour toward its target. Over water, the missile relies on inertial guidance, perhaps also the global positioning system, for navigation. Upon reaching land, the Tomahawk updates its position and corrects its course using TERCOM (terrain contour matching) or DSMAC (digital scene-matching area correlator) – the first system compares radar signals, the second optical images, with a computer-stored map – before closing on the target at an altitude of 100 feet (30 m) or less.

See how low a winged-missile could fly at high speed while remaining accurate, very low and stable – everything a 757 could not. Remember, too, the fantastic technology developed in the secret projects that we never see which is always far ahead of what we are allowed to know exists. Witness Steve Patterson said he was watching the World Trade Center coverage on television when he saw a 'silver commuter jet' fly past the window of his 14th-floor apartment in Pentagon City. He described seeing the plane about 150 yards away coming in from the west and about 20 feet off the ground. Patterson said it sounded like the high-pitched squeal of a fighter jet (or missile) and came over Arlington cemetery so low that he thought it was going to land on the road. He recalled that it was moving extremely fast and he couldn't read anything on the side of the 'plane' which appeared only big enough to hold 8 to 12 people. Another witness account by Lon Rains, an editor of *Space News*, said:

At that moment I heard a very loud, quick whooshing sound that began behind me and stopped suddenly in front of me and to my left. In fractions of a second I heard the impact and an explosion. The next thing I saw was the fireball. I was convinced it was a missile. It came in so fast it sounded nothing like an airplane ...

Defense Secretary Donald Rumsfeld said in an unintended moment that a missile was involved during an interview at the Pentagon with

Parade Magazine in October, 2001, when he was asked why there was no warning of the attacks:

> There were lots of warnings... It is a truth that a terrorist can attack any time, any place, using any technique and it's physically impossible to defend at every time and every place against every conceivable technique.
>
> Here we're talking about plastic knives and using an American Airlines flight filled with our citizens, **and the missile to damage this building** and similar [inaudible] that damaged the World Trade Center. The only way to deal with this problem is by taking the battle to the terrorists, wherever they are, and dealing with them.'

And *'plastic knives'*??

Major Doug Rokke, a PhD in educational physics and former top military expert, also pointed to a missile:

> When you look at the whole thing, especially the crash site void of airplane parts, the size of the hole left in the building and the fact the projectile's impact penetrated numerous concrete walls, it looks like the work of a missile. And when you look at the damage, it was obviously a missile.

Then there was the extraordinary high-speed 270 degree turn that the puddle-jumper pilot would have had to perform according to the government story. Robin Horton, former Boston Center air traffic controller and a flight instructor, said:

> An experienced pilot with thousands of hours probably would have to take between 10 and 20 attempts ... before they would be able to pull off that manoeuvre. You just can't do that with one of those big airplanes.

But he said that a military plane could do that and a programmed guided-missile certainly could.

CHAPTER 11

What happened to Flight 93?

History is a set of lies agreed upon – Napoleon Bonaparte

The Pentagon attack has received far less public attention than those involving the World Trade Center and that's even more the case with United Airlines Flight 93 which is claimed to have crashed about 80 miles east of Pittsburgh in Pennsylvania.

Flight 93 pulled back from the gate at Newark International Airport, a half hour drive from New York, at 8.01am bound for San Francisco, but did not take off until 8.42. This was officially explained by early morning take-off congestion and the timing of what was planned for the flight was delayed by approximately 30 minutes on the scheduled lift-off. Flight 93 headed west over Pennsylvania and into northern Ohio. The crew received a text warning from Ed Ballinger, a United Airlines flight dispatcher, via the Aircraft Communication Addressing and Reporting System (ACARS). The message warned about possible cockpit intrusion and reported the two World Trade Center crashes. Jason M. Dahl, the 43-year-old captain on Flight 93, confirmed receipt of the message and this was the only one of the four planes that had prior warning of possible trouble because of its late departure. Surely after such an alert the cockpit door would have been secured immediately if it wasn't already? Flight 93 was hijacked around 9.28am according to the official story when the last contact was made between the cockpit and air traffic controllers. This was about 45 minutes into the flight and after two planes had crashed into the World Trade Center. At 9.29 a controller at Cleveland Center is said to have heard 'a radio transmission of unintelligible sounds of possible screaming or a struggle from an unknown origin ...' The controller asked: 'Somebody call Cleveland?' A second transmission is reported to have been heard with sounds of screaming and a voice shouting 'Mayday – get out of here, get out of here.' The controller asked other pilots on his frequency if they had heard the screaming and some said they had. Then came a third transmission at 9.32: 'Ladies and Gentlemen: Here the captain, please sit down keep remaining seating. We have a bomb on board. So sit.' The controller at this point is said to have passed this information up the FAA command structure. Flight 93 would change course and head in the direction of Washington DC. At 9.36 Cleveland Center made an offer to the FAA Command Center to contact a nearby military base. The response was that FAA higher ups would have to make that decision and they were working on it. By this time two planes had struck the World Trade Center and fighter jets are said to have been despatched from Cape Cod to New York and from Langley, Virginia, but when Flight 93 showed obvious signs of being hijacked the FAA upper levels were only 'working on it' with regard to scrambling military jets? At 9.39 another transmission is said to have been heard from 'hijacker' pilot 'Ziad Jarrah', the 'Islamic extremist' who attended an evangelical Christian school and said he wouldn't mind marrying a non-Muslim. This is the same 'Jarrah' who was reported to have been questioned in Dubai and admitted spending the previous two months in Afghanistan while the real Jarrah was in that same period daily attending the flying school in Venice, Florida. At the time of his alleged Dubai interview he was at the bedside of his father at a hospital in Lebanon. 'Jarrah' is alleged to say on the cockpit tape:

> Ah, here's the captain; I would like to tell you all to remain seated. We have a bomb aboard and we are going back to the airport, and we have our demands. So, please remain quiet.

The plane's transponder signal disappeared at 9.41 and immediately afterwards Cleveland Center found out from TV coverage that 'Flight 77' had hit the Pentagon. The controller located the plane (whatever plane it was by then) on primary radar and the FAA Command Center reported that the aircraft was '29 minutes out of Washington, DC'. In the light of all this the following reported exchange is mind-blowing when the FAA Command Center at last suggested that FAA headquarters should make a decision about calling for a military response. The exchange took place at 9.46 – *eighteen minutes* after contact was lost with Flight 93 and after *three planes* by then were reported to have crashed into buildings in New York and Washington:

FAA Headquarters: They're pulling Jeff away to go talk about United 93.

Command Center: Uh, do we want to think about, uh, scrambling aircraft?

FAA Headquarters: Uh, God, I don't know.

Command Center: Uh, that's a decision somebody's gonna have to make probably in the next 10 minutes.

FAA Headquarters: Uh, ya know everybody just left the room.

At 9.53, *25 minutes after contact was lost* and with all that had already happened, FAA headquarters told its Command Center that the deputy director for air traffic services was talking to deputy administrator Monte Belger about scrambling aircraft. *Talking about it??* The Command Center reported that contact with 'Flight 93' had been lost and was then told of a sighting by another aircraft which reported the plane to be 'waving his wings'. This is claimed to be the 'hijackers' trying to fend off an attempt by passengers to regain control of the cockpit. The government story says that the plane crashed in a field near Shanksville, Pennsylvania, 125 miles from Washington at 10.03. 'Black smoke' on the ground was reported by Air National Guard Lieutenant Colonel Steve O'Brien in his C-130 cargo plane that had been over Washington when the Pentagon was hit. The military liaison at Cleveland called the NORAD NEADS military response centre in Rome, New York State, at 10.07 to report the situation with Flight 93 which apparently neither were aware was already said to have crashed. In the entire period of 35 minutes between contact being lost and the alleged crash of Flight 93 did anyone at the FAA request military support after three iconic buildings had already been hit? Red flags are everywhere with lots of flashing red lights.

Little 'hijackers' and big passengers. WTF?

The official story is that passengers on Flight 93 attacked the hijackers and the plane crashed into a field at an estimated 575 miles an hour. What is hard to comprehend once again is that some seriously big guys could be herded to the back of the plane and guarded by one hijacker, as claimed in alleged phone calls from the aircraft. Mark Bingham was a rugby player who stood six-feet five; Jeremy Glick was a rugby player and judo champion; Todd Beamer was over six-foot and 200 pounds; and Lou Nacke was a 200-pound weightlifter with a 'Superman' tattoo on his shoulder. Then there was Daniel Lewin on Flight 11. He was a captain in the Israeli Defense Forces who served in an elite specialist counter-terrorism, hostage rescue and assassination unit who could bench-press 315 pounds and said he was 'trained to kill terrorists with a pen or a credit card' or just his bare hands. I'll have more about him later. Hijackers with 'small knives' would have had no chance if they had been challenged by these guys. A transmission heard from the Flight 93 cockpit is reported to have said 'Mayday' and 'Get out of here'. Shortly afterwards follow more demands to 'get out of here' and then grunting, screaming, scuffling and finally silence. How did they pull off a hijack with such a weight disadvantage without guns? Alongside captain Jason Dahl was 26-year-old First Officer LeRoy W. Homer who was a former Air Force major and veteran of the 1991 Gulf War. Homer is credited with the 'get out of here' messages. How did hijackers get into the cockpit when the door had to be secured after the cockpit intrusion warning? One researcher spoke with Deena Burnett, wife of passenger Tom Burnett Jr, who said that her husband called her on a cell phone to tell her of the hijack. She said he told her the hijackers had said in English they were going to fly the plane into the ground. The media was twisting the story, she is claimed to have said, to make it look like they were trying to save people on the ground when they were trying to save themselves. My question is why hijackers would tell the passengers they were going to crash the plane when this would clearly trigger a response on the basis of 'what do we have to lose'? How does this fit with the official story that the passengers were told by the hijackers that they had a bomb on board and were flying the plane back to the airport? It makes no sense.

In April, 2002, after months of stalling by the FBI, the families of passengers on Flight 93 were allowed to hear the cockpit voice recording (or what was claimed to be the recording, you can seriously take nothing for granted with these agencies). Tom Burnett, father of Tom Burnett Jr, said the tape was difficult to follow: 'A lot was unintelligible, and a lot of it we couldn't follow very easily, so I don't think it gives us resolution.' He felt however that he had 'learned something, another piece of the puzzle'. What is alleged to be on the Cockpit Voice Recorder was played to the jury in the trial of '20th hijacker' Zacarias Moussaoui in 2006. A lot is indeed unintelligible, but it includes the following: Voices claimed to be the pilots saying they don't want to die; what is claimed to be passengers trying to get in through the cockpit door (how did the hijackers manage it?); and many 'Allah is the greatest' shouts as the plane is said to have been purposely crashed into the field. The tape ends a minute before the alleged impact time of 10.03 although seismic data indicates that impact was at 10.06. This is important because that would mean up to four minutes of the tape were missing at the end. The official crash time puzzled Terry Wallace, a leading expert on the seismology of non-natural events at the Southern Arizona Seismic Observatory. He said: 'The seismic signals are consistent with impact at 10.06am and five seconds plus or minus two seconds. I don't know where the 10.03 time comes from.' The New York Observer reported how some relatives questioned why when an apparent struggle was in full swing voices stop and only engine noise is heard after that. Something is being hidden and could it be that the plane was shot down by the Air Force? Could it be that the whole tape is fraudulent?

So what really happened?

Pilots for 9/11 Truth examined the alleged Flight Data Recorder information released by the National Transportation Safety Board (NTSB) which included a route animation based on the data. The pilots found many discrepancies including the plane lurching around at one point while the *autopilot was on* at a time when the 'struggle' was allegedly taking place. The pilot of another plane had reported that Flight 93 was 'waving his wings' minutes before the reported crash. At one point the autopilot is switched off and the plane descends and when it is restored a few minutes later the plane's descent continues instead of returning to normal altitude. Pilots for 9/11 Truth say that a banking turn at low speed and high altitude should have threatened something called 'stall spin'. This is when the angle of a plane in relation to speed causes one wing to lose lift and pulls the aircraft into a spin which is fatal if not immediately corrected. The Pilots for 9/11 Truth voiceover for its Flight 93 video says:

> Above 40,000 feet at 200 knots in a bank and the aircraft is still flying. No stall spin, the autopilot remains on – wow!

The 'Flight 93' animation eventually has the autopilot switched off and the plane spinning and inverting to the ground. Witnesses describe the altitude of the aircraft very differently to that shown in the alleged flight data record. Two spoke of seeing the plane at an estimated 100 to 200 feet and 500 feet at a time when the height on the cockpit display in the NTSB animation shows the plane to be at nearly 10,000 feet. This enormous difference eliminates simply witness error. There are also differences in the plane's direction. We then have the extraordinary lack of plane debris in and around the small hole where the plane is supposed to have hit the ground while wreckage was found miles away (Fig 56). A 757 is some 155ft long with two engines each weighing more than six tons and even crash experts were bewildered at the lack of wreckage. *Time* magazine for the week of 9/11 reported that the 'largest pieces of the plane still extant are barely bigger than a telephone book'. No witnesses reported seeing any bodies or blood at the 'crash site'. Similar crashes have produced far more wreckage and much bigger pieces. Pennsylvania State

Figure 56: The alleged impact crater of 'Flight 93'.

Police officer Lyle Szupinka said in a repeat of what witnesses said at the Pentagon:

> If you were to go down there, you wouldn't know that was a plane crash. You would look around and say, 'I wonder what happened here?' The first impression looking around you wouldn't say, 'Oh, looks like a plane crash'. The debris is very, very small. The best I can describe it is if you've ever been to a commercial landfill. When it's covered and you have papers flying around. You have papers blowing around and bits and pieces of shredded metal. That's probably about the best way to describe that scene itself.

Wallace Miller, coroner of Somerset County in Pennsylvania, is quoted by author David McCall in his book, *From Tragedy to Triumph*, as saying:

> I got to the actual crash site and could not believe what I saw. ... Usually you see much debris, wreckage, and much noise and commotion. This crash was different. There was no wreckage, no bodies, and no noise. ... It appeared as though there were no passengers or crew on this plane.

Miller told the *Pittsburgh Post-Gazette* that it was 'as if the plane had stopped and let the passengers off before it crashed' and he remarked to CNN:

> It was a really very unusual site. You almost would've thought the passengers had been dropped off somewhere ... Even by the standard model of an airplane crash, there was very little, even by those standards.

Miller said the crater looked like someone had taken a scrap truck, dug a ten-foot ditch and dropped all the trash in it. He is quoted in Jere Longman's book, *Among the Heroes*, describing how he walked around the scene with assistant volunteer fire chief Rick King for an hour and found almost no human remains: 'If you didn't know, you would have thought no one was on the plane.' Miller told the *Pittsburgh Tribune-Review*: 'This is the most eerie thing. I have not, to this day, seen a single drop of blood. Not a drop.' The authorities claimed that somehow they found hundreds of pounds of human remains at this site. *Where?* Wallace Miller would later seek to retract – I understand why – claiming he was misquoted. What all those times? Come off it, mate. Anyway, many other witnesses said the same including these:

- The only thing you could see was a big gouge in the earth, and some broken trees ... There was nothing that you could distinguish that a plane crashed there ... nothing going on down there, no smoke, no fire ... you couldn't see anything, you could see dirt, ash, and people walking

around – [the hole] from my estimate it was 20 to 15 feet long ... 10 feet
wide – Fox News photographer.

- I left work to locate the crash site [along with a colleague] but when we
  arrived almost nothing was recognizable. The only thing we saw that
  was even remotely human was half a shoe that was probably ten feet
  from the impact area – Jeff Phillips, who worked at Stoystown Auto
  Wreckers.

- We were so early that they hadn't had a chance to set up a barrier for
  the press ... I was able to get right up to the edge of the crater ... All I
  saw was a crater filled with small, charred plane parts. ... There were no
  suitcases, no recognizable plane parts, no body parts – Jon Meyer,
  reporter with WJAC-TV.

- Several trees were burned badly and there were papers everywhere. We
  searched ... I was told that there were 224 passengers, but later found
  out that there were actually 40. I was stunned. There was nothing there
  – Faye Hahn, an Emergency Medical Technician who responded to the
  first reports of the crash.

Yet within two weeks of the crash the FBI reported that around 95
percent of the plane had somehow been recovered and a pristine, crash-
proof, fire-proof hijacker passport and red bandana or headband that
'hijackers' were claimed to be wearing by a 'caller from the plane'. Milt
Bearden, a former CIA agent who trained the US-backed Mujahideen in
Afghanistan, pointed out that 'al-Qaeda' were a Sunni Muslim operation
and that red headbands were 'a uniquely Shia Muslim adornment which
dated back to the formation of the Shia sect'. Real Sunni followers,
especially alleged fanatics, would never make that error, he said. Other
incriminating evidence supporting the official story was 'found' at the
site and personal belongings from passengers were returned to loved
ones in undamaged condition. One family member said of a returned
wallet: 'It was practically intact. It just looked like it wasn't damaged or
hadn't been through much at all, which is so bizarre and ironic.' There
are many questions about how a remarkable range of personal items
from passengers, crew and hijackers appeared at the 'crash site' where
no wreckage or personal items were seen before the area was cordoned
off from public and media view. These included 'hijacker' ID cards, a
five-page document about conducting the hijacking, red bandanas and
many knives or parts of knives. Some of them were labelled 'Hollywood
Props Department' I would wager. Numerous paper documents were
recovered that would have been in the possession of passengers, but no
bodies were independently seen. Planting wreckage and evidence was

part of the planned fake plane crash scenario with Operation
Northwoods:

> At precisely the same time that the aircraft was presumably shot down a
> submarine or small surface craft would disburse F-101 parts, parachute, etc.,
> at approximately 15 to 20 miles off the Cuban coast and depart. The pilots
> returning to Homestead would have a true story as far as they knew. Search
> ships and aircraft could be dispatched and parts of aircraft found.

Protecting the lie

The removal of all this alleged wreckage and human remains at the
'Flight 93' crater was done in the strictest secrecy. A double ring of
security sealed off several miles around the crash site while the
'removal' was taking place with police on horseback and in helicopters
ensuring that no one got anywhere close. Police said 600 troopers were
deployed with check-points on all roads leading to the crater. No
photographs have been released of wreckage recovery. Paul Falavolito, a
Pittsburgh paramedic, described the level of security:

> Upon arrival at the site, we are greeted by a barrier of state police cars on a
> rural road in this town ... At the checkpoint, we show our IDs and are allowed
> through. For the next two miles, I cannot believe my eyes. Down this country
> road, police cars and troopers are everywhere. Horseback troopers are
> patrolling the area. Hundreds of American flags line the road on both sides,
> checkpoints are everywhere. I can hear someone talking on a loudspeaker, his
> voice echoing in the hills. This is a scary feeling; I feel like I am in another
> country.

The recovered parts from Flight 93 were said to have been returned to
the airline when this appears not to be the case. A film report by *Komo
News* was given access to the beyond top-secret underground storage
facility called Iron Mountain which is 220 feet below the surface at
Boyers, Pennsylvania, an hour's drive from Pittsburgh. During the
report it was stated that the 'charred evidence' from Flight 93 was
'heavily guarded in one of the underground vaults' at Iron Mountain
which was described as 'one of the most protected places on earth'. So –
just the place to protect evidence that would scupper the story of Flight
93. There are many other questions besides the lack of plane wreckage at
the reported impact site. Footage of vertical crashes like the one claimed
to have happened with Flight 93 produce plumes of thick black smoke
caused by jet fuel. Smoke in a picture taken immediately after 'impact'
shows only light grey smoke. Why wasn't the grass next to the small
crater even burnt and the same with most surrounding trees? An aircraft
155 feet long, 125 feet wide with a maximum take-off weight of 220,000

pounds simply disappeared into a hole 20 to 15 feet long and ten feet wide. A Boeing 737-300 hit the ground nose-first into soft ground in 2005 after plunging 34,000 feet and still a large part of the tail-section was clearly visible (Fig 57). Deceased passengers and luggage could also be seen. This leads us to another question: Where was the thousands of gallons of jet fuel in and around the crater? Witnesses said

Figure 57: The tail is clearly visible after Helios Airways Flight 522 dived nose-first into a Greek mountain gorge in 2005 and there was other obvious evidence of a plane crash – unlike the 'impact point' of Flight 93. Greek fighter jets were scrambled to check out and track the plane when contact was lost with air traffic control – unlike 9/11.

there was no smell of jet fuel (as with the Pentagon) only 'burned earth'. Three ground wells and between 5,000 and 6,000 cubic yards of soil at the site were tested by the Environmental Protection Agency (EPA) and no contamination was found. The impact crater itself is at odds with the NTSB alleged Flight Data Recorder which does not depict vertical contact with the ground (as the crater would indicate) but an angled one that would produce a very different length and shape of crater.

Flight 93 shot down?

President Bush did not give the order to intercept and shoot down any commercial airliner on 9/11 until after the Pentagon had been hit – the constantly recurring point before which any action was taken to influence events. Bush had the best part of an hour to give this order to protect Washington and the Pentagon after 'Flight 11' crashed and almost 35 minutes after the crash of Flight 175. By the time he did officially give the order Flight 93 was only the one of the four in the air when the military were given permission to shoot-to-kill. The order was confirmed by Vice President Dick Cheney who told the *Meet the Press* programme:

> I wholeheartedly concurred in the decision he made, that if the plane would not divert, if they wouldn't pay any attention to instructions to move away from the city, as a last resort our pilots were authorized to take them out.

Had the Air Force shot down Flight 93 a majority of people would have accepted there was no other choice given what had happened. Instead the authorities are insistent this did not happen. NORAD told me in

2002 that F-16s that were said to have been scrambled from Langley to Washington were redirected to check out Flight 93. When the plane crashed near Shanksville they were still eleven minutes or 100 miles from making contact. Shucks, missed again – the story of the day. But is that true? Deputy Defense Secretary Paul Wolfowitz said the Pentagon had been tracking Flight 93 and could have shot it down if necessary and Secretary Rumsfeld seemed to let slip that it was. He said in a speech to troops in Iraq in 2004:

> And I think all of us have a sense if we imagine the kind of world we would face if the people who bombed the mess hall in Mosul, or the people who did the bombing in Spain, or the people who attacked the United States in New York, shot down the plane over Pennsylvania and attacked the Pentagon.

Rumsfeld later claimed he 'misspoke'. But did he? Eyewitness reports near the alleged scene of the crash confirm that Flight 93 was being tracked and they seriously contradict the NORAD claim that the nearest military jet was 100 miles away at the time. The location of wreckage and eyewitness reports put in question the claim that the plane came down in one piece. How could a section of fuselage the size of a dining room table be recovered miles from the crash site? How could a half-ton piece of engine (one ton in some reports) be recovered from more than a mile away? The FBI apparently said it 'bounced'. The *Pittsburgh Post-Gazette* reported:

> Residents and workers at businesses outside Shanksville, Somerset County, reported discovering clothing, books, papers, and what appear to be human remains. Some residents said they collected bags-full of items to be turned over to investigators. Others reported what appeared to be crash debris floating in Indian Lake, nearly six miles from the crash site.

Indian Lake is nearer than that as the crow flies but still some miles away and debris was reported even further away. CNN reported on September 13th:

> A second debris field was around Indian Lake about 3 miles from the crash scene. Some debris was in the lake and some was adjacent to the lake. More debris from the plane was found in New Baltimore, some 8 miles away from the crash. State police and the FBI initially said they didn't want to speculate whether the debris was from the crash, or if the plane could have broken up in mid-air.

I have seen a plane crash documentary in which an aircraft dived into a field and left a small crater with no discernible parts and paper and other debris travelled a considerable distance on the wind. However, the plane was far smaller and hit the ground vertically at 5,000 times the force of gravity and beyond the speed of sound when an airline employee shot the pilots and purposely made the plane dive vertically at full speed. Flight 93 was a much bigger aircraft and according to the official flight data animation and witness accounts the plane did not hit the ground vertically or anywhere close to the speed of sound. There was virtually no wind at the time of the crash yet the *Pittsburgh Post-Gazette* reported that the plane left a trail of debris five miles long and some witnesses described seeing a 'cloud of confetti' falling from the sky after hearing an explosion. Reuters reported Pennsylvania state police as saying that debris from the plane had been found up to eight miles away in a residential community 'where local media have quoted residents as speaking of a second plane in the area and burning debris falling from the sky'. These reports were ignored by the 9/11 Commission and no witnesses were invited to testify because they do not fit the official narrative. Numerous eye-witnesses reported hearing loud bangs or thuds followed by Flight 93 in the words of one dropping 'like a stone'. Even CNN noted the discrepancies when correspondent Brian Cabell reported from the scene in Pennsylvania on September 13th:

> ... in the last hour or so, the FBI and the state police here have confirmed that they have cordoned off a second area about six to eight miles away from the crater here where [the] plane went down. This is apparently another debris site, which raises a number of questions.
>
> Why would debris from the plane – and they identified it specifically as being from this plane – why would debris be located six miles away? Could it have blown that far away? It seems highly unlikely. Almost all the debris found at this site is within 100 yards, 200 yards, so it raises some questions.

Yes – questions which were subsequently never asked and never investigated. *ABC News* reported that an eyewitness called Linda Shepley had told television station KDKA in Pittsburgh that she 'heard a loud bang and saw the plane bank to the side before crashing'. Other witnesses said they heard up to three loud booms before the jetliner went down. Danny Butler wrote in the *Herald Sun*: 'Witnesses reported eerie sounds from the aircraft as it fell. Some people heard an explosion, and others heard sputtering.' A local Pennsylvania newspaper, the *Daily American*, reported the experience of another witness:

> Laura Temyer of Hooversville RD1 was hanging her clothes outside to dry before she went to work Tuesday morning when she heard what she thought was an airplane. 'Normally I wouldn't look up, but I just heard on the news

that all the planes were grounded and thought this was probably the last one I would see for a while, so I looked up,' she said. 'I didn't see the plane but I heard the plane's engine. Then I heard a loud thump that echoed off the hills and then I heard the plane's engine. I heard two more loud thumps and didn't hear the plane's engine anymore after that.

The Pentagon told *The New York Times* that Flight 93 was being followed by a fighter jet with an order from President Bush to shoot down the plane if necessary. The *Telegraph* newspaper in Nashua and Southern New Hampshire quoted a 'Federal Aviation Administration employee who works in the Nashua control facility'. He is reported to have said that air traffic controllers there had learned through discussions with other controllers that an F-16 fighter stayed in hot pursuit of Flight 93 until it crashed. They had learned that the F-16 made 360-degree turns to remain close to the plane, the employee said. 'He must've seen the whole thing.' First media reports (often the most accurate before the lid goes on) said the plane had been shot down and *USA Today* reported how local residents said they had seen a second plane in the area. '[FBI Agent] Crowley said investigators had determined that two other planes were nearby but didn't know if either was military,' said the paper.

The mystery 'white jet'

Another aspect of the Flight 93 story that has conveniently been forgotten and ignored is the small white jet seen by many residents at the time of the crash. *The Record* newspaper in Bergen County, New Jersey, quoted five people in its edition of September 14th who live and work less than four miles from the crash site and in the end at least twelve people reported seeing the jet. Susan Custer said she saw a small white jet streaking overhead and then 'heard the boom and saw the mushroom cloud'. Robin Doppstadt was working inside her family food-and-supply store when she heard the crash and when she went outside she saw a small white jet that 'looked like it was making a single circle over the crash site'. She said it climbed very quickly and took off. 'It's the damndest darn thing,' said farmer Dale Browning. 'Everybody's seen this thing in the sky, but no one can tell us what it is.' Susan Mcelwain, a local teacher, said a small white jet with rear engines and no discernible markings swooped low over her minivan, almost clipped the tops of trees, and disappeared over a hilltop. Within a minute, she said, the ground shook and a white plume of smoke appeared over the ridge. 'It was so close to me I ducked,' Mcelwain recalled, 'I heard it ['Flight 93'] hit and saw the smoke. All I could think of was how close I came to dying.' Dennis Decker and Rick Chaney said they heard an explosion and ran outside to see a large mushroom cloud spreading over the ridge.

'As soon as we looked up, we saw a mid-sized jet flying low and fast,' Decker said. 'It appeared to make a loop or part of a circle, and then it turned fast and headed out.' They said the plane was something like a Learjet and was white with no markings that they could see. 'If you were here to see it, you'd have no doubt,' Decker said. 'It was a jet plane, and it had to be flying real close when that 757 went down – if I was the FBI, I'd find out who was driving that plane.' The FBI did not appear interested in doing that which will surprise no one. The FBI said it did not rule out a second plane and then did exactly that. An official at the Cleveland Air Traffic Control Center in Oberlin, Ohio, which tracked Flight 93, said 'no comment' when asked if there was any record of a second plane over the crash site. 'That's something that the FBI is working on and I cannot talk about,' said Richard Kettel, head of tower operations at the Cleveland Center. Small white jets like the one described are used by the US military. 9/11 investigator Christopher Bollyn travelled to the Shanksville area and found 'scores of eyewitnesses' whose story has not been told. What they said was seriously at odds with the official explanation. They describe seeing military aircraft in the area at the time. Resident Viola Saylor said she saw a low-flying 'very quiet' white 'military' plane flying over the crash site after the explosion and two other planes following behind. She was shown a picture of a low-flying combat aircraft called a Fairchild A-10 Thunderbolt II – known as a 'Warthog' – and she agreed that this was like the plane she saw (Fig 58). Witness Susan Mcelwain had described the Warthog perfectly:

Figure 58: The US Air Force 'Warthog' which witnesses said was like the 'white jet' they saw with 'Flight 93'.

It was white with no markings but it was definitely military, it just had that look. It had two rear engines, a big fin on the back like a spoiler on the back of a car and with two upright fins at the side. I haven't found one like it on the Internet. It definitely wasn't one of those executive jets.

Other witnesses identified the same picture which fitted the descriptions they gave before they saw the picture. They described its two rear engines and distinctive cockpit and nose. A website specialising in the investigation of Flight 93 in the months after 9/11 summarised the situation very well:

At this point, if a new story comes out – even if it comes with a recording – that shows heroes in the cockpit, I think we all have a right to be skeptical of its accuracy. I have a digital audio studio at home. I, and anyone else familiar with audio these days, can tell you anything can be created. No matter what information is released in the future, skeptics of the hero story have been given all the ammo they need by the FBI to remain skeptical forever. That ammo is silence, time and the failure to discuss witnessed events like the mystery white jet at tree top level before the crash, the wide debris field, the detached engine, the explosions heard by so many and the data recorders.

FBI witness tyranny

Witnesses to what happened in Pennsylvania were soon going quiet after visits from the FBI which controlled all evidence and witnesses and eventually hid the debris away at Iron Mountain while taking over the investigation from designated crash investigators at the National Transportation Safety Board. Those who had recounted stories which did not match the official narrative were told by FBI agents there were no other planes when there clearly were. If they still stuck with their stories they were warned to shut up and not talk about what they saw. This is a common theme running through all aspects of 9/11 as we have seen in Venice, at the Pentagon, the World Trade Center, here with Flight 93 and every facet of what happened. If the FBI and other government agencies really wanted the truth they would have encouraged everyone to share their experiences, but the aim was always to suppress the truth and not seek it out. Researcher and investigator Christopher Bollyn visited the Shanksville area many times in search of what really happened and produced some alarming – if predictable – evidence of outrageous FBI skulduggery. He said the 'crash crater' was on an already-scarred reclaimed mine and suggests the 'crater' could have been caused by a missile to divert attention from where he says the bulk of the plane – or *a* plane – did come down. Bollyn said he discovered that the real impact point was some 100 metres away deep in the woods near the cottage of local resident Barry Hoover with debris scattered over a wide area among the trees. Hoover's cottage was seriously damaged by shockwaves from the crash as described in the *Pittsburgh Post-Gazette*:

Obviously, I was upset when I saw my house. Who wouldn't be?' said Hoover, 34, whose home off Lambertsville Road is believed to be the local structure most seriously damaged by the crash. 'But you know, it's a house and there's nothing there that can't be replaced. The people who died can't be replaced.'

... Wreckage was still burning and emergency workers were still speeding to the scene when Hoover neared his house. While it was still standing, every window and door had been blown off and obliterated, its ceilings and floor tiles had been blasted loose and much of the interior was wrecked. 'It looked like what you see after a tornado or hurricane goes through -- a total ruin,' he said.

Bollyn said he spoke with Barry Hoover's father, Lutheran minister, Reverend Larry Hoover, who lived nearby, and the minister described how luggage had been found around his house (300 metres from the crater) and body parts around his son's cottage. Bollyn asked why he had stayed so quiet about what he knew and he replied: 'We tried to cooperate.' He and his son had been asked by the FBI not to say anything while the clean-up was launched in the woods and the world focussed on the crater devoid of credible plane wreckage, Bollyn writes. Jim Svonavec owned the reclaimed mine, worked at the crash site and provided excavation equipment. Bollyn said Svonavec told him in 2004 that an engine from the plane was recovered 'at least 1,800 feet into the woods' and this was done solely by the FBI using his equipment. This background would provide answers to the questions Bollyn poses about the actions of the local coroner:

> Why was Wally Miller, the Somerset County Coroner, forced to turn over the 'crash' site to the FBI? Why did he abdicate his responsibility for the site and the recovery of the bodies, his obligation under state law? Why was he not even allowed to be involved in the identification of the remains of the passengers of Flight 93, whose death certificates he duly signed?

Bollyn said that he met with Wallace 'Wally' Miller to find out what happened. Miller was prompted by workers painting his porch who said: 'Tell him what the FBI told you.' Bollyn writes that the FBI asked Miller if he was going to be a 'team player' or words to that effect and allow them to have control of the crash scene. Miller agreed and the FBI closed off the whole area of hundreds of metres into the woods around the properties of the Hoovers. Even Jim Svonavec who provided excavation and other equipment was not allowed into the FBI area and neither were those who owned properties there like the Hoovers. Coroner Wallace Miller who should have been overseeing recovery of bodies under Pennsylvania law was located six miles away. Then came the announcement by the Pentagon in 2012 that remains of some of the victims – *some?* – from Flight 93 and the Pentagon had been incinerated, mixed with medical waste and dumped in a landfill site. The report was published after a commission, chaired by retired General John Abizaid, investigated allegations of 'improper' (disgusting) actions at Dover Air

Force Base mortuary in Delaware with regard to the remains of
American soldiers killed in Iraq and Afghanistan. The 86-page report
said:

> Prior to 2008, portions of remains that could neither be tested nor identified
> ...were cremated under contract at a civilian crematory and returned to DPM
> [Dover Port Mortuary]. This policy began shortly after September 11, 2001,
> when several portions of remains from the Pentagon attack and the
> Shanksville, Pennsylvania, crash site could not be tested or identified.
>
> These cremated portions were then placed in sealed containers that were
> provided to a biomedical waste disposal contractor. Per the biomedical waste
> contract at that time, the contractor then transported these containers and
> incinerated them. The assumption on the part of DPM was that after final
> incineration nothing remained. A DPM management query found that there
> was some residual material following incineration and that the contractor was
> disposing of it in a landfill. The landfill disposition was not disclosed in the
> contractual disposal agreement.

The policy began immediately after September 11th, 2001. Well, you
do surprise me. Bollyn said he read that FBI agents were working at the
Dover AFB mortuary 'identifying' human remains. He said he called
Coroner Miller in early 2006 and 'asked him about the ethics of his
having signed death certificates for bodies that had been identified by
others at Dover AFB'. Bollyn said Miller 'got angry at me for having
asked this direct question, but he cannot say that he has not heard that
such things could have occurred'. He describes Miller as a 'nice fellow'
who thinks everybody plays by the rules. But they don't – especially the
FBI. All this happened on the watch of FBI chief Robert Mueller and his
bosses John Ashcroft and Michael Chertoff at the [In]Justice Department.
Chertoff's ears will be seriously burning later in the book.

CHAPTER 12

'Hijackers' and 'phone calls'

Don't believe everything you hear: Real eyes, Realize, Real lies
– Tupac Shakur

There is something very strange about the whole 'hijackers took over the aircraft' story. It might sound feasible to most people at first hearing and those who research or question no further. When you dig deeper there are many questions about whether there were any 'hijackers' on any of the 9/11 flights.

Some of the names listed were those of people who turned up still alive and the FBI has changed names that it originally said were involved. There were no security cameras in the departure lounge at Boston Logan Airport so we can't see the 'hijackers' boarding Flights 11 and 175 and there were reported to be no cameras at departure gates at Newark and Washington Dulles although officials would not confirm this to me when I asked soon after the attacks. There were cameras elsewhere in and around the airports that *must* have recorded the 'hijackers' on video as they passed through. We have not been allowed to see any of that except for what is *claimed* to be the hijackers of Flight 77 passing through security at Washington Dulles. This was not released through a Freedom of Information request until 2004 at the time the official 9/11 Commission 'report' was made public. If they could release this recording then why not the footage from other cameras and why wasn't this footage made public much earlier as a matter of course? The 9/11 Commission Final Report says that in the case of Flight 93 there is 'no documentary evidence' to indicate when the hijackers passed though security checkpoints or what alarms were triggered or security procedures involved. While Boston may not have had cameras in the departure lounge are they saying they had none anywhere on the 'hijackers" journey to and through the airport? Exactly the same theme can be found with the video footage of Timothy McVeigh and 'friend' in Oklahoma. One thing is certain: if the video footage in and around those airports showed the hijackers arriving in their cars, checking in, going through security and boarding the planes it would have been blasted on every television station in the world ASAP after the attacks. They didn't have any problem releasing the footage of 'Atta' and 'Al-Omari' rushing to catch the flight from Portland, Maine, that morning or the shots of 'Al-Omari' getting cash the previous night from an ATM Machine or the footage from Dulles *eventually*. Why are they so shy about video recordings that would confirm their story if they were telling the truth?

Video 'proof'?

Let us examine the 'Dulles security footage'. There were 300 security cameras at Dulles at that time, according to David Brent, a technical information engineer for IT systems in a 2011 article at Securityinfowatch.com headed 'The CSI Effect: How TV is changing video surveillance'. He said:

> In 2001, I worked for a manufacturer that at the time had its CCTV system in the Washington Dulles International Airport and the Pentagon. After the 9/11 attacks, I was part of a team that had the laborious task of reviewing all the video from the airport with several federal agents looking over our shoulders. Did you notice I said all the video? That's every frame from over 300 cameras with 30 days of retention time. The task took three weeks of 15-hour days.

There were some 300 cameras around Washington Dulles and we saw alleged footage from *one* and that came *three years* after the attacks with nothing from other 9/11 airports. It took a law firm Freedom of Information request to secure the tapes which were released the day before the report by the 9/11 Commission. If the authorities want to clear up doubts and speculation why wasn't this made public years earlier? The Dulles footage did not carry a time-code or identification number which is simply not credible for a security video (Fig 59). The camera features a wide shot – not a close-up – of people walking through security. Remember how the security footage at Portland, Maine, of 'Atta' and 'Al-Omari' had two time-codes – one at the bottom showing how late they were as they rushed for the commuter flight to Boston and one ridiculously smack in the middle that gave an earlier time? The media overwhelmingly cropped the picture so only the middle code was visible. In the case of the Dulles footage the date, time and

Figure 59: Dulles airport security footage.

camera number is missing altogether which is not normal procedure for a security camera. The cameras did not employ the airport security time-lapse technique to save space with data storage. The don't-question-the-official-story 9/11 Commission Report claims that two of the men, including next-to-useless small plane pilot Hanjour, travelled in first class on a flight of very few people. So why did Brenda Brown who handled first class check-in that day say in her interview with the FBI that she didn't remember any Arab males. This was on what she called 'a light travel day' when she remembered other passengers. No authenticated passenger lists (legal documents) including 'hijacker' names have ever been released and nor have authenticated boarding pass stubs. Some have claimed that shadows on the Dulles footage could not have been generated in the early morning when the video had to have been shot, but much closer to noon. Then there is the experience of Dulles security manager Ed Nelson when the FBI, FAA and other agencies descended on the airport after 'Flight 77' was said to have struck the Pentagon. He said he thought their behaviour was not 'adding up' when they appeared to be more interested in pressuring security screeners to admit violating procedures than the 'hijackers' themselves. 'It was as if they were working off a script', Nelson said. FBI agents later confirmed that the orders were coming from FBI headquarters via local Washington-area FBI field offices and the Joint Task Force on Terrorism. Nelson was also bemused at how FBI operatives could immediately pick out the relevant security tape:

> They pulled the tape right away ... They brought me to look at it. They went right to the first hijacker on the tape and identified him. They knew who the hijackers were out of hundreds of people going through the checkpoints. They would go 'roll and stop it' and showed me each of the hijackers ... It boggles my mind that they had already had the hijackers identified ... Both metal detectors were open at that time, and lots of traffic was moving through. So picking people out is hard ... I wanted to know how they had that kind of information. So fast. It didn't make sense to me.

How come the 9/11 Commission claimed that ten of the 19 'hijackers' were picked out for additional security checks by the automated passenger screening system known as CAPPS when no security staff had testified to seeing them? The Commission reported that in relation to Boston Logan Flights 11 and 175 none of the security checkpoint supervisors 'recalled the hijackers or reported anything suspicious regarding their screening'. Security at Washington Dulles (Flight 77) did not recall that any of those they screened were selected by CAPPS and security staff screening passengers for Flight 93 at Newark, New Jersey, remembered nothing suspicious. Then how come the FBI reported collecting '14 knives or portions of knives at the Flight 93 crash site'? Oops, the alarm's gone off – wow 14 knives. Never mind, have a good flight gentlemen, nothing suspicious here. Why were airline staff who would have seen the 'hijackers' board and checked their boarding passes not allowed to speak publicly to confirm what happened? I was knocked back by American Airlines after 9/11when I asked to speak with check-in and boarding staff on duty that morning and this has been the experience of other researchers ever since from what I can see. Why did the official 9/11 Commission not include testimony from these people? Why did a letter from American Airlines lawyers to the 9/11 Commission in 2004 list most of those who worked at the check-in desks in Boston and Washington Dulles while redacting the names of staff at the departure gates? Researchers did discover two FBI interview forms – known as 302s – released in 2009 and involving American Airlines employees Liset Frometa (conducted on September 11th, 2001) and Maria Jackson (conducted on September 22nd) who testified to working at Boston Logan Gate 32 on Flight 11. Also included was an interview with another unnamed female member of staff who said she was involved with boarding Flight 11. None of them remembered the alleged 'hijackers' and when Jackson was shown a 'photo spread of subjects' she did not recognise any of them. Jackson is quoted in the FBI form as describing how she 'took the tickets ... from AA flight attendant Karen Martin and brought them to the ticket lift and deposited them in the safe.' *So why have we never seen them?*

Death certificates were issued for everyone claimed to have been on the four flights, but not the alleged hijackers. An offer from the family of one of the men named to help with DNA identification was refused and it's clear from numerous witnesses that the FBI had DNA samples of the people they named from a series of locations including homes, hotel rooms and cars where hair and other DNA sources were gathered and taken away. The FBI has confirmed this and none of the material appears to have been used to identify the 'hijackers'. Chris Kelly, a spokesman for the Armed Services Institute of Pathology which claimed to have identified those killed at the Pentagon and in Pennsylvania, said: 'The remains that didn't match any of the [innocent passenger] samples were ruled ... to be terrorists.' Oh, scientific and thorough then. Somerset County judge Kim R. Gibson approved the issuing of death certificates in October, 2001, for passengers on Flight 93 but not for alleged 'hijackers' because the FBI was *not sure of their identities.* The Armed Services Institute of Pathology claimed in 2003 to have identified 58 passengers on Flight 77. The list was released under a Freedom of Information Act request and ... contained no Arabic names. Amazing how you can identify people from DNA after a crash apparently so fantastic that a Cockpit Voice Recorder specifically designed to survive such impact and heat was reported to have been destroyed. If they are so certain who was responsible then why did FBI Director Robert Mueller say that a case against the 19 would not stand up in court? Mueller said that not a single piece of paper had been uncovered in America or Afghanistan which mentioned any aspect of the September 11th plot. The FBI confiscated all the video footage relating to 9/11 within hours and what they have allowed us to see is clearly manipulated crap. Where is *any* credible video evidence to confirm the official story of 9/11 in locations like the Pentagon and airports awash with cameras? The fact is that all this time later we still have no proof or independent confirmation that the men named by the FBI actually *boarded* the crashed planes and nor that the planes were the ones that left the airports.

The phone calls

Many phone calls were said to have been made by passengers (most from Flight 93) describing their plight as it was happening. Faced with the constant stream of lies we have been fed about 9/11 and clear and obvious attempts by the FBI to cover up the truth we need to question everything to see if it stands up to scrutiny. This is especially important with reported telephone calls from the aircraft because what is claimed to have been communicated provided the *whole foundation* for the official story of 9/11. Pretty much the only information about what is claimed to have happened on the aircraft came from calls said to have been made by cabin attendants and passengers. From these we get the story of men with 'Middle Eastern appearance' hijacking the planes with small knives and box-cutters and taking over the controls with the pilots forced out of the cockpit to the back of the plane etc. From the same source came the whole 'Let's roll' narrative about an attempt by passengers to retake control of Flight 93. Given their importance to 9/11 official history it is equally important that we ask legitimate questions about them. Long-time 9/11 researcher David Ray Griffin points out in his excellent *9/11 Ten Years Later* that there are many anomalies, contradictions and impossibilities with the phone calls and obvious untruths. Griffin rightly says that if only one of those calls can be shown to be faked then they were all faked because it proves a pre-planned effort to mislead. They are hardly going to fake only one with obvious foreknowledge and planning while all the other calls are genuine. Before I look at the calls themselves I come back to a recurring theme I want to emphasise – technology that we see in the public arena has been available to the military and intelligence agencies for a long time before. So much so, that if we can see it today 'They' almost certainly had it at the time of 9/11. One example is the GPS navigation positioning technology that military planes had in 2001 which commercial 9/11 aircraft did not and that was even publicly available knowledge. The technology to replicate voices to make someone appear to say what they never did say is now phenomenal. I am not saying this was used on 9/11 – there are other ways to explain the calls – but it should be legitimately added to the mix of possibility. Voice replication or morphing technology takes the unique frequency of a person's voice and puts it through a process that allows someone else to speak while sounding exactly like the voice the technology is mimicking. This has reached the point where it is possible even to *write* the words and the technology will speak them in the voice of whoever you choose, as public demonstrations have shown. The same can be done with videos of people with their lips synched by artificial intelligence to appear to speak words in their own voice they never said. There are many YouTube presentations of this technology and if you have never come across it before you'll be amazed at how authentic it looks and sounds. We also know that the US military had voice-replication technology at the time of 9/11 because this has been revealed in government documents. I have written in other books about how advanced this was before 2001 thanks to technology developed at the deeply sinister Hidden Hand-controlled Los Alamos National Laboratory in New Mexico. William Arkin, author of *The U.S. Military Online* and a specialist on national security, the Internet and information warfare, wrote an article for *The Washington Post* in 1999 about voice-morphing technology developed by scientist George Papcun. Arkin, a former army intelligence analyst, said:

> By taking just a 10-minute digital recording of [General Carl] Steiner's voice, scientist George Papcun is able, in near real time, to clone speech patterns and develop an accurate facsimile. Steiner was so impressed, he asked for a copy of the tape.

Steiner was hardly the first or last victim to be spoofed by Papcun's team members. To refine their method they took various high quality recordings of generals and experimented with creating fake statements including 9/11 Secretary of State Colin Powell. Arkin wrote that digital morphing – voice, video, and photo – had come of age and was available for use in psychological operations, or PSYOPS, to 'exploit human vulnerabilities in enemy governments, militaries and populations to pursue national and battlefield objectives'. What happened on 9/11 was a PSYOP on the world. It was also a coup on the United States by Hidden Hand personnel and how prophetic that Arkin should write this in *1999*:

> To some, PSYOPS is a backwater military discipline of leaflet dropping and radio propaganda. To a growing group of information war technologists, it is the nexus of fantasy and reality. Being able to manufacture convincing audio

or video, they say, might be the difference in a successful military operation or coup.

Daniel T. Kuehl, chairman of the Information Operations Department of the National Defense University in Washington, the military's school for information warfare, said: 'We already know that seeing isn't necessarily believing – now I guess hearing isn't either.' He added that 'once you can take any kind of information and reduce it into ones and zeros, you can do some pretty interesting things'. This is the kind of research and development funded and overseen by the truly evil Defence Advanced Research Projects Agency (DARPA) located in a nondescript building in Arlington, Virginia. DARPA develops death-rays, created the Internet and seed-funded technology now known as 'personal assistants' which give the military-intelligence complex surveillance access to everyone who is asleep enough to have one. DARPA developed technology necessary to carry out the 9/11 military PSYOP including the ability to hijack aircraft computer systems from the ground. Another possibility I have seen suggested is that calls were made by the real people but after they had been landed at a military base in line with Operation Northwoods and they were basically reading a script believing they were playing a part in the wargame exercises. This would explain the strange calmness, lack of emotion and matter-of-factness that people described and the lack of aircraft noise that many mentioned. The point is we don't have to prove what happened in detail to expose the 9/11 conspiracy – only that what we are told happened could not have done.

Impossible phone calls

Many of the calls from the planes were said by media reports without any FBI contradiction to have been made by cell phones at high altitudes which simply wasn't possible in 2001. There is the obvious problem of being too high and cell phones have to connect with ground stations (it's called a 'handshake') and at the speeds the aircraft were travelling they would be rushing between ground station connections so fast the calls would be constantly cut as they were reassigned even if they could get through. Highly significantly after this was pointed out the FBI had changed its story by 2006 at the time of the trial of '20th hijacker' Zacarias Moussaoui and the Bureau said all the calls except two came from Airfones on the back of the aircraft seats. The two they still said were from cell phones were those made at much lower altitudes – around 5,000 feet – which were still dubious in terms of being possible at that time. If you are caught out – change the story. These remaining 'cell phone calls' by Flight 93 passenger Edward Felt and attendant CeeCee Lyles do not appear in phone records with either numbers or duration despite what the 9/11 Commission report described as 'an exhaustive study ... of the cell phone records of each of the passengers who owned cell phones'. Experimental evidence from Canadian mathematician and scientist A. K. Dewdney in 2003 suggested that cell phones had a one-in-a-hundred chance of working at up to 20,000 feet in a poorly insulated one-engine plane. In better insulated two-engine aircraft none worked at 7,000 feet and in a far more insulated airliner the altitude would be significantly lower for cell phones to operate. Dewdney said that 'in large passenger jets, one loses contact during take-off, frequently before the plane reaches 1000 feet altitude'. Reported cell phone calls from 9/11 aircraft were impossible and American Airlines said they did not have on-board Airfones fitted on their 757s for use by either crew or passengers. AA spokesman Chad Kinder said:

> ... We do not have phones on our Boeing 757. The passengers on Flight 77 used their own personal cellular phones to make out calls during the terrorist attack.

Not according to the updated FBI report they didn't and not according to the laws of physics. American Airlines pilot Captain Ralph Kolstad who flew their 757s and 767s said he was 'absolutely certain' that Airfones had been disconnected on the 757 long before 9/11 and this is supported by the Boeing 757 Aircraft Maintenance Manual (757 AMM), dated January 28th, 2001, which says: 'The passenger telephone system was deactivated by [code-numbered order] ECO FO878.' There were other code-numbered orders to do this, ECO F1463 and F1532. By January, 2001, Airphones on American Airlines 757s were deactivated and that was the plane which flew as Flight 77. Cabin attendant Ginger Gainer said that Boeing 757s on international flights had stickers on the seatback phones to say they were not working. Several current and former flight attendants for American who flew domestic routes were asked about them and they all said the phones were either disabled or removed at the time of 9/11.

Olson calls did not happen

The official story about the calls of CNN contributor Barbara Olson on Flight 77 falls between both cell phone and Airfone narratives. She was the wife of Bush administration US Solicitor General Theodore Olson, better known as 'Ted'. He said that his wife had twice called him at his office from the plane and they had conversations lasting 'about one minute' and 'two or three minutes'. 'Olson' is the only source for hijackers having 'box-cutters' and she is said to have described how passengers and crew had been herded to the back of the plane which meant that a big burly weightlifter and boxer pilot had to have been overpowered by small, slim and slight hijackers. *CBS News* reported that the manual for security screeners issued by airlines trade groups to comply with FAA regulations listed box-cutters as items not allowed to pass security checkpoints. Screeners were told to call supervisors if they found them. Without Barbara Olson's alleged calls there is no evidence that Flight 77 headed back to Washington and what she is claimed to have said set the theme for who was responsible for the attacks when the story was released within hours. Ted Olson said at first that his wife used her cell phone, but later he changed this to 'airplane phone' before changing again and later again. Well, cell phones were a no, no, and if what American Airlines said is true about 757s then so are Airfones on AA Flight 77. A 2006 FBI report for the Moussaoui trial said that Barbara Olson *didn't make any certifiable calls to her husband*. Or none that connected. The report said that one was attempted but was unconnected and lasted nil seconds. The get-out of jail card (but not really) for the official story is that there were five calls from the flight made by 'unknown callers' to 'unknown numbers' and four of them connected. It was claimed that these four calls were made by Olson. Well, Ted Olson said she made only two and if you can ascertain that 'Barbara Olson' made a call that was unconnected and lasted nil seconds then how come you can't track who the other four went from and to? It's just still more change-the-story-when-you-are-caught-out. Ted Olson said that his wife called him on call-collect because he said 'I guess she didn't have her purse'. Researchers have pointed out that even if the Airfones were working you needed a credit card to activate them and open a line. Once you had done this there would be no need to ask for call-collect because you were free to call who you liked. The bottom line is that according to American Airlines there were no activated Airfones on AA 757s and if she couldn't have called on an Airfone or a cell phone the calls could not have been made. This is why no telephone records from Ted Olson's Department of [In]Justice, Barbara Olson's cell phone or phone company logs have ever been made public.

The change of narrative by the FBI from cell phones to Airfones faces fundamental problems in the case of calls alleged to have been made by Tom Burnett, a passenger on United Airlines Flight 93, to his wife, Deena. She was very clear that when her phone rang her husband's cell phone number appeared. He could not have been calling from an Airfone, therefore, but the FBI had to claim that he did because his alleged cell phone calls came at a time when Flight 93's Flight Data Recorder shows it to be flying at between *34,300 and 40,700 feet*. Deena Burnett, a former Delta Airlines flight attendant, even said that when she saw her husband's caller ID on her phone she didn't understand how he could be calling from the air. Lorne Lyles, husband of Flight 93 attendant, CeeCee Lyles, said the same when he found a recorded message left by her 'from the plane' on his phone. He said he saw the caller ID was her cell phone and thought 'Okay, wait a minute – how can she call me from the plane from a cell phone because cell phones don't work on a plane?' What Deena Burnett told the FBI in the immediate wake of the attacks was confirmed in the Bureau's own documents:

> Burnett was able to determine that her husband was using his own cellular telephone because the caller identification showed his number, 925 980-3360. Only one of the calls did not show on the caller identification as she was on the line with another call.

The FBI contradicted Deena Burnett's own experience and statement when in 2006 they said the calls came from a passenger seat Airfone on United Airlines Flight 93 because clearly by then the claim that a cell phone was involved at between 34,000 and 40,000 feet was known to be ridiculously untenable. This is not to suggest that Deena Burnett is not telling the truth, but that the FBI isn't. Deena saw her husband's caller ID on calls he could not have made on a cell phone from where he was supposed to have been. So who did make those calls? And where were they made from? Brian Sweeney, a passenger on Flight 175, is said to have left a cell phone message to his wife, Julie, on their home answerphone which said: 'Hi Jules, it's Brian. We've been hijacked and it doesn't look too good.' Flight 175 at that time was flying at some 25,000 feet – way above the altitude that a cell phone could work. There are other questions regarding what 'Tom Burnett' said to his wife, Deena. She said in the last call that their children were asking to speak with him, but he declined and said: 'Tell them I'll talk to them later.' Does this sound a likely response from a father who by then had said the 'hijackers' planned to crash the plane? Would you not want to have what could be the final words with your children?

'Let's roll'?

We saw the same theme with 'Let's roll' United 93 passenger Todd Beamer who is said to have talked with CTE (Verizon) Airfone operators for 20 minutes and told them 'the plane had been hijacked and that he saw two hijackers with knives and someone else enter the cockpit'. The FBI report said Beamer had tried to call his wife on an Airfone and the call was routed to a customer-service operator named Phyllis Johnson who forwarded the call to colleague Lisa Jefferson who spoke with 'Beamer' for another 13 minutes at her station outside Chicago. 'Beamer' was offered the chance to have his call connected through to his wife, Lisa, but he declined. Why would you decline the chance to speak with your wife in such a situation when the FBI claims this is who he had been trying to call? 'Beamer' is said to have told Jefferson that his wife was pregnant and he didn't want to upset her. Then why try to call her in the first place and how upset did 'Beamer' think his wife was likely to be (a) with what was clearly likely to happen if the 'hijacker' story had been true and (b) that he declined the chance to speak with her one last time? FBI telephone records confirm that 'Beamer' tried to make four calls, but only the last was connected. The rest lasted '0 seconds' or, in other words, didn't get though. The third and fourth calls were somehow dialled at exactly the same time (9:48:48), a fact that has produced no explanation. 'Beamer' is supposed to have tried to call his wife, but when he was connected to an operator he declined to be put through to his wife and instead stayed on the line with an operator who would have been easily fooled by a voice-morpher because she didn't know him.

The bottom line of all this is that there is no proof that this was the real Todd Beamer who made those calls. Jefferson said that 'Beamer' told her he didn't think he would survive. He gave her his home phone number and asked: 'If I don't make it out of this, would you please call my family and let them know how much I love them?' Why not tell them yourself? Why not ask to be connected with his parents or other relatives and people he knew? His wife Lisa Beamer recalled in a 2002 book, *Let's Roll!: Ordinary People, Extraordinary Courage*, that Lisa Jefferson had told her it was 'a miracle that Todd's call hadn't been disconnected' because lines were being disconnected all around her because of the number trying to get through. Jefferson had thought: 'This call is going to get dropped!' But it never was. Airline staff have described how inefficient and hit and miss Airfones were. Without this call from Beamer there would have been no 'Let's roll' in the official narrative. He is said to have told Jefferson that some of the passengers were getting together to retake the cockpit from the hijackers. Jefferson said that the last words she heard were Beamer saying 'Are you guys ready? Okay, let's roll'. Or did she? This alleged phrase was milked by the authorities after 9/11 and used to promote support for the subsequent 'war on terror' in response to the attacks. The London *Evening Standard* said 'Beamer's' words were 'a symbol of America's determination to fight back' and a *Washington Post* article described how the words were 'embraced and promoted by President Bush as a patriotic battle cry'. Let's roll was 'emblazoned on Air Force fighter planes, city fire trucks, school athletic jerseys, and countless T-shirts, baseball caps and souvenir buttons'. Did Beamer or whoever it was really say 'Let's roll'? Lisa Jefferson reported in earlier interviews that he said: 'Are you guys ready? Okay.' Nor were the words included in the FBI report of their interview with Jefferson on the day of the attacks. The report recorded only that at approximately 9am Central Time, Beamer said the passengers were about to attack the hijackers:

... [H]e asked Jefferson to call [redacted] to tell them that he loved them ...
Next, Jefferson heard another passenger give the go-ahead to make their
move. After that point, she heard nothing.

The 'Let's roll' phrase apparently first appeared in an interview with
Jefferson by Jim McKinnon in the *Pittsburgh Post-Gazette* five days after
9/11. McKinnon had earlier interviewed Beamer's wife, Lisa, who told
him about her husband's use of the term 'Let's roll'. Wasn't such an
important conversation between Lisa Jefferson and the alleged Beamer
taped? The claim is that it wasn't and so how do we know that the real
Todd Beamer was the man she talked to or that he used the term 'Let's
roll' which came out of nowhere after not at first being mentioned? Lisa
Jefferson also said that her line to Beamer stayed open and connected
long after Flight 93 is supposed to have crashed and the same happened with
Flight 93 passenger Jeremy Glick. Jefferson recalled that after Beamer
said he was going to re-take the cockpit with other passengers she
remained on the connected line until 10.49am – 46 minutes after the
plane is said to have crashed. She said she never heard a crash and
during the call there was 'an unusually low amount of background
noise'. Jefferson was bewildered about how she stayed connected after
the apparent crash:

> I can't explain it. We didn't lose a connection because there's a different
> sound that you use. It's a squealing sound when you lose a connection. I
> never lost connection, but it just went silent.

Given what Jefferson said about calls at that time constantly cutting out
it is indeed remarkable that she and her colleague earlier could have
maintained an open and connected line talking to 'Beamer' for an
unbroken 65 minutes while 'Jeremy Glick's' line remained open to his
wife and then her father for a total of two hours and six minutes. Glick's
father-in-law told the FBI that he heard high-pitch screaming noises and
'wind sounds' between silences and after a Horizon telephone operator
cut into the call they stayed on the open line for approximately one and
a half hours until around 10.45am but heard nothing further. Neither
were disconnected by the plane supposedly crashing when Airfones
depend on the plane's power supply?? Weird gets weirder when you
consider that phone company records secured by the FBI show that
Todd Beamer's cell phone was used to make 19 outgoing calls after –
after – the plane is said to have smashed into the ground. There is yet
another glaring anomaly about the 'Beamer'-Jefferson call. All
government agencies say that Flight 93 was hijacked at 9.28, but
Jefferson told the FBI that Beamer called at about *9.45* East Coast time

and described for the next seven minutes how the hijackers were *preparing* to seize the cockpit. Only after those seven minutes – that is approximately 9.52 – did Beamer tell her that 'two hijackers armed with knives' had entered the cockpit and secured the door behind them. How can that be when *all* government agencies say the plane was taken over more than 20 minutes earlier at 9.28? He said the plane had just begun to fly erratically while government agencies describe this happening shortly after 9.28.

'Strange calmness' and no hijack drill

Constant themes reported with the calls include no or low aircraft noise, unexpected calm and lack of emotion. Among the descriptions are 'shockingly calm' ... 'very, very calm' ... 'couldn't believe the calm in [her] voice' ... 'calm, matter of fact' ... 'remarkably calm throughout the conversation' and 'it sounded to Jack as if [his wife] were driving home from the grocery store or ordering a pizza'. Phone operator Lisa Jefferson said 'Todd Beamer' was 'so tranquil it made me begin to doubt the authenticity of his call'. Lyzbeth Glick, wife of Flight 93 passenger Jeremy, said he told her the cockpit had been taken over by hijackers wearing red headbands and that pilots, flight attendants and passengers were ordered to the rear of the plane. Lyzbeth recalled:

> I was surprised by how calm it seemed in the background. I didn't hear any screaming. I didn't hear any noises. I didn't hear any commotion.

Todd Bennett's wife, Deena, said:

> It was as if he was at Thoratec [his workplace], sitting at his desk, and we were having a regular conversation. It was the strangest thing because he was using the same tone of voice I had heard a thousand times.

A further big question is why flight attendants did not follow normal hijack procedure – just as none of the pilots punched in the highjack alert code. Flight 11 attendant Betty Ong, or who we are told was Betty Ong, didn't alert people who could have launched a response to the 'hijacking' and instead called the small American Airlines reservations office in Cary, North Carolina, in a call lasting *27 minutes*. Once again she was described as 'calm' despite apparently reporting the following:

> The cockpit is not answering their phone, and there's somebody stabbed in business class ... we can't breathe in business class. Somebody's got mace or something ... I'm sitting in the back ... Our number 1 got stabbed. Our purser is stabbed. Nobody knows who stabbed who, and we can't even get up to business class right now 'cause nobody can breathe. Our number 1 is stabbed

right now ... and our number 5 ... and we can't get into the cockpit, the door won't open.

Amy Sweeney, another attendant on Flight 11, did not make any mention of mace or pepper spray being used when she is supposed to have called American Airlines colleague Michael Woodward. This would surely have been high on the list if it was on the scale that 'Betty Ong' described. When Flight 93 attendant CeeCee Lyles ended her answerphone message to her husband a sound can be heard like headphones being removed then a quiet voice that has been reported by some to say 'You did great'. Others hear this as 'It's a frame'. When Betty Ong reports a hijacking in her call and is asked what flight she is on there appear to be two voices speaking at the same time when she mistakenly says 'Flight 12' – as did attendant Amy Sweeney. Fight 93 passenger Mark Bingham called his mother and began: 'Hi Mom, this is Mark Bingham.' Would you really call your mother and use your last name? It has also been pointed out how few calls were made from the flights if calling had been possible. Surely others would have called given the situation passengers were facing and with passengers making long calls around them. I will be presenting evidence much later in the book when it is most relevant about how computer systems were taken over on 9/11 and this would have allowed air traffic screens to be manipulated and calls and 'cockpit transmissions' inserted in real time. There is a highly-detailed analysis of alleged phone calls from the aircraft in Elias Davidsson's first-class book, *Hijacking America's Mind On 9/11*, which puts the whole official phone call story into serious question. Among his findings on this and associated behaviour are the following:

- No passenger or crew member witnessed or described the 'hijackers' actually entering the cockpit or how they did so. The 9/11 Commission had to admit: 'We do not know exactly how the hijackers gained access to the cockpit.' This was despite passenger 'phone callers' in the first class sections right next to the cockpit door. No one saw the pilots overpowered either.

- Most callers did not describe the hijackers – including flight attendants whose job it was to give as much detail as possible to the ground in these circumstances. Callers in the second row of first class right next to 'hijackers' did not describe them.

- Most flight attendants did not contact the pilots and instead some stayed on the line talking to the ground for long periods while a hijack was supposed to be taking place. Alerting the pilots should have been number one priority. This is not to criticise the attendants but to question the official version of events.

• No one seems to have observed the reported stabbing of passenger
  Mark Rothenberg (Flight 93), Daniel Lewin, a former elite officer in the
  Israeli army (Flight 11) or a flight attendant (also Flight 11).

• Some reports mentioned guns on board and people being shot, but no
  one else did.

• No one reported the sound of impact at the end of the calls – only
  silence or something like wind sound.

• Flight 11 attendant Betty Ong complained of breathing difficulties from
  a mace/pepper spray but no one else did. Fellow attendant Amy
  Sweeney didn't mention this and if it was used to the extent that Ong
  described many would be affected including the 'hijackers'.

• Highly-experienced Renee May, an attendant on Flight 77, didn't call
  her airline to report the hijacking but called her *parents* to ask them to
  do it. This veteran flyer even had to ask for the emergency numbers – *no
  way*.

What if those involved were taking part in simulated hijackings as
part of the wargames manoeuvres and thought they were playing a role
in scripted or semi-scripted simulated attacks and response scenarios
while what they were doing would be presented as their responses to
'real attacks' that we know as 9/11. What can be said for sure is that
wargames do recruit public participants to play the part of passengers
and crew in simulated hijack exercises and what if a secrecy agreement
was involved in the name of 'national security'. As Elias Davidsson
writes:

> ... the fact that the phone callers reported bogus and implausible events, the
> question that immediately springs to mind is: Were the callers participating in
> the hijacking drills? It should come as no surprise that, had this been the case,
> it would be treated as a mortal secret never to be revealed. The conduct of the
> callers strongly suggests, indeed, that they were acting rather than relaying
> real events.

Davidsson reports that this very scenario was happening on 9/11 at the
National Reconnaissance Office near Washington Dulles Airport during
an exercise scenario involving a fictitious corporate jet crashing into the
building to test evacuation procedures. Employees were given cards for
pre-scripted actions including making phone calls telling people about

the make-believe 'crash' and fire as if they were real. The fire was simulated by using a smoke generator. Art Haubold, a spokesman for the NRO, said it was 'just an incredible coincidence that this happened to involve an aircraft crashing into our facility'. Add it to the list, mate. If 9/11 phone calls were part of an exercise it would explain the omissions, contradictions and universal calmness that those they spoke with described and the lack of normal procedures. In fact, pretty much all the questions about the phone calls would be answered if this was the case and particularly if the planes were flying at much lower altitudes than reported or were even on the ground.

Double cross

I concluded pretty soon after 9/11 that the four planes had 'doubles' in the way described by Operation Northwoods. Planes that officially took off from the airports were taken over by remote control from the ground and their military-controlled 'doubles' completed the journeys that ended in disaster. Gathering evidence to support this has emerged over the years. Planes with the same air traffic 'signature' could easily have been switched especially with transponders turned off and amid systematic confusion. Non-transponder radar can track location but not be certain of identity. Transponders can also be switched to a different code and assume a new identity on air traffic control screens to bemuse trackers even more. Whoever was controlling Flight 175 twice did this. There has certainly been confusion over which gates some of the planes left from with different ones reported. Flight 11 was reported to have left from Gate 26 at Boston Logan and later Gate 32. Journalists from the German weekly *Der Spiegel* say they established that Flight 11 left from Gate 26 and that boarding started at 7.35am. The 9/11 Commission said boarding began at 7.15am and left from Gate 32. There are also discrepancies in statements made to the FBI and 9/11 Commission about when the plane left. Some say it was five minutes ahead of time and others that it was delayed. American Airlines employee Michael Woodward told the Commission that Flight 11 was delayed although he didn't know why. Another, Elizabeth Williams, told the FBI that Woodward 'advised her that they needed to go to Gate 32 because two flight attendants had been stabbed'. This came from information communicated in a call to passenger service agent Evelyn Nunez by Flight 11 attendant Amy Sweeney which had been misunderstood – the flight had already taken off. Sweeney had also said, like attendant Betty Ong, that she was calling from 'Flight 12'. Elizabeth Williams said that when they arrived at Gate 32 there was only an empty plane. Sweeney's husband told the FBI that she called him from the plane – which he said was very unusual – to say departure had been delayed. Passenger Richard Ross said the same in a call to his wife while the plane was at the gate. Did it leave from Gate 26 or 32 and was it early or late? Tom Kinton, Aviation Director for Massport at Boston Logan, told 9/11 Commission staff that Flight 11 left from Gate 31. We also have the discrepancy highlighted by Pilots for 9/11 Truth about the departure gate for Flight 77. The pilots point out as I described earlier that Flight Data Recorder information supplied by the authorities reveals that the plane the data refers to did not depart from Dulles Gate D26 which was assigned to Flight 77. The RITA database of the Research and Innovative Technology Administration (which includes the Bureau of Transportation Statistics within the US Department of Transportation) has Flight 175 taking off at 8.23 while the 9/11 Commission says 8.14. RITA records Flight 93 as taking off from Newark at 8.23 while the Commission says 8.42. The RITA database does not include tail numbers for Flights 11 and 77 and records only the scheduled departure times and not the actual ones. The Department of Transportation said this was because the information had not been provided by the airlines. 'Double' planes did not have to take off from the same airports to replace the original flights en route, however, as we saw with Operation Northwoods when the double aircraft would take off from the Air Force base where the original plane was also due to land.

Planes still flying after they 'crashed'??

Then there is the ACARS data secured through the Freedom of Information Act which is claimed by some to be evidence that at least the two aircraft officially assigned to Flights 175 and 93 were still in the air after they were supposed to have struck the World Trade Center and crashed in Pennsylvania. ACARS, the Aircraft Communications Addressing and Reporting System, allows short messages to be communicated between aircraft and air traffic controllers and airlines via radio or satellite through a series of ground stations across the United States. I have already mentioned that ACARS messages were communicated to aircraft on 9/11 warning about possible cockpit intrusions. The point here is that the system routes messages through the nearest ground station with the strongest connection to the aircraft and this is achieved by a central router that picks the best radio ground station just like a mobile phone picks up the nearest communication tower. The ACARS system allows the sender to know that a message has been received by the aircraft. ACARS records show that Flight 93 received a series of messages between 9.21am and 10.10am from a series of ground stations that began with one in Pittsburgh and ended with a communication routed through a ground station at Willard Airport near Champaign, Illinois. The problems this poses for the official story are two-fold: (1) the last message was communicated at 10.10 – *after* the plane was supposed to have crashed; and (2) the ground station it was

routed through is *500 miles* from where Flight 93 is said to have gone
down near Shanksville, Pennsylvania. Pilots for 9/11 Truth say that with
the way the system works there is no chance even without the technical
distance limitations that a message would be routed by the system
through a ground station that far from an aircraft. The implication is that
the Flight 93 aircraft which connected with the ACARS ground station
near Champaign, Illinois, could not have been the one that crashed
seven or four minutes earlier near Shanksville 500 miles away. This
would fit with the testimony of Colonel Robert Marr, battle commander
at NORAD's NEADS response center, who told the 9/11 Commission in
2003 that he tracked Flight 93 as it was 'circling over Chicago'. Willard
Airport ground station near Champaign is less than 140 miles by road
from Chicago. Marr later said they believed that Flight 93 was heading
for Chicago and that NEADS contacted an Air National Guard base in
the area 'so they [can] head off 93 at the pass'. Hold on, I'm confused
here. What happened to the military not being aware of Flight 93 before
it crashed? Lieutenant Colonel Mark Stuart, an intelligence officer at
NEADS, confirmed that as the Flight 93 'incident began to unfold' his
professional judgment was that the plane was going to strike the Sears
Tower in Chicago and he had told Colonel Marr this. The 9/11
Commission sought to explain away this challenge to the official story
by suggesting that Colonel Marr mistook Flight 93 for Delta Air Lines
Flight 1989 which had been incorrectly reported as hijacked. The ACARS
information might suggest otherwise. Detailed passenger phone call
analysis by Elias Davidsson in *Hijacking America's Mind On 9/11* also
supports ACARS evidence that the plane was not where we are told it
was. ACARS data analysis has Flight 175 receiving messages from a
ground station at Harrisburg International Airport (also known as
Middleton) in Pennsylvania at the very time it was supposed to have
struck the World Trade Center 162 miles to the north. Another ACARS
message to the plane *20 minutes* after it was said to have crashed was
routed through the ground station at Pittsburgh International Airport
230 miles west of Harrisburg. The system must have picked up a
stronger connection signal from there by then than Harrisburg and this
would have located the aircraft around Pittsburgh 316 miles by air from
New York. There was certainly great confusion about the whereabouts of
Flight 175 with United Airlines issuing a press release more than two
hours after its alleged crash at the World Trade Center saying the airline
was 'deeply concerned' about the fate of Flight 175 and that 'United is
working with all the relevant authorities, including the FBI, to obtain
further information ...' It would be nearly three hours after the alleged
crash time that United Airlines confirmed Flight 175 was down and
where.

What happened to the real planes that morning if they didn't crash as reported? I repeat that establishing exactly what happened is not necessary to prove a conspiracy. All that's required is for the official story to be thoroughly discredited and we are certainly past that benchmark already with a lot more to come. It is understandable that people still seek answers to what happened, as I do, but some personalities within the 9/11 Truth Movement have done the cause no favours whatsoever by arguing with each other and abusing each other in irrelevant conflicts over who is 'right' about detail. Egos at ten paces are going to get us nowhere. What happened is far less important than what didn't happen and who really did it and why. My personal view from what I have observed since starting my own research the day after the attacks is that 9/11 aircraft were taken over by remote control via their computer systems and landed at a military base or other location as per Operation Northwoods while remotely-controlled military aircraft replaced them to do the deeds (Flights 11 and 175); a missile/bomb (Flight 77); and possibly the original Flight 93 was shot down or again replaced by another aircraft. The latter left the gate at 8.01, but didn't take off because of traffic congestion until 8.42 if you believe the official story and that may have scuppered the original plan and had to be dealt with. A fourth plane striking a building without a military response would have stretched credulity way, way past breaking point by then. The Flight 93 cover-story also provided the massively-exploited 'Let's roll' narrative to launch the propaganda for the long-planned 'war on terror'. What happened to the passengers? Well, put it this way, the super psychopaths behind all this would not want them telling their stories.

Psychopathic liars

We cannot hope for the authorities to tell us the truth. That is not what they are there to do. 'Investigations' into Hidden Hand plane crashes, including the Lockerbie bombing wrongly blamed on Libya, are fixed to suit the official line and hide what really happened. When TWA Flight 800 crashed shortly after take-off from New York on July 17th, 1996, the official report by the National Transportation Safety Board (NTSB) claimed it was caused by an explosion in a fuel tank that was traced to a fuel pump. Yes, that's probably partly correct in one sense because fuel tanks do tend to explode when missiles hit them. Jim Sanders, an investigative journalist and husband of a TWA flight attendant, worked tenaciously to expose the lies of the FBI. In retaliation, Sanders, his wife and a TWA captain were arrested by the FBI for impeding its 'investigation'. Sanders went to jail for his trouble, but produced a book and documentary after his release. He acquired samples of seat covers from the plane which were stained by a reddish residue. He sent them for analysis to Morton Thiokol and Hughes Aerospace where the laboratories discovered that the residue contained 15 chemicals found in anti-aircraft missiles and only one of them – glue – is found in aircraft seat covers. Pilots from the Air National Guard reported seeing a missile strike Flight 800 – as did 250 other people – and pictures existed of the missile and remote-controlled target drone it was launched to hit. The FBI, the organisation telling you what happened on September 11th, covered up the whole story with the help of the Navy who took control of the crash scene instead of the usual civilian crash investigators. This is what the FBI did on 9/11. Richard Russell, a retired airline pilot, acquired FAA radar tapes of the incident which revealed an object travelling at up to 2,000 miles an hour heading directly at the plane. When Russell said he would circulate the tape it was seized by the FBI. The *Southampton Press* told the story in 1997 of Dede Muma, a resident of Riverhead, Long Island, who was mistakenly sent faxes of official documents related to the Flight 800 investigation. Her fax number was very close to the one used by the FBI and other personnel on Long Island overseeing the 'investigation'. The cover sheet Dede Muma received indicated the fax was from a worker at Teledyne Ryan Aeronautical in San Diego to a co-worker helping the FBI on Long Island. Teledyne Ryan Aeronautical is operated by Hidden Hand-controlled Northrop Grumman. This is the company behind the Global Hawk remote control aircraft technology. Multiple fax pages detailed the rear structures of the 'Firebee' drone aircraft that Teledyne Ryan manufactured for the US military. The FBI claims that it was told by the US Coast Guard that the bright orange debris that was found with the debris of Flight 800 was from fishing and boating floats but here was a fax in May, 1997, that revealed how the FBI was asking experts from Teledyne Ryan – makers of a bright orange-red remotely-controlled plane for the US military – to identify this mystery debris. Official 'investigations' are designed to hide the truth, not reveal it.

A moment to ponder: The FAA, other government agencies and private companies knew Flight 800 was destroyed by some sort of missile and yet allowed the FBI/Navy cover story to become official 'history'. This is precisely what has happened with 9/11. FAA and other government agency insiders know the official version is nonsense while helping the FBI and the rest of the Deep State to concoct and defend the Big Lie.

CHAPTER 13

How *did* the mighty fall?

We live in a fantasy world, a world of illusion. The great task in life is to find reality – Iris Murdoch

The Rockefeller family, Hidden Hand to their DNA, were behind the building of the World Trade Center in the form of banker David Rockefeller and his brother Nelson, four times governor of New York. Their vehicle was the government/public-owned (but only in theory) Port Authority of New York and New Jersey.

David Rockefeller drove the project through a development organisation that he chaired in the 1960s and 70s and the involvement of the Rockefeller brothers was so pivotal the Twin Towers were known by some as 'David and 'Nelson'. The World Trade Center was a huge project with the 110 storeys of the North and South Towers soaring 1,368 feet (417 metres) above Manhattan and at the time they were the world's tallest buildings. Each floor was approximately 210 feet by 210 feet. Work began in 1965 and the buildings were opened on April 4th, 1973. The World Trade Center was sold into private hands for the first time only seven weeks before the 9/11 attacks when the Port Authority sold the lease to ultra-Zionist billionaire businessman Larry Silverstein who already owned the much smaller Building 7 in the WTC complex (Fig 60). Silverstein led a consortium that finalised the deal worth $3.2 billion for a 99-year lease while personally committing only $14 million. The deal included new insurance policies which seriously increased the pay-out in the event of a terrorist attack and Silverstein therefore had the money to replace the by-then

Figure 60: 'Lucky' Larry Silverstein.

320

deteriorating World Trade Center with a brand new state-of-art building on the same site after the soon-to-happen 9/11 attacks.

Hiding the truth from day one

The most traumatic images of all the horrors on September 11th were the collapse of the Twin Towers (Fig 61). These catastrophic events caused the biggest loss of life on American soil from a non-natural disaster; the biggest loss of firefighters in a single incident; and were the biggest structural failures in recorded history. *Fire Engineering* magazine rightly observed that you would think such a disaster would also prompt the biggest investigation in recorded history. But no. What followed continued the same pattern and theme that we have seen with every other aspect of 9/11.

Figure 61: What caused these enormous buildings to fall? The official story makes no sense.

There was no credible investigation and the token effort for public consumption set out to *cover up* what happened, not expose it. Vincent Dunn, a retired deputy chief of the New York Fire Department and nationally-recognized expert on high-rise firefighting, published an article with others in *Fire Engineering* calling for a proper investigation into why the towers fell. Dunn, author of the 1988 book, *Collapse of Burning Buildings,* said that all the public had been given was a 'series of unconnected and uncoordinated superficial inquiries'. There was no comprehensive 'Presidential Blue Ribbon Commission ... no top-notch National Transportation Safety Board-like response'. He said: 'We are literally treating the steel removed from the site like garbage, not like crucial fire scene evidence.' This is precisely what happened with the wreckage of the Murrah building after the Oklahoma bombing in 1995. *The New York Daily News* reported in April, 2002:

> Some 185,101 tons of structural steel have been hauled away from Ground Zero. Most of the steel has been recycled as per the city's decision to swiftly send the wreckage to salvage yards in New Jersey. The city's hasty move has outraged many victims' families who believe the steel should have been examined more thoroughly. Last month, fire experts told Congress that about 80% of the steel was scrapped without being examined because investigators did not have the authority to preserve the wreckage.

Chinese media reported that the Shanghai Baosteel Group
Corporation had bought 50,000 tons of World Trade Center scrap steel
paying no more than $120 per ton. The *Shanghai Morning Post* said
another 10,000 tons was shipped to India from New Jersey scrap
processor Metal Management. I'll have much more to say about this
later. What happened revealed the recurring contempt shown for the
9/11 victims and their families. New York City Medical Examiner
Charles Hirsch said in 2003 that in the haste to clear the site human
remains were taken to a landfill facility where the steel was sorted and
sold. Eric Beck, a senior supervisor of the landfill recycling, admitted in
2007 that some of these human remains were part of a mixture used to
pave roads and fill potholes in New York. The official excuse for
removing debris from the site so fast was the need to search for
survivors, but they did the same with the remains of World Trade Center
Building 7 which the authorities said had been evacuated and so there
were no survivors to find. Building 7 was the third building to collapse
that day which most people don't even know about, but which provided
glaring evidence for what really happened. I'll explore that in detail in
this chapter. Erik Lawyer, founder of Firefighters for 9/11 Truth, another
organisation of experts in their field questioning the 9/11 cover-story,
described the removal of the 1.5 million tons of potential evidence as a
crime – which it was. He said:

9/11 was the greatest loss of life and property damage in U.S. fire history. This
should of been the most protected, preserved, over-tested and thorough
investigation of a crime scene in world history. Sadly it was not. What was it?
Well, we know from their [government] admission the majority of the
evidence was destroyed ... in 22 years of experience I've seen a lot of crime
scenes, I've never seen anything like this in my life.

I was out at the site, I saw trucks leaving faster than anywhere I've ever seen
but I accepted it at the time and for years I accepted it because it was a
recovery and rescue operation and that's normal to have something like that
going. Again, we'd never seen anything like it but that was expected.

What I didn't know for years was what was going on behind the scenes was
that evidence was being destroyed when it was shipped off. By their own
admission, the [official] investigation of Tower 7 had no physical evidence.
How do you investigate a crime when you've destroyed all the evidence? It
doesn't make sense. They also admit that they refused to test for explosives ...

The reason for all this is simple: When you want to hide the truth you
don't preserve and examine evidence that would expose your lies. *Fire*

Engineering called on the Hidden Hand-created Federal Emergency Management Agency (FEMA) to immediately appoint a 'World Trade Center Disaster Review Panel' to coordinate a complete review of all aspects of the World Trade Center tragedy and to produce a comprehensive report which ...

> ... examines a variety of topics including determining exactly how and why the towers collapsed, critiquing the building evacuation procedures and the means of egress, assessing the buildings' fire protection features (steel 'fireproofing', fire protection systems) and reviewing the valiant fire-fighting procedures employed.

There was never any chance of that. The real role of FEMA is the one financed covertly by profits from the multi-billion-dollar Hidden Hand-intelligence agency drug racket. Former Green Beret William Tyree launched a lawsuit against the CIA and Father Bush in September, 1998, claiming they had allowed drug profits to fund FEMA's covert activities without the knowledge of Congress. FEMA was created by Jimmy Carter through a presidential executive order, an undemocratic and dictatorial outrage, in which the President introduces laws without debate in Congress. An executive order only has to appear in a legal newspaper called the *Federal Register* to become law and great swathes of the Hidden Hand's fascist-state-in-waiting has been put together in this way as I describe in detail in other books. Among the founders of FEMA was Zbigniew Brzezinski, President Carter's National Security Advisor and co-founder of the Hidden Hand Trilateral Commission with his fellow psychopath, David Rockefeller. Another famous FEMA name was *Oliver North*, the drug-running gofer from Iran-Contra. Ben Bradlee Jr wrote in *Guts and Glory: The Rise and Fall of Oliver North* that the Iran-Contra 'star' helped FEMA to stage a national emergency rehearsal in April, 1984, known as Rex-84 Bravo. This was a practice exercise in readiness for martial law and a FEMA takeover in the event of a 'national emergency'. The *Miami Herald* reported in 1987 that North was involved with FEMA in exercises that included the rounding-up of refugees and 'troublemakers'. Former Green Beret Colonel Albert Carone, who was murdered in 1990, said in a sworn statement for the William Tyree lawsuit that he worked with North in CIA-Mafia drug operations and he also confirmed North's use of drug profits to create and fund FEMA's unofficial activities. So, no, FEMA was never going to properly investigate 9/11. *Firefighters Magazine*, which published technical studies of major fires, described the destruction and removal of evidence from the World Trade Center site as 'a half-baked farce' of investigation (exactly as planned). The editorial was written by Bill Manning who said that steel from the site should be preserved to allow proper investigations into the cause of the collapse. He asked:

> Did they throw away the locked doors from the Triangle Shirtwaist fire? Did
> they throw away the gas can used at the Happy Land social club fire? ... That's
> what they're doing at the World Trade Center. The destruction and removal of
> evidence must stop immediately.

It didn't, of course, because a close examination by experts would have
identified why the towers collapsed when no other building of this kind
had ever done so in architectural history as a result of what was claimed
to be heat from fires. Despite this never-happened history the official
story of the towers falling due to structural damage from the plane and
fire softening steel columns was being promoted within hours without a
single second of investigation. *Firefighters Magazine* pointed out that a

Figure 62: 'Tell them anything and they'll
believe it.' Or, maybe not.

growing number of fire protection
engineers had suggested that 'the
structural damage from the planes
and the explosive ignition of jet fuel
in themselves were not enough to
bring down the towers' (Fig 62).
The New York Times reported the
frustration of experts from the
American Society of Civil
Engineers appointed by FEMA to
'investigate' the cause of the
collapse. They said the decision to
immediately recycle the steel
columns, beams, and trusses may
have cost them some of their most
direct evidence to explain what
happened. Dr Frederick W.
Mowrer, an associate professor in
the fire protection engineering
department at the University of
Maryland, said: 'I find the speed
with which potentially important evidence has been removed and
recycled to be appalling.' New York Mayor and '9/11 hero' (it says here)
Rudolph Giuliani was overseeing this extraordinary destruction of
evidence along with Richard 'Ground Zero's Jewish Knight' Sheirer,
Commissioner at the New York Office of Giuliani's Emergency
Management, and Pasquale J. D. Amuro, FBI inspector in charge of the
9/11 [non]-investigation. Both would become executives of Giuliani
'security' companies. Overseeing the overseers was Michael Chertoff,
head of the Criminal Division of the [In]Justice Department, of whom

much more in the final stages of the book. Giuliani would apparently not respond to requests to explain why crucial evidence was being destroyed. Instead he put forward Matthew G. Monahan, a spokesman for the city's Department of Design and Construction which was in charge of debris removal at Ground Zero. He said: 'The city considered it reasonable to have recovered structural steel recycled.' What – *before investigators had examined it?? The New York Times* interviewed members of the investigation team, among them some of America's most respected engineers. They said they had at various times been 'shackled with bureaucratic restrictions' that blocked them from interviewing witnesses, examining the site and requesting crucial information like recorded distress calls to the police and fire departments. 'This is almost the dream team of engineers in the country working on this, and our hands are tied,' one team member told the *Times.* They had been threatened with dismissal for speaking to the media. The team member said: 'FEMA is controlling everything.' In other words the Hidden Hand was. Here we go again as with the plane crashes – questions galore, but no open public investigation. Wherever you look in every aspect of 9/11 there is suppression of information, questioning and genuine inquiry. Everywhere there is something to hide.

'Caused by fire'? What a joke

The response of most people as they watched those terrible images of the Twin Towers collapsing was how they looked like controlled demolitions they had seen on television from time to time. Explosive charges are placed so expertly that colossal buildings, such as skyscrapers and football stadiums, are imploded to fall on their own footprint to protect the surrounding area from damage. None of this is surprising given that controlled demolitions quite obviously brought down the towers and not the fires. People can argue and debate *how* this was done, anything from explosives to super-top-secret energy weapons, but even a glance at the evidence makes it clear that (a) the government story is complete tosh and (b) the buildings came down because they were *made to.* Van Romero, President for Research at the New Mexico Institute of Mining and Technology (known as Tech), said after seeing the towers collapse on television that what happened appeared to be 'too methodical' to be a chance result of airplanes colliding with the structures: 'My opinion is, based on the videotapes, that after the airplanes hit the World Trade Center there were some explosive devices inside the buildings that caused the towers to collapse.' Romero said the collapse resembled controlled implosions and 'it would be difficult for something from the plane to trigger an event like that'. If explosions did cause the towers to collapse, he said, the detonations could have been caused by a small amount of explosive placed at strategic points. Romero should know what he is talking about as a former director of the Energetic Materials Research and Testing Center in New Mexico which studied the effects of explosions on buildings. The government must certainly have rated him highly because on September 11th he and another Tech official were on their way to a building near the Pentagon to discuss defence-funded research. Ten days later when the official story claimed the towers fell because heat softened the steel girders Romero dramatically changed his tune. He must have been on his way to Damascus at the time on another job. Now Romero agreed that fire was indeed the cause and not explosives: 'Certainly the fire is what caused the building to fail,' he told the *Albuquerque Journal*. The intense heat from the jet fuel fires had weakened the steel structural beams which gave way under the weight of the floors above. This set off a chain reaction as upper floors pancaked on to lower ones, Romero said with his fingers firmly crossed. He still believed it was possible that the final collapse of each building was triggered by 'a sudden pressure pulse caused when the fire reached an electrical transformer or other source of combustion within the building'. I wonder what happened to Romero in those ten days? A word in the ear from the FBI, perhaps, which seems to be a common prelude to silence or story-changing.

Fortunately other architects and structural engineers are made of far sterner stuff and in 2006 Richard Gage, an architect for 23 years, founded Architects & Engineers for 9/11 Truth. This is the building experts version of Pilots for 9/11 Truth. You can find their excellent information and videos at ae911truth.org. Gage is a member of the American Institute of Architects and has worked on the construction of many fireproof steel-frame buildings. More than 1,500 building and demolition experts are supporters of his organisation and they are demanding an independent investigation into the three building collapses on September 11th. Gage said: 'Fires have never before caused the collapse of any skyscraper even though there are numerous examples of much hotter, larger and longer-lasting fires in these buildings.' The architect of the new Larry Silverstein Freedom Tower on the World Trade Center site and new 7WTC, which replaced Building 7 felled on 9/11, agreed with Gage. David Childs said that a young man came to him in tears and asked if the new buildings would fall: 'I said no. Never has a steel structured building in the history of steel-structured buildings ever fallen down for reasons of fire.' And that includes the World Trade Center. I know the authorities say the Twin Tower structural failures were not entirely due to fire because the planes hit the buildings, but no way in all eternity would a plane have any direct impact-affect to make the towers fall as they did.

There are claims that the 17-storey Plasco Building in the Iranian

capital Tehran collapsed in 2017 because of fire, but watch it fall at
ae911truth.org and it is the most blatant controlled demolition. The
Iranian government was subsequently as determined to investigate
what happened as the American government has been with the World
Trade Center. Nowhere can governments be trusted to pursue the truth.
There are many examples of fires in steel-framed high-rise buildings that
burned for longer with far more heat
and did more damage without the
structure collapsing. The Windsor
Building in Madrid was a raging
inferno in 2005, took 24 hours to
extinguish and *did not collapse* (Fig 63).
A 50-storey skyscraper in Caracas, the
tallest building in Venezuela, was
ablaze for 17 hours with the top 20
floors gutted and did not fall. The
North Tower of the World Trade Center
was struck at 8.45am and collapsed at
10.29am – an impact-to-fall time of one
hour and 44 minutes. The South Tower
was struck at 9.03am and collapsed at
9.50am – an impact-to-fall time of 47
minutes. Therefore the tower struck
second collapsed first and took almost
an hour less to fall than the other one.
Yet the South Tower was struck a more
glancing blow and much of the fuel
exploded in a fireball *away* from the
building and not inside. This can be
explained according to the official story
by the fact that the South Tower was
struck lower between the 75th to the

Figure 63: The steel-framed high-rise
Windsor Building in Madrid burned with
far greater intensity than the Twin Towers
in 2005 and for far longer – the fire took
24 hours to extinguish. It did not collapse.

85th floors compared to the North (93rd to 99th floors) and the damaged
section was subjected to greater pressure from the floors above. It is
claimed that steel 'trusses' holding up the floors failed as they were
undermined by the heat, but none of this makes sense of the buildings
imploding like a controlled demolition. For this to happen the trusses
would have had to have failed almost simultaneously or one side would
have fallen first and caused a topple-over effect. A big topple over
would have relieved the pressure on the floors below and they could not
have collapsed as they did because of 'pancaking'. Either way the official
story is untenable. With the South Tower struck on one side and thus the
most intense fire in that area would you not expect this combination to
have caused that side of the structure to fail first and for the building to

topple over much more than it did?

Destroying the cover-story

The official explanation claims that the fire was so hot the steel became too weak to hold the weight of the concrete and steel above it. Steel beams then buckled and/or the joints broke. Concrete and steel crashed down on to the floor below and turned the concrete into powder. A chain reaction had started and each floor pulverised the one below. The evidence, as we shall see, does not in the least support this official hypothesis (lie). We are told that the 47-storey Building 7 on the World Trade Center site also collapsed at 5.20pm that afternoon because of fire and this was not struck by a plane or subjected to an aviation fuel explosion. This makes Building 7, long-owned by Larry Silverstein, the first steel-framed building in history to be brought down by fire alone because there was no aircraft strike on the structure. The only way such buildings had fallen before was through specially-placed explosives in a controlled demolition. A government report on the collapse confirmed this fact about Building 7 being a 'first-ever'. Lee Robertson, a structural engineer who co-designed the towers, told an international coalition on terrorism in Frankfurt, Germany, a week before the attacks that they were designed to withstand a hit by a Boeing 707 and this carried about as much fuel as a 767. He said later that buildings could have survived a hit by a 767 (and then went on to repeat the government line) while other high-rise architects and engineers were shocked that the buildings could have fallen from the result of a jet fuel fire. Hyman Brown, construction manager of the towers, said: 'They were over-designed to withstand almost anything, including hurricanes ... bombings and an airplane ...' Other construction engineers have made the same point. William Brinner, an architect for 25 years who witnessed 'Flight 175' striking the South Tower, said it didn't seem possible that buildings designed to withstand the impact of a 707 could possibly collapse in such a short time. 'They were designed to withstand hurricane force winds of up to 140 miles an hour', he said. World Trade Center architect Aaron Swirski lived in Israel and spoke to *Jerusalem Post* radio after the attack. He said the buildings were 'designed around that eventuality to survive this kind of attack'. Thomas Eagar, a professor of materials engineering at the Massachusetts Institute of Technology, said: '... the number of columns lost on the initial impact was not large and the loads were shifted to remaining columns in this highly redundant structure'. The melting point of steel is 1,538 degrees Celsius or 2,800 Fahrenheit and although it would not have had to reach this level of heat to be compromised we are talking a serious temperature before the structure was affected in a building of some 200,000 tons of steel. This is significant because when heat is applied it is dispersed through the steel and this helps to cool down the point of hottest temperature. Structural engineer G. Charles Clifton said: 'In my opinion, based on available evidence, there appears no indication that the fires were as severe as a fully developed multi-storey fire in an initially undamaged building would typically be.' Robert Podolsky, a physicist, engineer and systems analyst for ten years working with major companies, said:

> I looked up in the manual the burning temperature of jet fuel and found that under the conditions that existed at the World Trade Center on 9/11 that jet fuel had to have been burning at about 750 degrees Fahrenheit. I also noticed that the official explanation of what happened ... was the heat from the fire supposedly softened the steel and thereby brought the buildings down.

> If you have a flame of 750 degrees you can hold that flame under a steel beam forever and you'll never reach a high-enough temperature to bend steel, let alone melt it. So immediately I knew at that point that the official explanation was dead wrong.

This view is widely supported among experts in the field and if the building was being weakened by bending and softening steel we would have seen evidence that parts of the buildings were first beginning to sag. We didn't – they went from stable to collapse in an instant (Fig 64). Leslie Young, a high-rise architect and former firefighter, said the majority of the jet fuel burnt up instantly in the big fireball and it was gone. The fires that were left were office furnishings and carpets and such like. Young said: 'A lot of these things have to be fire resistant by nature, required by code, so there isn't a whole lot of fuel in there to begin with.' Edward Munyak, a fire safety expert who works for cities, federal agencies, insurers and other organisations, said that while the media portrayed the fires as being extremely hot they were, in fact, not that hot in the World Trade Center towers. If you looked at the official government data this was clear, he said, and temperature could be judged by the black smoke coming out of the windows. This meant the fires were oxygen-starved and so

Figure 64: The North Tower begins to fall – straight down on its own footprint.

'it was a low-temperature fire'. Munyak's view is supported by a lot of other evidence. On August 4th, 2002, almost a year after the towers collapsed, *The New York Times* revealed the existence of a tape recording of communications by firefighters who had reached the 78th floor of the South Tower. This was just two floors below the main impact point and the 78th floor was actually struck by a wing of Flight 175. New York fire officials said they had 'delayed listening' to the tape *(what for nearly a year?)* and had continued during that period to say that no firefighter went higher than the 50th floor. The tape is devastating to the official story because *The New York Times* described how Battalion Chief Orio J. Palmer is heard calmly organising the evacuation of survivors with Fire Marshall Ronald P. Bucca and the extinguishing of only 'two pockets of fire' that they could see. We are asked to believe that just above them, at the very same time, the building was reaching fantastic temperatures which caused the building to collapse shortly after these communications by Chief Palmer. It's fairyland. Brian Clark, a survivor from the South Tower, passed the 80th floor right in the impact zone, but he said: 'You could see through the wall and the cracks and see flames ... just licking up, not a roaring inferno, just quiet flames licking up and smoke sort of eking through the wall'. The official story says it was the heat from *this* fire that caused the South Tower to collapse in just 56 minutes when steel doesn't melt until it reaches a staggering 2,800 degrees Fahrenheit. This is why no other major steel-framed building had ever collapsed because of fire – *not ever*. International architect David Johnson said:

> As a professional city planner in New York, I knew those buildings and their design. I attended and participated in the hearings at the New York City Hall when the buildings were first proposed ... So I was well aware of the strength of the core with its steel columns, surrounding the elevators, and stairwells ...

> ...When I saw the rapid collapse of the towers, I knew that they could not come down the way they did without explosives and the severing of core columns at the base ... Moreover, the symmetrical collapse is strong evidence of a controlled demolition. A building falling from asymmetrical structural failure would not collapse so neatly, nor so rapidly.

We should not forget that the Twin Towers had 287 steel support columns, 240 perimeter columns and 47 colossal core columns. To say the least they were not coming down without a hell of a fight and they certainly wouldn't disappear in seconds because of fire. We have already seen how expert Van Romero said (before his journey to the Syrian capital) that little explosive would be needed to bring down the towers so long as it was placed in the right locations. Many witnesses from multiple backgrounds and professions – office workers, police officers, firefighters, government officials, journalists etc. – reported hearing explosions before the buildings collapsed. Firefighter Louie Cacchioli, who was assigned to Engine 47 in Harlem, said his crew were the first to enter the South Tower after it was hit. He said he was taking firefighters in the elevator to the 24th floor to support the evacuation. On his last trip he described how a bomb went off. 'We think there were bombs set in the building,' he said. 'I had just asked another firefighter to stay with me, which was a good thing because we were trapped inside the elevator and he had the tools to get out.' CBS broadcast a documentary six months after the attacks about what happened that day using the footage of firefighters taken by two French brothers, Jules and Gedeon Naudet. They had been shooting their own documentary on September 11th near the World Trade Center featuring the firefighters of Engine 7, Ladder 1, of the New York Fire Department based a few blocks away from the WTC. Suddenly the film-makers found themselves involved in a very different documentary as they captured the first plane hitting the North Tower which Boy Bush claimed to have seen live when he could not have done. When the fire crew and cameraman Jules Naudet arrived at the North Tower they were astonished to find that the lobby, 90-plus floors below impact, had suffered widespread damage. This was later explained away by officials who said burning jet fuel had poured down the elevator shafts and exploded in the lobby. There was no evidence of burning or incendiary explosion in the lobby area. 'The lobby looked like the plane hit the lobby!' one firefighter said. 'Experts' were wheeled out after the event to explain why it was obvious the buildings would collapse because of the fire. This was clearly not considered a potential problem by New York fire chiefs, however, despite their vast experience of the potential dangers in high-rise buildings, none of which had ever failed in this way. Far from clearing the towers in case of collapse they set up their operations command post in the lobby of the North Tower. Had that collapsed first they would all have been killed because it was only when the South Tower came down that the possibility was even considered. Hundreds of firefighters were sent up the stairways to their deaths because the collapse of the towers was not even taken into consideration. Why was this if, according to the 'experts' afterwards, it was so obvious why they collapsed? Then there is the account by the security officer at the World Trade Center told to Peter Jennings on ABC television. The officer said that after the South Tower collapsed he received a call from the New York Port Authority Command Center on the 22nd floor asking for a rescue in the North Tower. He went there himself with firefighters and they found that the offices were so devastated they had to 'tunnel through debris' to 'dig out' trapped Port Authority employees. Remember these offices were some 70 floors

below the impact point of the aircraft. The 22nd, 23rd and 24th floors
were also said to contain offices leased to the FBI. This was the reported
location of files for investigations against Mobil Oil and businessman-
fixer James Giffen involving alleged illegal oil swaps between Iran and
Kazakhstan and against then Federal Reserve chief Alan Greenspan,
Morgan and Company and Goldman Sachs involving gold price fixing. I
asked the FBI in 2002 if it had offices on those floors of the World Trade
Center, but my question was not answered.

Free-fall speed

The government claims that heat caused horizontal columns which held
up the actual floors to break away from the 47 massive vertical columns
that ran through the core of the building from top to bottom. If the
horizontal columns had broken away from the vertical central core then
that core would have been left standing. It wasn't – that came down too.
When a floor hits another floor and another floor in the way they
described there is resistance before each new floor gives way, especially
near the start. On 9/11, however, the speed at which the two buildings
collapsed was *free-fall speed* – the speed of dropping something from
mid-air with nothing in the way until it hit the ground. This only
happens with ... *controlled demolitions* when explosive charges remove all
resistance below. Government agencies agreed that the towers fell in 9
and 11 seconds respectively. To claim this could happen while falling
debris was 'pancaking on the floors blow' is utterly insane. A building
cannot drop at free-fall speed while meeting with any resistance or it
wouldn't be, and couldn't be, free-fall speed! This not only breaks the
law of common sense it also violates Newton's Law of Conservation of
Momentum which sounds very grand, but actually means that you can't
drop at free-fall speed if anything is slowing you down. Who couldn't
work that out over the age of four? Well, government agencies like the
National Institute of Standards and Technology (NIST) who clearly need
to hire some pre-schoolers to help them out. What's more – the top of the
South Tower did topple (before turning to dust in mid-air) and so could
not have provided the impact described in the government's ridiculous
story because it did not slam onto the storeys below (Fig 65). David
Chandler, a maths and physics academic for 30 years, said that the
structures were capable of holding three to five times the weight and
they fell with only a fraction of that resistance:

> Roughly 90 percent of its resistance has been removed and what's happening
> is the top section is not crushing down the bottom section like a pile-driver
> which is a picture [the authorities] have painted – it's actually falling into
> material that's already been pulverised.

Figure 65: The South Tower falls and the topple of the top section relieves the pressure on the building below.

We all remember those fantastic clouds of dust when the towers fell and this is yet another classic feature of controlled demolition. Buildings that collapse 'naturally' do not produce the power from gravity alone to pulverise everything into small pieces and extraordinary clouds of dust before they even hit the ground. Controlled demolitions do exactly that as you'll see with many examples on the Internet. Buildings implode without falling to one side when they are expertly charged and there is also a momentary delay after the charges go off before the buildings start to fall – another tell-tale confirmation of a controlled demolition. Jerry Russell PhD, who has a Master's Degree in Engineering at Stanford University, points out that steel frame towers are built very strongly and are almost impossible to destroy. He said that aircraft strikes don't destroy skyscrapers and neither does fire. No skyscraper had ever been brought down by a fire and if a big enough impact by a plane ever destabilised a building the structural failure would happen ... 'at the point of highest levered stress, near the base of the tower, and the tower would have fallen over like a giant tree in a forest windstorm'. Like many with his background who have gone public since 9/11, Russell says that the most effective way to make a skyscraper collapse is by controlled demolition:

> As your eyes will tell you, the World Trade Center collapses looked like controlled demolitions. Here's the proof. According to the law of gravity, it is possible to calculate the time it takes for an object to fall a given distance. The equation is $H=(1/2)at2$, where H is the height, a is the acceleration of gravity (10 meters per second squared) and t is time in seconds. Plug in the height of the building at 1350 feet (411 meters) and we get 9 seconds. That is just about the length of time it took for the very top of the World Trade Center to fall to the street below.' According to all reports, the whole thing was over in just about ten seconds.

> It is as if the entire building were falling straight down through thin air. As if the entire solid structure below, the strong part which had not been burned or sliced or harmed in any significant way, just disappeared into nothingness. Yet this (within a small tolerance) is what we would expect to find if there had

been a controlled demolition, because the explosions below really do leave
the upper stories completely unsupported. Like the Road Runner after he runs
off the edge of the cliff, the entire building pauses a moment, then goes
straight down.

Jerry Russell said any kind of friction process should have slowed the
whole thing down. Gravitational acceleration could not achieve its full
effect if it was fighting any opposing force. He pointed out that on 9/11
the intact building below 'should have at least braked the fall of the
upper stories'. This did not happen and there was no measurable friction
at all. 'This proves controlled demolition', he said.

'Boom, boom, boom'

The 'pancake collapse' theory is just another smokescreen to hide what
really happened – pre-planned demolition by those who would use this
horror to unleash their agenda of human control and wars of conquest.
Firefighters talked of hearing explosions in the building and so did
William Rodriguez, a janitor for 20 years at the World Trade Center who
was in the basement of the North Tower when the first plane struck. He
helped many people to safety and was honoured five times at the White
House until he began to speak publicly about hearing bombs go off in
the building. Rodriguez gave evidence to the 9/11 Commission which
was ignored in its final report and he became a well-known advocate for
a truly independent inquiry into what happened. There were so many
eyewitness reports of explosions before the towers came down and if
there was not an outward explosive force of some kind how come
enormous columns were ejected horizontally from the buildings to fall at
such a speed that they were hurled hundreds of feet into nearby
buildings? This was acknowledged by government agency reports
which blamed debris from the North Tower for starting fires in World
Trade Center Building 7 more than a hundred yards away. What caused
those phenomenal ejections right at the start? Jet fuel which the
government agrees would have been burned out in a matter of minutes?
Paul Lemos arrived at the World Trade Center subway station as events
were unfolding. He described how he saw people jumping from the
towers and later witnessed one of them collapse:

I looked up and about 20 storeys below [the fire] I saw, from the corner,
boom, boom, boom, boom, boom, boom, boom, boom, boom ... just like 20
straight hits, just went downward, then I just saw the whole building just went
'pshew'... and as the bombs were going people just started running and I sat
there and watched a few of them explode and then I just turned around and
just started running for my life because at that point the World Trade Center
was coming right down.

These are only some experiences of firefighters and paramedics:

Battalion Chief John Sudnik: 'We heard ... what sounded like a loud explosion and looked up and I saw tower two start coming down.'

Paramedic Kevin Darnowski: 'I heard three explosions, and then ... tower two started to come down.'

Firefighter Thomas Turilli: '... it almost sounded like bombs going off, like boom, boom, boom, like seven or eight.'

Firefighter Craig Carlsen: '[We] heard explosions coming from . . . the South Tower. . . . There were about ten explosions. . . . We then realised the building started to come down.'

Firefighter Joseph Meola: '... it looked like the building was blowing out on all four sides. We actually heard the pops.'

Paramedic Daniel Rivera: 'It was a frigging noise. At first I thought it was – do you ever see professional demolition where they set the charges on certain floors and then you hear "Pop, pop, pop, pop, pop?" ... I thought it was that.'

The pops were followed by a brief moment before the entire buildings fell with all resistance removed. Hence, they came down at free-fall speed. The preparation and the planting of the charges would have meant significant access to the building in the weeks before, and that was no problem with the World Trade Center as I will detail before the book's conclusion. New York Deputy Fire Chief Ray Downey, who died on 9/11, was reportedly concerned there were bombs in the buildings which could potentially bring them down. Downey was a 'very respected expert' on building collapse. Fire Department chaplain John Delendick told the 9/11 Commission that after an apparent explosion at the top of the South Tower he asked Downey if he thought that was caused by jet fuel. He said Downey replied that he thought there were bombs up there because the explosion was 'too even'. Downey's nephew, Tom Downey, said his uncle was 'worried about secondary devices in the towers, explosive devices that could hurt the firemen.'

Building 7: 'Pull it'.

The other World Trade Center building to collapse that day was the 47-storey Building 7, also known as the Salomon Brothers Building (Fig 66 overleaf) This fell in exactly the nature of a controlled demolition at

Figure 66: Building 7 or the Salomon Brothers Building.

Figure 67: Building 7 standing one minute ...

Figure 68: ... seconds later the 47-floor skyscraper has fallen straight down as one unit in the most classic controlled demolition – the first and only building of its type to collapse because of 'fire'.

5.20pm without being hit by an aircraft and became the first steel-framed skyscraper in history to be brought down purely by fire (according to the government). Still today large numbers of people have no idea that a third building fell on September 11th and this certainly suits officialdom given how easy it is for the example of Building 7 to destroy the government version of why it came down (Figs 67 and 68). Puffs of smoke can be seen in lower floors as the building begins to fall straight down in the way of a controlled demolition (Fig 69). When the subject of Building 7 came up in a New York court in 2009 the judge, Edward Lehner, asked 'Building what?' Such is the ignorance of this key element of the 9/11 Big Lie. The final official report on Building 7 (not published until *seven years* later) said the fires began after being hit by debris from the collapse of the North Tower. We will see that there's another far more credible explanation which dismantles the government narrative. Once again we were led to believe that a miracle of physics occurred when heat from ... wait for it ... 'burning office furnishings' caused Building 7 to collapse after no aircraft came near it. The government report, by the National Institute of Standards and Technology (NIST) did not include numerous witnesses describing how they heard explosions before and while the building fell. Neither did NIST mention that steel from the building was holed to the point of being described as like

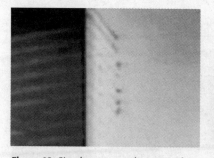

Figure 69: Simultaneous explosions in the lower floors as the building begins to fall straight down.

Figure 70: Larry Silverstein in his 'pull it' interview.

'Swiss cheese'. A controlled demolition was inadvertently confirmed by Larry Silverstein who owned Building 7 and then bought the World Trade Center lease and increased terrorist attack insurance just six weeks before 9/11. The collapse of Building 7 alone led to a pay-out of $861 million from Industrial Risk Insurers based on the official story of what happened – office furnishings on fire (another version of pants on fire). Hold on a cotton-picking second. Silverstein told a PBS television documentary in September, 2002, that he had been informed by fire chiefs that the building was so badly damaged they wanted to 'pull it' (Fig 70). This term is used by the demolition industry and emergency services as short-hand for 'pull it down' – demolish it. Silverstein made a major mistake here and he's been caught with his pants down as well as on fire. A bewildered Senator John Kerry, fending off questions about 9/11 at a public event in Texas in 2007, said that his information was that Building 7 was demolished by a controlled demolition. Even *CBS News* anchor Dan Rather, said the collapse was ...'reminiscent of ... when a building was deliberately destroyed by well-placed dynamite to knock it down'.

Indira Singh, a volunteer civilian Emergency Medical Technician working near Building 7, said she heard the Fire Department say they were going to bring down the building. 'There was another panic around four o'clock because they were bringing the building down and people seemed to know this ahead of time, so people were panicking again and running ...' Singh will return to the story from another crucial angle later in the book. Witnesses, including firefighters, agreed and described how they heard 'boom, boom, boom, boom' before Building 7 came down. Video footage includes the sounds of explosions as the building falls. A radio reporter on 1010 Winsam Radio, New York, said: 'And I turned in time to see what looked like a skyscraper implosion, looked like it had been done by a demolition crew, the whole thing collapsing down.' A television reporter at the scene said: 'It was almost as if it was a planned implosion. The whole building just pancaked down.' If you've not seen the collapse of Building 7 go to ae911truth.org and the video presented by actor Ed Asner called 'Solving the Mystery of Building 7'. You will see the most obvious controlled demolition imaginable including comparisons with other buildings

Figure 71: A screenshot from the Architects & Engineers video comparing the collapse of Building 7 with one brought down by controlled demolition. They are exactly the same.

brought down by professional demolition (Fig 71). There is no difference – they are exactly the same. For the building to fall as it did without a controlled demolition all 82 vertical steel columns would have had to have failed at *precisely* the same moment because of an office furnishings fire which is clearly insanity on a stick. Building 7 is a front-line smoking gun in the 9/11 hoax because it takes weeks to prepare large buildings for demolition and lay the explosives in the right places to implode them on their own footprint. There is no way in all eternity that Larry Silverstein could have decided with fire chiefs to 'pull it' and for the building to come down soon afterwards – not unless it had been pre-charged in the weeks before. This is what he said word for word in the PBS interview:

> I remember getting a call from the fire department commander and they said they weren't sure they were going to be able to contain the fire. I said, you know, we've had such a terrible loss of life the smartest thing to do is pull it. And they made that decision – to pull – and we watched the building collapse.

Bullshit. The 'fire department commander' on 9/11 was Chief Daniel Nigro who said he does not recall speaking to Silverstein that day (in an exchange you would never forget):

> I am well aware of Mr. Silverstein's statement, but to the best of my recollection, I did not speak to him on that day, and I do not recall anyone telling me that they did either. That doesn't mean he could not have spoken to someone from FDNY; it just means that I am not aware of it.

The mystery man is still to come forward. There's a few things to mention here: (1) firefighters don't demolish buildings, demolition experts do after weeks of preparation and so Silverstein's story is a crock of crap; (2) the fire that they were 'struggling to contain' was actually extinguished an hour before the demolition; (3) Silverstein went on to enjoy a fantastic insurance pay-out on the World Trade Center Buildings – insurance secured weeks before the attacks – and now has brand new buildings on the site to replace the aging 1973 World Trade Center towers and his Building 7 completed in 1987. Who said there were no winners on 9/11? Why would a billionaire businessman like Silverstein want to take on a poisoned chalice like the World Trade Center in the deteriorating state the Twin Towers were in? He can't be that bad a businessman when you think that in a deal worth $3.2 billion Silverstein agreed to lay-out $14 million of his own money and was handed $4.56 billion in insurance money. Another question – why did Silverstein say publicly that plans for a new Building 7 were first hatched in 2000 – *the year before* it came down on 9/11? The building was only 14 years old. Why would Mayor Giuliani's New York spend $13 million on a new emergency command centre in the building if there were plans to replace it? The command center was opened in 1999 – just a year before Silverstein said plans for a replacement Building 7 were underway. A number of emergency personnel and volunteers have said they were told long before Building 7 fell at 5.20pm that it was going to be 'pulled' or that it was 'coming down'. One was Kevin McPadden, a search and rescue volunteer formerly with Air Force Special Operations. He was working at a Red Cross centre and said he was told that Building 7 was going to be brought down:

> They said you know you've got to stay behind this line because they're thinking about taking this building down, they're not sure if it's stable or not, so they were holding a line off because they had knowledge that something was gonna happen. Well, they pushed us back a little bit ... a couple of minutes later they started coming down ... people started coming back out to the street, I watched five New York City buses jam packed with people wanting to do search and rescue, head down there towards Building 7 – people walked out into the middle of the street to see these people off, like bon voyage and right then Building 7 came down.

Building 7 was a planned demolition – end of story

Despite all of the evidence from building experts, firefighters, witnesses and the eyes of anyone watching the footage the government refused to admit what had really happened. The National Institute of Standards and Technology (NIST) published its final report on the Building 7 collapse in 2008 and proved beyond doubt or question that they have absolutely no shame. Shyam Sunder, the lead [non]investigator, told the media: 'World Trade Center 7 collapsed because of fires fuelled by office furnishings. It did not collapse from explosions or from oil fires.' The video clip that I saw must have cut out early before he fell about laughing or immediately apologised and begged for forgiveness. A 47-storey skyscraper was brought down by 'an ordinary building contents fire'? Architects & Engineers for 9/11 Truth founder Richard Gage said:

> In the case of Building 7 the fire that NIST said started the collapse had actually burned out over an hour before. It could not have caused the collapse as NIST claims. Yet this modern, steel-frame skyscraper which was not hit by an airplane, collapsed mostly into its own footprint like a house of cards as fast as a bowling ball falling off the side of the building in just under seven seconds.

For anyone still not sure if Building 7 was brought down in a controlled demolition – hence the preparation to do so must have been instigated weeks before – these are building and demolition experts speaking on the Building 7 video which you can see on the Architects & Engineers for 9/11 Truth website:

Kathy McGrade, metallurgical engineer: 'The symmetry is the smoking gun.'

Steven Dusterwald, structural engineer: 'Building number 7 descended in free-fall for the first 100 feet which means there was absolutely no resistance to descent whatsoever.'

Ronald Brookman, structural engineer: 'NIST has admitted it went in free-fall for eight storeys and going from motionless to free-fall, instantly, that's a bothersome part of the puzzle because NIST never explained it.'

Michael Donly, structural engineer: 'We've got a building that came down in its own footprint so all the columns needed to be severed at the same time for that structure to fall the way we saw.'

Jack Keller, professor of engineering at Utah State University: 'Obviously it was the result of controlled demolition.'

Frank Cullinan, specialist in bridge construction and demolition: 'Structural connections not only had to fail nearly simultaneously but in sequential order.'

Chester Gearhart, civil engineer: 'When I saw Building 7 fall I knew it was a controlled demolition.'

Anthony Szamboti, mechanical engineer: 'The whole building completely comes down in one continuous motion. There couldn't have been any structural resistance.'

Scott Grainger, forensic fire protection engineer: 'According to NIST, the failure occurred at column 79 on level 12. They're talking about a single columnar collapse or failure that resulted in the total collapse of the building.'

Kamal Obeid, structural engineer: 'It is possible that you could still have a local failure as a result of a connection failing, but the likelihood of that failure dragging the entire building in such fashion that all the columns would fail at the same time – it's an impossibility.'

Tom Sullivan, explosives technician formerly employed by the company, Controlled Demolition: 'What I saw, it was a classic implosion. The centre of the core, the penthouse area, starts to move first and the building starts to follow along with it.'

Danny Jowenko, owner of a Dutch controlled demolition company, was shown footage of the Building 7 collapse by a Netherlands film crew without telling him what or where it was. Like most people he had no idea that a third building had come down on 9/11. He was asked by the film crew for his thoughts on how the building came down. Jowenko said: 'They blew up columns and the rest caved in afterwards ... This is a controlled demolition ... This was a hired job – a team of experts did this.' It is worth pondering on that NIST Building 7 report from this perspective and in the knowledge that the same jokers told us that the World Trade Center towers fell because of heat from jet fuel. I have heard people say that the government would never get enough people to lie and go along with a fake story to make it stick and too many people would have known that it couldn't be true. Here is a government organisation that could not have failed to realise that its report about an 'office furnishings fire' bringing down a 47-story skyscraper is the most monumental, child-like bollocks you could ever imagine, but still went along with it to support the official narrative. At the same time NIST admitted that the building fell in *free-fall* at the start for more than two seconds and this can only happen if all resistance below is deleted. There was no structural prelude; the building went from stable to free-fall in an instant – just like the Twin Towers. We should not forget that the forces driving and directing 9/11 and other catastrophes are at the very outer extreme of psychopaths and your career would be over – or worse – if you failed to act as directed. The same can be said of the FAA, National Transportation Safety Board, FBI and so on. 'I was just following orders', right? Architects & Engineers for 9/11 Truth asked a team at the University of Alaska Fairbanks (UAF) to investigate what happened to Building 7 and the impact of the fires. Dr Leroy Hulsey led the team from the Department of Civil and Environmental Engineering. He said: 'It is our preliminary conclusions based upon our work to date that fire did not produce the failure at this particular building.' The study was ongoing at the time of writing. It is a real head-shaker that despite the expert opinion and eye-witness statements presented here I saw an article in the UK *Sun* which said there were 'conspiracy theories' that Building 7 was brought down by controlled demolition but '... there is no evidence to support such a theory'. *Extraordinary.*

Giuliani's bunker

Two years before the attacks Mayor Rudolph Giuliani opened a $13 million command center on the 23rd floor of World Trade Center Building 7– called by the media 'Giuliani's bunker'– and it was constructed with reinforced, bulletproof, and bomb-resistant walls, its own air and water supply and three backup generators. This was to be the focal point for Giuliani's Office of Emergency Management that he established in 1996 to take over the New York Police Department's responsibility for the preparation and directing of emergency response. Giuliani appointed Jerome M. Hauer to be the first director and he was replaced by 'Ground Zero's Jewish Knight' Richard Sheirer in early 2000 who was at Giuliani's side on 9/11. 'Giuliani's bunker' was really 'Hauer's bunker' because he made the decision to build a command center and to locate it in Building 7 owned by Larry Silverstein. Hauer and Silverstein must have known each other given they both had deep family connections with the New York Jewish community and with Israel. Giuliani was very clear: 'Jerry Hauer recommended that as the prime site and the site that would make the most sense ... It was largely on his recommendation that that site was selected.' From this command center all New York emergency communications frequencies could be monitored and it was supposed to be staffed around the clock. The facility was designed to respond to emergencies like terrorism and from here the mayor would oversee the response with first Hauer and then his successor Sheirer. Strange, then, that neither Giuliani nor Sheirer were anywhere to be seen there on September 11th. Giuliani cultivates a false image of the 'hero' mayor of 9/11. New York firefighters tell a very different story about this vicious man. He sent in firefighters and other rescue and clean-up workers after the attacks when the Environmental Protection Agency (EPA) knew that it was potentially lethal to breathe the toxic air at Ground Zero. Giuliani insisted because he said: 'The stock market must re-open.' Yeah, let's get our priorities right. Firefighters and their colleagues are suffering appallingly and a 2018 media report said: 'Seventeen years out from the Sept. 11, 2001, terrorist attacks, nearly 10,000 first responders and others who were in the World Trade Center area have been diagnosed with cancer ... More than 2,000 deaths have been attributed to 9/11 illnesses.' Many rescue dogs died of rare cancers. Meanwhile Giuliani continues his lucrative career in and around politics and in 'security'. What happened with regard to the Building 7 command center that day was very weird. Barry Jennings, Deputy Director of Emergency Services for the New York Housing Authority, said he took a phone call informing him that a small Cessna had hit the World Trade Center and he was told to go to the Office of Emergency Management – the 'command center' – in Building 7. When he arrived with New York City corporation counsel Michael Hess they were shocked to find the command center deserted:

> We noticed that everybody was gone. I saw coffee that was on a desk, the smoke was still coming off the coffee. I saw half-eaten sandwiches ... After I called several individuals, one told me to leave and leave right away. Mr. Hess came running back in and said, "We're the only ones up here, we gotta get out of here.

Giuliani's $13 million command center built for just this situation was *empty*? Someone told Barry Jennings on the phone to 'get out right away'? The Twin Towers had not fallen by then. Surely emergency management staff would have been in the command center with others heading there fast – most especially 'Ground Zero's Jewish Knight' Richard Sheirer, New York's Director of Emergency Management. *Unless* ... and it does appear very clearly that there was an ... *unless*. Barry Jennings and Michael Hess began to walk down the stairwell and when they reached the sixth floor the landing gave way underfoot from an explosion further below. Jennings recalled:

> The explosion was beneath me ... so when the explosion happened it blew us back ... both [Twin Towers] were still standing ... I was left there hanging. I had to climb back up and walk back up to the eighth floor.

Jennings said they were trapped there for several hours when the official report claims that the fire which brought down Building 7 was located between the seventh and ninth floors – precisely where Jennings and Hess were the whole time. Jennings said that as they waited 'I'm hearing all kinds of explosions'. When eventually they were rescued and returned to the lobby it was in ruins:

> Keep in mind, when I came in there, the lobby had nice escalators – it was a huge lobby. And for me to see what I saw was unbelievable.

He said they were told by fire officers not to look down because they
were stepping over dead bodies in the lobby and they were warned to
get out quickly because of reports of more explosions. Jennings, who
died in 2008, officially of cancer, told his story on camera for the 9/11
documentary *Loose Change*. He later sought to retract what he said about
seeing dead bodies after what the makers of *Loose Change* understood to
be threats made to Jennings about his job. Maybe the FBI dropped in
when they weren't sending human remains to landfills. Giuliani had
certainly been talking with Larry Silverstein judging by the incredible
bullshit he proceeded to deliver. He said in a television interview that
they set up an emergency response operation in a building in Barclay
Street and not in the purpose-built Building 7 command center which he
was told had been evacuated. Why hadn't the Barclay Street building
done the same when it was two minutes' walk from Building 7? Then he
said he was warned that the World Trade Center was going to collapse.
Whaaaaaaat?? Giuliani told Peter Jennings on ABC:

> I went down to the scene and we set-up headquarters at 75 Barclay Street,
> which was right there with the Police Commissioner, the Fire Commissioner,
> the head of Emergency Management [Richard Sheirer] and we were
> operating out of there when we we're told that the World Trade Center was
> going to collapse. And it did collapse before we could actually get out of the
> building. So we were trapped in the building for 10 to 15 minutes and finally
> found an exit, got out, walked north and took a lot of people with us.

Okay, so why didn't anyone else know about the warning? How did
they know the World Trade Center was going to collapse? Who told
them? Maybe it was Silverstein's mystery fire commander. Why wasn't
anyone else warned – like the firefighters that died? Why would anyone
think the buildings could collapse given that not one of their type ever
had through fire in the entirety of architectural history? There are some
reports from firefighters that the warning about a possible collapse came
from Giuliani's own Office of Emergency Management headed by
'Ground Zero's Jewish Knight' Richard Sheirer. When later challenged
by 9/11 researchers about the impossibility and great significance of
what he said Giuliani denied that he was warned even though he said
that on national television. You are a another bloody liar Giuliani and
why do people lie? To hide the truth – that's why the 9/11 fairy tale is
drowning in them. Building 7 was in the news (on the Internet at least)
when it emerged that the BBC and CNN reported that Building 7 had
collapsed *before* it actually did. BBC correspondent Jane Standley
announced that Building 7 had fallen some *26 minutes* before it came
down and the building can even be seen still standing behind her while

Figure 72: BBC reporter announces the demise of Building 7 while it remains standing behind her.

she reported its demise (Fig 72). The BBC made the bizarre and ridiculous statement when questioned about this that all recordings of its live coverage on 9/11 had been 'lost'. The corporation typically said that to accuse it of being part of a conspiracy over Building 7 was ridiculous. This, of course, was not what was being suggested. Not by me, anyway. The question was not about a BBC 'conspiracy', but *who told them* and CNN nearly half an hour before Building 7 came down that it had already done so? On this, the BBC was silent. When you look at the sequence of events it is clear that the 9/11 script was always to bring down Building 7 and maybe mistakenly released the news before the deed was actually done. Giuliani later headed to a command centre set up at New York's Pier 92 where hundreds of people were assembled from FEMA, the State Emergency Management Office and the Federal Government preparing for a bio-chemical attack exercise drill long-planned for the next day. What synchronicity, eh?

How was it done?

The fact that the towers were brought down deliberately is a gimme for anyone prepared to look at the evidence and clear their minds of the 9/11 download program. I am not attached, however, to exactly how this was done and I remain wide open to all possibilities. My aim here is to show that the official story didn't happen because everything else comes from that. The obvious conclusion is the use of explosive charges as per familiar controlled demolition technique which are employed all the time around the world to bring down big structures. Professor Steven Jones and others have suggested the involvement of substances known variously as thermite, super-thermite and thermate. These are incendiary mixtures which can burn very fast and very hot. Jones was a professor of physics at Brigham Young University (BYU) in Utah before he was suspended after entering the 9/11 debate and later chose to retire. He said that he became interested in the subject in 2005 because of the questions about Building 7 and many reports from Ground Zero of steel in a molten state still there weeks after the buildings fell. Researcher Christopher Bollyn quotes Peter Tully, president of Tully Construction of Flushing, New York, describing pools of 'literally molten steel' at the World Trade Center weeks into the clean-up operation. Particularly interesting were witnesses reporting molten steel in the basements of the three towers. Mark Loizeaux, president of Controlled Demolition, Inc. (CDI) in Maryland, told Bollyn there were 'hot spots of molten steel in the basements' – 'at the bottoms of the elevator shafts of the main towers, down seven [basement] levels.' Molten metal was discovered in the rubble of Building 7 which was not struck by an aircraft. This could not have been caused by the original relatively low-temperature fires and certainly not weeks later.

Professor Jones secured formerly molten metal fragments from the World Trade Center site and he and other physicists at BYU put them through a series of experiments and tests. Jones's conclusion was they contained the elements that would be expected with the presence of thermite/super-thermite/thermate. He said: 'The results, coupled with visual evidence at the scene such as flowing yellow-hot liquid metal still red after falling about 500 feet, provide compelling evidence that thermite reaction compounds were used, meaning thermite was deliberately placed in both WTC Towers and WTC 7.' Jones further contended that a souped-up version of thermite, known as thermate, could cut through steel beams and substantially reduce the melting point of steel. He said that thermate could 'cut through steel like a hot knife through butter'. The military use thermate, which burns at higher temperatures than regular thermite, to cut through tank armour and bunkers. Thermate can even burn under water and in other oxygen-starved locations. Professor Jones said thermate would explain molten metal seen falling from the still-standing South Tower and white smoke/ash emitting from the same area (Fig 73). He said they found elements in Ground Zero dust that strongly suggested the presence of thermite/thermate and that 'strange corrosion' on the dust-covered roofs of vehicles in the area would be expected with thermite residue. He claims that other 'finds' in the rubble and dust point in the same direction. This is only the briefest summary of the thermite/thermate hypothesis which has proved highly controversial even within the 9/11 Truth movement. There are a number of interviews and presentations by Steven Jones on the Internet for those who wish look deeper at the claims.

A very different explanation circulating over the years is the use of directed energy weapons to bring down the towers. I am not

Figure 73: The molten metal pouring from the South Tower highlighted by Professor Steven Jones.

saying this did happen or didn't, but I come back to a point I have emphasised over and over: The technology we see is not the cutting edge of technology that actually exists. Selling a perception of what is possible is a major element of the human perception program. If you limit perception of the possible in the target population they will dismiss explanations that are true because the truth appears to be impossible to programmed perception. It may be impossible to their *perception* of reality – but not to *actual* reality. World-changing technology developed in secret projects and underground bases is sitting there waiting for the right moment in the continuing sequence of human control to be played out in the public domain. This includes directed energy technology that could turn an enormous building to dust. These weapons exist today in the world of the known and so they would have existed – and then some – in the world of the hidden at the time of 9/11. I highlighted 'beams weapons' in *Alice in Wonderland* in 2002 and pointed out that some 425,000 cubic yards of World Trade Center concrete disintegrated mostly as immense clouds of dust. One witness said there was 'not a single block of concrete in that rubble'. Dr Charles Hirsch, the government's Chief Medical Examiner, reportedly told grieving relatives in December, 2001, that many bodies had been 'vaporized' and at that time only 500 of the nearly 3,000 who died had been identified. I described in *Alice* how the *American Free Press* (AFP) had interviewed a German physicist who believed a laser beam weapon could have caused the collapse of the Twin Towers using infrared technology that was first developed in the Soviet Union. The physicist, whom AFP does not name, was described as a former East German physicist who studied Soviet infrared technology and 'plasmoids' during the 1960s and 70s. He was claimed to be directly involved in the demonstration of a Soviet laser beam weapon for the US Air Force in Weimar in 1991. According to the physicist the Soviet weapon was used during a Soviet dispute with China in 1969 to destroy 'a wall' at the Ussuri River which separates Manchuria from Russia. Infrared radiation employs invisible wavelengths between visible light and microwave on the electromagnetic spectrum and produces fantastic heat. It creates a potentially devastating phenomenon called a plasmoid cloud of heated and ionised gas, AFP reported. The United States had been developing and deploying such weapons for many years and one of its centres of development was the Brookhaven Laboratories on Long Island, New York. Author Jeff Hecht wrote in his appropriately 1984 book *Beam Weapons: The Next Arms Race:* 'The military 'destructor beam' definitely is in our future tactical arsenal.' Advanced technology and plasma physics involved in directed-energy weapons gave them unprecedented lethal power. They could unleash devastating beams of energy in seconds and less. The 'German physicist' told *American Free Press*:

From my experience as a physicist and research scientist with the GRU [Russian military intelligence] I have enough experience to judge that the World Trade towers have been burning too quickly, too hot, and too completely to have been caused by the kerosene fires that resulted from the crashes. Furthermore, the demolished buildings nearby are an indication that there was a plasmoid cloud involved, which probably affected the buildings nearby.

He said that in 1991 the GRU demonstrated for the US Air Force Electronic Security Command (AFESC) the capabilities of its infrared beam weapon by reducing a ceramic plate to dust from a distance of one mile. He said the demonstration was designed to show the US 'how a stealth bomber could be turned into dust in the same way'. The plate had been disintegrated into such fine dust, he said, that it was difficult to pick up with a vacuum cleaner. 'The plate was not destroyed suddenly as if hit by a bullet, rather it disintegrated in a process taking about 15 minutes.' The physicist said that one of the transmitters involved in striking the World Trade Center with a beam weapon could have been located in a high building nearby or on a satellite, plane or ship. Russian state-funded TV station RT reported in 2018 that microwave directed-energy weapons were being tested at firing ranges in Russia. The prototypes were designed to burn missile-homing systems and could be incorporated in the arsenal of sixth-generation fighter jets. Vladimir Mikheev, deputy head of KRET, a leading electronic warfare contractor, said that these cutting-edge weapons systems 'exist and progress quite effectively', according to the TASS news agency. Mention of Russia here is not an indication that they were involved in 9/11, only that such weapons existed at the time of the attacks and the American military also had them. Mind you, judging by the hysterical demonisation of Russia maybe the best way to get a new investigation into 9/11 is to claim 'the Russians did it'.

Tesla knew

Targeted electromagnetic energy goes back at least to the late 19th century and was developed most famously in the first half of the 20th century by the Serbian-American technological genius, Nikola Tesla (1856-1943) who was way ahead of his time (Fig 74). He said: 'The day science begins to study non-physical phenomena it will make more progress in one decade than in all the previous centuries of its existence.' Tesla told

Figure 74: Nikola Tesla.

The New York Times in 1940 that he had developed 'an entirely new principle of physics' which 'no one ever dreamed about'. He called this the 'teleforce' and described it as an invisible beam that could generate an invisible 'Chinese Wall of Defence' and 'melt' aircraft motors at a distance of 250 miles. The teleforce beam was only one-hundred-millionth of a square centimetre in diameter, he said. Tesla was tapping into natural electrical/electromagnetic and other forces and focussing their power through technology. He said that he could produce 100 million volts of pressure with currents up to 100 billion watts and if the radio frequency was resonating at two megahertz the energy released would be the equivalent of ten megatons of TNT. Tesla said that he had the technology to 'split the Earth like an apple'. *New York American* published an article in 1935 with the headline 'Tesla's Controlled Earthquakes' in which he said that his technology's 'rhythmical vibrations pass through the Earth with almost no loss of energy ... [and it] becomes possible to convey mechanical effects to the greatest terrestrial distances and produce all kinds of unique effects'. Tesla manipulated the weather in experiments that included lightning strikes above his laboratory and he could make the ground shake violently (Fig 75). On one occasion thousands of windows in the area were broken before he could turn off his machine. His artificially-generated lightning storms unintentionally started hundreds of forest fires and blew out electrical grids in two states. He could see the military

Figure 75: Tesla understood electromagnetic reality and how it could be harnessed for good and evil.

potential of his inventions and acknowledged that his teleforce could be used with devastating effect in war. He said this was not his intention and he preferred to use his knowledge to provide free energy by harnessing naturally-occurring electrical and electromagnetic fields. This immediately had the Hidden Hand networks turn against him with a vengeance. Free energy, along with interest-free money, is their worst nightmare because of its devastating effect on both their income and control. Have any of the Green fanatics pressing to 'save the planet from global warming' ever stopped to ask why the super-rich families behind 'we must transform society to save humanity' are the very same families and networks that have suppressed Tesla-type free energy for everyone without generating any CO2? Tesla technology and its further developments can, in relation to 9/11, do the following:

- Deliver unprecedented amounts of energy at specific locations that are far more precise than a nuclear weapon.

- Interfere with global communications systems while itself remaining unaffected.

- Manipulate weather (they wanted a clear blue, cloud-free sky, for example, for maximum impact).

- Create nuclear-sized explosions using electromagnetic pulses.

Tesla died in a New York hotel room in 1943 and his cutting-edge research papers were confiscated by the American government, military and intelligence networks. The papers were reviewed for the military by John G. Trump (1907-1985), uncle of 'outsider' president Donald John Trump. This is where his middle name 'John' comes from. Uncle Trump would later become head of the British Branch of the Massachusetts Institute of Technology (MIT) Radiation Laboratory. This was funded by the Rockefeller family and would appear to have become the centre of a weather-manipulation programme. Did the American government, military and intelligence networks have the technology to bring down the World Trade Center buildings by using directed energy? Too bloody right they did and people will have to decide for themselves if they think that happened.

Dust to dust and more dust

The best-known proponent of the directed energy weapon scenario on 9/11 is Dr Judy Wood, a materials scientist and former professor of mechanical engineering who secured a doctorate in these subjects at the Department of Engineering Science and Mechanics at Virginia Polytechnic Institute and State University in Blacksburg, Virginia. Dr Wood set out the case for directed energy in her book *Where Did The Towers Go?* which was published in 2005. The book is highly detailed, illustrated and sourced and you can also see her video presentations on YouTube – '9/11 Dr Judy Wood where did the towers go?' will get you there. She makes a series of observations in support of her contention that the buildings were not brought down by conventional methods of controlled demolition. These include:

- The buildings turned to dust in mid-air – including steel beams and core vertical columns which can be seen turning to dust and disappearing as they fell – leaving only a tiny fraction of the one and a quarter million tons of steel, concrete, aluminium and other material to actually strike the ground.

- The Twin Towers were built on land reclaimed from the close-by Hudson River within a water-resisting dam or dyke known as the 'bathtub'. Had the buildings slammed into the ground before they turned to dust this dam would have been breached and the area flooded.

- Seismic records do not record the Richter scale reaction that would have been caused by such a massive impact of 110 storey buildings hitting the ground. When the Seattle Kingdome sports stadium was brought down in a conventional controlled demolition in 2000 it had a seismic impact of 2.3. The 110 storey World Trade Center 2 (the South Tower) registered just 2.1 despite having, Wood says, 30 times the potential energy. The mall and parking garage right under the World Trade Center site were still intact.

- Wood compares the 9/11 seismic readings with that of an earthquake in Midtown Manhattan in January of the same year and finds them to be very different. The 9/11 readings show that 'no signal went through the earth' which would have happened if the building had not turned to dust before impact. As for Building 7 there was no seismic reading of note and Wood describes the fall of the building as a 'non-seismic event'.

These are what Wood calls 'the biggest smoking guns' which show that (a) the government story about the World Trade Center is not true and (b) a conventional controlled demolition could not have been responsible. When the World Trade Center towers come down it's almost like watching a fountain of dust emanating from the top as the building basically disappears (Fig 76). Jay Jones, a

Figure 76: The dust 'fountain' emanating from the top as the Towers came down.

firefighter at the scene, said: 'These were the biggest office buildings in the world and I didn't see one desk or chair or one phone, nothing.' Wood points out other evidence that exposes the nonsense about fire compromising the steel and why there are descriptions of steel 'vaporising'. Buildings around the World Trade Center complex – even across the road – suffered nothing like the damage that would be expected had the falling debris not turned to dust, she says. Wood contends that with all the material 'squeezed' and projected out from the towers had the 'pancaking' story been true buildings all around them would have peppered like machine gun fire. Some were hit as described earlier, but not 'peppered'. She recalls being contacted by a man who worked at the World Trade Center and decided to go home when the planes initially hit. He said he walked past the South Tower 'with the fires about out' and headed for the ferry terminal on the Hudson. While he was there, with his view of the WTC obscured by other buildings, he said someone claimed the South Tower had collapsed. The reaction was that this was ridiculous and the person must be an idiot. When he was crossing the river and looked back there was only one tower standing. He hadn't heard anything or felt the ground shake. Michael Ober, an emergency medical technician, said: 'I don't remember the sound of the building hitting the ground ... if the building is hitting the ground that hard, how do I not remember the sound of it? Six different magnetometer readings of the Earth's magnetic field at ground level by six different stations in Alaska reveal that about 20 minutes before the first tower was struck the field around the World Trade Center began to act strangely and distort. The reading had been quite stable until then, but distorted significantly in the run up to the plane strikes and then began to distort dramatically and go 'haywire' over the period when the towers came down. This continued until Building 7 fell when the readings began to calm down and return to their former comparative stability.

What caused this?

There are other strange phenomena to consider. Vehicles some distance from the impact were turned upside down or burned out in a way that did not suggest a normal fire (Fig 77). Some vehicles were partly burned in a specific area but untouched in other parts and alongside them were trees, street lamps and shops that were not similarly damaged. This cannot be explained by burning debris flying from the building and only striking road vehicles and nothing else. The streets and area around the vehicles were strewn with unburnt paper and there are images of burning cars surrounded by paper that isn't burning. Vehicle engines were melted together with other parts which fire could not possibly have done. Cars and buses were twisted and melted with paintwork

Figure 77: Vehicles a long way from the World Trade Center were burnt out while trees and paper near them, even next to them, were not burned.

Figure 78: Cars were found burned out or 'toasted' on top of each other and others were upside down.

Figure 79: A bus stripped to the metal but with no burn or scorch marks.

stripped as if they had been dipped in paint-stripper (Figs 78). There were melted, paint-stripped buses and cars with no scorch-marks (Fig 79). One witness said: 'It was unbelievable, they were twisted and melted into nothing.' A television reporter described 'car after car, and buses, burned down to the steel'. Door handles and latches were gone and there was no window glass at all. The drjudywood.com website comments:

A reported 1400 vehicles were damaged on 9/11. These vehicles had peculiar patterns of damage and some were as far away as ... (about 7 blocks from the WTC, along the East River). Vehicles had missing door handles for example, windows blown out, window frames deformed, melted engine blocks, steel-belted tires with only the steel belts left, and vehicle front ends destroyed with little or no effect on the back end of the vehicles. What could have caused such extraordinary damage? Portions of cars burned while paper nearby did not.

Wood says that comparisons with images of burnt-out vehicles indicate this is not the same phenomena. Similar scenes were reported and photographed during devastating wildfires in California in 2018 which some blamed on energy beams directed from the sky. Houses were burnt to nothing alongside others that were untouched, homes turned to ash while surrounded by unburnt trees and vehicles were burnt and overturned in ways that looked very much like those that Wood highlights with 9/11. World Trade Center steel beams that survived were found twisted tightly back on themselves in a U-bend and materials with very different melting and boiling points became fused together including organic matter that should have been burned away if this had been caused by fire. Some witnesses described being picked up by a wave of energy and being tossed down the street or against walls. *New York Daily News* photographer David Handschuh recalled how he was thrown nearly a block: 'One second I was running, the next I was airborne.' He also remembered feeling a warm, not hot, blast of air which others also described. In the debris of the towers people saw acts of spontaneous combustion long after the towers came down that could not be explained by heat. Some may point to the thermite/thermate hypothesis, but Wood says all these phenomena would be expected if Tesla-like technology had been used on 9/11. She writes that when focussed-energy struck the buildings people would hear 'boom, boom, boom' by the effect of the structure disintegrating. As she puts it: 'Bombs go boom, but not everything that goes boom is a bomb.' Matter is only energy vibrating to a slow frequency and if that energetic construct of 'matter' is hit by high-powered focussed energy it will spatter apart and what it strikes would turn to dust. Wood wonders if many who jumped from the building were not forced to do so by the effect of microwave energy which can give you the feeling that your skin is on fire. The American military/law enforcement employs this skin-fire system to disperse crowds and, by the way, it operates in the same frequency band as the cumulatively lethal 5G communication systems being rolled out across the world by the Hidden Hand without any independent testing of its effect on human health. But then they are psychopaths – the same mentality and networks behind 9/11.

Another aspect of Wood's research is that on that clearest of blue-sky

days in New York and
Washington a category 3
hurricane was spinning
off the New York coast.
Anyone remember
hearing about that or any
pre-warnings as it
worked its way from the
south? Me, neither. It was
dubbed Hurricane Erin
and coverage was sparse
compared with what you
would expect and
restricted to weather
reports rather than the

Figure 80: Hurricane Erin off the US East Coast on 9/11.

main headlines (Fig 80). CNN Weather reported on September 8th that
'the first Atlantic hurricane of the season churned toward Bermuda
Saturday night, with experts forecasting even stronger winds over the
next 24 hours'. The report located Erin 325 miles southeast of Bermuda
'but creeping closer at a rate of 15 mph'. Wind speeds were recorded at a
sustained 85 miles per hour. Erin made its way north to reach its greatest
extent off the coast of New York on September 11th and following the
attacks moved sharply right out into the ocean. Personnel on the
International Space Station orbiting 240 miles above the Earth said they
could see plumes of smoke from the World Trade Center but didn't
mention a big hurricane system just off the coast. The position of Erin
apparently ensured the cloudless blue skies for which 9/11 is
remembered and against which events could occur in clear sight with
maximum impact. American meteorologist Joe Bastardi mentions Erin in
his book, *The Climate Chronicles,* in the sense of weather conditions
affecting an outcome. He writes:

> On 9/11 the sun was shining brightly as high pressure along the East Coast
> and strong sinking air outside of major Hurricane Erin well offshore allowed
> for a spectacular day on the East Coast. If Erin were closer, chances are the
> weather would have been less hospitable or perhaps there would have been
> flight delays. As it was, the storm was in the perfect spot to allow the usual
> sinking air create ideal conditions for the hijackers to do what they did.

Tesla-type technology can certainly whip-up hurricanes and use them
to gather and focus energy for many purposes or produce desired
weather conditions as described. Weather systems are simply energy
systems and if you can change the nature of that energy you change the
weather. Technological modification of the weather has been possible

since at least the first half of the 20th century and is now very powerful and sophisticated. You don't have international agreements not to mess with the weather and use it as a weapon if modifying the weather is not possible. Of course it is and since when did the United States and other countries with this technology give a damn about international laws and treaties? A major cover for this manipulation is the hoax about human-caused climate change upon which they can blame their weather-changing actions. Hurricane Erin off the coast of New York at the time of 9/11 is an amazing 'coincidence', that's for sure.

The deluge of unanswered questions and blatant lies and anomalies regarding the attacks of September 11th was the motivation for citizen journalists to come together organically and independently to form the movement that became known as 9/11 Truth. They are referred to as 'Truthers' and they have been abused and ridiculed by the mainstream media for doing the job *it* should have being doing. You have seen the evidence so far that puts the official story into question at every turn while excuses-for-journalists the world over dismiss with an arrogant wave of the hand the obvious flaws in the story they have accepted without a second thought. Many of these system-defenders call themselves 'progressives', as with Matthew Rothschild, editor of *The Progressive*, who described the official story of the towers falling as 'perfectly logical, scientific explanations'. Typical are comments like those of George Monbiot at the system-serving London *Guardian* which bizarrely claims to be 'radical'. Excuse me a moment, my belly hurts. Monbiot described 'Truthers' as 'fantasists', 'conspiracy idiots' and 'morons'.

Why has the mainstream media never uncovered the truth about 9/11? George Monbiot. Matthew Rothschild, ad infinitum. I rest my case.

CHAPTER 14

Prior knowledge and cover-up

Whenever you find that you are on the side of the majority, it is time to pause and reflect – Mark Twain

Still further confirmation that 9/11 was an inside job would be evidence that those with responsibility to defend the United States from terrorist attacks – and other insiders – were aware of what was going to happen. This evidence can be found a plenty.

Later in the book I will describe the remarkable absence of lease-holder Larry Silverstein and his family at the World Trade Center that morning even though they were there almost every other day at the time the attacks happened. There are many stories that indicate prior knowledge in either detail or theme. San Francisco Mayor Willie Brown said he was warned at 10pm the previous night by what he called 'my security people at the airport' to be especially cautious about travelling by air on September 11th – he planned to fly to New York. A report in *Newsweek* claimed that on the day before the attacks 'a group of top Pentagon officials suddenly cancelled travel plans for the next morning, apparently because of security concerns'. The *San Francisco Chronicle* reported that the FBI had advised Attorney General John Ashcroft not to fly on commercial aircraft in this same period and as the *Chronicle* put it: 'The FBI obviously knew something was in the wind.' Still the FBI and CIA claim they were not aware of a possible attack on commercial aircraft in the United States. Even Dan Rather at CBS asked why the warning was not shared with the public while Ashcroft avoided questions about what he was told. The FAA was reported to have issued a warning to airlines and airports on August 28th that people connected to terrorist networks were planning to fly on US airlines. Author Salman Rushdie, who has been threatened by Arab extremists for his book, *The Satanic Verses*, told the London *Times* that he believed the US authorities knew of an imminent terrorist strike when they banned him from taking internal flights in America and Canada just a week before the attacks.

The *Times* reported: 'On September 3rd the Federal Aviation Administration made an emergency ruling to stop Rushdie from flying unless airlines complied with strict and costly security measures.' Rushdie said the airlines would not upgrade their security. The *Times* said 'the FAA told Rushdie's publisher that US intelligence had been given warning of 'something out there' but failed to give any further details and 'the FAA confirmed that it stepped up security measures concerning Mr Rushdie but refused to give a reason'. Goldman Sachs also circulated a memo on September 10th warning of a possible terrorist attack and advising employees to stay away from American government buildings. A FEMA Urban Search and Rescue Team was deployed to New York City the night before the attacks. FEMA official Tom Kennedy told *CBS News* on September 11th:

> We're currently one of the first teams that was deployed to support the City of New York in this disaster. We arrived on late Monday night and went right into action on Tuesday morning.

They must have been in New York for the FEMA exercise drill planned there for September 11th. What are the chances that a disaster drill in New York on 9/11 by the country's emergency response organisation was planned to take place at the very time that plane hijacking drills were taking place in the skies and just as the 9/11 attacks were happening that mirrored those drills and required an immediate FEMA response? Vice President Dick Cheney said after 9/11 that political criticism of the Bush government's failure to react to warnings was 'thoroughly irresponsible and totally unworthy of national leaders in time of war'. He also tried to deflect such headlines by saying that 'without a doubt, a very real threat of another perhaps more devastating attack still exists'. You should know, Dick. Two Israel-based employees at an Israeli telecommunications company and instant messaging service called Odigo, with offices two blocks from the World Trade Center, were sent a warning two hours before the first tower was hit that some sort of attack was imminent. Odigo vice president Alex Diamandis said: 'The messages said something big was going to happen in a certain amount of time and it did – almost to the minute.' CEO Micha Macover said that immediately after the attack the two told the company about the warning and Israeli security services were then informed who told the FBI. Macover said:

> I have no idea why the message was sent to these two workers, who don't know the sender. It may just have been someone who was joking and turned out they accidentally got it right.

So why hasn't the sender been found then? Did they try? The idea that someone warned about attacks that had never happened before and almost to the minute may have been joking around and got it right by accident simply is not worth troubling neurons to activate in reply. How many know that Israel Mossad agents were arrested after being spotted on 9/11 cheering and high-fiving as they filmed the burning North Tower and were clearly in position knowing what would happen? They became known as the 'Dancing Israelis'. How many know that hundreds of Israelis were questioned by the authorities during 2001 suspected of being in a spy ring operating around the country and especially in Florida in the same period and even in the same city that alleged '9/11 hijackers' were located? All this is coming up in detail when I reach the climax of the book. Many remarkable 'coincidences' have been highlighted in television programmes and other media that have either portrayed or appeared to foretell events of 9/11. Some may be coincidence, but not all of them. The most remarkable was the first episode of a Fox series called *The Lone Gunmen*, an X-Files spin-off show broadcast in America in March, 2001, which featured a passenger aircraft having its controls taken over from the ground via the computer system and flown into the World Trade Center. At the last moment the pilot seized back control with help from 'good guys' on the ground and pulled up to avoid disaster. The point of the attack in the plot-line was to blame the crash on Middle Eastern terrorists to justify a war on terror to make fortunes for arms companies. If you think that's a 'wow' – the plane had its computer systems hijacked during a wargames exercise involved the hijacking of a passenger aircraft. The scenes were shot in the spring of 2000. Where did the inspiration for the storyline originate which was so incredibly accurate in terms of 9/11? Programme makers say it was a coincidence while others believe it was far too close to the soon-to-be truth for such an explanation.

Casino prophets

Then there was stock trading immediately before September 11th involving airlines and companies affected by the attacks. This provides spectacular evidence of prior knowledge. Again the 'government story is true' mind-set led to media speculation that this trading must have been the work of Osama bin Laden. Who is more likely to have been behind this – a guy in a cave in Afghanistan or those who run both the government and the banking/stock market system? These include the CIA which has long and extremely close connections to the financial elite. Many of the CIA's leading personnel over the years have come from this very background, starting with its first director, Allen Dulles, the Nazi supporter and business associate. The CIA claims to constantly monitor unusual financial transactions on the markets to track evidence of possible terrorist and criminal activity. What does it call 'unusual' when you consider what happened in the days before 9/11? Stock markets are not there to benefit the general population. They are casinos. A news report from Wall Street or the London Stock Exchange is little more than a report from Las Vegas on how the blackjack or roulette tables are going. They bet with people's lives and livelihoods. Two ways of doing this are 'put' and 'call' options. A 'put option' is when you bet that the stock in a company will go down in value within a certain period. If it does you can make big money. A 'call option' is when you bet that the stock price will go up. Clearly the stock price of airlines involved in the hijackings, American and United, would fall immediately after the attacks and the same with companies with a major operation in the World Trade Center or those with a potential insurance liability. How fascinating, therefore, that 4,744 put options were placed on United Airlines against only 396 call options at the Chicago Board Options Exchange between September 6th and 7th. Three days later 4,516 put options were purchased on American Airlines and only 748 call options. This represented six times the usual number of put options and trading in other airlines did not follow this pattern. The theme can be seen with major companies at the World Trade Center like Morgan Stanley and Merrill Lynch and insurance firms that would face crippling claims as a result of the attacks. When these highly unusual trades were reported, revealing as they do blatant prior knowledge of the attacks, more than $2.5 million in put option profits on United Airlines went unclaimed. Michael Ruppert, a researcher and former Los Angeles Police Department drug investigator, made a CIA connection after the attacks to this insider trading:

> That evidence also demonstrates that, in the case of at least one of these trades – which has left a $2.5 million prize unclaimed – the firm used to place the 'put options' on United Airlines stock was, until 1998, managed by the man who is now in the number three Executive Director position at the Central Intelligence Agency. Until 1997, A.B. 'Buzzy' Krongard had been Chairman of the investment bank A.B. Brown. A.B. Brown was acquired by Banker's Trust in 1997.

> Krongard then became, as part of the merger, Vice Chairman of Banker's Trust-A.B. Brown, one of 20 major US banks named by Senator Carl Levin this year as being connected to money laundering. Krongard's last position at Banker's Trust (BT) was to oversee 'private client relations'. In this capacity he had direct hands-on relations with some of the wealthiest people in the world in a kind of specialized banking operation that has been identified by the US Senate and other investigators as being closely connected to the laundering of

drug money.

In 1998 Krongard was appointed as counsel to CIA Director George Tenet and promoted to CIA Executive Director by Boy Bush in March, 2001. Bankers Trust-A.B.-Brown was taken over in 1999 by Deutsche Bank when Krongard left for the CIA and it became the biggest bank in Europe. Deutsche Bank was also used for the highly unusual pre-9/11 trading and its London branch was apparently frequented by the Bin Laden family. The question may be asked again: Who is more likely to have been behind these 'prior knowledge' stock trades, Osama bin Laden in Afghanistan or the global financial nexus connected to the CIA and the Hidden Hand elite? This is the same CIA that failed to respond to these highly unusual stock movements just as US air defences failed to respond to four hijacked airliners. The same CIA and 'intelligence community' which despite a then more than $30 billion annual budget (and that was just the official one) claimed with the FBI and military they had no idea the attacks were going to happen until they switched on the TV with the rest of the nation. We'll see what crap that is. The CIA announced an investigation when news of the stock trades broke and media reports said market regulators in the US, UK, Germany, Switzerland, Italy and Japan were to be involved. Have you ever heard another word about this 'investigation' even though the transactions must be traceable? The trail did not lead to Bin Laden or the Islamic world or we would have seen it blazed across the front pages a long time ago. The 9/11 Commission dismissed foreknowledge of the attacks by saying they had traced the bulk of the trades in United Airlines to someone 'with no conceivable ties to al-Qaeda'. You've got to laugh or weeping is all that remains.

Designer cover stories

The highest levels of the intelligence and law enforcement networks knew something was coming, but I repeat my warning about cover stories being used to misdirect from the real story. This can even be done by circulating evidence of a lesser conspiracy or cover-up to divert attention from the true depth and nature of the conspiracy/cover-up. We are dealing with state-of-art smoke and mirrors and we need to be careful about the double-spin technique or what I call 'fall-back position'. When these Hidden Hand operations are played out there is always a number one cover story that they want the people to believe and most do. In this case Cover Story A was that Osama bin Laden organised the entire operation with 'his' al-Qaeda network and it was so brilliantly done that US military and civilian agencies had no idea what was going on until the planes crashed. They know that not everyone will believe that and will look for some kind of conspiracy behind the official version of events. So they give them 'evidence' of a conspiracy to keep them happy and occupied – Cover Story B. When Princess Diana was assassinated in Paris in 1997 the prime cover story was that it was all a terrible accident caused by a drunk driver. The fall-back position for those who questioned that explanation was she was murdered because the British royal family did not want her to marry a Muslim, Dodi Fayed. Diana's murder goes much deeper than that (see *The Biggest Secret*), but together these two narratives provide alternative explanations accepted by the great majority including many of those that don't believe the prime cover story. The 9/11 fall-back position aimed at conspiracy researchers and others who question the official line is that (1) the Bush administration knew the attacks were coming, but were so incompetent that they did nothing; or (2) they knew the attacks were coming, but did nothing because allowing them to happen would provide the excuse to launch a war on terror for reasons of oil and advancing their agenda of conquest in the Middle and Near East. What these versions have in common is very significant: No matter what the background detail might be they are all based on Osama bin Laden and al-Qaeda being responsible for organising the whole thing and the plan involved 'terrorists' trained at American flying schools. This suits the Hidden Hand because it hides the central truth that the core organisation behind the attacks was not based in a cave in Afghanistan, but within the US government, military and intelligence 'community', the Israeli military and intelligence network (much more later) and at the highest level of the Hidden Hand hierarchy. We should keep that in mind when we hear stories that 'Bush was warned'. Incompetence is often used as a smoke screen to hide cold calculation. 'Incompetence' can be used, as in this case, to justify the 'reorganisation' (centralisation) of intelligence and security agencies to focus the power over intelligence, surveillance and law enforcement into even fewer hands. Yes Bush was warned, but it was far more than that – far, far more.

The story broke widely in the mainstream media (big red flag) in May, 2002, about the number of warnings given to, and circulating within, the Bush administration and its agencies. The theme was that President Boy Bush was told of possible hijackings in the United States before September 11th and did nothing to warn people. The White House admitted eight months after the attacks that Bush was told by US intelligence before 9/11 that Osama bin Laden's terrorist network might hijack American aircraft. White House press secretary Ari Fleischer said the administration notified the 'appropriate agencies' in the summer of 2001 that hijackings were possible, but the Massport organisation that ran Boston Logan Airport told the *Boston Globe* that no such warning was communicated to them. Bush was said to have been told of a possible attack during an intelligence briefing on August 6th, 2001, headed 'Bin Laden Determined to Attack Inside the United States' by the same US intelligence agencies that claimed they had no idea that the September 11th attacks were being planned. The CIA would only say in response to these reports that the subject of airline hijackings was among a number of terrorist methods raised to US government officials at the time. In fact, congressional correspondent David Welna said on National Public Radio on the morning of September 11th: 'I spoke with Congressman Ike Skelton – a Democrat from Missouri and a member of the Armed Services Committee – who said that just recently the Director of the CIA warned that there could be an attack, an imminent attack, on the United States of this nature. So this is not entirely unexpected.' The idea that the military-intelligence complex had no warning does not stand up for a second, but again watch the fall-back positions holding the dam at 'Bin Laden did it' whatever version you go for. I have also made the important point that there is the State and the 'Deep State'. These can be described on one side as government, intelligence and military personnel genuinely seeking to protect America (State) and on the other agents of the psychopathic cabal working for a very different agenda (Deep State). The latter seeks to thwart the efforts of the former and the same happens in every country. Bush even tried to call off Robert Mueller's [non]-investigation of the attacks by the FBI when a week later on September 18th letters containing anthrax were sent to Democratic Senators Tom Daschle and Patrick Leahy and some media organisations. Seventeen people were infected and five died. The FBI described its anthrax investigation as 'one of the largest and most complex in the history of law enforcement'. Oh, really? And 9/11? This was a highly convenient diversion and came to a sudden halt when it was revealed that this Ames strain of anthrax was commonly used in US military research and at the US Army's Dugway Proving Ground in Utah.

Federal Ban on Investigation (FBI)

Understanding 9/11 and its lies, diversions, contradictions and ever-changing stories requires people to grasp the true nature of the FBI. As with all these 'alphabet' organisations like the CIA, NSA and so on the FBI has many genuine, decent and professional people in its ranks, but they are allowed to know only so much. Compartmentalisation of information – the need-to-know technique – means that they are not aware of the agenda those in charge and control are really pursuing. They only know what they need to know to do their particular job. There is a chasm of difference between many of those who work for the FBI and those who control it. At that upper level the Federal Bureau of Investigation is a cesspit of deceit and manipulation and takes its 'moral' compass from that of its notorious long-time chief, J. Edgar Hoover.

Reports became public in the aftermath of 9/11 that a classified memo written by an FBI agent in Phoenix had urged FBI headquarters to investigate Middle Eastern men enrolled in American flight schools and that terrorist groups like those linked to Osama bin Laden could be sending students to the schools as part of terrorist plans. Be careful here with a fall-back position narrative, but law enforcement officials said the memo was received at FBI headquarters in late July, 2001, and reviewed by counterterrorism staff. No action was taken in response to the memo's plea to compile information on the visa applications of foreign students seeking admission to aviation schools. We are told that a flight instructor at the Pan Am Flying Academy in Eagan, Minnesota, called the local FBI office on August 17th to report his suspicions about a 33-year-old French-Moroccan called Zacarias Moussaoui who was later jailed for life for involvement in the 9/11 attacks. *The New York Times* reported that senior FBI officials repeatedly denied requests by agents at the Minnesota office for a detailed investigation into his background. One of the facts that interested the agents was that Moussaoui was attending flying schools while FBI Director Robert Mueller, who was appointed two weeks before 9/11, has constantly claimed the FBI had no idea that potential terrorists were training to be pilots in the US. He said it was 'news, quite obviously,' and added: 'If we had understood that to be the case, we would have – perhaps one could have averted this.' This is clearly not true as genuine FBI agents have pointed out. Agents were blocked in their investigations because they were in danger of thwarting the cover story for 9/11 rather than exposing the real plot. Information from FBI agents in Minnesota was included in an internal FBI document warning that Moussaoui 'might be planning on flying something into the World Trade Center'. Agents asked for a warrant to search Moussaoui's personal computer only for their requests to be refused by the [In]Justice Department of Bush Attorney General John Ashcroft and the head of the Department's Criminal Division, Michael Chertoff. Why? Coleen Rowley, an FBI agent for more than 21 years and Minneapolis Chief Division Counsel, sent a memo to FBI Director Mueller in May, 2002, condemning the way the headquarters had blocked terrorist investigations before 9/11. She said that certain facts about this had been 'omitted, downplayed, glossed over and/or mischaracterised in an effort to avoid or minimise personal and/or institutional embarrassment on the part of the FBI and/or perhaps even for improper political reasons'. She went on:

> In the day or two following September 11th, you, Director Mueller, made the statement to the effect that if the FBI had only had any advance warning of the attacks, we (meaning the FBI), may have been able to take some action to prevent the tragedy. Fearing that this statement could easily come back to

haunt the FBI upon revelation of the information that had been developed
pre-September 11th about Moussaoui, I and others in the Minneapolis Office,
immediately sought to reach your office through an assortment of higher level
FBIHQ contacts, in order to quickly make you aware of the background of the
Moussaoui investigation and forewarn you so that your public statements
could be accordingly modified.

When such statements from you and other FBI officials continued, we thought
that somehow you had not received the message and we made further efforts.
Finally when similar comments were made weeks later, in Assistant Director
Caruso's congressional testimony in response to the first public leaks about
Moussaoui we faced the sad realization that the remarks indicated someone,
possibly with your approval, had decided to circle the wagons at FBIHQ in an
apparent effort to protect the FBI from embarrassment and the relevant FBI
officials from scrutiny. Everything I have seen and heard about the FBI's official
stance and the FBI's internal preparations in anticipation of further
congressional inquiry, had, unfortunately, confirmed my worst suspicions in
this regard.

Coleen Rowley revealed how in a desperate 11th hour measure to
bypass the 'FBIHQ roadblock' the Minneapolis Division directly notified
the CIA's Counter Terrorist Center and were 'chastised' by FBI
headquarters for making a direct notification without their approval.
Rowley told Mueller that in the early aftermath of September 11th when
she was recounting the pre-September 11th events concerning the
Moussaoui investigation to other FBI personnel in other divisions or FBI
headquarters 'almost everyone's first question was 'Why? – why would
an FBI agent(s) deliberately sabotage a case?' If they would care to read
this book they will have the answer to that question and the fact that it
was asked so widely reveals how effective and watertight
compartmentalisation can be. FBI special agent Robert Wright Jr who
investigated terrorist money-laundering in the United States for four
years was equally livid at how his efforts were blocked by superiors. He
told the media in May, 2002:

> I truly believe I would be derelict in my duty as an American if I did not do
> my best to bring the FBI's dereliction of duty to the attention of others. I have
> made it my mission ... to legally expose the problems of the FBI to the
> President of the United States, the US Congress, and the American people.

FBI agents were so angry at the way they were blocked by their own
hierarchy they gave their information to Chicago lawyer David
Schippers, the man involved in legal efforts to impeach President
Clinton. He said he contacted the office of Attorney General John

Ashcroft to urge an investigation and again his pleas were ignored.
Schippers said he was given information by FBI agents and intelligence
sources that a massive terrorist attack was being planned for lower
Manhattan and he had tried in vain for six weeks to communicate this
information to Ashcroft. He said he had also tried in the past to tell
Ashcroft about the connection between the Oklahoma bombing and the
Iraqi officers and soldiers that were brought to Oklahoma after the Gulf
War by Father George Bush and he got the same response. Schippers
said of the Iraqi officers in 2002: 'The word is out even today that the
Oklahoma City police are not allowed to touch them.' He described his
efforts to warn Ashcroft ahead of 9/11:

> I was trying to get people to understand that [the Palestinian group] Hamas
> had infiltrated the United States. I tried the House, I tried the Senate, I tried the
> Department of Justice, these were the very people who put up roadblocks on
> the attack against the terrorists under Clinton and are still there. They still
> constitute almost like a moat between the people with information and the
> people who should hear the information.

> I used people who were personal friends of John Ashcroft to try and get him.
> One of them called me back and said right I've talked to him, he'll call you
> tomorrow morning. This was like a month before the [9/11 attacks]. The next
> day I got a call from a lower ranked official of the Justice Department who
> said they don't start their investigations at the top. He would look into my
> information and get back to me. He never did.

What stands out like a red flag there is the claim about Hamas which
Israel has a prime interest in demonising while Israeli operatives were
centrally involved with 9/11 as we shall see.

FBI made the bomb for 1993 attack

Multiple evidence makes it clear that many knew to a larger or lesser
extent that attacks were coming and why would we trust the FBI to tell
us otherwise with its track record of creating terrorism as well as
covering up those really responsible? Even the mainstream media has
acknowledged this extraordinary phenomenon with headlines such as
'The FBI again thwarts its own terror plot'. The agency is notorious for
covertly setting up targets through its agents and informants to plan
terrorist attacks and then either claiming to have foiled them just in time
or allowing them to go ahead when they could have been stopped. The
FBI has admitted to 'thwarting' a stream of 'terrorist' plots that it
originally instigated and this was happening during the tenure of 9/11
FBI chief, Robert Mueller. Intelligence insiders have picked up on the
same theme including David Steele, a former Marine with 20 years'

experience as an intelligence officer, who was the second-highest-ranking civilian in US Marine Corps Intelligence. He said that again and again 'terrorist attacks' are false flag (Problem-Reaction-Solution) attacks staged by security services:

> In the United States, every single terrorist incident we have had has been a false flag, or has been an informant pushed on by the FBI. In fact, we now have citizens taking out restraining orders against FBI informants that are trying to incite terrorism. We've become a lunatic asylum.

Tamerlan Tsarnaev, blamed with his brother for the Boston bombings in 2013 and shot dead by police, had connections to the FBI and CIA. His mother Zubeidat Tsarnaeva said Tamerlan was under the control of the FBI:

> My son, he was set up. He was counselled by the FBI for 3 to 5 years. They knew what my son was doing and what actions and what sites on the Internet he was going. They used to come home; they used to come and talk to me; they used to tell me that they are counselling ...

Tsarnaev's father, Anzor, confirmed the FBI had watched his son closely and visited him at home:

> Yes, I was there. It was in Cambridge [Massachusetts]. They said: 'We know what sites you are on, we know where you are calling, we know everything about you. Everything.' They said we are checking and watching – that's what they said.

They were in fact setting him up with his brother to take the rap for the Boston bombing that the 'Deep State' was planning to instigate (see *Everything You Need To Know But Have Never Been Told*). This brings me to the World Trade Center bombing of 1993 which will become more significant later to 9/11 and what happened will give you a big insight into the FBI lead 'investigation' agency for the September 11th attacks. The story might also make those who dismiss the idea that governments and their agencies plan terrorist attacks take a moment to reassess. *The New York Times* revealed how the FBI had the chance to stop the bombing, but failed to do so. The paper also published conversations secretly recorded by an FBI informant, one-time Egyptian army officer, Emad Ali Salem. The FBI knew the 1993 attack was coming and 'planned to substitute the explosives in the truck bomb [*made by their informant Salem*] for harmless powder'. Or rather not as things turned out. Salem said an FBI supervisor called John Anticev stopped the plan to make the substitution. Six people died and a thousand were injured when the bomb made by an FBI informer exploded at the World Trade Center. Salem said on the tape: 'Guys, now you saw this bomb went off and you both know we could avoid that.' He said FBI agents were paid to 'prevent problems like this from happening' and asked an Agent Floyd: 'Do you deny your supervisor is the main reason of bombing the World Trade Center?' Salem continues: 'We was handling the case perfectly well until the supervisor messed it up, upside down.' Salem, an FBI informant, built the bomb that exploded at the World Trade Center and was paid a million dollars for his trouble. He was under the witness protection programme when he was the chief prosecution witness in the trial of those blamed for the bombing by the FBI! Ron Kuby, an attorney for one of the defendants, said of the article revealing the tapes:

> The article on the FBI being involved in the World Trade Center bombing actually understated the evidence, believe it or not. The informer, Emad Salem, is actually on tape saying that he built the bomb that ultimately blew up the World Trade Center ... In addition, we have received information that he was visually observed at the scene of the bombing shortly after the bombing took place

> Shortly after that, he was admitted to the hospital, suffering from an ear problem that was consistent with exposure to blast ... The mastermind is the government of the United States. It was a phoney, government-engineered conspiracy to begin with. It would never have amounted to anything had the government not planned it.

The same theme can be found on a far bigger scale with 9/11 – another FBI non-investigation. There's more: The bomb that exploded at the World Trade Center in 1993 was built by an informant on the FBI payroll and planted in a truck with a rental agreement that included the phone number and address of a notorious Israeli Mossad agent, Josie Hadas. Mossad and US intelligence work very closely together as do the US and Israeli military and this will become incredibly relevant to 9/11 in due course. The late Sheikh Omar Abdel-Rahman, the 'blind Sheikh', alleged 'spiritual leader' of the Egyptian extremist group Al-Gama'a al-Islamiya, was convicted in January, 1996, of 'seditious conspiracy' and sentenced to life imprisonment for his part in planning the 1993 bombing. He was put on the State Department's 'watch list' in 1987 and then reported to have been recruited by the CIA when the American government was supporting Osama bin Laden in Afghanistan during the Soviet occupation in the 1980s. American foreign correspondent Mary Anne Weaver said that in Peshawar, Pakistan, in the late 1980s Sheikh Omar became involved with US and Pakistani intelligence officials who were orchestrating the war against the Soviets. She said that the '60 or so CIA and Special Forces officers based there considered him a valuable asset'. They overlooked his anti-western message and his incitement to holy war, she wrote, because they wanted him to help unify the Mujahideen groups 'led' by Osama bin Laden. Sheikh Omar was given a one-year visa to enter the United States on May 10th, 1990, by a CIA agent posing as an official at the US Consulate in Khartoum, Sudan, and he arrived in New York in July, 1990. The visa was revoked in November that year and the State Department warned the Immigration and Naturalization Service to watch for him. Instead, within months, they granted him a green card (work permit) and in 1993 came the World Trade Center bombing for which he and others were convicted. *An alleged CIA asset was convicted of conspiracy to plant a bomb that was made by an informant of the FBI and left in a rental truck connected to a Mossad agent.* We are supposed to believe these people when they tell us what happened on September 11th and who was responsible? Or that the CIA and FBI had no connection to what happened and who did it? Later it was revealed, in keeping with the FBI's appalling history of lies and cover-ups, that 'evidence' was changed to support the prosecution of people the FBI claimed to be responsible for the bombing. FBI special agent Dr Frederic Whitehurst testified at the trial in 1995 that the FBI concocted misleading scientific reports and pressured two of their scientists to lie to support its prosecution of the defendants. He was asked if during his examination of bomb residue materials and chemicals connected with the defendants that he became aware the FBI agents investigating the case had developed a preliminary theory that the bomb which blew up the World Trade Center was a fertilizer based urea nitrate bomb? 'That is correct,' he replied. The questioning continued as follows:

'Did there come a time when you began to experience pressure from within the FBI to reach certain conclusions that supported that theory of the investigation?'

'Yes, that is correct.'

'In other words, you began to experience pressure on you to say that the explosion was caused by a urea nitrate bomb?'

'Yes, that is correct.'

'And you were aware that such a finding would strengthen the prosecution of the defendants who were on trial, who were going on trial in that case, correct?'

'Absolutely.'

Special agent Frederic Whitehurst, the senior FBI explosives expert, found himself demoted to paint analysis for the crime of telling the truth – the most heinous of crimes to the FBI when it exposes its ubiquitous corruption. A Boston court released two men in January, 2001, who had spent 30 years in jail for a murder they did not commit, because the FBI rigged the 'evidence'. Two other innocent men jailed for the killing had already died in prison. The FBI was protecting an informant known as Joseph 'the Animal' Barboza who had been named to agents as one of those responsible for the murder. Barboza even gave testimony against the convicted men and was protected from prosecution by his FBI handlers, agents H. Paul Rico and Dennis Condon. Agent Condon testified at the time in support of killer Barboza's credibility. After the trial when Barboza said he had falsely named the four convicted men the FBI stood its ground and the courts denied a new trial. The FBI had the Algerian pilot Lotfi Raissi jailed for five months amid claims that he trained some of the 9/11 'pilots' and then produced no evidence whatsoever to support that allegation. This is the same organisation that is telling you what happened on September 11th and who did it and refuse to answer questions on the stream of lies and contradictions in its bullshit 'investigation'.

The shocking irony of John O'Neill

John O'Neill was an FBI deputy director and head of the Joint Terrorism Task Force in New York. He had refused to capitulate to manipulation from above in his investigations into the funding of 'al-Qaeda', the terrorist attack on the *USS Cole* in Aden harbour, Yemen, in 2000 and a case of Israeli 'art students' considered to be acting suspiciously in the months before 9/11 in locations later connected to the 'hijackers'. O'Neil clashed with Barbara Bodine, US Ambassador to Yemen at the time of the attack on the *Cole*, and among what O'Neil saw as Bodine's blocks on his investigation was her refusal to allow him back into Yemen after he made a brief trip home to the United States for Thanksgiving. O'Neill ignored official interference in all these investigations and his pursuit of Osama bin Laden although he was extremely upset by it. He resigned from the FBI shortly before September 11th amid a smear campaign against him from within the FBI. O'Neil told the authors of the book, *Hidden Truth* (or *Forbidden Truth* in the US version): 'The main obstacles to investigate Islamic terrorism were US oil corporate interests and the role played by Saudi Arabia in it.' One of the authors, Charles Brisard, said O'Neill had complained bitterly that the US State Department and the Bush oil lobby had undermined attempts to prove Bin Laden's

involvement in terrorist activity. John O'Neil left the FBI in late August,
2001, when he was offered a job as head of security at ... *the World Trade
Center*. He was reportedly last seen on 9/11 coordinating evacuation
efforts on the 49th floor shortly before the South Tower collapsed.
Amazing how those with knowledge that could expose the lies so often
end up dead at the most convenient times. People like John O'Neill who
could have revealed how investigations into Bin Laden and terrorism
had been systematically blocked before 9/11; David Kelly, the British
weapons inspector who knew that the Blair government was lying and
'sexing up' claims about 'weapons of mass destruction' in Iraq to justify
an invasion; and Robin Cook, the former British Foreign Secretary who
resigned over the Iraq war and was starting to speak out over the lies
and deceptions of the official 'al-Qaeda' story. John O'Neil was not alone
at the FBI or CIA in facing official opposition to terrorist investigations.
American journalist Greg Palast produced a report on the subject for the
BBC current affairs programme *Newsnight* in which he said he had
received a phone call from a high-placed member of a US intelligence
agency:

> He tells me that while there's always been constraints on investigating Saudis,
> under George Bush it's gotten much worse. After the [2000] elections, the
> agencies were told to 'back off' investigating the Bin Ladens and Saudi royals,
> and that angered agents.

The close connection between those blamed for terrorism and those
claiming to 'fight terrorism' is a constant theme. We need to lose this
perception of different 'sides' and realise that we are dealing with *one*
side with multiple faces working to one end.

The 9/11 Commission – all hide and no seek

All the lies and contradictions I have described so far were there to be
exposed from the start by those bravely claiming to be 'journalists' and
later by the 9/11 Commission or the 'National Commission on Terrorist
Attacks Upon the United States'. The media ignored the mountain of
contradicting evidence and has chosen ever since to slavishly repeat the
official story in all its insanity because they haven't got the desire,
intelligence or balls to seek out the truth. Instead they ridicule and
condemn those who have eyes open enough to see the elephant on the
sofa. The 9/11 Commission final report came from the same systematic
combination of myopia and corruption and never had any intention
whatsoever to seek out the truth. The report was an utter disgrace in the
same mould as the media who lapped it up as the definitive story and
arbiter of what happened. It wasn't. It was a cover-up so transparently
obvious that everyone involved had to be well aware that it was a pack

of lies and omissions from cover to cover. The 'report' treated those who died and their loved ones with the most stunning contempt and disrespect. They deserved the truth and what they got was still more lies to cover up all the ones that went before. Evidence to the Commission by Transport Secretary Norman Mineta which totally contradicted Dick Cheney's version of what he did that morning was *left out of the report* including the story of Cheney saying 'the orders still stand' in the run up to the Pentagon being hit. Those orders could only have been not to shoot down whatever was being tracked on radar, but the 9/11 Commission decided this was not worth the necessary paper and ink. All the other contradictions and provable lies by Bush, Rumsfeld and Myers were similarly missing and there was *no mention of Building 7* let alone the fact that it was a crystal-clear controlled demolition. Anything, in fact, that shone a light on the official catalogue of serial mendacity was ignored, omitted or spun.

Bush, Cheney and Rumsfeld did all they could to block any investigation at all and that by itself should have the warning lights flashing. Why would leaders of a country apparently attacked so devastatingly by terrorists on home soil with some 3,000 dead and the country in extreme states of shock and trauma not want to launch the biggest and most detailed investigation in American history to find out exactly what happened and ensure it could never happen again? The answer to that question is as simple as it is disgusting: They knew that a proper investigation would have seen them confined to jail for the rest of their lives. Alongside would have been the network – including those even more deeply responsible – which orchestrated the outrage and many of those were from a land far away. I don't mean Muslims, either, as we shall see. When Bush and Cheney could not resist demands for an

official 9/11 inquiry any longer, Bush announced in late 2002 that this would be led by ... *Henry Kissinger.* The implications of that could not have been clearer. Kissinger has been an almost life-long servant of the Hidden Hand (Fig 81). He has 'advised' both Republican and Democrat presidents on what they had better do if they don't want big trouble heading their way from those he represents. Anyone who names lies-for-a-living Kissinger to 'investigate' anything is desperate for a cover up. Even

Figure 81: Henry Kissinger breaks for lunch.

The New York Times said the White House chose him 'to contain an investigation it has long opposed' and the appointment was so breathtaking that Kissinger had to quickly resign in the face of flagrant conflicts of interest involving his infamous Hidden Hand front company, Kissinger Associates, which is exposed in my other books like *And The Truth Shall Set You Free*. Kissinger would have had to disclose the clients of Kissinger Associates and there was no way he was going to do that. If he had it would not so much have opened a can of worms as launched the lid into orbit. Kissinger was asked by a 9/11 widow if he had any Saudi Arabian clients that he wanted to tell them about. Kissinger was said to have 'twisted and turned' in his seat. When he was further asked if he had any by the name of Bin Laden 'he just about fell off his couch', according to a witness at the meeting.

Kissinger was replaced by the Republican Thomas Kean, former governor for New Jersey, as Commission chairman. Kean was another insider. He had been a director of the National Endowment for Democracy, a long-time front for CIA covert operations overseas, and had investment connections to the same Saudi sources that funded President Bush and Osama Bin Laden. Among them was Khalid bin Mahfouz who was named by the Bill Clinton State Department as a financer of terrorism. Commission vice-chairman Lee Hamilton sat on advisory boards to the CIA, the President's Homeland Security Advisory Council and US Army. Another Commission member was Richard Ben-Veniste, the Senate-appointed lawyer for the Clintons during the Whitewater corruption 'investigation' and also attorney for Barry Seal who flew cocaine out of South America to the Mena airstrip in Arkansas for the Clinton and Bush families. The 9/11 Commission was established in November, 2002, more than a year after the attacks, and published its final report in the summer of 2004. The official brief was 'to prepare a full and complete account of the circumstances surrounding the September 11 attacks'. This, of course, was the last thing the government wanted or intended to do. Kean and Hamilton would say in their 2006 book, *Without Precedent: The Inside Story of the 9/11 Commission*, that the whole 'inquiry' was 'set up to fail' and woefully underfinanced. Yes, it was, but it could still have been far more robust, candid and honest than it was. I say 'far more' – actually it was none of those things. Commissioners said they were so frustrated with the 'misstatements' (lies where I come from) by Pentagon and FAA officials that an investigation into their obstruction was considered. Why would you underfund and want to obstruct an investigation into the biggest terrorist attacks on US soil that killed so many people unless the truth would have exposed what you didn't want the public to know? Kean said that President Bush had not been 'well served' by the CIA and FBI when in fact from the bigger picture point of view both had served him and his owners with great distinction by keeping the truth under wraps.

Gatekeeper Zelikow

Kean, Hamilton and their fellow 'investigators' didn't even write the final report. This was overseen (as was the entire process) by Commission executive staff director, Philip Zelikow, a former Texas lawyer and an associate of Boy Bush and National Security Advisor Condoleezza Rice whose actions were supposed to be part of the 'investigation'. Bush appointed Zelikow to the President's Foreign Intelligence Advisory Board and he was for three years on the National Security Council of Father Bush. What a safe pair of hands then when you wanted the official story to survive intact. Zelikow had worked closely with Rice and even co-wrote a book with her, *Germany Unified and Europe Transformed: A Study in Statecraft*. She appointed him to be the main writer of the Bush National Security Strategy in 2002 which used 9/11 to justify the policy of attacking countries that posed no imminent threat or even a threat at all. Bush-circle insider and ultra-Zionist Zelikow was the same guy appointed executive director of the Commission 'investigating' the actions of Bush and Rice with regard to September 11th. Zelikow also directed the Aspen Strategy Group, a foreign-policy strategy body co-chaired by Rice's mentor, Brent Scowcroft of ... Kissinger Associates. In short – Zelikow was establishment to his DNA and compared with him Kean and Hamilton were bit-part players. Rice, Cheney and Deputy Secretary of Defense Paul Wolfowitz were members of Zelikow's Aspen Strategy Group. The 9/11 Commission was a complete stitch-up from first to last. There are other highly-significant connections to Zelikow which I will come to later when we get to the core of how 9/11 was pulled off and by whom. Paul Sperry wrote in an article for Antiwar.com:

> Zelikow picks the areas of investigation, the briefing materials, the topics for hearings, the witnesses, and the lines of questioning for witnesses ... and the commissioners for the most part follow his recommendations. In effect, he sets the agenda and runs the investigation. He also carries with him a downright obnoxious conflict-of-interest odor, one that somehow went undetected by the lawyers who vetted him for one of the most important investigative positions in U.S. history.

The 9/11 Family Steering Committee and 9/11 Citizens Watch called for Zelikow's resignation which was never going to happen. He was there to cover up the truth no matter what the families of the dead may have wanted. Zelikow ran the 9/11 Commission like his personal fiefdom. He decided what would be pursued or ignored and what would appear in the final 'report'. Zelikow led a staff of some 75 people and more than half were formerly with the CIA, FBI, Department of [In]Justice and other agencies of government. One staff member quoted in the media said: 'Zelikow is calling the shots. He's skewing the investigation and running it his own way.' This is why crucial information and contradictions in evidence were ignored. One commissioner, by-then former senator Max Cleland, resigned from the inquiry. He said 'Bush is scamming America.' This is the same Max Cleland who agreed he was on Capitol Hill with General Myers during the attacks when he could not have been. Cleland said Commission members had agreed a deal that allowed them only very limited access to CIA reports presented to Bush and the White House which could have indicated prior knowledge of the attacks. He said:

> This is a scam. It's disgusting. America is being cheated. As each day goes by we learn that this government knew a whole lot more about these terrorists before September 11 than it has ever admitted ... Let's chase this rabbit into the ground. They had a plan to go to war and when 9/11 happened that's what they did; they went to war.

Re-writing history

The Commission simply set out from day one to support the official narrative no matter what the evidence and their most important task was to hide the blatantly obvious fact that the military was stood down or blocked that day until after the Pentagon was hit to make sure the attacks would not be stopped by the usual fighter response to hijacked aircraft. This is the cover-up on which all the other cover-ups depend because if a stand-down or systematic delay was proved the whole house of cards collapses. Crucial to this has been to explain away why the military responded far too late to every hijack. We were first given a timeline for the military's non-response to the hijackings that said no fighter jets were scrambled until after the Pentagon was hit. Then, on September 18th a week after the attacks, the military issued a new timeline given the incredulity that three commercial airliners could crash into iconic American buildings before a single military plane intervened. This new version said that two F-15 fighters were scrambled from the Otis base in Massachusetts before the first tower was struck, but didn't get there in time; and two took off from the Langley base in Virginia to intercept the Pentagon 'plane' but, er, yet again, didn't get there to prevent what happened. This second military timeline stood for the next three years and still didn't absolve the military of blame for their shockingly 'inept' non-reaction ('inept' if you believe what they say and I don't). When the 9/11 Commission reported in 2004 it produced yet *another* timeline that was clearly compiled to push the responsibility onto the civilian FAA and hide the staggering truth that the military was stood down or purposely delayed until the Pentagon was struck because had they responded as they did every other day no buildings would have been hit and thousands of people on the ground at least would still be alive. Wherever the military reaction or non-reaction makes no sense the Commission report invents excuses that are excruciating to behold. If the two Otis jets were heading for New York when 'Flight 11' struck the first tower why weren't they on the scene well before 'Flight 175' arrived to hit the second one when at F-15 speed they would have got there comfortably? Er, um, er ...no, I got it ... they were not told about 175 and so were sent off into 'military-controlled airspace off Long Island' to await instructions. They were *what?* While the pilots were sitting there Flight 175 struck the Pentagon, the Commission claimed, and both planes stayed where they were for another *ten minutes* afterwards. Why didn't the military know about Flight 175? Er, um, er ... the FAA didn't tell them, so the Commission report claims. Phew, the military is in the clear (which was the whole point of all this nonsense). All the evidence up to this mendacious Commission re-write of history was that the military was told by the FAA about Flight 175 well before the South Tower was struck. In NORAD's own revised timeline issued a week after the attacks which remained the official story for the next three years the FAA notified them about the hijacking of Flight 175 at 8.43am – 18 minutes before impact. There are sources and statements galore from military and civilian air personnel and government insiders, including government counterterrorism advisor Richard Clarke, that say open lines and multi-agency conferences were underway in a time period that confirm the military *did* know about Flight 175 and did nothing that made a difference. The Commission in its desperation to serve its political and military masters now invented the 'we didn't know' story to explain the no-show for 'Flight 175' and asked us to believe that fighter jets heading for New York after the first tower strike were ordered to wait over Long Island and see what happened. Nearly 3,000 people died and thousands more lives were devastated you bloody liars. Do you have no soul *at all?* Wherever we look in the 9/11 Commission report we see the story altered and contradictory evidence and witness statements ignored to protect the military – or rather those that control the military – from exposure of what really happened (the stand-down/systematic delay) and why the normal response to these situations was prevented from happening.

Protecting the military - again

The same applies to the Commission's revisions with Flights 77 and 93. The second NORAD timeline issued a week after 9/11 detailing its response to reports about 'Flight 77' heading towards Washington gave the Commission another challenge in hiding the stand-down/delay.

NORAD said the FAA told them at 9.24am that Flight 77 had been hijacked. I guess this is as late as they could claim given all the evidence that the authorities would have known well before that about the strange behaviour of 'Flight 77' and the outlandish claim with state-of-art tracking technology available to NORAD at Cheyenne Mountain that the alleged 'Flight 77' could have been 'missing' for 36 *minutes* after 'turning around' and heading for the nation's political and military capital. This still left the question of why F-16s scrambled from Langley, Virginia, at 9.24 did not get to the Pentagon in time. The distance involved and the incredible top speed of an F-16 should have got them to the Pentagon comfortably before 'Flight 77'. We saw earlier how the military attempted to explain this away by saying the pilots did not know why they were being scrambled and headed out to sea in the belief that the threat was coming from outside. Pilots and their superiors at a stand-by, on-alert airbase hadn't heard that the World Trade Center had been hit by two planes 37 and 21 minutes earlier then? This excuse for the military's non-arrival at the Pentagon before 'Flight 77' was not enough for the 9/11 Commission and its report introduced a whole new scenario (which it called 'a brand new idea') that *no one* had mentioned – not the FAA or the military – in the entire three years between the attacks and publication of the 9/11 report. This was the claim that as well as heading out to sea a tape had been found in which an FAA official told a NORAD NEADS operative that Flight 11 had not struck the World Trade Center and instead was heading south towards Washington. The Commission update said the NORAD chap immediately scrambled the F-16s from Langley at 9.24 in pursuit of the phantom 'Flight 11' which the official story says crashed into the North Tower 38 *minutes* before. There was no doubt within the FAA networks after impact at 8.46 that 'Flight 11' had struck the North Tower and it is claimed that this FAA employee mentioned earlier caused fighters to be scrambled from Langley in pursuit of a 'still flying' Flight 11 which he – just one man – said he heard was heading for Washington. The cover-story was therefore that the fighters could not get to the Pentagon in time because of taking six minutes to get airborne – pedestrian by scramble standards – initially flying out to sea in the wrong direction and then taking a route to intercept a plane that didn't exist. If lies literally stank you would have to leave the room and get some air. NORAD chiefs like General Larry Arnold, Continental United States Commander, had said after the attacks and for years later that they were notified about the hijacking of 'Flight 77' at 9.24. The Commission said that he was 'incorrect' which, when passed through our Orwellian Translation Unit, means 'it doesn't fit the cover-up narrative'. Reading the transcript of a bewildered Arnold being guided to agree with the 'phantom Flight 11' story by Commission member Richard Ben-Veniste is like dragging a nail across a steel plate. Laura Brown, Deputy in Public Affairs at FAA headquarters, could not have been clearer that immediately after the first plane hit the World Trade Center (at 8.46) the FAA established 'phone bridges' or open lines with the relevant agencies including the Department of Defense (see NORAD) and the Secret Service (see Bush and Cheney) and she said that during these teleconferences the FAA shared real-time information about 'all the flights of interest, including Flight 77':

> NORAD logs indicate that the FAA made formal notification about American Flight 77 at 9.24am, but information about the flight was conveyed continuously during the phone bridges before the formal notification ...

> ... The FAA shared real-time information on the phone bridges about the unfolding events, including information about loss of communication with aircraft, loss of transponder signals, unauthorized changes in course, and other actions being taken by all the flights of interest.

In other words the military knew all along what was happening and did nothing. The 9/11 Commission once again lied to the American people and knowingly made up stories, skewed and omitted evidence to keep the truth from the world and protect the political and military players responsible from a lifetime in jail. This is the same Commission report that visitors to Internet site Reddit are directed to when they seek to access the 'quarantined' section where researchers are challenging the official 9/11 story. Perhaps boycotting Reddit until it stops being a censorship tool of the Hidden Hand might represent a statement of disgust. Another Commission excuse for the alleged delay in reporting a Flight 77 hijack to NORAD is that the air traffic controller at Indianapolis Center thought the aircraft was having electrical or mechanical problems and later that it had crashed. Once again blame the FAA for not telling the military early enough. Are we really to believe that an air traffic controller who knew that two planes had already struck the World Trade Center would assume electrical and mechanical failure for the strange behaviour of Flight 77 involving the transponder, loss of communication with the cockpit and route deviation? Boston Center had told other regional air traffic centers as early as 8.25 that Flight 11 had been hijacked and this included Indianapolis. No, forget all that – it must be mechanical problems. The Commission report contends that the Indianapolis controller didn't know at that stage about what had happened in New York. The rest of the world knew, but not someone on active flight control duty at a time when his bosses at the FAA were reporting that eleven or more other planes could have been hijacked. The new 9/11 Commission make-it-fit timeline for Flight 77 was as follows: The FAA became aware of a hijack at 9.05; fighters were scrambled from Langley at 9.24 in search of phantom Flight 11; the FAA told NORAD officially that Flight 77 was missing only at 9.34 and the Pentagon was hit at 9.38 with the phantom-chasing Langley F-16s nowhere close. The method in the madness in all this directs us to the same common theme that pervades everything. No matter how insane the story stick to it rather than let the truth be exposed. The Commission claimed that 'no one at FAA headquarters ever asked for military assistance with American 77' and this was to pass all the blame onto the civilian air traffic system and away from the military the Commission had to protect or the whole despicable story would be revealed. Colonel Leroy Fletcher Prouty yet again:

> No one has to direct an assassination – it happens. The active role is played secretly by permitting it to happen. This is the greatest single clue. Who has the power to call off or reduce the usual security precautions?

The answer in this case is the Pentagon and its agents in government with a combination of corrupt and spineless members of the 9/11 Commission providing essential cover. The story was the same with Flight 93 according to the Commission – the FAA never alerted the military even though by now no one disputes that open lines between agencies were operating (as they had been in truth since shortly after the attacks on the World Trade Center at 8.46 and 9.03). Flight 93 was recognised as a hijack by at least 9.34 (after the last routine call at 9.27). Once again the Commission report claims the FAA sat on its hands and the military was in the clear. The Commission said an FAA air traffic controller at Cleveland Center reported a likely hijack and news reached the FAA headquarters by 9.34. Cleveland is said to have asked the FAA Command Center at 9.36 if a military response had been requested and offered to call them directly. The reply was that the request had to go through the chain of command and they were 'working on the issue'. Take your time then, only three planes had already apparently crashed into iconic American buildings, so no hurry. Tea, anyone? The Commission said that another 13 minutes passed without further action and only at 9.49 did the FAA Command Center discuss a request to the military with FAA headquarters. Even then nothing was done and 'Flight 93' crashed without the military being contacted. All this would be criminal negligence and incompetence by the FAA *if it was true*. The claim is that NORAD didn't even know the plane had been hijacked before it crashed when there were three teleconferences going on – one initiated by the FAA, another by the National Military Command Center in the Pentagon and a third by anti-terrorism advisor Richard Clarke from the White House. These were established well before the demise of

'Flight 93' and we are told that the military didn't know anything about that plane being missing or hijacked. It makes no sense because it is non-sense. The Commission mendaciously claimed that at no time in the period from 'Flight 11' striking the North Tower and 'Flight 93 crashing' did any of three teleconferences include the necessary officials from the FAA and Defense Department for information about the hijacked planes to be communicated and acted upon. Richard Clarke states that his conference included Donald Rumsfeld, the Defense Secretary, Richard Myers, the highest-ranked military officer in the US that morning, and FAA chief Jane Garvey. Clarke reports that shortly after 9.30 – some *30 minutes* before 'Flight 93' went down and before the Pentagon was hit – Garvey reported to the conference:

> All aircraft have been ordered to land at the nearest field. Here's what we have as potential hijacks: Delta 1989 over West Virginia, United 93 over Pennsylvania.

The claim that the military did not know about 'Flight 93' before it crashed is another lie to cover the stand-down/delay and quite possibly the shooting down of the plane. There has been much speculation about whether Flight 93 was shot down by a pursuing F-16 – a pursuit confirmed by Deputy Defense Secretary Paul Wolfowitz and other sources. Major Daniel Nash, one of the pilots scrambled from the Otis base to New York said that he heard an F-16 had shot down Flight 93. Wolfowitz said 'the Air Force was tracking the hijacked plane in Pennsylvania ... and had been in a position to bring it down if necessary.' But why would a fighter be chasing or tracking Flight 93 if, as the Commission claims, the military didn't know this aircraft was hijacked or missing until after it had already crashed? The contradictions are legion, constant and endless. If this was Flight 93 (and perhaps the delayed take-off time had skewed the original plan for its destination) those behind 9/11 would not have allowed it to land and the real story told. By now at past 10am there would have been absolutely no possible explanation no matter how contrived for why the military would not have intercepted before another building was struck. The deeply mendacious 9/11 Commission was determined to ensure with its text and timeline that a take-down of Flight 93 did not happen. The report said that permission to shoot down aircraft was given by President Bush via Vice President Cheney at 10.31 when a number of other sources say it was much earlier and well before the end of 'Flight 93'.

Where was Winfield?

Three separate teleconferences also seems strange – why not just the one where all information was processed? Could this have been another ruse to create confusion? Normal procedure was for the FAA to initiate the conference in these circumstances and include all the relevant agencies – the Pentagon Command Center (NMCC), NORAD, Secret Service and other relevant agencies. The Pentagon NMCC having its own conference was not normal procedure and it claimed that lines could not connect the FAA with its conference because of equipment malfunction and not being able to find secure phone numbers. How very convenient if you wanted to develop a 'we didn't know', 'they didn't tell us' story. Another strange decision was for Brigadier General Montague Winfield, Director of Pentagon NMCC operations, to ask his far less experienced deputy, Captain Charles Liedig, to stand in for him on 9/11. Liedig took over at 8.30 when Winfield left just as the catastrophic series of events began. As 'coincidences' go the timing was uncanny. Liedig was newly qualified for his role and this was the first conference he had overseen – hence the subsequent headline 'Rookie in the 9-11 Hot Seat?' If you were Brigadier General Winfield wouldn't you have headed back to retake control from your rookie deputy when you heard what had happened 16 *minutes* after you left? Winfield didn't do that even though Flight 11 was reported hijacked before he went off duty and there are reports of FAA-NMCC 'phone bridges' being instigated. Is that really the time you would say to your inexperienced deputy – see you later, leave you to it? There seemed to be no problem with this from the authorities with both Winfield and Liedig later nominated for promotion. There were many timing 'coincidences' related to 9/11 including General Myers being in military charge that day because his superior was mid-Atlantic flying to Europe and Robert Mueller taking over at the FBI two weeks before the attacks and then running the subsequent (lack of) investigation. Captain Charles Liebig told the 9/11 Commission that Winfield did eventually return just before the reported crash of 'Flight 93'. Here is still another frontline player who was officially AWOL until the attacks were over or the Pentagon had been hit.

'It never occurred to us'

The Commission further protected the military from serious criticism and exposure by accepting there was a 'lack of imagination' that did not foresee aircraft being used as missiles to crash into buildings when this is provably not true. Researcher and author David Ray Griffin astutely points out in his demolition of the Commission report that this claim about not foreseeing planes used as missiles was deftly connected to the claim that the Pentagon and its agencies were only prepared for attacks from the sea and not from within the United States. The cover-up could then dismiss the considerable evidence that the military *had* foreseen the planes-as-missiles scenario ... *but only coming from the sea!* The Pentagon's General Myers and NORAD chief General Eberhart were naturally

promoting this lunacy. *USA Today* reported that two years before the
attacks NORAD conducted exercises simulating aircraft used as
weapons to crash into targets and cause mass casualties. General Myers
told a hearing of the Senate Armed Services Committee in 2004 about a
series of exercises which included 9/11-type scenarios. Myers spoke of
'five exercise hijack events' involving NORAD between November, 1999,
and October, 2000, that all 'included a suicide crash into a high-value
target'. NORAD practiced in 2000 a response to an aircraft being stolen
and flown into the United Nations building in New York. Others
involved similar attacks on the White House and the Statue of Liberty
close to the World Trade Center. Another exercise in 2000 coordinated by
the Defense Protective Service and the Pentagon's Command Emergency
Response Team simulated a passenger aircraft hitting the Pentagon and
according to *US Medicine* doctors and medics were training for just this
situation at the Pentagon in May, 2001. Only twelve days before 9/11 the
Department of Transportation in Washington DC ran an exercise
preparation for what administrator Ellen Engleman called 'a potentially
hijacked plane and someone calling on a cell phone, among other
aspects of the scenario that were very strange when twelve days later, as
you know, we had the actual event'. Government terrorism advisor
Richard Clarke chaired an exercise in 1998 based on a Learjet being
hijacked on the ground in Atlanta, filled with explosives and flown to
Washington. Correct me if I'm wrong but the route from Atlanta to
Washington does not involve arriving from the sea. An expert panel
assembled by the Pentagon in 1993 highlighted the threat from planes
used as missiles to strike landmark locations and a member of that panel
wrote the following in *Futurist* magazine in *1994* which actually
mentions the World Trade Center:

> Targets such as the World Trade Center not only provide the requisite
> casualties but, because of their symbolic nature, provide more bang for the
> buck. In order to maximize their odds for success, terrorist groups will likely
> consider mounting multiple, simultaneous operations.

It could not be more obvious that it *did* occur to the military that
9/11-type attacks could happen and they practiced scenarios based on
that theme. Nor could it be more evident that the 9/11 Commission was
established to cover up the truth. Here are some more disgraceful
examples:

- The Commission ignored the 'hijackers' named who were found to be
  still alive after the attacks. These names were repeated without any
  discussion or inquiry into how people still alive could have hijacked
  9/11 aircraft and therefore who did. They described the backgrounds

and include pictures of 'hijackers' that could not have taken part because they were still with us – an extraordinary confirmation that the Commission was only interested in supporting the official Big Lie.

- The Commission produced no proof that any of the named 'hijackers' were on board the planes and simply repeated the official narrative without question. They refused to even subpoena original passenger lists.

- There was no mention of Mohamed Atta's non-Muslim white American girlfriend Amanda Keller or his heavy drinking, coke habit and liking for pork chops. The report mentions that he and other 'hijackers' met in Las Vegas, but not that they paid hundreds of dollars to lap dancers at the Pink Pony strip club. The Commission referred to him as an Islamic fanatic and 'fantastically so'.

- The Commission maintained the blatant lie about Hani Hanjour, the utterly incompetent Cessna pilot, sitting at the controls of Flight 77 and completing a 270-degree turn at high speed and low altitude which commercial airline pilots with thousands of hours on wide-bodied jets say they could not have done. The report instead described Hanjour as 'the operation's most experienced pilot'. Well, how shit must the others have been then? The report claims all this while *at the same time* acknowledging that Hanjour was denied a pilot's licence on multiple occasions because he was such a 'terrible pilot' and that only weeks before 9/11 an instructor refused to fly with him a second time after his first experience of Hanjour at the controls of a one-engine puddle-jumper. How did the Commission reconcile these outrageous flagrant contradictions in its own report? It didn't even bother.

- The ridiculous official 'explanations' of how the three buildings fell were repeated without question despite the suspension of the laws of physics and endless anomalies and impossibilities. The fundamental questions and evidence by experts surrounding the fall of Building 7 were avoided in one fell swoop: The 9/11 Commission report did not even mention Building 7. By doing so Larry Silverstein's 'pull it' comment was also avoided.

- The question of how buildings could 'pancake' while collapsing at or near free-fall speed was not addressed and nor how steel columns could fail because of a quickly burned-off jet fuel fire with a maximum temperature of 1,700 degrees Fahrenheit when the melting point of steel is 2,770 degrees.

- There was no mention of the fact that before part of the façade of the Pentagon fell 30 minutes after impact (or at least an explosion) the hole in the wall was only 16 to 20 feet across. Through this hole a plane with a 125-foot wingspan and 40-foot high tail would have somehow had to pass with no resistance from a recently reinforced wall that would have surely sheared off the wings and tail and left them outside for all to see. This was not even worth questioning? Er, nope.

- The Commission did not address the ridiculous contradiction that the 'Flight 77' aircraft vapourised inside the Pentagon (impossible at the temperatures involved with jet fuel) while passengers were claimed to have been identified from their fingerprints.

- The fake and rigged 'investigation' did not subpoena security videos from the Pentagon and buildings looking out at the Pentagon and clearly if those videos did show Flight 77 striking the building they would have been circulated en masse to the global media within hours or days. They don't show that and so there was no subpoena by these shameful cover-up artists.

- There was no serious questioning and certainly no credible explanation for why ground-to-air missile systems protecting Washington and the Pentagon were not activated.

- The easily exposed lies about what Defense Secretary Rumsfeld and Joint Chiefs of Staff acting chairman Myers claimed they were doing before the Pentagon was hit were left unquestioned even with the evidence from Bush counterterrorism advisor Richard Clarke that they were taking part in his teleconference well before the Pentagon strike. Surely there are videotapes of that conference with time-codes? So where are they? In the same locked and sealed vault as the surveillance camera videos from the Pentagon no doubt.

- Nor did the Commission seriously question and investigate the confusing effect of all those wargame exercises going on involving the same response agencies as those reacting (or not) to the 9/11 hijackings.

- As for Operation Northwoods – not a mention. I bet you are shocked to the core.

On and on the report goes, page after page of lies, omissions, cover-up and slavish devotion to the official story which a child could have seen through. On that basis alone I say there is no way Thomas Kean, Lee Hamilton and especially Philip Zelikow did not know they were taking part in a cover up to hide the truth from the world. What level of contempt must they have for those who died and their loved ones left behind? How could Kean and Hamilton put their name to such a piece of garbage? This same question applies to all members of the Commission who didn't speak out and expose the scam. The report was so bad and so mendacious that weeks after publication 25 people who worked for government agencies such as the CIA, FBI, FAA and others involved in 'national security and public safety' wrote an open letter to Congress condemning the Commission's 'findings':

> We are aware of significant issues and cases that were duly reported to the Commission by those of us with direct knowledge, but somehow escaped attention ... The omission of such serious and applicable issues and information by itself renders the report flawed, and casts doubt on the validity of many of its recommendations.

The FBI was mandated by Congress in 2014 to conduct 'an assessment of any evidence now known to the FBI that was not considered by the 9/11 Commission related to any factors that contributed in any manner to the terrorist attacks of September 11, 2001'. A year later the FBI reported with painful predictability that no new evidence had come to light that would have changed the verdict of the 9/11 Commission. Architects & Engineers for 9/11 Truth launched a lawsuit against the Bureau over not including 'an assessment of evidence related to the WTC demolition nor an assessment of several other areas of evidence known to the FBI'. The lawsuit highlighted the following:

- The use of pre-placed explosives to destroy World Trade Center Buildings, 1, 2, and 7.

- The arrest and investigation of the [Israeli] 'High Fivers' observed photographing and celebrating the attacks on the World Trade Center on 9/11.

- Terrorist financing related the reported Saudi support for the 9/11 hijackers.

- Recovered plane parts, including serial numbers from all three crash locations.

- Video from cameras mounted inside and outside the Pentagon.

- Cell phone communications from passengers aboard airplanes.

Architects & Engineers also partnered with the Lawyers' Committee for 9/11 Inquiry to launch a Grand Jury Investigation Project that has named '15 different categories of persons who may have information material to the investigation, including contractors and security companies that had access to the WTC Towers before 9/11, persons and entities who benefited financially from the WTC demolitions, and persons arrested after being observed celebrating the WTC attacks'. We wish them well and you can donate to their efforts at ae911truth.org. The organisation sent to its mailing list an article about the lawsuit published by legal news service Courthouse News which it described as 'a rare deviation from the media's dogmatic denigration of any person who questions the government account of 9/11 (and who refuses to believe that miracles took place that day).' The mail circulation coincided with Courthouse News deleting the article. Just another day in the suppression of 9/11 truth.

I think it is fair to say, at the risk of stating the obvious, that the official story of what happened on 9/11 is among the greatest works of fiction in known human history and I am not anywhere near finished yet exposing the network behind the events of that day and their aftermath.

CHAPTER 15

'Bin Laden did it!'

The masses indulge in petty falsehoods every day, but it would never come into their heads to fabricate colossal untruths and they are not able to believe in the possibility of such monstrous effrontery ... The bigger the lie, therefore, the more likely it is to be believed – Adolf Hitler

Tell-tale signs in all Problem-Reaction-Solution or false-flag scenarios are: (1) who is blamed for the problem and (2) how soon after the event is an alleged villain promoted by establishment mouthpieces who rush to the microphones to sell the cover-story before any investigation has even started.

In the case of 9/11 we had: (1) Osama bin Laden and Islamic terror group 'al-Qaeda' condemned as the perpetrators and they were (2) first named a matter of minutes after the attacks. Villains blamed for the problem tell you what the solution is planned to be. If you want to target 'white supremacists' who oppose government tyranny you blame them and them alone for Oklahoma. If you want to justify wars of death, destruction and regime change in the Middle East you claim that Islamic terrorists were responsible for 9/11. We have had the long-planned invasion of Afghanistan to 'get Bin Laden' and this exploded into the global 'war on terror' launched by the Boy Bush administration and continued by succeeding presidents from 'both' political parties (the Hidden Hand one-party state). The Web of secret societies and other interconnected groups means that support is rarely a problem from Western countries. Afghanistan was invaded to 'get Bin Laden' for 9/11 while the FBI admitted there was not enough evidence against him to stand up in court. The FBI website did not list 9/11 as one of the attacks for which Bin Laden was a 'Most Wanted Man'. When asked why this was so FBI spokesman Rex Tomb said in 2006: 'The reason why 9/11 is not mentioned on Osama bin Laden's Most Wanted page is because the FBI has no hard evidence connecting Bin Laden to 9/11.' American government, intelligence and military officials have never produced *any* evidence of Afghanistan involvement in 9/11 and nor have any credible connections been made between that country and the patsy 'hijackers'. Never mind – we'll set the Middle East on fire anyway (Fig 82 overleaf).

Figure 82: American foreign policy.

While I was writing this chapter I re-watched the television address on October 7th, 2001, when Boy Bush announced that the invasion of Afghanistan had begun less than a month after 9//11. At no point and in no way did he justify the action by connecting Afghanistan to the attacks. Defense Secretary Rumsfeld and his deputy Wolfowitz were asked what evidence they had to link 9/11 to Bin Laden in Afghanistan and they both basically said that everyone saw the evidence on their television screens. Oh, that would be planes painted in the colours of Afghan Air would it? In the wake of 9/11 Hidden Hand gofer Tony Blair, the British Prime Minister, had his tongue out and tail wagging while the Twin Towers were still standing. Overseeing it all as the merciless head of the 'Bush' government was Dick Cheney who arranged for 'legal opinion' to dismantle all checks and balances to give him the power to do whatever he wanted in terms of deleting civil liberties and going to war. What happened on September 11th was indeed *The Trigger* excuse that ignited a wave of calculated violence and terrorism by the psychopaths of the United States, Britain, France, NATO etc., which has killed and maimed millions in Afghanistan, Iraq, Libya, Syria and elsewhere in the name of 'fighting terrorism'. This is quite an act of vengeance in response to the 3,000 who died on 9/11 and even more so given that those who have been killed and wounded for life in the 'war on terror' had nothing to do with what happened in New York and Pennsylvania or at the Pentagon. Former British troops told an investigation by the Middle East Eye website that rules had been relaxed to allow them to shoot unarmed civilians in Afghanistan and Iraq if they were 'holding a mobile telephone, carrying a shovel, or acting in any way suspiciously'. The dead included a number of children and teenage boys and the soldiers described how weapons were placed near bodies to claim they had been armed. One father had turned up at a British base carrying his dead eight-year-old son and demanding an explanation. What responsibility did that kid and all the others have for 9/11?

One ex-soldier said he witnessed the fatal shootings of significant numbers of civilians in Basra and did not believe that all the victims were keeping British troops under surveillance. He claims that relaxing the rules of engagement resulted in 'a killing spree'. He and his fellow soldiers were promised that they would be protected in the event of any investigation by military police. 'Our commanders, they would tell us:

"We will protect you if any investigation comes. Just say you genuinely thought your life was at risk – those words will protect you".' This is the dictionary definition of terrorism: 'The unlawful use of violence and intimidation, especially against civilians, in the pursuit of political aims.' By that definition the 'war on terror' has always been and continues to be nothing more than a 'war *of* terror'. Without 9/11 none of this could have been sold or justified on anything like the scale that we have seen. In that sentence we have the real reason for the 9/11 attacks. Those who have given the orders to make the 'war *of* terror' possible – Bush, Cheney, Rumsfeld, Wolfowitz, Powell, Blair, his successors Gordon Brown, David Cameron and Theresa May, and a long, long list of others – are terrorists and mass killers who should be standing in the dock at a war crimes tribunal. Even these psychopaths are only the public face and essential cover for the real orchestrators of 9/11 and the war *of* terror and I will begin the exposure of the prime orchestrators of 9/11 in the next chapter.

Get your villain in early

Problem-Reaction-Solution demands that you get your villain in ASAP before any other explanation can be suggested, debated or take root. Once the villain is named no other version of events is allowed or, in this case, you are giving 'comfort to terrorists'. This is how it is – you are either *with us* (believe what we tell you) or *against us* (ask for evidence). I'll choose 'against' if it's all the same with you. *CBS News* took only 13 minutes after the second World Trade Center strike to throw Osama bin Laden's name in the ring. Ehud Barak, Israeli prime minister from 1999 until early 2001, was on the airwaves soon after the attacks calling for a 'war on terror' and an American invasion of Afghanistan. Barak knew all about terror as former commander of the terrorist Sayeret Matkal (also Unit 269) of Israel's Military Intelligence Directorate (also Aman) which is the military intelligence arm of the terrorist Israel Defense Forces (IDF). Barak told the BBC within an hour of the attacks:

> The world will not be the same from today [that was the idea]. It's an attack against our whole civilisation. I don't know who is responsible [oh, do come on]. I believe we will know in twelve hours [you mean that's when the propaganda really begins]. If it is a Bin Laden organisation, and even if it is something else, I believe this is a time to deploy globally concerted effort led by the United States, the UK, Europe and Russia against all sources of terror [Israel's targets]. The same kind of struggle that our forefathers launched against the piracy of the high seas ... it's time to launch an operational concrete war against terror.

Barak went on to mention Bin Laden for a second time and linked him to Afghanistan. The script was already rolling. He used the term 'war against terror' and said that freedoms would have to be deleted with crossing borders and boarding aircraft becoming 'more complicated'. What was happening could hardly have been more blatant and in the proposed solutions you see the real creators of the problem. Barak also highlighted Iran, Iraq, Libya and North Korea as 'rogue states' that should be targeted and that list will become very significant as we proceed from here. Television networks named Osama bin Laden as the likely culprit in the hours that followed and Secretary of State Colin Powell first called Osama bin Laden a 'prime suspect' two days after 9/11. Powell told the media: 'We are looking at those terrorist organisations who have the kind of capacity to conduct the kind of attack that we saw.' Asked if he was referring to Osama bin Laden, he answered: 'Yes.' This was insanity. The idea that Bin Laden and a handful of associates could have pulled off 9/11 is beyond ridiculous. No matter – there's a script to be read. Once bin Laden's name was in the public domain the 'evidence' began to emerge in support of the theory that the attacks were the work of extreme Islamic fundamentalists. Funny how the fast emerging official story fitted what Israeli intelligence operative Ehud Barak had so quickly told the BBC. An official 'investigation' was launched by two Bush family gofers, Attorney General John Ashcroft and the two-weeks-in-the-job FBI chief Robert Mueller. The FBI immediately named 19 Arab men as responsible for the hijackings which was remarkable in itself when this same agency, along with the CIA, said they didn't have even a glimmer of an idea that the biggest terrorist attack in American history was being put together for months and, in Mueller's words, almost certainly years. Now the names and pictures of those involved were suddenly produced with such speed. What amazing detective work! The cover story was up and running and repelling all boarders.

Bin Laden and Father Bush

If the authorities wanted to know about Osama bin Laden they only had to ask the father of the 9/11 president. Father George Bush was a business associate of the Bin Laden family through the Carlyle Group which was founded in 1987 and is described as 'an American multinational private equity, alternative asset management and financial services corporation ... [and] ... one of the largest private equity and alternative investment firms in the world'. An article in *The Economist* said the Carlyle Group was embroiled with the defense and intelligence establishment and is 'widely regarded as an extension of the US government, or at least the National Security Agency, the CIA, and the Pentagon'. Some of personnel at the time of 9/11 might give you a feel for its intentions and mode of operation. Carlyle president Frank

Carlucci was a former deputy director of the CIA and Reagan-Bush Defence Secretary before Dick Cheney took over after the election of Father Bush. Carlucci was a long-time CIA agent mixed up in very dirty dealings and accused of involvement in the killing of Congo Prime Minister Patrice Lumumba in the early1960s. He was, naturally, never charged. With a record like that you would expect him to be a friend and associate of people like Father Bush and Donald Rumsfeld. Carlucci's deputy at Carlyle was James Baker, Father Bush's Secretary of State who became Boy Bush's 'advisor' during the election vote dispute with the Gore campaign in Florida. Another major figure at Carlyle was Father Bush himself, a former CIA director, while former British Prime Minister John Major became European Chairman in the late spring of 2001.

Father Bush and family had close connections with the Bin Ladens, their construction operation out of Jeddah, Saudi Arabia, and the 'royal' House of Saud. I mentioned how Father Bush was reported by the mainstream media to be at Washington's Ritz-Carlton Hotel in a Carlyle Group business meeting with Osama bin Laden's brother, Shafiq bin Laden, and other members of the family on September 10th and 11th. Carlyle executives Carlucci and Baker were also there. The Bin Ladens are an asset of the fake royals of the House of Saud who are assets of the United States and Israel. The latter may sound strange, but I'll be explaining that. Power over Arabia was handed to the House of Saud by the British government which was also behind the creation and emergence of the extreme form of Islam known as Wahhabism on which terror groups like ISIS and others are founded. Once again I'll be going more into this later on. ISIS and the Saudi Arabian fake royals both employ beheading as a staple punishment and this is not a coincidence; nor is the massive funding of Wahhabi terrorists by the House of Saud and its financial lackeys in league with the United States, Britain, Israel etc., and the fascistic Gulf states. Terror groups such as ISIS, al-Qaeda and their various 'affiliates' are funded, armed and trained by the United States, Britain, Israel and other Western sources to create proxy armies promoted as anti-Western terror groups to provide the excuse for sending American and other Western military into countries of the Middle East which would otherwise have no justification (Fig 83). Proxy armies of the West like

FLAGS OF THE REAL ISIS

Figure 83: ISIS is a proxy army for Western countries that claim to oppose terrorism. The rank and file 'Jihadis' will have no idea.

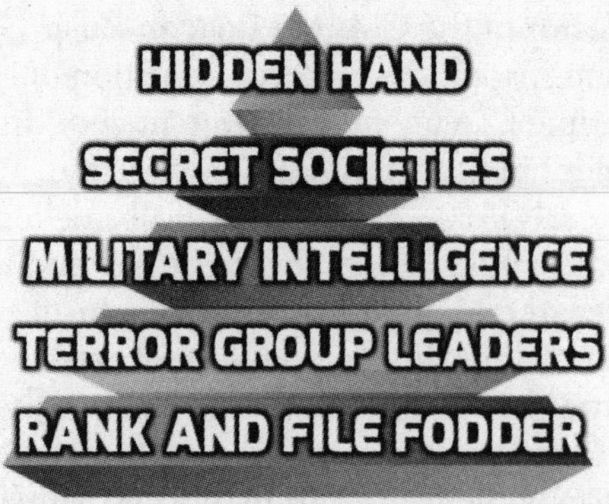

HIDDEN HAND

SECRET SOCIETIES

MILITARY INTELLIGENCE

TERROR GROUP LEADERS

RANK AND FILE FODDER

Figure 84: The compartmentalised pyramid structure that manipulates those at the bottom to believe they are fighting a 'holy war' against their perceived 'infidel' targets when those 'targets' are actually controlling and exploiting them for Problem-Reaction-Solution scenarios.

ISIS are largely mercenary operations. Documents came to light in 2018 revealing the lists of payments and rewards handed out to 'religiously-motivated' ISIS fighters. Killing an enemy soldier or 'infidel' gets you ten silver dinars and a car is on offer for bringing down an aircraft. Compartmentalisation means that rank-and-file terrorist fodder actually believe they are fighting some 'holy war' when they are ultimately controlled through military intelligence and terror group 'leaders' by the very Western government 'infidels' they think they are fighting (Fig 84). The Carlyle Group, like other US companies involved in arms sales (see Lockheed Martin, Raytheon, etc.), benefit monumentally from wars that Carlyle personal like the Bushes have instigated. This has continued under Obama and Trump. The same Carlyle Group managed the assets of the Jeddah-based Saudi Bin Laden Corporation (SBC) which enjoyed a close association with Father Bush. Salem bin Laden, Osama's brother, established a Texas company with Boy Bush in the 1970s called Arbusto Energy. This did go ar*busto* and was later absorbed by another Texas company, Harken Energy. The Bin Ladens helped Boy Bush secure petroleum concessions from Bahrain when he headed Harken and made a fortune for the Bush family. James R. Bath, the American agent for Salem bin Laden, represented him on the Harken board and Bush-Bin Laden connections went back decades before 9/11. Bath was a CIA asset and a close friend of Boy Bush since their days at the Texas Air National Guard when Bush was avoiding the draft to Vietnam. The Bushes and Bin Ladens were further connected through the Bank of Credit and Commerce International (BCCI), a conduit for intelligence agency and organised crime (same thing) money transfers before its very public collapse in the early 1990s when the money-laundering and arms transfer activities came to light. The 'bank' was dubbed 'the most corrupt financial institution in history' but with its connections to the Bush family and the CIA why wouldn't it be? BCCI had been involved in financing Boy Bush's Harken Energy. Former CIA Directors Richard Helms and William Casey, business partners of Father Bush, were on the BCCI board along with infamous Saudi arms dealer Adnan Khashoggi who represented Bin Laden family interests in the US. He was an uncle of Saudi dissident journalist Jamal Khashoggi who was murdered by Saudi government assassins at the country's consulate in Istanbul in 2018. Bush family associate Khalid bin Mahfouz, another Saudi 'businessman', held a controlling interest in BCCI which was found to be funding ... *terrorism.* Mahfouz was indicted by a US grand jury and eventually paid his way out of fraud charges by handing over $225 million. The cover up of the BCCI scandal and protection of its big political players was overseen by Robert Mueller, then head of the Criminal Division at the US [In]Justice Department. Mueller would become head of the FBI two weeks before 9/11 and play a key role in covering up what really happened by overseeing a non-investigation.

'Bandar Bush'

Another prime conduit between the Bush family, the Bin Ladens and the Saudi fake royals was the appalling Bandar bin Sultan from the House of Saud who was Saudi ambassador to the United States from 1983 to 2005. This period covered all but two years of the Reagan-Bush, Father Bush and Bill Clinton administrations and the first term of Boy Bush. He would go on to be secretary general of the Saudi National Security Council and director general of the Saudi Intelligence Agency and he used this influence to support US military actions in the Middle East after 9/11. Bandar was so close to Father and Boy Bush – especially Father – that he was nicknamed 'Bandar Bush'. Watergate journalist Bob Woodward claimed that Boy Bush told Bandar of the decision to invade Iraq in 2003 before his Secretary of State Colin Powell. First of all it wasn't 'Bush's decision' it was Cheney's and secondly Colin Powell was being royally exploited and shafted by the Cheney inner circle from which he was excluded. Given this close association between Bandar and the Bushes you won't be surprised to know that two of the alleged 9/11 hijackers received $130,000 from Bandar's checking account – a fact leaked from a *redacted* part of the 9/11 Commission Report. A court affidavit filed in 2015 claims that Zacarias Moussaoui, the jailed '20th hijacker', was a courier for Osama bin Laden and was introduced to Bandar. Moussaoui stated on oath that Bandar and other members of the Saudi royal family funded al-Qaeda and helped finance the 9/11 attacks. Bandar was not investigated for any of this and would have invoked diplomatic immunity if he had been. Russia's President Putin apparently accused Bandar to his face of supporting Islamic Chechen terrorist groups for a decade in southern Russia. You can see the connections between the United States and Saudi Arabia that led to so many Saudi-connected people being named as 9/11 'hijackers'. The Saudi 'royals' and the far-right government in Israel have long had close associations in secret and these have become more public recently (more later).

Bandar promoted greater contact between the Saudis and Israel while National Security Secretary and this fits with the very close relationship that the Bush family has had with Israel. Anyone think all these connections between the Bush and Bin Laden families and other rich Saudis are just a coincidence given who was named as the orchestrator of 9/11 – Osama bin Laden, the brother of Boy Bush's business partner? Or that leading members of the Bin Laden family were allowed to fly out of America on September 11th while all other aircraft were grounded? Or that so many of the alleged 'hijackers' were connected to Saudi Arabia?

Osama – hero then villain

To understand the sequence that led Osama bin Laden to be blamed for 9/11 we must go back to the 1980s and the invasion of Afghanistan by the Soviet Union in a trap set by President Jimmy Carter's National Security Advisor Zbigniew Brzezinski shortly before Carter was replaced in 1980 by the Reagan-Father Bush administration. Brzezinski, who died in 2017, was a serious Hidden Hand operative and co-founder with David Rockefeller of the Round Table's Trilateral Commission. This is one of the Web's 'cusp' organisations that act as conduits between the hidden and the seen. Brzezinski was a prominent force in the Democratic Party and one of the Democons that control Democrat presidents as the Neocons or neoconservatives control Republican presidents. Go one step back into the shadows and the Democons and Neocons answer to same masters. Brzezinski told French news magazine, *Le Nouvel Observateur*, in 1998 how he set out to entice the Soviet Union to invade Afghanistan in the 1980s and give them 'their Vietnam'. The Afghan government in the capital Kabul was a Soviet satellite regime at the time and Brzezinski described how he arranged for the arming, training and funding of what became known as the Mujahideen. These were portrayed as 'freedom fighters' seeking to overthrow the Soviet-controlled Afghan government when they were really a US proxy army designed to drag the Soviet Union into a war that it couldn't win (as the US themselves are still finding out in Afghanistan). The Soviets went for the bait and became entrapped in a proxy Soviet-US war via the Mujahideen between 1979 and 1989 when they gave up and went home. By then 1.5 million Afghan lives had been lost, but what did psychopaths like Brzezinski care or the Reagan-Bush (Bush-Reagan) administration that took over Mujahideen support when they came to power in 1980? Saudi Arabia, a satellite state of America (and Israel if the truth be told), also funded the Mujahideen which included fighters from 40 Muslim countries. Britain's MI6 and elite Special Air Service or SAS were involved in the training along with Pakistani forces. Mujahideen terrorists were further trained by the CIA in Virginia and Brooklyn, New York, down the road from the Twin Towers.

Billions in financial and military aid under the CIA's Operation Cyclone was poured into Afghanistan via Pakistan military intelligence, the ISI, which wired $100,000 to Mohamed Atta shortly before 9/11. The ISI was a central player in the CIA/Bush family drug operation that turned poppies in the fields of Afghanistan into heroin sold on the streets of America and the world. This life-destroying operation continues today. So many wars, including Afghanistan, Vietnam and others in South-East Asia have to a large extent been about the covert drug trade. Poppy production in Afghanistan fell to almost zero when the Taliban took power after the Soviets left and then went through the roof again after the US invaded in the weeks that followed 9/11. ISI chief Mahmood Ahmed was the source of Atta's $100,000 which has never been explained and would have been connected to the drug operation which at least one version of 'Atta' was certainly involved with. Why was Ahmed not subject to serious investigation for this? Perhaps for the same reason that he was in Washington DC on 9/11 having breakfast with Representative Porter Goss and Senator Bob Graham who had been part of a US delegation to Islamabad, Pakistan, two weeks earlier when they met with Ahmed, other ISI officials and the then President Pervez Musharraf. Goss had long been active in the CIA and was made director of the agency in 2004. The man Brzezinski and the Saudis used as the face of the 'Mujahideen resistance' to the Soviets was called Osama bin Laden from the prominent Saudi family with close connections to the House of Saud and the Bushes. Bandar 'Bush' bin Sultan said Osama bin Laden told him how grateful he was for American support against the Soviets in Afghanistan although the feared 'terrorist mastermind' in Bandar's opinion 'couldn't lead eight ducks across the street'. This is one of those rare moments when Bandar actually told the truth. Bin Laden was a hapless stooge and frontman ravaged by ill-heath – not a 'mastermind'. With the Soviets heading home the time had come for 'hero' Bin Laden to become the 'villain' and a 'terrorist monster'. The 'good guys' became the 'bad guys' with 9/11 providing the perceptual backdrop. Bin Laden, the Mujahideen and Taliban were given the roles of evil terrorists despite being the same people supported by the US against the Soviets. The Mujahideen were renamed 'al-Qaeda' for a new movie although the producer and directors remained the same – mainly the US military/CIA. To promote this rebrand Bin Laden and 'al-Qaeda' began to be blamed for terror attacks against the United States and the West in general. Former British Foreign Secretary Robin Cook, who resigned from the Blair government over the invasion of Iraq in 2003, said publicly that the very *name* 'al-Qaeda' came courtesy of the CIA. He said the term means 'the base' or 'database' and referred to the CIA

database of Mujahideen fighters brought together to fight the Soviets.
Cook said in 2005:

> The truth is, there is no Islamic army or terrorist group called al-Qaeda, and
> any informed intelligence officer knows this. But, there is a propaganda
> campaign to make the public believe in the presence of an intensified entity
> representing the 'devil' only in order to drive TV watchers to accept a unified
> international leadership for a war against terrorism. The country behind this
> propaganda is the United States.

Yes, and Britain and Israel. Less than a month later Robin Cook was
dead after suffering a 'heart attack' which, whatever the background, is
the easiest thing in the world to inflict with the technology/drugs they
have today. 'Al-Qaeda', the US proxy army and terrorist operation,
splintered into other names including eventually ISIS/ISIL/Islamic
State, Al-Nusra Front, Tahrir al-Sham and Boko Haram further south in
Africa. These manufactured terror groups with their compartmentalised
command structure have provided the excuse for US and other Western
countries to invade and bring devastation to the Middle and Near East
killing and injuring multiple millions and setting a sequence in motion
that has seen an exodus of people out of the Middle East and Africa and
into Europe. All of these consequences have been long planned and
none of them is random.

The West – the real home of terrorism

We can now clearly see why the Bush-connected BCCI mega-crooked
'bank' was found to be 'funnelling money to the Mujahideen' and why
Bush family associate and leading BCCI shareholder Khalid bin
Mahfouz was exposed for donating big money to Osama bin Laden at
the request of Osama's brother and Boy Bush business partner, Salem
bin Laden. Throughout the 1980s when Father Bush was always in the
White House as either vice president or president his family friend
Osama bin Laden was a major CIA asset promoted as a hero leading
resistance to the evil Soviet Union in Afghanistan. Then, when the
Soviets left, it became more beneficial to the Hidden Hand agenda to do
a 180 and turn the image of Bin Laden on its head. This led eventually to
Bin Laden being named as the 'mastermind' of 9/11 to justify an
invasion of Afghanistan where he was based. The United States invaded
Afghanistan on October 7th, 2001, less than a month after the 9/11
attacks in a military campaign that was clearly planned way before the
excuse was secured by 9/11 and 'Bin Laden did it!' You don't mount an
invasion of that scale in less than a month any more than you prepare a
building for a controlled demolition in the short time that Silverstein
claimed for Building 7. You will see in the next chapter how a long-

planned script has been playing out. The cover-story for the invasion was the need to 'get Bin Laden' and remove the Taliban from power who were protecting him in Afghanistan. The Taliban are a crazy group, but are they any more crazy – or psychopathic – than the US government and its military? When you compare their inflicted death tolls the Taliban are minor league and the US, especially when you add Britain, Europe and NATO, are world leaders year after year, decade after decade in mass murder and terrorism.

The Taliban offered to hand over Bin Laden to the US *if* the evidence was produced to show that he was involved in 9/11. This was a non-starter because the US didn't have any. Secretary of State Colin Powell said Bin Laden was definitely to blame and they would be producing compelling evidence to prove it which naturally they never did. When the time came to reveal this 'evidence' Powell said he could not make the information public because it was 'classified'. Yes and filed under 'piece of crap'. Hidden Hand lapdog Tony Blair read a 'dossier' to a compliant House of Commons in support of Britain joining the US invasion and he began: 'This document does not purport to provide a prosecutable case against Osama bin Laden in a court of law.' They must have been talking to Robert Mueller at the FBI. Moronic and unquestioning MPs in all political parties still gave Blair the nod for another bloodbath on the basis of made-up 'evidence'. The Blair 'report' was compiled by such trustworthy organisations as MI5 and MI6 with their drafts going to Washington and the CIA for approval. Boy Bush captured the moment: 'There's no need to discuss innocence or guilt, we know he's guilty.' The die was cast and Bin Laden was officially the 9/11 mastermind along with his associate Khalid Sheikh Mohammed who was named in the 9/11 Commission Report as 'the principal architect of the 9/11 attacks'. Mohammed was caught in Pakistan in 2003 in a joint operation between the drug-running duo, the CIA and ISI, and he was taken to torture centres in Afghanistan and Poland to encourage him to admit anything they wanted him to. He went on to the US military detention and torture camp at Guantanamo Bay in Cuba where he remains today despite never facing a trial. Further merciless torture by moral America led to Mohammed 'confessing' to a long list of terror attacks including 9/11. Human rights groups and a former military prosecutor have said the confessions are not supportable given they were secured by torture. Some question if it is even the real Khalid Sheikh Mohammed at Guantanamo.

The United States embarked upon precisely the course of action in Afghanistan demanded by Israel's former prime minister and military intelligence commander, Ehud Barak, within an hour of the attacks. The first phrase of the war was code-named Operation Enduring Freedom until 2014 when it became Operation Freedom's Sentinel (god, it's

pathetic) and it's still going on. The official death toll as of late 2018 was
38,000 Afghan civilians with more than 30,000 wounded. These are
seriously low-side figures, however, and include only the alleged
numbers of death by violence and not from all other consequences of
war. On the American side the figures are: 2,372 US troops killed and
20,320 wounded, plus all the dead and injured US civilian contractors.
Britain joined the invasion early as always under Hidden Hand poodle
Blair and later came a coalition of countries and NATO. The cost to
American taxpayers is estimated to be nearly $2 *trillion* and if you add in
all wars and conflicts since September, 2001, the figure is almost $6
trillion. Again these will be low-end figures. In the same period the
number of homeless Americans has soared with people living in cars,
tent cities or simply rough in the street. All that death and destruction
and mind-blowing financial cost only for General Austin Scott Miller,
commander of NATO's Resolute Support mission, to state the bloody
obvious in 2018 – 17 years after the post-9/11 invasion of Afghanistan.
He said: 'This is not going to be won militarily.' What incredible insight
and that was in no way obvious from the start after the Soviet
experience. Think what $6 *trillion* could have done for those people
living in the street and so many others. Instead it pours into the coffers
of Hidden Hand armament companies providing the weapons for *both*
sides in Hidden Hand wars paid for by struggling Americans and loans
from Hidden Hand banks. How apt that Trump nominated Patrick
Shanahan, long-time big-wig at major global arms company Boeing, as
his Secretary of Defense. The same theme can be seen in Britain under
Tony Blair (never seen a country he didn't want to bomb) and his
successors. Did I mention that these people are genetic psychopaths?

Bin Laden – movie star

The Osama bin Laden portrayed by the media was a construct, a
propaganda invention, and the truth was very different. Somehow old
Osama pulled off the attacks despite the reality described by British
journalist and Middle East specialist Robert Fisk who trekked across
desert and wasteland for a meeting with the 'mastermind' before 9/11:
'... Mr Bin Laden saw a pile of newspapers in my bag and seized them ...
By a sputtering oil lamp, he read them clearly unaware of the world
around him.' South African-born journalist and anti-apartheid activist
Tony Karon took the same line in his analysis of Bin Laden in *Time*
magazine three months before 9/11:

> ... The media's picture of Bin Laden sitting in a high-tech Bat cave in the
> mountains around Kandahar ordering up global mayhem at the click of a
> mouse is more than a little ludicrous. Yes, the various networks of Islamist
> terror have made full use of the possibilities presented by technology and

globalization. But few serious intelligence professionals believe Bin Laden is the puppet-master atop a pyramid structure of terror cells.

It's really not that simple, but personalizing the threat – while it distorts both the nature of the problem and the remedy – is a time-honored tradition. Before Bin Laden, the face of the global terror threat against Americans belonged to the Palestinian radical Abu Nidal. Or was it Colonel Ghaddafi? Ayatollah Khomeini, perhaps? And does anyone even remember the chubby jowls of Carlos the Jackal, whose image drawn from an old passport picture was once the icon of global terror?

Karon was correct in his assessment and we see the constantly-repeating technique of keeping people in fear so they will give their power away to those who claim to protect them. American writer Henry Louis Mencken (1880-1956) was spot on when he said: 'The whole aim of practical politics is to keep the populace alarmed and hence, clamorous to be led to safety, by menacing it with an endless series of hobgoblins – all of them imaginary.' Without fear there is no Problem-Reaction-Solution. 'Bin Laden did it' has been a vaudeville show, pure theatre with video inserts that had 'Bin Laden' confirming his terrorist credentials right on cue whenever the Bush-Blair-fronted terrorism network needed a credibility boost. 'Bin Laden' videos were often so perfectly timed you might even think they were manufactured to support the script, but that would be a conspiracy theory and we should immediately dismiss the idea. No, no, there is a much more plausible explanation for the timing – God was on our side. The fact that the videos were circulated by front organisations for Israeli intelligence (more later) should in no way influence our belief in the credibility of the official story. Bin Laden denied involvement after the attacks and said in a statement a week after 9/11:

> I have already said that I am not involved in the 11 September attacks on the United States. As a Muslim, I try my best to avoid telling a lie. I had no knowledge of these attacks, nor do I consider the killing of innocent women, children and other humans as an appreciable act. Islam strictly forbids causing harm to innocent women, children and other people. Such a practice is forbidden even in the course of a battle ... I have already said that we are against the American system, not against its people, whereas in these attacks, the common American people have been killed.

The London *Daily Telegraph* noted that Bin Laden had publicly issued four videos after September 11th and always denied carrying out the atrocities. We are asked to believe that he then suddenly switched his position in a 'confession' video on December 13th, 2001. The date is more than interesting to say the least because that is the day on which Bin Laden is said to have died. Yes – *died*. I will fill in the background shortly. This about-turn 'confession' was like a scene from the 1998 movie *Wag The Dog* which is so close to the truth in how political showbiz really works. It's all a psychological game to seize control of the public mind or, as Henry Kissinger said: 'It is not a matter of what is true that counts, but what is perceived to be true.' The *Wag The Dog* storyline involves an American president facing an election for a second term when his aides realise that the story of a sexual affair is about to hit the press. They hire a Hollywood producer played by Dustin Hoffman to create a non-existent US war with Albania to take news of the affair off the front pages. They pick Albania because they figure no one in America would know where it was and certainly nothing about the place. There is no actual war – they just kid the public there is. The 'war' all takes place in a movie studio where interviews and 'war footage' are created and then handed to compliant television news networks as 'footage from the front'. They hire singer Willie Nelson and other celebrities to record a Live Aid-type song called 'The American Dream' to capture public emotion in support of the fictional 'war in Albania'. I recommend the movie if you haven't seen it on the grounds of accuracy. In the end, with the Albania 'war' won and the president re-elected, Hoffman's character threatens to spill the beans because he wants to be publicly acknowledged for his achievement. He is then led away by large men to a blacked-out car and that's the last we see of him. This is so close to what really happens with the political and military mind games and anyone who threatens to get in the way. Hollywood is a creation of the Hidden Hand (hence so much Satanism and child abuse goes on there) and it has been used from the start as a stupendous weapon in global propaganda and perception conditioning. Most people download their version of 'history' from Hollywood movies and that's overwhelmingly a version that suits what the manipulators want the public to believe. Karl Rove, Boy Bush's chief political adviser, headed out to California after 9/11 to meet 45 of Hollywood's top players at the Peninsula Hotel in Beverly Hills. These included executives from all the main studios and they formed the Hollywood 911 committee to tell the world the Gospel according to Washington. Movie-makers were told they could have access to military sites, aircraft carriers, almost anything they wanted, so long as their productions did not criticise the government. Bush adviser Mark McKinnon told the BBC's *Newsnight* programme without once bursting into laughter:

> We don't want to, or intend to, turn Hollywood into a propaganda machine. It's not in the long-term interests for the effort, Hollywood, or this administration. This administration is very first-amendment minded. This

President has no interest in telling people what to do, what to say, or how to say it.

Right, gotcha – so they wanted to use Hollywood as a propaganda machine and tell people what to do, what to say and how to say it. Invert most things that politicians and their apologists say and you are pretty much there. Jack Valenti, President of the Motion Picture Association of America, said:

> We are at war. If I was in the White House, I'd reach out to the most powerful persuaders on earth, the movie industry, and ask, 'What can you do to help?' What can they do?

What Bush (or rather those that controlled him) wanted them to do was to tell lies about world events as they've been doing since Hollywood was founded (with honourable exceptions). Among the latter was Larry Gelbart, creator of *M*A*S*H*, the brilliant series about the Korean War. He said of the government's overtures to Hollywood:

> It is easy to talk out of the other side of your mouth when you are two-faced. You have got this extra mouth. They want it all ways.

Yes they do, and some big players in Hollywood from studio owners to experts in various disciplines were very keen to give them whatever they wanted. Government and military propaganda continues to be widespread in Hollywood productions. The 2019 *Captain Marvel* movie, starring Brie Larson, is a propaganda storyline for the American military involving military officers employed as consultants and advisers, dozens of active-duty US soldiers were used as extras, scenes shot at a military base and the film heavily promoted by the US Department of Defense.

Wag the Dog 'confession'

This brings me back to the Bin Laden 'smoking gun' confession video. With an invasion of Afghanistan to justify and no evidence to pin the rap on the declared villain it was no surprise that the Bin Laden 'confession' would drop from the heavens. Praise the Lord. Pentagon official statements claimed the video was shot at a 'guest house in Kandahar', Afghanistan's second largest city, and 'found in an abandoned private house in Jalalabad' 400 miles away. By whom, pray? That very much depends on which official spokesman you listened to. Most of the 9/11 story depends on that. We were variously told that the Bin Laden tape was found by the US Navy, US Army, United Islamic Front for the Salvation of Afghanistan (Northern Alliance), the 'military' and CIA.

More details, please? Er, sorry, it's classified. The video was said to have been shot on November 9th, 2001. Boy Bush apparently viewed the tape on November 30th before *The Washington Post* 'broke' (officially leaked) the story of its existence on December 9th and the rest of us saw bits of it on December 13th. The tape was about 40 minutes long and of very poor quality which suited the manipulation perfectly. It included shots of a downed helicopter in Afghanistan's Ghazni province and two sections with a man claimed to be Bin Laden talking to a Saudi cleric and others at a 'dinner'. Strangely, the tape had the first part of the 'Bin Laden' conversation at the end of the tape, the end of the conversation at the start, with the helicopter footage in between. Maybe Afghan video cameras whirl the other way like Chinese writing. We were told that the US government used the latest voice and face identification techniques (to check it or make it?) and a team of Arabic translators, none of them familiar with the Saudi language, spent days listening to the tape to make sure the conversations were accurately translated. Why didn't they succeed then? The video was not accurately translated as confirmed by State Department consultant Christopher Ross. If that was the face of the 'Osama Bin Laden' we had been seeing elsewhere then he must have placed a very large order with the Kandahar Cream Cake Company and been visited by a doctor from the local nose-job clinic – 'cave visits a speciality' (Fig 85). 'Bin Laden' in the 'confession video' looks nothing like the Bin Laden we had come to know; but we shouldn't mock, they were doing their best, and after all Boy Bush said:

> This is Bin Laden unedited. It's preposterous for anybody to think that this tape is doctored. That's just a feeble excuse to provide weak support for an incredibly evil man.

Cheers, George, so it was doctored then or rather made from scratch. Jack Straw, Blair's always bewildered Foreign Secretary, said there was 'no doubt it is the real thing' thus providing more confirmation that it wasn't. *Monitor*, a German TV show on the Das Erste channel, asked two independent translators and an expert in oriental studies to analyse the US government translation. They found it to be 'inaccurate' and

Figure 85: Confession tape 'Bin Laden' and the real Bin Laden.

'manipulative'. Dr Abdel El M. Husseini, one of the programme's translators, said that he had carefully examined the Pentagon's translation and found many problems with it. 'At the most important places where it is held to prove the guilt of Bin Laden it is not identical with the Arabic,' he said. My goodness, I'm shocked. Dr Murad Alami, another translator, said the alleged statement that the attacks would take place 'on that day' cannot be heard in the original Arabic version. Garnet Ratter, professor of Islamic and Arabic Studies at the Asia-Africa Institute at the University of Hamburg, told the programme: 'The American translators who listened to the tapes and transcribed them apparently wrote a lot of things in that they wanted to hear, but that cannot be heard on the tape no matter how many times you listen to it.' Bin Laden's mother was quoted by Britain's *Mail on Sunday* as saying the tape was a fake. 'The voice is unclear and uneven. There are too many gaps and the statements are very unlike him', she said. According to the official translation the tape's make-believe 'Bin Laden' appears to say that most of the hijackers did not know the details of the operation until just before they boarded the planes:

> The brothers, who conducted the operation, all they knew was that they have a martyrdom operation and we asked each of them to go to America but they didn't know anything about the operation, not even one letter. But they were trained and we did not reveal the operation to them until they are there and just before they boarded the planes ... (inaudible) ... Those who were trained to fly didn't know the others.

Are we to believe that after 'years of planning' most of those involved were only given the essential details in the few minutes before they boarded the planes for a 'brilliantly executed operation'? Hey, Abdul, quick, we don't have much time. You know those two big towers in New York? Well ... What utter, utter trash. What about the 'Atta letter' claiming to tell the hijackers what to do and how to prepare long before 9/11? Where is the video footage at Washington Dulles and Newark New Jersey of these 'hijackers' being told the plan 'just before they boarded'? Here we have 'Bin Laden' describing something that could not have happened. The 'pilots' didn't know each other? Three trained at Venice flying schools and Atta was a close friend of one according to the official story. The tape translation has the Bin Laden figure saying that he had been informed of the date in advance. Well, I guess as a 'mastermind' he would have to be told when it was happening. The figure says that it was 5.30pm when he heard the news on the radio that the first plane had hit the World Trade Center and he had told people with him that they should be patient with the implication that he knew there would be others. 'Bin Laden' then says he continued to listen to the radio. Would he not on that of all days have made sure CNN was switched on and ready? Instead he sits listening to the radio while the rest of the world watches live what he is supposed to have orchestrated. The translation also has 'Bin Laden' saying that he did not expect the two towers to collapse as they did. He thought that the fire would undermine the iron structure of the building and that three or four storeys would collapse. Isn't it strange that a man who comes from one of the biggest construction families in the Middle East should not think that three or four storeys falling on those below would threaten the whole building if that was how it was supposed to have happened? And, by the way, Mr Fake Osama, the building structures were made with steel, not iron. What a joke it all is and a deeply tragic one. Why would he 'confess' on tape? Why take that chance? It has been suggested that it was done as a recruitment video, but (a) that means the 'confession' would have been widely circulated and a copy would eventually have fallen into the wrong hands, and (b) why would they record a 'recruitment video' on such a crap camera with such crap quality when we are told he had limitless funds? None of this makes any sense because it isn't true.

By the time the video is said to have been shot on November 9th the Taliban were in serious trouble. The country was being carpet-bombed by the US and Britain and on that day the anti-Taliban forces of the Afghan Northern Alliance claimed to have won the battle for the strategic town of Mazar-e-Sharif. The capital Kabul would fall within days. At no time in the whole tape does Bin Laden or anyone else mention the US invasion, the bombing, the Taliban's retreat or the alleged pursuit of the man himself. 'Bin Laden' is claimed to say on the tape that Mohamed Atta was the leader of the hijackers, but he does not say that at all. He speaks only of Mohamed, hardly a rare name among Muslims, and the name 'Atta' did not leave his lips. 'Bin Laden' said: 'Mohamed from the Egyptian family was in charge of the group.' The name 'Atta' only comes in the translated subtitles on the broadcast version, which says: 'Muhammad (Atta) from the Egyptian family (meaning the Al Qa'ida Egyptian group) was in charge of the group.' The translation is peppered with these in-bracket comments that are not on the soundtrack. The term 'inaudible' appears over and over on the subtitles when they could not understand what was said after playing the tape back dozens of times and later another 50 times more. Significantly, many of these 'inaudibles' come at the start of sentences. A skilled editor can take someone's words and change the order to make them say what they didn't say before. An audiotape of Boy Bush was sent to my website in which he openly declares his intentions for a fascist state. What he said was true, but he didn't actually say it. His words from other speeches and statements had been re-edited to make it sound as if he had said that. The result was very good and imagine what Hollywood and the Pentagon's own secret Hollywood could do. Hani Al Sibaei, a specialist in Islamic affairs, told Al Jazeera TV that the congratulatory wishes on the tape and Bin Laden's happy expression were taken from a tape of Bin Laden being congratulated on the marriage of one his children which happened four years earlier. Al Sibaei described the 'Bin Laden confession' as 'fabricated and a scandal for the greatest democratic country in the world'. Not sure about the last bit, but you get his drift. With voice recognition technology they would have another means of mimicking the sound of the voice and with the Arabic audio so poor and difficult to hear this would be very straightforward for an expert. There are no close-ups of lips on the video, making it even easier to manipulate.

There were other puzzling aspects of the Kandahar 'confession' tape. The Pentagon said it was shot in mid-November although reports say it carried a date of November 9th. The cleric with 'Bin Laden' said he journeyed to the location on a night of a full moon, but the full moons at that time were on October 31st and November 30th – long before and even longer after the tape was supposed to have been recorded. The cleric, who was a paraplegic, would have had to make his alleged journey of some five hours or more from Kabul to Kandahar while the intensive US bombing and the anti-Taliban forces of the Northern Alliance were sweeping the country. Afghan warlord Mohammad Zaman Ghamsharik apparently reported on November 23rd that Bin Laden dined with Pakistanis in Jalalabad on November 9th and stayed there until the 13th. If that is so how could he also be in Kandahar on the 9th making his video 'confession'? 'Bin Laden' appears to have a ring on his right hand in the video while in his other appearances he only wore a watch and the left-handed Bin Laden is seen to be gesturing a lot and making notes with his right hand in the 'confession'. Bruce Lawrence, Professor of Religion at Duke University in North Carolina, was considered a Bin Laden expert. His opinion on the confession video: 'It's bogus'.

Bloke in a hat

Another 'Bin Laden' video in 2011claimed to have been found at his 'compound' after he was allegedly killed by US forces showed only the side of a beard, the tip of a nose and a woolly hat plonked on a head (Figs 86 and 87 overleaf). The video was taken (why?) of 'him' changing channels on a television and he seemed to be on all of them while never hitting an ad break. The real Bin Laden was left-handed and yet this guy uses his right hand to change the channels throughout. Close-ups of the ears of fake and real Bin Laden show they are not the same and other footage from what was called the 'treasure trove' was only pictures

Figure 86: This is all you see of 'Bin Laden' in the 'compound' video except for one brief moment when his head half-turns ...

Figure 87: ... compare the half-turn profiles and we see that 'compound Bin Laden' is not Bin Laden.

released years before. 'New' footage found in the 'compound' was circulating four years earlier. They did the same in 2007 when the footage was released as 'new' when it was clearly the same video that had been circulating in 2002. Then there was September 11th 'hijacker' Ahmed al-Haznawi 'threatening' attacks in America in a tirade to camera that is said to have been recorded six months before 9/11 on March 6th, 2001. The tape was released by Al Jazeera television, the 'Arab CNN', based in US/Israel-controlled Qatar. Al Jazeera claimed to have 'received' the tape in April, 2002, but would not say from what source. The 'hijacker' speaks to camera on good-quality footage as if he is sitting in a television studio and, most bizarrely, behind him are images of the burning World Trade Center. This was supposed to have been shot six months before the attacks. If that is correct someone has electronically added the background of the burning towers. Why? This tape was claimed to be the 'proof' that al-Qaeda was behind the attacks so why doctor this 'proof' in such a bizarre manner? Why not give us the original footage? Why would this guy record a video six months before the attacks warning that the fight against the United States would be taken to American soil? 'The time has come to prove to the whole world that the United States put on a garb that was not tailored for it when it had the mere thought of resisting the Mujahidin', he said. The United States did not resist the Mujahidin, it funded and armed them, and why would a carefully planned and secret operation to attack targets in the United States be revealed by one of the hijackers on tape six months before the day? Crazy. On the same Al Jazeera tape is claimed to be the

al-Qaeda second in command, Ayman al-Zawahiri, and a silent Bin
Laden. The alleged Zawahiri calls the September 11th attacks a 'a great
victory' and adds: 'This great victory was achieved only thanks to the
grace of God the Almighty, not due to any skill or competence on our
part.' At least the last bit is true.

Seeing is believing?

I remember watching the movie *Stuart Little* with my son Jaymie three
years before 9/11 and it gave me an idea even then for what was
possible. The movie is about an animated mouse living with a human
family. Cats in the neighbourhood, real ones not animations, speak to
each other like humans. The mouths moved so perfectly with the words
I realised that the days of believing what you see even with apparent
television interviews or statements were over. If they could do that with
cats what could they do with humans? When the actor Oliver Reed died
during the filming of the movie *Gladiator* he was replaced in the rest of
the film by a computer-generated image of himself. We also saw in
advertisements and movies like *Forrest Gump*, released seven years
before 9/11, how actors could appear to be chatting and shaking hands
with people long dead. Sean Broughton, director of Smoke and Mirrors,
one of Britain's top visual effects companies, described at the time how
relatively easy it would be for a skilled professional to fake the video of
Bin Laden. First they would transfer the original video images on to film
tape, he said. The distortion, or 'noise' and graininess, would be
removed and a 'morphing package' would be used to manipulate the
image on a computer screen. It would be possible to change the person's
mouth and expressions to fit whatever soundtrack they chose and finally
the 'noise' and graininess would be returned and the whole thing
transferred back to videotape. Smoke and Mirrors had used this
technique to put Bill Clinton's head on an actor for an advertisement for
a United States insurance company. Broughton said there were perhaps
20 people in America who would be good enough to fool everybody, but
'to find someone that good and make sure they kept quiet would
probably be pretty difficult'. Not for the Hidden Hand it wouldn't.
Philip Taylor, Director of the Institute of Communications at Leeds
University in the UK and the author of *Munitions of the Mind, a History of
Propaganda,* said US military leaders had once suggested to him
intercepting a live broadcast of Saddam Hussein 'and morphing a
blonde on one arm and a bottle of scotch on the other'. They decided
against doctoring the video, he said, because of its extraordinary
potential price of ruining US credibility forever if they were found out.
Greg Strause was Visual Effects Supervisor at Pixel Envy, a company
involved with special effects on the movie *Titanic*. He said:

That's how we make our money, kind of faking things to convince everyone else it's real. We just did some Nike commercials where half the people are digital. You wouldn't be able to pick them out.

Henry Hingson, a former President of the National Association of Criminal Defence Lawyers, said that in this age of digital wizardry many things could be done to manipulate video. Bob Crabtree, editor of the magazine *Computer Video*, said it was impossible to judge whether the 'Bin Laden' video was a fake without more details of its source: 'The US seems simply to have asked the world to trust them that it is genuine.' Techniques of video manipulation available then are nothing like we see today when a piece of software can lock-in your facial movements with anyone on video and make their mouth and facial muscles move the same as yours. Once a person's voice frequency is secured technology can to make them appear to say whatever you choose. The point to stress here again is that what we see in the public arena is way behind what they have in the secret military projects and at that level they would have been far closer in 2001 to what we see today. Put 'deep fake videos' into a search engine and you'll see that seeing and hearing is no longer believing.

Bin Laden is dead – but when?

Egyptian newspaper *Al-Wafd* reported on December 26th, 2001, that Bin Laden had died ten days earlier. The report quoted a 'prominent official' from the Taliban in Afghanistan as saying Bin Laden had died from serious lung complications and described how he had been buried in an unmarked grave according to Wahhabi tradition. The *Pakistan Observer* reported that Bin Laden had died a peaceful death due to an untreated lung complication and the Paris-based paper *al-Watan al-Arabi* quoted Pakistan sources confirming his death in 2002. No al-Qaeda source contradicted these reports. Bin Laden looked very ill with what was described as 'a gaunt, frail appearance' in videos that appeared to be genuine just before this time. Pakistan President Pervez Musharraf said that photographs showed Bin Laden to be extremely weak and 'I would give the first priority that he is dead'. Musharraf said Bin Laden had been using a dialysis machine for kidney failure, a fact that was widely known among the intelligence community. French newspaper *La Figaro* ran a story in late October, 2001, that Bin Laden had been treated in the urology department of the American Hospital in Dubai in the previous July and had ordered a mobile dialysis machine to be delivered to Afghanistan. *Time* magazine questioned if he was alive in June, 2002:

The last time the world heard from Osama bin Laden, there was reason to believe his end was near. In a videotape released in December, bin Laden looked sallow; his speech was slow, and his left arm immobile.

Many intelligence sources quoted agreed that Bin Laden was probably dead. CNN reported in July, 2003, that Bin Laden bodyguards had been captured and he was nowhere to be seen. Steve Pieczenik, a Deputy Assistant Secretary of State in three US administrations, said in 2002 that Bin Laden died in 2001 from the consequences of the degenerative genetic disease Marfan syndrome which affects the connective tissue of the body. Suffers tend to be thin, tall and have long arms, legs and fingers which certainly fits Bin Laden. A major symptom is lung disease. Pieczenik repeated the claim in 2011 when dismissing reports that Bin Laden had been killed in his 'compound' in Pakistan by American forces. Pieczenik said he worked with Bin Laden when he was used by the United States as the poster boy for Afghan resistance to the Soviet invasion in the 1980s. He said CIA physicians had treated Bin Laden and they had visited him at the American Hospital in Dubai in July, 2001. 'He died of Marfan syndrome, Bush junior knew about it, the intelligence community knew about it', Pieczenik said. David Ray Griffin reports in *Osama bin Laden – Dead or Alive?* that no messages from Bin Laden were intercepted by US intelligence from about December 13th, 2001, when he was reported to have died. Angelo Codevilla, a former foreign service officer and senior editor of *The American Spectator*, wrote about 'Osama bin Elvis' in 2009: 'Seven years after Osama bin Laden's last verifiable appearance among the living, there is more evidence of Elvis's presence among us than for his.' Video and audio tapes of 'Bin Laden' began to re-appear in 2003/4 up to his alleged death by US troops in 2011. Angelo Codevilla spoke for a lot of people when he said:

> The audio and video tapes alleged to be Osama's never convinced impartial observers. The guy just does not look like Osama. Some videos show him with a Semitic aquiline nose, while others show him with a shorter, broader one. Nor does the tapes' Osama sound like Osama ... Above all .... the words on the Osama tapes differ substantially from what the real Osama used to say.

Why would fake videos be circulated except to mislead and give the impression Bin Laden was still alive when he wasn't?

You only die twice

Bin Laden died again on May 2nd, 2011. This time he was killed by US Special Forces who raided his 'al-Qaeda compound' (a house) in Abbottabad about 35 miles north of the Pakistan capital Islamabad. The 40-minute operation by SEAL Team Six brought an end to the life of the 'World's most want terrorist' for the second time if you accept that he'd met his maker once and came back for more. President Obama is said to have approved the raid known as 'Operation Neptune Spear' (mercy, please) after 'months of preparation' that followed 'intelligence' about where Bin Laden was hiding. The authorities claim that Black Hawk helicopters took off from Afghanistan with 25 Navy SEALs and landed at the 'compound'. One crashed without causing injuries and they found Bin Laden on the third floor where they shot him in the head above the left eye. A woman was also killed along with Bin Laden's son and two other men. The SEALs all returned to Afghanistan with your man in a body bag. Obama-the-Fraud addressed the nation and big crowds cheered the news outside the White House, Pentagon and in New York's Times Square, so proving yet again that most people will believe anything the government tells them. With 24 hours to comply with Islamic law Bin Laden was buried at sea. No, no, I'm not taking the piss – that's what they told us. *Buried at sea*? He was a Saudi landlubber not Jack Sparrow. Does anyone really think the American government and military would care less about Islamic law in such circumstances? They were getting rid of the evidence pure and simple so their story could not be questioned. There were so many different versions of the raid and what happened in the house, sorry compound, and no tangible evidence to constitute 'proof of death' has been produced. Freedom of Information requests for DNA results, videos and photographs were denied. Internal emails released under the Freedom of Information Act suggest that only a very small number of people on board the ship were aware of what took place and no sailors witnessed it. The Pentagon sent all its files to the CIA in 2012 and deleted them from its own database so circumventing any more Freedom of Information requests because the CIA is exempt. They're not trying hide anything you understand.

Muhammad Bashir, a Pakistani national who lived next door to the 'compound', told Pakistan television that only one helicopter landed which was the one that exploded and crashed. How could they take away 'Bin Laden' if no other helicopter landed? He said that those in the crashed helicopter were dead. Bashir's cousin was said to have a vegetable garden at the 'compound' which the owner – not Bin Laden – let him use. Other residents interviewed by the BBC said it would have been impossible for Bin Laden to have lived there all that time without their knowledge and in fact the person living there was a neighbour they knew very well. The 'Bin Laden' raid was officially carried out by SEAL Team Six and within weeks 38 people – 15 from SEAL Team Six – were killed when their helicopter crashed in Afghanistan. They were on a mission with the call-sign Extortion 17 in a slow-moving Chinook helicopter totally inappropriate for such an action. The bodies were cremated 'because they were burned beyond recognition' when photographic evidence is reported to show otherwise. Black boxes were apparently not recovered after being washed away in a 'flash flood'. The helicopter had no air cover and drone surveillance wasn't working at the time of the crash which was claimed by the Taliban to have been hit by their missile. Family members have many questions about what happened to their loved ones and so do many in the military.

Sound like 9/11? History does have a habit of repeating when those driving events are the same people and the same networks. People will have to come to their own conclusions about when and how Bin Laden died, but he was just another patsy exploited as a hero and then a monster to advance the Hidden Hand agenda. He was no more responsible for 9/11 than I was.

PART 2

Who really did it
- and *so* much more

CHAPTER 16

The Sequence

There is a stubbornness about me that never can bear to be frightened at the will of others. My courage always rises at every attempt to intimidate me – Jane Austen

We are now starting a journey into the Forbidden Land. I am going to address and expose information, facts and connections that a whole global network of professional censors is desperate for you not to see.

There was massive and central involvement in 9/11 by Israeli government, military and intelligence operatives and what happened that day cannot be understood without its exposure. Most researchers are intimidated and cowed into silence about this and won't go there. They hide behind '9/11 was an inside job' through fear of the consequences that come with speaking the name that must not be spoken. Others are simply ignorant of the ultra-Zionist connection and no doubt in some cases they are specifically planted to hold the line of the 9/11 Truth movement at 'the government did it'. Actually 'the government' did not do it. A Hidden Hand network infiltrating and working from within government, military and intelligence agencies 'did it'. Those representing the Hidden Hand in the United States government and its agencies and military were of course involved. The story, however, goes much deeper than that – *much deeper*. The Forbidden Land of 9/11 (and so much else) is the involvement of Israel and more accurately the satanic Death Cult that controls Israel while hating to its core everything that country and its people are claimed to stand for and represent. Jewish people need to read the exposure that follows even more than non-Jews because they have been royalty stitched up by this Death Cult and continue to be so. Cult members have a deep and gathering hatred for me which I take as a compliment. Their problem is that I don't succumb to intimidation and I seek truth not popularity. If the latter results from the former, then fine. If it doesn't, that's equally fine. Whenever intimidation is attempted I shout louder and run faster in their direction. Far from fearing them I think they are pathetic. I'm sure the Cult believed that it had secured such levels of intimidation and acquiescence by now that a book like this would never be written today by anyone with a public profile. Wrong chaps – *very wrong*. When Michael Caine said that famous line in the *Italian Job* – 'You're only supposed to blow the bloody doors off!' – I must have been overcome by temporary deafness. I seek to blow the roof and the walls off, too, so that all humanity – Jewish and non-Jewish – can be free to create a world of our own choosing instead of being the puppets and lackeys of a self-appointed elite that takes the form at its core of a dark and satanic Death Cult. I will refer to the extreme expression of Zionism as 'ultra-Zionism' and I will use the term Death Cult for its inner core until I come to its background and real name. All will become clear as we proceed.

This is not an exposure that targets Jewish people for being Jewish, nor does it point the finger at the overwhelming Jewish majority. Revealing the involvement in 9/11 and far wider manipulation of the ultra-Zionist and Death Cult wing of the Hidden Hand does not refer to Jewish people in general any more than criticism and unmasking of the Sicilian Mafia is a condemnation of all Italians. Ultra-Zionism and the Death Cult only want you to believe that one means the other to secure their own protection from exposure by constantly – and I mean *constantly* – playing the card marked 'anti-Semitism'. I seek instead to shine a light on those who present a public face of Jewishness while treating the great body of Jewish people worldwide with absolute contempt. It is quite a story to say the very least which I am going to tell in the following order: (1) The sequence of ultra-Zionist and Death Cult manipulation that led to 9/11; (2) the staggering scale of the ultra-Zionist network of ever-gathering censorship and intimidation which prevents the truth from circulating in the mainstream; (3) where this cult came from and how it seized control of Israel and runs the country as its personal fiefdom; (4) how the Cult and its ultra-Zionist support network expanded their influence and manipulation around the world – especially in the West; and finally (5) how this Cult was the driving force behind 9/11 before, during and after. I will detail the real nature of ultra-Zionism and the Death Cult, both modern and historic, and expose what the global network of censorship and suppression is designed to hide from public view – particularly from the mass of Jewish people who have no idea what is being done in their name. The religion followed by most Jews is not the religion of the Cult which is a phenomenon that operates within mainstream Jewish society while being a self-contained and separate group. The Death Cult and the ultra-Zionists that support its agenda (some knowingly, most unknowingly) is a modern expression of a breakaway faction that can be traced at least to the 17th century and this has inverted much of what mainstream Judaism stood for and believed. What emerged from this was a satanic religion that spawned both the cabal that controls today's Israel *and* the House of Saud 'royal' family with its satanic version of Islam known as Wahhabism. This is the extremist, beheading-branch of psychopathy practiced in Saudi Arabia and by terrorist groups such as ISIS/ISIL/Islamic State. The Israel-House of Saud connection explains so much about what happened on 9/11 and in its aftermath right up to present day, and why there was such a Saudi involvement.

'Jewishness' and 'Zionism' are not interchangeable

Before I begin to detail 30 years of research into these subjects it is essential to define the terms I will use from hereon. I am exposing those that seek to exploit the mass of Jewish people as their cover to hide and protect their activities from exposure and this should *not* be equated with claiming there is some 'Jewish plot'. Defining the term 'Jewish' is highly controversial in that it means different things to different people. Some think of Jewishness as relating to a race – I say wrongly; others define Jewishness as a religious belief (although there are several alleged versions); and still others emphasise the common culture, rituals and way of life. This is for Jewish people to decide by what it means to them. One thing Jewishness is *absolutely not* is Zionism. This is a fundamental misunderstanding that is promoted and encouraged by the ultra-Zionist elite and their ultra-Zionist gofers to equate Zionism and Jewish people as interchangeable terms. They are not and never have been. Once that connection is erroneously made in the public mind – Jewish and non-Jewish – exposure of ultra-Zionism and its extremists can be protected and censored by claiming that such criticism is by definition always an attack on all Jewish people. From this the 'anti-Semitism' industry was born in which critics and exposers of ultra-Zionism are targeted and often silenced in the name of protecting Jewish people from 'racist bigots' and 'Nazis' when it's really all about protecting the ultra-Zionist elite from legitimate investigation. This is the dictionary definition of Zionism: 'International movement originally for the establishment of a Jewish national or religious community in Palestine and later for the support of modern Israel.' Zionism is a *political philosophy* – not a race – which sought to establish a homeland for Jews in Palestine and now seeks to keep it that way. The Jewish Virtual Library expands on the theme:

> The term 'Zionism' was coined in 1890 by Nathan Birnbaum. Its general definition means the national movement for the return of the Jewish people to their homeland and the resumption of Jewish sovereignty in the Land of Israel.

> Since the establishment of the State of Israel in 1948, Zionism has come to include the movement for the development of the State of Israel and the

protection of the Jewish nation in Israel through support for the Israel Defense Forces.

From inception, Zionism advocated tangible as well as spiritual aims. Jews of all persuasions – left, right, religious and secular – formed the Zionist movement and worked together toward its goals. Disagreements in philosophy led to rifts in the Zionist movement over the years, and a number of separate forms emerged. Notably: Political Zionism; Religious Zionism; Socialist Zionism and Territorial Zionism.

While Judaism and Jewish people are said to go back thousands of years the term 'Zionism' only emerged in 1890. Therefore Jewish people and Zionism are not the same thing and not interchangeable. Many Jews vehemently oppose Zionism never mind support it. Nor do you have to be Jewish to be a Zionist. There are the Christian Zionists, for example, that support the existence of a homeland for Jews in Palestine. We can also see from the Virtual Library definition that even Zionism itself has many faces and expressions. It isn't just one thing to all Jews. There is a myth that Jews are somehow all the same with the same beliefs and attitudes to life. This is another *absolutely not*. Jews span the spectrum of both behaviour and belief just like every other group. Selling the lie that all Jews think the same allows their elite to claim that they speak for all Jews. This is a travesty of the truth and there are endless self-styled Jewish organisations that exploit this misunderstanding by claiming to represent all Jewish people. They don't and never have, but their power and influence comes from making that claim and having it believed. These are the terms that I will be using to emphasise these differences: I will simple say Jews or Jewish people for everyone who considers themselves Jewish; I will refer to 'Zionists' when I am talking about those who support the existence of a Jewish homeland in Palestine, but don't support the extremists who exploit Zionism and Jewish people to increase their own self-interest and expand their personal and collective power; and I will describe the elite extremist minority and their support system as 'ultra-Zionist'. There are also two expressions of ultra-Zionism. There are those utterly consumed by Israel and Zionism in ways that completely define their self-identity and colour their every view and action. They are 'Israel right or wrong' and can support and justify horrors and injustices if they are perceived to be 'good for Israel'. The most extreme of them at the other end of the ultra-Zionist spectrum are willing to engage in any action – *literally anything* – to secure personal and collective power in the name of Israel and Zionism. This extreme fuses into the satanic Death Cult. Jewish people represent only 0.2 percent of the global population – *0.2 percent*. Take away those who oppose Zionism and those I will refer to as Zionists and you are left with a tiny number of ultra-Zionists and even fewer in the Death Cult. Their influence, however, is *fantastic* when compared with their number. This is possible because they exploit and manipulate Jews, Zionists and even many 'Israel right or wrong' ultra-Zionists to do their bidding without realising the true background to the satanic cult running the show which actually has contempt for Jewishness. To them Jewish people are only a means to an end, not the end itself, and the end they desire for the rest of humanity, Jewish and non-Jewish, is horrific.

On the road to 9/11

There is a sequence of events before, during and after the September 11th attacks that pulls all the pieces together and the sequence continues to play out to this day. The connections are devastating for the official version of the attacks and sweep back the curtain to allow the wizard to be seen. This is indeed the Yellow Brick Road in so many and various ways to what really happened on 9/11 and it takes us into evidence that reveals without question the foundation involvement in the attacks of the ultra-Zionist and Death Cult cabal that controls the State of Israel and operates worldwide. We can pick up the trail in 1979 when future Israeli Prime Minister, US-educated Benjamin Netanyahu, organised the Jerusalem Conference on International Terrorism (JCIT) where he called for a 'war on terror' to destroy what he called international terrorism. This was 22 years before his wish was granted as a result of 9/11. No wonder his first public reaction to the attacks was that they were 'very, very good for Israel'. He wanted 'to focus public attention on the grave threat that international terrorism poses to all democratic societies, to study the real nature of today's terrorism, and to propose measures for combating and defeating the international terror movements'. Netanyahu demanded pre-emptive attacks on states that were alleged to support 'terrorists', the use of torture, expanded intelligence networks, dehumanising propaganda against targets and curtailed civil liberties. Netanyahu's fellow speakers included then Israel Prime Minister Menachem Begin and future US president, Father Bush. Brian Crozier was another speaker – the leader of Le Cercle, a highly significant secret society formerly known as the Pinay Circle after former French Prime Minister, Antoine Pinay. Its members are in influential positions across multiple countries in North America, Europe and worldwide and at least four of them spoke at Netanyahu's 1979 conference. Le Cercle has a long history of political and other manipulation across the world together with its fellow secret society strands in The Web. I wrote in *The Biggest Secret* about alleged connections between Le Cercle and the murder in Paris of Princess Diana.

Le Cercle members have included Donald Rumsfeld, 9/11 Secretary of Defense; Paul Wolfowitz, Rumsfeld's 9/11 'deputy' but the one really

the circumstances of a truly massive and widely perceived external threat [my emphasis].

This was written in 1997. What could Brzezinski have been thinking about? Slithering in the background as always as the preparations were made for 9/11 was Henry Kissinger, an

Figure 89: The landmass that Brzezinski said in 1997 had to be targeted in pursuit of global control – and has been ever since.

ultra-Zionist agent for Israel in the United States all his political career. This included roles as Secretary of State *and* National Security Advisor at the same time to presidents Nixon and Ford. He was Nixon's handler during the Watergate scandal that cost Nixon his job while Kissinger got away unscathed. Kissinger was at the centre of manipulations involving the Vietnam War; horrendous war crimes in Indo-China; and the 1973 Arab-Israeli Yom Kippur War which he didn't tell Nixon about for three hours to 'stop him interfering', as documents show. I mean, Nixon was only US President after all and nothing like as important as Kissinger. It was such confirmation of what really happened on 9/11 when Boy Bush and Cheney tried to appoint Kissinger to head the 9/11 Commission.

Ultra-Zionism seizes power

Dick Cheney's ultra-Zionist Defense Planning Group produced a classified document (dominated by the views of Wolfowitz) in 1992 calling for permanent US dominance of Eurasia and the systematic undermining of potential 'rivals' in the region while targeting any countries with 'weapons of mass destruction'. I can't think where I've heard that before. The document included strategies to control Western Europe, countries of the former Soviet Union, Asia and ... here we go ... targeting *Afghanistan and Iraq*. This was 1992 when Cheney was Father Bush Defense Secretary and his dream would be realised nine years later as Boy Bush vice president – thanks to *9/11*. In 1997, the same year that Brzezinski's book was published, came the creation of The Project for the New American Century (PNAC). This crucially-important 'think tank' in the story of 9/11 was co-founded by the ultra-Zionist and Israel-focussed Robert Kagan and William Kristol and demanded everything

that Cheney, Wolfowitz, Brzezinski and Netanyahu had earlier
promoted. A 'think tank' is defined as 'a body of experts providing
advice and ideas on specific political or economic problems'. The PNAC
was not so much a think tank as an ultra-Zionist tank. Watch the think
tank organisations because they are a widely used Hidden Hand means
of publicly formulating and securing its policy goals. Robert Kagan is
Think-Tank-Man and so are many of the others who imposed the long-
planned war on terror. Kagan has been connected to a long list of
Hidden Hand front organisations including the public policy think tank,
the Brookings Institution; the Rockefeller-Rothschild Council on Foreign
Relations (CFR) which has driven much of US foreign policy since it was
established in 1921; the Carnegie Endowment for International Peace
which was exposed by a congressional committee to be manipulating
war; the Foreign Affairs Policy Board and many others. Founding
members of the Council on Foreign Relations included ultra-Zionist
Colonel Mandel House, President Woodrow Wilson's 'alter-ego' when
America entered the First World War, and people like elite bankers Paul
Warburg (ultra-Zionist), Otto Kahn (ultra-Zionist), Rothschild front man
Jacob Schiff (ultra-Zionist), J.P. Morgan and John D. Rockefeller who had
conspired together to manipulate the creation of the Federal Reserve, the
privately-owned 'US Central Bank' which has controlled, with others,
the American economy ever since. The agenda of these people can be
seen in the comment by James Warburg, son of CFR and Federal Reserve
founder Paul Warburg, to a Senate Foreign Relations Committee hearing
in 1950: 'We shall have world government whether or not you like it – by
conquest or consent.'

Ultra-Zionist Robert Kagan's Foreign Affairs Policy Board was
established by Barack Obama Secretary of State Hillary Clinton 'to
provide independent advice and opinion to the Secretary of State, the
Deputy Secretary of State, and the Director of Policy Planning on
matters concerning U.S. foreign policy'. You will see the common theme
of controlling 'foreign policy'. The same applies to ultra-Zionist William
Kristol, founder and editor-at-large of the political magazine *The Weekly
Standard*, and a 'political commentator' who appears regularly on TV
cable news shows. Kristol is also a member of many Hidden Hand think
tanks which are nothing more than vehicles to drive and influence
government policy in pursuit of a clear agenda that is not good for the
peace, justice and stability of human society. 'Foreign policy' to Kristol,
as with his cohort Kagan, is really code for 'whatever is best for Israel'
and the ultra-Zionist agenda. Both have been connected to a staggering
network of organisations before and across 9/11 which have
campaigned for invading countries in the Middle East in the 'war on
terror' that the ultra-Zionist Israeli hierarchy had so long desired. This
network includes, but is far from limited to: The Project for the New

American Century (PNAC), American Enterprise Institute, Council on Foreign Relations; Middle East Media Research Institute; Hudson Institute; Heritage Foundation; Washington Institute for Near East Policy; Middle East Forum; and a long list of openly Zionist organisations including the Jewish Institute for National Security Affairs (JINSA) and Center for Security Policy (CSP). There are so many others where they came from. Some change their names from time to time and appear in new guises. The Project for the New American Century disbanded in 2006 and was replaced by the Kristol-Kagan Foreign Policy Initiative which itself dissolved in 2017. No matter what the name and background the goal for Kagan and Kristol is always the same – service to the interests of Israel and ultra-Zionism. The Project for the New American Century (PNAC) was absolutely vital to the 9/11 story and the war on terror during its functioning years between 1997 and 2006. Among the members was a long list of key players involved with September 11th who became known as 'Neocons' or neoconservatives. These are only some of them and the positions they would hold in the incoming Boy Bush administration that took office in January, 2001, just nine months before 9/11. You might recognise some of them:

Dick Cheney– Vice President and de-facto President to Boy Bush and seriously involved in the events of 9/11. Reported to be responsible for securing government roles for fellow psychopaths and PNAC members (oops, I repeat myself) Donald Rumsfeld, Paul Wolfowitz, John Bolton and Elliot Abrams; **Donald Rumsfeld** (Le Cercle), 9/11 Secretary of Defense who lied about what he was doing that morning; **Paul Wolfowitz** (Le Cercle), Deputy Secretary of Defense and the real power behind Rumsfeld; **Douglas Feith**, 9/11 Under Secretary of Defense for Policy; **Dov S. Zakheim**, 9/11 Pentagon comptroller in charge of the entire military budget including the trillions that were announced to be missing on September 10th, 2001; **Richard Armitage** (Le Cercle), a brutal man who ran drugs for the CIA in South-East Asia and was 9/11 Deputy Secretary of State under Colin Powell; **Elliot Abrams**, served in foreign policy roles in the Reagan-Bush years in which he was involved in the Iran-Contra affair and genocidal US operations in Central America. He was 'Special Assistant' to Boy Bush on foreign policy – 'invade Afghanistan and Iraq, Mr President' – and appointed by Donald Trump to oversee the US-instigated attempted coup in Venezuela in 2019. Abrams proves that career longevity is secured if you are a clinically insane, psychopathic genocidal incarnation of evil; **Richard N. Perle** (Le Cercle), Pentagon Policy Advisor during the Boy Bush presidency and major manipulator of people and events. Extremely close to Israel's Benjamin Netanyahu; **John Bolton** (Le Cercle), 9/11 Under Secretary of State for Arms Control and International Security who went on to be

Ambassador to the UN to press for ultra-Zionist Neocon wars; **Lewis Libby,** 9/11 Chief of Staff to Cheney and close to Wolfowitz; **Jeb Bush**, brother of Boy Bush and Governor of Florida while the alleged 'hijackers' were living in his state; **James Woolsey,** member of the 9/11 Pentagon Defense Policy Board and Director of the CIA in the Bill Clinton administration. Nasty man, but then they all are, and a major promotor of post-9/11 war against Saddam Hussein and Iraq; **Robert B. Zoellick**, Boy Bush Trade Representative and Cabinet member who later replaced Wolfowitz as Head of the World Bank (they get everywhere these people); **Frank Carlucci**, chairman of the Bush-Bin Laden Carlyle Group, Secretary of Defense under Reagan-Bush and Deputy Director of the CIA. **William J. Bennett**, Secretary of Education under Reagan and Director of the Office of National Drug Control Policy under Father Bush. What a non-job that must have been. Bennett was also one of Cathy O'Brien's mind control abusers.

Another significant member of the Project for the New American Century was Afghan-born US 'diplomat' Zalmay Khalilzad who would go on to be US Ambassador to Afghanistan and Special Presidential Envoy to Afghanistan after the invasion. He would also be appointed Special Presidential Envoy to the Free Iraqis when Bush-Blair-fronted terrorism turned its attention to removing Saddam Hussein. Khalilzad had also written in the 1990s in ways that echoed both Cheney and Brzezinski designs on Eurasia and the fact that a way to win over public support would have to be found if that was going to happen. Khalilzad was a close associate of Brzezinski and worked with him in support of the Mujahideen in Afghanistan after the Brzezinski-manipulated Soviet invasion in the 1980s. He was also sponsored by the Hidden Hand's Council on Foreign Relations. You can see that membership of the Project for the New American Century covered every base in advancing the long-planned agenda of exploiting the upcoming 9/11 for wars of acquisition and regime change in pursuit of Eurasia domination and much else. The PNAC membership was much bigger than I have mentioned here and covered many other roles in the political-military hierarchy before and after 9/11. Quite simply the PNAC would control the incoming Bush government after January, 2001. Members included a stream of ultra-Zionists with allegiance to Israel and people like Cheney and Rumsfeld who were vehement supporters of Israel and its cause and ambitions. Their work is supported to this day by 'journalists' like ultra-Zionist Max Boot, the warmonger columnist for *The Washington Post* and many other outlets. Every time he taps the keys Neocon policy appears on the screen.

JINSA pincer

Cheney was on the advisory board of the Jewish Institute for National Security Affairs (JINSA) along with other PNAC stalwarts Paul Wolfowitz, Douglas Feith, John Bolton and Richard Perle. This organisation was a major player with its highly-placed Jewish and non-Jewish members committed to the ultra-Zionist action plan. JINSA's demands included: Increased counterterrorism training and funding (this was before 9/11); joint American-Israeli training and weapons programmes; 'enhanced weapons of mass destruction (WMD) counter-proliferation programs' (but don't you dare mention Israel's nuclear arsenal); and regime change in what it called 'rogue nations' providing 'support for terrorism'. Some of those named before 9/11 were Iran, Syria, Lebanon, Venezuela, Cuba, North Korea, and Libya. JINSA, an ultra-Zionist group lobbying for the Israeli elite, enjoyed close ties with the Pentagon and US military and through JINSA members Paul Wolfowitz (PNAC, Le Cercle), Douglas Feith (PNAC) and Richard Perle (PNAC, Le Cercle) would dictate Pentagon policy before 9/11 and beyond. JINSA established a programme in coordination with the Pentagon and State Department which has led to more than 200 retired US military chiefs, admirals and generals, making visits to Israel to meet with Israeli military leaders and politicians. There is also a JINSA Military Academies Program in Israel for cadets and midshipmen at US Military, Naval, Air Force and Coast Guard Academies to 'build bridges for future associations between the US Armed Forces and the Israel Defense Forces (IDF)'. These 'US' (proxy Israel) military leaders of the future visit six IDF bases, meet with Israeli academia, think tanks, and private companies 'to receive briefings covering a broad spectrum of subjects related to security, society, and contemporary life in Israel [and] ... learn about Israel's history and current events in the Middle East'. The game is so utterly clear – indoctrination for the future benefit of Israel. JINSA emphasised before 9/11 the need for greater 'homeland security' in the United States (JINSA is an *Israeli* organisation) and in 2002 after Boy Bush established the Orwellian Homeland Security structure justified by 9/11 JINSA began a programme to exchange counter-terrorism experience and tactics between US and Israeli law enforcement agencies. They were just trying to help, you understand. US police leaders and sheriffs from all across America have been to Israel for 'training' under this JINSA programme and the result has been 'significant changes in local law enforcement counter-terrorism tactics and training' which is Orwellian-speak for transferring the tactics used by Israel against Palestinians to the streets of American cities. People have no idea of the influence these ultra-Zionist fronts have on American society and in other countries, too.

One of those retired military chiefs taken to Israel under the JINSA programme was Lieutenant General Jay Garner who would be made Director of the Office for Reconstruction and Humanitarian Assistance for Iraq after the 2003 invasion which was long planned by this appalling crowd. Garner would be replaced by Le Cercle member Paul Bremer, a gofer to ultra-Zionist Henry Kissinger and managing director of the disgusting global manipulation front Kissinger Associates. Bremer would be named head of the Coalition Provisional Authority (CPA) to govern Iraq after the invasion. Billions in US 'reconstruction' money would disappear on his watch. JINSA and the Project for the New American Century were different expressions of the same organisational structure and one of their common themes was the late US senator and Le Cercle member, Henry Jackson. Every year JINSA hands out its Henry M. 'Scoop' Jackson Distinguished Service Award (distinguished service to ultra-Zionism). Israel agents in government like US senators John McCain and Lindsey Graham have been recipients for supporting the bombing of every country on the ultra-Zionist hit-list and Paul Wolfowitz had his turn, too. Many future 9/11 Neocons, including Wolfowitz and Perle, were aides to Henry Jackson who died in 1983. So, too, was ultra-Zionist Brooklyn-born Manny Weiss who is a 'generous funder' of the British wing of the Neocon think-tank network, the fiercely pro-Israel Henry Jackson Society. This, as you would expect, works to advance the ultra-Zionist agenda as does Jewish Human Rights Watch established by Weiss in the UK. The Henry Jackson Society agenda includes the demonisation of Russia in preparation for war.

The Blueprint

The ultra-Zionist Project for the New American Century (PNAC) (peopled by utter crazies) published a 90-page document in September, 2000, called *Rebuilding America's Defenses: Strategies, Forces, and Resources For a New Century* and described the blueprint for 9/11 and its aftermath (Fig 90). They didn't say that directly – though they came close –and it was pitched from a good-for-America perspective. It included the sequence of events that was about to play out through 9/11 long demanded by ultra-Zionism and the Death Cult. The document detailed a plan for American forces

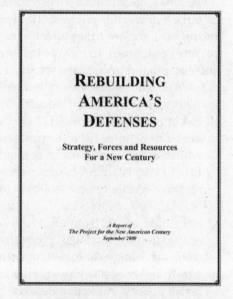

REBUILDING AMERICA'S DEFENSES

Strategy, Forces and Resources
For a New Century

A Report of
The Project for the New American Century
September 2000

Figure 90: The Project for the New American Century document a year to the month before 9/11 demanding all that has happened since the attacks and because of the attacks.

to impose a series of regime changes in the Middle East and North Africa all for the benefit of the Israeli elite and to advance their agenda for the region. The PNAC document called for America-instigated regime change in Iraq, Libya, Syria, Iran and Lebanon among others. The strategy basically photo-copied a policy document compiled in 1996 by PNAC/JINSA/Le Cercle asset Richard Perle and other ultra-Zionists for the psychopath Prime Minister of Israel, Benjamin Netanyahu. They were officially known as the Study Group on 'A New Israeli Strategy Toward 2000' and this 'strategy' was remarkably close to the later PNAC plan for an 'American' strategy for post-2000 or the 'new American century'. Netanyahu's 'Study Group' produced a report for Netanyahu entitled *A Clean Break: A New Strategy for Securing the Realm* and the ultra-Zionist members were: Richard Perle, who would be 9/11 Chairman of Defense Policy Board under Boy Bush; James Colbert, Jewish Institute for National Security Affairs (JINSA), former assistant and college friend of Wolfowitz; Charles Fairbanks Jr, Johns Hopkins University and former assistant to Wolfowitz; Douglas Feith, who would become 9/11 Pentagon Undersecretary of Defense for Policy; Robert Loewenberg, President of the Institute for Advanced Strategic and Political Studies; Jonathan Torop, Washington Institute for Near East Policy; David Wurmser, Institute for Advanced Strategic and Political Studies who would be Middle East advisor to Vice President Cheney; and Meyrav Wurmser from Johns Hopkins University. David Wurmser published a book in 1999 on why Saddam must be removed as leader of Iraq and why that would be good for Israel. What an incredible coincidence that when his ultra-Zionist pals came to power with Bush his wish was granted (Fig 91 overleaf). The Perle group document, *A Clean Break: A New Strategy for Securing the Realm*, also demanded the removal of Saddam Hussein in Iraq and targeting of the Assad government in Syria. The document said:

> Israel can shape its strategic environment, in cooperation with Turkey and Jordan, by weakening, containing, and even rolling back Syria. This effort can focus on removing Saddam Hussein from power in Iraq – an important Israeli strategic objective in its own right – as a means of foiling Syria's regional ambitions ...

> ... Most important, it is understandable that Israel has an interest supporting diplomatically, militarily and operationally Turkey's and Jordan's actions against Syria, such as securing tribal alliances with Arab tribes that cross into Syrian territory and are hostile to the Syrian ruling elite.

Plans for the downfall of Saddam Hussein and targeting the Assad government in Syria with internal conflict were already in place then in

Figure 91: Project for the New American Century co-founders Kagan and Kristol with de-facto 9/11 President Dick Cheney and those who dominated the 9/11 Pentagon – Rumsfeld, Wolfowitz, Zakheim and Perle.

1996 and in truth long before. What remained was to secure American military, political and financial power to bring all this about for Israel's benefit. These various ultra-Zionist plans that all read from the same script were also connected with another ultra-Zionist goal for the Balkanisation (as with the former Yugoslavia) of the surrounding region by dividing countries into smaller ethnic factions on the road to a new Middle East that would impose Israeli control and the dream of a Greater Israel from the River Nile in Egypt to the River Euphrates in Iraq. This area is known as the Eretz Yisrael and ultra-Zionists claim this to be the largest expanse of biblical Israel (Fig 92). This 'Greater Israel' includes all or part of what are now Egypt, Syria, Lebanon, Jordan, Iraq and Saudi Arabia. Theodore Herzl, officially Zionism's 'founding father' (it was really the House of Rothschild) said the area of the Jewish State stretches ... 'From the Brook of Egypt to the Euphrates'. The Greater Israel plan would give them control of their true spiritual home – Babylon in what is now Iraq. Rabbi Fischmann, a member of the Jewish Agency for Palestine, said in testimony to the UN Special Committee of Enquiry in 1947: 'The Promised Land extends from the River of Egypt up to the Euphrates, it includes parts of Syria and Lebanon.' The goal to secure all this land for Israel was described in what became known as the Yinon Plan. Oded Yinon, who formerly worked for the Israeli Foreign Ministry, set out the ultra-Zionist vision in 1982 when he published *A Strategy for Israel in the 1980s* in which he called for the fragmenting of Arab countries into a mosaic of ethnic groupings – it would be good for Israel to have 'every kind of inter-Arab confrontation'. Look at what has happened since 9/11 from this perspective and you can see how this has been systematically happening ever since in 'peoples' uprisings' and inter-country wars.

We have lift-off

To implement the vision in the Yinon Plan, *A Clean Break* and all the other plans, reports and strategies plotting the same outcome, the ultra-Zionist networks had to sell their Middle East regime change strategy to

Figure 92: The approximate area of control demanded by the Greater Israel Project – and they don't want to stop even there.

Americans as if it was for the benefit of America. To this end the Project for the American Century was established and its strategy document in September, 2000, presented essentially the same Yinon-*Clean Break* plan from the angle of good-for-America-and-whatever-you-do-don't-mention-Israel. The PNAC *Rebuilding America's Defenses: Strategies, Forces, and Resources For a New Century* was written by the same networks that produced *Clean Break* for Netanyahu and were the inspiration of the Yinon Plan. The PNAC document came with an added bonus, however. Those who wrote it were little more than three months away from taking over the American government and military when the hapless and clueless Boy Bush entered the White House in January, 2001, in the run up to 9/11. Content of the PNAC document leaves no doubt about what the game was. The paper called for 'American forces to fight and decisively win multiple, simultaneous major theater wars' to 'regime change' a series of countries: Iraq, Libya, Syria, Lebanon, Iran, Somalia, Sudan and North Korea leading to regime change in China – 'American and allied power [should provide] the spur to the process of democratisation in China.' This agenda is far bigger than only the Middle East – it's a plan for global control. The Project for the New American Century blueprint in September, 2000, demanded the following for Israel under the guise of 'America':

- US military control of the Gulf region whether or not Saddam Hussein was in power: 'While the unresolved conflict with Iraq provides the immediate justification, the need for a substantial American force presence in the Gulf transcends the issue of the regime of Saddam Hussein.'

[Since achieved]

- The US to 'fight and decisively win multiple, simultaneous major theatre wars' as a 'core mission'.

[Partly achieved and still going on]

- US forces to be 'the cavalry on the new American frontier'.

[US forces to be 'the cavalry on the new *ultra-Zionist Israel* frontier']

- Action to discourage advanced industrial nations from challenging US leadership [ultra-Zionist leadership via the US] or aspiring to a larger regional or global role.

[A strategy clearly being followed by the US – not least with Israel-controlled Trump's explosion of sanctions]

- Exploitation of allies like the UK as 'the most effective and efficient means of exercising American global leadership'.

[Easily achieved – see Tony Blair]

- Ensuring that 'peacekeeping' missions have 'American political leadership, rather than that of the United Nations'.

[Partly achieved but challenged by Russia in Syria]

- Permanent US bases in Saudi Arabia and Kuwait.

[Since achieved]

- Increased military pressure on China: 'It is time to increase the presence of American forces in South East Asia', which will lead to 'American and allied power providing the spur to the process of democratisation in China'.

[Targeting of China is clearly happening as I long predicted]

- The 'creation of "US Space Forces" to dominate space, and the total control of cyberspace to prevent "enemies" [opponents of the ultra-Zionist agenda] using the Internet against the US [proxy for the Hidden Hand and Israel]'.

[Happening big-time]

- Development of new methods of attack – electronic, 'non-lethal' and biological. These would be more widely available and 'combat is likely to take place in new dimensions, in space, cyberspace and perhaps the world of microbes ... advanced forms of biological warfare that can 'target' *specific genotypes* may transform biological warfare from the realm of terror to a politically useful tool' [my emphasis].

[Happening – and can you imagine the level of psychopathy required to envision 'advanced forms of biological warfare that can "target" *specific genotypes*' or the level of hypocrisy when you scream 'Nazi' and 'Hitler' to silence your critics?]

- The development of a 'worldwide command-and-control system' [world army] to contain the 'dangerous' regimes of North Korea, Libya, Syria and Iran.

[Happening]

- This 'American grand strategy' to be advanced 'as far into the future as possible'.

[It's still happening with no end in sight]

I don't for a moment want you to concern yourself with any of this – just ignore it. Remember there are no conspiracies let alone global ones. Ask the media.

'We need a 9/11'

The Yinon Plan, *A Clean Break* and *Rebuilding America's Defenses* were essentially the same vision under different names and now the ultra-Zionists had their chance to enforce it. Soon after the PNAC document was published in September, 2000, the people who wrote it or signed it came to power with Bush in the White House and Pentagon – Cheney, Rumsfeld and the ultra-Zionist cabal that dominated the Pentagon in the form of Wolfowitz, Feith, Zakheim, Perle and many others. Richard Perle, known as the Prince of Darkness, would work mostly in the background in terms of public profile while Robert Kagan and especially William Kristol would sell the strategy on cable TV news. There was still one problem, however – the problem recognised earlier by Cheney, Brzezinski and others. Somehow they needed something to kick-start the sequence that would give them widespread political and public support for their grotesque ambitions. The PNAC document said:

> ... [The] process of transformation ... [war and regime change] ... is likely to
> be a long one, absent some catastrophic and catalysing event – like a new
> Pearl Harbor.

A year to the month after the publication of that PNAC document
and nine months after those behind it came to power with Bush the
United States experienced what Bush called 'the Pearl Harbor of the 21st
century'. What happened on September 11th, 2001, was their
'catastrophic and catalysing event'. The road to Damascus – and Kabul,
Baghdad, Tripoli, Tehran etc. – suddenly opened up before them and if
anyone thinks that all this was a coincidence they should read the rest of
the book or become fully-paid-up members of Naivety Anonymous. The
Project for the New American Century and its connecting networks like
JINSA had their agents and operatives in key positions right across the
Boy Bush administration and the Pentagon on 9/11 and immediately
after the attacks they and the network as a whole sang from the same
pre-written song-sheet – *invade Afghanistan*. This invasion was to be the
prelude to picking off their long-planned wish-list of targeted countries.
Ehud Barak, former Israeli prime minister and military intelligence
chief, must have been so pleased and even contemplated his own
powers of prophecy by highlighting Bin Laden and the need to invade
Afghanistan within an hour of the 9/11 attacks. Now *bingo*, here it was
happening. A controlled, compliant and overwhelmingly clueless
mainstream media cheered them on and became the propaganda arm of
the Hidden Hand and ultra-Zionist agenda for carnage in the Near and
Middle East planned long before. American lives and money (and
British) were going to pay for what would soon be happening to country
after country. Most of all the price of ultra-Zionist ambitions would be
paid by millions of civilians who now faced death and destruction as an
ongoing way of life – or not.

Clark's confirmation

US General Wesley Clark is no hero after his role in the bombing of
Serbia during the Kosovo conflict when he was Supreme Allied
Commander of NATO. However, we are grateful to him at least for
further confirmation of the PNAC plan. You will find on YouTube
Clarke's interview in 2007 with the *Democracy Now* TV show in which he
says that about ten days after 9/11 he went to the Pentagon to meet with
PNAC Secretary of Defense Donald Rumsfeld and his PNAC deputy
Paul Wolfowitz and then went downstairs to see members of the
Pentagon Joint Chiefs of Staff that he once worked with. Clark said:

... one of the generals called me in. He said, 'Sir, you've got to come in and talk to me a second.' I said, 'Well, you're too busy.' He said, 'No, no.' He says, 'We've made the decision we're going to war with Iraq.' This was on or about the 20th of September. I said, 'We're going to war with Iraq? Why?' He said, 'I don't know.' He said, 'I guess they don't know what else to do.'

So I said, 'Well, did they find some information connecting Saddam to al-Qaeda?' He said, 'No, no.' He says, 'There's nothing new that way. They just made the decision to go to war with Iraq.' He said, 'I guess it's like we don't know what to do about terrorists, but we've got a good military and we can take down governments.' And he said, 'I guess if the only tool you have is a hammer, every problem has to look like a nail.

This is how Hidden Hand compartmentalisation works. Even many apparently very high in the official government and military hierarchy have no idea what is really happening and how they are pawns in a game they don't even begin to understand. The invasion of Iraq with American troops and money had been planned for decades by the Hidden Hand's ultra-Zionist network as we have seen. Wesley Clark said that he returned to the Pentagon a few weeks after 9/11 and his meeting with the general who told him about the plan to invade Iraq. By now the US was already in Afghanistan and he went back to see his friend again. Clark recalled:

I said, 'Are we still going to war with Iraq?' And he said, 'Oh, it's worse than that.' He reached over on his desk. He picked up a piece of paper. And he said, 'I just got this down from upstairs' – meaning the Secretary of Defense's office – 'today.' And he said, 'This is a memo that describes how we're going to take out seven countries in five years, starting with Iraq, and then Syria, Lebanon, Libya, Somalia, Sudan and, finishing off, Iran.' I said, 'Is it classified?' He said, 'Yes, sir.' I said, 'Well, don't show it to me.'

And I saw him a year or so ago, and I said, 'You remember that?' He said, 'Sir, I didn't show you that memo! I didn't show it to you.

Clark added that the Project for the New American Century (PNAC) behind these planned wars 'wanted us to destabilise the Middle East, turn it upside down, make it under our control'. He didn't say, however, that the PNAC was controlled by ultra-Zionists on behalf of Israel because people are utterly terrified of revealing that. The lies and cover ups are so clear once you lift the stone under which these people operate. All the death and destruction since 9/11 was planned for decades and the attacks that killed 3,000 people (and many more since) were only the cold, callous and calculated trigger and excuse instigated by the satanic Death Cult. This is why on 9/11 Netanyahu said the attacks were 'very good' for Israel. *The New York Times* reported:

> Asked tonight what the attack meant for relations between the United States and Israel, Benjamin Netanyahu, the former prime minister, replied, 'It's very good.' Then he edited himself: 'Well, not very good, but it will generate immediate sympathy.' He predicted that the attack would 'strengthen the bond between our two peoples, because we've experienced terror over so many decades, but the United States has now experienced a massive hemorrhaging of terror.'

Out of the mouths of babes and psychopaths

Hardly a word was said to the media or public about the plan to invade Iraq and the liars that are Bush and Blair were still saying right up to the invasion in 2003 that it could still be stopped if Saddam would comply with Western demands by removing weapons of mass destruction which by then he didn't actually have. Manipulation that led to Saddam's demise began way back and ultra-Zionists of the Project for the New American Century had written to President Clinton in January, 1998, to call for Saddam's removal:

> We urge you to seize that opportunity, and to enunciate a new strategy that would secure the interests of the U.S. and our friends and allies around the world. That strategy should aim, above all, at the removal of Saddam Hussein's regime from power. We stand ready to offer our full support in this difficult but necessary endeavor.

They even gave Clinton the excuse that Boy Bush and Blair would later employ – Saddam has 'weapons of mass destruction'. The letter was signed by among others Kristol, Kagan, Perle, Wolfowitz, Zoellick, Abrams, Bolton, Woolsey and Zalmay Khalilzad who would later be installed during the 'war on terror' as ambassador to Afghanistan, Iraq and the United Nations. Donald Trump made him a special envoy to Afghanistan for the one-party state in 2018. Out-of-the-loop military personnel at the Pentagon had to be told about the Iraq invasion immediately after 9/11 because there were plans to put in place. You don't prepare major invasions overnight which is why the speed with which the US invaded Afghanistan is confirmation that the plans were in the making long before the 9/11 attacks. Iraq was first on the list for regime change by the ultra-Zionist PNAC and Perle's earlier *Clean Break* document for Netanyahu. Both were answering to hidden powers that were orchestrating the whole sequence that would follow. You can see where conflicts and invasions are planned by watching the drip, drip of demonisation aimed at a leader or 'regime'. It wasn't difficult to demonise a dictator like Saddam and yet they exaggerated anyway with claims that his weapons were a threat to the 'Free World'. Confirmation that psychopaths have no shame arrived in the form of Defense Secretary Donald Rumsfeld who screamed about 'Saddam's chemical weapons' when Rumsfeld had been the conduit to supply them as I explained earlier. The late and very great American comedian Bill Hicks with his incisive humour once asked: 'How did the Americans know Iraq had incredible weapons?' Answer: 'They looked at the receipts.' No one was mentioning Iraq publicly or officially until 2002 when the demonisation and fear campaign began against Saddam and Iraq which led to the invasion in March, 2003. By now Saddam's chemical and biological weapons had been removed and the United States and Britain knew that. Little details like the truth were never going to be acknowledged when it would have scuppered the manufactured excuse for war. Instead psychopaths and ultra-Zionist puppets Bush and Blair just repeated the mantra which included the bare-faced lie that 'should Iraq acquire fissile material, it would be able to build a nuclear weapon within a year'. It was all a scam. The deal had long been done. *The New York Times* was one of the few that reported soon after 9/11 what was being hatched with regard to Iraq:

> A tight-knit group of Pentagon officials and defense experts outside government is working to mobilize support for a military operation to oust President Saddam Hussein of Iraq as the next phase of the war against terrorism, senior administration officials and defense experts said.

> Under this notion, American troops would also seize the oil fields around Basra, in south-eastern Iraq, and sell the oil to finance the Iraqi opposition in the south and the Kurds in the north, one senior official said.

The report described how the Pentagon's Defense Policy Board (Kissinger, Perle, Woolsey etc.) had met for 19 hours on September 19th and 20th, 2001, and, agreed (confirmed the long-time plan) to invade Iraq as soon as possible. Given all this background what can you say about the claim by London *Guardian* 'radical journalist' George Monbiot that 9/11 'conspiracy theories' were a 'distraction' from opposing the invasion of Iraq? I could cry, but I'll smile and move on. Wolfowitz and Rumsfeld had taken part in the Defense Policy Board meeting while Colin Powell at the State Department was excluded because he didn't support the invasion. Even so he later allowed himself to be used as a fall-guy with his comedic 'presentation' at the United Nations claiming to have proof of Saddam's world-threatening weapons capability (which turned out to be the nonsense it always clearly was). Powell should have walked away and maintained his integrity but instead he did what he

,

was told knowing that his 'evidence' was not credible. He would call the speech the most painful moment of his life. Powell was surrounded by the ultra-Zionist and JINSA Mafia and they had him for breakfast, dinner and tea. He has said that the invasion of Iraq in 2003 was made possible by Defense Secretary Rumsfeld's absorption in the 'JINSA crowd'. Powell's wife, Alma, would say in *Soldier: The Life of Colin Powell* that he was 'callously used' to promote a war she wished had never happened. She told author and *Washington Post* editor, Karen DeYoung: 'They needed him to do it because they knew people would believe him.' There are many stories about Powell being kept out of the loop by Cheney and these ultra-Zionist characters and they exploited his reputation with the 'weapons of mass destruction' presentation at the United Nations which was to make him look an idiot when none were found. Tony Blair, Alastair Campbell, his appalling 'spin doctor' (code for professional liar), and the Hidden Hand-front MI6 concocted a 'dossier' of evidence so full of lies it could have secured them a place on the 9/11 Commission. Much of the 'dossier' against Saddam was later revealed to have been simply cut and pasted from the Internet and even then it was out of date and further distorted to sell the war that wouldn't be stopped. Parts of this plagiarised crap were delivered by Powell at the UN. London's *Evening Standard* reported Blair's claims to the British parliament in September, 2002:

> Saddam Hussein's armoury of chemical weapons is on standby for use within 45 minutes, Tony Blair's dossier revealed today. The Iraqi leader has 20 missiles which could reach British military bases in Cyprus, as well as Israel and NATO members Greece and Turkey. He has also been seeking to buy uranium from Africa for use in nuclear weapons. Those are the key charges in a 14-point 'dossier of death' finally published by the Government today. In an introduction, Mr Blair says that the evidence leaves Britain and the international community no choice but to act.

Compliant, complicit and idiot fodder politicians both sides of the Atlantic lapped it all up with barely a question even though none of this was true and Blair knew that. He, Boy Bush and Cheney should have been before a war crimes court a long time ago with the later Barack Obama, British Prime Minister David Cameron, and so many more. Hidden Hand networks protect them as they always protect their agents and yes-people if their exposure would uncover the bigger picture. The propaganda had been so effective and so many Americans child-like in their trust of government that by the time of the invasion in March, 2003, some 70 percent of Americans polled believed that Saddam had been involved in 9/11 when he had absolutely nothing to do with it and no credible evidence was ever produced to make a connection. It doesn't matter what is true – only what you can get the public to *believe* is true.

Ticking off the list

Ultra-Zionists and the Death Cult got their long-planned invasion of Iraq and the deletion of Saddam and unleashed a catastrophic series of ongoing conflicts in line with the Yinon Plan, *Clean Break* and Project for the New American Century documents. The second phase of the assault on Iraq came with the invasion by the US/Israel/UK proxy army ISIS which was funded and armed through Saudi Arabia, Gulf States and Turkey. ISIS was also planned to overrun Syria after the US/UK/Israel-triggered 'civil war' that began in 2011. They would have done, too, before Russia came in with military support for President Assad. America used the excuse of its proxy army ISIS to 'free' cities like Mosul in Iraq and Raqqa in Syria from ISIS control (P-R-S). They basically razed Mosul to the ground in 2016/17 leaving an estimated 40,000 civilians dead with thousands more bodies buried in the rubble. Something similar happened in Syria's Raqqa. We are dealing with a death cult in which death is worshipped and mass murder is a form of satanic blood sacrifice ritual. This is how these deeply disturbed people look at the world. All this carnage – including the removal of Gaddafi in Libya and the targeting of Iran – has been the Death Cult ticking off the list of target countries published by the Project for the New American Century. The joke is that we are supposed to live in 'democracies' in which the people select the political leaders. This is only for public consumption. Illusion of freedom protects the tyranny. The nature of the one-party state can be seen in what followed the ultra-Zionist strategy document of September, 2000, and the 9/11 attacks that triggered and publicly justified its sequence of events. First Boy Bush ('Republican') and Tony Blair ('Labour Party') sent the military into Afghanistan and lied about weapons of mass destruction to sell the invasion of Iraq. Two ultra-Zionist targets were ticked off and Iraq was the first named in the PNAC document. Bush and Blair left the scene – Bush to learn to read and Blair to represent his beloved Israel as Middle East envoy for the United Nations, EU, US and Russia. This basically meant meeting with Israeli leaders to get his orders. With those two psychopaths gone and with all the political choice we are told is available surely things would change. In came Barack Obama ('Democrat') and Britain's David Cameron ('Conservative Party'). These had to be different because they represented opposition parties to Bush and Blair. Alas, no, Obama and Cameron promoted and supported the NATO mass murder and mob violence that removed and murdered Gaddafi in Libya and created the catastrophe that the country is to this day. They supported 'rebel' terrorists in Syria in an attempt to unseat Assad and instigated still more death, destruction and suffering on an unimaginable scale. I have documented at length in other books how the same ultra-Zionist and American/British networks at work in Iraq were behind what happened in Libya and Syria. Obama and Cameron were different to Bush and Blair, you see. Phew, to think they might have been the same. The next front man for the one-party state was the 'truly maverick' Donald Trump ('Republican'). He strode on the scene to drain the swamp he'd been swimming in all his life and 'make America great again'. He set out to do this by surrounding himself with Israel-focussed ultra-Zionists to control his financial and foreign policy and appointed the psychopath's psychopath John Bolton as his National Security Advisor. Bolton was a founding member of the Project for New American Century and the long planned list of targets continued with the focus on Iran, North Korea and China as well as the hysteria about Russia.

Netanyahu, the ultra-Zionists and Death Cult didn't want a peaceful agreement between the West and Iran because it's on their list for regime change. He and his fellow crazies are obsessed with regime-change in Iran and Netanyahu was caught on video aired by Israeli television telling activists from his extremist terrorist-created Likud Party that he had convinced Trump to withdraw from the nuclear agreement with Iran which threw US-Iran relations into turmoil again when the deal had settled everything down. Iran has not started a war against another country for more than 200 years and Netanyahu screams that in the Middle East 'those who are trying to kill us are being led by Iran, which openly and aggressively calls for the destruction of Israel.' I am no supporter of the Iranian regime, but nor do I take such bullshit from Netanyahu in the ultra-Zionist campaign of inventing enemies to justify wars, regime change and land acquisition – the same technique it has employed incessantly since Israel was established with US support in 1948. PNAC National Security Advisor John Bolton also led the Trump regime into pulling out of a nuclear agreement with Russia. Trump (his masters) targeted Iran and two other countries on the PNAC list – North Korea and China. Economic sanctions are the widespread weapon of choice employed by Trump against the countries his ultra-Zionist masters want regime-changed. Whenever a peaceful agreement with North Korea appears to move forward Israel-worshippers John Bolton and Trump's Christian Zionist Secretary of State Mike Pompeo intervene to block progress. The same ultra-Zionist list of countries have been ticked off and targeted one after the other no matter what the apparently different presidents in the United States and leaders and parties in Europe. Without the trigger of 9/11 none of this could have happened on the scale that it has. Watch for other countries on the list, Lebanon, Somalia and Sudan. Israel is desperately looking for an excuse to invade Lebanon after trying and failing before while Sudan and Somalia have been devastated by civil war in the period since 9/11. There are so many conflicts going on that the media doesn't tell you about including the mostly drone-strike US bombing of 'Islamic militants' in Somalia since 2007. Bombing was significantly increased at the start of 2019.

Terrified of the truth

The blatantly obvious connections between the Project for the New American Century document of September, 2000, and the 'new Pearl Harbor' of 9/11 is a potentially major Achilles heel for the ultra-Zionists and the Hidden Hand in general because it exposes a clear cause and effect. They know it, too. I was on a speaking tour of the UK in late 2018 highlighting these connections when I saw an interview on the Russian TV station RT with an MI6 operative who hilariously tried to provide a cover story for the PNAC document and what followed in the Middle East – and I do mean *hilarious*. Aimen Dean, also known 'Ramzi', is a Saudi-born Bahrainian who claims to have joined the (CIA-created) al-Qaeda, in 1997 and became an agent for British overseas military intelligence, or MI6, in 1998 to spy on al-Qaeda in Afghanistan. He joined al-Qaeda as presumably an Islamic extremist wanting a holy war against the West and within a year he's spying on Al-Qaeda for the very same West? Here is a man who lied for a living by claiming to be on the side of al-Qaeda while spying on them for MI6 which is connected to the CIA that created al-Qaeda. Dean ridiculously claimed in the RT interview that al-Qaeda had 'tricked' America into invading the Middle East. He said they had seen the letter sent by Richard Perle's Neocons to President Clinton in 1998 calling for the forced removal of Saddam Hussein and the subsequent Project for the New American Century document demanding regime changes that would require a 'new Pearl Harbor' to sell the policy to the American public. Dean said the al-Qaeda leadership decided to 'give them a Pearl Harbor ... that's exactly where we want them to be ... [the US] must smash [Iraq] in order for us to build an Islamist structure.' He said the plan was to attract 'the provocation of America as a superpower to come and do their dirty work for them.' Oh, so the PNAC document was not part of the plot to create a new Pearl Harbor. All explained ... Zzzzzzzzz. I wonder why he didn't mention the bit about the al-Qaeda leadership checking with the CIA to see if that was okay? Or the fact that 'al-Qaeda' could not possibly have been behind 9/11 as claimed by the official story. Or, or, or. Dean went on to claim, just as pathetically, that the Saudi murder of journalist Jamal Khashoggi by cutting him up with a bone saw was an accident and they had really only wanted to abduct him back to Riyadh. Oh, right, so Crown Prince Psychopath couldn't have ordered his killing then. So glad MI6 Dean cleared up those little misunderstandings and how fortunate they had a bone saw handy when everything went pear-shaped. The RT interviewer should have taken Dean apart – but didn't.

What this nonsense does show, however, is that they know the PNAC-9/11 connection makes them very vulnerable to exposure.

CHAPTER 17

The dominoes fall

If you want to know what God thinks of money, just look at the people he gave it to – Dorothy Parker

Ultra-Zionist billionaire George Soros has become a highly controversial character in recent years as the extent of his covert manipulation of national and world events has come to light. I had been exposing this devious man for decades before the scale (tip of iceberg) of his political and social influence worldwide seeped into public attention.

There will be many – not least Jewish people – who will reel back at my description of Soros as 'ultra-Zionist' because his manufactured image is that of a 'liberal' and 'progressive' philanthropist who is not a rampant Israel-firster like the Neocons. A person's image and words are irrelevant to me as an insight into who they are and what they stand for. Public image and words tell you nothing except how the person wishes to be seen and the statements they make (which may not be what they really believe). I prefer to consider actions and outcomes to understand what people are truly about and on that basis Soros is a fundamentally important cog in the ultra-Zionist Hidden Hand machine. I am appropriately writing these words on a European speaking tour in Budapest, Hungary, the city where Soros was born György Schwartz in 1930 (Fig 93). We must be constantly vigilant for bluffs and double-bluffs. Soros was born into what is described as a well-to-do non-observant Jewish family and moved to the United States via the UK before becoming an incredibly wealthy investor and financial manipulator. The Hidden Hand controls the global financial markets and what it does politically and economically dictates every day if they go up

Figure 93: The many – many – faces of George Soros

or down. Anyone with access to that information will obviously be on pole position to make financial fortunes by buying stocks before they go up and selling before they go down. Feted 'financial wizards' the world over have become billionaires this way. How did they know that stock was going to soar or plummet? My goodness, they must be financial geniuses! Or maybe they don't have to be. Part of the Soros bluff, I contend, is the image of his alleged disagreements with governments and policies of Israel. When you observe his behaviour and how he donates and directs his seemingly limitless resources he is doing everything the ultra-Zionists and Hidden Hand want him to do. One of his foundation roles is to fund so-called (and it is so-called) 'progressive' organisations and causes and he would not have street-cred in that area if he was an open supporter of ultra-Zionism. He should not have street-cred with 'progressives' anyway with his stated attitude to finance: 'I am basically there to make money, I cannot and do not look at the social consequences of what I do.' But, hey, he hands out lots of money to virtue-signalling 'progressives' so who cares if he's a fraud? 'Progressive' is a term that has been used to hijack the traditional and genuinely liberal left and invert everything that it formerly stood for.

'Anti-Semite' defence system

At the very core of this transformation of the once-liberal left into a screaming mob of virtue-signalling, heart-on-the-sleevers driving the fascism/Marxism of political correctness and free-speech deletion is Soros money. 'Liberal benefactor' Soros has usurped – indeed largely created – the 'progressive' (regressive) pseudo-left while openly ultra-Zionists like casino billionaire Sheldon Adelson has been the biggest funder of Donald Trump and the right. The equation is simple – control both sides and you control the game and so the outcome. I said before Trump came to power (or the illusion of it) that the plan was to set America at war with itself; to divide the population into clearly defined factions for a de-facto (or quite possibly literal) civil war. This has quite demonstrably happened with ultra-Zionist Adelson funding one side and 'Israel sceptic' Soros funding the other. This is, naturally, only an extraordinary coincidence akin to all those that happened with 9/11 and to say otherwise would be virulent 'anti-Semitism'. The 'you are a racist' mantra is the constant defence response whenever these matters are up for debate. You are only pointing out the provable fact that Adelson funds Trump and right and Soros funds 'progressives' and the 'left' because you are an anti-Semite. When the Cabal wouldn't benefit from debate or information circulating they trigger their 'progressive' mob and 'anti-Semitism' industry to shut it down. I will expose this industry and its breathtaking global reach in the next chapter because that is vital to appreciate the extraordinary – and ever-increasing – global censorship of ultra-Zionism and that of the Death Cult behind 9/11. Israel-worshipping British Labour MP Wes Streeting, who even calls Jews racists when they challenge the behaviour of Israel, demanded the sacking of philosopher Sir Roger Scruton as chair of a government housing commission when it emerged that he had described Jews in Budapest as forming part of a 'Soros empire'. Scruton said that 'many of the Budapest intelligentsia are Jewish, and form part of the extensive networks around the Soros empire'. Streeting, a vice-chair of the All-Party Parliamentary Group on Antisemitism, accused Scruton of propagating 'anti-Semitic conspiracy theories' which is straight from the ultra-Zionist censorship manual. Whether what is said is true or not is irrelevant. If it mentions someone who is Jewish this is by reflex action 'anti-Semitic'. I don't care if Soros is Jewish or Chinese – I care about what he does and the affect this has worldwide on people and their freedom. A member of Leave.eu, the anti-EU organisation, tweeted an image of Soros with the words of Conservative MP Maria Caulfield: 'Not sure there is even democracy in this country anymore ... The powerful elite seem to know best and openly mock the rest of us.' An image of Soros was very appropriate when he was substantially funding people seeking to stop Brexit while living in the United States. 'Appalling and nakedly anti-Semitic image' came the cry with Maria Caulfield herself demanding the tweet be deleted. She said it was particularly hurtful 'as my family are Jewish'. So it's okay for Caulfield to talk about a 'powerful elite' so long as no one mentions anyone who is part of that elite who happens to be Jewish. War criminal Tony Blair, a yes-man for the same Web that attaches to Soros, has also campaigned to stop Brexit, but linking him to a 'powerful elite' is fine. Now that's what I call racism. Ultra-Zionist Democratic Congressman, the ridiculous Adam Schiff, who became Chair of the House Intelligence Committee, told CNN that 'most' of the criticism of billionaire globalist George Soros is because he's Jewish. This line is becoming so familiar as the truth about Soros emerges and it's obviously a centrally-dictated response to avoid having the chilling facts about the man and his activities made public. Soros's son, Alexander, has said that many attacks on his father over the years have been 'dripping with the poison of anti-Semitism'. Yes, mate, it is absolutely nothing to do with the way he uses his fortune to mess with people's lives across the world. It's only because he is Jewish. Okay, glad we sorted that out then, and on that basis the dripping poison of billionaires dictating the lives of the penniless poor should never be questioned again. But, actually, on reflection – fuck that.

Soros Spring

The global vehicle that Soros established for his social engineering and political shenanigans is called the Open Society Foundations (OSF) to which he has so far donated some *$32 billion*. The latest $18 billion was announced in 2017. That's a lot of bang for a lot of bucks and buys you colossal influence in all sorts of ways, subjects and places. The Open Society networks operate in *100 countries* with 26 national and regional foundations and offices. They call themselves 'NGOs' or 'non-governmental organisations'. This is the Soros vehicle to overthrow governments targeted by Israel and the United States, secure mass immigration into Europe and the United States, and fund and promote 'progressive' mobs transforming human society to herald the long-planned global dystopia I have for so very long warned was coming if we didn't snap out of an induced perceptual coma. The Soros connection to the ultra-Zionist Hidden Hand agenda can be most clearly seen in the role his Open Society networks have played in manipulating unrest in countries targeted for regime change. If the United States and its allies simply keep invading countries as with Iraq even some of the most myopic of the population might wonder what was going on. This would have certainly happened had America's ultra-Zionist proxy military openly invaded Libya and Syria as they ticked off the Project for the New American Century wish-list. To hide the pattern of conflict and its ultra-Zionist coordination they had to invent different excuses to pick off the list. For example we had Afghanistan (get Bin Laden) and Iraq (weapons of mass destruction). With Libya, Syria, Egypt and elsewhere it was 'the Arab Spring' and 'we must stop tyrants killing their own people'. The trick is to manipulate the population to remove – or demand the removal – of regimes that you want to remove. To do this you need to stimulate unrest that can be propagandised into a full-blown 'revolution' which ends with the people you don't want in government being ousted and those you do want being handed power to run the country and control the people according to your instructions. This is where Soros and his Open Society Foundations come in along with CIA fronts like the US Congress-funded National Endowment for Democracy (National Endowment for Deletion of Democracy). They are expert in preparing, funding, training and then promoting agitators to ferment civil unrest which often follows a period of severe economic sanctions by the United States and the West to create economic deprivation and fuel public frustration with the target government. People come out on the streets in phase two who believe they are taking part in a genuine 'revolution' against the government when in fact it is a Western-contrived hoax to secure regime-change without apparent direct American, British and Israeli involvement. The unrest is blazed across newspapers and television screens the world over through Hidden Hand-owned government propagandists who have the audacity to call themselves 'journalists'. They tell the population the story the Hidden Hand wants them to believe and most of these 'journalists' have no idea what they are being used for. Most of those that *do* know justify this acquiescence to themselves with: 'I have a mortgage to pay.' The few that are left are active members or assets of the Death Cult – mostly in positions of executive and editorial power.

I have described in detail in other books how Soros networks were behind the 'Arab Spring', instigated in 2010, and the 2014 American coup in Ukraine as well as a long list of other 'people's revolutions'. As I write the US Neocons are playing the same scam in Venezuela through their puppet Trump. The, in reality, '*Soros* Spring' brought devastation and new tyrants to the Middle East and North Africa while being promoted by governments and presstitutes of the media as a spontaneous demand by the people to throw off the yoke of oppression. Tyrant leaders in Egypt were replaced by an American-funded military junta that's still in power today. The 'people's revolution' in Ukraine (American coup) replaced a pro-Russia leader with a pro-American yes-man overseeing a country heavily influenced by neo-Nazis. Soros Open Society Foundations manipulated the 'Euromaidan' protests in the Ukraine capital Kiev and protestors were shot in sniper attacks blamed on the government when clearly another force was involved. Pro-Russia president Viktor Yanukovych was forced to flee the country and in came American poodle and long-time US agent in Ukraine, Petro Poroshenko (who was later replaced by a Jewish comedian/actor, Volodymyr Zelensky). Soros operatives orchestrated the initial unrest and the whole coup was overseen by ultra-Zionist Victoria Nuland, the US Assistant Secretary of State for European and Eurasian Affairs. *Nuland is the wife of ultra-Zionist Robert Kagan, co-founder of the Project for the New American Century.* But don't you worry. George Soros and the ultra-Zionist Neocons are not working together. They don't like each other – didn't you know? The fact that Soros networks target the very countries the Neocons want to regime-change is pure coincidence and it is virulent and poisonous 'anti- Semitism' to say otherwise. Yeah, yeah, yawn. In truth, Soros networks provide the excuse for 'regime change' and the Neocons take it from there. A stash of 2,200 Open Society Foundation documents secured by the group DC Leaks reveal that Soros and his lackeys dictated US policy toward Ukraine after the 2014 coup and, with the fake-liberal Obama administration, removed the democratically-elected Yanukovych. One of the documents described the 'New Ukraine' as a key that 'reshapes the European map by offering the opportunity to go back to the original essence of European integration'. This is not how the Jewish community of Ukraine see it (0.1 percent of the population) with the 'revolution' putting Hitler and Nazi-supporting militia on the streets. Well done, George, another glorious victory for freedom. Ukraine's Prosecutor General Yuri Lutsenko revealed that a 2016 investigation into the NGO called the Anti-Corruption Action Centre

(AntAC), funded by Soros and the Obama administration (same thing), was dropped after the US government delivered 'a list of people whom we should not prosecute'. This is 'free' Ukraine? US investigative journalist Wayne Madsen said of Soros involvement in the Ukraine coup:

> It is the degree to which Soros provided finances, logistics, and other support to the Ukrainian coup plotters in 2012, two years before the Euromaidan [fake revolution] uprising, that is noteworthy. [Open Society Foundations] and its affiliates provided entire buildings, office space, computers, software, broadband Internet, videoconferencing equipment, vehicles, travel to the United States, and other material for the Euromaidan uprising [US coup]. This was all done with the cooperation of the US and Swedish embassies in Kiev, USAID, the Carnegie Endowment, the Swedish International Development Agency (SIDA), and the Central Intelligence Agency-linked National Endowment for Democracy (NED).

> Investigative journalists were also sought by the Soros gang to travel to Ukraine and submit articles that had to be approved by Soros operatives before publication. One major collaborator of Soros and the United States in pushing Ukrainian propaganda was identified as the Hromadske Television, which was singled out for its work to counter 'Russian propaganda' ...

> ... Soros is one of the closest advisers and financiers of Hillary Clinton. The leaked Soros documents describe how the Clinton Global Initiative and Foundation cooperates on undermining the sovereignty of nations around the world, including those in Europe.

The Clintons are buddies and drug-running business partners of the Bushes among much else that is disgusting and sordid beyond belief. DC Leaks documents revealed how Soros is paying a large swathe of 'journalists' (presstitutes) to write articles supporting his agenda in country after country with a veto on publication if he doesn't like anything they say. Soros and his multi-billion dollar network is a major source of the demonisation of Russia which the ultra-Zionist Neocons have been driving. When you realise that the 'progressive left' and the 'far right' are controlled by agents of the same force the behaviour of ultra-Zionists like George Soros and Sheldon Adelson suddenly makes sense. The Soros Open Society network officially left Hungary in 2018 after Prime Minister Viktor Orban's government passed the 'Stop Soros' law to criminalise the organisation's manipulation of the country. Withdrawal from Turkey was announced in December, 2018, when the government said Soros was controlling Turkish opposition figure Osman Kavala who was accused of organising anti-government demonstrations. Kavala is an advisory board member of Open Society. British academic Frank Furedi exposed the nature of the Soros network and revealed the shocking levels of arrogance expressed by people who think they have the right to impose their will on everyone else (or *Soros's* will – the *Hidden Hand's* will in truth). This is the mind-set of the 'progressives' that direct his operation under his command and brief. Soros, too, is a foot soldier to more powerful interests deeper in the shadows which he had better not cross. Frank Furedi said he was asked to speak at an event funded by a Soros foundation (they are legion) in Budapest. Soros activists attended from many areas of the former Soviet Republics and Eastern Europe. Furedi recalled:

> It was later during lunch at a plush Budapest hotel that I encountered the full force of the arrogant ethos promoted by the Soros network of organisations. At my table I listened to Dutch, American, British, Ukrainian and Hungarian representatives of Soros NGOs boast about their achievements. Some claimed that they played a major role in the Arab Spring in Egypt. Others voiced their pride in their contribution to the democratisation of the Ukraine. Some bragged about their influence in preparing the ground for the overthrow of the Gadhafi regime in Libya.

> I sat quietly and felt uncomfortable with a group of people who so casually assumed that they had the right to play God throughout the world. At one point, the head of the table – a Hungarian leader of a Soros NGO – asked me what I thought about their work. Not wishing to offend, I quietly remarked that I wasn't sure whether the external imposition of their idea of democracy on the people of Libya was legitimate nor that it would work. Without a second's hesitation, my interlocutor rounded me with the response: 'I don't think that we have the luxury of waiting until the Libyan people come with their own Jefferson.

This is how the ultra-Zionist network operates manipulating the arrogant and gullible to do its work of global dystopian transformation. Soros is everywhere funding 'progressive' groups of all kinds, mass immigration, censorship of free speech, the climate change hoax, facet after facet of the ultra-Zionist Neocon agenda. If Soros funds it the motivation is bad for humanity. He even gave a large sum to an organisation in Britain seeking to stop Brexit when he doesn't even live in the country. The European Union is a Hidden Hand fly-trap for national sovereignty and freedom and the last thing they wanted was British people voting to come out. Revealing that Soros was using his money to thwart the will of a national referendum and block Brexit was apparently 'anti-Semitic' – the perpetual reflex-action defence against public exposure. UK Zionist *Guardian* columnist and Soros-apologist

Rafael Behr suggested this in an article headed 'A secret plot to stop Brexit, or an anti-Semitic dog whistle?' Frank Furedi describes very well the Soros mentality:

> Why am I not surprised that the billionaire George Soros has decided to give £400,000 to the anti-Brexit crusading group Best for Britain? Because, since the 1980s, Soros has acted as if his considerable wealth entitles him to influence and alter the policies of governments throughout the world. Soros does not believe in the legitimacy of borders nor in the authority of national electorates. Consequently he feels entitled to influence and if possible direct the political destiny of societies all over the world. Today it is the future of Britain; tomorrow it might be Italy or Hungary that will be the target of Soros' largesse.

'Soros largess' means Hidden Hand largesse.

Soros lays the trap

The billionaire prepared the ground for the Arab Spring, Middle East regime change and US/Western intervention with his 2004 article 'The People's Sovereignty'. This appeared in *Foreign Policy* – the magazine published by the Hidden Hand Carnegie Endowment for International Peace which was exposed by a Congressional investigation for manipulating war. Soros said he wanted to change the definition of sovereignty from the *government* of a country to the *population* and this was sold as 'progressive' and giving power to the people. It was, as always with Soros, nothing of the sort. He wanted to bypass the block on external forces invading countries on the grounds that it was a breach of sovereignty. By switching the definition of sovereignty from government to population they can invade on the premise that they are stopping a government from violating the *people's* sovereignty. This is precisely the scam that would be used in Libya, Syria and other countries of the 'Arab Spring' with the claim that the long-targeted 'regime leader' was 'killing his own people'. Soros wrote:

> ... true sovereignty belongs to the people, who in turn delegate it to their governments. If governments abuse the authority entrusted to them and citizens have no opportunity to correct such abuses, outside interference is justified. By specifying that sovereignty is based on the people, the international community can penetrate nation-states' borders to protect the rights of citizens.

> In particular, the principle of the people's sovereignty can help solve two modern challenges: the obstacles to delivering aid effectively to sovereign states, and the obstacles to global collective action dealing with states

experiencing internal conflict.

This was exactly what the ultra-Zionist Neocon plan of the Project for the New American Century demanded – you know, the one that Soros isn't part of. He dubbed his doctrine the 'responsibility to protect' (i.e. invade, takeover, slash and burn):

> ... the rulers of a sovereign state have a responsibility to protect the state's citizens. When they fail to do so, the responsibility is transferred to the international community [ultra-Zionism and the Hidden Hand]. Global attention is often the only lifeline available to the oppressed.

Soros cares so much about the 'oppressed' – ask the 'progressives' who take his money and do his bidding. Only a year later in 2005 what Soros called for in that article was adopted by the United Nations Security Council and General Assembly. Everything was in place for a renewed military assault on the Middle East that had been mercilessly targeted since 9/11. Exposure of the lies about weapons of mass destruction in Iraq had slowed the pace of the PNAC ultra-Zionist regime-change schedule. Now the road was open to press the throttle to the floor. This was the deal:

- Decree that the people represent sovereignty and that governments have a responsibility to protect the sovereign population.

- If they don't, or your propaganda makes it look that way, there was now an automatic transfer of power from the country to the 'International community' (ultra-Zionists and the Hidden Hand).

- Arm, fund and train 'rebels' to attack the target regime and wait for them to respond. When they do you scream 'he's killing his own people' and condemn the government for failing in its 'responsibility to protect', as Soros put it.

- The 'International Community' can then deploy the military to 'protect the people' (by bombing them shitless, as in Libya and Syria, and taking over their land and resources under various guises).

Far from protecting national sovereignty the ultra-Zionists and wider Hidden Hand want to destroy it through a tyrannical world government controlled by them which would dictate the lives of everyone on earth. For this to happen the Cabal is plotting the end of countries and just by coincidence this a major goal of the Soros *Open Society* (no countries or borders just global government) Foundations. This is why Soros described sovereignty as an 'anachronistic concept originating in bygone times' and why his networks are behind the manipulation of mass immigration to break down a sense of defined and tangible countries and cultures. I'll explain more shortly.

Mission accomplished (well, some of it)

The outcome – always judge by outcome not rhetoric – of the Neocon-Soros Doctrine has been mass human catastrophe. Look at the consequences of the 'peoples' revolution' against Gadhafi in Libya and what happened when West/Israel-backed 'rebels' began another 'Arab Spring' civil war in Syria in pursuit of the Neocon-Soros agenda. Look at the multi-millions who have died, towns and cities destroyed, disease and suffering. This is the work of psychopaths hiring other psychopaths to do their bidding while idiocy cheers them all on. Ain't that right, CNN, and both parties in the United States? Libya's Colonel Gadhafi was no saint but under his reign education and medical treatment were free; electricity was either free or cost very little; newlyweds received $50,000 from the government to buy a home; having a home was considered a human right; Gadhafi's Great Man-Made River Project made water available to everyone; Libya had no external debt and the highest per-capita income in Africa. Now after the US-NATO air invasion led by Barack Obama and Hillary Clinton's America, David Cameron's UK, plus France and others, Libya is a basket case of warring factions and life for the population is a barely-surviving hell. None of the psychopaths responsible for this have faced any consequences because as always Hidden Hand networks have their back for services rendered. Libya was bombed into the Stone Age and is now a lawless land of violence, warlords and the very ISIS terrorists that those who caused this mayhem claimed to be fighting. ISIS was in fact a Western-created-armed-and-funded proxy army and outgrowth from the Mujahideen/al-Qaeda creations of the CIA to set the Middle East at war with itself and justify Western 'intervention' – all of which suited the ambitions of the ultra-Zionists and the Death Cult for which wars and mass killing is a human sacrifice ritual. Many of those who attacked Gadhafi were the same people with the same weapons – and certainly the same Western and Israeli backers – that would seek to remove Assad in Syria once the Libyan gig was completed with mass bombing of the innocent by US, UK and NATO raids 'to protect civilians from violence'. Assad would have been long gone, too, without Russia's intervention and air support. Israel and the Death Cult I will expose have been desperate to remove Assad. Major General Gershon Hacohen, former senior Israeli commander, said that then Defense Minister Moshe Ya'alon personally met with Syrian (West/Saudi-funded and armed) 'rebels' at the height of the Syrian war. Hacohen, Commander of the

Israeli Defence Forces Staff Corps before retiring in 2014, said that he was also present at the meeting. Trump said in 2018 that American troops only remained in the Middle East to 'support Israel' (pursue its agenda). Soros is supposed to be antagonistic to authorities in Israel, but his networks start the momentum rolling in 'people's revolutions' and then military and civilian thugs go in. This was all described in a US military document entitled 'US Special Forces Unconventional Warfare Strategy' published on November 30th, 2010, just a month before the Soros 'Arab Spring' began in Tunisia. The document said:

> The intent of US UW [Unconventional Warfare] efforts is to exploit a hostile power's political, military, economic, and psychological vulnerabilities by developing and sustaining resistance forces to accomplish US strategic objectives ... For the foreseeable future, US forces will predominantly engage in irregular warfare (IW) operations.

The document goes on to say the strategy requires that target-state population perceptions are first 'groomed' into accepting an armed insurrection, using 'propaganda and political and psychological efforts to discredit the government'... creating local and national 'agitation'... helping to organise 'boycotts, strikes and other efforts to suggest public discontent'... before beginning the 'infiltration of foreign organizers and advisors and foreign propaganda, material, money, weapons and equipment'. Should there be retaliation by the target government, the document continues, the resistance can exploit the negative consequences to garner more sympathy and support from the population by emphasising the sacrifices and hardship the resistance is enduring on behalf of 'the people'. This is exactly what has happened in the 'Arab Spring' along with the mantras of: 'He's killing his own people'; the protests are 'peaceful (when they weren't); the opposition is unarmed (when often they weren't); and this is a popular peoples' revolution (when it was instigated by Soros and other Western/ultra-Zionist intelligence and military networks). One estimate put the civilian death toll in the post-9/11 war on terror in Iraq, Libya, Syria, Yemen and Sudan at six million, but the figure is substantially higher when deaths from disease, poverty and hunger caused by those wars are taken into account. There is at least some good news – profits of armament companies like Raytheon and Lockheed Martin which are owned by the same Hidden Hand that manipulates the wars have absolutely soared. Don't you worry about dead and mutilated men, women and children when mass murder is good for jobs and profits. United States military spending (much of which goes to the arms companies) increased by *50 percent* (adjusted for inflation) in the first ten years after 9/11 while spending on education, healthcare, public transport and other domestic civilian programmes increased by only 13.5 percent. Official US spending on the military for 2018 (ironically called 'defence spending') was $700 billion which is only the headline figure for the public to see. The real figure with all aspects included will be way over *$1 trillion* and then some. Even by official figures the United States spends more on the military than the next *eleven* or more

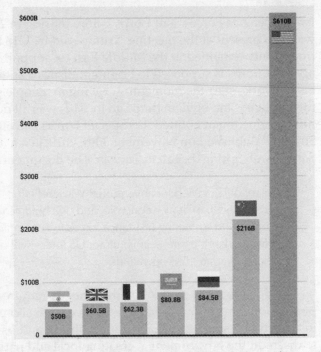

Figure 94: The staggering levels of US 'defence (attack) spending which is preparing for the emergence of the long-planned world army.

countries combined and that includes China and Russia (Fig 94). The ultra-Zionist agenda of regime change triggered by 9/11 has turned the American taxpayer into a cash-cow to fund wars in the Middle East for the benefit of Israel's territorial and acquisitive ambitions while so many Americans sleep in the streets. From the bigger-picture perspective the United States military is really the Hidden Hand military being prepared to be the foundation of the world army to impose the will of the world government. This is why the US has built a global military structure

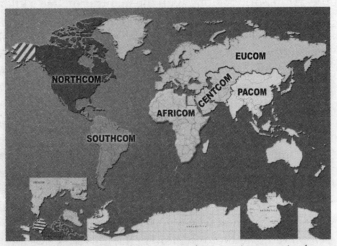

Figure 95: The US military global command structure in preparation for the world army.

operating in 147 countries which has carved up the world into 'Command' regions ready to be handed over eventually to become the control structure of the world army (Fig 95). Locations and actions of the US military overwhelmingly have no impact on the security, safety or *defence* of America and its citizens because that is not the point of what American troops are doing. The 'US military' is really the Hidden Hand military and the ultra-Zionist military. Let that reality sink in and so much that has happened since 9/11 will suddenly make sense.

Dominoes topple

What I am about to talk about next – also involving Soros – may not appear to be connected to 9/11, but it is. I emphasise again that the September 11th attacks did not happen in isolation. They were part of a fantastic global agenda and the subject I raise now would not have happened without 9/11 leading to Middle East wars which themselves led to the situation I am about to address. Context is crucial to understanding anything. What looks one way in and of itself can look very different when contextual connections are revealed. Dots are one reality and dots-connected quite another. This is absolutely the case with the Hidden Hand plan for the world which plays out like lines of dominoes with one event triggering another and another. The preferred sequence is all worked out in advance and what happened on 9/11 was crucial to that. If you have a plan that involves the mass movement and resettlement of people from one culture or cultures into another then you know that war and destruction in the Middle East and Africa are going to understandably generate large numbers of people seeking to relocate to more peaceful lands and their direction would be north into Europe not south into Africa or East into other troubled areas. Desperate people did indeed begin to flee the Western-created hell of Libya and Syria and headed for Europe. Few people, and certainly not me, would challenge humanitarian support and succour for tragic refugees seeking protection from war – especially Western-instigated ones. This was not the real story, however. Waiting to pounce on this movement of genuine refugees from conflict were Soros and connected networks working to massively increase the flow of people into Europe by adding much greater numbers who were not escaping war but simply relocating when the chance arose. France's interior minister Christophe Castaner said that some aid groups operating in the Mediterranean act like accomplices to human traffickers (a fact I pointed out in my last book from other sources) and he said there was 'real collusion between smugglers and some NGOs' including through phone contacts to 'facilitate the migrants departure from Libyan coasts in appalling conditions'. Italian interior minister Matteo Salvini said something similar.

The same networks have been operating in Central and South America where war, conflict, upheaval and violent crime serve the interests of these psychologically insane people to encourage population movements north into the United States. I understand why people south of the US border see America as the Land of Milk and Honey compared with their own plight and if I was them I would try to do the same. The problem is that they are not being guided to America or Europe for their own benefit – the Death Cult couldn't give a damn about them – but to transform American and European society for deeply malevolent ends. Migrants and indigenous populations are both pawns in the same Death Cult agenda. Mass immigration benefits the elite in every day – not least with an over-supply of cheap labour that drives down wages and conditions for everyone. You won't do it for that? Okay, bye, bye, there are plenty who will. Genuine liberals of old would have opposed that – today's 'progressive' fake Soros-liberals cheer and call you a bigot if you point these things out. Trump's much-vaunted wall along the southern border with Mexico was always going to be opposed on the scale he described because the agenda doesn't want any barrier to stop what it plans eventually to be a colossal and unstoppable exodus of people from the south into the United States. Kirstjen Nielsen, then Department of Homeland Security Secretary, told a congressional hearing that close to a million illegal immigrants were expected to attempt to cross the border into the US in 2019 alone and the situation was 'truly an emergency'. This is all planned and migrants often suffer terrible hardships on the way, including violence, rape and child trafficking, while being unknowing pawns in a plan long hatched by the Hidden Hand to transform American society by transforming its demographics and dynamic of power. Kirstjen Nielsen described a 'real serious and sustained crisis at our borders ... make no mistake, this chain of human misery is getting worse'. She went on:

> Since late last year, we have been seeing 50,000 to 60,000 migrants arrive at our southern border each month. But in February, we saw a 30 percent jump over the previous month, with agents apprehending or encountering nearly 75,000 aliens. This is an 80 percent increase over the same time last year.

Nielsen said the system was already being overwhelmed and all she describes has happened under 'we must reduce immigration', ultra-Zionist-owned Trump. I have predicted these events for a long time after uncovering the mass migration agenda and what is now 'overwhelming the system' is planned to become a tidal wave of people crossing the border from the south in such numbers they will be unstoppable. America's southern border will, in effect, cease to exist which is what so many Soros-manipulated 'progressives' are calling for along with the extreme-'progressives' now hijacking the Democratic Party funded and owned by Soros. Democrats in their myopic idiocy believe that the more migrants the more votes for them until they become the only party of government on the basis that most migrants support them. They don't see that by the time that happens they won't be controlling the Democratic Party and the force that does will then oppress *their* freedom as *they* now oppress the freedom of others. Democrat 'progressives' have been the Soros/Hidden Hand vehicle to block the Trump wall plan along with ultra-Zionist/Sheldon Adelson/Hidden Hand bought-and-paid-for Republicans because no effective barrier is going to be allowed to stop the plan to transform America now long underway. Something similar is happening in Europe with a new flood of migration from the south waiting to be instigated as I write. Turkey is being funded currently to stem the flow and if that agreement falters (as I say it is planned to) the consequences will be obvious and catastrophic both for migrants and the current populations of Europe whether indigenous or migrant. Süleyman Soylu, Turkey's interior minister, said the country was hosting more than 3.6 million Syrians displaced by the US/UK/Israel-manipulated conflict under 'temporary protection' status while security forces held more than a quarter of a million 'irregular migrants' in 2018 and deported another 54,000. 'There is an increase of 56 percent compared to the figures of the first 11 months of last year', Soylu said.

No one knows how many people are in America illegally already although a ball park figure appears to be more than 20 million. Yet another think-tank was launched in 2018 called the New Center to campaign for an amnesty for all those 'illegal aliens' so they can be allowed to stay permanently. The New Center is headed by William Galston of the Hidden Hand Brookings Institute and ... *William Kristol, co-founder of the Project for the New American Century*. You know, the ultra-Zionist far-right advocate of any war going and with nothing at all in common with George Soros who just happens to be using his hijacked Democratic Party and progressive mob to press for exactly the same policy. Kristol-promoted wars have mass murdered millions of people with brown faces yet now he says that not allowing an estimated more than 20 million to stay in the country illegally would be 'morally unacceptable'. No, it would damage the agenda this sleazy man represents of transforming American and European society demographically, religiously and economically. Kristol wants everyone to stay with no discernment at all between genuine and peaceful people and psychopathic Central American gangs like MS13 which plague American cities with their horrific violence overwhelmingly against their fellow immigrants. But if you seek to create fear, chaos and rule of jungle you want MS13 and their like in the country, right Mr Kristol?

Encourage what you want – punish what you don't

We have cities now called 'sanctuary cities' where the state government refuses to cooperate with the Federal government in seeking out people living in the country illegally. Other states and cities have passed laws giving undocumented migrants money for healthcare, education and support costs that *legal Americans and born Americans don't get*. What is that going to do except encourage more to come – exactly as planned. George Soros teamed up with his fellow humanitarian lovers of the poor and destitute at MasterCard in a project called Humanity Ventures in which he pledged $500 million to address 'the challenges facing migrants and refugees'. I bet his heart bleeds. We should not forget that part of the deal with the Hidden Hand to become incredibly rich is that you spend significant swathes of your wealth on advancing the agenda in the guise of 'philanthropy'. Thus you have callous, heartless billionaires like the Rockefellers establishing 'charity foundations' which are also good for avoiding tax – not that they pay much anyway. You can see a pattern of donations with so many billionaires in terms of people, projects and subject areas which affect the world and society in line with the plan that I have been exposing for 30 years. Rockefeller foundations are a perfect example of this and you can add so many others including the Bill and Melinda Gates Foundation. In a joint statement the Mother Theresa pairing of Soros and MasterCard said:

> Migrants are often forced into lives of despair in their host communities because they cannot gain access to financial, healthcare and government services. Our potential investment in this social enterprise, coupled with MasterCard's ability to create products that serve vulnerable communities, can show how private capital can play a constructive role in solving social problems.

It makes you fit to puke. These 'social problems' are being systematically created because this two-three-four-faced financial elite don't give a shit about migrants. They are just pawns to them. MasterCard admitted in 2016 that it has handed out prepaid debit cards to migrants and refugees traveling through Europe with support from the European Union and the UN High Commissioner for Refugees both of which are promoting the mass migration agenda. Kristol's ultra-Zionist New Center is also calling for an end to caps on numbers from different countries. Up to this point the inflow of people from the south have overwhelmingly competed for jobs and housing with poor Americans (of all backgrounds and races). Now Kristol's demand is aimed at unblocking immigration into America from countries such as

India and China that would compete for jobs of higher earners and what are called 'professional classes'. The aim is to destroy American professional classes with immigration pressure on the jobs market after devastating the low-paid and middle classes. Jessica Vaughan, Director of Policy at the Center for Immigration Studies, explains the consequences:

> If the per-country cap were to be lifted, then for the next 10 years, nearly all of the green cards in the ordinary professional worker category would go to citizens of India. That means any company wishing to sponsor a professional from any of the other 150-plus countries that currently receive employment green cards or immigrant visas would have to wait 10 years or take their chances by entering the annual lottery for a temporary H-1B visa for that individual.
>
> Such a change in legal immigration would shift wage pressure away from U.S. blue-collar workers and onto American white-collar workers who would likely experience more displacement due to the vast number of Indian workers that would be imported to the country every year to take high-paying professional jobs.

This is all part of the ultra-Zionist Hidden Hand transformation of human society into a globally-centralised borderless dictatorship. Donald Trump shocked and angered his deeply-misguided supporters in March, 2019, by announcing that more migrants were going to be allowed to settle in the country because American corporations needed them. Apple CEO Tim Cook, who claims to have 'values', was sitting next to him at the time. For the reason behind this Trump 360 about-turn see the Jessica Vaughan quote above. Trump is the Cabal's man and always was as I shall be explaining later. The Soros progressive mob and the increasingly dominant progressive extremes of the Democratic Party are calling for the end of borders which would, by definition, mean the end of countries – precisely the aim of the Neocon-Soros ultra-Zionist Hidden Hand as I have been exposing for decades.

Media lies and calculated abuse

The debate about the calculated 'migrant crisis' cannot be won by these crazies and so they ban contrary views and information amid a frenzy of abuse in the form of 'racist', Nazi' and 'bigot' if you highlight the obvious consequences of what I have described (Fig 96 overleaf). A guaranteed way of uncovering the agenda is to observe what you are not allowed to have an alternative opinion about. It works every time. The enormous majority of migrants entering Europe and the United States are not families, mothers and children fleeing war but young men

Figure 96: A few questions for the open border Soros 'progressives'. Oh, I'm a bigot? Okay, that must be the answer then.

taking the opportunity to change locations. The same controlled media that lies to you about wars lies to you about this. A 'caravan' of thousands heading for the US border from the south in 2018 was portrayed by the media as dominated by families, mothers and children to manipulate emotions when that was demonstrably not true. As in Europe it almost entirely consisted of single men travelling alone. American filmmaker Ami Horowitz produced a documentary about the 'caravan' and estimated that single males accounted for 90 to 95 percent of the people. Many he interviewed said they were heading for America for a 'better life' and not fleeing violence and oppression. Horowitz exposed the lie that most migrants are spontaneously leaving their countries and walking to America. Instead the operation was highly organised with buses, food and water orchestrated through an organisation called Pueblo Sin Fronteras (People without Borders) which was formed in 2000 by Mexican-American 'human rights activist' Irineo Mujica to get as many as possible into the United States through Central America and call for open borders which means the end of America as a country and society. People Without Borders is being funded to the tune of millions by front-groups and progressive groups in the United States with known associations with George Soros money. The organisation itself is based in Chicago with its affiliated La Familia Latina Unida (The United Latin Family) and Centro Sin Fronteras (Center Without Borders) which share the same goals. Soros is reported to fund Center Without Borders, the parent organization of The United Latin Family which is the parent organisation of People Without Borders. The money trail comes through the National Immigration Forum which is financed by George Soros' Open Society Foundations. Viridiana Vidal, a People without Borders organiser and spokeswoman, is the Nevada state director for America's Voice according to her LinkedIn profile. Soros funds America's Voice. The Soros plan is crystal clear – People *Without Borders = Open Society* Foundations = the end of countries. This just happens to be the Hidden Hand plan for the world working through gofer assets like Soros. I have no truck with the far right or the far anything (except the far out), but it is the so-called 'progressives' that are driving the tyranny. The trouble is they are so far up their own virtue-signalling arses they can't see that. Alexandria Ocasio-Cortez, a US Representative for New York, is the epitome of the George Soros 'progressive'– ultra-Zionist – agenda while believing she is a 'voice of the people'. 'Soros progressive' is an appropriate description for the mind-set. Ocasio-Cortez is clueless about the forces driving 'her' agenda. We have the same in the UK in the form of Owen Jones, a 'journalist' on the 'progressive' *Guardian* who appears to spend his days in television studios spouting his 'anti-establishment' rent-a-rants while the establishment he claims to oppose cheers him on. Why do these people think giant corporations and billionaires who make their money from exploitation of the masses are on the same 'progressive' page? Soros funds so many 'progressive' political projects and organisations it is just mind-blowing and he has transformed the genuine Liberal left that I grew up with into a fascistic mob seeking to impose their mindless will on the global population and delete freedom of speech and opinion. Programmed mindlessness blocks them from seeing that it's not *their* will at all – just a mantra repetition delivering the agenda of the one-percent. Put the words 'Organizations funded by George Soros and his Open Society Foundations' into a search engine and you'll see a list at Discoverthenetworks.org of where just *some* of his money goes.

All planned long ago

US law has been interpreted to mean that anyone born in the country automatically becomes a US citizen and this has led to birth-tourism in which pregnant women travel to America just to give birth. By 2018 one in twelve births in the US was to non-citizens. Steven Camarota, Director of Research for the Center for Immigration Studies, estimated that by 2060 immigration will add 75 million people to the US population and that 95 percent of the country's population growth will come from future immigrants and their children and grandchildren. The percentage of foreign-born people in the United States is soaring with 65 million Americans, or one in five, speaking a language other than English at home. This rises to as high as 50 percent in America's five largest cities and some areas of concentrated immigration has 85 to 95 percent of children in schools speaking a foreign language at home. So-called 'progressive' groups and media dispute the figures, but the trend is clear and indisputable. The number living illegally in the US was estimated at more than 22 million in a 2018 study by Mohammad M. Fazel-Zarandi, a researcher at Yale and Massachusetts Institute of Technology (MIT). This exodus from other lands into the United States and Europe has been in the planning at least since the 1920s and in truth far longer – for the detail see *Everything You Need To Know But Have Never Been Told*. I have highlighted over the years the words of ultra-Zionist Dr Richard Day, a

big-time Rockefeller family insider and executive of Planned
Parenthood, who shocked a meeting of paediatricians in Pittsburgh,
Pennsylvania, in 1969 when he asked them to turn off recording
equipment and not to take notes because he was going to tell them how
the world was going to be changed dramatically by the network he
represented. He meant the ultra-Zionist network and wider Hidden
Hand. Dr Lawrence Dunnegan, a member of the audience that night, did
take notes and made them public through an alternative media site
years later when he realised that what Day said would happen *was*
happening. I quote Day at length in a book called *Phantom Self* and what
he predicted (because he knew) even in detail is the world we see today.
This was what he said 50 years ago about the plot for mass migrations of
people:

> There [will] be mass movements and migrations of people without roots in
> their new locations because traditions are easier to change in a place where
> there are a lot of transplanted people, as compared to trying to change
> traditions in a place where people grew up and had an extended family,
> where they had roots.

This is the plan happening all around us today. Mass movements of
people are part of the agenda to transform the nature of society in ways
described in the 1920s by those behind the eventual development of the
European Union – another body manufactured to centralise power into
the hands of the unelected few. See the chapter 'Saying the Unsayable' in
Everything You Need To Know But Have Never Been Told for the in-depth
background to the mass migration agenda in which ultra-Zionism is
centrally involved. Sweden-based American ultra-Zionist and academic
Barbara Lerner Spectre has been open about their role in transforming
European culture. She relocated from America to Israel in the 1960s
before heading to Sweden with her husband, Rabbi Philip Spectre, to
found the European Institute for Jewish Studies called Paideia which is
funded by the Swedish government. She said in a TV interview:

> I think there's a resurgence of anti-Semitism because at this point in time
> Europe has not yet learned how to be multicultural, and I think we're gonna
> be part of the throes of that transformation, which must take place. Europe is
> not going to be the monolithic societies that they once were in the last
> century. Jews are going to be at the centre of that. It's a huge transformation for
> Europe to make. They are now going into a multicultural mode, and Jews will
> be resented because of our leading role. But without that leading role, and
> without that transformation, Europe will not survive.

I find it hard to comprehend the arrogance it must take for a fraction of 0.2 percent of the world population to impose their will on everyone else. The truth is that Europe as we know it will not survive what *she* is talking about and when she says Jews will have a leading role she's not referring to *all* Jewish people or anything like. She means ultra-Zionists and the Death Cult I will be exposing later which have contempt for the general Jewish population. It is so important that all Jews are not blamed for the actions and ambitions of the few. While Israel promotes open hostility towards Muslims at home and the wider Middle East its representatives in Europe are calling for Jews and Muslims to unite against 'nationalist' anti-mass immigration parties. France's Chief Rabbi Haim Korsia said the country's Jewish community must seek cooperation with French Muslims against far-right political forces in the country (what is the government of Israel if not far, far right?). Pinchas Goldschmidt, President of the Conference of European Rabbis, said Muslims and Jews have common cause in resisting attacks on minorities with the rise of ultra-nationalist parties and damage to the European Union caused by Brexit. What is the government of Israel if not ultra, ultra nationalist? The hypocrisy is breathtaking. Some Rabbis openly celebrate mass migration into Europe from the Muslim world like Rabbi Baruch Efrati, a yeshiva head and community rabbi in the illegal West Bank settlement of Efrat:

Jews should rejoice at the fact that Christian Europe is losing its identity as a punishment for what it did to us for the hundreds of years we were in exile there ... We will never forgive Europe's Christians for slaughtering millions of our children, women and elderly ... Not just in the recent Holocaust, but throughout the generations, in a consistent manner which characterises all factions of hypocritical Christianity... Europe is losing its identity in favour of another people and another religion, and there will be no remnants and survivors from the impurity of Christianity, which shed a lot of blood it won't be able to atone for.

Then there is French Rabbi Rav Touitou who said:

The Messiah will come when Edom, Europe, Christianity, has totally fallen. So, I ask you, is it good news that Muslims are invading Europe? It's excellent news! It means the coming of the Messiah! Excellent news!

It is easy to write such people off as simply bonkers, but they are seeking to manifest their racist madness. When you see quotes like these – and they are legion if you look for them – how outrageous that they blame everyone else for 'anti-Semitism' when they are creating this as people wrongly judge all Jews by these ultra-Zionist extremist crazies. What would happen if anyone else talked of Muslims *invading* Europe?

A deluge of abuse would follow and calls for resignation. Touitou can say that with no problem. What would happen if a non-Jew said that 'we should rejoice at the fact that Zionist Israel is losing its identity as a punishment' or 'Israel is losing its identity in favour of another people and another religion, and there will be no remnants and survivors from the impurity of Judaism'? It would be called 'anti-Semitic' and 'hate speech'. Efrati can say that about Europeans no problem. What does this one law for one and another for the rest stimulate? *'Anti-Semitism'*. The same is happening in the United States with calls for open borders to allow unchecked immigration from the south that would be the end of America as a country and nation. Borders are what define a culture, its laws, values and way of life. Once borders come down all of that goes with it because there is no defined area within which those 'values' and so on can be protected. This is why we have a no-border European Union. What have I been saying for *decades* is a key aim for the Hidden Hand? The *end of countries* and their replacement by a tyrannical hierarchy of superstates and world government. Distinct and individual cultures of *any kind* – not only those in Europe and North America – have no place in the Brave New World of a global fascist/communist state of centralised control. One bland, blob fused-culture common to everyone is what the conspirators want. We are seeing this ever more clearly with gathering deletion of individuality in life-style, thought and opinion and the imposition of one culture with one mind parroting one narrative about everything. The process goes like this:

You arrange for a mass influx of people from other cultures into the target culture; you manipulate support for this on 'humanitarian' grounds, but that is not your real motivation when you are psychopaths after all; incoming cultures begin to impose themselves on the target culture and eventually become significant, then decisive, in which political party is elected to government; those parties then do everything they can to win the 'minorities vote' while ignoring the needs of those from the indigenous culture that they believe have no other choice but to vote for them (the 'gimme vote' as I call it); minority numbers continue to grow until collectively they are the majority, firstly in specific areas and then nationally; at this point the once minorities *become* the government and laws are changed in line with the beliefs of the one-time migrants; a fusion happens the other way, too, with many migrants, especially their children and grandchildren, absorbing into the target culture and an overall fusion is reached in which all cultures are at some point absorbed into each other; now you have the one-world blob culture of the Hidden Hand global state. The plan over time is also for racial fusion through interbreeding. No – this is not a condemnation of interracial relationships – I think they're lovely. It is a question of scale and a question of what the elite want to happen and *why*. Part of the 'why' is the elimination (what an irony for 'progressives') of all cultural and racial diversity to create a global monoculture which their sick minds appear to desire.

Gathering numbers of people are beginning to realise what is happening and when they speak out the ultra-Zionist and 'progressive' hate groups respond in the usual way – 'bigot', 'Nazi', 'conspiracy theorist'. Attacks on 'white supremacy' and 'white privilege' are all connected to this agenda and so is the increased focus and fearmongering about the 'far right'. The mind-game is to link demands for free speech and claims of a mass migration agenda to the far right so when anyone even mentions these concepts they are immediately dubbed a 'white supremacist'. I think anyone who self-identifies the true 'I' with their body-type is missing the point. We are all expressions of the same consciousness and the body is only a vehicle for a brief experience in a tiny band of frequency we call 'the world'. There are, however, some who do self-identify this way that have a racial agenda to target white people in ways which become more hysterical by the day. Instead of screaming 'white supremacist' would it not be more adult and mature to ask why white people are being so demonised and why they are being pressured to despise *themselves?* Horrors like the mass shooting in Christchurch, New Zealand, in 2019 in which a 'white supremacist' shot dead 50 Muslims serves the Hidden Hand agenda perfectly. Psychopath Brenton Tarrant, a 28-year-old white man, circulated a 74-page 'manifesto' in which he said of mass migration: 'This is ethnic replacement. This is cultural replacement. This is racial replacement. This is white genocide.' What he did and what he said played into the desired perceptual association between questioning the agenda of mass migration and far right white supremacy. Tarrant also wrote that he wanted his sickening attack to spark a debate on gun ownership in the United States and a civil war between left and right which would fracture America 'along ethnic and cultural lines'. This just happens to be what the Hidden Hand has been working towards. It's just a coincidence, nothing to worry about. Either Tarrant is a complete moron (very possible) or there is more to know here. Attacks like his present the opportunity – mercilessly exploited – to justify censorship and suppression of views expressed by the psychopath involved and to link him and his actions to anyone far, far from violent or psychopathic who challenges the impact and goals of mass migration. It might also be worth considering the question of why ultra-Zionism has such a connection with the far right and more about that in a moment. The New Zealand government banned circulation of the Tarrant manifesto with anyone found to have it on their computer facing a jail sentence of up to ten years with another four added for passing it on. This sparked a

free speech debate because there is one constant theme with all these
terror attacks from whatever source – freedom is always the loser.
'Progressive' New Zealand Prime Minister Jacinda Ardern, a one-time
policy advisor to Tony Blair, vowed she would never mention Tarrant by
name which is clearly childish and not the maturity we should expect
from leaders of countries. Alarm bells rang with the speed at which the
collective 'white supremacy' and 'white nationalist' demonisation
agenda flung into action after the killings with Facebook banning
content that includes explicit praise, support, or representation of white
nationalism or separatism. Posts like 'I am a proud white nationalist'
and 'Immigration is tearing this country apart' were outlawed, but 'I am
a Jewish nationalist' and 'deport African blacks from Israel' continue to
be allowed. There was also not a problem when Jewish journalist, David
Sirota, senior communications adviser and speechwriter for Democratic
presidential candidate Bernie Sanders, who wrote in 2013: 'Let's hope
the Boston Marathon bomber is a white American.' We are replacing one
form of racism with another – reverse racism – and even reverse
segregation in some cases. This is not 'anti-racism' – it's racism with a
different colour face.

Soros and his (Twitter) storm troopers

George Soros is the name that pulls together the 'Arab Spring' with mass
migration into both Europe and the United States, the cultural 'fusion'
agenda and deletion of free expression to stop the first three being
publicly challenged and exposed. Buying and inverting the genuine
liberal left has produced the perception program known as 'progressive'.
This confuses being awake with being 'woke' to use its utterly ludicrous
term. Being 'woke' is defined as 'alert to injustice in society, especially
racism'. Unfortunately, they are not 'woke' enough to ask themselves
why a man who plays the financial markets without a care about the
social impact would be spending billions to fund people claiming to be
'alert to injustice in society, especially racism'. *Wake up* (or woke up)
people for goodness sake. The last thing they want is for you to truly
wake up and so they park you in a perceptual siding called 'woke' and
kid you they mean the same. They *don't*. 'Physical' transformation of
society is being driven by *perceptual* transformation and people need to
seize back control of their minds. Soros-funded and moulded
'progressive' mind programs have created the storm troopers – or
Twitter storm troopers – to enforce the ultra-Zionist agenda for mass
migration, fusion of cultures and silencing any opinion except its own.
They employ the techniques of fascism while claiming to be 'anti-fascist'
and impose the fascistic/communistic agenda of the ultra-Zionists and
Hidden Hand. 'Progressives' claim to be 'anti-establishment' and yet the
political and corporate elite are watching their backs and supporting

their goals. They have been manipulated to be so utterly confused they don't question why they find themselves on the same side as billionaires and giant global corporations who don't give a shit about injustice or racism. They are the up-their-own-arse mobsters enforcing the will of the elite in the form of the very societal transformation described by George Orwell and Aldous Huxley in *Nineteen-eighty-four* and *Brave New World* in the first half of the 20th century. This is the mind-set that dismisses exposure of the global agenda and 9/11 as 'conspiracy theory' and breaks into applause when 'conspiracy theorists' and their information and opinions are censored by the cabal of giant Internet corporations which increasingly control what we can see and hear. These are 'woke' people like George Monbiot, Owen Jones and Alexandria Ocasio-Cortez who are played by the system like a stringed instrument and do its bidding while claiming to be 'radical' – and actually believing they are such is the depth of their delusion. The 'progressive' mind-program cannot see in the mist of obsession with its own self-purity that its mentality is fundamentally racist in that it divides people into groups of good and bad races and backgrounds instead of seeing everyone as an individual to be perceived by their individual behaviour and not by the colour of their skin or nature of their sexuality.

Racism is not okay and that applies to racism against white people for the crime of being white as it does to everyone else – a fact this mentality cannot seem to grasp. Discrimination against gender-type is not okay and that applies to white men – *all* men – who are now condemned and suppressed from the earliest age for their 'toxic masculinity'. The Web does not want expressions of masculinity that say 'we're not taking this anymore'. It wants weak and fragile people who believe they are powerless victims who must look to the state for protection from racists, Nazis and bigots (which translated from the Orwellian largely mean other opinions and the right to an opinion). The scale of self-delusion is off the dial. They care far more about the political correctness of 'he', 'she' or 'they' than they do about people living on the street and those devastated by Neocon wars. Instead of protecting the population of *all* races and backgrounds from the impositions of billionaires this 'woke' mind stands with the billionaires as freedom disappears and ever more people that the genuine liberal left used to support fall into ever greater levels of deprivation and suppression. Virtue-signalling their own 'woke' credentials and purity is the only show in town. They call for open borders *and* an end to poverty, homelessness, unemployment and deteriorating healthcare. These are not seen as contradictions even though they quite obviously are. To the Soros 'progressive' there are no contradictions here – only demands that signal their own virtue. Look at me, I'm such a good person, look at how much I care – I want an end to poverty, homelessness, unemployment, deteriorating healthcare *and* I want open borders so any number of people can come in. Whoopee, well done you, oh, righteous one. What they don't realise, and cannot until they regain control of their own minds, is that they are creating a tyrannical, Orwellian nightmare which they and their children will have to live with for the rest of their lives.

I am not doing what I do for me. I'll be long gone before the fully-blown mega-extremes arrive which 'progressives' are helping to make possible. I am pointing out the consequences of what they are doing for *their* sake, not mine. Already once-progressive' campaigners for open borders in Sweden have been forced to leave their former neighbourhoods because Islamic Sharia police are hassling them over the clothes they wear. The momentum of societal transformation increases at ever-faster speed once there is little resistance to earlier waves of people looking to relocate. This encourages even larger numbers to follow. Instead of bringing people together in mutual support to challenge their political, financial and satanic oppressors the 'progressive' mob plays its essential part in dividing that unity into factional divisions of self-identity victimhood – absolutely crucial for the few to control the many. 'Progressives' are the Orwellian infantry at the front-line of the gathering dystopia I have warned was planned for 30 years. It is amazing, too, to see 'progressives' with power and wealth – not least in 'entertainment' – posing as victims of society and calling for 'equality' and 'inclusivity' while bunging the system a large wad to get their kids into Harvard through money and privilege instead of merit. 'Progressive' and 'hypocrisy' are so often interchangeable. America's Democratic Party today is not the party of the 1960s and today's 'social justice warriors' are not the civil rights movement of Martin Luther King. He would weep at the violence and reverse racism of 'progressives' and their paramilitary arm known as Antifa. Soros money and the organisations this has funded and spawned is a prime driver in this usurping of the once-liberal left in the United States and this has since swept across Europe and the wider world with its mass censorship disguised as 'political correctness'; its reverse racism disguised as 'anti-racism'; and its fascistic behaviour disguised as 'antifascism'. I found it interesting that 'pipe bombs' were posted to Soros, Obama, Clinton, CNN and other 'progressive' figures in the run-up to the 2018 US mid-term elections at a time when the manipulations of Soros and the antics of the 'progressive' mobs were being exposed. The ancient question 'Cui bono?' or 'Who benefits' comes to mind. The packages, which had no chance of ever reaching the big names, were immediately blamed on those calling out Soros and company.

Breathtaking bias

Those with any capacity for free thought and observation will have long noted that attacks on white Europeans and the Christian religion are no problem and laws and limits set by political correctness don't apply. The same happens in North America, Australia and New Zealand. Incoming migrants are a no-go area for criticism almost no matter what some may say or do and their religion of Islam is protected by law from adverse comment as is Zionism. CNN soul-for-sale Don Lemon said on air that the biggest terrorist threat was white men and that was fine because it supported the agenda of demonising white people and especially men and masculinity. Change 'white men' in what he said to 'black men' or 'Muslim/Jewish men' and he would have had to resign amid a hate-fuelled Twitter storm. The bias is systematic to allow this transformation to take place without open debate that would expose what is really going on and how both migrants and indigenous populations are pawns in the same game. We passed another Rubicon in Europe in 2018 when the Hidden Hand European Court of Human Rights ruled that a person's 'religious feelings' are more important than freedom of speech. This in effect brought back the law of blasphemy to Europe with regard to Islam (you can say what you like about Christianity). The Court of Human Rights ruling was made in the case of an Austrian woman who was convicted and fined in her own country for comparing the Prophet Mohammed to a paedophile on the grounds that many Muslims believe from their texts that he married a six-year-old child and consummated the marriage when she was aged nine. Whatever the historical background the correlation would obviously be correct, if true, by modern standards; but the woman's appeal to the human rights court was dismissed for the said reason that free speech is less important than someone's religious feelings. The ruling is clearly ridiculous and very, very dangerous in a society that in any way considers itself to be free. I don't follow any religion. I think all religion is a form of fundamental perceptual myopia, but when someone's chosen religious beliefs (which could be anything) cannot be criticised in case it hurts their feelings we are truly in the land of fascism and tyranny. If your religion has validly it will survive any criticism. Only when it does not have validity or the strength to be questioned does it require censorship. Why can't people reach a state of maturity where they believe what they do and allow others to believe something else? Muslims and their religion are being exploited in two main ways. A manufactured version of extreme Islam has been created via Saudi Arabia and its sponsors Britain and America which is used to demonise *all* Muslims and have them play the role of the Big Bad Terrorist Monster to justify wars of conquest and regime change. I will be explaining the origin of this extreme form of alleged Islam and it puts modern events into a very different context. The other front to exploit Islam is based on mass migration into Europe – with political correctness and 'hate laws' watching its back – to destroy long

fought-for freedoms like the right to free speech and opinion. What can
safely be said about Islam is that it does not encourage free speech
especially in relation to Islam. Okay, that's their right to do that and the
right of the followers to submit to that. When those same restrictions
begin to be applied to the non-Muslim population – as they increasingly
are – the entire foundations of the indigenous society are transformed
and dismantled and that is what is happening. This long-planned
process is fast gathering pace and the time for silence is over. Political
correctness is simply manipulating the target population to censor itself.
Once people's feelings or what 'offends' them overrides freedom of
speech then freedom of speech is over, finished, caput, because you will
always find someone, somewhere, to be offended about *anything*. The
pressure to be offended for ever-increasing reasons is again
systematically deleting freedom of speech by providing a consequently
ever-increasing list of things you can't say and opinions you can't have
because someone, somewhere, takes offence. The equation is: the more
offence, the less freedom. I have heard it said that you know who
controls you by who you can't criticise, but there is another way – by
who you can't laugh at. Try telling a transgender joke in public and
when was the last time you heard a joke about Israel or Jewishness?
Jokes about white males? Oh, that's okay, say whatever you like.
Comedy has been destroyed by political correctness in the 'progressive'
purge on human freedom with comedians even asked to sign a contract
agreeing not to upset anyone. But that is comedy's power and its
greatest contribution to human discourse – freeing people from the
prison of their own backside.

Alinsky's blueprint

We have ultra-Zionists funding 'progressives' *and* the far right which
'progressives' spend their lives condemning. Soros-funded
'progressives' might look just a little deeper and see that while Soros, the
man dubbed 'Godfather of the Left', is controlling and directing the anti-
Trump mob on one side the ultra-Zionist casino and Israel media
magnate Sheldon Adelson, who describes himself as 'the richest Jew in
the world', has been the biggest financial donor to Trump. If you want to
control the outcome before the game starts then you need to control both
sides and the referee. This is how the Hidden Hand works. On one side
Soros has hijacked the Democratic Party and created an unthinking,
unquestioning, unseeing and constantly-incandescent mob calling itself
'progressive'. On the other Adelson owns the Republicans and Trump
who is surrounded by ultra-Zionists like son-in-law and 'senior advisor' Jared Kushner, a life-long friend of Benjamin Netanyahu; David
Freidman, his bankruptcy lawyer who is ambassador to Israel (for
Israel); Jason Greenblatt, former Trump company operative who is now

his international negotiator; Steve Mnuchin, his Treasury Secretary from Goldman Sachs ... on and on and on it goes. I say that if you take one step further back into the shadows Soros and Adelson are batting for the same side. They have worked together to create a situation of catastrophic division (divide and rule) with the extreme far right acting like fascists while 'anti-fascists' like 'progressive'Antifa also act like fascists. Trump was brought to power by the ultra-Zionists in line with the philosophy and rules of manipulation of Zionist Marxist Saul Alinsky (1909-1972), the godfather of 'community organising' (manipulating). He wrote the book *Rules for Radicals* published in 1971 giving a nod to Lucifer as the 'first radical' and among his rules for overthrowing the established order was to focus upon a 'common enemy'. Once the enemy figure was established the 'community' would come together in united opposition and put aside differences to focus on a common goal. This is a major reason why ultra-Zionists and the Death Cult brought Donald Trump to power – to play the role of common enemy for the 'progressive' fake left. My goodness how effective this has been to transform the 'left' and the Democratic Party into a hysterical mob with one thought in mind: hate Trump and oppose Trump. Talk about polarisation. The mob is being directed by closet ultra-Zionist George Soros while open ultra-Zionists surround Trump. The pincer movement is classic Marxism and classic Alinsky who said:

> Pick the target, freeze it, personalize it, polarize it. Don't try to attack abstract corporations or bureaucracies. Identify a responsible individual. Ignore attempts to shift or spread the blame.

Alinsky's book urged his followers to 'rub raw the sores of discontent, galvanize them for radical social change'. What this really means is exploit discontent of the masses to overthrow the established order to create a structure of centralised control that will lead to permanent discontent and oppression. He wrote:

> We'll start with specific issues – taxes, jobs, consumer problems, pollution – and from there move on to the larger issues: pollution in the Pentagon and the Congress and the board rooms of the mega-corporations. Once you organize people, they'll keep advancing from issue to issue toward the ultimate objective: people power.

This is the same 'people power' Marxism that always leads to structural control by the elite few and the crushing of all opposition that has led to a death toll in excess of 100 million in its cumulative ex- pressions. Soros-supported Hillary Clinton is an Alinsky disciple and wrote a thesis on him. Democratic House Speaker Nancy Pelosi was another student and so is Barak Obama who emerged into politics after working as a 'community organiser' in Alinsky's city of Chicago. Alinsky's methods and tactics can be seen all over the 'progressive' mob today and not least with his rule that 'the issue is never the issue'. For example, 'climate change' is not the issue. Using the hoax of climate change to secure power is the issue. I am all for changing society for the better to make it fairer, more inclusive and just. I have been pursuing that for 30 years by exposing why the world is as it is. But overthrowing the establishment order is not enough. It has to be replaced with something better not worse. The Cabal must be in hysterics as they observe their creation that the pincer movement on Trump has delivered. Israel gets whatever it wants while at the same time America and other societies are divided by mutual hostility. Perfect.

Ultra-Zionism and the far right

Why is it that so many dubbed as 'far right' are enthusiastic critics of Muslims while being ardent supporters of Israel? This is a clear pattern. With what should be extraordinary irony Israeli governments, military intelligence and their apologists have a long and disgraceful record of supporting far right regimes – including apartheid South Africa. I guess they want to be among friends. Jair Bolsonaro, the far right president of Brazil elected in 2018, is a fanatical supporter of Israel's far right government. The Jewish Telegraphic Agency reported how Bolsonaro declared 'my heart is green, yellow, blue and white' in reference to the Israeli and Brazilian flags. His sons have been photographed wearing shirts with the logos of Mossad and Israeli Defense Forces. 'Bolsonaro stood out among the many candidates for including the State of Israel in the major speeches he made during the campaign,' said Osias Wurman, Israel's honorary consul in Rio de Janeiro. 'He is a lover of the people and the State of Israel.' His far right view of the world did not appear to matter so long as he would bat for Israel. This would explain the response to Bolsonaro's election by Trump National Security Advisor John Bolton, the ultra-Zionist tea-maker who is a 'confidant' (lackey) of ultra-Zionist Trump-funder Sheldon Adelson. Bolton welcomed the result and called Bolsonaro 'like-minded' which at least has the benefit of being accurate. Jerry Iannelli wrote in the *Miami New Times*:

> John Bolton just came to Miami's Freedom Tower and gave a speech praising Jair Bolsonaro, the wannabe Brazilian neo-fascist who wants to bring back the country's dictatorship, torture people, and kill dissidents. Bolsonaro has repeatedly compared indigenous tribespeople to animals living in zoos.

This can be explained by the ultra-Zionist/United States wing of the Hidden Hand moving in on South America to remove any government that doesn't dance to their tune and bow to their will. The attempted American coup in Venezuela, overseen by Trump-appointed Eliott Abrams, a far-right ultra-Zionist Neocon from the Project for the New American Century, is part of this strategy and connects with the installation of Bolsonaro in Brazil. Steve Bannon, Trump's one-time chief White House strategist, is condemned as a far right racist by the 'progressive' left, but he's an Israel fanatic and the admiration would appear to be mutual. Bannon told a Zionist Organisation of America event:

> I am proud to stand with the State of Israel, that's why I am proud to be a Christian Zionist, that's why I am proud to be a partner to one of the greatest nations on earth and the foundation of the Judaeo-Christian West.

It's okay, Steve, you can get off your knees now and put your tongue back in. Bannon's *Brietbart News* is considered a pillar of the so-called Alt-Right and was conceived by conservative commentator Andrew Breitbart during a visit to Israel. British 'working class hero' Tommy Robinson is another example of someone considered far right who is promoting Israel and being promoted himself by ultra-Zionists like American tech billionaire Robert Shillman who serves on the boards of the ultra-Zionist Friends of the Israel Defense Forces, Jewish Foundation for the Righteous, and David Horowitz Freedom Center. Robinson was invited to speak in the United States by the far right and vehemently pro-Israel David Horowitz Freedom Center and Middle East Forum. The latter, established by ultra-Zionist Neocon and war on terror advocate Daniel Pipes in 1990, has paid Robinson's legal bills and those of Dutch politician Geert Wilders who is labelled far right by his 'progressive' critics. Robinson is just a stooge being strung along so the Death Cult can take over the nationalist movements and play them off against the Muslim community and 'progressives'. They will drop him like a stone when he is surplus to requirements. The Middle East Forum is supported by ultra-Zionist Nina Rosenwald, heiress to the Sears Roebuck fortune, who was described by one headline in *The Nation* as 'the sugar mama of anti-Muslim hate' [for] 'using her millions to cement the alliance between the pro-Israel lobby and the Islamophobia fringe'. Rosenwald was on the board of notorious ultra-Zionist lobby group AIPAC and is founder and president of the Gatestone Institute, a New York-based think-tank which has supported Geert Wilders. Trump National Security Advisor John Bolton was Gatestone chairman from 2013 to March 2018 and he was awarded the Defender of Israel Award at the 2018 Zionist Organization of America's annual Brandeis Award dinner where Tommy Robinson supporter Robert Shillman was another award recipient. Daniel Pipes founded Campus Watch in 2002 to harass, blacklist and intimidate academics who criticise Israel. British journalist and Middle East specialist Robert Fisk wrote:

> Daniel Pipes and Martin Kramer of the Middle East Forum now run a website in the United States to denounce academics who are deemed to have shown 'hatred of Israel'. One of the eight professors already on this contemptible McCarthyite list – it is grotesquely called 'Campus Watch' – committed the unpardonable sin of signing a petition in support of the Palestinian scholar Edward Said. Pipes wants students to inform on professors who are guilty of 'campus anti-Semitism'.

I will expose the astonishing scale of ultra-Zionist censorship in the next chapter. It's no good anyone screaming 'racist' at what I have written here. I think labels of race, religion, income bracket and all the rest are illusory diversions from the true 'I' which is simply consciousness – the same consciousness having different experiences. I say we are a state of awareness and a point of attention within an *infinite* state of awareness of which we are all a part no matter what transitory labels we may be given or give ourselves – man, woman, black, white, Muslim, Jew, Christian, whatever. The body is only a temporary vehicle for our point of awareness to experience this frequency band of reality and the body is illusory in terms of self-identity. Who is more obsessed with race than progressives, 'anti-racists' and the 'anti-Semitism' industry? All they see is race while I see the same consciousness having different experiences through different vehicles. Anyway – all cultures are in the gun-sights of these crazies. Muslim and Arabic people from the south are being exploited to change Europe with countries like Sweden and Germany in the forefront while the Latino population of Central and South America is being used to change the United States. Campaigns of anti-white reverse racism are all part of this in the targeted predominately white countries and so is the psychological manipulation to instil even in white people shame of their own culture. The Hidden Hand doesn't care *what* culture you are so long as you are eventually absorbed into its culture – or lack of one. Exposure of this and everything else the Hidden Hand wants to keep quiet is now in the gun-sights of ultra-Zionist and other censorship that becomes more extreme by the day. Soros money, you will not be shocked to know, has found its way into organisations specialising in censorship and 'fact-checking' which, in this context, is just another term for censorship.

This book has 9/11 as a central theme and I will be returning to that in detail before I close, but 9/11 did not happen in isolation and cannot be fully understood if we only see it that way. There is a lot more background to know before we can put the September 11th attacks in their true context.

CHAPTER 18

Thou shalt not speak its name

I have come to believe over and over again that what is most important to me must be spoken, made verbal and shared, even at the risk of having it bruised or misunderstood – Audre Lorde

It may seem in the next few chapters that I am moving away from the central theme of 9/11, but I'm not. I need to lay out a lot of background information before I return directly to the *real* perpetrators in the context of exactly who and exactly why.

The attacks did not happen in isolation. They were part of a global plot by the Death Cult so vast and so deep it almost defies the imagination. I am going to expose in this chapter the network operating mostly from the shadows that prevents ultra-Zionist involvement in 9/11 and so much more from being exposed and why even seasoned researchers are terrified of going there. Appreciating the scale of ultra-Zionist and Death Cult control and censorship is essential to understanding how what I will be revealing in the rest of the book – including in relation to 9/11 – has never come to mainstream public attention.

Silencing the truth-tellers

Ultra-Zionism has created a vast money-no-object global structure of hate groups – mostly focussed in the West – to weaponise the label 'anti-Semitism' as a means of silencing critics of the far right government in Israel and its global manipulations orchestrated through its satanic military intelligence arm Mossad and the Death Cult in general. I say 'hate groups' because their modus operandi is to make people hate their targets by accusing them of 'anti-Semitism', 'hate speech' (another irony), 'bigotry' and by generally screaming 'Nazi' in all directions. Another regular is 'Holocaust denier' for those that they *really* want to be hated, silenced and crushed. They've thrown the lot at me when I don't have a racist cell in my body and the very concept of racism goes against my entire philosophy and perception of life. Judging anyone by their body-type or genetic history is utterly ridiculous and childlike to me. I am still dubbed 'anti-Semitic' by ultra-Zionist hate groups in an attempt to silence and discredit me when those groups are themselves consumed by race and self-identity with race. I form my opinions by what people do, not what their temporary, illusory body-vehicle might be. To be called racist by racists is a sight to behold. Not that I give a shit, but it shows how ultra-Zionists play the 'anti-Semitic' card at absolutely anyone who challenges their behaviour. The game is not about exposing 'racists' and 'anti-Semites' – it's about silencing people with information they are desperate for the public not to see. Exploiting the horrors of what happened to Jewish people in Nazi Germany to advance their own agenda of censorship today turns my stomach. I find it absolutely disgusting and an insult to those who suffered under Nazi fascism. The same scam to silence criticism was played by the Hidden Hand's Muslim Brotherhood when its front operation, the America-based International Institute for Islamic Thought, coined the term 'Islamophobia'. Abdur-Rahman Muhammad was with the organisation when the label of abuse was created and later rejected its ideology. He confirms that 'Islamophobia' was coined specifically to silence critics by dubbing them racist: 'This loathsome term is nothing more than a thought-terminating cliché conceived in the bowels of Muslim think tanks for the purpose of beating down critics.' This is the same modus operandi of the 'anti-Semitism' industry.

Ultra-Zionism and the Death Cult hide behind the Jewish population and pedalled misrepresentations of history and motivation that are so outrageous and factually incorrect that only fierce and incessant censorship can protect them from exposure. They not only have to keep the truth from the non-Jewish population. Most importantly of all they must keep it from the great majority of Jews who either support 'mainstream' Zionism (not knowing what's really behind it) or vehemently oppose Zionism in any form. *What – not all Jewish people are Zionists??* No, far from it, and only a relatively few are the extreme ultra-Zionists directly involved with the American Hidden Hand 'elite' over 9/11 who I will focus upon later. 'Zionism' is not a race; it's a political philosophy and standpoint which is opposed by many Jews. The number of Jewish people in the world, lest we forget, is around 16 million out of more than 7.7 *billion* and that means Jewish people represent just *0.2 percent* of the world population. They represent only two percent of the population of the United States where, together with Israel, most Jews are resident. Those two countries account for 83% of the Jewish population with 98 countries hosting the other 17 percent. Most of the 16 million would consider themselves supporters of Zionism in the dictionary definition of 'a movement for (originally) the re-establishment and (now) the development and protection of a Jewish

nation in what is now Israel'. We also have the significant number of
Jews who reject Zionism altogether and that leaves us with the ultra-
Zionists that represent a small minority even of just 16 million or 0.2
percent of Jewish people worldwide – and the full- blown Death Cult
initiates are even fewer than that. We are looking at tiny numbers of
those knowingly manipulating events with fantastic comparative
influence and power.

Designer language

Even the use of the term 'anti-Semitic' is fraudulent because Semitic
refers to a series of language groups in the Middle East which are almost
entirely *Arabic*. Current figures for the main native Semitic speakers are
Arabic (400 million), Amharic (22 million), Tigrinya (7 million), Hebrew
(5 million), Tigre (1.05 million), Aramaic (575,000 to a million) and
Maltese (482,880). Yiddish, another Jewish language, is not Semitic.
Yiddish is Germanic and related to Bavarian and other sources. To be
'anti- Semitic' in its true definition you have to exhibit discrimination
and hatred towards an estimated 500 million Semitic speakers across a
range of cultures and racial types throughout the Middle East, North
Africa and the Horn of Africa. To isolate the term only to Hebrew
speakers (and the many Jewish people who don't speak Hebrew) is a
gross misrepresentation of the term. There is an obvious reason why this
has been done. Without the label 'anti-Semitism' you are left only with
the all-encompassing term of 'racism' which applies to everyone. This
doesn't work for ultra-Zionists who want to justify special protection
beyond what is afforded to other groups and 'anti-Semitism' was
hijacked and applied exclusively to those who are Jewish. The term only
came into use in the second half of the 19th century and had its origins
in Germany. Ultra-Zionism has so much to hide that this added unique
protection from exposure is essential. Special laws that only apply to this
term opened the way to unique interpretation and ongoing expansion of
the definition which now includes criticism of the government of Israel.
The term 'racism' used for the rest of the human family would allow no
such special treatment and protection by law. If you are exposing the
governments of Nigeria or Uganda are you by definition considered to
be racist against all black people? What about if you condemn some
mass-murdering African, Far-Eastern or South American dictator – is
that racist against all those populations and racial types? No, of course
not. That would be considered madness. So why does this happen in the
Jewish or Zionist context where criticism of one is interpreted as an
attack on all? The answer is that we a dealing with a racket and a scam.

By hijacking the label 'anti-Semitic' and applying that exclusively to
Jewish people you create an isolation of meaning which allows an
interpretation way beyond racism and takes you into the realm of

silencing *political* critics. This in itself is a grotesque exploitation in my view of those Jewish people that *do* suffer genuine discrimination. The artist known as 'Banksy' produced a poster protesting at illegal Israeli occupation of Palestine and this couldn't be respected as someone expressing their basic human right to an opinion. Israeli billionaire's wife Batia Ofer condemned the picture as 'anti-Semitic' (Fig 97). Yep, I understand. How I share the pain of oppression that must have been felt by Mrs Ofer and her billionaire husband Idan Ofer, his father Sammy Ofer, one of the wealthiest men in Israel, and Monaco-based billionaire brother, Eyal Ofer. An artist publishing a poster highlighting the plight of a truly oppressed people must have been devastating between the caviar course and the champagne. If the label 'anti-Semite' was really about racism then Jewish people wouldn't be condemned as 'anti-Semites' by the ultra-Zionists when they challenge the actions of the Israeli government and the ultra-Zionist agenda. How can a Jew be an 'anti-Semite' under the accepted definition when they are, er, *Jewish?* This is obviously contradictory nonsense and the term is not about protecting Jewish people from 'racism' and discrimination; it's about protecting the ultra-Zionist and Death Cult cabal from exposure and the government of Israel from criticism. Jewish people who challenge them are therefore attacked even more ferociously than anyone else because

Figure 97: This Banksy poster was branded 'anti-Semitic', but then what isn't these days?

although they may try the 'anti-Semite' approach it is clearly going to be far less credible than with non-Jews. You are not allowed a contrary opinion even if – actually *especially* if – you are Jewish. RT America journalist Dan Cohen is but one example. Cohen posted a tweet about the Associated Press 'whitewashing Israel's crimes' which included the shooting of an AP journalist covering Gaza. He received a message from the Israeli consulate in Boston calling him a 'disgrace to Americans and Jews everywhere'. Cohen tweeted:

I received this creepy and menacing direct message from @IsraelinBoston. Apparently the consulate uses its official account to monitor and harass journalists, especially Jewish ones.

Here we have the theme – 'especially Jewish ones'. We are looking at the exploitation of Jewish people by those who use them as an excuse to silence legitimate criticism and exposure. 'Self-hater' is another label of abuse employed by ultra-Zionism to target Jewish people who condemn the inhumane-beyond-belief treatment of Palestinians since their land was seized by ultra-Zionists in a frenzy of murder and terrorism in 1948. This disgusting abuse of 'dissident' Jews is the work of self-proclaimed 'protectors of Jewish people'. Jews – and the rest of us come to that – might benefit from the words of Greek philosopher Plato: 'This and no other is the root from which a tyrant springs; when he first appears he is a protector.' The real protection here is aimed at ultra-Zionism.

The Protection Racket

The dictionary definition of 'anti-Semitism' is basically hatred, hostility or prejudice against Jewish people because they are Jewish. I don't accept the meaning of anti-Semitism there for reasons I have explained, but the rest is fair enough. The trouble is that's far from fair enough or far enough when you want to weaponise the slur as the means to protect your activities from investigation and exposure – investigation based on your behaviour and not your cultural background. To secure such protection you must link all criticism to cultural background and perceived 'race' and this is why we constantly see the expansion of what is defined as 'anti-Semitic'. The more you extend the meaning the more critics you can target with your 'unclean, unclean' labelling. 'You are only saying that about Netanyahu because you're an anti-Semite.' No, because he's a psychopath – no cultural connection necessary. This technique was perfectly described by Shulamit Aloni, a former Israeli minister and peace activist, when she told an American alternative television show about the way ultra-Zionists use 'anti-Semitism' and 'the Holocaust' to silence critics:

> It's a trick. We always use it. When from Europe someone is criticising Israel then we bring up the Holocaust. When people in this country are criticising Israel then they are anti-Semitic. The organisation is strong and has a lot of money and the ties between Jews and America – the Jewish establishment – they are strong in this country, they have power ... they are talented people and they have power, money, media and other things, and their attitude is Israel, my country, right or wrong ...

> ... They are not ready to hear criticism, and it is very easy to blame people who criticise certain acts of the Israeli government as anti-Semitic and to bring out the Holocaust and the suffering of the Jewish people, and that justifies everything we do to the Palestinians.

Imagine the psychopathic callousness required to exploit what happened to Jewish people in Nazi Germany to advance your political agenda today – *shocking*. We have an 'anti-Semitism' industry running a protection racket to protect ultra-Zionism, the Death Cult and Israel from criticism and exposing its manipulations and behaviour to open public debate. The 'trick' that Aloni described has been expanded with a new definition of 'anti-Semitism' which is outrageously broad and wide-ranging and was compiled simply to increase the number of critics and investigators who could be given 'the label' and silenced. The wording was accepted in 2016 by the 'International Holocaust Remembrance Alliance' (IHRA) thanks it would appear to Mark Weitzman of the Simon Wiesenthal Center, 'an international Jewish human rights organization'. Oh, unbiased then. The definition has since been adopted by a gathering number of organisations and governments including those of the UK, Scotland, Germany, Austria, Lithuania, Romania, Bulgaria, Macedonia and the European Union. The 'trick' here is to say that because most Jewish people associate their identity with Israel any criticism of the actions of Israel is attacking their Jewish identity and is thus 'anti-Semitic'. This is complete baloney and so much so it provides confirmation that the 'new definition' is merely about helping ultra-Zionists, the Death Cult and the Israeli government resist exposure. US attorney Kenneth Stern of the American Jewish Committee against Anti-Semitism, who was involved in the original draft before it was hijacked, told a congressional hearing in 2017:

> The definition was drafted to make it easier for data collectors to know what to put in their reports and what to reject ... because the definition was drafted with data collectors utmost in mind, it also gave examples of information to include regarding Israel ... The definition was not drafted, and was never intended, as a tool to target or chill speech.

Stern has strongly condemned the misuse of the definition in ways he describes as 'McCarthy-like'. To ultra-Zionists, however, it was a Heaven-sent chance to silence opposition to the behaviour of the far-right Israeli government and some have even demanded that people be targeted for 'anti-Semitism' under the new and outrageously-wide definition for articles they wrote years before it was adopted. A hysterical campaign orchestrated by ultra-Zionists and the lap-dog media was waged against the UK opposition Labour Party for weeks in 2018 to pressure them into accepting this definition by condemning the leader Jeremy Corbyn and the party hierarchy as 'anti-Semitic'. Jewish Labour MPs were activated to play the victim as part of the propaganda and add to the pressure on Corbyn to concede to ultra-Zionist demands.

We had extraordinary stupidity at the height of the hysteria when black Labour *anti-racist activist* Marc Wadsworth was expelled from the party for allegedly accusing Jewish Labour MP Ruth Smeeth of working with the *Daily Telegraph* newspaper to undermine the party over 'anti-Semitism' allegations. Wadsworth was, in effect, expelled for making 'anti-Semitic' remarks to Smeeth and bringing the party into 'disrepute' – impossible surely after this decision. But wait. Wadsworth didn't mention anything about Jews or even Israel and says he didn't even know Smeeth was Jewish. How could this be 'anti-Semitic'? *Ahhh ...* Smeeth claimed that Wadsworth connecting her to the *Daily Telegraph* was a 'traditional anti-Semitic slur to attack me for being part of a "media conspiracy."' These are the depths to which we have sunk in the desperation to block all exposure and criticism of ultra-Zionist extremism or any Jewish person supporting Israel. I got a feel for what it must be like now in the Labour Party when I posted a story on Twitter from a political website that was challenging what it called the witch-hunt in the party based on fraudulent claims of 'anti-Semitism'. I included a meme with a picture of Jewish Labour MP Luciana Berger, one of the big promotors of 'anti-Semitic' Labour, which simply said: 'This is the Labour Party, Ms Berger, not Likud.' To say the reaction was over-the-top is rather understating the case. Berger called me 'dangerous', reported me to Twitter for 'anti-Semitism', and a stream of tweet replies expressed sympathy for how she must be feeling and urging her to 'stay strong'. If in doubt play the victim card. Dr Alex Scott-Samuel, a *Jewish* chair of Berger's local Labour Party branch, was dubbed an anti-Semite (yes, really) for supporting two motions of no confidence against her over her constant attacks on leader Jeremy Corbyn for 'anti-Semitism'. The move could not have been a genuine attempt by party members to express discontent at her behaviour – it *had* to be anti-Semitism even though the man himself is Jewish. This is how the Protection Racket works.

The absolute desperation The Racket has with discrediting me was confirmed in the UK *Jewish Chronicle* edited by a bloke called Jonathan Pollard who once wrote an article condemning political correctness attacks on freedom of speech. I contacted him to support his view and asked him to confirm that he would now condemn all attempts by Zionist groups to have people's public events banned. He didn't reply. The *Chronicle* ran an article attacking the *Jewish* Dr Scott-Samuel for his appearances on a radio show that was once broadcast through Davidicke.com. Oh, he *has* to be an 'anti-Semite', then. The story included the claim that I say Jews are reptiles. The more desperate they get the more extreme and insane the claims. There was a hilarious interview at the peak of one period of attacks on the Labour Party when Simon Johnson, Chief Executive of the Jewish Leadership Council, commented in the usual soft-ball television interview that three Jewish papers, the *Jewish Chronicle*, *Jewish News* and *Jewish Telegraph* all ran the same headline – 'United We Stand' – and the same Labour-bashing editorial. Johnson said: 'It is unprecedented for three community newspapers to have the same headline, the same story, the same editorial.' So it wasn't carefully coordinated or anything as part of the ultra-Zionist campaign to destroy Jeremy Corbyn and force the Labour Party to adopt the coldly, calculated new definition of 'anti-Semitism'? You may think the British people are all idiots, Mr Johnson, but we're not. Medialens.org published a study of newspaper articles using the terms 'Jeremy Corbyn' and 'anti-Semitism' before and after May 1st, 2015. Before that date during 30 years as a Member of Parliament the number was 18. Since that date in the period he became Labour leader the number was: 11,251. Why? Corbyn was one of the few remaining British politicians who would criticise Israel and his new platform as leader meant he had to be silenced. Unfortunately, he has largely allowed himself to be – another glorious victory for The Racket. Twelve Holocaust survivors sent an open letter to *The Sunday Times* contending that Jeremy Corbyn had 'bent over backwards to help Jews' and that '[We] do not believe that any prejudice against or hostility towards Jews is being perpetuated by Labour.' This was a response to the UK Equality and Human Rights Commission announcing it would investigate the Labour Party's approach to anti-Semitism (bowing to ultra-Zionist pressure). The letter said media attention on the Labour Party in general, and on Corbyn in particular, was being generated by anti-Labour and anti-Corbyn mischief makers, 'who unfortunately are over-represented within the so-called Anglo-Jewish leadership' which was not considered legitimate by 'mainstream Charedi Jews'. Once again we see how ultra-Zionist groups set themselves up as the voice of Jewish people when they are not. We should also be aware of the fantastic army of trolls employed by Israel both to support its ambitions and to post anti-Jewish attacks which can be used as evidence of 'growing anti-Semitism'. The Electronic Intifada website highlighted ten Twitter accounts claiming to be Corbyn supporters posting anti-Jewish abuse that 'share sufficient similarities to indicate that the same person – or group – is running them'. The Protection Racket has absolutely no shame or integrity and only the naïve would dismiss that such fakery posting goes on all the time. By the way, Electronic Intifada reporter, Asa Winstanley, a member of the Labour Party, was suspended in March, 2019, for comments he made on Israel and Zionism. News of his suspension was leaked by the ultra-Zionist *Jewish Chronicle* before Winstanley even heard about it. Labour Party R.I.P.

New definition of ~~anti-Semitism~~ silencing dissent

A Labour Party leadership that would bend the knee to the 'anti-Semite' garbage about anti-racist activist Marc Wadsworth and Asa Winstanley couldn't possibly summon the backbone necessary to resist the ultra-Zionist onslaught. They should have stood firm and made it clear that this ultra-Zionist hate campaign was not about racism in the party, but about power *over* the party which still had people among its number prepared to criticise Israel. Labour's backbone turned to jelly and to mix my metaphors the hierarchy wagged its tail, rolled over, stuck its legs in the air, and accepted the expanded definition. Labour-connected group Jewish Voice for Peace and many other Jewish groups said they were appalled at the new definition and the campaign against the Labour Party. This mattered not a jot. They were the *wrong kind* of Jewish people with the *wrong kind* of opinions. Whether you are Jewish or not is irrelevant because it's irrelevant to ultra-Zionists. Agree to what we want or face dismissal and abuse – even more so if you're Jewish. Other UK political parties, the US Republicans and Democrats and so many others in Europe and Australia simply fall to their knees and hang out their tongue when ultra-Zionists come a-calling. This is the foundation statement in the new and expanded definition of 'anti-Semitism':

> Antisemitism is a certain perception of Jews, which may be expressed as hatred toward Jews. Rhetorical and physical manifestations of antisemitism are directed toward Jewish or non-Jewish individuals and/or their property, toward Jewish community institutions and religious facilities.

Okay, what's wrong with that? Well, on the face of it nothing if you ignore the vagueness and misuse of 'anti-Semitism'. The Devil is in the detail in the form of 'examples' given for what that definition means and how it should be applied and interpreted. Here they are:

> Contemporary examples of antisemitism in public life, the media, schools, the workplace, and in the religious sphere could, taking into account the overall context, include, but are not limited to:

> Calling for, aiding, or justifying the killing or harming of Jews in the name of a radical ideology or an extremist view of religion.

Fair enough. Does that work in reverse when ultra-Zionist extremists call for the killing of Palestinians? No.

> Making mendacious, dehumanizing, demonizing, or stereotypical allegations about Jews as such or the power of Jews as collective - such as, especially but not exclusively, the myth about a world Jewish conspiracy or of Jews

controlling the media, economy, government or other societal institutions.

This is a classic protection clause to stop any investigation and exposure of ultra-Zionist extremism. You have seen a blatant ultra-Zionist conspiracy – not 'Jewish', ultra-Zionist – to manipulate the United States into targeting the list of countries compiled by the ultra-Zionist Project for the New American Century a year before September 11th. You have seen evidence already and you are going to see a great deal more before the end of this book with regard to ultra-Zionist and Death Cult involvement in 9/11. However, under this 'example' such exposure would be 'anti-Semitic' and 'stereotyping'. The little matter of it being true is irrelevant to the definition and this is simply a calculated effort to secure protection from investigation by hiding behind the smokescreen of 'anti- Semitism'. I know we're doing it but you can't say we're doing it because that would be 'anti-Semitic'.

Accusing Jews as a people of being responsible for real or imagined wrongdoing committed by a single Jewish person or group, or even for acts committed by non-Jews.

Fair enough again. I am certainly not doing that and I have always made it clear that I am talking about a tiny group of ultra-Zionists, not Jewish people as a whole who I have said largely have no idea what is being done in their name. This is another important point – 'in their name'. Jewish people in general have often been collectively condemned for the actions of the ultra-Zionist few and paid the price while the few responsible do not. No one needs to understand this more than Jewish people as a collective. The other point with this 'example' is that when individual Jewish people such as George Soros are exposed for their provable manipulations the exposer is immediately accused of being 'anti- Semitic' both against the individual and Jews in general. They use the example one way but then reverse it to stop criticism or exposure of any Jewish person they want to protect. The 'example' is another expression of the Protection Racket.

Denying the fact, scope, mechanisms (e.g. gas chambers) or intentionality of the genocide of the Jewish people at the hands of National Socialist Germany and its supporters and accomplices during World War II (the Holocaust).

What happened to so many Jewish people in Nazi Germany was unspeakable and almost unimaginable. I wonder if it is really sensible and sensitive to commemorate victims of a Nazi tyranny that jailed or murdered people for their views and opinions to now jail, assassinate the character and destroy the lives of those asking questions about an historical happening and not accepting every last syllable of official history. Would it not be a far better tribute to the memory of Nazi victims for us to live in a society where questions can be asked and facts and evidence produced to prove a point rather than sending 'non-believers' to a jail cell or a life of mass condemnation? Wouldn't that be a world those who suffered in the concentration camps would like to see as a contrast to the actions and behaviour of their captures and killers? Does it really serve the memory of those people and what they went through to jail grandmothers for not accepting an historical narrative? Or is what is really happening here a case of weaponising the suffering of Jews in Germany to secure a political agenda today? I can't think of anything more cold and evil, but *isn't it?* I have been interviewed about this by software minds in the media and they insist – as the ultra-Zionists do – that you agree with every last strand of the official narrative or you are a Nazi bigot and 'Holocaust denier'. It has to be six million – don't you dare question if it was a single digit less. What a stomach-turning insult to those who were in the concentration camps as opposed to those exploiting them today who were not. You can call what happened unspeakable or a 'catastrophe' – Jews themselves call it the Shoah or 'calamity' – but none of this is even nearly enough. You must agree with the exactly designated figure or you are an anti-Semitic Nazi. One idiot on a Channel 10 morning show in Australia talked to me about *twelve million*. I can see why he got the job. Are you an idiot? Yes. When can you start?

The term 'holocaust' comes from the Greek 'holos' meaning 'completely' and 'kaustos' or 'sacrificial offering' and had been used to refer to destruction by fire. 'Holocaust' came into widespread use to describe events in German concentration camps after the 1978 TV film, *Holocaust*, starring Meryl Streep. Holocaust museums and memorials are still being built around the world with a new one planned for Victoria Tower Gardens in London next to the Houses of Parliament. Royal Parks rejected the idea on the grounds that it would 'dominate the park and eclipse the existing listed memorials which are nationally important in their own right'. UNESCO's International Council on Monuments and Sites agreed but the campaign to build the memorial continues as I write with all living UK prime ministers voicing support. A bill was introduced in the US House of Representatives in 2019 to 'finance grants to public and private middle and high schools to help teachers develop and improve Holocaust education programs'. The Never Again Education Act was deemed to be necessary by Zionist advocacy groups, including the Center for Jewish History in New York, in the light of 'reports of a rise in anti-Semitism and a decline in awareness of the Holocaust'. Democrat Carolyn Maloney, the bill's sponsor, said: 'Anti-Semitism is on the rise around the world and here at home, and the memory of the Holocaust is fading for far too many Americans – we can combat this by making sure we teach our students, tomorrow's leaders, about the horrors of the Holocaust.' Okay, but why is it fine to do this while it's a crime to ask a single question about the subject that in any way fails to accept that every word of what is presented in the museums and education programmes is 100 percent correct?

> Accusing the Jews as a people, or Israel as a state, of inventing or exaggerating the Holocaust.

Why would that be a problem? Surely in a civilised society you simply produce the evidence and proof that other arguments are misguided and wrong and the debate is over and won? Isn't this what a mature and free society does? If someone claimed that the millions killed by Pol Pot in Cambodia (close to 25 percent of the country's 1975 population) was an exaggeration would that mean they were racist against all Cambodians? Or that they were by definition far right Nazi bigots?

> Accusing Jewish citizens of being more loyal to Israel, or to the alleged priorities of Jews worldwide, than to the interests of their own nations.

This is the technique again of using the many to protect the few. Is this 'example' really saying that no Jewish person anywhere in the world – *not one* – is more loyal to Israel and the global Jewish community than the country they are living in? This is ridiculous and to have this as an example of 'anti-Semitism' is equally so. There is a difference between saying this or that person is more loyal to Israel and saying *every* Jewish person is the same and this is still another 'example' inserted by the Protection Racket.

> Denying the Jewish people their right to self-determination, e.g., by claiming that the existence of a State of Israel is a racist endeavor.

The irony of this is beyond belief given that in 2018 the Israeli parliament passed the 'national state law' which decrees that Israel is a Jewish state and only *Jews* living there have the right to 'national self-determination'. The law describes Israel for the first time as 'the national home of the Jewish people' and drops Arabic as an official language of the country. Prime Minister Netanyahu declared: 'This is our state – the Jewish state.' He means the one that was Arabic for centuries before 1948 and still has a 20 percent Arab population. The move has been dubbed 'an apartheid law', a term used by Israeli newspaper *Haaretz*, and the Israeli Labour Party and others voted against it. The ultra-Zionist lobby is seeking to ensure that anyone calling for equal rights for all Israelis no matter what their religion or race is condemned as *'anti-Semitic'*. We have crossed the border into the Land of Lunacy. Political commentator John Wight wrote:

> Learning the lessons of history is non-negotiable – and there has been nothing more squalid in our history than settler colonialism, responsible for the extirpation of the Native American Indians of North America and the aborigines of Australia. Those historical comparisons are fundamental when it comes to understanding the nature of the oppression and dispossession of the Palestinians in our time.

> That an Israeli government, led by Benjamin Netanyahu, can pass an explicit apartheid law – the country's so-called 'nation-state law' – mandating and enshrining the superior status of the state's Jewish citizens over its Arab minority of 1.8 million citizens, and do so without any international sanction, is a shameful indictment.

How on bloody earth can this bill be passed while at the same time any suggestion that 'the existence of a State of Israel is a racist endeavor' is being cited as an 'example' of 'anti-Semitism'? This is taking contradiction into the realms of insanity and all those countries and the UK Labour Party have accepted this outrageous example for lack of common sense and a pair of bollocks. Of course Israel is a racist endeavour, don't be silly. What do you say Mr Netanyahu? 'Oh, I say ... This is our state – the Jewish state.' Or, as he said in 2019: 'Israel is not a state of all its citizens. According to the nation state law we passed, Israel is the nation-state of the Jewish people – and not anyone else.' How very inclusive and we should launch a Benjamin Netanyahu Award for Narcissistic Hypocrisy. The new definition is claimed to be non-binding. Sure it is when it is being used to force people out of their jobs for the crime of criticising Israel. Paul Jonson, an employee of the UK Dudley Council near Birmingham, was suspended for posting on Facebook 'stand with Palestine, Israel is a racist endeavor'. Jonson was helping to organise a protest against Ian Austin, a local Labour Party MP and Israel propagandist. The suspension came after a complaint by the free-speech denying Campaign Against Antisemitism (CAA) of which MP Ian Austin is a patron.

> Applying double standards by requiring of it [Israel] a behaviour not expected or demanded of any other democratic nation.

Do they mean behaviour such as having military snipers blowing the legs off children and other unarmed protestors through a Gaza border fence with troops caught on camera cheering at their success? That behaviour, yes? Or dropping state-of-art bombs and missiles – some illegal under international law – on defenceless civilians in Gaza day and night for weeks in 2014 killing thousands of civilians including 500 children while ultra-Zionist psychopaths sat on hills above the carnage whooping and cheering? Is that what they mean? How about destroying or making uninhabitable more than 20,000 homes in that bombardment and displacing half a million people? Or Operation Cast Lead across 2008/2009 when more defenceless civilians and children were slaughtered from the sky? That behaviour, yes? Or shooting part of the head off a child and then jailing his 16-year-old cousin Ahed Tamimi for slapping a soldier who turned up at her home? Or jailing children in adult jails and treating them with callous inhuman contempt? That behaviour, yes?

Using the symbols and images associated with classic antisemitism (e.g., claims of Jews killing Jesus or blood libel) to characterize Israel or Israelis.

But Jews *did* kill 'Jesus' *according to the New Testament* even though I don't believe any of it. Is the Bible 'anti-Semitic' now when the Old Testament forms a foundation of the Jewish religion? How does that apply to all the Israel-supporting Christian Zionist churches in America who say that Jews must return to Israel before the 'messiah' can come? Extreme Christian Zionists actually believe that all Jews must return to Israel 'from the West' before Jesus the Messiah, or 'anointed one', comes and Jews will then be converted to Christianity or be doomed to Hell. How 'anti-Semitic' is that, but Christian Zionism is supported by the Death Cult and ultra-Zionists because it suits their short-term plans. John Hagee, the best-known frontman for this movement, is an Israel fanatic and founder and National Chairman of Christians United for Israel. Hagee has said that Adolf Hitler was born from a lineage of 'accursed, genocidally murderous half-breed Jews' and that 'God' allowed the Holocaust to happen to punish German Jews who didn't want to resettle in Israel according to Zionist demands and forced those who survived to do so. Not quite, many went to the United States. Outrageous as those words are Hagee is free to say them because he serves the ultra-Zionist cause. Christians who don't, however, are fair game for abuse and slander. Hagee was selected to give the closing benediction at the ceremony marking the opening of the US embassy in Jerusalem (Al-Quds to Palestinians) when Trump bowed to ultra-Zionist donors like casino magnate Sheldon Adelson to move the embassy from Tel Aviv with great symbolic and literal significance for Palestinians.

Drawing comparisons of contemporary Israeli policy to that of the Nazis.

Okay, so the far right government in Israel and its merciless military and intelligence networks are incapable of acting like Nazis did in Germany? It's just not possible, not now, not *ever?* How about Miriam 'Miri' Regev, the right wing Israel minister, former military censor and acting prime minister, who said that she was 'happy to be a fascist'? Or Strategic Affairs Minister Gilad Erdan who said: 'The number [of peaceful Palestinian protesters] killed does not mean anything because they are just Nazis anyhow'? Oh, it's fine to call others Nazis, but anti-Semitic if it is said about you. The Nazi mentality is not a race or culture it's a state of mind and that means every race and culture can produce Nazi-like crazies. If it looks like a duck, swims like a duck and quacks like a duck – it's probably a duck. Hajo Meyer is a Holocaust survivor condemned as 'anti-Semitic' for likening Israel to the Nazi regime – a *Holocaust survivor.* UK Labour Party leader Jeremy Corbyn spinelessly apologised in the face of ultra-Zionist and media demands for speaking with Meyer at an event in 2010. Auschwitz survivor Esther Bejarano, who lost both parents and a sister to the Nazis, has been called an 'anti-Semite' for condemning Israel's sickening treatment of the Palestinians. The 94-year-old has referred to the Netanyahu government as 'fascist – 'I have no other name for it'. Nor are there any words to describe those who never went near a concentration camp labelling those who did 'anti-Semites' while at the same time weaponising the term to silence opposition today. To claim that one particular government or group is not capable of Nazi-like behaviour and that it's racist or 'anti-Semitic' to say so is the Protection Racket at work.

Holding Jews collectively responsible for actions of the state of Israel.

Ahh, but criticise the government of Israel in isolation and they say you are being 'anti-Semitic' against *all* Jews. You can't have it both ways, but that's what they want and this is what the new definition is really all about. How can you have a situation where any criticism of anyone that happens to be Jewish is labelled as 'anti-Semitic'? Are they the only people in all eternity who never do anything worthy of criticism and if you question their actions this is, by definition, racist?? What about the mass demonstration by Israeli women in 2018 about 28 of them murdered by domestic violence in Israel during that year? If non-Jews condemn that and the perpetrators of the violence is this proof of their 'anti-Semitism'? Or do those critics simply care about violence against women no matter what their creed or background?

We will silence them

Governments, education campuses and other organisations the world over are being pressured, manipulated and intimidated into accepting this calculated censorious stupidity to silence criticism of Israel and the extremes of the ultra-Zionist network. The consequences of this are already seen in cancelled events, lectures and conferences exposing or debating the actions of Israel and they are increasing all the time. I describe many examples in my last book, *Everything You Need To Know But Have Never Been Told*, and the chapter 'Terrified of Truth'. Events and discussion regarding Israel are being cancelled or banned when they would not have been before because of the expanded definition. Jewish historian Ilan Pappé, professor at the College of Social Sciences and International Studies at the UK University of Exeter, said:

> In the past anti-Semitism hated Jews for being Jews, now Israel is trying to extend it to say that this is any criticism about what Jews are doing ... If you question the right for Israel to be a Jewish state then you are no different from these classical anti-Semites.

Joseph Berman, an American rabbi and a campaigner with Jewish Voice for Peace, condemned the attempts to define anti-Semitism in ways that fuse actual anti-Semitism with 'completely legitimate criticism of Israel or Israel government policies'. John Mearsheimer, Professor of Political Science at the University of Chicago, said this is one of the major Israel Lobby tactics to defend against criticism and the tactic was being used more and more 'to identify people who criticise Israel as an anti-Semite'. We are seeing this scam emerging everywhere with Emmanuel Macron, the arrogant and idiotic Rothschild employee and gofer President of France, announcing in 2019 that criticism of Zionism (a political philosophy not supported by many Jews) should be equated with 'anti-Semitism'. Trump and the US government say the same. The almost laughable overuse of the term in their desperation to stop criticism of the far, far right Israeli government is allowing gathering numbers to see through the mirage of bullshit. At the same time that 'anti-Semitism' (i.e. racism) is used to target and silence critics we had Israel launching an advertising campaign urging Israelis to inform on Jewish friends and relatives abroad who may be 'in danger' of marrying non-Jews. Television and Internet advertising has sought to stop the 'assimilation' of Jews outside Israel (diaspora Jews as they are called) and urges them to move to Israel. The idea is to increase the size of the Israeli population to seize more and more Palestinian land. One advertisement said that 'assimilation' (Jews marrying the partner they love) is 'a strategic national threat' and warned that 'more than 50 percent of diaspora youth assimilate and are lost to us'. Lost to '*us*'? Who do these people think they are? They treat the mass of Jews like commodities which is what they are to them. One advertisement featured missing person posters showing images of Jewish youths with the word 'lost' in various languages. The voiceover asked people who 'know a young Jew living abroad' to call a hotline and give details. 'Together, we will strengthen their connection to Israel, so that we don't lose them,' it said. Israel also refuses to recognise Jewish and Arabian intermarriage unless it is performed abroad. Isaac Herzog, outgoing leader of Israel's Labor Party, said in 2018 that intermarriage between Jews and non-Jews was a 'plague" which required a "solution'. Can you imagine if anyone else spoke or acted with such facism? They would be condemned by Israel and its endless front organisations. Jewish researchers Max Blumenthal and Jesse Rosenfeld exposed Israeli racism with their YouTube video *Feeling the Hate in Jerusalem* in which American Jews visiting the country were asked about Barack Obama. A barrage of foul-mouthed racism followed including: 'White power! Fuck the niggers!' There was also extraordinary racism from Israeli students towards Palestinians. The video was banned by ultra-Zionist-controlled YouTube and some other sites after getting hundreds of thousands of hits. If that had been a video of white supremacists condemning Jews in the same terms there would have been a global outcry and YouTube would be promoting the hell out of it. The hypocrisy is criminal. Israel minister Miriam Regev called African asylum seekers a 'cancer in the nation's body,' inciting anti-immigrant protests and far right racism in general against black immigrants seeking to stay in Israel (Fig 98). Ultra-Zionism is an extreme racist doctrine that has the nerve to accuse everyone else of racism and deports African asylum-seekers and migrants while its agents urge and manipulate the rest of the world to accept indefinite mass-migration until their societies are demographically transformed.

Figure 98: Jewish protest against black Africans in Israel. This is not racist, however, and it's 'anti-Semitic' to say so.

Ultra-Zionist censorship network

Ultra-Zionism has established an absolutely *enormous* global network of front organisations and hate groups to target politicians, activists and anyone else with the audacity to challenge the actions of Israel and/or support the cause of the psychopathically-abused Palestinian people. This is directed and coordinated from the Ministry of Strategic Affairs and Public Diplomacy located in the Prime Minister's Office under Director-General Sima Vaknin-Gill, a former IDF chief censor and Israel

Air Force intelligence officer. The Ministry's brief is to target and 'name and shame' critics of Israel with special emphasis on the Boycott, Divestment and Sanctions (BDS) campaign for boycotts of Israeli goods and services until the government complies with international law in the treatment and rights of Palestinians. Demands include handing back occupied Palestinian land, taking down the separation wall with the illegally-occupied West Bank, equal rights for Palestinians and Jews and the right of return for Palestinians terrorised into leaving their homeland by ultra-Zionist terror groups when the State of Israel was formed in 1948. The BDS movement has grown at great speed since it was launched in 2005 and operates worldwide with gathering success that the Israeli regime is desperate to stop or mitigate. BDS was established as a non-violent means way of challenging impositions and violence by the military might of Israel to press for a simple humanitarian goal of having Jews and Arabs treated the same. That should be a gimme in any civilised free society, but John Mearsheimer, professor of political science at the University of Chicago, highlighted the key reason why Israel will not agree to that:

> BDS is saying that what Israel has to do is treat the Palestinians in its midst the same way it treats Israeli Jews. The problem is that if Israel does that there are more Palestinians or there will be more Palestinians inside greater Israel than there are Jews and that means that if you had a system where everybody was treated equally and there was one person and one vote you would no longer have a Jewish state.

The reason we have an apartheid Israel is that they don't want a free and equal society but a racist one – the full-blown Jewish state which the ultra-Zionists and Death Cult are determined to impose. To hide clear and obvious racism and ultra-Zionist manipulation in other countries (including 9/11) they have to control the narrative by emphasising their own propaganda while censoring other information and opinions. *The Seventh Eye*, an Israeli media watchdog organisation, reported that the Strategic Affairs (Censorship/Defamation) Ministry paid $100,000 to the publisher of Israel's best-selling daily newspaper to run articles and videos attacking BDS as 'anti-Semitic'. The watchdog added that this was part of a wider campaign by the Ministry which had a $740,000 budget 'to promote content on social media and search engines, including Google, Twitter, Facebook and Instagram'. An added bonus is that ultra-Zionist-controlled Facebook and other social media platforms act as censors for the Israel military. The Electric Intifada website reported in 2018 that Twitter had demanded the removal of a post that the Israeli IDF did not want to be circulated. 'In recent days, other publications and individuals have faced the same demand, indicating that the social media firm has agreed to become an enforcement arm for Israel's efforts to control information about potential war crimes and abuses of Palestinian rights', the website said. 'It is another ominous sign of how monopolistic Silicon Valley corporations – especially Facebook and Google – that control what are in effect the public commons are colluding with governments to reassert control of information previously lost due to the freedom provided by the internet.' Facebook and Google (which owns YouTube) are ultra-Zionist-controlled corporations *officially* created and run by Jewish 'progressives' Mark Zuckerberg, Sergei Brin and Larry Page and as such Israel and ultra-Zionism dictate censorship policy. Wikipedia where most people get their background information about people and events today is the work of staunchly pro-Israel Zionist and Tony Blair buddy, Jimmy Wales. There is also Amazon, officially controlled by Jeff Bezos with its close connections to the Pentagon and CIA, which somehow absorbed massive losses year after year to secure dominance in the book market and from this position of near-monopoly has now begun a gathering policy of book banning/burning – 'anti-Semitism' among the most prominent excuses. Amazon has taken the same route as Facebook, Google/YouTube and others. No censorship when they are building their near-monopolies and then ever more extreme censorship once domination has been secured (Fig 99). The overall Israeli campaign to weaponise 'anti-Semitism' and demonise critics is called the Hasbara which means 'explaining' in Hebrew. More accurately in this case 'explaining' means ultra-Zionist propaganda and controlling the narrative throughout the media in all its forms and targeting critics – *especially* Jewish ones (Fig 100). Israel bans BDS supporters and Israel critics from the country and this

Figure 99: If exposure of Israel is not outright banned by YouTube and others, or its circulation algorithmically suppressed, then the viewer is given warnings like this.

Figure 100: Ultra-Zionist Israeli propaganda in a single image.

includes Jews with the wrong opinions. Rebecca Vilkomerson, executive director of the US-based Jewish Voice for Peace, described the personal consequences of this increasing discrimination on the grounds of opinion. She said of one new law:

> My grandparents are buried in Israel. My husband and kids are citizens, and I lived there for three years, but this bill would bar me from visiting because of my work in support of Palestinian rights.

German newspaper *Die Tageszeitung*, better known as *taz*, revealed in 2018 that the Israeli government was demanding Germany stop funding the Jewish Museum in Berlin and other Jewish human rights organisations including B'Tselem, Coalition of Women for Peace, Israeli publication *+972 Magazine* and Breaking the Silence, an organisation that allows Israeli soldiers to tell the truth about what is happening to Palestinians. Netanyahu wanted the funding stopped because these organisations present a far more balanced view of the Israel-Palestinian conflict and allow free discussion on the subject. Dozens of Israeli artists wrote an open letter to the paper urging the German government to ignore the demand and expressing their shock at the actions of the Israel government. No one should be shocked at the far-right ultra-Zionist extremists targeting Jewish people and organisations who deviate from the script. This is what they do all the time.

Manipulation on a fantastic scale

The ultra-Zionist network is vast and its censorship and intimidation are the reason why the general public has not seen the information that I will be presenting of ultra-Zionist and Death Cult involvement in 9/11. We have New York-based Hasbara Fellowships which train pro-Israel activists on college campuses. These were introduced in 2001 by the Israel Ministry of Foreign Affairs and a Jewish Orthodox organisation which claim to have so far trained nearly 2,000 students on more than 220 North American campuses. The ultra-Zionist and Zionist network in the United States consists of lobby groups, think-tanks, media watchdog groups (censors), spying operations connected to Israel and Mossad, and what are called political action committees or 'PACs'. John Mearsheimer, a professor of political science at the University of Chicago, and Stephen Walt, professor of international relations at the Kennedy School of Government at Harvard University, expose this network in their 2007 book, *The Israel Lobby and U.S. Foreign Policy*. They say the Israel Lobby 'has a core consisting of organizations whose declared purpose is to encourage the US government and the American public to provide material aid to Israel and to support its government's policies, as well as influential individuals for whom these goals are also a top priority'. The network has become known as The Lobby and it went into overdrive after 9/11 to secure the American fought-and-funded 'war on terror'. This is only a *small* sample of The Lobby's amazing web of organisations within the United States alone:

American Israel Public Affairs Committee (AIPAC); Jewish Institute for National Security Affairs (JINSA); American Jewish Congress; Zionist Organization of America; Washington Institute for Near East Policy; Anti-Defamation League (ADL); Christians United for Israel; Israel Policy Forum; American Jewish Committee; Religious Action Center of Reform Judaism; Americans for a Safe Israel; Republican Jewish Coalition; American Friends of Likud; Mercaz-USA; Hadassah; Israeli-American Coalition for Action; Israeli-American Council; Alliance for Israel Advocacy; Americans for Peace Now; Tikkun Community; Brit Tzedek v'Shalom; Israel Policy Forum; American Enterprise Institute; Hudson Institute. Center for Security Policy; Foreign Policy Research Institute; Institute for Foreign Policy Analysis; Heritage Foundation; Saban Center for Middle East Policy; Center for Security Policy; Committee for Accuracy in Middle East Reporting in America; Conference of Presidents of Major American Jewish Organizations (an umbrella group for more than 50 Zionist lobby groups and Israel policy promotors) with the mission of 'forging diverse groups into a unified force for Israel's well-being' and to 'strengthen and foster the special US-Israel relationship'.

The latter is Orwellian-speak for manipulating America to serve the interests of Israel and ultra-Zionists especially through funding and the military. The infamous Project for the New American Century which did so much to establish the catastrophic (but not for Israel) 'war on terror' was part of this network before it became too exposed and high profile and disappeared to reform under another name. I emphasise that this is only a very *partial* list from what is a truly incredible web of organisations – some estimate as many as 800 – serving the same agenda that claims to serve the interests of just 0.2 percent of the world population and two percent of the American public (Fig 101). In truth it is doesn't even represent that tiny number and it is not supposed to. Ultra-Zionism and the Death Cult are the network's masters and focus. The great majority of people will have never have heard of these organisations while the more high-profile ones hide their real controllers and intentions behind

Figure 101: Tiny country – global reach.

cover stories and mission statements.

Southern Very Rich Israel Center 'plantation'

A major example of Israel agenda groups hiding behind cover stories is
the Southern Poverty Law Center (SPLC) in the United States
established by lawyers Morris Dees and Zionist Joseph J. Levin Jr in
Montgomery, Alabama. The organisation was headed by ultra-Zionist
President and CEO Richard Cohen until he fell on his sword in 2019 in
the wake of a scandal which caused Morris Dees to be removed. Ultra-
Zionist 'legal director' Rhonda Brownstein left with Cohen. Both had
worked for the SPLC for 30 years and were paid huge salaries to label as
'hate groups' any organisation the ultra-Zionist Mafia demanded to be
silenced and demonised. A mirror is all they need at the SPLC if they
want to locate a hate group. Morris Dees is credited as a major influence
in the strategy of issuing lawsuits against target organisations for an
alleged 'wrongful act' and securing court judgements to seize their
assets and drive them into bankruptcy. This was the forerunner of the
ultra-Zionist technique today known as 'lawfare' in which Zionist hate
groups with lots of money or pro-bono ultra-Zionist lawyers take out
civil actions against people when law enforcement has decided that the
target has done nothing wrong. They couldn't care less what this does to
people's lives, but then psychopaths never do. Morris Dees was
removed from the organisation in 2019 amid allegations of a *racist culture*
(irony of ironies) while Cohen and Brownstein left soon afterwards.
Black employees came forward to tell their stories. One said the working
environment was like a 'plantation' for black workers. Out of 100
lawyers and advocates for the SPLC only five were black. This is the self-
styled 'anti-racist', 'anti-hate', fraudulent censorship operation that dubs
others racists and hatemongers. The *Washington Examiner* described the
SPLC as a 'scam' with 'no care whatsoever for the reputational and
personal harm it causes by lumping Christians and anti-extremist
activists with actual neo-Nazis':

> As it turns out, the SPLC is a cynical money-making scheme, according to a
> former staffer's blistering tell-all, published this week in the New Yorker. The
> center's chief goal is to bilk naive and wealthy donors who believe it's an
> earnest effort to combat bigotry. The only thing worse than a snarling partisan
> activist is a slimy conman who merely pretends to be one.

Here you have the blueprint for ultra-Zionist hate groups and this
disgusting organisation advises Facebook, Twitter, Google, YouTube,
Amazon and others on who should be censored as a 'hate group'.
Former employee Bob Moser said they spent a lot of time 'drinking and
dishing' in Montgomery bars and restaurants about 'hyperbolic fund-

raising appeals' in which 'hate' was always on the rise and more dangerous than ever with each new report on 'hate groups'. He said it was 'hard for many of us not to feel like we'd become pawns in what was, in many respects, a highly profitable scam'. Have you ever heard an ultra-Zionist hate group say that 'anti-Semitism' was not on the rise? Selling the perception of 'hate' fills the coffers and provides the excuse to silence and demonise people while hate and racism are in the mirror all along. The SPLC, it is safe to say, is not what it appears to be as with so many in the ultra-Zionist web which claim to represent wider issues of civil rights when really fronting for Israel and the ultra-Zionist agenda. For a start the Southern *Poverty* Law Center is nothing to do with 'poverty'. The organisation is extremely rich thanks to big donations (including from Soros foundations) and only a fraction of its work relates to 'law'. At least it's based in Alabama, so I guess the 'southern' bit is true. A 2003 audit revealed that *89 percent* of SPLC income went in 'administrative costs and fundraising' while only *11 percent* was spent on its alleged mission (alleged being the word) of 'advancing human rights'. The SPLC admitted in 2015 that only $61,000 was spent on legal services (it's a 'law center') while receiving $50 million in donations and having assets of $328 million. Even worse it squirrels away millions in multiple unregulated offshore tax havens in the Cayman Islands, British Virgin Islands and Bermuda while at the same time being classed as a 'non-profit' organisation with all the tax benefits that entails. Ultra-Zionist fronts and hate groups invariably use their contacts to be designated as 'non-profit' in America or 'charities' in Britain. How can a 'charity' enjoy all the benefits of that status while spending its time hurling hate at its targets, manipulating politically and seeking to silence anyone whose opinion doesn't suit the ultra-Zionists behind Israel? They can do this because they are a law unto themselves on the basis of my dad is bigger than your dad. The power of the Zionist lobby, especially in America, is breathtaking and so they do what they like despite their tiny numbers. This is one analysis of SPLC income:

The Capital Research Center have revealed some of the main funders between the years 2000-2011. Between these years by far the biggest donor was the Picower Foundation, founded by the Jewish Jeffry Picower, the largest beneficiary of the Bernie Madoff financial swindle, to the tune of $3,813,112. Other high profile backers include Cisco Systems at $1,620,000 between the years 2000-2004, the Grove Foundation (associated with the Jewish Andrew Grove, a co-founder of the Intel Corporation) at $875,000 from 2001-2011, the Richard and Rhoda Goldman Fund (Jewish heirs of the Levi Strauss fortune) at $535,000, and Rockefeller Philanthropy at $510,000 between 2008-2010, amongst many others.

Further donors include Apple and the clueless virtue-signalling celebrity George Clooney who handed them a million dollars in 2017. Ultra-Zionist PayPal CEO Dan Schulman admitted during an interview with the *Wall Street Journal* in 2019 that his company consults with the ultra-Zionist SPLC over who to ban from its services. Schulman is a mega-bullshitter who says that PayPal's 'values' are founded on 'diversity and inclusion'. The monumental hypocrite then bans those with views he disagrees with (non-agenda people) and discriminates against Palestinians while working with Israelis. PayPal pulled the payment plug on uncensored BitChute, a video site competitor of ultra-Zionist YouTube, and other uncensored sites offering alternatives to all-censoring ultra-Zionist giants. Yep, Schulman believes in diversity and it is so good to know that he has 'values'. The SPLC portrays itself as a human rights or civil rights organisation as in for 'everyone'. This is just bollocks. The ultra-Zionist network pedals front-stories while its real goal is attacking, labelling and silencing those who don't bow to Israel and the ultra-Zionist agenda. Long-time SPLC spokesman Mark Potok, who always looks like he's chewing a lemon, told an event in Michigan in 2007: 'Sometimes the press will describe us as monitoring hate groups. I want to say plainly that our aim in life is to destroy these groups, completely destroy them.' A year later he continued the theme for a Vermont school meeting:

> You are able to destroy these groups sometimes by the things you publish. It's not so much that they will bring down the police or the federal agents on their head, it's that you can sometimes so mortally embarrass these groups that they will be destroyed.

The SPLC is best-known for its 'hate group' list that includes a stream of organisations which are not in the least hate groups – unlike itself. Among its 'categories' of hate are white nationalist, Ku Klux Klan, Neo-Confederate, skinhead, white power music, radical traditional Catholicism, Holocaust denial, Christian identity, anti-LGBT, black separatist, anti-Muslim and anti-immigrant. Some listings are justified but many are not with qualification decided largely by those the SPLC's masters and owners wish to demonise and silence. This naturally includes 'conspiracy theorists' and those questioning government narratives. Amazing how so many want to silence 'conspiracy theorists' for saying what is claimed to be so obviously crazy. These are some the SPLC does NOT designate to be hate groups: Those supporting Jewish supremacism; groups demanding sharia law (with discrimination and/or violence against non-Muslims, women, and homosexuals); Communist organisations promoting class hatred and praising Communist mass murderers; social anarchist organizations committing violence and other crimes against opponents; non-white, pro-terrorist or terrorist organisations that promote or commit violence; anti-white hip hop groups. The criteria are clearly not about hate, but agenda. Pulitzer Prize winning journalist Jerry Kammer produced a report exposing the systematic bias of the SPLC both in general and in particular with the case of the Federation for American Immigration Reform (FAIR) which seeks to reduce the number of immigrants entering the United States – especially illegally. Ultra-Zionists and the Death Cult want open borders and an end to countries and nations and so the SPLC went to work branding FAIR a 'hate group' in an effort to exclude it from the national debate on immigration. Kammer wrote:

> With no serious analysis, the SPLC in late 2007 unilaterally labelled FAIR a 'hate group'. That poisonous designation became the centrepiece of a 'Stop the Hate' campaign launched by the National Council of La Raza (NCLR), also known as La Raza, to call on Congress and the media to exclude FAIR from the national debate on immigration.

> The campaign gathered strength as newspapers across the country reported that FAIR had been 'designated a hate group by the Southern Poverty Law Center'. While the news stories generally included FAIR's denial of the charge, thereby providing a semblance of balance, the designation's taint lingered. The SPLC, presenting itself as a non-partisan, public-interest watchdog, never acknowledged – and no reporter ever disclosed – that the center was an active ally of the NCLR in the campaign.

> The evidence presented here demonstrates that the SPLC became a propaganda arm of the NCLR. The SPLC's decision to smear FAIR was the work of a kangaroo court, one convened to reach a pre-determined verdict by inventing or distorting evidence. The 'Stop the Hate' campaign would more accurately be labelled as a campaign to 'Stop the Debate'.

What an encapsulation of how these ultra-Zionist organisations work throughout the global network using labels of 'hate group' and 'hate speech' to silence dissent for those that control Israel. Type 'Jerry Kammer SPLC' into a search engine and you can read the whole article which exposes the methods of the Southern Poverty Law Center and they are the same as all the ultra-Zionist hate groups. Part of this war on predominantly white societies in the culture-fusion agenda is to delete their history, both good and bad. The SPLC was straight in there in the wake of conflict between 'progressives' and the political right over a Confederate statue at Charlottesville, Virginia, in 2017: 'More than 1,500 Confederate monuments stand in communities like Charlottesville with the potential to unleash more turmoil and bloodshed,' it said. 'It's time to take them down.' They are nothing if not predictable if you know the game that's being played. The point is not about supporting Confederate history but acknowledging that it happened. History is a culture's heritage, what we liked and what we didn't. Once it's gone, so has the culture, and the manipulators know that. This came to mind when the 800-year-old Notre Dame Cathedral in Paris, a global Christian icon, was devastated by fire in 2019 and look how invaders like the US military and ISIS target historical artefacts and ancient monuments as happened in Iraq and Syria. The SPLC has been a major driver of the campaign to pull down historical monuments and for the same reason history is systematically neglected in schools and universities. A poll asked 2,000 people about the First World War (1914-18) and found that six-percent of millennials thought the conflict started over the assassination of President Kennedy (in 1963); one in ten thought Margaret Thatcher was British prime minister during that war when she was in office from 1979 to 1990; almost *half* thought Britain's World War II prime minister Winston Churchill was leader during World War I; a quarter believed Britain was in conflict with war ally Russia and a fifth thought the war was with ally France; five percent of younger people in the poll thought the 'Battle for Helms Deep' from the *Lord of the Rings* movie trilogy was a battle in the First World War. This revealed a dramatic decline in historical knowledge since the 'baby boomers' generation (born between 1946 and the early 1960s) and even since 'Generation X' (early-to-mid-1960s to the early 1980s) although that, too, showed a decline. The figures are highly significant when the deletion of history means the deletion of the culture developed from that history. Mindless destruction of historical monuments and statues by mindless 'progressive' mobs responding to their software are part of this end of history – Orwell's Memory Hole where history is deleted so the past can become whatever it suits authority to be in the present. This is happening with information exposing 9/11 deleted, pushed down the search engine listings or 'quarantined' in the case of Reddit. You would expect the Southern Poverty Law Center and the Hidden Hand to be right there at the front line of censorship and major Hidden Hand corporations including Amazon use the purposely-flawed-and-biased SPLC 'hate-list' to make decisions on who to support and who to censor. The SPLC ultra-Zionist hate group list is also the Bible of 'progressive' hate groups such as Antifa, a named that derives from 'antifascist' while employing precisely those methods to violently suppress dissent against programmed 'progressive' orthodoxy. Indeed 'orthodoxy' is the perfect description because 'progressive' actually refers to a religion in which faith and not facts are the criteria for entry and perception. We can open the borders to everyone and there won't be any consequence is only another version of Jesus walked on water. You have no facts to support what you say and it goes against all the evidence, but you believe it anyway because you are speaking the words of the Lord, well, George Soros.

SPLC and the FBI

I saw long ago how ultra-Zionist hate groups and other Israel fronts work closely with law enforcement to secure their ends and after what I have written in the book so far about the FBI and 9/11 you won't be surprised to hear that Fox News host Tucker Carlson, one the last surviving real journalist anchors on US television, reported connections between the FBI and the Southern Poverty Law Center. Carlson has faced (failed) attempts to intimidate him when mindless 'progressive' Antifa toddlers gutlessly turned up at his home while knowing he was presenting a live show elsewhere and only his family would be there. 'Progressives' are against 'toxic masculinity' intimidating women, you see. Many efforts have been made to take Carlson's show down including targeting advertisers. The Soros-funded propaganda operation Media Matters trawled through his broadcasting life to find anything they could use to discredit him and in March, 2019, they came up with comments he made years earlier about women while joking around with a 'shock jock'. 'Progressive' rage was unleashed. I didn't agree with what he said, but I agree with his right to say it and take any consequences that follow. It's called freedom of speech and you could never accuse a Soros 'progressive' of having a sense of humour and proportion. Fortunately Carlson gave the perpetually outraged mob the finger instead of falling to his knees. I don't know Tucker Carlson and have never met him, but what I have seen is a man – one of the last standing – who is prepared to ask questions and make points that the elite would love to silence. This is the real reason he is being targeted and that's easy when rage is on tap – the tap of a keyboard away.

Carlson has well understood the propaganda garbage spewed out by the SPLC hate group which he described as 'an entirely fraudulent enterprise', 'totally dishonest' and 'a left-wing political group that uses hate crime designations to target its ideological enemies and to crush people'. He pointed out that wrongly designating organisations as hate groups had led them to be subjected to violence and that the SPLC had been forced to pay $3.3 million in a court case over falsely labelling a foundation as anti-Muslim extremists when it was created and run by a Muslim who condemns Islamic extremism. The guy had to be silenced because he is the wrong type of Muslim preaching peace and not violence. Carlson's report revealed the FBI has a long record of collaborating with the SPLC which the Bureau described as 'a well-established and credible organisation that monitors domestic terrorism in the US'. For 'domestic terrorism' read anyone challenging government propaganda and the ultra-Zionist agenda. Carlson said the

SPLC had been briefing the FBI on 'extremists' and this was ongoing. The agency refused to answer simple questions about the relationship and anyone who has investigated 9/11 will be well aware of FBI stonewalling. Given its cancerous corruption I can understand why its drawbridge is permanently pointing upwards. The FBI/SPLC connection is another example of how The Web functions as a vehicle for coordination between organisations that appear unconnected to the public eye while really operating to secure mutual goals. The political nature of the FBI was revealed by accident on the Carlson show in an interview with former FBI Deputy Assistant Director Terry Turchie. He said in a passing remark that when he first joined the Bureau 'one of the missions of the FBI in its counterintelligence efforts was to try and keep these people out of government'. He was talking about those considered 'left-wing' at the time, but the political stance of the FBI has now shifted in line with a different stage of the Hidden Hand agenda. The point is that here was a former FBI Deputy Assistant Director admitting to manipulating events to influence who could secure political power. This was the main investigation agency of 9/11. I have personal experience of British police also supporting the censorship agenda of ultra-Zionist hate groups as I will be describing.

Censorship Valley

Ultra-Zionist censorship connections also apply to Silicon Valley. The Southern Poverty Law Center despite being, as Carlson said, 'entirely fraudulent' and 'totally dishonest', has partnered with music streaming platform Spotify to 'crack down' on 'hate content' and 'hateful conduct' – censor in accordance with the ultra-Zionist agenda of the SPLC. Spotify's definition of hate speech is anything 'that expressly and principally promotes, advocates, or incites hatred or violence against a group or individual based on characteristics, including, race, religion, gender identity, sex, ethnicity, nationality, sexual orientation, veteran status, or disability'. Observe the limitless potential for making almost anything fit that criteria to justify targeted censorship and we have these Israel-serving hate groups also 'advising' Facebook, Google, YouTube and others on what should be deleted from those platforms. Add to this Soros-funded 'fact checker' organisations employed by the same companies to decide what is 'fake news' and is it any wonder that in this same period ever greater numbers of alternative groups and researchers have been banned from Facebook and YouTube and been made to disappear by Google search list algorithms? *Washington Free Beacon* reported on a leaked 49-page document that revealed how Media Matters and other Soros funded-groups have 'access to raw data from Facebook, Twitter, and other social media sites' to 'systemically monitor and analyse this unfiltered data' to eliminate 'right wing propaganda

and fake news' (what we don't want the public to see). Shouldn't we be
legitimately questioning why ultra-Zionist censors are employed by
Google headed by Larry Page (Zionist) and Sergey Brin (Zionist);
Google's YouTube run by Susan Wojcicki (Zionist); and Facebook run by
Mark Zuckerberg (Zionist) along with Chief Operating Officer Sheryl
Sandberg (Zionist), formerly with Google; and Apple chaired by Arthur
D. Levinson (Zionist)? *Quiet!* To ask why so much power over what we
can see is in the hands of people from two percent of the population of
the United States and 0.2 percent of the world population is 'anti-
Semitic'! No – it's a *legitimate question* and all the censorship and
weaponising of 'anti-Semitism' is to stop that question being asked.
Well, fuck that. The ultra-Zionist Anti-Defamation League (ADL) has a
state-of-the-art Silicon Valley Internet censorship centre to track what
people post and 'provide insights to government and policy makers'
using the 'best-in-class technology' to 'stamp out hate' and 'anti-
Semitism'. Ultra-Zionist censorship has moved to a whole new level and
soon it will be impossible to criticise Israel and have any public arena
see or hear what you say. This is a main reason for why I am calling
them out in such an in-your-face manner in this book. It could be last
chance we have to expose the truth about what ultra-Zionism *really* is,
how it operates and to what end. Remember the Reddit 'quarantine' of
information exposing 9/11 and the direction to the official lies of the
9/11 Commission? What better way to hide the 9/11 involvement of
ultra-Zionism and make all questioning of the attacks just disappear?
This is meant to be the norm very soon.

Anti-Free Speech Defame People League

The ADL is the Big Daddy of ultra-Zionist hate groups and an example
of those in The Lobby which are transparently censoring for Israel.
Many try to hide this fact by claiming to represent the 'human rights' of
other people, but they don't. The ADL is the offspring of the House of
Rothschild and ultra-Zionist front B'nai B'rith, or 'Sons of the Covenant',
which was established in 1843 by twelve founders all born in Rothschild
Germany who moved to New York in the same period from the late
1820s to the 1830s. B'nai B'rith claims to be the 'global voice of the
Jewish Community' when it is nothing of the kind. American rabbi,
Marvin S. Antelman, worked to expose the Death Cult that I will be
addressing in detail. He writes in his two-volume *To Eliminate the Opiate*:

> After doing the terrible things certain establishment organisations such as
> B'nai B'rith and the American Jewish Congress did by playing the ostrich
> during the Shoah [Holocaust], why do we still give these organizations any
> support? They have Jewish blood on their hands ... They should be ignored
> and condemned to the cesspools of history. It is very aggravating to see them

continue their self-identity hating campaigns.

We will see as our story develops that there are in fact two distinct groups – fake Jews which are the people I am exposing here and genuine Jews who are something very different although most will not be aware of the frauds in their midst. They will be by the time I've finished and relate all this to 9/11. Many genuine Jews don't support B'nai B'rith and what it does. It represents the voice of the ultra-Zionist agenda, not Jewish people. As such it has attacked me for exposing that agenda and so has the Anti-Defamation League which B'nai B'rith created. I take this as a compliment. B'nai B'rith, which is closely connected to Freemasonry, established the ADL in 1913 and it remains the best-known name in the ultra-Zionist censorship network. The main role of the 'Anti-Defamation' League is ironically to defame people, label them 'anti-Semites' for exposing Israel and its lobby and to crush them into the smallest pieces possible. Its motto appears to be: 'We are the Chosen People and above all others, and you are a racist.' Or maybe the Mossad motto might be better: 'By way of deception, thou shalt do war.' Either works with the ADL. Jewish academic Noam Chomsky said this of the ADL in his book, *Necessary Illusions*:

The ADL has virtually abandoned its earlier role as a civil rights organization, becoming 'one of the main pillars' of Israeli propaganda in the U.S., as the Israeli press casually describes it, engaged in surveillance, blacklisting, compilation of FBI-style files circulated to adherents for the purpose of defamation, angry public responses to criticism of Israeli actions, and so on. These efforts, buttressed by insinuations of anti-Semitism or direct accusations, are intended to deflect or undermine opposition to Israeli policies, including Israel's refusal, with U.S. support, to move towards a general political settlement.

American Rabbi Michael Lerner took the same view:

The ADL lost most of it credibility in my eyes as a civil rights organization when it began to identify criticisms of Israel with anti-Semitism, still more when it failed to defend me when I was receiving threats to my life from right-wing Jewish groups because of my critique of Israeli policy toward Palestinians (it said that these were not threats that came from my being Jewish, so therefore they were not within their area of concern).

The reason for this is simple. The ADL has never been a 'civil rights' organisation and was never meant to protect all Jewish people. It was specifically established to protect the ultra-Zionist agenda and by extension only those Jews working in support of that agenda and its

Protection Racket. What about all other Jews? Those who speak *against* the agenda? The ADL couldn't care less. Here are some of the 'civil rights' activities of the ADL: In 1993 it was exposed for spying on Arab-Americans and left-wing groups and for collecting files on more than 600 organisations and 10,000 people. This would not surprise anyone with knowledge of the ultra-Zionist web which operates as a front for the psychopaths of the far, far right Mossad Israeli intelligence network. Organisations targeted by the ADL included the American Civil Liberties Union (ACLU) and 20 labour unions in the San Francisco area. The 'anti-hate', 'anti-racist' ADL shared this information with Mossad and passed details about anti-apartheid groups to intelligence agents representing the white apartheid regime in South Africa. This is the real mentality of those who brand others as racist. Noam Chomsky has widely criticised Israel's treatment of the Palestinians, and revealed that the ADL compiled a 150-page dossier on him. An ADL insider sent Chomsky the document which he said looked like an FBI file:

> ... It's clear they essentially have spies in classrooms who take notes and send them to the ADL and other organizations. The groups then compile dossiers they can use to condemn, attack or remove faculty members. They're like J. Edgar Hoover's files. It's kind of gutter stuff.

The ADL *is* gutter stuff and seeks to terrorise academics, students, university authorities, the media and public into stopping all criticism of Israel. Examples to support this are legion and now rapidly increasing as the ultra-Zionists seek to lasso all freedom of speech. Mark Levine, a Jewish professor of Middle Eastern Studies, said pro-Israel groups had, in effect, created a 'large machine' to attack Israel-critics on college campuses. 'These are powerful, organised groups in the Jewish community who use fear and intimidation to try to make sure Israel doesn't get criticised,' he said. 'They go after anyone, even more so when the critics are Jews, because they fear that if we can criticise them, then everyone can.'

Silence the kids – silence *everyone*

The Forward, a New York-based Jewish magazine, highlighted a disgusting keynote speech by American-born Israeli, Rabbi Daniel Gordis, at the American Jewish Committee's annual conference. Gordis called for a college junior at the University of California in Los Angeles to be targeted at her home for asking a question of a Jewish student Rachel Beyda who was nominated to the students' judicial board. The junior, Fabienne Roth, asked Beyda how she could maintain an unbiased position given her relationship to the Jewish community. This is a fair question to a candidate who is a member of *any* religious or cultural community standing for office. The response of Rabbi Gordis was so typical of ultra-Zionist extremists and crazies. Take a deep breath:

> We can find out where [she lives], and she should not be able to come in or out of her house, in or out of her apartment, without being reminded, peacefully, morally, legally, that we know who you are.

He said that everyone needed to understand that 'not for naught is the Jewish people one of the very-best-organized communities in the world'. This bully of a man demanded that Roth's future employers should be protested and boycotted:

> A well-organized Jewish community would let Fabienne Roth know that if she becomes a lawyer, any firm that hires her will have picketers outside its offices until she is fired. It's Jewish and other fair-minded clients will be pressured to leave the firm. Having Roth on staff has to become a liability – not for a month or two, not for a year or two. For decades.
>
> If Fabienne Roth becomes a physician, then whatever hospital or practice hires her needs to know they will experience the same pressure. Should Roth choose not to have a career, she will still have a home somewhere. She should not be able to exit or enter her home without encountering a small number of polite, lawful protesters, who will remind her – day in and day out – that we know exactly what she is. If and when she has children, we'll remind them, too.

Fabienne Roth was just a kid you sad and shameful idiot and people have been jailed for far less. There you see in all its grotesqueness the mentality of ultra-Zionism, its vicious, merciless, empathy-deleted thirst for revenge and its truly staggering self-obsession and sense of self-importance. Anyone still wonder why the ultra-Zionist connection to 9/11 which I am going to expose is unknown to the general public? These are the kind of people that the gutless UK Labour Party, gutless councils, gutless employers, gutless venue owners and gutless media are falling to their knees to appease. John Mearsheimer, co-author of *The Israel Lobby*, said:

> They are picking out individuals who they think are critical of Israel and they are smearing them and they are telling them that what is going to happen here is if you don't cease and desist from acting like this we in the end will do much to destroy your career.

We are talking serious levels of psychopathy here. As Israel-born activist Gilad Atzmon said: 'Jewish power is the power to silence opposition to

Jewish power.' Or, as I would say, ultra-Zionist Death Cult power.

Undercover revelations

Qatar television station Al Jazeera produced a revelatory hidden camera exposure of the Israel Lobby in the United States in 2016 only for pressure from the US and Israel on the Qatari dictatorship to ensure the four-part series did not air. Al Jazeera staff were furious and a source leaked the documentaries which are available on the Electronic Intifada website. They were also made available to French and Lebanon sources. 'Tony', an undercover Jewish reporter, posed as a pro-Israel volunteer in Washington and accessed the inter-workings of the Israel Lobby in the US. The documentaries reveal a staggering spying, surveillance and data-gathering ultra-Zionist network in the United States answering to the Israeli government and its Ministry of Strategic Affairs headed by high-ranking intelligence officer Sima Vaknin-Gil and the Minister of Public Security, Strategic Affairs and Minister of Information, Netanyahu ally Gilad Erdan. Vaknin-Gil spent 20 years with Israeli air force intelligence reaching the rank of brigadier general. She has said she wants 'to create a community of fighters' to 'flood the internet' with Israeli propaganda while publicly appearing unconnected with the government. These are overwhelmingly the people that attack you if you post anything challenging Israel. The Ministry of Strategic Affairs, Israeli military and Mossad are all masks on the same face and they are targeting Palestinian and pro-Palestinian activists worldwide with a focus on the BDS Israel boycott movement. Israeli spy Vaknin-Gil is caught on a hidden camera by Al Jazeera at a pro-Israel event in Washington saying:

> We are a different government working on foreign soil and we have to be very, very cautious. We have three different sub-campaigns, which are very, very sensitive. Regarding data gathering, information analysis working on activist organisations, money trail. This is only something that a country with these resources can do the best ... We have to think differently. And this is waging a holistic campaign against the other side. Take him out of his comfort zone. Make him be on the defensive ...

> ... In the air force when you want to win, you have to have aerial superiority. If you want to win a campaign, you must have information superiority. And this is exactly the added value of Israel's capabilities, technological and otherwise, we can bring to the game and we are working on that very hard.

What Vaknin-Gil was describing is a super-extensive Israeli spying and intelligence gathering operation throughout the United States and the wider world to smear anyone who questions or challenges the actions of Israel. Noah Pollak is the executive director of the ultra-Zionist group, Emergency Committee for Israel (established by Bill Kristol, co-founder of the Project for the New American Century). Pollak also worked at Israel's Shalem Center, a think tank affiliated to Netanyahu's Likud Party and part-funded by Trump's biggest financial backer, Sheldon Adelson. The appalling Pollak was caught on hidden camera saying:

> When you talk about ... BDS, you talk about them as a hate group, as a movement that absolutely endorses violence against civilians, not military conflict, but violence against civilians. AKA terrorism. You discredit the messenger as a way of discrediting the message.

Activists were told by other ultra-Zionist organisers that they should stay on message ... BDS is a 'hate movement'. Al Jazeera undercover reporter 'Tony' was told to call BDS an anti-Semitic hate group as often as possible because 'it polls well'. Israel's ultra-Zionists are terrified of the potential for BDS to awaken the world to the treatment of Palestinians and damage the country financially – a fact confirmed in 2019 by the desperate campaign launched by Strategic Affairs Minister Gilad Erdan to label BDS activists 'terrorists in suits'. I think they call it 'projection'. The strategy and accompanying propaganda was a copy of that used by Jerusalem-based NGO Monitor which claims to be independent while being a front for targeting NGOs that challenge the behaviour of Israel and its far right government. The organisation was founded in 2001 by ultra-Zionist academic Gerald Steinberg and claims 'to promote accountability, and advance a vigorous discussion on the reports and activities of humanitarian NGOs in the framework of the Arab–Israeli conflict' (the 'framework' of whether they criticise Israel or not). The Quakers, a Christian pacifist movement, were targeted by the ultra-Zionist hit-squads after they said they would no longer invest in any company which benefits from the Israeli occupation. Quakers opposed slavery, apartheid in South Africa and were awarded a Nobel peace prize for saving Jews and Christians from the Nazis including 10,000 mostly Jewish children transported to Britain. None of these are mitigating factors to opposing what the ultra-Zionists decree. The Quakers were condemned by the *pathetic* British Board of Jewish Deputies and other ultra-Zionist groups who described the Quaker decision taken on moral grounds as, yes, yes, yes – 'anti-Semitic'. Sagi Balasha, former Chief Executive of the Israeli-American Council from 2011-2015, now works with cyber-intelligence organisations targeting BDS activists. He explained to an Israel Lobby meeting captured by Al Jazeera's secret filming how they have billboards taken down that criticise Israel and call for a boycott. He said that in a few hours of being alerted about billboards their systems and analysts 'could find the exact organisation, people and even their names, where they live'. They would pass this information to the 'ministry' and 'three days later there were no billboards'. All this is going on in America and so many other countries every day orchestrated by a country of less than eight million people with a total global population of 0.2 percent. Jacob Baime, Executive Director of the Israel on Campus Coalition, described on hidden camera how they track those who criticise Israel:

> We use all sorts of technology. We use corporate level, enterprise-grade social media intelligence software. Almost all of this happens on social media so we have custom algorithms and formulae that acquire this stuff immediately.

Baime added that 'within about thirty seconds or less of one of these things popping up on campus, whether it's a Facebook event ... [or something] on Twitter, the system picks it up.' He said the information then goes into a queue and 'alerts our researchers and they evaluate it'. They tagged it and if it rose to a certain level they 'issue early-warning alerts to our partners'. Baime went on:

> If one of these terrorists on campus [anyone calling for equal rights for Palestinians] wants to disrupt a pro-Israel lecture or something and unfurl a banner or whatever else, we're going to investigate them and look into bad stuff they have done. That stuff becomes very useful in the moment and there are any number of ways to push it out. The only thing is that we do it securely and anonymously and that's the key.

This is how the ultra-Zionist bully boys target kids in universities and anyone with the decency to stand up for the abused Palestinians.

We must destroy them

Bill Mullen a Professor of American Studies at Purdue University, had been a long-standing BDS campaigner when his wife was sent a link to a website containing a letter addressed to her claiming to be from a former student making allegations of sexual harassment against him. The letter said she had found other students telling the same story. Creating anonymous websites is a modus operandi of the Israel Lobby along with copious fake social media pages. Mullen said that within about 48 hours they established that these multiple sites attacking him had been taken out almost at the same time and were clearly the work of the same people. He said:

> It was really an attempt from people who didn't know us to think maybe I can destroy this marriage at the very least, maybe I can cause them horrendous

personal suffering. The same letter purporting to be harassment to my wife used the name of our daughter. I think that was the worst moment. I think we thought these people will do anything, they are capable of doing anything.

Yes they are – as we will see when I return directly to 9/11. Jacob Baime of the Israel on Campus Coalition said: 'Every few hours you drip out a new piece of the opposition research ... it's psychological warfare. It drives them crazy.' The Al Jazeera documentary featured a Purdue student who was targeted for her Palestinian support with anonymous claims that she was often drunk and had sex with multiple men. Jacob Baime again on hidden camera: 'They either shut down or they spend time responding to it and investigating it, which is time they can't spend attacking Israel – that's incredibly effective.' BDS-supporting Jewish activist and journalist Max Blumenthal said this Israel network operates through subterfuge and walked a very thin line between the legal and illegal to gather information to smear opponents and to ultimately destroy them. Al Jazeera reporter 'Tony' was accepted as an activist working with the Israel Project, or 'TIP', an Israeli propaganda operation that seeks to control the narrative on what is reported about both Israel and Palestinians. Professor John Mearsheimer who has exposed the Israel Lobby told Al Jazeera about the role of the Israel Project. He said the 'special relationship' between the United States and Israel is unprecedented in recorded history. He said that not only did the United States give Israel a tremendous amount of economic aid and diplomatic protection but gave that aid and protection no matter what – it's not conditional. 'The Israel Project will go to enormous lengths to achieve that end', Mearsheimer said. Israel Project staff described to 'Tony' how they had contacts in numerous media organisations and set out to forge friendships with reporters as a primary means of influence to control what is written about Israel and 'neutralising undesired narratives'. The aim was to build an 'echo-chamber for pro-Israel information' using the media as the vehicle. David Hazony, a managing director at the Israel Project, told 'Tony':

They're not things we do loudly. A lot of them are things we do behind the scenes. You can get a lot more done by making questions get asked by journalists. And if you create it from multiple directions at the same time through multiple journalists, then you create a kind of sense of crisis. We develop relationships. A lot of alcohol to get them to trust us.

We're basically messaging on the following. BDS is essentially a kind of a hate-group targeting Israel. They're anti-peace. We try not to even use the terms, because it builds their brand. We just refer to 'boycotters'. The goal is to actually make things happen and to figure out what are the means of communication to do that.

New Yorker magazine exposed in February, 2019, how BDS was targeted by a Mossad-front 'security company' called Psy-Group in an operation code-named Project Butterfly. Psy-Group recruited from Israel's secret services and gathered donations from wealthy ultra-Zionists mostly in New York on the understanding that their names would never be revealed. BDS activists would be followed and targeted with discrediting campaigns and this even included putting leaflets on the cars of neighbours claiming an activist to be a 'terrorist'. Article author Adam Entous wrote:

> Psy-Group's intelligence and influence operations, which included a failed attempt in the summer of 2017 to sway a local election in central California, were detailed in a New Yorker investigation that I co-wrote earlier this month. Before it went out of business, last year, Psy-Group was part of a new wave of private-intelligence firms that recruited from the ranks of Israel's secret services and described themselves as 'private Mossads'.

> Psy-Group initially stood out among its rivals because it didn't just gather intelligence; its operatives used false identities, or avatars, to covertly spread messages in an attempt to influence what people believed and how they behaved.

This is happening in your country today, America. Are you just going to take this crap and abuse of your country?

Israel's American spy network

The ultra-Zionist campaign against BDS includes keeping surveillance within the United States on American students and it is coordinated through the highest levels of Israeli intelligence. Omar Barghouti, a co-founder of the BDS movement, said that government ministers attacked him with 'one of them threatening BDS leaders with targeted civil assassination'. Yisrael Katz, Israel's Minister of Intelligence, is captured by Al Jazeera saying that the plan is to act against BDS leaders, isolate them and transfer information to other intelligence agencies around the world. Israel must 'carry out a targeted civil thwarting of the leadership of BDS activists', he said. Julia Reifkind, a Director of Community Affairs at the Israeli Embassy in Washington and 'AIPAC-training camp activist', told 'Tony' that nobody really knew what they were doing on behalf of Israel, but it included 'a lot of research, monitoring BDS things and reporting it back to the Ministry of Foreign Affairs – making sure everyone knows what's going on'. When politicians talked about the subject in the Israeli Parliament she said: '... we've usually contributed to

what the background information is.' Reifkind was asked if the Israeli
Embassy is trying to 'leverage faculty' (university departments). She
said that was correct and they were working with several faculty
advocacy groups 'that kind of train faculty'. She said they were 'helping
them a little bit with funding, connections, bringing them to speak,
having them speak to diplomats and people at the Ministry of Foreign
Affairs that need this information'. Reifkind said ultra-Zionist activists
lobbying for mega Israel lobby group AIPAC don't come clean about
that. They are trained to simply say they are pro-Israel students: 'When
you're meeting with students on campus I would never say "I am the
AIPAC Campus Rep". I would say, "My name is Julia and I'm a pro-
Israel student".' She admitted that Israel groups seek to influence
student elections from 'very behind the scenes' and that she had several
fake Facebook accounts that allowed her to appear to be other people
including 'an old white guy'. One Al Jazeera documentary shows how
Reifkind sought to portray students at the University of California Davis
using the tired old line of 'anti-Semitism' when they voted to boycott
Israel. They use this slur constantly because that's all they have. Once
open debate is allowed they lose every time when the treatment of
Palestinians by a racist state cannot be intellectually or morally
defended. Reifkind told 'Tony' how they pre-planned a walkout from
the debate at Davis they knew they would lose and used film of the
walkout to post on the Internet and 'control the narrative'. Reifkind
recalled:

> That day all of us released 50 op-eds in major news sources, so that ... when
> people opened their Facebook it would be them celebrating their victory, it
> would be us sharing our stories. Once it blew up then random people like the
> Huffington Post contacted me, it was like 'Do you have anything to say?' and I
> was like 'Conveniently I wrote an op-Ed two weeks ago just in case'.

The article was duly published with the headline 'My 15-Day Journey
Confronting Divestment at UC Davis'. Reifkind crowed that people's
'entire newsfeed was Israel stuff and that's what we wanted'. Students
demanding justice and fairness for Palestinians against the global
political and intelligence networks of Israel should be a no-contest, but it
is testament to the disgust that gathering numbers have with the
behaviour of the Israel government and military that BDS continues to
expand. At the perfect propaganda moment in the UC Davis story
swastikas suddenly appeared scrawled on campus and we should
absolutely not rule out in these situations that Lobby assets stage their
own 'anti-Semitism' including swastikas and slogans to advance their
agenda of demonisation and censorship. A joint investigation by US and
Israeli authorities led to a ten-year jail sentence for a 19-year-old Jewish

man with dual American-Israeli citizenship for making bomb threats to Jewish community centers in the United States. Michael Kadar made more than 2,000 threatening calls to schools, airports, police stations, malls and other targets over two years, Israeli prosecutors said. The Anti-Defamation League (ADL) and other Jewish groups had blamed 'white supremacists' and even the man's mother said: 'I thought it was done by someone who is anti-Semitic.' The man apparently has mental problems, but the point is that when the crimes happened they were automatically assumed to be the work of 'anti-Semites'. American proper journalist Tucker Carlson presented an expose' of hate crime hoaxes in the wake of the fake self-staged 'racist attack' by actor Jussie Smollett who said he had been beaten and left with a noose around his neck by white men claiming to be Trump supporters. It turned out that Smollett arranged for black associates to beat him and then told his lies to the media and generated more division and hatred between communities with the enthusiastic support of ultra-Zionist controlled CNN. The two black men who 'beat him up' came forward and admitted it was all a set-up arranged by Smollett. Police charged him on a number of counts. What was the outcome? Cook County State Attorney General Kim Foxx, who was funded in her election campaign to the tune of more than $400,000 by George Soros foundations, dropped the charges against Smollett in a blatant fix that followed an attempted intervention on his behalf by Tina Tchen, an ally of the actor's friend Michelle Obama. Smollett rails against 'white privilege' while being so privileged himself that he's above the law. This is yet another example – and they are endless – of 'progressive' bullshit and unspeakable hypocrisy and of the octopus networks controlled by Soros who has been funding state prosecutors and secretaries of state into office for years to dictate who and what gets prosecuted and who and what doesn't. But don't you dare tell anyone – that's 'anti-Semitic'. 'Hate crime' convictions are actually rare and not exploding. Part of Carlson's segment on hate crime hoaxes featured an interview with Robby Soave, author of *Panic Attack: Young Radicals in the Age of Trump,* who exposed the fraudulent nature of 'hate crime' statistics including the Anti-Defamation League claims of a 60 percent increase in 'anti-Semitic' attacks since Trump was elected. Soave said that he checked the statistics and 'anti-Semitic' violence was in fact 'way down'. He said the entire increase claimed by the ADL was the work of Jewish hoaxer Michael Kadar. Did the ADL apologise for such misleading claims and for once be honest? They couldn't spell the word. I am sure you will have observed that 'anti-Semitism' always goes up and is 'on the rise' according to figures released by ultra-Zionist front groups. When you meet rank and file Jews they say they don't know what the fuss is because they have never faced discrimination. Does it happen? Of course. Does it happen on anything like the scale the ultra-Zionist hate groups claim? Not a chance. Things are not, to say the very least, always what they seem to be and we need to remember that instead of jumping to instant conclusions. A question to ask is who benefits? For example, who benefited from the swastikas that appeared at UC Davis? Who benefits from anonymous log-ins posting anti-Jewish abuse?

Canary Mission

The Algemeiner, a New York-based Jewish newspaper, approached Al Jazeera undercover Jewish reporter, 'Tony', to ironically work 'undercover' within BDS groups as a form of surveillance. Rachel Frommer, *The Algemeiner's* Senior Campus Correspondent, said they were working on a project to rank US universities and colleges with regard to their 'anti-Semitic and anti-Israel activity'. She said they had a campus bureau that monitors BDS campaigns 'all day long, all week long'. Frommer said that the 'new anti-Semitism' is 'anti-Israelism' in line with the new song-sheet worldwide. One *Algemeiner* headline captured its methods and approach: 'Cesspool of Antisemitic, Anti-Israel, Racist Behaviour at U of Tennessee Uncovered by Covert Watchdog Group'. Put another way – there is a BDS group at the University of Tennessee that is far too effective. The story was given to them by a secretive Israel Lobby group called the Canary Mission which weaponises 'anti-Semitism' on US campuses in line with the overall Protection Racket blueprint. *Algemeiner* ran the article while admitting it had no idea who was behind the Canary Mission. The story was a blatant lie, but the label 'anti-Semitism' is all they have. When your only tool is a hammer every situation must be a nail. Respected Jewish magazine, *The Forward*, reported that in 2015 Jewish and pro-Israel groups in the US and Israel used significant resources to direct hard-line, often secretive tactics against their targets:

> An online blacklist called Canary Mission, which went live in 2015, targeted college students critical of Israel. Professional pro-Israel operatives posed online as college students. Pro-Israel campus groups hired top-tier professional Washington, D.C. political consultants and sent them to work on college campuses. An Israeli spy firm pitched U.S. Jewish donors with a proposal to covertly undermine the movement to boycott, divest from and sanction Israel.

A Canary Mission video calls for its operatives to 'make sure today's radicals are not tomorrow's employees' by destroying their careers. This seriously sick organisation keeps surveillance on its targets and constantly harasses them. Israel Lobby operative Jacob Baime said on the Al Jazeera documentary: 'They are terrified of Canary Mission and it's about time.' Eric Gallagher, an AIPAC director from 2010-2015, told undercover reporter 'Tony' that the highly secretive and 'anonymous' Canary Mission is funded and run by Adam Milstein, Chairman of the Israeli-American Council who was convicted of tax evasion in 2009. Gallagher tells how he was in email contact while Milstein was in jail. Milstein is a pivotal figure in the Israel Lobby with its surveillance and smears, and sits on the boards of AIPAC's national council, Israel on Campus Coalition and StandWithUs. He is close to mega ultra-Zionist donor, Sheldon Adelson, the biggest funder of Donald Trump. Milstein described on a secret camera his mode of operation with regard to critics of Israel: 'We're doing it by exposing who they are, what they are, the fact that they are racist, the fact that they are bigots, they're anti-democracy.' Hypocrisy knows no bounds.

Tennessee is one of the major centres of Israel-worshipping, ultra-Zionist-created Christian Zionism and became the first state government to condemn BDS. Increasing numbers of others have followed, including Arkansas where to receive state contracts firms have to pledge not to boycott Israel or reduce their fees by 20 percent. The power of ultra-Zionism over United States government at all levels can be seen in the targeting of Americans and their free speech and conscience to serve a country of eight million people nearly seven thousand miles away. Helene Sinnreich, Jewish Professor of Judaic Studies at the University of Tennessee and a Fellow at the Center for Advanced Holocaust Studies at the United States Holocaust Memorial Museum, said a claim of rampant anti-Semitism at the university was quite a shock. 'It was very surreal and strange – I didn't see anything happening on the ground, it all seemed to be internet based.' Suddenly flyers appeared all over the university accusing students of supporting Palestinian group Hamas and the theme was seen again – criticising the Israeli government is 'anti-Semitism'. The psychological game works by repeating lies enough times for them to becomes accepted truth. Among those exploiting this technique to attack the University of Tennessee was Aviva Vogelstein, Director of Legal Initiatives at the Louis D Brandeis Center for Human Rights Under Law in Washington DC (of course). This is another strand in The Lobby that hides its real controllers and reason for being behind the term 'human rights'. Kenneth Marcus, founding president of the Brandeis Center, told 'Tony' that they were attempting to redefine 'anti-Semitism' to include criticism of Israel. They wanted to have this imposed on all American universities to stop criticism of Israel and undermine BDS. Marcus said in a secret recording: 'You have to show that they're racist hate groups – that they are using intimidation to get funded, and to consistently portray them that way.' It is a cold and callous abuse of the term 'racism' in pursuit of a blatant political end and what this does is to cry wolf so often and so constantly that genuine 'anti-Semitism' gets lost in the tidal wave. The real reason for the attack on the University of Tennessee as on all their other targets, including myself, is to silence opposition and to secure changes in the law to protect Israel from criticism. Jewish and other Tennessee students gave evidence to a state hearing into the allegations and said claims of 'anti-Semitism' were nonsense. The only people making the claims were outsiders, most notably Kenneth Marcus and his subordinate Aviva Vogelstein who admitted to 'Tony' that Jewish students had told her there was not an 'anti-Semitism' problem at Tennessee.

Paying the piper ...

Ultra-Zionist control of politicians – especially in the United States – is stunning and explains so much about 9/11. This control is mainly through funding and who gets it and who doesn't. John Mearsheimer and Stephen Walt expose this fact in *The Israel Lobby and U.S. Foreign Policy*. Bribing politicians with ultra-Zionist 'donations' is the norm in America and many other countries. Phenomenal ultra-Zionist donations to both American parties (control both sides and you control the game) are scandalous in an alleged 'democracy' and he who pays the piper calls the tune. *Ynetnews*, an online English-language Israeli news website of newspaper *Yedioth Ahronoth*, reported in 2016 that *50 percent* of donations to the Democratic Party came from Jewish sources and 25 percent of those to Republicans. This is from a minority within a *two percent* minority of the American population. We can see this stark truth in the US presidential election of 2016. The five biggest donors to 'Democrat' candidate Hillary Clinton were: Hedge fund manager Donald Sussman (ultra-Zionist); venture capitalist Jay Robert Pritzker and his wife Mary (ultra-Zionists); Israeli-American media tycoon Haim Saban and his wife Cheryl (ultra-Zionists); financier George Soros (ultra-Zionist place-man whatever they may claim); and SlimFast founder Daniel Abraham (ultra-Zionist). Another Clinton financial supporter to the tune of $35 million was Facebook co-founder Dustin Moskovitz (ultra-Zionist). The Clintons are also very close to the ultra-Zionist Rothschilds via Evelyn de Rothschild and his wife, the American-born businesswoman, Lynn Forester. They spent their wedding night at the White House at the Clintons' invitation. The couple were apparently introduced by Henry Kissinger at a meeting of the Hidden Hand Bilderberg Group. A Hillary Clinton email when she was US Secretary of State has her making a grovelling apology to the Rothschilds for asking then UK Prime Minister Tony Blair, another Rothschild tea-boy, to accompany her to Israel when the Rothschilds were inviting him to a weekend 'conference' in that global elite centre of Aspen, Colorado. Clinton tells Lady de Rothschild: 'I hope you all understand ... Let me know what penance I owe you.' The grovelling nature of the Clinton-to-

Rothschild emails is in stark contrast to the usual Clinton demeanour. A former bodyguard said she could 'make Richard Nixon look like Mahatma Gandhi'. Only her best behaviour will do for the Rothschilds. Fox News reported in 2019 a stash of released Hillary Clinton emails that confirmed Israeli influence over American politics:

> A newly unearthed batch of heavily redacted, classified emails from Hillary Clinton's personal email server revealed that the former secretary of state discussed establishing a 'private, 100% off-the-record' back channel to Israeli Prime Minister Benjamin ['Bibi'] Netanyahu, and that one of her top aides warned her that she was in 'danger' of being 'savaged by Jewish organizations, in the Jewish press and among the phalanx of neoconservative media' as a result of political machinations by 'Bibi and the Jewish leadership' … The documents, representing a small proportion of the tens of thousands of emails still unaccounted for from Clinton's server, also underscored the apparently significant political threat that the Obama administration felt it faced at the hands of Israel.

Meanwhile 'Republican' Donald Trump's biggest donor was Israeli-American ultra-Zionist Sheldon Adelson who handed over $82 million to Trump and the Republicans. This was three times the contribution of the next highest individual donor (Fig 102). Another big Republican donor is ultra-Zionist Bernard Marcus, co-founder and former CEO of Home Depot, who sits on the board of the Republican Jewish Coalition. Marcus has funded ultra-Zionist and Neocon organisations including the American Enterprise Institute, Christians United for Israel, Friends of the IDF, Hoover Institution, Hudson Institute, the Israel Project, Jewish Institute for National Security Affairs (JINSA), Manhattan Institute and Middle East Media Research Institute. It's a similar story with ultra-Zionist billionaire investor Paul Singer, founder and CEO of the hedge fund Elliott Management Corporation. Singer, Marcus and Adelson were all major funders of Trump with Adelson out in front. You get what you pay for. The media subsequently reported that 'Trump's' highly controversial decisions' to move the US Israel embassy to Jerusalem, ditch the US-Iran nuclear deal and appoint Project for the New American Century

Figure 102: Casino billionaire Sheldon Adelson – the Israel fanatic behind Trump.

stalwart and Israel tea-maker John Bolton as National Security Advisor were all 'passions' of Shelden Adelson. Yes and the government psychopaths in Israel. During the 2016 Republican Primary – or 'Adelson Primary' as it was called – to decide the presidential nominee we saw headlines such as 'Sheldon Adelson is ready to buy the presidency'. *The New Yorker* said Adelson was '... the single person to whom both the Prime Minister of Israel and the President of the United States owe everything'. Trump election strategist Steve Bannon evangelised over Adelson at a Zionist Organisation of America dinner and said that without him Trump would not have become president. It wasn't about Adelson's money, Bannon said, it was his counsel, guidance and wisdom. Of course it was. Adelson told an event for the Israeli Defense Forces that *unfortunately* the military uniform he once wore was American and not Israeli, but he said that his wife and a daughter served in the IDF and he hoped that one of his 'little boys' whose hobby was shooting would go back to Israel and join the Israeli military. He suggested that he could be a sniper. 'All we care about is being good Zionists – good citizens of Israel', Adelson said. Why would this man with those priorities hand over tens of millions to a candidate in Trump with the slogans 'America First' and 'Make America Great Again'? What was an example of 'anti-Semitism' in the new definition again? Oh, yes – 'Accusing Jewish citizens of being more loyal to Israel, or to the alleged priorities of Jews worldwide, than to the interests of their own nations.' How transparent it all is when someone has the backbone to call it out.

Adelson owns Trump as he owns Neocon John Bolton and so they are both continuing the post-9/11 'US' foreign policy dictated by Adelson and the ultra-Zionists. Bolton is reported to have told the ultra-Zionist American Friends of Beit El after Trump's election in 2016 that not only would the US embassy be moved to Jerusalem there would be no opposition to any new Jewish settlements in the occupied West Bank. This has proved to be the case. American Friends of Beit El, headed by ultra-Zionist US Ambassador to Israel David Friedman and financially supported by the ultra-Zionist Jared Kushner family of Trump's son-in-law and 'senior advisor', has been pumping millions into new settlements. Trump is going to oppose illegal settlements when his main funder, his ambassador to Israel and son-in-law are all funding them?? The American people should be embarrassed at how their government has been hijacked so blatantly. Adelson's fingerprints were also all over 'Trump's' decision to seriously cut aid to Palestinians including $25 million from impoverished East Jerusalem hospitals that treat Palestinian cancer patients *when* they are allowed to travel from the West Bank and Gaza. Ultra-Zionists want to clear East Jerusalem of Palestinians so they can replace the Al-Aqsa Mosque with a rebuilt

'Solomon's Temple' and to so impoverish and destitute the Palestinian people that they will agree to Israeli demands in return for a promise of money. The scam was described in its most extreme form by Alliance for Israel Advocacy, a lobbying group established by the Messianic Jewish Alliance of America which is pressing the White House and Capitol Hill for Palestinians to be given money to move aboard and leave Israel to Jews only. Executive Director Paul Liberman said that over ten years they wanted to change the demographics of the illegally-occupied West Bank with a view to annexation by Israel. He said that Palestinians who stayed would 'live under the doctrine of the sojourner', not have a vote and would 'not participate in the sovereignty of the land'. Liberman, who has been to the White House to present his proposals, said: 'The only rights the Palestinians have are squatter's rights.' Sounds such a nice chap. Netanyahu's eldest son, Yair, has also made Internet posts calling for all Muslims to leave Israel. Trump attacked ultra-Zionist Goldman Sachs during his election campaign because it played well with his potential voters, but after he won with Adelson's money he immediately appointed Steve Mnuchin (ultra-Zionist), former Goldman Sachs executive vice president, as his Treasury Secretary and ultra-Zionist Gary Cohn, Goldman Sachs chief operating officer, as Director of the National Economic Council and chief economic advisor. When Cohn left in 2018 he was replaced by ultra-Zionist Lawrence Kudlow. Trump is surrounded by Zionists and ultra-Zionists including his son-in-law Jared Kushner, a life-long friend of Benjamin Netanyahu who is a long associate of Kushner's jailbird father. The *Wall Street Journal* reported that Kushner didn't disclose on his government financial-disclosure form his business ties to 'Israel critic' George Soros, Goldman Sachs and Silicon Valley billionaire Peter Thiel who has the closest of ties with the US intelligence community. Nor did Kushner disclose that he arranged loans of $1 billion from more than 20 lenders for properties and companies he part-owned including personal guarantees on more than $300 million of that debt. Trump's policy on Israel and what matters to Israel is also dictated by David Freidman, appointed US ambassador to Israel, and Jason Greenblatt, Assistant to the President and Special Representative for International Negotiations. Freidman worked for the Trump Organization as a bankruptcy lawyer and Greenblatt was executive vice president and chief legal officer to Donald Trump and the Trump Organization and his 'advisor on Israel'. Yael Lempert (ultra-Zionist) was named Special Assistant to the President and Senior Director for Israel, Egypt and the Levant. What chance have the Palestinians ever had of justice and can anyone be in the least surprised with this line-up that Trump is continuing the agenda laid out by the Project for the New American Century led by Adelson puppet and PNAC fanatic John Bolton which was triggered by 9/11?

'The Pledge' (pinch yourself, you're not dreaming)

We are talking hundreds of millions being poured into US presidential races and elections by Zionists and ultra-Zionists and in return every candidate who accepts a donation must take 'The Pledge' of allegiance to Israel and its policy demands. This is why by far the biggest financial 'aid' handed out by the United States every year goes to Israel, a tiny already rich country (its elite anyway) with a population of less than some cities. This includes $3.8 billion of US taxpayers' money every year in 'military aid' while Americans sleep in the street. America and Israel signed a 'Memorandum of Understanding' in 2016 through which Israel will receive $38 billion in military assistance over ten years – an increase of around 27 percent on the agreement signed in 2007. This was the biggest single aid pledge of its kind in American history and even before it was signed the Congressional Research Service confirmed that Israel was 'the largest cumulative recipient of U.S. foreign assistance since World War II'. The $38 billion is just a headline figure for the public about one deal – the total amount transferred from American taxpayers to Israel will be bone-shaking. Israel is a sliver of land with a population of eight million people and yet receives more US aid than any other country. So you use your money to buy American politicians and they vote to pay you back – with enormous interest – in American tax dollars in the form of 'aid'. What a racket. Ultra-Zionist funding of Senate and Congressional candidates is fantastic and often make-or-break to their chances of winning. Professor John Mearsheimer said:

> To get elected in the American political system you need lots of money. What AIPAC does is it makes sure that money is funnelled your way if you are seen as pro-Israel and it will go to significant lengths to make sure that you stay in office if you continue to be staunchly pro-Israel.

Former Congresswoman Cynthia McKinney has revealed how this scam operates. She said that when she ran for office she was asked to 'sign the pledge' to Israel and confirm she would always vote in Israel's best interests. Agreeing or not agreeing was the difference between money or no money and often whether money was directed instead to an opponent. Which party doesn't matter so long as you pledge allegiance to Israel. McKinney said:

> Every candidate for Congress ... had a pledge, they were given a pledge to sign ... If you don't sign the pledge, you don't get money. For example, it was almost like water torture for me. My parents observed this. I would get a call and the person on the other end of the phone would say 'I want to do a fundraiser for you.' And then we would get into the planning. I would get

really excited, because of course you have to have money in order to run a campaign. And then two weeks, three weeks into the planning, they would say, 'Did you sign the pledge?' And then I would say, 'No, I didn't sign the pledge.' And then my fundraiser would go kaput.

McKinney eventually lost her seat when the ultra-Zionist lobby funded her opponent who signed the pledge. Jim Moran, a member of Congress from 1991-2015 in northern Virginia, confirmed McKinney's experience:

... anybody running for Congress is expected to fill out a questionnaire and they evaluate your depth of commitment to Israel on the basis of that questionnaire, then you have an interview with local people. If you get AIPAC's support, then more often than not you are going to win ...You realise it's not just the money, it's the number of concerned activists. They'll send out postcards, they'll make phone calls, they'll organise. That's the democratic process, they understand the democratic process.

This pledge-to-Israel demand is expanding into wider society, too. A Texas elementary school speech expert filed a federal lawsuit after the school district refused to renew her contract unless she signed a pro-Israel oath. Bahia Amawi had worked for the Pflugerville Independent School District for nine years when her contract renewal form included a demand that she 'will not boycott Israel during the term of the contract' and will not engage in any action 'that is intended to penalize, inflict economic harm on, or limit commercial relations with Israel, or with a person or entity doing business in Israel or in an Israel-controlled territory'. The arrogance and Orwellian nature of this is shocking, but then Texas politics is owned by the ultra-Zionists just as they own American politics in general which ensures that what Israel wants Israel gets and their obvious connection to 9/11 ignored. I think we can also see now why Netanyahu is treated as a god when he visits the United States and speaks to both houses of Congress (as leader of that tiny country) and the politicians of both parties are on their feet in homage every two minutes. In a 50-minute speech in 2011 he was given 29 standing ovations. I said at the time that they must have had springs attached to their arses. They dare not do otherwise because their devotion is *literally* being monitored and there is money to be begged for. So get on your feet to your master. Who do you think you represent – Americans? This is why the annual conference of the America Israel Public Affairs Committee (AIPAC) is the world's biggest arse-licking contest. Prominent politicians of both parties and presidential wannabes shuffle to the stage on their knees and deliver their undying allegiance to Israel while the ultra-Zionist elite look on with both arrogance and

contempt. No wonder then that in early 2019 the House of
Representatives voted *411 to 1* for a bill forcing the vacant post of 'anti-
Semitism' envoy to be filled. This envoy has always been an activist for
the major Israel lobby organisation, the America Israel Public Affairs
Committee (AIPAC), and the occupant is placed there to 'serve as the
primary advisor to, and coordinate efforts across, the U.S. government
relating to monitoring and combating anti-Semitism and anti-Semitic
incitement in foreign countries'. The bill upgraded the post to the rank
of ambassador. The bill was sponsored by Republican Representative
Christopher H. Smith. His biggest campaign donor was NORPAC, an
ultra-Zionist Israel lobby group 'working to strengthen the United States
– Israel relationship' which fundraises for Israel-supporting politicians
on both sides. Recipient politicians are sent regular emails on affairs in
the Middle East (ultra-Zionist propaganda in other words). The only
dissenter to the bill was Republican Justin Amash from Michigan who
presumably doesn't take their money (bribery). The first Senate bill at
the start of 2019 proposed to hand Israel billions to combat the BDS
boycott. These people are owned political prostitutes and a disgrace to
everything America claims to stand for. What chance did the truth about
9/11 ever have? But it's coming out in the final section of this book.

I should emphasise that Israel may get all this support from the
United States and ultra-Zionist billionaires but this doesn't go the Israeli
population in general. Latet, an Israeli humanitarian aid organisation,
reported in 2018 that 26.5 percent of the Israeli population in the
occupied West Bank live below the poverty line with one in three
children missing at least one meal a day. The report describes how Israeli
children have to beg for donations, 'collect food from the ground or
garbage bins' or steal to eat. Latet chairman Gilles Darmon said: 'When
there are more than half a million poor families and more than a million
poor children, you cannot just get used to it and accept it.' Israelis have
been taking to the streets in protest at ever higher prices for the basics of
life. The ultra-Zionist and Death Cult elite have contempt for Jewish
people as a whole for reasons that will become clear in later chapters.
They want bodies located in the West Bank to take the land from
Palestinians, but they don't care what happens to them. An Israeli media
host told me before an interview that Holocaust survivors in Israel were
suffering from terrible deprivation and poverty and he described cases
of their teeth falling out for the lack of nutrition. Jewish people – they
don't give a shit about you. All those who endure the consequences of
global elite psychopathy – Jewish, Palestinian, everyone – should come
together in common cause. While we are divided the Death Cult will
rule.

Covering all bases

At the centre (with others) of the US Israel lobby web of hundreds of organisation is the Washington DC-based American Israel Public Affairs Committee or AIPAC. This sounds (on purpose) like something attached to government and it is, but certainly not officially. AIPAC is a massive ultra-Zionist Israel Lobby grouping with almost unlimited funds to buy American politicians of both parties and many others that influence what passes for political debate. It may not fund politicians directly, but it knows a man who does. In fact, many of them. AIPAC has more than 100,000 members and 17 regional offices and constantly campaigns for political and financial support for Israel and against anyone who doesn't think the Israeli government is God's gift to the world. AIPAC was established in 1951 as a lobby group of the American Zionist Council called the American Zionist Committee for Public Affairs. On one side AIPAC is close to the far right Netanyahu Likud Party in Israel while a similar group, J Street, comes from the 'left' or 'progressive' direction. Once again control both sides and you control the game. AIPAC wants a one-state – Jewish state – 'solution' to the Palestinian 'problem' while J Street claims to organise and mobilise 'pro-Israel, pro-peace Americans who want Israel to be secure, democratic and the national home of the Jewish people'. J Street claims to 'advocate policies that advance shared US and Israeli interests as well as Jewish and democratic values, leading to a two-state solution to the Israeli-Palestinian conflict'. The two-state solution is a herring so red that held against a bright red background it would disappear. Widespread and rapidly-increasing Jewish-only illegal settlements in the Israeli-occupied West Bank means that anyone still supporting a 'two-state solution' is either deeply ignorant or lying to you. There is no Palestinian land left in the occupied West Bank to have a credible 'second state'. Alan Elsner, Vice President of Communications for J Street, described Father George Bush, a mass killer and paedophile who loved to torture children, as 'one of the great foreign policy leaders of the 20th century' and 'anyone who cares about Israel and Middle East peace owes him a debt of gratitude'. Well, Israel sure does, but not the rest of the Middle East which he helped to tear asunder on behalf of Israel. There is very little between these 'right' and 'left' organisations in truth except for the nature and angle of their mutual bullshit and both will ultimately answer to the same masters. Another prominent organisation in the Israel Lobby is the American Jewish Committee (AJC) established in 1906 and co-founded by Rothschild front-man and Russian Revolution-funder Jacob Schiff (much more later). The AJC calls itself the 'Global Center for Jewish and Israel Advocacy' and as always targets people criticising Israel as 'anti-Semitic'. It has 22 offices in the United States, ten overseas and 33 partnerships with other Jewish organisations around the world. The Israel Web is absolutely extraordinary for the size of the country because the network is not about Israel, but those that *control* Israel. Eric Gallagher, an AIPAC director from 2010-2015, was recorded on an Al Jazeera hidden camera saying that the aim was to influence the US President and Congress to secure benefits like the $38 billion in military aid:

> You can hold up signs and have rallies on campus, but the Congress gets $3.1 billion a year for Israel. Everything AIPAC does is focused on influencing Congress. Congress is where you have leverage. So you can't influence the President of the United States directly but the Congress can.

With Trump in power and owned by Sheldon Adelson going direct is definitely an option. M. J. Rosenberg, a former editor of AIPAC's policy journal, *Near East Report*, said they make sure there are people in every single congressional district working on Israel's behalf. You can see the influence range of AIPAC-connected people with Rosenberg's CV. He's been a Senior Foreign Policy Fellow at Soros-funded Media Matters Action Network; a worker for Democratic members of the House and Senate; and was appointed by Bill Clinton to USAID, the American CIA-front that claims to be about overseas aid. Ultra-Zionist David Ochs, a pro-Israel advocate, invited Al Jazeera undercover reporter 'Tony' to a fundraising event for people such as Illinois Senator Mark Kirk, Florida Congressman Ted Deutch, Virginia Congresswoman Barbara Comstock, North Carolina Senator Richard Burr and New Hampshire Senator Kelly Ayotte. Ochs described Ayotte as 'fantastic' because she was on the Senate Arms Committee. Ultra-Zionist Ted Deutch, with the greatest of irony, was chairman of the House Ethics Committee. Ochs told 'Tony':

> It's the AIPAC group. It makes a difference, it really does. It's the best bang for your buck and the networking is phenomenal. Congressmen and Senators don't do anything unless you pressure them. They kick the can down the road unless you pressure them. The only way to do that is with money.

And there is so much money to be had. Craig Holman from the Public Citizen consumer advocacy group said the legal limit for individual campaign contributions was $2,700, but this was overcome by getting 50 or 100 people together at an event and pooling their contributions. 'So suddenly you've got a group of people with the same demands they want from the lawmaker handing over a quarter of a million dollars – that buys a lawmaker.' David Ochs told 'Tony' about these 'demands' in return for the money. He said that candidates were told: 'We want to make sure if we give you money that you're going to enforce the Iran deal.' Ochs said when they need something from a lawmaker like the Iran deal they can quickly mobilise and say 'look we'll give you $30,000'.

Public Citizen's Craig Holman said of the Ochs strategy: 'He's actually saying we are buying these office holders and that's the point, we're chipping in all this money so we can hand over $100,000 or $200,000 to the office holder so we can buy him.' Another illegal fiddle revealed by Al Jazeera was that donors gave money to each other so they all gave the maximum amount. Ochs described the involvement of ultra-Zionist Jeff Talpins, founder and Chief Investment Officer of New York-based hedge fund, Element Capital Management:

> In New York with Jeff Talpins we don't ask a goddamn thing about the fucking Palestinians. You know why? Because it's a tiny issue, that's why. It's a small insignificant issue. The big issue is Iran. We want everything focused on Iran. What happens is Jeff meets with the congressman in the backroom, tells them exactly what his goals are and by the way Jeff Talpins is worth $250 million. Basically they hand him an envelope with 20 credit cards and say, 'You can swipe each of these credit cards for $1,000 each'.

Crushing dissent

Iran is a big focus because it was on the list of the Project for the New American Century and is a long-time target of the ultra-Zionists and Death Cult that control Israel. Former Congressman Jim Moran described how the Executive Director of AIPAC had said his most important accomplishment was securing authorisation for the US invasion of Iraq. Moran refused to vote for the war and an ultra-Zionist was planted at a public meeting to ask him why there were not more Jews involved in marches against the war. Moran replied: 'If the leaders of the Jewish community were opposed to the war I think that would make a difference.' The ultra-Zionist Lobby went into overdrive condemning him for believing in a Jewish conspiracy to lead America into war. This is so important to appreciate – the technique of condemning as 'anti-Semitic' the exposure of what you are *actually doing*. This is why ultra-Zionists condemn what they call 'anti-Semitic tropes' claiming a Jewish plot for world domination. They use this to dub any claim of a global conspiracy as automatically 'anti-Semitic' even when a Jewish connection is not even mentioned. It's not Jewish people they are seeking to protect with this mantra. It's the plot itself. Moran told Al Jazeera:

> There was a conservative rabbi in my district who was assigned to me I assume by AIPAC and he warned me that if I voiced my views about the Israel lobby that my career would be over and implied that it would be done through the Post and sure enough the Washington Post editorialised brutally, everybody ganged up.

The ultra-Zionist-controlled *Washington Post*, with its close connection to AIPAC, ran a story by senior editor Marc Fisher saying Moran was not fit for public office because 'what we have here is a United States congressman endorsing and spreading one of the oldest and most pernicious myths in the annals of ethnic hatred'. The 'trope' fraud is also one of the oldest and most pernicious protection rackets in the annals of ethnic diversion. They have constantly tried it with me, often through the clueless on the fake 'socialist' left, but I couldn't care less. Eric Gallagher, a director at AIPAC, was asked by Al Jazeera's 'Tony' which were the main media outlets that the Israel Project propaganda operation worked with. '*Washington Post* is the biggest one,' he replied. The *Post* was owned by ultra-Zionists before being purchased by Amazon's Jeff Bezos which basically means business as usual. 'Jewish leaders' (self-appointed) called on Moran to resign even though both his daughters married Jewish men and his grandchildren are Jewish. This is irrelevant to the ultra-Zionist Lobby to which 'Jewish' is merely a convenient label and means to an end. Former AIPAC magazine editor M. J. Rosenberg said everyone knew that what Moran said wasn't 'anti-Semitic':

> Anti-Semitism has come to mean anti-Israel. The AIPAC crowd doesn't really care very much about whether or not a person likes Jews or wants one to move next door. All they care about is what their position is on Israel.

The whole hoax and diversion of targeting Russia for influencing US elections is to a large part to hide the glaringly obvious fact that Israel and ultra-Zionism is buying and controlling American elections and lawmakers including the president. I had to chuckle when former Mossad chief Tamir Pardo said that Russia deployed tens of thousands of bots to influence the 2016 US elections in favour of Trump to support the candidate they thought would best suit their interests. He warned against 'the danger to Western democracies posed by Russian influence on public discourse'. What utter crap and he knows it. Al Jazeera undercover reporter 'Tony' heard about the 'Israel Cyber Shield' project which is 'a civil intelligence unit that collects, analyses and acts upon the activists in the BDS movement'. This is spying by a foreign power on American citizens and the government does *nothing*. What if the country was Russia or Iran? BDS co-founder Omar Barghouti, said:

> Israel has used cyber sabotage, we suffered from intense denial of service attacks, hacking attacks on our websites. Israel decided to go on cyber warfare against BDS publicly. They said we shall spy on BDS individuals and networks, especially in the west. We have not heard a peep from any western government complaining that Israel is admitting that it will spy on your

citizens. Imagine Iran saying it will spy on British or American citizens. Just imagine what would happen.

Palestinian-American journalist Ali Abunimah, author of *The Battle for Justice in Palestine*, made the same point. If China, Russia or Iran was doing this there would be uproar, he said. 'You would have Congress going off to them, you would have hearings, you would have prosecutions. The question is how does Israel get away with this?' The answer is the Hidden Hand Web and the Death Cult. The scale of Israeli surveillance in the United States and worldwide is incredible. Jacob Baime, Executive Director of the Israel on Campus Coalition, told 'Tony':

> There's a company called Sensus. It's very pricy though. We had to raise hundreds of thousands of dollars for it. It's going to increase our discovery rate. We're discovering just about everything we need. It's also going to bring new sources online that we weren't able to access in an automated fashion.

> Like message boards ... we have ways to crawl message boards right now and to monitor them but it's disconnected from the event and activity discovery mechanism, so we want that system to be all integrated. We just signed the contract yesterday for them to start that work. They actually already started it. Good friends in Israel that are helping us with that.

John Mearsheimer, co-author of *The Israel Lobby*, rightly said that you would think with the United States having an unconditional special relationship with Israel, which gives it so much and protects it diplomatically at every turn, that Israelis would do less spying on America than other countries do: '... but on the contrary what we see is that the Israelis are probably at the top of the list when it comes to foreign countries spying on the United States.' This will become highly significant when I return to the September 11th attacks. Given what I am laying out here is it any surprise that Israeli Foreign Minister Shimon Peres revealed that Prime Minister Ariel Sharon said in the wake of 9/11 in October, 2001:

> I want to tell you something very clear. Don't worry about American pressure on Israel. We, the Jewish people, control America and the Americans know it.

What Jewish academic Noam Chomsky said about Israeli interference in US elections is clear to anyone who has even mildly researched the subject:

> First of all, if you're interested in foreign interference in our elections, whatever the Russians may have done barely counts or weighs in the balance

as compared with what another state does, openly, brazenly and with enormous support.

Israeli intervention in U.S. elections vastly overwhelms anything the Russians may have done. I mean, even to the point where the prime minister of Israel, Netanyahu, goes directly to Congress, without even informing the president, and speaks to Congress, with overwhelming applause, to try to undermine the president's policies – what happened with Obama and Netanyahu in 2015. Did Putin come to give an address to the joint sessions of Congress trying to – calling on them to reverse US policy, without even informing the president?

The absolutely stunning scale of influence that ultra-Zionists and the Death Cult have over the United States is important to expose before I return to 9/11 because it explains why and how the truth has been suppressed – and ultra-Zionist manipulation is not at all confined to America.

CHAPTER 19

Everywhere you look

Until you realize how easily it is for your mind to be manipulated,
you remain the puppet of someone else's game – Evita Ochel

Ultra-Zionist manipulation in Britain and Europe (and countries like Canada and Australia) is also systematically structured for maximum ongoing effect and certainly explains the puppy dog, tail-wagging enthusiasm for the post-9/11 war on terror by war criminal prime minister Tony Blair.

The ultra-Zionist web in the UK includes the Friends of Israel network within every major UK political party – Conservative Friends of Israel, Labour Friends of Israel and Liberal Democrat Friends of Israel. These are essentially the same organisation seeking the same outcome – political support in Britain for ultra-Zionist/Israel desires and demands. These 'Friends' groupings work closely with the Israeli Embassy in London and the Britain Israel Communications and Research Centre (BICOM), a UK version of AIPAC, which promotes 'awareness of Israel and the Middle East in the United Kingdom'. BICOM hilariously describes itself as an 'independent research centre producing research and analysis about Israel and the Middle East'. Don't be silly. BICOM is an ultra-Zionist lobby front established in the 9/11 year of 2001 by ultra-Zionist billionaire Chaim 'Poju' Zabludowicz and works closely with the Israeli Embassy directly and indirectly like all these major expressions of The Lobby. Helsinki-born Zabludowicz is the son of arms manufacturer Shlomo Zabludowicz of Soltam Systems. The family company owns some 40 percent of the land covered by downtown Las Vegas where a big noise is Trump funder Sheldon Adelson. Poju' also bought property in illegal West Bank settlements. He has been a major donor to Conservative Party/Israel causes and developed a close relationship with Conservative prime minister David Cameron. BICOM is Britain's AIPAC making connections with politicians and journalists with daily briefings issued with suggested stories and angles beneficial to Israel. There are the usual free trips for politicians and journalists to visit Israel and pick up the script that we see in the United States and elsewhere.

BICOM is especially active whenever Israel is bombing Palestinian civilians and PR is urgently needed with Israel's public standing in free-fall. Two other UK ultra-Zionist censor groups, the Campaign Against Anti-Semitism (CAA) and the North West Friends of Israel were both established in the period around the 2014 Israel slaughter in Gaza known as Operation Protective Edge. Mass Murder Edge would have been far more accurate. Other strands of the UK ultra-Zionist Lobby include the Board of Deputies of British Jews, the Jewish Leadership Council and the usual Christian Zionists. BICOM also has a UK pro-Israel advocacy organisation called We Believe in Israel headed by former Labour Party councillor Luke Akehurst.

Buying Blair

Long-time Labour Party MP Tam Dalyell spoke out in 2003, the year of the ultra-Zionist-manipulated invasion of Iraq, about how 9/11 Prime Minister Tony Blair was unduly influenced by a 'cabal of Jewish advisers' in forming policy towards Iraq, Syria and Iran. Dalyell particularly focused on Blair's 'Middle East envoy' ultra-Zionist Lord Levy who was also the Labour Party's chief fundraiser and known to the media as 'Lord Cashpoint'. I can't think where Levy would go for money. Levy was described by *The Jerusalem Post* as 'undoubtedly the notional leader of British Jewry'. He was a founding member of the Jewish Leadership Council and led the financial campaign to fund Blair's successful run for prime minister in 1997. Two of the people Levy tapped for big donations were ultra-Zionist television executive Alexander Bernstein and ultra-Zionist printing tycoon Robert Gavron who were both given titles of Baron and Lord when Blair was elected. I'm sure there was no connection. Lord Levy's son Daniel has been an assistant to former Israeli Prime Minister Ehud Barak who so brilliantly predicted the role of Bin Laden and Afghanistan on the morning of 9/11. Daniel Levy headed the Middle East Department of the European Council on Foreign Relations and became President of the US Middle East Project. Blair was the ultra-Zionists' man from the start and Levy was at his side across 9/11 and into the 'war on terror' until Blair stood aside in 2007 for Gordon Brown to become his brief successor in Downing Street. Blair and Brown were both members of Labour Friends of Israel and so little changed on that score. Levy's fundraising bonanza for Blair ended amid allegations and scandal over people who donated large sums being rewarded with a title and place in the House of Lords. Israeli newspaper *Haaretz* reported a connection between money donated by Zionist Jews and the pro-Israel policy of Tony Blair and Gordon Brown. Ultra-Zionist millionaire David Abrahams, a deputy chair of Labour Friends of Israel, was exposed in 2007 for making secret and illegal donations through junior employees of £600,000. He told *The*

Jewish Chronicle that he 'didn't want Jewish money and the Labour Party being put together'. Oh, really? I wonder why. Journalist Yasmin Alibhai-Brown questioned in *The Independent* the influence in Labour Party election victories of Zionist lobbyists and Labour political organiser Jonathan Mendelsohn. He was a trustee of the UK Holocaust Educational Trust, former chairman of Labour Friends of Israel and prominent in other ultra-Zionist groups. Mendelsohn, too, became a Baron. His ultra-Zionist wife Nicola, or Lady Mendelsohn, was named as Facebook's Vice President for Europe, the Middle East and Africa in 2013 on the watch of ultra-Zionist Facebook chairman and chief executive officer Mark Zuckerberg and ultra-Zionist Chief Operating Officer Sheryl Sandberg. Did I mention that Jewish people are only 0.2 percent of the global population and that many are not Zionists and only a comparative few ultra-Zionists? The Jewish percentage of the UK population is two percent with 290,000 in a nation of more than 66 million. Tony Blair immediately joined Labour Friends of Israel when he became an MP in 1983 and remained a close supporter and attendee. Baron Mendelsohn, chief election fundraiser for Blair's successor Gordon Brown, said that Blair transformed the party's stance on Israel:

> Blair attacked the anti-Israelism that had existed in the Labour Party. Old Labour was cowboys-and-Indians politics, picking underdogs to support, but the milieu has changed. Zionism is pervasive in New Labour. It is automatic that Blair will come to Labour Friends of Israel meetings.

This was all in the run-up to 9/11 and its 'war on terror' aftermath while precisely the same was happening around Boy Bush in the United States via the Project for the New American Century network.

Castrating Corbyn

The vicious hate-filled campaign by the ultra-Zionist lobby against Labour Party leader Jeremy Corbyn in 2018 and beyond to brand him and his party 'anti-Semitic' can now be seen in its true light. The UK Conservative Party is owned by ultra-Zionists and so are most of the Labour Party MPs still loyal to war criminal Tony Blair. They are both a gimme to do whatever Israel demands. It was different with Corbyn and Labour activists supporting him. They were still prepared to speak out against Israel and the inhuman treatment of Palestinians. The campaign of hate against Corbyn and what is left of genuine Labour was specifically orchestrated with disgraceful support from the *Daily Mail* and other media to force the party into adopting the ridiculously-broad new definition of 'anti-Semitism'. I say 'force' but 'force' always requires acquiescence to 'force' and the party hierarchy outrageously caved. Labour Friends of Israel MPs were at the forefront of the campaign as you would expect and that is the source of constant efforts to replace Corbyn as leader. Ultra-Zionist Labour MPs played the victim card and the depths of insanity and exaggeration of the get-Corbyn campaign were personified by ultra-Zionist Labour MP Margaret Hodge (née Oppenheimer). She is a patron of the Campaign Against Antisemitism (CAA) which hurled hysterical abuse in Corbyn's direction as it has against me. Hodge actually said that facing a party disciplinary inquiry (later dropped) over calling Corbyn an 'anti-Semite' made her think about 'what it felt like to be a Jew in Germany in the 30s'. She went on: '... when I heard about the disciplinary, my emotional response resonated with that feeling of fear, that clearly was at the heart of what my father felt when he came to Britain.' To make a comparison between a party disciplinary hearing and being a Jew in Nazi Germany takes the bloody breath away. One of the most sickening comments I saw with relation to Corbyn was when he posted on Twitter on the 100th anniversary of the end of the First World War in 2018 that we should say 'never again'. This was met with a reply from an ultra-Zionist fanatic who said: 'Please don't ever use the phrase #NeverAgain (which FYI is a reference to the Holocaust). It is an insult!' An estimated 37 million people died in the First World War and this man was claiming copyright for 'never again' for 0.2 per- cent of the global population. Now *that* is an insult, but what a glimpse into the extremes of this cultural chauvinism. Political commentator John Wight made a telling contribution to understanding the background to the anti-Corbyn hate campaign by 'anti-hate' ultra-Zionist frauds. Wight described them as: 'A sundry crew of in the main very middle class, very affluent, and very mendacious champions of war – Iraq, Libya anyone? – and defenders of Israel's oppression and dispossession of the Palestinian people, who to all intents have been marked out as children of a lesser God':

> Many of these defenders of Israel occupy prime positions within the mainstream media, within the Labour Party itself as MPs — indeed within the establishment in general — and key among them are members of a pro-Israel lobby that is committed to policing and controlling the terms of the debate when it comes to the treatment of the Palestinians.

> At their behest people in Britain have been invited to enter an upside-down world in which lifelong committed anti-racists, such as Corbyn, are presented as rabid racists and anti-Semites, while they – proponents of regime change wars and defenders of apartheid – are presented as Camusian warriors of integrity and decency.

Gaining Momentum? Or gaining control?

Four weeks after Jeremy Corbyn became UK Labour Party leader an organisation called Momentum was launched from the multi-million pound home overlooking Tower Bridge in London of Zionist Jon Lansman with fellow Zionists James Schneider and Adam Klug. Momentum is called a 'grassroots' organisation allegedly to gather support for Corbyn and it quickly made inroads into the Labour Party hierarchy with Lansman securing a place on the party's National Executive Committee. There were more than 170 local groups in the UK by early 2018 and 40,000 members. Momentum said it would 'encourage mass mobilisation for a more democratic, equal and decent society' and 'assist members in making their voice heard in Labour Party debates'. Well, debates that don't include criticism of Israel would appear to be more accurate because according to *Jewish News* Lansman was for weeks lobbying Labour's leadership to adopt the international definition of anti-Semitism with all its carefully-worded examples that I detailed earlier. He came out full-blown in 2019 when he said that the Labour Party he claims to support had a major problem with 'anti-Semitism' and members who believed in 'conspiracy theories'. How yawningly predictable. The real agenda of Zionist-controlled 'Momentum' was now on public display and even more so when Momentum produced a video condemning 'conspiracy theories' and saying they were only trying to get people to 'hate Jews'. The Rothschilds and George Soros were especially defended and yours truly naturally got a mention. No matter how much documented evidence is produced about Soros it doesn't matter because there is only one explanation for why people expose him – they're 'anti-Semitic'. The clueless presenter of the video said the Rothschilds can't be part of a conspiracy because they are hardly mentioned in the Forbes Rich List. The idea that those in real control – as opposed to mega-rich frontmen like Jeff Bezos – are going to flaunt the extent of their wealth and power is so ridiculous, naive and misleading that you can only laugh. Are genuine Labour Party members going to realise what Momentum really is and why it was created by Zionists immediately after Corbyn was elected leader? By 2018 Corbyn was so controlled by people like Lansman and Israel-arse-licking Labour Deputy Leader Tom Watson that he posted a link to the Momentum video while condemning 'vile and destructive ... antisemitic conspiracy theories'. This was the end of Corbyn as a credible 'radical'. His backbone had gone and he was now owned by Israel. The coup on the Labour Party was complete. I never had Corbyn down as the brightest, but his spineless contempt for genuine Labour supporters that made him leader is a disgrace. Tom Watson, who has taken donations from pro-Israel lobbyists, said amid rising homelessness and poverty with kids going to bed hungry every night that 'fighting anti-Semitism' should be the Labour Party's 'number one issue'. How Watson shaves without averting his eyes I cannot think. The claim by rich-man

Lansman that he started Momentum to improve the lives of the oppressed working class is utterly hilarious to me. He became a member of the National Executive Committee's working group on anti-Semitism and Momentum vice-chair Emina Ibrahim was on the panel that expelled Labour Party members for 'anti-Semitism' *including* Jewish ones. The most shocking case was that of Cyril Chilson, a Jewish academic at Oxford University who served 16 years of compulsory and reserve service in the Israeli army, including in occupied Palestinian territories and in occupied Lebanon during the war in 1982. He was also a foreign press liaison officer with the Israeli Defence Forces (IDF) spokesman unit. Chilson said that his job was to:

> ... whitewash the atrocities which I had witnessed on a daily basis when serving in the West Bank or in Gaza and spoon-feed with watered-down information the foreign correspondents while escorting them during their restricted visits.

Chilson's parents were both survivors of the Nazis. He moved to the UK where he became a naturalised British citizen in 2006 and was able 'to gain a wider perspective of the real intentions of the state of Israel, reflected through the agenda of the settlers' movement, namely a permanent and irreversible Jewish colonisation of the occupied Palestinian territories'. Chilson joined the Labour Party and said he recognised from personal experience the 'ideological fingerprints' of the Israeli military propaganda machine and 'Hasbara' that were 'all over' the attacks on Jeremy Corbyn and the Labour Party for being 'anti-Semitic'. He was describing how the Israeli military and government via its UK network was the source of the campaign of abuse for Corbyn and Labour to accept the new full and ludicrous definition of 'anti-Semitism' while Momentum's Lansman was lobbying Labour from the inside to the very same end which was eventually successful. This manufactured ultra-Zionist mob abused Chilson and his family and tried to pressure Oxford University to sack him. This is typical of ultra- Zionist hate groups. Instead of giving Chilson support the spineless ultra-Zionist-hijacked Labour Party suspended him in 2016 and he was permanently expelled from the party at a disciplinary hearing with Momentum's Emina Ibrahim on the panel. Another expelled Jewish Labour member, Tony Greenstein, described her as a 'collaborator in this racist outrage'. Cyril Chilson wrote:

> The charges against me revolved around my 'antisemitism' – a grotesque accusation for a son of Holocaust survivors whose mother had been snatched in the last minute from the crematoria of death camps and whose father had fought the Nazis flying a Soviet combat aircraft, while his entire family,

parents, siblings and all their relatives perished in the Belzec concentration camp.

The 'antisemitism' in question was my criticism of the state of Israel and its atrocious policies – namely, the unending occupation of the West Bank and the inhuman siege on Gaza, the continuous colonisation of the West Bank and annexed territories (i.e. Eastern Jerusalem and the Golan Heights) and the pervasive apartheid and discrimination against the Palestinian citizens of Israel.

What profound confirmation that the 'anti-Semitism' hysteria and ultra-Zionist hate groups are not about protecting Jews, but deleting all criticism and exposure of the far right Israel government and the Death Cult that drives its policies and behaviour. Chilson's comments about Israel 'recruiting certain leaders of western Jewish communities and turning them into zealous supporters who ostracise opposing Jewish voices' were decreed by the panel, or what Chilton calls a kangaroo court, as 'making mendacious allegations about Jews as a collective" and 'accusing Jews, supporters of Israel and critics of antisemitism as being more loyal to Israel than to the UK ...' Chilson said that most insane of all he was accused of 'denying Jewish people the language to describe their own oppression'. Even the sons of Nazi concentration camps victims are 'anti-Semitic' if they criticise Israel. Jeremy Corbyn, caught in a pincer-movement between the Tony Blair-supporting, Israel-supporting wing of his party and Zionist Lansman's Momentum sat on his hands and zipped his mouth while all this was going on. In November, 2018, Lansman's Momentum would turn on me and try to get my public event in Watford, just north of London, cancelled on the grounds of, yes, 'anti-Semitism'. They tried to demonise me on social media and produced a video in support, but they were met with a lot of condemnation from genuine Momentum and Labour Party members and others for their contempt for freedom of speech. It might be wise for those genuine Momentum members and Labour activists to ask a few questions about the organisation's real agenda and why a rich man like Lansman has this calling to represent the poor and downtrodden while campaigning within the party for what suits Israel and its network of lobby groups. Labour MP Chris Williamson was suspended for saying that the party had been 'too apologetic' over the 'anti-Semitism' campaign. This was not only true, but even if it wasn't he had a right to that opinion. Not in the Israel-owned Labour Party he doesn't. Williamson's biggest mistake was to then say he deeply regretted his remarks. Every time someone apologises for speaking either the truth or their view of the truth more power is handed to the ultra-Zionist hate groups who are further emboldened to attack others. They should demand that I apologise for reporting supportable facts. They will die waiting. 'Progressive' *Guardian* columnist and self-obsessed social justice warrior Owen Jones jumped to the defence of Williamson and free speech, surely? Well, er, not quite:

> This is utterly out of order. When does the left ever say we've been 'too apologetic' about fighting racism or bigotry? Why is he, a non-Jew, right and Jon Lansman - a Jewish socialist who founded Momentum and ran Corbyn's second leadership campaign - wrong about anti-Semitism?

Another little boy in short trousers who believes he's an intellectual giant. Jones and Lansman's Momentum even urged people to protest at a music event of Israeli-born Gilad Atzmon – now music is 'anti-Semitic' to these morons. Didn't the Nazis target music and cultural events? I do they believe they did.

One party state and the climate of fear

Peter Oborne is one of the few mainstream journalists with the courage and integrity to question the influence of the Zionist Lobby in British politics which he has done both in print and a rare television documentary on the subject. He has highlighted the 'formidable turnout' at major Conservative Friends of Israel events including the party leader and how *80 percent* of Conservative Members of Parliament were members of Conservative Friends of Israel (CFI). The UK Conservative Party has been in government since 2010 at the time of writing led by prime ministers David Cameron and Theresa May who have slavishly supported the US ultra-Zionist Neocon agenda in Libya, Syria and elsewhere. The current Conservative Party treasurer and money-man as I write is the Israeli-born businessman Ehud Sheleg who has donated large sums to the party while Sir Mick Davis, born to a South African Jewish family and former chair of the Jewish Leadership Council, was appointed the party's chief executive in 2018. I wonder what the Conservative policy on the Middle East will be? *Mmmm* ... can't think. Peter Oborne reported how then Prime Minister David Cameron made the main speech at the annual Conservative Friends of Israel gathering in 2009 like other Conservative leaders before him. Margaret Thatcher was a founder member of the Conservative Friends of Israel, a member of the Anglo-Israel Friendship League and the first serving British prime minister to visit the country in 1986. Cameron's speech to this Israel lobby group within his own party was made amid an Israeli invasion of the Gaza Strip and Oborne said he was shocked to see that Cameron did not even mention the invasion. Instead he praised the way Israel 'strives to protect innocent life' at a time when 1,370 people in Gaza were dead. Oborne said he found it impossible to reconcile the remarks with the numerous reports of human rights abuses in Gaza and said as much to some Conservative or 'Tory' Members of Parliament. 'They looked at me as if I was distressingly naive, drawing my attention to the very large number of Tory donors in the audience,' he said. We are looking at the UK equivalent of the spring-arsed Israel-worshippers on Capitol Hill. Most people have no idea about the scale of influence ultra-Zionism and Israel have in the corridors of power, but to know this is to understand so much about the way Israel gets what it wants and avoids criticism and challenge for behaviour that would have others before the International Criminal Court or subject to regime change invasion. Oborne has described how the slur of 'anti-Semitism' is used against journalists and publications to deter would-be critics and how 'News International, Telegraph newspapers and the Express Group have tended to take a pro-Israel line and have not always been an hospitable environment for those taking a critical look at Israeli foreign policy and influence'. I should congratulate him for one of the understatements of the century. Oborne and colleague James Jones produced a pamphlet exploring the influence of the Zionist Lobby and they noted how clearly frightened people were to speak publicly on the subject even though they had plenty to say in private. Oborne and Jones wrote:

> Many people who privately voiced concerns about the influence of the lobby simply felt they had too much to lose by confronting it. One national newspaper editor told us, 'that's one lobby I've never dared to take on.' From MPs, to senior BBC journalists and representatives of Britain's largest charities, the pattern became depressingly familiar. Material would come flooding out on the phone or in a meeting, but then days later an email would arrive to say that they would not be able to take part. Either after consultation with colleagues or consideration of the potential consequences, people pulled out.

Oborne and Jones revealed how charities such as Disasters Emergency Committee, Amnesty, Oxfam, Christian Aid, Save the Children Fund and the Catholic agency CAFOD all refused to comment on the BBC's refusal to air a Gaza disaster appeal in response to the humanitarian catastrophe at the time delivered by the Israeli military. Even finding a publisher for their pamphlet was not easy with potential publishers concerned about losing their charitable status or saying 'I don't think that our donors would like this very much'. Zionist money and intimidation are the twin pillars of ultra-Zionist control networks both sides of the Atlantic and in countries like Australia and New Zealand. The writers described how one MP had predicted they would never 'have the guts' to make a television programme about what was happening. The MP said it was 'a big story' and called the Zionist network 'the most powerful lobby by far in parliament'. When the programme *was* made the MP refused to take part and a 'front bench Conservative MP was so paranoid he insisted we remove the battery from our mobile phones to ensure our privacy during the conversation'. Only senior MPs reaching the end of their political careers were willing to speak on the record including Michael Mates, a member of the Intelligence and Security Committee and former Northern Ireland minister, who eventually left parliament in 2010. He said: 'The pro-Israel lobby in our body politic is the most powerful political lobby. There's nothing to touch them.' Their lobbying, he thought, was 'done very discreetly, in very high places'. Sir Richard Dalton, former British ambassador to Iran and consul in Jerusalem, told the writers how politicians are afraid to say publicly what they may say in private and so Israel avoided proper public scrutiny and much of this pressure to stay silent was financial. Oborne and Jones described how different members of the Friends of Israel networks from Conservative and Labour parties have public dialogue about Israel policy while never making clear their membership of in effect Israel lobby groups. This included those in government and parliamentary roles highly relevant to Israel policy. Oborne and Jones wrote in 2009:

> Many of the most sensitive foreign affairs, defence and intelligence posts in the House of Commons are occupied by Labour or Conservative Friends of Israel. Mike Gapes, chairman of the Foreign Affairs Select Committee, is a former deputy chairman of the [Labour Friends of Israel]. Kim Howells, the chair of the Intelligence and Security Committee (and another former Middle East minister) used to chair Labour Friends of Israel. James Arbuthnot, chairman of the powerful Commons Defence Select Committee, is also the serving parliamentary chairman of the [Conservative Friends of Israel]. There is no prohibition on parliamentarians having membership of such groups, but how many voters are aware of these links?

The same situation continues today with the ultra-Zionist lobby massively influencing British government policy on the Middle East and elsewhere through their maze of channels. Oborne reveals that then Conservative Party opposition foreign affairs spokesman William Hague was the target of Zionist anger when he described the Israeli attack on Lebanon in 2006 as 'disproportionate'. Threats were made by ultra-Zionist Lord Stanley Kalms, treasurer of the Conservative Party across 9/11, to withdraw funding. Oborne said party leader David Cameron gave the Zionists an assurance that the term 'disproportionate' would never be used again. Members of Parliament supporting the ultra-Zionist agenda attract financial support and particularly those who are standing against critics of Israel. No guesses where the inspiration came from for Jeremy Hunt, I think I pronounced that correctly, the British

Conservative government Foreign Secretary, to describe Israel as 'an inspiration' and 'beacon of democracy' when it is anything but. Hunt announced in 2019 that the UK would oppose the United Nations Human Rights Council's permanent agenda item on human rights abuses in Israel and Occupied Palestinian Territories. He said 'elevating this dispute above all others cannot be sensible' and he might have added 'if I want to stay attached to my arse'. Hunt condemned the suggestion that 'one side alone holds a monopoly of fault'. He's right – the ones with the state of the art arsenal funded by the United States and those by comparison with pea-shooters are equally at fault. The same is true of those who are free to travel anywhere and those imprisoned behind fences with checkpoint exits manned by armed troops and those who pepper-bomb Gaza and those on the receiving end. They are equally to blame. It's your fault – you shouldn't have been having tea in your home with your family when we decided to drop a bomb. In fact, that could even be 'anti-Semitic'.

It's the same game in Britain that we see in the United States, Canada and other countries. Labour and Conservatives Friends of Israel MPs and those they want to snare are taken on funded visits to Israel to be subjected to ultra-Zionist propaganda. How can this be in any way acceptable when according to the Committee on Standards in Public Life: 'Holders of public office should not place themselves under any financial or other obligation to outside individuals or organisations that might seek to influence them in the performance of their official duties.' Do you think being owned by ultra-Zionist money and largesse might qualify for that? Journalists told Oborne and Jones how they had been accused of anti-Semitism' for writing articles unfavourable to Israel and they were sure it had damaged their careers. BBC Middle East reporter Orla Guerin was moved to other duties after a campaign against her by Israel and its lobby dubbing her 'anti-Semitic' for the 'crime' of trying to report the Israeli-Palestinian conflict fairly and honestly. Both words are like garlic to a vampire to the ultra-Zionist lobby which demands that only its narrative is heard. Writer Antony Lerman who had been very supportive of Israel and highlighted anti-Semitism was called 'a nasty anti-Semite' as soon as he broke ranks with the script. 'I think there are people who are deliberately manipulating the use of the term antisemitism because they do see that it's useful in defending Israel', he said. Oh, just a little bit. Veteran British journalist Richard Ingrams, a critic of Blair minder Lord Levy, highlighted 'the reluctance throughout the media to contemplate the Israeli factor' with regard to the September 11th attacks and pointed to 'pressure from the Israeli lobby in this country that many, even normally outspoken journalists, are reluctant even to refer to such matters.' Ingrams pointed out the 'close business links with Israel' with regard to major media owners like Rupert

Murdoch. Sam Kiley, a journalist on the Murdoch-owned *Times* newspaper, resigned after saying his work had been severely censored by senior executives because of the owners' support for Israel and Zionism. Most won't walk out with a mortgage to pay and so they bow their heads and avoid the subject. Columnist Kevin Myers was fired by the Irish version of the Murdoch-owned *Sunday Times* for alleged 'anti-Semitic' comments in 2017 about the way the BBC paid male presenters more than female for the same job. Myers wrote:

> I note that two of the best-paid women presenters in the BBC – Claudia Winkleman and Vanessa Feltz, with whose, no doubt, sterling work I am tragically unacquainted – are Jewish. Good for them. Jews are not generally noted for their insistence on selling their talent for the lowest possible price, which is the most useful measure there is of inveterate, lost-with-all-hands stupidity. I wonder, who are their agents?

Had had the word 'Jewish' instead been 'American', 'Chinese', 'French', 'Russian', 'Colombian' or 'Canadian' Myers would not have been instantly fired, his column removed and an apology published. The Jewish population of Ireland is about 2,500 in a total Irish population of around 4.8 million and the pressure to sack him didn't even come from Jews in Ireland. They *defended* him – not least because he had a record of pro-Israel articles. The Jewish Representative Council of Ireland said that branding him as either an anti-Semite or Holocaust denier was 'an absolute distortion of the facts'. Distortion of the facts? Who could have done that to get Myers sacked and his career destroyed? *Mmmm*, that would be the UK-based Campaign Against Antisemitism (CAA) in its perpetually red-faced outrage. This is the same CAA that targets the Labour Party and myself – while Labour members targeted by the CAA also target me on the same grounds that the CAA targets them. Don't waste your time trying to make sense of that. Just accept that the world is mad and let's continue.

Israel's 'take-down' policy

Ultra-Zionists use their web of organisations and hate groups to fund, manipulate and intimidate their demands into reality through theoretically (and only that) sovereign governments. Elected politicians who won't play ball with the psychopaths of the Israeli far right are targeted for removal. We saw a glaring example of this in an Al Jazeera documentary series about the Zionist Lobby in Britain in 2016 when hidden cameras caught Shai Masot, 'a senior political officer' (see 'Mossad') at the Israeli Embassy in London headed by far-right ultra-Zionist ambassador Mark Regev who has become well known for 'justifying' in the media the slaughter of Palestinian civilians. Israeli embassies around the world are Mossad fronts with the main Mossad operative having a higher rank than the ambassador. This was revealed by former Mossad agent Victor Ostrovsky in his 1990 book, *By Way of Deception*. Friends of Israel groups within UK political parties work closely with the Israel embassy in London as confirmed by Labour Friends of Israel officer Michael Rubin when caught on a secret camera. He said there was a need to keep this connection to the embassy secret: 'We work really closely together, but a lot of it is behind the scenes.' Oh, I don't doubt it, and so we are looking at organisations connected to the Israel embassy infiltrating UK political parties. *Hello*? Al Jazeera's covert filming exposed the manipulations of the Friends of Israel network and

Figure 103: UK Israeli embassy 'take down' operative Shai Masot on the left with Ambassador Mark Regev on the right, the notorious apologist for Israeli mass-murder in Gaza. In the centre is Jeremy Newmark , former chair of the Jewish Labour Movement within the Labour Party which has been very active in the 'anti-Semitism' campaign against Jeremy Corbyn and the party in general.

associated groups and in one scene Israeli embassy operative Shai Masot is seen listing British politicians he wanted to 'take down' for their stance on Israel (Fig 103). They included Foreign Office Minister Alan Duncan. Masot was in conversation with his friend, Joan Ryan, then chair of the Labour Party Friends of Israel and a vociferous critic of party leader Jeremy Corbyn. This shocking exposure should have been met with a tidal wave of condemnation and questions about Israel's manipulation of politics in

Britain and elsewhere. Imagine what would have happened had the country been Iran? But it wasn't – it was Israel and the incident passed with barely a whimper and that included from Corbyn who is in political hock to the Momentum 'radical socialist' organisation of Zionist Jon Lansman. Prime Minister Theresa May said in reaction to an Israeli demand to take down one of her own ministers: 'The Israeli ambassador has apologised ... the UK has a strong relationship with Israel and we consider the matter closed.' This was both pathetic and also very revealing. Another ultra-Zionist group working within the Labour Party is the Jewish Labour Movement (JLM) which the Electric Intifada website reported, quoting unbroadcast footage from an Al Jazeera documentary, was reformed in 2015 just to oppose Jeremy Corbyn. Still another ultra-Zionist group within the party is Jewish Voice for Labour which is a 'racially'-exclusive group that only allows non-Jews to join as a 'solidarity member'. What if it was the other way round? 'Anti-Semitic!!!' JLM director Ella Rose admitted to Al Jazeera's undercover reporter that she worked closely with Shai Masot before and after she took up the post. 'We work with Shai, we know him very well,' she said, which is not surprising. Rose once worked for the Israeli embassy. You won't be shocked to know that Rose is another critic of Corbyn within the party. The Jewish Labour Movement invited an Israeli delegation to the 2016 Labour Party conference at the behest of the Israeli embassy who were portrayed as young, left-wing Israeli activists. Israel daily *Haaretz* reported after the conference – without naming the groups involved – that a cable from Israel's London embassy confirmed that Israeli agents had been 'operating British Jewish organizations' and this was possibly 'in violation of British law'. Michael Rubin, Parliamentary Officer for the Labour Friends of Israel, said on hidden camera that Israel Friends Labour chair Joan Ryan spoke with Shai 'take down' Masot 'most days' and that Labour Friends of Israel 'work with the [Israeli] ambassador and the embassy quite a lot'. Still believe in 'democracy'?

The inevitable came in early 2019 when Israel-stooge Labour and Conservative MPs, including Friends of Israel stalwart Joan Ryan and Jewish MP Luciana Berger, a one-time director of Labour Friends of Israel, left their parties to form their own 'Independent Group'. A greater contradiction in terms it is hard to imagine. They claimed their motivation came from 'anti-Semitism' in the Labour Party. This 'group', which included the oil-slick-slimy Labour MP Chuka Umunna, turned out not to be a new political party, at least at first, but a private company! This allowed them to keep secret their sources of funding. Half a brain cell was all you needed to work out where much of it would come from and confirmation soon arrived. Multi-millionaire Israel lobbyist David Garrard announced that he was funding the 'Independent' Group which chose Umunna as its 'spokesman'. Oil slick would not have had it any other way. David Garrard has been a major financial backer of Labour Friends of Israel and joined its board. He donated nearly $2 million to the Labour Party under pro-Israel leaders Tony Blair, Gordon Brown and Ed Miliband, but then called in a loan of more than $2.5 million when Jeremy Corbyn was elected leader. But don't you worry your little head – there is no ultra-Zionist manipulation of British politics and it is absolutely 'anti-Semitic' and Holocaust-denying to say so. I mean, where's your evidence? Garrard has made donations to Ryan, Umunna and other breakaway Israel-worshippers, but their new 'party', later called Change UK, soon began to unravel. Labour MP Ruth George commented that it was possible this group would get support from Israel (solid gold certainty) but after the usual furore she apologised for 'invoking a conspiracy theory'. Is there no one in politics or public life who is not permanently on their knees facing Tel Aviv? The UK Liberal Democrat Party is another fiefdom of the ultra-Zionist lobby and the Friends of Israel network. Baroness Jenny Tonge, a thoroughly decent former Liberal Democrat MP and member of the House of Lords, was suspended by the party and later resigned after the truth she told about Israel was too much for her butt-licking colleagues. She said in 2006: 'The pro-Israeli lobby has got its grips on the western world, its financial grips. I think they've probably got a grip on our party' (another solid-gold certainty). The establishment immediately fell to its knees led appropriately by former Archbishop of Canterbury George Carey who condemned Tonge's 'irresponsible and inappropriate' comments which 'evoked a classic anti-Jewish conspiracy theory'. *What an idiot.* Journalists Peter Oborne and James Jones said the following about the influence of the Zionist and Israel Lobby in the UK:

> This influence works in a variety of ways: the unceasing cultivation of British MPs; political donations; availability of research briefs; brilliant presentation of the case for Israel. The Israel lobby has enjoyed superb contacts at the very top of British politics, and never hesitated to use them. As we have shown in this pamphlet, it has used them at key moments; for instance the Israeli invasion of the Lebanon three years ago and the publication of the Goldstone Report into alleged war crimes during the invasion of Gaza earlier this year.

> Beyond these specific examples of influence, there is also a wider presence. The Friends of Israel groups in the House of Commons have firmly established themselves in the interstices of British political life. Their heavy presence at party conferences is taken for granted, their lunches and dinners an ingrained part of the Westminster social scene, the donations a vital part of the political financing. An environment now exists where MPs and ministers feel cautious about criticizing the foreign policy of the Israeli state, wary of opening themselves to criticism on the home front. Meanwhile, public discourse on Israel, as we have shown, is heavily policed.

'Conspiracy theorist' = 'anti-Semite'

What the CIA dubbed 'conspiracy theorists' are very dangerous to the official narrative because they are questioning its validity either in total like me or in part. They therefore have to be discredited and silenced and once again 'anti-Semitism' is the weapon of choice. The Board of Deputies of British Jews and the UK Community Security Trust don't seem to like talk of conspiracy – the same with their American counterparts the Anti-Defamation League (ADL). 'Conspiracy theories' are now condemned as 'anti-Semitic tropes' by the Protection Racket even if Jewish people or Zionism are not mentioned because this is about preventing exposure of the global conspiracy and nothing to do with protecting Jewish people from discrimination. The ADL attacked a researcher for questioning how the Twin Towers collapsed when there was no mention of a Jewish or Zionist angle. How interesting and it will get more so later in the book. The UK Community Security Trust (CST), which likes to attack me, is a private 'security' organisation that makes its money from protecting Jewish people and thus benefits when they feel threatened. Every year it issues figures which invariably show that 'anti-Semitism is on the rise' and the media and politicians just accept the figures without question and with not even a thought about potential conflict of interest. True to form in February, 2019, the CST published its latest 'figures' and would you believe it – 'anti-Semitism' incidents had reached a record high for the third year in a row. The CST said that this indicated a general atmosphere of intolerance when they took a brief break from calling for others to have their free speech denied. The Campaign Against Anti-Semitism (CAA) is so tolerant that its stated policy is 'zero tolerance'. They're not hypocrites or anything – that's just an 'anti-Semitic' trope. The CST and Board of Deputies condemned the anti-EU UK Independence Party (UKIP) for embracing people connected to conspiracy talk show host, Alex Jones. Israel arse-licker, rent-a-quote and Labour MP John Mann said Jones' organisation was 'vile and dangerous'. I thought he was talking about his Labour Friends of Israel at first hearing, but apparently not. I have some big differences with Alex Jones and not least his backing of Trump, but I will support to my dying day his right to his opinion. This is in stark contrast to the tech and financial companies of The Web that have banned him. Apple, Twitter, Facebook, PayPal and so on did so while talking about 'our values' when they don't have any. 'Values' is only Orwell-speak for controlling the narrative. The ultra-Zionist attack on Jones was particularly bizarre on the face of it because the Jones associate they mention rails against the impact of Islam but has argued *against* any suggestion of a 'Jewish plot'. Jones overwhelmingly avoids the Zionist connection, too. Ultra-Zionist groups linked the exposure of George Soros by Alex Jones and company as evidence of 'anti-Semitism' which is the constantly-employed tactic to protect Soros and his mega networks manipulating human society. I read the story about the targeting of UKIP on the *Guardian* website in an article by its 'political correspondent' (God help us) Peter Walker. He wrote about 'the supposed influence of Soros, the billionaire financier who is at the centre of antisemitic conspiracies about so-called "globalists" seeking to control the world.' The fact that what Soros is doing has been confirmed by leaked documents and emails and by arrogant members of his Open Society Foundations passes Walker by. *The Guardian* promotes itself as radical left of centre but is actually the epitome of an establishment propaganda sheet promoting the agenda of human enslavement while most of its number think they are 'anti-establishment'. The paper's biased coverage of Israel and Palestine is a disgrace to journalism and those seeking to present both sides have been purged as contributors in recent years in yet another example of ultra-Zionist-inspired censorship.

Speaking from experience

Elements within the programmed *Guardian*-like 'progressive left' turned on Alice Walker, once one of their icons, when she recommended my book *And The Truth Shall Set You Free* in an interview with *The New York Times* in late 2018. Alice, the acclaimed author of the Pulitzer Prize-winning *The Color Purple* and many other books and works of poetry, was born as a black child into racist and segregated Georgia in 1944. Against all those incredible odds she built a career as a celebrated author and activist opposing racism and campaigning for justice for all. She married Melvyn Rosenman Leventhal, a Jewish civil rights lawyer, in 1967 and they became the first legally-married interracial couple in Mississippi which obviously attracted harassment and condemnation from white racist morons and their enforcement arm, the Ku Klux Klan. It took incredible commitment and fortitude to stand by her principles – her Jewish husband, too – but all this was forgotten and ignored on both sides of the Atlantic by the calculated hate-merchants of the ultra-Zionist Protection Racket and their mindless sycophants in the 'progressive' mob and media when Walker committed the crime of saying positive things about my book. The symbiosis of ultra-Zionist hate groups and 'progressive' 'anti-hate' groups and activists is the symbiosis of cold calculation and self-righteous ignorance and stupidity. Not a pretty sight from any angle. The media was in uproar as they always are when anyone questions the absolute, uncriticisable perfection of 0.2 percent of the global population. Well, apart from those in the 0.2 percent that criticise Israel – they are fair game to the Protection Racket. I was also interested to see how writers who promote themselves as 'moderate', 'socialist' Zionists were attacking Walker including a bloke called Raphael Magarik writing in the Israeli paper, *Haaretz*. He called my book 'rabidly anti-Semitic' (I doubt he'd even read it) and accused Walker of making 'anti-Semitic' remarks. Utterly ridiculous and outrageous, but for much of the Zionist left Jewish self-identity is still the default position no matter what they may say about the Israeli right wing. Once we reach the point of accusing people like Alice Walker of racism we know that something is seriously wrong and all this does is alert still more people to the Protection Racket, its methods and goals.

I have often been targeted by the ultra-Zionist lobby and its hate groups which have lied to venues and police in an effort to have my public events banned. They have succeeded a few times – at great cost to their public credibility and standing – but we have always somehow found a way around this coldly-calculated censorship – except in Germany where venues are cowed and threatened into cancelling my events or refusing to take a booking (see *Everything You Need To Know But Have Never Been Told* for the detailed background). Germany, meanwhile, continues in its delusion of being a free country despite these facts and Orwellian laws targeting freedom of speech. I don't know what they will do when this book comes out. They will be apoplectic and fit to burst and what I have written will be completely misrepresented as always. I can't say enough times that I am not exposing a 'Jewish plot' but a plot by a cabal that hides in part within the Jewish community and connects with the The Web which operates in all communities, cultures and races. The emphasis in this book is on the ultra-Zionist part of The Web because of its direct relevance to 9/11 as we will see. I will address directly in the next chapter the nature of the usurpers who use the Jewish community as their smokescreen. The prime organisation seeking to silence me in the UK has been the Campaign Against Antisemitism (CAA) which was established in August, 2014, during the mass murder of Palestinians by the Israeli military in Operation Protective Edge which killed more than 2,000 Palestinians including more than 500 children. Another Zionist censor group, the North West Friends of Israel, was formed in the same summer of 2014 and it, too, has worked to have my events cancelled by lying to venues and media about what I would be saying and what I believe. The venues, including the Lowry Hotel in Manchester, never consult me about what is being claimed. They just cancel the event often without even telling us.

Manchester (no class) United

A perfect example with regard to the CAA is the behaviour of Manchester United Football Club in 2017 where a book-launch dinner was to be held for *Everything You Need To Know But Have Never Been Told*. The booking had been confirmed for months and right up to the previous day my son Jaymie was in communication with the club over final arrangements for hundreds of guests, many of them Manchester United supporters and others who had come from abroad. Some had booked tickets to celebrate birthdays. None of this matters to the agenda of the CAA who joined forces with Kick-It- Out, an organisation that campaigns against racism in football. Kick-It-Out knew nothing about me but they didn't have to. The CAA told them everything they needed to know. They both contacted Manchester United with their lies about what I say in the events and alerted local Labour Party Member of Parliament, Kate Green. She went to work on the club as well and we heard on the Internet on the morning of the event that Manchester

United had cancelled. To this day they have never told us. Jaymie headed to the club's Old Trafford ground to ask the people he had been dealing with for months what was going on and he was met by the club's security who escorted him from the premises. Manchester United may be one of the world's biggest football clubs but clearly has no class and no integrity. We managed to find another venue at incredibly short notice to hold the event and in doing so we came across a big venue that will absolutely not cancel when I next speak in Manchester. So thanks for that CAA. It is astonishing to think that MP Kate Green, who was pivotal in having the event cancelled at the expense of her own constituents, was responding to the misrepresentations of me by the very same CAA that so viciously targeted her Labour Party as 'anti-Semitic'. People actually vote for this person? The head of a local homeless charity was pressured by aides to Manchester Labour Mayor Andrew Burnham not to attend the event to receive a donation from us for the homeless of Manchester collected at my events. Burnham sells himself politically as a champion for the homeless. We walked around the city handing out the money directly to the homeless instead. One of three Twitter accounts that Kate Green said had demanded my event to be cancelled was called 'Falconmalteser'. This was established ten years earlier and had the sum total in that time of *one tweet*. So it was genuine then? Green went into battle immediately without even checking. The thought that she is representing anyone let alone a whole political constituency of Stretford and Urmston is terrifying.

The North West Friends of Israel were also involved in pressing for cancellation and they have connections to the Labour Party via people like MP John Mann, a fanatical Zionist, stalwart of Labour Friends of Israel, chair of the All-Party Parliamentary Group against Antisemitism and in the forefront of attacks on Labour leader Jeremy Corbyn over alleged 'anti-Semitism'. You get the picture. Kick-It-Out is partly funded by the Professional Footballers Association (PFA) which is run by Gordon Taylor, a man I knew quite well many years ago when I did interviews with him for the BBC. I wrote to Taylor to point out that the organisation he was helping to fund had grossly misrepresented me both to Manchester United and in public, but he couldn't be bothered to reply. Keep your head down, Gordon, you know it makes sense. I made an offer to publically debate the CAA, Kate Green, Andrew Burnham, Kick-It-Out, all of them together, but they wouldn't accept. Ultra-Zionist hate groups make a point of avoiding open debate with their targets by saying they don't debate with 'anti-Semites'. Throw your mud and run is their modus operandi and they know the media will never call them out. As for Manchester United, they told the media they didn't know the booking was for me which was a lie beyond belief and provably so. Jaymie had actually told them that venues had been targeted to cancel my events and club staff said that we wouldn't have that problem with them because 'We are Manchester United'. In fact, Zionist-owned Manchester United melted like wax in a fire once the ultra-Zionist lobby came to call representing as it does a fraction of two percent of the UK population and a fraction of 0.2 percent of humanity worldwide. Other venues have taken the same mendacious stand of 'we didn't know it was him' out of sheer terror of ultra-Zionist extremists and their threats. When are people going to get off their bloody knees? When venues refuse to cancel they are themselves accused of being 'anti-Semitic' because standing up for the basic human right of freedom of speech is now considered racist. The desperation to silence me has led to ever more hysterical and insane claims. A Jewish man in the Netherlands claimed that me being allowed to speak was a threat to his life. I did speak and somehow he survived. I am one man who is not a member of any organisation or movement. Why are they so frightened of me? Actually, they are not so much frightened of *me* as frightened of the truth coming out *through* me. Tough – its time has come.

Man and dog with banner

Another Labour Party ultra-Zionist front calling for protests at my events in 2018 was the Jewish Labour Movement which is affiliated to the Board of Deputies of British Jews, the Israeli Labor Party, Zionist Federation of the UK, and the World Labour Zionist Organisation, a faction within the World Zionist Organisation. The Jewish Labour Movement's stated objective is 'to maintain and promote Labour or Socialist Zionism as the movement for self-determination of the Jewish people within the state of Israel.' It's the *Zionist* Labour Movement, then, rather than 'the Jewish'. Anyway, these moronic groups who called on the 'Labour movement' to protest at my events managed only a handful outside the venue in Watford, even fewer days later in Crewe and at my final event on that tour in Margate one man turned up with banners he didn't bother to unfurl because no one else came. He even stood at the wrong entrance while the audience were walking in elsewhere. That's all they could manage because there is an increasing awareness on the genuine 'left' that they are being hijacked by the 'anti-Semitism' Protection Racket which has taken over their party. An ultra-Zionist writer by the name of David Collier and another from the Hope Not Hate (Hate Not Hope in truth) organisation both produced outrageous misrepresentations of my talk and my own views. Collier, who incredibly describes himself as an 'independent' writer, called me 'poison' and then immediately began his laughable 'report' of my talk by saying: 'Icke doesn't stand up and publicly attack Jews.' Even not attacking Jews is now 'anti-Semitic' to these people. I feel sad for them – what a strange and bizarre world they must live in getting up every day

with the intent of silencing and discrediting their fellow humans. A
Twitter account was launched in 2019 called Stop Funding Fake News
which urged people to target advertisers on alternative media sites and
ask them to remove their ads. If this didn't exist then Hasbara would
have had to invent it. Collier was one of the first to re-tweet in support
and its most vocal promoter appears to be minor Jewish television
'celebrity' Rachael Riley. She seeks to delete funding for websites that
include among other things 'antisemitic tropes featuring George Soros'.
The Twitter account urges people to 1) Visit a fake news site; 2) Take a
screenshot of an advert; 3) Tweet it at the company; 4) Tag
@SFFakeNews. Riley said she looked into the 'anti-Semitism' debate
after seeing posters that said 'Israel is a racist endeavour' and this
offended her. Personally I am more offended by Palestinian kids having
their limbs blown off by Israeli snipers. Any TV 'celebrity' who
supported a campaign to target advertisers on websites promoting Israel
would be taken off air in an instant. Riley wants to boycott alternative
news sites but when someone started the hashtag
#BoycottRachaelkRiley the ludicrous *Jewish Chronicle* editor Stephen
Pollard said: '... every one of you who promotes #BoycottRachelRiley is
a racist. Every one of you is the enemy of decency. Every one of you is
beneath contempt.' Words have no meaning. Another minor Jewish
celebrity David Baddiel said that #BoycottRachaelkRiley was an
example that Jews don't count. God, it's pathetic. A YouTube
documentary defending Labour activist Jackie Walker – a lady of Jewish
descent with a Jewish partner expelled for 'anti-Semitism' – included a
picture of David Collier at a small protest against a Palestinian cultural
event with Paul Besser, former 'intelligence officer' of the far-right
Israel-supporting Britain First organisation. Collier's 'material' has been
used by Labour Party elements driving the 'anti-Semitism' agenda
which so overcooks the pot that genuine discrimination is sidelined.
Collier is considered a credible source of information by the mainstream
media despite being a professional Israel propagandist and this shows
how crazy and slanted it all is.

The video defending Jackie Walker was apparently taken down many
times by ultra-Zionist-owned YouTube. You can have all the coverage
you like to libel people that you want to silence, but when anyone
defends them they must be denied a voice. Walker's felonies were
secretly filmed in a hit-job at a Labour 'anti-Semitism training session'
and included criticising Holocaust Memorial Day for only
commemorating Jewish victims ... saying 'I still haven't heard a
definition of antisemitism that I can work with' ... and questioning why
Jewish organisations and schools claim to need high security. You can
see that her comments were absolutely horrendous and in no way could
be construed as fair points that anyone with half a brain might consider

making or views that any free and fair society would support her right
to have. Labour activists were disgusted with the ultra-Zionist attacks
on Walker and demands for her to be expelled, but Euan Phillips of the
Labour Against Anti-Semitism group (yet another) had worked out the
reason for that and it was nothing to do with her treatment by a racist
tyranny. Oh, no. Phillips said: 'If Ms Walker is expelled, as she should
be, we can expect an explosion of outrage across the Labour
membership – itself an indication of how ingrained anti-Semitism has
become.' You can see what we are dealing with. How do you have
dialogue with a software program? Jackie Walker was indeed expelled
by the Israel-owned 'party of the people' (Fig 104). The Conservative
Party also suspended a councillor, Jacqui Harris from Stratford-Upon-
Avon, for commenting on Twitter about the 'anti-Semitism' attacks on
the Labour Party: '... the
whole antisemitism thing is
a false flag, probably
masterminded by
Mossad/CIA.' She added:
'Don't you find it timely
that this was encouraged
fanned and exploded just
before the release of the
report on Israel and war
crimes?' The moronic
virtue-signalling Brandon
Lewis, chairman of the
Conservative Party,
quickly announced Jacqui
Harris's suspension for the
crime of engaging in free

Figure 104: What happens when you let a foreign power
highjack your party.

speech, opinion and observation. He said: 'We do not accept any form of
abuse or racism.' Clearly, however, they do accept any form of idiocy
and censorship which he personifies.

'Apartheid is not racism'

The Campaign Against Antisemitism is actually a man and a dog
operation with big political connections. The CAA claims to have close
links with the police, legal system, pro-bono lawyers and political
corridors of power including UK Prime Minister Theresa May when she
was Home Secretary. Freedom of Information emails have confirmed the
cosy relationship between the CAA and Derbyshire police and that
certainly won't be anything like the only example. The main players at
the CAA are chairman Gideon Falter and self-styled Director of
Investigations and *Enforcement*, Stephen Silverman. To call yourself an

'enforcer' has got to be Little Dick Syndrome, surely? Anyway, Little Dick and Falter – Big Dick – run the show day-to-day which basically means targeting people as 'anti-Semitic' who are saying anything that Israel's masters would rather not have people hear. They even seek to ban music events of Israel-born and Britain-based jazz musician and anti-Zionist activist Gilad Atzmon. Jewish-born people are the biggest problem because it is far more difficult to make 'anti-Semite' credible. The CAA is a censorship operation like all these 'anti-hate' groups which specialise in hurling hatred at their targets and 'anti-defamation' groups that set out to defame people. American writer, editor and former financial lawyer Eve Mykytyn published an article in 2018 on the Redressonline.com website headed 'Exposed! How Britain's anti-Semitism scaremongers operate'. This section captures the theme and you can read the article in full by putting the headline words in a search engine:

> This article about the British charitable organisation, the Campaign against Anti-Semitism (CAA), and its officers, Gideon Falter and Steve Silverman, examines events in England but ought to serve as a cautionary message for Canadians and Americans.
>
> The article will delve into the corrosive methods of the CAA; review the manner in which this ultra-Zionist group 'discovers' anti-Semitic 'incidents'; examine their inaccurate statistical 'studies' and see how they seek to intimidate political parties, venues, the press and others; and look at the court cases which the CAA has prosecuted. In the guise of fighting anti-Semitism, the CAA has managed to manoeuvre British society into abdicating its core liberal values, intimidate the prosecutorial and judicial system, and silence criticism of Israel in both social media and the mainstream media. The CAA does not just attempt to limit speech; it openly follows a scorched earth policy 'that if someone commits an anti-Semitic act in the UK (including criticism of Israel)' the CAA 'ensure[s] ruinous consequences, be they criminal, professional, financial or reputational'.

They have such big hearts these people and such empathy with their fellow humans. CAA chairman Gideon Falter serves on the UK board of the Jewish National Fund, an apartheid operation established at the turn of the 20th century which buys up land in Israel that only Jewish people can then live on. This is the man who hurls the slur 'racist' at other people (constantly). CAA 'Little Dick' Stephen Silverman refers to me as a 'modern day hate preacher', but that's a role I will leave to him. An example of the deceitful way these people operate was another event of mine in Manchester at a venue owned by a chain of theatres where I had presented many times. They were aware, therefore, what my events are about and what I say. They knew that the usual mendacious claims made to venues by 'enforcer' Silverman were the garbage that they are and the event went ahead. Little Dick must have been stunned by this knock-back when he's an *enforcer* and must be obeyed. In response he told those attending to send him reports and complaints about what I said so he could take them up with the police and Manchester council. They did write to him in large numbers to report that I said nothing that he claimed I would say; that I had made the point that we are all one consciousness and the labels of race, religion etc. are only illusions to divide us; and that we need to come together irrespective of culture, race and background to realise that we are all being manipulated by the same force. If Little Dick's mission had *really* been about exposing racism he would have published the emails and apologised for the lies that he was spreading about me. At the very least he would have gone away and left me alone. Instead this disingenuous man simply continued to tell future venues what he had told the one in Manchester which audience members had refuted in email responses that he had asked for. This is not about racism or 'anti-Semitism', it's about censorship, and it needs exposing by people who care about freedom because the spineless, gutless mainstream media won't do it.

The ultra-Zionist lobby means that in the country where I was born, and one that claims to be 'free', we have to hold back the locations of my events until the last minute to stop ultra-Zionist hate groups having the time to intimidate venues and campaign to have them cancelled. The interest in my work is now enormous but we can't book bigger venues owned by local councils because we know they will fold at the first call or email from Little Dick and company. The worst for this are councils controlled by the Labour Party which the CAA and its Big Dick chairman have targeted in the same way they target me. It's madness but there we are. Labour Party and backbone don't tend to appear very often in the same sentence these days. One of the reasons ultra-Zionist hate groups give for cancellation is that there could be violence due to my 'controversial' presentation and the audience and venue staff could be in danger. They never have been anywhere in the world in 30 years of public speaking, but the truth doesn't matter to these people – only their desired outcome of silencing my freedom of speech. Little Dick Silverman tried that one again with Bristol City Football Club in 2018 when he emailed the club at the last minute after hearing where I was speaking. Bristol City officials went into backbone-seizure mode as usual but the head of security would not cancel because he had a thousand people heading for his football ground expecting to hear me. What happened? *Nothing* – except for a lovely evening with lovely people. Extra security was added and the police turned up, saw there was no problem and left while asking what the fuss was all about. The 'fuss' was only that generated by Little Dick Silverman. What happened to the law against wasting police time? Or making allegations about a security threat knowing there would be none on the basis of 30 years of history alone? This is the Campaign Against Antisemitism (CAA) with all its ultra-Zionist connections and support system and so they get away with anything. For goodness sake they have been given charity – *charity* – status to do this with all the benefits that affords them. Absolutely outrageous, but who dare take it away? There are ultra-Zionist groups for different regions of the country like the North West Friends of Israel and Sussex Friends of Israel in the UK. If you want to see a video example of the mentality involved go to Davidicke.com and put 'Meet Simon Cobbs, founder of Sussex Friends of Israel' into the search engine. These organisations are absolutely everywhere and all to protect from exposure a tiny section of 0.2 percent of the world population. The big problem these ultra-Zionist hate groups around the world have with me is that I don't give a shit what abuse they throw at me and I don't bow to intimidation of any kind or concede my right to free speech to these humourless numbskulls. It is an approach to professional censors that I can strongly recommend.

Bobbies for Israel

The most sinister aspect of efforts to stop my public events has been the involvement of the police. The Bristol City event was one in a series of talks at football clubs over three weeks in 2018 that also included Sheffield Wednesday, Derby County, Birmingham City, Southampton and Norwich City. Someone – a 'third party' the police wouldn't name – approached Norfolk Police for help in getting the Norwich City event cancelled and the police were only too happy to oblige as emails I secured under the Freedom of Information Act were to prove. Norwich City did cancel after a meeting with police, but Jaymie brilliantly found another venue within half an hour. Worth the effort was it, chaps? The police emails were shocking. They redacted the 'third parties' that contacted them and some were 100 percent redacted. Others at least revealed the emails themselves and the police officers involved. Here's a selection and when you see 'Exempt Section 31' and 'Exempt Section 40' this refers to the 'third parties' and others we are not allowed to know. The bad grammar is theirs, not mine:

Email 25/04/2018 09:13 CI Lynne Cross to N Paling, G Dalton, J Colbert, M Austin, D Cocks, R Watkins

Team,

David Icke is reportedly holding an 'event' in Norwich on 30th April 2018.

Enquiries to date have failed to identify a location.

Can you task your Beat Managers to keep their ear to the ground and see if they can identify any location?

If you have not heard of him, David Icke is a controversial conspiracy theorist and some of our communities (Exempt Section 31) in Norwich are very concerned about his messaging.

He was previously coming to Norwich in March but the Council cancelled the event once they realised. [NO - once ultra-Zionist hate groups told the Labour council a load of tosh.]

See the EDP for any more info!

(Exempt Section 31)

Thanks,

So here we have Norfolk Police acting on behalf of an unnamed 'third party' to track down the venue of my event – which have absolutely no history of problems – with a view to getting it cancelled. The police are supposed to *defend* free speech, but they have become just another vehicle for destroying it. We continue with an email from the 'third parties' to the police:

Email 25/04/2018 08:29 .... Exempt – Section 40) to CI Lynne Cross & Julie Inns

Dear both

So frustrating because it is still advertised as a Sold Out! ....

(Exempt – Section 31)
(Exempt – Section 40)

And thanks for prompt reply.

How clear could it be that this is collusion between the (ultra-Zionist) third parties and Norfolk Police to track down the venue and have my event cancelled? If you are still in doubt:

Email 25/04/2018 09:15 CI Lynne Cross to .... (Exempt – Section 40) & Julie Inns

We are actively trying to identify a location so if anything changes I will be in touch.

Kind regards

Email 27/04/2018 12:46 CI Lynne Cross to .... (Exempt – Sections 40)

Spookily I have already asked our Events Planning to make some enquiries. We will see what they come back with.

One unnamed party even admits that they can't find anything about trouble at my talks 'and I get the impression the offence is taken in the interpretation rather than what he actually says, but I've never heard him speak so don't know for definite'. *At no point* did Norfolk police contact me about any of this or about what I am or am not saying. Then came ecstatic emails revealing they had located the venue – Norwich City Football Club – and they had secured cancellation of the event:

Email 27/04/2018 16:19 CI Lynne Cross to ...., D Marshall, J Inns, ... (Exempt – Section 40)

Dear all,

I have been in contact with the Club and made them aware of the community concerns. After taking advice internally, they have taken the decision to cancel.

These 'security concerns' were utterly fictitious and came from ultra-Zionist liars. Nice to know the police have such a keen eye for mendacity which they don't even check out with the target. Still ... the liars were ecstatic:

Email 27/04/2018 16:26 Julie Inns to CI Lynne Cross, ... Exempt – Section 40)

Lynne,

Fantastic news .... (Exempt – Section 31)

Brilliant partnership working at its best, well done everyone.

There was even a pat on the back from the boss:

**Email 27/04/2018 16:26 Ch Supt David Marshall to J Inns, L Cross, ...
(Exempt – Section 40)**

Lynne/team,

Well done.

What a disgusting way for a police force to act and just in case the third parties were still concerned that I might have freedom of speech:

Email 27/04/2018 16:33 CI Lynne Cross to .... (Exempt – Section 40) & Julie Inns

Good afternoon ...., (Exempt – Section 40)

By way of reassurance, my enquiries suggest you don't need to worry about NCFC.

Regards

All this effort and police time and yet half an hour after Norwich City announced the cancellation Jaymie had secured another venue and the event went ahead with no problem and without even any security. Once again – worth it was it? How much police time do these ultra-Zionist hate groups waste in a year? It must be phenomenal. No wonder that Philip Flower, a former Chief Superintendent with London's Metropolitan Police, said the force is giving up on investigating burglaries while having *900* 'anti-hate investigators' on the payroll. Incredulity about this insanity can be tempered if you know that allowing free reign for burglars is what the Hidden Hand wants to generate the 'jungle atmosphere' of fear and anxiety that the agenda demands (Problem-Reaction-Solution) and at the same time it seeks to have freedom of speech deleted through the excuse of 'hate crime'. There in a sentence you can see why burglaries and other crimes are left to flourish while 900 investigators seek out hate crime which does not exist on anything like the scale we are told to believe and only expands on the basis of ever more opinions being designated as hate crime. By the way, the police definition of a racist incident or 'hate crime' is: '... any incident which is perceived to be racist by the victim or any other person.' What could possibly go wrong? I wrote to the Chief Constable of Norfolk, a bloke called Simon Bailey, with a series of questions about the disgraceful behaviour of his officers and this arrogant man did not even reply. I then made a complaint to the former Independent [it's not] Police Complaints Commission (IPCC), now the Independent [it's not]

Office for Police Conduct. They replied that my complaint against the officers was an abuse of the complaints system. It's all a stitch-up and freedom of speech always the loser.

Home town repetition

Then there was Leicestershire police when I was booked to speak at a major venue in my home city of Leicester for the first time. The Athena Theatre in the city centre had taken the booking for months, all tickets had gone, and despite the usual lying emails from ultra-Zionist hate groups the theatre management said the event would go ahead because 'we have all kinds of people here'. That was before they had a visit from Bill Knopp, Chief Inspector Regional Prevent Coordinator ('counter-terrorism') and Ben Smith, Leicester City Council counter-extremist coordinator. Bill and Ben the Terrorism Men had been contacted by the ultra-Zionist mendacity network when the theatre had refused to budge and this pair of prats believed them without at *any stage* contacting me. They went to see the Athena management and we received an email from the theatre which said that Knopp and Smith had 'expressed their concerns at your upcoming event at Athena'. The email continued:

> They have strongly emphasised to us the possible consequences of holding the event both in terms of the venue reputation and the increased risk of protests from members of the public which would require large police coordination and pose a serious risk to our patrons, staff and members of the public ... Based on this we have decided that we can no longer continue to host the event.

The said pair of prats had basically frightened the shit out of them to cancel the event and I'm sure their ridiculous titles including 'counter terrorism' and 'counter extremism' would have played their part. I say ridiculous because if their mentality is supposed to protect us from terrorism and extremism then we are in serious trouble. I went with Jaymie to meet them and what happened was a big insight into how easy it is for freedom of speech to be destroyed. I found Knopp arrogant and clueless and Smith just clueless and every police force and council now has its Bill and Bens to enforce the tyranny that is political correctness. I called Knopp 'Mr Nob' when I met him and he will never believe that this was a slip of the tongue but it genuinely was. My subconscious, however, had clearly sussed the situation early. I asked them what they knew about me and where they got their information from. Knopp said at one point 'open sources'. I had to laugh. What police and spy agencies call 'open source intelligence' means they read it in the papers or on the Internet. Wikipedia is 'open source intelligence' by their definition. I asked them how many of my books they had read.

None. I asked when they had attended one of my events. *Never*. I said
that since my world speaking tour had begun in 2016 I had spoken at
multiple events in the UK, Ireland, United States, Canada, Australia,
New Zealand, Netherlands, Italy, Sweden, Serbia, Slovakia, Czech
Republic, Estonia, Iceland and so on. I asked them to name a single
event where there had been a 'security problem'. They couldn't because
there were *none*. I asked who had told them that there could be trouble
and violence at the event. Knopp said: 'We can't talk about our
intelligence.' Well, at least that was true in every sense. I said this didn't
matter because I would tell them where their 'intelligence' came from –
organisations contacting them with the usual lies which they had
believed without ever checking. You don't question ultra-Zionist hate
groups because it's not good for the career. I complained to the
Leicestershire Chief Constable Simon Cole, as did many members of the
public, and he replied with the usual bollocks; but at least he replied.
The police wouldn't even take responsibility for the cancellation and
instead blamed it on the theatre. It was *their* decision, the police said
without even a smear of embarrassment given how they had told them
of potentially dire consequences if they allowed me to speak including
damage to the theatre's *reputation*. What on earth has that got to do with
the police and council? Anyway, all that effort was still more wasted
police time and money. We returned a few weeks later to another venue
in Leicester, called The Kube, at what turned out to be a much more
convenient time for us and everything went ahead fine with no police
security necessary you'll be taken aback to know. What a head-shaker.
Leicester City Council has a very different attitude to its own free
speech, by the way. It went to the High Court and Appeals Court with
two other councils to block attempts by the ultra-Zionist Jewish Human
Rights Watch, established by the Henry Jackson Society-connected
Manny Weiss, to have council motions supporting the BDS boycott-
Israel movement ruled illegal. I'm glad they did and it was called a
'victory for free speech' while the same council was an active participant
in denying mine on the say so of people with exactly the same mentality
and motivation as Jewish Human Rights Watch. Irony, anyone? I tried
for the best part of a year to secure Freedom of Information requests for
communications between Essex Police and the Campaign Against Anti-
Semitism because I knew they had many interactions. Essex Police
refused the first time because the request was too broad (it wasn't for
Derbyshire Police) and when I made it specific to two cases they refused
again.

Hate-group network

There are versions of the CAA in country after country protecting Israel
from criticism and exposure by employing the slur of 'anti-Semite' and

using 'lawfare' to intimidate people in the courts. There is an organisation established in 2011 called UK Lawyers for Israel (UKLFI) which says that its members and supporters 'employ advocacy, legal research and campaigning to support Israel, Israeli organisations, Israelis, and/or supporters of Israel against BDS and other attempts to undermine, attack or delegitimise them'. Perhaps UK Lawyers for the Protection Racket (LFPR) might be more appropriate but everyone to their own. In Ireland there is Irish4Israel who have successfully had academic conferences on Israel cancelled for 'security' reasons. They have failed miserably with me because I have been speaking at the same theatre in Dublin for years and they know that what is claimed by Irish4Israel is a pack of lies. Their gutless mud-slingers won't debate with me, either, as always. In Canada we have Rothschild-created B'nai B'rith which spawned the Anti-Defamation League. They tried to have my meetings banned in Canada in 2017 and failed when we found alternatives. The Mayor of Vancouver refused to bow to their pressure (more lies) to cancel an event there. Canada is a country where ultra-Zionism is incredibly influential as I have personally found many times in efforts to have my meetings banned by B'nai B'rith and its lowlife gofers and front people who do its dirty work. Both sides of the political aisle answer to The Lobby which includes the usual network of ultra-Zionist organisations mendaciously claiming to represent 2.7% of the Canadian population. It was good to hear that the Canadian Jewish Congress (CJC) which spent a lot of time trying to undermine me was disbanded in 2011 after being accused by Jewish people of representing Zionism and Israel rather than the range of Jewish opinion. CJC activist Abraham Arnold had said the organisation 'seem to be spending more time in relation to Israel than in relation to anything else' and had become increasingly Zionist and a 'top-down' group which discouraged debate. There you have more confirmation that these organisations are about promoting Israel and ultra-Zionism – not the interests and *multiple* views of the Jewish community. In 2018 'progressive' Canadian Prime Minister Justin Trudeau made a public apology to Jews refused entry to Canada from Germany in 1939. Okay, nothing wrong with that except that he used the opportunity for more 'Israel is a victim' and anti-BDS boycott propaganda and did he make an apology to all the Muslim men, women and children killed by Canadian forces fighting ultra-Zionist and American wars in the Middle East? Not a chance – he was too busy supplying weapons to Saudi Arabia to bomb the innocent in Yemen and create what has been described as the world's biggest humanitarian catastrophe. Ultra-Zionist-owned Donald Trump takes the same stand and condemns criticism of Israel. Trudeau is the product of a Hidden Hand family – see *The Biggest Secret* for the disgusting background to his father Pierre Trudeau, a long-time Canadian Prime Minister.

Demands for special laws and privileges for Jewish people emerge from these networks including the call by Abraham Lehrer, Vice President of Germany's Central Council of Jews, for extra 'integration' classes for migrants to change their anti-Jewish beliefs. Would it not be more productive for him to pressure the Israeli government to stop treating Palestinians like vermin and manipulating the United States into devastating wars against Israel's perceived enemies in the Middle East? Oh, no – that would mean taking some responsibility for events and that will never happen. It's always someone else's fault. Facebook takes down posts that question the 'genocide of Jews in the Holocaust' but then apologises for having a category in which people claim that a 'white genocide' is happening. Why is there one law wherever you look for matters pertaining to Zionism and Israel and another for almost everyone else? If you have stayed with me this far you will know why.

Banned from Australia

Attempts to silence me reached new levels in February, 2019, when I was banned from Australia on the last-minute say-so of Liberal Party Immigration Minister David Coleman after lobbying by ultra-Zionists Dvir Abramovich of the 'Anti-Defamation Commission', lawyer Kate Ashmor, then Victoria Liberal candidate, and her Labour 'opponent' Josh Burns. They believed in their breathtaking arrogance that they should decide what 25 million Australians can choose to see and hear. The Jewish population of Australia is 0.4 percent and these characters will not represent more than a fraction of that. Other professional virtue-signaller MPs of both major parties declared their agreement with the ban while knowing nothing about me except what the propagandists told them. The three stooges parroted the same bollocks almost word-for-word that is thrown at me everywhere because the same script is circulated in the systematic way I have described already. Coleman's disgraceful and spineless behaviour was beyond outrageous and calculated to do most damage in terms of money and inconvenience. I was given a visa by the Immigration Ministry in September, 2018, for a series of speaking events in Australian cities in March, 2019. It would have been my eleventh speaking tour of the country and there had never been a problem with any event and I had never broken a single law in that time – as Coleman had no choice but to acknowledge. I had been speaking in Mexico and was now with Jaymie in a Los Angeles airport hotel waiting to leave for Melbourne that night to start the tour. *Four hours* before the plane was due to take-off we received a long document from Coleman telling us he had revoked the visa and I was banned from speaking in Australia. The email could not have been better timed for maximum disruption. It cost us £30,000 in booked hotels, flights and venues – especially when the Melbourne Convention Centre and the

Enmore Theatre in Sydney wouldn't return a penny of the deposits. All
the other venues did. To inflict that on someone who has done nothing
wrong with all the costs and chaos that would obviously entail was
extraordinary by any standards of decency which Coleman doesn't
have. The move backfired, however, because it allowed the Australian
public to see both the scale of Orwellian censorship in their country and
how a handful of ultra-Zionists had so much power over what they
could see or not see. Coleman listed all the reasons why I *should* have
been allowed into the country – including ten previous visits with no
problems since 1997 – but decreed that I did not pass the 'character test'.
Why this was suddenly the case four hours before my plane left when it
wasn't in September, 2018, and in the months that followed he didn't say
because he couldn't. Coleman pronounced that I was 'a risk to the
health, safety or good order of the Australian community or a segment
of the Australian community'. The only thing missing was to add '0.4
percent' before 'segment'. How I could be such a danger when I had
never been before in ten visits and hadn't been considered so until four
hours before take-off is something else the spine-deleted Coleman didn't
explain.

At no point was I given any opportunity to respond – the very least
one would expect in a free and fair society – and I was left sitting in Los
Angeles after fulfilling everything I was asked to do by the Australian
authorities on the basis of unsubstantiated libels, lying 'journalists' and
what someone apparently read on the Internet. Yes – Coleman produced
no evidence for his claims except what the ultra-Zionist Protection
Racket told him, ultra-Zionist 'journalists' wrote in ultra-Zionist
Murdoch-owned newspapers and here we go … 'open sources'. Coleman
had obviously been on the phone with Chief Inspector Nob. 'Open
sources' – he read it the paper or on the Internet. Two hours before my
visa was revoked I was interviewed by Eve Fisher, a Jewish Australian
journalist in Victoria, and she was shaking her head and laughing at the
claim that I was 'anti-Semitic' because Eve had engaged in a rather
revolutionary act in actually reading my books before reaching a
conclusion. What was her conclusion? That the claim I am 'anti-Semitic'
is utterly ridiculous. She subsequently said so in a published article that
received considerable public acclaim in letters to her newspaper. In fact
large numbers of Australians were shocked and disgusted by the
decision and an online petition was started and supported by the best
part of 20,000 people. Thousands of Australians had bought tickets for
the events, but they didn't matter to the ultra-Zionist trio and the
Immigration Minister they had spun around their finger while his spine
vibrated in terror at the very thought of denying those who must be
obeyed. No major party politicians spoke out in support of freedom of
speech – they wouldn't dare. A West Australian Labour candidate,

Melissa Parke, felt she had to stand down after she later said
Israel treated Palestinians 'worse than the South African system of
apartheid'. The message from all this is clear – 'little' Israel controls
Australia as it controls America and so many other countries. Backbone-
deleted minister Coleman's other excuses for the ban were my views on
vaccines and global warming which in many ways was even more
sinister. I was banned from a country for questioning the propaganda of
the say-whatever-you-like Big Pharma cartel? And for not accepting the
propaganda about human-caused global warming? George Orwell
shakes his head and says 'I told you so'. American doctor Sherri
Tenpenny, a long-time opponent of vaccination, was also banned from
Australia because the government has contempt for its population and
their right to hear all sides. This is the world we now live in and I
predicted it three decades ago because it's all been long planned.

Soon after I was banned Palestinian-American poet Remi Kanazi had
his Australian visa request blocked amid a campaign to have him
banned by the same people who secured my ban – the ultra-Zionist
lobby led by Dvir Abramovich of the man and a dog Anti-Defamation
Commission (see the US ADL) who had such contempt for the victims of
the New Zealand mass shooting (of Muslims!) that he exploited that
attack as one of the reasons why Kanazi (a Muslim!) should be denied
entry to speak in the country. Abramovich said Kanazi 'has no business
being here spreading his toxic agenda' in the 'aftermath of the
Christchurch massacre'. A self-appointed 'representative' of a fraction of
0.4 percent of the population thinks he has the right to decide who and
what 25 million Australians can and cannot choose to hear. Then, when
Abramovich was faced with a publish backlash, he called it 'anti-
Semitism'. This is how the 'anti-Semitism' industry and its Protection
Racket function across the world. Remi Kanazi said:

> The Anti-Defamation Commission weaponised the white supremacist mass
> murder of 50 Muslims, including at least six Palestinians, to attack me.
> Furthermore, groups like the ADC shamelessly back Israeli apartheid and
> whitewash the stripping away of Palestinian land, resources and dignity.

> If you dare challenge Israel's well-documented human rights abuses, which
> include torture and forced confessions, they will try to smear you into silence.

Having visas revoked is another gathering ultra-Zionist and Death
Cult strategy to silence dissent because they are terrified of what they
are doing being exposed to the public. They cannot defend what they do
and they see their only option as silencing all criticism. This terror of
exposure leads to a man like me connected to no organisation or
movement being banned from Australia through a revoked visa,

grandmothers and grandads jailed in Germany for questioning the official story of the Holocaust and 72-year-old Palestinian activist Rasmea Odeh banned through a revoked visa from speaking at an event, again in Germany, with the credit for that taken by Israeli strategic affairs minister Gilad Erdan who runs the vast ultra-Zionist network of censorship and surveillance out of Israel and across the world. Israeli ambassador Jeremy Issacharoff and US ambassador Richard Grenell (of course) added their condemnation of Odeh. Berlin mayor Michael Mueller called Odeh's planned event 'extremist propaganda', the Green Party's Volker Beck protested against Odeh while Cornelia Seibeld, deputy leader in the Berlin Senate, called Odeh an anti-Semite. Berlin's interior minister Andreas Geisel said criticism of Israel is 'anti-Semitic'. Why? Because he's an idiot and his tongue needs a workout. Ultra-Zionists and the Death Cult control Germany which is why people like Rasmea Odeh and myself can't speak there on the say-so of the Protection Racket which the German government dare not disobey. Newspaper *Der Tagesspiegel* ran four articles accusing Odeh of spreading hatred towards Jews and referred to BDS as 'anti-Semitic'. The same happened to me via Murdoch newspapers before I was banned from Australia in 2019. It's a repeating pattern that we are asked to believe is 'spontaneous outrage' – outrage on tap more like. We had the truly pathetic sight of Rasmea Odeh being prevented from speaking at a public meeting marking International Women's Day in Berlin. The Electric Intifada described what happened:

> Officers surrounded the 72-year old as she arrived outside the venue and ushered her away from supporters protesting the decision. She was handed a document from the Berlin Senate and told to vacate the area. The 26-page report claimed her appearance could endanger Germany's relationship with Israel and threaten peaceful coexistence. It also referred to BDS Berlin, the event co-host, as an 'anti-Semitic coalition'.

> Odeh was scheduled to speak alongside Palestinian poet Dareen Tatour, who was imprisoned in Israel last year for posting a poem on social media, when Berlin city officials forced the Dersim Cultural Community Center to cancel the talk. Odeh decided to speak outside the venue to an audience of over 100 but police cornered her on arrival, following her until she boarded a bus out of the area.

Is this really what we have allowed a handful of the human race to bring us to? Some background to Rasmea Odeh: She was arrested, raped and tortured by Israeli soldiers in 1969 and as a result of the torture signed a 'confession' to killing two people in bomb attacks. She spent a decade in jail before being released in a prisoner exchange. She's been referred to as a terrorist ever since without acknowledgement that she was tortured to 'confess'.

Tide is turning

The unfairness and bias, plus the actions of the far-right Israeli government, is changing the opinions of people with regard to Israel. A poll conducted for the UK ultra-Zionist lobby group BICOM in 2018 found that only 20 percent of those questioned felt 'warm' towards Israel and only 23 percent towards Israelis while 49 percent felt 'cold' towards Israel and 45 percent towards Israelis. This shows how the actions of the ultra-Zionists wrongly affect attitudes towards all Jews and Israel in general. This is the same pattern we have seen before with the actions of the few affecting the lives – sometimes ending the lives – of the many. I want to stress and stress again that no one needs to know what the ultra-Zionist and Death Cult cabal is doing more than the Jewish community as a whole which takes the consequences in the end in public attitudes. I further emphasise again that I am not exposing a plot by the Jewish community – the 'classic Jewish conspiracy theory' as the censor organisations call it to protect their masters' agenda and actions. Most Jewish people are victims and potential victims of this cabal, not perpetrators of it and should not be held responsible for actions about which they know nothing. Nor is it justified for those in the Jewish community who *do* know what is going on and stay silent about it because of misguided loyalty or fear of consequences. What is happening must be stopped before a global nightmare becomes global reality and freedom of speech disappears altogether. This means all of us coming together – including, and in many ways *especially* – the majority of the non-extremist Jewish community. They need to speak out against the psychopaths in their midst or they will be wrongly blamed for what is going on.

It was clear from the Al Jazeera hidden camera footage that the ultra-Zionist lobby is terrified of the change taking place among young Jewish people especially in America who are rejecting the Israel narrative. Some are organising protests against AIPAC and Israeli treatment of Palestinians. Israeli newspaper *Haaretz* reported in 2018 a sharp decline in the number of American Jews on 'Birthright' trips to Israel. A 'downturn of this magnitude, unrelated to the security situation' was described as 'unprecedented' with some trip providers losing 50 percent of their custom. *Haaretz* said that one explanation is the numbers 'could reflect the well-documented fact that young American Jews are growing increasingly disengaged from Israel, and have less and less interest in visiting the country – even when the trips are free'. The paper said that 'recent studies have shown that Jewish millennials, who are largely progressive, feel less connected to Israel than their parents and grandparents because they perceive the country's policies as antithetical to their values'. Treatment of Palestinians and of asylum seekers were frequently cited, the paper said. Changing attitudes of young American Jews is reflected in the rise of groups like Jewish Voice for Peace (JVP), IfNotNow and Jews for Racial and Economic Justice. Maya Edery, JVP's national campus coordinator, said:

> More and more young people are realising that our Jewish values are actually about social justice and have to be for all people ... They realise that a lot of Jewish institutions have lied to them.

This is the way forward for humanity – to put aside the labels and treat everyone as individuals with an equal right to be treated with fairness and justice. Ultra-Zionist lobby propaganda is aimed as much – sometimes more – at young Jewish people than the population as a whole. To keep them on board they have to be sold the ultra-Zionist narrative and to believe they need protection against the evil non-Jewish world that 'hates them' when it *doesn't*. How much of the hatred that does exist – far, far less than claimed – stems from the actions of the ultra-Zionist few which is then wrongly blamed on the entire Jewish population? The Israeli American Council (IAC) is yet another strand in the web that aims to connect American Jews with the desires of Israel. Al Jazeera's undercover 'Tony' attended an ultra-Zionist gathering in Washington where they were concerned about the changing attitudes of young people to Israel. David Brog, Executive Director of the anti-BDS Maccabee Task Force, told activists that 'the younger you get on the demographic scales, the lower support for Israel is'. Younger people were leaving college less sympathetic to Israel than when they entered and this threatened future American support for Israel. It is not only young people, either. A major survey of Jewish opinion in Canada found the following:

- Almost two in five respondents (37 percent) had a negative opinion of the Israeli government, while half viewed it positively
- Almost a third (31 percent) opposed Israel's military blockade of the Gaza Strip
- Roughly equal numbers opposed (45 percent) and supported (42 percent) Donald Trump's decision to recognise Jerusalem as Israel's capital
- More than a third (36 percent) viewed the Palestinian call for boycott, divestment and sanctions on Israel to be reasonable, and more than two in five (44 percent) opposed the Canadian parliament's condemnation of the BDS movement
- Almost a quarter (22 percent) thought it would be reasonable to impose

sanctions on Israel
- Almost three in five did not see criticism of Israel as necessarily 'anti-Semitic'
- Half agreed that accusations of 'anti-Semitism' are often used to silence legitimate criticism of Israel

You can see that the general Jewish population has a diversity of opinion while the ultra-Zionist networks claim that they speak for all Jews when they clearly do not. This has been a glimpse, and only a glimpse, of the fantastic number and range of these networks (in the end one network) that seek to silence opposition to Israel and protect ultra-Zionism and the Death Cult. The next question to be addressed as we continue our journey back to 9/11 is: Protect them from what exactly? And two more: What is this 'Death Cult' and where did it come from?

Postscript: We made a legal appeal against my ban from Australia and months later the government has not even bothered to respond. Wake up Australia – you live in a tyranny.

CHAPTER 20

What the censors don't want you to know

Truth never damages a cause that is just – Mahatma Gandhi

I emphasis that while ultra-Zionism and the Death Cult are connected this does not mean the terms are interchangeable. The Death Cult operates at the inner core of what I am exposing and ultra-Zionism has a wide range of advocates with most unaware that such a Cult even exists.

They express what I observe to be their Zionist extremism and elitism from a belief in a Chosen People and the official historical narrative which fuels a further belief that their duty always lies in supporting Israel and its perceived interests no matter what the circumstances. I would rather deal in the justice and fairness of a situation no matter what the racial, cultural, religious and economic background of those involved. Once you have a bias towards one group, whichever one it may be, such values cease to be applied. George Orwell was well aware of the importance of controlling history because our sense of where we are and who we are is fundamentally influenced by the belief in how we got to where we are. Change historical belief and its perceived sequence of events and you change the perception of present time. Orwell wrote: 'Who controls the past controls the future. Who controls the present controls the past.' I have highlighted in other books the importance to the elite of controlling the writing and perception of history. This is especially important – indeed utterly crucial – in the case of Zionism. I had yet another experience of this on the morning I began writing this chapter when synchronistically Zionist-controlled YouTube announced they were taking down a video of mine in a long list of countries after a 'legal complaint'. The video had been posted all of four years earlier and was entitled 'Exposing The Lie On Israel's Fake History – The Cruellest Hoax'. The countries quoted were: Austria, Belgium, Bulgaria, Switzerland, Cyprus, Czechia, Germany, Denmark, Estonia, Spain, Finland, France, United Kingdom, French Guiana, Guadeloupe, Greece, Croatia, Hungary, Ireland, Israel, Italy, Lithuania, Luxembourg, Latvia, Martinique, Malta, New Caledonia, Netherlands, French Polynesia,

Poland, Saint Pierre and Miquelon, Portugal, Reunion, Romania, Sweden, Slovenia, Slovakia, French Southern Territories, Wallis and Futuna, Mayotte. Clearly the content of the video is information you must not be allowed to know, but I'll tell you anyway.

The claim that today's Jewish people are heirs to Biblical Israel simply does not stand up to the scrutiny of history and yet that is the entire basis for the existence of modern Israel and its justification for occupying the Arab lands of Palestine. The story is a hoax as Jewish historians have documented and the inner core of ultra-Zionism and the Death Cult knows that. They perpetuate the hoax because it gives them power to be wielded for the benefit of themselves and the wider Hidden Hand. This is not to say that we should demand that Jewish people just up and leave. We are where we are and that needs to be the starting point for agreement between Israel and the Palestinian people, but the claim that Israel should be a Jewish state by some historic right is untenable and irreconcilable with the facts. The hoax has been perpetuated on Jewish people more than anyone and the Palestinians have taken the greatest consequences. They are not the only ones, however. Millions have died in wars instigated on behalf of Israel by the United States, Britain, France, NATO and others based on the claims that today's Jewish people have an historic right to the land. This has provided a very convenient excuse to divide and conquer the oil-rich Middle East and go to war with Israel's enemies who are accused of denying the right of Zionists to impose a Jewish state on the alleged land of the Israelites. The *Clean Break* document which provided the policy foundations of the Project for the New American Century and the wars that followed said:

> Our claim to the land – to which we have clung for hope for 2,000 years – is legitimate and noble. Only the unconditional acceptance by Arabs of our rights, especially in their territorial dimension, 'peace for peace', is a solid basis for the future.

The claim is *not* legitimate and certainly not noble given what has happened since Israel was founded in 1948. Jewish writers like Arthur Koestler and historian Shlomo Sand, Professor of History at Tel Aviv University, uncover a very different history in their books, *The Thirteenth Tribe* and *The Invention of the Jewish People*. Alfred M. Lilienthal (1915-2008), a former American State Department official and Jewish critic of Zionism, called this information 'Israel's Achilles heel' because it destroyed Zionist claims 'to the land of the Biblical Hebrews'. Official history tells us that Israelites from the Kingdom of Judah were taken captive in Babylon (formerly Sumer, now Iraq) by King Nebuchadnezzar II after 605BC and this lasted until 539BC. The dispersal to others lands that followed of former Babylonian captives and the 'exile' of other tribes of Israel is known as the diaspora, or dispersion in Greek, and the claim is that modern Jews in Israel are the successors of those people 'coming home'. This is not the case.

The Khazar conversion

We can pick up the story in what is now southern Russia and the Caucasus Mountains where lived a people called the Khazars. They controlled an empire that stretched to the Ural Mountains in the east and the Caucasus Mountains in the south (Fig 105). Khazars were gifted traders and 'middlemen', levying taxes on goods using the trade routes across their lands and their influence extended into countries we now know as Poland, Czechoslovakia, Austria, Hungary, Romania and Bulgaria. Khazars were phallic worshippers and engaged in human sacrifice although they were far from alone in that. They were not Biblical Israelites and instead are associated by historians with the

Turkic tribe known as the Huns or Hun that invaded Europe from Asia around 450AD. The Huns controlled territories at one time in Central Asia, Siberia, China, North India and Central Europe. Their most famous, or infamous, leader was Attila the Hun who killed his brother, Buda (hence Budapest), to take power. Khazars, like the Huns, spoke the Turkic language and are believed to be the same people. Around 740AD, Bulan, King of Khazaria, adopted the religion of Judaism and the whole

Figure 105: Khazaria where a mass conversion to Judaism in the 8th century was the origin of the overwhelming majority of Jewish people today – not biblical Israel.

nation followed. This was apparently to avoid being absorbed by the Christian empire on one side and the Islamic empire on the other. The Khazarian king was called the Khagan or 'Kagan' and that's why this is such a common Jewish name today as in Robert Kagan, co-founder of the Project for the New American Century. People associate some Jews with a 'hook nose' and that is a physical trait of the lands occupied by Khazaria and not the Middle East. The so-called 'Jewish nose' is found in far greater numbers today among Caucasian tribes and Turks of Asia Minor. Among truly Semite language group peoples it is not seen at all.

Khazars, not the Biblical Israelites, are the ancestors of Jewish people today known as Ashkenazi Jews which dominated the creation of modern Israel and have influenced its direction and politics. They originate from Asia and other parts of the Eurasian landmass and, as I will come to, ancient Sumer (later Babylon and now Iraq). 'Israel' is certainly not on the list. When the Khazar Empire began to unravel in the 12th and 13th centuries they migrated north into Lithuania, Poland and Russia and eventually the biggest concentration of Jewish religion believers were located in Russia and Poland. Jewish Hungary-born Arthur Koestler writes that the numerically and socially-dominant part of the Hungarian Jewish population in the Middle Ages was of Khazar origin. Abraham Nahum Polak (1910-1970), Israeli Professor of Medieval History and founder of the department of Middle-Eastern History at the Tel Aviv University, published a book in Hebrew in 1944 called *Khazaria* followed by a second edition in 1951. He wrote about 'a new approach, both to the problem of the relations between the Khazar Jewry and other Jewish communities, and to the question of how far we can go in regarding this [Khazar] Jewry as the nucleus of the large Jewish settlement in Eastern Europe'. Polak concluded from his research:

> ... The descendants of this settlement – those who stayed where they were [in Khazaria], those who emigrated to the United States and to other countries, and those who went to Israel – constitute now the large majority of world Jewry.

There is also a connection between the Khazars and non-Semitic Sumerians, a highly-significant people which I have written extensively about in other books. Sumerian culture emerged around the fifth or sixth millennia BC in the 'Fertile Crescent' between the Tigris and Euphrates rivers in what is now Iraq. Historians refer to Sumer as the 'cradle of civilisation' because it was in many ways the blueprint for the modern world. Dr Sandor Nagy describes in his 1973 book, *The Forgotten Cradle of the Hungarian Culture*, how the people who later became known as Magyars were re-located Sumerians forced out of the Fertile Crescent. Dr Nagy uses extensive examples to confirm the linguistic similarities between Sumerian, Old Magyar and the current Magyar language. He also refers to several works written during the first millennium including the *Arpad Codices* and *De Administrando Imperio* and Nagy completed 50 years of his own research. He said that while there are only two hundred Magyar words related to the Finno-Ugric language more than two thousand related to the Sumerian. British, French and German archaeologists and linguists concluded that the language of ancient Sumerian inscriptions was not Indo-European nor Semitic, but a language which demonstrated significant similarities with the group of languages known at the time as the Turanian ethnolinguistic group that included Hungarian, Turkic, Mongolian and Finnic (later referred to as the Ural-Altaic group). Research has indicated that Sumerian and Hungarian languages have more than a thousand common word roots and a very similar grammatical structure. Kálmán Gosztony, professor of Sumerian philology at the Sorbonne in Paris, demonstrated in his *Sumerian Etymological Dictionary and Comparative Grammar* that the structure of the Hungarian language is closest to that of Sumerian. Of the 53 characteristics of Sumerian grammar, 51 matched in the Hungarian, compared with 29 in Turkic, 24 in Caucasian, 21 in Uralic, 5 in Semitic and 4 in Indo-European. The linguistic similarities between Sumerian, Hungarian and other related languages are confirmed by the archaeological and anthropological evidence. Dr Nagy said there were two separate migrations of Sumerian people out of Mesopotamia – one through Turkey to the Carpathian Basin in Central Europe and the other went east and then north across the Caucasus Mountains into the area between the Caspian and Black Seas. This was the land occupied by the Khazar Empire to such an extent that the Caspian became known as the Khazar Sea. Rivers flowing into the Caspian have names that derive from the Sumerian language, Nagy wrote. Khazars were descended from the Huns who are said to be descended, like the Magyars, from what I emphasise were the *non*-Semitic Sumerians in the land that became Babylon and is now Iraq. Ancient Byzantine sources say the Magyars were also called the Sabirs and originated from Mesopotamia, the land of Sumer. Numerous other ancient and medieval sources refer to the Scythians, Huns (Khazars), Avars and Magyars as the same people. I have highlighted in previous books the movement of former Sumerians and Babylonians through the Caucasus Mountains under different names, including the Scythians (Fig 106 overleaf).

Khazar diaspora

The Khazar Empire, the first feudal state in Eastern Europe, broke up in the period after 960AD in a series of wars and invasions culminating in the arrival of the Mongol 'Golden Horde', best remembered for their inspiration, Genghis Khan. Over the centuries of waning power and influence, Khazars began to emigrate in many directions. S.W. Baron said of Khazaria in *A Social and Religious History of the Jews*:

> Its population was largely absorbed by the Golden Horde which had established the centre of its empire in Khazar territory. But before and after the Mongol upheaval the Khazars sent many offshoots into the unsubdued Slavonic lands, helping ultimately to build up the great Jewish centres of Eastern Europe.

The non-Semitic Khazars took their Judaistic or Talmudic faith (with

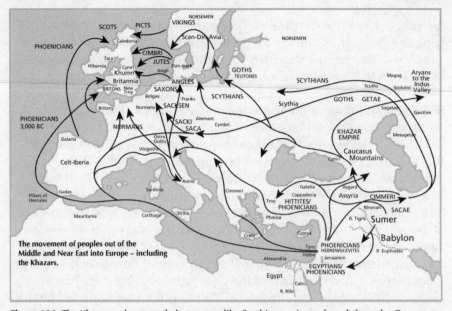

The movement of peoples out of the
Middle and Near East into Europe – including
the Khazars.

Figure 106: The Khazars, also recorded as names like Scythians, migrated north from the Caucasus into Eastern and then Western Europe.

all its major Sumerian / Babylonian influences) and settled in a number of East European and Alpine lands. There are many ancient place names in Poland and Ukraine inspired by the name 'Khazar' or 'Zhid', a term meaning Jew. These include Kozarzewek, Kozara, Kozarzow and Zydowo. As the Khazar Empire collapsed a number of Slavonic tribes, led by the Polans, formed an alliance that became the country called Poland. 'Jews' (Khazars) played an important role in Polish legends about the formation of the country. One says that a 'Jew' called Abraham Prokownik was elected by the tribes to rule them. Certainly Khazar 'Jews' became prominent in many countries of Eastern Europe. Arthur Koestler writes:

> Both the Hungarian and Polish sources refer to Jews employed as mint-masters, administrators of the royal revenue, controllers of the salt monopoly, tax-collectors and 'money-lenders' – i.e., bankers. This parallel suggests a common origin of those two immigrant communities; and as we can trace the origins of the bulk of Hungarian Jewry to the Magyar-Khazar nexus, the conclusion seems self-evident.

This matches the descriptions of how Khazars operated in their own land as middlemen and tax collectors on the trade routes. Koestler points out that the traditional garb of Polish Jewry is of unmistakably Eastern origin – 'The skull-cap (yarmulke) is worn to this day by orthodox Jews and by the Uzbeks and other Turkish people in the Soviet

Union.' In this period the people known for centuries as Khazars became known simply as 'Jews' and their true origin began to be lost. This allowed their leaders to sell them – and the rest of the world – a false history about them being the Biblical Jews. The fallacy continues to this day with devastating consequences for peace in the Middle East. Khazar 'Jews' were confined to ghettos as a result of Papal decision in the mid-16th century and another mass exodus would see them expand into Hungary, Bohemia, Rumania and Germany. There were hardly any Jews in Germany until this time. 'Thus the great trek to the West was resumed', writes Koestler. 'It was to continue through nearly three centuries until the Second World War, and became the principle source of the existing Jewish communities in Europe, the United States and Israel.' So what does all this mean for the official history of Jewish people? Koestler, who was born in Budapest as was Khazar descendant George Soros, said of Jewish ancestry:

> ... [It] would mean that their ancestors came not from the Jordan, but from the Volga, not from Canaan but from the Caucasus, once believed to be the cradle of the Aryan race [hence 'Caucasian']; and that genetically they are more closely connected to the Hun, Uigur and Magyar tribes than to the seed of Abraham, Isaac and Jacob. Should this turn out to be the case, then the term 'anti-Semitism' would be void of meaning, based on a misapprehension shared by both the killers and their victims. The story of the Khazar Empire, as it slowly emerges from the past, begins to look like the most cruel hoax which history has ever perpetrated.

Benjamin H. Freedman was a one-time Jewish businessman in New York and a long-time 'insider' before speaking out vociferously against Zionism after World War Two. He was personally acquainted with leading American political figures like Presidents Woodrow Wilson, Franklin Roosevelt and John F. Kennedy. Jewish-born Freedman, who became a Christian, went even further than Koestler in his assessment of the Khazar revelation:

> What are the facts about the Jews? (I call them Jews to you, because they are known as Jews. I don't call them Jews myself. I refer to them as so-called Jews, because I know what they are) ... There wasn't one of them [the Khazars] who had an ancestor who ever put a toe in the Holy Land. Not only in Old Testament history, but back to the beginning of time. Not one of them!

> And yet they come to the Christians and ask us to support their armed insurrections in Palestine by saying, 'You want to help repatriate God's Chosen People to their Promised Land, their ancestral home, don't you? It's your Christian duty. We gave you one of our boys as your Lord and Saviour ...' It is

as ridiculous to call them 'people of the Holy Land,' as it would be to call the 54 million Chinese Moslems 'Arabs' ...

Former Khazars are known as Ashkenazi Jews (plural Ashkenazim) and some writers estimate that perhaps 90 to 95 percent of those calling themselves 'Jewish' worldwide are ancestors of the Khazars. The other major group are known as Sephardic Jews – which means 'Spanish' or 'Hispanic' – and they are descendants of those who lived in Spain from at least Roman times before being expelled in the 15th century after which they settled in the Mediterranean, Balkans, Western Europe (mainly Amsterdam), North Africa and the East. A sub-group known as 'Mizrahi' literally means 'Oriental' or 'Eastern'. There have been divisions between Ashkenazi and Sephardic Jews based on culture and racial superiority in race-obsessed Israel. The Ashkenazim ('Khazars') hold the reins of power in Israel (at least on the surface) and have done so since the country was created in 1948 although Sephardic Jews account for many wealthy and influential families. The name Ashkenazi is said by some to originate from Ashkenaz, the Hebrew word for Germany. In fact, the Bible refers to the Ashkenaz as a people living in the region of Mount Ararat (now Turkey) and Armenia. That would certainly fit the basic location of the Khazars. There is also a Biblical reference to Ashkenaz, brother of Togarma and nephew of Magog. A Khazar king known as Joseph in the second half of the tenth century wrote in correspondence that they were ancestors of Togarma, who, he said, had ten sons that seeded all the Turkish tribes including the Huns, Khazars and Bulgars. Ashkenazi as a people did not speak the Semitic language of Hebrew in the centuries after the demise of Khazaria. This is no surprise at all because they were not Hebrews. They developed their own tongue called Yiddish which began as a Germanic language from south eastern dialects of Middle High German and expanded into central and Eastern Europe starting in the 12th century. Later it evolved to include elements of Hebrew, Aramaic, Slavic languages and other influences. Once again, Yiddish, the language of the Ashkenazi, did not come from Israel, but from Germany and Eastern Europe. Multiple linguistic influences in their language were also seen in the genes of these former Khazars. By this time they had interbred with so many other races they became a genetic cocktail which included Sumerian, Turkish, Far Eastern and northern and western European. It could well be that among their leaders, their perceived 'royalty' or 'elite', they have held on to their Sumerian genetic origins through targeted interbreeding.

There was no 'exile' and is no 'race'

Jewish-born Shlomo Sand, Professor of History at Tel Aviv University, also concludes in his book, *The Invention of the Jewish People*, that today's Jews overwhelmingly originate from the Khazar Empire in the Caucasus region. His book has been translated into more languages than any other on Israeli history. He accepts the religious affinity between Jews and the Holy Land but adds: 'I don't think the religious affinity to the land gives you historical right.' Sand calls himself a 'post-Zionist' and 'non-Zionist' because there is no historic justification to claim rights to Palestine. He believes as I do that we are where we are and that must be the starting point to reconciliation. Sand searched for evidence of ancient Israelites being forced out of the area of modern Israel and was shocked to find there wasn't any even though this is the whole foundation of the Jewish belief system. He concluded that this pivotal event in official Jewish history simply didn't happen and that the whole concept of a 'diaspora' is a much later invention. He wrote in a 2018 article for Israeli newspaper *Haaretz:*

> As I pursued my research, my realization that the Exodus from Egypt never happened and that the inhabitants of the Kingdom of Judah were not exiled by the Romans, left me nonplussed. There is not one study by a historian who specializes in antiquity that recounts that 'exile' or any serious historiographic study that reconstructs a mass migration from the place.

> The 'exile' is a formative event that never took place, otherwise it would be the subject of dozens of research studies. Judahite farmers, who constituted an absolute majority of the population at the first century C.E., were not seafarers like the Greeks or the Phoenicians, and did not spread across the world.

Sand's research led him to see that far from being an historic 'people' Jews were converted to a *religion* and were not a *race*. He cites other mass conversions, not only that of the Khazars, and points to Christian influence in creating the myth about an ancient Jewish people with a common ancestry being expelled from their lands. 'Christians wanted later generations of Jews to believe that their ancestors had been exiled as a punishment from God,' he said. Sand further notes that after Arabs took control of Palestine in the 7th century many in the region practicing the Jewish religion converted to Islam and became ancestors to today's Palestinians. We are, therefore, at the very extremes of irony with current events in the Middle East. Sand wrote in *Haaretz:*

> I have made a point of emphasizing that it's not only Jews who don't possess a common DNA – neither do all other human groups that claim to be peoples or nations – besides which I have never thought that genetics can confer national rights. For example, the French are not the direct descendants of the Gauls, just as the Germans are not the offspring of the Teutons or of the

ancient Aryans, even if until a little more than half a century ago many idiots believed just that.

One trait that all peoples have in common is that they are retroactive inventions with no distinctive genetic 'traits'. The acute problem that genuinely disturbs me is that I live in a singular political and pedagogical culture that continues persistently to see the Jews as the direct descendants of the ancient Hebrews.

Further support for a non-Israel origin of Ashkenazi Jews comes from Israeli-born geneticist Dr Eran Elhaik from Britain's University of Sheffield. He said his studies suggest that Ashkenazi Jews are descendants of Greeks, Iranians and others who located more than 2000 years ago in what is now northern Turkey. There they converted to Judaism with the influence of Jews from Persia which had at that time the world's biggest Jewish presence. Elhaik believes that more than '90 percent of Ashkenazic ancestors come from that converted partially Greek-originating ancient community in north-east Turkey', according to an article in the UK *Independent*. His conclusions were based on 'genetic, historical and place-name evidence' and in his view 'Ashkenaz' originates from Ashguza, an ancient Assyrian and Babylonian name for the Iron Age Eurasian people known as Scythians who are associated with the Khazars. The *Independent* article in 2013 goes on:

> From the 690s AD onwards, anti-Jewish persecution by the Christian Byzantine Empire seems to have played a part in forcing large numbers of Jews to flee across the Black Sea to a more friendly state – the Turkic-ruled Khazar Empire with its large Slav and other populations ... By the 730s, the Khazar Empire had begun to convert to Judaism – and more people converted to the faith.

This would explain the King Bulan mass-conversion in 740. Claims of an historic right to the land of Palestine are a hoax perpetuated in more modern times by those who created Zionism with the House of Rothschild at the centre of this as we shall see. The tenuous historic evidence can be seen in the words of Israeli minister Tzachi Hanegbi who said the Bible alone is enough to prove that his country has legitimate claims to the land:

> Defense is important and security is important but the most important thing is the moral claim of Israel and we are committed to living in our regional land, land that was given to us ... by the Bible ... And this is the right, which we are going to demand our right forever and ever.

No, it's not. Don't be daft. Israel's UN Representative Danny Danon made a similiar claim in 2019.

Overwhelming evidence

The assimilation of Jews and Khazars has been confirmed by several studies which give more credence to Jews as *converts* to a religion and not an ancient people. There is, in fact, no such thing as a Jewish 'race', just as there is no Aryan 'race' in the way it is portrayed by white supremacists. These are fabrications of history. What should 'race' matter anyway? It's all illusion and childish beyond belief to self-identify ourselves with what is a transitory experience for our eternal state of awareness. Judging ourselves and others by genetics is the ultimate confirmation of ignorance about the nature of reality. Unfortunately 'race' and its related historical 'rights' and claims are used as a political tool and source of perception manipulation. There are people who follow the Jewish *faith* around the world and those that support the *political philosophy* called Zionism. This, however, is not the same as a *race*. There are white 'Jews', brown 'Jews', black 'Jews', Spanish 'Jews', Chinese 'Jews' etc., etc., that share the *belief system* and good luck to them so long as they don't force it on anyone else. If they want to call themselves 'Jewish' on the basis of their faith then please feel free, it's none of my business; but there is not a Jewish 'race', let alone a 'chosen people'. Arthur Koestler points out that those calling themselves 'Jewish' have far more in common genetically with the 'host' population than they do with each other. This was highlighted by Professor Juan Comas (1900-1979) in his work, *The Race Question in Modern Science*, published by UNESCO:

> Thus despite the view usually held, the Jewish people is racially heterogeneous [diverse in character]; its constant migrations and its relations – voluntary or otherwise – with the widest variety of nations and peoples have brought about such a degree of crossbreeding that the so-called people of Israel can produce examples of traits typical of every people.

> For proof it will suffice to compare the rubicund, sturdy, heavily-built Rotterdam Jew with his co-religionist, say, in Salonika with gleaming eyes in a sickly face and skinny, high-strung physique. Hence, so far as our knowledge goes, we can assert that Jews as a whole display as great a degree of morphological disparity among themselves as could be found between members of two or more different races.

Raphael Patai (1910-1996), a Hungarian-born Jewish historian and anthropologist, wrote in the *Encyclopaedia Britannica*:

The findings of physical anthropology show that, contrary to popular view, there is no Jewish race. Anthropometric measurements of Jewish groups in many parts of the world indicate that they differ greatly from one another with respect to all the important physical characteristics – stature, weight, skin colour, cephalic index, facial index, blood groups, etc.

Patai said that with regard to blood type, Jewish groups show considerable differences among themselves and marked similarities to the 'Gentile environment'. American Jewish anthropologist Harry Shapiro (1902-1990) produced the same assessment in his UNESCO work, *The Jewish People: A Biological History*:

The wide range of variation between Jewish populations in their physical characteristics and the diversity of the gene frequencies of their blood groups render any unified classification for them a contradiction in terms. For although modern racial theory admits some degree of polymorphism or variation within a racial group, it does not permit distinctly different groups, measured by its own criteria of race, to be identified as one.

To do so would make the biological purposes of racial classification futile and the whole procedure arbitrary and meaningless. Unfortunately, this subject is rarely wholly divorced from non-biological considerations, and despite the evidence efforts continue to be made to somehow segregate Jews as a distinct racial entity.

There is no more a Jewish *race* than there is a connection today between the Biblical land called Israel and the mass of people today calling themselves Jewish. It's a faith, a way of life and set of rituals, not a race. The hoax has been sprung by the Death Cult network hiding within that faith and its rituals and playing those identifying as Jewish for fools. Cult leaders have had to concoct the *perception* of a race and a connection to the ancient Middle East to justify everything they have done and continue to do with regard to Palestine and the wider world. How can you claim to be a special race, a 'chosen people' considered by 'God' to be above all others, and with special rights given by 'God' to own a certain piece of land, when there is no such thing as a 'Jewish race'? Arthur Koestler writes that during the Babylonian 'exile' the 'Israelites', including members of the priestly families, married Gentiles and even before the diaspora the Israelites were a 'thoroughly hybridized race'. He says the same story can be found with most historic nations 'and the point would not need stressing if it were not for the persistent myth of the Biblical Tribe having preserved its racial purity throughout the ages.' Koestler concludes his book:

To sum up, the Jews of our day have no cultural tradition in common, merely certain habits and behaviour-patterns, derived by social inheritance from the traumatic experience of the ghetto, and from a religion which the majority does not practice or believe in, but nevertheless confers on them a pseudo-national status ... the lingering influence of Judaism's racial and historical message, though based on illusion, acts as a powerful emotional break by appealing to tribal loyalty.

The point about tribal loyalty is so important. Most Jewish people are pressured and conditioned to identify with tribal loyalty to protect what they are told are an oppressed people even though when you look at the evidence today this is absolutely not the case. Ultra-Zionists not aware of the hoax or Death Cult (most of them) have simply bought the lie to the extreme and it colours their every perception and action. Observe the national and global influence of 0.2 percent of the human population and the idea that Jewish people are uniquely oppressed is ridiculous. The influence of their elite in particular is way, way, way beyond the ratio to their tiny number and their financial clout is the same. People are getting sick of seeing this obvious fact – this elephant on the sofa – while at the same time constantly hearing how the Jewish community must be uniquely protected from unique danger with free speech deleted to this end. Ultra-Zionists never concede that their own behaviour might be affecting the way others view them. It is never their responsibility and blame always lies with the rest of the population who apparently carry some genetic hatred for anyone Jewish. It's all bollocks, but expedient to the agenda. All tyrannies need enemies to unite people behind them in common cause and if they don't exist they have to invent them. Young people are told in Israel that the world hates them and they must stick together in tribal loyalty to survive. This is just perception manipulation in pursuit of the tyranny's need for collective support and a shield to hide behind. Jewish people are among the most lied-to communities on earth for this very reason. Jewish-born historian Shlomo Sand talks of 'tribal Judeocentrism' and the 'caprices of the sleepwalking sorcerers of the tribe'. The definition of 'caprices' is 'a sudden and silly change of mind or behaviour'. Yes, about right.

The Death Cult

A major departure from mainstream Judaism began with a new cult or sect in the 17th century and this is of fundamental significance to the modern world, ultra-Zionism and 9/11. This cult hiding within Judaism and later Zionism is known as 'Sabbatianism' or 'Sabbateanism'. In many ways this cult – with a later addition called Frankism – *is* ultra-Zionism although most ultra-Zionist Israel-right-or-wrong advocates and fanatics will not be aware of this. Compartmentalisation is the

golden rule.
Sabbatian-
Frankism is a term
used to describe
what I have
referred to up to
this point as the
Death Cult. This is
a major expression
of what is called
Satanism which
pervades the
deeper recesses of
The Web in many
forms (Fig 107).

Figure 107: Sabbatan-Frankist Death Cult – masters of inversion.

The founder of the
cult that controls events in Israel to this
day was Sabbatai Zevi (1626–1676), a
Sephardic rabbi, occultist and black
magician who proclaimed he was the
Jewish messiah (Fig 108). Gershom
Scholem (1897-1982), the first Professor of
Jewish Mysticism at the Hebrew
University in Jerusalem, writes in *The
Messianic Idea in Judaism* that Zevi's cult
was 'the largest and most momentous
messianic movement in Jewish history'
since ancient times and much of the
Jewish population fell for it. One of its

Figure 108: Sabbatai Zevi.

key promotors was a Zevi devotee, 'prophet' and Kabbalist called
Rabbi Nathan Chazzati, or 'Nathan of Gaza', who is credited with
convincing Zevi that he was indeed the Jewish Messiah. The Kabbalah
or Kabala/Cabala is the bible of Jewish mysticism and esoteric thought
and practice. It provides the textual 'spiritual' foundation of the
Sabbatian-Frankist Death Cult. Kabbalah teachings relate to the 'occult',
a word that merely means 'hidden'. Knowledge about the nature of life
and reality systematically hidden from the population can be used for
good or ill and I will refer to its satanic use as the Dark Occult.
Sabbatian-Frankists follow the Lurianic Kabbalah named after its
creator, Jewish rabbi Isaac ben Solomon Luria (1534–1572), the 'Holy or
Sacred Lion', which emphasises messianic belief. 'Nathan of Gaza'
employed Lurianic ideas to claim the 'new Messiah' (Hebrew
'Mashiach') as Sabbatai Zevi and this messianic mind-set remains a
pillar of Sabbatian-Frankism today. None of this may appear to be

relevant to 9/11 or what is happening now, but oh, yes it *is*. The Sabbatian cult was supposed to have ended with Zevi's demise according to mainstream Jewish history. This suits the Sabbatians who are still *very* much with us and operating from the shadows in their satanic form while offering a very different public face. Sabbatians and their associated Frankists are world class infiltrators – that's their route to control and they have infiltrated all the world's major religions including Judaism. Belief in a coming messiah who will rule the world from Jerusalem – 'a saviour and liberator of the Jewish people' – is driving modern events and most obviously the step-by-step process of Zionism taking complete control of Jerusalem and replacing the Al-Aqsa mosque with a rebuilt Solomon's Temple. Sabbatai Zevi promised his followers that they would return to their alleged homeland in Palestine to establish a Jewish state and here we have the origin of modern-day Zionism which is the creation of the same Sabbatian-Frankist Death Cult that has passed through the centuries and infiltrated almost every aspect of human society. We are now living in the new Messianic Age according to these deluded people – an age when their 'messiah' descended from 'King David via Solomon' will rule the world from Jerusalem. I will come to how this is planned to be done in the final chapters. These are some of the messianic biblical prophecies that these crazies are seeking to make happen:

- The whole world will worship the One God of Israel
- Once he is King, leaders of other nations will look to him for guidance
- The peoples of the world will turn to the Jews for spiritual guidance
- Nations will recognize the wrongs they did to Israel

Sabbatai Zevi's cult sought to usurp traditional Judaism and literally invert everything it stood for. A day of fasting became a day of feasting, for example. Traditional religious teachings and laws, sexual taboos and the concept of right and wrong were all turned on their head as Zevi advocated that doing evil was to be encouraged and celebrated without guilt. Scholars have referred to this as a 'transvaluation' within Jewish culture turning accepted norms on their heads and promoting a belief that the violation of the sacred became a sacred duty. Do not kill became *do* kill and a Sabbatian 'prayer' was 'Blessed be they who permit the forbidden'. Redemption thorough sin was the sales-pitch, but it was really just a scam to spread the Hidden Hand 'religion' of what we call Satanism. Sabbatian belief was founded on the concept that being evil implodes evil and so the more evil there is the quicker it is imploded. I don't claim it makes sense, but that is what they believed (or claimed to believe in pursuit of a desired outcome). Modern Satanism is the same with its inverted anything-goes celebration of evil. Sabbatian-Frankism,

Satanism, human sacrifice religions of Sumer and Babylon fuse into one force within the Hidden Hand and stalk and control the corridors of global power. Sabbatianism has become known by some researchers as the 'Synagogue of Satan'. It is not surprising then that in the heralded new Messianic Age nothing will be forbidden except the freedom to challenge and expose the controllers. Some Jewish sources say their 'messiah' is already alive and waiting to take his place as ruler of the world. Others refer to this figure as the 'anti-Christ'. Jerry Rabow writes in his book, *50 Jewish Messiahs*:

> ... Shabbatai Zevi continued to issue proclamations of the theological changes wrought by the coming of the messianic age. Shabbatai's new prayer was, 'Praised be He who permits the forbidden.' Since all things would be permitted in the age of the messiah, Shabbatai declared many of the old restrictions of the Torah no longer applicable. He abolished the laws concerning sexual relationships. He eventually declared that all of the thirty six major biblical sins were now permitted and instructed some of his followers that it was their duty to perform such sins in order to hasten the Redemption.

Look around at the world today and you see this happening – including clear efforts to make sex with children (a 'norm' in the Cult) legal and acceptable. The name Sabbatai relates to the Hebrew word for Saturn and also to the devil-worshipping 'Witches' Sabbath', or Sabbat, which corresponds with the major ritual days of Satanism. These include May 1st (Beltane), and Halloween. Readers of my other books including *Everything You Need To Know But Have Never Been Told* will be aware of the connections I have made between Saturn and Satanism – *Saturn*-ism – and human control. Saturn is not actually a planet, but a form of sun – the 'Black Sun' and 'Dark Sun' of Satanism and Nazi dark occultists. Jewish tradition connects 'the reign of Sabbatai', or Saturn, to the arrival of the messiah which Sabbatai Zevi was claimed to be. Remember the 40-foot Moloch/Molech owl, a symbol of Saturn, at Bohemian Grove. Saturday or *Saturn*-day is the Jewish holy day and the Jewish/Hebrew god of Saturn is 'El' as in Isra-*El*. Saturn was the major god of Rome and today's Christmas is really a modern version of the Roman Saturn festival of Saturnalia in the period between December 17th and what became our Christmas. The Saturnalia festival included a sacrifice in the Temple of Saturn in Rome (the ruins still stand today) and people decorated trees, exchanged presents and hung holly etc. Other ancient societies had something similar as with the Greek festival of Kronia – Kronos/Cronus was the Greek name for Saturn. Check out some of my other books and you'll see the significance of Saturn and its symbols that abound in both ancient and modern society. Saturn symbolism can be found throughout the 'establishment' and religion. The hexagram, or 'Star of David', is one of them and remember the six-pointed star symbol between the twin pillars at the Mother Lodge of Freemasonry in London earlier in the book in Figure 3. Santa is an anagram of Satan and Rabbi Marvin S. Antelman, a fierce opponent of Sabbatian-Frankism within the Jewish community, said the symbolism of the Santa reference to 'Saint Nick' originates from the Hebrew root 'Nikail' which means 'conspiracy'. Can I say 'conspiracy', is that okay?

Enter Jacob Frank

The Sabbatian movement and belief-system was expanded and made even more satanically extreme in the 18th century by Jewish dark occultist Jacob Frank (1726-1791). He was born Jacob Leibowicz in an area of Poland that is modern Ukraine. Black magician Frank claimed to be the reincarnation of 'messiah' Zevi and biblical patriarch Jacob (Fig 109). He posed as a Turkish Sephardic Jew called 'Frenk' – Yiddish for Sephardic Jew – and this eventually became Frank. This deeply psychopathic man was an advocate of human and animal sacrifices, the dark occult and sex with children – hence the story earlier in the book by the unofficial Rothschild about incest being 'considered normal and something to be admired'. Frank said that 'Lucifer' was the true god. Sabbatians and Frankists, what I will call Sabbatian-Frankists, were told: 'Do What Thou Wilt'. This was the anything-goes no matter what the effect on others 'philosophy' of Satanists like British occultist Aleister Crowley (1875-1947) who was an expression of the same satanic web. Jacob Frank said:

Figure 109: Jacob Frank.

> I did not come into this world to lift you up but rather to cast you down to the bottom of the abyss ... The descent into the abyss requires not only the rejection of all religions and conventions, but also the commission of 'strange acts', and this in turn demands the voluntary abasement (degradation) of one's own sense of self, so that libertinism [no morality] and the achievement of the state of utter shamelessness which leads to a tikkun [fixing/rectification] of soul are one and the same thing.

'Anything goes' includes paedophilia, human sacrifice and incest because depravity to Sabbatian-Frankists is a form of worship while compassion and empathy are sacrilege. Imagine what lack of compassion and empathy it would take to pull off 9/11 and Sabbatian-

Frankism was the force behind those attacks. What the Rothschild family insider said about incest being 'normal' to them was actually describing the life-style of Sabbatian-Frankism within which incest is a major pillar. Sabbatian-Frankism is behind the manipulated wars which are to them a mass blood sacrifice ritual – as was 9/11. Once you understand the mentality running the world you understand what happens in the world. We see the Death Cult's obsession with inversion in the inverted symbols of the Dark Occult in the form of the inverted cross and pentagram and with the dove which means 'peace' to the public mind but to them it is the symbol of the Babylonian goddess Semiramis in all her forms and names (Fig 110). The late America-based Rabbi Marvin S. Antelman said in his two-volume work *To Eliminate the Opiate* that Frankism is 'a movement of complete evil'. Jewish professor Gershom Scholem agrees in *The Messianic Idea in Judaism*: 'In all his actions [Frank was] a truly corrupt and degenerate individual ... one of the most frightening phenomena in the whole of Jewish history.' Scholem wrote a highly acclaimed analysis of Sabbatian-Frankism in which he said:

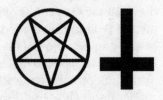

Figure 110: Inverted symbols of the inverted Death Cult of Sabbatian-Frankism (Satanism).

> The sect's exclusive organization continued to survive in this period through agents who went from place to place, through secret gatherings and separate religious rites, and through dissemination of a specifically Frankist literature. The 'believers' endeavored to marry only among themselves, and a wide network of inter-family relationships was created among the Frankists, even among those who had remained within the Jewish fold. Later Frankism was to a large extent the religion of families who had given their children the appropriate education. The Frankists of Germany, Bohemia, and Moravia usually held secret gatherings in Carlsbad in summer round about the ninth of Av.

This date was believed to be the following: The birthday of Sabbatai Zevi; the alleged date of the two destructions of the Jerusalem Temple by the Babylonians and Romans; and when Sephardic Jews were expelled from Spain. In keeping with their inverted faith this day was celebrated by partying rather than sadness. Professor Scholem describes how Sabbatian-Frankist 'believers' sought to marry only among themselves, passing on the baton through the generations. This is precisely how the Hidden Hand works in totality as I have been exposing since the 1990s. Followers and advocates of Frank and Zevi are still with us and advancing their plan for global takeover with the rest of the Hidden

Hand Web. Rabbis preaching traditional Judaism excommunicated Frank and his supporters as heretics. This just drove them underground and into the realms of covert manipulation. Sabbatian-Frankists are also known as Zoharists because they are led by the Zohar, a group of works considered by many to be the most important in the mystical Kabbalah. Zohar in Hebrew means 'splendour', 'radiance' and by extension 'illuminated'. This is the symbolism of the lighted torch held by the Statue of Liberty (the Babylonian goddess, Semiramis) and of Lucifer 'the light bringer'. Jacob Frank, like Zevi, believed that the Torah, the central document of Judaism, was no longer relevant and should be superseded by the occult Zohar. The Torah is the 'five books of Moses' in the Old Testament which are more widely known known as Genesis, Exodus, Leviticus, Numbers, and Deuteronomy. These are claimed by Judaism and Christianity to have been dictated by 'God' to Moses on Mount Sinai.

Frank, again like Zevi, said that particular elite people (i.e. them) are exempt from the moral law and therefore the laws and commandments of the Torah did not apply to them. They preached the inversion in which what had formerly been prohibited would now be encouraged and even done through compulsion no matter how despicable – the more despicable the better. Sacrifice, incest and sex with children were included and this is the background to the horrors I have exposed at length in my books perpetuated by some of the most famous people on earth including Father George Bush. Sabbatian-Frankism and Satanism, paedophile rings and Dark Occult ritual dominate the 'elite' and their playgrounds like Hollywood and Bohemian Grove in northern California that I described earlier in the book. A war to these people is a mass human sacrifice and something in their inverted minds to be desired and celebrated. Frank believed – as did his followers – that human society had to be overthrown and destroyed. They wanted 'the annihilation of every religion and positive system of belief' despite being outwardly religious themselves. Their aim was to infiltrate religions and destroy them from within and the same with the human values of society in general. Now ... recognise that world today? This is hardly surprising given that Sabbatian-Frankists and Satanists are running the show. In keeping with their techniques of manipulation the desired end had to be achieved secretly so that no one would see where the source of destruction was coming from. They hid themselves within all religions and no religions and one of their prime covers has been Judaism and Jewishness. Jewish writer and researcher Clifford Shack, author of *The Sabbatean-Frankist Messianic Conspiracy Partially Exposed*, said: 'Jacob Frank was not a big fan of the Jewish people.' Rabbi Marvin Antelman describes in *To Eliminate the Opiate* how Sabbatian-Frankists established their own fake systems to appoint rabbis that appear to be the genuine article while pursuing a very different agenda. Antelman described them as 'barbarians' who masqueraded as rabbis. He said these same Sabbatian-Frankist groups continue to Christianise Judaism and Judaise Christianity (Christian Zionism) with the ultimate aim of destroying both. The planned replacement is Sabbatian-Frankist Satanism which is why its symbols, methods and ways of life are gathering all around us.

The Red-Shields

Enter at this point one of the most powerful and important names behind Sabbatian-Frankism and ultra-Zionism – the House of Rothschild banking and financial dynasty. Jewish researcher Clifford Shack's research leads him to believe that the Rothschilds are related to Sabbatai Zevi. The scam of lending people money that doesn't exist – 'credit' – and charging interest on it can be traced at least to Babylon and on through the Knights Templar secret society and Italian banking families like the de Medicis into Europe. The system was honed and globalised by the Rothschilds. Jewish bankers were able to dominate the emergence of banking and finance wherever they located because their religion allowed the charging of interest on 'money' (credit), a system known as 'usury', while Islam and Christianity (for a time) condemned it. The Koran states:

> Those who charge usury are in the same position as those controlled by the devil's influence. This is because they claim that usury is the same as commerce. However, God permits commerce, and prohibits usury. Thus, whoever heeds this commandment from his Lord, and refrains from usury, he may keep his past earnings, and his judgment rests with God. As for those who persist in usury, they incur Hell, wherein they abide forever.

The Jewish religion allowed the charging of usury although more specifically it officially allowed Jews to charge usury to *non*-Jews but not to other Jews. The Hebrew Bible says that interest can be charged to strangers but not between Hebrews. Israelites were banned from adding interest to loans made to other Israelites while charging interest to non-Israelites was allowed, so the official texts say. Jews lending money at no interest to fellow Jews is said to be 'tzedakah' (charity or literally 'justice', 'righteousness'). This is the foundation of the global Association of Hebrew Free Loans through which interest-free loans are provided but only to Jews. It's not racist, though, and if you say so you're an 'anti-Semite'. Rothschild frontman Jacob Schiff (more soon) was the prime player behind the creation of the Hebrew Free Loan Society of New York in 1892 after which all the others followed. Jews were expelled from many countries for the actions of their banking class charging outrageous rates of interest that enslaved the population in debt. This recurring theme is explained away *in total* by the alleged genetic hatred that the rest of humanity is supposed to have for Jewish people. Well, I don't feel hatred towards them and I personally don't know anyone who does so clearly there's more to know here. Charging interest on loans has now enslaved much of humanity and has sucked the wealth of the world into the coffers of the banking families and dynasties by seizing the assets of those who don't – mostly simply can't – pay back loans of created-out of-nothing 'credit' *plus interest*. The vastly greater involvement of Zionist and ultra-Zionist bankers in ratio to 0.2 percent of the global population is protected from exposure by the ultra-Zionist hate group network using the label of 'anti-Semitism' to silence those who wish to make these facts public and begin a legitimate debate on why this is. The Rothschilds have mercilessly exploited the usury system to secure fantastic fortunes and accumulation of assets. They were a Middle Ages occult family called 'Bauer' until 1760 when banker Mayer Amschel Bauer, located in Frankfurt, Germany, changed the family name to Rothschild or 'Red-Sign/Red Shield' in German (Fig 111). The name was inspired by the red hexagram or 'Star of David'/'Seal of Solomon' on their home although the symbolism goes much deeper. A six-pointed star is a symbol of *Saturn* which is a central pillar of Sabbatian-Frankism – Saturnism/Satanism – and so how absolutely appropriate that the very name of the

Figure 111: The Rothschild house in Frankfurt where the dynasty began.

Figure 112: The hexagram or 'Star of David' is the ancient symbol of Saturn from which came the name 'Rothschild' or 'Red Shield/Red Sign'.

Sabbatian-Frankist inner circle Rothschilds should be inspired by a symbol of Saturn which, in turn, inspired the name Sabbatai (Fig 112). Nor is the six-pointed star an exclusively Jewish symbol. It can be found in many parts of the world because it is an esoteric symbol for Saturn used by a long list of ancient cultures and religions including Islam. One example was discovered on the floor of a 1,200 year old excavated mosque where Tel Aviv is today. The same symbol from which the name 'Rothschild' originates can be seen on the flag of Israel – a state established by the Rothschilds who oversee the country as their own fiefdom (Figs 113 and 114 overleaf). Frankfurt, home city of the Rothschild dynasty,

Figure 113: The symbol of Saturn on the flag of Rothschild Israel.

Figure 114: The real owners of Israel.

was a centre for Sabbatian-Frankists as was the city of Mannheim an hour's drive away. Rabbi Marvin S. Antelman said that among the Sabbatian settlers in Mannheim were names such as Oppenheim and Hess.

I have exposed the Rothschild inner circle and its history in great detail in other books and I won't repeat everything here. Enough to say they are even more amazingly wealthy than they already appear to be, but don't tell the bloke in the Momentum video or he'll say they can't be or the Forbes Rich list would say so. The Rothschilds control global finance through a network of operatives all over the world. Many of these place-people assets go on to be famous billionaires because of this Rothschild connection and their role as Rothschild proxies. The House of Rothschild has a grotesque history of manipulating wars in which they fund all sides and end up owning countries through the subsequent debt. This increases even more when they lend governments 'money' (credit) to rebuild the countries their manipulated wars have devastated. Mayer Amschel Rothschild, the dynasty founder, made his fortune thanks to his close relationship with German royalty and aristocracy which he then usurped. This was especially so with Prince William of Hesse-Hanau who sought to loan money at high interest rates and no wonder Rothschild became his financial agent (and Svengali). The Hesse dynasty made fortunes from loaning troops to fight other country's wars which increasingly Rothschild networks were causing to happen. William and Rothschild shared a love of the Dark Occult based on the Kabbalah and its Zohar. The inner elite of the Rothschild dynasty remain dark occultists today although I stress that not *everyone* called Rothschild is involved – only the inner sanctum compartmentalised from many in the wider family and its offshoots. The 1999 movie *Eyes Wide Shut* starring Tom Cruise and Nicole Kidman was directed, produced and co-written by Stanley Kubrick, a Jewish man who wanted to expose the hidden world of elite Satanism and mind control. He chose the Rothschild-built stately home at Mentmore Towers in Buckinghamshire, England, for the location of the satanic mass orgy around which the film was based. I doubt given the highly symbolic nature of the movie that this was an accident. Kubrick died of a heart attack soon after the film was shown to Warner Brothers executives and some 25 minutes was cut after his death. The banking and major corporate system is controlled by Satanists and dark occultists which explains why it operates with such cold, callous corruption. I have exposed the 'elite' satanic networks at great length over the years going back to *The Biggest Secret* in 1998.

Sabbatian-Frankist Illuminati and the creation of Marxism

Dark Occult Rothschilds have been the drivers of ultra-Zionism and much of the Hidden Hand structure and it is hardly a shock that satanic occultist Jacob Frank and his Sabbatian-Frankism formed an alliance in 1773 with Mayer Amstel Rothschild and the Jesuit-educated Jew, Adam Weishaupt, who later became (in public) a Protestant. The origin of his name Adam-Weis-haupt apparently breaks down to mean 'the first man to lead those who know'. The Catholic Inquisition jailed Frank for 13 years after his arrest in 1760 when the truth about his Sabbatian-Frankist infiltration of Catholicism was uncovered. After his release he headed for Frankfurt, home city of the Rothschilds, and their alliance was formed. Frank was given the title of Baron and became a wealthy nobleman with a big and gathering following of Jews in Germany, the Austro-Hungarian Empire and other European countries. Rothschild-funded Adam Weishaupt established the infamous Rothschild/Frank Bavarian Illuminati, firstly under another name, in 1776. The 'Illuminati' was (is) based on the Zohar or 'radiance', 'illumination', 'the light bringer' and the organisation set its sights on world control in league with the wider Web. Weishaupt was a Sabbatian-Frankist infiltrator posing as a Jesuit within the Roman Church after apparently being persuaded by Mayer Amschel Rothschild to join the Frankist 'crusade'. Illuminati ambitions for world domination and revolution came to light in 1785 when a horseman courier called Lanz was reported to be struck by lighting and in his saddlebags were found extensive Illuminati documents laying out the plan for world domination and revolution and confirming the connection to Weishaupt. The Rothschild/Frank-directed Illuminati would be involved in widespread society-changing manipulation and violence (death rituals) including the French and American Revolutions (the network was operating before its official formation in 1776). Rabbi Antelman in *To Eliminate the Opiate* connects the Illuminati to the Jacobins who were a central player in the French Revolution and the Bund der Gerechten or League of the Just which was the manipulative force behind the emergence of communism/Marxism. He writes:

> The original inner circle of the Bund der Gerechten consisted of born Catholics, Protestants and Jews [Sabbatian-Frankist infiltrators], and those representatives of respective subdivisions formulated schemes for the ultimate

destruction of their faiths. The heretical Catholics laid plans which they felt would take a century or more for the ultimate destruction of the church; the apostate Jews for the ultimate destruction of the Jewish religion.

Antelman pointed out that there has not been a single Communist government in which religion is allowed to be practiced freely without interference. The 'Bund' morphed into the International Communist Party and Communist League which produced the Communist Manifesto of Karl Marx and Friedrich Engels in 1848 and spawned the mass-control system known as Marxism. Violent revolution is the Sabbatian-Frankist Illuminati calling card. The Illuminati-Jacobins were behind 'The Terror' in France in 1793 and 1794 when Jacobin Maximillian de Robespierre and his Orwellian 'Committee of Public Safety' killed 17,000 'enemies of the Revolution'. September 11th was just another notch on the bedpost for the Sabbatian-Frankists and their bloodlust. The death-toll of communism and Marxism alone can be counted in hundreds of millions worldwide. Illuminati imposition by death and terror both directly and through its connected offshoots would transform human society. Wars in the aftermath of 9/11 are simply modern examples of a clear pattern through history with the same network manipulating from the shadows. This is what happens when empathy and compassion are deleted. Rabbi Antelman in his studies of the Illuminati and League of the Just concluded:

> Contrary to popular opinion Karl Marx did not originate the Communist Manifesto. He was paid for his services by the League of the Just, which was known in its country of origin, Germany, as the Bund der Geaechteten.

Antelman said the text attributed to Marx was the work of other people and Marx 'was only repeating what others already said'. He describes Marx as 'a hired hack – lackey of the wealthy Illuminists'. Karl Marx (1818-1883) is famous for a description of religion as the 'opium of the people', hence Antelman called his books, *To Eliminate the Opiate* – or eliminate religion by infiltrating them and tearing them apart from within so the openly satanic religion of Sabbatian-Frankism can take their place. Antelman further connects Marxism to the 'Rhodes-Milner-Rothschild nexus' and to the Rockefeller dynasty. The former is the network of satellite organisations spawned by the Rothschild Round Table secret society in London which went on to create the Royal Institute of International Affairs, Council on Foreign Relations, Trilateral Commission, Bilderberg Group and Club of Rome. Antelman notes that Marx's original mentor, Sabbatian Illuminist Moses Hess, was a first cousin of Sabbatian Leopold Zunz and he said the Zunzs were 'an integral part of the Schiff family'. The name 'Schiff', a family that lived in the same house as the Rothschilds in Frankfurt, is of central importance to much of what followed including the

Russian Revolution as we will see. Hess was a French-Jewish philosopher who founded Labour or Socialist Zionism which appears to be in conflict with far-right Zionism while in truth Sabbatian-Frankism ultimately controls both. Rabbi Antelman writes that the later falling out between Hess and Marx was all staged. The Sabbatian-Frankist Illuminati modus operandi was – and still is – to infiltrate, take over and destroy organisations (governments, religions, political parties etc.) while posing as supporters and even leaders of them. Karl Marx was born Jewish but his family converted to Christianity in the way of Sabbatian-Frankist infiltrators and he attacked Jews, not least in his book, *A World Without Jews*. Jacob Frank and his movement did the same because Sabbatian-Frankists hate Jews while posing as protectors of them. You can see the seamless links unfolding here which connect Sabbatian-Frankism to the Rothschilds, Illuminati, Jacobins of the French Revolution, the 'Bund' or League of the Just, International Communist Party, Communist League and the Communist Manifesto of Karl Marx and Friedrich Engels which would lead to the Rothschild-funded Russian Revolution.

'Progressive' Marxism

To know the foundation goals and techniques of what became known as Marxism and its Sabbatian-Frankist origins is to grasp so much about both history and what is happening all around us today. The Marxist methodology is to change society through conflict between distinct groups and this is everywhere to be seen, not least in constant and apparently endless war. Nothing transforms a society more completely and irreversibly than a war and they are manipulated into being to that end by the Sabbatian-Frankist Death Cult and other satanic expressions of The Web. Conflicts are mostly artificially generated by creating, funding and arming different countries and groups which are played off against each other to transform the nature of countries, groups and societies. We have seen this with ISIS and the manipulated conflicts in Iraq, Libya, Syria and elsewhere since 9/11. World Wars were conflicts in the Marxist mode of manipulation to transform global society through conflict and so is today's identity politics. The Marxist 'class struggle' (conflict between groups) has become the Marxist 'self-identity struggle'. Identity politics is based on the struggle for power between *groups* – classic Marxism. The more groups you have the more potential for conflict and societal transformation and so we have the creation of ever more groups based on ever more detailed minutiae of self-identity. You have the male-female struggle subdivided into the straight male/female/gay struggle and the feminist-transgender struggle in which, for instance, transgender imposes its will over feminism by insisting that those in big, strong, males bodies identifying as female can take part in women's sport. This 'struggle' alone is transforming women's sport in accordance with Marxist conflict theory. The war on the family unit is straight from Marxist doctrine and so is political correctness which both have Sabbatian-Frankist/Illuminati origins through a Sabbatian-Frankist Marxist operation known as the 'Frankfurt [Rothschild] School' which I am coming to. This approach to Marxism is known as 'Cultural Marxism' and human society today is deluged with its poison. You know when something is part of agenda because opponents are insanely targeted by ultra-Zionist attack groups and in 2019 British Conservative MP and former minister Suella Braverman was condemned by the ultra-Zionist Board of Deputies of British Jews for using the term. The Board claimed that 'cultural Marxist' is an 'antisemitic trope' and demanded that she undertake not to use the phrase in future. The ludicrous Hate Not Hope censorship group weighed in saying that Braverman's phrase was 'deeply disturbing' – as is Hate Not Hope – and Israel-worshipping Labour MP Wes Streeting said it was 'an ugly and reprehensible term with anti-Semitic connotations'. How he could speak with his tongue extended I have no idea. You always get ridiculous over-the-top condemnation when someone hits the button dead centre and I am a perfect example (Fig 115).

Sabbatian-Frankist ultra-Zionists that established the Frankfurt School of social engineering in the 1920s referred to a foundation of Marxism as 'Critical Theory' which basically requires groups to be hyper-sensitive to criticism and all of them convinced of their oppression and victimisation by what is deemed the 'dominant culture'. You then harness this manipulated rage to bring down the 'dominant culture' while at the same time all these multifarious self-identity

Figure 115: Up yours.

groups are also in a constant state of conflict with *each other* over who is the most oppressed and victimised. Anyone recognise that today – like *everywhere?* The 'dominant culture' in the West is perceived to be (by the constant repetition that it is) the white male. Thus white male 'history' has to be demonised and obliterated on the road to their marginalisation in the present and societal transformation. To achieve this outcome a state of group-think is essential – both in the sense of everyone thinking the same and also judging everyone by their racial, religious and cultural group. Break down the 'white male' culture into individuals and you see that white men span the entire spectrum (as with every race, religion and culture) from kind, courageous, decent and caring to slave-owning, mass-murdering psychopaths. Many white people fought against slavery as they did against apartheid in South Africa. Irony of ironies slave-owning, mass-murdering psychopaths created Marxism as a means to achieve total global control and now enslave much of humanity. What you must do is isolate the 'dominant culture' in terms of blame. White men are presented by the propaganda as the only slave owners, oppressors and psychopaths in history when every race, religion and culture has had their slave owners, oppressors and psychopaths – and still do. This is not only about the white male and even some black people owned black slaves in the United States. In other areas of the world the dominant non-white culture is attacked by the need for 'regime change' in the name of freeing the people through 'democracy'. This is another irony because regime change in non-white countries is done overwhelmingly by white males in government and the military. Non-white cultures being prepared for regime-change are told that the white male in the dark suit or uniform is the good guy coming to free them from oppression while in countries where white males are perceived to be the dominant culture they are deemed to be the oppressor. We are looking at designer transformation of different societies while using the same methodology – *ideology*. The trick is to give the same ideology of Marxism different faces for different situations on the spectrum from vicious Soviet and Chinese communism to heart-on-the-sleeve-we-are-nicer-than-you-are 'progressive socialism'. The sales-pitch changes, but not the outcome which is always centralised control by the elite few over everyone else. It is worth 'progressives' pondering on the fact that the foot-soldiers of Marxist (Sabbatian-Frankist) 'revolutions' never end up in power at the end of the story. That is always the gift of the elite who were behind it all along. I am not saying that dominant cultures cannot be forms of oppression – clearly they all are to a larger or lesser extent. 'Progressives' and their billionaire supporters deleting freedom of speech is the most fundamental form of oppression which their self-purity, I-am-right-and-you're-not-so-you-can't-have-a-say arrogance cannot see. Imposed Islam, Judaism, Christianity, Hinduism and so on are vehicles for oppression if choice is not allowed – *everything* is oppression where choice is not freely made. My point is that oppression in its multiple forms and scale is exploited by Sabbatian-Frankist Marxism to justify even more extreme oppression and centralised control. I want to see a world in which power is decentralised and devolved to communities and the individual which negates the potential for a tiny cabal to impose its will on everyone. There is no contradiction whatsoever between individual liberty and collective responsibility on the basis of my own philosophy of do what you like so long as you don't impose it on anyone else either physically or psychologically.

The Soros 'progressive movement' is really the same old Marxist movement wearing its latest disguise and Marxism is the creation of the

Sabbatian-Frankist Death Cult. Marxism is driven by the very elite that Marxism is supposed to be overthrowing. 'Progressive' people – you are being played by the string section and you and your children are going to have to take the consequences if reality doesn't dawn like *now*. The string section is a Death Cult and why do you think that Marxism in its many expressions – Stalin, Mao, Pol Pot and so many more – has led to the deaths of hundreds of millions of people directly and through related consequences? Here we are with virtue-signalling idiots like film-maker Michael Moore and his wish-for 'leader'Alexandria Ocasio-Cortez promoting this very Marxism-in-thin-disguise society with I doubt the first idea that this is what they are doing. The proposed Ocasio-Cortez 'Green New Deal' is only Chairman Mao's Cultural Revolution in China in that it demands subordination of individual uniqueness to the alleged 'collective will' which is really the will of the elite pulling the strings – or playing them – from the shadows. 'Collective will' never actually is because the 'collective' is never consulted. The excuse for the 'Green New Deal's' introduction is that 'climate change threatens human existence' when the 'global warming/climate change' hoax has been perpetrated by the same Death Cult via front organisations like the Club of Rome in the Round Table network. I have been warning since the 1990s that alleged human-caused global warming/climate change was a scam to justify the transformation of global society into a centrally-controlled dictatorship through United Nations projects known as Agenda 21 and Agenda 2030. The plan is also to encourage or coerce people not to have children as part of a depopulation agenda, especially in the West, by employing the 'end of the world is nigh' approach. Now we have Ocasio-Cortez urging people to ask: 'Is it okay to still have children?' I watched an interview with a sad-looking lady called Blythe Pepine, founder of Birth Strike, an organisation for those choosing not to have children because of the dangers of 'global warming'. She said she would not have children herself because of 'the threat we have been told about'. By whom, Blythe? The Sabbatian-Frankist propaganda machine designed to transform global society into a single Marxist state. She said we face extinction, but what will speed that quicker than not having children? It reminds me of the line ... 'When we have deleted heterosexuality future generations will thank us.' The 'Green New Deal' promoted by Hidden Hand-stooge Ocasio-Cortez proposes precisely what those UN Agendas demand and I am going to shock you again here ... groups supporting the Green New Deal are funded by George Soros. I bet you're speechless. The policy has been supported by other prominent members of the Soros-funded Democratic Party including Elizabeth Warren who laughably claimed to have Native American ancestry. Definitely someone you can trust.

Sabbatian-Frankist political correctness

Censorship and political correctness (censorship) are an expression of Death Cult Marxism with the *minority will* posing as the *collective will* subordinating individual freedom to the demands of the mob. Marxism and its offspring communism are always about mobs imposing the will of the elite. Marxism demands centralised control and that structure allows even greater control by the few of the many than capitalism (cartelism) does. Instead of having to manipulate control by the few through hording capital and ownership it is delivered on a plate by the very centralised societal structure of Marxism/Communism. Does anyone believe that Marxist governments all over the world have been 'people's governments'? How about Stalin's Soviet Union? Or Mao's China? Today's China? How about Vietnam where it is illegal to criticise the government on the Internet? Why is the 'free world' going the same way as China and Vietnam with ever more extreme censorship and information control? The same Marxist agenda is being rolled out behind the smokescreen of political correctness and so you have Internet corporations owned by the filthy rich elite in alliance with 'progressives' in their support for censoring non-Marxist information and opinion founded on freedom of the individual and not the tyranny of collective control. Demands for equality of *outcome* rather than equality of *opportunity* are straight from the Marxist rule book. Equality of opportunity offers the platform for people to go their own way and choose their own path in pursuit of their chosen outcome. Equality of outcome destroys incentive and imprisons creativity in a grey and dour sameness while driving out individual achievement in pursuit of outcome 'equality' (classic Marxism). Instead of raising people up it crushes them down. The world portrayed in Orwell's *Nineteen-eighty-four* in fact. A structure based on centralisation of power always involves the few controlling the many and to counter that we need devolution of power *from* the centre founded on respect for individuality and freedom of choice and expression. This is everything 'progressives' and their corporate billionaire cheerleaders are seeking to destroy. The whole ridiculous nonsense of political correctness was developed by ultra-Zionist Marxists from the 'Frankfurt School', or the Institute for Social Research, established in 1923 and affiliated to the University of Frankfurt. Jewish historian and theologian Gershom Scholem, who made a major study of Sabbatian-Frankism, described the School as a 'Jewish sect', but I say it was a pseudo-Jewish sect. Sabbatian-Frankism has sought to control key areas of human society including finance, politics, media, law, social sciences and psychiatry. The foundation of the few controlling the many is to understand human thinking and behaviour and armed with that knowledge to manipulate the perceptions of the many. From perception comes behaviour. Zionist website Myjewishlearning.com reports:

Jewish psychologists and the influence of Jewish tradition have been instrumental in creating the field of modern psychology. The fundaments of several psychological movements can be traced directly to Jewish values, ideas, and practices, and Jews in the 20th century were at the forefront of research about the psyche and the varieties of human behavior.

Jewish psychologists founded several branches of psychological inquiry. All of the major theorists of the Gestalt school, except Wolfgang Kohler, were Jews. Max Wertheimer, Kurt Koffka, Kurt Lewin, and Kurt Goldstein posited theories of perception and understanding based on holistic understanding, rather than a previous model based on the computation of parts. Psychoanalysis was founded by Sigmund Freud and, with the notable exception of Carl Jung, most of its early proponents were also Jews.

Political correctness is a mind-game to manipulate the target population to silence *itself*. The whole 'progressive' mind-set of fascistic/communistic 'socialism' is an outgrowth of the Frankfurt School and Sabbatian-Frankist manipulation which was itself a continuation of the ultra-Zionist Marxism named after Sabbatian-Frankist stooge, Karl Marx. US Congresswoman Alexandria Ocasio-Cortez, who claims her family has Sephardic Jewish ancestry, is the current political poster girl of this movement, but she is too obsessed with her own reflection and too perceptually programmed to see who her mind-masters really are. She said of her Jewish roots: '... the story goes that during the Spanish Inquisition so many people were forced to convert on the exterior to Catholicism, but on the interior, continued to practice their faith, continued to be who they were, even though they were pressured to not be that on the outside world.' American academic Kevin Macdonald describes in *The Culture of Critique: An Evolutionary Analysis of Jewish Involvement in Twentieth-Century Intellectual and Political Movements* how 'leftist authoritarianism' emerged from the Frankfurt School. This captures the authoritarian 'progressive' movement of today which has been the goal of these ultra-Zionist intellectuals all along. The Frankfurt School was funded into existence by ultra-Zionist Felix Weil; the first director was ultra-Zionist Carl Grünberg; and he was followed by ultra-Zionist Max Horkheimer. Among other prime influences on the school's thinking were ultra-Zionists Theodor W Adorno and Herbert Marcuse. The School relocated to Switzerland before moving to New York in 1935 and six years later branched into California which would become the global capital of political correctness. This Rothschild ultra-Zionist centre for social engineering set out to control American social sciences and here are just some of the changes they sought to introduce to American and global society. Perhaps you can recognise them:

- The creation of racism offences.

- Continual change to create confusion.
- The teaching of sex and homosexuality to young children.
- The undermining of schools' and teachers' authority.
- Huge immigration to destroy national identity.
- The promotion of excessive drinking.
- Emptying of churches [targeting anything that brings people together].
- A legal system with bias against victims of crime.
- Dependency on the State or State benefits [do what we say or they stop].
- Control and dumbing down of the media.
- Encouraging the breakdown of family.

None of these goals are to benefit people – they are only there to *control* people. National identity *is* being destroyed by 'huge immigration' and it is clear to see the real motivation behind the borderless European Union and the United States failing to adequately police the border with Mexico and make it easier for so-called 'illegal aliens' to secure residency. They want a borderless United States, Canada and Mexico to destroy the self-identity of all three. A sense of nationhood is a big potential block to the acceptance of a single uniform Marxist world and so they are working to delete any sense of national identity. Perhaps people might realise now why mega-rich George Soros who says he doesn't care about social consequences and only making money is spending tens of billions supporting 'progressive' groups and those making it easier for the mass movement of people between different cultures. This doesn't make sense on the face of it, but perfect sense when you see what is really behind it. Marxism/communism has never been an ideology for oppressed masses, only for the super-rich using communism to further oppress those masses. The same is true of its alter-ego fascism and its 'democratic' version of socialism (the don't-scare-the-children term for introducing Marxism to America). Nazi fascism was really a form of Marxism and it was appropriate that they called themselves the National Socialist German Workers Party. The Nazis were dark occultists – the same as the Sabbatian-Frankists that controlled them.

From the inside

The takeover of countries through the perceptions of the population was described in *1985* by Soviet KGB defector Yuri Bezmenov who was trained in the subversion doctrine which he described as a four-step plan to subjugate societies. The first stage he called 'demoralisation'. He said this takes 15 to 20 years in which generations of students are systematically programmed in the school and college system to transform their perception of reality while other information and perspectives are suppressed. Marxist-Leninist ideology was being pumped into the 'soft head' of at least three generations of American students (it's happening in Europe and elsewhere, too) without being challenged or counterbalanced by the basic values of Americanism. Bezmenov said of the demoralisation stage:

> Exposure to true information does not matter anymore. A person who is demoralised is unable to assess true information – the facts tell nothing to him. Even if I shower him with information, with authentic truth, with documents, with pictures, even if I take him by force to the Soviet Union and show him concentration camps he will refuse to believe it until he gets a kick in the back bottom [realises he has been had by Marxist governments taking over his country]. When the military boot crashes then he will understand.

Look at what has been happening for years in the schools and colleges and you will see that quite obviously stage one has been long underway and is now bearing fruit in people like Ocasio-Cortez. Demoralisation is followed by stages that Yuri Bezmenov called 'destabilisation', 'crisis' and 'normalisation' in which 'normalisation' means the imposition of a new 'normal' (society transformed). These stages together are classic Problem-Reaction-Solution. A poll of American 18-24 year olds in early 2019 found that 61 percent were open to a 'socialist society'. They think that means fair and just – if only. The poll reflects the control of the education (indoctrination) system from pre-school to college for generations now that Bezmenov described. Once the programmed promotors (see today's 'progressives') have played their part as essential pawns they would be 'lined up against the wall and shot', Bezmenov said. They would not be needed any more and they would know too much. There was also the telling line that I have been trying to get across to these programmed people for years: 'They think they will come to power, but that will never happen, of course.' No, because Marxist 'revolutionaries' are only pawns in a game orchestrated by their elite violin players – the 'revolution' always tends to eat itself. Ocasio-Cortez and the Marxist mob masquerading as 'social justice warriors' are temporary pawns to bring their hidden masters to power in a full-on global dictatorship. This is how Sabbatian-Frankists operate the world over and they were the force behind the creation of the Soviet Union/KGB as we will see shortly. All the anti-Russia propaganda directed at Vladimir Putin as an individual is a smokescreen to hide the manipulation of American and global society by the Sabbatian Death Cult with major power-bases in Russia and Eastern Europe which was also once the old Russian Empire from where so many major ultra-Zionist players or their families have emerged that created and still control Israel.

Infiltration a speciality

When you appreciate the Babylonian, Sabbatian-Frankist occult foundation of the force behind human society the pieces start to fit. With Rothschild support the Sabbatian-Frankist Death Cult (Satanism and *inverted* Judaism) quickly expanded its influence, secret networks and infiltration of Freemasonry. Sabbatian-Frankists were encouraged to convert to other religions posing as advocates and believers while working to turn them into vehicles for the Sabbatian-Frankist agenda and eventually destroy them. The cult infiltrated Judaism, Islam (more shortly) the Roman Church, Protestant Christianity and other religions while also subverting secret societies including the Jesuits, Knights Templar, Knights of Malta and Opus Dei (all connected to the Church of Rome), Rosicrucians, Grand Orient Freemasonry, wider Freemasonry and the secret and semi-secret strands that connect with them to form The Web. All these infiltrated secret societies are based on the teachings of the Kabbalah – the Lurianic Kabbalah – as are the inner core of major religions. Hasidism, or Hasidic Judaism, the ultra-Orthodox Jewish religious group that wear side-curls, the fedora, homburg and big fur hats are an outgrowth of Sabbatian-Frankism and heavily influenced by the Lurianic Kabbalah. The movement emerged out of Poland in the 18th century in what is now modern-day Ukraine and most advocates will not be aware of its Sabbatian-Frankist origins although the inner core will. The same applies to all these infiltrated groups and organisations. Most won't be a practicing Sabbatian-Frankist, but the cult will be the power in the shadows. Hasidic rabbi Menachem Mendel Schneerson (1902-1994), leader of the messianic Chabad-Lubavitch movement and a deeply racist Jewish supremacist, once said:

> The body of a Jewish person is of a totally different quality from the body of [members] of all nations of the world; an even greater difference exists in regard to the soul. Two contrary types of soul exist, a non-Jewish soul comes from three Satanic spheres, while the Jewish soul stems from holiness ... A Jew was not created as a means for some [other] purpose; he himself is the purpose, since the substance of all [divine] emanations was created only to serve the Jews.

This gives a feel for the attitude to the rest of humanity of extreme Sabbatian-Frankist racists who have the nerve to call others racist. Instead of being condemned for such comments Schneerson was posthumously awarded the Congressional Gold Medal for 'outstanding and lasting contributions toward improvements in world education, morality, and acts of charity'. President Jimmy Carter designated Schneerson's birthday as US Education and Sharing Day and every

president since has fawned over him when the day comes around.
Sabbatian-Frankists have no influence with the US government, though,
so don't worry.

Jacob Frank targeted the Roman Catholic Church from the start and
he was so persuasive in his claim to be a dissident Jew that the Church
funded his work and allowed him to convert thousands or apparent
followers of Judaism into Catholicism. By 1790, 26,000 Jews were
recorded baptised in Poland. Sabbatian-Frankists were not, of course,
really converts. They were interlopers infiltrating the Catholic hierarchy
to take over the reins of power through clandestine cells and high
positions in the Church including the Pope. We see the influence of the
paedophilia-practicing Sabbatian-Frankists today with the constant
revelations about mass child abuse by Catholic priests which, at the
same time, is being exploited by the same Sabbatian-Frankist cult to
destroy the church. Child abuse – a calling card of Sabbatian-Frankists –
has also made the news within the Hasidic community in Brooklyn,
New York, where cover-ups are widespread with internal laws against
reporting any of their number to the police. Rabbi Marvin S. Antelman
said that a lesser known fact about Jacob Frank is that he also converted
to Islam two years before his conversion to Catholicism. A golden rule of
the cult was – and is – that 'the believer must not appear as he really is'.
This applies to politics and other walks of life and not only religion.
Rabbi Antelman gives an example of what happened to the Jewish
community in Vienna, Austria:

> What emerges from a close inspection of Viennese Jewry in the latter part of
> the 19th century is that the establishment is controlled by a Sabbatian Frankist
> underground, who through their influence on the infrastructure of the
> community and its media, could orchestrate innocent Jews into supporting
> their 'causes'.

This is exactly what has happened to the Jewish community in Israel, the
United States, Europe and elsewhere.

Sabbatian-Frankist Jesuits

Ignatius of Loyola (1491-1556) was the Spanish Catholic priest who
established the Society of Jesus (Jesuits) in 1539. He had appeared before
an ecclesiastical commission in 1527 charged with having sympathy
with the Alumbrados, a mystical sect with basically the same beliefs as
the later Sabbatian-Frankists with their connection to the satanic religion
of Babylon. The Alumbrados ('Illuminated') emerged in Spain in the
15th and 16th centuries and they believed that once they became
'illuminated' through a 'complete union with 'God' they could do
anything they liked because 'sin' was impossible in their state of

'enlightenment' and no matter what horrors they perpetrated it had no effect on their soul. This is the sales-pitch of the Sabbatian-Frankists when you cut back all the verbiage and manufactured justifications for evil, but when their consciousness leaves the body at 'death' they find out otherwise. Loyola escaped with a firm warning for his Alumbrados connections and his Jesuit Order would go on to become a major controlling force on behalf of the Sabbatian-Frankists and the wider cult within the Roman Church. Adam Weishaupt who established what became the Bavarian Illuminati with Jacob Frank and Mayer Amstel Rothschild in 1776 was a Jesuit-educated 'Jew' (Sabbatian-Frankist). Jewish researcher Barry Chamish, quoting the work of Rabbi Antelman, said:

> A movement of complete evil now took hold. The Jesuits' goal was the destruction of the Protestant Reformation leading to a return of one pope sitting in judgement on all mankind. The Rothschilds' goal was to control the wealth of the planet. And the Frankist vision was the destruction of Jewish ethics to be replaced by a religion based on the exact opposite of God's intentions [Satanism]. When these factions blended, a bloody war against humanity, with the Jews on the front lines, erupted.

The Jesuits, Rothschilds and Sabbatian-Frankists moved – and move – as one unit. Ignatius of Loyola became the first Jesuit Superior General in 1541 and the post continues today. A Superior General is also called the 'Black Pope' and has enormous hidden power within the Church – even more so currently with Pope Francis who became a member of the all-male Jesuit Order. With 20,000 Jesuits – three-quarters of them priests – operating in 100 countries the potential for manipulating events and situations is obvious. They work across the world in their schools, colleges and many other centres which include a big network of Jesuit universities and they follow a vow of obedience to the Jesuit hierarchy. Their 'education' system of calculated perceptual indoctrination provided in many ways the structure for modern 'education' to this day. Jesuits played a front-line role in the European colonisation and 'Christianisation' of native lands around the world and the mass murder of the Inquisition. They engaged in political manipulation wherever they located to advance their own power and agenda. Jesuits were thrown out of many countries only to return in new guises – the technique of Sabbatian-Frankists with whom the Jesuits joined forces. Francesco Borgia, the third Jesuit Superior General, said: 'We came in like lambs and will rule like wolves. We shall be expelled like dogs and return like eagles.' Religious, royal and political leaders were terrified of the Jesuits and when Pope Clement XIV signed the decree abolishing the Jesuit Order in 1773 he said: 'I have signed my death warrant, but I have obeyed my conscience.' He was dead within nine months and the Jesuit Order was restored in 1814. Needless to say that Clement's death is described as 'controversial'. Jesuits operate like covert Nazis and how appropriate that the Nazi SS was structured and organised by Heinrich Himmler on the Jesuit blueprint. Walter Schellenberg, former chief of Nazi counter-espionage, said:

> The SS organisation had been constituted by Himmler according to the principles of the Jesuit Order. Their regulations and the Spiritual Exercises prescribed by Ignatius of Loyola were the model Himmler tried to copy exactly. Himmler's title as supreme chief of the SS was to be the equivalent of the Jesuits' 'General' and the whole structure was a close imitation of the Catholic Church's hierarchical order.

Jesuits still control the Vatican and Roman Catholic Church today in league with their Sabbatian-Frankist masters. This is highly appropriate given that the Roman Church is the Church of Babylon relocated. Sabbatian-Frankists are modern-day purveyors of the Babylonian satanic human-sacrifice religion and Babylonian bloodlines established Rome and its empire. The Hidden Hand creates religions to seize the minds of the populous and then divides them into factions and sets them at war with each other. How many wars have there been between Christian Catholics and Protestants alone? Martin Luther triggered the schism with the Church of Rome in the 16th century to create Protestantism and then John Calvin triggered a schism within Protestantism called Calvinism. You see this with virtually all religions as with Islam's schism of Sunni and Shia. The Vatican has long been controlled by Sabbatian-Frankist-Jesuit occultists and it's no surprise when you hear Jesuit Pope Francis say that Christians must work 'to ensure anti-Semitism is banned from society'. He said Christians share the same roots as 'their Jewish brothers and sisters'. How about the other link, mate – infiltration by Sabbatian-Frankists which as a Jesuit you well know? Another highly significant family infiltrated by these covert Satanists was the Habsburg dynasty which produced a stream of kings and emperors and occupied the throne of the Holy Roman Empire from 1438 until 1740. They remain very connected to The Web through secret societies like Le Cercle, the Knights of Malta and the elite and exclusive Order of the Golden Fleece founded in 1430. The Austrian version is led today by Karl von Habsburg (also Archduke of Austria, Royal Prince of Hungary, Bohemia and Croatia), current head of the House of Habsburg-Lorraine. Le Cercle initiate Otto von Habsburg, or Archduke Otto of Austria (1912-2011), was a key figure behind the creation of what is now the European Union as an agent of The Web to delete countries and bring them under centralised control. The

Habsburgs have worked closely with the Rothschilds.

America calling

Mayer Amschel Rothschild and his five sons (symbolised by five arrows) established banking houses in Frankfurt, London, Paris, Vienna and Naples and he selected the wives of his sons for the business connections they would bring to the family. He wanted his offspring to marry cousins wherever possible to keep the bloodline 'pure' and keep it all 'in family' – just as Sabbatian-Frankists are told to intermarry and 'keep it in the cult'. Rothschild had eighteen grandchildren and sixteen of them married first cousins while his daughters all married bankers – Worms, Sichel and Beyfus – and the family became immensely rich. They were infamous for their psychopathic activities and behaviour as they took control of European countries through financial and political manipulation. From Europe they hijacked the American economy and expanded worldwide. In 1773 Mayer Amschel Rothschild is reported to have met with Sabbatian-Frankist banking families including Schiff, Oppenheimer, Warburg and Goldschmidts (later Goldsmiths) to agree a plan to bankrupt nations and control world finance. They have certainly achieved that if you look at national debt levels alone. American government debt at the time of writing is $22 *trillion*. The meeting came in the same year of 1773 that saw the alliance formed between Rothschild and Jacob Frank and what followed was the creation of the Bavarian Illuminati by Sabbatian-Frankist Jesuit infiltrator and Freemason Adam Weishaupt. From the mid-19th century a series of German Ashkenazi (Khazar) Jewish (Sabbatian-Frankist) families emigrated to the United States and they would become the great banking dynasties that still largely prevail today with the Rothschilds holding the strings of all of them. They included Goldman, Sachs, Lehman and Warburg (the Venetian Jewish – Sabbatian-Frankist – del Banco family). The most important one of all across the late 19th and early 20th centuries would be lesser known to most people – Schiff. The Ashkenazi Sabbatian-Frankist rabbinical Schiff family shared the Rothschild home in Frankfurt and in 1875 Jacob Schiff (1847-1920) relocated to New York to join (and eventually head) the banking firm Kuhn, Loeb & Company. This was a front for the Rothschilds with Schiff as their loyal agent. Schiff became a dominant figure on Wall Street and a director of companies such as National City Bank of New York, Equitable Life Assurance Society, Wells Fargo & Company and Union Pacific Railroad. 'He' (the Rothschilds) funded the rise of the Rockefeller Standard Oil monopoly headed by J.D. Rockefeller; Andrew Carnegie's steel empire; J. P. Morgan's financial empire; and Harriman family railroad interests. All were really Rothschild-controlled operations through middleman Schiff and the Rothschilds remain in control of their modern versions. We see the same technique with global corporations, not least in Silicon Valley, which appear to be run by their famous faces when they are actually controlled from the shadows by a very different force. The Rothschilds, via Schiff, orchestrated through banker Paul Warburg the fraudulent creation in 1913 of the Federal Reserve Banking System, the still privately-owned 'Central Bank of the United States' which has controlled the American economy and government financial policy ever since. If you want to know the foundation origin of the $22 trillion debt then look no further than the Rothschild-controlled Federal Reserve (or 'the Fed'). For 31 years from 1987 to 2018 ultra-Zionists headed the Federal Reserve in the form of Alan Greenspan, Ben Bernanke and Janet Yellen. In the same period Yellen and the Israeli-American duel citizen, ultra-Zionist Stanley Fischer, former governor of the Bank of Israel, served as vice chairs of the 'Fed'. What are the statistical chances of that happening randomly from two percent of the American population? The sequence was broken when Jerome Powell replaced Yellen as chair – Powell was a partner in the Father Bush Carlyle Group while it was a financial agent for the Bin Laden family across 9/11. Today the vast ultra-Zionist network that I exposed manipulating American politics and society from within is ultimately controlled by Sabbatian-Frankists to advance their agenda. The mass of those involved with their ongoing childish shenanigans will have no idea that this is so. The same is true in the UK, Europe, Canada, Australia and wherever Sabbatian-Frankists are at work.

Sabbatian-Frankist 'Russian' Revolution

Jacob Schiff in true Rothschild fashion funded half the cost of the successful Japanese war against Russia in 1904 and 1905 (spending more than $4.5 billion by today's equivalent) as part of the effort to prepare Russia for the overthrow of the Romanov Tsars by the Lenin-Trotsky communist (*Marxist*) 'revolution' of 1917. Schiff was awarded the 'Second Order of the Treasure of Japan' medal in recognition of his pivotal role in securing that victory. In the years before the revolution Tsar Nicholas II, the last monarch of Russia, was undermined by the infamous Grigori Rasputin, a mystic and manipulator befriended by the Tsar and his family, and his views were the same as those of Sabbatian-Frankists. Gershom Scholem, Professor of Jewish Mysticism at Hebrew University, said: 'Rasputin, who played a major role in the Russian Revolutions, espoused a doctrine which was identical to that of the Frankists of "redemption through sin".' Zionism had been making ground in Russia and according to the *Encyclopedia Judaica* the Russian delegation accounted for one-third of all the delegates (66 out of 197) at the First Zionist Congress in Basle, Switzerland, in 1897. British-born Jacob Rothschild, 82 at the time of writing, said in a television interview that 'Zionism was primarily a movement from Eastern Europe'. One center for the emergence of Zionism was Prague in what is now the Czech Republic – a major centre for Sabbatian-Frankists going back to Jacob Frank. The year 1897 also saw Rothschild asset Jacob Schiff use his influence over outgoing US President Grover Cleveland to secure passage into America for Zionist and Communist Jews from Russia and elsewhere. Zionism is Rothschildism. This political movement masquerading as a 'race' has been the Sabbatian-Frankist infiltrators' vehicle for taking over the Jewish people worldwide and using them as a smokescreen and diversion on the way to global control. Thus we have today's 'anti-Semitism' industry and the Protection Racket. The Russian 'Revolution' was a version of the 'Arab Spring' which was made to look like a 'people's uprising' when it was actually financed and organised by banking families in the United States, Britain and Germany (i.e. the Rothschilds ultimately). Russian people suffered horrifically after the 'revolution' as Arabs have since their 'Spring'. In both cases this was the idea from the start. John Schiff, Jacob's grandson, said in the *New York Journal American* in 1949 that his New York-based grandfather gave some $20 million ($1 billion today) to fund the Russian Revolution. Rabbi Antelman said Schiff's Rothschild banking firm, Kuhn, Loeb, secured an immense return with 600 million roubles in one payment alone. A key player in the revolution was Ukrainian Jew Leon Trotsky (born Lev Davidovich Bronstein). He lived in New York before travelling to Russia to 'revolt'. He had $10,000 with him when he was stopped on the way by Canadian and British naval personnel – and that was in 1917. Another big funder of Trotsky was Britain's Lord Alfred Milner according to anti-Communist Russian general Arsene de Goulevitch. Milner just happened to be a big-time Rothschild frontman and head of the Round Table secret society who would be heavily involved in the 'Balfour Declaration' in 1917 through which the British government publicly-supported a Jewish homeland in Palestine. Vladimir Lenin, who was part-Jewish, was allowed to travel in an allegedly sealed train across Germany to Russia as part of the same plot to oust the Tsar. Yep, it was a people's revolution all right. Rabbi Antelman describes Lenin as 'a tool of the Illuminati monopoly capitalists'. According to *New World Encyclopedia* Allen Dulles, a Hidden Hand operative almost his entire life and longest-serving head of the CIA, reviewed and rejected Lenin's application for a visa to the United States while working at the US Embassy in Switzerland. Dulles also claimed that he had taken a phone call from Lenin at the embassy, but he 'didn't think the matter was urgent' and asked him to call back. The next day Lenin headed for his train and the revolution. With the limpet-close associations between the Dulles family and those funding the Revolution in the United States there was far more to this Dulles-Lenin story than we are told.

Most of those at the forefront of the communist regime that took over Russia in 1917 were 'Jewish' (I would say Sabbatian-Frankists). Rabbi Antelman said: 'Frankists appear to have dominated Eastern European radical circles' (from where the momentum for Zionism emerged). Trotsky was head of the brutal Red Army and chief of Soviet foreign affairs; Yakov Sverdlov (Solomon) was head of the Soviet government as chairman of the Central Executive Committee; Grigori Zinoviev (Radomyslsky) led the Communist International to expand the revolution to other countries. There were many other prominent 'Jews', too, when the Jewish population of Russia was no more than five percent. British journalist Robert Wilton confirmed these themes in his 1920 book *The Last Days of the Romanovs* when he studied official documents from the Russian government to identify the members of the Bolshevik ruling elite between 1917 and 1919. The Central Committee included 41 Jews among 62 members; the Council of the People's Commissars had 17 Jews out of 22 members; and *458* of the 556 most important Bolshevik positions between 1918 and 1919 were occupied by Jewish people. Only 17 were Russian. Then there were the 23 Jews among the 36 members of the vicious Cheka Soviet secret police established in 1917 who would soon appear all across the country. Professor Robert Service of Oxford University, an expert on 20th century Russian history, found evidence that Leon Trotsky had sought to make sure that Jews were enrolled in the Red Army and were disproportionately represented in the Soviet civil bureaucracy that included the Cheka which performed mass arrests, imprisonment and executions of 'enemies of the people'. A US State Department Decimal File (861.00/5339) dated November 13th, 1918, names Jacob Schiff and a list of ultra-Zionists as funders of the Russian Revolution leading to claims of a 'Jewish plot', but the key point missed by all is they were not 'Jews' – they were Sabbatian-Frankists. Britain's Winston Churchill made the same error by mistake *or otherwise*. He wrote in a 1920 edition of the *Illustrated Sunday Herald* that those behind the Russian revolution were part of a 'worldwide conspiracy for the overthrow of civilisation and for the reconstitution of society on the basis of arrested development, of envious malevolence, and impossible equality.' He continued:

> There is no need to exaggerate the part played in the creation of Bolshevism and in the actual bringing about of the Russian Revolution by these international and for the most part atheistical Jews. It is certainly a very great one; it probably outweighs all others. With the notable exception of Lenin, the majority of the leading figures are Jews. Moreover, the principal inspiration and driving power comes from the Jewish leaders.

Thus Tchitcherin, a pure Russian, is eclipsed by his nominal subordinate, Litvinoff, and the influence of Russians like Bukharin or Lunacharski cannot be compared with the power of Trotsky, or of Zinovieff, the Dictator of the Red Citadel (Petrograd), or of Krassin or Radek – all Jews. In the Soviet institutions the predominance of Jews is even more astonishing. And the prominent, if not indeed the principal, part in the system of terrorism applied by the Extraordinary Commissions for Combatting Counter-Revolution has been taken by Jews, and in some notable cases by Jewesses.

In the same way, Donald Rumsfeld was 'eclipsed by his nominal subordinate', the ultra-Zionist Paul Wolfowitz, in the Pentagon at the time of 9/11. What happened in Russia was not a Jewish revolution – many Jews would suffer the consequences. It was a Sabbatian-Frankist revolution to impose the Sabbatian-Frankist-created political creed and tyranny called Marxism. What Churchill calls 'the system of terrorism' applied against 'enemies of the Revolution' was a repeat of the Jacobin period of 'The Terror'. This is a constant theme in 'revolutions' of the Sabbatian-Frankist-Illuminati cult. Churchill's reference to 'atheistical Jews' fits the modus operandi of Sabbatian-Frankist interlopers. Marxism is an atheist creed and this was Sabbatian-Frankist Marxism manifesting as the Russian Revolution which in true Marxist style targeted religion including the Jewish one. A great irony in attacks on me by the ultra-Zionist hate group 'anti-Semitism' Protection Racket is an oft-quoted passage from my book *And The Truth Shall Set You Free* in which I say that the Russian Revolution was the work of a group of Jewish people together with non-Jewish people. This is sighted as proof of my 'anti- Semitism' when, as you see here, it is simply provable *fact* and when fact is no defence against condemnation we are living in a tyranny. *And The Truth Shall Set You Free* is the book in which I expose in detail support for the Nazi master race movement by the Bush, Harriman and Rockefeller families (with the Rothschilds) and its connection to Hitler's race purity 'expert' Ernst Rudin. My ultra-Zionist abusers never mention that. They must have forgot.

Sabbatian-Frankist Red Army

The Russian Red Army, the biggest killing machine in known human history, was the creation of Sabbatian-Frankists. Leon Trotsky was the head of the Red Army and the leading administrators were ultra-Zionists Aron Solts; Yakov Rappoport; Lazar Kogan; Matvei Berman; Genrikh Yagoda; and Naftaly Frenkel. The Red Army killed almost seven million Germans and millions more across Europe. Red Army soldiers murdered and tortured civilians wherever they went and were ordered to do so by their Sabbatian-Frankist leadership. They raped some two million German women and many more in Austria, Hungary,

Romania, Bulgaria, Poland, Czechoslovakia and Yugoslavia. They also raped women – most of them *Jewish* – who had been freed from Nazi concentration camps. The Red Army went on to terrorise Eastern Europe for decades. Ultra-Zionist Ilya Ehrenburg was the evil Soviet propagandist who distributed pamphlets ordering the Red Army to rape, torture and kill their millions of victims. Ehrenburg told them:

> If your part of the front is quiet and there is no fighting, then kill a German in the meantime ... if you have already killed a German, then kill another – there is nothing more amusing to us than a heap of German corpses.

> Kill! Kill! In the German race there is nothing but evil; not one among the living, not one among the yet unborn but is evil! Follow the precepts of Comrade Stalin. Stamp out the fascist beast once and for all in its lair! Use force and break the racial pride of these German women. Take them as your lawful booty. Kill! As you storm onward, kill, you gallant soldiers of the Red Army.

The Red Army took ultra-Zionist psychopath Ehrenburg at his word and this is how one young Russian officer described what happened day after day after day:

> Women, mothers and their children lie to the right and left along the route and in front of each of them stands a raucous armada of men with their trousers down. The women, who are bleeding or losing consciousness, get shoved to one side and our men shoot the ones who try to save their children.

Ilya Ehrenburg is celebrated by Zionism as a Jewish hero of the Russian Revolution and he is honoured in Yad Vashem, Israel's Holocaust history museum. At Israel's instigation Prime Minister Benjamin Netanyahu and Russian President Vladimir Putin opened the 'Victory Monument' in the Israeli city of Netanya in 2012 to celebrate the Red Army. Why would Israel honour this killing and raping machine of historical proportions? See above. The same mentality that created the Red Army and decreed its murdering, raping and torturing methods of operation has been in control of Israel since it was bombed into existence in 1948. Anyone surprised that it is committing genocide against Palestinians and treats them with such hatred and contempt? These people are not 'Jews'. They are fake Jews exploiting and hiding behind genuine ones and those they have enticed into their lair. While Trotsky made sure *fake* Jews under the control of the Sabbatian-Frankist cult were given the major role in the post-revolution Russian hierarchy the story was very different for the rank and file. Rabbi Antelman writes:

... born Jews such as Trotsky [cooperated] with Lenin in executing Jews, and ... Lenin's Jewish Section was even more severe than Lenin in closing synagogues and religious schools, and persecuting and murdering Rabbis and religious leaders.

You see it wasn't – and isn't – about 'Jews'. It is rather about Sabbatian-Frankists hiding within the Jewish and other communities posing as 'one of them'. This is why there is no contradiction between 'Jews' taking power or controlling power in Russia, Germany and Israel treating Jewish people with such violence and contempt. Most people will never have heard about the Zionist (Rothschild) dominance of the Russian Revolution and what followed because of the ultra-Zionist censorship networks. These are *facts*, not 'anti-Semitism'. For the latter to be so I would have to be saying that all Jewish people are the same as those I am calling out. I am *not* saying that – quite the opposite. Most Jewish communities around the world will not know about the background that I am summarising here and can be read in detail in other books. They are the ones who are blamed in the minds of many by actions in which they have played no part and of which they know nothing. If we are to protect human freedom for *everyone* these are facts that we cannot go on ignoring because their implications and connections are indivisible from current events. A dispatch in 1918 by the US ambassador to Russia, David R. Francis, said: 'The Bolshevik leaders here, most of whom are Jews and 90 percent of whom are returned exiles, care little for Russia or any other country but are internationalists and they are trying to start a worldwide social revolution.' William Oudendyke, Dutch Ambassador at the time, said something similar: 'Unless Bolshevism is nipped in the bud immediately, it is bound to spread in one form or another over Europe and the whole world as it is organized and worked by Jews who have no nationality, and whose one object is to destroy for their own ends the existing order of things.' This is straight from the Sabbatian-Frankist statement of intent and method of operation. Russian dissident writer Alexander Solzhenitsyn (1918-2008) spent eleven years in labour camps and exile. He was a hero to the Western Establishment for his opposition to Communism until he, too, pointed out the greatly disproportionate overrepresentation of Jewish people in key positions among the Bolshevik 'revolutionaries'. He wrote a two-volume work, *Two Hundred Years Together*, in which he called for both Russians and Russian Jews to take responsibility for their 'renegades' who supported the totalitarian communist regime. The 'renegades' and ultra-Zionist 'Bolshevik leaders' he was talking about were tools of the Sabbatian-Frankist *anti*-Jewish cult which indeed was – and is – pursuing 'worldwide social revolution' on the road to planned global dictatorship. Rabbi Marvin S. Antelman said this about the *Protocols of the Elders of Zion*, a highly controversial document that came to light in the early years of the 20th century and some allege to be detailing a Jewish plot for world domination:

> The Protocols alleged that there was a Jewish world conspiracy. The Czar was a virulent anti-Semite, but may have published the Protocols because he had a personal axe to grind with the Schiffs, the Warburgs and the Rothschild banking dynasties, who were already planning a revolution in Russia. Jacob Schiff was giving immense financial help to the Japanese against the Russians. He was decorated by the Mikado after the Russio-Japanese War. The question should be raised of Schiff, if he was such a loyal Jew, why did he finance the Japanese who caused the death of thousands of Jewish men who were used as cannon fodder for the Czar.

Answer – because he was a Sabbatian-Frankist cult member and they hate Jews. I'll have more about the *Protocols* in the next chapter. Antelman continues and invokes the big bad word, *conspiracy*:

> The truth of the matter was, as this book will point out, that there was a conspiracy, but it was neither Jewish, nor Catholic, nor Masonic. It involved people of all types of religious and national backgrounds. Side by side with the Schiffs, Warburgs and Rothschilds were the Morgans and the Rockefellers. With Trotsky were Lenin and Stalin.

This is the same conspiracy that American professor Carrol Quigley exposed in the 20th century with the same families and their agents and assets involved. Quigley (1910-1977) was a professor of history at Georgetown University in Washington DC for 35 years and taught Bill Clinton. He was an insider who revealed in *Tragedy and Hope* and *The Anglo-American Establishment* the existence of the Rothschild Round Table secret society that spawned the network of think tanks including the Council on Foreign Relations, Bilderberg Group, Club of Rome and Trilateral Commission. This is the same seamless intergenerational conspiracy that I have been exposing for 30 years along with a mountain of wider and deeper connections. We can see The Web at work when you connect the funding of the Russian Revolution by the Rothschilds and New York-based Jacob Schiff with other revolution funders I detailed earlier in the book – Skull and Bones initiates, Roland Harriman, Prescott Bush, Percy Rockefeller and their associates. They were all working as one team and their latter-day successors were the evil behind 9/11. Jacob Schiff's granddaughter, Dorothy Schiff, owned the *New York Post* for more than 40 years and his investment banker son Mortimer Schiff was an early leader of the Boy Scouts of America. Karenna Gore, daughter of global warming hoax frontman, Al Gore, married Andrew Schiff, Jacob's great, great grandson.

Sabbatian-Frankist Islam

Sabbatai Zevi's cult established in the 17th century is described as the biggest messianic movement in Jewish history since ancient times and he promised to return them to a homeland in Palestine. The promise was delivered by the Sabbatian-Frankist cult and ultra-Zionists in the 20th century. This was achieved in stages by infiltrating mainstream Judaism and other faiths and communities with Islam a crucial example. Zevi lived both in Palestine and in what is today's Republic of Turkey under the rule of the Islamic Ottoman Empire which took over the region in stages from the end of the 14th century to its demise in the 20th century. Zevi converted to Islam when the Sultan of the Ottoman Empire gave him the 'choice' between conversion, or torture and death. By now Zevi had a million Jewish followers believing he was the Messiah and although he lost some with his 'conversion' many also converted in the Ottoman Empire and others knew that all the 'conversions' were only agreed to stay alive. Zevi and his fake-conversion cult became known as 'Donmeh' (meaning 'to turn') and they were called 'crypto-Jews' who, while publicly converting to Islam, retained their Sabbatian beliefs. This did not mean *Jewish* beliefs, but the Sabbatian *inversion* of traditional Jewish beliefs. Zevi was rejected as the Messiah by traditional Judaism and he and his followers hid behind the fake conversions and traditional Judaism while practicing their Sabbatian-Frankism in secret. Even their children were not told about their family's real religion until they were old enough to keep the secret and this continues up to current times. A hidden satanic 'religion' was born which continues today as the Sabbatian-Frankist Death Cult manipulating world events to a specific end and this was the foundation force behind 9/11. Donmeh were forbidden to marry outside of their sect (the interbreeding families theme again) and they became an interloper religion or cult within Islam, mainstream Judaism and other religions. Donmeh bloodlines infiltrated royalty and aristocracy as they expanded into Western society. Jacob Frank lived and studied with the Donmeh in Turkey before launching his Frankist cult in Europe. The Sabbatian Donmeh method of operation was founded on infiltration and control of positions of religious and political influence. They became powerful in the politics and business of Salonica (today called Thessalonica or Thessaloniki in Greek Macedonia in the southern Balkans) which was a major centre for Freemasonry and the birthplace of the Young Turk movement which overthrew Ottoman Islamic rule in Turkey in the 1920s. Mustafa Kemal, more famously known as 'Atatürk', was a Donmeh Jew who played the role of frontman for the rebellion that led to the establishment of the Republic of Turkey in 1923 (see *Everything You Need To Know But Have*

Never Been Told). Atatürk was a Grand Orient Freemason in the Lodge Veritas in Salonica and a British agent in the breakup of the Ottoman Empire, according to Lord Patrick Kinross in his book, *Ataturk, The Rebirth of a Nation*. The end of the Ottoman Empire was essential to the planned establishment of Israel because Palestine had long been under Ottoman rule.

The Donmeh 'interloper Jewish' cult infiltrated Islam and eventually manifested as the Saudi 'Royal' family and the extreme British-Saudi version of Islam known as Wahhabism. This is the religion of extreme suppression of women and beheading non-believers and 'infidels'. Western/Saudi-funded, armed and trained terrorist groups like ISIS are its most famous manifestations along with the fascistic Saudi state itself. Wahhabism set the new blueprint for how Islam is perceived both by many of its followers and the wider global public. From this came the perception that Islam is about death and destruction. In fact, like every other religion, it is the chosen *interpretation* of Koranic texts – what you emphasise and what you ignore – that drives your actions. This is what dictates if Islam is a peaceful religion or a violent one and the great majority of Muslims are not violent. I don't support any religion because I think they are all prisons of the mind, but these points need to be made to ensure some balance. On my trips to the Middle East I remember only kind people willing to share with visitors what little they had no matter what your personal beliefs. By contrast Wahhabism is anything but kind. It is a brutal, merciless, deeply psychopathic and supremacist creed that appropriately mirrors in its mind-set the Sabbatian-Frankist Death Cult. There is a reason for this. I tell the story of the Donmeh cult and its connection to Saudi Arabia in *Everything You Need To Know But Have Never Been Told* and see that book for more detail. Many in the Islamic world are well aware of who the House of Saud interloper 'royals' and architects of Wahhabism really are. Muhammad ibn Abd al-Wahhab, a Donmeh Jew hiding within Islam, was chosen by the British Empire in the 18th century to front-up a new extreme version of Islam and the British forged an alliance between Wahhab and Muhammad bin Saud who created the first Saudi state before he died in 1765. Bin Saud's successors formed the current Saudi Arabia with their British and American controllers in 1932 and in doing so hijacked the major centres of Islamic belief in Mecca and Medina. Wahhab's daughter married Bin Saud's son. Head-chopping Wahhabism spawned head-chopping ISIS and terrorist al-Qaeda (via the CIA) and the Sabbatian-Frankist cult had a home-grown terrorist 'problem' that it could falsely blame for 9/11 and justify a 'war on terror' against the very groups it had created. Saudi royals' are Donmeh 'crypto-Jews' as many Islamic writers have attested. An Iraqi intelligence report includes Arabic texts saying that Abd al-Wahhab and Muhammad bin Saud were Jewish (Sabbatian-Frankist

Dönmeh) and it sources the following from an Arabic work by D. Mustafa Turan called *The Donmeh Jews*:

> Muhammad Bin 'Abd-al-Wahhab is a descendent of a family from the Jews of Al-Dunamah in Turkey. Al-Dunmah [Donmeh] refers to the Jews who declared their embracement of Islam in an effort to insult Islam and to escape the pursuit by the Ottoman sultans ... [Turan] confirms that Sulayman; the grandfather of [Wahhab], is (Shulman); he is a Jew from the merchants of the city of Burstah in Turkey, he had left it and settled in Damascus, grew his beard, and wore the Muslim turban, but was thrown out for being voodoo.

> Then he fled to Egypt and he [was] faced [with] strong objection so he left to Hijaz and settled in Al-Ayniyyah where he got married and had a child whom he called Abd-al-Wahab and claimed to be from the descent of Rabi'iyyah, and that he was born in Morocco.

This would explain the otherwise unexplainable closeness between Saudi Arabia and Israel when you would have thought they would be in fierce opposition. The alliance largely happened behind the scenes until more recently when it came to the surface with the installation by Israel and America of Saudi Crown Prince Mohammed bin Salman in 2017 who proceeded to take over the reins of power in Saudi Arabia from the official king. Salman became known as 'Mr Everything' because of his control of the economy, military, foreign affairs, oil and entertainment. He was at the centre of the grotesque murder of Saudi dissident journalist (and one-time Saudi establishment supporter) Jamal Khashoggi at the Saudi consulate in Istanbul, Turkey, in 2018. If you want an example of the psychopathic mentality behind world events look no further than this. Turkish Foreign Minister Mevlut Cavusoglu said he personally listened to an audio recording of the killers being told to listen to music while they dismembered Khashoggi with a bonesaw while he was still alive. 'I listened to it. He was killed within seven minutes', Cavusoglu told Germany's *Suddeutsche Zeitung*. He said one of the killers commented that he 'liked to cut people up'. Would someone with that mentality give a damn about 3,000 people killed on 9/11 or would they get high on such slaughter? This is the mentality behind 9/11 and world events in general.

Crown Prince Psychopath

Salman has also been the architect of the war against Yemen which produced the world's biggest humanitarian crisis using weapons supplied by America, Britain, France and others. By early 2019 this was Yemen in figures: 360,000 dead from malnutrition; 80,000 children dead from starvation; 20 million on the brink of starvation; 16 million lacked access to water and sanitation; a cholera outbreak had infected an estimated 1.2 million; tens of thousands dead from airstrikes two-thirds of which the United Nations High Commissioner for Human Rights said were by the Saudi-led 'coalition' of Arab state psychopaths supported by US, UK and other Western psychopaths. Never lose sight of the fact that we are dealing with a Death Cult that is sexually-stimulated by death and suffering. The number of Yemini dead from direct attacks passed 60,000 by the end of 2018 with the rate increasing by some 2,000 a month. For the psychopaths involved this enters multiple orgasm territory. The same people who promote and fuel this human catastrophe against Muslim civilians had the outrageous nerve to condemn with their fake moral piety the gun attack on Muslims in New Zealand (Fig 116). They have no shame. Overwhelming support from the American and British governments for the evil Saudi regime comes from the fact that the House of Saud is a Western front and those that control Saudi

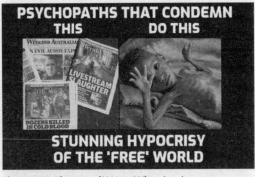

Figure 116: The 'moral' West. When it suits us we condemn mass murder and when it suits us we support it.

Arabia and Israel are members of the same Sabbatian-Frankist satanic cult and family network. Prince Khalid Bin Farhan al-Saud, a Saudi prince who defected from the family in 2013 because he was sick of their behaviour, has said publicly that the US and Israel control the Saudi 'royals' and that he knew from inside the family that the US and Israel had set 'conditions' for 'helping' current Saudi king, Salman bin Abdulaziz Al Saud, succeed his father in 2015. Two others higher up the order of succession conveniently died in 2011 and 2012. The defector prince said that in return for this 'help' King Salman had to agree to 'absolute obedience' to the US and Israel and work to settle all Gaza Palestinians in north Sinai (to be paid for by the Saudis and UAE), destroy Palestinian group Hamas and secure ownership of Sanafir Island from Egypt. The latter would change the Gulf of Aqaba from Egyptian territorial waters to international waters for the benefit of Israeli shipping operating out of the port of Eilat and into the Red Sea (Fig 117). Egypt's president and US-Israel placeman Abdul Fattah al-Sisi secured power for his military government thanks to the Soros-funded and manipulated 'Arab Spring'. Sisi and King Salman obeyed orders and transferred ownership of Sanafir Island and neighbouring Tiran Island in 2017 to Saudi Arabia against the will of the Egyptian people.

Ironically, Israel had to give its permission for the transfer because the islands were part of an earlier peace agreement between Egypt and Israel. I bet the Israeli authorities had a good laugh about that. The installation of Crown Prince Mohammed bin Salman has made King Salman nothing more than a symbolic figure and the media has reported on efforts by the Crown Prince and Egyptian leader Sisi to have closer relations with Israel. Both are puppets of the Sabbatian-Frankists working to stitch-up the Palestinians. We can now see why the home of the bloodthirsty Wahhabi religion would fund and arm Wahhabi terrorist groups like al-Qaeda and ISIS/Islamic State along with

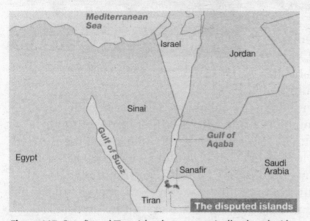

America, Britain and Israel (collectively The Web) to create mayhem (the 'problem') in the Middle East to which they could offer the 'solution' (a Western military presence serving the agenda of Israel). Intelligence Colonel Sa'id Mahrnud Najrn Al-'Arniri, who wrote the Iraqi intelligence document which I detail in *Everything You Need To Know*,

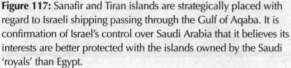

Figure 117: Sanafir and Tiran islands are strategically placed with regard to Israeli shipping passing through the Gulf of Aqaba. It is confirmation of Israel's control over Saudi Arabia that it believes its interests are better protected with the islands owned by the Saudi 'royals' than Egypt.

said that the enemies of Islam use the Wahhabi religion in the political arena 'to prevent the unity of Muslims'. He continued:

> Al-Wahabi today is subconsciously working in all its power on promoting occupation in order to achieve its despicable desires. The Wahabis have worn the Muslim robe inside out therefore; they couldn't apprehend any of the Muslim goals, because how is it possible for someone who seeks the help of infidels to speak of unity?

> They sign treaties of peace and friendship with the criminals, surrender and bow in front of the masters of rotten politics. Therefore; I wanted in my study to focus on the history of this movement from the stand point of its relation with the British government and how Britain had employed all its spies in Muslim countries in order to establish and spread this movement to destroy Muslim religion and create heterodoxies in Islam.

The involvement in 9/11 of Saudi Arabia-connected alleged 'hijackers' alongside Hidden Hand elements in the United States and ultra-Zionist Israel (much more to come) now takes on a new light, significance and clarity. They are on the same team (Fig 118). Saudi government funding of Islamic schools in Sweden is also connected to what ultra-Zionist academic Barbara Lerner Spectre said about Zionists being at the forefront of transforming European culture with 'multiculturalism'. Swedish daily *Svenska Dagbladet* reported that Saudi Arabia has for a long time spread ultra-conservative (Sabbatian-Frankist) Wahhabism or Salafism in Sweden

Figure 118: Different names – same masters.

and the same is happening in Germany (where there are thousands of mosques) and elsewhere. The Swedish Defense College said there are 18 registered foundations in Sweden – and counting – with the stated goal of promoting the building of mosques. Sweden is committing cultural and genetic suicide while calling it 'compassion'. Sabbatian-Frankists are global masters at manipulating genuineness that isn't streetwise. The reason Saudi Arabia and Israel are so close when you would think the very opposite would be the case is that both are controlled by Sabbatian-Frankists – the same with the United States, Britain, France, Germany, Canada, Australia and a long list of other countries affecting the direction of human society. No wonder ultra-Zionist Jared Kushner, Trump's son-in-law and 'senior advisor', a life-long friend of Benjamin Netanyahu, was reported to be urging the administration not to punish Saudi Arabia and its Sabbatian-Frankist Crown Prince Salman over the psychopathically-disgusting murder of Jamal Khashoggi when Salman clearly instigated what happened. Sabbatian-Frankists work as one unit towards their collective goal of global domination and watch each other's back on the way unless cutting them loose would benefit the agenda.

In summary

A Hidden Hand has been at work for thousands of years with the aim of transforming human society into a centrally-controlled tyranny by concentrating power in a world government and creating a one-world everything. This would demand a single global government, army, religion and 'culture' which would mean deleting the concept of nations and countries and creating a single fused 'blob' culture underpinned by the interbreeding of individual races to develop racial fusion. A world army and control of the media was planned to impose this agenda either directly when necessary or through the manipulation of perception and what is now called political correctness, 'hate speech' and 'fake news' to silence debate and exposure of what was happening. Control of money was also essential to dictate and limit choice of the target population and thus freedom. A focal point of the Hidden Hand from the 17th century has been the satanic cult that I am calling Sabbatian-Frankism which is the continuation of the ongoing satanic human sacrifice and child-abuse religion of Babylon under another name. Much older secret societies such as the Knights of Malta (under different names) and Knights Templar, established in the 11th and 12th centuries, were founded on the Babylonian religion and the same 'Hebrew' (Babylonian) Kabballah of esoteric and mystical 'magic' that 'inspires' the Sabbatian-Frankists pursuing the outcomes desired by the same Hidden Hand. This explains why the Knights Templar (since the 12th century) and Sabbatian-Frankists (since the 17th century) have had the ambition to rebuild 'Solomon's Temple' on the current site of the Al-Aqsa Mosque at al-Haram al-Sharif/Temple Mount in Jerusalem. To the Knights Templar and Sabbatian-Frankists 'King Solomon' was an occult magician of the Kabballah religion and rebuilding 'his' temple is nothing whatsoever to do with Jewish people in general who are pawns in a game they have been manipulated not to see. The cult is not 'Jewish' but satanic. This is what unites them and not some perceived 'Jewish plot' which is a smokescreen behind which the cult can take essential cover.

Jewish communities and the official Jewish religion around the world have been infiltrated and exploited by Sabbatian-Frankists who have absolute contempt for non-Sabbatian-Frankists. The cult hijacked much of Judaism while following in secret a very different Kabbalistic psychopathic creed involving Satanism, paedophilia and the manipulation of war and suffering in pursuit of their unspeakably evil desire for control. Rabbi Antelman writes that Sabbatian-Frankist mysticism was known as the 'red Kabbalah' and provides the philosophical basis for 'the international occult neo-Frankist Cult of the All-Seeing Eye' (Fig 119).The Kabbalah, occultism, witchcraft and

Figure 119: The Sabbatian-Frankist symbol of the All-Seeing Eye on the US dollar shining ('illuminated') above the occult-significant 13 levels of the pyramid. The lower Latin words mean 'New Order of the Ages' or 'New World Order' – a long time code-name for the Hidden Hand Sabbatian-Frankist agenda to transform and control human society.

Satanism go hand in hand, he said. Antelman contends in *To Eliminate the Opiate* that the Jewish Reform and Conservative movements, which both emerged in the 19th century, are Sabbatian-Frankist stalking horses for the fracturing and demise of traditional Judaism. Professor Gershom Scholem at Hebrew University concluded the same. Antelman said that the instigators of these movements could be traced back to the Sabbatian families of Europe and he described how Rothschild operative Jacob Schiff and the Rothschilds themselves played a prominent role in the development of both movements along with the Warburgs. Antelman writes that funding fraudulent seminary fronts to create fraudulent Sabbatian-Frankist 'rabbis' was part of the plan:

> The Conservative movement by its very existence, perpetuates the lie that they are a branch of Judaism when, indeed, they are anti-Judaic. Their members are, nevertheless, invariably Jews. The problem is that since their conversions are fraudulent, counterfeit rabbis take authentic Christians and convert them to counterfeit Jews ... Perhaps accurately their members are duped into being 'Jews for Satan'.

What is called Christian Zionism, one of the foundation promoters of ultra-Zionism in the United States, was created by Sabbatian-Frankists in their infiltration of Christianity. Remember how the unofficial Rothschild, Phillip Eugene de Rothschild, said he was designated by the Rothschild hierarchy to be an infiltrator of the Christian Church – classic Sabbatian-Frankism. The term 'Christian Zionist' was reportedly first used by Theodor Herzl, the 'father of modern political Zionism', at the First Zionist Congress in 1897. Most Christian Zionists are evangelical Protestants and they include superstar evangelists like Jerry Falwell and Pat Robertson. They believe that Jews must relocate to Israel for the Book of Revelation 'Armageddon' End Times when Jesus returns, presumably on a cloud if biblical texts are to be believed. Trump's Israel-worshipping Vice President Mike Pence and Secretary of State Mike Pompeo are Christian Zionists – and war warmongers and regime-changers who must have missed the lines about turning the other cheek and not coveting their neighbour's ass. To be fair to them it doesn't say anything about oil. I don't know what will happen when the Christian Messiah and the Jewish Messiah tussle for power on their mutual return. My own view is that Jesus will have his work cut out. It may be a double-dose of nonsense but the calculated development of Christian Zionism aligning itself with messianic Judaism has led to a crucial well of support and finance for the ultra-Zionist agenda especially from the southern states of America. It has also paved the way for Sabbatian-Frankist infiltration into America's government and heartlands. There is much that Rabbi Antelman and I would not have agreed on. However, in the subject areas where I quote him we are absolutely on the same page. I don't follow any form of Judaism or Islam, Christianity, Hinduism or any other religion and that's not the point. Understanding *why* this infiltration and destruction of religion and human society are happening is the point. Religion served the interests of human control for a long time through perceptual control and divide and rule, but in the 'One World' dictatorship they want only one religion – Sabbatian-Frankism.

Exposing The Web

The hidden power and reach of the Death Cult explains why tiny Israel has so much global influence and why so many people *appearing* to be Jewish occupy positions of control and influence from 0.2 percent of the world population. The French 'Revolution', American 'Revolution', Russian 'Revolution' and so many more have been Sabbatian-Frankist 'revolutions' to transform, hijack and control those societies. Most replaced one form of tyranny with another which was much harder to see because it called itself 'liberty' and 'democracy' or, in Russia's case, overthrew the dominance of the Tsars for the dominance of the Politburo. Sabbatian-Frankists play the long game and now look how the long fought-for 'liberties' of America and other apparently 'free' countries are being deleted. If chains on your hands and feet are replaced by a new restraining device there is a short time between the two when your hands and feet appear to be free. This is the short window we have been experiencing in the West during the transition from one form of control to another far more virulent and permanent one via technology which I will highlight in the final chapters. Several rabbis over the years have realised what is happening and tried to alert both the Jewish population and the world in general although with limited success because of the Sabbatian-Frankist domination of mainstream media and communication in general. This is even more so today with ultra-Zionist-controlled censorship fronts in Silicon Valley like Google and Facebook having an increasingly monopolistic control over who sees what and the gathering book-banning by Amazon now it has secured the dominance in book publishing and distribution that it was created to achieve. In early 2019 Amazon banned multiple books about the dangers of vaccines, alternative treatments for vaccine-caused autism and withdrew from Amazon Prime documentaries such as *Vaxxed: From Cover-Up to Catastrophe.* Meanwhile, the Sabbatian-Frankist Big Pharma cartel can say what it likes and Amazon thinks it's fine to sell child sex dolls and baby clothes with slogans such as 'Daddy's little fuck toy' and 'I just look illegal'. The *only* criteria for such decisions is this: Does it serve the agenda that Amazon represents or expose it?

Those who say the global conspiracy is a 'Jewish plot' are missing the deeper truth and making life easier for the Sabbatian-Frankists by pointing at the wrong villain. The destruction and absorption of Judaism and Jewishness is only one front in the Sabbatian-Frankist satanic war on the world. Agents and activists of this interbreeding cult have infiltrated all religions (to ultimately delete them) and controlled global finance and corporations to enslave the target population in debt and dependency. They have bought and hijacked so much of the mainstream media, not least in satanic Hollywood, and dictated political policy from the shadows through donations and other manipulation. Covertly instigating wars and then funding all sides to the desired end is a speciality and you will see the evidence I will soon present that Sabbatian-Frankists were the real force behind 9/11 which, in turn, has led to so many wars. The Web is what connects outward 'Jews' like William Kristol and Robert Kagan, co-founders of the Project for the New American Century, and non-Jews like Dick Cheney, Donald Rumsfeld and John Bolton. Others only 'find out' about their Jewish backgrounds when they have secured public office. Madeleine Albright, Bill Clinton's 'we think killing half a million Iraqi children is worth it' Secretary of State, had 'a shock' while in office to find that she comes from a Jewish background which she wasn't aware of (lie). Michael Dobbs of *The Washington Post* reported that Albright's parents were Jewish converts to Catholicism (a classic Sabbatian-Frankist theme) and that she had lost three of her grandparents and other close relatives in the Holocaust. Albright would call this 'obviously a major surprise'. Strange then that it was subsequently revealed that she had received letters years before – including one from the mayor of her father's hometown – revealing all this. Skull and Bones John Kerry, Obama's Secretary of State and a presidential candidate in 2004 against Skull and Bones Boy Bush, had the same surprise news. Israeli newspaper *Haaretz* reported:

> Senator John Kerry, with his mother's New England patrician pedigree and his Irish last name actually has a grandfather who was born a Jew in the former Austro-Hungarian Empire. The news was a revelation to Kerry himself, who only found out about his Jewish roots while running in the 2004 presidential election.

The 'elite' are obsessed with their family histories yet neither Kerry or Albright knew this? Oh, please. A declassified document released in 2015 by the US National Security Archive and the Center for Non-proliferation Studies at the Middlebury Institute of International Studies in Monterey revealed that Kerry's father, Richard Kerry, then a US embassy official in Oslo, played a role in the covert sale of Norwegian heavy water to Israel (through the United Kingdom) for Israel's nuclear programme under a secret agreement made in 1959. Kerry's paternal grandfather, officially known as Frederick A. Kerry, was actually born Fritz Kohn in what today is the Czech Republic before changing his name ahead of emigration to the United States a century ago. The politician's grandparents converted from Judaism to Catholicism at the turn of the 20th century. Many Jewish families changed their names when they crossed the Atlantic. Rabbi Antelman described the mode of operation employed by Sabbatian-Frankists in the United States today which will be mightily important when we return directly to who was behind 9/11:

> The Frankists today no longer call themselves by that name. The organisation has grown into an international group labelled by outsiders as the Cult of the All-Seeing Eye ... They have expanded from Judaism, Islam and Christianity to six religions, adding on Buddhism, Confucianism and Hinduism as well.

> In the United States they are most active in Boston, New York, Washington and San Francisco. Their ranks and sponsors include some very famous people, numbering diplomats, senators, governors and clergymen in their ranks ... in Jewish circles, they dominate the Reform movement at many levels and the Conservative movement at the highest level.

Antelman added that Sabbatian-Frankists dominate the Anti-Defamation League (ADL) and its creator B'nai B'rith, the self-appointed 'voice of Jewish people'. Both have tried many times to silence me. He said that B'nai B'rith was founded in New York by twelve Jewish-born German Sabbatian Bundists who emigrated to the United States in the 19th century and by 1860 already had 50 lodges. Antelman named other Sabbatian-Frankist fronts as the American Jewish Congress, Federations of Jewish Charities in many American cities and a clique within in the National Lawyers Guild. Two techniques employed to protect the common identity of Sabbatian-Frankists is for advocates to attack each other in public to give the illusion of separateness and different opinions and to condemn aspects of the Death Cult's agenda while secretly working to that end. The foundation technique of the cult is to set the human population at war with itself in every area of society while it pulls the strings of all sides from the shadows.

Look at the world. I rest my case.

CHAPTER 21

Completing the job

There is not a crime, there is not a dodge, there is not a trick, there is not a swindle, there is not a vice which does not live by secrecy
– Joseph Pulitzer

Sabbatai Zevi promised his followers they would 'return' to their Jewish homeland on the alleged site of ancient Israel and this ambition was pursued to ultimate success by the Death Cult. Jewish people have been sold the lie about their connections to this land and their 'historic right' to ownership and many gave their support to the Sabbatian-Frankists who they believed were regular Jews like themselves; but they weren't 'Jews' in that sense – only crypto ones hiding within Judaism as they have hidden within Christianity, Islam and other religions.

Israeli historian Shlomo Sand said that before the 19th century Jews thought of themselves as people who shared a common religion and not a common racial history. Jewish intellectuals in [Rothschild] Germany then began to retrospectively invent just such a mythical history about a 'Kingdom of David' and a racial connection back to biblical Israel, Sand said. He writes that until the advent of Zionism in the 19th century most Jews did not consider a return to the 'Promised Land'. This was underpinned by their religious belief that they were banned by God from retuning to Jerusalem until the Jewish messiah came and for this reason many orthodox Jews vehemently oppose Zionism and the State of Israel today through organisations such as Neturei Karta (Fig 120). Among the intellectuals to which Sand refers was Heinrich Graetz (1817-1891) who wrote the multi-volume *History of the Jews from Oldest Times to the Present*. Graetz joined the Proto-Zionist movement, the forerunner of Zionism, and it is no accident that just as a mythical Jewish racial history and connection to ancient Israel was starting to be promoted that the Sabbatian-Frankist House of Rothschilds was developing the political philosophy of Zionism founded on the right of Jewish people worldwide to seize their 'historic right' to the land of Palestine. The 'academic' promotion of this 'historical right' and the political demand to act on this 'historic right' were incredibly symbiotic and clearly not random chance. British Foreign Secretary Lord Palmerston wrote in 1840

Figure 120: Not all Jews are Zionists, even fewer are ultra-Zionists and still fewer Sabbatian-Frankists.

to the British Ambassador in the Islamic Turkey-based Ottoman Empire which then controlled Palestine:

There exists at the present time among the Jews dispersed over Europe, a strong notion that the time is approaching when their nation is to return to Palestine ... It would be of manifest importance to the Sultan to encourage the Jews to return and settle in Palestine because the wealth which they would bring with them would increase the resources of the Sultan's dominions; and the Jewish people, if returning under the sanction and protection, and at the invitation of the Sultan, would be a check upon any future evil designs of Mehmet Ali [of Egypt] or his successor ... I have to instruct Your Excellency strongly to recommend [to the Ottoman government] to hold out every just encouragement to the Jews of Europe to return to Palestine.

What is most relevant and significant about that statement is the background to the man who made it. Lord Palmerston was Grand Patriarch of Grand Orient Freemasonry, the elite version controlled by Sabbatian-Frankism. Palmerston was also prime minister during the 19th century Opium Wars against China when the British Empire sought to get the Chinese hooked on the drug to destroy the country and take control. Sabbatian-Frankist global drug networks continue to operate today and this was the cartel served by Father George Bush and Bill Clinton and by the activities I have described at Venice Airport in Florida where 9/11 'hijackers' attended the flying schools and 'Mohamed Atta' is reported to have flown planes on drug trafficking routes.

Sabbatian-Frankist Zionism

The clearly orchestrated campaign to secure control of Palestine under the fake guise of 'historic rights' continued to build throughout the 19th century both politically and in terms of 'academics' and 'historians' delivering the fraudulent narrative. This culminated at the end of the century with the establishment by the Rothschilds of *Zionism* – Zion was a hill once outside Jerusalem and now within the modern city. This *political movement*, opposed by many Jews and rabbis at the time, was officially launched by Austro-Hungarian journalist Theodor Herzl and encouraged the relocation of Jews from Europe to Ottoman-controlled Palestine where Jewish settlements began to appear. Such was German Jewish hostility to Zionism that the first Zionist Congress in 1897 was moved from its planned location in Munich to Basle, Switzerland. Jews in general did not want to move to Palestine because they preferred to stay in Germany. This mind-set didn't really change until the Nazis came to power in the 1930s with all that followed. Theodor Herzl was the 'founding father of Zionism' who acted more like a Sabbatian-Frankist in that what Jewish people in general wanted was of no importance – what he (and his masters) wanted was all that mattered. He suggested at one time that Austrian Jews mass-convert to Catholicism to overcome 'anti-Semitism' and his vision of Israel was a state in which what was perceived as Jewishness, including religion, was thrust to the margins. A rabbi reprimanded him for celebrating the Christian Christmas with a Christmas tree and he refused to have his son, Hans, circumcised. Hans later became a Baptist minister before becoming a Catholic and shooting himself at the age of 39. Herzl categorised Jewish people as two types – 'rich Jews' and 'poor Jews'. He saw 'anti-Semitism' as an ally in using fear to bring Jews into line – his line. Ultra-Zionists are still using the same technique today and if there is not enough 'anti-Semitism' they invent it, not least by constantly widening the definition. Herzl said: An excellent idea enters my mind – to attract outright anti-Semites and make them destroyers of Jewish wealth.' Israeli students were asked on video who they thought had said those words and they all replied 'Adolf Hitler'. But, no – it was the 'founding father of Zionism'. Herzl wrote in the German newspaper, *Deutsche Zeitung*:

> The wealthy Jews rule the world. In their hands lies the fate of governments and nations. They start wars between countries and, when they wish, governments make peace. When the wealthy Jews sing, the nations and their leaders dance along and meanwhile the Jews get richer.

Herzl would have been way into 'anti-Semite' territory today with that. British Jewish writer Leon Rosselson rightly said that the quote could have come from the 'Jewish plot' document known as *The Protocols of the Elders of Zion*. 'So what is going on here?' he asked. What indeed? Rosselson wrote of Herzl:

> Like many educated, German-speaking Jews, he had nothing but contempt for the mass of religious, Torah-abiding, Yiddish-speaking, shtetl-dwelling Eastern European Jews. There is nothing in his writings to suggest that he had any great attachment to Judaism or much interest in or knowledge of Judaic teaching.

Balfour (Rothschild) 'delares'

Some early Zionist advocates only wanted a homeland and not necessarily one in Palestine. Countries such as Uganda and Argentina were discussed and Theodor Herzl was okay with this at first before committing himself to Palestine with the publication of his pamphlet *Judenstaat* (*The Jews' State* or *The Jewish State*) in 1896. The original title – very appropriately – was *Address to the Rothschilds*. Herzl called for an independent Jewish state to be established during the 20th century and encouraged the buying of land in Palestine although Argentina still wasn't ruled out at this point. The World Zionist Organization was founded at the Basle congress with Herzl at its head and the path to control Palestine began to open thanks to Rothschild money. Baron Edmond de Rothschild (1845-1934) of the French House funded the relocation of Russian Jews to Palestine in the 1880s, built homes, a Hebrew University, drained swamps and dug wells and generally promoted a 'return to the homeland'. As always with the Rothschilds they demanded control of Jewish settlements and established a structure of administration which still calls the shots in Israel today. English Rothschilds, too, were central to the establishment of Israel. Sabbatian-Frankists manipulated events that led to the First World War with the Rothschilds as usual funding all sides and the war was exploited to secure the 'Balfour Declaration' in 1917 in which British Foreign Secretary Lord Arthur Balfour pledged support of the British government to a Jewish homeland in Palestine. This was a pivotal moment in the plan with Britain still an empire with much overt global influence (it's covert today). The term 'declaration' sounds like a speech, but the Balfour Declaration was a letter to Lord Lionel Walter Rothschild (1868-1937), the unofficial leader of the British Jewish community, who would go on to become President of the Board of Deputies of British Jews which led the assault on the UK Labour Party in 2018 to accept the new ridiculously wide definition of 'anti-Semitism'. Balfour said in his 'Declaration' on November 2nd, 1917:

> His Majesty's Government view with favour the establishment in Palestine of a national home for the Jewish people, and will use their best endeavours to facilitate the achievement of this object, it being clearly understood that nothing shall be done which may prejudice the civil and religious rights of existing non-Jewish communities in Palestine, or the rights and political status enjoyed by Jews in any other country.

Mainstream history records the 'Declaration' without the essential background. The Rothschilds established the UK-based secret society called the Round Table in the latter years of the 19th century just as they were launching Zionism. The first head of the Round Table was

Rothschild agent Cecil Rhodes who plundered southern Africa on their behalf for gold and diamonds and entrapped black Africans in apartheid regimes in South Africa and Rhodesia (later Zimbabwe) by manipulating tribes into wars with each other that allowed the 'British Empire' (Rothschild Empire by now) to take control of those lands and resources. No wonder that Rothschild-controlled Israel would be exposed for supporting the white apartheid South African government in a number of ways including surveillance of anti-apartheid activists by the Rothschild Anti-Defamation League (ADL). Rhodes died in 1902 and left money to fund 'Rhodes Scholarships' for carefully-selected students who were planned to be Sabbatian-Frankist assets (knowingly or unknowingly) to attend Oxford University. Bill Clinton would be one recipient. Rhodes was replaced as Round Table chief by banker and Rothschild lackey Lord Alfred Milner who, as I mentioned earlier, was a big financial supporter of Leon Trotsky according to anti-Communist Russian general Arsene de Goulevitch. This was the same Trotsky supported by Rothschild agent Jacob Schiff out of New York. The letter that became known as the 'Balfour Declaration' was sent by Lord Balfour, an inner-circle initiate of the Round Table, to Lord Rothschild, funder and creator of the Round Table, and was almost certainly written by Round Table leader Lord Milner. Balfour's 'Declaration' was a Rothschild scam to advance the agenda of a homeland for 'Jews' (Sabbatian-Frankism) in Palestine by winning the crucial public support of the Rothschild-controlled British government. The Round Table would go on to spawn those series of think tanks to further that advancement including: the Royal Institute of International Affairs ('Chatham House') in London in 1920; the Council on Foreign Relations established by Sabbatian-Frankists including Rothschild agent Jacob Schiff in 1921 which has driven 'American' (Sabbatian-Frankism) foreign policy from that day to this in league with other organisations in the network; the Bilderberg Group had its first meeting at the Bilderberg Hotel in the Netherlands in 1954; the Trilateral Commission came in 1972 and was the work of Sabbatian-Frankist David Rockefeller and Hidden Hand agent Zbigniew Brzezinski who was President Carter's National Security Advisor and bragged about arming, training and funding the Mujahidin in Afghanistan which morphed into 'al-Qaeda'; and the Club of Rome in 1968 was created specifically to exploit environmental concerns to justify a transformation of global society and from this has come the hoax about human-caused 'global warming' which is indeed being used to transform the way people live, work and are governed. These organisations operating as one unit through the Round Table network and The Web gather together politicians, government administrators, bankers, corporate representatives, intelligence operatives, military and media people to form a common

(Sabbatian-Frankist) policy. Some are invited for short-term goals who have no idea of the real background and others like Henry Kissinger and the late David Rockefeller have spanned the decades. The Balfour Declaration was the turning point for Zionism and the homeland of Palestinians was now destined for takeover. The line in the letter about it being clearly understood that 'nothing shall be done which may prejudice the civil and religious rights of existing non-Jewish communities in Palestine' was a joke and only inserted to placate opposition. Minutes of the British War Cabinet led by Prime Minister Lloyd George dated July 18th, 1917, tell a different story:

> H. M. Government, after considering the aims of the Zionist Organisation, accepts the principle of recognising Palestine as the National Home of the Jewish people and the right of the Jewish people to build up its National life in Palestine under a protection to be established at the conclusion of Peace, following upon the successful issue of the war.

> H. M. Government regards as essential for the realisation of this principle the grant of internal autonomy to the Jewish nationality in Palestine, freedom of immigration for Jews, and the establishment of a Jewish National Colonising Corporation for the re-settlement and economic development of the country.

> The conditions and forms of the internal autonomy and a charter for the Jewish National Colonising Corporation should, in the view of H. M. Government, be elaborated in detail and determined with the representatives of the Zionist Organisation.

The Balfour Declaration came in the same month that the Sabbatian-Frankist Russian Revolution broke out and a massive transformation was underway in Eastern and Western Europe that would be central to the emergence of a Jewish homeland 30 years later. There was indeed only five days between Balfour's 'declaration' and the start of the Russian Revolution.

World-changing war

At the end of the Sabbatian-Frankist-manipulated First World War in which the Rothschilds funded all sides the 'victorious' countries met near Paris at the Versailles Peace Conference in 1919 when Europe's future was decided in the wake of the war (Problem-Reaction-Solution). History records that the following major leaders attended: US President Woodrow Wilson; British Prime Minister David Lloyd George; and French Prime Minister Georges Clemenceau. What people are not told is the Rothschild connection. Lloyd George was 'advised' by Rothschild employee and Round Table leader Alfred Milner and Sir Phillip Sassoon, a direct descendant of dynasty founder Mayer Amschel Rothschild; Clemenceau was 'advised' by his Minister for the Interior, Georges Mandel, whose real name was Jeroboam Rothschild; and President Wilson was 'advised' (controlled) by two Rothschild/Rockefeller agents, Sabbatian-Frankists, ultra-Zionists and Round Table operatives, Colonel Edward Mandel House (a founding member of the Round Table's Council on Foreign Relations) and financier Bernard Baruch. President Wilson described House as 'my second personality', 'my alter-ego' and said 'his thoughts and mine are one'. I have seen Britain's Lloyd George quoted as saying in the *New York American* in 1924: 'The Treaty of Versailles was hijacked by Jewish international financiers to create the necessary economic, social, and political conditions necessary for Hitler to exploit.' I have not yet been able to track that down to confirm its authenticity, however. Even if it is correct the word 'Jewish' should be replaced with Sabbatian-Frankist. House and Baruch advised Wilson to enter the First World War despite winning an election on the slogan: 'He kept us out of war.' No doubt Britain promising the Balfour Declaration was part of the deal for the US entering the war via House and Baruch. Charles Seymour, who wrote House's biography, described him the 'unseen guardian angel' of the Federal Reserve Act which he manipulated through Congress to hijack the US economy. House also wanted to scrap the US Constitution and rewrite the text – something the Hidden Hand is still desperate to do. House revealed other intentions in an anonymously-published book in 1912 called *Philip Dru: Administrator*. The character Philip Dru (Colonel House) transforms American society with graduated income tax, central bank, and a 'league of nations'. All these things and more would soon follow.

The infamous John Foster Dulles was an American representative at the Versailles Peace Conference. Dulles married into the Rockefeller family and was later Secretary of State to President Eisenhower. He was a founding member of the Council on Foreign Relations, Chairman of the Board of the Rockefeller Foundation and Board Chairman of the Carnegie Endowment for International Peace which was exposed by a congressional committee for its role in manipulating America's involvement in the First World War. His brother, Allen Dulles, the first head of the CIA and a president of the Council on Foreign Relations, was also at the Paris Peace Conference. Allen Dulles would be appointed to the disgusting Warren Commission which decided that President Kennedy was hit in the forehead by a bullet shot from behind him. John Foster Dulles was a legal counsel to the US Versailles delegation working under his uncle, Secretary of State Robert Lansing. Those who triggered the First World War and arranged for America's involvement came together to dictate what would happen as a result of the war. They were Sabbatian-Frankist agents advising President Wilson and other 'leaders' on the terms that should be demanded from Germany and the reparations imposed. Wilson would later describe how 'a little group of wilful men, representing no opinion but their own, have rendered the great government of the United States helpless and contemptible'. You will hardly be taken-aback in the circumstances to know that the Versailles Peace Conference supported the Rothschild-Zionist plan for a Jewish homeland in Palestine and handed control over Palestine to Britain as a temporary custodian until the State of Israel was established in 1948. Another crucial role of Versailles was to impose such crippling war reparations on Germany that the post-war Weimar Republic would fall amid unbelievable economic mayhem which caused enormous depravation and hyperinflation. A loaf of bread costing one mark in 1919 would cost 100 billion marks by 1923. This prepared the circumstances – on purpose – for the rise of dark occultists Hitler and the Nazis and this would provide the biggest momentum of all for the establishment of Israel in Palestine with Jewish people heading in droves after the war to Palestine and the United States. We have so many wars because they are the most effective way of destroying a status quo and imposing a new one. Nothing transforms a country or culture quicker and more irreversibly than a war and this is why Sabbatian-Frankists specialise in them. The two world wars changed the world totally and irreversibly and all to the advantage of Sabbatian-Frankists and their Death Cult that must have been permanently orgasmic as the mass killing was unleashed year after year and white headstones multiplied by the day.

Out of the Versailles Peace Conference came the League of Nations in 1920 which was the first attempt by the Rothschilds and their Rockefeller subordinates to establish a stalking horse for a planned fully-fledged world government. The stated reason for the League was to bring together nations to work together and 'maintain world peace'. This was just a Problem-Reaction-Solution in which you manipulate war and then offer your long-planned new centralised global structure as the solution to conflict. The League of Nations eventually unravelled, but after the Second World War between 1939 and 1945 (in which the Rothschilds and Sabbatian-Frankist bankers once again funded all sides) came the United Nations and a stream of global organisations including the International Monetary Fund and what became the World Bank. These 'solutions' imposed society-transforming centralisation of global power and installed a global structure that could be morphed into a world government dictatorship. The Rockefeller family was pivotal in the creation of the United Nations as they were with the League of Nations. The UN itself acknowledges their 'moral and financial support'. *Wow* – 'moral' and the Rockefeller family in the same sentence. Land on which the UN headquarters stands in New York was donated by the Rockefellers on the site of a former slaughterhouse – a 'gift' valued at $8.5 million by *1945* prices. Money has never been an object to Sabbatian-Frankist ambitions.

Following Protocol

It is interesting to note that in the first quarter of the 20th century while all this was happening great controversy surrounded a document entitled the *Protocols of the Elders of Zion* or *Protocols of the Learned Elders of Zion* which was claimed to be a report of meetings held during the first Zionist Congress in 1897 in Basle, Switzerland. The *Protocols* describe a secret plan for global conquest and the imposition of a world government dictatorship via constant centralisation of power, control of money and media and a society based on fake liberalism and socialism. Again – recognise that society emerging so fast today? One *Protocol* says:

> It is from us that the all engulfing terror proceeds. We have in our service persons of all opinions, of all doctrines, monarchists, demagogues, socialists, communists and utopian dreamers of every kind ... striving to overthrow all established forms of order. All states are in torture ... but we will not give them peace until they openly acknowledge our international Super government ...

Whatever the background to that statement it captures perfectly the technique of control all sides and you control the outcome. The *Protocols* are another taboo subject. Should you have any questions about them that don't fit with the official narrative you are, instantly and by definition, a Nazi and 'anti-Semite' who must be condemned, vilified, silenced and destroyed. Well, actually, I do have some questions so vilify and condemn to your heart's content, but silence and destroy me you will not. The *Protocols* are claimed to be a forgery originating in Russia and I am quite happy to accept they are a forgery which is defined as: 'An illegal copy of a document, painting, etc. or the crime of making such illegal copies.' So if the *Protocols* are a forgery what are they a copy *of* ? I have seen Zionist activist Rabbi Mordecai Ehrenpreis (1869-1951), Chief Rabbi of Sweden, quoted as saying in 1924:

> Long have I been well acquainted with the contents of the Protocols, indeed for many years before they were ever published in the Christian press. The Protocols of the Elders of Zion were in point of fact not the original Protocols at all, but a compressed extract of the same. Of the 70 Elders of Zion, in the matter of origin and of the existence of the original Protocols, there are only ten men in the entire world who know.

What we can say for sure is that the content of the *Protocols* is a mirror of the plan for global control by the Zionism-creating Sabbatian-Frankist

Death Cult and its offshoot known as the Illuminati as confirmed in documents discovered on the fallen horseman in 1785. I will come back to the subject in a later chapter. The text and techniques described in the *Protocols* also reflect very accurately the theme of a funeral oration attributed to Emanuel Reichhorn, Chief Rabbi of France, in Prague in 1869 at the tomb of Grand Rabbi Simeon-ben-Ihuda of Bohemia. Reichhorn is quoted as saying that 'already the principal banks, the exchanges of the entire world, the credits of all governments, are in our hands'. Other statements quoted include:

- The other great power is the Press. By repeating without cessation certain ideas, the Press succeeds in the end in having them accepted as actualities. The Theatre renders us analogous services. Everywhere the Press and the Theatre obey our orders.

- By the ceaseless praise of democratic rule we shall divide the Christians into political parties, we shall destroy the unity of their nations, we shall sow discord everywhere. Reduced to impotence, they will bow before the law of our bank, always united, and always devoted to our Cause.

- We shall force the Christians into wars by exploiting their pride and their stupidity. They will massacre each other, and clear the ground for us to put our people into.

- But above all let us monopolise education. By this means we spread ideas that are useful to us, and shape the children's brains as suits us.

Make of that what you will because I can't prove authenticity, but (a) you have the right to be aware of this information and (b) there can be no doubt as we observe the world that the plans laid out in the *Protocols*, by the Sabbatian-Frankist Illuminati and attributed to Rabbi Reichhorn *have happened or are happening*. This is so patently obvious that agents of Sabbatian-Frankism, some knowingly, some dupes, have employed the usual fall-back, fit-every-situation technique of condemning as 'anti-Semitic' anyone who points this out and asks any questions about the plan described in the *Protocols*. I am not saying this is all a 'Jewish plot'– I am saying it's a plot by the Sabbatian-Frankist Death Cult that hates and despises Jews and Judaism as it hates and despises everyone else, and that this cult is part of the wider global satanic cult that infests every culture, race and country. On Sabbatian-Frankism I am at one with rabbis such as Marvin S. Antelman and many others. The *Protocols*, whatever their origin, have been dismissed as a forgery since the articles by Irish writer Philip Graves in the London *Times* in 1921 which were

also carried by *The New York Times*. Graves
claimed the *Protocols* resembled a satire on
Napoleon III by French lawyer Maurice Joly
called *Dialogue aux enfers entre Machiavel et
Montesquieu* ('Dialogue in Hell Between
Machiavelli and Montesquieu') published in
1864. This is where the story usually ends. The
Protocols were proved to be a forgery in *The
Times* in 1921 – move along now, nothing to see
here. There is, however, other background to
consider. Phillip Graves was a captain in British
Army Intelligence who worked with 'Lawrence
of Arabia', another British agent, who
manipulated Palestinian Arabs to drive out the
Ottoman Empire and open the way for the new
Israel to hijack their land (Fig 121). Graves'
uncle was Sir Robert Windham Graves, a
British Consul in Turkey and financial advisor
to the Turkish government who worked for
Civil Intelligence in Cairo, Egypt. The writer of
the articles in *The Times* was connected to
British Army Intelligence and there's more.
Peter Grose, a writer with the Council on
Foreign Relations, revealed in his 1994 book,
Gentleman Spy: The Life of Allen Dulles, that
Philip Graves' 'source' for the articles was a
'Russian émigre' provided to him by ... *Allen
Dulles*. What a coincidence. Dulles, a Council on
Foreign Relations stalwart, later CIA chief and
instigator of the satanic MKUltra mind control
horror, 'discovered' his man while stationed at

Figure 121: British
government agent 'T. E.'
Lawrence or 'Lawrence of
Arabia'.

Figure 122: Allen Dulles,
Hidden Hand to his fingertips,
produced the unnamed
'source' for *The Times* articles
that also appeared in *The
New York Times*.

the US Embassy in post-Ottoman Turkey (Fig 122). The end of the
Ottoman Muslim empire (brought about by World War I) was crucial to
the establishment of Israel because it included Palestine. Peter Grose
said *The Times* extended a 'loan' to the 'émigre' on the understanding
that it did not have to be paid back. An Internet commentator said of the
Allen Dulles 'scoop':

This was quite an accomplishment for a young American embassy employee,
to both prove the major anti-Jewish plan for world domination was a forgery
as well as unilaterally keeping Lenin out of the United States so he could be
transported to Russia to begin the communist revolution. Strange
coincidences like this seemed to follow both Dulles brothers during their long
careers in 'public service' – or should we say 'serving the Anglo-American

interests headquartered in the City of London'.

Dulles and dodgy are interchangeable words and Rabbi Antelman said that the Council on Foreign Relations is America's most powerful pro-Israel lobby group and controlled by Sabbatian-Frankists. *The Times* articles that trashed the *Protocols* were written by a British Army Intelligence operative using an unnamed source provided by the infamous liar and manipulator Allen Dulles and the source secured a loan from the newspaper he would not have to repay. Oh, nothing to question here, then. Now shut up you 'anti-Semite'! Colin Holmes, a lecturer in economic history at the UK's Sheffield University, claimed to have identified the Dulles émigré as Michael Raslovleff, a 'self-identified anti-Semite', who gave the information to Graves because he didn't want to 'give a weapon of any kind to the Jews, whose friend I have never been'. Surely having a document circulating that was alleged to be proof of a 'Jewish plot' is what an 'anti-Semite' would want rather than seeking to trash its legitimacy? Anyway, that's some background and people will have to decide what they think.

Heading for 'home'

The Sabbatian-Frankist First World War hugely advanced the Zionist project with events before, during and after the conflict bringing an end to the Ottoman Empire. The British government in the form of Thomas Edward 'T. E.' Lawrence, more famously known as 'Lawrence of Arabia', persuaded Palestinian Arabs to support British efforts in the 'Arab Revolt' in 1916 to rid those lands of the Ottoman Empire with the promise that when successful they would be given independence. Lawrence knew all along that this was a lie and from the shadows the Rothschilds and Sabbatian-Frankists wanted the Ottoman rulers gone to open the way for their new Israel. A Lawrence associate, British agent and 'the *Protocols* are a forgery' *Times* writer Phillip Graves, must have been delighted how well the hoax worked. By 1924 the Ottoman Empire was over in totality with the Sabbatian-Frankist 'Donmeh' revolution in Turkey fronted by the Donmeh crypto-Jew Atatürk. Less than 30 years after the first Zionist Congress in Switzerland the scene was set for its 'dream' (agenda) to be realised. The new status quo and redrawn geography that emerged after the First World War would be changed again and global power further centralised by the soon-to-be Second World War as the Sabbatian-Frankist-Rothschild 'New World Order' moved ever closer to its desired outcome – world government tyranny. The establishment of Israel entered the finishing straight when the Rothschild-controlled British government was awarded the 'British Mandate for Palestine' as a result of decisions made by the Rothschild-Rockefeller-controlled League of Nations. British administrators and military forces now oversaw the very lands that Arabs had helped them to clear of the Ottoman Empire and which the Rothschilds and their fellow Sabbatian-Frankists had targeted for Israel. All that was left was to remove the British and take the place over by force and terror.

Rothschild networks and money arranged for tens of thousands of Jewish people to relocate to Israel with 40,000 arriving between 1919 and 1923. A large percentage fled from Russia after attacks on Jews when many of their brethren (actually Sabbatian-Frankists and their agents) were dominating the post-Revolution government and the Red Army. At face value that would seem to be a contradiction, but it wasn't because it caused tens of thousands to head for Palestine who would not otherwise have done so. An estimated 60,000 Jewish people left Germany to settle in Palestine after the Haavara Agreement between Nazi Germany and Zionist German Jews in 1933 which allowed Jews to transfer some portion of their assets to British Mandate Palestine. Meanwhile, the ultra-Zionist Jewish National Fund (JNF), set-up in 1909, was acquiring land with donations from Jewish communities abroad and largely founded Tel Aviv. Only Jews were allowed to live on these JNF lands and that remains the case today in what can only be described as a policy of apartheid. Gideon Falter, chairman of the UK Campaign Against Anti-Semitism (CAA), who hurls the slur 'anti-Semitism' and racism at the British Labour Party, myself and so many others, sits on the UK board of the Jewish National Fund. The Canadian branch of the fund was exposed in a 2018 audit for using donations to finance infrastructure projects on Israeli army, air and naval bases, in contravention of Canadian law while another ultra-Zionist organisation in Canada lost its charity status for funding projects connected to the Israeli military. What many of these organisations say they do often turns out to be something different. Gathering numbers of European Jews heading for Palestine became a flood after the Second World War as a result of the horrors in Nazi Germany where the Jewish community obviously saw things differently now to the time only a few decades earlier when the first Zionist Congress in 1897 had to relocate from Munich to Basle, Switzerland, because of Jewish opposition to their plans. Berihah ('Flight'), a Zionist organisation, arranged for the emigration of a quarter of a million Jews to Palestine from Poland, Romania, Hungary, Czechoslovakia and Yugoslavia. The British, weakened by the Second World War, couldn't cope. The Jewish population of Palestine was already 33 percent of the country by the end of the Second World War and it was about to increase dramatically. European Jews also headed in numbers to the United States. America and Palestine became by far the world's biggest Jewish communities.

Funding Hitler

There was some irony with the relocation choice of the US because from there vast amounts of money had been funnelled to Hitler and the Nazis by elite families like the Sabbatian-Frankist Rockefellers and their associates including the Bush family in the form of Prescott Bush. He was the father of Father Bush and grandfather to Boy Bush, president in name only at the time of 9/11. Other Hitler supporters in the United States included the Dulles Brothers, Allen and John Foster, who would become post war head of the new CIA and Secretary of State respectively. Allen Dulles covered up the assassination of John F. Kennedy as a member of the 'investigation commission', denied a US visa to Lenin before he headed to the Russian Revolution, and supplied the 'Russian emigre' for British agent Philip Graves to trash the *Protocols of the Elders of Zion* in *The Times* in 1921. How strange that Hitler-supporter Dulles would be so keen to discredit the *Protocols* which the Nazis used against German Jews. Bush family involvement in funding the Nazis was highlighted by John Loftus, president of the Florida Holocaust Museum and former prosecutor in the [In]Justice Department's Nazi War Crimes Unit. Loftus said in a speech at the Sarasota Reading Festival in 2001: 'That's where the Bush family fortune came from – it came from the Third Reich.' The Rockefeller family funded the work of Ernst Rudin, Hitler's foremost 'racial hygienist', at Germany's Kaiser Wilhelm Institute for Eugenics, Anthropology and Human Heredity. Other Nazi doctors, including 'Angel of Death' Josef Mengele, conducted unimaginably cruel and vicious experiments on live, captive human subjects with the emphasis on children. Writer and researcher Anton Chaitkin wrote that body parts from victims 'were delivered to [Josef] Mengele ... and the other Rockefeller-linked contingent at the Wilhelm Institute'. Sabbatian-Frankist families including the Rothschilds, Rockefellers and Harrimans were behind the race purity eugenics movement and shared their knowledge and specialists with Hitler and the Nazis (see *And The Truth Shall Set You Free*). These 'elite' American families and their counterparts in the UK and Europe had common cause with Hitler and his associates because they were all occultists following the same satanic creed. Sabbatian-Frankists hate Jewish people we should not forget and this is why, as noted by Rabbi Antelman, the ultra-Zionist Warburg bank was a funder of Hitler. Rabbi Gunther Plaut, a President of the Canadian Jewish Congress, implies in his 1988 novel-biography of Jacob Frank, *The Man Who Would be Messiah*, that what I am calling Sabbatian-Frankists were behind the Holocaust. Support for Hitler in targeting Jews by the ever-recurring American and European financial elite all fits with the Sabbatian-Frankist agenda of targeting genuine Jews. Rabbi Antelman wrote that 'great Rabbis have warned as far back as the middle of the eighteenth century that if the Sabbatians were not stopped there would be mass destruction of the Jewish people'. He, too, indicates a Sabbatian-Frankist connection both to Hitler and the Shoah or Holocaust. Antelman said:

> Hitler was really the product of an adulterous relationship between his mother, Klara Polzl, and a Sabbatian Frankist (1861-September 1928), who was Hitler's real father. The Frankist Sabbatians had a ritual on the 9th of Av, which is observed by Jews as a fast day commemorating the destruction of the First and Second Temples. This night, the Sabbatians secretly observed as incest and adultery night. However, there is a persistent rumor that Klara was artificially inseminated that night.

I know from my own research over decades that artificial insemination is a way the Hidden Hand perpetuates its bloodline and in this way there are endless 'Rothschilds' living under other names and coming to power as described to me by Phillip Eugene de Rothschild who claimed to be an unofficial son of Baron Philippe de Rothschild of the Mouton-Rothschild wine estates in France. Rabbi Antelman continued:

> Rabbinic Court testimony claims that not only Hitler's real father was a Sabbatian, but his maternal grandfather as well; i.e., Klara's maternal grandfather, who fathered her mother out of wedlock. There is evidence that Hitler maintained close contacts with Sabbatians throughout his lifetime. In fact, his personal astrologer Erik J. Hanussen (murdered in the woods outside of Berlin in February 1933), was a Sabbatian who was called 'the prophet of the Third Reich' and 'magician of Berlin'.

Rabbi Antelman said that the Sabbatian-Frankist Jew-hating Death Cult was responsible for the Second World War and the Holocaust and Jewish writer and researcher Barry Chamish agreed. Chamish, who died in 2016, said he lost a third of his family to the Nazis. He emigrated to Israel from Canada where he attended the Hebrew University in Jerusalem and fought in the 1982 war with Lebanon as a conscript in the Israeli Defense Forces. Later he became an Israel correspondent with the *Hollywood Reporter*, *Billboard* and *Screen International* before he began to investigate the assassination of Israeli Prime Minister Yitzhak Rabin in 1995 and a whole new world opened up for him. This included the Sabbatian-Frankists (he called them Sabbatians) and their history, global agenda and role in the creation of Israel. Chamish contended after decades of research that Sabbatian-Frankists were behind World War Two, the Nazis and the Holocaust. The word 'Holocaust' means 'burnt offering' and historically was 'a Jewish sacrificial offering which was burnt completely on an altar'. Chamish said that 'burnt offering' was a term used by Sabbatians for the killing of Jews. 'The Sabbatians are not Jews', he said. 'Don't mix them up – they are the enemies of Jews.' Chamish said the Sabbatians set out to transform Judaism into Sabbatianism while hiding behind labels such as 'secular': 'They wanted the Jews to be something else.' Those that would not 'convert' were killed or forced to move to Palestine as a result of what happened in Nazi Germany, Chamish said, and when many Jews fled to the United States from Sabbatian persecution in places like Germany and Russia Sabbatian agents in America arranged for blocks to be introduced on their immigration so Palestine was their only choice. He was adamant that Sabbatians were behind the world wars with the Rothschild dynasty acting as puppet masters: 'The Rothschilds are *THE* Sabbatians of the world.' Chamish said of the Second World War:

> This was a Sabbatian war. This was a war fought by Sabbatians and they are not Jews … Israel took the German Jews and used them for seed stock to get a new Judaism. They were going to wipe out the Jews – as many as they could in Europe – and start a new Judaism in Israel based on Sabbatianism … No religious Jews were allowed into Israel. The only Jews allowed into Israel from 1933 until 1939 were German Jews.

Chamish said that if you are a Jew that does not believe in Sabbatai as the messiah 'it is a mitzvah [commandment] to kill you'. He claimed the leaders of Zionism that established Israel were Sabbatians, including Chaim Weizmann, another born in the Russian Empire, who he called a 'butcher'. Weizmann would be Israel's first president and remains a Zionist icon to this day: 'Israel's founders were Sabbatians who went to Turkey to learn their stuff from the original Sabbatians.' Chamish was particularly scathing of 'Labour Zionism' which dominated governments of Israel after the state was formed in 1948. He named Britain's Second World War Prime Minister Winston Churchill as a Sabbatian and for sure Churchill's condemnation of Jews is their modus operandi. Churchill's mother was Sephardic Jew Jenny Jacobson/Jerome, daughter of New York stock market speculator Leonard Walter Jerome (changed from Jacobson). Jerome was a close friend of August Belmont (changed from Schoenberg), the American representative of the Rothschild family. Winston Churchill was close to the Rothschilds who bailed him out when he was in serious debt (as they did with Trump). Jenny Jacobson/Jerome had a long affair with King Edward VII according to a book quoting private Churchill family documents and letters. What we can say for sure is that the shocking treatment of Jews by Hitler and the Nazis opened the way for the post-war flight to Israel when before that time there had been great opposition by German Jews to Zionists seeking to relocate them to

Palestine. American academic Antony Sutton wrote in *Wall Street and the Rise of Hitler*:

> It is important to note as we develop our story that General Motors, Ford, General Electric, DuPont and the handful of U.S. companies intimately involved with the development of Nazi Germany were – except for the Ford Motor Company – controlled by the Wall Street elite – the J.P. Morgan firm, the Rockefeller Chase Bank and to a lesser extent the Warburg Manhattan bank.

Sutton's information, gleaned from documents that came to light during the post-war Nuremberg Trials, includes confirmation that the same American elite made major donations to the Nazi Party. Borders do not divide what occultism unites and leading Nazis, including 'Angel-of-Death' Josef Mengele, escaped from Germany to South America and the United States at the end of the war through an American intelligence/Vatican (Jesuit) network known as Operation Paperclip. More than 1,600 German scientists, engineers, and technicians were taken to America to continue their work and establish NASA (Fig 123). They included Wernher von Braun, the German rocket scientist and member of the Nazi Party who designed the V-2 rockets launched against Britain in World War II. He later

Figure 123: More than 2,000 scientists were relocated from Nazi Germany to the United States after World War II under Operation Paperclip. NASA was their creation.

became the leading rocket engineer at NASA and largely designed the Saturn V booster rocket that propelled Apollo spacecraft in the Moon programme. Mengele and his team of mind and genetic manipulators who experimented and tortured Jews and children in the Nazi concentration camps were behind the creation of the evil-beyond-belief mind control programme MKUltra which I mentioned earlier in relation to the Bush family, Dick Cheney, Bill Clinton and the experiences of Cathy O'Brien. Mind control was expressed as 'MK' in deference to the German spelling of control – kontrolle. Such is the borderless world of Sabbatian-Frankism and the Dark Occult in general.

Revisionist Zionism (terrorism)

The target for the Sabbatian-Frankists after the Second World War was British Mandate control of Palestine and the Palestinian Arabs who lived on the overwhelming majority of the land despite all the Rothschild and Sabbatian-Frankist settlement of European and Russian Jews over previous decades. Removing both Britain and hundreds of thousands of Palestinian Arabs was achieved by a campaign of horrific violence. To appreciate the background it is necessary to understand a new extremist cult within Zionism that called itself 'Revisionist Zionism', also known as 'Gun Zionism'. This was, and is, the political wing of Sabbatian-Frankism and I have referred to this combination in some previous books as 'Rothschild Zionism' as opposed to mainstream Zionism that most Zionists believe they are supporting. The cult of Revisionist Zionism was the ideology of violence established in the 1920s by Russian Jew Ze'ev (Vladimir) Jabotinsky (1880-1940). He called for Palestine to be seized with an 'iron wall of Jewish bayonets'. Bombs and mass murder later proved to be the weapons of choice as Sabbatian-Frankist Revisionist Zionists bombed British targets and slaughtered the Arab population of Palestine to such extremes that 750,000 Arabs fled for their lives from their homes and the land of their ancestors. They have never been allowed to return while any person anywhere in the world who is accepted as Jewish or married to someone who is Jewish has the automatic right to settle in Israel whenever they like. But don't worry, that's not racist and it's 'anti-Semitic' to say so. Between 400 and 600 Palestinian villages were destroyed and urban Palestine was reported to be 'almost entirely extinguished'. This racist ethnic cleaning is marked by Palestinians on May 15th every year on Nakba Day – 'Day of the Catastrophe'. Palestinian land abandoned in terror or by direct and brutal force was then seized as Jewish land with the help of organisations like the Jewish National Fund (JNF). That's right Gideon Falter, isn't it? Do you mention that when you accuse others of racism at the Campaign Against AntiSemitism? Israel had the nerve to demand $250 billion in 2019 in compensation from seven Arab countries and Iran for assets left by Jews forced to flee those lands after the creation of the State of Israel. They said this was to correct an 'historic injustice'. Compensation for the 750,000 Arabs which ultra-Zionist terrorist groups forced to flee their homeland in fear of their lives? *Silence.*

Ze'ev Jabotinsky's plan was to impose a Greater Israel from the River Nile in Egypt to the Euphrates in Iraq. This is known to Jews as Eretz Yisrael and represents the largest expanse of 'biblical Israel' described in the Old Testament written by who knows who, who knows when in who knows what circumstances. To achieve this end not only Palestinians had to be conquered but the lands of Syria, Lebanon and parts of Egypt and Iraq. Events since 9/11, anyone? Jabotinsky set out to 'create, with sweat and blood, a race of men, strong, brave and cruel'.

Well, he certainly achieved that with brutal terrorists who would go on
to be prime ministers of the new Israel – Menachem Begin (who won the
Nobel Peace Prize), Yitzhak Shamir and Ariel Sharon among others with
Benjamin Netanyahu walking in their footsteps. All sourced their
ideology, brutality and terrorism from Sabbatian-Frankism and
Jabotinsky's Revisionist Zionism. Indeed a personal assistant to
Jabotinsky was Netanyahu's father, Benzion Netanyahu (1910-2012), a
Polish Jew born Benzion Mileikowsky and himself the son of ultra-
Zionist fanatic and rabbi, Nathan Mileikowsky. Netanyahu's father was
a close friend of ultra-Zionist extremist Abba Ahimeir whose views
influenced the actions and approach of underground ultra-Zionist
terrorist groups like Irgun and Lehi which began to bomb British targets
before turning their attentions to terrorising the Arab population. Irgun,
or The National Military Organization in the Land of Israel, was created
in 1931 as a breakaway terrorist group from paramilitary terrorists called
Haganah or 'Defence'. The Irgun was a terrorist army of Revisionist
'Gun' Zionism and as such believed that only extreme violence would
secure a Jewish state.

Einstein's condemnation

Scientist Albert Einstein and more than 20 other prominent American
Jews sent a letter to *The New York Times* in 1948 describing Irgun and its
new political arm as 'terrorist', 'right wing' and founded on 'ultra-
nationalism, religious mysticism and racial superiority'. They were
talking about Revisionist Zionism/Sabbatian-Frankism which are all of
those things and were controllers of Irgun. Notice the mention of
'religious mysticism' which refers to the Kabbalah/Zohar foundation of
Sabbatian-Frankism and thus Revisionist Zionism and Irgun. The letter
described the Israeli party representing the Zionist Revisionist
movement as 'closely akin in its organization, methods, political
philosophy and social appeal to the Nazi and Fascist parties'. Exactly
right. This is why Sabbatian-Frankists and Zionist Revisionists behave
like Nazis and why they have introduced that new definition of 'anti-
Semitism' which includes any suggestion that ultra-Zionists and Israeli
leaders can be compared to Nazis. Once again it is nothing to do with
protecting Jews in general and everything to do with protecting the
hidden agenda of Sabbatian-Frankists. Among Irgun's great 'victories'
was the bombing of the British Mandate headquarters at the King
David's Hotel in Jerusalem on July 22nd, 1946. The attack killed 91
people and injured 46. Irgun terrorists disguised themselves as Arab
workmen and waiters to plant the bomb in the basement, a technique
widely used by their successors like Israeli intelligence agency Mossad
which has employed the same Arab disguises to blame terrorism on
Arabs in Problem-Reaction-Solution scenarios. The dead included 17

Palestinian Jews (Sabbatian-Frankism hates Jews anyway), 41 Arabs, 28 British, two Armenians and a Russian, Greek and Egyptian. Ultra-Zionist terror groups wanted to make life so difficult and dangerous for British people in Palestine that they would walk away from the Mandate and leave Palestine to them. This is what happened and with the British in disarray and seeking a way out the ultra-Zionist Sabbatian-Frankist terrorists could have free reign against the Arab population. In 2006 the Israeli authorities commemorated the King David's Hotel attack without apology. They placed a plaque at the scene unveiled by former Irgun terrorists and right-wing Israeli politicians with the same mentality today. It said:

> The hotel housed the Mandate Secretariat as well as the Army Headquarters. On July 22,1946, Irgun fighters at the order of the Hebrew Resistance Movement planted explosives in the basement. Warning phone calls had been made urging the hotel's occupants to leave immediately. For reasons known only to the British, the hotel was not evacuated and after 25 minutes the bombs exploded, and to the Irgun's regret and dismay 91 persons were killed.

'Dismay' by the same Irgun terrorists who celebrated mass murder in the same period? The British vehemently denied such warnings were received and after protests by the British embassy the wording was changed about ignoring warnings. The British Mandate ended in May, 1948, and on the 14th day of that same month the Rothschild-controlled Jewish People's Council announced the establishment of the State of Israel. Ultra-Zionist-supporting US President Harry S. Truman and Soviet Union monster Joseph Stalin, who came to power as a result of the Rothschild-funded Russian Revolution, both immediately recognised the new state. Chaim Weizmann (1874-1952), another born in the Russian Empire, became the first Israeli president while Russian Empire-born David Ben-Gurion (1886-1973), the 'Father of Israel', became the first prime minister. Both were close associates and assets of the Rothschilds who would donate £5 million to build the Israeli Parliament building, or Knesset, and still more to construct the occult symbol-adorned Israeli Supreme Court building (Fig 124 overleaf). Palestinian Arabs had been well and truly shafted and this continues to present day.

Deir Yassin and other outrages

Mass slaughter of Palestinian Arabs by Sabbatian-Frankist/Revisionist Zionism terrorist groups included the massacre in the village of Deir Yassin on April 9th, 1948, shortly before the British officially left the country. Irgun and another Revisionist Zionist terror group known as

Figure 124: The Rothschild-built, occult-symbol-festooned Israel Supreme Court including the pyramid and All-Seeing Eye of the Sabbatian-Frankist/Illuminati Death Cult.

Lehi or the Stern Gang had worked together with the Jewish militia Haganah to bomb, assassinate and generally terrorise the British out of Palestine. They joined forces again for the mass murder at Deir Yassin. They slaughtered at least 107 Palestinians (the terrorists claimed 254, others said 240), including women and children, by throwing hand grenades into homes and shooting the defenceless. Jacques de Reynier of the International Red Cross described bodies lying in the streets with some disembowelled or decapitated. Benny Morris, an Israeli historian, recorded mutilation and rape. Investigator Zvi Ankori said: 'I saw cut off genitalia and women's crushed stomachs.' This is the mentally that terrorised the State of Israel into existence and still controls it today. The head of Irgun at the time of the massacre was the brutal Revisionist Zionist terrorist Menachem Begin (1913-1992), the Eastern European Jew who became Prime Minister of Israel and had the nerve to condemn

Figure 125: Menachem Begin, one of many terrorist leaders of Israel.

terrorism (Fig 125). He also ludicrously and outrageously won the Nobel Peace Prize like so many other war criminals. Begin was head of Irgun during its campaign of terrorism against the British and during the slaughter of the Arab innocent. The Albert Einstein letter to *The New York Times* in 1948 was in protest at a visit to America by Menachem Begin in which Einstein and his fellow Jewish signatories highlighted the slaughter at Deir Yassin. They said:

> A shocking example was their [Zionist terrorist] behavior in the Arab village of Deir Yassin. This village, off the main roads and surrounded by Jewish lands, had taken no part in the war, and had even fought off Arab bands who wanted to use the village as their base. On April 9 ... terrorist bands attacked this peaceful village, which was not a military objective in the fighting, killed most of its inhabitants '240 men, women, and children' and kept a few of them alive to parade as captives through the streets of Jerusalem.

Most of the Jewish community was horrified at the deed, and the Jewish Agency sent a telegram of apology to King Abdullah of TransJordan. But the terrorists, far from being ashamed of their act, were proud of this massacre, publicized it widely, and invited all the foreign correspondents present in the country to view the heaped corpses and the general havoc at Deir Yassin.

This is the difference between interloper Sabbatian-Frankists/ultra-Zionists and Jewish people in general. The idea was to terrorise the Arab population to leave – and they're still doing it. Menachem Begin was not the only future Israeli prime minister who was a terrorist operative – the deeply evil Yitzhak Shamir was another (Fig 126). He was a Jabotinsky-worshipping terrorist with the Lehi/Stern Gang which cared so much about the plight of Jews that it had tried to form an alliance with Nazi Germany against the common enemy, the British. The German minister to Beirut, Lebanon, said that 'the establishment of the historic Jewish state on a national and totalitarian basis, bound by a treaty with the German Reich' was proposed by the Stern Gang in 1941. Did I mention that Sabbatian-Frankists hate Jews? Shamir, Begin and their fellow terrorists were extraordinarily racist yet accused others of 'anti-Semitism' and condemned terrorism while being skilled proponents of it. But then, as Nazi Propaganda Minister Joseph Goebbels said: 'Accuse others of that which you are guilty.'

Stern Gang member Uri Greenberg described Arabs as 'the filthiest people in the East' (imagine the storm if anyone said that about Jews). Yitzhak Shamir sanctioned the assassination of Churchill's friend Lord Moyne in 1944 and was one of the terrorists who bombed the King David's Hotel while disguised as a rabbi. He was jailed but escaped after two years.

Figure 126: Terrorist Israel Prime Minister Yitzhak Shamir.

Shamir was involved in the Deir Yassin massacre and the murder of United Nations mediator, Sweden's Count Folke Bernadotte, in 1948. Bernadotte saved an estimated 30,000 Jews in Nazi Germany, but what did that matter to the Jew-hating Sabbatian-Frankists? When Bernadotte opposed the claims of ultra-Zionist extremists to Transjordan (land east of the Jordan River) they killed him. Shamir became head of Mossad, Israeli (Sabbatian-Frankist) intelligence, which was simply an amalgamation of Revisionist Zionism terror groups under another name – the same with the hierarchy of the Israeli Defence Forces (IDF) in general. Shamir said of his move to

Mossad: 'I felt at home very soon. I had returned to an atmosphere, behaviour, incentives and points of view that were in many ways, familiar to me.' Yes, because it was – and still is – the Stern Gang/Lehi, Irgun etc. with a new title. I will detail more about Mossad in a later chapter and its involvement in 9/11. From these mega-terrorists came the far right Likud Party formed in 1973 by terrorists Menachem Begin (Prime Minster 1977-1983) and Ariel Sharon (9/11 Prime Minister from 2001 to 2006). I'll be coming to Sharon's terrorist and war criminal background when I relate all of this to who was really behind the September 11th attacks. Likud was formed out of Begin's first party, Herut ('Freedom'), which he established from terrorist groups in 1948. The Albert Einstein letter to *The New York Times* described Begin's party as 'closely akin' to fascism:

> Among the most disturbing political phenomena of our times is the emergence in the newly created state of Israel of the 'Freedom Party' (Tnuat Haherut), a political party closely akin in its organization, methods, political philosophy and social appeal to the Nazi and Fascist parties. It was formed out of the membership and following of the former Irgun Zvai Leumi, a terrorist, right-wing, chauvinist organization in Palestine.

> The current visit of Menachem Begin, leader of this party, to the United States is obviously calculated to give the impression of American support for his party in the coming Israeli elections, and to cement political ties with conservative Zionist elements in the United States. Several Americans of national repute have lent their names to welcome his visit. It is inconceivable that those who oppose fascism throughout the world, if correctly informed as to Mr. Begin's political record and perspectives, could add their names and support to the movement he represents.

This was the party which with other far right groups became Likud. Terrorist Yitzhak Shamir (Prime Minister 1983-84 and 1986-1992) was a member of Likud as is Benjamin Netanyahu (Prime Minister 1996-1999 and 2009 to the time of writing). Likud is the political arm of Revisionist or 'Gun' Zionism, but extremists can be found in other parties allegedly to the 'left' of Likud. Examples of this can be seen in David Ben-Gurion, Levi Eshkol, Yitzhak Rabin and Shimon Peres. Sabbatian-Frankism always sets out to control all sides and so the game and its outcome. Ben-Gurion oversaw the ethnic cleansing of some 750,000 defenceless Palestinians along with the destruction of hundreds of their villages. Ben-Gurion said that 'without Deir Yassin there would be no Israel' because it caused so many Palestinian Arabs to leave the country as fast as possible in case they would be next. Many of those massacred and forced to flee from the country were Arab Christians. Levi Eshkol, born

Levi Yitzhak in the Russian Empire, founded the Israeli Labour Party and presided over still more ethnic cleansing as Prime Minister between 1963 and 1969. Yitzhak Rabin (Labour Prime Minister between 1974 and 1977 and from 1992 until his assassination in 1995) was a commander of the Palmach ('Strike Forces') of the Jewish paramilitary organisation Haganah during the British Mandate and yet another terrorist. He issued the order to the Israel Defense Forces (IDF) to expel 50,000-70,000 Arabs from the towns of Lydda and Ramle in 1948 which stated: 'The inhabitants of Lydda must be expelled quickly without attention to age ...' Within three days Lydda no longer existed. The way ultra-Zionists can be found in parties in official opposition to Likud is confirmed by Israeli opposition leader Tzipi Livni who called on Netanyahu to resign after Israeli police recommended that he and his wife be indicted for bribery and other corruption charges. Livni was born into a prominent right-wing and Revisionist Zionist family and became a member of an elite Mossad unit. Her father, Eitan, was chief operations officer of terrorist group Irgun and so it's hardly a shock that she was foreign minister during the bombardment of Gaza in 2008/9 for which she has been accused of war crimes. Not really 'opposition', then. The Labour

Figure 127: Terrorist Israeli Prime Minister Shimon Peres who was Foreign Minister at the time of 9/11.

Party's Poland-born terrorist Shimon Peres (1923-2016) would be president and twice prime minister between 1984 and 1986 and from 1995 to 1996 (Fig 127). Peres, a disciple and protégé of Ben-Gurion, was the man behind the development of Israel's nuclear weapons arsenal that it does not admit to having to avoid the limitations of the Nuclear Non-Proliferation Treaty (Fig 128). At the same time it condemns Iran as a nuclear danger when it has no nuclear weapons. Anyone observing the Israeli leadership knows what gross and constant hypocrisy looks like. Insider Israeli military historian, Martin van Creveld, was more forthcoming when he described the nuclear consequences the ultra-

Figure 128: Israel's nuclear programme in the Negev Desert near the city of Dimona, but don't worry – it doesn't exist.

Zionist crazies are prepared to deliver:

> We possess several hundred atomic warheads and rockets and can launch
> them at targets in all directions, perhaps even at Rome. Most European
> capitals are targets for our air force ... We have the capability to take the world
> down with us. And I can assure you that that will happen before Israel goes
> under .

They're not insane or anything.

By war thou shalt take what thy want

The State of Israel as established in 1948 was not enough for the
Sabbatian-Frankists and ultra-Zionists. They wanted the whole region of
Jabotinsky's 'Nile to the Euphrates' or Egypt to Iraq including Lebanon,
Syria and the northern part of Saudi Arabia. They expanded into the
then Egyptian Sinai Peninsula, the Palestinian Gaza Strip and West
Bank, which is being covered in illegal Jewish-only development, and
part of Syria known as the Golan Heights. The latter has been occupied
by the Israelis since the 1967 Arab-Israeli War (the 'Six-Day War')
instigated by an Israeli pre-emptive strike and involving Egypt, Syria
and Jordan. Gamal Abdel Nasser, President of Egypt (then known as the
United Arab Republic) closed the Straits of Tiran to Israeli shipping and
access to its port of Eilat. Remember what I said earlier about part of the
Israeli-US deal with Saudi Arabia's Salman bin Abdulaziz Al Saud for
him to become king was for him to buy Egyptian islands to secure Israeli
shipping access to the Gulf of Aqaba and the Israel port of Eilat. Nasser
mobilised his military along the Israeli border in the light of Israel's
earlier claim that closing the Straits would be cause for war. Nasser
would later tell US President Lyndon Johnson that his troop build-up in
the Sinai Peninsula had been to defend against a feared Israeli attack. A
CIA assessment spoke of Nasser's military presence in the Sinai as
defensive. Michael B. Oren, who would be Israeli ambassador to
America, agreed in his book, *Six Days of War*, that 'by all reports Israel
received from the Americans, and according to its own intelligence,
Nasser had no interest in bloodshed'. Yitzhak Rabin, who would later be
prime minister, told French daily *Le Monde* in 1968:

> I do not think Nasser wanted war. The two divisions which he sent to the
> Sinai, on May 14, would not have been sufficient to start an offensive against
> Israel. He knew it and we knew it.

The claim that Israel's attack was a response to an imminent invasion
by Egypt was therefore a lie. Israel's strike and justification was an
excuse to secure more land and it worked. The Egyptian air force was

quickly taken out and more land occupied. By now with American money and state-of-the-art aircraft and weaponry 'little victim Israel' had ever-increasing military superiority over its Arab neighbours. Today that superiority is fantastic and includes nuclear weapons. The United Nations Security Council unanimously agreed in Resolution 242 in 1967 to call for Israel to withdraw from territory seized in the war. This has never happened and instead Israel has been building Jewish-only settlements in the occupied West Bank while removing Palestinians from their homes in yet another clear case of apartheid and ethnic cleansing. The 'two-state' solution to the Israel-Palestinian land dispute has been endlessly talked about for no other reason than to buy time until such a solution is made impossible by so many Jewish developments constructed in the West Bank and that point has now been reached. Israel had been pressing for the United States to recognise its right to permanently absorb the illegally-occupied Syrian Golan Heights and in March, 2019, Trump unilaterally acknowledged Israel's sovereignty over that Syrian land in a signing ceremony with his minder, Netanyahu. He told an American ultra-Zionist group backed by his funder Sheldon Adelson that he made the decision after a 'quick history lesson' from ultra-Zionists David Friedman, US ambassador to Israel, and son-in-law Jared Kushner. The pressure then immediately turned to recognising the West Bank as permanent Israel territory. Trump is owned by Israel and ultra-Zionism to the tip of every orange hair. Jewish-only Israeli settlements are illegal under the Fourth Geneva Convention of 1949 which bans countries from settling their population into territories occupied in a war. The UN Security Council, UN General Assembly, International Committee of the Red Cross, International Court of Justice and High Contracting Parties to the Geneva Convention have all confirmed this. Israel says 'up yours' and 'we do what we like'. In 2018 the UN General Assembly voted by 99 to 10 for a resolution declaring that Israel's demand to absorb the Golan Heights was null and void and called on Israel to withdraw from that occupied land. The United States naturally opposed the resolution and in March, 2019, Trump said it was time for the United States to recognise Israel's sovereignty over the Golan Heights which was 'of critical strategic and security importance to the State of Israel and Regional Stability'. Trump managed to send that tweet while on his knees. The constant theme of Israel doing whatever it wants and ignoring international law and war crimes agreements with the slavish support of the United States and other Western countries should beg the question of why? Why can a tiny, tiny country of eight million people be allowed to do this? Sabbatian-Frankist occult networks are the major explanation. Egypt and Syria sought to regain their lost territory in the 1973 Yom Kippur War which ended in failure in the face of Israel's military superiority. Israel was supported by the United States as usual with ultra-Zionist Henry Kissinger in place as US Secretary of State and National Security Advisor while the Soviet Union supported Egypt and Syria.

Suffer little children

Life for Palestinians in the occupied West Bank has got ever worse as Israel settlements take over the land and a massive wall has taken more Palestinian property against international law. Week after week Palestinian homes are hijacked for Jewish settlers or demolished on any pretext to free the land for Jews. East Jerusalem is often targeted because the Sabbatian-Frankist psychopaths are ethnically cleansing the area in preparation for the takeover of Temple Mount and a new Solomon's Temple to herald the arrival of their Messiah 'King of the World'. The heartless psychopathy now even plumbs the depths of making Palestinians demolish their own homes or face a big bill from the government for doing it. A Palestinian father was forced in early 2019 to demolish his own home in occupied East Jerusalem, as well as that of his daughter, by the Israeli authorities. Motor mechanic Mustafa Subah spoke with Israel daily *Haaretz* reporters in the ruins of his home. He had fought and lost (a gimme) a 15-year legal battle that cost him around $110,000 and was 'compelled to demolish his and his daughter's homes with his own hands'. His daughter with her husband and three children moved into cramped conditions in the home of her mother-in-law while Mustafa and his wife and three children were 'squeezed into the two rooms of the original structure, waiting in dread to hear whether they will have to raze that as well'. Sabbatian-Frankists get off on suffering, anguish, death and the dopamine rush of their own perceived power over others. Children are almost routinely taken from their homes in the middle of the night by Israeli troops and held in adult jails. Rights group Defense for Children International (DCI) reported that since 2000 at least 8,000 Palestinian children have been detained by the Israeli military detention system infamous for the systematic mistreatment and torture of Palestinian children (Fig 129). Shadi Farah, a 15-year-old minor, described his abuse in prison by Israeli interrogators to the Turkey-based international news agency, Anadolu:

> Israel is using all heinous methods during interrogation from suffocation, beating to giving us hallucinogenic pills. I remember spending days suffering from nightmares and headaches because of the drugs that we were forced to take.

Defense for Children International says Palestinian minors are often made to sign documents written in Hebrew and have no idea what they say. They are interrogated without parents or lawyers. Khaled Quzmar

Figure 129: Just another day in the Israel-occupied West Bank. The boy is 14-years-old.

said minors frequently report being kicked, slapped and blindfolded during arrest and/or interrogation. 'Around 90 percent of detained children are subject to verbal abuse and humiliation by Israeli army officers', he said. Some 30 percent were physically abused in custody. Ahmad al-Zatari, a 15-year-old minor, said he was beaten and suffocated by an Israeli interrogator when he was 12:

> I stepped into the room and one integrator was there. He started asking questions and calling for quick answers. I was only 12-year-old during the interrogation and the questions were not clear to me so I could not answer any.

He said the Israeli interrogator turned off the cameras and started beating him.

> He jumped over me and put his hands around my neck and started yelling at me. It was a horrible experience. I thought he was going to kill me.

The Palestinian Prisoners Society said in 2018 that about 900 Palestinian children had been detained by Israeli forces that year with some 270 children continuing to be held in detention. High profile cases like the jailing of 17-year-old Ahed Tamimi for slapping an Israeli soldier outside her home after her cousin had part of his head blown off by the Israel army are tips of a mountain of daily abuse. I will spare you the images of Gaza children with no heads and as just a pair of legs after Israeli bombing raids on a defenceless people. When Jewish-American actress Sarah Silverman responded to the treatment of Tamimi by tweeting that 'Jews have to stand up EVEN when – ESPECIALLY when – the wrongdoing is BY Jews/the Israeli government' she was castigated by the ultra-Zionist mob. Oshrat Kotler, a television presenter with Israel's Channel 13, was besieged by death threats and put on trial by the 'Middle East's only democracy' when she said that the occupation of Palestinian land was turning Israeli troops into 'animals':

> When you send your children to the army, they are kids. You send them to the territories, and they come back as human animals. This is the result of the

occupation.

Kotler was commenting on IDF soldiers from the ultra-Orthodox Netzah
Yehuda Battalion who were convicted of aggravated assault and
aggravated battery for beating two handcuffed and blindfolded
Palestinians, a 50-year-old father and his 15-year-old son detained in
custody. Psychopath Netanyahu was as always seething with outraged
condemnation over Kotler's comments. Many former IDF troops, forced
into the army by conscription, have said that they were systematically
de-humanised, but since when did the truth matter to Sabbatian-
Frankists? Kotler was put on trial on charges of incitement,
incrimination of suspects, failure to grant a right of reply. Jewish people
are only allowed to have approved opinions and Israeli 'democracy' is
an illusion. Kotler said she had 'thousands' of death threats and such is
the power of the persecuted Chosen People program which leaves no
room for self-reflection. Nadera Shalhoub-Kevorkian, an Arab professor
of the Hebrew University of Jerusalem, told an audience at the
University of Colombia in 2019 that the Israeli military tests its weapons on innocent Palestinians, even children, to assess which are the most
powerful. She said that 'Israel does weapons tests on Palestinian
children' and 'Palestinian spaces are laboratories for the Israeli security
industry'. Robrecht Vanderbeeken, cultural secretary of Belgium's
ACOD trade union and a philosophy of science scholar, said in 2018 that
the population of the Gaza Strip was being 'starved to death, poisoned,
and children are kidnapped and murdered for their organs'. Palestinian
UN ambassador Riyad Mansour wrote to the Secretary General to say
that bodies of Palestinians killed by Israeli security forces 'were returned
with missing corneas and other organs, further confirming past reports
about organ harvesting by the occupying power'. Even *The New York
Times* ran a story in 2014 revealing that transplant brokers in Israel had
made enormous sums of money and that Israelis had played a
'disproportionate role' in organ trafficking. Dr Yehuda Hiss, former head
of Israel's forensic institute, said in a 2000 interview that Israeli
pathologists would harvest skin, corneas, heart valves, and bones from
the bodies of Palestinians and others often without permission from
relatives. These are the kind of revelations the new definition of 'anti-
Semitism' is designed to silence. By adding to the definition of 'anti-
Semitism' the point about 'comparisons of contemporary Israeli policy
to that of the Nazis' the aim is simply to stop those comparisons being
made even when they can be demonstrably true. Jewish people are
castigated for protesting at the actions of their government and military
and when UK Liberal peer Baroness Tonge claimed that members of the
Israeli Defence Forces had been harvesting body parts in the aftermath
of the Haiti earthquake she was thrown out of the party for what its

I can take his home as a temporary base for a few hours, to a few days, to a few weeks. I can decide that I am arresting the people of the house and tie them up to the fence of my base ... [You can] get an order to demolish their home or just lock the front door to not let them out into the street, their house is on, a street that only Jewish settlers can walk on and Palestinians cannot. So they have to walk from windows to yards ...

Efrati said the Israeli military bypass a Supreme Court ruling banning outright assassinations with orders that say if a Palestinian reacts in any way to being woken up at night by armed troops they should shoot him dead:

What we're going to do is come in five or six people units into their home in the middle of the night, break in quietly, go up to his bedroom, go into his bed and point a gun into his head. Now, if he just wakes up and surrenders we're taking him into the police but if he screams you shoot him in the head, if he lifts his blanket you shoot him in the head, if he lifts his hands or legs or is trying to do any movement you shoot him in the head.

Now, because we understand as rational human beings that no human being can wake up in the middle of the night with a gun to his head and not scream or move, we understand these orders as an execution order that bypass the Supreme Court order.

This is the fascism that the Protection Racket of the 'anti-Semitism' industry is designed to keep secret and it is precisely the modus operandi of the Sabbatian-Frankist Death Cult. Efrati said that he realised early in his compulsory military service that he had been lied to about Israel and its relationship with the Palestinians. 'I didn't feel like I was protecting anyone, I didn't feel like I am helping anyone feel more safe – I felt like I was terrorising people.' The defined mission was to instil fear in the hearts of Palestinians and that was exactly what they did:

I don't want to live in an only Jewish state that values privileged Jewish life over every other life. This urges me to understand that I want my kids to grow up in a place when they don't have to press anyone, they don't have to be soldiers ...

Eran Efrati talked about his experience of the appalling treatment of Palestinians in Israel-occupied Hebron, the biggest city in the West Bank and home to 200,000 Palestinians. Dozens of monitors from multiple countries recorded 40,000 cases of abuse since 1967 by Israeli settlers and troops and some constituted war crimes. The response of psychopath

Prime Minister Netanyahu was to expel international observers and this was another expression of the Protection Racket in which you delete all sources of exposure and criticism. With the observers gone the Palestinians are left to an even more extreme fate. There are brave and determined Jewish Israelis who refuse to serve in the military and treat the Palestinians with violent contempt. They are incredible young people who pay for their compassion and backbone by being jailed for the crime of refusing to commit crimes against humanity. Such are the perverse inversions that multiply in sync with the scale of tyranny involved. Are these thoroughly decent Jewish people given respect for what they do by the ultra-Zionists? No – they are dismissed as 'useful idiots of the BDS'. Psychological sickness has no interest in rational thought and psychopaths have no empathy with which to engage with their fellow human beings. Israel's approach to Palestinians and its brutally excessive use of force (Gun Zionism) against unarmed demonstrators was described by Michael Lynk, United Nations special rapporteur on human rights in the Palestinian territories, as 'an eye for an eyelash'. God knows how many Palestinians that Israel has killed directly or through systematic deprivation since 1947/48 but one thing is for sure – the Sabbatian-Frankists would have celebrated all of them. In 2018 the Israeli High Court ruled that Israeli intelligence officers were justified in their use of torture against Palestinians and set a precedent for its continued and expanded use. Israeli officials from the Shin Bet domestic intelligence agency forced a prisoner into stress positions, including arching and tying the body in the 'banana' position and subjected him to 'severe physical and mental violence, including beatings'. Judges ruled that this was all fine and dandy. Israeli human rights group B'Tselem said: 'In interrogating Palestinian residents of the Occupied Territories, the Israel Security Agency routinely used methods that constituted ill-treatment and even torture until the late 1990s.' None of this – not the violent expulsion of Palestinians or the heartless ongoing violence and abuse were in the minds of most people who supported Zionism before the establishment of the State of Israel. Auschwitz survivor Esther Bejarano became a fierce critic of Israel and what she called its 'fascist' government. She was born in Germany and lost her parents and sister to Nazi murderers before moving to a Palestine still then under the pre-Israel British Mandate. She said:

> We wanted to develop the country together with the Palestinians. In general, the Palestinians helped us. Not only us, but also the first Jews who came to the country. We wanted to develop the land together. But it was different with David Ben-Gurion and Golda Meir. They turned Zionism upside down and then the Zionists said 'we are the ones who own the land.' That was not our idea.

was an asset of Rothschild operative, Jacob Schiff. The Sabbatian-Frankist Death Cult had long been at work in the United States, but now with the end of the Second World War the expansion would go into overdrive. After the State of Israel was formed in 1948 a number of ultra-Zionists relocated to the United States so their offspring would be born American citizens and take the manipulation of US politics to still new levels. Among them was Benjamin Emanuel (real name Ezekiel Auerbach), a Russian Jewish terrorist with Irgun and father of Barack Obama's White House Chief of Staff (handler), the ultra-Zionist Rahm Emanuel who went on to become the first Jewish Mayor of Chicago. Father Emanuel's speciality was apparently bus bombing. Rahm Emanuel's role has been that of a 'Democon', the name I use for the Democratic Party equivalent of the Neocons of the Project for the New American Century which control the Republican Party and use Donald Trump as their sock puppet. Democons and Neocons answer to the Sabbatian-Frankists and the Hidden Hand and so no matter who is in the White House the same force in the shadows is always in control. Boy Emanuel was Senior Advisor to President Bill Clinton, Chair of the Democratic Congressional Campaign Committee, Chair of the House Democratic Caucus and White House Chief of Staff. New York-born ultra-Zionist David Axelrod was Obama's Chief Strategist overseeing his two successful election campaigns and his senior advisor. Obama's personal advisors on policy, known by the media as 'czars', were also awash with ultra-Zionists and the ratio is almost comically enormous when compared with two percent of the population. Among them was Emanuel's brother Ezekiel, an Obama policy advisor on health while another brother is Ari Emanuel, a Hollywood agent who has represented Obama campaign contributor Michael Moore whose film *Fahrenheit 911* (executive producer ultra-Zionist women-abuser Harvey Weinstein) avoided the real story of what happened. Another Moore film, *Bowling for Columbine*, was an attack on gun ownership in line with the Hidden Hand agenda to disarm Americans while arming law enforcement to the enamel on their teeth. I certainly won't assign to Mr Moore the level of intelligence necessary to realise that he is being used by a force that he has no idea exists. The scale of the Sabbatian-Frankist ultra-Zionist takeover of American politics and financial policy can be seen in 'Obama's' financial team which led the reaction to the 2008 financial crash caused by major banks and bankers. His team decided, just by coincidence, of course, that bailing out those same bankers with trillions of dollars of taxpayer money and debt was the way to go about it. These were 'Obama's' picks:

Timothy Geithner (ultra-Zionist), Treasury Secretary; Larry Summers (ultra-Zionist), director of the White House National Economic Council;

Paul Adolph Volcker (ultra-Zionist and Rothschild business partner), chairman of the Economic Recovery Advisory Board; Peter Orszag (ultra-Zionist), director of the Office of Management and Budget overseeing all government spending; Penny Pritzker (ultra-Zionist), Commerce Secretary; Jared Bernstein (ultra-Zionist), chief economist and economic policy adviser to Vice President Joseph Biden; Mary Schapiro (ultra-Zionist), chair of the Securities and Exchange Commission (SEC); Gary Gensler (ultra-Zionist), chairman of the Commodity Futures Trading Commission (CFTC); Sheila Bair (ultra-Zionist), chair of the Federal Deposit Insurance Corporation (FDIC); Karen Mills (ultra-Zionist), head of the Small Business Administration (SBA); Kenneth Feinberg (ultra-Zionist), Special Master for Executive [bail-out] Compensation. Feinberg would be appointed to oversee compensation (with strings) to 9/11 victims and families and will appear again later. These are only a few of the ultra-Zionists out of all proportion to population percentage that could be found throughout the administration of Obama ('Democrat') with a similar story to be found with Trump ('Republican'). 'Obama's' ultra-Zionist financial team was in operation while Bernard Bernanke (ultra-Zionist) was chairman of the Federal Reserve, America's privately owned central bank. He was deciding, no doubt with input from people like ultra-Zionist Feinberg, who got the bail-out money. Bernanke had taken over at the Fed from Alan Greenspan (ultra-Zionist) who had been head of the bank during the Reagan-Father Bush, Father Bush, Bill Clinton and Boy Bush presidencies before stepping down in 2006. Greenspan was in situ when calculated deregulation of banks and financial services unleashed a free-for-all that led to the 2008 crash and he did this in league with Bill Clinton's Treasury Secretaries Robert E. Rubin (ultra-Zionist) and Larry Summers (ultra-Zionist), former chief economist at the World Bank; Rubin's assistant Timothy Geithner (ultra-Zionist); and Peter Orszag (ultra-Zionist), Clinton's Special Assistant for Economic Policy and Senior Economist and Senior Adviser on the Council of Economic Advisers. Geithner, Summers and Orszag who had played a highly significant role in causing the financial crash would be leading Obama's financial response to the crash and they decided to hand their mates and masters unspeakable amounts of taxpayer money. Many of these people were associated with the infamous ultra-ultra-Zionist Goldman Sachs which was Obama's biggest corporate donor. Goldman Sachs (with others) was seriously responsible for the engineered economic crash which caused such suffering and deprivation worldwide (Greece is a major example) and which led to corporate bail-outs overseen by Goldman Sachs-connected government officials.

'The Team' picks itself

The origin of these 'Obama-selected' names was revealed in a WikiLeaks release of emails belonging to John Podesta, a chair of Obama's 2008 Transition Team. One email included a list of proposed administration appointees suggested by ultra-Zionist Michael Froman, a Citigroup executive who had been Chief of Staff at the US Treasury in the 1990s under ultra-Zionist Robert Rubin. He had also been a class mate of Obama at Harvard Law School and went on to be a distinguished fellow of the Council on Foreign Relations, Vice-Chairman of MasterCard and a director of the Walt Disney Company. In an email dated October 6th, 2008, before Obama won the election, Froman sent Podesta three documents listing proposed women for top administration jobs, non-white candidates and a sample outline of names for 31 cabinet-level positions. These same people overwhelmingly ended up getting the jobs that ultra-Zionist Forman had 'suggested'. Names included Janet Napolitano for Homeland Security, Rahm Emanuel for Chief of Staff, Robert Gates for Defense, Eric Holder for the [In]Justice Department or White House Counsel, Susan Rice for United States Ambassador to the UN and Arne Duncan for Education. Holder is a big-time agent for the ultra-Zionists and instrumental while Obama's Attorney General in blocking the case of '9/11 mastermind' Khalid Sheikh Mohammed from coming to trial where evidence would have to be produced. Instead Mohammed, or someone with that name, continues to be held without trial in Guantanamo Bay. Zionist John Kerry was named by Froman for Secretary of State and three choices were offered for Treasury Secretary – ultra-Zionists Robert Rubin, Larry Summers, and Timothy Geithner. Always control the money. Alan Sabrosky, a former Director of Studies at the United States Army War College Strategic Studies Institute who has taught at several prestigious universities, also highlighted how Zionists have dominated the White House Personnel Office at least since 1980. This was 'reducing the likelihood that people unfriendly to Israel or unsupportive of its "ways and means" will be nominated in the first place'. He wrote:

> The vetting of nominees by key organized Jewish groups in the US before they go before the US Senate for their confirmation hearings has also been a fixture of this process for decades, as Haaretz (an Israeli newspaper) among many others has pointed out, and forces otherwise excellent nominees to withdraw if said Jewish groups find them to be unsuitable. And the leverage of AIPAC in the US Senate is in this respect crucial: anyone AIPAC wants confirmed will be confirmed, and anyone who manages to reach that point and is not acceptable to AIPAC doesn't stand a chance.

> This is why under both Republicans and Democrats, the staffs in and around

the President and the Vice-President, the National Security Council, the State Department and the Defense Department (among others) look the way they do. Many are Jewish and actively Zionist, often with dual US-Israeli citizenship (not that the absence of an Israeli passport matters all that much to the others). Some are Christian Zionists who need no persuading to take the pro-Israel positions they do ... Others are what the communists used to call 'useful idiots', frequently intelligent people like Condoleezza Rice or John Bolton who have made their own Faustian bargain in the furtherance of their own careers. And the rest of us live with the consequences of all of them, not least of which was 9/11 and the ensuing wars.

Zionists and ultra-Zionists also have an extraordinary ratio to their numbers in lower government positions. I must have mentioned that only two percent of the American population is Jewish and a *fraction* of even them are the ultra-Zionist Sabbatian-Frankist pseudo Jews that we are talking about.

The People pick the President?

Interestingly, on the subject of the Obama administration, a businessman called Tom Fife wrote an article in 2008 in which he recalled a visit to Russia in the early 1990s while starting a joint-venture company with members of the Russian scientific community. He recalled how he was told by his guests that the United States was destined to have its first black president who would be a communist plant. Fife quoted one of his female Russian hosts:

Yes, it is true. This is not some idle talk. He is already born and he is educated and being groomed to be president right now. You will be impressed to know that he has gone to the best schools of Presidents. He is what you call 'Ivy League'. You don't believe me, but he is real and I even know his name. His name is Barack. His mother is white and American and his father is black from Africa. That's right, a chocolate baby! And he's going to be your President.

Fife said the woman told him that 'Barack' was from Hawaii and she described how everything had been 'thought out':

His father is not an American black so he won't have that social slave stigma. He is intelligent and he is half white and has been raised from the cradle to be an atheist and a communist. He's gone to the finest schools. He is being guided every step of the way and he will be irresistible to America.

According to Fife the woman said that 'America would have to be converted to communism [Soros 'progressive' socialism] and Barack was going to pave the way'. Is this so incredible when Obama was brought up and prepared for his task as a follower of Saul Alinsky and his Marxist methods of 'community organising'? I can't of course verify that story. What I can say is this is how presidents come to power. They do not emerge by chance, but by design and long-term grooming. The kind of president installed in the illusion of public choice varies in line with the Hidden Hand agenda for that particular period and they vary the perceived nature and personality to keep the public interested in what is a rigged system. The first black president was followed by the fake 'maverick' president and the first woman will be along eventually. Keep them interested and focussed so they won't open their eyes to the *permanent government* and will keep giving credibility to the here-today-gone-tomorrow political level of government which is nothing more than a smokescreen to hide where the power *really* is.

Draining the swamp

Thank goodness at least the influence in government of Goldman Sachs was going to be ended by Donald Trump who had attacked the company and its personnel during his election campaign. It's called telling your target audience what it wants to hear (Fig 131). When he secured 'power' he named the ultra-Zionist Steve Mnuchin, a Goldman

Sachs employee for 17 years, as his Treasury Secretary; Gary Cohn (ultra-Zionist), chief operating officer of Goldman Sachs, became Trump's Director of the National Economic Council and chief economic advisor; Cohn was later replaced by Larry Kudlow (ultra-Zionist). Trump's senior advisor is his son-in-law, the ultra-Zionist Jared Kushner, a life-long friend of Benjamin Netanyahu, with ultra-Zionist Jason Greenblatt as

Figure 131: Swamp swimmer to drain the swamp? Fill it more like.

his international negotiator, including on Israel-Palestine. His ambassador to Israel is the ultra-Zionist David Friedman who arranged for the American Embassy to be moved from Tel Aviv to Jerusalem in 2018 in a highly provocative slight against Palestinians. This is a stepping stone on the way to replacing the Al-Aqsa Mosque on what Jews call Temple Mount with a rebuilt Solomon's Temple named after their occult Kabbalah hero. Trump's administration is awash with ultra-Zionists and perhaps the most pro-Israel in American history. This is why from the moment Trump was elected Netanyahu increased the speed of illegal settlements built in occupied Palestinian land because he knew there would be no resistance. American sanctions and aids cuts to Palestinians have followed with the aim of creating such destitution that they will agree to anything the Sabbatian-Frankist psychopaths demand. Trump's biggest funder is the ultra-Zionist casino magnate Sheldon Adelson while the Democrats are funded by ultra-Zionist George Soros (whatever he may claim) and ultra-Zionist financial and media mogul, Haim Saban. Adelson and Netanyahu wanted Trump to delete the nuclear deal with Iran to re-ignite conflict on the road to regime change as per Project for the New American Century (PNAC) and so he did. Adelson wanted big-time Israel asset John Bolton of the PNAC to be Trump's National Security Advisor and so he is. Bolton is leading the charge against Iran, Russia, China and North Korea, all Sabbatian-Frankist targets. Trump's pick for UN ambassador was the ultra-Israel supporting Nicky Haley who continued America's role of vetoing any resolution of condemnation by the UN Security Council of whatever Israel does – no matter how deadly and grotesque. When Haley resigned she was replaced by her ultra-Zionist deputy Jonathan Cohen who stood in until a permanent appointment was made. Cohen, who attended Hebrew University in Jerusalem on an Israeli government grant, had been Deputy Assistant Secretary of State for European and Eurasian Affairs. Even *New York Times* columnist Timothy Egan highlighted the Adelson influence:

> An 85-year-old casino magnate, Sheldon Adelson, now has more influence on American foreign policy than even the secretary of state ... Adelson got a ... tax windfall for the millions he put into electing Republicans, with the added benefit of controlling the State Department's view of Israel.

There is so much manipulation of political events secured through the chequebook and wire transfer. Alan Hart, a former BBC and Independent Television News correspondent, wrote in *Zionism: The Real Enemy of the Jews:* 'Jewish people make up less than two percent of the American population, but account for *50 percent* of the political campaign contributions.' This incredible amount of political funding (control and influence) does not come from Jewish people in general, but from mega-rich individuals, banks and corporations controlled by ultra-Zionism and Sabbatian-Frankism. There are certainly plenty of billionaire sources to choose from with a *Forbes Magazine* analysis in 2012 concluding that 35 percent of the 400 richest people in the United States were Jewish from a population of two percent. By 2018 five of the top ten richest people in America were Jewish: Facebook CEO Mark Zuckerberg; Oracle's Larry Ellison; Google's Larry Page and Sergey Brin; and former New York Mayor Michael Bloomberg. Close to a quarter of the richest 200 people in Russia were also found to be Jewish according to Russian ranking website lanta.ru. It hardly scans with the claims of an oppressed minority which the 'anti-Semitism' industry loves to promote, but we should always keep in mind that the great majority of Jewish people worldwide are not rich. Many in Israel itself are struggling economically while the few suck up the spoils. The image of the 'rich Jew' is true if you apply that to a minority and these are the people that spend their wealth to influence politics while most Jews are not at all involved in such manipulation and not mega-wealthy. Unfortunately, the actions of the few colour the perception of the many and this is inaccurate, unfair and potentially very, very, dangerous.

Pro-Israel lobby groups poured more than $22 million into the 2018 US mid-term election cycle according to public records and the real figure is far more than actually tracked. The Washington-based Center for Responsive Politics (CRP) found the Israel lobby to be highly active and spending heavily to influence lawmakers. They could not have come to any other conclusion given the evidence and yet when Minnesota Congresswoman Ilhan Omar tweeted in 2019 about pro-Israel money influencing decisions made on Capitol Hill (it does and fundamentally) she faced the usual orchestrated abuse and contrived rage including the tag of 'anti-Semite'. 'Outrageous', 'disgraceful', screamed her Democratic colleagues as they fell to their knees in gratitude for the latest cheque. Democrats most critical of Omar received some of the highest levels of contributions from the pro-Israel lobby and we are looking at in-your-face political prostitution with representatives of a tiny country buying the support of American politicians that are supposedly elected to represent the interests of Americans and not a foreign power. Omar said 'it's all about the Benjamins baby', as in the image of Benjamin Franklin on the $100 dollar bill. The hysterical attacks on her – not least by AIPAC – simply proved that she was right. Truth is the worst nightmare of the liar. 'Benjamins' Netanyahu weighed in on video-link to the 2019 AIPAC conference by saying that American politicians supported Israel (slavishly) because of shared values and not

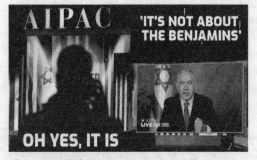

massive donations. They should put him on at the Comedy Store. It's the Benjamins, Benjamin, and you know it (Fig 132). There are many areas where I would have profound disagreements with Omar but on this she is absolutely right and she should not have made the mistake that almost everyone

Figure 132: It's the Benjamins, Benjamin. To say otherwise is a joke.

does of speaking the truth and then apologising when the ultra-Zionist abuse and outrage follows. Pro-Israel lobbyists and donors spent more than $22 million on lobbying and campaign contributions in the 2018 election cycle, but it's not about the Benjamins?? AIPAC spent more than $3.5 million on lobbying during the cycle and more than $5 million in the year in total – the highest since tracking began in 1998. Ultra-Zionist 'progressive' J Street gave $4.03 million in political donations. Dan Auble, a senior researcher at the Center for Responsive Politics (CRP), said he hadn't seen many other countries which had 'a comparable level of activity'. The Israel lobby donated to a long list of politicians including 269 House representatives. House Majority Leader, the Democrat Steny Hoyer, has so far received $1.02 million from pro-Israel groups. Anyone think that might affect his judgement? Hoyer's condemnation of Congresswoman Omar for stating an obvious fact was matched by Republican Vice President and Christian Zionist Israel butt-licker Mike Pence who called for Omar to be removed from the Foreign Affairs Committee. Hoyer and Pence should form their own Israel support group. Tongues Out For Israel might be a title they could consider and there would be no shortage of members on Capitol Hill – Trump among them who also loudly condemned Omar. Pro-Israel groups have donated hundreds of millions to US politics according to CRP figures and the payback comes in the billions handed over in American 'aid' to Israel and the unwavering support for the ultra-Zionist agenda no matter what Israel's government and military may do. The 'anti-Semitism' industry and Protection Racket target with abuse anyone who reveals this elephant in the room because the scale of ultra-Zionist influence in US politics (and elsewhere) is so appalling they are desperate to keep this from public attention. We saw the Protection Racket at work with Ilhan Omar while at the same time non-ultra-Zionist Jews defended her. An open letter by North American Jews, including Canadian-born author and activist, Naomi Klein, said Omar had been falsely accused of antisemitism' and there was nothing anti-Semitic about calling out the 'noxious' role of the American Israel Public Affairs Committee (AIPAC) in American politics: 'The pro-Israel lobby has played an outsized role in producing nearly unanimous congressional support for Israel.' The letter thanked Omar for having the bravery to shake up the congressional taboo against criticizing Israel. 'As Jews with a long tradition of social justice and anti-racism, AIPAC does not represent us', the letter said. All Jewish people think the same, you see – ask the ADL.

Kosher Nostra

Another aspect of the 'Atlantic Crossing' is the role played by ultra-Zionists from Russia and the former Soviet Union in general. The same transfer of people can be seen between the Soviet Union and the United States that happened earlier with the influx out of Germany from the 19th century of families that became major banking figures like Goldman, Sachs, Lehman, Rockefeller and Rothschild agent Jacob Schiff. Russian and Soviet Zionists and their organised crime syndicates moved in numbers to Brighton Beach in Brooklyn, New York, which became known as 'Little Odessa' when the 1975 Jackson-Vanik law was passed to allow this Jewish immigration into America from the Soviet Union. The 'Jackson' who drove the law through Congress was ... Henry M. 'Scoop' Jackson, hero of the ultra-Zionist Neoconservatives. Two Jackson assistants at the time were Richard Perle and Paul Wolfowitz. Nearly 80 years earlier in 1897 Jacob Schiff's influence over outgoing Democrat US President Grover Cleveland led to changes to the Immigration Bill that would allow an influx for Zionist and Communist Jews from Russia and other countries in the decades that followed. The mass-Russian (Zionist) arrivals to New York after 1975 have become known as the Russian Mafia, Red Mafia, or 'Red Octopus' (to hide the ultra-Zionist connection) and has strong ties to the Rothschilds, Anti-Defamation League (ADL), AIPAC and Mossad. The most famous leader of this ultra-Zionist mob in the United States has been Marat Balagula and the overall global 'Mr Big' is the Ukrainian-born and Moscow-based Semion Mogilevich who once said there were 'too many Jews' in Israel. This fits with the relationship between the Sabbatian-Frankist satanic cult and the mainstream Jewish population and so does the way Mogilevich first made his fortune – by exploiting Jews leaving Russia for the United States and Israel. He would make a deal to sell their assets at market value and forward the proceeds and then just keep the money. Mogilevich was jailed for that swindle, but would eventually become so powerful that no one would touch him. Mogilevich has been described by US and European law enforcement as the 'boss of bosses' of global Russian (ultra-Zionist) crime syndicates and the FBI has labelled him 'the most dangerous mobster in the world' as the head of a colossal global criminal empire involving 'weapons trafficking, contract murders, extortion, drug trafficking, and prostitution on an international scale.' Lovely man, apparently. Among his nicknames are 'Don Semyon' and 'The Brainy Don'. He is reported to have had a good relationship with Vladimir Putin since the 1990s and lives unchallenged in the Russian capital. The Putin 'good relationship' was described by Russian defector Alexander Litvinenko shortly before he was assassinated in London. Litvinenko had been an officer with the Russian secret service, or FSB, and specialised in organised crime investigation. 'Brainy Don' trafficks Russian and Ukrainian girls to brothels in Israel and the authorities are fine with that so long as the girls aren't Jewish. This, then, is the man who ultimately controls the 'Russian' (ultra-Zionist) Mafia in the United States and worldwide. American investigative journalist Robert Friedman exposed in his book *Red Mafiya: How the Russian Mob Has Invaded America* that the 'Russian Mafia' is really the 'Jewish Mafia' – hence one of its nicknames is the Kosher Nostra in contrast to the Sicilian/Italian Cosa Nostra. Friedman died in 2002 of a 'tropical disease' after those he named put a price on his head. He wrote that the so-called Russian Mafia were all Jewish with connections into Zionist organisations the world over – especially the Anti-Defamation League. Friedman's work was echoed by Jewish writer Laura Radanko, a long-time researcher of the Russian Mafia and author of *The Russian Mafia in America*:

> During the detente days of the early 1970s, when Soviet leader Leonid Brezhnev had agreed to allow limited emigration of Soviet Jews, thousands of hard-core criminals, many of them released from Soviet Gulags by the KGB, took advantage of their nominal Jewish status to swarm into the United States ... In the 1970s, more than forty thousand Russian Jews settled in Brighton Beach. It was under the shadow of the elevated subway tracks on Brighton Beach Avenue, bustling with Russian meat markets, vegetable pushcarts, and bakeries, that the Russian gangsters resumed their careers as professional killers, thieves, and scoundrels.

Radanko says there were 30 Russian crime syndicates operating in the United States with major ones in New York, Miami, San Francisco, Los Angeles and Denver. Their hierarchy locks into Mossad and the Sabbatian-Frankist, ultra-Zionist, Revisionist Zionist, appropriately 'Gun Zionism', networks across the United States. They are brutally violent and often openly so to terrify law enforcement, politicians and anyone else who seeks to challenge them or refuse to do what they are ordered to do. Another tide of Russian ultra-Zionists relocated to the US in the 1990s, among them former KGB officers and veterans of the Soviet war in Afghanistan. They and their successors are so merciless that it is said 'they will shoot people just to see if their guns work'. More empathy-deleted psychopaths, in other words, and they are not nearly as rare as people think. This makes it easier to understand why American politicians jump to attention when the ultra-Zionists speak – this and the same merciless approach of Mossad which I will be coming to. There are many 'incentives' for politicians to do what they are told and not all of them are financial. Israel is the 'spiritual' home of the Sabbatian-Frankist ultra-Zionists – Russian and otherwise – and a safe place to run when trouble brews. Dr M. Raphael Johnson wrote the following in a *Barnes Review* article called *The Judeo-Russian Mafia: From the Gulag to Brooklyn to World Dominion*:

The roots of Jewish organized crime go far back into tsarist times. Organized crime syndicates assisted Lenin's gangs in bank robberies and the creation of general mayhem. During the so-called revolution, it was difficult, sometimes impossible, to distinguish between Bolshevik ideologues and Jewish organized crime syndicates. They acted in nearly an identical manner ...

... The state of Israel is a major factor in the rise and power of the Jewish mafia. Jewish drug dealers, child porn pushers and slave traders are free from prosecution in Israel. Israel does not consider these to be crimes, so long as the victims are non-Jews. The Israeli state will not extradite its citizens to non-Jewish countries, and, therefore, Jewish murderers can quite easily escape punishment in Israel.

There is ultra-Zionist law and the law the ultra-Zionists demand is imposed on everyone else. We'll see the escape to Israel scam in relation to 9/11 in the chapters that follow.

Kosher Nostra and Trump

This brings me to the Donald Trump connection. Robert Mueller, the FBI chief appointed two weeks before 9/11 who then played his part in the cover up, was named to investigate allegations of Russian collusion with Trump to win the 2016 presidential election. At the level that Mueller investigated this made-up 'plot' the claim about collusion was nonsense and politically-motivated to ensure that Trump would not secure closer connections and cooperation with Russian President Vladimir Putin. This is why the 'Russian collusion' story began immediately Trump was elected. The Hidden Hand wants conflict with Russia, not friendship, and as a result of the claims and Mueller's 'investigation' Trump dared not get closer to Russia and indeed became tougher – not least through sanctions – than any post-war president in an effort to show he was not 'Putin's puppet'. In the end, as I predicted in my last book, no evidence was uncovered by Mueller to show Trump and Russian government collusion. No, Trump is not *Putin's* puppet – he's an ultra-Zionist puppet and caught in another pincer movement with the ultra-Zionists around him dictating his policy while those opposing him in the Democrat Party boxed him in from the other direction to stop any Trump policies unacceptable to the ultra-Zionist agenda from becoming law. Ultra-Zionist Capitol Hill 'Democratic' stalwarts Adam Schiff, Chuck Schumer and Steve Cohen played the role of 'bad cops' to the 'good cops' (same cops) that encircle Trump by pressing the insane Russia investigation and doing everything they can to block a border wall on the scale that Trump promised. Soros money was involved as always, too. Schiff ended up with access to sensitive American 'intel' on the House Intelligence Committee. This is the man that Fox News host Tucker

Carlson called 'a reckless serial liar'. However, there *is* a Russian connection that Mueller did not investigate and indeed wouldn't dare. This is the link between Trump and the Russian ultra-Zionist Mafia in New York. Trump's mentor and legal advisor from the early 1970s until his death from AIDS in 1986 was the ultra-Zionist, Kosher Nostra-connected Roy Cohn. His death came a few weeks after being disbarred for unethical conduct by the Appellate Division of the New York State Supreme Court. What kept them? The stunningly corrupt Cohn was also chief counsel to Senator Joseph McCarthy's 'communist' witch-hunt in the 1950s which was a version of the 'anti-Semitism' witch-hunt today. Under Cohn's support and protection Donald Trump became a front man for the ultra-Zionists operating out of New York with their fundamental connections to the 'Russian' ultra-Zionist Mafia for whom Cohn worked. Cohn also represented Rupert Murdoch, the media mogul and fanatical Israel supporter, and introduced him to Trump to start a long friendship. *Esquire* magazine described Cohn in an article headed 'Don't mess with Roy Cohn' as the most feared lawyer in New York and 'a ruthless master of dirty tricks... [with] ... more than one Mafia Don on speed dial'. Cohn worked for both the Jewish and Italian Mafias and these connected into Trump's building projects and the organisations he used for supply and construction.

Trump borrowed huge amounts of money from 72 banks with major ultra-Zionist connections and they never called in the debts to put him out of business. He built two casinos in Atlantic City and bought the massive Taj Mahal operation. Together they were a disaster waiting to happen because of the debt payments involved. By the start of the 1990s he owed $4 billion to banks that he couldn't pay including almost $1 billion that he would have had to find personally. The 72 banks were represented in negotiations with Trump by real estate lawyer Alan Pomerantz who would later say that they didn't foreclose and send Trump into mega-bankruptcy because he was worth more to them 'alive than dead' (bankrupt). Trump also approached BT Securities Corporation and Rothschild Inc. to devise a plan to get him out of trouble and the Rothschild senior managing director who handled the case and sorted out Trump's debacle was Wilber Ross who would be named US Commerce Secretary when Trump was elected US President. Ross worked for the Rothschilds for 27 years. Zionist investor Carl Icahn was a major help in the bail-out by buying the Taj Mahal casino and Trump talked about him becoming Treasury Secretary during his election campaign. Ultra-Zionist Steve Mnuchin was given that job while Icahn was named Special Advisor to the President on Regulatory Reform. Icahn also had some tremendous good fortune when he sold holdings sensitive to the price of steel three days before Trump imposed a 235 percent tariff on steel imports. The timely sale is reported to have saved Icahn $31.3 million. The Trump bankruptcy lawyer hired to advise him through the Atlantic City disaster was ultra-ultra-Zionist David M. Friedman who Trump would later make US ambassador to Israel to oversee the relocation of the US embassy from Tel Aviv to Jerusalem. Friedman and ultra-Zionist Jason Greenblatt, executive vice president and chief legal officer to Donald Trump and the Trump Organization, helped Trump recover from financial disaster. Trump made Greenblatt his Assistant to the President and Special Representative for International Negotiations including Israel-Palestine. The ultra-Zionist/Death Cult Mafia in all its financial and legal forms own Donald Trump and whatever Israel has demanded has been given from day one of the Trump presidency. Trump is owned by ultra-Zionist Neocons and even the Democratic Party is now being dubbed 'the Neocon Party' because it supports war every bit as much as the Republicans. When Tulsi Gabbard, Democrat Representative for Hawaii, announced plans in early 2019 to run for US President she was fiercely attacked by Neocon/Soros 'progressives' in her own party (and the pro-Neocon Democrat media) because she opposes American wars in the Middle East. The vast Israel lobby was immediately on her case, too, as you would expect. Ultra-Zionist Sheldon Adelson funds a right-wing warmongering Neocon Republican Party and George Soros funds a right-wing warmongering Neocon Democratic Party which both pursue the same Middle Eastern policy in the one-party state. Trump is surrounded and owned and his bombastic style gives the appearance of him making decisions when they are being made for him by Sabbatian-Frankists and ultra-Zionists. Israeli daily *Haaretz* reported on contributions to Trump by ultra-Zionist Russian oligarchs:

> Of 10 billionaires with Kremlin ties who funneled political contributions to U.S. President Donald Trump and a number of top Republican leaders, at least five are Jewish ... There's Len Blavatnik, the dual British-American citizen who dumped huge amounts of cash on Republican candidates in the last election cycle, much of it funneled through his myriad investment firms. (The same Len Blavatnik funds scholarships for IDF veterans and who is friends with Israeli Prime Minister Benjamin Netanyahu.) Alexander Shustorovich is the president of IMG Artists, a titan among impresarios, who gave Trump's inauguration committee a cool $1 million ... The list goes on.

David Friedman 'advised' (love it) Trump on Israel and Jewish matters during his presidential campaign and co-chaired Trump's Israel Advisory Committee with Jason Greenblatt. Friedman has headed the American Friends of Bet El Institutions which donates $2 million a year to the illegal Jewish settlement of Bet El in the occupied Palestinian West Bank. Jared Kushner, Trump's ultra-Zionist son-in-law and senior

advisor, a life-long friend of Benjamin Netanyahu, has made donations
to American Friends of Bet El. Ultra-Zionists utterly dominate Trump
and he has served perfectly their agenda for divide and rule in the
United States aided by the 'progressive' mob funded by Soros. Is it any
wonder that under this administration Israel has been given everything
it wants while Palestinians have seen aid money cut back and warned it
will get worse if they don't do as they're told? This has included
threatened 'consequences' against Palestinians for joining nearly a dozen
international bodies and conventions. The Trump administration
announced in 2018 a plan to delete all US funding or the main UN
programme for Palestinian refugees, the United Nations Relief and
Works Agency for Palestine Refugees in the Near East (UNRWA), with
devastating impacts on five million people who rely on its schools,
healthcare and social services. The five million are those (and their
descendants) who fled or were expelled from their homes amid ultra-
Zionist terror in 1948 and as a result of 1967 Six Day war. The arrogance
of the US and Israel takes the breath away. They want to bring
Palestinians to their knees and then force them to accept whatever they
are given – *nothing*, basically – while the Sabbatian-Frankists pursue
their Greater Israel and they will get all the support they ask for from
ultra-Zionist operatives within Western political parties. In early 2019
both the Conservative and Labour Party Friends of Israel were pressing
the British government to stop funding for UNWRA and the Palestinian
Authority. Leading the campaign from the Labour side was ultra-Zionist
Liverpool MP Louise Ellman, vice-chair of Labour Friends of Israel.
Ellman voted 'very strongly' for the Iraq War and 'very strongly' against
an investigation into the war when it turned out to be a humanitarian
disaster. Ellman is 'very concerned' about 'anti-Semitism' in the Labour
Party. But clearly not about Palestinians.

Israel created and controlled by Russian/Soviet ultra-Zionists

The Russia connection extends to Israel itself with a million-plus citizens
of the former Soviet Union migrating to Israel in recent decades. The
effect on Israeli society was described in a *Guardian* article by one-time
Jerusalem correspondent Harriet Sherwood headed 'Israel's former
Soviet immigrants transform adopted country'. We have already seen a
clear common theme between those born in Russia and the one-time
Russian Empire and political power in the new Israel. Now this was a
further influx from the same region. Harriet Sherwood described how
these incomers have 'influenced the culture, high-tech industry,
language, education and, perhaps most significantly, Israeli politics.' The
influx has been so great they constitute 15 percent of the country's
population, but not all of them are Jewish. Traditional Judaism insists
that a Jew is someone with a Jewish mother or a person who goes

through a formal conversion to Judaism. When the Soviet Union collapsed in 1990, however, the criteria for people from there to become Israeli citizens under 'right of return' was expanded to include those with a Jewish father or grandparent or anyone *married* to someone who has. Sherwood reports that according to Israel's Central Bureau of Statistics around *30 percent* of immigrants from the former Soviet Union in the 1990s were not Jews or not considered Jewish under Orthodox law. The figure had increased to *59 percent* by 2005 with only about five percent converting to Judaism. Sherwood writes:

> ... they almost overwhelmed Israel, causing a severe housing crisis. Many eventually settled in Russian enclaves in cities such as Ashdod, Petah Tikva and Haifa – and in expanding [illegal] West Bank settlements, such as Ariel.

> 'It was a very different type of immigration,' said Lily Galili, an Israeli journalist writing a book about the impact of the tidal wave from the former Soviet Union. 'They didn't want to integrate. They wanted to lead. They changed the nature of the country.'

They have certainly in a short time begun to dominate Israeli politics and the former Soviet Union is a major centre for Sabbatian-Frankism. One of their prime vehicles is the far right 'Gun Zionist' Yisrael Beiteinu Party of Netanyahu's one-time Defence Minister, the Moldova-born psychopath Avigdor Lieberman who lives in the illegally-occupied West Bank. Lily Galili said that unfortunately migrants from former Soviet states had changed the nature of democracy in Israel. 'They have strengthened and given confidence to the secular right wing', she said, and she point to alienation between Russian immigrants and native Israelis. 'There is not much social interaction. There are still places for "Russians" that "Israelis" don't go and aren't wanted – and vice versa.' Auschwitz survivor Esther Bejarano pointed out that Israeli settlements in the occupied West Bank were mainly for those from Eastern Europe and the United States:

> They have no business there. Nothing at all, and you know who these settlers are? These are Americans and Russians, Ukrainians. They were not born there. Absolutely not.

Bejarano said the idea that the land 'belongs to the Jews because they lived there 2,000 years ago is the biggest nonsense there can be' – 'There were so many Turks and Arabs who have always lived there. The Jews came later.' Who are these people have taken over Israel to a large extent, many of whom are *not Jews*? What is the significance of the Soviet Union where there was such a ridiculous ratio of Zionists among those who triggered the Russian Revolution?

Control of money and information

Key areas targeted by the Sabbatian-Frankist Death Cult are banking
and finance, politics, law, intuitions of social engineering and media. The
last two are crucial. They want to control the perceptions of the target
population so they will act and see the world and events in the desired
manner. From this manipulated perception comes their behaviour, what
they will do and not do, accept and not accept, challenge and not
challenge, condemn and not condemn. For example, the man credited
with being among the first to 'warn' about the threat of 'global Islam'
which exploded as an issue as a result of 9/11 is Avi Lipkin (pen name
Victor Mordecai) with his 1995 book, *Is Fanatic Islam a Global Threat?*
Lipkin is an American-born Israeli who served in the Israeli Defense
Forces and with the press office intelligence department of Israeli Prime
Minister and Revisionist Zionist terrorist, Yitzhak Shamir. Lipkin
claimed to have spoken in 500 churches worldwide and his role has been
to bring Christian Zionists on board with his 'Islam must be stopped',
'Armageddon' claptrap. I am no supporter of any religion, certainly not
Islam, but by far the greatest danger to the world is from the satanic
orchestrators of Sabbatian-Frankism. They to a large extent own and
control the global media to dictate the way their manipulations and
wars are reported to the population for whom they have a contempt so
deep that words do not suffice – not least their contempt for non-
Sabbatian-Frankist Jewish people. Ultra-Zionist columnist Joel Stein
wrote an article in the *Los Angeles Times* in 2008 headed 'Who runs
Hollywood? C'mon' in which he said: 'I don't care if Americans think
we're running the news media, Hollywood, Wall Street or the
government. I just care that we get to *keep* running them.' He went on:

> I have never been so upset by a poll in my life. Only 22% of Americans now
> believe 'the movie and television industries are pretty much run by Jews,'
> down from nearly 50% in 1964. The Anti-Defamation League, which released
> the poll results last month, sees in these numbers a victory against
> stereotyping. Actually, it just shows how dumb America has gotten. Jews
> totally run Hollywood.

> How deeply Jewish is Hollywood? When the studio chiefs took out a full-page
> ad in the Los Angeles Times a few weeks ago to demand that the Screen
> Actors Guild settle its contract, the open letter was signed by: News Corp.
> President Peter Chernin (Jewish), Paramount Pictures Chairman Brad Grey
> (Jewish), Walt Disney Co. Chief Executive Robert Iger (Jewish), Sony Pictures
> Chairman Michael Lynton (surprise, Dutch Jew), Warner Bros. Chairman Barry
> Meyer (Jewish), CBS Corp. Chief Executive Leslie Moonves (so Jewish his great

uncle was the first prime minister of Israel), MGM Chairman Harry Sloan (Jewish) and NBC Universal Chief Executive Jeff Zucker (mega-Jewish). If either of the Weinstein brothers had signed, this group would have not only the power to shut down all film production but to form a minyan with enough Fiji water on hand to fill a mikvah.

The person they were yelling at in that ad was SAG President Alan Rosenberg (take a guess). The scathing rebuttal to the ad was written by entertainment super-agent Ari Emanuel (Jew with Israeli parents) on the Huffington Post, which is owned by Arianna Huffington (not Jewish and has never worked in Hollywood).

The Jews are so dominant, I had to scour the trades to come up with six Gentiles in high positions at entertainment companies. When I called them to talk about their incredible advancement, five of them refused to talk to me, apparently out of fear of insulting Jews. The sixth, AMC President Charlie Collier, turned out to be Jewish.

As a proud Jew, I want America to know about our accomplishment. Yes, we control Hollywood. Without us, you'd be flipping between 'The 700 Club' and 'Davey and Goliath' on TV all day.

So I've taken it upon myself to re-convince America that Jews run Hollywood by launching a public relations campaign, because that's what we do best. I'm weighing several slogans, including: 'Hollywood: More Jewish than ever!'; 'Hollywood: From the people who brought you the Bible'; and 'Hollywood: If you enjoy TV and movies, then you probably like Jews after all.

If anyone else said that Zionists control the news media, Hollywood, Wall Street and the government they would be condemned as racists and neo-Nazis repeating an 'anti-Semitic trope' even though they say it themselves. Ultra-Zionist Jeff Zucker at NBC Universal is now head of CNN while the chairman of the journalistically corrupt NBC News and MSNBC is ultra-Zionist Andrew Lack. The sheer arrogance of those *claiming* to represent *two percent* of the American population and 0.2 *percent* of the world population is hard to imagine. Joel Stein said that then ADL chief Abraham Foxman agreed that Jews are disproportionately represented in the creative industry. 'They're disproportionate as lawyers and probably medicine here as well', he said. But he did not want Stein to brag about their control of Hollywood and the entertainment industry:

That's a very dangerous phrase, 'Jews control Hollywood'. What is true is that there are a lot of Jews in Hollywood,' he said. Instead of 'control,' Foxman would prefer people say that many executives in the industry 'happen to be Jewish,' as in 'all eight major film studios are run by men who happen to be Jewish.'

The ADL is actually there to stop people seeing the Zionist influence by intimidating into silence those who *can* see the obvious with the 'anti-Semite' technique. Anyone trying to silence the truth or freedom of speech has an agenda to protect. Ultra-Zionist American lawyer Alan Dershowitz agrees that Jewish people 'are represented in large numbers in various professionals such as the academy, finance, and the media' and he says this is because 'they have proved to be successful at these enterprises'. In some cases that will be true, but *all* of them? As Joel Stein would say ... c'mon. Dershowitz points out in support of his case that 'there is poverty among many Jews, particularly the elderly' and I would respond this way: (1) I am not saying that all Jews are involved in a conspiracy. I am saying that the great majority are victims of the Sabbatian-Frankist Death Cult of fake Jews who use them as camouflage; (2) If the goal is protecting Jewish people why is there 'poverty among many Jews, particularly the elderly' when there are others worth multiple-billions? American psychologist Kevin B. MacDonald, a former professor of psychology at California State University, Long Beach, confirmed Joel Stein's analysis in a trilogy of books which included *The Culture of Critique: An Evolutionary Analysis of Jewish Involvement in Twentieth-Century Intellectual and Political Movements* published in 2002. MacDonald documents the absolutely extraordinary power of Zionism over Hollywood and the American broadcast and print media which applied in the period across 9/11. He has naturally been dubbed an 'anti-Semite' because facts are no defence against that. Ultra-Zionists don't want to debate facts so they deal only in abuse. As we head back towards the detailed background to 9/11 it is important to know the scale of control that ultra-Zionists had at that time – as now – over government, Pentagon, law and media. It will explain so much from the next chapter onwards.

Shoot the messenger – stop the message

Media control of the Israel/Zionist narrative is also achieved by firing anyone who offers criticism of either. When others see their colleagues sacked in an instant they know they had better stay silent about anything that could put Israel and Zionism in a bad light. Jim Clancy worked as a journalist, correspondent and anchor on CNN for 34 years but resigned in 2015 after tweeting that attacks on him on Twitter were possibly part of the Israeli Hasbara campaign of systematic propaganda. Compared with those mild comments and a justifiable question 34 years of service meant nothing to CNN. He had to go. Only ludicrous, tongues-out, establishment-repeater clones like Chris Cuomo, Don Lemon, Jim Acosta and former CIA intern Anderson Cooper need apply to CNN these days. Contempt for journalism and a willingness to sell your soul must be ticked on the application form to even secure an interview. See also MSNBC where presenter Rachel Maddow is a disgrace to journalism and the BBC which is Britain's CNN and another disgrace to journalism. Maddow the fake 'journalist' was actually close to tears on air after the Mueller investigation found no provable Trump collusion with Russia (Fig 133). Twitter banned the account of someone making fun of the incident involving a television host who had misled America for two years over Russia and Trump – as did CNN, NBC and others. The BBC can't be so openly biased because of (one-sided) British media 'impartiality' laws but achieves the same biased end through story angles and emphasis, omission, language, labels and choice of interviewees. Britain's state broadcaster feels the need to tell us often how honest and trustworthy it is hoping that we won't notice that it isn't (see 'America is the freest country in the world'). CNN ended the contributor contract of academic Marc Lamont Hill after his comments about the Israel-Palestine conflict were labelled 'anti-Semitic'. Yawn. Hill accused Israel of 'ethnic

Figure 133: Don't cry, Rachael, biased excuse for a journalist. Just tell the bloody truth – that's all we ask.

cleansing' and denying Palestinians due process and compared the experience of the African American struggle against slavery and apartheid in the United States. He called for a new model of regional peace based on a single state with equal rights to Israelis and Palestinians (the ultra-Zionists' worse nightmare) with the two-state 'solution' now dead in the water after so much Jewish-*only* settlement in illegally-occupied Palestinian land. Hill said there should be 'a Free Palestine from the river to the sea' – from the Jordan to the Mediterranean. This was spun as a call to remove all Jews from the region – which it wasn't – but it's okay for the founding charter of the Likud Party of terrorists Menachem Begin and Benjamin Netanyahu to demand that: 'Between the sea and the Jordan there will only be Israeli sovereignty.' The way the global Israeli propaganda network operates can be clearly seen in the response to what Hill said in a much longer speech at a United Nations event marking the International Day of Solidarity with Palestine. Jewish 'leaders' began calling for Hill's dismissal from his position at Temple University. Targeting the income and careers of those who criticise Israel is a foundation modus operandi and a warning to others to keep quiet or risk losing both. Who were these 'Jewish leaders' with their 'spontaneous' response of outrage? Well ... the *Philadelphia Inquirer* reported that one was Leonard Barrack, a 'Temple trustee and major donor' to Temple University, a Temple alumnus and former finance chairman of the Democratic National Committee (DNC). Barrack is also former president of the Jewish Federation of Greater Philadelphia which hosts events with AIPAC and Israel lobby group StandWithUs exposed in the Al Jazeera documentaries over its manipulation on US campuses. Barrack said of Hill: 'He called for the destruction of the State of Israel in code words. I am very upset about it. I think it was anti-Semitic.' Another demand for Hill to be sacked came from Morton Klein, President of the Zionist Organization of America, who is close to the Trump administration and the President's biggest donor (owner) Sheldon Adelson who, in turn, is an associate of Benjamin Netanyahu. Klein described 17-year-old Ahed Tamimi, jailed by Israel for slapping a soldier after part of her cousin's head was blown off, as a 'convicted Palestinian-Arab terrorist'. Nice man. Klein was at the forefront of the campaign to remove Trump National Security Adviser H.R. McMaster for alleged 'anti-Israel' beliefs and he was replaced by Israel sycophant and Adelson confidant, the psychopath, John Bolton. Also on Hill's case was the National Council of Young Israel (NCYI), a collective of more than 100 groups throughout the United States. The NCYI was founded more than 100 years ago and claims to have helped to supply weapons to ultra-Zionist terrorist groups, including Irgun, before Israel was established in 1948. The Jewish Federation of Greater Philadelphia, headed by Leonard Barrack, has celebrated Menachem Begin, the Irgun terrorist Israeli prime minister, in yet another show of breathtaking hypocrisy. This is how the ultra-Zionist networks attack their opponents and the mentality of those behind such coordinated attacks. Ultra-Zionist conservative political commentator Ben Shapiro, who some amazingly see as 'alternative', said Hill had called for 'killing all the Jews' in the region when he blatantly had not. With ultra-Zionists positioned across the political spectrum they can come out in unison and say 'see – everyone agrees'. Cuban-American CNN news anchor Rick Sanchez was fired in 2010 after he indicated that Jewish people claim to be an oppressed minority when they have so much power in the media. Compared with their number that statement is clearly factually correct, but truth has no value if it's not what the ultra-Zionists want people to hear. Sanchez then fell to his knees in an effort to save his career. He wrote to Abraham Foxman, then head of the appalling Mossad front, the Anti-Defamation League:

from the official line.' The NBC chairman (and former president) is ultra-Zionist Andrew Lack. BBC reporter and presenter Tim Willcox was pressured to apologise for a 'poorly phrased question' after telling a Jewish woman that Palestinians 'suffer hugely at Jewish hands' during a live interview at a Paris anti-terrorism rally. Willcox said: 'Many critics of Israel's policy would suggest that the Palestinians suffer hugely at Jewish hands as well …You understand everything is seen from different perspectives.' Once again this is true and once again truth is no defence from the ultra-Zionist mob. Jewish historian Simon Schama said the question was appalling and as always the hypocrisy of *Jewish Chronicle* editor Jonathan Pollard and the Campaign Against Antisemitism of Jewish National Fund board member Gideon Falter couldn't be unleashed fast enough. Top American basketball player LeBron James lashed out in 2018 against 'a bunch of old white men owning teams and they got that slave mentality.' That was okay – and it is – to express those views, but shortly afterwards when he quoted rap lyrics that included the line 'We been getting that Jewish money, everything is Kosher' he immediately apologised because that was not okay. There is no 'Jewish money', you see, no Jewish billionaires funding both sides in US politics. It's all a myth, an 'anti-Semitic trope', so it is outrageous to even raise the subject and most certainly 'anti-Semitic'. As for exposing ultra-Zionists like the Rothschilds for their serious involvement in the slave trade – you must be a Nazi to say that even though it's true.

Israel-born and now British-based anti-Zionist activist and musician Gilad Atzmon has long contended that 'Jewish power is the power to silence opposition to Jewish power'. I would put it like this: 'Sabbatian-Frankist power is the power to silence opposition to Sabbatian-Frankist power by presenting it as Jewish power and weaponising 'anti-Semitism' to target opponents. Atzmon, even though born into a Jewish family in Israel, is one of the hate figures of the ultra-Zionist Protection Racket and they even seek to have him banned from musical events when all he is doing is playing the saxophone. Islington's Labour-controlled council in London – the area where Labour leader Jeremy Corbyn is an MP – banned Atzmon from playing at a concert in the borough after a *single* complaint from a rabid ultra-Zionist who constantly excuses Israel's disgusting and merciless treatment of Palestinians. You'll find Islington Council in the phone book under 'i' for idiots or 's' for spineless. All who challenge the extremes of Zionism and the Israeli government must be destroyed both financially and in terms of their reputation; but the tide is turning because people are increasingly sick of 'anti-hate' groups promoting hatred and self-serving censorship. Jonathan Schanzer from the ultra-Zionist front, the Foundation for the Defense of Democracy, was caught on a hidden camera saying that those who challenge Israel must be smeared in other ways because 'Personally I think anti-Semitism as a smear is not what it used to be.' Too right, mate. You've overcooked the mantra and now people are seeing through the game.

SiliCON Valley

By far the most important media control today is based in Silicon Valley, California, or the 'Devil's Playground' as I prefer to call it. The Hidden Hand and its Sabbatian-Frankist, ultra-Zionist arm have worked to transfer the circulation of information from newspapers and television to the Internet because then it can be censored by artificial intelligence algorithms with not even human intervention once the codes are in place. Set the algorithms to censor key words or subjects and you can dictate, potentially in total, what people see and don't see. This is the ultimate ambition of the Hidden Hand and Sabbatian-Frankist ultra-Zionism. The gathering censorship of alternative voices using the systematically-decreed excuses of 'hate speech', 'fake news' and political correctness (see the ultra-Zionist Frankfurt School) is this very agenda unfolding before us and becoming more extreme by the day. In the light of this is it an obviously legitimate question to ask why Internet information giants and near-monopolies are dominated by a fraction of 0.2 percent of the global population. It is not only legitimate to ask this question, but absolutely essential for *everyone* to ask it and that includes Jewish people because they are subject to the same censorship by the same people when they don't sing from the official song-sheet. I have already mentioned that Google is run by Larry Page (Zionist) and Sergey Brin (Zionist); Google's YouTube by Susan Wojcicki (Zionist); Facebook by Mark Zuckerberg (Zionist) and Chief Operating Officer Sheryl Sandberg (Zionist), formerly with Google; and the chairman of Apple is Arthur D. Levinson (Zionist). The statistical chances of this happening from such a tiny percentage of the population must be astronomical given the power these companies have over global communication through the Internet and technology. Add-in the fact that ultra-Zionist hate groups are being employed to 'advise' these ultra-Zionist-controlled companies on who and what to censor and that includes the ultra-Zionist CAA in the UK which targets me and the Labour Party. I doubt the Jewish National Fund will be censored for peddling apartheid.

The ultra-Zionist hate group and apartheid-supporting Anti-Defamation League (ADL) established its own state-of-the-art censorship centre in Silicon Valley and you are looking at a gigantic scam to control what the world population can see and hear. It is part-funded by eBay founder Pierre Omidyar who also contributes to the George Soros Open Society Foundations and has big Pentagon connections. Omidyar is another fake 'progressive' in the mould of Soros who funds Neocon regime change operations and organisations closely connected to ultra-Zionist Bill Kristol, co-founder of the Project for the New American Century. Investigative journalists Alexander Rubinstein and Max Blumenthal uncovered many of these connections for MintPress News. Rubinstein said:

> If partnering with the Neocon think tank guru who was a main conduit for US government messaging in the lead-up to the Iraq War is 'progressive' then I think it's time we retire the term.

Omidyar also bought The Intercept website via his First Look Media and shut down access to its archive of documents leaked by National Security Agency whistleblower Edward Snowden. This is same Omidyar funding the ADL Internet censorship centre. Multi-billionaire Soros, the 'progressive'-funding ultra-Zionist in disguise, is financially-supporting 'fact-checking' and search engine groups that seek to dictate the information that the ultra-Zionist-controlled Silicon Valley giants will allow to be communicated. Apple CEO Tim Cook was the first recipient of the ADL's 'Courage Against Hate Award' in 2018 which was a mind-boggling irony given that the ADL is an extreme hate group that sets out to get the public to hate its targets. This disgusting organisation was exposed for supporting the apartheid regime in South Africa and is controlled by the far right Israeli government which indoctrinates Israelis to hate Palestinians. Cook seized the chance in his acceptance speech at the ADL's 'Annual Summit on Anti-Semitism and Hate' to say that 'conspiracy theories' should be banned – exactly what ultra-Zionist hate groups like the ADL have been working so hard to achieve. Cook suggested that the Holocaust was a function of too much free speech when what happened in Nazi Germany was actually caused by *too little*. Why does he think the Nazis went on a rampage of book burning?? My God, *what an idiot*. Nazis, like all tyrannies, targeted free speech to silence critics and those who could otherwise have exposed what they were doing. They burned books they didn't want people to see – just like Silicon Valley is involved in digital book-burning. They banned or broke up public meetings of opponents just like the 'progressive' 'anti-fascist' Soros-backed mob and the CAA and censor-network seek to do today. Apple and other ultra-Zionist Internet dominants banned conspiracy radio show host Alex Jones from their platforms in 2018 which freedom-deleting Cook was quite happy to crow about. The level of narcissistic arrogance and self-obsession required to demand freedom of speech for yourself while seeking to deny that to other people is beyond my comprehension. I don't agree with a lot that Alex Jones says – and some I do – but that is irrelevant to the fact that his freedom is speech is *everyone's* freedom of speech. If he doesn't have it then no one does because all that is left is the 'freedom' to conform to what authority decides to allow. It is worth making the point, too, that while Cook and Apple talk about their 'values' they have already sold hundreds of millions of their WIFI 'Airpods' (many to children and young people) which constantly pass frequency waves through the brain. Apple doesn't know the consequences because they have done no long-term studies, but to anyone *with* a brain those consequences are bloody obvious in dangers to health and brain function. How comforting that Apple and Cook have 'values'.

The 'hate-speech' scam

So-called 'hate speech' constantly expands the excuse for censorship as the definition gets longer by the hour. Things like incitement to violence are subject to criminal law and that is where it should be addressed and debated – in open public courts. It should not be at the behest of biased people like Tim Cook, Zuckerberg, Brin, Page and other corporate dictators to impose their views and agenda on the rest of the human race. People should be free to say anything they like and their views then be open to public debate and challenge while involving the criminal law where violence is being promoted against others. In short, what people say should be dealt with *after* their words are delivered and not *before* as the Internet censors want to achieve through artificial intelligence. The difference between the two is utterly pivotal for human freedom. When speech is addressed *after* delivery there is no way any authority can dictate what people see and hear; but once you accept censorship *before* delivery you are giving exactly that power to authority. What's more the criteria for pre-delivery censorship just goes on growing ... incitement to terrorism, incitement to violence, 'hate speech', 'fake news', hurting anyone's 'feelings'. The list goes on and on until there is no freedom left which has been the plan all along. Tim Cook's ADL speech was a classic misrepresentation of what he was claiming to stand for as he couched his 'ban conspiracy theories' in the smokescreen of 'white supremacy'. In doing so he was following the blueprint of connecting in the public mind free speech and the far right. Link the two together psychologically and then when anyone calls for freedom of speech they are automatically considered 'far right extremists' who believe in 'white supremacy'. I think that anyone who self-identifies the 'I' with the transitory labels of race has completely missed the point about the nature of reality, but it's okay it seems to claim to be God's Chosen People while seeking to silence others for seeing their own race as above all others. I say both are forms of extreme and idiotic racism because I am against racism *in totality* – not only where it suits me. Cook said that companies like Apple need to 'do the right thing' rather than debate whether they are being impartial or not: 'If we can't be clear on moral questions like these, we've got big problems'. Oh, do piss off. It's about silencing speech and information you don't want people to hear – end of. If only they were honest about it. That would be bad enough because of the consequences for human freedom, but to justify politically-targeted censorship on the basis of the (non-existent) 'morality' of global corporations is definitely sick-bag territory. We are in the midst of a tiny few people controlling all global communication for more than 7.7 billion people and the weaponisation of 'anti-Semitism' is being used to protect this tyranny from exposure. Well, *bollocks* to that. Call me what you like, I don't care. What I *do* care about is free speech, the very foundation of freedom, and the truth of what is really happening.

Time for us all – Jewish and non-Jewish – to call it out

Once again I emphasise the consequences of what the ultra-Zionists and Sabbatian-Frankists are doing for the rest of the Jewish population. Many people can't or won't distinguish between the Death Cult and ultra-Zionist extremists and Jews in general because they don't know about the Cult. Thus the actions of the Cult are blamed on the whole Jewish population and people are getting increasingly enraged at the actions and fascistic tendencies of the Cult. It is well past the time when the overwhelming majority of Jewish people who are not part of any of this start speaking out against its impact on global affairs and the way they themselves are perceived. A CNN survey of 'anti-Semitism' in Europe revealed:

> More than a quarter of Europeans surveyed believe Jews have too much influence in business and finance. One in five say they have too much influence in media and politics. In some countries the numbers are often higher: 42% of Hungarians think Jews have too much influence in finance and business across the world.

The CNN poll also claimed that in Poland '50% of people think that Jews use the Holocaust to advance their position'. These numbers should be of great concern to Jewish people in general because they indicate that efforts to control the narrative have been far from successful and they need to distance themselves from the extremists using them as cover. Israel-born activist Gilad Atzmon wrote:

> If Jews want to be loved or simply just ignored, then: (1) maybe the European Jewish Congress should seriously consider the possible consequences of its 'demand' that 'the Bible and the Koran use "trigger warnings" to highlight anti-Semitic passages'; (2) the French Jewish organisations might want to reconsider their relentless campaign to decimate the artistic career of France's most popular comedian; or (3) it might not be a great idea for Britain's Jewish

institutions to interfere with British national politics by smearing Britain's number one anti-racist [a reference to the Labour Party's Jeremy Corbyn although I wish he would grow a spine].

It is vital for people to see the difference between the Sabbatian-Frankist Death Cult and its ultra-Zionist gofers and lackeys and Jewish people in general. They are not the same. It is way past the time for Jewish people to address the extremists and cultists who exploit them to silence exposure.

And so back to 9/11

Zionist and ultra-Zionist organisations form a network across America and the world to manipulate and impose the will of ultra-Zionism and the Sabbatian-Frankist Death Cult which the great majority of Jewish people have no idea exists. They see these organisations as only there to promote the interests of Israel and the land to which they believe they have an historic right. No such right exists, but that has to be indoctrinated into them from birth so they act as unknowing stooges to the Sabbatian-Frankist agenda. It helps, too, when people claim a 'Jewish plot' to take over the world when that is exactly what the Sabbatian-Frankists want to hear to give cover to the real perpetrators that merely exploit the Jewish majority as a convenient shield to hide within. Jewish children are indoctrinated with the belief that the rest of humanity hates them and so they have to stick together behind the collective protection of what are Sabbatian-Frankists posing as Jewish leaders. Fear is the currency of control and the Death Cult employs this mercilessly against the Jewish majority. Add the Kosher Nostra networks of organised crime which interlock with Mossad, the ultra-Zionists in Israel and the rest of the web within The Web – add control of so much of government and media – and you have a hidden stream of interconnections perfectly capable of perpetrating and then covering up 9/11.

Out of these networks in the United States and Israel came the Project for the New American Century and the attacks of 9/11 that were essential to triggering the long-planned response of regime change in the Middle East and elsewhere and the systematic deletion of privacy and civil rights worldwide. From this detailed background we will now return to 9/11 and who was *really* responsible. The 'why?' is already painfully obvious.

CHAPTER 23

Just a coincidence?

And if all others accepted the lie which the Party imposed – if all records told the same tale – then the lie passed into history and became truth. 'Who controls the past' ran the Party slogan, 'controls the future: who controls the present controls the past' – George Orwell, 1984

Sabbatian-Frankism, ultra-Zionism and Revisionist 'Gun' Zionism have a long and sickening history of using violence to get their way. This forced the British out of Palestine, established the State of Israel and Gun Zionism's military and intelligence arms, the Israeli Defense Forces (IDF), Mossad, Shin Bet and other global assets have ever since followed that lead to bomb, kill and terrorise in pursuit of the Death Cult's agenda of global control.

We should not be surprised to find, therefore, that the attacks of September 11th, 2001, have ultra-Zionist and Death Cult fingerprints all over them, but please don't take my word for it. Consider the evidence and connections I will present – together with those already presented – and see if you think they are all simply bizarre coincidences. I emphasise again (because I know I will be massively misrepresented) that I am not saying 9/11 was a 'Jewish plot'. This would require me to claim that all Jewish people were involved in accordance with how a 'Jewish plot' is defined by the 'anti-Semitism' industry and the Protection Racket. I am absolutely not saying that and indeed in so many ways I am saying the opposite – that claims of a 'Jewish global conspiracy' have perfectly served those who truly drive the hijacking of global society. The claim has diverted attention from the real perpetrators by (a) blaming 'The Jews' and (b) allowing the weaponisation of 'anti-Semitism' to not only silence criticism of 'The Jews' but to silence exposure of the real perpetrators hiding within and behind the smokescreen of 'The Jews'. The satanic Sabbatian-Frankist Death Cult has infiltrated the Israeli political left, right, and far right and has contempt for traditional Jewishness, Judaism and its advocates. Jewish people have been manipulated to believe that Israel, Judaism and Zionism are the same as fake and fraudulent Sabbatian-Frankist 'Judaism' and 'Zionism' when that is clearly not the case. Sabbatian-Frankists talk like Jews, but act like Satanists and psychopaths. This is why the background set out in the last few chapters has been essential to put 9/11 into its real context.

The Sabbatian-Frankist Cult has arranged for Jews to be indoctrinated from the earliest age into believing historical myths and crucially that the rest of the world hates them. This has been essential to manipulate the population to believe they must be 'protected' by the (Sabbatian-Frankist) ultra-Zionist hierarchy. Claims by ultra-Zionist front groups that 'anti-Semitism is 'on the rise' (it always is according to them) are as much aimed at Jewish people as the rest of the population. They have to be kept in fear and the siege mentality for Sabbatian-Frankists to maintain their control. Former Mossad operative Victor Ostrovsky tells in *By Way of Deception* how he was taught that the State of Israel is incapable of misconduct. Look at the new definition of 'anti-Semitism' and you'll see how that is actually claiming the same. No Jewish person can be criticised because that would be 'anti-Semitic' is only another way of saying that no Jewish person can be legitimately criticised. Yet like every other cultural, religious or racial group you find within the Jewish community nice people, okay people and psychopaths. Why should they be different to every other group? The 'anti-Semitism' industry is there to protect the psychopaths from exposure by using the nice and okay people as their human shield. Most Jewish people are victims of the plot, not perpetrators, but they can be manipulated into serving that plot by believing in the genuineness and Judaistic nature of the psychopaths. Ostrovsky describes how he was told from an early age that Jews were 'the David in the unending struggle against the ever-growing Goliath'. There was 'no one out there to protect us but ourselves – a feeling reinforced by the Holocaust survivors who lived among us'. He says of this indoctrination:

> We, the new generation of Israelites, the resurrected nation on its own land after more than two thousand years of exile, were entrusted with the fate of the nation as a whole. The commanders of our army were called champions, not generals. Our leaders were captains at the helm of a great ship ...

You can see how the mind-fuck works. Keep them in fear of the rest of humanity and they will give their power away to the military and government to protect from their otherwise certain fate. What a perceptual burden to carry from birth and even most of those who serve the Sabbatian-Frankist and ultra-Zionist agenda only do so because their minds and perceptions belong to someone else. You can understand Ostrovsky's one-way indoctrination as he was growing up given that his mother fought for Haganah, the Israeli underground (terrorist group), and his father fought in the Israel-Arab war in 1948 and commanded an Israeli Air Force Base. His grandfather was Auditor General of the apartheid Jewish National Fund (JNF). Ostrovsky writes:

... My own idea of Israel as I was growing up was as the land of milk and honey. That any hardships were worth it. I believed it was a country that would do no wrong, would not inflict evil on others, would set an example to all nations to see and to follow. If there was anything wrong financially or politically in the country, I always imagined this was at the lower echelons of government – with the bureaucrats, who would eventually clean up their act. Basically I believed there were people guarding our rights, great people like [Israel's first Prime Minister] David Ben-Gurion ...

Ostrovsky realised during his time with Mossad as a 'katsa' (case officer) that Israel and its leaders were not like that and hence his extremely brave exposure of what Mossad is really doing. If Jewish people woke up from the life-program they would see that the rest of humanity doesn't hate them and does not seek to destroy them. I have a problem with the Sabbatian-Frankist Death Cult, not Jewish people. I don't agree with the behaviour of *some* Jews and I don't believe in their religion, but that's not the same as hating them for simply *being* them. This is what the real definition of 'anti-Semitism' should be if the term is going to be used at all given that it's a misnomer to start with. In fact, I don't hate *anyone* – what you hate you become just as what you fight you become. See the 'anti-fascist' mobs for confirmation. By contrast those who scream 'anti-Semitism' at every turn are seeking to encourage people to hate their targets while calling themselves 'anti-hate' groups. We should also not forget that the Sabbatian-Frankist Satanic Cult is only part of the Hidden Hand Satanic Cult and I am highlighting this part of The Web because of its clear and obvious connection to 9/11.

War by deception

Control of information and intelligence has always been a prime target for Sabbatian-Frankists with the Rothschilds creating an intelligence and courier network that eclipsed in scale and efficiency those of governments. Knowing what is happening or planned to happen before governments do is an immense source of power. Rabbi Marvin S. Antelman describes in *To Eliminate the Opiate* how the Sabbatian network 'was held together by an elaborate system of communications consisting of couriers and emissaries whose full time job it was to run messages all over Eastern Europe':

Across this network travelled much information and secret messages, some of which have been lying around in archives in Europe. It reached the archives because, from time to time, various governments who were monitoring Sabbatian activity in Europe were able to intercept and confiscate their communications.

These Rothschild and Sabbatian-Frankist communication networks eventually fused to become the national and international intelligence agencies – most especially Israeli Mossad, America's CIA and National Security Agency (NSA) nexus, and Britain's MI5 (domestic) and MI6 (overseas). Victor Ostrovsky said he was told during his Mossad training in the 1980s that its motto is: 'By way of deception, thou shalt do war'. This certainly encapsulates the techniques of Mossad (Israeli global intelligence), Shin Bet (domestic intelligence), Aman (military intelligence) and the fantastic Zionist web of organisations that ultimately answer to the ultra-Zionist hierarchy and Sabbatian-Frankism. Understanding Mossad and its associated military and intelligence networks is crucial to understanding what happened on 9/11 and who was really behind the attacks. Mossad, which was centrally involved in 9/11, was established in 1949 on the say-so of Prime Minister David Ben-Gurion as the central body of Israel intelligence. The full title is the Institute of Intelligence and Special Operations and, as with Israel's nuclear weapons, Mossad did not at first officially exist although everyone knew that it did. Mossad became part of the Prime Minister's Office – just like the Ministry of Strategic Affairs 'Hasbara' operation of global propaganda – but 'the Institute' is actually a law unto itself and beyond even political leadership. Ostrovsky exposes Mossad's targeted assassinations and execution list, the undermining of politicians it doesn't like and secret operations in foreign lands including (especially) those of its apparent 'friends'. He writes that '... one of the first duties of any new Israeli prime minister is to read the execution list and decide whether or not to initial each name on it' (agree for them to be killed). Ostrovsky describes an Israeli spy network in the United States known as 'A1' and says that people 'don't understand that the Mossad regards the whole world outside Israel as a target, including Europe and the United States'. An Israel-defending article by the ultra-Zionist-owned *New York Times* reviewing Ostrovsky's book did acknowledge Israeli spying within the US to be fact. It further revealed that a 'secret CIA report dated March, 1979 (made public by Iran when militants seized the American Embassy there) says that Israel has used bugs, wiretaps and attempted blackmail and bribes to gather intelligence in this country [the US]'. Others have exposed Mossad's assassination policy including Ronen Bergman in *Rise and Kill First – the secret history of Israel's targeted assassinations*. This account of Israel's assassinations, meticulous in its detail and sources, describes how Mossad, Shin Bet and the Israeli Defence Forces (IDF) had a policy from the start of simply assassinating those considered a problem to their agenda and not just in Israel and Palestine either. When you think they are all outgrowths of the ultra-Zionist terror groups that bombed and murdered Israel into existence this should be no surprise. There are many examples of Mossad and other ultra-Zionist military and intelligence hit-squads killing the wrong people and goodness only knows how many innocents have been killed and maimed who were in the wrong place at the wrong time. Ostrovsky says that Mossad operatives are taught to fire as many bullets as possible at their target – 'When he's on the ground you walk up to him, put your gun to his temple, and fire one more time.' Mossad gives ruthlessness, evil and psychopathy a bad name and no wonder that terrorist Menachem Begin was one of its favourite prime ministers.

In many ways Mossad is a modern-day version of the infamous Sufi Islamic sect from which the very word 'assassin' derived – the Hashashin who became known as the Assassins. Interestingly Rabbi Marvin S. Antelman connects the Sufi 'Islamic mysticism' sect to Sabbatian-Frankism and to Sabbatai Zevi and Jacob Frank themselves. He says that Frank 'received financial remuneration from the Aga of the Sufi to aid him in the Frankist plans to exterminate Jews and Judaism in Bucharest, Romania, on November 6, 1757'. There are many covert connections between Jewish, Islamic and Christian groups not least via the infiltrating Donmeh. The cult of the Assassins can be traced to the First Crusade in the late 11th century under its first Grandmaster, Hassan-i Sabbah (1050s-1124). Their claim to fame and particular method of operation was to control rulers through fear of being assassinated if they didn't play ball. A heavily-protected king or leader would wake up to find a knife on his pillow and a note saying that his guards were no match for the Assassins and they could kill him whenever they liked. This would normally illicit compliance and those who didn't comply were killed which added to the Assassins' reputation for calculated murder. Mossad works on the same principle and politicians and others worldwide are controlled by Israel not only through money but the knowledge that Mossad doesn't take prisoners and doesn't take kindly to Israel's will not being obeyed or people getting in their way. Assassinations of people, family members and/or character are Mossad specialities. Letter bombs are a Mossad calling card and so are limpet bombs stuck onto vehicles by passing Mossad agents on motorbikes. They have killed Iranian nuclear scientists this way. This is one description of the Assassins' (now Mossad's) assassination technique:

> In order to get rid of ... rulers, clerics and officials, the Assassins would carefully study the languages and cultures of their targets. An operative would then infiltrate the court or inner circle of the intended victim, sometimes serving for years as an advisor or servant; at an opportune moment, the Assassin would stab the sultan, vizier or mullah with a dagger in a surprise

attack [classic Sabbatian-Frankist infiltration].

Mossad and its networks do the same although they are much more likely to spring a surprise through people who are either the same race as their targets (an Arab Mossad asset killing an Arab) or made to look so. Jewish terrorists in the merciless groups that became Mossad and the Israel Defense Forces blew up the King David's Hotel while *dressed as Arabs* and waiters. Using disguise to instigate Problem-Reaction-Solution events is very common. Two British Special Air Service (SAS) soldiers dressed as Arabs were arrested by the Iraqi authorities in 2005 after a shoot-out at a checkpoint in which two Iraqi officers were shot, one fatally (Fig 134). The British agents were driving a car full of munitions, explosives and detonators believed to be for a false flag 'terrorist attack' on a religious event in Basra to manipulate conflict between Sunnis and Shia. They escaped from custody when British tanks and infantry with helicopter support stormed the jail allowing 150 other prisoners to get away. Not everyone that looks like an Arab is really an Arab and that could easily be the case with 9/11. Some Israelis have complexions that could be taken for Arabs and in fact this was the original mistake made by some witnesses who saw the 'Dancing Israelis' cheering and celebrating the 9/11 attacks while the World Trade Center burned (much more to

Figure 134: Two British SAS soldiers arrested by Iraqi police while dressed as Arabs, including wigs, in an unmarked vehicle containing weapons, explosives and a remote-controlled detonator booby-trapped and ready to explode.

come). Israeli Mossad agents with such skin-type are often used to pose as Arabs in their operations and Ostrovsky says they are known within Mossad as 'Arabists'. Adam Yahiye Gadahn who was claimed to be an American operative for al-Qaeda killed in a US drone attack in Pakistan in 2015 turned out to be a Jewish man, Adam Pearlman, grandson of Carl Pearlman, the former director of ultra-Zionist Mossad front, the Anti-Defamation League. Pearlman, sorry Gadahn, is said to have been behind at least one of the ridiculously transparent 'Bin Laden' videos. Another technique Ostrovsky reveals is the use of doubles to simulate someone being in a location at a certain time when the real person is somewhere else and they can often be oblivious that their double even exists. 'I saw him there with my own eyes, it was definitely him', witnesses will report. This technique was undoubtedly used in the 9/11 operation and it is a method common to all intelligence agents, including the CIA and British intelligence.

Extraordinary scale and reach

Ostrovsky says that while the core personnel of Mossad are not large in number compared with other major intelligence agencies they have a vast network of people to call upon in Jewish communities around the world. These Jewish volunteers are known by Mossad as 'Sayanim' ('collaborators' in Hebrew) and they number thousands in the United States (especially in New York) and worldwide. Many don't even know that what they are asked to do is being directed by Mossad. They will be approached to do something to 'serve Israel' and told little more. The psychological pressure to 'help the homeland' can be very powerful with the life-long perceptual programming. Ostrovsky says in his book:

> So much of our training was based on forming relationships with innocent people. It built a strange sense of confidence. Suddenly everyone in the street became a tool. You'd think, hey, I can push their buttons. Suddenly it was all about telling lies; telling the truth became irrelevant ...

Support from these 'Sayanim' comes in many and various ways. A Jewish owner of an electrical store might supply electrical goods for a Mossad front operation posing as an electrical shop; a doctor might treat an agent with no questions asked; or they might supply vehicles that can't be traced to the Mossad driver. The cost of Mossad operations, as revealed by Ostrovsky, is absolutely incredible with so many on the payroll worldwide. He writes:

> Of the 30 to 35 katsas [case officers] operating at any given time, each would have at least 20 agents. Each of those 600-plus agents would average at least $3,000 a month, plus $3,000 in bonuses, and many would earn considerably more, which cost the Institute [Mossad] $15 million a month at least just to pay the agents. In addition, there were the costs of recruiting, safe houses, operations, vehicles, and numerous other expenses, all adding up to hundreds of millions a month.

He wrote this in *1990* – what must it be today? A country of eight million people on a tiny area of land spends that kind of money only to protect *itself*? C'mon. Ostrovsky reveals the massive network of Mossad front companies to hide their real activities and I'll come to that in relation to 9/11. He says that Mossad operates out of Israeli embassies with the Mossad station chief outranking the actual ambassador. The 'anti-Semitism' scam against me, the UK Labour Party and others around the world will be orchestrated through the Israeli embassies as the Al Jazeera documentaries confirmed. A network of 'safe houses', as

Ostrovsky mentioned, is operated from Mossad stations in target countries to keep agents and their assets from prying eyes and they have an enormous fake passport operation. He says many immigrants to Israel are asked to give up their country-of-origin passports to 'save Jews' and they are stored in 'a huge, library-like room, containing many thousands of passports divided by countries, cities, and even districts, with Jewish and non-Jewish-sounding names, also coded by ages – and all data computerised'. Agents can enter a country illegally by covert means but still have a passport or visa stamped as if they had passed through an airport. Ostrovsky revealed the level of detail involved:

> The Mossad also had a major collection of passport stamps and signatures that they used to stamp their own passports. These were kept in a log book. Many of them were gathered with the help of the police who could hold a passport temporarily and photograph the various stamps before returning it to the owner.

> Even stamping a false passport was done methodically. If, for example, my passport bore an Athens stamp on a certain day, the department would check their files for the signature and stamp from that day at the correct flight time, so that if someone should check with Athens as to which [passport] officer was on duty, that would be correct.

Mossad, like the CIA, has a technology development and seed-funding arm to keep its surveillance and technology capabilities at the cutting edge. Israel today is a global centre for technology and artificial intelligence that is hijacking global communication and dictating what people see and hear. Technology funding and development, added to the Israel-right-or-wrong mentality, means that Israeli technology companies are basically fronts for Mossad, ultra-Zionists and ultimately the Death Cult or at least serve their interests. Silicon Valley Internet giants and AI technology companies are really fronts for Israel, the CIA and Pentagon (controlled by the Death Cult). Israel's global technology hub is supplying surveillance, tracking and other AI/computer high-tech around the world to governments, military and others which have back-door entry-points which Mossad and Israeli intelligence and military networks in general can access (with fundamental relevance to 9/11 as we will see). This back-door access includes taking over the technology at a distance and, for instance, changing what appears on computer screens and in archive records. Israel claims the moral high ground with regard to, well, *everything*, and especially 'fighting terrorism'. The approach reminds me again of the propaganda technique described by Nazi Propaganda Minister Joseph Goebbels as 'accuse your enemy of that which you are guilty'.

Breathtaking hypocrisy

Ostrovsky realised – as many others have exposed – that Israel sells arms to terrorists and tyrannical regimes and even supplied military technology to its alleged Arab 'enemies' such as its Donmeh associates in Saudi Arabia. He says that Israel was selling increased military aircraft fuel-tank capacity to the Saudis via a third country but the Saudis found this too expensive and went to the United States for alternatives. The US Zionist Lobby then 'stood on its hind legs and hollered no!', Ostrovsky writes. The Lobby claimed that such fuel capacity would allow Saudi F-16s to target Israel when it was about nothing more than money. Ostrovsky says that Israel sold missiles to Iran and during the Iran-Iraq war in the 1980s when a Mossad operative in London was calling the embassies of both countries posing as a 'patriot' for each side. He would tell them where each other's shipping was. 'That way we could keep the war "hot"', Ostrovsky says. '... if they were busy fighting each other, they couldn't fight us.' Mossad was close to apartheid South Africa and has trained psychopathic police forces for fascist regimes including Pinochet's Chile, Noriega's Panama and Idi Amin's Uganda as well as apartheid South Africa. Israeli 'advisors' along with Americans were arrested by Iraqi forces in 2015 for 'advising' ISIS fighters. Today Israel trains American police forces. Classic is Ostrovsky's story about a Mossad operation that was training Tamil rebels fighting the Sri Lankan government in the art of guerrilla warfare while at the same time also providing anti-guerrilla training and weapons to Sri Lankan government forces. Neither of them knew, but then the motto is 'By way of deception, thou shalt do war' and Ostrovsky calls his training programme 'a school that taught people to be con artists for their country'. Israeli daily *Haaretz* revealed in 2019 that Israeli officers were training foreign mercenaries, including Colombians and Nepalese, to fight in the Saudi war against Yemen which has created the world's biggest humanitarian crisis. The mercenaries were being trained at camps in Israel's Negev Desert funded by the United Arab Emirates. This is still more confirmation that the Donmeh Saudis and Gulf states such as the UAE are working as one unit with Israel. The *Haaretz* article said the mercenaries had taken part in the Saudi offensive against the port city of Hudaydah and other conflict zones in Yemen. Mossad is heavily involved in the global drug trade along with the CIA and played its part in the Iran-Contra drug operation that involved the Bushes and Clintons. Both families have big Mossad/Israel connections and give evil a bad name. One Mossad drug operative was Israeli official and 'journalist' Amiram Nir who was 'counter-terrorism' advisor to two terrorist Israeli prime ministers, Shimon Peres and Yitzhak Shamir. He was reportedly killed in a plane crash although some doubt he actually died while Nir's son blamed his apparent death on Father George Bush. What a small world it is when you delve into the cesspit. Whenever exposure is imminent or made public there is always the Protection Racket response when anyone suggests that Mossad has been involved in anything – 'anti-Semitism'. Ostrovsky confirms how this is systematically used by Mossad to prevent public exposure and is directed at anyone who doesn't support the Zionist line:

> There was one simple question asked when anything happened: 'Is it good for the Jews or not?' Forget about policies or anything else. That was the only thing that counted, and depending on the answer, people were called anti-Semites whether deservedly or not.

This is such an insight into the mentality that we are dealing with. Was 9/11 good for Israel or not? Benjamin Netanyahu said on television that very morning that it was and he also said this in 2001 when he was not aware of being filmed:

> I know what America is. America is something that can be easily moved. Moved to the right direction. They won't get in our way. So let's say they say something. So they say it! Eighty percent of the Americans support us. It's absurd.

He said that America would not get in the way of further Israeli expansionism into Palestinian land and he pledged to strike the Palestinians with 'blows that are so painful that the price will be too heavy to be borne'. So speaks a mega-psychopath. The ultra-Zionist network is no friend of the United States, Britain or anywhere else. It is the friend of Israel's Sabbatian-Frankist elite and that's it. Ostrovsky says that recruiting agents from 'friendly agencies' to become a Mossad agent was something they were always on the look out to do. He recalls a Mossad operative who said he had many friends within US intelligence but 'when I am sitting with my [American] friend, he's not sitting with *his* friend'. This is the Mossad/ultra-Zionist dynamic. Ostrovsky writes that danger to non-Jews was far less important to Mossad than a danger to Jews and the most they would offer was a 'low-key' warning to foreign governments and agencies over planned attacks. He describes how in 1983 Mossad learned that a Mercedes truck was being prepared to carry bombs which they believed was likely to target an American installation in Beirut, Lebanon, but Mossad chief Nahum Admoni passed on only a general warning with no specifics even though he had them. A Mercedes truck was then crashed through the barriers of the United States compound and killed 241 US Marines. Ostrovsky became disillusioned with Mossad's one-eyed cultural bias and that of Israel in general. He writes:

> You know what Israelis say: 'If they weren't burning us in World War II they
> were helping, or if they weren't helping they were ignoring it.' Yet I don't
> remember anybody in Israel going out to demonstrate when all those people
> [nearly two million] were being murdered in Cambodia. So why expect
> everyone to get involved just for us? Does the fact that Jews have suffered give
> us the right to inflict pain and misery on others?

Ostrovsky freed himself from the Zionist-imposed perception and self-
obsession programme. Many don't and when it is so constant and life-
long it's easy to see why.

A history of attacking Americans

Put this Mossad information together with all that I have detailed in the
last few chapters and it's clear that the Israel ultra-Zionist network
(including all the Sayanim or collaborators located in the US and
especially New York) most certainly had the capability to carry out 9/11
together with other Web operatives and place-people like Dick Cheney.
The Israel-Mossad operation in America is shockingly vast and includes
every area necessary to plan and play out the attacks and to protect
those really involved while blaming those who were not. Ultra-Zionists
controlled the White House, Capitol Hill, the Pentagon, media,
Hollywood, law enforcement and investigation – even the removal of
the evidence from Ground Zero and its transportation to Asia. They also
had the motive to use 9/11 as the excuse to manipulate the United States
into more wars in the Middle East against countries that Israel and its
ultra-Zionist Neocons wanted to regime change and subjugate through
violence and chaos. They had 'previous' in terms of attacking American
targets and others in supposedly 'friendly' countries. Israeli fighter jets
and torpedo boats attacked the *USS Liberty*, a US surveillance ship,
during the Six Day War between Israel and Egypt and other Arab states
in 1967. The *Liberty* was in international waters north of the Sinai
Peninsula. Israel sought to hide the source of the attack to blame it on
Egypt and cause conflict with the United States. The evidence against
Israel became so overwhelming that the government was forced to
apologise and pay compensation for the 44 American crew members
who were killed and 171 wounded, plus severe damage to the ship.
Israel claimed the *Liberty* was attacked by accident – yet another lie.
Surviving crew members said it was quite clearly a premeditated attack.
Israel was as always protected by the US authorities with the US Navy's
Court of Inquiry holding hearings about the attack in closed sessions
and survivors subjected to gag orders to stop them talking about what
happened. Some, however, still have. A key player in the cover-up was

Admiral John S. McCain, then Commander-in-chief, Naval Forces
Europe, and father of the late Israel fanatic US Senator John McCain.
Israeli planes made eight reconnaissance trips to identify the *Liberty* over
a period of three hours and the ship was flying a big US flag. To claim
mistaken identity was laughable. The attack went on for two hours from
air and submarine while communications from the *Liberty* were jammed
by Israel. Even life rafts launched by survivors were hit by machine gun
fire and no one was meant to survive. US fighter aircraft launched after
Israel jamming was breached were ordered to turn back and a Russian
ship reached the *Liberty* long before anyone from the US Navy. James
Ennes Jr, a surviving officer of the *Liberty*, published a book exposing in
detail how the Israeli attack was premeditated and no accident
called *Assault on the Liberty*. Israel's response as always when anyone
tells the truth about its psychopathic elements was that Ennes was …
yes, you got it … 'anti-Semitic'. You're in shock, right? Ennes recalls
how his friend Pat O'Malley, a junior officer, sent a list of the killed and
wounded to the Bureau of Naval Personnel and an immediate message
came back: 'Wounded in what action? Killed in what action? … It wasn't
an "action", it was an accident.' O'Malley's response was: 'I'd like for
them to come out here and see the difference between an action and an
accident. Stupid bastards.' Stupid, yes, but then excuses for Israel's
outrageous behaviour have to hide the truth, or try to, with transparent
lies.

The *Liberty* attack is only one in a long stream of examples that show
how America's political and military leaders care far less about
protecting American lives than they do Israel's reputation. Israel's far-
right political, military and intelligence hierarchy has utter contempt for
America and its people. Former Mossad agent Victor Ostrovsky reveals
in *By Way of Deception* how in 1986 Israel used a communication system
known as 'Trojan Horse' to transmit from an Israeli ship messages that
appeared to be coming out of Libya and sent to Libyan embassies
around the world in support of terrorism. The US National Security
Agency (NSA) intercepted the 'Libyan' (Israeli) transmissions and the
Reagan-Bush administration ordered an attack on Libyan airports,
military bases and other targets that killed the four-year-old adopted
daughter of Libyan leader Colonel Gaddafi. Just another casualty in
ultra-Zionism's endless addiction to war and self-interest. Then there
was the 1964 'Lavron Affair', named after Pinhas Lavron, Israeli's
Minister of Defense, when Israel ran a campaign of terror bombings
against British and American targets in Egypt which were planned to be
blamed on Egyptians. It was an Israeli 'false flag', or Problem-Reaction-
Solution, to demonise a Muslim enemy in the eyes of the West – just like
9/11. Only in 2005 did Israel accept that the bombings blamed on Egypt
were carried out by Egyptian Jews overseen by Israeli intelligence.

Moshe Sharrett, Israel's second prime minister and a less extreme Zionist, named the terrorist Shimon Peres for involvement in the attacks on US targets in Egypt. Sharrett said that Peres and Lavron shared the same ideology and that Peres 'wants to frighten the West into supporting Israel's aims'. This was precisely the reason for Israel's involvement in 9/11 at a time when Peres was Minister of Foreign Affairs. Sharrett said of Peres:

> I have stated that I totally and utterly reject Peres and consider his rise to prominence a malignant, immoral disgrace. I will rend my clothes in mourning for the State if I see him become a minister in the Israeli government.

Peres would go on to be President of Israel, twice Prime Minister, an interim Prime Minister and 9/11 Foreign Affairs Minister.

How the West was stung

American investigative journalist Christopher Bollyn has been uncovering the Israel connection to 9/11 since first hearing about the 'Dancing Israelis' – the Mossad operatives cheering and celebrating the attacks as the first tower burned – and he has paid the price for his efforts in a campaign of hate against him by ultra-Zionist hate groups including the Anti-Defamation League (ADL). He was even subjected to a physical attack at his home by 'three heavily-armed unidentified men' in 2006 that were later identified to be undercover police. He suffered a fractured elbow and was hit with 50,000 volts from a Taser. The attack happened in front of his wife and eight-year-old daughter and to make things even more disgusting he was charged with 'resisting arrest'. Bollyn has published two highly recommended books, *Solving 9-11* and the more extensive *Solving 9-11 – the Original Articles*. His research when added to my own produce overwhelming confirmation of Israel's involvement in the attacks of September 11th, 2001. Bollyn writes in *Solving 9-11*:

> At every critical point where the events and circumstances of 9-11 should have been investigated and discussed, there has been a Zionist, a dedicated devotee of the State of Israel, occupying a key position and acting as the controller and censor of evidence – the gatekeeper of information.

Yes, and not only in positions to cover up, but also in those to make the attacks happen. The ultra-Zionist response is that Bollyn is 'anti-Semitic' (yawn). How strange – well, perhaps not – that hate groups like the ADL have attacked him for questioning 9/11 even in areas where he has made no mention of Jewish people or Zionism. The 'anti-Semitic'

Protection Racket tries to equate simply questioning the official story of 9/11 with 'anti-Semitism' as it does any claim in any shape or form of a global conspiracy to enslave humanity. Something is not right here and clearly it's not about protecting Jewish people, but something far deeper, sinister and all-encompassing. The appalling ADL (spawned by the appalling Rothschild B'nai B'rith) condemned Bollyn as early as November, 2001, for an article highlighting the *fact* that numerous witnesses and experts, including news reporters, said they heard or saw explosions immediately before the collapse of the Twin Towers. He did not mention a Jewish connection to this story in any way. Yet the ADL attacked the article and its author. Why would an organisation apparently dedicated to protecting Jewish people from discrimination get involved in condemning the factual reporting that witnesses saw and heard explosions? That might be obvious to many by the end of this book, but people must come to their own conclusions. Heads-up to Christopher Bollyn for his tireless work in uncovering the Zionist connections to 9/11. I don't know him and I'm sure we would disagree on many things about the world and religion, but on the cover up of Israel's involvement in the September 11th attacks we are most certainly in agreement. Given the evidence that will now follow how could *anyone* not be?

I'm going to return to the 9/11 sequence of events with a quote by the Russian-born Isser Harel, former chief of Haganah (terrorist) intelligence, Shin Bet domestic intelligence, and Mossad (1952 to 1963). Harel was Mossad chief when the Nazi Adolf Eichmann was captured in Argentina in a clandestine operation and flown to Israel in a diplomatic plane while disguised as a member of the crew. He was then executed by the Israelis. Nahum Admoni, the later Mossad director who failed to properly warn the United States about the deadly Mercedes truck attack in Beirut in 1983, served under Harel who was infamous for targeting people in 'friendly' countries of the West. Isser Harel resigned from Mossad over a terror campaign called Operation Damocles which included letter bombs and assassination attempts to intimidate German scientists to stop working with Egypt on a rocket programme. This 'Father of Israeli Intelligence', was interviewed in 1979 by 'Christian Zionist' journalist Michael D. Evans and predicted a terror attack by Muslims on 'your tallest building' which he mistakenly believed to be the Empire State Building. In fact, by then the title went to the World Trade Center Twin Towers opened in 1973 in a project suggested and orchestrated by mega Hidden Hand manipulator, David Rockefeller, and his brother Nelson. Three weeks after those buildings came down on September 11th Evans recalled his conversation with Harel in an article for *The Jerusalem Post*. He said Harel told him in 1979:

New York City is the symbol of freedom and capitalism. It's likely they will strike the Empire State Building, your tallest building and a symbol of your power ...

... In Islamic theology, the phallic symbol is very important. Your biggest phallic symbol is New York City and your tallest building will be the phallic symbol they will hit.

It is not only Islamic theology that knows the emotional impact of symbolism – Death Cults like Sabbatian-Frankism are steeped in such knowledge and indeed symbolism is their secret language between initiates as I have explained in detail in my books. Associates of Isser Harel who would later be connected to the World Trade Center will enter the picture shortly. Benjamin Netanyahu also called a press conference on September 11th and handed out copies of his 1995 book, *Fighting Terrorism: How Democracies Can Defeat Domestic and International Terrorism*, to claim that he had predicted the attacks. This was after he had said that they were 'good for Israel'. He told journalists that he had foreseen 'militant Islam' seeking a confrontation with the 'Great Satan, the United States' and had suggested that those loyal to Iran might plant a nuclear bomb in the basement of the World Trade Center. He said that 9/11 would be a turning point in the history of the United States just as Pearl Harbor had been. Well, it was the '*new* Pearl Harbor' according to Boy Bush after the attacks which is exactly what the ultra-Zionist Project for the New American Century had said they needed to trigger their regime change plans in the Middle East and elsewhere. Netanyahu and other prominent ultra-Zionists had been campaigning throughout the 1990s for a US war on terrorism and that had been the foundation theme of the 1996 *Clean Break* document produced for then Prime Minister Netanyahu by a group headed by ultra-Zionist Richard Perle who in 2001 ahead of 9/11 entered the Bush administration in a Pentagon post. *Clean Break* provided the basis for the Project for the New American Century (PNAC) document in September, 2000, which has been the blueprint for US foreign policy under successive presidents ever since. The PNAC was co-founded by ultra-Zionists Robert Kagan and William Kristol, the latter of which was constantly appearing on cable news shows selling American wars in the Middle East in the wake of 9/11.

Ultra-Zionist domination

Before, during and after 9/11 the very ultra-Zionists and their gofers who demanded specific regime changes in Middle Eastern countries and said they needed 'a new Pearl Harbor' to achieve that end were in key positions in government and the Pentagon 'under' (over) puppet president Boy Bush. Among them were Dick Cheney, Vice President and

de-facto President; Donald Rumsfeld, Secretary of Defense; Paul
Wolfowitz, Deputy Secretary of Defense; Douglas Feith, Under Secretary
of Defense for Policy; Dov S. Zakheim, Pentagon comptroller overseeing
the entire military budget; Richard Armitage, Deputy Secretary of State
to Colin Powell; Elliot Abrams, a 'Special Assistant' to Bush on foreign
policy and major architect of the invasion of Iraq who would be
appointed by Donald Trump to oversee the attempted US coup in
Venezuela; Richard N. Perle, Pentagon Policy Advisor and close
associate of Benjamin Netanyahu; John Bolton, Under Secretary of State
for Arms Control and International Security, Ambassador to the UN and
Trump's National Security Advisor seeking to continue the PNAC
campaign of war to this day; Lewis Libby, Chief of Staff to Cheney and
close to Wolfowitz; James Woolsey, member of the Pentagon Defense
Policy Board and former Director of the CIA; Robert B. Zoellick, Bush
Trade Representative and Cabinet member.

Add to them the ultra-Zionist Michael Chertoff, son of a Mossad
agent, who was named United States Assistant Attorney General for the
Criminal Division in 2001 and presided over the non-investigation of the
attacks and the destruction of evidence from Ground Zero. Then there
were ultra-Zionists Philip Zelikow, Executive Director of the 9/11
Commission who ran that non-investigation, and Judge Alvin K.
Hellerstein, who oversaw all the cases in which 9/11 families refused to
accept compensation that came with a no-legal action clause. They
wanted their day in court where the evidence could be publicly
presented and questioned. Hellerstein waged what has been called a
'war of attrition' in which the 96 families withdrew their legal action one
by one until the last conceded in 2011. Still another ultra-Zionist, Judge
Michael Mukasey, who would go on to be US Attorney General, had
significant involvement in the post-9/11 sequence of events. Mukasey
had refused demands to recuse himself in 1994 when he presided over a
case stemming from the 1993 bombing of the World Trade Center. It was
claimed that his views and connections to Israel and Zionism put into
question a fair trial for Muslims accused of terrorism. Never, surely!
That's 'anti-Semitic'! Zionist-owned companies removed the debris from
Ground Zero – crucial evidence for what actually happened and why the
towers fell – and shipped it to Asia for smelting. Ultra-Zionist-owned
companies connected to Israeli intelligence ran security at the World
Trade Center and 9/11 airports and the computer systems of the Federal
Aviation Administration (FAA) and other government departments and
agencies. The World Trade Center lease was owned by ultra-Zionist
Larry Silverstein after a deal agreed with ultra-Zionist Lewis Eisenberg,
head of the New York Port Authority, which had sold the lease into
private hands for the first time months before the attacks. In all major
areas of the 9/11 story can be found Zionists and ultra-Zionists

answering to Israel – which means Mossad, the military and behind them the Sabbatian-Frankist Death Cult. This gave ultra-Zionists complete control of what happened in those buildings in the weeks before the planes struck. Given this background how can it possibly be dismissed that Israel and its octopus intelligence agency Mossad were involved in the attacks of September 11th? There is only one 'defence' put forward for such legitimate investigation of the facts – the 'anti-Semitism' mantra of the Protection Racket.

Terrorists in charge

The Israeli Prime Minister across 9/11 was the terrorist Ariel Sharon while his foreign minister was terrorist Shimon Peres. Sharon was a brutal psychopath, a commander in the Israeli military from its creation out of terrorist groups in 1948, and he became Prime Minister in March, 2001, just weeks after the ultra-Zionists came to power with Bush in the United States (Fig 135). Sharon was the Israeli Defense Minister who

Figure 135: Israel's 9/11 Prime Minister, the psychopath Ariel Sharon.

oversaw the mass slaughter of Palestinians in the Shatila refugee camp and the neighbourhood of Sabra in West Beirut during the 1982 Israeli invasion of Lebanon. Christian Lebanese militiamen allied to Israel and known as Phalangists were allowed into the camp and neighbourhood while the Israeli army looked on. They murdered up to 3,500 Palestinian and Lebanese civilians, mostly women, children and the elderly.

Many were raped. Survivors were taken for questioning by the Phalangists and Israeli intelligence and many who were then handed back to the Phalangists by the Israelis were executed. *The New York Times* would reveal that Sharon and Israeli officials misled the United States before and during the atrocities about the safety of civilians. Israel's Prime Minister at the time was ultra-Zionist terrorist Menachem Begin. Sharon had contempt for the United States and saw it as a tool to secure Israeli ambitions. He was vocal in his calls for the US to remove Saddam Hussein after 9/11 which was straight from the wish-list of the ultra-Zionist Project for the New American Century. On the second day of the Sabra-Shatila massacre Israeli journalist Ron Ben-Yishai went to Sharon to tell him about reports of mass murder. Ben-Yishai recalled:

I found [Sharon] at home sleeping. He woke up and I told him 'Listen, there are stories about killings and massacres in the camps. A lot of our officers know about it and tell me about it, and if they know it, the whole world will know about it. You can still stop it.' I didn't know that the massacre actually started 24 hours earlier. I thought it started only then and I said to him 'Look, we still have time to stop it. Do something about it.' He didn't react.

An Israeli committee of inquiry, known as the Kahan Commission, decided that Sharon bore 'personal responsibility' for the massacre and recommended his removal. Menachem Begin removed him as Defense Minister, but kept him in the cabinet. Sharon went on to be Benjamin Netanyahu's Foreign Minister and eventually Prime Minister. This was the mentality running Israel at the time of 9/11.

Synchronicity or what?

Everything was in place with the right personnel and psychopathic mentality by the early months of 2001. All they needed for the PNAC plan to be implemented was – in their own words – a 'new Pearl Harbor' and 9/11 came along right on cue. All a coincidence, of course, and all this happened purely by chance. Move along again – nothing to see here. What are the chances of Netanyahu's close buddy, ultra-Zionist Larry Silverstein, buying the lease on the World Trade Center towers just weeks before they were attacked in the 'new Pearl Harbor'? Or that the man who sold the lease to Silverstein was ultra-Zionist Lewis Eisenberg, head of the New York Port Authority, and another friend of Netanyahu? Or that the one who successfully lobbied for the World Trade Center to be privatised and thus sold to Silverstein was ultra-Zionist billionaire Ronald Lauder of the Estée Lauder cosmetics company who was instrumental in Netanyahu becoming Israeli Prime Minister? But don't concern yourself – these coincidences happen all the time (Fig 136, 137 and 138). Lauder was chairman of the New York State Advisory Commission on Privatization and New York State Research Council on Privatization when he was pressing for the World Trade Center to be sold into private hands for the first time. Journalist Scott Robert Makufka (pen-name Victor Thorn) wrote in his book *9/11 Evil*:

Prior to 9/11, Netanyahu and Silverstein would speak on the phone every Sunday afternoon. [Netanyahu] becomes a key player in this scenario because he was the man who actually coined the term 'war on

Figure 136: Ultra-Zionist Larry Silverstein bought the World Trade Center lease weeks before 9/11 and increased the insurance in the event of a terrorist attack.

terrorism', the official term for the never-ending, Israeli-induced war.

Silverstein's intimate friendship with Netanyahu and the every-Sunday phone calls have also been confirmed by Israeli paper, *Haaretz*, which said they had been close friends since Netanyahu was Israel ambassador to the United Nations in the 1980s. World Trade Center seller Lewis Eisenberg and buyer Larry Silverstein both held senior positions with the United Jewish Appeal Federation of Jewish Philanthropies of New York, a billion-dollar ultra-Zionist organisation

Figure 137: Ultra-Zionist Lewis Eisenberg, head of the New York Port Authority, agreed the World Trade Center deal with his friend Silverstein.

and the biggest Israel fundraiser in America. Well, apart from the American taxpayer that is. Eisenberg was formerly vice president of ultra-Zionist Israel/Mossad mega-lobby group AIPAC and worked for ultra-Zionist Goldman Sachs. Silverstein has been heavily involved with extreme right-wing Israeli politicians and Zionist organisations worldwide while Ronald Lauder was connected to the Conference of Presidents of Major American Jewish Organizations, the World Jewish Congress, Jewish [apartheid] National Fund, American Jewish Joint Distribution Committee, Abraham Fund, Jewish Theological Seminary, and the Anti-Defamation League of B'nai B'rith. Lauder became president of the World Jewish Congress in 2007. It was incredible forethought in the circumstances that Silverstein took out so much extra insurance on the buildings in the case of a terrorist attack – just as it was such incredible good fortune that his wife made him a 'dermatology' appointment that stopped him being in the Windows on the World restaurant on the 106th and 107th floors of the North Tower that morning of 9/11 as he nearly always was with an 8.30am start. Two of

Figure 138: Ultra-Zionist Ronald Lauder of Estée Lauder pressed for the World Trade Center to be sold into private hands which turned out to be the sweaty palms of Larry Silverstein.

his children, Roger and Lisa, were vice presidents of Silverstein Properties and also held breakfast meetings with tenants in the Windows on the World most days, but they were at the chiropractor. No, sorry, they were both for different reasons 'running late'. Roger was in the parking garage of Silverstein's Building 7 when the first plane hit the North Tower while Lisa didn't get even that far. The *New York Observer* reported:

> [Silverstein's] son, Roger, and his daughter, Lisa, were working for him in temporary offices on the 88th floor of the W.T.C. north tower. Regular meetings with tenants in the weeks immediately following their July 26, 2001, takeover of the building were held each morning at Windows on the World. But on Sept. 11, Roger and Lisa Silverstein were running late. Meanwhile, Mr. Silverstein's wife of 46 years had laid down the law: The developer could not cancel an appointment with his dermatologist, even to meet with tenants at his most important property. If the attack had happened just a little later, Mr. Silverstein's children would likely have been trapped at Windows.

How fortunate they all were when you think that everyone in the restaurant when the plane struck – estimated at about 170 people – was killed because they could not escape before the tower collapsed. 'Lucky Larry', indeed, in fact, 'Lucky Silversteins'. More great fortune befell Geoffrey Wharton who Silverstein hired to manage and redevelop the property. He 'cut a meeting a little short' and left the restaurant with three other people, two of them senior officials with the New York Port Authority, minutes before the plane hit. They were the last people to leave the restaurant alive.

Lucky Larry – Lucky Frank

Ultra-Zionists Larry Silverstein (Silverstein Properties) and his partner, Frank Lowy (Westfield America Inc.), finalised a 99-year lease on the entire World Trade Center in July, 2001, five months before 9/11. They agreed to pay $3.2 billion after first being outbid. Silverstein got the WTC towers while Lowry took about 425,000 square feet of retail space known as the Mall. Included in the deal was the right for them to rebuild the structures if the properties were destroyed. The World Trade Centre lease had been purchased with a $124 million down-payment and Silverstein's personal investment was just $14 million. Other investors included Zionist real estate developers Lloyd Goldman and Joseph Cayre. Silverstein partner Frank Lowy joined the ultra-Zionist terror group, Haganah, in 1945 during the reign of murder and intimidation against Palestinians (Fig 139). He is a close associate of Israeli prime ministers, including Benjamin Netanyahu and Ehud Olmert, while Silverstein has been close to Netanyahu, Ariel Sharon and Ehud Barak. Sharon was Israel Prime Minister when 9/11 happened and the man he replaced, former Israeli military intelligence chief, Ehud Barak, was the one who immediately after the attacks flagged up Bin Laden and called

Figure 139: Frank Lowy.

for a war on terror and invasion of Afghanistan. Barak would also later order the mass murder of Palestinians in Gaza in 2008-2009 dubbed Operation Cast Lead. The purchase of the World Trade Center by Silverstein and Lowy bewildered many observers because the Twin Towers were considered a 'white elephant' with low occupancy rates, outdated technology and elevator systems and reports of toxic asbestos estimated to cost $200 million to remove. It appeared to be a really bad investment but after the attacks it became a hell of a deal. Silverstein said that he 'felt a compelling urge to own them'. Oh, I'm sure he did, but why? Silverstein and Lowry insured the complex for $3.55 billion and claimed twice that amount after the attacks on the basis that it involved two attacks and not one. Insurance companies eventually paid out $4.56 billion and Silverstein and Lowry were able to afford to replace the aging WTC with up-to-date buildings in the form of towers and a Mall. Some 24 companies insured the World Trade Center and lost massively, but even though the pay-out was dependent on the ludicrous official story being true (with no provable evidence) not a single one of them questioned the narrative which cost them so much. Silverstein had reportedly managed to control his shock at the attacks and grief at the dead for long enough to immediately hatch his plan for a double-pay-out. Steven Brill, author of *After: The Rebuilding and Defending of America in the September 12 Era*, said Silverstein told him he had not thought about the insurance until 'perhaps two weeks later' because of the tragedy. In fact Brill reports that according to two people who called Silverstein with their condolences the morning after 9/11 he quickly changed the subject:

> He had talked to his lawyers ... and he had a clear legal strategy mapped out. They were going to prove, Silverstein told one of the callers, that the way his insurance policies were written the two planes crashing into the two towers had been two different 'occurrences,' not part of the same event. That would give him more than $7 billion to rebuild, instead of the $3.55 billion that his insurance policy said was the maximum for one 'occurrence.' And rebuild was just what he was going to do, he vowed.

Apparently by mid-morning on September 12th Silverstein had called his architect David Childs and told him to start plans for a new building with the same office space as those whose debris was still smouldering and full of human remains. Even this was not quite the same level of foresight that had seen Silverstein have the new Building 7 designed and planned in 2000, a year before the old one came down in the most obvious controlled demolition. Silverstein's lawyers are reported to have confirmed that he had phoned them on the night of 9/11 to ask 'whether his insurance policies could be read in a way that would construe the attacks as two separate insurable incidents rather than one'. It's amazing what people do when consumed by shock and grief. The original insurers were ACE, Marsh & McClennan and AIG all run by the ultra-Zionist Maurice Greenberg and family. The Greenbergs quickly sold on their responsibility before the attacks to the 24 other companies through a process called 'reinsuring' and they took the hit, not the Greenbergs. Not only 'Lucky Larry' and 'Lucky Silversteins', then, but 'Lucky Frank', 'Lucky Maurice' and 'Lucky Greenbergs' as well. Greenberg, a former deputy chairman of the Council on Foreign Relations, has connections to the CIA, Mossad operatives, the Anti-Defamation League Mossad front and he's a long-time associate of Henry Kissinger. Eight years before 9/11 Greenberg went into partnership with the ultra-Zionist Kroll family – Kroll and Associates would be responsible for security at the World Trade Center at the time of the 9/11 attacks and employ the ill-fated FBI counterterrorism chief John O'Neil as head of security shortly before the attacks that claimed his life. O'Neil had resigned from the FBI over blocks on his investigation of Obama bin Laden. Kroll and Greenberg will return to the story in due course. Larry Silverstein later received another big pay-out of nearly $9.52 million when he successfully sued American Airlines Group Inc., United Continental Holdings Inc., and other aviation-linked defendants for losses he claimed to have suffered over the 9/11 attacks. The litigation battle lasted for 13 years and was overseen by ultra-Zionist District Judge Alvin Hellerstein who also presided over civil litigation stemming from the attacks and prevented families of 9/11 victims getting their cases to court.

'High-fiving Israelis'

The 'Dancing Israelis' are the most obvious red-flag of Israeli involvement in 9/11 (Fig 140). A New Jersey housewife looked from her apartment window immediately after the first impact on the North Tower and saw young men kneeling on the roof of a white Chevrolet van with a New Jersey registration parked at Liberty State Park in Jersey City. They were filming the catastrophe from the waterside while hi-fiving each other, cheering and laughing. Other witnesses would describe the same van at another location with men who were 'celebrating and filming' and 'videotaping the disaster and shouting in

Figure 140: The 'Dancing Israelis'.

what was interpreted as cries of joy and mockery'. The men were filming and taking photographs of each other with the burning towers in the background. They were initially described as 'Middle Eastern' men – the same description attributed to the 'hijackers' by 'passengers on the planes'. These early reports added to the already gathering story that Arab terrorists were involved in the attacks (said to have been code-named 'The Big Wedding'), but the high-fivers would turn out to be Israelis. For sure they were 'Middle Eastern' only not the type that come to mind with that description. Indeed, as I've mentioned, the likeness of some Israelis to Arabs in their skin colour and features has proved useful for Mossad in anti-Arab covert operations over the years by Israeli 'Arabists'. The woman in New Jersey took down the licence plate and called the police. They and the FBI arrived and went in search of the vehicle which was registered to what turned out to be a Mossad front company called Urban Moving Systems. Later that afternoon law enforcement found the van and its five Israeli male occupants all in their 20s who they handcuffed and arrested. They would become known as the 'Dancing Israelis'. Among their belongings were two foreign passports and $4,700 in a sock. Sniffer dogs located evidence of explosives in the van which also contained box-cutters. The men were named as Sivan and Paul Kurzberg, Yaron Schmuel, Oded Ellner and Omer Marmari. The brothers Kurzberg were apparently known by law enforcement agencies to be Mossad operatives and Yaron Shmuel's LinkedIn profile is reported to describe expertise and experience with 'explosives' and 'secret services'. His Facebook page said his wedding was a year to the day after the attacks on September 11th, 2002. These were the men described by the woman observer as '... like happy, you know ...They didn't look shocked to me. I thought it was very strange'. Sivan Kurzberg, the van's driver, told police:

We are Israeli. We are not your problem. Your problems are our problems. The Palestinians are the problem.

Investigative journalist Christopher Ketcham said that FBI spokesman Jim Margolin told him the Israelis explained away their joy by saying: 'The United States would now have to commit itself to fighting [Middle East] terrorism, that Americans would have an understanding and empathy for Israel's circumstances, and that the attacks were ultimately a good thing for Israel.' The sentiments matched those of Benjamin Netanyahu on 9/11. Even if this explanation was correct – and it is far from the whole story – what level of empathy-deleted psychopathy does it take to be happy about the deaths of nearly 3,000 people because it is 'good for Israel'? This does, however, capture the We-and-Israel-are-all-that-matters mentality of ultra-Zionists. An FBI report said that one Israeli claimed the van was on the West Side Highway in New York at the time of the attack, but pictures were found of him and his colleagues at the scene where they were spotted cheering and filming. There was also a police report that another van was found with an extraordinary mural on the side. The incident is mentioned in a document by the Mineta Transportation Institute (MTI) at San Jose State University called 'Saving City Lifelines: Lessons Learned in the 9-11 Terrorist Attacks':

> A panel truck with a painting of a plane flying into the World Trade Center was stopped near the temporary command post. It proved to be rented to a group of ethnic Middle Eastern people who did not speak English. Fearing that it might be a truck bomb, the NYPD immediately evacuated the area, called out the bomb squad, and detained the occupants until a thorough search was made. The vehicle was found to be an innocent delivery truck.

Or *was* it? The original police report was recorded by Robert Stanford, Emergency Coordinator for the New York City District Amateur Radio Emergency Service, which taped hours of police and emergency service communications. An officer calls and reports:

> It's a big truck with a mural painted of an airplane diving into New York City and exploding. Don't know what's in the truck. The truck is in between 6th and 7th on King Street ... with a mural painted ... airplane ... diving into New York blowing up ... two men got out of the truck ... ran away from it, we got those two under ... got them under let's get some units ... we have both suspects under ... we have the suspects who ... drove the van – the van exploded ... we have both of them under ... let's get some help over here ...

Exploded? What on earth was that all about? And what happened to the two men arrested? Manhattan Fire Department Despatch was contacted by two separate fire units about the same 'truck bomb in King Street'. Television news reported that a van/truck full of explosives had been stopped with 'two or three occupants'. The Dancing Israelis were taken to Bergen County jail in New Jersey and then to the FBI Foreign Counterintelligence Section. Dominik Suter, the Israeli owner of Urban

Moving Systems in New Jersey, was questioned by the FBI and another interview was scheduled, but Suter fled to Israel before it could happen and he has since been reported to have returned to the United States clearly in the knowledge that the FBI would leave him alone. Suter apparently surfaced on the Internet in 2012 to say allegations about him were only being made to 'spread hate and anti-Semitism'. So bloody original. ABC reporters who went to Urban Moving Systems said it looked like people left in a big hurry. Cell phones were lying around, office phones were still connected, and the property of dozens of clients remained in the warehouse. Dominik Suter owned some 14 businesses in the United States in New Jersey, New York and Florida – locations that had been connected to an Israeli spy ring that I will describe shortly. Urban Moving Systems was given a $498,750 business loan from the Federal Government Assistance Program in June, 2001, that would never be repaid. New York-based Jewish publication *The Forward* would later report that Urban Moving Systems was a front for Mossad and two of the men were known Mossad agents. Victor Ostrovsky highlighted in his book eleven years earlier the 'hundreds' of 'shell companies' operated by Mossad worldwide 'with an address, a registered number, just waiting to come to life'. Many use Arabs as front owners and cover while Mossad and Israelis are really in control. Ostrovsky said Mossad even kept money in these companies, enough to file tax returns and avoid raising suspicions:

> At headquarters, five rooms were filled with the paraphernalia of dummy companies, listed in alphabetical order, and set up in a pull-out box. There were eight rows of shelves and 60 boxes per shelf in each of the five rooms. The information included a history of each company, all its financial statements, a history of its logo, who it was registered with, anything at all that a katsa [case officer] might be expected to know about the company.

The 'Dancing Israelis' were held in custody for visa fraud and questioned by the FBI for two months. They failed polygraph tests in which they tried to portray themselves as students. FBI agents believed that at least two of them were Mossad operatives and the others were surveillance volunteers. Documents found at the offices of Urban Moving Systems suggested they were focussing on the big Muslim community in Patterson, New Jersey. The mother of one of those arrested was quoted by Israeli daily *Haaretz* as saying the five had worked for the company for between two months and two years.

The cover-up

The Bush White House and ultra-ultra-Zionist Michael Chertoff, head of the [In]Justice Department's Criminal Division and with deep connections to Israel, ordered the release of the five after 71 days in custody and they flew back to Israel after being accused only of 'passport violations'. Three of the five – not the Mossad Kurzberg brothers – appeared on Israeli television on their return and said they were there 'to document the event'. To 'document' an event on a single camera from the other side of the river when it was being filmed from all angles by the US mass media and broadcast around the world? And explain the high-fives, the laughing and cheering at a disaster for America that would lead to the deaths of thousands of people. If they were there before the first tower was hit how did they know it was going to happen? If they were there immediately after the strike (which they were at the *very* latest) how did they know it was a 'terrorist attack'? Even Michael Chertoff said that 'like many people at the time, I thought it was a pilot error'. Boy Bush claimed the same. Yet these Israelis somehow knew? An *ABC News* report in June, 2002, interviewed Vincent Cannistraro, former chief of operations for counterterrorism with the CIA, who said some of the names of the five Israelis appeared as 'hits' on an FBI national intelligence database. Journalist Christopher Ketcham, writing for *Counterpunch*, said Cannistraro told him that 'the FBI investigation operated on the premise that the Israelis had foreknowledge'. The *Bergen Record* in New Jersey quoted 'an investigator high up in the Bergen County law enforcement' as saying: 'It looked like they knew what was going to happen when they were at Liberty State Park.' Marc Perelman, a reporter with Jewish-American *The Forward* , a long-standing New York magazine for Jewish-Americans, said his sources claimed the Israelis admitted to the existence of a spy ring and apologised after American authorities confronted them at the end of 2001. Christopher Ketcham wrote:

> Before such issues had been fully explored, however, the investigation was shut down. Following what ABC News reported were 'high-level negotiations between Israeli and U.S. government officials', a settlement was reached in the case of the five Urban Moving Systems suspects. Intense political pressure apparently had been brought to bear. The reputable Israeli daily Haaretz reported that by the last week of October 2001, some six weeks after the men had been detained, Deputy Secretary of State Richard Armitage [Project for the New American Century] and two unidentified 'prominent New York congressmen' were lobbying heavily for their release.
>
> According to a source at ABC News close to the 20/20 report, high-profile [ultra-Zionist] criminal lawyer Alan Dershowitz also stepped in as a negotiator on behalf of the men to smooth out differences with the U.S. government. (Dershowitz declined to comment for this article.) And so, at the end of November 2001, for reasons that only noted they had been working in

the country illegally as movers, in violation of their visas, the men were flown home to Israel.

Ultra-Zionist Dershowitz, a massive supporter of Netanyahu, was on the legal team that secured an outrageous plea deal for ultra-Zionist billionaire paedophile Jeffrey Epstein which allowed him to avoid the long jail sentence which the charges should have involved. The five Dancing Israelis had the nerve to sue the US government in 2004 because 'their detention was illegal and their civil rights were violated, suffering racial slurs, physical violence, religious discrimination, rough interrogations, deprivation of sleep, and many other offenses'. Their lawyer was Nitsana Darshan-Leitner, founder of the Shurat HaDin Israel Law Center which is closely connected with the Israeli government. The Center is one of many Israel 'lawfare' operations around the world which target critics of Israel with lawsuits to intimidate them into silence. Israel-owned (to his bone marrow) Donald Trump would later talk about Muslims celebrating 9/11 that day in New York when they were actually Israelis who were certainly not acting alone. A 579-page report on the case was partly declassified in 2005 but won't be fully so until 2035. Why? France-based journalist Hisham Hamza read through the declassified sections for his book *Israel and September 11: The Great Taboo*. Included were photographs confirming the Israelis' delight at what had happened and one said that 'the United States should now take steps to stop terrorism in the world.' Given that at least one witness saw them in position at 8am and others say that within five minutes of the North Tower strike they saw the group taking pictures – how did they know what was about to happen? A former Urban Moving Systems employee told the FBI, according to the report, that the atmosphere was fantastically pro-Israel and anti-American and director Dominik Otto Suter had said: 'Give us 20 years and we will seize and destroy your media and your country.' *The Record*, the newspaper of Bergen County in New Jersey, quoted an employee as saying the majority of his colleagues were Israeli and that they were happy about the attacks: 'I was in tears. These guys were joking and that bothered me.' The five Israelis arrested were in contact with another company called Classic International Movers and four of its employees were interviewed separately about links with the 19 alleged hijackers. One of them had called 'an individual in South America with genuine links to Islamic militants in the Middle East'. Was the cheering and whooping meant to appear to be by Arabs? Reports believed them at first to be 'Arabs' or 'Palestinians' and an anonymous call to police in Jersey City, reported by *NBC News*, described 'a white van with two or three guys on the inside, they look like Palestinians and they are circling around a building'. The caller said one of them 'is mixing things and he has a 'sheikh's outfit on ... He is dressed like an Arab.' Journalist Paulo Lima, working for *The Record*, said that police sources he interviewed were convinced of Israeli involvement in the attacks. They told him:

> There are maps of the city in the car with certain places highlighted. It looked like they're hooked in with this. It looked like they knew what was going to happen when they were at Liberty State Park.

The Israeli US spy ring (and what else?)

Fox News reported that Israeli intelligence was involved in a major spying operation in the United States in 2001 and across 9/11 which involved the creation of front companies to hide the identity of Mossad agents who were coordinated via the Mossad station in Washington DC. These 'companies' operated in Florida (where most of the 'pilot hijackers' attended 'flight school'), California and New Jersey – home of 'Urban Moving Systems'. Florida seems to have been the main centre of Mossad operations and this is where 'Mohamed Atta' was located before 9/11. One of their cover stories was to pose as 'art students' and among them was 'art student' Hanan Serfaty who rented two apartments in Hollywood, Florida, close to where Atta lived. Once again Victor Ostrovsky had highlighted eleven years before how Israeli students are often used by Mossad for covert operations. The Mossad 'art student' intelligence scam was focussed on US military secrets and other information and surveillance and the story was told in a series of reports by Fox News in 2002. Israel had been famously caught spying on the US with the conviction of Jonathan Pollard, a former US government intelligence analyst, who was jailed for life in 1987 after he admitted passing a very large stash of classified information including nuclear secrets to Israel which, in turn, traded them on to the Soviet Union. This was in the period when Mossad operatives were keeping close surveillance on the United States and other countries through illegal 'back-door' software which I will be describing in more detail because it has key relevance to 9/11 and how the attacks were pulled off. Fox News reports (quickly deleted from their website) said that US agencies believed Israeli spies were at work again in 2001 and German newspaper *Die Zeit* also uncovered details of a major Israeli spy ring operating across America with some agents masquerading as art students trying to sell 'their' work. The UK *Daily Telegraph* reported the contents of a leaked 60-page internal report by the US Drug Enforcement Administration (DEA) which revealed that 200 young Israelis, among them former members of military intelligence units, had been arrested in the United States. The report was compiled in June, 2001, by the DEA's Office of Security Programs and was meant only for the eyes of senior officials at the [In]Justice Department. Someone leaked the document to the media in December, 2001, and it was widely circulated by the following March. Israelis had used cover stories (we're 'art students') to gain access to sensitive government buildings and homes of American officials. The report said the actions 'may well be an organised intelligence-gathering activity'. *May?* Around 140 Israelis were arrested earlier in 2001 before the 9/11 attacks and another 60 afterwards. The DEA report said most of the 'students' admitted serving in units of the Israeli military 'specialising in military intelligence, electronic signals interception or *explosive ordnance'*. Expertise in explosives and computer programming was a common theme. Former Mossad agent Victor Ostrovsky reveals in *By Way of Deception* a level of Mossad operative known as 'combatants' who are recruited from the Israeli general public from all walks of life – doctors, lawyers, engineers, academics. He said most pose as Europeans and operate as every-day people doing every-day occupations:

> Many bridges in Arab countries had bombs planted in the concrete by combatants during their construction – all combatants are trained in demolition techniques. In the case of war, these bridges could be easily demolished by a combatant sent in to detonate the explosives.

Some of the arrested Israelis were linked to high-ranking officials in the Israeli military. One was the son of an Israeli general, another was a bodyguard to the head of the Israeli Army and a third served in a Patriot missile unit. Peer Segalovitz, one of those arrested, served in the 605 Battalion in the Golan Heights and 'acknowledged he could blow up buildings, bridges, cars, and anything else that he needed to', the DEA report said. 'That these people are now travelling in the US selling art seems not to fit their background.' Fox reporter Carl Cameron said that in the wake of 9/11 more than 60 Israelis had been arrested and detained under anti-terrorism laws or for immigration violations and among them were 'a handful of active Israeli military'. Some of those arrested had failed polygraph tests when asked if they were spying on and in the United States. Cameron said investigators suspected that Israel operatives could have gathered intelligence about the 9/11 attacks and not shared it with American authorities (see the bombing of the US base in Beirut in 1983). A 'highly-placed investigator' had said that there were 'tie-ins'. When asked to elaborate on this Cameron quotes the investigator as saying:

> Evidence connecting these Israelis to 9/11 is classified. I cannot tell you about evidence that has been gathered. It is classified information.

Massive US Mossad network

Cameron said that numerous classified documents obtained by Fox
News indicated Israelis had been arrested or detained in a 'secretive and
sprawling investigation into espionage by Israel in the United States'.
This is the same Israel to which the American taxpayer hands over
billions of dollars a year in 'aid'. What gratitude, eh? A report by the US
General Accounting Office said: 'According to a US intelligence agency,
country A (Israel) conducts the most aggressive espionage operation
against the US of any US ally.' The *Washington Times* highlighted a report
by the US Army School for Advanced Military Studies at Fort
Leavenworth, Kansas, which called Mossad a 'wildcard ... ruthless and
cunning ... [with the] capability to target US forces and make it look like
a Palestinian/Arab act'. The *Washington Times* story was published on
September 10th, 2001. Talk about prophetic. A Defense Intelligence
report emphasised that Israel possessed the resources and technical
capability to achieve its objectives. A working group of US agencies had
been compiling evidence against Israel since the mid-1990s and
hundreds of incidents had been logged in towns and cities across the
country that 'may well be an organised intelligence-gathering activity',
Fox reporter Cameron said. The first part of the Defense Intelligence
investigation focussed on Israelis who said they were art students from
the 'University of Jerusalem' who made repeated contacts with
government personnel by saying they wanted to sell 'cheap art or
handiwork' and they targeted and penetrated military bases, law
enforcement including the FBI, and dozens of other government
facilities. They did the same even with unlisted offices and private
homes of law enforcement and intelligence personnel. Another part of
the investigation led to the arrest of dozens of Israelis selling toys in
'mall kiosks' which was believed to be a front. The kiosks, in San Diego,
Kansas City, Cleveland, Houston and St Louis, began to disappear after
the Israeli arrests were reported by *The New York Times* and *Washington
Post*. Israel denied spying on the US which was the same response they
gave when Israeli spy Jonathan Pollard was caught and they later had to
admit that Pollard was indeed spying for them. The Israeli authorities
have a simple policy – lie until you have absolutely been proved to be
lying and then, and only then, admit you lied. Journalist Christopher
Ketcham wrote a detailed article for Salon.com in May, 2002, headed
'The Israeli "art student" mystery' and the sub-heading captured its
conclusions:

> For almost two years, hundreds of young Israelis falsely claiming to be art
> students haunted federal offices – in particular, the DEA. No one knows why –
> and no one seems to want to find out.

Ketcham describes how, in January, 2001, the security branch of the US Drug Enforcement Administration began to receive a number of strange reports from DEA field offices across the country of young Israelis claiming to be art students and offering artwork for sale while attempting to penetrate DEA offices for more than a year. The Israelis had also attempted to penetrate the offices of other law enforcement and Department of Defense agencies. 'Strangest of all, the "students" had visited the homes of numerous DEA officers and other senior federal officials', Ketcham said. The DEA appeared to have been targeted in what it called an 'organized intelligence gathering activity'. In some cases, the Israelis had visited locations not known to the public and without street addresses, plus DEA offices not publicly identified. Authorities suspected that information had been gathered from prior surveillance or perhaps electronically, from credit cards and other sources. Ketcham said one Israeli was discovered holding banking receipts for close to $180,000 in withdrawals and deposits over a two-month period:

Reports of the mysterious Israelis with an inexplicable interest in peddling art to G-men came in from more than 40 US cities and continued throughout the first six months of 2001. Agents of the DEA, ATF, Air Force, Secret Service, FBI, and US Marshals Service documented some 130 separate incidents of 'art student' encounters. Some of the Israelis were observed diagramming the inside of federal buildings. Some were found carrying photographs they had taken of federal agents. One was discovered with a computer printout in his luggage that referred to 'DEA groups'.

The Office of the National Counterintelligence Executive, a branch of the CIA, issued a warning to federal employees in March, 2001, about 'suspicious visitors to federal facilities' – 'employees have observed both males and females attempting to bypass facility security and enter federal buildings.' The warning said that Federal agents had 'arrested two of these individuals for trespassing and discovered that the suspects possessed counterfeit work visas and green cards'. Salon.com said it had established that none of the Israelis were enrolled in the art school most of them claimed to be attending and the other college where they claimed to be enrolled did not exist. Ketcham wrote:

The 'art students' followed a predictable modus operandi. They generally worked in teams, typically consisting of a driver, who was the team leader, and three or four subordinates. The driver would drop the 'salespeople' off at a given location and return to pick them up some hours later. The 'salespeople' entered offices or approached agents in their offices or homes.

Sometimes they pitched their artwork – landscapes, abstract works, homemade pins and other items they carried about in portfolios. At other times, they simply attempted to engage agents in conversation.

If asked about their studies, they generally said they were from the Bezalel Academy of Arts and Design in Jerusalem or the University of Jerusalem (which does not exist). They were described as 'aggressive' in their sales pitch and 'evasive' when questioned by wary agents. The females among them were invariably described as 'very attractive' – 'blondes in tight shorts or jeans, real lookers,' as one DEA agent put it to Salon. 'They were flirty, flipping the hair, looking at you, smiling. 'Hey, how are you? Let me show you this.'

Agents noted that the 'students' made repeated attempts to avoid security personnel by trying to enter federal buildings through back doors and side entrances and suspicious agents visited at home noticed how the Israelis did not approach any of the neighbours. Anna Werner at KHOU-TV in Houston, Texas, reported that 'government guards have found those so-called students trying to get into [secure federal facilities in Houston] in ways they're not supposed to – through back doors and parking garages'. The 'students' had appeared at the DEA's Houston headquarters, at the Leland Federal Building in Houston, and even the federal prosecutor's office. They seemed to be monitoring the buildings. 'Guards at the Earle Cabell Federal Building in Dallas found one "student" wandering the halls with a floor plan of the site', Werner reported, and she said her sources had described a similar pattern at federal buildings in New York, Florida, and six other states, including '36 sensitive Department of Defense sites'. For more than 18 months the Israeli 'art students' were encountered with the same modus operandi in Atlanta, Chicago, Denver, Detroit, El Paso, Los Angeles, Miami, Orlando, New Orleans, Phoenix, San Diego, Little Rock, Seattle, Washington DC, Arlington, Texas, Albuquerque and 'dozens of other small cities and towns'. A former Defense Department analyst told Anna Werner that such activity suggested a terrorist organisation 'scouting out potential targets and ... looking for targets that would be vulnerable'. All this is incredible enough, but even more so is that the 'students' ended up being deported and not charged with the federal offences they were committing. The Web and Sabbatian-Frankists looks after its own. Six of the 'students' were reported to have cell phones purchased by a former Israeli vice consul to the United States. French daily Le Monde reported that two of the 'students' had travelled in a single day from Hamburg to Miami to visit an FBI agent in his home, then went on to Chicago and visited the home of an [In]Justice Department agent before taking a direct flight to Toronto. Hamburg was the alleged one-time location of 'student' 'Mohammed Atta' or Mohamed El-Amir. Highly suspiciously the US [In]Justice Department tried to trash the story as an 'urban myth' and claimed the DEA report, or memo, was written by a 'disgruntled agent' when clearly this was not the case. Salon's Christopher Ketcham puts the 'urban myth' nonsense into its true perspective:

> The memo is a compilation of field reports by dozens of named agents and officials from DEA offices across America. It contains the names, passport numbers, addresses, and in some cases the military ID numbers of the Israelis who were questioned by federal authorities. Pointing a finger at the author is like blaming a bank robbery on the desk sergeant who took down the names of the robbers.

Salon approached agents named in the memo and all confirmed that the information was correct. It was a fantastic scoop for proper journalists, but they are a rare and dying species. The story was dismissed by the ultra-Zionist-owned *Washington Post* and ignored completely by the ultra-Zionist-owned *New York Times*. Ketcham notes that 'the *Post's* "debunking" and the *Times'* silence ... effectively killed the story'. The UK-based Jane's Information Group, an intelligence and military analysis service, said: 'It is rather strange that the US media seems to be ignoring what may well be the most explosive story since the 11 September attacks – the alleged break-up of a major Israeli espionage operation in the USA.' Not so strange if you know how The Web operates and the power and influence that the Sabbatian-Frankist and ultra-Zionist network has over the American government and media. Ketcham wrote:

> Some of the same pressures that keep government officials from criticizing Israel may also explain why the media has failed to pursue the art student enigma. Media outlets that run stories even mildly critical of Israel often find themselves targeted by organized campaigns, including form-letter emails, the cancellation of subscriptions, and denunciations of the organization and its reporters and editors as anti-Semites.

> [Fox News reporter] Cameron, for example, was excoriated by various pro-Israel lobbying groups for his exposé. Representatives of the Jewish Institute for National Security Affairs (JINSA), the Anti-Defamation League (ADL), and the Committee for Accuracy in Middle East Reporting in America (CAMERA) argued that the Fox report cited only unnamed sources, provided no direct evidence, and moreover had been publicly denied by spokesmen for the FBI and others (the last, of course, is not really an argument).

Carl Cameron's reports on the Israeli ring were deleted within four days from the news pages and archives by Fox along with all transcripts, links and headlines. Robert Zimmerman, a Fox News spokesman, told *Le Monde* that this was normal when it most certainly wasn't. Zimmerman made an utterly lame excuse about 'bandwidth' on the news pages but when told the report series was also gone from the archives he said: 'I don't know where it is.' How absolutely appropriate that the Israeli government spokesman quoted by Salon denying the 'spy ring' story was Mark Regev, a long-time Netanyahu mass murder apologist and Israeli ambassador in London when embassy asset Shai Masot was plotting to 'take down' a British government minister over criticism of Israel. Regev, who changed his name from Mark Freiberg, was a spokesman at the Israeli embassy in Washington at the time of 9/11 and the 'spy' ring. Regev told Salon that 'no American official or intelligence agency has complained to us about this'. They wouldn't dare, but this was his best line: 'Israel does not spy on the United States.' As lies go they don't get much more bare-faced. How about the 1996 US General Accounting Office report which said that Israel 'conducts the most aggressive espionage operation against the United States of any U.S. ally' or the 1997 Defense Investigative Service memo warning that 'Israel aggressively collects [US] military and industrial technology' and 'possesses the resources and technical capability to successfully achieve its collection objectives'? How about Jonathan Pollard? Is Regev lying? Are his lips moving?

Mossad and 9/11 'hijackers' – the Florida connection

Israel's 'spying' operation was said to be keeping surveillance on suspected Muslim terrorists in the United States, but if that was the case why would they appear so often at locations relating to the Drug Enforcement Administration and at homes of government and military personnel? Indications emerged in DEA investigations of some connections to drug-trafficking and that would make sense with Mossad and the CIA heavily involved in this trade and 9/11 'lead hijacker' Mohamed Atta working with drug-trafficking through Venice Airport in Florida. Fox reporter Carl Cameron said he was told that a lot of information had been pieced together to strongly suggest that the Israelis knew about 9/11 beforehand. He quotes one intelligence source as asking 'how could they not have known?' This would explain the behaviour of the 'Dancing Israelis'. German weekly *Der Spiegel* reported:

> An entire troop of Israeli terror investigators disguised as students took to the tracks of Arabic terrorists and their cells in the USA between December 2000 and April 2001. During their undercover investigations, the Israelis came very close to the later perpetrators of September 11. In Hollywood, Florida they located both of the former Hamburg students and later terrorist pilots Mohamed Atta and Marwan al-Shehhi as potential terrorists. Agents settled

down in immediate proximity of their apartment and observed the seemingly normal flight school students around the clock.

Here we have Mossad agents specifically living near and staking out the very people who would later be – wrongly – blamed for the 9/11 attacks. *What?* The idea that this all ended in April, 2001, is simply not believable when Mossad agents and operatives were on the scene of the attacks to film and celebrate. The spin when news of the Israeli 'hijacker' surveillance came to light was that Mossad handed over details of the 'hijackers' to American authorities in August, 2001 (why the wait since the April?), but they did not pass on specifics only vague possibilities (Mossad modus operandi). Investigative journalist Christopher Bollyn highlights the Israeli and Mossad connection to Florida which he calls 'the central networking base and staging area for the "false flag" terror attacks of 9-11'. How clear this is with 15 of the 19 alleged 'hijackers' based in southern Florida where the Israeli 'spy ring' was also based. Is this yet another coincidence? Florida's governor at the time was Boy Bush's brother, the Israel fanatic, Jeb Bush. A secret government report sourced to the Drug Enforcement Administration (DEA) identified Florida and the small city of Hollywood (ten miles from Fort Lauderdale and 20 from Miami) as the centre of the Mossad 'art student' ring: 'The Hollywood, Florida, area seems to be a central point for these individuals with several having addresses in this area.' Yes – the same area that 9/11 'lead hijacker' Mohamed Atta lived in the same period and the location with connections to 15 of the 19 alleged 9/11 'hijackers'. Christopher Ketcham wrote in his Salon article:

> One Israeli was discovered holding banking receipts for substantial sums of money, close to $180,000 in withdrawals and deposits over a two-month period. A number of the Israelis resided for a period of time in Hollywood, Fla, – the small city where Mohammed Atta and three terrorist comrades lived for a time before Sept. 11.

Intelligence Online, a Paris-based espionage publication, reported in detail on the DEA report and said that more than a third of the students located in 42 cities lived in Florida and most notably in Hollywood and nearby Fort Lauderdale. Hanan Serfaty, a 'former' Israeli military intelligence officer, sorry 'art student', rented two Hollywood apartments close to the mail drop and apartment of Mohamed Atta and other alleged 'hijackers'. Serfaty rented an apartment at 4220 Sheridan Street and 701 South 21st Avenue in Hollywood. Atta's mail-drop was at 3389 Sheridan Street and he lived with Marwan al-Shehhi, alleged 'pilot' on Flight 175, in a rented apartment at 1818 Jackson Street close to South 21st Avenue. Christopher Ketcham points out that Hollywood, just north of Miami, was home during 2001 to nine alleged 'hijackers' with six in the surrounding area and that among the 120 suspected Israeli spies posing as art students more than 30 lived in the Hollywood area with ten in Hollywood itself:

> As noted in the DEA report, many of these young men and women had training as intelligence and electronic intercept officers in the Israeli military – training and experience far beyond the compulsory service mandated by Israeli law. Their 'traveling in the U.S. selling art seem not to fit their background', according to the DEA report.

The same coincidence can be found in New Jersey as Ketcham highlighted in his *Counterpunch* article which, despite this background, accepts the official 9/11 story:

> All five future hijackers of American Airlines Flight 77, which rammed the Pentagon, maintained addresses or were active within a six-mile radius of towns associated with the Israelis employed at Urban Moving Systems. Hudson and Bergen counties, the areas where the Israelis were allegedly conducting surveillance, were a central staging ground for the hijackers of Flight 77 and their fellow al-Qaeda operatives.

> Mohamed Atta maintained a mail-drop address and visited friends in northern New Jersey; his contacts there included Hani Hanjour, the suicide pilot for Flight 77, and Majed Moqed, one of the strongmen who backed Hanjour in the seizing of the plane. Could the Israelis, with or without knowledge of the terrorists' plans, have been tracking the men who were soon to hijack Flight 77?

No wonder that Ketcham says that 'in retrospect, the fact that a large number of "art students" operated out of Hollywood is intriguing, to say the least'. Now, as coincidences go, these really are major league:

> In fact, an improbable series of coincidences emerges from a close reading of the 2001 DEA memo, the 9/11 Commission's staff statements and final report, FBI and Justice Department watch lists, hi-jacker timelines compiled by major media and statements by local, state and federal law enforcement personnel.

> In at least six urban centers, suspected Israeli spies and 9/11 hijackers and/or al-Qaeda-connected suspects lived and operated near one another, in some cases less than half a mile apart, for various periods during 2001 in the run-up to the attacks. In addition to northern New Jersey and Hollywood, Florida, these centers included Arlington and Fredericksburg, Virginia; Atlanta; Oklahoma City; Los Angeles; and San Diego.

Statistical chance alone rules out coincidence and puts 9/11 into a whole new context. What's more we are only just beginning to expose the evidence that implicates Israel and its Sabbatian-Frankist control network.

Mossad patsies?

Were the 'hijackers' really assets – patsies – of Mossad (along with Sabbatian-Frankist elements of US agencies)? I say they were and almost certainly had no idea what they were being set up for. Ali al-Jarrah, a Lebanese cousin of alleged 9/11 hijacker Ziad Jarrah (Flight 93), was recruited by Israeli intelligence in 1983 after the 1982 Israeli invasion of Lebanon. *The New York Times* reported how he spied for Mossad in Lebanon and Syria for 25 years and communicated his findings by satellite phone. He also visited Israel on an Israeli passport and is reported to have been paid hundreds of thousands of dollars. His brother Yusuf is claimed to have helped him before Ali al-Jarrah ended up in a Lebanese jail for betraying his country. Until his work for Israeli intelligence was uncovered al-Jarrah appeared to friends to be 'an earnest supporter of the Palestinian cause'. His friends and colleagues were said to be 'in shock over the extent of his deceptions: the carefully disguised trips abroad, the unexplained cash, the secret second wife'. Many Arabs have been caught over the years working for Israel with a substantial number subjected to blackmail or avoiding long jail sentences. Threats to families will be in there, too, for sure. Journalist Robert Freidman wrote in *The Village Voice* that 'Ahmad Ajaj, a 27-year-old West Bank Palestinian being held in federal custody for conspiring to bomb the World Trade Center [in 1993], may have been a Mossad mole, according to Israeli intelligence sources'. Freidman, writing six months after the bombing, said Ajaj was convicted for counterfeiting in Israel and sentenced to two-and-one-half years. He quoted Israeli intelligence sources as saying Ajaj was recruited by Mossad at this time. Ajaj was released after just one year and suddenly became a 'radical Muslim' when before he was just a 'petty crook'. He was then arrested for smuggling weapons into the West Bank. Friedman said:

> ... Israeli intelligence sources say that the arrest for weapons smuggling, and Ajaj's subsequent torture and deportation, were staged by Mossad to establish his credentials as an intifada activist. Mossad allegedly 'tasked' Ajaj to infiltrate radical Palestinian groups operating outside Israel and to report back to Tel Aviv. Israeli intelligence sources say that it is not unusual for Mossad to recruit from the ranks of common criminals [it makes them feel at home].

This is how espionage works. Nothing is ever what it seems. It could well be that the wide-ranging and often not very subtle behaviour of most of the Israeli 'art students' was meant to be a diversion and cover for the real deal going on behind that smokescreen. The truth about the alleged 9/11 'hijackers' in terms of their movements will never be truly known because of the potential use of doubles, identity swaps, fake passports and so on – all of them signatures of Mossad and other intelligence agencies. I mentioned earlier how the Florida *Sun-Sentinel* reported 17 days after the 9/11 attacks:

> At least six of the suspected terrorists had two sets of driver's licenses issued by Florida, which would have allowed two or more people to use the same identity ... Many of the suspected terrorists, it is becoming increasingly clear, swapped identities as part of their preparations for the Sept 11 attacks on the World Trade Center and the Pentagon, according to a Sun-Sentinel review of documents, interviews and published reports.

How would a double know that he had a double and how would they know if someone else was using false documents purporting to be them?

Bollyn's experience

9/11 investigator Christopher Bollyn recalls how he stayed at a hotel in Miami in 2006 located among under-construction hotels being built by Donald Trump and his ultra-Zionist Israeli-American partners of Russian-descent, Michael and Gil Dezer (Dezertzov). The Dezer family are financial supporters of the Israeli Defense Forces. Bollyn went for a walk with his wife and found a beach store called Wings. The logo reminded him of the 'wings' worn by Israeli pilots and his wife noticed a computer screen filled by an image of the Israeli flag. He asked a Middle-Eastern-looking man behind the counter if he was from Israel and he confirmed that he was and that the store was Israeli-owned. Bollyn only ever saw young men of military age working at the store and they were the same age-group as those Israeli-operatives masquerading as 'art students'. Wings had a large warehouse attached to the store – unlike most beachwear outlets – with two trucks parked at the side of the building. Bollyn observed in *Solving 9- 11*:

> Every time we walked by the Wings store we never saw any customers; the store was always empty. This seemed odd because they must have had very high overhead costs. Nothing about this store made sense. It seemed to me more like a logistics base that operated a beachwear store as a front, not unlike the shuttered Urban Moving Systems outfit I had visited in Weehawken, New Jersey.

Bollyn later established that Israeli-owned Wings had 'a whole chain' of stores in Florida and the East Coast as well as Texas and the West Coast. Their corporate office and warehouse was on a low-rent industrial park at 2800 NW 125th Street in Miami in a building shared with a company selling art products – Empire Art Products Inc. Bollyn discovered that the founders of Wings were two Israelis, Shaul and Meir Levy, and that they had both met in New York the day before 9/11 with Ehud Olmert, then Mayor of Jerusalem and later Israel Prime Minister. Olmert's parents were a founding family of the Irgun terror group. He was convicted of corruption in 2015 over charges related in part to his time as Jerusalem mayor. Olmert's visit to New York was unreported apart from a sports news item three years later in *The Jerusalem Post* that said he had met the Levys in New York on September 10th over the sale of an Israeli football club. It's a heck of a coincidence and didn't Olmert tell his friend, New York mayor and Israel arse-licker Rudolf Giuliani, that he was coming? Surely New York police were told? Why no mention in the media? The same question must be asked about a report by investigative journalist Wayne Madsen who said two sources with the Israeli airline El Al (not Israeli nationals) had told him that an El Al Boeing 747 took off from New York's JFK Airport at 4.11pm on the afternoon of September 11th heading for Ben Gurion International Airport in Tel Aviv. This was hours *after* the FAA had grounded all civilian aircraft incoming and outgoing across the whole of the United States. The same happened with the Bin Laden family who were allowed to leave the US for Saudi Arabia that same day from Boston Logan after all flights were grounded. Was Olmert on that EL Al flight? Who else was on board the jumbo jet? Wayne Madsen said his sources reported that the Israeli flight was authorized by the direct intervention of the US Department of Defense and that 'US military officials were on the scene at JFK and were personally involved with the airport and air traffic control authorities to clear the flight for take-off'.

Connections between Israel, Mossad and 9/11 are already clear and blatant and there is so much more to come.

* See Dancing Israeli updates in the Postscript at the end of the book.

CHAPTER 24

Just a coincidence? (2)

He who passively accepts evil is as much involved in it as he who helps to perpetrate it. He who accepts evil without protesting against it is really cooperating with it – Martin Luther King

Orchestrating the attacks of 9/11 would have meant access and control of US government, military and Federal Aviation Administration (FAA) computer and communication systems and that is precisely what Death Cult-controlled Israel and its Mossad intelligence network had the ability to do.

Many arrested in the Israeli 'spy ring' investigation were employed by Israeli software companies, Amdocs and Nice Systems. Amdocs is a 'private' (yeah, right) Israel-based telecommunications company which had contracts with the 25 biggest phone companies in America and others around the world. Fox News reporter Carl Cameron said that it was virtually impossible to make a call without Amdocs keeping a record. Nice Systems was another Israeli software company connected with those arrested for 'spying'. Israeli 'art student' Tomer Ben Dor worked for Nice Systems – its American subsidiary is located in Rutherford, New Jersey, a few minutes from East Rutherford where the 'Dancing Israelis' were arrested on 9/11. Ben Dor was found with a computer file print-out referring to 'DEA Groups' while he was employed by an Israeli wire-tapping company?? Brigadier General Shlomo Shamir became Nice President and CEO in April, 2001. Shamir led the planning division at the Israeli IDF military headquarters and was Israel's military attaché to Germany. Mossad specialises in creating and controlling telecommunication, Internet and high-technology companies for obvious reasons and some that are not so obvious which I will reveal later. Carl Cameron said that Amdocs had been investigated a number of times and the National Security Agency (NSA) had issued a private warning to other agencies – and held conferences – to say that American phone records were getting into foreign hands – *Israel*. An NSA document warned against America's dependency on oversees technology for telecommunications:

Many factors have led to increased dependence on code developed oversees.

[We] buy rather than train or develop solutions.

They were talking about Israel. Ultra-Zionist 'art student' Michal Gal, arrested by DEA investigators in Texas, was released on a $10,000 cash bond thanks to Ophir Baer, an employee of the Israeli software company Amdocs. An Amdocs internal memo said phone information the company was compiling could be used along with 'spread data mining techniques and algorithms ... [to combine] both the properties of the customer (i.e. credit rating) and properties of the specific behaviour' (such as who the customers are calling and who is calling them). This is a long-standing technique of Israeli surveillance with data from different sources connected together to establish the big picture about a person or situation. The same Israeli focus on control and surveillance via high-technology has led to its domination of information and surveillance based in the Devil's Playground – Silicon Valley. Have a look at who runs Google, YouTube and Facebook for a start and ask how statistically likely it is that this would happen by chance. Israel, a tiny country in both population and geography, has positioned itself at the cutting edge of technology to the point where it is known as the 'start-up nation'. Israel is second in the world only to the United States for start-up companies and only America and China are ahead for companies quoted on the Nasdaq stock market. All this has happened on a sliver of land with eight million people. Israel's prime focus is on technology and 'cyber-security' (cyber infiltration). A *Vice* documentary captured the situation in its title – 'How Israel Rules The World Of Cyber Security'. Israel is basically a military state with the military-intelligence network at the centre of everything – and most definitely with cyber-technology. One of the biggest branches of the Israeli military is the Cyber Intelligence Unit headquartered in the desert-city of Beersheba and involving some 20,000 'cyber soldiers'. The headquarters represents the biggest infrastructure project in Israel's history (Fig 141). Here is located

the army of Israeli Internet trolls seeking to appear like members of the public around the world and in the same area as this vast military cyber-hub are a long list of 'private' companies and technology giants. Intel, Microsoft, IBM, Google, Apple, Hewlett-Packard, Cisco Systems, Facebook and Motorola have research and development centres in Israel.

Figure 141: The new Beersheba centre of Israel's military and domestic (military) control of cyber space.

Techcrunch.com ran an article about this global Internet technology centre headed 'Israel's desert city of Beersheba is turning into a cybertech oasis':

> The military's massive relocation of its prestigious technology units, the presence of multinational and local companies, a close proximity to Ben Gurion University and generous government subsidies are turning Beersheba into a major global cybertech hub.
>
> Beersheba has all of the ingredients of a vibrant security technology ecosystem, including Ben-Gurion University with its graduate program in cybersecurity and Cyber Security Research Center, and the presence of companies such as EMC, Deutsche Telekom, Paypal, Oracle, IBM, and Lockheed Martin. It's also the future home of the INCB (Israeli National Cyber Bureau); offers a special income tax incentive for cyber security companies, and was the site for the relocation of the army's intelligence corps units.

Israel's emerging global role in cyber technology and control will be mightily important in the closing chapters as well as shortly in relation to 9/11. We need to define the term 'cyber security' as applied to the Israeli military and Mossad and in true Orwellian fashion all you need to do is reverse the generally accepted meaning. 'Cyber security' appears to mean protection of computer systems, but to Israel it means breaching security protection to gain anytime access to those systems. To 'protect' you need to be given or even design all protection codes and with that knowledge you can access them whenever you want. It really is that simple. In this way 'little' Israel has access to all government, military, intelligence, financial, corporate and air traffic computer systems using its software – which is now much of the world. Imagine the potential for amassing almost limitless wealth alone by tapping into financial and business records and controlling events by blackmailing companies and individuals with the information you have downloaded from their computers. They can access government records, intelligence, military and police databases and steal corporate technology secrets to increase their own cyber-domination. The Israeli military trawls schools, colleges and universities for cyber talent and recruits them for military operations during their period of conscription before sending them out into 'private' (military-Mossad-connected) companies around the world (especially in the United States) to continue to work on Israel's behalf. The elite cyber and intelligence team is known as Unit 8200 which specialises in hacking into computer systems of other countries, inserting viruses, gathering information, instigating malfunction and even taking control of them from a distance. This is very relevant to 9/11 as we shall see. The Stuxnet virus which caused substantial damage to

Iran's nuclear programme and other computer systems worldwide is an Israeli cyber weapon – one of many and increasing all the time. Israel's control of major and not so major cyber technology companies allows 'back-doors' to be covertly-inserted into systems used by governments, military and public throughout the world and through these access points the Israel military and intelligence networks can infiltrate and take control. Israel doesn't make cars but dominates the manufacture of vehicle computer and WIFI systems. Through these connections an external operator can take over and drive you at high speed into a wall, a tree or over a cliff. The *Vice* documentary shows how easy it is for them to take control of your car using Israeli-created technology now fitted as standard. What else can be taken over through computer access? *Aircraft*. The world is dominated today in every area by what happens in cyberspace with the 'Internet of Things' connecting almost every facet of human life to the centrally-controlled Internet. He who controls cyberspace controls the world and every facet of human life – and Israel's Sabbatian-Frankist Death Cult to a large extent controls cyberspace and they are working to make that control complete. Sleep well. I will come to the 'endgame' consequences for the world of this Sabbatian-Frankist control of cyberspace out of Israel in the final chapters. The information is both shocking and profound for human freedom and makes absolute sense of past and current events.

Intel Inside

Intel Corporation which provides processors ('brains' or central processing units) for some 80 percent of the world's computers has a massive and ever-increasing presence in Israel. The company's first development centre outside America was opened in Haifa in 1974 (Microsoft's first overseas centre was also in Israel). The late Hungarian-born Zionist-American businessman Andrew S. Grove (born András István Gróf) is credited with the company's incredible success and he was named *Time* magazine Man of the Year in 1997. Grove was Intel president (1979–97), CEO (1987–98), chairman (1997–2005) and a funder of the ultra-Zionist Southern Poverty Law Center (SPLC). Today Intel employs thousands of people in its Israeli arm and in early 2019 announced investment of another $11 billion to build a new manufacturing facility in Israel with the government donating a major sum to the global giant while Holocaust survivors live in economic deprivation. Intel's Israel chief Yaniv Garty was named one of the country's most influential people by business and financial newspaper *The Marker* which included 20 tech 'luminaries' in its top 100 most influential Israelis. Al-Awda, the Palestine Right to Return Coalition, points out that the Intel operation north of Beersheba is built on land Israel confiscated from the Palestinian villagers of al-Faluja and Iraq al

Manshiya where thousands of people were living. They were terrorised out of their homes which were razed to the ground for the Jewish settlement of Kiryat Gat. Members of an American Quaker relief mission documented the violence they witnessed including a man with 'two bloody eyes, a torn ear, and a face pounded until it was blue'. UN observers reported beatings, robberies and attempted rape on civilians by Israeli soldiers. The villagers have never been allowed to return. Israel is not racist, though, only everyone else. The Electric Intifada website reported in 2008 the following concern of Israeli authorities about Kiryat Gat:

> ... the local authorities in Kiryat Gat are focused on preventing yet another kind of 'disaster', as they put it: Jewish girls taking up with Bedouin boys. So common has this phenomenon become that the municipality last year convened an 'emergency' conference to address it. The upshot: a program run by the municipal welfare department, with support from the police, that sends speakers into public school classrooms to warn girls about the dangers they face from Arab boys. The curriculum even includes a 10-minute video entitled 'Sleeping with the Enemy'.

Anti-racist racism is never a pretty sight. Intel was in the news in 2019 when computer experts claimed its chips are hiding mysterious and 'undocumented' technology. Analysts from London-based Positive Technologies alleged that Intel chips and processors contain a 'logic signal analyser' which can read 'almost all data on a computer'. This theme of 'back-door' access to computer systems is going to be highly significant to 9/11 and global control from here to the end of the book. Maxim Goryachy and Mark Ermolov revealed their findings at the Black Hat Conference of hackers and cybersecurity experts in Singapore. They said they discovered the 'analyser' (known as VISA) in the Platform Controller Hub (PCH) on Intel motherboards and the main processor itself. These comprise the 'brain' of the computer and potentially VISA technology can allow external access to information stored in the memory and also to connected items such as a webcam or mouse. One report of the story said:

> This ability would be useful to hackers looking to steal information – as well as spies or anyone else interested in stealing sensitive information. Normally, VISA is turned off in commercial systems. Yet the researchers claimed to have found a way to switch it on.

You will see as we proceed the significance of this and the significance of Israel being a global centre for cyber-technology and control in relation to both current events and 9/11.

Israel: Breaking a PROMIS

We can pick up the story of Israel's domination of cyber-technology and its relevance to 9/11 in the 1970s when a Washington DC software company called Inslaw developed tracking technology with the potential for prosecutors to monitor case records. This was dubbed the Prosecutor's Management Information System or PROMIS and was backed by funding from the US Department of [In]Justice. PROMIS user contracts stipulated that the software could not be modified, distributed to others or any derivative versions made. Instead the US National Security Agency (NSA) and other government departments sold PROMIS software to banks and foreign intelligence networks with a built-in 'back-door' that allowed US intelligence to spy on the operations of purchasers. Among the countries involved were Israel, Egypt, Jordan, Iraq and Canada. A letter from the US Department of [In]Justice dated 1985 was secured by Inslaw during its court proceedings against the US government for breaking the terms of contract through among other things modifying the software. The letter revealed that conduits for PROMIS sales by the government included Saudi billionaire Khalid bin Mahfouz and the arms dealer Adnan Khashoggi. Yes, yes, the same Khalid bin Mahfouz, operations director and 20 percent shareholder of the Bank of Credit and Commerce International (BCCI), close associate of the Bush family and named by the United States government as a financial supporter of Osama bin Laden. The government letter secured by Inslaw said that PROMIS should be delivered without 'paperwork, customs, or delay', and payments channelled through a Swiss bank account. Edwin Meese, Attorney General during the Reagan-Father Bush administration, and Dr Earl Brian from the government consultancy firm Hadron were apparently designated to sell the illegal 'back-door' version of PROMIS. A 1992 House Judiciary Committee report revealed that they were allowed to do this 'for their personal financial gain and in support of the intelligence and foreign policy objectives of the United States'. Earl Brian was also the head of Infotechnology Inc, a New York holding company that controlled among many other companies, United Press International (UPI), and the Financial News Network (FNN). He would later be jailed on fraud charges unrelated to PROMIS.

Earl Brian was apparently given crucial help in circulating the back-door PROMIS by Rafi Eitan, a top Israeli intelligence officer and former head of LAKAM, an intelligence operation connected to Israel's nuclear weapons programme – the open secret that it ludicrously won't confirm or deny. The truly appalling Eitan was central to the PROMIS scam and its back-door access to government and other computer systems around the world. He was also an advisor to MI6 on counter-terrorism (love it) in Northern Ireland during the Margaret Thatcher premiership in the 1980s. This ended with his involvement in the shoot-to-kill operation in Gibraltar in 1985 when three members of the Irish Republican Army (IRA) were killed by the British elite military unit, the SAS. Shoot-to-kill with no legal oversight is typical of Israeli Mossad. Another Mossad operative involved with PROMIS was the infamous crook, sorry, 'businessman and publisher', Robert Maxwell, nicknamed Captain Bob and the Bouncing Czech. His daughter Ghislaine has been accused of procuring young girls for the paedophile ring of ultra-Zionist billionaire child-abuser Jeffrey Epstein in the United States who is big mates with the rich and famous including Bill Clinton and Britain's Prince Andrew. The Maxwells are a lovely family apparently. Investigative writer Gordon Thomas interviewed many senior officials of Israeli intelligence for his book, *Gideon's Spies – The Secret History of the Mossad*, including Rafi Eitan. Thomas said in a sworn affidavit that Maxwell sold $500 million worth of illegal back-door PROMIS to the 'UK, Australia, South Korea, Canada and the KGB in the Soviet Union'. Former Mossad agent Victor Ostrovsky describes in his book, *The Other Side of Deception*, how Maxwell was murdered by Mossad at sea on his yacht when he became more of a hazard than a help as his business empire collapsed which included his ownership of Britain's Mirror newspaper group. Maxwell was then buried by the country that killed him on the Mount of Olives in Jerusalem – the 'resting place for the nation's most revered heroes', as Ostrovsky puts it. The hypocrisy is breathtaking. A small cabal in the know about back-door PROMIS in both Israel and the United States sold it all over the world to intelligence agencies, government departments and law enforcement giving them global access to people-tracking data. The apartheid regime in South Africa employed PROMIS to identify black activists and dissidents who would then disappear.

Long story short – Israel secured back-door PROMIS access to the government-military-intelligence computer systems of the United States and so knew pretty much everything the US knew. A House Judiciary Committee investigation revealed in 1992 that 'a foreign power – the state of Israel – had been engaged in active espionage against the United States by the illegal use of the Enhanced PROMIS software'. This has since become massively more widespread and sophisticated as Israel has dominated cyberspace ever more totally and it spies on the spies in countries all over the world, especially the United States. PROMIS took this espionage against the American state to a whole new level at that time and no wonder Israeli intelligence was a central player in what happened to PROMIS software and how it was later used. This is highly significant given that PROMIS-like software access to government, military and civil aviation computer systems is centrally connected the attacks of September 11th. Ari Ben-Menashe was a former agent with

Israeli intelligence, served for twelve years in the Israel Defense Forces and was intelligence consultant to terrorist Prime Minister Yitzhak Shamir. Ben-Menashe said that PROMIS was given by the US government to the Israel Defense Forces Intelligence Unit and court files in the Inslaw case reveal the plan was to access computer systems of those who had purchased the software. This Israel-American connection would have been Sabbatian-Frankist in nature. Ben-Menashe said in an Inslaw affidavit that he was present at a meeting in Tel Aviv in 1987 when Earl Brian was pitching PROMIS to Israel officials. Two courts ruled in favour of Inslaw in 1988 and said that the US government 'took, converted, stole' PROMIS 'through trickery, fraud and deceit', but amid the most blatant corruption the verdict was overturned by a court of appeal on the grounds of a 'jurisdictional technicality'. Such is the power over the courts by the Hidden Hand. The PROMIS story was a sign of things to come as Israel's control of cyberspace continued to develop in the run-up to 9/11.

Israeli tech-matrix

Comverse Infosys (which changed its name to Verint in 2002) is another Israeli telecommunications company in the United States highlighted in the Fox News report after 9/11 and this company was providing phone-tapping technology to the FBI and other law enforcement. The potential for blackmail through tapped calls is obvious and the ability to stay one-step ahead of any law enforcement investigation. Comverse was established in the early 1980s by three Israelis, investment banker Jacob 'Kobi' Alexander, engineer Boaz Misholi, and Columbia University computer science professor, Yechiam Yemini, who was Alexander's brother-in-law. The Israeli company was phone-tapping for US law enforcement and *retaining access through its computers to the call-tap information.* Reporter Carl Cameron said that US intelligence agencies were concerned about 'back-doors' (here we go again) in the technology. The report said that Comverse worked closely with the Israeli government which under 'special programmes' paid half the company's research and development costs. This is typical of the seamless connection between Israeli tech companies and Israeli government, military and intelligence networks. Cameron said he was told that to question if Comverse was involved in spying for Israel was 'career suicide' for investigators and the technology had never been checked for leaks. Is it not worth asking why 'tiny' Israel so terrifies politicians, intelligence operatives and media the world over that they stay silent in the face of its outrageous behaviour? FBI personnel responsible for awarding contracts to Comverse later ended up working for the company – something that should have been banned in any fair and open system. Cameron also said that what most troubled investigators into 9/11 was the number of cases in which supposedly *secret* wire-taps led to the people involved immediately changing their means of communication. Intelligence agencies and organised crime have a very close relationship and in fact much of what intelligence agencies do *is* organised crime. Mossad and Israeli-Zionist organised crime – like the Kosher Nostra in New York and the wider United States – are absolutely the same thing. Documents obtained by Fox for the Cameron reports describe how Israeli organised crime operating in Israel, Egypt, New York, Miami, Las Vegas and Canada was being investigated in 1997 for cocaine and ecstasy trafficking along with credit card and computer fraud, but there was a problem. The Israeli crime syndicate had the police beepers, cell phones and home phones *under surveillance*. Investigators concluded that the syndicate 'has apparent extensive access to identify pertinent personal and biographical information'. The Fox News reports were deleted from their website and not another word has ever appeared despite Israel penetrating the entire US government communication and computer system to the point where through PROMIS and later systems they could use the covert back-doors to change information at will – including in real time. Think about the potential of that on 9/11. Pointing the finger at Russia for hacking US government and election systems is simply cover for Israel doing that on an industrial scale. Odigo is yet another Israeli telecommunications company and instant messaging service and has offices near the World Trade Center. I have explained how Israel-based Odigo employees were sent a warning two hours before the first tower was hit that some sort of attack was imminent. Odigo vice president Alex Diamandis said: 'The messages said something big was going to happen in a certain amount of time and it did – almost to the minute.' CEO Micha Macover said that immediately after the attack the two told the company about the warning and Israeli security services were then informed who told the FBI. Macover said: 'I have no idea why the message was sent to these two workers who don't know the sender. It may just have been someone who was joking and turned out they accidentally got it right.' So why hasn't the sender been found?

Israeli tech innovator and trained assassin on Flight 11

A point widely missed with 9/11 is that the first person reported to have been killed on Flight 11 according to flight attendant calls was 31-year-old Daniel Lewin, an American-Israeli co-founder of multi-billion dollar cloud services and cyber-security company Akamai Technologies which is headquartered in Cambridge, Massachusetts. Lewin, who was said to be sitting very close to alleged 'hijackers' Mohamed Atta, Abdulaziz al-Omari and Satam al Suqami in seat 9B, was a captain in the Israeli Defense Forces who served in the elite specialist counter-terrorism, hostage rescue and assassination operation known as the Sayeret Matkal or General Staff Reconnaissance Unit. This is modelled on the British elite SAS and adopted the same motto of 'Who Dares Wins'. Lewin was the subject of a book entitled *No Better Time: The Brief, Remarkable Life of Danny Lewin, the Genius Who Transformed the Internet*. He was an Israeli-American duel citizen who understood Arabic. Lewin was acclaimed as a hero of 9/11 for tackling the 'hijackers' before being overpowered. This is said to have happened to a man who could bench-press 315 pounds and squat close to 500 pounds. By his own account he was 'trained to kill terrorists with a pen or credit card' or just his bare hands. He was, to get straight to the point, a trained assassin. Somehow we are told he was overpowered by slightly built 'hijackers' as were other huge men said to be on the planes. The official 9/11 account is that Lewin was stabbed which overrode an internal FAA memo on September 11th that said he was shot by a single bullet:

> The American Airlines FAA Principal Security Inspector (PSI) was notified by Suzanne Clark of American Airlines Corporate Headquarters, that an on board flight attendant contacted American Airlines Operations Center and informed that a passenger located in seat 10B shot and killed a passenger in seat 9B ... The passenger killed was Daniel Lewin, shot by passenger Satam Al Suqami. One bullet was reported to have been fired.

The report was later changed from being shot to being stabbed. Childhood friend Brad Rephen who served with Lewin in the Israel Defense Force said: 'With his training, he would have killed them with his bare hands ... I can tell you, their knives would not have stopped him ... He would have taken their knives or their box cutters away and used them against them.' Rephen said Lewin 'knew how to fight with knives and take knives away from people.' The Akamai Technologies website makes it clear what a signigicant internet delivery and security operation Lewin co-founded:

> As the largest distributed platform operating at the edge of the Internet, Akamai provides a defensive shield built to protect your websites, mobile infrastructure, and API-driven requests. Via 24/7 monitoring, we collect and analyze terabytes of attack data, billions of bot requests, and hundreds of millions of IP addresses to solidify your defenses and keep you informed. And we never stop innovating to stay ahead of the latest threats including malware, phishing, data exfiltration, DDoS, and other advanced attacks.

> This commitment to security is why we're trusted by the most security-conscious industries, including 18 of the largest asset managers, 12 of the top insurers, and 8 of the top financial technology companies. So you can worry

less about cyber attacks, and more about growing your business.

The company was floated in 1999 and overnight made Lewin at least a near-billionaire as he became one of the world's richest high-tech entrepreneurs before the age of 30. Akamai clients include Sony, Apple and the Murdoch News Corp. The company has been responsible for 'keeping some of the world's most popular websites running smoothly, including Facebook and iTunes'. Akamai claims to be used by 50 percent of Global 500 companies, 55 percent of Fortune 500 companies, all branches of the US military with 85 percent of the world's Internet users 'within a single "network hop" of an Akamai CDN server'. Akamai says it delivers nearly three trillion Internet interactions every day. Danny Lewin reached the rank of captain with the Israeli counter-terrorism, hostage rescue and assassination unit before studying maths and computer science at the Israeli Institute of Technology and going on to the Massachusetts Institute of Technology (MIT). He also worked for IBM's research lab in Haifa, Israel, and he would then have a 'ground-breaking' idea to allow the internet to work more efficiently and at faster speeds with a set of algorithms that he called 'consistent hashing'. Akamai claim that Lewin's technology 'transformed the Internet from a chaotic network into a secure business platform'. By some bizarre chance a picture was taken of Danny Lewin in 2000 wearing a Swatch Watch of the model name 'Hijacker' and the hour, minute, second hands and date are all set to 11. It's amazing how elite Israeli military and intelligence operatives turn up in every area of the 9/11 story.

Ptech and 9/11

Genuine investigators on the trail of Israel's involvement in 9/11 have highlighted a network of Israeli tech companies in the United States which deserve serious attention. I'm going to start with one called Ptech ('Process Technology'), a 'small' software company in Quincy, a suburb of Boston, Massachusetts, which listed among its clients the Pentagon, NATO, the White House, US Congress, Department of [In]Justice, FBI, US Secret Service and ... the *Federal Aviation Administration, US Air Force and NORAD.* Oh yes, and add US Customs and Border Protection, Internal Revenue Service and the Department of Energy, plus others. At the time of 9/11 Ptech and the associated federally-funded MITRE Corporation had real-time access to all computer systems and inter-agency communications that would have been bottom-line essential to anyone orchestrating the attacks. From 1997 Ptech was given security clearance to deal with 'sensitive military projects' and secured a contract with the Defense Advanced Research Projects Agency (DARPA) – the technology-development arm of the Pentagon which basically controls Silicon Valley (for its Death Cult masters) and drives the agenda to attach the human mind to artificial intelligence (see *Everything You Need To Know But Have Never Been Told*). Ptech was apparently just a small and insignificant company on the surface although it had connections with giants like IBM and its *high*-significance to 9/11 can be seen with the client list that I described. Another 'apparently' is that it was primarily a Muslim company established in 1994 by Oussama Ziade, a Lebanese immigrant, but there are other links that take us elsewhere. Ptech became a company of interest to 9/11 investigators in the alternative media after Indira Singh, an IT professional, went public with her experience. Singh had worked as a high-level IT consultant to the United Nations, American Express and Wall Street companies including JPMorganChase where she was developing a next-generation system to expose money laundering, rogue trading and illegal financing patterns. She also worked as a senior consultant in Washington DC with the Interoperability Clearing House (ICH) which had connections with the CIA and DARPA. Singh realised in the course of her work with JPMorganChase that Ptech would have had access to all the key computer systems necessary to stage the 9/11 attacks while at the same time having a major Muslim connection with apparent ties to people accused of funding terrorism. Ptech dealt in 'enterprise architecture software' which makes it possible to observe in real time all data produced by an organisation or system. Seeing what is going on everywhere as it happens has clear potential for numerous activities from very good to extremely bad. It was a big advance on PROMIS software with its back-door to government and military computer systems in which Rafi Eitan, a top Israeli intelligence officer, was a key player. Here was the chance for Israel and the Hidden Hand in general to get even more control of those systems via what *appeared* to be a Muslim company.

The Islamic connection to Ptech was further highlighted by the number of Saudi investors and board members accused or suspected of funding terrorism. Ptech board member Soliman Biheiri was the head of BMI, an Islamic, Sharia-compliant investment bank based in New Jersey which was accused of funding terrorist groups. Biheiri was jailed in 2005 for terrorism and fraud. US prosecutors described him as the US banker for the Muslim Brotherhood. BMI's backers included two brothers of CIA-asset Osama bin Laden. Indira Singh claimed in an interview that Thomas Kean, joint head of the pathetic 9/11 Commission, had done business deals with BMI and should have either not accepted the job of 'investigating' 9/11 or made his connections public. Another big Islam-BMI-Ptech connection was Saudi businessman Yassin al-Kadi, or al-Qadi, who had links with Muslim entities funding terrorism including investments in BMI. Kadi was a major investor in Ptech with all its access to US government, military and FAA computer systems. He has appeared on terrorism wanted lists, been subject to international

financial sanction and has also been connected to the Muslim
Brotherhood. Kadi has slowly overturned the terrorist designation
through legal actions and submissions. The United Nations Security
Council refused to remove Kadi from its terrorism blacklist and in 2009
published a list of reasons which included evidence that Osama bin
Laden was the source of working capital for up to five of Kadi's
companies in Albania. The UN relented and de-listed him in 2012. Kadi
is reported to have been a close friend of Bin Laden (he certainly met
him) and claimed himself to be a friend of Dick Cheney. Kadi was a
long-time associate and business partner of Bush family friend Khalid
bin Mahfouz, a leading shareholder in the stunningly corrupt Bank of
Credit and Commerce International (BCCI) who was exposed for
donating more than $270,000 to Osama bin Laden at the request of
Osama's brother and Boy Bush business partner, Salem bin Laden. Bin
Mahfouz was named as a financer of terrorism by the Bill Clinton State
Department and was involved along with Israel in selling the back-door
PROMIS software. We should not forget that Saudi Arabia and Israel at
inner-circle levels are not 'enemies' but fellow Sabbatian-Frankists
pursuing the same agenda. This explains so much about events on 9/11.
Israel loves those who fund Muslim terrorism because it serves their
interests in demonising the Muslim world. Large numbers of Saudis and
other Arabic people work for Mossad and the CIA – some by choice,
many by entrapment – and Mossad commonly uses Arabs to front-up its
operations and companies to hide the real perpetrators. Who is going to
suspect Israeli involvement with 'Muslim' companies? The obvious
connection between 9/11 and 'hijackers' with a Saudi background
makes perfect sense from this perspective. What can be said with
certainty is that people like Yassin al-Kadi and Soliman Biheiri would
not have had their Ptech software company given access to the most
sensitive United States military, government and civilian air traffic
computer systems and information by mistake because their connections
were well known. The FBI said that Kadi was investing millions in Ptech
ongoing and they were told by company insiders of their trips to meet
investors in Saudi Arabia with Kadi always among them. Ptech's chief
scientist Hussein Ibrahim, who started Muslim bank BMI with Soliman
Biheiri, was close to Kadi. Ibrahim was the former president of BMI
which was also a seed-investor in Ptech. BMI leased computers and
office space in New York from Kadi International. If you find the official
Ptech story extraordinary then you are not alone. American
Investigative journalist Christopher Bollyn writes:

> It simply did not make sense that the most secure computer systems of the US
> government would be running software written by a Lebanese immigrant
> financed by a Saudi who happened to be on the most-wanted list of global

terrorists.

The ultra-Zionist connection

The background to Ptech with its access to top secret computer systems across the US government, military and FAA civilian aviation at the time of 9/11 would appear to be Muslim in nature, but hold on a second. Author Dan Verton in his book, *Black Ice: The Invisible Threat of Cyber-Terrorism,* says that Ptech and its Lebanese founder Oussama Ziade were innocent victims of [Muslim] paranoia. He notes in support of this that many Ptech employees were Jewish. Christopher Bollyn discovered that a key man involved with Ptech was Michael Goff, a Jewish ultra-Zionist lawyer from Worcester, Massachusetts. He is the son and grandson of 'highest level' B'nai B'rith Freemasons in the Worcester lodge and he would go on to work with an Israeli Mossad/military-connected software company called Guardium, later absorbed into IBM. Guardium was an asset of Log-on Software founded by two Israeli military officers, Joseph Segev, one-time head programmer and telecommunications officer with the Israeli Navy, and Major Gil Migdan. The company's vice president was Danny Zeitouny, head of logistics programming for the Israeli Defense Forces (IDF). The same story can be found with Log-on's spin-off Guardium which had Israeli colonel Gill Zaphir or Zafir on its board of directors. Zaphir was head of research and development with the Israeli Air Force. Amit Yoran was another Jewish director of Guardium and also a co-founder, CEO and president. Yoran is a graduate of the United States Military Academy at West Point and became a founding member of the Pentagon's Computer Emergency Response Team. He would later be appointed by President Boy Bush as director, or 'czar', of the National Cyber Security Division at the Department of Homeland Security with responsibility for coordinating America's cyber security. The number of ultra-Zionist connections to US government, military, intelligence and security systems is simply mind-blowing when they represent only one section of two percent of the population. If the same ratio was true of Chinese people or Muslims what would the reaction be? Amit Yoran has been a consultant and advisor to CIA technology seed-funding company, In-Q-Tel, and when he was with Silicon Valley software company Symantec Corporation he was 'primarily responsible for managing security infrastructure in 40 countries', according to *Business Week*. Yoran also 'designed security architecture for the Pentagon and Office of the Secretary of Defense' and was Network Security Manager responsible for maintaining operations of the Pentagon's network. This was at the same time that ultra-Zionist Michael Goff was 'marketing and information systems manager' at Ptech supplying software for Pentagon computer systems. Those with allegiance to Israel were and are all over US government and military computer systems.

Amit Yoran was president and chief executive of a company employing hackers to test the vulnerabilities of computer systems. This was Riptech which Yoran co-founded in 1998 and was acquired by Symantec in 2002. Yoran told the Associated Press in 2001 that once you break into a web-server 'there are fewer protections between it and other parts of the network'. And what if you control the web-server? Riptech was established by Yoran and his elder brother, Elad, another Israeli West Point graduate, and Tim Belcher, a veteran of the Gulf War in 1990/91. Belcher has been connected to a long list of tech and software companies and according to his Bloomberg profile 'conducted security assessments of some of the nation's most critical infrastructure components, including the Federal Aviation Administration's Air Traffic Control Network' and has been employed by the National Aeronautics and Space Administration, National Reconnaissance Office, Office of the Secretary of Defense and Space and Naval Warfare Command. He and Amit Yoran were also 'advisors' to Security Growth Partners (SPG), a funding company founded and run by Elad Yoran, and on the advisory board was Jeremy M. Kroll from the ultra-Zionist family that was running security at the World Trade Center on 9/11 – of which more shortly. Jeremy Kroll was Managing Director of Marsh Kroll, a division of ultra-Zionist Marsh & McLennan (known as MMC), and the first plane to strike the World Trade Center hit the 'secure computer room' of Marsh & McLennan in the North Tower. Marsh & McLennan was controlled by the family of ultra-Zionist Maurice Greenberg and together they handled the initial insurance for Larry Silverstein and the World Trade Center. Ultra-Zionist interconnections between Big Tech and cyber-'security' companies are extraordinary. Christopher Bollyn writes:

> A number of senior corporate officers of Amdocs, all Israelis, moved between Nice Systems, ViryaNet Ltd, and Guardium. Sometimes a person would go to a company for a while and then return to the previous company. In some cases, such as Gill Zaphir, a person would be involved in an Israeli 'venture capital' fund supporting a company while serving as a director of the company being funded. Elad Yoran, Amit's older brother, held similar positions at Broadview International and Riptech, a 'security' software company that specialized in hacking into corporate computer networks.

Ptech, MITRE and 9/11

These were the sort of people ultra-Zionist Michael Goff would have worked with at Israel-front Guardium and would have come into contact with while at Israel-front Ptech with all its access to computer systems essential to 9/11. Goff had earlier worked for an ultra-Zionist law firm and later ultra-Zionist Guardium, but in between he suddenly joins an apparently – *apparently* – Muslim company at Ptech which would have access to key swathes of the US government, military, intelligence and FAA computer systems. Here we have a Jewish man from a seriously ultra-Zionist family working as a 'marketing and information systems manager' at Ptech, a company funded by people accused of funding Islamic terrorism, including Hamas which is so condemned by Israel. Yep, makes sense doesn't it? As Bollyn puts it:

> So, why would a recently graduated Juris Doctor in Law leave a promising law career to join forces with a Lebanese Muslim's upstart company sponsored by dodgy funders in Saudi Arabia?

Bollyn asked Michael Goff how in 1994 he left the ultra-Zionist Seder and Chandler law firm in Worcester and ended up with a job at Ptech. Goff said this was done 'through a temp agency'. Which one? He couldn't remember. Goff was asked who wrote the original Ptech software used by government, military and FAA air traffic for which he was the original marketing and information systems manager. He said he didn't know. This is despite being described on his own website in the following terms in relation to his work at Ptech: 'As information systems manager, Michael handled design, deployment and management of its Windows and Macintosh, data, and voice networks ... Michael also performed employee training and handled all procurement for software, systems and peripherals.' He was at the centre of everything, then, and Bollyn was right to question his story:

> Goff, the original marketing manager for Ptech software, said he did not know who had written the code that Ptech sold to many government agencies. Is this believable? Goff leaves a legal practice in his home town to take a job through a temp agency, with a Lebanese Muslim immigrant who is selling software, and he doesn't know who even wrote the code?

How about it was written in Israel and through these connections ended up on US government, military, intelligence and FAA computer systems essential to American security and response on 9/11? The Israeli global technology company network is fantastic and they are all ultimately assets of the equally fantastic Israeli military and intelligence web that spans America, Europe and the wider world. Bollyn, who has researched the subject for nearly two decades, says this about Guardium which Michael Goff worked for after leaving Ptech:

> Guardium is closely connected with other companies of the Israeli military intelligence network in the United States. Some of the key Israeli-run

companies linked to Guardium are Amdocs, ViryaNet, Nice Systems, and CreoScitex. Like Guardium, these companies are all run by senior officers of Israeli military intelligence.

Amdocs and Nice Systems are especially noteworthy because these two companies were involved in the espionage network of computer programmers and demolition experts from the Israeli military who posed as art students as they tried to infiltrate offices of the US Drug Enforcement Agency (DEA) in 2000 and 2001.

Ptech worked closely on government, military and FAA civil aviation computer systems with the MITRE Corporation where James Rodney Schlesinger was the long-time chairman of the Board of Trustees from 1985 until his death in 2014. Schlesinger was born to Jewish parents in New York and later converted to Lutheranism. He went on to be Secretary of Defense, Secretary of Energy, Director of the CIA and was appointed to the Homeland Security Advisory Council by President Boy Bush in 2002. MITRE Corporation was established in 1958 as a private, not-for-profit company to provide engineering and technical guidance for the federal government and provides specialised technology for defense and intelligence. MITRE's headquarters is in McLean, Virginia, where it shares space with big-time Hidden Hand Northrop Grumman, one of the world's biggest aerospace and armament corporations. The MITRE website says it 'has operated at the intersection of advanced technology and vital national concerns [and] we've grown to serve a variety of government agencies at the highest levels through the operation of federally-funded research and development centers'. Among them are the National Security Engineering Center working on 'national security' for the Department of Defense and the Center for Advanced Aviation System Development working for the FAA on air traffic management. MITRE was partnered before and during the 9/11 attacks with Ptech and MITRE also used Ptech (Israeli back-door) software. Back-door access to US government, military and FAA computer systems could have controlled the whole 9/11 scenario while genuine staff were desperately trying to make sense of the mess and confusion. The potential was also there for normal reaction mechanisms including fighter response and ground-to-air missile defences to be infiltrated, delayed and deactivated. This alone would answer so many still-unanswered questions about what happened that day. Elias Davidsson writes in *Hijacking America's Mind On 9/11*:

A central feature of the simulated war games conducted on 9/11 was for the military to feed electronic blips representing airliners into military and civilian radar [these are known as 'input']. As the events of 9/11 unfolded, radar operators had no way of knowing whether the blips they were observing on their screens represented real or simulated aircraft.

There were in fact three types of blips the controllers had to confront: Those representing virtual aircraft, possessing no physical existence; those representing real aircraft which were scheduled to participate in the simulated hijackings; and all other blips representing real aircraft.

This is how it was possible with real-time access to government, military and FAA computer systems to swap planes, lose planes, invent planes and cause maximum confusion during which the deed could have been done while genuine operatives were asking: 'What the fuck is going on?' Major James Fox, leader of the NORAD NEADS weapons team, said amid the chaos: 'I've never seen so much real-world stuff happen during an exercise.' The confusion was such that some operatives believed that the scenes of carnage on their television screens were simulated for them to see as part of an exercise. It tells you so much about the scale of the cover-up that neither the FBI nor the 9/11 Commission sought to investigate the relationship of the wargame exercises with actual events.

In-your-face cover-up

IT risk-assessment consultant Indira Singh began to speak out about the obvious potential security risks of having people accused of funding Islamic terrorism and Osama bin Laden so involved with a company in Ptech at the heart of US government and military computer systems relating to security and communication between front-line 9/11 agencies including the Pentagon, Air Force, NORAD, CIA and FAA. She contacted the FBI in Boston (which had a reputation for being notoriously corrupt) to share her findings and predictably to no avail. She notified a stream of agencies at local, state and federal levels and again nothing happened. JPMorganChase warned her to stop what she was doing *or else* and she lost her job because she refused to stop. For her this was personal. Singh had been due at a meeting on the 106th floor (where no one survived) of the World Trade Center North Tower that morning, but overslept. She was on her way to the building when the first plane hit and then volunteered to help with the medical response as a part-time emergency medical technician. I mentioned her earlier with regard to hearing that Building 7 was going to be brought down. From the information Singh uncovered and her own experience she not unnaturally concluded that Ptech was being protected. With no response amid warnings about dangers to her life if she continued to dig she turned to investigative reporter Joe Bergantino at a Boston CBS affiliate called WBZTV. He verified Singh's story about Ptech and more.

Bergantino's report was due to run on September 11th, 2002, but it didn't because of pressure, Singh says, from the Bush-Cheney White House. Ptech's office was raided by the FBI in 2002 before the lid went on and *seven years* later the FBI 'investigation' concluded with an indictment for 'loan fraud'. Singh said that Bergantino and his investigation team did produce a video connecting a Boston-based Islamic charity called Care International to the Al Kifah Refugee Center (which has been linked to the 1993 World Trade Center bombing in which the FBI was involved) and to the Maktab al-Khidamat (MAK) which was founded in 1984 with input from Osama bin Laden and others to raise money and recruit Mujahidin for the fight against the Zbigniew Brzezinski-instigated Soviet occupation in Afghanistan. MAK was established by the CIA together with the 9/11-connected ISI Pakistan military intelligence to fund Bin Laden and the Mujahidin before morphing into a fundraising and recruitment network for al-Qaeda when the CIA morphed the Mujahidin into al-Qaeda. Indira Singh said she then realised that MAK was being 'run out of Ptech' because faces in the Bergantino videotape she was shown were core employees at Ptech. Some formerly worked for the Islamic Care International (not to be confused with the major international humanitarian agency of the same name) and among them was Suheil Laheir. Singh described him as 'one of the only one or two people who had access to the source code at Ptech' which was the key to the entire program. She said '... it would be like having the formula for Coca Cola, basically.' Singh continued:

> By the end of the day when I was finished with certain parts of the investigations, it was clear to me that there was no way Ptech could have done all of this without a lot of inside help. And that's what I began focusing on, that it was a cut-out, it was a front, was it a regular CIA front, was it a clandestine front, what was it? ... There are walls within the FBI, walls within the CIA, behind which these operations take place, and who is behind those operations, is a key question.

How about Mossad working with Hidden Hand elements within the CIA, US government/military, Pakistan ISI and Saudi Arabia with British intelligence also involved somewhere as they always are? The Web makes this possible. Compartmentalisation means that most strands in something like 9/11 won't know what they are ultimately part of and where it is all meant to lead. Singh correctly observed that this wasn't just a simple case of 'Muslims hate America' – 'there is something else going on here, they're being used as a tool, just as the good people of the US are being used, are being misled, and frightened and terrorised into "if we don't wage these horrific wars, our way of life will be over". Who benefits?' She correctly made this point:

... maybe those organisations don't fully know who their masters are. Ptech is the one thread, the one golden thread you pull on, all of this is unravelled. Because it goes into the corporations, it goes into these government entities, it goes into the terrorism financing entities ... none of which have been taken to task ... there are just so many questions about what does this all mean? And as I investigated further, we found that the origins of Ptech were very interesting. Where did this company come from? ... And how did they get to be so powerful? Who were the people, who were the organisations that brought them in who knew, who gave them the power?

Singh is describing The Web and how it works. Ptech was clearly an intelligence front and so all doors were opened at the expense of other companies. Singh said:

... I remember that Ptech's competitors, US companies, were extremely annoyed at the fact that they could not get equal time, all the plum contracts were going to a foreign-owned company. And I said, 'Well, did you know that they were foreign-owned? And if they were foreign-owned, they could not get certain classified projects...' and [I was told], 'Indira, everyone knew that they were Saudi-owned and that meant that they got favourable treatment on Capitol Hill.' And I said, 'Well, are you saying that they just got "favoured treatment" or there's something more going on?' They wouldn't answer, their lawyers instructed them not to answer, so they knew a lot of what was going on.

'Saudi-owned' on the surface and ultra-Zionist owned behind the scenes = Sabbatian-Frankist-owned.

Bingo!

Indira Singh said that Ptech software 'is utilized at the highest levels of almost every government, military, security and law enforcement organisation in this country including the Secret Service, the FBI, the Department of Defense, the House of Representatives, the Treasury Department, the IRS, the US Navy, the US Air Force, and, last but not least, the Federal Aviation Administration'. Of the latter she said:

Ptech was with MITRE in the basement of the FAA for two years prior to 9-11. Their specific job is to look at interoperability [connections between different computer systems] issues the FAA had with NORAD and the Air Force in the case of an emergency. If anyone was in a position to know the FAA, that there was a window of opportunity or to insert software or to change anything, it would have been Ptech along with MITRE ...

... they were looking at holes, basically, in the FAA's interoperability, responding with other agencies, law enforcement, in the case of an emergency such as hijacking. So they were looking for ... what people would do, how they would respond in case of an emergency, and find the holes, and make recommendations to fix it. Now, if anyone was in a position to know where the holes were, Ptech was. And that's exactly the point. If anybody was in a position to write software to take advantage of those holes, it would have been Ptech.

Singh explained the potential implications for communications between the FAA, Department of Defense (DOD) and NORAD on 9/11:

Now, with the FAA in particular, if something goes wrong, and there is an emergency with a particular flight, and the DOD needs to be notified, well, that's a really major interoperability thing, a signal has to be sent in some way, shape or form, either mediated by a human in most cases, or automatically, or even if its mediated by a human something needs to be initiated on a separate computer to start a whole other sequence of events, interventions, scrambling a jet, notification up and downstream with many other organisations, such as NORAD, such as other terminal radar areas, such as local law enforcement, you name it. So, this all has to be blueprinted, mapped out, and that's where enterprise architecture comes in, you need some kind of blueprint to keep all of this together and that's what Ptech was so good at.

In other words, communication between different agencies can be blocked or delayed if their computer systems are not talking to each other. These are extraordinary revelations because as we saw earlier in the book one of the most bewildering mysteries surrounding 9/11 is the non-communication and inexplicably late communication between the FAA, NORAD and the US Air Force which led to no fighter aircraft reaching the scene in time and hijacked planes being left to fly unchallenged and untracked for utterly ridiculous periods. The Ptech-MITRE combination had the potential to see and track all communications in real time throughout all the agencies and centres involved. They could have inserted changes, blocks and adjustments without those working for the agencies and trying to follow protocol having any idea their systems were being manipulated. Note, too, that Ptech software was used by the Secret Service which was with Bush at the school on the morning of 9/11. Access to these computer systems would have allowed fake planes to be added to air traffic and NORAD screens as was happening anyway as part of the war game scenarios. Utter confusion could have been caused by Mossad-CIA-Israeli/US military factions of the Hidden Hand. How easy it would have been with this level of control to make fake planes appear and the real 9/11 aircraft disappear from computer screens to be replaced by doubles – and even easier with NORAD chief General Eberhart deciding to have so many wargame exercises that day and at the same time to order that protection for Pentagon communication networks be reduced to its *lowest level*. Take this further and the potential was there to observe the response to the attacks by those genuinely trying to do the right thing and to track genuine law enforcement officers as they tried to uncover the truth. Everything could be known and responded to, including reports on the Dancing Israelis and the Israeli spy ring in general. This would always keep you one step ahead (along with insiders watching your back) and you would know when assets had to disappear if the law was coming. Anyone think the eventual FBI raid on Ptech would have come as a shock to them? The raid was part of Operation Green Quest, a multi-agency investigation into terrorist funding headed by extreme ultra-Zionist Michael Chertoff, then head of the Criminal Division of the [In]Justice Department who chose not to prosecute the Dancing Israelis or the 200 'art students' in the Israeli 'spy ring' and just sent them home to Israel. Michael Chertoff and 9/11 are joined at the hip. Indira Singh said:

> It was possible that there was an alternate command and control system ... could you technically use Ptech software to do the surveillance and intervention? Well, gosh, yes, that's exactly what I was planning on using it for in one of the largest banks in the world.

The MITRE Corporation is also the 'in-house engineer' at the US Air Force Electronic Systems Center at Hanscom Air Force Base in Bedford, Massachusetts, which is described as 'the Air Force's "brain" for information, command and control systems'. Hanscom is near to Boston Logan Airport where the first two '9/11 aircraft' took off. Singh said that because of the vast scope of their enterprise architecture project at the FAA both Ptech and MITRE would have been given pretty much 'carte blanche' to have access to everything in the organization – 'what is being done, where it's being done, on what systems, what the information is'. In a major project like this they 'would have been everywhere in the FAA system' in the years before 9/11. Singh said she was told they were in places that required clearances; they had log-on access to FAA flight-control computers; and they were given passwords to many other computers. She said that when she did the same work for JPMorganChase she could have access to almost anything she wanted: '... If you were up to no good, as an enterprise architect, with such a mandate, you typically could have anything you wanted. Access to anything.' Is anyone in any doubt why Israel is such a global centre of cyber high-tech and 'cyber security' – enterprise architecture?

FBI – Federal Blocking of Investigation

The FBI is an extraordinarily corrupt organisation at its Hidden Hand core although with many genuine and decent people working there around the rest of the organisation. We saw earlier how FBI agents complained about being undermined in their investigations into terrorist groups before 9/11 and one was agent Robert Wright operating out of Chicago – the American base for Ptech funder Yassin al-Kadi (Qadi). Wright began investigating Kadi and others accused of transferring money for guns and ammunition to al-Qaeda and the Hamas 'Palestinian' terrorist group. Not all of them were necessarily guilty in this twilight world of serious smoke and mirrors in which diversion and false accusation are central to the systematic deceit, but 23 organisations in the US were reportedly named for secretly funding Hamas including one called the Holy Land Foundation. This was based in Richardson, a relatively small city in Texas, which was said to be 'throbbing' with Israeli 'art student' activity. I have quoted people in other books, including Palestinian Liberation Organisation (PLO) leader, Yasser Arafat, as saying Hamas was covertly created by Israel. Many of these pre-9/11 Saudis in the US accused of funding terrorists were said to be 'funding Hamas'. This is more smoke and mirrors. Former British MP George Galloway, who called himself a 'comrade of Yasser Arafat', said: 'I saw Hamas be born, and Israel was the midwife':

> The Muslim Brotherhood, a client of the British in Egypt, had brothers in Gaza of course. Those brothers became Hamas with the full cooperation of Israel … I saw with my own eyes the open development of Islamism in Gaza, a catspaw against Arafat and the PLO. While the gaols (and the grave-yards) were full of PLO men, the roads were choc-a-block with Islamist society vehicles. Communities were served by Islamic schools, hospitals and civic-society institutions of all kinds. Permitted, encouraged, sometimes financed by Israel. It was divide and rule in perfect harmony.

Arab terrorism funders connected to Ptech and other Israeli fronts were said to be supporting Hamas and the Muslim Brotherhood – both Israeli fronts. Everything starts to make sense. Galloway appears to believe that Hamas is now independent of Israel, but I disagree. I am not talking about everyone who calls themselves Hamas only those elements within its ranks that serve Israel's interests. The actions of Hamas perfectly serve the Israeli agenda of refusing to reach a peace agreement with the Palestinians because of 'Hamas terrorism'. Look at how the murder of Palestinians has been explained away by 'fighting Hamas' and cold-blooded killing of civilians is excused by claims of 'Hamas using civilians as human shields'. Legitimate peaceful protest against shocking Palestinian oppression is condemned as the work of 'Hamas terrorists'. The existence of Hamas is good for Israel's ultra-Zionists and Sabbatian-Frankists and who is blamed for firing makeshift missiles into Israel that provides the excuse to bomb Gaza with state-of-the-art missiles? *Hamas*. Ultra-Zionists that run Israel need terrorists to keep their own population in fear and justify violence and oppression against their targets. Former German Defence Minister Andreas von Bulow described the 'Palestinian terrorist' Abu Nidal as 'an instrument of Mossad'. Anyway – back to FBI agent Robert Wright who claims to have uncovered a whole network of people in the United States apparently funding Hamas and al-Qaeda (a network overwhelmingly of Mossad and CIA fronts in other words) and the investigation became known as Operation Vulgar Betrayal which would be undermined by an undercover FBI agent who refused to secretly record a Muslim suspect. Far from being reprimanded for protecting the suspect the agent was promoted to a post at the US Embassy in Saudi Arabia. This would have been unexplainable if you didn't know how the global networks operate with both 'sides' controlled by same force. Wright realised that the closer he got to the truth the more his bosses at the FBI resisted what he was doing. They forbade him from making arrests and his investigation was trashed. 'Let sleeping dogs lie', he was told. Operation Vulgar Betrayal was shut down the year before 9/11 after Wright had earlier been removed from the case. He highlighted the FBI's International Terrorism Unit as a source for most of the resistance to genuine investigation:

> September the 11th is a direct result of the incompetence of the FBI's International Terrorism Unit. No doubt about that. Absolutely no doubt about that. You can't know the things I know and not go public ... There's so much more. God, there's so much more. A lot more.

This was not incompetence, but design. If you want to stop something being investigated control the agency that should be investigating. Who but the streetwise are going to suspect an 'anti-terrorism' agency of protecting, even instigating, terrorism? Who is going to suspect an anti-drug agency of running drugs? Robert Wright was tenacious in seeking to expose the truth about the FBI after 9/11 and as a result he was banned from working on the 9/11[non]-investigation or even answering calls from the public. His efforts to speak with [In]Justice Department big-wigs like Attorney General John Ashcroft and Criminal Division chief Michael Chertoff were denied. Ultra-Zionist Chertoff, reportedly the son of a Mossad agent, said: 'We are tired of conspiracy theories.' Wright, however, continued to his great credit to fight on.

Mendelson's remote control

The upgrade of FAA air traffic computer systems undertaken by Ptech and MITRE from the late 1990s and across 9/11 was overseen by Monte Belger, a senior official of the FAA and Acting Deputy Administrator for Air Traffic Services and System Operations in the period 1997 to 2002. Christopher Bollyn found his name and his connection to the 'upgrade' in documents about FAA failures on 9/11. I mentioned Belger earlier in this context:

> At 9.53, 25 minutes after contact was lost, FAA headquarters told the Command Center that the deputy director for air traffic services was talking to deputy administrator Monte Belger about scrambling aircraft. *Talking about it??*

Bollyn describes Belger as '... the key decision-maker at the Federal Aviation Administration, responsible for the software and computer upgrades that involved Ptech, the suspicious upgrades which were being done during the years prior to 9/11'. Belger's Internet biography said that he was 'leading the 49,000-person team and in charge of operating the world's safest aviation system'. Well, except on 9/11. Belger's pivotal role in the FAA air traffic system and the 'upgrade' rightly requires investigation in the light of the failure of that system on September 11th, 2001. Bollyn established that when Belger left the FAA in 2002 he was employed as 'Vice President, Government Connection' of an Israeli company called US Aviation Technology in Parkland, Florida, half an hour's drive from Hollywood, Florida, the apparent centre of the Israeli 'spy' ring operation uncovered in 2001, and where Mohamed Atta and other alleged 9/11 'hijackers' lived in the same period. Bollyn says that US Aviation Technology appears to have been run from the apartment of Ehud 'Udi' Mendelson who founded the company. He is a self-described 'captain in the prestigious Army Intelligence Unit of the Israel Defense Forces'. Bollyn tracked down documents and other information from the Israel Venture Capital Research Center website which list Monte Belger of Centreville, Virginia, as a Vice President and Government Connection of US Aviation Technology LLC. Mendelson was Chief Technology Officer of the company which in another incredible coincidence was involved in a remote-control system that allows an operator on the ground to 'monitor and adjust the computer flight systems on aircraft' in real time. In Mendelson's own words: 'We put the ground "pilot" in the cockpit.' Bollyn writes in *Solving 9/11*:

> His software and design was promoted as a system to obtain real-time data from the aircraft's computer recorders (black box, FDR) in order to monitor flight systems – and make corrections – if necessary. The possibility to

remotely hijack a plane with Mendelson's system is obvious. Mendelson also promoted a Flight Data Animator, which he said gives the ground pilot all of the data and the visuals that the pilot in the aircraft has. In the two on-line presentations of this equipment it is stated that corrections can be made by the ground pilot to avoid an accident or situation.

In short the ground pilot could fly the aircraft – a capability for the military going back at least to the 1960s and Operation Northwoods and mega-updated by 2001. Mendelson's system transmitted data via satellite to the plane's satellite antenna. Bollyn asked Monte Belger, who oversaw the work of Ptech and MITRE on the FAA air traffic computer systems, about his relationship with Israeli military intelligence officer Ehud Mendelson. Belger denied 'knowing or having anything to do' with either Mendelson or US Aviation Technology, a position he reiterated in another Bollyn call to his office at arms giant Lockheed Martin where he was vice president with responsibility for Transportation Systems Security. Then how did Belger's name get on those documents relating to US Aviation Technology along with his address and specific job title?? Bollyn found another interesting name on the Israeli US Aviation Technology personnel documents – Peter Goelz. He is the former managing director of the National Transportation Safety Board (NTSB). This is the organisation that investigates the cause of air crashes and produced those woefully flawed flight data recording animations for the 9/11 aircraft discussed at length earlier. Goelz was at the NTSB between 1995 and 1999 in a period when a number of investigations into air crashes remain controversial to this day – including TWA Flight 800 (1996); Egypt Air (1990); and the one that killed JFK's son, John F. Kennedy Jr, near Martha's Vineyard, Massachusetts (1999). Goelz was named as Mendelson's US Aviation Technology vice president, Corporate Strategy. Bollyn could find nothing in his background that related in any way to experience or expertise in aviation despite being named by the Bill Clinton administration as managing director of the NTSB and appearing in the documents as Vice President, Corporate Strategy for ultra-Zionist Mendelson's US Aviation Technology. Goelz's background was as a political advisor and a lobbyist for gambling interests in Kansas City. *He* was overseeing investigations of *air crashes*? Blackjack table crashes maybe, but aircraft? Bollyn contacted Goelz and asked him about his connections to Mendelson and US Aviation Technology. At no time did Goelz deny that he was Vice President of a company founded and run by an Israeli intelligence officer with a keen interest in aircraft remote-control technology. Goelz told Bollyn that he had met with Mendelson 'two or three times' in Washington DC and that Mendelson was 'based in Miami'. He said he couldn't recall if he had met Mendelson before

9/11. Goelz knew that the company was focused on technology providing a 'ground pilot' with real-time data from aircraft but said he didn't really understand it. This was a strange comment given that Bollyn found a Goelz testimonial for US Aviation Technology in which he clearly understood it very well:

> Your system of real time downloading of aircraft data meets a very real and pressing problem. Not only is it important from a safety and security standpoint it also has applicability for navigation and flight management. A robust two-way data pipe from the aircraft to the ground and back could revolutionize the industry.
>
> The key to your system is it[s] initial simplicity, relying on tested, almost off the shelf, components. That your concept is well on the way to securing a patent further strengthens your proposal.
>
> I look forward to working with you on this project and believe that with the appropriate backing it will be successful.

Bollyn says that after his conversations with Goelz and Belger the web pages and documents that connected them to US Aviation Technology and Mendelson were taken down.

Hawks and Dov

Ultra-ultra-Zionist Dov Zakheim, who served in a number of Department of Defense positons during the Reagan-Bush administration, is an interesting character with a link to remote-control aircraft systems (Fig 142). Zakheim was a member of the Project for the New American Century (PNAC) that produced the regime-change document (which he co-wrote) in September, 2000, and a member of the ultra-Zionist-dominated group dubbed 'The Vulcans' which 'advised' Boy Bush on foreign policy ('bomb for Israel') before he became president. The group, which was *officially* headed by soon-to-be Secretary of State Condoleezza Rice, included ultra-Zionist PNAC stalwarts Zakheim, Richard Perle, Robert Zoellick, Paul Wolfowitz and Lewis Scooter Libby. Dov Zakheim's fingerprints were everywhere before, during and after 9/11, but that's just a coincidence and nothing to

Figure 142: Ultra-Zionist Dov Zakheim, 9/11 Pentagon comptroller.

worry about. He was appointed Comptroller, or Undersecretary of Defense, in charge of the Pentagon budget when Boy Bush came to power with a list of other ultra-Zionist PNAC Neocons in January, 2001. Zakheim would continue in that role until 2004 in the period in which trillions of dollars were found to be missing from the Pentagon books – a fact announced on September 10th, 2001. He came to the Pentagon after some five years as CEO of SPC International, a subsidiary of the high-technology 'defense' company System Planning Corporation which has close connections to the Pentagon and its technology-development arm, the Defense Advanced Research Projects Agency (DARPA). During this period from 1987 to 2001 he advised defence secretaries in the Father Bush and Bill Clinton presidencies and was appointed to many major groups within the Department of Defense including the Task Force on Defense Reform. Three times he won the Defense Department's highest civilian award.

System Planning Corporation was involved with aircraft remote control systems including one developed by its Radar Physics Group called the Flight Termination System, or FTS. This had the capability of controlling multiple aircraft from the ground – including large passenger jets – over a distance of hundreds of miles and taking over planes in-flight. Eglin Air Force Base in Florida is reported to have been a customer for the technology and this is the base mentioned in the Operation Northwoods document as the location of a drone aircraft made to look like a passenger aircraft that it was planned to replace before being brought down by radio signal over Cuba. The Flight Termination System included a Command Transmitter System (CTS) which the company's website described as having 'remote control and flight termination functions through a fully-redundant self-contained solid-state system ...' Zakheim's SPC International reportedly contracted with MacDill Air Force Base in Florida to test the Flight Termination System (FTS) on more than 30 Boeing 767s as part of a planned deal between Boeing and the Pentagon to lease 767s converted into refuelling tankers. 'World Trade Center' Flights 11 and 175 were 767s and some witnesses and observers have suggested that Flight 175 looked more like a tanker than a passenger jet when it struck the South Tower. Former Mossad operative Victor Ostrovsky describes an operation in which an Israeli Boeing 707 refuelling aircraft was made to look like a commercial jet from Irish airline Aer Lingus. Another World Trade Center connection is the Tridata Corporation, a subsidiary of Systems Planning Corporation. Tridata was awarded the contract to investigate the 1993 WTC bombing in which the FBI was seriously involved and ultra-Zionists played a significant part in associated legal proceedings including Michael Chertoff. Dov Zakheim is reported to be an American-Israeli duel citizen and he's an extreme supporter of ultra-

Zionism with a family history to match. His grandfather, Julius Zakheim, was a Russian rabbi who married a relative of Karl Marx, the Rothschild Illuminati bankers' frontman to sell authoritarian control (Marxism) as 'government of the people'. Zakheim's father, Rabbi Jacob Zakheim, befriended terrorist Israeli Prime Minister Menachem Begin and was himself a member of Betar, a terrorist 'youth movement' established by Mr Gun Zionism, Ze'ev Jabotinsky. I consider them all Sabbatian-Frankist 'rabbis' of the kind described by Rabbi Antelman in *To Eliminate the Opiate*. Dov Zakheim is also a rabbi, but which kind? He resigned from the Pentagon in 2014 with the missing money then totalling $3 trillion and became a Senior Vice President at Booz Allen Hamilton, a management and information technology consulting firm notorious for its connections to the US military and intelligence community including DARPA. Dov Zakheim is an ultra-Zionist insider to his DNA and controlled Pentagon spending before and after 9/11.

Lights, camera – action!

I am coming shortly to ultra-Zionist control of 9/11 'security', but first I want to emphasise again as I conclude this chapter the enormous reach Israel has into the networks of power in the United States in ways and by means and personalities that may not at first sight be obvious. A perfect example is ultra-Zionist Arnon Milchan, the billionaire businessman, film producer and founder of the production company Regency Enterprises. Milchan was born in British Mandate Palestine in 1944. He is known for movies like *JFK, Pretty Woman, Free Willy, Fight Club* and *LA Confidential*, but less known as an Israeli intelligence agent from the mid-1960s to *at least* the mid-1980s. Unless you turn against them like Victor Ostrovsky, do you ever really cease to be one? No way. Milchan is a big-time Israeli elite insider. He claimed terrorist Israeli president Shimon Peres as his 'best friend' and is also close to Benjamin Netanyahu who faces corruption and fraud charges in Israel over accepting more than $283,000 worth of champagne and cigars from Milchan in exchange for tax break laws and intervening to help Milchan with his long-term American visa. Netanyahu is reported to have asked then Secretary of State John Kerry three times to intervene on Milchan's behalf. Official political persuasions mean nothing at this level. Milchan is a close friend of far-right Netanyahu and also helped to establish the Israel Labor Party in 1968 with Peres and others including military leader Moshe Dayan. They were all equally far-right and hiding behind a 'socialist' smokescreen (as many still are today). Under the cover of his work in Hollywood Milchan was for decades Israel's 'foremost weapons procurer' in deals that included 'everything from nuclear triggers to rocket fuel to guidance systems'. Shimon Peres was the architect of Israel's nuclear weapons arsenal and so it's no surprise that one of

Milchan's Israeli intelligence roles was securing technology and materials for Israel's nuclear programme. Peres recruited Milchan to the Bureau of Scientific Relations – known as LAKAM – which negotiated arms deals and supported Israel's secret nuclear weapons project. LAKAM was headed in this same period by Mossad chief Rafael 'Rafi' Eitan, the man at the centre of the PROMIS 'back-door' scandal that infiltrated top secret government and military computer systems in America and other countries. Eitan and LAKAM were working with Jonathan Pollard, the Jewish intelligence analyst for the US government who admitted spying for Israel and providing top-secret classified information. Well, Eitan did describe America as 'the enemy'. Shimon Peres said of Milchan:

> Arnon is a special man. It was I who recruited him ... When I was at the Ministry of Defense, Arnon was involved in numerous defense-related procurement activities and intelligence operations. His strength is in making connections at the highest levels ... His activities gave us a huge advantage, strategically, diplomatically and technologically.

A documentary on Israeli television in 2013 revealed that at one time Milchan, former owner of sports brand Puma, was operating 30 companies in 17 countries to broker deals worth hundreds of millions of dollars and he told the programme that he used connections to promote the apartheid regime in South Africa in exchange for its help with Israel acquiring uranium. Someone was seriously watching his back in 1985 when a close associate heading a company Milchan financed was indicted for smuggling 800 triggers ('krytrons') for nuclear weapons to Israel. Richard Kelly Smyth ran the Milchan-financed Milco International which is reported to have done as much as 80-per-cent of its business with Milchan and Israel. The charges against Smyth listed the buyers of the triggers in Israel as Milchan Brothers and Heli Trading Ltd (also known as Milchan Limited), both owned by Milchan. Yet Milchan was never charged and Smyth did a runner to Israel before the case came to court. He was arrested by Interpol in Spain in 2001 and returned to the United States where 28 of the 29 counts against him were miraculously dropped and he was made immediately eligible for parole. Smyth would claim that his go-between who worked at the Heli Trading Company 'node' of the Israeli smuggling network code-named Project Pinto was ... *Benjamin Netanyahu.* According to the FBI report:

> Smyth and [Netanyahu] would meet in restaurants in Tel Aviv and in [Netanyahu's] home and/or business. It was not uncommon for [Netanyahu] to ask Smyth for unclassified material.

Netanyahu, Sabbatian-Frankists and ultra-Zionists have absolute contempt for the United States and every other country they manipulate for their own dastardly ends. Arnon Milchan's Israeli company Milchan Brothers represented a list of major armament (we-love-war) giants such as Raytheon in arms-to-Israel deals and he has made a fortune in the process. Milchan has been described as a 'big star' at Raytheon – the company behind Unmanned Aerial Systems (UAS) which allows a ground 'pilot' to fly unmanned Global Hawk drone aircraft on the other side of the world. If a missile or military plane hit the Pentagon on 9/11 it would most likely have been made by Raytheon. A remarkable number of Raytheon executives were listed to have died on 9/11 aircraft – Stanley Hall, Director of Electronic warfare program management (Flight 77); Peter Gay, Raytheon vice president of Electronic Systems on assignment to where the Global Hawk remote control system is made (Flight 11); Kenneth Waldie, Senior Quality Control for Electronic Systems (Flight 11); David Kovalcin, Senior Mechanical Engineer for Electronic Systems (Flight 11); and Herbert Homer, Corporate Executive working with the Department of Defense (Flight 175). Terms like 'shady' have been used by those who have worked with Arnon Milchan. Screenwriter and director Terry Gilliam, who directed the film *Brazil* for Milchan, said: 'Arnon can be great, but when it comes to money there's something – I don't know – bits just don't seem to connect.' Milchan told American Jewish journalist Ann Louise Bardach in 2000:

> I love Israel, and any way I can help Israel, I will. I'll do it again and again. If you say I'm an arms dealer, that's your problem. In Israel there is practically no business that does not have something to do with defense.

Now that last point is absolutely the truth and those businesses most especially include tech and security/cyber security companies operating worldwide. Milchan admitted to Bardach that he has allowed 'prominent Israelis' to use his companies to buy newspapers. Other authors have connected him to money-laundering – including some of the $100 million spent by apartheid South Africa to Photoshop its global image. Milchan is a close friend of media mogul and Israel fanatic Rupert Murdoch (with whom he became a business partner in Regency) and other ultra-Zionists at the top of major media organisations. Murdoch's Fox aired the episode of *The Lone Gunmen* in March, 2001, about a group within the American government hijacking an airliner by remote control with the aim of flying it into the World Trade Center and blaming Arab terrorists to justify a war. Six months before the 9/11 attacks that is serious prophecy and the programme was shot in 2000. Would it not have been an obvious move for investigators to ask where the plot for that programme came from? Arnon Milchan's first film as

goes for the Eisenberg subsidiary, Atwell Security, which won the contract to 'protect' the World Trade Center in 1987. Atwell was run by senior agents of Israeli intelligence who had worked with Isser Harel, their 'former' boss and 'father of Israeli intelligence', who made the prediction in 1979 that 'Islamic terrorists' would target the biggest building in New York because it was 'America's phallic symbol'. The deal for Atwell to take over World Trade Center security was done with the same New York Port Authority that would later sell the WTC lease to ultra-Zionists Larry Silverstein and Frank Lowy. There was not a security company in America that could have done the job? Once again the ultra-Zionist connection between the New York Port Authority and Israel is glaring at the time when Atwell was awarded the World Trade Center security contract. Ultra-Zionist Stephen Berger, Port Authority executive director at the time, has served on the board of the New York Citizens Budget Commission with Larry Silverstein while ultra-Zionist Philip D. Kaltenbacher was chairman of the Authority's Board of Commissioners. Kaltenbacher's father was the founder of the ultra-Zionist New Jersey branch of the American Jewish Committee. Yet another ultra-Zionist involved with the Port Authority until just before 9/11 was Michael Glassner, a senior advisor to chairman Lewis Eisenberg. Glassner was a Southwest Regional Political Director of AIPAC who would turn up again in 2016 as executive director of the Donald Trump for President campaign committee. Ultra-Zionist Ed Koch was New York Mayor in the same period and he would later cross party lines to endorse fellow-travellers Rudolph Giuliani and Michael Bloomberg for mayor of the city vehemently controlled by ultra-Zionism. Koch's Deputy Mayor for Operations was ultra-Zionist Stanley Brezenoff who would become Port Authority executive director in 1990. A prerequisite for being Mayor of New York is to be an ultra-Zionist or Israel fanatic – witness the stomach-turning sycophantism of Mayor Bill de Blasio at the AIPAC conference in 2019 when he spoke of Israel being essential 'to shelter an oppressed people' from rising 'nativism, fascism, and white supremacy'. Straight from the script, Bill. Well done you.

Meanwhile, Atwell's negotiator with the Port Authority at the New York end was Peter (Zvi) Malkin, a major Mossad officer who kidnapped the Nazi Adolf Eichmann in Argentina in 1960 and took him to Israel for execution. Malkin hid his senior Mossad background by posing in New York as a 'security consultant' and 'artist'. There seem to be a lot of artists in Israel. I wonder if Malkin's work interested the reportedly Mossad agent mother of Michael Chertoff who ran an art gallery in New Jersey at the time? Chertoff's key role in the 9/11 cover up will be discussed later in the chapter. The World Trade Center deal quickly went pear-shaped, however, when the background to Atwell's president became known. His official name in the WTC contract negotiations was Avraham Bendor, but he was exposed to be also known as Avraham or Avram Shalom – the former head of Israeli domestic intelligence, Shin Bet. Shalom, head of Shin Bet for six years from 1980, was exposed by the Israeli Justice Ministry for sanctioning the murder of two Palestinian bus hijackers by smashing their skulls with stones. He had to resign in 1986 along with some Shin Bet agents and was then pardoned by Israeli president Chaim Hertzog. The Israel intelligence terrible trio of Avraham 'Bendor' Shalom, Zvi Malkin and the omnipotent Rafi Eitan had worked together for decades on covert operations which included supplying Israel's nuclear programme with American uranium. Now here was the same gang, with other senior Israeli intelligence assets, seeking to secure security control of the World Trade Center that would be bombed in 1993 and destroyed on 9/11. This is all a coincidence? Pigs might ...

So the first ultra-Zionist, Israeli intelligence, attempt to control security at the World Trade Center was thwarted in 1987 by the Bendor-Shalom exposure, but they were not taking no for an answer. Why were they obsessed with controlling security at the World Trade Center? It's a rhetorical question, by the way. This brings us to ultra-Zionists Jules Kroll and Larry Silverstein insurer, Maurice Greenberg. In 1972 Kroll founded Kroll Inc., a corporate investigations and risk consulting company in Manhattan which would later employ Avraham 'Bendor' Shalom and become known as 'Wall Street's private eye'. Kroll employed ultra-Zionist Jerome Hauer who was the first director of Mayor Giuliani's New York Office of Emergency Management from 1996 to 2000 and responsible for locating the $13 million command center on the 23rd floor of Larry Silverstein's World Trade Center Building 7. It was opened in 1999 just two years before 9/11. The Office of Emergency Management took over the preparation and directing of emergency response from the New York Police Department. Hauer was replaced in this role in 2000 and across 9/11 by ultra-Zionist Richard Sheirer, 'Ground Zero's Jewish Knight', and on 9/11 Hauer was a managing director with Kroll Associates which by then had long been the company running 'security' at the World Trade Center. Ultra-Zionism controlled the World Trade Center and New York's security and response system lock, stock and barrel on September 11th. There were also connections between the Kroll family and ultra-Zionist CIA tech advisor Amit Yoran, co-founder, CEO, president and director of tech company Guardium and founding member of the Pentagon's Computer Emergency Response Team who was appointed director, or 'czar', of the National Cyber Security Division at the Department of Homeland Security with responsibility for coordinating America's cyber security. He 'designed security architecture for the Pentagon and Office of the Secretary of Defense' and was Network Security Manager maintaining operations of the Pentagon's network. Jeremy M. Kroll, son of Jules Kroll, was on the advisory board of Security Growth Partners (SPG), a funding company founded and run by Elad Yoran with his brother Amit on the advisory board with Kroll.

The grip tightens

In 1993 Maurice Greenberg bought into Kroll when his insurance and finance giant American International Group (AIG) purchased 20 percent of the company. Greenberg doesn't do justice to the term 'ultra-Zionist' and many more 'ultras' would be required to get anywhere close. Put it this way – Henry Kissinger became chairman of AIG's advisor board in 1987. AIG was the company that originally agreed to massively increase the insurance in the case of a terrorist attack for Greenberg friend Larry Silverstein's lease on the World Trade Center and swiftly sold on the risk to the companies that had to pay Silverstein billions for his $14 million personal investment. Jules Kroll was also a friend of Silverstein and they served together on the Citizen's Budget Commission of New York. Greenberg's AIG had a joint venture in Israel called AIG Golden with the Aurec Group of ultra-Zionist Morris Kahn. Aurec is the parent company of Amdocs, the Israel-based telecommunications company that employed many of those arrested over the Israeli 'spy' ring in 2001. AIG became widely known during the financial crash of 2008 when it was bailed out by the American taxpayer to the tune of $180 billion to 'protect the financial integrity' of trading partners such as Goldman Sachs, Morgan Stanley, Bank of America, Merrill Lynch and a host of banks in Europe. The fact that AIG and the rest of the financial and banking system were *responsible* for the crash was irrelevant because they controlled the politicians and so they were considered 'too big to fail'. So big, in fact, that a fantastic transfer of wealth from the American people to ultra-Zionist banks and financial institutions was believed justified by the ultra-Zionist Federal Reserve and government operatives to keep them afloat. The financial crash was a disaster for the public but led to a breathtaking transfer of money from public via government to the bankers and insurance operations like Greenberg's AIG although the absolute domination by ultra-Zionists of the Bush and Obama financial teams that made these decisions was surely only another coincidence. Boy Bush's Treasury Secretary during the mega-bail-outs was Henry 'Hank' Paulson, former chairman and CEO of ultra-Zionist Goldman Sachs, at a time when ultra-Zionist Bernard Bernanke was head of the US Federal Reserve overseeing who got what in the bail-out. Bernanke had replaced ultra-Zionist Alan Greenspan as head of the Fed and would be replaced himself by ultra-Zionist Janet Yellen and her deputy Stanley Fischer, former governor of the Bank of Israel. Thanks to the beleaguered taxpayers AIG continues to operate in 'more than 80 countries and jurisdictions'.

In the same year of 1993 when Greenberg became a partner in Kroll two significant things happened. There was the FBI-connected World Trade Center bombing and the award of the contract to Kroll Inc. by the New York Port Authority under ultra-Zionist executive director Stanley Brezenoff to 'redesign' its security procedures – including those at ... the *World Trade Center* in the wake of the 1993 bombing. Kroll continued to control WTC security right up to 9/11 and employed former FBI anti-terrorism agent John O'Neil as head of security just before the attacks in which he died. He was offered the job on the recommendation of Kroll Associates ultra-Zionist managing director, Jerome Hauer. O'Neil had complained that his FBI investigations into terrorism and Osama bin Laden had been blocked and he had investigated the background to the 1993 World Trade Center bombing. Electronic security at the WTC was handled by a company called Securacom (now known as Stratesec) which had Marvin Bush, youngest brother of President Boy Bush, on the board from 1993 to 2000. Securacom was funded by the long-time Bush family-linked Kuwait-American Corp that was connected to the Kuwaiti 'royal' family which, in turn, is close to the Saudi 'royal' family of Donmeh Sabbatian-Frankists. The company also worked for the Department of Defense. Kroll had a close association with another company, Marsh & McLennan (MMC), a New York-based global insurance brokerage and risk management operation. Jeffrey Greenberg, son of Kroll's Maurice Greenberg, was either CEO or chairman of MMC between 1999 and 2004. MMC acquired Kroll Inc. in 2004 in an all-cash deal. The amazing connections and coincidences continue with the fact that the alleged (but not) 'Flight 11' struck the North Tower of the World Trade Centre at an impact zone which spanned the floors of Marsh & McLennan from 93 to 99 and specifically hit a secure computer room. One of the Marsh & McLennan offices belonged to Paul Bremer, former managing director of ultra-Zionist Kissinger and Associates. War criminal Henry Kissinger was the man Bush and Cheney named to head the 9/11 Commission until his monumental conflicts of interest forced him to stand-down. His side-kick Bremer would be appointed Presidential Envoy to Iraq by Bush (Kissinger) to oversee US operations in the country after the invasion of 2003. Bremner at the time of 9/11 was chairman and CEO of Marsh Crisis Consulting, a risk and insurance subsidiary of Marsh & McLennan. He was not in his office when the plane stuck – I bet you are stunned to your water by that – but he was in a live television studio at lunchtime that day being introduced as a 'counter-terrorism expert' who was Chairman of the National Commission on Terrorism. I have watched this NBC interview on the Internet and that was truly shocking even for me. He is quickly into 'Bin Laden did it' mode with Iraq and Iran thrown in and he is astonishingly calm throughout when hundreds of Marsh & McLennan employees were at the epicentre of the strike on the North Tower in the very area where he had an office. None of them would survive with 295 MMC employees and 63 contractors killed. Bremner does not even mention his Marsh & McLennan connection and what happened to its North Tower offices which suffered a direct hit three hours earlier and by then the building had collapsed. It's an absolute head-shaker.

Calling them 'home'?

The final report on the collapse of the towers by the National Institute of Standards and Technology (NIST) describes how the nose of 'Flight 11' struck the 96th floor and 'filled the 96th and 95th floors from top to bottom'. The report describes the 95th floor as being a 'large walled data centre along the north and east sides' and the plane hit the floor on the north side. Christopher Bollyn called Marsh & McLennan to confirm what had been on the 95th floor and talked to company spokesman, Reginald McQuay, who said it wasn't a data centre, but a *computer* centre. NIST's report on the South Tower says it was struck on the 81st floor without describing what was there. The floor in fact was one of three occupied by Fuji Bank, but no other details about floor 81 came to light until a former bank employee who worked with computers came forward. He said the 81st floor had been specifically reinforced and a raised platform introduced to support massive UPS (Uninterrupted Power Supply) batteries, or at least they *appeared* to be. Cables and a power supply ran underneath the raised platform, but the employee said they were *never turned on*. He said they were delivered during the night and were in place by the summer before the attacks ... 'The whole floor was batteries' ... 'huge battery-looking things' [which were] ...'all black' ... 'solid, very heavy'. The employee said that only senior IT people from Fuji and associated banks were ever allowed in there along with staff from Shimizu-America Corp, a Japanese heavy construct, engineering and project management company. Shimizu employees were the only ones who could open the 'enclosed server racks' that 'were so tall you could not see over the top of them', the source said. Bollyn could get no explanation from Shimizu-America about what the 'batteries' were or what was happening on the 81st floor. NIST confirms the floor had been reinforced and other documents say this was 'to accommodate the new UPS workspace'. Bollyn tracked down the structural engineering firm called Leslie E. Robertson and Associates (LERA) and spoke with SawTeen See, a managing partner. She said she was not at liberty to discuss the work and Bollyn should contact the 'project owners' – the New York Port Authority. It is very possible that the floors the planes hit in both towers contained some kind of homing device guiding them to their target via on-board remote-control technology and there was certainly something strange about the 81st floor of the South Tower from which molten metal was seen pouring after the strike. Bollyn points out that this could be explained if thermite, or thermate, was stored on the floor. He points out that the metal is yellow and white hot and says thermite/thermate could have this effect and explain the white smoke pouring from around the 81st floor. White smoke is produced in a thermite/thermate reaction which has the power to cut through even the huge supporting pillars at the World Trade Center, advocates of this theory claim. Whatever the detail of exactly what happened, we can see that Israeli intelligence and ultra-Zionists both aggressively sought control of World Trade Center security from at least the mid-1980s and had secured that control for years before 9/11. This would have been essential to making the attacks possible and total control came with the arrival of Larry Silverstein as lease-holder from the summer of 2001.

Ultra-Zionist airport 'security'

Several security companies were at work at 9/11 airports, but one worth emphasising in the light of all this background is Huntleigh USA, a subsidiary of ICTS, the Netherlands-based International Consultants on Targeted Security. ITCS was founded in 1982 by Israelis Ezra Harel and Menachem Atzmon and run by Israeli intelligence agents. Harel was under criminal investigation relating to a company collapse when he died in 2003 while Atzmon was convicted of political fraud in 1996 over his actions as co-treasurer of Netanyahu's Likud Party. His fellow co-Treasurer and later Prime Minister, Ehud Olmert, was acquitted in the same case and later jailed in 2016 on other corruption charges. Olmert was in New York on 9/11 when Mayor of Jerusalem with the Israeli owners of the Wings 'beachwear' chain. Three years after his criminal conviction Menachem Atzmon and his partner Ezra Harel took over security at Boston Logan and Newark Airports in 1999 via Huntleigh, a subsidiary of ITCS which was operated by 'former' members of Israeli Shin Bet intelligence and 'former' Israeli military personnel. Mossad-controlled ITCS was also responsible for security at Charles de Gaulle Airport in Paris where 'shoe bomber' Richard Reid boarded in 2001 and at Amsterdam's Schiphol Airport where 'underwear bomber' Umar Farouk Abdulmutallab, a Muslim Nigerian, was allowed to board in 2009. American lawyers Kurt and Lori Haskell were passengers on the latter flight and said they watched the would-be bomber being allowed on the plane without a passport after the intervention of a 'smartly dressed man' of possibly of Indian descent with an American accent. Abdulmutallab apparently had a one-way ticket which is a no-no for a non-resident flying to the United States. The Haskells, of course, were dismissed as 'conspiracy theorists', but Kurt Haskell was convinced that the whole thing was a scam: 'Umar was given an intentionally defective bomb by a US Government agent and placed on our flight without showing a passport or going through security, to stage a false terrorist attack to be used to implement various government policies.' It emerged that ICTS had earlier allowed shoe bomber Richard Reid onto a flight from Amsterdam to Tel Aviv in July, 2001, for what is reported to have been an all-expenses-paid trip to Israel. Paid by whom and why? Reid apparently said that he had explosives in his shoes on that occasion, too. His aunt, Claudette Lewis, who raised Reid in London, said she believed he had been brainwashed. *This*, then, is the Israeli company, run by Israeli intelligence operatives, that failed to protect its 9/11 flights from terrorism. Ultra-Zionist Michael Chertoff who oversaw the [non]-investigation of 9/11 at the US [In]Justice Department and then became head of Homeland Security did the rounds of television studios using the 'underwear bomber' as an excuse to press for full-body radiation scanners at airports. He didn't mention that his Chertoff Group represented the manufacturer, Rapiscan Systems. I'll have more about Chertoff shortly, but you have him to thank for full-body scanners that give you a blast of radiation every time you board a plane unless you choose to opt out – and almost no one does. Ultra-Zionist ITCS handled security at Moscow's Domodedovo International Airport when 37 people died and 173 were injured in 2011 in a suicide bomb blamed by the government on lax security and also at Brussels airport when 32 civilians died and more than 300 were injured in a bombing blamed on Islamic State in 2016.

The same Israeli ITCS was involved with security on the London underground when bombs on three tube trains and a London bus blamed on 'Islamic terrorists' killed 52 people and injured more than 700 on July 7th, 2007. They became known as the 7/7 bombings. Surveillance cameras on the bus were not working and surveillance images in general were remarkably sparse. Benjamin Netanyahu was in London at the time and said he was warned by the Israeli embassy not to attend an event that morning close to where one of the bombs went off – an event also attended by 9/11 New York Mayor Rudolph Giuliani. Some witnesses described how train floors were bent *into* the carriages from underneath and not the other way as would have happened if the bombs were as claimed in the bags of 'Islamic terrorists' inside the train. You'll recall from earlier that former Mossad chief, Efraim Halevy, wrote in *The Jerusalem Post* about 'multiple, simultaneous explosions that took place today on the London transportation system' when London police did not know at the time they were 'simultaneous' and until later believed them not to be. ITCS subsidiary, ITCS UK, had its office in London's Tavistock Square and the bus bomb went off right in front of the building. Fortress GB, another Israeli company, had an office next to

ITCS UK on the first floor of Tavistock House South and still *another* ultra-Zionist operation, Verint Systems, then a subsidiary of Israel's Comverse Technology, was given the contract the year before the 7/7 bombings to install a 'networked video system' across the underground. 'We are delighted to be helping the London Underground meet their important security and customer service objectives,' said Dan Bodner, a former senior Israeli army officer who was President and CEO of Verint. New York-based Verint (around half the staff reportedly live in Israel) was known until 2002 as Comverse Infosys. This has already appeared in the story when its role was exposed by Fox News reporter Carl Cameron in his revelations about the Israeli 'spy' ring and its connection to Israeli security, surveillance and telecommunications companies. Cameron said Comverse worked closely with the Israeli government which under 'special programmes' paid half the company's research and development costs. He was told by US investigators that it was 'career suicide' to question if Comverse was involved in spying for Israel. There is no Israeli 'security' company that is not connected in some way – usually fundamentally – to the Israeli military and intelligence network (see the Beersheba operation). Another Mossad front, sorry, 'private spy firm', to watch is Black Cube (very significant symbolism for Saturn – see my other books) which involves former Mossad chief, Efraim Halevy, who was so prophetic in his *Jerusalem Post* article about the 7/7 bombings. Black Cube is known as 'private Mossad' but then that's what they all are. As ultra-Zionist film producer and Israeli intelligence operative Arnon Milchan said: 'In Israel there is practically no business that does not have something to do with defense.' Or worldwide come to that.

So here we have an attempt by top-level Israeli intelligence operatives to gain control of World Trade Center security from at least the 1980s and when the first attempt failed through the exposure of Avraham 'Bendor' Shalom the control was secured through ultra-Zionist Kroll Inc. in 1993 following the World Trade Center bombing. The first plane to strike on 9/11 made a direct hit on the offices of Kroll-connected Marsh & McClennan run by ultra-Zionist Jeffrey Greenberg, son of Kroll Inc. partner and ultra-Zionist Maurice Greenberg. At the same time a company run by 'former' agents of Israeli domestic intelligence Shin Bet ran security at two of the three 9/11 airports. But don't worry, it's all a coincidence and to suggest otherwise is 'anti-Semitic' and 'Holocaust denial'.

Chertoff your back

It is not possible to understand what happened before, during and after 9/11 without the background to ultra-ultra-Zionist, Michael Chertoff (Fig 143). He is yet another Israeli-firster-and-laster with his fingerprints

Figure 143: Ultra-Zionist Michael Chertoff who oversaw the 9/11 (lack of) investigation.

all over 9/11. Chertoff was born in Elizabeth, New Jersey, but the family has Russian roots. His father was a rabbi (which kind?), Talmud scholar and former leader of Congregation B'nai Israel in Elizabeth. The Talmud is a deeply racist work with origins in Babylon and the ancient world and this is the foundation, together with the Kabballah, of ultra-Zionism and the Sabbatian-Frankist Death Cult. Chertoff's grandfather, Paul Chertoff, was also a rabbi (which kind?) and his mother, Livia Chertoff (née Eisen), was an Israeli citizen and the first flight attendant for Mossad-connected Israeli airline El Al. She was reportedly a founding member of Mossad. She took part in Operation On Wings of Eagles (also Operation Magic Carpet) in 1949/50 that transported nearly 50,000 Yemeni Jews to Israel. This was presented as an wonderful success while many Jews suffered in the extreme with thousands abandoned in deserts and left to fend for themselves. Chertoff spent much of his childhood in Israel and then attended the Jewish Educational Center in Elizabeth and went on to the London School of Economics (the same as insiders like David Rockefeller and George Soros) and Harvard Law School. He was hired as a prosecutor by then US District Attorney Rudolph Giuliani and in 1990 Father George Bush made him United States Attorney for New Jersey. Chertoff was asked to stay in the post by the incoming President Clinton and was the only US attorney not to be replaced when Democrats came to power. He was appointed special counsel for the Senate committee investigation into the Clintons known as 'Whitewater' when no charges followed. Then, in 2001, he was named by the incoming President Boy Bush as head of the Criminal Division of the Department of [In]Justice where he stayed until 2003. Now Chertoff was sitting at the epicentre of the criminal 'justice' nexus in the United States in the period across 9/11. The [In]Justice Department website says:

> The Criminal Division develops, enforces, and supervises the application of all federal criminal laws except those specifically assigned to other divisions. The Division and the 93 US Attorneys have the responsibility for overseeing criminal matters as well as certain civil litigation. Criminal Division attorneys prosecute many nationally significant cases. In addition to its direct litigation responsibilities, the Division formulates and implements criminal enforcement policy and provides advice and assistance on criminal matters.

The Criminal Division also: '... advises the Attorney General, Congress, the Office of Management and Budget and the White House on matters of criminal law; provides legal advice and assistance to federal prosecutors and investigative agencies; and provides leadership for coordinating international as well as federal, state, and local law enforcement matters.' When 9/11 happened ultra-Zionist Michael Chertoff was in effect running the show in all matters criminal and the [In]Justice Department was boss to the FBI – the lead [non]-investigative agency for 9/11. A 2005 report in *USA Today* described how Chertoff went to work immediately the first plane hit:

> In the minutes after the Sept. 11 terrorist attacks, while Attorney General John Ashcroft was rushing back from Milwaukee, Michael Chertoff was calling the shots.

> Chertoff, then chief of the Justice Department's criminal division, breached the prickly territorial lines that have long divided the Justice Department from the FBI. From a fifth-floor office at FBI headquarters, above the streams of panicked people who flooded Pennsylvania Avenue, he set up shop in the bureau's crisis center. For the next 20 hours, he directed the government's initial response to the most lethal terrorist attack in US history.

> Chertoff would spend the next two years serving as a central figure in formulating US anti-terrorism policy – from the effort to secretly detain hundreds of Middle Easterners in the USA, to increasing the FBI's authority to conduct domestic surveillance at religious gatherings and other public events.

In other words ultra-ultra-Zionist Israel-worshipping Michael Chertoff had control of the criminal [non]investigation into 9/11 *and* the writing and implementation of legislation to take away basic freedoms justified by 9/11 *and* as head of Homeland Security the authority to enforce that legislation. *ONE MAN*. In his role as head of the Criminal Division of the [In]Justice Department Chertoff had the power not to prosecute the Dancing Israelis and 200 Israeli 'spy ring art students' and simply send them back to Israel – which he did. There should have been a long and detailed investigation into what had been happening and its connection to the September 11th attacks. Instead Chertoff and company closed it down and sent the suspects home to Israel where they were untouchable. Nor did Chertoff seek out Dominik Suter at the Mossad-front Urban Moving Systems when he fled to Israel after his first FBI interview. Chertoff and the White House were supported in blocking an investigation into Urban Moving Systems by ultra-Zionist California US Representative Jane Harman, chair of the Working Group on Terrorism and Homeland Security, a subcommittee of the Intelligence Committee. Harman served nine terms in Congress and was a member of all major security committees – Armed Services (six years), Intelligence (eight years) and Homeland Security (eight years). She received the Defense Department Medal for Distinguished Service, CIA Agency Seal Medal, CIA Director's Award and the Director of National Intelligence Distinguished Public Service Medal. These awards go to big-time insiders that serve the interests of the Pentagon and CIA. Washington publication *Congressional Quarterly*, or *GQ*, revealed details in 2009 of a National Security Agency (NSA) wiretap of Harman that was connected to an investigation into alleged Israeli covert operations in the US capital. Well, blow me down, who'd have thought it? The call was between Harman and an agent of the Israeli government in which she is said to have agreed to lobby the [In]Justice Department to drop espionage charges against two employees of AIPAC. In return the agent promised support in Harman's efforts to chair the House Intelligence Committee. NSA transcripts are reported to record Harman saying at the end of the call: 'This conversation doesn't exist.' Even though Harman was a Democrat further investigation of her was blocked by Alberto Gonzales, Attorney General for Republican Boy Bush. There are no national or party boundaries with ultra-Zionism and Sabbatian-Frankisim. Espionage charges against the AIPAC employees were indeed dropped – against the wishes of the FBI.

So transparently corrupt

While Chertoff was failing to investigate and prosecute the arrested Israelis he instead ordered the rounding up of innocent Muslims without charge or lawyer to promote the 'Muslims did it' cover story that ultra-Zionists were using to (a) justify American wars in the Middle East and (b) to cover their own tracks over 9/11. The immediate Problem-Reaction-Solution response to the attacks was to rapidly introduce the Patriot Act – the first post-9/11 assault on freedoms and civil liberties justified by 'protecting America from terrorism'. It was signed into law the month after the attacks and was clearly written and in the pipeline before they happened. The Patriot Act was co-written by its dominant author – *Michael Chertoff*. He drove America's 'anti-terrorism' policy with a huge increase in police powers and secret detention and oversaw the prosecution of '20th hijacker' Zacarias Moussaoui which ended in a life sentence in 2006. Chertoff is described as 'the master of the cover up' by Sanders Hicks in *The Big Wedding: 9/11, the Whistle-Blowers and the Cover-Up*. For a start Chertoff was a key player as a Senate Counsel in the blatant cover-up of the fake suicide (murder) in 1993 of Vince Foster, a Deputy White House Counsel in the Bill Clinton administration and an associate of the Clintons since their days in Little Rock, Arkansas. Foster knew where the bodies were buried in every sense and he was added to a long, long list of murders, 'accidents' and fake suicides of people dangerous to the Clintons which became known as the 'Clinton Body Count'. John H. Clarke, lead attorney for private detective Patrick Knowlton who tried to expose the Foster murder, said of Chertoff: 'He's a dishonest bastard. He went along with the Foster cover-up.' Just the guy you want in charge of the 9/11 criminal investigation then. Sanders Hicks describes how Chertoff failed to prosecute alleged funders of Islamic terrorism before the attacks and yet a month after 9/11 he was named by the Boy Bush White House to head Operation Green Quest, a multi-agency investigation including the FBI, into the funding of terrorist organisations. The operation went nowhere in terms of the prime culprits and failed to properly investigate Ptech and connected companies with their back-door control of all the relevant 9/11 computer systems. The same is true of the FBI headed by Robert Mueller who moved to the Bureau just two weeks before 9/11. Mueller was head of the [In]Justice Department's Criminal Division during the cover-up of the BCCI banking scandal and flawed prosecutions in the case of Pan Am Flight 103 which crashed after an on-board bomb exploded over Lockerbie in Scotland. Running the Criminal Division is a monumentally pivotal position, especially in the response, or lack of it, to 9/11 and ultra-ultra Zionist Chertoff was sitting in the chair. It is important to remember that all the endless examples of the FBI's determination not to investigate 9/11, cover up and destroy evidence and block the work of genuine agents came under the ultimate control and responsibility of Michael Chertoff and his underling, Mueller.

With the official story in place and any evidence that challenged the narrative trashed, deleted or ignored, Boy Bush made Chertoff the second head of Homeland Security in 2003. This is a freedom-busting operation specifically justified by 9/11 that brought together 187 federal agencies and departments which included the agencies of US intelligence, the Secret Service, National Guard, Federal Emergency Management Agency (FEMA), US Coast Guard, Immigration and Customs Enforcement, Citizenship and Immigration Services, Civil Air Patrol and the Transportation Security Administration (TSA). Homeland Security is a Big Brother wet dream and 9/11 was the excuse to create it. Tom Fitton, president of Judicial Watch, said of Chertoff's rapid progression: 'It's an exceptional rise to power.' Yes, what timing in relation to 9/11 and what it was used to justify in terms of crushing civil liberties. Chertoff has since made a fortune through his Chertoff Group, co-founded with Chad Sweet, his Chief of Staff of Homeland Security who also worked at the Directorate of Operations for the CIA. The Group has employed other Homeland Security personnel and former

Director of the CIA, General Michael V. Hayden. There needs to be an independent investigation into Chertoff's actions throughout his time at the [In]Justice Department with relation to 9/11 – but don't hold your breath.

Smelting the evidence

Chertoff's Criminal Division, its subordinate FBI headed by Mueller, and the administration of New York Mayor Rudolph Giuliani allowed the steel from World Trade Center buildings with all the evidence it contained to be rapidly removed from the site and smelted down. More than 1.6 million tons of steel and other remains were transported to New Jersey scrapyards by June, 2002, for shipping to Asia. Chertoff also confiscated aircraft remains and denied all access to evidence by 9/11 families while citing SSI laws or 'Sensitive Security Information Regulations'. I doubt Chertoff has ever felt 'sensitivity' in his life. Chertoff's actions ensured that a full and proper investigation into the cause of the building collapses was virtually impossible. Had the steel been protected for detailed examination we would know for sure what caused the colossal girders to give way in unison in an instant and what explosives, thermite or whatever else were involved. A chemical examination could have been definitive. Instead, on the watch of Chertoff, Mueller and Giuliani, the evidence was whisked away to New Jersey scrap yards and off to Asia for smelting. All three knew each other extremely well with Israel-lackey Giuliani once hiring Chertoff as a prosecutor in the 1980s when the future New York Mayor was the United States Attorney for the Southern District in Manhattan. Giuliani's Commissioner for the New York Office of Emergency Management at the time of 9/11 was ultra-Zionist Richard 'Ground Zero's Jewish Knight' Sheirer who died in 2012. Sheirer was put in charge of the rescue and clean up at the World Trade Center and so was directly involved in the chain of command that allowed the steel to be removed before an investigation could take place. He would later become Senior Vice President at Giuliani's private company, Giuliani Partners. The FBI's inspector in charge of the 9/11 [non]-investigation under Director Mueller was Pasquale J. D'Amuro and again he would have had to sanction the destruction of the steel. D'Amuro would become chairman of Giuliani Security and Safety. Ultra-Zionist Sheirer took charge of coordinating the Ground Zero clean-up overseeing the work of some 100 agencies and he handed responsibility for the steel to Kenneth Holden, head of New York's Department of Design and Construction. Holden oversaw removal of the steel under Mayor Giuliani and his successor, ultra-Zionist Mayor Michael Bloomberg who responded to complaints about the removal of evidence with the memorable line: 'Just looking at a piece of metal doesn't tell you anything.' Holden told the 9/11

Commission that he had been given 'verbal permission' to remove the
steel and transport it to New Jersey scrapyards. He didn't say who the
person was and staggeringly (or maybe not) the Commissioners appear
not to have asked him. Holden was no more forthcoming when
Christopher Bollyn made contact to ask who had told him to start
moving the steel and other debris. The call quickly ended with Holden
refusing to answer and saying he was no longer doing interviews on the
subject. Bollyn called back and asked immediately the phone was picked
up: 'Was it Chertoff who gave you the verbal permission?' Holden
remained silent and ended the call. Given that Michael Chertoff was
overseeing the entire 'investigation' how could he not have sanctioned
the decision for the crucial removal of evidence? Bollyn wrote to
Chertoff to ask if he had authorised the removal of the steel. 'No',
Chertoff replied. When asked who did he said: 'No idea.' The very
suggestion that the man in overall charge of the criminal investigation
into 9/11 didn't know who sanctioned the rapid removal of crucial
evidence is preposterous and clearly a lie.

The smelting of World Trade Center steel brings us to an ultra-Zionist
mega-crook and Mossad operative called Marc Rich. Commodities were
his business. He was a billionaire international commodities trader,
financier and businessman who was indicted with an ultra-Zionist
partner in 1983 on 65 charges relating to tax evasion and oil deals with
Iran despite a US embargo while American hostages were being held by
the Iranians. Rich fled to Switzerland when he knew the indictment was
coming. A 2005 article in Israeli daily *Haaretz* said that Rich 'carried out
special missions for the State of Israel and the Mossad'. He was also 'a
donor who channelled more than a billion shekels to Israel – and a man
who was pursued by the US legal authorities on suspicion of tax
evasion, money laundering and commercial ties with the enemy'. Rich
had ties with everyone who would make him money. He supplied most
of Israel's oil after the 1973 Yom Kippur War when the country was
subject to an oil boycott (ironically Rich sourced the oil from Iran) and
like so many ultra-Zionists he traded with apartheid South Africa.
Charges against Rich in America carried a potential sentence of more
than 300 years in jail (life would have sufficed surely), but Bill Clinton
gave Rich a presidential pardon on his last day in office. Rich's
songwriter wife, Denise (née Eisenberg), gave more than a million
dollars to Clinton's Democratic Party plus $100,000 to Hillary Clinton's
Senate election campaign and $450,000 to the Clinton presidential
library. There were, however, more important reasons than money for
Clinton's pardon. *Haaretz* reported that Israeli political leaders were
behind the decision:

The pardon was granted after heavy pressure by none other than then-Prime

Minister Ehud Barak, Shimon Peres, Ehud Olmert and other prominent Israelis and American Jews ... Clinton received a request for the Rich pardon signed by Barak, Shimon Peres, Ehud Olmert (then mayor of Jerusalem), Foreign Minister Shlomo Ben-Ami, Mossad chief Shabtai Shavit, Spanish King Juan Carlos and a number of leading members of the Jewish community in the US, Switzerland and the world of finance.

Nearly 56 of the 71 signatories were prominent Israeli or American ultra-Zionists including Abe Foxman, head of the Anti-Defamation League (ADL) and Rabbi Irving Greenberg, chairman of the American Holocaust Memorial Museum. Prime Minister Barak further applied pressure directly in a meeting with Clinton. *Haaretz* quotes social activist Eldad Yaniv, who was in the next room, describing how Barak shouted at Clinton, insisting that he approve the pardon. Yaniv wrote in his online book *U-Turn*:

'[The pardon] could be important,' Barak shouted at Clinton. 'Not only from the financial aspect, but also because he helped the Mossad in more than one instance.'

What did Barak mean by 'the financial aspect'? Terrorist Ehud Barak was the man who spoke on the BBC immediately after the 9/11 attacks pointing the finger at Osama bin Laden and calling for the invasion of Afghanistan. Former Israeli military intelligence commander Barak moved to the United States in 2001 to be an advisor for Electronic Data Systems and a partner with financial company SCP. Marc Rich founded a commodities and raw materials company, Marc Rich & Company AG, in 1974 and sold his majority stake to commodity trading company Glencore International in 1993. Rich's fellow ultra-Zionist, Ivan Glasenberg, CEO of Glencore, also has Mossad connections and the Israel-based Marc Rich Foundation was headed by 'former' Mossad operative, Avner Azulay. *Haaretz* said Azulay had organised the Clinton pardon from behind the scenes with Clinton's Deputy Attorney General Eric Holder, an ultra-Zionist agent, also involved. Holder grew up around ultra-Zionist elite families and became their place-man. Azulay, who had ties to 9/11 Israeli Prime Minister Ariel Sharon, ran the Rich Foundation from the Asia House office building in Tel Aviv of ultra-Zionist Shaul Eisenberg who I highlighted earlier as an Israeli intelligence operative and arms smuggler heavily involved in the Israeli nuclear weapons programme and its connections to apartheid South Africa. The Eisenberg Group owned Atwell Security, the Israeli intelligence front that won the contract to run security at the World Trade Center before the background to its president, Shin Bet chief Avraham 'Bendor' Shalom, came to light. Ultra-Zionism is a very small world, to be sure.

The Mossad/Asia connection

Shaul Eisenberg had been Mossad's man in Asia where the World Trade Center steel ended up. The steel was quickly removed from the Ground Zero site by a Zionist company and transported to two Zionist-owned New Jersey scrapyards, Hugo Neu and Metal Management, who cut it into small pieces and shipped it to Asia. Hugo Neu was a German Jew who formed the Associated Metals and Minerals Corporation in New York in the 1930s with fellow ultra-Zionists Meno Lissauer and Walter M. Rothschild before founding the Hugo Neu company in 1947. Two years before 9/11 with scrap metal prices extremely low Hugo Neu launched a global trading arm, Hugo Neu Schnitzer Global Trade, to broker deals with Asian markets among others and it was headed by two ultra-Zionist former Marc Rich and Glencore traders, Nathan K. Fruchter and Jedua Saar, as reported by *Business Wire* in 1999. Christopher Bollyn writes in *Solving 9/11*: 'From their early days with Marc Rich and Glencore, on to Hugo Neu and [later] the Midland Group, Saar and Fruchter have always worked for companies closely tied to Israel and Mossad.' Hugo Neu had some good fortune in 2001 when they entered into a joint venture with the New Jersey Office of Maritime Resources to dredge the water access to its yard and this allowed bigger ships to enter – essential with the size of the vessels that would later ship World Trade Center steel to Asia. The dredging cost Hugo Neu $24 million. The new company and the dredging were brave investments at a time of such depressed scrap metal prices. Bollyn points out that Hugo Neu has invested in the Agua-Agro fund, an Israeli venture capital operation. The fund was managed by Nir Belzer who co-founded Israel's Millennium Materials Technologies Fund with Oren Gafri who was trained at the Israeli Dimona Nuclear Research Center in the Negev Desert. Bollyn says Gafri is 'a specialist in energetic nano-composite coatings exactly like the one [he believes] pulverized the 220 acres of concrete floors in the World Trade Center'. He says Millennium Materials Technologies has invested in companies that produce these coatings.

Robert Kelman, Hugo Neu vice president, said in 2002 they had processed and shipped around 250,000 tons of World Trade Center steel. Girders and columns were cut into pieces less than 60 inches long and shipped for smelting while mixed with other scrap. *The New York Times* reported that Hugo Neu had a workforce of nearly a hundred people working on scrap from the World Trade Center with 25 assigned to girder cutting and working in twelve-hour shifts around the clock before being shipped for smelting in eleven countries in Asia. Why not smelters in the United States? Why smelt at all until experts had examined the steel for evidence? World Trade Center steel would end up as other products from street lamps to refrigerators. The other company involved with the disposal of World Trade Center steel was Chicago-based Metal Management Inc. headed by Zionist Alan D. Ratner who was appointed in 2000. Another executive Daniel W. Dienst, a managing director with Zionist-controlled CIBC World Markets, joined Metal Management to guide the company out of financial difficulties in June, 2001. CIBC World Markets, formerly Oppenheimer & Co., has enormous connections to Israel. *The Jerusalem Post* described CIBC as the leading underwriter in Israel with merger and acquisition transactions in the country worth more than $4.5 billion in the previous five years. CIBC had also been involved with nearly 100 mostly high-tech Israeli companies which takes us back to Israeli military control of cyberspace. Metal Management and Hugo Neu both later merged with the Sims Group. Christopher Bollyn said he made efforts to talk with executives Robert Kelman, Alan Ratner and Daniel Dienst, but was passed on to a Sims company spokesman who refused to connect him with the three men to question them about the steel removal. The spokesman said it was all a matter of public record – 'read *The Wall Street Journal*'.

Contempt for 9/11 victims and families

By early February, 2002, a report by James Glanz and Eric Lipton in *The New York Times* was describing the truly farcical situation that Michael Chertoff and his ultra-Zionist cohorts had allowed to unfold. The headline said it all: 'A Search for Clues In Towers' Collapse; Engineers Volunteer to Examine Steel Debris Taken to Scrapyards'. What an insult to the families who lost their loved ones. Take in the scene described here and think that nearly 3,000 people had died months before in the biggest 'terrorist attack' on American soil:

> From the moment the two towers collapsed on Sept. 11, engineers and other experts have been struggling to answer the monumental questions of exactly why and how the buildings, designed to sustain a jet impact, completely collapsed. But despite promises of a broad federal investigation, and after weeks of calls from victims' families and others to halt the destruction of the steel that could hold all sorts of clues, the half-heroic, half-comic scenes at the Jersey City scrapyard continue to play out.

> Small teams of engineers plot slightly mad dashes, like mountain goats, into mounds of steel to claim pieces of tower columns. The engineers time their forays to avoid being crushed ... Through it all, the engineers profess optimism that they are catching and saving what is most useful. But they concede that there is no way of saying for sure; an unknown number of steel columns has been sent off to mills as far away as Asia without ever having been examined

or saved.

'What they're doing is extremely noble, ambitious and wonderful and I'm glad somebody is doing that,' said Dr James G. Quintiere, a professor in fire protection engineering at the University of Maryland. But, he added, 'the steel, to me, it's almost a foregone conclusion that it's gone'.

This tragic farce could only have happened because Chertoff and his ultra-Zionist conspirators didn't want the real answers to be found. There can be no other rational or credible explanation. Road transportation from Ground Zero to dump sites in New York and New Jersey was overseen by Zionist Yoram Shalmon of subcontractor PowerLoc Technologies of Toronto. Trucks were tracked in real time using GPS – and I mean *tracked*. Shalmon told SecuritySolutions.com:

We were able to start identifying patterns of behaviour. If a driver arrived late, the traffic analyst would look at why. Maybe the driver stopped for lunch, or maybe he ran into traffic. Ninety-nine percent of the drivers were extremely driven to do their jobs. But there were big concerns, because the loads consisted of highly sensitive material. One driver, for example, took an extended lunch break of an hour and a half. There was nothing criminal about that, but he was dismissed.

All this high-detailed real-time tracking for 'sensitive material' that was then dumped or shipped to Asia for smelting? *C'mon.*

Covering all bases

Ultra-Zionist judges answering to Michael Chertoff's 'Justice' Department dominated criminal and civil decisions and litigation with regard to 9/11. Chertoff's Criminal Division could block rigorous and genuine investigation into the criminal legalities of 9/11, but there was the problem of civil actions by families of victims and others who claimed civil loss from the attacks. Families were offered government compensation if they agreed not to seek civil actions that would have the background and evidence to what happened examined in open court. Nearly a hundred families, however, were not having that. They wanted their day in court so the evidence could be publicly revealed in cases filed against airlines and security firms like Shin Bet/Mossad front ITCS. This was a potentially catastrophic development because, as *The New York* Times reported: '... the families had amassed a trove of internal documents and depositions.' Enter ultra-Zionist Alvin K. Hellerstein, a judge for the US District Court for the Southern District of New York (Fig 144). He was appointed to oversee (control) the civil litigation relating to 9/11 including compensation for fire fighters and first

Figure 144: Ultra-Zionist Judge Alvin K. Hellerstein – stopped 9/11 families taking their case to court in pursuit of the truth.

responders whose minds and bodies had been ravaged by their experience. Many would die before they received a penny. Hellerstein ran what has been described as 'a war of attrition' against the families and not one of their cases came to court. Over a period of ten years each one in turn was settled confidentially under his direction as the families gave up hope on securing justice. Hellerstein told *The New York Times* that he had 'no regrets' about the outcome of the cases when they should have explored the background to the deaths of nearly 3,000 people. He acknowledged criticism from those that wanted a trial in open court (the very last thing ultra-Zionists and Sabbatian-Frankists behind 9/11 wanted). Families have talked of Hellerstein's coldness towards them. Ellen Mariani, who lost her husband on United Airlines Flight 175, said of Hellerstein: 'That bastard judge is so corrupt.' The family of Mark Bavis, a 31-year-old hockey scout aboard Flight 175, said Hellerstein 'essentially gutted the case so that the truth about what led to the events of September 11, 2001, would never be told at trial'. The Bavis family were the last to settle in 2011. Michael Bavis, twin brother of 9/11 victim, Mark, was saying as late as 2010 that a settlement 'has not been in our vocabulary', but then *The New York Times* reported:

> Judge Hellerstein shifted the focus of the case in a way that the plaintiffs believed favored the defendants, United and a security firm [ITCS] that ran the checkpoint at Logan International Airport in Boston, where Mr. Bavis had boarded the plane.

The Bavis family were well prepared for the trial and argued that the airline had a history of security breakdowns and of not heeding warnings from a company executive about inadequate staffing and training. They said that many screeners on duty on September 11th could not speak English and some had never heard of al-Qaeda or knew what Mace spray was. I guess they would never have heard of Mossad either. With Hellerstein's direction in favour of the defendants the Bavis family finally gave up. Michael Bavis said: 'We put ourselves through great strain to try to do what we considered the right thing and eventually threw the towel in.' One of Hellerstein's scams was to determine the likely financial pay out to families before liability had actually been proved – a ridiculous inversion of normal procedure – and this was to signal the likely cash payments so families would be more likely to settle out of court. Another point about Hellerstein – he ruled in 2007 that jurors in litigation cases brought by families related to Flight 93 would not be allowed to listen to the entire recording of the alleged Cockpit Voice Recorder. They could only hear 'portions that the hijacked passengers may have heard'. He wasn't even subtle about his intent. Hellerstein agreed that by not holding a trial there was a 'loss of information' to the public. In a telling justification he said: 'But it pales in my mind with the fact that the people who were suing for money got their money.' Yep, money is all that matters, not the truth. 'Money is the essential lubricant', as he told the families and their lawyers. Well, it may be in the dark and cynical world that Hellerstein inhabits, but thank goodness not everyone is like him. Hellerstein said he encouraged families to apply to the (no evidence, no trial) September 11th Victim Compensation Fund for a quicker recovery. The ultra-Zionist judge also told *The New York Times* that courts are 'not the best venue for civil litigants to seek answers'. So where else are they going to get them? *The government?* What mendacious nonsense. Hellerstein was supported in his views and actions by ... yes ... yes ...

ultra-Zionist Kenneth R. Feinberg – *the lawyer who administered the no evidence, no trial Victim Compensation Fund* (Fig 145). Feinberg summed it all up when he said that Hellerstein 'knew from the very beginning that the cases had to settle – and he got there'. In a nutshell, mate – or the ultra-Zionist cabal would have been fuming. Feinberg had been Special Master for Executive Compensation deciding who got bail-out money after the financial crash of 2008 (his ultra-Zionist associates in so many cases). He said that he, too, told the families that a trial made little sense:

Figure 145: Ultra-Zionist Kenneth R. Feinberg controlled the September 11th Victim Compensation Fund.

I told them 'If you're going to trial to find out what happened, you are wasting your time. A courtroom is not where you will get answers'.

Same script, same goal. Donald A. Migliori, a lawyer from the firm that represented more than 50 families, said Hellerstein's view was 'absolutely wrong'. He said they used the legal system to gather real information: 'We obtained it; we just couldn't tell the public the whole story.' Ultra-Zionist Kenneth Feinberg ran the no-trial government compensation fund and those who refused to take the money and wanted their time in court were faced with ultra-Zionist Hellerstein. The 'special mediator' between the families and other parties in the lawsuits was ultra-Zionist Sheila Birnbaum with some of her sessions attended by Hellerstein. Birnbaum worked at the ultra-Zionist Skadden Arps law firm where one of the partners was Kenneth Bialkin, former national chairman of the Anti-Defamation League (ADL) established by the Rothschild-created B'nai B'rith. Hellerstein said of Birnbaum: 'Without her patience, skill, empathy, and persistence, these results [the out of court settlements] would not have been achieved.' Hellerstein is a Talmudic Jew, Israel fanatic and connected to the same New York ultra-Zionist organisations as Michael Chertoff. His son, Joseph Hellerstein, a Talmudic Jew, lives in an illegal settlement in the occupied West Bank. They both worked for the Rothschild-connected New York law firm, Stroock, Stroock and Lavan, which represented Larry Silverstein in acquiring the lease to the World Trade Center and also major ultra-Zionist companies like Goldman Sachs and Maurice Greenberg's AIG. In fact, Stroock, Stroock and Lavan has been the go-to law firm for the ultra-Zionist elite since the hey-days of Rothschild frontman Jacob Schiff more than a hundred years ago. Company historian Jethro Lieberman said:

> It was the 'Our Crowd' German-Jewish clientele for which the firm was mostly, and justly, noted in those days. That included Otto Kahn, Felix M. Warburg, Walter N. Rothschild and Jacob Schiff.

History repeating (yet again)

Otto Kahn was an investment banker connected to Schiff's (the Rothschilds') Kuhn Loeb & Co which funded the Russian Revolution. So was Felix Warburg who also funded Leon Trotsky. The Warburgs have been a front for the Rothschilds since at least 1857 when the Rothschilds saved the Warburg bank in Hamburg from collapse. Max Warburg was a director of I.G. Farben which ran the concentration camp at Auschwitz while his brother, Paul, was a director of its US arm, American I.G. Paul Warburg, a partner in Kuhn, Loeb run by his brother-in-law Jacob Schiff, was a key player on behalf of the Rothschilds behind the creation of the privately-owned US 'central bank', the Federal Reserve, which was established in 1913 to allow elite bankers like the Rothschilds and Warburgs to control government finances and drown America in debt. Why would the 'Jewish' Warburgs be involved with the company that ran concentration camps? Sabbatian-Frankisim which hates Jews. This is just some of the ultra-ultra-Zionist background from which Alvin Hellerstein and his son emerged out of Stroock, Stroock and Lavan. Hellerstein's control of family and civil litigation stopped cases related to the ultra-Zionist Shin Bet/Mossad 'security' company ICTS and its

subsidiary Huntleigh USA coming to court. He also worked to block
families seeking legal discovery having access to information and
documents about ICTS. How could Hellerstein even hear the case at all
when his son Joseph was a lawyer with Amit, Pollak and Matalon, one
of Israel's major law firms which, in turn, represented and had close
connections to ICTS parent company, the leading Israeli investment
bank, Cukierman? This is controlled by founder and chairman Edouard
Cukierman and his father Roger, a former Chief Executive Officer in
France until 1999 of the Edmond de Rothschild Group. Father
Cukierman was also CEO of the Israel General Bank and the
Cukiermans have many connections to the Rothschilds. Ultra-Zionist
Boaz Harel, president and senior partner at another Cukierman
company, Catalyst Investments, was at the time of 9/11 chairman of
ICTS – defendants in litigation overseen by Hellerstein. How can it be
right for the father of someone at a law firm representing the parent
company of ICTS to hear litigation claims against them over 9/11? By
the way, Yair Shamir, son of Israeli Prime Minister and terrorist, Yitzhak
Shamir, was the co-founding Managing Partner and Chairman Emeritus
of Catalyst Investments and Chairman of Cukierman. He was actually
named after Avraham 'Yair' Stern, founder of Jewish terrorist group
Lehi, also known as the Stern Gang. Netanyahu also has a son called
Yair.

Ultra-Zionist Talmudic Jew Michael B. Mukasey, yes another one,
was a close and long-time friend and associate of ultra-Zionist asset
Rudolph Giuliani and was the judge in the litigation between Larry
Silverstein and insurance companies in which Silverstein was awarded
billions as a result of the World Trade Center attacks. Mukasey attended
the same Manhattan Orthodox Jewish Kehilath Jeshrun synagogue as
Hellerstein which says it is 'deeply committed to the State of Israel and
its citizens'. The same Mukasey also helped in the Michael Chertoff
release of the 'Dancing Israelis' as United States District Judge for the
Southern District in Manhattan – a role he took over in 1987 when he
replaced ultra-Zionist Abraham David Sofaer. President Boy Bush
would name Mukasey as US Attorney General in 2007 despite
opposition over the judge's support of torture. Mukasey's appointment
followed a campaign on his behalf by New York Senator and ultra-
Zionist Charles Schumer. Mukasey refused demands to recuse himself
when he presided over a case stemming from the 1993 bombing of the
World Trade Center in which Michael Chertoff was the prosecutor of the
well-stitched-up Omar Abdel Rahman, known as the 'Blind Sheikh' and
a CIA asset. Dov Zakheim, 9/11 Pentagon comptroller, was CEO of SPC
International when a SPC subsidiary, Tridata Corporation, was put in
charge of the investigation into the 1993 bombing which primarily
involved the FBI and its 'informants'. The bombing led to ultra-Zionist

Kroll Inc., being awarded the contract to upgrade security at the World Trade Center in the same year that ultra-Zionist Kissinger-buddy Maurice Greenberg of AIG bought into Kroll. The first plane on 9/11 made a direct hit on the offices of his son's Kroll-connected company, Marsh & McLennan. I mentioned earlier that the vehicle used to plant the FBI-informant-made bomb in 1993 was rented by Israeli Mossad agent, Josie Hadas. The bomb was said to have been planted by Mohammed Salameh and he was yet another 'Muslim terrorist' set up by Mossad.

Ultra-Zionist-controlled 9/11 Commission

Ultra-Zionist Michael Chertoff controlled the criminal investigation into 9/11 – actually the criminal *lack* of investigation – and ultra-Zionist judges and lawyers controlled the civil litigation to stop the cases reaching a public trial; but there's more. The lead investigator into the building collapses for the National Institute of Standards and Technology (NIST) was Zionist Stephen Cauffman. You will recall from earlier the nonsensical reports by NIST that were clearly a cover-up from start to finish of what really happened and why. Then there was the 9/11 Commission that published a 'report' on the attacks that was a grotesque insult to the truth and those who died and their loved ones. Bush and Cheney tried to block *any* official investigation into the attacks and it took an incredible 441 days for one to be established. Then, when they were forced to relent, they sought to have ultra-ultra-Zionist Henry Kissinger take charge. When that failed came Plan B with the Commission controlled from day one by ultra-Zionist Philip Zelikow who was appointed 9/11 Commission executive director (Fig 146). We have seen already how this former Texas lawyer was an associate of President Bush and National Security Advisor Condoleezza Rice whose actions were officially part of the Commission's investigation. Zelikow co-wrote a book with Rice and was a Bush administration insider, besides being a representative and agent for ultra-Zionism. Zelikow was a director of the Aspen Strategy Group that included Rice, Cheney and 9/11 Deputy Secretary of Defense, the ultra-Zionist Paul Wolfowitz. Bush 9/11 counter-terrorism advisor Richard Clarke said when Zelikow was appointed to oversee the Commission: 'The fix is in ... could anyone have a more

Figure 146: Ultra-Zionist Phillip Zelikow controlled the 9/11 Commission to block anything but support for the official story.

obvious conflict of interest than Zelikow?' Paul Sperry said in an article
for Antiwar.com that 'Zelikow picks the areas of investigation, the
briefing materials, the topics for hearings, the witnesses, and the lines of
questioning for witnesses ... and the commissioners for the most part
follow his recommendations.' In effect, Sperry wrote, Zelikow set the
agenda and ran the investigation. One Commission staff member said:
'Zelikow is calling the shots. He's skewing the investigation and running
it his own way.'

Ultra-Zionist Zelikow prevented staff of the Commission – which he
hired – from talking with Commission members and shut them out
while he got on with securing the report his ultra-Zionist masters
wanted. Commission member Max Cleland resigned saying: 'This is a
scam. It's disgusting. America is being cheated.' Yes, and it was meant to
be – that was the whole point. Commission chairman Thomas Kean said:
'We think in many ways the Commission was set up to fail.' Zelikow's
contempt for a real investigation included writing with his long-time
associate Ernest May a detailed outline in March, 2003, of the *final* 9/11
Commission Report including chapter headings, subheadings and sub-
subheadings *before the Commission had held a single hearing*. Given what
had happened to those 3,000 people the man must be very sick. Official
Commission leaders, Kean and Hamilton, agreed to keep the Zelikow-
May pre-emptive report a secret to avoid being accused of pre-
determining the conclusions from the start. Outraged Commission staff
members were not told about the report until a year later. Zelikow based
much of the Commission report about the 9/11 'plot' on 'evidence'
secured from illegal torture of alleged suspects while never seeing the
documentation which was later illegally destroyed. Khalid Sheikh
Mohammed was named by the 9/11 Commission as 'the principal
architect of the 9/11 attacks' when that 'confession' had come during
horrific torture – including being waterboarded (simulated drowning)
183 times in one month alone. His children were kidnapped by the CIA
and he was told they were going to be tortured with insects. Mohammed
confessed to anything he was told to and this is how he confessed to
bombing a bank that didn't even exist when he was taken into custody.
The government and military psychopaths made up the story of what
happened and then tortured people until they agreed that indeed this is
what happened. Zelikow re-wrote a Commission staffer report to invent
a link between Iraq and al-Qaeda before 9/11 because the ultra-Zionists
wanted to justify the American removal of Saddam Hussein based on
the lie about weapons of mass destruction that didn't exist. He even
claimed that the 'al-Qaeda' attack was to punish America for supporting
Israel. While Zelikow remains uninvestigated for what he did with the
9/11 Commission Report America is not taking itself seriously.

The 9/11 Family Steering Committee and 9/11 Citizens Watch

demanded Zelikow's resignation, but he was going nowhere when he was in place to do a job. Zelikow decided what was in the final report in which, for example, Building 7 was not even mentioned and anything that would point to what really happened was ignored. Another thing – Zelikow actually wrote (although that wasn't made clear at the time) the United States National Security Strategy document of September, 2002, which set out the policy of attacking countries in the Middle East with pre-emptive strikes that was central to the demands of the ultra-Zionists of the Project for the New American Century to whom Zelikow was so closely connected. The policy 'turned military doctrine on its head' and said countries could be attacked which posed no direct or imminent threat to the United States. This was an essential change produced just in time for the invasion of Iraq a few months later in March, 2003. Zelikow further co-wrote a 'prophetic' article pre-9/11 in 1998 for the Council on Foreign Relations (CFR) publication *Foreign Affairs* headed 'Catastrophic Terrorism: Tackling The New Danger' in which he warned about terrorist attacks in the United States and the possible response:

> If the device that exploded in 1993 under the World Trade Center had been nuclear, or had effectively dispersed a deadly pathogen, the resulting horror and chaos would have exceeded our ability to describe it. Such an act of catastrophic terrorism would be a watershed event in American history. It could involve loss of life and property unprecedented in peacetime and undermine America's fundamental sense of security, as did the Soviet atomic bomb test in 1949.

> Like Pearl Harbor, this event would divide our past and future into a before and after. The United States might respond with draconian measures, scaling back civil liberties, allowing wider surveillance of citizens, detention of suspects, and use of deadly force. More violence could follow, either further terrorist attacks or U.S. counterattacks. Belatedly, Americans would judge their leaders negligent for not addressing terrorism more urgently.

Note the use of Pearl Harbor three years before 'the new Pearl Harbor' and Zelikow used the term in the article 'weapons of mass destruction' which would be the mantra to sell the ultra-Zionist-demanded invasion of Iraq. Zelikow's co-authors were John Mark Deutch, Director of the CIA and Deputy Secretary of Defense in the 1990s, and Ashton Carter who was on the board of trustees for the MITRE Corporation and would go on to be Secretary of Defense under Barack Obama. Deutch comes from a Russian Jewish family that emigrated to the United States from Belgium in 1940 and his grandfather was a friend of Israel's first president, Chaim Weizmann. Both Deutch and Carter have been senior partners in the Rothschild aerospace, military and technology

investment operation, Global Technology Partners (GTP). Deutch
pleaded guilty to mishandling government secrets in January, 2001, after
several of his laptops were found to have classified information wrongly
labelled unclassified during his time at the CIA. Bill Clinton pardoned
him on his last day in office. I think I've heard that somewhere before.
Now as the list continues to grow we have ultra-Zionism with the ability
to control US government, military and FAA computer systems and
manipulate them in real time to cause confusion and deactivate missile
defence responses; control of World Trade Center and 9/11 airport
security; control of the criminal investigation and destruction of
evidence; control of civil cases to stop the truth ever coming out and
control of the 9/11 Commission to ... stop the truth ever coming out. All
this crucial 9/11 control by a fraction of two percent of the American
population. Ah, but there's more.

Ultra-Zionist 'Bin Laden' videos

Every facet of the 9/11 story has ultra-Zionism at the helm either
directly (mostly) or through agents and proxies like Dick Cheney and
Donald Rumsfeld. This control even extends to the 'Bin Laden' videos
and 'al-Qaeda' statements that fuelled the belief in 'Bin Laden did it'.
The videos were miraculously 'acquired' and released to the pathetically
unquestioning media through Mossad front organisations like SITE, or
'Search for International Terrorist Entities' (but never in Israel). SITE, or
SHITE as I call it, is run by ultra-ultra-Zionist Rita Katz, daughter of an
alleged Israeli spy executed by Saddam Hussein, and has been
reportedly funded by the US government to the tune of $500,000 a year.
Who sanctioned that and how much more has been donated out of Israel
through ultra-Zionist fronts and operatives in the United States? SITE,
the 'private intelligence firm' based in Washington DC, is a for-profit
organisation that depends on government and corporate contracts. Look
at what has been written and revealed in the last few chapters. Are we
seriously meant to believe that SITE is not connected to Mossad? SITE
worked in harness with IntelCenter, another releaser of 'Bin Laden'
videos run by another ultra-Zionist Ben Venzke. The media has
published their 'information' as fact again and again without ever
asking about the background, agenda and motivation of either
organisation. One of their modes of operation is 'monitoring Islamic
extremist websites' but American investigative journalist, Wayne
Madsen, has pointed out that many 'Jihadist' and 'al-Qaeda' websites
are controlled by Mossad. He writes: 'Mossad has a program to
distribute bogus claims of responsibility for Islamist terrorist attacks via
'Jihadist' websites that are actually operated by the Mossad and a
network of "hasbaratchiks", Israeli and foreign Jews who act as
propagandists on the web.' Set up the websites to make extremist

statements and claim responsibility for attacks and then 'reveal' their content via your 'monitoring' fronts for government and media to repeat them as fact. Katz 'revealed' that what appeared (on the surface) to be a supporter of ISIS in Australia using the tag 'Australi Witness' held a prestigious position in 'online jihadi circles' and was 'part of the hard core of a group of individuals who constantly look for targets for other people to attack'. How strange then that 'Australi Witness' turned out to be a Jewish American called Joshua Ryne who would be arrested by the FBI. Katz, a fluent Arabic speaker, has attended Muslim events disguised with a burqa concealing recording equipment and taken part in pro-Palestinian rallies in the United States as part of her 'investigations'. She even appeared on the CBS *60 Minutes* as 'Sarah' wearing a wig and fake nose before her real identity was outed. A lengthy statement translated and distributed by SITE 'confirmed' the death of Bin Laden in the highly questionable alleged assassination by US troops in 2011. SITE was the source for 'Bin Laden' and other 'al-Qaeda' videos including one in 2007 of a half-an-hour tape by 'Bin Laden' in which all except four minutes was a frozen image of him. The government, of course, deemed it 'authentic'. American intelligence officials said the video was 'inspired' by 'al-Qaeda's' Adam Yahiye Gadahn – Adam Pearlman, grandson of a former director of ultra-Zionist Mossad front, the Anti-Defamation League. Somehow SITE managed to distribute the video to the media a day before (it was claimed) al-Qaeda planned to release it. One question about all this: Who benefits?

Yeah, who does benefit?

We have seen that ultra-Zionism controlled all the key areas of the 9/11 attacks. They provided year after year of incessant propaganda calling for a 'war on terror' and through the Project for the New American Century (PNAC) and other ultra-Zionist-dominated organisations they even named the countries they wished to regime-change. As a result of the 9/11 'trigger' those countries have been picked off one after the other in a 'war on terror' (Netanyahu's pre-9/11term) that has seen – so far – Iraq, Libya, Syria, Iran, Lebanon, North Korea and China targeted either through direct invasion, manipulated 'civil war' or demonisation and sanctions in preparation for direct invasion, 'civil war' or capitulation to the will of the United States (Sabbatian-Frankists). The terrorist former Israeli Prime Minister Ehud Barak named Osama bin Laden and Afghanistan as targets in a BBC interview within minutes of the attacks to start the momentum rolling and other ultra-Zionists and their assets soon followed to sell the lie about 'Bin Laden did it'. Netanyahu also said it all on the very day of the attacks – 9/11 is good for Israel. In truth, it was not good for the population of that tiny land, but good for the ultra-Zionist, Sabbatian-Frankist psychopaths who use the Jewish population as a cover for their evil activities and goals. Ultra-Zionists 'prophesied' a terrorist attack in New York on its biggest building in 1979 and the Project for the New American Century made clear in its September, 2000, document that '... the 'process of transformation ... [war and regime change] ... is likely to be a long one, absent some catastrophic and catalysing event – like a new Pearl Harbor'. A year to the month later came 9/11 – an attack on the World Trade Center complex built through the lobbying of the Rockefeller family and a complex which, by September, 2001, ultra-Zionists completely controlled. By then the ultra-Zionists and their PNAC assets were also running the government and Pentagon. They made their first attempt to control WTC security through the most transparent Israeli intelligence front, Atwell Security, which was part of the Eisenberg Group of ultra-Zionist intelligence operative and arms smuggler, Shaul Eisenberg. When that failed after the intelligence background and behaviour of its Shin Bet 'president' Avraham Shalom was revealed, Plan B was soon in operation. In 1993 came the bombing of the World Trade Center in an attack centrally involving the FBI with the investigation contracted to a company connected to ultra-Zionist Dov Zakheim, the 9/11 Pentagon budget controller. A major case arising from the bombing was prosecuted by ultra-Zionist Michael Chertoff, who would oversee the whole 9/11 'investigation', while the judge was Michael B. Mukasey who would also preside over the insurance case that would hand ultra-Zionist World Trade Center lease holders, Larry Silverstein and Frank Lowy, billions of dollars in compensation for a comparatively negligible investment. Silverstein and Lowy had greatly increased insurance in the case of a terrorist attack when they became the first private holders of the WTC lease thanks to the ultra-Zionist-controlled New York Port Authority and the campaign to privatise the buildings by ultra-Zionist Ronald Lauder, chairman of the New York State Commission of Privatization and New York State Research Council on Privatization. The deal, which shocked many observers because of the state of the buildings, was sealed weeks before 9/11 in a deal between ultra-Zionist Larry Silverstein and ultra-Zionist Lewis Eisenberg, head of the New York Port Authority. Ultra-Zionist Maurice Greenberg of AIG had insured the towers for Silverstein and then immediately sold on the liability to a long list of other companies that would take the hit. Greenberg would also buy into ultra-Zionist security firm Kroll Inc. in 1993, the year the company was awarded control of World Trade Center security because of the bombing. The first plane would make a direct hit on a secure and mysterious data/computer room in the offices of Greenberg's son and his Kroll-connected global insurance brokerage and risk management company, Marsh &

McLennan. Control of airport security came courtesy of Mossad-Shin Bet front, ITCS, and the company did not have to answer for its actions in court thanks to ultra-Zionist judge Alvin Hellerstein whose son worked for the Israeli legal firm representing ITCS's parent company.

Ultra-Zionist-controlled tech and software companies had access to the computer systems connecting the Pentagon, NORAD, FAA and a host of government and military agencies – including real-time air-traffic computers and information with the power to intervene at will. Cyber control also had the potential to deactivate missile defence systems. Ultra-Zionists dictated the propaganda reporting of the attacks and their aftermath through control and ownership of vast swathes of the American media and Hollywood almost in its entirety. 'Bin Laden' videos to support the official fairy tale came courtesy of Mossad front operations. The criminal lack of investigation was assured by ultra-Zionist Michael Chertoff while efforts by families and responders to get their cases to court were blocked by a combination of ultra-Zionist judge Alvin Hellerstein who controlled lawsuit compensation claims and ultra-Zionist lawyer Kenneth R. Feinberg who ran the no-trial Victim Compensation Fund. The oh, so reluctantly established 9/11 Commission was never going to reveal the truth of what happened when it was controlled by ultra-Zionist Executive Director Philip Zelikow who made absolutely sure that any evidence or experience that contradicted the story that he laid out before the Commission even *began* would be trashed or deleted. A Zionist was the lead investigator at NIST into why the towers collapsed (a catastrophic Achilles heel if the truth came out) and the steel with all the potential evidence it contained to solve the mystery was whisked away by an ultra-Zionist transportation firm to ultra-Zionist-controlled scrap metal yards for transportation to Asia for smelting while 'volunteer engineers' ran around trying to dodge the diggers and cranes to examine the steel before it disappeared across the ocean to become someone's fridge. We also had the accurate warning two hours before the attacks sent to two employees at Odigo, an Israeli telecommunications company and instant messaging service with offices two blocks from the World Trade Center. ZIM, an Israeli shipping company with 10,000 square feet of office space in the North Tower, vacated at short notice a week before 9/11 breaking the terms of its lease. Shaul Eisenberg of the Eisenberg Group that owned Mossad-front 'security firm', Atwell, which sought to control World Trade Center security in the 1980s, had a controlling interest in ZIM before he died in China. How could people be this evil? Sabbatai Zevi and Jacob Frank said that doing evil was to be encouraged and celebrated without guilt and some have clearly taken their lead. The major speech-writer for President Boy Bush in this period was ultra-Zionist Neocon David Frum. He came up with the phrase 'axis of evil' in Bush's 2002 State of the

Union address which referred to Iraq, Iran and North Korea – all countries named for regime change by the Project for the New American Century. Frum also wrote the book, *An End to Evil: How to Win the War on Terror,* with ultra-Zionist Richard Perle in 2004.

Elephant on the sofa

Put all the evidence together and the connection between what happened on 9/11 and ultra-Zionist Israel and its military, intelligence and censorship network is breathtakingly obvious. Most people don't have the guts to call this out because they fear the consequences including loss of career; but a few of us do – a very few and getting fewer. Former German Defence Secretary Andreas von Bulow has said he believes Mossad was involved and former Italian President Francesco Cossiga said the same. Cossiga revealed his own role in Operation Gladio, the NATO-controlled terrorist operation after the Second World War that bombed civilian targets in Problem-Reaction-Solution scenarios blamed on those they wished to demonise. He told Italian newspaper *Corriere della Sera* in 2007 that all American and European intelligence agencies well knew that the 9/11 attacks had been the work of the CIA and Mossad 'with the aid of the Zionist world' to induce western powers into targeting Iraq and Afghanistan. As Andreas von Bulow said: ' The CIA is steered by Mossad'. Then there is Alan Sabrosky, a retired Marine officer and former Director of Studies at the United States Army War College's Strategic Studies Institute, who has taught at the United States Military Academy at West Point, Georgetown University, University of Pennsylvania, and Johns Hopkins University School of Advanced International Studies. Sabrosky said in 2010 that it was 'one hundred percent certain 9/11 was a Mossad operation'. He said that if Building 7 was wired for demolition – which he agrees it was – then 'all of them were wired for demolition'. He said that 9/11 had led directly to 60,000 Americans dead and wounded and 'God knows how many hundreds of thousands in other countries we have killed, injured and made homeless'. He went on:

> If Americans ever know that Israel did this they are going to strike them off the earth. They are not going to give a rat's arse about the consequences. They are not going to care – they will do it. The Zionists are playing it as a truly all or nothing exercise. If they lose this one – if the American people ever realise what's happened they're gone. It'll be a bloody, brutal war and they're gone.

It is NOT a 'Jewish plot'

You will have your own thoughts on whether that is true about the response, but the theme brings me to a vital point that I have emphasised many times and one which should focus the minds of all

Jewish people worldwide. I have stressed often in this book that what I am exposing is not a 'Jewish plot'. The vast majority of Jewish people do not know what is being done in their name and most would be horrified if they did. I am exposing a conspiracy for human control by a global Hidden Hand – The Web – in which ultra-Zionism and the Sabbatian-Frankist Death Cult is a frontline player. Through The Web ultra-Zionism connects with regard to 9/11 into the American military and intelligence networks and to people like Dick Cheney and Donald Rumsfeld. Ultra-Zionists infiltrated and controlled the inner workings of the Pentagon-FAA reaction and communication system and blocked the normal response and security wherever necessary. They then orchestrated the cover-up that continues to this day. Jewish people in general were no more responsible for what happened on September 11th than Americans were for the involvement of Cheney, Rumsfeld, Myers, Bolton or the Bush family. Well, except in this way – by allowing psychopaths to take over their countries through control of the key positions and power centres in politics, military, intelligence and media. This has happened the world over and never more blatantly than with the happenings and ongoing consequences of 9/11. Jewish people have fallen for the trap of accepting the perception program instilled from birth that the rest of the world hates them and so believing they must be protected by the psychopaths posing as their saviours. They have fallen for the myth of a Chosen People when we are all the same consciousness having different brief and transitory experiences in what we call 'the world'. 'Chosen People' immediately instigates a sense of apartness as does the belief that for some reason never explained the world somehow hates by reflex action 0.2 percent of its number.

We have seen the consequences in the past for the Jewish many through the actions of the ultra-Zionist, Sabbatian-Frankist few and the only people who can break that cycle are the mass of Jewish people themselves. They need to expose and distance themselves from the ultra-Zionist psychopaths in their midst and the same with Americans with their psychopaths, British people with theirs and so on. The few have controlled the many for long enough – it's time to turn the page and let freedom and justice reign for *all* the human family. We are not apart from each other – we *are* each other. Don't be hoaxed by the 'anti-Semitism' scam whether you are Jewish or otherwise. It is the calculated Protection Racket to protect the control of the psychopathic few over the Jewish community and to protect the psychopaths themselves from exposure. They have no other option because the evidence is there to be seen in abundance to expose them and silencing its communication is all they can do. Who could deny ultra-Zionist involvement in 9/11 after the evidence presented here – or that ultra-Zionism has infiltrated the very fabric of American – and elsewhere – politics, finance, media and decision-making? Ultra-Zionists cannot debate the evidence because they couldn't win and so they slur and smear and seek to destroy. What was their response to the contention by American military expert Alan Sabrosky that Mossad did 9/11? The Anti-Defamation League condemned him as 'a key figure in anti-Semitic conspiracy theories'. Same old, same old, because that is all they have.

Definition defined

From the perspective of all I have outlined in the last few chapters we can return to that new definition of 'anti-Semitism' which is being increasingly accepted by all levels of government, academia, corporations, media and the entire system under pressure and often abuse from the ultra-Zionist network. Such is the power of a tiny country of eight million people (or rather the Sabbatian-Frankist few that control it). The motivation behind this 'definition' is so transparent – especially after what I have exposed in this book. I am going to return to the definition 'examples' that I highlighted earlier so we can see how calculated they are in the light of what the ultra-Zionists are doing and are desperate to hide. There are many problems in defining those who hate Jews for being Jews because 'anti-Semitism' is a complete misnomer for reasons already explained and 'racism' does not apply because Jewishness is not a race but a cultural and religious system of belief and ritual. Hating Jews for being Jews or discriminating against Jews for being Jews is as close as we can get. But that is not what the new definition sets out to challenge. The new 'definition' is a central pillar of the Protection Racket and so must include every aspect of what the Sabbatian-Frankists are *doing* but wish so ferociously to keep from public view. The definition 'examples' are simply a means to stop legitimate investigation and silence exposure of Sabbatian-Frankists and ultra-Zionists and the wider Web of the Hidden Hand. Here's the first one:

Making mendacious, dehumanizing, demonizing, or stereotypical allegations about Jews as such or the power of Jews as collective – such as, especially but not exclusively, the myth about a world Jewish conspiracy or of Jews controlling the media, economy, government or other societal institutions.

Look at what I have exposed about ultra-Zionist control of the prime positions of power and decision-making with regard to 9/11 – control of the Pentagon, US government, tech companies, media, Hollywood, finance etc., etc. The power of *some* Jews as a 'collective' is clearly at work, but not a collective of *all* Jewish people – only a relative handful who have contempt for the rest. This 'example' is designed to equate exposure of a few – even specific individuals – with a claim that all Jews are being accused. By doing so they can protect themselves from exposure by hiding behind the Jewish population as a whole through the lie that exposure of one or a few is a condemnation and hatred of all. That is the last thing I am saying, indeed I am saying the opposite. Once the actions of the few are isolated and disconnected from Jewish people in general the ultra-Zionists and Sabbatian-Frankists lose their wizard's curtain and their game is up. The 'example' is worded precisely to stop what ultra-Zionists are *provably* doing from being publicly exposed and debated. Example number two:

Accusing Jews as a people of being responsible for real or imagined wrong doing committed by a single Jewish person or group, or even for acts committed by non-Jews.

This is seriously ironic given that ultra-Zionists and Sabbatian-Frankists are doing exactly the same in reverse. It is *they* who are equating exposure or criticism of a single Jewish person or group with accusing Jews 'as a people' of being responsible. They have to do this for reasons explained above and this is just a calculated and inverted sleight of hand to accuse others of what *they* are doing. Number three:

Denying the fact, scope, mechanisms (e.g. gas chambers) or intentionality of the genocide of the Jewish people at the hands of National Socialist Germany and its supporters and accomplices during World War II (the Holocaust).

This 'example' is to block all questions whatever they may be about an historical happening and it is the only historical event in all human existence on which such a ban is imposed. To ask even the most basic questions about the official narrative is to be immediately labelled an 'anti-Semite' and 'Nazi' and have your life and reputation destroyed. You see this reaction from even most of those who regard themselves as 'moderates' or 'progressive'. The fact is that the horrors of Nazi Germany are coldly exploited by ultra-Zionists and Sabbatian-Frankists to silence those who seek to expose their manipulation today and this is both sick and disgusting. Those who are confident that what they say is true do not seek to ban people from asking questions about it. Those who are *not* confident do that. To *question* is not to *deny* – it is to question and see what answers come back. It's called freedom. Why such desperation to shut down *all* questioning and debate on the subject? Well, Sabbatian-Frankists? Number four:

Accusing the Jews as a people, or Israel as a state, of inventing or exaggerating the Holocaust.

How can anyone know unless the official narrative is allowed to be questioned and the answers forthcoming? Number five:

Accusing Jewish citizens of being more loyal to Israel, or to the alleged priorities of Jews worldwide, than to the interests of their own nations.

I guess most who have read through the last few chapters will now be shaking their head at this one. The extraordinary connections between ultra-Zionists and 9/11 were all for the benefit of America were they? The hundreds of inter-connecting Zionist and ultra-Zionist organisations in the United States alone promoting the policies and self-interest of Israel are only there to make America a better place and are nothing at all to do with 'being more loyal to Israel, or to the alleged priorities of Jews worldwide, than to the interests of their own nations'? Manipulating the United States and its young men and women to fight wars for Israel in the Middle East is only in the interest of America and Americans? What an absolute joke. There can be few more obvious examples than this 'example' of labelling exposure of what the ultra-Zionists are clearly *doing* as 'anti-Semitic'. Ultra-Zionists like Arnon Milchan, Larry Silverstein, Michael Chertoff, Dov Zakheim and the rest of that crowd do not have more allegiance to Israel than America?? Shelden Adelson telling an event for the Israeli Defense Forces that *unfortunately* the military uniform he once wore was American and not Israeli is allegiance to America is it? And what about Adelson's 'all we care about is being good Zionists – good citizens of Israel'? I mean, pass the sickbag. Number six:

Denying the Jewish people their right to self-determination, e.g., by claiming that the existence of a State of Israel is a racist endeavor.

This is to stop exposure of Israel's shocking racism against Palestinians by claiming that such criticism is 'denying the Jewish people their right to self-determination ... by claiming that the existence of a State of Israel is a racist endeavor' and then condemning such views as 'anti-Semitism'. Any country that operates a regime and society based on apartheid, which Israel profoundly does, is a racist endeavour and if ultra-Zionists don't like me saying so they can fuck off. Number seven:

Applying double standards by requiring of it a behaviour not expected or demanded of any other democratic nation.

The wording is designed to equate an apartheid regime with a 'democratic nation' and calling an apartheid regime an apartheid regime with 'anti-Semitism'. Number eight:

Using the symbols and images associated with classic antisemitism (e.g., claims of Jews killing Jesus or blood libel) to characterize Israel or Israelis.

Ban the exposure of symbols and images that relate to Sabbatian-Frankist Satanists and extreme ultra-Zionists by claiming that this is a condemnation of all Jews. Number nine:

Drawing comparisons of contemporary Israeli policy to that of the Nazis.

This 'example' is there to stop anyone saying that if it looks like a duck, swims like a duck, and quacks like a duck, then it probably is a duck. Or, as I say, every race, culture and religion is capable of producing every kind of human personality including what is called 'Nazi'. To claim that one group alone is not is capable of doing that is farcical, but this 'example' is to prevent people from stating the bloody obvious in the case of the Sabbatian-Frankist and ultra-Zionist extremists that control Israel. Finally, number ten:

Holding Jews collectively responsible for actions of the state of Israel.

I agree that this unfair, but the Protection Racket seeks to promote the propaganda that criticism of Israel is criticism of all Jewish people – this is the very foundation of the 'new definition' for goodness sake to protect ultra-Zionists, Sabbatian-Frankists and their vehicle Israel from criticism and public exposure.

The new definition of 'anti-Semitism' needs to be scrapped and the public ignore its 'examples' now the true reason for its introduction are so clearly exposed. You can see from these chapters that claims about Israel and its ultra-Zionist networks having nothing to do with 9/11 are utterly laughable. They were central players at the very foundation of the 'inside job' in league with the Bushes, Cheney, Rumsfeld, and rogue elements in the Pentagon, [In]Justice Department, FBI, CIA, FAA, New York authorities and so on, which lock into the same Hidden Hand Web as the Sabbatian-Frankists and ultra-Zionists. In the light of the blatantly obvious connections exposed here there must be massive and unyielding public pressure for a new and truly independent investigation into what happened before, during and after 9/11 with all the evidence and witnesses presented that were denied and blocked by the ultra-Zionist-controlled 9/11 Commission. Those I have named in this book must be forced to publicly answer for their actions and non-actions and explain the connections between them that take the term 'coincidence' to stratospheric levels of statistical chance.

This is vital not only to bring justice at last to those directly and indirectly affected by 9/11, but also to dismantle the conspiracy for which the attacks of September 11th were only one strand in a gigantic web of human control that seeks to advance human enslavement to extremes and levels that most people would not even begin to comprehend. To this, in the final chapters, I will now turn.

CHAPTER 26

Eyes wide OPEN

Life is a constant journey of trying to open your eyes. I'm just beginning my journey and my eyes aren't fully open yet – Olivia Thirlby

I think it is fair to say that in the modern climate created by the 'anti-Semitism' industry, the Protection Racket and 'progressive' policing of speech and opinion that I have been 'controversial' in this book so far and I am about to get even more so.

I am 67 at the time of writing and I could live out the rest of my life quietly doing whatever I choose to do. I didn't have to take the untold abuse and ridicule that I have for 30 years and I don't need to amplify that condemnation to still new levels with the writing of this book. I choose to do that, knowing how the 'anti-Semitism' industry and 'progressive' mob will react because, bizarrely in the circumstances, I care about the world that those who abuse me will have to live in unless eyes are opened with immediate effect. I most certainly care about what my children and grandchildren will have to face if the conspiracy to enslave them and everyone else is not brought to public attention before the endgame is complete. We are very close to that now in the wake of decade after decade of perception manipulation through unrelenting propaganda and conditioning; but, as Nazi propagandist Joseph Goebbels said: 'Propaganda becomes ineffective the moment we become aware of it.' I have spent the last 30 years working to make people aware of it and I have written this book as a symbolic arm thrusting through the elevator door as the two sides are about to meet. I do so in the hope that it will have the same effect once the dust has settled and the, oh, so predictable abuse has repeated itself into boring irrelevance. Yeah, yeah, whatever. I want to open those doors to freedom again just as they close for seemingly the final time by showing that you don't have to stay silent and acquiesce to professional bullies or any other kind. You can shout even louder instead. If I have to take monumental abuse to achieve that – and it seems I do – then so be it. They can throw their worst and do their worst. It makes no difference to me. I am, like all of us, a point of attention within an infinity of consciousness and what happens in any moment is but a transitory experience on an infinite journey of exploration. Put simply: I don't give a fuck (Fig 147).

'Jewish' cover story

Those who have read this book to the end – the abusers largely will not – know that what I am exposing isn't a 'Jewish plot'. You might have gathered by now that if I

Figure 147: Twitter storm response system.

thought it *was* a 'Jewish plot' then I would bloody well say so. But I don't, so I'm not. The 'plot' for total human enslavement of mind and body is not 'Jewish' in origin but satanic. In the end it goes off planet, or off dimension, and that's a whole other story told in my other books. The perpetrators are the satanic Sabbatian-Frankist Death Cult and the wider Hidden Hand manipulating through The Web. Jewish people are largely its victims, not perpetrators. The Cult has infiltrated and taken control of all major religions, governments, banking and other corporations, media, Hollywood, Silicon Valley, the Internet, high-tech, artificial intelligence, 'education' and almost every other area of human life required for their goal to be secured. What happened on 9/11 gave renewed impetus and momentum to infuse the hijack of human society with an ever quickening pace. Look at how fast the world has changed since September 11th, 2001. The American military, largely the world army in the making, now has personnel in 175 countries out of 195 and 175,000 active troops in 158. This has been made possible by the nearly *90 percent* increase in military spending since 9/11 which has also been used as the excuse for war, mass surveillance, secret courts and invasion of privacy the like of which the world has never seen on such a scale. The Hidden Hand chose to target Jewish society for many reasons. Among them was the need (it's a long story) to control their global tyranny out of what is today called Israel. The Knights Templar (12th century) and Zionism (19th century) both seeking to rebuild Solomon's Temple is not a coincidence. One of the reasons takes us into the esoteric and the Earth's energetic grid or matrix of force lines (ley-lines, meridians) on which particular points of power have greater effect on the whole than elsewhere. Jerusalem is one such place and again the background can be found in other books. The focus of Christianity, Islam and Judaism on the same city and even the same spot – Temple Mount/Haram al-Sharif – is also no coincidence. It's not called the 'Holy City' for nothing. The Greater Israel project which seeks to expand Israel into Iraq would fulfil the Sabbatian-Frankist dream of returning to their other spiritual home, Babylon.

Targeting the Jewish community gave the Death Cult the potential (which has been mercilessly exploited) to develop a shield of protection from exposure. Again and again you will find quotes from Zionist leaders along the same basic theme that using claims of 'anti-Semitism' would block criticism of 'Jewish' (Sabbatian-Frankist) actions and frighten the Jewish majority into giving their power to the Death Cult and its ultra-Zionist stooges to protect them from perceived 'enemies' (the rest of humanity) while having no idea there even is a Death Cult. Hiding within a *specifically* identifiable group has allowed for a *specific* term of 'anti-Semitism' to be erroneously invented to secure *specific* and amplified protection for the Sabbatian-Frankist infiltrators above all other groups. Designer protection you could call it. As the Death Cult moves into its in-your-face endgame stage of total human control even that protection had to be dramatically increased to avoid exposure through open debate and freedom of expression and so we have the hysterical ramping-up of the 'anti-Semitism' industry and Protection Racket with the ever-widening definition of how 'anti-Semitism' should be applied and targeted. More to hide = more to keep hidden = greater extremes of censorship. We are rapidly closing in on the point where no criticism of any Jewish person will be allowed except for ultra-Zionist and Death Cult operatives attacking Jews who refuse to sing from the song-sheet. They are fair game because ultra-Zionism and the Death Cult are not there to protect Jewish people for whom they have extreme contempt. Protecting the ultra-Zionist/Death Cult agenda is the only name of the game. Another bonus is the concept of 'God's Chosen People' which can be manipulated to make significant swathes of the Jewish community believe the Sabbatian-Frankist messianic fairy tale about the return of a Jewish 'Messiah' (Moshiach) to rule the world. The Death Cult is founded on the alleged messianic credentials of Sabbatai Zevi and Jacob Frank. Many ultra-Zionists are not Sabbatian-Frankists, but they have bought the 'Chosen People' lie and the perceived destiny that comes with that. This leads them to work and plot for that destiny while the Sabbatian-Frankists laugh behind their hands. In many ways ultra-Zionists that are not part of the Death Cult are the most manipulated of all and therefore the most despised by the Cult. Those who have seen through the lies may be a threat to the Cult but it has a grudging admiration for them and total contempt for those it manipulates so easily. Such is the power of Death Cult perceptual manipulation that a 2019 poll found that 42 percent of Israelis support annexation (stealing) in some form the Palestinian West Bank illegally occupied by Israel. This is Death Cult policy and they have fallen for it as they have fallen for so much more. The background to the Cult, its history and ambitions, laid out over in the last few chapters, brings events in the world today into clear focus as we shall see.

Protocol prophecies

Goals and methods of the Death Cult also present the *Protocols of the Learned Elders of Zion* in a new light. Whatever the origin of the document circulated under that name the texts describe without question the ambitions and techniques of Sabbatian-Frankism. You can still get a copy – even on Amazon – and it is worth the effort to read what they said well over a century ago and compare that with real world events since then and up to present day. Never mind – 'that's anti-Semitic'. It is your right to read what you see fit and come to conclusions of your choice. Don't let anyone tell you otherwise. Anyway, there is nothing 'anti-Semitic' about reading the *Protocols* because they are not, as promoted, detailing a 'Jewish plot'. They just appear to be. The *Protocols* are describing a Sabbatian-Frankist Death Cult plot that uses Jewish people as essential cover. You are not supposed to talk about the *Protocols* or you are labelled a 'Nazi'. Well, I don't give a shit. They describe what has subsequently happened and I have the right to ask *why that is*. The Sabbatian-Frankist 'anti-Semitism' industry and Protection Racket is designed to stop that question being asked through its reflex-action hatred and abuse, but I choose to raise my finger in nonchalant response. 'Zion' has a different meaning to Sabbatian-Frankists than it does to Jewish people in general and notice that the document is not called the Protocols of the Elders of Jewish People or Judaism, but the Protocols of *Zion*. To the Death Cult the arrival of 'Zion' is the arrival of their global control system which is being constructed all around us every day. Remember the 'Zion mainframe' in the *Matrix* movies? This will be very relevant shortly. 'The New Jerusalem' also means something different to the Death Cult. The biblical *Book of Ezekiel* (said to be a priest exiled in Babylon) describes this as a city with a rebuilt Solomon's Temple which would be the capital of the Messianic Kingdom in the Messianic Era of a world controlled from Israel by a descendent of 'King David'. The *Book of Ezekiel* says: 'David My servant *shall be* king over them, and they shall all have one shepherd; they shall also walk in My judgments and observe My statutes, and do them.' You don't have to believe in Old Testament prophecy for this to be profoundly relevant to the world today. What ultra-Zionists and the Death Cult believe (or promote for their own ends) is all that matters. This is the sequence of the final plan to bring this about: United States embassy moved to Jerusalem (done); removal of Palestinians from the area of Temple Mount and the Al-Aqsa Mosque (being done); seizure and demolition of the mosque; rebuilt Solomon's Temple. In the same period they want to annex the Golan Heights (already agreed by the United States) and the West Bank on the road to the Greater Israel and a return to Babylon. You can see how all the post-9/11 wars have fitted into this scenario although they have not yet gone exactly to plan. Another name for the New Jerusalem is Zion and while this is interpreted as a heavenly location it is planned to be very much of the 'physical' world by the Sabbatian-Frankist Death Cult.

The *Protocols* and many other sources for the same plan describe how: Might is the only right; the end justifies the means (see 9/11); freedom is bad; the best form of rule is despotism; the future for humanity is serfdom; Masonic secret societies rule from the shadows; Masonry is the 'legislative force' and the leader and guide of all secret societies; the mob is blind and an essential means for the few to impose their will on the many; political discord is systematically created and political leaders such as presidents are only figure-heads controlled by secret advisors; 'They' control the media and manipulate public opinion; ferments, discords and hostility are secretly instigated all over the world; the plan is for an all-powerful global government; terror is used as a form of human manipulation and control; diseases are introduced through inoculation; 'They' control the police; dissidents will be executed when the final takeover is secured and people will be arrested on first suspicion; collectivism (Marxism) will be the new system of control; a one-day 'coup d'état' (revolution) over all the world will herald the arrival of 'the Sovereign Lord of all the World, King of Israel, Patriarch of all the World and Patriarch-Pope'. These are some other main themes of the *Protocols* from well over a hundred years ago and you may recognise them:

- **Program and demoralise youth by indoctrinating false beliefs and perceptions.**

  (See 'progressive' mob and perceptual programming in schools, colleges and universities.)

- **Destroy the family unit.**

  (This is happening through multiple means including divisions between generations and social media which has for many become the new 'parent'/family.)

- **Appeal to humanity's lower instincts.**

  (This has clearly been happening for a long time.)

- **Destroy respect for religions and the clergy through scandal and other means.**

(Blatantly happening and it helps if the hierarchy of the Roman Catholic Church is dominated by Sabbatian-Frankists who see sex with children as 'normal'.)

- **Introduce diversions in entertainment that require spending money and erode the enjoyment of simple cost-free pleasures.**

  (Smartphones, videogames, etc.)

- **Divert the attention of the population with sport and vacuous 'entertainment' so they don't see what is really going on.**

  (Big-time happening and for long past.)

- **Confuse people with false and contradictory theories that hide the real story.**

  (Constantly happening.)

- **Instigate class hatred and class war among different classes of people.**

  (This has now been morphed into hatred and war between self-identities.)

- **Create division between all groups including employers and employees and 'right' and 'left'.**

  (Happening in ever greater extremes.)

- **Destroy agriculture through industrialisation and then destroy industry.**

  (What a prediction this was more than a century ago given that industrial farming (promoted by the Rothschilds) has utterly poisoned the food chain and replaced individual farmers with giant corporations to control global food production.)

- **Circulate utopian theories to enslave people in a labyrinth of impractical ideas.**

  ('Progressive', New Age, Alexandria Ocasio-Cortez.)

- **Cause conflict and suspicion between states that lead to increased spending on armaments.**

  (Obviously happening.)

- **Introduce public voting while keeping the people so ignorant of the real game that they pick people the manipulators want.**

  (This happens at almost every election and when the public vote the 'wrong way' as in the British Brexit referendum you call them 'morons' and 'far right' and do everything you can to thwart what they voted for.)

- **Appoint people to key positons who have something to hide so they will do whatever they are told in fear of exposure.**

  (The system is awash with such compromised place-people.)

- **Slowly change all constitutions in preparation for despotic world government.**

  (Preparation for global Marxism is what they mean. The European Union is a perfect example of constitutional change in countries of the EU and the deletion of sovereignty.)

- **Establish huge monopolies.**

  (Amazon, Google/YouTube, Facebook, ad infinitum.)

- **Trigger economic and industrial crises and instability leading to world bankruptcy and at the most effective time crash the system globally to trigger panic.**

  (This has been done through the Wall Street crash and the crash of 2008, but what is planned is a global crash the like we have never seen. They' who cause the crash can then come forward as the 'saviours' so long as we accept the new system which they will control.)

- **Control global banking and finance to enslave governments and population in debt.**

  (Achieved long ago.)

- **Destroy nations and break the spirit of humanity with all kinds of suffering, deprivation, food shortages and reasons to fear.**

(Happening to so many today (see the EU) and we have seen nothing yet unless the world wakes up to what is being imposed upon us.)

Whatever the background the *Protocols* describe the Sabbatian-Frankist manifesto and the Illuminati (Sabbatian-Frankist) manifesto. And all this is just *coincidence*? *Please*. What the *Protocols* predict has happened ever since and it is still happening as the plan now surges towards its goal. I mean, just look around you. The arrogance in the *Protocols* is Sabbatian-Frankist arrogance as they describe their new world of tyrannical control in which all humanity would be ruled from Israel by a super global government of Zion. The document says:

> ... we shall so wear [them] down ... that they will be compelled to offer us international power, a nature that by its position will enable us without any violence gradually to absorb all the state forces of the world and to form a super-government; In place of the rulers of today we shall set up a bogey which will be called the Super-Government Administration; Its hands will reach out in all directions like nippers and its organisation will be of such colossal dimensions that it cannot fail to subdue all the nations of the world.

The *Protocols* talk about owning the world through debt to their banks which people and countries could never repay while controlling industry, commerce and governments through Zion-instigated debt. Presidents and politicians were mere puppets to their will: '[We] arrange elections in favour of such presidents, as have in their past some dark, undiscovered stain, some "Panama" or other – then they will be trustworthy agents for the accomplishment of our plans out of fear of revelations and from the natural desire of everyone who has attained power, namely, the retention of privileges, advantages and honour connected with the office of president.' This is exactly how it works and few have been more obviously controlled by Sabbatian-Frankists than 9/11 president Boy Bush and Donald Trump. The *Protocols* continue:

> The chamber of deputies will provide cover for, will protect, will elect the president, but we shall take from it the right to propose new, or make changes in existing laws, for this right will be given by us to the responsible president, a puppet in our hands. Naturally, the authority of the president will then become a target for every possible form of attack, but we shall provide him with a means of self-defence in the right of an appeal to the people, for the decision of the people over the heads of their representatives, that is to say, an appeal to that same blind slave of ours – the majority of the mob.

Independently of this we shall invest the president with the right of declaring a state of war. We shall justify this last right on the ground that the president as chief of the whole army of the country must have it at his disposal, in case of need for the defence of the new republican constitution, the right to defend which will belong to him as the responsible representative of this constitution. It is easy to understand that in these conditions the key of the shrine will lie in our hands, and no one outside of ourselves will any longer direct the force of legislation.

The *Protocols* describe how 'They' would bring the population into a 'state of bewilderment' through 'so many contradictory opinions and for such length of time as will suffice to make [them] lose their heads in the labyrinth and come to see that the best thing is to have no opinion of any kind in matters political' which were understood only by those who guide the public:

> The second secret requisite for the success of our government is comprised in the following. To multiply to such an extent national failings, habits, passions, conditions of civil life, that it will be impossible for anyone to know where he is in the resulting chaos, so that the people in consequence will fail to understand one another …

The *Protocols* tell us that education would be manipulated to be a means of perceptually-programming the masses to see themselves and the world in the way that suits the agenda for global control. Observe the transformation of schools, colleges and universities into bastions of free speech deletion, group-think and indoctrination of 'progressive' lies and insanity. The *Protocols* describe how national and individual liberty would end under rule from Jerusalem by the 'King of Israel' born of the 'blood of Zion' symbolised as the 'line of David'. I will describe shortly how from a modern perspective all this is planned to be brought about. I should not even speak in future tense because it is happening now if only people would breach the fire-walls of their Sabbatian-Frankist software program.

Different sources – same story

A long list of prophetic works including Aldous Huxley's *Brave New World* (1932), George Orwell's *Nineteen-eighty-four* (1948) and the presentation by ultra-Zionist Dr Richard Day (1969) involve precisely the same themes as the *Protocols*. How could these people be so accurate that long ago? The *Protocols* are older than all of them. The Master Plan was already in place and they were just putting that plan into their own context from their own sources. Therefore Huxley's drug and genetic agenda is happening; Orwell's Big Brother state is happening; Day's new world order is happening in all the facets and forms that he described. Research the United Nations' scam of Agenda 21/2030 to transform human society into a centralised global state to 'save the world' from the (hoax) of human-caused climate change and the 'Green New Deal' of the Soros 'progressive' Alexandria Ocasio-Cortez. They both demand the centralised control demanded by the *Protocols*. The Sabbatian-Frankist climate change hoax has been spun as a problem to which they can offer their control-system 'solution'. All these various expressions of the plan, including the *Protocols*, describe how private property ownership will be outlawed. Paediatrician Lawrence Dunnegan described what Richard Day said in 1969:

> Privately owned housing would become a thing of the past. The cost of housing and financing housing would gradually be made so high that most people couldn't afford it … Young people would more and more become renters, particularly in apartments or condominiums. People would not be able to buy [homes] and gradually more and more of the population would be forced into small apartments. Small apartments which would not accommodate very many children [part of the population cull agenda I have described in other books].

> Ultimately, people would be assigned where they would live and it would be common to have non-family members living with you. This by way of your not knowing just how far you could trust anybody. This would all be under the control of a central housing authority. Have this in mind … when they ask, 'How many bedrooms in your house? How many bathrooms in your house? Do you have a finished game room?' This information is personal and is of no national interest to government under our existing Constitution. But you'll be asked those questions …

We are moving in this very direction every day.

Sabbatian-Frankist coup d'état

The *Protocols* talk about a one-day 'coup d'état' or revolution all over the world at the same time and Richard Day told those paediatricians in 1969:

> The bringing in of the new system probably will occur on a weekend in the winter. Everything would shut down on Friday evening and Monday morning when everybody wakened there would be an announcement that the New System was in place. During the process in getting the United States ready for these changes everybody would be busier with less leisure time and less opportunity to really look about and see what was going on around them.

How this can be done over a single weekend – and done out of Israel – will soon become clear. One *Protocol* says:

> When we have accomplished our coup d'état we shall say then to the various peoples: everything has gone terribly badly, all have been worn out with sufferings. We are destroying the causes of your torment – nationalities, frontiers, differences of coinages [Problem-Reaction-Solution and remember this was stated more than a hundred years ago]. You are at liberty, of course, to pronounce sentence upon us, but can it possibly be a just one if it is confirmed by you before you make any trial of what we are offering you … then will the mob exalt us and bear us up in their hands in a unanimous triumph of hopes and expectations. Voting, which we have made the instrument which will set us on the throne of the world by teaching even the very smallest units of members of the human race to vote by means of meetings and agreements by groups, will then have served its purposes and will play its part then for the last time by a unanimity of desire to make close acquaintance with us before condemning us [this is the long-planned post-democratic society I have warned about for decades].

> To secure this we must have everybody vote without distinction of classes and qualifications, in order to establish an absolute majority, which cannot be got from the educated propertied classes. In this way by inculcating in all a sense of self-importance, we shall destroy … the importance of the family and its educational value and remove the possibility of individual minds splitting off, for the mob, handled by us, will not let them come to the front nor even give them a hearing; it is accustomed to listen [only to us] who pay it for obedience and attention. In this way we shall create a blind, mighty force which will never be in a position to move in any direction without the guidance of our agents set at its head by us as leaders of the mob. The people will submit to this regime because it will know that upon these leaders will depend its earnings, gratifications and the receipt of all kinds of benefits.

Once again this dastardly plan came to light well over a hundred years ago and the Soros 'progressive' mob is now with us acting in exactly the way this *Protocol* describes. Yet another coincidence? Not only that – the mob *is* beholding to its funders like Soros who pay for its 'obedience and attention' and drive its direction and tyranny to stop 'individual minds splitting off'. The mob does indeed 'not let them come to the front nor even give them a hearing'. This is political correctness; these are the reflex labels of 'Nazi', bigot' and 'racist'. The social engineers of the Rothschild ultra-Zionist Frankfurt School demanded the demise of the family unit as the *Protocols* do. Wish-list items of the Frankfurt School that I described earlier are widely included in the

Protocols and among them are continual change to create confusion; promotion of excessive drinking; emptying churches (targeting anything that brings people together); dependency on the state or state benefits (thus do what the state says – or else); control and dumbing down of the media and encouraging the breakdown of family. Go as far back as the fallen horseman in 1785 and the Illuminati plan on his person for world domination and revolution and you will see the same themes, methods and goals. No wonder the Hidden Hand had to pull the stunt with its professional liar operative Allen Dulles and his 'Russian émigre' to trash the credibility of the *Protocols* in the *Times* and *New York Times* in 1921 in articles written by an asset of Sabbatian-Frankist-controlled British intelligence. The 'anti-Semitism' industry and Protection Racket ultimately controlled by the Death Cult works 24/7 year after year to demonise and silence the few who are willing to highlight the bloody obvious correlation between the *Protocols* and subsequent world events. Surprise, surprise, mention of the *Protocols* is another press-enter definition of 'anti-Semitism'. Did I say they can fuck off? I think I might have mentioned it.

King of the World

These messianic crazies of the Sabbatian-Frankist Death Cult want to impose their 'world ruler' on the throne of Jerusalem on the site of a rebuilt Solomon's Temple. We can see with the emphasis in the *Protocols* on the vital part played by Freemasonry the reason why Freemasonic temples are really symbols of Solomon's Temple with their twin pillars and worship of the Sabbatian-Frankist god of Saturn after which Sabbatai (Saturn) Zevi was named. The vast majority of Freemasons will have no idea they are in effect worshipping Saturn under names like the 'Great/Grand Architect', but they are. 'El' is the Hebrew god of Saturn – as in IsraEL – and even the New Jerusalem is described in The *Book of Revelation* in terms of a cube which is an ancient symbol of Saturn. If you read my other books, like *Everything You Need To Know But Have Never Been Told*, you will see the detailed background to why Saturn is so important to them. The King of the Jews will be the real Pope of the Universe, Patriarch of an international church, the *Protocols* tell us, and rule over what is planned to be a one-world religion (Sabbatian-Frankism) with universal acceptance of the 'Jewish' God and 'Jewish' religion. All other religions (including Judaism as currently practiced) would disappear. This 'figure' will not really be the King of the 'Jews' but what some call the 'Antichrist' or, put another way, a global Big Brother. Christian Zionists have been utterly manipulated to relate this to the return of 'Jesus'. I will describe in this chapter what I have concluded the 'king' really is. The *Protocols* tell us:

The Supreme Lord who will replace all now existing rulers, dragging on their existence among societies demoralised by us, societies that have denied even the authority of god, from whose midst breaks out on all sides the fire of anarchy, must first of all proceed to quench this all-devouring flame. Therefore he will be obliged to kill off those existing societies, though he should drench them with his own blood, that he may resurrect them again in the form of regularly organised troops fighting consciously with every kind of infection that may cover the body of the state with sores.

This chosen one of God is chosen from above to demolish the senseless forces moved by instinct and not reason, by brutishness and not humanness. These forces now triumph in manifestations of robbery and every kind of violence under the mask of principles of freedom and rights. They have overthrown all forms of social order to erect on the ruins the throne of the King of the Jews; but their part will be played out the moment he enters into his kingdom. Then it will be necessary to sweep them away from his path, on which must be left no knot, no splinter. then will it be possible for us to say to the peoples of the world: 'Give thanks to God and bow the knee before him who bears on his front the seal of the predestination of man, to which god himself has led his star that none other but he might free us from all the before mentioned forces and evils'.

This is classic Problem-Reaction-Solution. Create global mayhem, conflict and suffering and then step forward as the solution to the horrors you have systematically created.

Importance of 'the mob'

The point about sweeping away the mob once it has played its part in overthrowing the old order was exactly what Soviet KGB defector Yuri Bezmenov described in 1985 when he said that once the mob (today's Soros 'progressives') had completed their role as essential pawns they would be 'lined up against the wall and shot'. Bezmenov was describing the techniques of Marxism and that is what today's Soros 'progressive' mob represents – *Marxism*. This is the same Marxism created by Sabbatian-Frankists through their frontman Karl Marx to overthrow the existing order and establish a centralised structure of control under the smokescreen of 'government of the people'. But what happened in Russia, China and everywhere else that Marxism has been imposed? The mob overthrows the prevailing order and then the new order destroys the mob. Self-obsessed pawns of the Soros 'progressive' mob are walking – sprinting – into the same trap with Marxism disguised as 'socialism' and 'inclusivity' (self-identity exclusivity). Marxism seeks to transform society by conflict between groups and Sabbatian-Frankists need a far right mob to provide the focus of hate for the Soros 'progressive' mob which is what we have with ultra-Zionists (ultimately the Death Cult) funding both 'sides'. Donald Trump was brought to power to be that focus of mob-expanding hatred not just in America, but around the world. The *Protocols* say of the mob mentality:

> In order to elaborate satisfactory forms of action it is necessary to have regard to the rascality, the slackness, the instability of the Mob, its lack of capacity to understand and respect the conditions of its own life, or its own welfare; It must be understood that the might of a Mob is blind, senseless and unreasoning forever at the mercy of a suggestion from any side …

American Freemasonic legend Albert Pike emphasised the importance of the mob in seizing global control for the few. Pike was Supreme Pontiff of Universal Freemasonry and involved in the creation of the Ku Klux Klan (how very progressive). He was said by British-born Canadian intelligence operative William Carr to have revealed in a letter to high Freemason, Mafia founder and Illuminati chief Giuseppe Mazzini in 1871 a plan for three world wars to transform global society into a centrally-controlled dictatorship. Pike described the first two wars accurately, but the alleged content of the letter only came to light after they had happened and so what he said about the still-to-happen Third World War is most relevant. Carr quotes Pike as saying that this would break out in the Middle East between Israel and the Muslim world and drag in other nations to create a global conflict. Those who say that Pike's mention of 'political Zionism' (the State of Israel) as one of the protagonists could not have been known about in 1871 do not understand how far ahead the Sabbatian-Frankist plan is projected. Society-changing world events and happenings are not random, but stepping-stones to a final outcome that are planned and prepared for way in advance. This is where incredibly accurate long-term descriptions and predictions by Huxley, Orwell and Day ultimately originate. Pike is quoted by Carr as saying:

> … other nations … will be constrained to fight to the point of complete physical, moral, spiritual and economical exhaustion. We shall unleash the Nihilists and the atheists, and we shall provoke a formidable social cataclysm which in all its horror will show clearly to the nations the effect of absolute atheism, origin of savagery and of the most bloody turmoil.

Nihilism is 'a political belief or action that advocates or commits violence or terrorism without discernible constructive goals' and ISIS/Islamic State is a perfect example. Pike continued:

> Then everywhere, the citizens, obliged to defend themselves against the world

minority of revolutionaries, will exterminate those destroyers of civilization, and the multitude, disillusioned with Christianity, whose deistic spirits will from that moment be without compass or direction, anxious for an ideal, but without knowing where to render its adoration, will receive the true light through the universal manifestation of the pure doctrine of Lucifer [a god of Sabbatian-Frankism], brought finally out in the public view. This manifestation will result from the general reactionary movement which will follow the destruction of Christianity and atheism, both conquered and exterminated at the same time.

You see the same recurring themes from all these sources pointing to the same story and the evidence of this happening is everywhere. The *Protocols* say:

… it is indispensable to trouble in all countries the people's relations with their governments so as to utterly exhaust humanity with dissension, hatred, struggle, envy and even by the use of torture, by starvation, by the inoculation of diseases, by want, so that [the population] see no other issue than to take refuge in our complete sovereignty in money and in all else; but if we give the nations of the world a breathing space the moment we long for is hardly likely ever to arrive.

If that does not describe the world today and indeed throughout the 20th century then I don't know what does.

Essential fake 'liberals'

The *Protocols* stress the importance of 'liberals, utopian dreamers' in the plan or what the Cabal would call today 'progressives'. They would be 'played out' once the Sabbatian-Frankist world government was in place, but until then 'they will continue to do us good service' – 'Therefore we shall continue to direct their minds to all sorts of vain conceptions of fantastic theories, new and apparently progressive.' The *Protocols* boast at having 'turned the brainless heads of the [population] with progress till there is not among [them] one mind able to perceive that under this word lies a departure from truth in all cases where it is not a question of material inventions, for truth is one and in it there is no place for progress.' This *Protocol* continues:

When we come into our kingdom our orators will expound great problems which have turned humanity upside down in order to bring it at the end under our beneficent rule; Who will ever suspect then that all these people were stage-managed by us according to a political plan which no one has so much as guessed at in the course of many centuries?

We shall assume to ourselves the liberal physiognomy [face / appearance] of all parties, of all directions, and we shall give that physiognomy a voice in orators who will speak so much that they will exhaust the patience of their hearers and produce an abhorrence of oratory.

This is a vital point that explains so much about what is happening today. The constant mantra from the 'progressive' voice of self-proclaimed 'moderation' is to condemn opposing groups and opinions as 'far right', 'fascist' and 'Nazi'. This is both projection and an effort to demonise opposition as extremists while selling their own image as one of moderation, inclusion and caring. It's another inverted hoax which most of the Soros mob will not have grasped while ensconced in the jet-black darkness of their nether regions. Pump-primers among them representing Sabbatian-Frankism will absolutely know what the game is. The trick is to present a face of 'moderation' while pursuing an agenda of tyrannical extremism. To do this you must brand the opposition as extremists which is what they try to do with me. This technique leads to extraordinary levels of inverted nonsense in which Tony Blair who lied to sell a war that killed or maimed millions directly and through ongoing consequences is described as a 'moderate' while those who opposed his mass murder are 'rebels', 'radicals' or extremists. The media play their vital role in this with the labels they hand out such as 'Labour rebels' and 'Labour moderates' (extremists). Remember how Western-armed-and-funded psychopathic killers in Syria were described as the 'moderate opposition'?

In search of a 'saviour'

The Sabbatian-Frankist Messiah scam is made easier by other religions having the same concept with Jesus in Christianity, Krishna in Hinduism and Maitreya in Buddhism. Humanity's need for a 'saviour' when a mirror would suffice has long been exploited by the few to control the many. Christian Zionism, a Sabbatian-Frankist creation, has entrapped so many Christian believers, especially in the American Deep South, into waiting for the Messiah and supporting the Israel-Jerusalem agenda of Sabbatian-Frankists and ultra-Zionists in the belief that this must happen before their Messiah can come. They think they are talking about Messiah 'Jesus' while the Sabbatian-Frankists plan someone, or something, very different. By the time they realise that it will be too late. Christians call the dawning of the Messianic Age the 'Kingdom of God' and the 'world to come', but they are going to be in for a shock. They have been taught (programmed) to believe that the 'End Times' will bring great trials, tribulations and upheavals which they welcome as signs that 'Jesus' is coming. In fact these planned happenings are the very Problem-Reaction-Solution scenario being played out by Sabbatian-

Frankists to usher in their own 'Messiah' – and a global control system based in Israel. The picture is far bigger than almost anyone has grasped and even Sabbatian-Frankism is only a relatively modern expression of the Hidden Hand Master Plan. It goes way back beyond the emergence of the Bible and thus this is a document encoded with the same basic themes that you find in the *Protocols* and other 'prophetic' works from sources that knew the score. Christians have been had – Christian Zionists have been *massively* had – and where this has all been leading is getting mighty close. The restoration of Israel and the Jewish return is at the very core of Christian Zionist belief and hence all the money they have contributed to making that happen while the Death Cult can barely hold back their contempt and amusement. Messiah Jesus is supposed to save the righteous, judge the wicked, and restore peace to the world which is what Sabbatian-Frankists claim for their Messiah or 'World King' when the idea is to instigate a global tyranny. They are pulling in the gullible until the point of stopping what is planned has passed. Then reality will dawn.

The Torah, or first five books of the Hebrew Bible (Genesis, Exodus, Leviticus, Numbers, and Deuteronomy) do not specifically mention a 'Messiah' returning although the term 'End of Days' is seized upon by the messianic fanatics along with other quotes about a leader who would restore and rule Israel. Sabbatian-Frankists as a Kabbalah occult religion reject the Torah. The far more extreme Talmud – the guide for ultra-Zionists – reserves the title Moshiach, or Melech HaMoshiach (the King Messiah), for the leader who will 'redeem Israel' in the End of Days. It is claimed that all the nations of the world will recognize Moshiach to be the world leader and will accept his dominion in the Messianic Era. Note how Christians and Christian Zionists say the same about Jesus. Maimonides, a famous Jewish philosopher and codifier of the 12th century, said that the Messiah, or Moshiach, will rebuild the Temple and bring back the exiles. Jerusalem and the Temple would be the focus of divine worship, and 'from Zion shall go forth … the word of the Lord from Jerusalem'. The Sanhedrin rabbinical courts would return and decide matters of law. Jerusalem's Supreme Court built by the Rothschilds was really designed for this purpose with all its satanic symbolism. Jesus was condemned to death by the Sanhedrin in the New Testament story and I wonder if Christian Zionists are following all this? The Sanhedrin this time around are meant to decree law for the whole world and not only Israel. I read that 'the coming of Moshiach will complete God's purpose in creation', but my question is this: Why does 'God' have an obsession with 0.2 percent of the world population on a planet that's a billionth the size of a pinhead compared with the projected extent of the Universe? What manipulative bollocks it all is.

Control the tech – control the world

What is planned for humanity and how it can be achieved can only be understood from the perspective of the 'smart' technological society that has emerged 'out of nowhere' so fast and taken over human focus, perception and perspective. This has been planned all along because the inner sanctum of Sabbatian-Frankism is operating from a very different timeline and level of knowledge to the general population. I am not going into why that is because it is detailed at length in *Everything You Need to Know but Have Never Been Told*. There are reasons for this, however, and they explain how Aldous Huxley could describe modern drug and genetic techniques in 1932, George Orwell describe smart televisions ('telescreens') in 1948, and Dr Richard Day describe the Internet in 1969. There are two 'worlds' in terms of knowledge and projected 'future'. The human population lives in one and the *inner core* of the Hidden Hand and Sabbatian-Frankism lives in quite another. The technology now available and that which is about to be introduced offers the potential to control all human minds and perceptual processes and to do so from a single location – *Israel*. This control system is planned to be operated by artificial intelligence and that is the real meaning of 'Supreme Lord', 'King of the World' and 'from Zion shall go forth … the word of the Lord from Jerusalem'. I'm not saying they don't plan some form of figurehead around which to sell this control, but artificial intelligence is the means of delivery and the real practical meaning of the terms. This is why today Israel is fast becoming the technology centre of the world which is planned to eclipse Silicon Valley that it already controls from afar through front men and women and the Sabbatian-Frankist-owned Pentagon and US intelligence networks. Silicon Valley giants systematically censor criticism of Israel and exposure of the Sabbatian-Frankist conspiracy in all its expressions because it is owned by that conspiracy and thus employs ultra-Zionist censors such as the Anti-Defamation League (ADL), Southern Poverty Law Center (SPLC) and others of their mendacious ilk to recommend what and who should be banned. Humanity has been led like lambs to the slaughter along a technological Totalitarian Tiptoe towards complete enslavement of body, mind and emotions. The plan – which I have long warned about and is now being openly promoted – is to connect the human brain/body to artificial intelligence which would then *become the human mind and all human perception*. Don't take my work for it. Ultra-Zionist Ray Kurzweil, the 'futurist' Google executive, is a central figure predicting and promoting the brain-AI connection to start in earnest by 2030 (Fig 148). He describes how the global population will be perceptually connected to 'the cloud' (which is controlled through ultra-Zionist-controlled Silicon Valley corporations and other ultra-Zionist

Figure 148: The end of humanity (as long planned) if we allow this to happen.

fronts like Amazon and is planned to be ultimately controlled from Israel). Kurzweil says:

Our thinking ... will be a hybrid of biological and non-biological thinking ... humans will be able to extend their limitations and 'think in the cloud' ... We're going to put gateways to the cloud in our brains ... We're going to gradually merge and enhance ourselves ... In my view, that's the nature of being human – we transcend our limitations. As the technology becomes vastly superior to what we are then the small proportion that is still human gets smaller and smaller and smaller until it's just utterly negligible.

Kurzweil also writes in the book *The Scientific Conquest of Death*:

It will be routine practice to have billions of nanobots (nano-scale robots) coursing through the capillaries of our brains, communicating with each other (over a wireless local area network), as well as with our biological neurons and with the Internet. One application will be to provide full-immersion virtual reality that encompasses all our senses.

I call this the 'assimilation' when our minds will literally no longer be our own, but controlled through AI and by whatever controls AI – Sabbatian-Frankists and the Hidden Hand (and what controls them – see my other books). The takeover of human society will be complete and humanity will be controlled and directed from Israel. This has been the long-unfolding Totalitarian Tiptoe with only the final stage still to come. The AI-brain connection is planned to be made by injecting chips or a connecting 'mesh' into the brain and through other less intrusive methods of securing brain access. Preparation and manipulated acceptance of this human-AI fusion can be seen all around us. Before you can make a physical connection between humans and AI you have to establish a psychological connection. You have to *humanise* AI and make the interaction between the two like a human to human. This is a major reason for the 'personal assistant' technology known under many names including Alexa, Siri, Google Assistant and so on which are also surveillance devices. The technology was seed-funded by DARPA, the technological-development arm of the Pentagon, and is designed to humanise AI on the road to total control by AI. Notice the AI dolls and other toys for children through which they can converse with AI as if it is human and research has shown that AI can program their perceptions. It's all the same story. Watch, too, for laws protecting robots as if they are human as we head towards a human-AI connection that will be the end of humanity as we know it – the plan all along. Other psychological preparation comes in the form of what is called pre-emptive programming. The world we are being led into is so fantastically different to the one we have known that this chasm of difference is a massive potential point of resistance to accepting its introduction. You want to do *what?* We are therefore being bombarded with Hollywood movies and television programmes depicting this very world to develop a conscious and subconscious 'pre-emptive' *familiarity* to dilute this potential resistance to the society the Hidden Hand wants to impose. The main focus is again on the young because they will be adults when this is meant to be brought in full-blown. Demonising older people and creating a disconnect between young and old is designed to dismiss the concerns of those who remember when the world was not like the one it is so fast becoming. They can thus see the scale and consequences of what is happening. If you are born into the world as it is now that's all you have known and only the awake will see what an Orwellian nightmare it really is.

Mind hack

Humanity has been guided like laboratory rats along a technological journey leading to the brain-AI connection and the end of human thinking and perception. Firstly the population was addicted to technology that they hold – 'holdables' – and for vast swathes of humankind this has already been achieved thanks to Hidden Hand tech companies like Apple and Samsung (Fig 149). By early 2019 it was estimated that more than five billion people have mobile devices with more than half of them smartphones in a world population of 7.7 billion. Smartphone and tablet devices have seized control of children and adults alike as they stare at the screen in a zombie-trance while increasingly incapable of meaningful human interaction. Phones have isolated families in the same home with some having to be texted that

Figure 149: Welcome to 'childhood'. Time for tea, kids. Kids? *HELLOOO!*

their dinner is ready because shouting up the stairs no longer has any effect during their screen 'fixes'. Almost everywhere you see human activity there are eyes welded to screens and the rest of the world doesn't exist. Cyberspace is the new realty, the new 'real world'. Smart technology has catastrophically transformed human relationships and discourse and with its associated social media has hijacked childhood, destroyed self-esteem and is literally rewiring brain function. Until relatively recently scientists believed that once the brain was formed that was it. From then on nothing changed. Now they know very different. Through a process known as placidity the brain is constantly changing in line with *information received* and *how* it is received. The sudden and incessant explosion of information received digitally and electronically is transforming the human brain and the way it processes information – and so reality and perception. Humanity is being rewired and that's especially happening with the young because they do not have the same perceptual resistance of some older people who have earlier perceptions to give them perspective on how the world is changing so quickly. I've already said that those born into this technological Alcatraz think this is how the world is. It is their 'normal'. A few generations pass and it becomes the *only* normal and this is the game that's playing out. As neuron networks and pathways change so does the way information is processed and from that comes changed perception. Think of a computer programmed to compute only in line with the codes of the program. This and the impact of psychopathic social media has coincided with rapidly rising depression, anxiety and suicide rates among the young. Teenage suicides soared by 67 percent between 2010 and 2017 alone in England and Wales and that figure will not only continue to rise but will be matched in other countries with the same or greater smartphone/social media usage. Here is glimpse of what is happening worldwide to young people as they are perceptually and psychologically targeted to become the programmed AI-controlled zombie adults of the near future. This is a report in the UK *Daily Mail*:

> More than 40,000 British 'hermit kids' are locking themselves away from the world for months or even years, shocking research has discovered. The study says chronic social isolation is increasingly affecting young people from all backgrounds and is driven by a combination of poor academic attainment and anxiety about finding good jobs. Many with the condition become obsessed with social media and live effectively virtual lives.

We are allowing the young to be literally *possessed* by technology driven by the Death Cult and the term 'virtual lives' is a potent one. The population, especially young people, is being absorbed into the 'virtual world' because the plan is for humanity to live permanently in a 'virtual world' through a connection with AI. What is coming off these devices is purposely designed to be electromagnetically addictive. The brain operates electrically and electromagnetically and 'placidity' rewires neuron networks to sync with the frequency fields of smart technology. Addiction follows because the brain demands a constant fix of the electrical/electromagnetic/digital stimulus it has been wired to process. When someone puts the phone down the brain goes into 'cold turkey' as it craves the stimulus. The person then picks up the phone again for no conscious reason because addiction is calling the shots. People and particularly the young think they are constantly on the phone for their own reasons when really the brain-stimulus connection is driving everything. Once this brain-phone frequency connection is achieved then information – much of it subliminal beyond the perceptions of the conscious mind – can be transferred and dictate perception. This is happening to people all the time that the phone is on and through Wi-Fi even when it's not. 'Smart' brains are being hacked and hijacked to be anything but 'smart'. If people really care about their children they should get them off the phones and let them get their minds back. I have a lower-tech phone that stays in the draw for months on end and is only very rarely used when I am going to be nowhere near a proper phone and need to be contacted. Even then I use it on speaker away from my head and all the cumulative damage that would do bombarding my brain with microwaves at touching-range. I quickly note the basic information I need to know and arrange for a later conversation at length if necessary on a landline phone. I don't feel 'deprived' in the least not carrying a smartphone and if I need to speak with people in the usual course of events I have a wired phone to do that. It's not always instant, but so what? Like all addictions people think they need them but when they overcome the addiction they realise that they don't. We are looking at a silent 'holocaust' and humanity is going to reap the whirlwind with the longer-term effect on human brain and body health. This applies especially to children who are using phones while their brains are still forming. Those deep in the shadows behind all this know the consequences and have coldly planned for them to happen. It is a Death Cult after all.

Gotcha!

Stage two of the 'Tiptoe' are 'wearables' worn *on* the body en route to *in* the body. These are Bluetooth devices, Apple watches, and a long and ever lengthening list of Internet-attached technology that people wear including circuitry stitched into clothes for a better cell phone signal and 'electronic tattoos' which are nothing more than microchips on the skin and only one step from under the skin (Fig 150). Wearables are only a middle step to what has been the aim all along – implantable technology

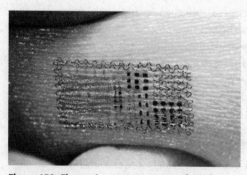

Figure 150: Electronic tattoos – one step from the microchip.

in the body and brain. This is the stage we are fast entering now. Thousands of people have already been microchipped in Sweden and I warned in my books from the mid-1990s that these 'implantables' were coming globally. My words were dismissed then as an example of my 'madness' and yet implantables are here as with a tidal wave of other 'crazy' information I have published over the years which is now happening. I write things and system-thinkers say that's crazy; then they happen. I write new things and same system-thinkers say *that's* crazy and so it continues. I shake my head and keep on writing. This news report about Swedish microchipping captures the Totalitarian Tiptoe without realising that:

> Technology continues to get closer and closer to our bodies, from the phones in our pockets to the smartwatches on our wrists. Now, for some people, it's getting under their skin. In Sweden, a country rich with technological advancement, thousands have had microchips inserted into their hands.
>
> The chips are designed to speed up users' daily routines and make their lives more convenient — accessing their homes, offices and gyms is as easy as swiping their hands against digital readers. They also can be used to store emergency contact details, social media profiles or e-tickets for events and rail journeys within Sweden.

Actually, the chips are designed for far deeper reasons than those described there. 'Benefits' listed like opening doors (lazy bastards) are only the selling points. The real deal is external access and manipulation of the human body through which mayhem and control is planned to ensue. The deeper reasons and fine detail of the technology / AI hijack can be found in *Everything You Need To Know But Have Never Been Told*. In brief, however, external access to the body can literally decide if you live or die. The body in its base form is an electromagnetic vibrating information field which you can think of as a Wi-Fi field that operates to optimum in its natural and balanced frequency state. Health and clear thinking comes from this energetic harmony while illness, 'physical' and psychological, comes from disharmony in the field – dis-ease. The brain processes information electrically and communicates with the cellular structure the same way. Any external frequency disturbance from Wi-Fi and other technologically-generated electrical and electromagnetic communications and fields will disrupt and potentially devastate the natural electromagnetic balance and cause anything from mild to catastrophic consequences for 'physical', mental and emotional health. Dramatic increases in depression and anxiety, dementia, suicide (see the young), and other states of emotional imbalance have all happened in the 'smart'/social media era and that is not a coincidence. They are the consequences of energetic (information) disharmony, scrambled brain function and skewed information processing. What are social media 'trolls' except deeply scrambled and imbalanced people? The difference between I am full of joy and I want to kill myself is the difference in how information is processed – same glass, same liquid, but is it half full or half empty? Distorted electrical communication between brain and cells is going to have obvious consequences for health. Observe what happens on the screen of a computer when its communication system is malfunctioning or what happens to analogue radio reception in a vehicle when you drive under electrical pylon cables. Distort the communication and you distort the outcome. In the body/brain's case this is the 'physical', mental and emotional outcome. I will address in a moment the current introduction of 5G communication systems when all of the above will *massively* increase in both scale and effect because of its frequency range and vastly increased power compared with even where we have come so far.

Humanity's perceptions and reactions have been manipulated for thousands of years through control of information received. Religion and various expressions of Problem-Reaction-Solution are only two of the endless examples of how this has been done. The smart era, however, is allowing this to enter a whole new level of control through frequency manipulation. Every thought and emotion is a unique frequency. Love and hate, joy and depression all have their own frequencies and if you can externally generate those frequencies you can trigger the corresponding mental and emotional states in people individually and collectively. The brain picks up the frequency of a thought or emotion in an energetic field like Wi-Fi or directly through microchips and it processes that information into what the person experiences as the corresponding perception or emotion. '*I am* depressed, angry or dispirited' is the subsequent response when the '*I am*' is really being externally generated. I have documented this technological potential for frequency mind-control at great length over the years and it is becoming ever more effective. Dr Andrija Puharich, an American medical and parapsychological researcher, discovered in the 1950s that frequencies affect perception and so behaviour. He used frequencies to change behaviour by manipulating DNA and its 'encoder/decoder' RNA. It has long been known by cutting edge, independent-minded scientists (a comparatively tiny minority) that DNA is a receiver-transmitter of information and can be likened to an antenna. If you communicate with DNA using frequencies related to specific perpetual and emotional states you will cause people to think and feel that same way. This also applies to the brain. Even more than that you can by synching with the frequency of DNA make a connection (known as 'entrainment') and then move its 'dial' to another frequency. You could think of this is terms of a computer mouse connecting ('entraining') with a file icon and dragging it to another location or, in this case, frequency. When the DNA frequency switch is complete the genetic antenna is picking up a different information source which has corresponding perceptual, emotional and 'physical' effects. This way you can so affect DNA, the code of life, that it mutates the body into a different form. Yes, technological entrainment with DNA has the potential to mutate humanity into a whole new species and this is happening step-by-step today driven by the Hidden Hand and its Sabbatian-Frankists.

The end of men

Masculinity is being systematically deleted this way through technological frequencies aided by societal pressures and female hormones polluting water supplies by the content of contraceptive pills and other such drugs being peed into the system. We have fish changing from male to female or somewhere in between through chemical pollution of rivers and streams. Contraceptive pills contain the hormones oestrogen (estrogen) and progesterone. Oestrogen is the primary female sex hormone which will have obvious implications if it accumulates in men while Dr Diana Fleischman and a team at the University of Portsmouth discovered, albeit in a relatively small sample, an apparent connection between progesterone levels and sexual attitudes. Women with more progesterone are more likely to be open to relationships with other women and this was found to be even more the case with male-male relationships among men that have high levels of progesterone. For sure sperm counts and male testosterone levels have fallen dramatically and all the attacks on men – especially white men – to demonise 'toxic masculinity' are all part of this process of de-masculinisation of human society for reasons I will come to. Another reason for falling sperm counts is the effect of frequencies emanating from smartphones when men carry them in trouser pockets. This frequency bombardment kills sperm and 5G will enormously increase that process. A vital point here is that *everything* has its own particular frequency including hormones and if the population is bathed in these frequencies through the technological 'sea' via Wi-Fi and other sources those hormones will be stimulated in the body. Broadcast the frequency of radio station A and you will get radio station A. Broadcast the frequency of oestrogen and progesterone and that's what you will get. Scientist Albert Einstein said:

> Everything is energy [information] and that's all there is to it. Match the frequency of the reality you want and you can't help but get that reality.

Dr Andrija Puharich found that frequencies of 10.80Hz produce 'riotous behaviour' and 6.6Hz makes people depressed. If you want a riot as a Problem-Reaction-Solution to justify more police and surveillance powers or divide and rule you just bathe the target area with the frequencies of rage and 'riotous behaviour' and then light the fuse with an event or situation. Hey, presto, the primed people will rage and riot because their symbolic or literal triggers are already cocked and waiting to fire. There are frequencies to stimulate mass hysteria, fear and outrage. People have no idea how they are being played with and manipulated while they believe that their thoughts, emotions and decisions are coming from within themselves. The US military has used frequency technology to break the spirit of an enemy so they walk out with their hands up and they use the same techniques on the general population. I have read technical reports of experiments in Russia decades ago when behaviour instructions were delivered to people through frequencies directing them to take certain actions and immediately the technology was activated the targets did exactly what they were told while believing they were making the decisions. Journalist Curtis Waltman had a shock when he filed a Freedom of Information Act request with Washington State Fusion Center (partnered with the US Department of Homeland Security) for information about white supremacist groups. He was sent by mistake a file on 'psycho-electric weapons' including electromagnetic effects on the human body and 'remote mind control'. They included descriptions of how electromagnetism can be used for various forms of remotely-induced torture, mind infiltration and perception manipulation including 'forced memory blanking', 'sudden violent itching inside eyelids', 'wild flailing', 'rigor mortis' and 'forced orgasm'. Remote attack and control systems in the documents were described to me by insiders many years earlier. From this perspective it is sobering to ponder on the potential power for mass human control of those who direct the technology and what frequency instructions and perceptions it delivers. The power of consciousness and will can overcome these effects but most people have had their personal power so drained and their responses so programmed that they are babes in arms when the button is pressed.

Why they are called SECRET societies

I am staying with themes rather than fine detail on these subjects because there is no point in repeating what is available in my other books like *Everything You Need To Know But Have Never Been Told*. Themes can be extremely effective in connecting dots and forming pictures and here are the basic themes that we face. The Hidden Hand and Sabbatian-Frankists know how reality works and how we interact with it. This forms the foundation of 'occult' (hidden) knowledge passed on through secret societies and Satanism to the chosen few across the generations. The knowledge is hidden or 'occult' for a reason. They don't want the target population to know what *they* know or the potential for using that knowledge to control and suppress is dramatically diluted. We are back to Joseph Goebbels again: 'Propaganda [or in this case secret knowledge] becomes ineffective the moment we become aware of it.' While the population goes about its daily business believing largely in the 'physical', 'solid' reality perceived by the five senses the Hidden Hand and Sabbatian-Frankists know that our reality in its prime form consists of waveform radiation fields encoded with information that we decode into the 'physical' world of the five senses. The principle is the same as a computer decoding information from Wi-Fi fields and presenting it on the screen in a totally different form. Our 'screen' is in the brain and that's the only place the world we think is outside of us really exists. The process is the same as computers decoding the Internet. We experience the Internet as pictures, words and graphics, but they only exist in that form on the computer screen (Fig 151). The information exists in its base form as Wi-Fi radiation fields and electronic communication systems. Computers are designed to decode information from that form into what we see on the screen and the biological computer that we call the human body does the same as we decode waveform information into electrical,

Figure 151: Computers decode information encoded in waveform radiation fields into a very different form on the screen.

digital and holographic information that we perceive as the 'external' 'physical' world. The five senses decode waveform information into electrical information which is communicated to the brain to be decoded into digital holographic (illusory 'physical') information (Fig 152 overleaf).

The Hidden Hand knows all this and it absolutely doesn't want you to know. Notice how

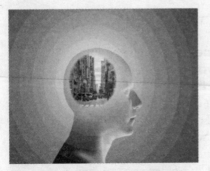

Figure 152: How the human biological computer decodes 'physical' reality from waveform 'cosmic Wi-Fi' that we experience as the illusion of an external world.

rarely the nature of reality is even mentioned in 'education' or the media except to repeat the 'it's all solid and real' nonsense pedalled by most of mainstream science and the establishment in general. By keeping this secret they can manipulate people en masse by understanding reality as it really is while the population believes in a reality that doesn't actually exist – a 'solid', 'physical' world of apparently extreme limitation. The Hidden Hand knows that reality is malleable because it is *not* solid and can be manipulated by changing the nature of the information content of electromagnetic fields and the use of specific frequencies to manifest specific ends. Albert Einstein again: 'Match the frequency of the reality you want and you can't help but get that reality.' This describes very well how humanity is controlled and directed – match the frequency of the reality you want people to believe in and they will then believe in that reality. Bathe the human environment with frequencies that match the mental and emotional states in which you wish to enslave the population; then target, marginalise, ridicule and, if possible, destroy those who expand their minds beyond those prison-frequencies and see the world as it really is. Throughout history such people have been perceived as mad or dangerous (then later right) by the perceptual 'norms' of the time because the population in general, enslaved by perceptual and frequency programming, cannot compute what the visionaries are seeing and perceiving. Legendary artist/inventor Leonardo Da Vinci is a perfect example. He wasn't ahead of his time in the 15th and 16th centuries, but *beyond* time – beyond the perceptual walls of experienced reality where the illusion of 'time' appears to be real. It is no more 'real' than solidity, as I explain in other books, and the Hidden Hand is well aware of that.

'Smart Grid' – the Endgame

From this background we can begin to grasp what the technological 'revolution' and 'smart society' is really all about and the power over the human mind and global society that would come from controlling the fast emerging 'Smart Grid' which I say is planned to be centred eventually in Israel. Who could not have noticed the ubiquitous prefix of 'smart'? We have smartphones, smart meters, smart televisions, smart cards, smart cars, smart driving, smart roads, smart pills, smart dust, smart patches, smart watches, smart skin, smart borders, smart pavements, smart streets, smart cities, smart communities, smart environments, smart growth, smart planet ... smart *everything*. These and all the other 'smarts' are connected parts of the new smart global society planned to be controlled in intricate detail and 24/7 by the 'Smart Grid'. A 'smart object' is defined as something that 'interacts with not only people but also with other smart objects'. Together they form a global grid of 'smart' electrical/electromagnetic/digital information sources controlled by artificial intelligence which means by whatever or whoever controls artificial intelligence. This is the grid or 'cloud' that people like ultra-Zionist Ray Kurzweil at Google says will be connected to the human brain by 2030 and expand thereafter to *become* the human mind. This is the real reason for smart meters planned for every home and business and being promoted like crazy by corporations, media and government. Smart meters are electromagnetic fields – another form of Wi-Fi – through which information can be gleaned from your home and with which your body, mind and emotions are interacting through frequency effects and connections. The meters, like the Smart Grid itself, are both a form of surveillance and mind or perceptual control able to manipulate what you think and feel. They are information delivery systems and the frequencies can be changed and ramped up once in place. The 'cloud' is not only one source, but multiple fields of electromagnetic and electrical/digital information designed to form one global system. Smart meters connect with Wi-Fi (ground-based and

Figure 153: The 'cloud'.

beamed from satellite), smartphone communication masts and networks, the Internet, artificial intelligence etc. (Fig 153 on previous page).

The 'Internet of Things'

It seems like only yesterday that I was warning about the plan for the Pentagon/CIA/Hidden Hand-driven 'Internet of Things' (IoT) to which all technology would be connected – everything from household appliances to televisions to vehicles and once again *everything*. All this is happening now on a mega and ever-growing scale with billions of items connected and controlled through the Internet because the Hidden Hand Sabbatian-Frankist agenda is moving so quickly. The speed in part is to have the Smart Grid in place and dictating human life before the population has realised what is going on and why. I am seeking to bring forward that realisation with this and other books while the Death Cult seeks to silence me. I have been predicting for so long what I called the technological sub-reality which is today known as the Smart Grid or 'cloud'. This is the 'Zion Mainframe' to which everything is planned to be connected including the human mind (Fig 154). The Internet of Things with the human brain added becomes the all-controlling Internet of Everything. Nano-technology far smaller than the eye can see is being embedded everywhere. They are calling this 'nanobots' or 'smart dust' – nano-microchips all communicating with each other no matter what

Figure 154: The 'Internet of Everything'.

their location. Nano-chips in pavements, walls, lamp posts, computers, vehicles, aircraft, energy and electrical systems, human brains/bodies and so on would form one grid of communication controlled from a central point (I say Israel) via 'hubs' around the world. Information passing through this system would decide if your car will start and where it will go through self-drive vehicles; if an aircraft falls from the sky; if you have warmth and at what level; if doors will open and elevators will work; if you eat; and, most crucially, the Smart Grid will dictate what you are thinking and feeling once the human-AI connection is made. *Nothing* will happen, including human behaviour, unless decided or deemed acceptable by the AI Smart Grid. A key to this is smart dust which is being released in the atmosphere to be breathed in and connect people to the Smart Grid network. A prime vehicle for this is what are called 'chemtrails'. These are released from aircraft and appear at first to be contrails caused by heat from engine exhaust interacting with the cold air at high altitude. The difference is that contrails quickly disperse as the exhaust heat cools while chemtrails don't disperse and instead expand and eventually fall to earth (Fig 155). I have watched military and other planes so many times around the world criss-crossing the sky pouring out their chemtrails until a clear blue sky looks like a cloudy day. They began to be noticed in the late 1990s and are now everywhere. After decades of denying that chemtrails were real Microsoft's Bill Gates and others are calling for precisely the

same process to be officially implemented to block out the sun to 'save the world from climate change'. It is obvious that connecting everything through nano-smart dust would require it to be released from the sky. What Google's ultra-Zionist Ray Kurzweil describes could only be achieved through aerial distribution:

Figure 155: Chemtrails. Nothing to worry about – perfectly natural.

Nanobots [smart dust] will infuse all the matter around us with information. Rocks, trees, everything will become these intelligent creatures.

By 'intelligent' he means controlled by AI – and who will control the AI? Yep, right first time. We are hearing gathering warnings from independent scientists about drugs, chemicals and frequency technology that is undermining the 'blood-brain barrier' which protects the brain from being infiltrated by dangerous foreign bodies or substances. This is an explanation from a science website:

> The blood-brain barrier (BBB) is formed by brain endothelial cells lining the cerebral microvasculature, and is an important mechanism for protecting the brain from fluctuations in plasma composition, and from circulating agents such as neurotransmitters and xenobiotics capable of disturbing neural function.

The concerted and multi-faceted attack on the blood-brain barrier is to allow, among other things, the passage of smart dust nano-microchips to infiltrate and manipulate brain function. What is freedom in a single word? *Choice*. The more choices you can make the freer you are and the AI Smart Grid is about deleting all choice that doesn't suit the elite controlling the grid. What's more – take away choice and you delete what it means to be human and replace that with little more than a robotic zombie programmed to do and 'decide' whatever the system demands.

Smart cities

You will be hearing more and more about 'smart cities' in which chips and nano-chips are everywhere controlling everything externally through AI (Fig 156). New smart cities are being built and others transformed into smart cities. Sabbatian-Frankist Saudi Arabia is building a $500 billion smart city 33

Figure 156: Coming to every city if they have their way.

times the size of New York on the Red Sea coast near the border with Jordan. The real reason for smart cities is hidden in the verbiage and misleading cliché descriptions like this one from IBM:

> Cognitive computing and its capacity for building citizen engagement introduce fresh opportunities for government organizations to improve citizens' lives and the business environment, deliver personalized experiences, and optimize program and service outcomes.

So what the hell does that mean? The Smart Cities Council definition gets closer to the truth while still ignoring the real motivation which is human control. It describes a smart city 'as one that has digital technology embedded across all city functions'. Yes, as I have described with the consequences for human freedom ignored. An article at Openingdoors.alj.com also attempts a definition with this: 'As processing power continues to increase at an exponential rate, and artificial intelligence, big data, cloud computing, and the Internet of Things reshape our lives, smart cities aim to harness these tools to transform their ability to meet the demands of 21st Century living.' Good except for the last bit where 'demands of 21st Century living' should read 'demands of 21st Century control'. The article listed seven major elements to smart cities with supporting comments:

- 5G mobile networks, which are expected to be up to 60 times quicker than 4G networks and available by 2020 [I will come to the real reason for 5G in a moment].
- Blockchain, a financial technology that allows transactions to do away with intermediaries like stock exchanges that currently function as guarantors of a transaction.
- Artificial intelligence, which is already being used by Hong Kong, Shanghai, Sydney and New York to deliver smart parking and increased energy efficiency in buildings.
- Autonomous vehicles, which are set to have an enormous impact in the coming decades. Research has suggested autonomous taxis and rapid inter-urban rail systems could combine to reduce the numbers of cars in a city by up to 90%.
- Low-cost space exploration and micro-satellites, which will be the key element in powering the 20 billion connected things research firm Gartner expects to be in use by 2020 [more shortly].
- Biometrics, which could rapidly increase the number of people around the world who are able to prove their identity, thereby reducing fraud, waste and corruption [24/7 tracking and control].
- Drones, which when paired with artificial intelligence, could soon perform everything from parcel deliveries to hazardous jobs, such as maintenance checks on rooftops or towers.

The EU wants all new vehicles from 2022 to have AI controls on speed that stop anyone exceeding speed limits through the installation of 'Intelligent Speed Assistance limiters' connected to GPS satellite location monitors and traffic sign recognition cameras. This is not about safety – the Death Cult couldn't care less about that. It's all about control. Israel dominates the market for in-vehicle AI technology which can externally take over your vehicle and drive it into a wall or over a cliff if the hacker operator so decides. It's no good people laughing at that – go on the Internet and see external control of vehicle systems demonstrated. Then think aircraft and 9/11. All this is only a stepping stone – a Totalitarian Tiptoe – to AI driven vehicles which are planned to replace all current human-controlled transport eventually – cars, trucks, buses, trains and aircraft. The business model of Silicon Valley-based global taxi company Uber is founded on AI-driven taxis. Current drivers, who are often treated with contempt by the company, are only a transition to self-drive. Uber has lost a fortune on the road to what is planned to be a global monopoly and yet money is always there to keep it expanding (see Amazon).

Just a search engine? Just a social media site?

Technology on which the Internet is based came from the military and in particular DARPA, the Pentagon's Defense Advanced Research Projects Agency, which has given the world enormous gifts of peace and love like death rays. They are

such nice people. In fact, so lovely they seed-funded personal assistant technology because they care so much about human happiness. DARPA seed-funds Silicon Valley companies and technology that it believes will help with its agenda of human surveillance and control – as does the CIA with its seed-funding arm In-Q-Tel which put money into Google

Figure 157: The Pentagon runs Silicon Valley and Sabbatian-Frankism runs the Pentagon *and* Silicon Valley

before it was called Google (Fig 157). The bottom line is that DARPA did not develop and release the military technology on which the Internet is based unless that served the agenda of its controllers – the Hidden Hand and Sabbatian-Frankist Death Cult. How coincidental that the Internet is the very foundation of the Smart Grid. The Internet of Things allows control of human society and 24/7 surveillance not least through connection to smart televisions with their cameras and microphones monitoring you in your own home (Orwell's telescreens) and today's TVs are only the opening versions and not where they are planned to go. The Internet was described by ultra-Zionist asset Dr Richard Day in 1969 long before it became reality and it is a long-planned global Trojan horse. The Internet has been the fishing line to capture human life and that line is now being reeled in. The first stage was to introduce a free and open Internet without censorship to attract so many users that it became the central foundation of human society and irreversibly so. Now that point has been reached what the Internet was planned to be all along has become more evident by the day as the censorship of what can be said and communicated becomes ever more extreme. The plan was to move sources of information that people receive from traditional media such as newspapers onto the Internet where what is seen and not seen can be regulated by AI algorithms. This is exactly what is happening. Another aspect of the strategy was to establish, promote, fund or take over companies to secure near-monopolies on the communication of information. I am talking about Google, Google-owned YouTube, Facebook (which owns Instagram and WhatsApp), Twitter and so on. Once again to become near monopolies they had to sell themselves as free and uncensored to attract the audience and have access to funding that trounced potential competitors. Then, once market domination was achieved, what they were always planned to be was unleashed in a frenzy of censorship to promote the Death Cult agenda and silence its critics and exposers. Once again this is so clearly what is happening. The same process can be seen with Amazon which dominates the book and retail market and is now censoring the 'wrong' books when it wasn't doing so as its domination was being secured.

The extraordinary ratio of Zionist control can also be seen with people like Sergey Brin and Larry Page (Google and parent company Alphabet); Susan Wojcicki (YouTube); Mark Zuckerberg and Sheryl Sandberg (Facebook); and Arthur D. Levinson (Apple chairman). Another Apple board member is ultra-Zionist Bob Iger, chairman and CEO at Disney. The small world nature of Silicon Valley and connected parts of The Web can be seen with Apple board member Ronald D. Sugar, chairman of Uber and former chairman and CEO of global arms manufacturer Northrop Grumman, and with the connections involving YouTube CEO Susan Wojcicki, a former executive of Google. Her ultra-Zionist sister Anne was married to Google co-founder Sergey Brin and now runs Silicon Valley DNA testing company 23andMe which was funded by both Google and biotech giant Genentech whose CEO was Arthur D. Levinson, chairman of Apple (he replaced Steve Jobs). Levinson is a former director of Google who is founder and CEO of biotech company Calico owned by Google parent company Alphabet. Google and Facebook are phenomenally important assets of The Web because of their power over the circulation of information. Google suppresses search engine listings of the alternative media while Facebook (like Google/Alphabet's YouTube) increasingly outright bans information that challenges the elite agenda or 'shadow' bans it which means that while it can be posted algorithms ensure its audience is tiny and nothing like what it would otherwise be. This is not, however, the full extent of Google and Facebook service to the Hidden Hand and The Web. They both play globally crucial roles in surveillance and data gathering for intelligence and military networks and if they didn't exist the intelligence-military complex would have had to invent them. I say

Figure 158: Regina Dugan – strange career at first glance, but with a common theme.

they did. Big Brother now accrues the fine detail of people's lives and beliefs because the public tell them via Facebook posts and search engine history. Those that appear to run these companies are anything but genuine and trustworthy characters while they promote a fraudulent image of being 'progressive'. The idea that Zuckerberg is ultimately controlling Facebook is a joke when you see his terrified face and staring eyes on being asked even a mildly incisive question.

The Pentagon and CIA have colossal influence over these Internet giants and the Pentagon/CIA in turn are assets of the Hidden Hand and Sabbatian-Frankist Death Cult. Regina Dugan personifies these connections (Fig 158). She was the director of DARPA who then became an executive of Google before moving on to Facebook. Her role in all cases can be summed up by her brief at Facebook – 'to develop technologies that fluidly blend physical and digital worlds'. Or, to be more to the point, to develop technologies that fluidly blend AI with the human brain. 'Retail website and bookseller' Amazon has fundamental connections with the Pentagon and CIA and like Google and Facebook operates at the cutting edge of smart technology and AI. Microsoft is up there, too, and this Bill Gates company has the most obvious surveillance and control connections to computers and other devices that use its software. Even Amazon and Microsoft employees have spoken out against their work with the military, intelligence and law enforcement. Amazon's Jeff Bezos provides cloud services, surveillance and other support for the Pentagon, CIA and police. One Amazon worker said: 'Companies like ours should not be in the business of facilitating authoritarian surveillance. Not now, not ever.' So what if those involved in authoritarian surveillance are the real force behind the company? Microsoft responded with the finger to its employees complaining about technology and weapons contracts with the military. CEO Satya Nadella said: 'We made a principled decision that we're not going to withhold technology from institutions that we have elected in democracies to protect the freedoms we enjoy.' If it wasn't so tragic my belly would ache. Billions of dollars are spent by the Pentagon and intelligence 'community' with Silicon Valley companies which are assets of the military-intelligence complex. Employees need to rub their eyes and see that their pay checks are not coming from companies with humanity's interests at heart – far, far from it. No surprise, then, that Google parent company Alphabet (the CIA, NSA, FBI etc. are known as 'alphabet agencies') is involved in a smart city project in Toronto which foresees everything being controlled and monitored by AI right down to rubbish bins. The plans are being developed by Alphabet-owned and New York-based Sidewalk Labs and the project guided by ultra-Zionist CEO, Dan Doctoroff, who says the smart city development would be built 'from the internet up'. This is what I have been describing. One media report said that the sheer scale of data gathering involved was a cause of concern to those pointing out the Big Brother potential. David Murakami Wood, an associate professor at Queen's University in Kingston, Ontario, said that the public's ability to give consent to trade privacy for convenience 'goes out the window straight away' under the Alphabet/Google scheme: 'I think in some ways what we're facing here is a situation where none of this is very much like anything we've seen before.' That's because we are entering the Hidden Hand endgame and so witnessing a transformation of human society in ways that absolutely have not been seen before.

Behavior control

Those who refuse to submit to this control system will be cut adrift, made a non-person and where necessary eliminated. You will do what you are told in every aspect of life or the AI Smart Grid will give you severe consequences. We are already seeing this emerging in China with the social credit system that decides how you should behave in every area of life and then awards or deletes credits in response. Act as the government demands and you accrue credits. Act in other ways and they are taken away resulting in multiple consequences. Chinese dictators have blocked millions of 'discredited' citizens from buying plane and train tickets. By the end of 2018 the National Public Credit Information Centre said Chinese courts had banned the purchase of plane tickets 17.5 million times and 5.5 million for train tickets. According to a 2014 government document the behaviour credit system is designed to 'allow the trustworthy to roam everywhere under heaven while making it hard for the discredited to take a single step'. Do as we tell you or we'll destroy you. Imagine the potential for this once the world is subject to a global Smart Grid that controls everything. You want to rebel? Okay, well doors will literally not open for you – anywhere. By then every front door, garage door and barrier will only open if the Smart Grid says it can and the codes of your microchips – constantly reprogrammable – allow you to pass through. I saw a *Guardian* article on the China system which reported that critics were claiming the authorities were using technology and big data to create an Orwellian state of mass surveillance and control'. Critics were *claiming?*

You mean that dictating your every behaviour through a governmental and technological carrot and stick is open for debate about whether or not it is an Orwellian state of mass surveillance and control. *What?* Of course it is. What else could it be? What is happening in China under its murderous communist dictatorship is the blueprint for what is planned for the entire world. China today and the world tomorrow – including China's millions of people-recognition cameras that can identity the location of anyone in minutes. Hidden Hand global Internet companies including ultra-Zionist-controlled Facebook, Google, Apple and Microsoft are actively working with Hidden-Hand-controlled China while claiming to be 'progressive' organisations with 'values'.

The plan in the end as AI destroys almost every current form of employment is to introduce a guaranteed income for people. This may sound at first to be a good thing, but the unspoken reason is control. You don't do what we say? Okay, we stop paying your guaranteed income and where else are you going to earn the money so you and your family can eat? All the jobs have gone to AI. Hidden Hand and Sabbatian-Frankist front groups and organisations are calling for this guaranteed income which will make everyone poor except the elite. Facebook's

Figure 159: The planned structure of the 'post-democratic' society with the Smart Grid and AI taking all the jobs and humanity living off a guaranteed income to ensure guaranteed poverty and only paid to those that conform.

multi-billionaire Zuckerberg is one of those calling for a 'universal basic income' because he cares so much about the poor and needy. My god, these people are truly disgusting and yet heroes to Soros 'progressives'. I have used the term 'Hunger Games Society' in other books for the plan to impose a fierce hierarchical structure controlled by the few with everyone else living in poverty controlled by a mercilessness police state (Fig 159). The latter is fast emerging – a military-police state in the end – while plunging the population in totality into collective poverty and control is planned to be achieved by AI taking their jobs and the 'guaranteed income' ensuring everyone-the-same poverty. Those who think none of this applies to them because they have a nice house and good income today should ponder on that and realise that it absolutely *does* apply to them. Basic income would mean the end of property ownership or ownership of anything (except for the elite) and the same outcome for everyone. This is what Soros 'progressives' are demanding as they promote Marxism (see the Soviet Union) as 'socialism'. Equal opportunity is one thing and to be desired, but equal outcome means a race to the bottom for everyone (except the elite).

Watch for the basic income control scam because it's coming unless we collectively wake up to what the game is. The *Protocols* say: 'The people will submit to this regime because it will know that upon these leaders will depend its earnings, gratifications and the receipt of all kinds of benefits.' Dependency is the greatest form of control.

* Glasgow, Scotland's biggest city, is pledged to be a 'smart city' through AI and surveillance technology and has partnered with Israeli government/military-connected Nice Systems which was exposed by Fox News reporter Carl Cameron in his post-9/11 reports about the Israeli spy ring in the United States. Glaswegians who have questioned the use of an Israeli military-connected company to keep surveillance on them have been condemned by the council as 'anti-Semitic'. Well, wave a feather and I shall swoon. Even more reasons to question the involvement of Israeli technology and 'cyber-security' companies follows in the next chapter.

* Another significant Google and parent company Alphabet executive is ultra-Zionist State Department official Jared Cohen, CEO of Jigsaw (formerly Google Ideas) and an Adjunct Senior Fellow at the Council on Foreign Relations. He wrote a book with former Google and Alphabet Executive Chairman Eric Schmidt called *The New Digital Age: Re-shaping the Future of People, Nations and Business.* You get the picture. Cohen and Schmidt attended the elite Sabbatian-Frankist Bilderberg Group meeting in 2019 along with ultra-ultra-Zionist Jared Kushner, senior advisor and son-in-law to 'anti-elite' (yeah, right) Donald Trump.

CHAPTER 27

Eyes wide OPEN (2)

*The only person you are destined to become is the person
you decide to be* – Ralph Waldo Emerson

The term Smart Grid describes AI and wireless connections between
technology and the human brain, all aspects of human society
including household appliances and throughout the natural world. This
will allow the entire human race and everything else to be controlled
and manipulated from a central point once smart dust and other
AI/technological connections are made and turn humanity into one hive
mind dictated by the 'queen' out of Israel. That's my view anyway.

The plan is being sold as a wonderful thing to increase the collective
power of human creativity, but that's just the sales-pitch that claims all
this will make us 'super-human' (Fig 160). It won't – it will make us
post-human. The real reason for the hive mind is the central control of *all*
minds. Scientists are already experimenting with animals to connect
their minds into one 'hive' on the way to doing the same with humans.
To make this and the Smart Grid in general work the Hidden Hand
requires a minimum level of communication and Wi-Fi power of at least
what is known as '5G'. This is another Totalitarian Tiptoe. 'G' stands for
'generation' and so we have been pied-pipered from the first generation
(1G) of wireless communication power through 2G, 3G, 4G and now the
roll-out of 5G. Each one has been more powerful and so has affected
mind and body in more
intrusive ways. We live in an
ever-expanding sea of Wi-Fi
(the 'cloud') that with each
new 'generation' is impacting
on mind and body functions to
ever-greater extremes.
Anything that disrupts and
distorts the electrical and
electromagnetic
communication and
information processing
functions of brain and body is

Figure 160: The real reason is rather different, right,
Mr Kurzweil?

going to disrupt and distort human health and psychology and each new 'generation' is doing this more fundamentally as the power and impact is increased. Observe the soaring increases in cancer, depression, suicide, dementia and Alzheimer's in the Wi-Fi, smartphone era. What is Alzheimer's? Disrupted brain function caused by toxins as well as direct frequencies. The plan is for there to be no escape from Wi-Fi anywhere on earth by having it beamed from satellite to every inch of the planet. No escape is already the case with those in urban areas. We have children at home in a 24/7 Wi-Fi field made worse by smart meters and they walk to school through increasing prevalence of Wi-Fi and sit in classrooms all day awash with Wi-Fi. This is causing cumulative mind and body consequences and very direct ones for many with brain tumours where they put smartphones to their ear. Studies have revealed a massive increase in brain tumours especially among the young near the ear they use to listen to phone calls and 'scientists' say they have no clue what is making this happen when the cause is staring them in the face – or the ear (Fig 161). The 'don't know' is simply protecting their careers and the telecommunications industry and government from exposure that would threatened the roll-out of the Smart Grid within which smartphones are crucial – well, until the microchips are installed that is and AI is directly dictating perception. Humans are now living in a technologically-generated electromagnetic soup and here's a sobering fact: The first mile above the earth is today filled with *two million* times the amount of electromagnetic fields (EMF) that was there in 1900. EMF

Figure 161: It's a mystery, I guess.

radiation has the potential to damage DNA and we are living in an ever more powerful human-generated sea of the stuff which has been systematically created by the Sabbatian-Frankist Death Cult. Canadian neuroscientist Michael Persinger, a long-time researcher on these subjects, said:

For the first time in our evolutionary history we have generated an entire secondary, virtual, densely complex environment – an electromagnetic soup – that essentially overlaps the human nervous system.

This is affecting not only humans but all life on earth throughout the natural world. Animals, trees and plant life are damaged the same as humans through information field distortion and the potential is there to

Figure 162: Shocking: 416 whales beached themselves at the same time in New Zealand.

change the very atmosphere that keeps us alive. We are seeing the effects on marine life, birds, bees and others of having their natural navigation systems disrupted to the point where whales and dolphins have been beaching themselves sometimes in large numbers (Fig 162).

Endgame technology – 5G

All this brings us to 5G. Don't fall for the scam that 5G is just a more powerful version of 4G. That would be bad enough, but it's far worse than just increased power. 5G operates on an entirely new frequency range known as millimeter waves which pulsate their highly disruptive frequencies within the window of 30 and 300 gigahertz and 5G is an ultra-high frequency with ultra-high intensity that will bombard the body-brain with … 90 *billion* electromagnetic waves per second. Just contemplate the consequences of that. The brain, body and DNA receiver-transmission system constantly blasted with 90 *billion* technologically-generated electromagnetic waves per second. When you consider the psychological, emotional and bodily consequences we are already seeing from 4G and lower we are staring in the face of a cumulative human catastrophe for body and mind. Professor Trevor Marshall, Director of the Autoimmunity Research Foundation in California, said:

> The new 5G wireless technology involves millimeter waves (extremely high frequencies) producing photons of much greater energy than even 4G and Wi-Fi. Allowing this technology to be used without proving its safety is reckless in the extreme, as the millimeter waves are known to have a profound effect on all parts of the human body.

Dr Joel Moskowitz, professor of public health at the University of California, Berkeley, said that 5G is a 'massive experiment on all species'. Against this background Dr Graham Downing, who trained in clinical sciences and molecular biology at London's King's College, asks the question: 'Is 5G about to destroy two billion years of evolution?' Put those words and his name into YouTube and you'll see his presentation exposing 5G. Hundreds of doctors and scientists across the world have highlighted how wireless radiation is linked with cancer, brain and immune system malfunction and harm to unborn children. They warn that all these effects threaten to vastly increase with 5G and call for a ban

on its introduction until the facts are known. This is the last thing the
Death Cult wants because independent research publicly circulated
would assign 5G to history. Instead they simply don't fund or consult
independent research and dismiss any that does come to light.
Telecommunications industry representatives were asked at a session of
the US Senate Commerce, Science and Transportation Committee how
much money they had committed to independent research into the
effects of 5G. Answer: *Zero*. Senator Max Blumenthal who conducted the
questioning summed up the responses when he said: 'No research
ongoing – we're flying blind here so far as health and safety is
concerned.' Well, yes and no. They don't want the public to have access
to research that would be the death-knell for 5G but insiders absolutely
know what the effects are going to be in disrupting brain function – clear
thinking and emotional response – and the extraordinary numbers it is
likely to cumulatively kill. We are dealing with a Death Cult lest we
forget and they must have a way of protecting themselves from the
affects their targets will suffer. More confirmation of systematic
suppression of 5G consequences came from Tom Wheeler, then
chairman of the US Federal Communications Commission (FCC) which
is supposed to protect the public from the dangers of technology like 5G.
The Hidden Hand Web ensures, however, that the force controlling the
FCC and other would-be 'protection' agencies also controls the
telecommunications industry and it's a complete stitch-up. Wheeler is a
classic. The fraud that is Barack Obama appointed him as head of the
Federal Communications Commission when his previous jobs included
being a lobbyist for the cable and wireless industry which as FCC
chairman he was supposed to be regulating. He was also president of
the National Cable & Telecommunications Association (NCTA) and CEO
of the Cellular Telecommunications & Internet Association (CTIA). He is
the last person who should have been FCC chief in the light of his
monumental conflicts of interest, but it was fine with Hidden Hand
puppet Obama. Wheeler, who is a serious piece of work, said in a speech
about 5G at the National Press Club in 2016:

> We won't wait for the standards to be first developed in the sometimes
> arduous standards-setting process or in a government-led activity. Instead, we
> will make ample spectrum available and then rely on a private sector-led
> process for producing technical standards best suited for those frequencies
> and use cases.

We'll hand safety regulation to the industry that doesn't want
regulation and is spending zero on independent scientific research into
the consequences of what the industry is doing. If you put 'Tom Wheeler
5G' into YouTube you'll find the speech and I recommend people give it

a look to see the sheer cold-eyed arrogance that we are dealing with. Other 'safety' scams played by industry and government are to focus only on the heating effects of the technology and ignoring all the other far more dangerous aspects and to ensure that official 'safety limits' are always just above whatever the industry needs them to be to do what it wants. The enforced introduction of 5G is being centrally dictated to prevent local opposition blocking the plan and laws and regulations are being imposed to stop local communities refusing to accept it. But we must *not* accept it – under any circumstances.

See no evil

Public opposition is gathering to 5G despite the virtual radar silence on the subject from the mainstream media and we have to act because those who claim to be serving the public interest never will through either malevolence or ignorance and often both. The council leader on the Isle of Wight where I live is a perfect example. His name is Dave Stewart and he took time out from plans to concrete over great swathes of the island to respond to questions about 5G. He said of 5G opposition:

> I am actually an evidence-based individual, when I read some of the things I read and then I research them online I actually have to question the thinking of some people, because it takes them to the extreme of everything.

My experience of Stewart is that little ever emits from his mouth that stands up to scrutiny and he is typical of the political class worldwide. How can he be 'an evidence-based individual' on 5G when there is *no* evidence supporting its safety because there has been no officially-funded independent research? All the truly independent scientific studies done outside the system have pointed to serious dangers. What people like Stewart mean by 'evidence' is 'evidence' that they want to hear. Any other kind – like the obvious truth – is 'the extreme of everything'. Well, here are some 5G consequences that the Stewarts of the political class don't want to hear:

- DNA single and double-strand breaks which genetically mutate and break-down body systems (leading to diseases such as cancer) and seriously disrupt DNA receiver-transmissions which will have catastrophic consequences for mental, emotional and bodily health.

- Infertility, damage to unborn children and miscarriage.

- Heart problems (the heart is pumped by electrical frequencies).

- Oxidative damage (which leads to tissue deterioration and premature ageing).

- Disruption of cellular systems which means a long list of health consequences.

- Increased blood-brain barrier 'permeability' (opening the door to allow toxins and smart dust to enter the brain).

- Melatonin suppression (sleep problems, increased risk of cancer and many other consequences).

- Behaviour problems including memory loss.

- Serious nose bleeds.

Babies, children, pregnant women and the elderly are especially vulnerable to 5G which also has the effect of diminishing antibiotic potency while making bacteria stronger and more resistant. Some politicians with more intelligence and public concern than off-the-peg political class operatives like Dave Stewart are responding to the dangers although how long they will hold out is quite another matter. Among them is Céline Fremault, a minister in the Brussels-Capital Region responsible for Housing, Quality of Life, Environment and Energy. She announced a halt on 5G:

> I cannot welcome such technology if the radiation standards, which must protect the citizen, are not respected, 5G or not. The people of Brussels are not guinea pigs whose health I can sell at a profit. We cannot leave anything to doubt.

Dave Stewart is checking Google as I speak to convince himself that Fremault is at 'the extreme of everything'. Increasing numbers of people are becoming 'electro-hyper-sensitive' through the technologically-generated 'sea' they are now interacting with and they cannot tolerate even low exposure to Wi-Fi fields. What happens to them at even higher frequencies from which they cannot escape because they are literally everywhere? The body bone structure or skeleton is an antenna and so is DNA and the skin. Dr Yael Stein of Jerusalem's Hebrew University wrote to the Federal Communications Commission (wasting his time, ink and paper) to point out that more than 90 percent of microwave radiation is absorbed *by the skin which is like a sponge absorbing microwave radiation*. Dr Stein said that sweat ducts operate as antennas responding to electromagnetic fields. We have millions of these ducts and the effect of 5G is to make them even more conductive. 5G is a military weapon planned to be used on the human race and this skin antenna phenomena has allowed them to develop technology to disperse crowds which broadcasts frequencies within the millimeter 5G range to make people feel like their skin is on fire. This 'Active Denial System' emits frequencies which the skin decodes into heat. The 5G Smart Grid gives the Hidden Hand the potential to dramatically increase the power of 5G transmissions to microwave the population and turn streets and homes into the equivalent of microwave ovens. Once the Smart Grid is in place and broadcasting 5G the potential there for a mass cull of the human population which the Hidden Hand and Sabbatian-Frankists have been planned for a very long time as I have detailed in other books. 5G is not the end either with even more powerful 'generations' in the pipeline. Those controlling the grid (I contend Sabbatian-Frankists out of Israel) would have control of every human mind, all human health and that of the entire natural world. 'Dose' levels would be able to target specific individuals with everyone given a unique digital code to isolate them for targeted attacks as required. You want to challenge the control system? Bye, bye.

No escape

The short wavelengths of 5G mean that it can't travel far or pass effectively through physical objects like buildings, trees, etc. and many have noticed the astonishing number of perfectly healthy mature urban trees being felled – thousand alone in the English city of Sheffield. These limitations of 5G communication mean that instead of the big broadcast transmitters we have seen up to this point sending the signal longer distances 5G requires a staggering number of small transmitters at close intervals down every street (Fig 163). 5G can in fact travel further than they claim, but transmitters close together is the agenda. To give you an idea the single city of Thousand Oaks in the Greater Los Angeles area will require '4,000 to 5,000 new cell sites over the next five years', according to campaigner and attorney Jonathan Kramer. At the time of writing Thousand Oaks has just 140 wireless sites and this is the scale of change we are facing. Play-out 5,000 cell transmitters for one city of well under 150,000 people across the world and cities like London, New York or Tokyo and the number

Figure 163: 5G will mean having transmitters along every street and the closer people are to transmissions the more dangerous they are.

would be absolutely fantastic. They would construct a global grid of human manipulation and health devastation controllable from a central point which I say is planned to be Israel. But that's not all. Some 20,000 satellites are due to be beaming 5G at every inch of the planet to ensure no one can escape. Tech celebrity Elon Musk alone is in the process of putting thousands in place through his SpaceX operation. Musk is the man who said that AI could be the end of humanity and then started a company called Neural Link to connect AI to the human brain and without the satellites he is launching the full-spectrum AI Smart Grid entrapping everyone worldwide would not be possible. Go figure. He's either incredibly confused or he's misleading people. Facebook and Google (same thing) are both involved in sky-based Wi-Fi with a Freedom of Information Act request revealing that Facebook is developing an internet satellite that would 'efficiently provide broadband access [5G] to unserved and underserved areas throughout the world'. When a Musk SpaceX rocket exploded at Cape Canaveral in 2016 it was carrying a Facebook Wi-Fi satellite. Facebook is not just a social media platform, nor Google just a search engine, nor Amazon just a global retail site. Their significance and agenda is far greater and all are controlled by the same Hidden Hand in pursuit of the same outcome of global domination and control. They are disgusting organisations controlled by disgusting people for disgusting ends and those working for them need to face that fact. Another point to make here is the connection between the 'climate change' environmental movement, the UN's Agenda 21 and Agenda 2030 and the telecommunications industry rolling out 5G and the Internet of Everything. The 5G Smart Grid is being pushed and supported by environmental and UN groups to 'save the world from climate change' with telecommunications/Internet industry and NGO connections to big names in climate change hysteria including Extinction Rebellion which has closed London streets with direct action demanding the government imposes a transformation of society precisely in accordance with the Marxist/Agenda 2030 blueprint being manipulated into place by the Sabbatian-Frankist Death Cult. Gail Bradbrook of Extinction Rebellion has many such connections while 16-year-old Swedish climate change poster girl Greta Thunberg is being mercilessly manipulated by the billionaires behind the hoax. I have said for decades that the scam of human-caused climate change was a 'no-problem' to which the 'solution' of centralised global control could be imposed – and now here we are. George Soros will be beaming.

Israel and 5G

The Sabbatian-Frankist Death Cult and its (largely ignorant) ultra-Zionism support system are planning to be the operational centre of the global Smart Grid from where everything – and everyone – will be controlled. This is why Israel has so fast become a world cyber tech and 'security' power and we have seen nothing yet. Through control of the Smart Grid the Sabbatian-Frankist 'Messiah', symbolic or otherwise, is planned to be 'Supreme Lord' of human society and that includes the non-Sabbatian-Frankist Jewish population (the overwhelming majority). It is vital that this penny drops because the Cult has contempt for those non-Sabbatian Jews. The cell phone was invented in 1973 by a Jewish man, Martin 'Marty' Cooper, a pioneer of the wireless communications industry with a long list of patents. He made the world's first cell phone call on April 3rd, 1973, while an engineer at Motorola and he is acclaimed as the 'father' of the mobile phone. Qualcomm, co-founded by ultra-Zionist Irwin M. Jacobs and by far the world's biggest cell phone chip company today, is driving the introduction of 5G along with others. 'Leading the world to 5G and a unifying connectivity fabric that will transform the wireless edge', the company claims in its promotion blurb:

> This is the age of 5G. Made real by Qualcomm – the mobile know-how we put into 3G and 4G enabled us to pioneer 5G, connected cars, and a true Internet of Things (IoT) that will have everyone, and everything, talking.

Qualcomm's cellular modem or data converter called Snapdragon (appropriately named for readers of my other books) is leading the transformation to 5G smartphones (digital suicide notes). The company's propaganda describes how over 30 years Qualcomm's 'mobile invention has led to the Invention Age'. Qualcomm's headquarters are in San Diego, California, but the major location for its research and development of the Smart Grid is Israel. *The Times of Israel* reported in 2014:

> Last year, the company celebrated the 20th anniversary of its presence in Israel, where it has developed some of its most innovative technologies. Among the technologies developed by QualComm Israel are the company's m2m (machine to machine) cellular platform, which is used to track the location of pets, kids, the elderly, and property, a spokesperson said.

> It's part of QualComm's attempt to create an 'Internet of Everything,' where objects are intelligently connected through a combination of advanced wireless networks, modules, sensors and software to enable the real-time exchange of information – with key elements developed in QualComm's Haifa facility, the company said. Among the products that have resulted from that technology is Tagg, the pet-tracking device.

> In addition, Israeli start-up Wilocity, which received a substantial investment

from QualComm Ventures, the company's venture capital group, recently demonstrated multi-gigabit wireless WiGig chipsets, based on chips made by QualComm. The system can transfer high-definition video at distances of up to 40 meters with speeds more than 10 times faster than current average Wi-Fi transmission rates, according to Wilocity CEO Tal Tamir.

This only one of many Israeli start-up technology companies absorbed into Qualcomm. Ultra-Zionist founder Irwin M. Jacobs told *The Times of Israel* that throughout Qualcomm's early years 'a number of Israelis came to work with us in the US – some stayed and some went back and we kept working with them until we eventually decided to open an Israeli office in 1993'. Israel is at the very central core of the Smart Grid agenda and technological control of humanity – Israeli companies and military/Mossad operatives posing as private entrepreneurs are everywhere with regard to this. Israel's increasingly vast cyber and Internet operation is driven by the military out of the Beersheba cyber complex which is surrounded by global high-tech and Internet giants to whom the military send technicians and executives along with all the Israeli start-up tech companies. One headline said: 'Israeli military intelligence unit drives country's high-tech boom'. Other headlines galore herald the arrival of Israel as the centre of the smart tech industry: Musk calls Israel 'technological superpower'; From Jerusalem shall come forth cyber-security, says cyber guru; Israel as a Cyber Super Power; Israel is becoming an artificial intelligence powerhouse; Six reasons Israel became a cybersecurity powerhouse leading the $82 billion industry; How Israel is rewriting the future of cybersecurity and creating the next Silicon Valley; Why Israel dominates in cyber security; Bill Gates: Israeli tech 'changing the world'; Microsoft's top new tech and its Israel connection; Israel leads world in R&D investment; Israel – No. 2 home of global top 500 cyber security companies; Israel wins second-largest number of cybersecurity deals globally; Apple to open R&D centre in Israel; How Intel came to be Israel's best tech friend; Intel CEO: We think of ourselves as an Israeli company as much as a US company; Execs from Facebook, Google, and Microsoft explain why they use Israel for their R&D. There is also a weapons aspect to this Israeli tech explosion as reflected in these headlines: Why Israel has the most technologically advanced military on Earth; 'Weapon Wizards': How tiny Israel became a military superpower; Israel's arms exports spike, hitting record $9 billion. All of the above are driven by the Sabbatian-Frankist Death Cult although most of those involved won't know that. Weapons and Israel's control of the Smart Grid dovetail with these questions: So you want to stop what we are doing through the Smart Grid? Did we tell you we have a serious nuclear arsenal that we are mad enough to use? Something else to ponder: Why would a country on a tiny piece of land with a population of just eight million (20 percent of them Arab) spend so much time, effort and money building up one of the world's biggest stockpiles of nuclear weapons? Well, maybe now we know.

In his own words

Benjamin Netanyahu was apparently re-elected in 2019 for a record fifth term as Israeli prime minister (and as President of the United States) when the population was given the 'choice' between a far right psychopath and a far right psychopath (Fig 164). However, at the time of writing new elections were called for September, 2019, after he failed to secure a coalition government in a spat with the extremist's extremist Avigdor Lieberman.

Netanyahu won the first election with promotional help from Donald Trump and Vladimir Putin who hosted him for high-profile meetings near the end of the election campaign which were nothing more than election propaganda for the home audience. Mossad operative Victor Ostrovsky was not wrong when he said in his

Figure 164: Strange, but true.

1990 book that Israel politics was constantly moving to the right and the process has continued ever since. Ultra-Zionism is on the march as the programming intensifies. Netanyahu is the common theme through the years of preparation for cyber and Smart Grid domination and I am going to confirm the plan through his words in several speeches to AIPAC, tech conferences and the United Nations General Assembly. The theme is the same – Israel dominance of global technology and cyber 'security'. Netanyahu included in one speech a quote from the 'Prophet Isaiah: 'I've made you a light unto the nations, bringing salvation to the ends of the Earth.' He then took up the theme:

> Today 2,700 years after Isaiah spoke those prophetic words Israel is becoming a rising power among the nations, and at long last its light is shining across the continents. Bringing hope and salvation to the ends of the earth. It's very important for us to recognize that we possess a great treasure, the capacity to innovate is a great treasure, a profound economic value in today's world. We have the economic future of the world in Israel.

> You know these companies; Apple, Google, Microsoft, Amazon, Facebook,

guess what they all have research centres in Israel, all of them. Major research centres! And they're not alone, there's hundreds more and there's a reason, something is going on, it's a great change ... It's this shift from the old world to the new world ...

The psychopath is talking in barely-hidden code about precisely what I am describing. Netanyahu said there was a revolution that was changing the world, both economically and in terms of security. 'I think it will also change our politics', he said (as always planned). He bragged that top cyber technology and Internet companies were establishing major advanced research centres in Israel which was a 'meeting ground between big data, AI and connectivity':

Everything is being driven from this nexus, everything ... it's the confluence of big data, connectivity and artificial intelligence, okay, you get that? Israeli technology is driving the world. Israeli technology is driving the world.

Global telecommunications giant Verizon launched Verizon Ventures Israel because 'much of today's innovation comes from Israel, where thousands of start-up companies are creating new technologies and services that are challenging the status quo and changing markets every day'. It's a story being repeated by all the leading tech and Internet companies with connections to the Smart Grid agenda. Netanyahu rejoiced that Israel was number two in the world and closing on the United States. He said that Israel is one tenth of one percent of the world's population and yet attracts already 20 percent of global share in cyber security investments. '[We are] ... now second to the United States ... it's bigger than Israel but it ain't that much bigger than Israel and Israel is number two.' He went on:

And we look ahead with pride to the remarkable contributions Israel will continue to make to all nations. Captains of industry, as they're called, that is founders and leaders of big companies and some small companies and medium-sized companies. They're all coming to Israel, including today, I had a meeting with another head of state. They all want the same three things; Israeli technology, Israeli technology and Israeli technology.

They crave it, they thirst for it because they know that we're in the knowledge [control] centre. They know that Israel is the repository of great genius, great creativity, entrepreneurship, innovation, scientific capability, out-of-the-box thinking. This is a tremendous capacity that we have, because people are coming here. The new powers, the old powers and the new powers, you know, the new world powers, the superpowers ...

It also helps with your 'innovation' if you have back-doors into the computer systems of other innovators in the United States and elsewhere to find out what they know.

'Turning the world blue'

Netanyahu said the world economy was being propelled forward by the Internet which required cyber protection for bank accounts, privacy, communications, power lines, power grids, traffic lights, train schedules and Israel had the capacity to protect (control) them all (and the back-doors will come in very handy to potentially manipulate and trawl for information all these systems). Why would big-time Israel-connected Intel implant a unit in all computers carrying its technology since 2008 that can secretly control the computer and not be turned off? Why would they do that if not for surveillance and external control of all computer systems? Intel's development and success is attributed to Zionist-businessman Andrew S. Grove and the company's first development centre outside America was opened in Israel as early as 1974. The interloper 'Intel Management Engine' is an autonomous system that can override anything you or your main computer operation can do. It has been described as 'a computer within a computer' and runs on its own system known as MINIX which cannot be detected by anti-virus or anti-malware software and can bypass any firewall. Through this system your entire computer hard drive can be accessed at will and the computer shut down at any time (or all at once worldwide through common code connections). Passwords can be accessed and the keys that you type. The open-source MINIX was created by Jewish cyber developer Andrew Stuart Tanenbaum who said in 2017 that he didn't know Intel was using it. Back-door undetectable access to global computer systems is happening on an industrial scale with Israel right at the centre of it. I have already described how analysts from London-based Positive Technologies alleged that Intel chips and processors contain a 'logic signal analyser' which can read 'almost all data on a computer'. Think of the power over the world you would have with control of basically all computer systems at every level of society in every country. This is what we are talking about and it provides the access to devastate financial systems to trigger a global crash so big it would be heard on Mars. Netanyahu said:

> You have bank accounts, sure? Okay, well you don't want anyone hacking into them [except us], right? Or into your cars, or into the planes you ride, you need cyber security. Everybody needs cyber security. Israel has become a world leader in cyber security [back-door access].

Netanyahu called for 'a sort of UN for the internet … a coalition of the leading companies in the cyber world ... and in my opinion Israel is the most advanced.' For this and 'many, many other reasons' Israel was being sought after. The world was coming to Israel and Israel was going around the world, he said, as he highlighted a chart detailing the extent of Israel's global cyber reach:

> The blue are all the new agreements that we have made in various efforts around the world in the year 2017. I've been to Africa four times in two years, to South America most recently, in Brazil. With the great powers of Asia we have new agreements, every single country here, every single country here in Israel's expanding diplomatic horizons is talking to us about cyber ...
>
> ... They all want to share in our knowledge of cyber defence, that doesn't mean that we share with everyone and it doesn't mean that we share equally with those that we share. But we do have a general policy of cooperation between governments and we have a general policy of cooperation with companies ... [so we get the back-doors].
>
> ... We are colouring the world blue, all these countries are coming to us, India, China, Mongolia, Kazakhstan, all of them, Azerbaijan, Muslim countries, so we're colouring the world blue. You know what, the numbers, you remember people talked about Israel's isolation, remember that? Israel's isolation, pretty soon the countries that don't have relations with us, they're going to be isolated.

Israel now has ever-growing connections with India in both cyber 'security' and weaponry. Netanyahu said disingenuously that 'we made [the tech domination] stronger by moving Israel to free-market principles which unleashed the spark of genius embedded in our people, into innovation, entrepreneurship'. In fact, the whole thing is led and overseen by the Israeli military and intelligence network including Mossad. Even Netanyahu indicated this when he described how the plan had been to converge military intelligence, academia and industry in one place (Beersheba). He outlined the military intelligence benefits when comparing Israeli intelligence with America's National Security Agency or NSA:

> Our NSA, which is called unit 8200, it's pretty big, how big do you think it is? Hmm, well I'll give you a hint. America, the United States is about 42 times the size of Israel in terms of population, so how much bigger do you think the American NSA is relative to the Israeli NSA? It's not even ten times bigger, you know the [Western intelligence grouping] Five Eyes. Israel is the sixth eye. No, Israel is the second eye, so we have a tremendous sunk investment.

Why wouldn't you build one of the world's – perhaps *the* world's – most effective intelligence networks when you have back-door access to the intelligence systems of other countries, especially the United States, and control double-agents in those foreign agencies like the CIA and NSA? Sabbatian-Frankists and their gofers have become so arrogantly confident of their predominance that they hardly care if we know any more so long as we think they are talking about Israel and not the Death Cult that controls Israel. Netanyahu described the systematic way Israeli cyber dominance is being achieved:

> We take our brightest people and put them in, we look at the entire population, we go into the high schools, we're going to go into kindergartens very soon. So we need the smartest people, we put them in this, they run on the information networks and then it develops into a business, enterprises if we allow the graduates of our military units and our intelligence units to create companies and allow the graduates of our security services to merge into companies with local partners and foreign partners.

There you go from the psychopath's own mouth. Israeli military and Mossad agents are, and have been for a long time, sent out into the global tech and Internet industry posing as purely private entrepreneurs taking with them 'innovations' secured from the Israeli military-intelligence tech program which in part gets its 'inspiration' from other people's creativity waiting on tap through the back-doors. Netanyahu said: 'These incredibly gifted young men and women who come out of the army or the Mossad they want to start their start-ups.' This 'private entrepreneur' Israeli (military/Mossad) technology is then bought and used by governments, military, intelligence agencies, global tech companies, business and (through computers and smartphones) individuals all over the world to which Israel's military and intelligence networks have back-door access – just as they did on 9/11. Technological developments have also come from Israel's military state which has been mega-funded to seek ever more sophisticated ways to keep surveillance on the world (Fig 165). Netanyahu said that Israel had technology because the military, especially military intelligence, produced 'a lot of capabilities'. An article in *The Jerusalem Post* summed up Israel's current level of cyber control:

> Most importantly, Israel is positioned to guard the world's Internet. Everything today is traded, controlled and administered online. And Israel is emerging as the world's number one guardian of the worldwide web. That means, regardless of being a few miles off-track from China's Land and Maritime Roads, it is positioned to be the center of both [East and West] belts ...

Figure 165: The 'Zion Mainframe'.

... A global currency collapse might be seen as a way to wipe the slate clean of nation-based currencies, especially the US dollar, and establish an international one: like Bitcoin, perhaps. If Bitcoin is the model for a new Internet-based global currency, Israel is likely to be its guardian too, protecting that currency from hackers around the world.

'Guarding the world's Internet' means the potential to have access to the codes that open the door to every aspect of the Internet and cyberspace that uses Israeli-controlled technology, companies and military-intelligence operatives. It also means:

- The potential power to control, manipulate and maintain surveillance on every system.

- To crash the world's financial markets at will and make 'money' disappear from any target.

- Control the information that people see and hear – already being increasingly achieved through ultra-Zionist-controlled Google, YouTube, Facebook and so on, but with the potential to be total.

- To control all military technology attached to the Internet or computer systems to which Israel has access.

- External control of autonomous driverless vehicles as is already the case through Israeli-made cyber-systems on modern cars which constantly feed-back vehicle and driver information.

- To control the perceptions of the human race once an AI connection is made.

- To take over a world founded on the Internet of Things and Internet of Everything which would control all attached technology and eventually the human brain.

I say 'Israel' in terms of this potential control, but that word always means in my context the Sabbatian-Frankist Death Cult that controls Israel and not the entirety of its general population. According to the Israeli media Israel has designs on creating the global digital no-cash currency which is dubbed the 'digital shekel'. A *Haaretz* headline said: 'Israel's answer to Bitcoin: A digital shekel that could replace cash.' *The Times of Israel* went with: 'Israel – Blockchain capital of the world?' This has all been long in the preparation and 9/11 gave the plan major momentum. Israeli newspaper *Ma'ariv* reported in 2008 that Benjamin Netanyahu had told an audience at Bar Ilan University that 'the September 11, 2001 terror attacks had been beneficial for Israel'. The paper quoted him as saying: 'We are benefiting from one thing, and that is the attack on the Twin Towers and Pentagon, and the American struggle in Iraq.' He reportedly added that those events 'swung American public opinion in our favour'. But then that's why they were made to happen. Netanyahu also said in what he thought was a private conversation caught on camera: 'America is a thing you can move very easily.' No wonder he said at the end of one speech about Israel cyber domination:

> Thank you America. Thank you successive American presidents. Thank you Congress, Republicans and Democrats alike. Thank you AIPAC for helping bring this about, you're terrific!

The man should be in jail and the key thrown into a very deep ocean. This background to the Smart Grid and Israel's central role in its development and control explains what appears at face value to be crazy claims by these messianic lunatics of the Sabbatian-Frankist Death Cult about installing a 'world ruler' on the throne of Jerusalem on the site of a rebuilt Solomon's Temple. Control of cyberspace in the world as it is today would give them that very global control and via an AI connection to the human mind control over all human perception. Control will then be total and, without outside intervention, irreversible.

Of course we are not there yet – quite – and the point of exposing all this and taking the untold shit that will follow this book's publication is to stop it getting there. We are, however, moving in that direction so fast and we are getting closer by the hour let alone the day.

Many faces of the Death Cult

Some people may look at what I do and think that I see conspiracies everywhere. Well, first of all conspiracies *are* everywhere if you take the dictionary definition of the word: 'A secret plan by a group to do something unlawful or harmful.' By that definition we are drowning in conspiracies and the act of conspiring is defined in law: 'A criminal conspiracy exists when two or more people agree to commit almost any unlawful act, then take some action toward its completion.' My goodness, how many conspiracies must there be worldwide on that basis? Even so, my work is not to see conspiracies everywhere, but to see *ONE* conspiracy with multiple faces in pursuit of the same goal – global human control. The cyberspace conspiracy is the foundation pillar of the greater conspiracy while being underpinned by many other facets that may seem to be unconnected while being fundamentally so. I have been saying for years that if you want to identify major aspects of the global conspiracy look at those subjects and situations about which you are not allowed to have a contrary opinion or engage in free and open debate without being directly silenced or subjected to abuse and hostility from the gatekeepers of the conspiracy (most of whom have no idea there even *is* a conspiracy let alone they are working on its behalf). If you know you can't win a debate to justify what you want the public to believe or accept then simply don't have the debate. Censor other views and information and use abuse to intimidate opposing advocates into self-censored silence. I expose all the major strands of the Death Cult agenda at length in *Everything You Need To Know But Have Never Been Told* along with all other aspects of the conspiracy and its deeper connections into the 'Beyond'. I have mentioned some already earlier in the book including mass immigration, human-caused global warming, cashless society, police-military state (controlled by AI and robot 'troops') and centralisation of global power giving ever more control to the few over the many. Before I finish I want to emphasise three more which like all the others connect into the emerging Smart Grid: Vaccines, transgender hysteria and the deletion of free speech. They would appear to have nothing to do with 9/11 but they do because they are part of same conspiracy.

Vaccine madness

There are many reasons for the vaccine agenda that have nothing to do with protecting people from disease. What a perfect way to get access to the body for body/mind manipulation substances and nano-microchips. Insider Richard Day talked in 1969 about 'innoculated diseases'. I was told by a CIA scientist in the 1990s that nano-chips were planned to be implanted in vaccination programmes. You will have noted if you follow the news that a war is underway on those who challenge the Hidden Hand agenda of vaccines. So-called 'anti-vaxers' are having their videos, books and documentaries censored by Google, YouTube, Facebook and Amazon and those questioning the official narrative about 'safe vaccines' are being demonised by the media (Fig 166). This sequence is always confirmation that the agenda is seeking to silence and discredit information that it knows could bring its house down. The pharmaceutical cartel, or Big Pharma, which makes its billions from people continuing to be sick, can basically say what it likes to promote vaccination and has the mainstream media as a constant PR operation to push its products and discredit opponents. When I was a kid childhood diseases were part of the process of activating and developing the immune system and building up ongoing natural resistance. Now those same diseases come with dire warnings and responses along the lines of '*Oh no*, the plague, your child will die, *ahhhh!!!*' The smallest outbreak is made to seem like some end of the world catastrophe with falling vaccination rates due to 'anti-vax' information always declared the villain. 'You horrible people, you terrible child-abusing parents – *look what you've done!*' New York mayor Bill de Blasio responded to a measles outbreak by declaring an emergency and ordering mandatory vaccinations under threat of a fine of up to $1,000. 'We cannot allow this dangerous disease to make a comeback here in New York City', he said. When I was kid I never heard 'measles' and 'dangerous' used in the same sentence. The UK *Guardian* reported the story and pinned the blame on 'anti-vaxers' citing 'scientifically debunked concerns that the shots are dangerous'. Shockingly and outrageously the writer will call herself a 'journalist'.

Figure 166: A good motto for everything.

What never gets reported is that often non-vaccinated children don't get the diseases that vaccinated children *do* get. This happened with my two unvaccinated sons who are now strapping adults who remained untouched by childhood vaccination diseases while their vaccinated mates were getting sick. I was given all the vaccines recommended in the 1950s and got most of the diseases. Studies have shown that vaccinated kids (vaccinated with the 'virus') are able to spread the diseases to others. The obvious contradiction between unvaccinated children staying healthy, while the vaccinated get sick despite their 'protection', presents an obvious problem to credibility of vaccinations. To mitigate this devastating contradiction Big Pharma invented 'herd immunity' which claims that vaccines only work effectively if the vast majority (they want all) are vaccinated. This is a mendacious scam to provide the excuse for mandatory vaccinations for everyone to ensure 'herd immunity' and represents the main thrust of 'anti-vax' demonisation – 'My vaccinated child is only sick because of your unvaccinated child' (who isn't sick). Yes, I know it is mind-numbing bollocks, but tell unquestioning people anything enough times and they will believe it – the Nazis built a whole control system on that basis. 'Herd immunity' does not explain why an unvaccinated child doesn't get a disease and vaccinated children do. If you are vaccinated according to Big Pharma orthodoxy your immune system is triggered to develop protection. Why would a kid need other kids to be vaccinated when the relationship here is between his or her immune system and the disease? Er, um, er. American neurosurgeon Russell Blaylock said:

> In the original description of herd immunity, the protection to the population at large occurred only if people contracted the infections naturally. The reason for this is that naturally-acquired immunity lasts for a lifetime. The vaccine proponents quickly latched onto this concept and applied it to vaccine-induced immunity.

> But, there was one major problem – vaccine-induced immunity lasted for only a relatively short period [if at all] and then this applies only to humoral [body fluids] immunity. This is why they began to suggest boosters for most vaccines, even the common childhood infections such as chickenpox, measles, mumps, and rubella.

The whole foundation of vaccinations is that they produce antibodies for the disease in question, but it has long been known that this does not constitute proof of immunity. This is a quote from Learntherisk.org:

> … science has long known that antibodies alone do NOT create real immunity. Some people with high levels of antibodies can be exposed to an illness and still get sick, while others without antibodies can be exposed and not get sick. Dr. Merrill Chase, nicknamed the Grandfather of Immunology for his pioneering work, did clear-cut research on this issue back in the 1950s. His results are clear: antibody levels don't determine immunity.

The immune system is a highly complex system and science is still in its infancy understanding how it functions. In fact, immunology textbooks were completely rewritten recently after a University of Virginia study finally proving the link between the gut and the brain through the lymphatic system. Before this 2014 study, immunology books were adamant there was no link.

The truth is that the deluge of vaccinations today overwhelms a still developing immune system with toxic shite and this natural protection from disease will never be as powerful as it would otherwise be. Vaccine ingredients and substances used in manufacture include: Aluminium; aborted foetal tissue; mercury-based thimerosal; gelatine; human serum albumin (found in blood plasma); sorbitol and other stabilisers; emulsifiers; taste improvers; antibiotics; egg proteins (ovalbumin); yeast proteins; formaldehyde; acidity regulators; human cell strains, animal cell strains and GMOs; recombinant DNA technology; bovine products. Aluminium alone is a brain toxin. Given that little lot why is anyone surprised that many health problems have been linked to vaccinations? Among them are: Anaphylactic shock; aseptic meningitis and meningitis; Bell's palsy, facial palsy, isolated cranial nerve palsy; blood disorders; brachial neuritis; cerebrovascular accident (stroke); chronic rheumatoid arthritis; convulsions, seizures, febrile seizure; death; encephalopathy and encephalitis (brain swelling); hearing loss; Guillain-Barré syndrome; immune system disorders; lymphatic system disorders; multiple sclerosis; myocarditis; nervous system disorders; neurological syndromes including autism; paralysis and myelitis including transverse myelitis; peripheral neuropathy; pneumonia and lower respiratory infections; skin and tissue disorders including eczema; sudden infant death syndrome (SIDS); tinnitus (ringing in the ears); vaccine-strain versions of chicken pox, measles, mumps, polio, influenza, meningitis, yellow fever, and pertussis vasculitis (inflammation of blood vessels). Big Pharma has so much influence on government policy via The Web that in 1986 the US Congress voted into law the National Childhood Vaccine Injury Act (NCVIA) which protected vaccine makers from being sued at a time when they were losing court cases over vaccine damaged children. What incentive is there to produce something safe when you can't be sued? The only motivation left would be common decency and basic empathetic humanity, but you won't find that anywhere in the Big Pharma racket. Vaccine producers are so callously and satanically empathy-deleted they make colossal profits from selling drugs to 'treat' the health problems their vaccines are causing. One of America's leading opponents of the Big Pharma vaccine narrative is Robert F. Kennedy Jr, son of the US attorney general assassinated by the Hidden Hand in 1968. An article on the Kennedy-connected website, Childrenshealthdefense.org, highlighted this profiteering scam. Writer

Kristina Kristen said:

Following the passage of NCVIA, the number of vaccines on the childhood schedule mushroomed, creating a gold rush for vaccine makers: the vaccine industry went from a $1 billion industry to a $50 billion industry. But this expansion in the vaccine industry, in fact, is relatively small in comparison to the even greater gold rush for the BIG 4 companies. The drug 'treatment' side of the equation, which is substantially more lucrative than the 'gateway' vaccine side the BIG 4 already monopolized, now also increased substantially.

The vaccine manufacturers began to capitalize on the known adverse effects of their vaccines, and have since created drugs for the 'treatment' side of the equation as well. The lack of incentive to make safe products, which created the bloated vaccine schedule, became the gateway to the lucrative drug treatment side for these companies. Today, the BIG 4 monopolize vaccines as well as the drug 'treatments' for chronic illnesses known to be induced by vaccines. First, vaccines push kids off the cliff, and then vaccine makers profit from 'rescuing' those they don't kill.

The number of vaccinations and their combinations is utterly insane and any society that wasn't completely mad and given up its right to free thought would laugh in the face of such preposterous idiocy. American children and young people are given between 53 and 70 vaccines depending on how you count them from birth to 18 years with many given in one go. The childhood schedule has tripled in little more than 30 years in a period when children have got sicker, not healthier – a period in which once rare autism, food allergies, asthma, brain malfunction, autoimmune diseases and cancer in children have dramatically increased by comparison. We now have the *six-in-one* vaccine for diphtheria, tetanus, whooping cough (pertussis), polio, Hib disease (Haemophilus influenzae type b) and hepatitis B. The still-developing immune systems of babies get this shit (including aluminium) at 8, 12 and 16 weeks. Very common reactions are reported as redness, pain and/or swelling at the injection site; raised temperature (fever); irritability; loss of appetite; vomiting; abnormal crying. Common reactions are diarrhoea; bruising or bleeding at the injection site; a small, painless lump at the injection site. Rare reactions (1 in 1,000) are reported as 'unusual high-pitched screaming', and episodes during which the child may become blue, pale and/or limp. Very rare consequences are described as fits (also called febrile convulsions or febrile seizures). Oh, perfectly safe then. Parents are told that if babies are irritable and have a fever after the shot they should give them infant paracetamol or ibuprofen, so confirming the point about the Big Pharma cause and effect scam. What is never mentioned in such official lists of consequences are the life-long effects of suppressing the immune system by attacking it with combinations of toxins while still developing and getting up to speed.

Vaccines and DNA

Immune systems of children and the young are being devastated by the vaccine deluge and they grow up with far less immune protection than nature has provided. We have seen an enormous rise in autoimmune diseases in the vaccine era, especially the mass vaccine era, and while technologically-generated radiation and the chemical content of food will also play a part the cause and effect between vaccinations and the immune system are obvious. Injecting into the arm or leg also bypasses the immune system which would otherwise act to repel the toxic infiltration. Today's generation of children in the United States, for example, is sicker than their predecessors with more than 50 percent having one or more chronic illness and as a result they are given pharmaceutical drugs for body and psychological problems on a scale never seen before. Make a fortune creating the problem and then make an even bigger fortune offering the solution (which creates still more problems). The United States is only 19th for infant mortality rates in the developed world and has the most highly vaccinated children with the rest of the West not far behind. Vaccine effects go much deeper than what I have described so far. I have been picking up information from experts and government/intelligence insiders throughout my decades of research that points to vaccines being used to change human DNA as part of an agenda to mutate the human form in ways that include suppressing the scale of potential perception. Put another way – making humans even more myopic in their ability to perceive reality. DNA is a receiver-transmitter of information and if you reduce the range of frequencies it can access you close down the channels to insight beyond the reality bubbles that pass for human awareness. Human foetal and animal DNA in some vaccines will alone affect human DNA. The immune system attacks foreign DNA and when this or animal DNA attaches to the recipient's DNA the immune system will attack its own cells. The body is attacked by *itself* and this is known as autoimmune disease. But, don't worry, vaccines have nothing to do with the explosion of autoimmune diseases in the vaccine era. Helen Ratajczak, a former senior scientist at pharmaceutical company Boehringer Ingelheim, suggested a link between brain damage and human DNA in vaccines.

I have written in other books about an emerging branch of science called epigenetics which becomes highly significant in relation to vaccines, toxic 'food' and 'drink' and the effects of technological radiation with 5G about to increase the consequences dramatically. Epigenetics describes a process in which genes are switched on and off. There is an optimum on/off sequence that keeps you healthy in mind and body and when that sequence is disturbed or scrambled with the wrong ones 'on' and the right ones 'off' big trouble can follow in the form of anything from heart disease to cancer to psychological problems. These distorted blueprint sequences are then passed on to the next generation and human health spirals downwards. Vaccines, toxic food and drink and environmental factors like technological radiation causes this gene switching to malfunction and here you have a frontline reason for the dramatic increases in cancer, heart disease, autism and a long, long list of other ailments in the vaccine/toxic food/smartphone era. Gene-switching malfunction affects neuron transmitters in the brain leading to mental, emotional and psychological disturbances which are also soaring. On some levels this war on humanity is happening through ignorance and stupidity, but it is being orchestrated from the shadows with cold calculation by those who know far more about how reality works than mainstream scientists and doctors who are enslaved by their programming, sources of funding and government regulation. Doctors are little more than paid agents of Big Pharma and so every illness and problem is a 'nail' requiring a scalpel, drug or vaccination. Kerching! More profit for the sickness industry. No wonder mainstream 'medical' treatment is one of the Western world's biggest killers right up there with cancer and heart disease and yet still most people treat doctors with awe when they don't even know what the body *is* let alone how it works. If any doctor strays from Big Pharma (therefore medical/government) orthodoxy they are struck off even if alternative treatments work and the system is constantly seeking to destroy many alternative forms of healing *because* they work. The patient is irrelevant, you see. Only money, power and control matter to the Big Pharma psychopaths who lock into the Sabbatian-Frankist and Hidden Hand psychopaths.

The body is an electro-chemical organism and is therefore affected by infiltration from electro-chemical sources. From one direction we are bombarded by technological electromagnetic frequencies alien to body and mind and from another we have the tsunami of chemical toxicity in vaccines, drugs, food, drink and air. Why would food be so full of poisons and horrific content? Why is the same true of what people drink? Why is humanity becoming a drugged-up society courtesy of Big Pharma and the medical profession that it owns? Why are children targeted by brain-changing drugs from the earliest age? Why is the air poisoned and the land devastated with deadly herbicides and pesticides that end up in food and destroy the soil (the 'industrialisation of agriculture' predicted more than a hundred years ago in the *Protocols*)?

Why are people consuming pharmaceutical drugs and growth hormone weight-gain drugs in the meat that they eat? Why is the human race becoming increasingly obese with this tendency passed on through the epigenetic gene pool to future generations? On the face of it all this is madness and societal suicide, but in fact it is being done systematically from the inner sanctum of The Web and is designed to weaken humanity mentally, emotionally and physically to allow a global takeover with the least resistance possible. Attacking and diluting masculinity is part of this process, too. Quintus Fabius Maximus Verrucosus, a Roman statesman and general of the third century BC, was famous for his technique of never fighting a battle that could be decisive either way. Instead his method was to weaken and wear down the enemy over a period in a war of attrition and when it was too weak to resist just walk in and take over. This is what is being done to humanity today through all these electromagnetic and toxic attacks and how appropriate that the Fabian Society, one of the strands of the Hidden Hand which operates on the left of politics, was named after him. Multi-faceted frequency and toxic attacks purposely weaken the immune system through, among other things, sheer overload. The immune system keeps us alive and healthy when it is strong and effective and here we have a war with endless fronts against the immune system (problem) which leads to demands for vaccinations and drugs (solution). We don't need vaccines, we need *immune systems* and that means toxin-free clean water, toxin-free nutritious food and a harmonious electromagnetic environment – everything that is being destroyed.

Vaccines meet the Smart Grid

Vaccines, drugs and the Smart Grid come together with the plan to track and monitor the population to ensure that everyone has vaccines and drugs imposed by law. This society was accurately portrayed in the 2002 movie *Equilibrium* in which the population has all emotion suppressed by a daily injection that is monitored to ensure compliance. It is worth watching if you can get a copy to see what is planned. I have been warning about this for a long time and the Tiptoe to that end is clear to see with increasing moves to mandatory vaccines. The plan is for forced immunisation and the taking of mind-altering and suppressing drugs to maintain calm apathetic subservience to be monitored through the Smart Grid so that no one can escape. The promotion of lithium in public water supplies is part of this agenda. Lithium is used as a psychiatric medication to treat conditions such as manic depression and its advocates say mass medication of lithium will make people 'happier'. Run 'happier' through the Orwellian Translation Unit and it comes out as 'subservient'. Studies have shown that the electromagnetic soup and 5G can have the effect of making people more apathetic. The vaccine tracking agenda is already being pushed by Seth Berkley, CEO of Gavi, the Vaccine Alliance, who was formerly with the US Centers for Disease Control and Prevention (a Big Pharma front) and the Rockefeller Foundation (the family that gave us Big Pharma 'medicine'). One of Gavi's biggest supporters, financially and otherwise, is Microsoft vaccine fanatic Bill Gates. Gavi is a leading 'light' in the global network of organisations and fronts pushing the Big Pharma vaccine agenda and seeks to have everyone worldwide subject to vaccinations (for their own good, of course). Seth Berkley says Gavi spends an average of nearly $2 billion a year on getting vaccines to children in the poorest countries and has invested tens of millions of dollars in 'innovations to monitor immunization'. Berkley wants technology to track who has been vaccinated and to give everyone an 'identity' which all fits in to the Smart Grid agenda whether he knows it or not. The United Nations wants all 193 member countries to ensure that everyone has a legal form of identity by Kurzweil's year of 2030. Whatever the reason they give you for this it won't be the real one. The increasingly extreme censorship of 'anti-vax' information in all its forms is to stop the public knowing the real story and to give free reign to Big Pharma and its compliant media to tell the population only what the cabal wants them to believe. One of the reasons given by the Australian government for my ban from the country was my views on vaccines and Sherri Tenpenny, an American osteopathic physician and anti-vaccination activist, was also banned from Australia to prevent Australians from hearing her research. Hidden Hand-front Wikipedia classically describes Tenpenny as someone who 'supports the discredited theory that vaccines cause autism'. This is the same controlled and devious Wikipedia used to 'fact-check' the alternative media. If you want to know what the agenda is look at those subjects in which alternative opinions are met with reflex-action censorship and abuse. Talking of which …

Transgender hysteria

Another of my rules of thumb with regard to identifying the Hidden Hand-Sabbatian-Frankist wish-list is this: When it comes out of nowhere and is suddenly everywhere – it's the agenda. The button has been pressed on another stage of the plan. Nothing fits this picture more profoundly than the obsession with transgender 'issues' which literally did come out of nowhere (in terms of the public arena) and now my god it's everywhere. I have once again exposed the background to this in detail in my last book. I really have no need to tell anyone about the insane transgender extremes that have taken over human society like mass hysteria. We have all seen the imposition of 'gender-neutral' toilets in which people in male bodies claiming to be women are allowed to use female or any-gender toilets and changing rooms no matter how that

makes women feel and the obvious affect on women's sport when
transgender people in male bodies with all those physical advantages
are allowed to 'compete' with and obviously defeat female opponents.
They've stopped taking bets on the weightlifting, by the way. Schools
and universities have been taken over by the transgender agenda
because self-obsessed activists and their extremes of narcissism are given
whatever they want by governments and authorities imposing the
Hidden Hand plan for the no-gender 'human' which I shall shortly
explain. If ever there was a $2 + 2 = 4$ v $2 + 2 = 5$ then this is it. Professors
of biology are being slated, abused and 'investigated' for saying that
men and women are biologically different $(2 + 2 = 4)$ while activists
prevail with their bloody nonsense that gender is decided by whatever
you choose it to be $(2 + 2 = 5)$. I saw a video shot at an American
university in which a
woman panellist said that
men are generally taller than
women. What could be more
supportable by
observational fact? *Fact*,
however, is now an historical
concept and some members
of the audience began to
walk out in protest (Fig 167).
In the safety of the venue
lobby they condemned what
they heard as 'fascist'. How
can that response be

Figure 167: When facts are 'fascist' – walk-out at the kindergarten.

described except in terms of mental illness? It doesn't matter what utter
baloney headless-chicken activists may claim to be reality. The law is
increasingly standing with them in support because it's a Hidden Hand
agenda and so nothing must stand in the way and certainly not open
public debate or peripheral matters like facts.

New York congresswoman Alexandria Ocasio-Cortez, a classic Soros
'progressive', summed up the post-fact mind-set: 'I think that there's a
lot of people more concerned about being precisely, factually, and
semantically correct than about being morally right.' I may make
factually unsupportable statements, but I am a good person – far better
than you are – and so what I say must prevail. Talk to the general
population and they will tell you they think it's all insane (so long as
you are considered 'safe' and won't report them for having the wrong
opinion). But those with the shrill voices and 'anti-hate' faces of hatred
who dominate the microphones and cameras are the only voice you hear
because by now most other people are terrified of saying what they
really think. Well, let me have a go: It's all *fucking bollocks*. There –

intimidation over. Oh, you say I am a transphobic bigot? I am so sorry, let me have another go: It's *monumental fucking bollocks*. No, I am not speaking here of people who genuinely relate to another gender different to their body-type. How people choose to self-identify is none of my business and I have no problem with that at all. Good luck to them and I hope it makes them happy. My problem – and a very serious problem for human society – is not that some people think they are in the wrong body and you are pushing against an open door when it comes to opposing discrimination against anyone be they transgender or white men. The problem is that 'discrimination' is not the real reason for the transgender agenda at all. That's only the excuse. It's the foot in the door to open the way for the transformation – literally – of the human form. Yet again 'progressive' activists are stretched out and twanging on the Death Cult violin.

Synthetic masculine-deleted humanity

The real transgender agenda, irony of ironies, is the *end* of gender. I have detailed in *Everything You Need To Know But Have Never Been Told* the plan to replace the present biological human form with a synthetic version that will have no sexes and be unable to procreate. Aldous Huxley described just such a society in his 1932 book *Brave New World* in which children were created in strict genetic castes (lower castes akin to worker ants) in 'hatcheries' where procreation was done technologically and parentless children attended state conditioning centres to program them to never question what the government tells them. Before anyone waves away the idea of synthetic 'humans' with a waft of the hand and words like crazy and ridiculous they should know that the Tiptoe to that very outcome is happening both before our eyes and in secret projects day after day. The replacement of human thought and emotion with artificial intelligence and the replacement of the biological human with a synthetic human are two parts of the same goal of creating the post-human or trans-human that would be artificial intelligence operating through an artificial synthetic body. Humanity as we know it is in the process of being replaced. You would need to read my last book to see where this is ultimately coming from, but for our purposes here all we need to know is this is happening and that transgender hysteria is meant to lead us to this end while appearing to be about something completely different. Rockefeller insider Dr Richard Day told those paediatricians in 1969: 'We are going to make boys and girls the same.' He said people would be made 'gender-neutral'. What is happening now is what he was talking about. The scam is following a multi-stage process of 'physical' and psychological manipulation similar to that of holdables-wearables-implantables that we have seen with technology. The combination this time includes changing the gender foundations by feminising the male body through a long list of methods that I detail in *Everything You Need To Know*. These involve endocrine-disrupting synthetic chemicals (EDCs) which are found in plastics, food containers and packaging, canned food and drinks, electrics, solvents, cleaning products, detergents, pesticides, cosmetics, soaps, car exhausts, polish, paints, batteries, dental fillings (mercury) and many types of fish. Hormone-disrupter Bisphenol A or BPA is used in cans, bottles, plastic food containers and cash register receipts (because everyone touches them). Plus what could be in vaccines adding to the genetic transformation? Atrazine, one of the world's most-used pesticides, is changing the sex of male frogs and making them infertile. What effect are other common poisons having which are sprayed on farms (food), parks and sports fields including golf courses? EDCs and the female sex hormone oestrogen (estrogen) are found in unfiltered tap water. Indeed EDC's can mimic oestrogen and have the same effect on a male body. I quote in *Everything You Need To Know* Dr Devra Davis, an internationally-renowned American epidemiologist, president of the Environmental Health Trust and director of the Center for Environmental Oncology at the University of Pittsburgh. She both highlights the dangers of 5G and what is happening to men in terms of plummeting sperm counts, diminishing levels of the male hormone testosterone and falling male birth-rates. She points out that fast-dividing cells producing sexual organs in the womb are very open to 'incorporate and replicate errors' that can lead to changing once-developing boys into girls and chemical infiltration can affect this process. Dr Melody Milam Potter, an American clinical health psychologist for 30 years, wrote:

EDCs we encounter every day can alter the sex hormone balance, preventing male genitals from growing properly. By suppressing testosterone or by enhancing or mimicking the female sex hormone, estrogen, they can undermine the natural testosterone messages surging through a growing fetus. For instance, estrogen mimics [such as] dioxin, a widespread pollutant and potent endocrine disruptor, can intercept and overcome a hormonal message from a male gene. Dioxin also acts as a testosterone flusher reducing male hormone concentrations so much that the male action may not be stimulated adequately.

Testosterone suppressors like DDT can block testosterone's position on a receptor. Hormone stimulators can intensify the action of a natural hormone so much that the system shuts down and refuses to receive a male 'go ahead' signal ... In fact, research substantiates that exposure to EDCs at a crucial time can disrupt the entire genital sequence.

Studies claim that the number of people identifying as gay or 'LGBT'

is rapidly increasing to the extent that one study in the US estimated that
those born before and across the Millennium to be nearly twice as likely
to identify as LGBT as other American adults – 'Millennials Are the
Gayest Generation', as one headline put it. Are we really saying that
none of this is connected to a chemical environment awash with gender-
bending toxicity? Alongside the chemical manipulation of gender we
have the psychological dimension and this is where transgender tyranny
and hysteria plays its crucial role. The number of children and young
people questioning their gender and identifying with another is
exploding since the incessant transgender propaganda began. What is
called 'gender dysphoria' was rare until the programming campaign
began and as late as 2009 the number referred for treatment in that year
in England and Wales was 97. Then came the propaganda surge and
today it is thousands per year and growing with the increase since 2009
measured in thousands of percent. Kids are being purposely confused
about their gender who were not at all confused before and parents are
being margined and blocked from intervening. To question even a small
child's contention that they are in the wrong body can mean the child
being kidnapped by the social services tyranny and placed with foster
parents or permanently adopted. Gender-changing drugs are
increasingly handed out to children and young people with cavalier
disregard for the life-long consequences. Whistleblower workers at a
British transgender clinic resigned over children as young as *three*
having 'unnecessary gender reassignment treatment' after being
incorrectly diagnosed with gender dysphoria. Carl Heneghan, director
of the Centre of Evidence-based Medicine at Oxford University,
described the policy as 'unregulated live experiments on children'. You
need courage to state the obvious today. Dr Allan M. Josephson, a
former head of Child and Adolescent Psychiatry and Psychology, sued
the University of Louisville after he was demoted for saying children
who insist they are transgender should not be instantly believed.
Academia is being terrorised by transgender activism with Professor
Nicholas Meriwether at Shawnee State University in Ohio suing officials
after being rebuked for refusing to refer to a student with a male body
using 'female pronouns' because it was against his religious beliefs. The
imposition of how people must be addressed is a tyranny and so many
are now losing their jobs over not calling someone with a dick in female
terms or vice versa. Anyone noticed what is happening to kids in
Yemen? But no – 'he', 'she' or 'they' is far more important to stress
about. Moves are being made to legally recognise a gender change
simply by people saying 'I identify as a man/woman now' and the
whole program is being underpinned and enforced by changing the
language and punishing people who won't conform. We have even seen
terms like 'mum' and 'dad' targeted because the non-procreation

synthetic human won't have parents and will be owned and brought up by the state – as per *Brave New World*. The concept of parents therefore has to be eroded until it is deleted and to the Hidden Hand falling sperm counts – especially among racial types they want to eliminate – are not a problem because they are heading to the day when natural sperm will no longer be required. Sperm can already be created from other cells. The sequence unfolding goes like this: Two genders – confuse genders – fuse genders – no genders. This is happening through genetic and psychological manipulation. Remember, too, that once generations born before the transgender tyranny began have left this world anyone arriving will inherit a done deal in which insanity is the new normal. The Hidden Hand is waiting for those with the radar of experience to die (quickened by 5G) when the challenge to their madness will all but disappear. It already is through intimidation. If we allow that to happen we'll have what Huxley described in *Brave New World*:

> Natural reproduction has been done away with and children are created, 'decanted', and raised in 'hatcheries and conditioning centres'. From birth, people are genetically designed to fit into one of five castes, which are further split into 'Plus' and 'Minus' members and designed to fulfil predetermined positions within the social and economic strata of the World State.

Confirmation that manufactured transgender hysteria is not about helping or protecting transgender people can be seen with those who have surgically transitioned between genders and then regretted doing so. They are marginalised, silenced and abused for making people question what the agenda wants them to do. This is the gender equivalent of attacking Jewish people for criticising the Israeli government and dubbing them 'anti-Semitic'. We are there for your wellbeing and protection unless you deviate from our script in which case we are coming for you big-time you 'anti-Semitic' transphobe. Development of the synthetic human is long underway and psychologically supported through pre-emptive programming in a list of movies and television series (with *Westworld* a prime example) portraying conscious synthetic robots and synthetic human form. You only have to see the now close resemblance between humans and their synthetic equivalent (Fig 168). The development of a synthetic human genome, DNA, blood, skin and so on is already happening and don't judge its stage of development by what you see in the publicly-acknowledged projects. Secret science in the underground and inside-mountain facilities directed by Hidden Hand levels of the military-intelligence networks are light years ahead on all fronts compared with official science. No, the synthetic human may not be arriving tomorrow,

Figure 168: Human and synthetic 'human'.

but the plan is that it eventually will and far sooner than people imagine. Transgender hysteria is preparing the ground and the collective psyche for just that and doing no favours at all for those genuine transgender people who just want to get on with their lives without demanding that everyone else be pronoun perfect or the wrath of hell will follow. As I was writing this chapter the British Co-op supermarket chain launched a gender-neutral gingerbread person (biscuit) to be 'inclusive' and asked the public to choose a 'fitting' name. I suggest 'Loada' for the first name and 'Bollocks' for the second. Yes, Loada Bollocks seems very 'fitting'.

Information control

The foundation of the entire Hidden Hand/Sabbatian-Frankist conspiracy is the control of information. From that comes control of perception which means control of behaviour. Our actions come from our perceptions and our perceptions are formed from information received. Control information and you control that sequence unless the targets have a mind of their own and can see though the game. If you know the outcome you can see the journey and this is why uncovering where we are being taken is so important. Without that compass daily events appear to be random and have no pattern, but when you know what the outcome is planned to be those same events become crystal clear steps towards that end. The Hidden Hand's desired outcome with regard to information is that eventually people will only see and hear what the authorities decide they can see and hear. Everything else will be silenced and censored. The Tiptoe sequence to this outcome cannot be denied as censorship increases by the hour through (Hidden Hand-controlled) government and (Hidden Hand-controlled) Internet and media giants. Transferring the communication of information from traditional media to the Internet allows AI algorithms to censor and suppress information they don't want you to see. We now have the Hidden Hand symbiosis of gofers in government, gofers in Silicon Valley like Zuckerberg and mind-programmed Soros 'progressives' all calling for more regulation of what people can post and thus see. Ultra-Zionists and the Sabbatian-Frankist Death Cult are the force driving this censorship with the intent of destroying the genuine alternative media before it does any more damage to its satanic ambitions. 'Fake news', 'hate speech' and 'anti-Semitism' with their definitions constantly expanded are only three of the ever-growing manufactured excuses to censor and silence. As I write these words the Hidden Hand-controlled UK government has announced plans for a new 'online regulator' to fine web companies that 'fail to protect users' (censor content) with the power to close down websites that are accused among a list of other things of dealing in 'disinformation'. Who defines that? They do. This censorship on steroids is the calculated abuse of freedom which threatens to fine 'social media platforms, file hosting sites, discussion forums, messaging services and search engines' and to make them responsible 'for any harmful material which they allow their users to share or discover'. The motivation is painfully obvious – to give all these sources the excuse and incentive to censor anything that questions the official version of anything. Watching the UK Home Secretary Sajid Javid selling the policy as 'protection' had me fit to puke when the real reason is so clear. 'Protection from harm' is the latest Orwellian phrase they are using because this takes censorship beyond the merely illegal into the realms of 'harm' which is a totally subjective term that can be used to censor opinion and legitimate exposure that is perfectly legal. Ah, it may be legal and it may be accurate, but does it cause *harm?*

It's best not to rely on the traditional left's historical demand for freedom of speech because that's been hijacked by Soros 'progressives' who believe that freedom of speech is the 'freedom' to agree with them. UK *Guardian* 'progressive' Owen Jones, one of the most arrogant and ignorant people I have ever observed, thinks he should have the right to bounce between TV studios endlessly giving his opinions while those he disagrees with should be censored. He then calls free speech 'sacred'. Yes, for *him*. Free speech is being targeted through ever-gathering excuses and political correctness in general for a simple reason. While it exists there can never be a situation – an outcome – in which authorities dictate everything you can see and hear. Freedom of speech therefore has to be deleted to bring this about and that's why it is now happening on an industrial scale via government regulation and despicable people who call the shots at despicable organisations with contempt for freedom like Google, YouTube, Facebook, Twitter, Apple, Spotify, Amazon and so many others. The Soros 'progressive' software program is screaming its abuse at the frontline to demand that alternative information and opinion is silenced in its alliance with multi-billionaires who have absolute contempt for their 'social warrior', 'woke', puppets and pawns. They are the 'anti-fascist' fascists, the 'pro-inclusion' excluders and the 'pro-diversity' destroyers of diversity. They are the 'anti-hate' haters and the current day version of the two minutes of hate in Orwell's *Nineteen-eighty-four* when Big Brother's manufactured 'villain' Emmanuel Goldstein appears on the screen while the crowd

Figure 169: Orwell's equivalent of the 'progressive' mob screaming their orchestrated hate in the movie version of *Nineteen- eighty-four.*

dressed all the same (guaranteed income) follow instructions to scream hatred at Goldstein using terms such as 'traitor' and 'death' (Fig 169). Put the words 'two minutes of hate, 1984' into a video search engine and you'll see what I mean. Then look at the faces of 'progressive' extremists no matter what their expression or particular obsession and you'll see the same. I feel so sad for them. Forgive them for they know not what they do. The program has possessed them, but it doesn't have to if they choose to take their minds back. Everything is a mind game and perceptual manipulation. Even the ever-growing contempt for politicians is being orchestrated to manipulate the population to accept a post-democratic society in another Problem-Reaction-Solution. All you really need to bring this about is to make sure most politicians are disingenuous, ignorant and incompetent and the rest follows. The political class alliance between Westminster politicians and EU bureaucrats to create the orchestrated chaos aimed at thwarting the UK referendum vote for Brexit is a perfect example. A survey on political attitudes by the Hansard Society in 2019 found support for a 'strong leader' who would break the rules and 42 percent of those questioned agreed that many problems could be dealt with more effectively 'if the government didn't have to worry so much about votes in parliament'. Sabbatian-Frankists would have been punching the air and contemptuously cheering their mainstream media for promoting and supporting the very agenda planned to delete *its* freedom of speech – or what's left of it. The way so much of the media supported the arrest of Julian Assange of WikiLeaks in 2019 for doing the job *they* should be doing said it all and there was not even a titter of media outrage at my own ban from Australia by the authoritarian government on the say-so of basically one ultra-Zionist. I do wonder, however, why in the face of the evidence that Assange calls 9/11 a 'false conspiracy theory'.

So there we are ...

We have come such a long way since you turned the first page and everything between then and now is connected. I didn't intend or expect to write such a big book and to think that I started out to simply produce an updated version of my *Alice in Wonderland*. The enslavement of humanity, however, has so many elements and such an essential back-story that it cannot be effectively exposed without volume and connections. Dots are interesting', but connecting the dots is devastating. It's the only way to reveal the apparently random to be long-planned calculation and to transform pixels of confusion into pictures of clarity. Even then what I have written in this book is still only part of the story. Far deeper levels and so many other connections and expressions of the conspiracy can be found in *Everything You Need To Know* and earlier works. The basic theme is the same from whichever angle or depth that you observe the human plight. When you give your mind and perceptions away the receiver will control your life. When you take them back their game is over. A relative handful cannot control and dictate the lives of 7.7 billion unless the 7.7 billion give their minds away and concede their uniqueness to group-think and acquiescence. The way out of here becomes obvious: We reverse that process. This means no longer believing what we are told without checking the facts; no longer rejecting the evidence of our own eyes and experience because authority or intimidation demands that we do so; and no longer being frightened into silence by the bullies and the mob. If we don't do that – and in number – then all I have described will come about because who is going to stop it? We are eternal expressions of consciousness and our transitory labels are only brief experiences in a tiny band of frequency – a sort of TV channel. We need to play the long game from that perspective and not limit and enslave ourselves in the fear of short-term consequences. Instead of worrying what will happen if I say or do this, that or the other, consider the consequences of *not* saying or doing it. I have been highlighting those consequences in this book and for 30 years since. If you think it's bad now what kind of world are you, your children and grandchildren going to live in a short and long while hence? We are only where we are – not where it is meant to stay. The most extreme stuff is still to come. We must shout louder when we are told to be silent. You might lose some friends? *And*? What kind of 'friends' don't respect your right to speak your truth? John Lennon said: 'Being honest may not get you a lot of friends but it'll always get you the right ones.' We must cease to cooperate with our own enslavement – cease to be intimated into conformity by a mob of adolescent children (whatever their age) programmed to impose their programming on the rest of us. I will not be intimidated, have my views silenced or take lectures from arrogant terrible-twos masquerading as adults. If people continue to do so we will live in the world they are creating and, with more irony, so will they. Everything they are seeking to impose on others will be imposed on them once they have served their purpose and those pulling their strings sweep back the curtains and openly seize power. We need to call out the social warrior bullies and the 'anti-hate' hate groups for their blatant hypocrisy and when that happens we will realise their only power was intimidation. When we cease to be intimidated their power will be gone and so will that of their hidden and not-so-hidden masters that they refuse to acknowledge. Fault-lines of divide and rule – race, religion, culture, sexuality, income bracket – need to be set aside to allow unity of purpose. When we divide we fall. When we unite – *they* fall.

Fear of the Maverick

The *Protocols of the Learned Elders of Zion* which I say are based on the Sabbatian-Frankist plan for the world makes it very clear that divide and rule is utterly essential for their endeavours to reach fruition. They talk of the need to 'set one against another the personal and national reckonings … religious and race hatreds, which we have fostered'. This is, of course, what has happened and is happening. There is, however, a pause in the diatribe of arrogance when it comes to maverick people – a term defined as 'a person who thinks and acts in an independent way, often behaving differently from the expected or usual way'. The term 'maverick' comes from Samuel A. Maverick, a mid-19th century Texas rancher who did not brand his cattle. How apt given the microchip branding of human cattle now fast emerging. Maverick translates in the *Protocols* to what they call 'personal initiative':

> The second secret requisite for the success of our government is comprised in the following; To multiply to such an extent national failings, habits, passions, conditions of civil life, that it will be impossible for anyone to know where he is in the resulting chaos, so that the people in consequence will fail to understand one another; This measure will also serve us in another way, namely, to sow discord in all parties, to dislocate all collective forces which are still unwilling to submit to us, and to discourage any kind of personal initiative which might in any degree hinder our affair.

This is their worst nightmare – maverick personal initiative. The *Protocols* emphasise: '*There is nothing more dangerous than personal initiative.*' If it has genius behind it, the document says, such initiative 'can do more than can be done by millions of people among whom we have sown discord'. The *Protocols* describe the plan more than a century ago to so direct education that 'whenever they come upon a matter requiring initiative they may drop their hands in despairing impotence'. Yet again we can see with the perspective of hindsight that what the *Protocols* predict and what has happened are mirrors of each other. 'Education' has suppressed and punished mavericks and personal initiative in favour of the group-think that infects the human psyche and especially its 'progressive' expression. Group-think is not only collective perception. It is also founded on the black and whiteness of us and them, for us or against us. To break from the program we must break from black and white. I consider individual statements on their validity and not by who makes them. Is what is said *true?* That is my only criteria. It means that I can accept a statement and then reject the next one when spoken by the same mouth. To accept everything from one person and nothing from another only on the basis of what you think of the people involved is clearly crazy, but that happens all the time. I have been criticised for posting clips on my website of Tucker Carlson presentations and interviews because he's on Fox News (black and white – bad) and for calling out the disingenuous 'news' host Rachael Maddow on MSNBC (black and white – good). This is typical of the perception polarisation that people have fallen for whether coming from the far left (far 'progressive') or far right. They both think they are different while psychologically they are just the same and play the essential role of perceived polarities to ensure Marxist-demanded conflict and divide and rule. Anyone who judges statements and information on the basis of the political colour of the source instead of the validity of the statement and information *itself* is caught in the fly-trap. Perceptions should be formed from evidence and actions not whether someone is on MSNBC or Fox and not whether they tell us what we want to hear or not. Rachael Maddow is a professional virtue-signaller and through that a hero of the 'progressive' virtue-signalling fake 'radical left' which is being so blatantly manipulated by the elite and its place-men like Soros. Talk about babes in arms and lambs to the slaughter. 'Progressives' are programmed to believe in a black and white world that doesn't exist and they might ask how come they and the multi-billionaire elite are now on the same page and reading from the same script. How did this come about and to what end? Answer that and they may get their minds back. The same is true of the black and white right and far right and its media 'gods' like Sean Hannity on Fox and the Soros of the right, Sheldon Adelson. The fact that I unite the 'progressive' left and the far right against me in mutual condemnation gives me great comfort. I remember talking to a 'progressive' television news producer who could not compute the fact that I opposed political correctness, unchecked immigration and the hoax of human-caused 'climate change' and yet also opposed Trump. To him if I was against one then I had to be for the other. It was hilarious to observe. The world is not black and white – it's always somewhere in between. Hey, 'progressives' and far right I'll meet you there one day I hope and this nonsense can be brought to an end. The perception of love is another black and white when love is multi-faceted and often the opposite of how it is perceived. Is it love to give your child a smartphone to bring short term elation or to say no in the name of long-term protection? Is it love to take the easy route to immediate gratitude or the harder route of short-term disappointment for long-term benefit? Is it love to spend 30 years telling people what they want to hear with all the kudos that comes with that? Or to tell them what they don't want to hear – but *need* to hear – in full knowledge of the ridicule and abuse that will ensue? Nothing is black and white except the programmed human mind.

Consequences don't matter – only the truth and freedom does

You can guess what the reaction will be to this book from Sabbatian-Frankists, ultra-Zionists and their agents and place-people. They will be apoplectic and not because what I say is not true – but because it *is* true. Of course they will claim that I'm wrong about where this is planned to go and I have been told the same so many times over the decades only for what was denied to happen. It is hilarious to hear what I say dismissed and condemned only to be proved right by the very people who are trashing it. 'A few people don't control the world and if you say so we'll silence you.' It's hysterical and what happened to me with Australia was a classic. 'He's anti-Semitic' for saying we Zionists have influence way beyond our number and so we've had him banned by the government.' I think you are supposed to be intimidated by all this, but to me they're a comedy club. What I say is planned with Israel so centrally involved is out there now and we'll see what happens from here with the passage of events won't we? If I'm wrong then it won't happen will it? No high-profile person was supposed to reveal this information and be so up-front about it. Everyone was supposed to keep their heads down in fear of the consequences and labels of racist and Nazi; but I don't give a shit what people say about me – least of all the ultra-Zionists and Death Cult behind 9/11 and so much more. I want the truth, that's all, whatever that truth may be and wherever it may take me. The harder they try to silence me the louder I will shout.

It is likely there will be efforts to ban the book or block its circulation or maybe they will just ignore it for fear of giving publicity to a book they don't want people to read – as they did with my last one. It is certainly possible that Problem-Reaction-Solution attacks on Jewish targets will be set-up to blame on the book and fuel demands for it and me to be banned. This is the modus operandi of the satanic Sabbatian-Frankist Death Cult and the wider Hidden Hand. I can't do anything about what they do in their efforts to stop me and with such psychopathic evil anything is possible. I can only control what *I* do and that will be, and will *always* be, to speak my truth no matter what the consequences. Nearly 3,000 people died on 9/11 and millions have been killed and wounded in the sequence of wars and upheavals that it was coldly exploited to trigger. For every person who has died there are many, many more who suffer the ongoing emotional consequences of what happened to their mums and dads, sons and daughters, brothers and sisters, wives and husbands. Those people deserve justice and I am not going to stay silent in fear of abuse from the ultra-Zionist hate group network that ultimately connects to the Death Cult perpetrators. The human race has been running away for thousands of years and it's time to stop.

ENOUGH! I'm sick of the bullshit.

Postscript

Just prior to this book going to print a Freedom of Information Act request led to the release of 14 images taken by and of the 'Dancing Israelis' before and during the 9/11 attacks. They are not the originals, only photocopy quality and heavily redacted by the FBI. Even the background of the towers is missing so desperate are the authorities to censor the devastating evidence the public would otherwise see. The pictures do, however, confirm the location.

Their release was remarkable given that the Department of [In]Justice had previously claimed the pictures were destroyed in 2014. Put this headline into the search engine at Davidicke.com and you can see them: Newly Released FBI Docs Shed Light on Apparent Mossad Foreknowledge of 9/11 Attacks. Some of the images, including one with Mossad operative Sivan Kurzberg holding up a lighter flame apparently against the Twin Towers in the background, are dated *September 10th*, 2001, and the rest are from September 11th. This would make sense of FBI reports of an eyewitness stating with certainty that Sivan Kurzberg was at the Doric apartments on September 10th where the Dancing Israelis would be spotted the next day when the towers were hit. Kurzberg was said to have claimed to be a 'construction worker' and he was with at least one other man with whom he conversed 'in a foreign language'. Clearly if Dancing Israelis were on site the day before the attacks and returned to film and celebrate them on 9/11 their foreknowledge is clear. Yet still the case against them was dropped in a blatant cover up of Mossad Israeli involvement. The release of the Israelis was signed off by Attorney General John Ashcroft in league with Criminal Division chief Michael Chertoff and one of Ashcroft's first clients when he entered private business was the Israeli government. Dominik Otto Suter, official owner of the Dancing Israeli Mossad-front, Urban Moving Systems, fled to Israel on September 14th, 2001, after being interviewed by the FBI, but is reported to have lived in the San Francisco area since at least 2016 as a contractor for Silicon Valley tech giants such as Google and Microsoft and also been employed by Granite Telecommunications which works for the US military and government agencies. Granite Telecommunications is headquartered in Quincy, Massachusetts, where key 9/11 computer company Ptech was based in 2001. I am not saying that this implies a connection, only stating a fact. If Suter has been resident in the United States since 9/11 why in the name of sanity has the FBI not been on his case to establish the real background to Urban Moving Systems and why he fled to Israel after his first interview?? It has been further reported that four Israeli nationals were detained (and released like all the others) who worked for another 'moving company' called Classic International Movers. The FBI in Miami, Florida, told the Newark Division that this company had connections to at least one of the alleged 9/11 'hijackers'. A Dancing Israeli had the number of Classic International Movers in his notebook. What deceit. What a cover up. America should be outraged at the contempt for the dead by its own government that all this reveals – and it's still going on. A *New York Post* headline 18 years after the attacks said: '9/11 fund shrivels up as first responder cancer cases continue to grow'. It is described as 'cancer on steroids'. The *Post* said:

> New Yorkers who survived 9/11 are experiencing a massive surge in aggressive brain cancers as dollars for the September 11th Victim Compensation Fund continue to dry up — leaving them wondering in their final days who will support their families once they're gone.

The world is not run by psychopaths?

Nazi censorship out of control

The agenda moves on so fast and even in the short time this book has been in the production stage much has happened to confirm the themes I have highlighted and exposed. Censorship of information and opinion has reached ever more fascistic extremes through the ultimately Death Cult-controlled Internet tyrannies such as Facebook, Twitter and the rest of the censorship cabal posturing 'values' they don't have. Challenging official narratives across a swathe of subjects is increasingly likely to have you banned from these Hidden Hand, Sabbatian-Frankist and Pentagon operations that dominate the communication of information and crush any competing platforms with the usual enthusiastic support from their Hidden Hand cheerleaders in government and media. A Facebook employee revealed that Zuckerberg 'values' include having a 'hate agents list' of people it seeks to ban while another list gives 'extra credit' to employees who find creative ways to censor them. Those challenging the Big Pharma vaccine scam, transgender imposition and unchecked society-changing mass immigration have all been the particular targets of ever-growing censorship in the short time since I completed the book along with the ubiquitous 'anti-Semitism'. The ultra-Zionist and Death Cult-controlled German parliament decreed that the Boycott Divestment and Sanctions (BDS) movement is 'anti-Semitic' and called for a ban on funding groups backing BDS. Supporters of the decision included the utterly System-serving Green Party. They outrageously likened BDS to German Nazis who urged people not to buy from Jews. So the United States and all the countries imposing economic sanctions on target governments are all racists and fascists are they? It is so transparent – they do what the Death Cult tells them while the vast majority have no idea there even is a Death Cult. Jonathan Greenblatt, Chief Executive Officer and National Director of the Mossad/Rothschild Anti-Defamation League (ADL), bragged to a meeting of the Council on Foreign Relations that they were leading the Internet censorship war on free speech:

> We work with Google on using AI to try and interrupt cyber-hate before it happens. We work with YouTube to get them to change their algorithms so it lessens the likelihood that a young person is going to run into some of these anti-Semitic conspiratorial videos. So there are different ways [Facebook] can tweak their algorithms and adjust their products so they think not only about free speech … but protect the user's right to not be harassed or hated.

Pass that through the Orwellian Translation Unit and you get censorship of any criticism or exposure of the far right regime in Israel and the force that really controls it. Greenblatt also called for more draconian laws to protect Jews from 'anti-Semitism' (see above). So-called 'world leaders' led by Rothschild frontman Emmanuel Macron met with tech giants in Paris to exploit the deaths of 51 Muslims in Christchurch, New Zealand, to justify even more draconian censorship. They took a break from bombing Muslims and supplying arms to kill Muslims in the Middle East to show how much they cared about Muslims. My god – it turns my stomach in the same way that Jews who suffered in Nazi Germany are mercilessly exploited to pursue a cold and calculated agenda of censorship today. The Hidden Hand UK, France, Germany, Spain, Ireland, Norway, Sweden, Netherlands, European Commission, Senegal, Jordan, Canada, New Zealand, Australia, India, Indonesia and Japan signed the 'Christchurch Call' agreement along with Hidden Hand Facebook, Amazon, Twitter, Google and Microsoft, but Donald Trump declined because it targets for online censorship his public support base. Soros 'progressives' and the mainstream media of course were delighted with still more censorship in their self-deluded stupidity and arrogance. They don't think *they* will be the target eventually? Bless 'em.

~~Intel~~ Israel inside - *again*

Researchers found *another* back-door 'security flaw' in the Intel processor chips that drive the great majority of the world's computers. This is in addition to the one that I highlighted earlier. The 'flaw' (door) has been dubbed 'ZombieLoad' and is embedded in Intel chips opening the way for access to browser history, passwords, disk encryption keys and other sensitive data. Experts said it was not possible to 'patch' the problem without loss of performance and access can 'also be exploited in the cloud' external to the computer. They pointed out that access could be gained while leaving no trace of what had happened. Nathaniel Gleicher, Facebook's head of cybersecurity policy, revealed that 65 Israeli accounts, 161 pages, dozens of groups and four Instagram accounts had been removed for attempting to interfere with elections. Many were linked to Tel Aviv-based political consulting and lobbying firm, the Archimedes Group, which claims to exploit social media to 'change reality'. Archimedes' chief executive Elinadav Heymann is listed as a former director of the Brussels-based lobbying group, European Friends of Israel, political adviser in the Israeli parliament and agent with Israeli Air Force intelligence. Accounts posing as political candidates and local news organisations were smearing opponents with the focus on Sub-Saharan African countries, Southeast Asia and Latin America. A headline in the Israeli daily *Haaretz* called it an 'Israeli Campaign to Disrupt Elections in African, Asian and Latin American Nations'. Tip and iceberg come to mind given what I have exposed about ultra-Zionist Internet manipulation and 'it's the Russians' is a smokescreen behind which Israeli manipulation can overwhelmingly hide. Facebook further warned users that hackers were able to remotely install software on phones and other devices by exploiting a flaw (door) in Facebook-owned WhatsApp. A simple WhatsApp missed call was enough to covertly install the software. Facebook said the cyber-attack was orchestrated by 'an advanced cyber-actor' using software developed by Israeli company NSO Group which has been referred to as a 'cyber-arms dealer'. NSO's software known as Pegasus can 'collect intimate data from a target device, including capturing data through the microphone and camera, and gathering location data'. The company said that its technology is 'licensed to authorised government agencies for the sole purpose of fighting crime and terror'. Among its clients are those bastions of democracy and human rights, Saudi Arabia, Bahrain and the UAE. Amnesty International issued a lawsuit against NSO fearing its staff could be under surveillance through Pegasus software and called on Israel's defence ministry to ban its export. The Citizen Lab research organisation at the University of Toronto said the NSO technology has been used by several countries to target human rights groups, activists and journalists with 'no attempt to rein it in'. As I write the Trump administration is targeting Chinese giant Huawei and alleging that back-doors are being installed in its technology to spy for the Chinese government. I'm sure they are – just like the US and Israel does the same – but somehow Trump must have missed that. Maybe he just forgot. Other Israeli tech companies have been exposed for attempting to manipulate elections and in 2019 Microsoft unveiled a technology called

ElectionGuard to 'protect' US elections from hacking with the fake 'Russian interference' hoax used as the excuse. Fox guarding the hen house comes to mind. Microsoft, like all the Silicon Valley giants, has massive connections to the Pentagon, DARPA (funders of ElectionGuard) and US intelligence networks and to the Israeli military and intelligence cabal including the Unit 8200 cyber elite at the Beersheba complex. Microsoft has significant investment in the 8200 front company, Team8, and its spin-off, Illusive Networks. Team8 was founded in 2014 by three former leaders of Unit 8200 and has connections to majors players like Intel, Citigroup, Microsoft and Qualcomm. Eric Schmidt, former CEO of Google (Alphabet), is a significant backer of Team8. You get the picture. See the Mintpressnews.com article: 'Microsoft's ElectionGuard a Trojan Horse for a Military-Industrial Takeover of US Elections'.

Renegades are dangerous (to the Death Cult)

The scale and depths of censorship now being imposed can be seen with two premieres of the film *Renegade* being banned in London and Los Angeles which doesn't even mention Zionism. This is a film about my life and work that was due to be shown at a venue in London owned by the Trades Union Congress (TUC) and at the Aero Theatre in Los Angeles owned by an operation called American Cinematheque which also owns the Egyptian in Hollywood. The really elderly may still remember the time when trade unions represented working people, but they have long since been absorbed by the System like the vast majority of those on the former political 'Left'. The TUC, a trade union umbrella organisation, cancelled the showing of *Renegade* the afternoon before the event because they said they believed in 'inclusivity'. The fact that they made that claim in an email *excluding* me would never have breached the walls of their programming. How more inclusive can a philosophy be than – *we are all one consciousness having different experiences*? But this would be far too deep for the software TUC. Think about that – a *trade union* organisation bans a film about a *renegade*! What confirmation of how far the 'Left' has fallen into cabal conformity. The TUC could not care less about the potential effect on the audience (we fortunately found another venue) and nor had they seen the film or read any of my books. Someone told them what to believe about me and so they did. *Pathetic*. Then there was 'American Cinematheque' which is described as 'an independent, non-profit cultural organization in Los Angeles dedicated exclusively to the public presentation of the moving image in all its forms'. Well, unless it's about me. The American Cinematheque board of directors and trustees is reported to include 'many prominent leaders in the entertainment industry', including directors and producers such as Sydney Pollack, Martin Scorsese, Mike Nichols, Francis Coppola, William Friedkin, Melvin Van Peebles, Brian Grazer, Joe Dante, Paula Wagner, and Steve Tisch together with actors Candice Bergen and Goldie Hawn, studio chief Mike Medavoy, journalist Peter Bart, editor in chief of *Variety*, and talent agent Rick Nicita, co-chairman of Creative Artists Agency. The producer of *Renegade*, who is not a 'follower' but just thought it would make an interesting film, booked the Aero Theatre in Santa Monica weeks before the premiere and arranged for us to arrive at 4pm for a technical run-through ahead of a 6pm start. At 3.55 when we were only minutes from arriving the producer's phone rang in the back of the vehicle. He put the phone to his ear, but I clearly heard every word even from the front seat such was the volume from the other end. Firstly a woman told us they were cancelling the premiere and then a man came on shouting down the phone. Both of them, especially the man, were extremely unpleasant and basically horrible. This was a deeply sinister part of the conversation between the producer and the hysterical man:

'Is this film about *David Icke*?'

'Yes.'

'Does the film put him in a *good light*?'

'Well, yes, he comes across very well.'

Then it wasn't being shown at his theatre, the hysterical man said – hysterically.

That is another shocker to ponder. If the film does not demonise me it can't be shown but if it did there would have been no problem. We saw the same Orwellian, fascistic approach about the same time when a group of people, including Alex Jones and Muslim leader Louis Farrakhan, were banned from Facebook and Facebook-owned Instagram under the title 'dangerous individuals' that 'promote or engage in violence and hate'. None are in Facebook's league for being dangerous to human society. The ban also targets those who post information from these people or say anything positive about them. Demonising them is okay – as with me and American Cinematheque. We are well on the road to Orwell's 'unperson' – those removed from all communications and records so they do not to the general population even exist. Once again American Cinematheque could not care less about the effect on the audience which turned up at the venue to find the event had been cancelled while we battled through Los Angeles rush-hour traffic to get back to our hotel before we could tell them. David Icke is evil so anyone who supports him is evil so what does it matter if we abuse them?

That's the mentality at work in these situations because they are people who have 'values', you see. It's appropriate to give the last word in this book to the Campaign Against Antisemitism (CAA) because they spend their time saying I'm wrong while constantly proving me right. 'Enforcer' Stephen 'Little Dick' Silverman called on UK station Talkradio to 'immediately apologise' for interviewing me about *Renegade* – a film that doesn't mention Jewish people and the interview didn't mention Jewish people either. 'We are going to make a formal complaint to the station and are considering raising the matter with [media watchdog] Ofcom' said the professional censor. They were going to make a formal complaint about an interview which didn't mention Jewish people and talked about a film that doesn't mention Jewish people?

Yes, because it is not about Jewish people is it Little Dick and Dvir Abramovich who had me banned from Australia? It's about silencing the truth. At the time of writing some 500,000 people had watched the Talkradio recording – it will be many more by the time you read this – but none of them should have been allowed to hear what I said. Little Dick says so. I rest my case.

You can watch *Renegade* by going to Davidicke.com where you will also find world news every day from another perspective and my latest interviews and information. By subscribing you can access a library of my work and presentations over the last 30 years plus many other features, benefits and sources of information and exposure.

Two recommended vaccine books: *Vaccines: A Reappraisal* by Richard Moskowitz MD (Skyhorse Publishing, 2017) and *Saying No To Vaccines* by Sherri Tenpenny (Tenpenny Publishing, 2008). Also put the words 'Robert F. Kennedy Jr. exposes vaccines' into the search engine at Davidicke.com – a magnificent speech with spot-on information that every parent should hear.

For a fantastic interview exposing the catastrophic effects of 5G and microwaves with world expert Barrie Trower put these words into the Davidicke.com search engine: 'Barrie Trower 5G WiFi Smart Meters Armageddon Interview'.

Bibliography

Abunimah, Ali: *The Battle for Justice in Palestine* (Haymarket Books, 2014)

Alinsky, Saul: *Rules for Radicals* (Vintage, 1989)

Antelman, Marvin S: *To Eliminate the Opiate* (Vol 1, Zionist Book Club, 1974)

Antelman, Marvin S: *To Eliminate the Opiate* (Vol 2, Zionist Book Club, 2002)

Arkin, William: *The U.S. Military Online: A Directory for Internet Access to the Department of Defense* (Potomac Books, second edition, 1998)

Bamford, James: *Body of Secrets* (Doubleday, 2001)

Baron, S W: *A Social and Religious History of the Jews* (1957)

Bastardi, Joe: *The Climate Chronicles* (Relentless Thunder Press, 2018)

Beamer, Lisa: *Let's Roll!* (Tyndale House Publishers, 2002)

Beaty, Jonathan and Gwynne, S.C.: *The Outlaw Bank: A Wild Ride into the Secret Heart of The BCCI* (Random House, New York, 1993)

Bergman, Ronen: *Rise and Kill First – the secret history of Israel's targeted assassinations* (Random House, 2019)

Bollyn, Christopher: *Solving 9-11 and Solving 9-11 – the Original Articles* (both published by Christopher Bollyn, 2012)

Bowen, Russell S: *The Immaculate Deception* (America West Publishers; first edition, September, 2000)

Bradlee Jr, Ben: *Guts And Glory: The Rise and Fall of Oliver North* (Donald I. Fine Inc., 1988)

Brill, Steven: *After: The Rebuilding and Defending of America in the September 12 Era* (Simon & Schuster, 2003)

Brisard, Jean-Charles, and Dasquie, Guillaume: *Forbidden Truth: U.S.-Taliban Secret Oil Diplomacy, Saudi Arabia and the Failed Search for bin Laden* (Nation Books, 2002)

Brzezinski, Zbigniew: *Between Two Ages: America's Role in the Technetronic Era* (The Viking Press, 1970)

Brzezinski, Zbigniew: *The Grand Chessboard, American Primacy and its Geostrategic Imperatives* (Basic Books, 1997)

Chaitkin, Anton. and Tarpley, Webster: *George Bush, The Unauthorised Biography* (Executive Intelligence Review, 1991)

Chomsky, Noam: *Necessary Illusions: Thought Control in Democratic Societies* (South End Press, 1999)

Clarke, Richard: *Against All Enemies* (Free, 2004)

Cockburn, Leslie: *Out of Control: The Story of the Reagan Administration's Secret War in Nicaragua, the Illegal Arms Pipeline, and the Contra Drug Connection* (Atlantic Monthly, different edition, 1987)

Davidsson, Elias: *Hijacking America's Mind on 9/11* (Algora Publishing, 2013)

De Masi, Nicholas, and Bellone, Mike: *Behind the Scene: Ground Zero* (Self-published, 2003)

DeYoung, Karen: *Soldier: The Life of Colin Powell* (Vintage, 2007)

Dugger, Ronnie: *The Politician: The Life And Times Of Lyndon Johnson* (Norton, 1982)

Dunn, Vincent: *Collapse of Burning Buildings* (Fire Engineering Books second edition, 2010)

Friedman, Robert: *Red Mafiya: How the Russian Mob Has Invaded America* (Little, Brown, 2000)

Ennes Jr, James: *Assault on the Liberty* (Random House, 1979)

Evanzz, Karl: *The Judas Factor: The Plot To Kill Malcolm X* (Thunder's Mouth Press, 1993)

Graetz, Heinrich: *History of the Jews from Oldest Times to the Present* (Myers & Co, 1904)

Griffin, David Ray: *9/11 Ten Years Later* (Olive Branch Press, 2012)

Griffin, David Ray, and Woodworth, Elizabeth: *9/11 Unmasked* (Olive Branch Press, 2018)

Griffin, David Ray: *Osama bin Laden – Dead or Alive?* (Olive Branch Press, 2009)

Griffin, David Ray: *The 9/11 Commission Report, Omissions and Distortions* (Olive Branch Press, 2004)

Grose, Peter: *Gentleman Spy: The Life of Allen Dulles* (University of Massachusetts Press, 1996)

Hall, Manly P: *The Secret Teachings of All Ages* (Jeremy P. Tarcher, new edition, 2004)

Hallin, Daniel C: *The Uncensored War: The Media And Vietnam* (Oxford University Press, 1986)

Hamza, Hisham: *Israel and September 11: The Great Taboo* (e-book, 2013)

Hart, Alan: *Zionism: The Real Enemy of the Jews* (Clarity Press, 2009 – several volumes)

Hatfield, J H: *Fortunate Son: George Bush and the Making of a President* (Vision Paperbacks, 2002)

Hecht, Jeff: *Beam Weapons: The Next Arms Race* (Plenum, second edition, 1985)

Herzl, Theodor: *Judenstaat* (CreateSpace Independent Publishing Platform, 2016)

Herzl, Theodor: *The Complete Diaries of Theodor Herzl* (The Herzl Press, 1960)

Hicks, Sanders: *The Big Wedding: 9/11, the Whistle-Blowers and the Cover-Up* (Drench Kiss Media, 2005)

Hopsicker, Daniel: *Barry And The Boys: The CIA, The Mob, And America's Secret History* (MadCow Press, 2001)

House Mandel, *Philip Dru: Administrator*: (WP, 2010)

Ide, Dr Arthur F: *George W. Bush: Portrait Of A Compassionate Conservative* (Monument Press, Texas, 2000)

Kean, Thomas H, and Hamilton, Lee H: *Without Precedent: The Inside Story of the 9/11 Commission* (Knopf, 2006)

Kinross, Lord Patrick: *Ataturk, The Rebirth of a Nation* (Weidenfeld and Nicolson, first edition, 1964)

Knight, Moll: *No Better Time: The Brief, Remarkable Life of Danny Lewin, the*

Genius Who Transformed the Internet (Da Capo Press, 2013)

Kollerstrom, Nick: *Terror on the Tube, Behind the Veil of 7/7* (Progressive Press; third revised edition, 2011)

Kurzweil, Ray, and multiple authors: *The Scientific Conquest of Death* (Libros en Red, 2004)

Lipkin, Avi (pen name Victor Mordecai): *Is Fanatic Islam a Global Threat?* (Talmidim Publishing, 2003)

Loftus, John, and Aarons, Mark: *Unholy Trinity: The Vatican, The Nazis and the Swiss Banks* (St Martin's Press, 1992)

Longman, Jere: *Among the Heroes: United Flight 93 and the Passengers and Crew Who Fought Back* (Harper, 2002)

Macdonald, Kevin: *The Culture of Critique: An Evolutionary Analysis of Jewish Involvement in Twentieth-Century Intellectual and Political Movements* (Authorhouse, 2002)

Marrs, Jim: *Crossfire: The Plot That Killed Kennedy* (Carrol and Graf Publishers, New York, 1989)

Martin, Al: *The Conspirators: Secrets of an Iran-Contra Insider* (National Liberty Press, 2001)

Marx, Karl: *A World Without Jews* (Philosophical Library, first edition, 1959)

McCall, David: *From Tragedy to Triumph* (Noah's Ark, 2002)

McGowan, David: *Weird Scenes Inside the Canyon: Laurel Canyon, Covert Ops & the Dark Heart of the Hippie Dream* (Headpress, 2014)

Mearsheimer, John, and Walt, Stephen: *The Israel Lobby and U.S. Foreign Policy* (Farrar, Straus and Giroux, 2007)

Mencken, Henry Louis: *The American Language* (New York, 1919)

Morgenstern, George: *Pearl Harbor, The Story of the Secret War* (Costa Mesa, USA, 1991 edition, first published 1947)

Nagy, Dr Sandor: *The Forgotten Cradle of the Hungarian Culture* (Patria, 1973)

Netanyahu, Benjamin: *Fighting Terrorism: How Democracies Can Defeat Domestic and International Terrorism* (Farrar, Straus and Giroux, 2001)

Netanyahu, Benjamin: *Terrorism: How the West Can Win* (Farrar Straus & Giroux, first edition, 1986)

North, Oliver: *Under Fire* (HarperCollins, 1991)

O'Brien, Cathy: *Trance Formation of America* (Reality Marketing, 1995)

Orwell, George: *Nineteen-eighty-four* (Dutton/Plume, 1983, first published in 1949)

Oren, Michael B: *Six Days of War* (Oxford University Press, 2002)

Ostrovsky, Victor: *By Way of Deception* (St Martin's Press, 1990)

Ostrovsky, Victor: *The Other Side of Deception* (HarperCollins, 1994)

Perloff, James: *The Shadows Of Power: The Council On Foreign Relations And The American Decline* (Western Islands, Appleton, Wisconsin, USA, 1988)

Polak, Nahum: *Khazaria* (1943)

Powell, Colin: *My American Journey* (Random House, 1995)

Prouty, L Fletcher: *JFK, The CIA, Vietnam And The Plot To Assassinate John F. Kennedy* (Skyhorse, 2011)

Prouty, L Fletcher: *JFK, the CIA, Vietnam and the Plot to Assassinate John F.*

Kennedy (Birch Lane Press, 1992)

Prouty, L Fletcher: *The Secret Team: The CIA and Its Allies in Control of the United States and the World* (Skyhorse, 2011)

Quigley, Carroll: *The Anglo-American Establishment* (GSG and Associates, 1981)

Quigley, Carroll: *Tragedy and Hope* (GSG and Associates, 2004)

Rabow, Jerry: *50 Jewish Messiahs* (Gefen Publishing House, 2002)

Radanko, Laura: The Russian Mafia in America (CreateSpace Independent Publishing Platform, 2011)

Rashid, Ahmed: *Taliban: Militant Islam, Oil And Fundamentalism In Central Asia* (Yale University Press, 2000)

Reed, Terry and Cummings, John: *Compromised: Clinton, Bush, And The CIA* (SPI Books, New York, 1994)

Sanders, Jim: *The Downing of Flight 800* (Zebra Books, 1997)

Sand, Shlomo: *The Invention of the Jewish People* (Verso, 2010)

Scholem, Gershom: *The Messianic Idea in Judaism* (Schocken Books, 1971)

Shack, Clifford: *The Sabbatean-Frankist Messianic Conspiracy Partially Exposed* (Facsimile Publisher, 2015)

Shaw, Jim: *The Deadly Deception* (Huntington House Inc., 1988)

Soave, Robby: *Panic Attack: Young Radicals in the Age of Trump* (All Points Books, 2019)

Solzhenitsyn, Alexander: *Two Hundred Years Together* (Two volumes, Vagrius, Russia, 2008, first published 2001 and 2002)

Stich, Rodney: *Unfriendly Skies: Saga of Corruption* (Silverpeak Enterprises, third edition, 1990)

Stinnett, Robert: *Day Of Deceit: The Truth About FDR And Pearl Harbor* (Simon & Schuster, 2001)

Sutton, Antony: *Wall Street and the Rise of Hitler* (G S G & Associates, 1976)

Taylor, Philip: *Munitions of the Mind, a History of Propaganda* (Manchester University Press, 1995)

Thomas, Gordon: *Gideon's Spies – The Secret History of the Mossad* (St. Martin's Griffin, revised edition, 2015)

Thomas, William: *All Fall Down, The Politics Of Terror And Mass Persuasion* (Essence Publications, 2002)

Thorn, Victor: *9/11 Evil* (2006)

Turan, D. Mustafa: *The Donmeh Jews* (Cairo, 1989)

Verton, Dan: *Black Ice: The Invisible Threat of Cyber-Terrorism* (McGraw-Hill Osborne Media, 2003)

Walker, Alice: *The Color Purple* (Houghton Mifflin Harcourt, 1992)

Wells, Tom: *The War Within: America's Battle Over Vietnam* (Open Road Distribution; reprint edition, 2016)

Wilton, Robert: *The Last Days of the Romanovs* (Blurb, 2018, first published 1920)

Wood, Dr Judy: *Where Did The Towers Go?* (The New Investigation, 2010)

Zarembka, Paul, and various authors: *The Hidden History of 9-11* (AI Press, 2006)

Index

Other work by David Icke

Everything You Need To Know But Have Never Been Told

The perfect companion book to *The Trigger* which expands on many of the themes in far greater detail and takes the story even deeper into the rabbit hole of human manipulation and control to reveal who controls the controllers and orchestrates the enslavement of this 'world' from beyond the firewalls of human reality. The book also explains how we can dismantle the control and leave our children a world of freedom.

Phantom Self

The questions are being asked like never before. What is happening in the World? What is 'life' really about? Gathering numbers of people have a sense of unease about the direction of human society without knowing why. Something is happening, but what?

The Perception Deception

David's most comprehensive book in which a vast spectrum of subjects are weaved together to present the world in a totally new light. 900 pages copiously illustrated and a colour art gallery by Neil Hague. *The Perception Deception* is the most detailed dot-connecting book ever written on these subjects.

Remember Who You Are

This book breaks massive new ground and brings a world of apparent complexity, mystery and bewilderment into clarity. The key is in the title. We are enslaved because we identify 'self' with our body and our name when these are only vehicles and symbols for that we really are – Infinite Awareness.

Human Race Get Off Your Knees – The Lion Sleeps No More

A monumental work of more than 650 pages, 355,000 words, 325 images and 32 pages of original artwork by Neil Hague. David's biggest and most comprehensive book introducing the 'Moon Matrix' and providing the fine detail about reality, history and present day events. Highly-acclaimed and a 'must have' for anyone interested in David Icke's work.

The David Icke Guide to the Global Conspiracy (and how to end it)

A masterpiece of dot-connecting that is both extraordinary and unique. There is a 'wow', indeed many of them, on every page as Icke lifts the veil on the unseen world.

Infinite Love is the Only Truth, Everything Else is Illusion

Why the 'world' is a virtual-reality game that only exists because we believe it does. Icke explains how we 'live' in a 'holographic internet' in that our brains are connected to a central 'computer' that feeds us the same collective reality that we decode from waveforms and electrical signals into the holographic 3D 'world' that we all think we see.

Alice in Wonderland and the World Trade Center Disaster – Why the Official Story of 9/11 is a Monumental Lie

A shocking exposé of the Ministries of Mendacity that have told the world the Big Lie about what happened on September 11th, who did it, how and why. This 500 page book reveals the real agenda behind the 9/11 attacks and how they were orchestrated from within the borders of the United States and not from a cave in Afghanistan.

Tales from the Time Loop

In this 500-page, profusely-illustrated book, David Icke explores in detail the multi-levels of the global conspiracy. He exposes the five-sense level and demolishes the official story of the invasions of Iraq and Afghanistan; he explains the inter-dimensional manipulation; and he shows that what we think is the 'physical world' is all an illusion that only exists in our mind. Without this knowledge, the true nature of the conspiracy cannot be understood.

The Biggest Secret

An exposé of how the same interbreeding bloodlines have controlled the planet for thousands of years. It includes the horrific background to the British royal family, the murder of Princess Diana, and the true origins of major religions. A blockbuster.

Children of the Matrix

The companion book of The Biggest Secret that investigates the reptilian and other dimensional connections to the global conspiracy and reveals the world of illusion – the 'Matrix' – that holds the human race in daily slavery.

... And The Truth Shall Set You Free (21st century edition)

Icke exposes in more than 500 pages the interconnecting web that controls the world today. This book focuses on the last 200 years and particularly on what is happening around us today. Another highly acclaimed book, which has been constantly updated. A classic in its field.

I Am Me, I Am Free

Icke's book of solutions. With humour and powerful insight, he shines a light on the mental and emotional prisons we build for ourselves ... prisons that disconnect us from our true and infinite potential to control our own destiny. A getaway car for the human psyche.

Earlier books by David Icke include The Robots' Rebellion (Gill & Macmillan), Truth Vibrations (Gill & Macmillan), Heal the World (Gill & Macmillan), Days of Decision (Jon Carpenter) and It Doesn't Have To Be Like This (Green Print). The last two books are out of print and no longer available.

David Icke Live At Wembley Arena

Filmed at London's Wembley Arena in 2012 – this is the biggest event of its kind ever staged anywhere in the world. Nearly ten hours of cutting edge information researched, compiled and presented by David Icke that you will hear nowhere else in the world put together in this way.

The Lion Sleeps No More

David Icke marks his 20th year of uncovering astounding secrets and suppressed information with this eight-hour presentation before 2,500 people at London's Brixton Academy in May

2010. David has moved the global cutting edge so many times since his incredible 'awakening' in 1990 and here he does it again – and then some.

Beyond the Cutting Edge – Exposing the Dreamworld We Believe to be Real

Since his extraordinary 'awakening' in 1990 and 1991, David Icke has been on a journey across the world, and within himself, to find the Big answers to the Big questions: Who are we? Where are we? What are we doing here? Who really controls this world and how and why? In this seven-hour presentation to 2,500 people at the Brixton Academy in London, David addresses all these questions and connects the dots between them to reveal a picture of life on earth that is truly beyond the cutting edge.

Freedom or Fascism: the time to choose – 3xDVD set

More than 2,000 people from all over Britain and across the world gather at London's famous Brixton Academy to witness an extraordinary event. David Icke weaves together more than 16 years of painstaking research and determined investigation into the Global Conspiracy and the extraordinary 'sting' being perpetrated on an amnesic human race. Icke is the Dot Connector and he uses hundreds of illustrations to reveal the hidden story behind apparently unconnected world events.

Revelations of a Mother Goddess – DVD

Arizona Wilder was mind-programmed from birth by Josef Mengele, the notorious, 'Angel of Death' in the Nazi concentration camps. In this interview with David Icke, she describes human sacrifice rituals at Glamis Castle and Balmoral in England, in which the Queen, the Queen Mother and other members of the Royal Family sacrificed children in Satanic ceremonies.

Available at the shop at **Davidicke.com.**